The Routledge Handbook of Mobilities

The twenty-first century seems to be on the move, perhaps even more so than the last, with cheap travel and more than two billion cars projected worldwide for 2030. And yet, all this mobility is happening incredibly unevenly, at different paces and intensities, with varying impacts and consequences, to the extent that life on the move might be actually quite difficult to sustain environmentally, socially and ethically. As a result 'mobility' has become a keyword of the social sciences, delineating a new domain of concepts, approaches, methodologies and techniques which seek to understand the character and quality of these trends.

This Handbook explores and critically evaluates the debates, approaches, controversies and methodologies inherent to this rapidly expanding discipline. It brings together leading specialists from a range of backgrounds and geographical regions to provide an authoritative and comprehensive overview of this field, conveying cutting-edge research in an accessible way whilst giving detailed grounding in the evolution of past debates on mobilities. It illustrates disciplinary trends and pathways, from migration studies and transport history to communications research, featuring methodological innovations and developments and conceptual histories – from feminist theory to tourist studies. It explores the dominant figures of mobility, from children to soldiers and the mobility impaired; the disparate materialities of mobility such as flows of water and waste to the vectors of viruses; key infrastructures such as logistics systems to the informal services of megacity slums; and the important mobility events around which our world turns, from going on vacation to the commute, to the catastrophic disruption of mobility systems.

The text is forward-thinking, projecting the future of mobilities as they might be lived, transformed and studied, and possibly, brought to an end. International in focus, the book transcends disciplinary and national boundaries to explore mobilities as they are understood from different perspectives, different fields, countries and standpoints.

This is an invaluable resource for all those with an interest in mobility across disciplinary boundaries and areas of study.

Peter Adey is Professor of Human Geography at Royal Holloway University of London. His research interests are located at the intersections of space, mobility and security and he is the author of several books including *Mobility* (Routledge, 2009).

David Bissell is Senior Lecturer and Australian Research Council DECRA Fellow in the Research School of Social Sciences at the Australian National University. His research examines how different forms of travel, from international air travel to urban commuting, are generating new forms of subjectivity, new political formations and new sensory configurations of contemporary life. He is co-editor of *Stillness in a Mobile World* (Routledge, 2011).

Kevin Hannam is Professor of Tourism Mobilities at Leeds Metropolitan University, UK, and Visiting Senior Research Fellow at the University of Johannesburg, South Africa. With John Urry and Mimi Sheller he is a founding co-editor of the journal *Mobilities*. He is the co-author of the recent books *Understanding Tourism* and *Tourism and India*. He is currently collaborating on a research project on walking, art and landscape.

Peter Merriman is Reader in Human Geography at Aberystwyth University. He is author of *Mobility, Space and Culture* (2012) and *Driving Spaces* (2007), and co-edited *Geographies of Mobilities: Practices, Spaces, Subjects* (2011) with Tim Cresswell. He is an Associate Editor of *Transfers: Interdisciplinary Journal of Mobility Studies*, and on the editorial board of *Mobilities*.

Mimi Sheller is Professor of Sociology and Director of the Center for Mobilities Research and Policy at Drexel University. She is the author or editor of seven books, including the forthcoming *Aluminum Dreams: The Making of Light Modernity* (MIT Press, 2014). She is founding co-editor of the journal *Mobilities* and Associate Editor of *Transfers*.

The Routledge Handbook of Mobilities

Edited by Peter Adey, David Bissell,
Kevin Hannam, Peter Merriman
and Mimi Sheller

LONDON AND NEW YORK

First published 2014
by Routledge
2 Park Square, Milton Park, Abingdon, Oxon OX14 4RN

and by Routledge
711 Third Avenue, New York, NY 10017

First issued in paperback 2017

Routledge is an imprint of the Taylor & Francis Group, an informa business

British Library Cataloguing in Publication Data
A catalogue record for this book is available from the British Library

Library of Congress Cataloging in Publication Data
The Routledge handbook of mobilities/edited by Peter Adey,
David Bissell, Kevin Hannam, Peter Merriman, Mimi Sheller.
    pages cm
  Includes bibliographical references and index.
  1. Human geography. 2. Migration, Internal–Social aspects.
  3. Social mobility. I. Adey, Peter.
  GF41.R68 2013
  304.8–dc23   2013022984

Typeset in Bembo
by Sunrise Setting Ltd, Paignton, UK

ISBN 13: 978-1-138-07144-5 (pbk)
ISBN 13: 978-0-415-66771-5 (hbk)

Contents

Contents

Contents

SECTION SEVEN
Introduction: Methodologies   **503**

Figures and Tables

Figures

Tables

Contributors

Sebastian Abrahamsson is working as a postdoc at the AISSR at the University of Amsterdam. His current work explores spatial and temporal figurations of food wasting practices in everyday life. He has published in *Social and Cultural Geography*, *Cultural Geographies* and *Science Studies*.

Peter Adey is Professor of Human Geography at Royal Holloway University of London. His research interests are located at the intersections of space, mobility and security and he is the author of several books including *Mobility* (Routledge, 2009).

Rachel Aldred is Senior Lecturer in Transport at the University of Westminster. She led the two-year Cycling Cultures research project and has published widely on cycling, as well as on topics including transport and disability, and cars and CO_2. Two current research projects explore how modelling can better address the need for a step-change in transport. Her personal blog is at rachelaldred.org.

David Bissell is Senior Lecturer and Australian Research Council DECRA Fellow in the Research School of Social Sciences at the Australian National University. His research examines how different forms of travel, from international air travel to urban commuting, are generating new forms of subjectivity, new political formations and new sensory configurations of contemporary life. He is co-editor of *Stillness in a Mobile World* (Routledge, 2011).

Nicholas Blomley is Professor of Geography at Simon Fraser University. He has a longstanding interest in the geographies of law, particularly property. He is the author of *Rights of Passage: Sidewalks and the Regulation of Public Flow* (Routledge, 2011).

Melissa Butcher is Senior Lecturer in the Department of Geography, Open University, UK. The focus of her research is transnational mobility, cultural change, intercultural competence and conflict in diverse urban spaces, emphasising questions of identity and belonging. Her recent publications include: *Managing Cultural Change: Reclaiming Synchronicity in a Mobile World* (Ashgate, 2011) and *Dissent and Cultural Resistance in Asia's Cities* (with S. Velayutham, Routledge, 2009).

Lily Cho is an Associate Professor of English at York University. Her recent publications on citizenship and mobility include 'Citizenship and the Bonds of Affect: the Passport Photograph,' *Photography and Culture* 2.3 (2009) and 'Stranger Intimacy: Anticipating Citizenship in Chinese Head Tax Photographs,' *Interventions* 15.1 (2013).

Georgine Clarsen teaches History at the University of Wollongong, Australia. Her research interests include the history of gender and automobility, and settler colonial mobilities as a distinctive constellation of mobility practices. She is a founding associate editor of the journal *Transfers: Interdisciplinary Journal of Mobility Studies*.

Deborah E. Cowen is Associate Professor in the Department of Geography at the University of Toronto. She is the author of *Military Workfare: The Soldier and Social Citizenship in Canada*, co-editor, with Emily Gilbert, of *War, Citizenship, Territory*, and co-editor of *Environment and Planning D: Society and Space*.

Tim Cresswell is Professor of History and International Affairs at Northeastern University, Boston. He is the author or editor of nine books including *Geographic Thought: A Critical Introduction* (2013), and *On the Move: Mobility in the Modern Western World* (2006).

Tim Dant is Professor of Sociology at Lancaster University, UK, and has published books on critical theory, the sociology of knowledge and material culture. His latest book is *Television and the Moral Imaginary: Society through the small screen* (Palgrave, 2012) and he is currently writing about the critical potential of phenomenology and the moral responsibility of materiality in relation to, among other things, guns, the repair of stuff, science in museums and theory of mind.

Adriana de Souza e Silva is Associate Professor at the Department of Communication at North Carolina State University (NCSU) and associate director of the Communication, Rhetoric, and Digital Media (CRDM) PhD program at NCSU. Dr. de Souza e Silva's research focuses on how mobile and locative interfaces shape people's interactions with public spaces and create new forms of sociability.

J.-D. Dewsbury is a senior lecturer in human geography at the University of Bristol. His research centres on bodies, performativity and the concept of the event in continental philosophy, with a focus on the performing arts. He is currently completing a book entitled *Performative Spaces: Subjectivity, Materiality and the Event*.

Colin Divall heads the Institute of Railway Studies & Transport History, a joint initiative of the UK's National Railway Museum and the University of York. Widely published in the histories of transport and of technology, he is currently working on a history of the marketing of discretionary mobility in Britain.

Iain Docherty is Head of Management and Professor of Public Policy and Governance at the University of Glasgow's Adam Smith Business School. His current research focuses on two major Research Council projects on sustainable transport and low carbon transitions. In 2011 he was appointed as one of the inaugural members of the Royal Society of Edinburgh's Young Academy of Scotland.

Martin Dodge is a Senior Lecturer in Human Geography at the University of Manchester, and his research focuses primarily on the politics of mapping technologies, new modes of geographic visualisation, and cultural understandings of urban infrastructures. He curated from 1997 to 2007 the well-known web-based *Atlas of Cyberspaces* and has co-authored three books analysing technologies: *Mapping Cyberspace* (Routledge, 2000), *Atlas of Cyberspace*

(Addison-Wesley, 2001) and *Code/Space* (MIT Press, 2011). He has co-edited four books on cartographic theory and mapping practice: *Geographic Visualization* (Wiley, 2008), *Rethinking Maps* (Routledge, 2009), *Classics in Cartography* (Wiley, 2010) and *The Map Reader* (Wiley, 2011).

Tim Edensor teaches cultural geography at Manchester Metropolitan University. He is the author of *Tourists at the Taj* (1998), *National Identity, Popular Culture and Everyday Life* (2002) and *Industrial Ruins: Space, Aesthetics and Materiality*, as well as the editor of *Geographies of Rhythm* (2010) and co-editor of *Spaces of Vernacular Creativity* (2009) and *Urban Theory Beyond the West: A World of Cities* (2011). Tim has written extensively on national identity, tourism, industrial ruins, walking, driving, football cultures and urban materiality and is currently investigating landscapes of illumination and darkness.

Rowan Ellis is a lecturer in Human Geography at the University of Edinburgh. Her research interests include urban political-ecology, class and caste politics, and urban marginality in South Asia. Her work appears in *Antipode*, *ACME*, *Professional Geographer*, *Scottish Geographical Journal* and in several edited collections.

Jason Farman is an Assistant Professor of American Studies and a Distinguished Faculty Fellow in the Digital Cultures and Creativity Program at University of Maryland, College Park. He is author of the book *Mobile Interface Theory: Embodied Space and Locative Media* (2012) and editor of *The Mobile Story: Narrative Practices with Locative Technologies* (2013).

James Faulconbridge is a Professor of Transnational Management in the Department of Organisation, Work and Technology at Lancaster University Management School. His research on mobility focuses, in particular, upon the way forms of mobility are used in global firms, with the role of business travel being of especial interest. He co-edited the book *International Business Travel in the Global Economy* (Ashgate, 2010).

Anne-Marie Fortier is Reader in Social and Cultural Studies at Lancaster University. Her research interests include migrant identities and belongings, multiculturalisms, nation formation, citizenship and migration. She is the author of *Migrant Belongings* (Berg, 2000) and *Multicultural Horizons* (Routledge, 2008), and co-editor of *Uprootings/Regroundings* (Berg, 2003). Her current research is on the citizenship naturalisation process in Britain.

Adrian Franklin is Professor of Sociology at the University of Tasmania, Australia. His research focuses on tourism, travel and mobilities, the sociology of nature, and collecting. He is the author of *City Life* (2010), *Tourism: An Introduction* (2003), and most recently *Retro: A Guide to the mid-20th Century Design Revival* (2013).

Malene Freudendal-Pedersen is Associate Professor at the department of Environmental, Social and Spatial Change at Roskilde University in Denmark, from where she also holds her PhD. She is part of the research group 'Space, Place, Mobility and Urban Studies' and has for many years been working within the field of mobilities with a specific focus on everyday praxis.

Gillian Fuller is a digital media specialist whose research focuses on the impact of digital cultures on the interaction and aesthetics of bodies, matter and data in space. She is co-author of *Aviopolis: A Book about Airports* (BDP: London, 2005). Her most recent book (with David Bissell), *Stillness in a Mobile World* (Routledge: London, 2010), is a collaboration between media theorists, human geographers, education theorists and artists. Gillian is Visiting Research Fellow at the National Institute of Experimental Arts, COFA, UNSW.

Zack Furness is Assistant Professor of Communications at Penn State University, Greater Allegheny and author of the book, *One Less Car: Bicycling and the Politics of Automobility* (Temple University Press, 2010). He is also editor of *Punkademics* (Minor Compositions, 2012) and co-editor of *The NFL: Critical/Cultural Perspectives* (Temple University Press, forthcoming).

Jennie Germann Molz is Associate Professor of Sociology at the College of the Holy Cross in Worcester, Massachusetts. She is the author of *Travel Connections* (Routledge, 2012), co-editor of *Mobilizing Hospitality* (Ashgate, 2007), and a founding co-editor of the journal *Hospitality & Society* (Intellect).

Eric Gordon studies civic media, location-based media, and serious games. He is a fellow at the Berkman Center for Internet and Society at Harvard University and an associate professor in the Department of Visual and Media Arts at Emerson College, where he is the founding director of the Engagement Game Lab (http://engagementgamelab.org), which focuses on the design and research of digital games that foster local civic engagement and enhance urban and democratic life.

Stephen Graham is an academic and author who researches cities and urban life. He is Professor of Cities and Society at the Global Urban Research Unit and is based in Newcastle University's School of Architecture, Planning and Landscape.

Kevin Hannam is Professor of Tourism Mobilities at Leeds Metropolitan University, UK, and Visiting Senior Research Fellow at the University of Johannesburg, South Africa. With John Urry and Mimi Sheller he is a founding co-editor of the journal *Mobilities*. He is the co-author of the recent books *Understanding Tourism* and *Tourism and India*. He is currently collaborating on a research project on walking, art and landscape.

Clare Holdsworth is Professor of Social Geography at Keele University, UK. Her most recent book, *Family and Intimate Mobilities* (Palgrave Macmillan, 2013), considers the interrelationships between family practices and mobility. She is also co-author of *Population and Society* (Sage, 2013).

Allison Hui is an Academic Fellow in Sociology at Lancaster University. Her research examines transformations in everyday life in the context of changing global mobilities, including considerations of social practices, tourism, leisure and migration. Her chapter was supported by a Postdoctoral Fellowship at Hong Kong Baptist University and a UK Commonwealth Scholarship.

K. Neil Jenkings has a doctorate in Sociology and is currently investigating 'The Value of the University Armed Service Units' following 'The Social Production of the Contemporary British Military Memoir' and 'Negotiating Identity and Representation in the Mediated Armed Forces', all ESRC-funded projects. He is a widely published scholar at Newcastle University, UK.

Ole B. Jensen is Professor of Urban Theory at Aalborg University, co-founder and board member of The Centre for Mobilities and Urban Studies (C-MUS), founder of the Mobility and Tracking Technologies Research Cluster (MoTT) and member of the Cosmobilities Task Force. Research interests are mobilities theory, urban theory and technology.

Roger Keil is Professor at the Faculty of Environmental Studies at York University in Toronto. He researches global suburbanization, cities and infectious disease, and regional governance. He is the editor of *Suburban Constellations* (Berlin: Jovis, 2013) and *Networked Disease: Emerging Infections and the Global City* (with S. Harris Ali, 2008).

Jonas Larsen is Associate Lecturer and research leader at the Department of Environmental, Social and Spatial Change. He has co-authored *Performing Tourist Places* (Ashgate, 2004), *Mobilities, Networks, Geographies* (Ashgate, 2006) and *Tourism, Performance and the Everyday: Consuming the Orient* (Routledge, 2010), (with John Urry) *The Tourist Gaze 3.0* (Sage, 2011), and co-edited *Digital Snaps: The New Face of Snapshot Photography* (I.B. Tauris, 2013).

Eric Laurier is Senior Lecturer in Geography and Interaction at the University of Edinburgh. Over a number of projects he has used video to study how people travel together in cars. 'Meet You at Junction 17' and 'Habitable Cars' were funded by the ESRC.

Stephanie Lavau is a Lecturer in Human Geography at Plymouth University. Her research interests include geographies of knowing and managing nature, biopolitics and the securing of biological life, and the intersections of scientific and other knowledge practices.

Debbie Lisle is a Senior Lecturer in International Relations in the School of Politics, International Studies and Philosophy at Queen's University Belfast. Her research explores how identity, difference, travel, mobility, visuality and culture intersect with global affairs and international security. She is currently exploring the relationships between tourism, war and geopolitics.

Orvar Löfgren is Professor Emeritus in European Ethnology at Lund University, Sweden. The cultural analysis and ethnography of everyday life has been an ongoing focus in his research. Central research fields have been studies of tourism, commuting and transnational mobility.

Glenn Lyons is Professor of Transport and Society and founder of the Centre for Transport & Society at UWE Bristol. He is now Associate Dean responsible for research within UWE Bristol's Faculty of Environment and Technology. Glenn's research has focused upon the role of information and communications technologies and services in shaping social practices and personal travel behaviour.

Juliana Mansvelt is a Senior Lecturer in Geography in the School of People, Environment and Planning, Massey University. She is author of *Geographies of Consumption* (Sage, 2005) and editor of *Green Consumerism: An A–Z Guide* (Sage, 2011). Juliana's recent research has involved interdisciplinary projects – examining the ways in which life-courses, living standards, mobilities and identities of older people are shaped in relation to consumption practices and choices.

Scott McCabe is Associate Professor of Tourism Management/Marketing at Nottingham University Business School. His research focuses on theorizations of tourist experience, social tourism and the benefits of tourism participation, marketing communications and technology in tourism marketing. He writes on qualitative methods, particularly the application of socio-linguistics in tourism.

Eugene McCann is a professor of geography at Simon Fraser University, Burnaby, BC, Canada. He studies the mobilization of urban policies, specifically those related to development and to public health. He is a co-editor, with Kevin Ward, of *Mobile Urbanism: Cities & Policymaking in the Global* Age (Minnesota, 2011).

Derek P. McCormack teaches in the School of Geography and Environment at the University of Oxford. He is the author of *Refrains for Moving Bodies: Experience and Experiment in Affective Spaces* (Duke, 2013), and has written widely on nonrepresentational theory and spaces of affect. He is currently working on a book project about balloons as atmospheric things.

Colin McFarlane is Reader in Urban Geography at Durham University. His research focuses on everyday life and infrastructures, especially in informal settlements, and on the politics of urban knowledge. He is currently writing the results of a research project on everyday sanitation politics in Mumbai. He is author of *Learning the City: Knowledge and Translocal Assemblage* (Wiley-Blackwell, 2011) and has published widely in journals including *Public Culture, Society and Space, Transactions of the Institute of British Geographers, Antipode, Urban Studies,* and *International Journal of Urban and Regional Studies.*

Peter Merriman is Reader in Human Geography at Aberystwyth University. He is author of *Mobility, Space and Culture* (2012) and *Driving Spaces* (2007), and co-edited *Geographies of Mobilities: Practices, Spaces, Subjects* (2011) with Tim Cresswell. He is an Associate Editor of *Transfers: Interdisciplinary Journal of Mobility Studies,* and on the editorial board of *Mobilities.*

Esther Milne is Head of Humanities, Arts and Social Sciences at Swinburne University in Melbourne, Australia. She researches the cultural and legislative contexts of celebrity production and the history of networked postal communication systems. She is the author of *Letters, Postcards, Email: Technologies of Presence,* published by Routledge.

Annemarie Mol is a professor of Anthropology of the Body at the University of Amsterdam. Her publications concern themselves with the multiplicity of reality, caring bodies, travelling technologies, feminist ways of writing and fluid theorising. She is currently working with a team and an ERC Advanced Grant on *Eating Bodies in Western Practice and Theory.*

Natalie Oswin is Assistant Professor of Geography at McGill University. Her publications include articles on South Africa's post-apartheid gay and lesbian movement, the cultural politics of heteronormativity in Singapore, and conceptual pieces on queer geographies. She is co-editor of the interdisciplinary journal *Environment and Planning D: Society and Space.*

Lisa Parks is Professor of Film and Media Studies and Director of the Center for Information Technology and Society at the University of California, Santa Barbara. She is the author of

Cultures in Orbit and co-editor of *Planet TV* and *Down to Earth*. She is finishing two new books: *Coverage: Aero-orbital Media after 9/11* and *Mixed Signals: Media Infrastructures and Cultural Geographies*.

Matthew Paterson is Professor of Political Science at the University of Ottawa. His research focuses on the political economy of global environmental change. He is currently working in particular on carbon market politics, and is preparing a new project on the cultural politics of climate change.

George Revill is Senior Lecturer at the Open University. His research concerns issues of landscape, technology, culture and identity. His current research interests bring issues of sound, mobility and landscape together. His most recent book, *Railway* (Reaktion Press, 2012), examines the railway as a cultural icon of modernity.

Noel B. Salazar is Research Professor in Anthropology at the University of Leuven. His research interests include mobility and travel, the local-global nexus, imaginaries of Otherness, culture contacts, heritage and cosmopolitanism. He is the author of *Envisioning Eden* (Oxford: Berghahn, 2010) and founder of Culture Mobilities Research (CuMoRe) and the EASA Anthropology and Mobility Network.

Kim Sawchuk is a Professor in the Department of Communication Studies, Concordia University. She holds a Concordia University Research Chair in Mobile Media Studies and co-directs the Mobile Media Lab – Montreal, with Dr. Owen Chapman. More on her research, teaching and creative interventions can be found at www.mobilities.ca.

Jon Shaw is Professor of Transport Geography with Plymouth University. He researches issues associated with mobility, transport policy and governance and he is widely published in the academic and policy literatures. His current research activity includes a large EU-funded project on the mobility needs of older people.

Mimi Sheller is Professor of Sociology and Director of the Center for Mobilities Research and Policy at Drexel University. She is the author or editor of seven books, including the forthcoming *Aluminum Dreams: The Making of Light Modernity* (MIT Press, 2014). She is founding co-editor of the journal *Mobilities* and Associate Editor of *Transfers*.

Paul Simpson is a lecturer in Human Geography in the School of Geography, Earth and Environmental Sciences, Plymouth University. His research focuses on the social and cultural geographies of everyday, artistic, and mobile practices and explores the complex situatedness of such practices in the environments in which they take place.

Dan Swanton is a Lecturer in Human Geography at the University of Edinburgh. His current research focuses on everyday multiculture and performances of race in mill towns in northern England; photography and wastescapes; and rethinking understandings of economy through performative accounts of steelmaking.

Cristina Temenos is a PhD Candidate in the Department of Geography at Simon Fraser University, Burnaby, BC, Canada. She studies urban social movements and policy activism related to drug policy reform and public health policy in European, North American, and

Caribbean cities. Her work on urban policy mobilities has been published in *Environment and Planning A* and *Geography Compass*.

Peter Thomas is an Honorary Research Fellow at the National Centre for Epidemiology and Public Health at the Australian National University. He has a PhD in human geography and since then has worked in research and policy fields relating to passenger transport.

John Urry is Distinguished Professor of Sociology and Director of the Centre for Mobilities Research, Lancaster University. Recent books include *Mobile Lives* (2010, with Anthony Elliott), The *Tourist Gaze 3.0* (2011, with Jonas Larsen), *Climate Change and Society* (2011), and *Societies beyond Oil* (2013). He is currently working on 'offshoring', post carbon futures and the mobility implications of 3D printing.

Phillip Vannini is Canada Research Chair in Innovative Learning and Public Ethnography and Professor in the School of Communication & Culture at Royal Roads University in Victoria, Canada. He is author of *Ferry Tales: Mobility, Place, and Time on Canada's West Coast* (Routledge, 2012), and editor of *The Cultures of Alternative Mobility* (Ashgate, 2009) and *Technologies of Mobility in the Americas* (Peter Lang, 2012).

Alex Vasudevan is a Lecturer in Cultural and Historical Geography at the University of Nottingham. His current research focuses on radical politics in Germany and the wider geographies of neo-liberal globalisation. He has published widely in journals such as *Antipode, Cultural Geographies, Environment and Planning D: Society and Space, Public Culture* and *Social and Cultural Geography*. He is currently working on a book for the RGS-IBG book series on the history of squatting in Berlin.

Rachel Woodward is Professor of Human Geography in the School of Geography, Politics & Sociology, Newcastle University, UK. Her research interests include military sociology; representations of and by military personnel in images and texts, including the military memoir; and the politics and effects of military activities in different environments and landscapes.

Introduction

Peter Adey, David Bissell, Kevin Hannam,
Peter Merriman and Mimi Sheller

Let us consider an image. In fact, let's take the picture on the front cover of this book and consider what we see. The train carriage immediately evokes a very mobile story, perhaps reminding us of the scene of everyday urban commuting. But it also evokes some of the more extensive, complex flows that criss-cross the globe. Its interior is sleek and shiny. The surfaces are not scuffed or dirty, but reflective, and it feels new and modern. It's difficult to identify where the train is because there are no definable signs of where or when the photograph was taken. This might be read as symbolic of trends in globalization, where a plethora of people, things, signs and images cross the globe in an increasingly homogeneous whirlwind. The carriage is uninhabited, no-one's home. Perhaps this is the archetypal non-place or 'placeless' place that lacks meaning or authentic social activity (Relph 1976; Augé 1995; Merriman 2004). Perhaps its emptiness evokes the serenity that commuters might crave on leaving work in the early evening. Perhaps the train is underground? As a subway or metro carriage it demonstrates the penetration of our mobility systems through rock and soil to different depths as well as different points on the earth's surface. The visual perspective is linear, the distant window is a vanishing point sucking us into the image and beyond. Indeed we could easily substitute the picture with the cover of Bill Gates's book *The Road Ahead*, depicting a clear highway shooting into the far distance, a metaphor for the information superhighway. We seem to be moving faster than ever before. The whole world is now your oyster. Opportunity is in the palm of your hand. Everything seems possible. Everywhere seems accessible.

Narratives of novelty, accessibility and speed-up might sound rather familiar. These narratives are incredibly powerful and they have profound effects. But they are often prone to exaggeration and caricature, obscuring other ways of thinking about mobility.

Despite the persistence of the idea that mobility might remove us from harm or place us on the road to prosperity, this opening paragraph presents a somewhat stereotypical account of the desirability and novelty of mobile life, which obscures the complexity and richness of what might actually be going on. It also repeats a series of popular, ideologically driven and prophetic scenarios about the ease and smoothness of globalization. Narratives of this kind imagined a future prospering by the undoing of national barriers and state intervention, the unhooking of individuals from social and cultural structures, and the telemediation of just about everything by burgeoning telecommunication systems such as satellite TV, mobile phones and the internet. Indeed, much of all this was written by extremely privileged people, ruminating on the frictionless world that they themselves inhabited without restriction and in luxury, while at the same time profiting from the dismantling of regulations over finance capital. Narratives of an ever-accelerated twenty-first century and abstract evocations and celebrations of speed and fluidity are certainly not what this handbook is about.

We are concerned with a series of rather different questions that grapple with how mobilities are changing the world in complex, subtle and powerful ways. For example, how have mobilities altered the structure of our societies and economies, and elicited different regulatory and governmental practices? How do mobilities challenge and threaten societies, perhaps through the fear of the illicit mobilities and security risks of transnational diseases, contraband and potential weapons, or simply through triggering a sense of uprootedness and the perception of constant flux? How do mobilities embody and generate incredibly stark inequalities: from the struggles of undocumented peoples, trafficked women, stowaways and border crossers, to the super-rich, business class and 'kinetic elites'? How have we become so reliant upon mobilities that, should they fail, our lives may be thrown into chaos? We are interested, in other words, in how changing mobilities have transformed the way we live: our practices, our relations, our senses and our desires. Rather than celebrating the pristine decontextualized modern machines and spaces that we might apprehend in the photo of the train carriage, we begin from a series of perspectives which have emerged within the social sciences, humanities and arts that approach mobility in a more critical, contextual and less superficial manner. This style of analysis is what has become known as mobility research, and this handbook seeks to bring together the best of this scholarship, introducing new empirical questions, anticipating futures for how we might move, and creating alternative research pathways we might pursue to account for mobility.

★　★　★

So if we can hold the image of the railway carriage in the backs of our minds, let us first trace how mobilities or 'new mobilities' research has emerged, before returning to the picture of the empty train carriage and thinking about other ways of interpreting it.

★　★　★

A large proportion of research on mobility has been inspired and influenced by a burgeoning paradigm of thought which first became identified with a 'mobilities turn' (Hannam *et al.* 2006) or 'new mobilities paradigm' (Sheller and Urry 2006). This provocative labelling was quite knowing, its authors aware that it perhaps marked a re-turn of sorts to a particular yet fragmented and often abstract concern with mobile life, albeit in quite a different way. In Geography, for example, the positivist models of spatial science always had mobility at their heart, except they became subject to behaviouralist models of decision making, or rational economic analyses of mobility as a variable of an equation to be inputted along with the 'friction of distance' (Cliff *et al.* 1974). In Sociology, mobility was often implicit in writing on issues as diverse as migration and assimilation (Jansen 1970), urbanization and suburbanization (Yago 1983). It was also present in many theories of modernization and development (Harrison 1988). Yet the trope of mobility was often more fully tethered to the idea of 'social mobility', referring to transitions through social hierarchies, and thereby losing something of its spatial resonance (Lipset and Bendix 1959). Furthermore, only certain mobilities were being talked about. Whilst the mobilities bound up with residential transformations and transnational migration received much attention, many other hugely significant mobilities were often neglected. The mobilities of tourism, for example, were marginalized and even derided as an unacceptable subject of academic enquiry, certainly not a serious object of knowledge claims (Franklin, this volume).

Within the mobility turn, by contrast, mobilities were explored in such a way that they did not appear as exceptional circumstances, functional tasks to simply overcome spatial detachment, or superfluous activities outside of scholarly pursuit. Rather, mobility became acknowledged as part of the energetic buzz of the everyday (even while banal or humdrum, or even stilled) and seen as a set of highly meaningful social practices that make up social, cultural and political life. New mobilities collectives saw the production of scholarship at particular sites, and through particular networks and research initiatives. These include the Cosmobilities research network in Europe and the Pan-American mobilities network, as well as key nodes located in specific institutions such as the Centre for Mobilities Research at Lancaster University, the Center for Mobilities Research and Policy at Drexel University, the Centre for Mobilities and Urban Studies at Aalborg University, the Research Centre Mobility and Transport at the Institute for Transportation at Technische Universität München, and the Transport and Mobility Laboratory at the École Polytechnique Fédérale de Lausanne. We could also highlight the formative influence of key events and conferences, such as the 'Mobilities' conference at Gregynog Hall in 1999, the 'Alternative Mobility Futures' Conference at Lancaster University in 2004, and the forming of the International Association for the History of Traffic, Transport and Mobility in 2003. Significantly, key journals have also taken shape, including *Mobilities* in 2006, and *Transfers: Interdisciplinary Journal of Mobility Studies* in 2011.

Mobilities researchers have sketched out new transdisciplinary research spaces between sociology, geography, history, anthropology, communication and cultural studies. The forging of these research spaces was assisted in part because of the pressure of internal critiques within individual research fields concerning the continued prioritization of fixity and stasis. James Clifford (1997) suggested that anthropologists needed to leave behind their preoccupation with social-cultural roots, and instead move closer to explorations of the 'routes' through which social and cultural forms are made and remade. What constituted the 'field' therefore transformed from a location to a set of relations that were multi-sited (Marcus 1998). The definition of culture transformed from something that was fixed in place to something understood as an amalgamation of mobile 'scapes' (Appadurai 1996). Within Anthropology and Geography the mobile body even challenged assumptions about the a priori dominance of representations and symbolism, demanding theories and approaches that were more attuned to practice and performances. Thus, Nigel Thrift began a research trajectory known as 'non-representational theories' that could attend to the praxis and experience of mobile life (Thrift 1996, 2007).

Within the 'new mobilities paradigm', the social was being reconfigured as mobile, with many aspects of social life, civil society, and political participation increasingly understood as being performed through mobilities. Mobilities sustained families, relationships, access and delivery to services, leisure, work and politics, bringing about material and discursive transformations to both urban and rural landscapes. Furthermore, 'new mobilities' perspectives sought to bring far more attention to both the empirical facts of mobility, and to precisely what was happening within the journey, through the movement from one place to another. How were different mobilities involved in making people's lives meaningful? How were these mobilities meaningful in and of themselves? How was all this mobility inherently uneven and unequal? And how might attending to such questions require different modes of analysis and critique? In many respects research on mobility shares something with notions of 'social mobility', which implies some kind of movement up and down socio-economic hierarchies of wealth, class and status, yet departs from it insofar as it is explicitly spatial and performative – in other words, emergent. Mobilities research would account for displacement geographically *and* socially, attentive to social progress and categorical advancement within 'power geometries' composed through class, race, ethnicity and gender. Subjects not only moved through geographic space, but were shaped by power relations of mobility and immobility, including rights to move, to enter, to dwell, to leave.

In attuning to the difference that space and place makes, mobilities research also became more cognizant of the rhythms and temporalities of mobile subject formation, including those of the researcher (Edensor 2010). The attention to mobilities offers us a substantive epistemological challenge: how to 'get a grip' on a highly differentiated mobile world. 'How are our modes of "knowing" being transformed by the very processes that we wish to study?' asked Hannam, Sheller and Urry (2006: 10). Just as anthropologists like Clifford and Marcus had shifted towards multi-sited fieldwork and a more dislocated sense of 'the field', other social scientists also had to grapple with what their research object actually was, and how it could be apprehended if it – and they – were in motion.

Such perspectives did not simply appear out of nowhere. Ontologically, mobilities research might be better apprehended not as some kind of discipline poacher, but rather as a force that animates fields, creating connections as it moves, while growing and benefiting from that diversity. Thus some of the initial impetus for mobilities research emerged in political-economic explorations of emerging practices of consumption, such as tourism. Post-structuralist nomadic theory helped to break the mould of theories that could not escape the structures and strictures of state formation, territorial power and identity norms (for example, in the works of Gilles Deleuze and Félix Guattari), whereas post-colonial and feminist thinking helped us to realize that 'we don't all have the same access to the road', undoing the bounded assumptions about race, ethnicity and gender (Wolff 1993: 235; Kaplan 1996). Theories and metaphors of the network and complexity provide powerful tools for considering the inter-relatedness and inter-dependencies of the mobilities of both people and things. Alternatively, the lures of phenomenology can move debates beyond the mere tracings of actants and networks to help us to understand how mobilities are actually experienced through bodies interacting with other mobile technologies and prostheses (see, for example, Seamon 1979; Manning 2009). This means accounting for how embedded and embodied mobilities are practised in minutely meaningful yet fully felt and viscerally realized sensations, moods and affects.

More established sub-disciplinary areas have also been brought to bear on mobilities. Migration and citizenship studies realized that their concerns with generalized issues of regulation and securitization at the scale of the city or nation needed to be combined with the more prosaic concerns of a walk down the street (Conradson and Latham 2005). Communications theory and cultural studies have examined the mobilities of data, media and information, and how they can come to replace, mediate and complement physical mobilities (Moores 2012). Different sorts of presence are now possible in our net localities, permitting quite different variations on that 'compulsion to proximity' (Boden and Molotch 1994).

Indeed, in spite of ostensible differences between fields such as tourism, migration and transport studies, 'new mobilities' seems to have been able to spark new avenues for research initiatives, contributing to a revitalization of existing disciplinary concerns. For example, transport geography and transport history have undergone substantive shifts, partly in response to the challenges laid down by mobilities research (see Shaw and Docherty, this volume; Divall, this volume). This is characterized by a much richer appreciation of the role of transportation in ordering societal patterns, cultures and ways of life, together with a renewed attention to the social shaping of transportation itself through perceptions, senses and habits which condition transport spaces, technologies and systems in different ways. Both transport geography and mobilities research have made substantive moves to accommodate one another and complement one another, evidenced in cross-disciplinary commentaries and papers in special issues of the *Journal of Transport History, Journal of Transport Geography and Transfers: Interdisciplinary Journal of Mobility Studies*.

Across these disciplinary, pedagogic and dissemination spaces, research methodologies themselves have, to different extents, undergone processes of transformation in response to mobilities. Some appear more able to insert themselves into the flow, in order to grasp a potentially unstable and ephemeral object of enquiry. Others explore the value of historical perspectives, for example where archives might tell us quite different stories of mobilities, windowing the contexts from which they have emerged. Others suggest we explore mobilities using complex data sets, looking at the qualculative traces a mobile body or object might leave, or complementing and triangulating qualitative techniques with quantitative techniques to generate intriguing as well as beautiful forms of mapping and visualization.

And so it is from these perspectives that we could find other inspirations and approaches for interpreting the railway carriage photographed on the cover, focusing on the specificity and detail of life on the move, its experiences, its differences, its cultures and its politics. So let us return to where we started and consider the image again.

First, we might consider that the train comes from somewhere. The image's snapshot belies the train's *history*, which might tell us much more about the institutional, societal and political context of this form of mobility. What were the broader conditions of possibility for this form of mobility, and why might they matter? What cultures of mobility have emerged around the train? We could interpret this photo using a range of different mobility approaches and perspectives, which might lead to questions about, for instance, the gender relations the train's mobility expresses or reinforces. Second, perhaps the image illustrates certain kinds of *qualities* of mobility. Its mobility seems frictionless, the ergonomic and machine-moulded almost-aerodynamic forms emphasizing its potential speed in opposition to much slower and more laborious forms of mobility, particularly in the context of urban transport. Yet the bench seats without armrests and red handgrips suspended from the ceiling suggest that this carriage is designed to pack passengers close together, prompting questions about the ethico-political terrain of being mobile in tight (and at times perhaps barely bearable) proximity (cf. Fujii 1999). On the other hand, the emptiness of the train in the photo may tell us less about our apparently hypermobilized world, and more about the importance of moments of stillness and quiet, even our vulnerability that is produced by mobility. Third, we get a sense that this form of travel is systemic and *infrastructural*. The railway constitutes a networked infrastructure upon which people's daily lives depend, but that infrastructure is also heavy, sunk and often invisible. Indeed, this particular mobility system's *materialities* are often under-analysed in mobility studies, unlike in transport history. We see oil-based plastics and aluminium and have the impression of speed and liquidity – qualities that have characterized narratives of mobility, communication and transportation over the last century and before (Sheller 2014). The oil in the very evident red plastic seats reminds us of the importance of this substance as *the* fuel of the twentieth century. Fifth, the photo's emptiness demands we ask who might inhabit these sorts of spaces. Who are the train's passengers? Who works to produce and keep moving the railway or subway system? Who are its *subjects*? Vitally, then, we must ask who depends on this kind of travel, how do they use it, and how might they inhabit this space in different places and at different times? Also, who might be excluded, or made invisible, by and from such modes, technologies and spaces of mobility? A train in rural England might be quite different to a train pulling out of the Chhatrapati Shivaji Terminus in Mumbai. Sixth, what role might this train play in mobility *events*? Is the train part and parcel of the everyday commute to work? Does it form the main mode of travel for vacationing or escaping a disaster or an intolerant regime? Can it become a potential space for acts of terrorism? Or, does the train's failure become part of an interruption, a disruption to the circulations of commuting and rhythms of everyday life, like the flooded railways disconnecting Lower Manhattan after Hurricane Sandy in October 2012? Seventh, how might we explore this site methodologically? How attuned are our research *methods* to mobilities – to grasping objects on the move? How easy might it be to research a train historically, from an archive? What records might exist about this now banal form of travel? These are important questions.

So, there are many different ways of looking at and reading different scenes, practices and spaces of mobility – and some of these might be represented in the image on our front cover. These seven themes gesture towards some of the different ways that mobilities researchers have approached the topic, but they have also been used to structure this handbook. The themes correspond with seven sections which cut across the major issues, concepts and case-studies within this broad field. While each section will be fronted with an editors' introduction that sets out the content and major themes discussed in the chapter, here we provide a more contextual explanation and rationale for how these areas of mobilities research have developed and come to matter.

Genealogies, philosophies and approaches

In many ways mobilities research appears to escape easy categorization and disciplinary straightjacketing. The 'paradigm' could be located at the intersection of concepts, the spatial boundaries of empirical sites and in the seams of academic disciplines. That said, even if we characterize mobilities research as being concerned with a combination of trajectories of thought, methods and approaches, this does not mean that we cannot focus on the role of particular academic and intellectual disciplines and contexts that have been instrumental in shaping the mobilities agenda, or examining how particular disciplines have themselves been transformed by mobilities research.

The first section of the book examines the specific disciplinary contexts from which mobilities research has emerged, and the traditions and trajectories of thinking which have often emerged from conversations and intellectual debates between disciplinary areas.

At first glance, mobilities research has been dominated by a relatively small number of traditional disciplines, particularly sociology and geography. This is perhaps not surprising, given that key themes germane to mobilities research, such as the socio-political practices of production and consumption, and the cultural economies of leisure, have been sustained concerns of both disciplines. Fusing these themes together, in Sociology John Urry's ground-breaking work on tourism helped to put mobility centre stage in the social sciences (Urry 1990). Post-colonial theorists and gender scholars have also shaped the trajectory of mobility studies. Taken-for-granted notions of 'home' and 'away' have been challenged in migration studies (Ahmed *et al.* 2003), for example, while the public provision of transport infrastructures would be questioned for their particular fulfilment of predominantly male commuting patterns (Uteng and Cresswell 2008).

Within Geography, humanistic researchers began to foresee mobility as almost an equivalent of the category of place, which meant that mobilities would no longer be considered as abstract, functional or instrumental, but saturated with significance and meaning for human experience (Tuan 1977). Indeed, geographers such as Nigel Thrift, Derek Gregory and others have illustrated the value of exploring shifting senses of movement and space in their histories of travel, mobility and modernity (Thrift 1990). Thrift was also beginning to advocate the analysis of a new 'structure of feeling' associated with mobility and, in doing so, was interested in examining new ontologies of mobility which he saw emerging in the nineteenth and early twentieth centuries, characterized by a changing landscape of 'speed, light and power' (Thrift 1994). Pre-figuring a body of work that would become known as 'non-representational theories' (Anderson and Harrison 2012), Thrift's excavation of the sensible, embodied and affective registers of mobility and technology inspired a series of interventions into practice- and performance-based theories of social action (Thrift 1996, 2007).

Highlighting the work of specific authors of course occludes the complexity of the field. What's more, it is difficult to locate the philosophies and approaches of researchers who are housed in particular departments and institutions but who work across boundaries and communities. Many different ideas have laid the groundwork or have provided the conditions of possibility for the emergence of a mobilities paradigm. As previously intimated, broader trends in social theory, and particularly developments in post-structuralist theory, were a significant part of the intellectual climate within which these ideas emerged. During the 1980s and 90s we witnessed a general move towards the analysis of discursive powers, along with a kind of 'nomadism' of thought. Evading the structures and strictures of political and social norms became a leitmotif of 'nomadic theory', just as post-colonial writings pushed attention towards the words of shifting perspectives out of colonial administration, the exilic energy of migrants moving along imperial networks, territorial disputes and forced displacement, as seen particularly in the work of Palestinian refugee Edward Said (2000, 2001).

While new research on mobilities appears to have had a major impact on disciplines such as Geography and Sociology, it would be a mistake to assume that mobilities research necessarily has an even geographical spread. For example, the way British sociologists understand mobility might be quite different to how sociologists understand it in the United States. Disciplines such as Geography have certainly proved sympathetic to this kind of work, and we see an enormous amount of scholarship published and represented in geography journals, conferences and workshops. But intra-disciplinary debates have at times been more fractious. Geography's sub-fields, such as transport geography, have sometimes had an uneasy relationship with 'new mobilities' work. But the situation is changing. We see co-authored special issues and journal articles that have tried to explore how transport geography and mobilities research might complement one another and speak out against their perceived differences (Bissell et al. 2011).

Far from remaining located within tightly defined disciplines, we see mobilities researchers engaging with wider disciplinary debates. For example, scholars in communications and media studies have deployed notions of mobility to examine communications networks, audiencing, presence, co-presence, tele-presence, the everyday life of media and mobility (Moores 2012; Morley 2000), the materiality of mobile communications (Packer and Wiley 2012), and emergent forms of mobile gaming (De Souza e Silva and Sutko 2009). In migration studies there is a growing appreciation of the mobilities perspective and a decentring of states and borders (Verstraete 2004; Blunt 2007; King 2012; Mountz 2010, 2011). In studies of Education, student mobilities have become a wide area of focus (Waters 2012), while in Anthropology there is a renewed interest in theorizing (im)mobilities in critical dialogue with the mobilities turn (Salazar and Smart 2011).

In the Humanities too we find that, in English and Literature studies, mobilities have been explored in African fiction, Victorian writing (Parkins 2009), travel writing (Chard 1999; Edwards and Grauland 2012) and even the plays of Shakespeare and Marlowe (Palmer 2005; Hopkins 2010). Thus from the written word to its dramatic performance, theatre and performance studies has provided a strong intellectual and practice-based groundwork for the relationship between mobilities, phenomenology and the limits of representation. We also see these disciplines turning to mobilities research in order to reconsider the role of 'site' and 'place' as taken-for-granted and somewhat stable categories in dramaturgical performance (Birch 2012; Wilkie 2012).

Alternatively, in other social science fields such as Criminology, International Relations and Environmental Studies, researchers consider mobilities in relation to Foucauldian notions of power, particularly through concepts such as 'circulation' within the apparatus of biopolitics, security and population controls (Aas *et al.* 2008; Bergman and Sager 2008; Khoo and Rau 2009). In these contexts, mobilities are explored in terms of the ways in which they are policed and governed, as how they cross borders and threaten, and how they relate to notions of cosmopolitanism.

Qualities

What might different mobilities have in common? Do they feel or seem similar? Do they display patterns that resemble one another? Does time move at the same pace? What does distance feel like? Strangely enough, many of these sorts of questions are rarely if ever posed outside of the singular concerns of an individual research project. The second section of the handbook explores the 'qualities' of mobility through a series of entries that address some of the most dominant characteristics of mobility that are often of peripheral concern within specific projects. Or, in other circumstances, such qualities are reduced to different sorts of conceptual orderings, such as power relations.

While Tim Cresswell's (2006) now familiar equation 'mobility = movement + meaning + power' has become quite a useful articulation of mobility as distinct from simply movement, perhaps we can start with another formula:

$$speed = distance/time$$

or

$$v = d/t$$

Drawing down mobility into equations like this only takes us so far, but this universal formula for calculating the speed of a moving object directs our attention to three important characteristics of mobilities: their speed, the distance they travel over or move through, and their temporalities. Thinking about mobilities in relation to speed has been quite problematic. Descriptions of fast and footloose mobilities like those at the start of this introduction have rightly been criticized for being rather sweeping, universal and indeed hyperbolic, as well as for their reliance on positivist and simplistically physicalist definitions of, amongst other things, speed. On the other hand, there has been research on speed – more specifically what Paul Virilio has labelled 'dromopolitics' – that has made significant moves to investigate the relationship between the speed of mobility and communications and the technologies and tactics of warfare and the mass media. Moreover, exploring relations of speed and slowness may reveal the filtering mechanism of the city gates, redolent of contemporary security regimes. But relations of speed also provide a way of examining inequitable distributions of wealth and social class which often reveal themselves through different patterns and degrees of velocity. Approaching speed in this way also tells us much about the subtle patterns and cadences of mobility, most notably their rhythms (see Edensor 2010; Vannini 2012).

Accounts of distance within mobilities research have undergone a transformation. Distance could be understood as a kind of 'friction' or impediment between locations. Distance gets in the way of the turnover time between production and exchange. It also gets in the way of getting things done or getting where one needs to be. But distance can also be approached in terms of perceptions and experiences, the far-off and the nearby, and what compels us to move. Certainly, mobilities researchers have examined people's 'compulsion to proximity' (Boden and Molotch 1994) – the demand for co-presence and forms of social and bodily contact in a specific location and at a particular time (Urry 2002). We see this compulsion underpinning many different kinds of mobility, from the 'trust' and rapport established through face-to-face meetings, which are essential to many working relationships, to the organization of a business, or the makeup of a family or personal relationships. What impels mobility is often proximity, whether to a person, place, idea, or even an object. Witness the remarkable queues for the latest Apple iPhone and its diverse social uses (Hjorth *et al.* 2012), or moments of pilgrimage to religious icons and relics (Coleman and Eade 2004). However, proximity is not the only way that mobilities are compelled. What's more, co-presence and proximity have changed or are changing quite significantly (Bissell 2013). Communication technologies allow us to establish co-presence or 'virtual proximity' at a distance (Urry 2002), while networked and location-aware mobile technologies facilitate quite intense forms of social engagement with a place or locality, not in spite of, but because of, communication from afar (Farman 2011).

The temporalities of mobilities have been absolutely central to these processes, as well as to how societies have made sense of moving through space. Some of the earliest research on the mobilities of the train, stagecoach and postal coach described how large-scale coordinated mobilities required standardized notions of time (Schivelbusch 1978). Giddens would evoke the train timetable's regulating role in encouraging not just one time-zone but the accurate measurement of time in all regions of the country. But it was more complicated than this. Historians such as James Nye have shown that time was not in fact universally produced by the timetable, but it required pumping, synchronizing and delivering to particular locations such as town squares, shop windows and public houses complying with alcohol licensing laws. The other story here is that mobility systems have altered our perceptions of time, so that the procession of temporality appears faster, or slower, or more intense, as has been detailed in the train's 'panoramic perception' (Schivelbusch 1978), elaborations of jet-lag (Gottdiener 2000) and notions of play (Roy and Hannam 2012).

The train on the front cover is interesting, here, because different scholars have considered the sorts of practices and social actions that are possible when moving. Taking these questions in the context of work and shifting economies, research on 'travel time' gives credence to the belief that some modes of mobility can actually enable different kinds of working while on the move, rather than prevent them (Lyons and Urry 2005). Laurier's work in relation to car travel has led many of these studies (Laurier 2004).

But perhaps the bigger issues underlying all this are more conceptual understandings of time, space and mobility which purport that the separation of these categories as formal primitives for action is nonsensical. The engagement of mobility with practices and habits, as well as technologies of coordination, would seem to support this view. Nigel Thrift's (2004) evocative discussions of 'movement-space' outline how our ontologies are being reworked by the emergence of ubiquitous computing and calculating background technologies. For Thrift, the remarkably mobile and complex environments in which humans now act and move – including synchronized transport, logistics and delivery systems, software-coded and mediated spaces – are nigh-on impossible to grasp. In order to navigate them we instead rely upon their delegation into environmental prostheses that do the coordinating of this movement-space for us. Movement is central to many contemporary understandings, experiences and technological productions of space, but Merriman has questioned whether such understandings of movement and mobility ultimately rely upon rather conventional scientific understandings which position space and time as primordial, foundational a priori backgrounds, dimensions, qualities or measures of position, extension and context. As he puts it, "why not position movement, rhythm, force, energy or affect as primitives or registers that may be of equal importance when understanding the unfolding of events, and why approach space and time as privileged *measures* for conceptualizing location, position and context?" (Merriman 2012a: 24; also Merriman 2012b).

Finally, the entries in this section are not about taking these qualities for granted, or presenting speed, distance and time as unproblematic in the sense of the moral and ethical questions mobilities throw up. Usually these questions are premised in terms of 'sustainability'. How will we survive in the future if we continue living and moving in the ways we have always done? Implying some degradation or loss, some commentators have asked whether mobilities will inevitably undermine the social and physical environment of the future, and if there will be some degradation as a result. Perhaps it is difficult to imagine any more pressing ethical question than the effect of mobility on the environment, although there has been a tendency to divorce environment and sustainability from the social, when, of course, they should be entwined. What these issues demand or imply is a responsibility for mobility, i.e. we should take responsibility for our mobile choices and decisions, and for the mobility politics and policies that we support, vote on or resist.

Spaces, systems and infrastructures

Mobilities, we might say, are often routed in networks because they follow and are facilitated by infrastructures that carry or mediate mobile subjects and things. There is a feeling of automaticity to some mobilities that do not require simple motive human force to move them, but are shunted and shuttled to and fro by systems of pipes and cables, copper wires and fibre-optics that deliver energy, information and services to our homes and other locations (Thrift and French 2002). Mobilities are seemingly techo-mediated and choreographed. They are 'entubulated' (Bissell and Fuller 2011) and restrained into the sorts of architectures the architect Paul Andreau became famous for in Paris-Roissy Airport. This kind of structuring of mobility – away from chaotic, aimless or 'free' movement – would even be used by Deleuze and Guattari (1988) as an exemplar of 'state power', striating space with hydraulic and legible pathways in order to administer and manage populations. Thus even a space apparently absent of infrastructure, such as the sea, is deeply overlain by a skein and system of navigation markers and international and geopolitical signatures, as Philip Steinberg (2001) has shown, just as mobile GPS technology relies on very distant satellite infrastructure for boats and ships to make their way.

That is not to say, however, that such a focus on infrastructure has been self-evident in the context of mobilities research. While the development of specific mobility infrastructures has been a focus for many transport historians, historians of technology and historical geographers, mobility infrastructures have been somewhat under-explored by social scientists focusing on contemporary mobility, in part because they remain hidden or 'sunk' underneath our roads and streets, and in-amongst the fibers of our buildings and homes (Graham and Marvin 2001). Infrastructures are often inaccessible and unknowable, being tucked away in hard-to-reach places. Some infrastructures are purposively secret or elite, or lie in impenetrable, secure spaces, being deemed to constitute the 'vital' infrastructures or systems of our societies (Collier and Lakoff 2008). Scholars such as Trevor Paglen and Bradley Garrett have made fascinating moves to explore these highly secret and militarized spaces, such as networks of extraordinary rendition, or simply those forgotten or hidden enclaves where the best infrastructural services are excluded from those who need them most. Aside from this more practical 'infiltration' of infrastructures of rendition/torture and elite network spaces, the scholarship of academics such as Stephen Graham and Simon Marvin has worked to 'reveal' or open out these sites to critical scrutiny. Indeed, if we cannot see or know these spaces, then how can we interrogate them politically?

Graham and Marvin's (2001) literally *ground*-breaking work explores how infrastructurally facilitated technological mobilities not only express but reproduce and even reinforce highly uneven relationships of power. In the manner of Massey's discussion of 'power-geometry' (Massey 1993), infrastructural access is not deemed to be a universal right, especially as many states and governments have withdrawn their role as the sole provider of infrastructure within the pillars of welfare policy. Rather, technological mobilities tend to be provided to the most well-off and privileged, while poor access, poor quality services or simply no access at all – whether to health care, other welfare services, voting, education or employment – may have detrimental effects upon one's life-chances and futures.

These kinds of 'technological mobilities' are frequently described as being ungrounded or superficial, but this overlooks the physicality of infrastructures which permit techno-mediated communication and appear to collapse distance and compress space. Early conceptions of the internet as some kind of frontier, 'wild west' or road to nowhere of limitless freedoms and virtual travel were incredibly seductive. And yet, while many researchers would question this sort of account of virtual space, far less seemed to be said about the physical infrastructure of servers, switches, satellites and the really 'grounded' hardware technologies through which data and information are sorted and processed. Grounding infrastructures is incredibly important because we gain a greater sense of the embeddedness of mobility infrastructures within semi-fixed and very real material settings and cultures. What's more, attending to the embeddedness of infrastructure can highlight the vulnerability of those systems and, moreover, the fragility of the kinds of mobile life that depend on them. What happens when our mobility systems break down, when infrastructures fail (Graham 2009)? In the past decade we've seen countless examples of network disruption. Hundred-mile-long traffic jams in China. Thousands stranded in the Astrodome in New Orleans during and after Hurricane Katrina. Hundreds of thousands stranded due to the ash cloud from the eruption of a volcano in Iceland (Birchnell and Büscher 2011). When mobility infrastructures like airports, roads and public transport systems fail, huge societal disruption is often the result, with very real implications for the survival of individuals and social structures.

It's not only in disaster zones that power outages, large-scale congestion or impoverished mobility systems can occur, either. Formalized mobility infrastructures are, to a certain extent, not the things all of us have the luxury of living with, despite our geographical proximity to them. Localities can be very easily 'bypassed' in terms of their access to infrastructural services. While some infrastructures might be very uneven in social distribution and quality, others are simply unattainable. In many parts of the global south infrastructure is not simply absent, but it is accessed 'informally'. This does not mean an urban poor making-do, but explicitly and deliberately living outside 'formal' legal regulations. For many, this is more than the exception of urban mobility politics but actually the rule (Gandy 2008; Roy 2005).

Materialities

This discussion of grounded infrastructures highlights the importance of the mobilities of a wide array of 'things' to mobilities research. Inspired by a 'material turn' across the social sciences and humanities – drawing upon post-humanist, relational and actor-network philosophies, as well as work in anthropology, sociology, archaeology, design and related disciplines – there has been a widespread rethinking (or re-feeling) of what the 'social' might be. Indeed, the refiguring of the social as mobile has led to a serious engagement with the role of material things (such as fuel or food) as mobile objects, exploring the emergence of complex assemblies of objects and bodies.

A now-classic example of this trend is John Law's description of the assembly of a fifteenth- and sixteenth-century Portuguese man-o'-war ship (Law 1986). Exploring the complex arrangement of the ship as a combination of men, ropes and rigging, masts and timbers, the ship is understood as a relatively immutable mobile. In other words, the ship's extraordinary mobility in Europe's imperial powers is due to its relative stability and its ability to hold together as a stable and reliable base for exploration and empire building. As a working unit, the organizational structure of the ship relied upon a coherent assembly of bodies, objects and hierarchies to move it. Should this organization break apart, the ship may as well break upon the rocks as it loses its capacity for navigation – in essence, it loses its organizational integrity to move from one place to the next. However, just as we can learn from informal infrastructures, networks can be improvised. The apparently fixed networks of an 'immutable mobile' can become mutable by tinkering, adjustment and change, creating flexibilities in the associations between and within objects. For instance, Law and Mol's (2001) example of a 'mutable mobile' is the Zimbabwean bush pump that achieved both mobility and flexibility as it moved between different places and in different contexts. Perhaps another example would be a virus or the mobilities of disease, which appear to change shape and mutate as they move across different spaces and between different organisms and species. Ironically enough, then, the non-human or inhuman mobiles that have enabled the provision or supply of water networks can also be threatening, as transgenic and zoonotic organisms piggy-back on aviation networks, commodity movements across borders, and infrastructure linking localities of communities in cities.

What all of these examples highlight is the formal and informal arrangement or organization of humans and technologies into what we might call 'systems'. One of the most obvious of these is what has become known as automobility. To describe automobility as a system does more than consider the embodied interaction between car, driver and passenger as a mutual imbrication of practices, habits, feelings, sensations and affects that we might associate with the feeling of car travel (Sheller 2004; Urry 2004). Of course, driving can be understood as a skill that we learn as we become or take on the role of the driver (Merriman 2009). Driving is clearly far more than a functional movement from A to B; the car is no mere utility. Automobility has meant social status. A fact of social mobility, the car has been rooted in all sorts of social and cultural life, from the drive-in cinema, food and road-side advertising to the growth of post-war consumerism and suburban living. The extent to which all this constitutes a system is important when we consider how something like automobile travel may be embedded within broader societal, economic systems of production and labour, industries and resources and entire service economies. According to authors such as John Urry, Kingsley Dennis and others, this leads to actors being 'locked-in' to these systems. In other words, systems such as that of the car have achieved such permanence that they have become almost obdurate. So it is not so much the fact that driving or car cessation is a difficult choice, but it becomes nigh-on unthinkable because of the lack of alternatives and its embeddedness within social life (Dennis and Urry 2009). The system of the car, therefore, has become incredibly difficult to shape or govern, although we are seeing the growth of car use and ownership faltering in some instances.

The problem and consequences of all this is that the system of automobility relies heavily upon the liquidity of not only capital but also fuel. It is oil that fuelled the twentieth century's extraordinary growth in car-based travel. And it is oil that criss-crosses the globe from oil fields in the Persian Gulf, Russia, North Sea, and potentially the Arctic. First, this means that some of our planet's dwindling resources are dedicated towards enabling our cars and aircraft to keep going. Second, it means that car travel and many other forms of automotorized mobility have not inconsiderable effects upon the environment and our residential and commuting patterns. From congestion to reductions in air-quality, urban heat island effects, smog and more, the car and more general societal reliance on oil has distinctive and potentially irreversible effects on our environments and public health.

Finally, the sense that these resources have been unlocked, sometimes from right under our feet, tells part of a much wider story about mobile ontologies – a feeling that the ground itself is moving. Of course we see stark reminders of this in disasters such as the Deepwater Horizon explosion and oil spill in 2010, when an estimated 4.9 million barrels (or 779 million litres) of oil spilled into the Gulf of Mexico – with extensive effects on tourism, animal and bird migration and the broader economy of the Southern coastal states of the United States. In other events, earthquakes under the ocean floor have created tsunamis that have destroyed towns and cities with their power. Attending to the complexity of the very mobile, fluid and often primal and volatile materialities of the environment is important, not least because it can help us to rethink more everyday senses of land and landscape, matter and environment through ontologies attuned to process, flow and drift. This may force us to attend to the simple matter of the matter upon which our mobile lives depend.

Subjects

One of the caricatures we opened the introduction with was that of the hyper-mobile individual. This figure is not new, referencing a longer history of mobile subjects that have drawn upon and fed into quite powerful ideologies of national progress and nation-state building. Some of the most powerful stories are the individualist and pioneering narratives associated with the 'narration' of the United States, or indeed more recent neo-liberal political and economic policies that seem to emphasize the flexibility of the mobile worker who crosses national territorial borders by enjoying relaxed visa regimes and 'flexible citizenship' (Ong 1999).

The mobile subject is certainly one of the new mobility paradigm's main objects of enquiry, and this section of the book features perspectives on a range of different embodied mobile figures, from soldiers to children. The diversity of subjects gestures towards an important corrective within the literature, where scholars are trying to represent the lives of mobile subjects who have been marginalized, excluded and displaced, and who are often sidelined within academic enquiry. Many mobility scholars are actively embracing and documenting the lives of mobile subjects and objects who have been silenced or marginalized, including women, the poor, the young and the old. What this adds up to is the recognition that mobilities are always multiple and differentiated. Or, rather, different subjects are often placed in quite different ways in relation to their mobility. This means that mobilities researchers seek to attend to the lives and experiences of mobile subjects, particularly the sorts of social structures and relations that produce highly uneven forms of mobility. Work on the mobilities of the super-rich has labelled the most extreme forms of mobility as being those of a 'kinetic elite'. Some of the leading contributions to the field explore what Doreen Massey (1993) calls a 'power geometry' that associates different subjects with different capacities to be mobile. In other words, Massey has led us to ask how the mobilities of some can depend on the (im)mobility of others.

Relational approaches to mobility teach us that mobilities almost never happen in isolation. Neither do mobilities necessarily imply singularity. Rather, mobilities often happen amongst collectives of people and things. Some mobilities seem entirely dependent on others (Ferguson 2009), so that we see mutual relationships of support and care within and outside familial structures such as the institutional provision of welfare. Research on the mobilities of care-givers provides remarkable insight into these possibilities.

Mobilities researchers have sought to explain the socialities of mobility and how social relations happen on the move, not least because mobilities often involve all manner of encounters that are sometimes quite difficult to predict or engineer. Perhaps this is what gives our public spaces their sense of bricolage and spontaneity, as well as moments of difficulty. For instance, recent examples of incivility and racist abuse on Britain's public transport system have been captured and circulated by video. Whether they rehearse longer histories of racial, religious and nationalist tension, new mixtures of cultures, races and faiths might spark their own eruptions of discord and even violence. What might emerge from these encounters of mobile publics in new configurations and intensities of mobility? Helen Wilson has called these 'passenger propinquities' (Wilson 2011), and they raise significant questions about how we travel together.

What happens to how we might think about the social or the political in these contexts? Moving about together can perhaps challenge our assumptions as to where our subjects are, or, indeed, who they are, as it feels as if something is in the air, moving or expressing the sentiment of a crowd on a busy transport system. We might remember moments of elation travelling back from a sporting event with other fans, or conversely how those encounters might seem strange and threatening. How do feelings appear to vibrate or resonate through mobile collectives (Bissell 2010)? Is that why they are so powerful in public gatherings and marches? Perhaps they are equally threatening. What gives emotion the power to seemingly hover like an atmosphere suspended between us? And to what extent might the things we travel with lend an agency to these situations?

Events

A great deal of research into events takes as a starting point spectacular mega-events such as sporting occasions like the recent Olympic Games in London with its related security concerns (Boyle and Haggerty 2009). However, when scholars talk about mobilities they often evoke a momentary or temporary event, or a series of memorable events: walking, driving, running, flying, cycling, passenger-ing, commuting, busking, sailing, boating, skiing, hunting. Mobilities are articulated in relation to, and as, a series of other sorts of social functions and pursuits, from travelling to work and numerous leisure activities, to going on holiday, leaving a country in search of work or sanctuary, or to hopping on a bus to get to the supermarket. Mobile events might appear to serve as contexts that provide meanings and purpose to a distinct action – from frantically leaving one's home to escape from a mudslide, to embarking on a protest march. In some cases, particular mobilities may be read as responses to unexpected, unexplained or 'natural' events and occurrences, although even 'natural disasters' are mapped out and rehearsed in emergency response plans and in auto-mated models. Other mobilities might seem more predictable or indeed controllable, but what is clear is that a broad range of experts and authorities are concerned with the movements of all manner of things – from commuters, migrants, criminals and the diseased, to illicit substances, nuclear materials, oil, animals, money and weather systems. And in all of these cases, becoming stuck, being bogged down, or being detected may also be a crucial event.

Events are also how our mobilities become articulated as meaningful activities within different systems and categories of knowledge. Considering mobilities as events enables mobility to be made legible as much more than an undifferentiated flow, but rather as iden-tifiable activities that might concern a particular organization or institution. For instance, Passenger Focus, a British passenger advocacy group, is concerned with and represents the rights of passengers on Britain's public transport systems. The commute is of primary con-cern to a group like this, as well as to different transport providers and corporations who direct most of their resources to highly profitable commuter journeys. Within the commute, an event like congestion may be regularly on the lips of the consumers whom Passenger Focus and other passenger interest and road users groups represent. This focused investment in the commuter can pose problems for those who want to move outside of this daily event for other purposes, such as accessing health care and social services outside of peak travel hours or in other locations. The International Organization for Migration (www.iom.int/) similarly researches, lobbies and writes strategic policy on the affairs of migration in an international context, especially in relation to migrant populations from outside the EU. Here we might reflect on the governance of events such as weddings. Weddings routinely involve complex orderings of mobility and proximity in the social, familial and religious obligations to travel to the event (Urry 2002). But frequently such events also involve mul-tiple governance assemblages – for example when a non-EU or non-US citizen seeks to marry an EU or US citizen. This can lead to the reconfiguring of a wedding as a series of multiple events, of multiple weddings in different geographical locations to gain the neces-sary paperwork rather than an event as a single point in time. Issues of love can thus become governmentalized (see Constable 2004; Mai and King 2009). The point is that identifying mobile events allows us to make sense of the technological systems that societies depend on and affect.

More broadly, an emphasis on the 'evental' character of mobilities shifts our focus from the subjects, infrastructures or systems of mobility as fixed entities to instead bring into view the performative practice of mobile actions, or indeed planned actions of non–mobility (including strikes). To stay still is also an event, as is to move voluntarily or involuntarily. We can ask: What instigates particular events? How are activity chains associated with mobilities strung together? And how does the organization of events of moving and staying shape social relations, influence infrastructure planning or challenge mobility regimes that govern who and what can move? When is mobility a necessary event, and when can it be deferred or replaced by virtual mobility? How is the mobilization of the event assisted by new mobile and locationally aware technologies? Ultimately, research itself becomes envisioned as an event, as mobility studies has brought into play new methodologies which seek to engage in a shifting and mobile field full of intersecting and transactional events.

Methodologies

Sheller and Urry's article 'The new mobilities paradigm' called for new research methods that could respond and prove sensitive to the demands of the mobility turn. Thus we have seen interactional and conversational analysis with people as they move; mobile ethnography involving itinerant movement with people and objects, including co-present immersion in various modes of movement; after-the-fact interviews and focus groups about mobility; the keeping of textual, pictorial, or digital time–space diaries; various methods of cyber-research, cyberethnography and computer simulations; imaginative travel using multimedia methods attentive to the affective and atmospheric feeling of place; the tracking of affective objects that attach memories to place; and finally methods that measure the spatial structuring and temporal pulse of transfer points and places of in-between-ness, in which the circulation of people and objects is slowed or stopped, as well as facilitated and speeded up (Hein *et al.* 2008; Büscher and Urry 2009; Büscher *et al.* 2011; Fincham *et al.* 2010; D'Andrea *et al.* 2011). Mobilities research methods have made definite efforts to either be 'on the move' or to 'simulate intermittent mobility' (Sheller and Urry 2006: 217). Furthermore, there has been an emphasis on improvisation, flexibility and novelty in approaches that have been somehow recombined or reapplied in more mobile settings.

It is sometimes unclear what the role of slower, sited or historical research methods might be in recent characterizations of mobilities research, although there has also been a growing interest in historical research on mobilities. For some scholars, innovation in 'mobile methods' is essential because of the weakness or failure of more conventional methods, but the danger is that we simply reduce mobilities research to a particular kind of social science research which relies upon participative and ethnographic methods and new technologies which seem to allow researchers to see, be or move with their research subjects and objects (Merriman, in press). Established methods such as archival research and interviews are not only useful, but also very diverse and ever-changing, and are frequently reworked and adapted to particular situations, providing insights into experiences or decision-making processes which may not be 'visible' or apprehendable on the ground. Thus, there has been detailed work to explore the representations and performances of driving, population movements and sea travel, and we should not forget that archives and libraries can also act as immersive settings of encounter and surprise.

There are further challenges to this evolving agenda. First, much more work has to be done to 'bridge the quantitative–qualitative divide' (Goetz *et al.* 2009). This is particularly important if the mobilities research agenda is to be able to do a number of things. While transportation and population geography and areas of migration studies have been able to make sense of longitudinal and quantitative data to establish frames of analysis along longer-term time horizons and vaster spatial scales, much mobilities research remains more attuned to smaller-scale processes and events, and thicker forms of description and interpretation. Recently, a few scholars have sought to explore approaches that can complement and triangulate different sets and sorts of data. This becomes particularly vital if we take seriously Thrift's assertion that so much of our world is being measured, anticipated and tracked through 'qualculation' – in real time (Thrift 2007). How might research get to grips with vast new data sets that express both qualitative and quantitative information, and how can researchers access data which is frequently seen to have a commercial and political sensitivity? How might research methods utilize recorded and real-time mobilities data through visualization techniques that make that data more accessible to lay or expert audiences? How might 'mashups' of different sorts of mobility information enable different sorts of perspectives? And given the disposition of public policy agendas and debates towards quantitative rather than qualitative data, should mobilities research engage these approaches more imaginatively when there is far more possibility to intervene in public policy debates that will reshape modes of transport decision-making and the future investments it might be critical of?

References

Aas, F., Hundhus, H. and Lomell, H. (eds) (2008) *Technologies of Insecurity: The surveillance of everyday life* (London: Routledge).

Ahmed, S., Castaneda, C., Fortier, A.-M. and Sheller, M. (eds) (2003) *Uprootings/Regroundings: Questions of home and migration* (Oxford and New York: Berg).

Anderson, B. and Harrison, P. (eds) (2012) *Taking-place: Non-representational theories and geography* (Aldershot: Ashgate).

Appadurai, A. (1996) *Modernity at Large: Cultural dimensions of globalization* (Minneapolis: University of Minnesota Press).

Augé, M. (1995) *Non-places* (London: Verso).

Bergman, S. and Sager, T. (eds) (2008) *The Ethics of Mobilities: Rethinking place, exclusion, freedom and the environment* (Farnham: Ashgate).

Birch, A. (2012) "Editorial: Site-specificity and mobility" *Contemporary Theatre Review*, 22(2), 199–202.

Birtchnell, T. and Büscher, M. (2011) "Stranded: an eruption of disruption" *Mobilities*, 6(1), 1–9.

Bissell, D. (2010) "Passenger mobilities: affective atmospheres and the sociality of public transport" *Environment and Planning D: Society and Space*, 28(2), 270–289.

Bissell, D. (2013) "Pointless mobilities: rethinking proximity through the loops of neighbourhood" *Mobilities*, 8(3), 349–367.

Bissell, D. and Fuller, G. (2011) "Stillness unbound" in D. Bissell and G. Fuller (eds) *Stillness in a Mobile World* (London: Routledge).

Bissell, D., Adey, P. and Laurier, E. (2011) "Introduction to the special issue on geographies of the passenger" *Journal of Transport Geography*, 19, 1007–1009.

Blunt, A. (2007) "Cultural geographies of migration: mobility, transnationality and diaspora" *Progress in Human Geography*, 31(5), 684–694.

Boden, D. and Molotch, H. (1994) "The compulsion to proximity" in R. Friedland and D. Boden (eds) *Now/here: Time, Space and Modernity* (Berkeley: University of California Press).

Boyle, P. and Haggerty, K. (2009) "Spectacular security: mega-events and the security complex" *International Political Sociology*, 3(3), 257–274.

Büscher, M. and Urry, J. (2009) "Mobile methods and the empirical" *European Journal of Social Theory*, 12(1), 99–116.

Büscher, M., Urry, J. and Witchger, K. (eds) (2011) *Mobile Methods* (London: Routledge).

Chard, C. (1999) *Pleasure and Guilt on the Grand Tour: Travel writing and imaginative geography 1600–1830* (Manchester: Manchester University Press).

Cliff A. D., Martin, R. L. and Ord, J. K. (1974) "Evaluating the friction of distance parameter in gravity models" *Regional Studies*, 8, 281–286.

Clifford, J. (1997) *Routes* (Cambridge, MA: Harvard University Press).

Coleman, S. and Eade, J. (eds) (2004) *Reframing Pilgrimage: Cultures in motion* (London: Routledge).

Collier, S. J. and Lakoff, A. (2008) "Distributed preparedness: the spatial logic of domestic security in the United States" *Environment and Planning D: Society and Space*, 26(1), 7–28.

Conradson, D. and Latham, A. (2005) "Transnational urbanism: attending to everyday practices and mobilities" *Journal of Ethnic and Migration Studies*, 31(2), 227–233.

Constable, N. (ed.) (2004) *Cross-Border Marriages: Gender and mobility in transnational Asia* (Pennsylvania: University of Pennsylvania Press).

Cresswell, T. (2006) *One the Move: Mobility in the modern western world* (London: Routledge).

D'Andrea, A., Ciolfi, L. and Gray, B. (2011) "Methodological challenges and innovations in mobilities research" *Mobilities*, 6(2), 149–160.

Deleuze, G. and Guattari, F. (1988) *A Thousand Plateaus* (London: Athlone).

Dennis, K. and Urry, J. (2009) *After the Car* (Cambridge: Polity Press).

De Souza e Silva, A. and Sutko, D. (eds) (2009) *Digital Cityscapes: Merging digital and urban playspaces* (New York: Peter Lang).

Edensor, T. (ed.) (2010) *Geographies of Rhythm: Nature, place, mobilities and bodies* (Farnham: Ashgate).

Edwards, J. and Grauland, R. (2012) *Mobility at Large: Globalization, textuality and innovative travel writing* (Liverpool: Liverpool University Press).

Farman, J. (2011) *Mobile Interface Theory* (London: Routledge).

Ferguson, H. (2009) "Driven to care: the car, automobility and social work" *Mobilities*, 4(2), 275–293.

Fincham, B., McGuinness, M. and Murray, L. (2010) "Introduction" in B. Fincham, M. McGuinness and L. Murray (eds) *Mobile Methodologies* (Basingstoke: Palgrave Macmillan) 1–10.

Fujii, J. A. (1999) "Intimate alienation: Japanese urban rail and the commodification of urban subjects" *Differences: A Journal of Feminist Cultural Studies*, 11(2), 106–133.

Gandy, M. (2008) "Landscapes of disaster: water, modernity and urban fragmentation in Mumbai" *Environment and Planning A*, 40, 108–130.

Goetz, A. R., Vowles, T. M. and Tierney, S. (2009) "Bridging the qualitative–quantitative divide in transport geography" *The Professional Geographer*, 61(3), 323–335.

Gottdiener, M. (ed.) (2001) *Life in the Air: Surviving the New Culture of Air Travel* (Lanham, MD: Rowman & Littlefield).

Graham, S. (ed.) (2009) *Disrupted Cities: When infrastructure fails* (New York: Routledge).

Graham, S. and Marvin, S. (2001) *Splintering Urbanism: Networked infrastructures, technological mobilities and the urban condition* (London and New York: Routledge).

Hannam, K., Sheller, M. and Urry, J. (2006) "Editorial: Mobilities, immobilities and moorings" *Mobilities*, 1(1), 1–22.

Harrison, D. (1988) *The Sociology of Modernization and Development* (London: Unwin Hyman).

Hein, J. R., Evans, J. and Jones, P. (2008) "Mobile methodologies: theory, technology and practice" *Geography Compass*, 2(5), 1266–1285.

Hjorth, L., Burgess, J. and Richardson, I. (eds) (2012) *Studying Mobile Media: Cultural technologies, mobile communication and the iPhone* (London: Routledge).

Hopkins, L. (2010) "Englishmen abroad: mobility and nationhood in Dido, Queen of Carthage and Edward II" *English*, 59(227), 324–348.

Jansen, C. J. (1970) *Readings in the Sociology of Migration* (Oxford: Pergamon).

Kaplan, C. (1996) *Questions of Travel* (London: Duke University Press).

Khoo, S.-M. and Rau, H. (2009) "Movements, mobilities and the politics of hazardous waste" *Environmental Politics*, 18(6), 960–980.

King, R. (2012) "Geography and migration studies: retrospect and prospect" *Population, Space and Place*, 18(2): 134–153.

Laurier, E. (2004) "Doing office work on the motorway" *Theory, Culture & Society*, 21(4–5), 261–277.

Law, J. (1986) "On the methods of long-distance control: vessels, navigation and the Portuguese route to India" in J. Law (ed.) *Power, Action and Belief: A new sociology of knowledge* (London: Routledge) 234–263.

Law, J. and Mol, A. (2001) "Situating technoscience: an inquiry into spatialities" *Environment and Planning D: Society and Space*, 19(5), 609–621.

Lipset, S. M. and Bendix, R. (1959) *Social Mobility in Industrial Society* (Berkeley: University of California Press).

Lyons, G. and Urry, J. (2005) "Travel time use in the information age" *Transportation Research A*, 39, 257–276.

Mai, N. and King, R. (2009) "Love, sexuality and migration: mapping the issue(s)" *Mobilities*, 4(3), 295–307.

Manning, E. (2009) *Relationscapes: Movement, art, philosophy* (London: The MIT Press).

Marcus, G. E. (1998) *Ethnography through Thick and Thin* (Princeton: Princeton University Press).

Massey, D. (1993) "Power-geometry and a progressive sense of place" in J. Bird, B. Curtis, T. Putnam, G. Robertson and L. Tickner (eds) *Mapping the Futures: Local cultures, global change* (London: Routledge) 59–69.

Merriman, P. (2004) "Driving places: Marc Augé, non-places and the geographies of England's M1 motorway" *Theory, Culture & Society*, 21(4–5), 145–167.

Merriman, P. (2009) "Automobility and the geographies of the car" *Geography Compass*, 3(2), 586–559.

Merriman, P. (2012a) "Human geography without time-space" *Transactions of the Institute of British Geographers*, 37(1), 13–27.

Merriman, P. (2012b) *Mobility, Space and Culture* (London: Routledge).

Merriman, P. (in press) "Rethinking mobile methods" *Mobilities*, doi: 10.1080/17450101.2013.784540.

Moores, S. (2012) *Media, Place and Mobility* (Basingstoke: Palgrave Macmillan).

Morley, D. (2000) *Home Territories: Media, mobility, and identity* (London: Routledge).

Mountz, A. (2010) *Seeking Asylum: Human smuggling and bureaucracy at the border* (Minneapolis and London: University of Minnesota Press).

Mountz, A. (2011) "Specters at the port of entry: understanding state mobilities through an ontology of exclusion" *Mobilities*, 6(3), 317–334.

Ong, A. (1999) *Flexible Citizenship: The cultural logics of transnationality* (Durham, NC: Duke University Press).

Packer, J. and Wiley, S. (eds) (2012) *Communication Matters: Materialist approaches to media, mobility, and networks* (London and New York: Routledge).

Palmer, B. D. (2005) "Early modern mobility: players, payments, and patrons" *Shakespeare Quarterly*, 56(3), 259–305.

Parkins, W. (2009) *Mobility and Modernity in Women's Novels, 1850s–1930s: Women moving dangerously* (Basingstoke: Palgrave Macmillan).

Relph, E. (1976) *Place and Placelessness* (London: Pion).

Roy, A. (2005) "Urban informality: towards an epistemology of planning" *Journal of the American Planning Association*, 71(2), 147–158.

Roy, S. and Hannam, K. (2012) "Embodying the mobilities of the Darjeeling Himalayan Railway" *Mobilities*, forthcoming.

Said, E. (2000) *Out of Place: A memoir* (New York: Vintage).

Said, E. (2001) *Reflections on Exile: And other literary and cultural essays* (New York: Granta).

Salazar, N. B. and Smart, A. (eds) (2011) "Anthropological takes on (im)mobility" *Identities: Global Studies in Culture and Power*, 18(6) i–ix.

Schivelbusch, W. (1978) *The Railway Journey* (Oxford: Blackwell).

Seamon, D. (1979) *A Geography of the Lifeworld* (London: Croom Helm).

Sheller, M. (2004) "Automotive emotions feeling the car" *Theory, Culture & Society*, 21(4–5), 221–242.

Sheller, M. (2014, in press) *Aluminum Dreams: Lightness, speed, modernity* (Cambridge, MA: MIT Press).

Sheller, M. and Urry, J. (2006) "The new mobilities paradigm" *Environment and Planning A*, 38, 207–226.

Steinberg, P. (2001) *The Social Construction of the Ocean* (Cambridge: Cambridge University Press).

Thrift, N. (1990) "Transport and communication 1730–1914" in R. A. Dodgson and R. A. Butlin (eds) *An Historical Geography of England and Wales (Second Edition)* (London: Academic Press) 453–486.

Thrift, N. (1994) "Inhuman geographies: landscapes of speed, light and power" in P. Cloke, M. Doel, D. Matless, M. Phillips and N. Thrift, *Writing the Rural* (London: PCP) 191–248.

Thrift, N. (1996) *Spatial Formations* (London: Sage).

Thrift, N. (2004) "Movement-space: changing domain of thinking resulting from the development of new kinds of spatial awareness" *Economy & Society*, 33(4), 582–604.

Thrift, N. (2007) *Non-Representational Theory: Space, politics, affect* (London: Routledge).

Thrift, N. and French, S. (2002) "The automatic production of space" *Transactions of the Institute of British Geographers*, 27, 309–335.

Tuan, Y.-F. (1977) *Space and Place: The perspective of experience* (Minneapolis: University of Minnesota Press).

Urry, J. (1990) *The Tourist Gaze* (London: Sage).

Urry, J. (2002) "Mobility and proximity" *Sociology*, 36(2), 255–274.

Urry, J. (2004) "The 'system' of automobility" *Theory, Culture & Society*, 21(4–5), 25–39.

Uteng, Tanu P. and Cresswell, T. (eds) (2008) *Gendered Mobilities* (Aldershot: Ashgate).

Vannini, P. (2012) "In time, out of time: rhythmanalyzing ferry mobilities" *Time and Society*, 21(2), 241–269.

Verstraete, G. (2004) "Technological frontiers and the politics of mobility in the European Union" in S. Ahmed, C. Castañeda, A. M. Fortier and M. Sheller (eds) *Uprootings/Regroundings: Questions of home and migration* (London: Berg) 225–50.

Waters, J. (2012) "Geographies of international education: mobilities and the reproduction of social (dis)advantage" *Geography Compass*, 6(3), 123–136.

Wilkie, F. (2012) "Site-specific performance and the mobility turn" *Contemporary Theatre Review*, 22(2), 203–212.

Wilson, H. (2011) "Passing propinquities in the multicultural city: the everyday encounters of bus passengering" *Environment and Planning A*, 43(3), 634–649.

Wolff, J. (1993) "On the road again: metaphors of travel in cultural criticism" *Cultural Studies*, 7(2), 224–239.

Yago, G. (1983) "The sociology of transportation" *American Review of Sociology*, 9, 171–190.

Section One

Introduction: Genealogies, Philosophies, Approaches

In an essay entitled 'Nietzsche, genealogy, history', the French philosopher Michel Foucault explains how genealogy is opposed to 'the search for "origins"' and the belief that one can 'capture the exact essence of things, their purest possibilities' (Foucault 1986, pp.77, 78). This incessant searching for origins and the exact point of emergence 'assumes the existence of immobile forms that precede the external world of accident and succession' (Foucault 1986, p.78); but in an ever-shifting, pluralistic and mobile world, could we ever recover 'a' moment of emergence, point of departure, or single history of events? Foucault's thinking brings us close to the later arguments of James Clifford, Paul Gilroy and others that, to understand cultures (including diasporic cultures), we need to trace the *routes* of cultural connection, flow and relation, rather than trace the *roots* of cultures (Clifford 1997; Gilroy 1993, 1995). Mobilities, cultures and identities can best be approached through an attention to routes and paths, flows and connections; and this anti-foundational (and frequently post-structuralist and anti-essentialist) critique of the search for origins could also be applied to attempts to reflect on the recent history of 'the mobilities turn' (Hannam *et al.* 2006) or 'new mobilities paradigm' (Sheller and Urry 2006).

The editors of this handbook have been to a number of conferences and workshops where attention often focused on the history and origins of mobilities research and the historical shifts implied by a Kuhnian language of 'paradigms' and 'turns'. Was there really a (wholesale) turn? How far and deep has the impact of this research been? Has it permeated mainstream social science and humanities research? Or can it best be called a new sub-, inter- or multi-disciplinary field? More fundamentally, is 'mobilities research' that new — whether in terms of its focus, theories or methods? For some academics, the announcement of a new paradigm or turn failed to acknowledge the many traditions of research on mobility, transport and communications, which could be seen to precede or underpin this new field. How should we understand the relationship between transport history, migration studies, transport geography, tourism studies, histories of travel writing, and this new field? Should mobility scholars work harder to situate their field or are they more specifically concerned with studying *new forms* of mobility or developing *new ways* of studying existing mobilities? If we were to trace the *routes* of mobility studies, we would almost inevitably find that specific individuals, publications, conferences, networks and organisations have been influential in shaping mobilities research, but it would be fruitless to try and identify the *origins* or *roots* of mobilities research, if this was even desirable.

This section is comprised of a series of contributions which collectively trace a genealogy of some of the different ways scholars have approached mobility and mobilities. The aim is not to be exhaustive, so instead we have commissioned chapters which examine how specific disciplines and traditions of thinking have engaged with concepts of mobility, as well as the influence of mobility studies on certain traditions of thinking. The section opens with a series of chapters on very different established traditions of thinking about mobility and movement, which trace how these different traditions have cultivated a rich seam of research on mobility, as well as how these areas have responded to recent research associated with the 'new mobilities paradigm'.

In 'Geography and Transport', Jon Shaw and Iain Docherty examine the impact of new mobilities scholarship on research within the long-established sub-discipline of transport geography. As an area of research that rapidly expanded alongside positivist traditions of spatial scientific research utilising quantitative methods in the 1950s and 1960s, transport geography has often been framed as a sub-discipline that remained largely unaffected by the philosophical influences of Marxism, humanism, feminism and post-structuralism – which reshaped much human geography during the 1970s, 1980s and 1990s – as well as the broader cultural turn within human geography during the 1980s and 1990s. And yet, as Shaw and Docherty show, transport geography has not been impervious to broader disciplinary trends that have shaped geography over the past forty years, with increasing numbers of transport geographers drawing upon qualitative methods and the work of mobilities scholars since the heyday of transport geography in the 1960s and 1970s. The past five years have seen an increasing dialogue and intersection of interests between scholars working in transport geography and mobility studies, and in order to highlight the kinds of multi-method and multiple-perspective studies which could engage with both traditions of thinking, Shaw and Docherty outline the diverse and complementary ways in which one could trace the geographies of the 10.44 train from Plymouth to London in the UK.

In the following chapter, Colin Divall outlines some of the major changes which have occurred in the field of 'transport history' over the fifteen years since 1998, when transport history was still dominated by the approaches of social and economic history, and the proto-typical study was a single-mode study of railways or canals in pre-twentieth-century Britain. Divall shows how developments in cultural history and mobility studies have led transport historians to focus as much attention on the consumption practices of transport users as the production of transport technologies, with recent work looking at air travel, car travel, the bicycle, walking and other modes, as well as broadening its focus to examine the subjectivities, representations and spaces of transport. In his position as the Head of the Institute of Railway Studies, a joint venture of the University of York and the UK's National Railway Museum, Divall has been in an almost unique position from which to reflect on the intersection of academic histories of transport and the representational imperatives and practices of transport museum curators and heritage practitioners, and he concludes his chapter with a call for academics to focus attention on what he calls the 'usable past'.

If there is a single discipline which has been most associated with the 'new mobilities paradigm' and 'the mobility turn', then it is most probably the discipline of sociology, marked by a series of land-mark articles and books in the early 2000s by sociologists Mimi Sheller and John Urry (Sheller and Urry 2000, 2006; Urry 2000, 2007). And yet, as Mimi Sheller suggests in her chapter on 'Sociology after the Mobilities Turn', many sociologists have been resistant to this newer body of work, and mobility studies appear to have gained more purchase in disciplines such as geography and transport studies. Sheller traces a genealogy of mobility studies within sociology, examining the work of early scholars on social mobility and urban morphology, as well as the emergence of recent research in which questions of history, power, friction, turbulence, capital, scale, practice, materiality, embodiment and rhythm have been coming to the fore. She also examines the key role of sociologists in developing new methodologies for understanding the ephemeral, embodied, and affective dimensions of mobility, a subject which is examined in more detail in Section Seven of this handbook.

In the fourth chapter Noel B. Salazar provides us with a critical insight into the ways in which anthropologists have approached the topic of mobility. The writings of prominent anthropologists such as Marc Augé (1995) and James Clifford (1997) have had a major influence on both theoretical and empirical research in mobility studies, but the long history of fieldwork, travel and ethnographic research undertaken by anthropologists also reveals the ways in which different practices of mobility underpin the practising of the discipline. In his chapter Salazar provides 'a short history' of anthropological engagements with 'ideas of mobility', tracing the distinctive methods anthropologists have used in their studies, as well as discussing traditions of research on borders and boundaries.

Within long-established fields such as transport history and transport geography there have been significant shifts in the philosophies, methods and conceptual approaches through which different kinds of mobility are often apprehended. Quantitative studies of mobility flows are ever-frequently joined (and in many cases replaced) by qualitative studies which trace the differential movements of people, ideas and things, and these shifts are particularly evident in the interdisciplinary field of 'migration studies', which is the subject of the fifth chapter, by Anne-Marie Fortier. Statistical patterns of international and internal migration have formed the core of many studies of migration, but with the increasing influence of social theory, cultural studies, post-colonialism, feminism, and political theory in debates surrounding migration, a wide range of new research questions and topics have come to the fore. In her chapter, Fortier shows how migration scholars have increasingly focused their attention on issues of diaspora, trans-nationalism, identity, citizenship, affect and social imaginaries, and she outlines the transformations in methodology which are associated with these conceptual shifts.

In the sixth chapter, Adrian Franklin traces the contours of the multi-disciplinary field of 'tourist studies', which he sees as springing from sociologies of leisure in the 1960s and 1970s. After discussing the emergence of tourism and leisure travel as fairly modern practices since the grand tours of the seventeenth and eighteenth centuries, organised tourism of the nineteenth century, and the emergence of mass tourism in the 1960s and 1970s, Franklin examines the different disciplinary perspectives which have cohered around this economic and cultural practice, whether by anthropologists, sociologists or geographers. While tourism studies is a diverse field, pursued by scholars interested in topics ranging from business, marketing and ecotourism, to tourist identities and embodiment, a subtle (though partial) cultural turn in tourist studies may be seen to predate the emergence of mobility studies, in part driven by John Urry's influential book *The Tourist Gaze* (Urry 1990).

The final two chapters in the section are on traditions of thinking – 'queer theory' and 'feminism' – which, on the face of it, may not appear to be primarily concerned with the phenomena of mobility. Tourism studies, migration studies, transport history and transport geography are, after all, primarily concerned with understanding particular forms and patterns of movement and mobility. The same cannot be said about 'feminism' and 'queer theory', or 'anthropology' or 'sociology', but as leading mobility scholars have gone to great efforts to emphasise, mobility 'is a thoroughly social facet of life imbued with meaning and power' (Cresswell 2006, p.4). The result, as mobility scholars and feminist theorists have argued, is that not everyone has the same capacity or ability to move, and neither do they have the same experiences of mobility. Feminists writing about mobility, displacement and nomadic theory were some of the first to highlight the differential politics of mobility (Wolff 1993; Kaplan 1996; McDowell 1996), while others have highlighted how issues of race, gender, class, sexuality, age, nationality, wealth and physical ability can all have an impact on our ability to move and our experiences of movement. In her chapter on 'Queer Theory', Natalie Oswin starts by outlining this concern with the differential politics of mobility, before highlighting the relative absence of queer theory and work on sexuality within mobility studies. After outlining the key dimensions of queer theory, Oswin then provides a detailed analysis of different 'queer mobilities', and how they have been influenced by global processes, national politics, migration, and urban and rural contexts.

Finally, in a chapter on 'Feminism and Gender', the mobility historian Georgine Clarsen provides a useful overview of the ways in which mobilities research has been animated by feminist theory. This can be located in research which has pursued the silences and omissions of women in the production of authoritative knowledge, such as in the ignored or maligned works of women travel writers. Clarsen also identifies mobilities research which has explored how women have been excluded from particular kinds of mobilities, public life and its opportunities, as can be seen in historical and contemporary accounts of public transport, buses, aviation, etc. Yet Clarsen also provides a crucial challenge to the mobilities agenda by asking whether the field has done enough. She argues that mobilities research should do more than just identify different kinds of 'gendered' mobility or silences in the accounts of disciplinary or scientific knowledge, advising that it should place those mobilities in their specific historical and discursive contexts, for not doing so 'can work to reinstall and naturalise those very power relations that feminists seek to understand and change'. Moreover, a 'critical' approach to mobility and gender would explore how both ideas of gender and notions of mobility are in fact produced through one another.

References

Augé, M. (1995) *Non-Places: Introduction to an anthropology of supermodernity*, London: Verso.

Clifford, J. (1997) *Routes: Travel and translation in the later twentieth century*, Cambridge, MA: Harvard University Press.

Cresswell, T. (2006) *On the Move: Mobility in the modern western world*, London: Routledge.

Foucault, M. (1986) 'Nietzsche, genealogy, history', in P. Rabinow (ed.) *The Foucault Reader*, Harmondsworth: Penguin, pp.76–100.

Gilroy, P. (1993) *The Black Atlantic: Modernity and double consciousness*, London: Verso.

Gilroy, P. (1995) 'Roots and routes: Black identity as an outernational project', in H. W. Harris, H. C. Blue and E. H. Griffith (eds) *Racial and Ethnic Identity: Psychological development and creative expression*, London: Routledge, pp.15–30.

Hannam, K., Sheller, M. and Urry, J. (2006) 'Editorial: Mobilities, immobilities and moorings', *Mobilities*, 1, pp.1–22.

Kaplan, C. (1996) *Questions of Travel*, London: Duke University Press.

McDowell, L. (1996) 'Off the road: alternative views of rebellion, resistance and "The Beats"', *Transactions of the Institute of British Geographers*, 21, pp.412–419.

Sheller, M. and Urry, J. (2000) 'The city and the car', *International Journal of Urban and Regional Research*, 24, pp.727–757.

Sheller, M. and Urry, J. (2006) 'The new mobilities paradigm', *Environment and Planning A*, 38, pp.207–226.

Urry, J. (1990) *The Tourist Gaze*, London: Sage.

Urry, J. (2000) *Sociology Beyond Societies*, London: Routledge.

Urry, J. (2007) *Mobilities*, Cambridge: Polity.

Wolff, J. (1993) 'On the road again: metaphors of travel in cultural criticism', *Cultural Studies*, 7, pp.224–239.

1

Geography and Transport

Jon Shaw and Iain Docherty

We sit writing these words on a ScotRail train service running along a newly completed stretch of line between Airdrie and Bathgate, in the Central Belt of Scotland. The line in question is the fourth rail link between Glasgow and Edinburgh and forms part of a larger investment programme to upgrade rail connectivity between the two cities and their hinterlands. This is not the first of our chapters or papers we have part-written on a train, and nor will it be the last. In addition to using our most common train journeys between Plymouth and London (Jon) and Glasgow and Edinburgh (Iain) to review lectures, respond to emails, catch up on reading or get through any number of other tasks, we occasionally meet up to make train journeys with the sole intention of exchanging research ideas or (as in this case) committing these ideas to paper. As transport geographers it seems odd now to think that until the last few years neither we nor our colleagues in the sub-discipline ever really gave much thought to making this practice of working on the move the object of systematic academic inquiry. We may well have been interested in the geography of the transport network on which we were travelling, or the regulatory environment that had influenced its extent and level of service, or the uneven spatial impact these have on economic development, or patterns of trip generation. Some of us would have made noises about particular gaps in the transport geography literature or suggested new research agendas (Hall 2004; Knowles 1993; Law 1999), but few would have dwelt beyond anecdote on the *experience* of travelling, or for that matter on how particular journeys are *represented* (Cresswell 2006). We would not have considered in any serious way the relationship between the 'travel space' – the bounded area in which individuals travel, such as a train carriage, bus or car – in which we found ourselves and our capacity for productive activity.

As is evident throughout this volume, work under the banner of mobilities has brought into sharp relief the significance of movement in human (and other) societies, especially in terms of its experience and representation. Much of what is now published moves far beyond the traditional interests of transport geographers, and this sometimes leads to transport geography being cast in an unflattering light by mobilities scholars. The stereotype of it being stuck in the analytical framework of spatial science surfaces from time to time as a counterpoint to the vibrant, extensive and agenda-setting approaches to movement typified by the mobilities paradigm. In reality, characterisations of transport geography as the domain of spatial scientists producing utilitarian analyses of 'rational mobile man' are wide of the mark, especially (but not exclusively) in relation to some of the more recent output that has been influenced by authors working to the mobilities agenda. The contents of the *Journal of Transport Geography (JTG)*, for example, now look rather more varied than they did a decade or so ago, and this is very much to the good. But it is also our contention that this influence should not necessarily all be one way: some of the very aspects on which much transport geography analysis is based retain purchase in the context of mobilities scholarship precisely because of their rootedness in transport networks and services, what puts them there, how they are governed and how they are used. No experience or representation of mobility can exist without the 'brute fact' (Cresswell 2006) of movement in the first place.

We expand upon these issues in what follows. First we trace the trajectory of transport geography from its antecedents though its heyday in the 1960s and 1970s to its most recent guise. With reference to a train journey taken regularly by one of us, we then consider the compatibility of transport geography with broader approaches to mobility scholarship. We bring together some final thoughts in a short concluding paragraph.

Transport geography

Before providing a short history of transport geography, we should first consider what it actually is. This is not as straightforward as it might at first appear; in much the same way that mobilities is a wide ranging, multifaceted and evolving set of approaches, transport geographers have over the years worked to different guiding principles and assumptions. Many of these now coexist, each exerting different levels of influence on individual (or groups of) researchers depending on their particular world view or conception of geography itself. Rodrigue *et al.* (2009) identify as important the geography of transport networks and the impact of these networks in determining wider human geographies. Goetz *et al.* (2003, 221) cast a wider net. "Transportation geography is the study of the spatial aspects of transportation." It also "includes the location, structure, environment and development of networks as well as the analysis and explanation of the interaction or movement of goods and people." They further emphasise the "role and impacts – both spatial and aspatial – of transport in a broad sense including facilities, institutions, policies and operations in domestic and international contexts." A final line adds to this list the "explicitly spatial perspective, or point of view, within the interdisciplinary study of transportation."

In that they appear in the same paragraph, Goetz *et al.*'s explicit references to spatiality and aspatiality seem contradictory, but others seeking to defend transport geography have been keen to play up the limitations that a spatial fixation can introduce. Hall (2010, 1) champions geography's role as an "integrating, synthesising facilitator" when "its profile as a distinctive spatial discipline per se is restrained." Still others (including ourselves, and see also Hanson 2003; Hoyle and Knowles 1998) have advanced more variations that include reference to the role of transport in the production and consumption of place. Perhaps the principal unifying theme to be distilled is that most transport geographers' work involves the privileging, or at least keen awareness, of movement and its significance in the broader geographical endeavour (Shaw and Sidaway 2011), but it probably remains true to say that analyses of the direct *experiences* and *representations* of movement remain relatively scarce in the transport geography literature (Keeling 2007, 2008, 2009).

Cresswell and Merriman (2011) note that calls for a keener awareness of movement within human geography can be traced back at least to the 1930s, when a 'dynamic geography' centred on the ideas of 'men and things moving' was put forward. Some years later Ullman

(1954, 311) asserted that because transport "is a measure of the relations between areas" it is "therefore an essential part of geography." There followed a 'heyday' period in which transport geography was at the forefront of cutting edge developments in geography (in many ways this was not dissimilar to the position in which mobilities finds itself in relation to the social sciences today). Some innovations from that period still resonate, albeit in rather a different context now. In *Geography as Spatial Interaction*, for example, Ullman critiqued geographical thinking for placing too much emphasis on areas and territories, and argued instead that more attention should be paid to "the effect of one area on another area, the connection between areas." In other words, he was pointing to the basic link between site and situation, finding that virtually no single place is economically or socially independent because it is bound up in a network of interaction and interdependency (Hesse 2010).

It was in the wake of the quantitative revolution, in the 1960s and 1970s, that transport geography enjoyed its highest profile (Preston and O'Connor 2008). Significant work on network analysis and mechanistic models was firmly rooted in positivism, and 'rational mobile man' – strongly related to 'rational economic man' – emerged to aid analysis through his assumed behaviour as "the distance minimiser" (Rimmer 1988, 175). While rational economic man would make 'optimum' economic decisions based on the cost of goods and services, his mobile equivalent would arrive at similar conclusions based on trip length, on the assumption that transport costs were directly proportional to distance. In explaining settlement patterns and industrial location, therefore, influential theoreticians such as Christaller and Weber placed transport costs at the heart of their analyses and thus transport geographers focused intently on searching for better means of dealing with the 'friction of distance'. Hanson (2003) points out that one such means is to increase speed – concepts such as time–space convergence (Janelle 1969) can be appreciated in this context – and in theory at least this can be delivered by better networks designed to link places together more effectively. Refining existing understanding of such connectivity thus required more and better network analysis and ever more sophisticated models. It all became a self-fulfilling prophecy. Textbooks of the time accordingly set about training the next generation of transport geographers in the same mould (e.g. Hay 1973; Lowe and Moryadas 1975; Taaffe and Gauthier 1973; White and Senior 1983).

In the economist- and engineer-dominated worlds of transport studies and policy making, the need for speed and the credibility of modelling remain surprisingly under-challenged, but human geography as a discipline moved on and many transport geographers were left behind (there is a lesson here for those working in the mobilities paradigm today). Partly this was because inter-disciplinary connections were maintained – indeed, Goetz (2006) has noted how it is often difficult for transport geographers to be taken seriously in the transport sector unless they speak the language of economists or civil engineers – but by pinning their colours so firmly to a particular approach and failing to engage with developments elsewhere in geography, many transport geographers became "trapped in by . . . [a] narrow emphasis on network analysis and mechanistic models" (Knowles 1993, 3). Of particular concern was that while much of this work was technically impressive, it was rather detached from wider socio–economic and political contexts (Rimmer 1978, cited in Taylor 1980). Good examples cited by Eliot-Hurst (1974) are Gauthier's study of highways in São Paulo and Taaffe's investigation into agricultural change in the Soviet Union following the arrival of the railway. While such work was illuminating it failed to explain "transportation developments within the framework of the very real exploitation of the Brazilian economy or of the political/ ideological struggles within a centrally planned economy" (512). Broader critiques about the quantitative revolution having generated masses of cleverly derived, but in terms of addressing troublesome social problems rather useless, techniques and information are of clear relevance here.

It would be wrong to say that this went unrecognised. Eliot-Hurst (1974) used his introduction to *Transportation Geography: Comments and Readings* to highlight shortcomings associated with a positivist approach focused on "measuring and explaining the objective façade and mechanical linkages of social reality." He argued that geographers "should not be content with merely outlining the 'objective' dimensions of economic and social patterns in space . . . To increase our understanding of the landscape we need also to incorporate 'subjective' dimensions of decision making, political frameworks, and governmental legislation" (4). Peter Rimmer (1988) added to calls for a more humanistic transport geography, and the emergence of time geography stemming from the ideas of Torsten Hägerstrand offered further scope to foreground *actual people* in studies of movement (see also Taylor 1980). But the mainstream of transport geography was slow to change, and the effect of this intransigence was amplified by the realisation among those working in other areas of the discipline that, in fact, transport costs were becoming a rather small element in the overall costs of production.[1] Distance may have remained a friction, but cheap oil was increasingly providing a lubricant. With ever more human geographers downplaying the role of transport in their analyses of social and economic patterns and systems (although one notable exception is David Harvey (1982) in *The Limits to Capital*), the influence and popularity of transport geography had inevitably – ineluctably – waned by the 1980s (Hall *et al.* 2006; Hanson 2003; Knowles 1993, 2009; Preston and O'Connor 2008). In perhaps the most damning critique by 'one of its own', Susan Hanson echoed Bryan Berry's comments about political geography by describing transport geography as a "quiet, some might say moribund, corner" of the discipline and wondered how "such an important area of inquiry [became] so marginalised."

Goetz *et al.* (2010, 327) have taken issue with Hanson's critique, suggesting that it is "not entirely accurate and is much too harsh an indictment of a subfield that has actually made significant progress in many areas." Others write of a 'revival' of transport geography's fortunes (Knowles 1993, 2009; Preston and O'Connor 2008). In the UK this has in part been manifest through the appearance of several new textbooks (Hoyle and Knowles 1992, 1998; Knowles *et al.* 2008; Tolley and Turton 1995) and the launch of the *JTG*. Across the Atlantic, Hanson's own *Geography of Urban Transportation* (Hanson and Giuliano 2004) has gone into its third edition and more general textbooks by Black (2003) and Rodrigue *et al.* (2009) have been published. A thoroughly international *Handbook of Transport Geography and Spatial Systems* (Hensher *et al.* 2004) also appeared as part of a broader book series. Interestingly, only Knowles *et al.*'s volume is predominantly qualitative in its approach and even then is not especially successful at engaging with mobilities work: in his review, Pooley (2008) observes that "repeatedly, the authors attempt to move beyond transport to engage with the mobilities agenda, but usually the two glide past each other and never become fully engaged."

It is in the production of research articles that the resurgence of transport geography has been most evident, at least in terms of volume of output. David Keeling (2007), in the first 'progress report' on transport geography to appear in *Progress in Human Geography* for 19 years, suggests that achievements in transport geography research were impressive in the 1990s and 2000s (although this does raise the question as to why no one had reported on them since 1988, but then we are as guilty as anyone else). Goetz *et al.* (2010) note that the number of paper and panel sessions at the Annual Meeting of the Association of American Geographers sponsored by the Transportation Geography Specialty Group rose from six in 1997 to 22 in 2007, and 225 transport-related articles appeared in the top 12 ranked geography journals in the decade from 1996. The *JTG* has moved from four to six issues per year and its impact factor has increased to over 2.5, partly as a result of its increasingly attracting papers from cognate disciplines.

Quantitative and modelling work remains strongly represented (see also Schwanen 2010), but an increasing amount of this work is informed by wide ranging concerns and some of it has a distinctly critical edge. For example, Selima Sultana's (2005) work on racial differences in commuting patterns has raised considerable interest; Mei-Po Kwan (1999, 2002) has used quantitative methods to investigate questions of gender, access, feminism and GIS; and Tim Schwanen and colleagues in The Netherlands have published their findings on commuting and the relationships between residential context and travel time (Schwanen *et al.* 2002). Indeed, a hallmark of Schwanen and Kwan's work is that it draws influences from a wide range of literature and they, more than many, seem capable of harnessing the power of quantitative approaches in ways that would be unfamiliar to traditional transport geographers.

Schwanen's extensive qualitative work also takes its place among a swiftly growing battery of transport geography publications showcasing the use of interview, travel diary, ethnographic, documentary and other methods that would be well-known to mobilities scholars. Topics addressed include transport governance, privatisation and deregulation, urban planning, accessibility, travel and ICT use, time geography, social exclusion, transport and travel history, marginalisation, and travel and gender (see Keeling 2007, 2008, 2009 for a detailed review of transport geographers' output over the past 20 years). The contents of the *JTG* increasingly reflect this and indeed now regularly include the work of mobilities scholars, most notably of late the 2011 special issue on *Geographies of the Passenger*, co-edited by Peter Adey, David Bissell and Eric Laurier.

Among the first of the mobilities papers to appear in the *JTG* was a piece by Juliet Jain and Glenn Lyons (2008) that drew upon multi-disciplinary literature to challenge the traditional view that travel time is a disutility or a burden (this view, a direct throwback to ideas of the friction of distance from the 1950s, remains common in the transport sector and is overwhelmingly influential in cost–benefit assessments of transport investment). Arguing instead that travel time can be seen as a 'gift', they showed how positive utility could be derived from using travel time as a period for transition (e.g. from work to home) or as 'time out' (e.g. for relaxing). Key to their argument were the nature and characteristics of the travel space in which journeys are made. Explicitly geographical in nature, travel space has been the subject of numerous studies (see Laurier 2004; Letherby and Reynolds 2005; Lyons and Urry 2005; Jain 2011; Watts 2008), and we refer to this concept now – in the form of a particular train that travels from Plymouth to London – as the basis for our discussion of potential connections and linkages between transport geography and mobilities scholarship.

The 10.44

Every weekday at 10.44 First Great Western's service from Penzance to London Paddington is timetabled to leave from Plymouth. One of us (Jon) uses this service about three times a month, and we both use it at least once a year. Despite the 1970s vintage of the rolling stock, the quality of the travelling environment is reasonably high, although standard-class coaches have been configured for commuter rather than long-distance services and in our experience it is much easier to work in first class than in standard class. Not only are there fewer distractions, but the amount of extra space is especially significant. Plymouth is the largest city on the route except Reading and London itself, but it is rather poorly connected to the capital by rail: the first direct westbound train arrives at 11.20 and services are often very heavily loaded. The fastest journey time for the 200-mile trip is three hours – this has been getting slower over the years — but most trains take closer to three and a half hours, and in part reflecting a 'need for speed' mentality Plymouth City Council's campaign to promote economic growth has highlighted the need for faster journey times. Given that getting from London to Plymouth by train takes longer than to any other major English city, this is not unreasonable, especially now the airport has closed, but major improvements are unlikely in the foreseeable future because planned electrification and new rolling stock elsewhere in the Great Western region will not reach the far south-west. Existing trains will continue to operate to Plymouth well into the 2020s, and so unless there is a major rolling stock upgrade the quality of the travel environment will deteriorate considerably (which of course will be all the more noticeable given the length of the journey).

More broadly, First Great Western is one of the 20 or so privately owned franchises who between them operate Great Britain's passenger train services. The costs of running the railway network are formidable and unit costs are 30 per cent higher than equivalent networks elsewhere in Europe (McNulty 2011). In 2006/07, government support peaked at more than £6 billion (Office of Rail Regulation 2011) and ministers are pursuing a policy of shifting more of the cost burden from taxpayers to passengers. This has resulted in some of the highest fares in Europe, although train travel continues to increase in popularity despite the recession; passenger journeys, at more than 1.3 billion in 2010/11 (Office of Rail Regulation 2011), are now at their highest levels since the 1920s, when the network was much more extensive. At the same time, capital investment in both England and Scotland has survived recent budget cuts. Electrification, new rolling stock, new stations and even new lines are being procured and will have sizeable impacts upon transport patterns and associated geographies in affected areas. The so-called 'High Speed 2', a new 200-mph line from London Euston to Birmingham, Manchester and Leeds, is also being taken forward despite complaints from nimbies in the Cotswolds privileging their own local-scale inconveniences over wider national-scale advantages.

To a mobilities audience, much of this kind of information — on train services, timetabling, privatisation, economic development, network characteristics, patterns of movement — might appear rather 'traditional' and getting away from the point of what was anticipated to be an ethnography of our journey (see Watts 2008). Certainly much of it could be associated with Cresswell's notion of the 'brute fact' of movement. Yet at the same time it should be apparent that this brute fact of movement is by no means reducible to the simple enumeration of passenger or goods flows. Even the most cursory of glances at the policy context in which the 10.44 operates reveals a great deal about linkages between the transport system and the society it serves and shapes. For example, one of the reasons that many journeys take longer on the Great Western network today than they did decades ago is the radically altered patterns of settlement and economic activity in the Thames Valley and beyond. Not only have end-to-end connectivity requirements changed, but the number of long-distance commuters from places like Chippenham, Swindon, Didcot and Reading has also hugely increased. This has implications for a privately owned train operator seeking to maximise revenue: every train that runs non-stop from London to Bristol cannot pick up fare-paying passengers from intervening stations. Thus, whereas in the 1970s trains from Bristol to London would, like the 10.44, have been limited-stop Inter-Cities, nowadays they have in effect been reduced to glorified commuter services. In the absence of investment to speed up trains between stations, time–space *divergence* rather than convergence has become the norm (see Knowles 2006).

All of this means that general structural shifts in society and the economy have both led to and interacted with specific changes in the transport industry to impact upon the geography of transport and travel in the Westcountry. In other words, the brute fact of movement is about very much more than just the brute fact of movement: it is at once intensely political and deeply embedded in broader socio-economic and political (not to mention environmental) processes and imperatives. Much of this was, of course, overlooked by previous generations of transport geographers, but equally it should not be forgotten by mobilities scholars concentrating on the experience and the representation of mobility.

A further glance at our notes from the 10.44 unearths points of relevance to these aspects of experience and representation. Take, for instance, their relevance to policy making. There is a long tradition of policy-driven work in transport geography – leaving aside for the moment debates about the influence and position of geography as a discipline in relation to key policy decisions (see Johnston and Sidaway 2004) – but certainly transport geographers who overlook the potential contribution of the mobilities literature to their work will miss out on key insights that could improve their policy analyses. Lyons and Urry's (2005) work on travel time use and Jain and Lyons' (2008) related considerations of the potential for travel time to be a gift both relate to how travel space can impact upon the productivity of time spent on the move. In essence, the more suited any given travel space is to the needs of travellers, the more 'productive' – however this may be defined (Jain and Lyons 2008)[2] – they are likely to be. It is difficult to create a travel space that suits all travellers' sometimes contradictory needs and desires, but we can speculate that a comfortable, relatively spacious, clean, wi-fi-enabled environment that encourages respect for fellow passengers and is configured in different zones for different types of passenger would be a good start.[3]

The UK Department for Transport is acquiring a fleet of new 'Intercity Express' trains and is arguably opting for as few carriages as it thinks it can get away with to move predicted flows of passengers between nodes. These flows are forecast to increase considerably as economic activity and settlement patterns continue to change and as journey times between London, Bristol and Cardiff are reduced as a result of new timetables and better train performance. We caution the Department against overlooking the quality of people's journey experiences. Focusing only on the 'brute fact of movement' (in response to predicted passenger growth) or the 'need for speed' (in response to Plymouth City Council and others) could result in a false economy. It might well produce a far better economic (and not to mention social and environmental) return to invest in more carriages capable of providing a far more comfortable journey, which in turn would enable much greater productivity on the move. In this context reductions in journey time will obviously be welcome as one part of a wider suite of overall improvements.

It may be that better journey experiences would also lead to a better representation of train travel. Although a recent survey rated Britain's railways highly in terms of consumer satisfaction in comparison to other European railways (European Commission 2011), and some positive media coverage of the railway industry in the light of HS2 has appeared in recent years, more familiar stories are of fare increases, overcrowding, poor punctuality and the like. In 2011 First Great Western was reported to be running all of the 10 most crowded services in London and the south-east, and the company was also the subject of a 'fares strike' by disgruntled commuters in Bristol some years before (BBC 2007; Meikle 2011). We wonder how far such negative news stories impact on the views of train travel not only of captive rail users such as commuters, but also those who use the train only rarely or, even more significantly, not at all.

Perhaps we are worrying about nothing, given the large-scale increase in passenger numbers experienced since the mid-1990s. But there is the potential – and from a sustainable transport perspective there is certainly the need – for even (and much) higher patronage growth. This would also need factoring into current plans for rolling stock orders, not to mention other capacity enhancement work around the network. And the effect of negative publicity for the railways can be felt in places, not just in trains. Negative press coverage of the far south-west's omission from the electrification programme can be interpreted as perpetuating a particular image of Plymouth and Cornwall as economic backwaters, the kinds of places associated with taking holidays rather than doing work. Herein lies a potentially irresolvable tension, of course, for the tourism industry has much invested in ideas of fun and relaxation defining the far south-west. In the event it is likely that all business people in the region would benefit from better rail services – and equally as importantly the *perception* of there being better rail services – to and within the region throughout the year.

Some thoughts on arrival

You will remember we started writing this chapter on the train between Glasgow and Edinburgh. On the way back from 'Auld Reekie', Iain retraced our earlier journey, and his travel experience was unremarkable. In many ways, this is how a journey should be. There was enough space on the train to read over the words we wrote on the outbound journey, and to make corrections as necessary. Hearing about the jams on the M8 certainly confirmed his view that rail is by far the best way to travel between Scotland's two biggest cities. Jon uncharacteristically took the train all the way back to Plymouth. It was cramped, uncomfortable and the vestibules smelt remarkably unpleasant; the train in question (a 'Voyager') was completely unsuitable for making a long journey and much of the time on the move was wasted. It resulted in what Lyons and Urry (2005) term a counterproductive journey, in that it had a detrimental impact on subsequent activities. Jon characteristically represented this journey in rather Anglo-Saxon terms to anyone who would listen, and has gone back to flying between the south-west and the Central Belt.

We are both acutely aware that in these cases our travel experiences, the way we represented them and the broader social, economic and environmental consequences they may have had were the direct result of economics, politics, policies, personalities and their approaches that conspire to produce the particular kind of railway we have in Great Britain. Had we been travelling in Germany or France our travel experiences and subsequent representations would probably have been completely different. On an ICE, we would never need to buy first-class tickets to guarantee a good working environment because the second-class carriages are much more spacious and comfortable. On a TGV, a journey of the distance between Edinburgh and Plymouth would only take about half the time of its British equivalent, although it would not be as comfortable as on an ICE. We could glean interesting insights from research into experiences and representations of journeys on these trains, but ultimately our work would be partial if we took no account of underlying issues associated with the brute fact of movement. While not so much of a problem with regard to the methodologies adopted for individual studies so long as they are located in a broader context, replicated across an entire body of work such partiality is clearly limiting. Any analysis of train journeys in Scotland, or the south-west of England, or indeed from anywhere to anywhere in any circumstances is likely to be most insightful and accomplished if it is grounded in a good understanding of all three of Cresswell's triumvirate of movement, experience and representation.

We have considered our examples (even if we have not outlined our own positionality in any great detail) from the perspective of transport geographers, but we have made use of some innovations associated with the mobilities approach to broaden and strengthen our discussion. There is nothing to suggest that those working in the mobilities paradigm should not apply the same logic to their own work. Indeed, criticising others for reducing the study of movement to an overwhelmingly utilitarian affair (see Spinney 2009) is entirely legitimate and has been very welcome, but then to underplay the 'traditional' aspects of mobility in subsequent analyses would at the very least represent something of a missed opportunity. What creates the particular conditions that dictate an individual's particular travel experiences? Why are travel experiences in some places better than they are in others? How will representations of certain travel experiences impact upon the likelihood of others seeking out the same journeys? Academic knowledge sometimes develops in a rather oppositional fashion, and while this encourages the exposure of weaknesses in the 'discarded' approach, it tends to ignore that usually this approach is not entirely without merit. Failure to acknowledge this merit is a mistake; in scholarship, as in life more generally, it is worth remembering that two wrongs don't make a right. Any programme of detailed investigation of the experience or representation of mobility will have more to say if 'traditional' issues associated with the brute fact of movement are taken seriously. The perspectives of transport geographers are more relevant to mobilities scholarship than some of its protagonists might think.

Notes

1 And some didn't necessarily see the need to change in any case. Goetz *et al.* (2010) note how, writing in the 1990s, Taaffe and Gauthier acknowledged the lack of transport geography underpinned by social theory, but "in a backhanded reference to the lack of stability of the various philosophical orientations (e.g. structuralism, structuration, realism, postmodernism, etc.), they state, "the rate of turnover has been remarkable: 'isms' have become 'wasms' at an impressive clip" (327).
2 Productivity need not necessarily be economic (in the sense of doing work) or indeed immediate (in the sense that the experience of a journey can 'spill over' into and have an effect on post-travel activities), but either way it will be positive, sometimes for the individual traveller and sometimes for others as well.
3 First Great Western make the best of their aged and constraining rolling stock to feature quiet carriages, a TV carriage, a family carriage in school holidays, and so on.

References

BBC (2007) 'Rail users vote for fares strike'. Available online at news.bbc.co.uk/1/hi/england/bristol/6269875.stm. Accessed 2 April 2012.

Black, W. (2003) *Transportation: a geographical analysis.* Guilford Press, New York.

Cresswell, T. (2006) *On the move: mobility in the modern western world.* Routledge, Abingdon.

Cresswell, T. and Merriman, P. (eds) (2011) *Geographies of mobilities: practices, spaces, subjects.* Ashgate, Farnham.

Eliot-Hurst, M. (1974) *Transportation geography: comments and readings.* McGraw–Hill, New York.

European Commission (2011) 'Survey on passengers' satisfaction with rail services'. Available online at http://ec.europa.eu/public_opinion/flash/fl_326_en.pdf. Accessed 3 April 2012.

Goetz, A. (2006) 'Transport geography: reflecting on a subdiscipline and identifying future research trajectories: the insularity issue in transport geography'. *Journal of Transport Geography* 14 (3) 230–231.

Goetz, A., Ralston, B., Stutz, F. and Leinbach, T. (2003) 'Transportation geography'. In Gaile, G. and Wilmott, C. (eds) *Geography in America at the dawn of the 21st century.* Oxford University Press, Oxford, 221–236.

Goetz, A., Vowles, T. and Tierney, S. (2010) 'Bridging the qualitative-quantitative divide in transportation geography'. *Professional Geographer* 61 (3) 323–335.

Hall, D. (2004) 'Towards a gendered transport geography'. *Journal of Transport Geography* 12 (3) 245–247.

Hall, D. (2010) 'Transport geography and new European realities: a critique'. *Journal of Transport Geography* 18 (1) 1–13.

Hall, P., Hesse, M. and Rodrigue, J.-P. (2006) 'Re-exploring the interface between economic and transport geography'. *Environment and Planning A* 38 (8) 1301–1308.

Hanson, S. (2003) 'Transportation: hooked on speed, eyeing sustainability'. In Sheppard, E. and Barnes, T. (eds) *A companion to economic geography*. Blackwell, Oxford, 468–483.

Hanson, S. and Giuliano, G. (2004) *The geography of urban transportation*. Guilford Press, New York.

Harvey, D. (1982) *The limits to capital*. Blackwell, Oxford.

Hay, A. (1973) *Transport for the space economy: a geographical study*. Macmillan, London.

Hensher, D., Button, K., Haynes, K. and Stopher, P. (2004) *Handbook of transport geography and spatial systems*. Elsevier, Oxford.

Hesse, M. (2010) 'Cities, material flows and the geography of spatial interaction: urban places in the system of chains'. *Global Networks* 10 (1) 75–91.

Hoyle, B. and Knowles, R. (1992) *Modern transport geography*. John Wiley, Chichester.

Hoyle, B. and Knowles, R. (1998) *Modern transport geography*. 2nd edition. John Wiley, Chichester.

Jain, J. (2011) 'The classy coach commute'. *Journal of Transport Geography* 19 (5) 1017–1022.

Jain, J. and Lyons, G. (2008) 'The gift of travel time'. *Journal of Transport Geography* 16 (2) 81–89.

Janelle, D. (1969) 'Spatial reorganization: a model and concept'. *Annals of the Association of American Geographers* 59, 348–364.

Johnston, R. and Sidaway, J. (2004) *Geography and geographers: Anglo-American human geography since 1945*. Hodder, London.

Keeling, D. (2007) 'Transportation geography: new directions on well-worn trails'. *Progress in Human Geography* 31 (2) 217–225.

Keeling, D. (2008) 'Transportation geography: new regional mobilities'. *Progress in Human Geography* 32 (2) 275–283.

Keeling, D. (2009) 'Transportation geography: local contexts, global challenges'. *Progress in Human Geography* 33 (4) 516–526.

Knowles, R. (1993) 'Research agendas in transport geography in the 1990s'. *Journal of Transport Geography* 1 (1) 3–11.

Knowles, R. (2006) 'Transport shaping space: differential collapse in time-space'. *Journal of Transport Geography* 14 (6) 407–425.

Knowles, R. (2009) 'Transport geography'. In Kitchin, R. and Thrift, N. (eds) *International Encyclopedia of Human Geography*. Elsevier, Oxford, 441–451.

Knowles, R., Shaw, J. and Docherty, I. (eds) (2008) *Transport geographies: mobilities, flows and spaces*. Blackwell, Oxford.

Kwan, M.-P. (1999) 'Gender and individual access to urban opportunities: a study using space-time measures'. *Professional Geographer* 51 (2) 211–227.

Kwan, M.-P. (2002) 'Feminist visualization: re-envisioning GIS as a method in feminist geographic research'. *Annals of the Association of American Geographers* 92 (4) 645–661.

Laurier, E. (2004) 'Doing office work on the motorway'. *Theory, Culture & Society* 21 (4–5) 261–277.

Law, R. (1999) 'Beyond "women and transport": towards new geographies of gender and daily mobility'. *Progress in Human Geography* 23 (4) 567–588.

Letherby, G. and Reynolds, G. (2005) *Train tracks: work, play and politics on the railways*. Berg, London.

Lowe, J. and Moryadas, S. (1975) *The geography of movement*. Houghton Mifflin, Boston.

Lyons, G. and Urry, J. (2005) 'Travel time use in the information age'. *Transportation Research Part A: Policy and Practice* 39 (2–3) 257–276.

McNulty, R. (2011) 'Realising the potential of GB rail. Report of the Rail Value for Money Study'. Department for Transport, London. Available online at www.dft.gov.uk/publications/realising-the-potential-of-gb-rail/. Accessed 3 April 2012.

Meikle, J. (2011) 'London Paddington station worst for overcrowded trains'. *The Guardian*. Available online at www.guardian.co.uk/uk/2011/aug/11/train-services-overcrowding-london. Accessed 2 April 2012.

Office of Rail Regulation (2011) 'National rail trends 2010–2011 yearbook'. ORR, London. Available online at www.rail-reg.gov.uk/upload/pdf/nrt-yearbook-2010-11.pdf. Accessed 3 April 2012.

Pooley, C. (2008) 'Review of transport geographies: mobilities, flows and spaces'. *Journal of Transport Geography* 16 (6) 443.

Preston, J. and O'Connor, K. (2008) 'Revitalized transport geographies'. In Knowles, R., Shaw, J. and Docherty, I. (eds) *Transport geographies: mobilities, flows and spaces*. Blackwell, Oxford, 227–237.

Rimmer, P. (1988) 'Transport geography'. *Progress in Human Geography* 12 (2) 270–281.

Rodrigue, J.-P., Comtois, C. and Slack, B. (2009) *The geography of transport systems*. Routledge, New York.

Schwanen, T. (2010) *The mobility multiverse.* Paper presented at the Annual Conference of the Association of American Geographers, Washington, DC.

Schwanen, T., Dijst, M. and Dieleman, F. (2002) 'A microlevel analysis of residential context and travel time'. *Environment and Planning A* 34 (8) 1487–1507.

Shaw, J. and Sidaway, J. (2011) 'Making links: on (re)engaging with transport and transport geography'. *Progress in Human Geography* 35 (4) 502–520.

Spinney, J. (2009) 'Cycling the city: movement, meaning and method'. *Geography Compass* 3 (2) 817–835.

Sultana, S. (2005) 'Racial variations in males' commuting times in Atlanta: what does the evidence suggest?' *Professional Geographer* 57 (1) 66–82.

Taaffe, E. and Gauthier, H. (1973) *Geography of transportation.* Prentice Hall, New Jersey.

Taylor, Z. (1980) 'Some comments on social transport geography'. *Progress in Human Geography* 4 (1) 99–104.

Tolley, R. and Turton, B. (1995) *Transport systems, policy and planning: a geographical approach.* Longman, London.

Ullman, E. (1954/1980) *Geography as spatial interaction.* University of Washington Press, Seattle.

Watts, L. (2008) 'The art and craft of train travel'. *Social and Cultural Geography* 9 (6) 711–726.

White, H. and Senior, M. (1983) *Transport geography.* Longman, London.

2

Mobilities and Transport History

Colin Divall

Mobilities – understood here to mean the flows of persons and things along with the immaterial circulation of information enabled by these flows – increasingly define how transport history is researched and written. This might seem an odd remark, given that transport is inherently involved with physical movement. But the shift to the language of 'mobilities' reflects a series of incremental conceptual and thematic developments since the 1990s in the way that historians and other scholars with an interest in the past, such as historical geographers and sociologists, industrial archaeologists, museum curators and transport-policy academics, understand and construct transport as an object of study. In particular, historical transport is now quite widely comprehended as a material (or socio-technical) culture functioning at and across a range of spatial scales from the local to the global. While such a schematic characterization leaves plenty of scope for further debate, there is an emerging consensus that it forms the basis for a flexible, open research programme constituting transport-cum-mobility history as a field marked by a common set of questions, themes and methodologies (Mom, Divall and Lyth 2009; Wilson 2010; Mom 2011). To borrow from the natural sciences, the term 'collaboratory' – a research centre without walls – signals a widespread desire for an intellectual community working across disciplinary and national boundaries and dedicated to showing how and why over the long term transport has produced the material mobilities of the present.

Whatever the labels, the pace of change has been impressive. As late as 1998 transport history – at least in the post-1945, Anglo-American tradition represented by the *Journal of Transport History*, then the only dedicated academic periodical in English – could still be described as a branch of social and economic history, albeit one in urgent need of an infusion of new ideas (Armstrong 1998, p. 103). In sum, the field was overwhelmingly defined by theoretical or thematic considerations drawn from economic, business or management, and labour history. Studies were almost always of single modes of transport, and there was a clear bias towards those underpinning the industrializing societies of the global north during the eighteenth and nineteenth centuries. Railways and inland waterways were particularly prominent, with far less attention given to roads, the air or the sea (although the last had been covered since 1989 by the *International Journal of Maritime Transport*): human-, wind- or animal-powered transport (excepting inland waterways) was largely missing. Nevertheless, these studies provided important insights into some of the political, legal, economic, social, cultural and even environmental factors underpinning the *production* of particular modalities of vehicular movement (the motion of trains, buses, cars, ships and so on) along with their flows of people, things and information: this combination of a specific mode and the flows it enables is a *transport system*. In this way these older ways of researching and writing transport history pioneered aspects of today's mobilities programme. Thus, for example, a good deal of attention was given to physical and social infrastructures – such as the politics and economics of developing railway networks (e.g. Simmons 1978) – and today's scholars who follow in these traditions continue to make significant points about how transport systems were conceived, built and operated in the past (e.g. Kostal 1994; Casson 2009).

But the old transport historiography tended to neglect users, as well as the ways in which they 'consumed' not only their own movement but also that of things and of information circulating by physical means. This last category most obviously included the likes of post and newspapers, but it also embraced the communication afforded by the interactions of people on the move. Of course, earlier scholars were well aware of these flows. But they usually conceptualized them far too narrowly from the perspective of today's mobilities programme, taking their theoretical cues from other fields of history. In sum, these scholars failed to recognize the irreducible nature of transport flows as simultaneously both meaningful and functional. Thus, for example, economic historians conceived mobility as no more than a functional means of moving from A to B, the demand for which was 'derived' from the pursuit of other, so-called higher-order goods and services. It was then easy to assume that economic metrics of aggregated flows captured the essence of transport usage. So, for example, starting in the 1960s with R. W. Fogel's pioneering work on US railroads, econometricians spent upwards of two decades attempting – with very mixed success – to quantify how much the substitution of rail for alternative forms of goods and passenger transport in the nineteenth century was worth to individual national economies (e.g. Fogel 1964; Hawke 1970). Similarly, business historians argued over how well managers of enterprises like railway companies or shipping lines tailored services to their usage by passengers and traders. These traditions continue to make important contributions to our understanding of the historical 'impact' of transport's aggregated flows (e.g. Leunig 2006; Crafts *et al.* 2008). But they need to be supplemented not only by a much more nuanced understanding of how users actively shaped flows, but also by a frank recognition that across history transport has played an essential role in constituting individuals, communities and societies in ways that go beyond the functional movement of goods and people.

A thematic shift in emphasis from the production to the consumption of transport along these lines was evident within the pages of the *Journal of Transport History* by 2003 (Lyth 2003; Mom 2003), the same year in which the International Association for the History of Transport, Traffic and Mobility (T²M) was founded. Chiefly building on academic initiatives across Europe, T²M provides a range of activities and outlets for scholars of any discipline who wish to study material flows as fundamentals of social life (Dienel and Divall 2009). Owing an obvious intellectual debt to the then-new mobility turn in the social sciences (e.g. Urry 2000) as well as to the growing influence of the well-established contextual history of technology (epitomized by the Society for the History of Technology (SHOT) and its journal *Technology & Culture*), T²M's research programme frames historical transport as interacting systems of meaning-laden physical flows and infrastructures which are irreducible to other social or technological processes.

This is an ambitious project still in need of a good deal of theoretical clarification and amplification, and this brief essay cannot explore all the possibilities. Nevertheless, nearly a decade after T²M's establishment, there are encouraging signs of a reasonably coherent trans-disciplinary, transnational and transmodal body of work. An important trend is the greater use – although not without substantial disagreements over which schools of thought are most appropriate – of concepts drawn from cultural theory; particularly those that relate material social processes and institutions (including those of economic development and political conflict) to the cultural forms that make social life possible. Discourses that explore consumption as a key element of modernity are particularly influential (Mom *et al.* 2009, p. 38). The single most important advance is the recognition that all forms of personal transport have been as imbued with socially inscribed meanings – the cultures of transport – as other forms of capitalist consumption. Here there are clear connections with John Urry's augmentation of Bourdieu's taxonomy of economic and cultural capital to include the 'network capital' afforded in part by access to personal transport, as well as with the work of cultural geographers like Tim Cresswell (Urry 2007, pp. 194–203; Cresswell 2006). In this way the field is sensitized to the cultural processes through which transport-cum-mobility interacts with the goals and interests of social groups and individuals. In other words, we come to see transport throughout history not just as a practice heavily informed by, and informing, power – earlier generations of historians were well aware of that – but as one in which the symbolic component of social life was critical to the constitution and exercise of that power.

In this context, it is a straightforward, if not entirely uncontroversial, step to understand the historical movements of persons as cultural acts or performances that were enabled, or took place within, the simultaneously social and physical (that is, technological) infrastructures we call transport modes. Thus historical mobilities can be understood as a bundle of three socio-technical dimensions constituting one another: mobility-subjects, mobility-objects and mobility-scapes, all of them defined through their physical–functional and symbolic–expressive relations with each other (Divall and Revill 2005; Beckmann 2001, pp. 593–594). Mobility-subjects are the individual and collective actors that used, were moved or were otherwise affected by transport's flows – in the case of railways, for example: passengers, traders, workers, luggage, viruses, trespassers on the tracks, companies and so on. Mobility-objects refer to the physical and ideal entities and processes that produced these flows: the hardware – vehicles (trains, locomotives, wagons) and their associated physical infrastructures (railway tracks, tunnels, stations) – as well as social-institutional factors like operating rules, management structures, statutory regulatory regimes, labour unions, conditions of carriage, and the railway by-laws and social conventions that govern passengers' behaviour. Mobility-scapes are the spatial and temporal frames in and through which flows occurred. The term comprehends the ways in which space and time were created, shaped, perceived, represented and performed (through movement and social interaction) within a transport system; we might, for instance, talk about somewhere being 'about an hour away by train', or a train being 'down the main relief track'. Adopting this schema, or something like it, helps to reframe historiography so that it becomes transmodal. In other words, the challenge is to find ways of understanding single-mode transport systems as elements in the ecology of competing and complementary modes – that is, the *transport regime* (Elzen 2005, p. 173).

The contents of the *Journal of Transport History*, the multi-lingual *TST* (*Transportes, Servicios y Telecomunicaciones*, founded in 2001) as well as T²M's annual (since 2009) *Mobility in History* and the inaugural 2011 issue of *Transfers* (an explicitly interdisciplinary but historically orientated periodical), demonstrate the new programme's strengths, weaknesses, aspirations and absences. (Historians of maritime transport maintain their own journal and international association, and largely shun the new ways of working (Wilson 2010; Jerolimov 2011).)

Chronologically, the field remains dominated by studies of the modern period, although this is much better balanced, with the twentieth century (or, more accurately, the decades after the First World War) now receiving as much, if not more, attention than the previous two. New scholarship on the early-modern, mediaeval and even earlier periods exists, but is not well integrated into the field (e.g. Adams 2007; Harrison 2004; Laurence 1999). This is a weakness because it is partly by looking to the feudal era (and its equivalents outside the global north) and even further back that we can gain a proper perspective on whether, and if so how and why, the near-global hegemony of capitalism in all its variants altered the essential characteristics of transport regimes.

Partly as a correlative of the chronological shift to the twentieth century, the long traditions of research on modes such as railways, inland waterways, coastal and deep-sea shipping are now more than matched by that on the dominant systems of inland and transnational transport of late-modernity in the global north: auto- and aero-mobility (e.g. McShane 1994; O'Connell 1998; Merriman 2007; Millward 2008; Pirie 2009). Such studies now commonly adopt the kind of cultural and spatial categories familiar from mobility studies, and this is also true of much of the work on older modes of transport. For example, the pioneering work of Wolfgang Schivelbusch (1986) and, before him (though far less widely acknowledged), Leo Marx (1964) defines a range of approaches to the study of the cultural categories through which railway travel has historically been represented and understood (e.g. Freeman 1999; Carter 2001; Welke 2001; Richter 2005; Beaumont and Freeman 2007; Revill 2011). All of this research is slowly being supplemented by studies of alternative – and even in some historical and geographical conjunctures, counter-hegemonic or 'subversive' – systems such as motor- and pedal-cycling or walking (e.g. Solnit 2000; Ishaque and Noland 2006; Norton 2008). Nevertheless, most research still focuses on a single mode, even if these are now much more commonly treated as elements of a transport regime. And it is exceptional to study how a particular kind of personal mobility – such as the everyday trips needed to maintain a family unit – changed or remained the same over the long term. Urban transport is the main exception to this criticism: the geographical focus provided by a town, city or peri-urban region seems to make it easier to study the trip rather than the means (e.g. Pooley, Turnbull and Adams 2005; Hepp 2003).

Geographical coverage is becoming better balanced as well, with scholars across more than 20 countries in all the inhabited continents working on historiographies at a range of spatial scales: local, regional, national, transnational. However, studies of specific national and sub-national territories in the global north still dominate. This work suggests that there have been many different historical pathways to 'mobilized modernity', especially as defined by automobilization, as well as some resistance to adopting faster and more individualized transport (Clarsen 2010; Presner 2007). But for all the persistence and present-day resurgence of older, even ancient transport systems like walking, it remains difficult to avoid the conclusion that these mostly survive within niches in a transport ecology overwhelmingly shaped by the mechanized modalities familiar from the long run of nineteenth- and twentieth-century history. The research emerging on the global south might prove this judgement too pessimistic: it already warns that the north's (heterogeneous) experience of the relationship between mobilization and modernization is not always adequate to explain events elsewhere (Mavhunga 2011; Dávila and Aranda 2011; Kim 2009). Moreover, the histories of well-established indigenous and 'subaltern' transport systems such as the hand-, pedal- and motor-rickshaws of the Indian sub-continent offer the prospect of radical alternatives to the car-dominated inland transport regimes of the global north (Whitelegg 1997, pp. 46–48; Divall 2011, p. 313; Mom 2011, p. 23).

Research on transnational flows of persons has disproportionately focused on tourists. International (and internal) tourism was a significant factor in the democratization of mobility in the nineteenth- and – particularly – the twentieth-century history of the north, with recent decades seeing a growing significance for the south, particularly for (from a European perspective) long-haul destinations such as south-east Asia and sub-Saharan Africa. But its importance should not be elevated above that of other flows across the centuries, such as nomadic movements, or the forced or semi-forced movements of people displaced by, for example, war, famine, religious persecution or economic circumstances. Studies of such flows do exist (e.g. Thorne 2011; Millward 2009, p. 139; Bhattacharyya 2005), but they are at present largely invisible to the field of transport-cum-mobility history. And mobility historians outside the maritime sector have so far not given much attention to the transnational flows involved in establishing, maintaining and dismantling empires (but see Pirie 2009), nor to the 'love miles' implicated in the trips made by migrant communities when returning to their original place of abode to visit friends and relatives. Transnational business travel is also largely ignored (Miller 2003; Divall 2012).

It is also very striking that in general terms personal mobilities dominate the historiography, almost to the exclusion of any systematic concern with the flows and exchanges of wastes, goods, intermediates and raw materials that have existed for as long as humanity and which were central to the (re-)globalization of the economy in the last century. In this regard, older ways of writing transport history were better balanced. Perhaps this neglect stems from the fact that these flows do not yield so readily to cultural and semiotic analysis, and thus scholars feel they run the risk of being labelled old-fashioned. In any case, a re-appraisal of the very considerable body of work by maritime historians is highly desirable, not least because shipping has always borne the brunt of global trade (Miller 2003, p. 4; Killingray, Lincoln and Rigby 2004; Jerolimov 2011). And, apart from some studies of air mail (e.g. Pirie 2009; Linden 2002), very little has been written about air freight (Pisano 2011; Millward 2010a, 2010b; Mom, Divall and Lyth 2009, pp. 34–37). In short, a historiography of the flows tied up in commodity chains is very urgently needed.

Sources

It is not hard to see why transport history is still often viewed through the prism of specific modes at the national or sub-national scale. In some countries long-established historiographies provide well-signed routes for further research. The quest for historiographical innovation, however desirable, can too readily cause the material conditions of academic practice to be ignored. Take, for example, the continuing popularity of single-mode studies. Sources are a key here since research on periods before living memory (and oral histories generate their own challenges) obviously does not offer the same opportunities as those on contemporary mobilities to study why, how and with what consequences people and things move. In particular, the historical supply of specific modes by large businesses, public utilities or government departments has helped – if not guaranteed – the survival in some countries of enough primary evidence to satisfy several generations of scholars. The use of this material is encouraged by the fact that there is financial support from sources other than the usual academic trusts and foundations – to some extent, scholarship follows the money.

But these sources rarely yield the kinds of insight into, say, the perceptual, sensual or emotional experiences of trips and journeys desired by scholars interested in the formation of the historical subjectivities of people on the move. Of course, scholars have long turned to alternative evidence such as the personal accounts found in diaries, or the representations (aural and visual as well as textual) of popular and high culture (e.g. Freeman 1999; Carter 2001). But the former sources are few in number and difficult to locate, and there are limits to how much our increasing knowledge of cultural archetypes can tell us about the actual emotions, feelings, perceptions and behaviours of the people who moved and, just as importantly, stayed still in the past. It requires ingenuity, tenacity and often no small measure of luck in conceiving of and locating sources that allow one to grasp something like the full complexity of human mobility across the generations. Perhaps here the increasing availability of digitized material over the internet makes it practical to mine large quantities of sources such as local newspapers for the snippets of evidence that collectively can make a difference.

Another potential resource is the large groups of (in the best sense of the words) amateur historians and enthusiasts. They make up one of the largest fields of voluntary historical activity in Europe, North America and elsewhere. Much of their work focuses on artefacts – not always just the vehicle – and often demonstrates impressive levels of specialist knowledge, albeit mainly about engineering and operations. Quite apart from the fact that mobility historians need to know about such things, the operation of heritage transport presents fascinating possibilities for exploring some of the sensual aspects of personal mobilities that are starting to interest scholars (Divall and Scott 2001, pp. 1–38, 159–188; Cooper 2011; Krebs 2011, p. 156). Museums are another major source of artefactual knowledge, embracing both voluntary and official discourses. Many museums – as evidenced by reviews in the periodicals already mentioned – increasingly think about how object-rich exhibitions might promote public debate about the relationship between past, present and future ways of moving (Divall and Scott 2001, pp. 39–113; Divall 2003). The research undertaken to support such activities often produces evidence such as oral histories of trips and journeys that could profitably be used by mobility historians. And sometimes – although not often enough – curators and others show how a thorough understanding of the design, construction and usage of transport artefacts can enhance appreciation of the social and cultural dimensions of historical mobilities (Wilson 2008; Votolato 2007). Moreover, as well as their objects, some museums have world-class collections of archival, aural, photographic, and popular- and high-art materials, far too little of which gets used by academics. The UK's National Tramway Museum is a good example of an under-utilized resource; it holds material on urban transport and planning extending far beyond the specific modal and national focus signalled by its name.

Conclusion: a 'usable past'

While the study of history stands as its own justification, the mobilities research programme should contribute more to debates about how in the future we shall move ourselves and our things. Inequalities of network capital around the globe, along with the high – and increasing – levels of ecological damage being caused by mechanized transport, demand no less. Tackling these matters requires not just more transport-cum-mobility history, but a 'usable past', a pragmatic, even instrumental approach to writing history framed by this imperative. Admittedly, this is difficult and dangerous territory, raising questions of how scholars relate to power, be it that of governments, state bureaucracies or corporations: but as Otis L. Graham observed nearly thirty years ago, 'it is much too late to debate whether history should serve power. Power answered that question a long time ago' (Graham 1983, p. 8). Thus the real challenge for the mobilities programme is to negotiate a 'political turn' that maintains the integrity of historical research while trying to ensure that its insights are used in the service of those who are disadvantaged by the present ways of moving or staying still (Divall 2010, 2011, 2012; Mom 2011, pp. 20–23).

Bibliography

Adams, C. (2007). *Land Transport in Roman Egypt: A Study of Economics and Administration in a Roman Province*. Oxford: Oxford University Press.

Amato, A. (2004). *On Foot: A History of Walking*. New York and London: New York University Press.

Armstrong, J. (1998). 'Transport history, 1945–95: the rise of a topic to maturity'. *Journal of Transport History 3rd ser.* 19, 103–21.

Beaumont, M. and Freeman, M. (eds) (2007). *The Railway and Modernity: Time, Space and the Machine Ensemble*. Oxford: Peter Lang.

Beckmann, J. (2001). 'Automobility – a social problem and theoretical concept'. *Environment and Planning D: Society and Space* 19, 593–607.

Bhattacharyya, G. (2005). *The Illicit Movement of People and Things*. London: Pluto Press.

Carter, I. (2001). *Railways and Culture in Britain: The Epitome of Modernity*. Manchester and New York: Manchester University Press.

Casson, M. (2009). *The World's First Railway System: Enterprise, Competition, and Regulation on the Railway Network in Victorian Britain*. Oxford: Oxford University Press.

Clarsen, G. (2010). 'Automobility "South of the West": toward a global conversation'. In Mom, G., Norton, P., Clarsen, G. and Pirie, G. (eds) (pp. 25–41).

Cooper, M. (2011). *Brazilian Railway Culture*. Newcastle upon Tyne: Cambridge Scholars Publishing.

Crafts, N., Leunig, T. and Mulatu, A. (2008). 'Were British railway companies well managed in the early twentieth century?'. *Economic History Review* 61, 842–66.

Cresswell, T. (2006). *On the Move: Mobility in the Modern Western World*. New York and Abingdon: Routledge.

Dávila, C. and Aranda, A. M. (2011). 'Mule, railroad, plane: a historiography of transport in Colombia'. In Norton, P., Mom, G., Millward, L. and Flonneau, M. (eds) (pp. 111–118).

Dienel, H.-L. and Divall, C. (2009). 'Changing histories of transport and mobility in Europe'. In Roth, R. and Schlögel, K. (eds) *Neue Wege in ein Neues Europa* (pp. 65–84). Frankfurt AM and New York: Campus Verlag.

Divall, C. (2003). 'Transport museums: another kind of historiography'. *Journal of Transport History 3rd ser.* 24, 259–265.

Divall, C. (2010). 'Mobilizing the history of technology'. *Technology & Culture* 51, 938–960.

Divall, C. (2011). 'Transport history, the Usable Past and the future of mobility'. In Grieco, M. and Urry, J. (eds) *Mobilities: New Perspectives on Transport and Society* (pp. 305–319). Farnham: Ashgate.

Divall, C. (2012). 'Business history, global networks and the future of mobility'. *Business History* 54, 542–555.

Divall, C. and Revill, G. (2005). 'Cultures of transport: representation, practice and technology'. *Journal of Transport History 3rd ser.* 26/1, 99–111. Revised version available online at www.york.ac.uk/inst/irs/irshome/papers/Cultures%20of%20Transport%20revised.pdf (accessed 19 April 2012).

Divall, C. and Scott, A. (2001). *Making Histories in Transport Museums*. London and New York: Leicester University Press.

Elzen, B. (2005). 'Taking the socio-technical seriously: exploring the margins for change in the traffic and transport domain'. In Harbers, H. (ed.) *Inside the Politics of Technology: Agency and Normativity in the Co-production of Technology and Society* (pp. 171–197). Amsterdam: Amsterdam University Press.

Fogel, R. (1964). *Railroads and American Economic Growth: Essays in Econometric History*. Baltimore: Johns Hopkins University Press.

Freeman, M. (1999). *Railways and the Victorian Imagination*. New Haven and London: Yale University Press.

Graham, O. (1983). 'The uses and misuses of history: roles in policymaking'. *The Public Historian* 5, 5–19.

Harrison, D. (2004). *The Bridges of Medieval England: Transport and Society 400–1800*. Oxford: Oxford University Press.

Hawke, G. (1970). *Railways and Economic Growth in England and Wales, 1840–1870*. Oxford: Clarendon Press.

Hepp, J. (2003). *The Middle-Class City: Transforming Space and Time in Philadelphia, 1876–1926*. Philadelphia: University of Pennsylvania Press.

Ishaque, M. and Noland, R. (2006). 'Making roads safe for pedestrians or keeping them out of the way?'. *Journal of Transport History 3rd ser.* 27, 115–137.

Jerolimov, D. (2011). 'Martime mobilities of North America'. In Norton, P., Mom, G., Millward L. and Flonneau, M. (eds) (pp. 85–94).

Killingray, D., Lincoln, M. and Rigby, N. (eds) (2004). *Maritime Empires: British Imperial Trade in the Nineteenth Century.* Woodbridge: Boydell and Brewer.

Kim, N. (2009). 'Transport in China before the industrial age: comparative research issues'. In Mom, G, Pirie, G. and Tissot, L. (eds) (pp. 141–147).

Kostal, R. (1994). *Law and English Railway Capitalism 1825–1875.* Oxford: Oxford University Press.

Krebs, S. (2011). 'Towards a cultural history of car sound(s)'. In Norton, P., Mom, G., Millward, L. and Flonneau, M. (eds) (pp. 151–156).

Laurence, R. (1999). *The Roads of Roman Italy: Mobility and Cultural Change.* London and New York: Routledge.

Leunig, T. (2006). 'Time is money: a re-assessment of the passenger social savings from Victorian British railways'. *Journal of Economic History* 66, 635–673.

Linden, F. (2002). *Airlines and Air Mail: The Post Office and the Birth of the Commercial Aviation Industry.* Lexington: University Press of Kentucky.

Lyth, P. (2003). 'Editorial: the *Journal of Transport History* at fifty and the shape of things to come. . .'. *Journal of Transport History,* 3rd ser. 24, unpaginated.

Marx, L. (1964). *The Machine in the Garden: Technology and the Pastoral Ideal in America.* New York and Oxford: Oxford University Press.

Mavhunga, C. (2011). 'Which mobility for (which) Africa? beyond banal mobilities'. In Norton, P., Mom, G., Millward, L. and Flonneau, M. (eds) (pp. 73–84).

McShane, C. (1994). *Down the Asphalt Path: The Automobile and the American City.* New York and Chichester: Columbia University Press.

Merriman, P. (2007). *Driving Spaces: A Cultural-Historical Geography of England's M1 Motorway.* Oxford: Blackwell.

Miller, M. (2003). 'The business trip: maritime networks in the twentieth century'. *Business History Review* 77, 1–32.

Millward, L. (2008). *Women in British Imperial Airspace, 1922–1937.* Montreal and Kingston: McGill Queens University Press.

Millward, L. (2009). 'Knitting a nation together: three themes in Canadian mobility history'. In Mom, G., Pirie, G. and Tissot, L. (eds) (pp. 137–140).

Millward, L. (2010a). 'One hundred years of flight in Canada: time for a change?'. In Mom, G., Norton, P., Clarsen, G. and Pirie, G. (eds) (pp. 145–150).

Millward, L. (2010b). 'The view from above: a year of aeromobility history'. In Mom, G., Norton, P., Clarsen, G. and Pirie, G. (eds) (pp. 205–210).

Mom, G. (2003). 'What kind of transport history did we get? Half a century of *JTH* and the future of the field'. *Journal of Transport History* 3rd ser. 24, 121–138.

Mom, G. (2011). '"Historians bleed too much": recent trends in the state of the art in mobility history'. In Norton, P., Mom, G., Millward, L. and Flonneau, M. (eds) (pp. 15–30).

Mom, G., Divall, C. and Lyth, P. (2009). 'Towards a paradigm shift? a decade of transport and mobility history'. In Mom, G, Pirie, G. and Tissot, L. (eds) (pp. 13–40).

Mom, G., Norton, P., Clarsen, G., and Pirie, G. (eds) (2010). *Mobility in History: Themes in Transport: T2M Yearbook 2011.* Neuchâtel: Éditions Alphil-Presses universitaires suisses.

Mom, G., Pirie, G. and Tissot, L. (eds) (2009). *Mobility in History: The State of the Art in the History of Transport, Traffic and Mobility.* Neuchâtel: Éditions Alphil-Presses universitaires suisses.

Norton, P. (2008). *Fighting Traffic: The Dawn of the Motor Age in the American City.* Cambridge, MA: MIT Press.

Norton, P., Mom, G., Millward, L. and Flonneau, M. (eds) (2011). *Mobility in History: Reviews and Reflections: T2M Yearbook 2012.* Neuchâtel: Éditions Alphil-Presses universitaires suisses.

O'Connell, S. (1998). *The Car in British Society: Class, Gender and Motoring, 1896–1939.* Manchester and New York: Manchester University Press.

Pirie, G. (2009). *Air Empire: British Imperial Civil Aviation, 1919–39.* Manchester: Manchester University Press.

Pisano, D. (2011). 'Recent aerospace historiography: a slow but steady revolution'. In Norton, P., Mom, G., Millward, L. and Flonneau, M. (eds) (pp. 95–103).

Pooley, C., Turnbull, J. and Adams, M. (2005). *A Mobile Century? Changes in Everyday Mobility in Britain in the Twentieth Century.* Aldershot: Ashgate.

Presner, T. (2007). *Mobile Modernity: Germans, Jews, Trains*. New York: Columbia University Press.

Revill, G. (2011). 'Perception, reception and representation: Wolfgang Schivelbusch and the cultural history of travel and transport'. In Norton, P., Mom, G., Millward, L. and Flonneau, M. (eds) (pp. 31–48).

Richter, A. G. (2005). *Home on the Rails: Women and the Railroad and the Rise of Public Domesticity*. Chapel Hill: University of North Carolina Press.

Schivelbusch, W. (1986). *The Railroad Journey: The Industrialization of Time and Space in the 19th Century*. Leamington Spa: Berg. Originally published in German, 1977, and in English, 1979.

Simmons, J. (1978). *The Railway in England and Wales, Vol. 1: The System and its Working*. Leicester: Leicester University Press.

Solnit, R. (2000). *Wanderlust: A History of Walking*. New York and London: Penguin.

Thorne, M. (2011). 'Assimilation, invisibility, and the eugenic turn in the "Gypsy question" in Romanian society, 1938–1942'. *Romani Studies* 21, 177–205.

Urry, J. (2000). *Sociology Beyond Societies: Mobilities for the Twenty-First Century*. London: Routledge.

Urry, J. (2007). *Mobilities*. Cambridge: Polity Press.

Votolato, G. (2007). *Transport Design: A Travel History*. London: Reaktion Books.

Welke, B. (2001). *Recasting American Liberty: Gender, Race, Law and the Railroad Revolution 1865–1920*. Cambridge: Cambridge University Press.

Whitelegg, J. (1997). *Critical Mass: Transport, Environment and Society in the Twenty-First Century*. London and Chicago: Pluto Press.

Wilson, G. (2008). 'Designing meaning: streamlining, national identity and the case of locomotive CN6400'. *Journal of Design History* 21, 237–257.

Wilson, G. (2010). 'The mobility paradigm and maritime history'. In Mom, G., Norton, P., Clarsen, G., and Pirie, G. (eds) (pp. 13–24).

3

Sociology after the Mobilities Turn

Mimi Sheller

Reflecting back on a little over a decade of research that has gathered under the banner of the "new mobilities paradigm" and "critical mobilities research," it is a good time to ask what impact it has had on traditional disciplines such as sociology. Although sociologist John Urry's work has been fundamental to challenging the "sedentarism" of sociological thought, sociology itself has been especially resistant to the "mobilities turn" as compared to other disciplines such as geography, transport studies and communication (though even in these disciplines the inroads are only partial). Following his book *Sociology Beyond Societies* (2000), Urry's 2001 article "Mobile Sociology" in the *British Journal of Sociology* was re-printed in their special 60th anniversary edition (Urry 2010) as being one of the most agenda-setting articles of the decade. Yet there is scant evidence of that impact within the discipline of sociology itself: much of the impact has been on adjacent fields.

Although Urry's approach has at times been equated with that of theorists of global fluidity or liquidity, it goes beyond a description of the contemporary world as more mobile than in the past. It also posits a relational basis for social theorizing that puts mobility at its center; a research agenda around the study of various complex systems, assemblages and practices of mobility; and it includes a normative move toward addressing the future of mobility in relation to ecological sustainability. While the epochal claims have been rejected by many sociologists or perceived as Eurocentric (see Sheller 2012), few of these latter trajectories have been seriously taken up within sociology.

Having co-founded the journal *Mobilities* in 2005, with the first edition published in 2006, the editors (Kevin Hannam, Mimi Sheller and John Urry) worked to establish a shift in thinking around mobilities that would influence a range of disciplines, including sociology. With full-text downloads from the journal growing from about 1500 in 2006 to 20,000 in 2011, the journal entered the Thomson Reuters Social Science Index with an impact factor of 1.238, ranking 28/65 in Geography and 12/23 in Transportation. Yet the journals with the largest number of citations of *Mobilities* articles are all within the discipline of geography. The presence of "mobility" as a strong theme in geography can be seen in the abstracts of papers presented at the recent annual meeting of the Association of American Geographers (2012), in which there were 95 papers with "mobility" listed as a keyword. In contrast, at the American Sociological Association conference mobility does not appear as a searchable topic area, and the only sessions with mobility in their title are concerned with social mobility – with only a handful focusing on educational mobility, job mobility or geographic mobility. Within the discipline of sociology, especially in the United States, it seems clear that the influence of new ways of thinking about mobilities has barely made a dent.

In the sociological literature the term "mobility" is usually equated with the idea of "social mobility," which refers both to individual movement up or down the scale of socio-economic classes and to the collective positional movement of social groups or classes. Dating back to the work of Alexis de Tocqueville and Emile Durkheim, sociology has been fundamentally concerned with the relation of social mobility to processes of social change and social stability. Elaborated by Russian sociologist Pitirim Sorokin in his 1927 book *Social Mobility*, this approach to structural sociology and stratification theory became especially influential in the United States. Seymour Martin Lipset and Reinhard Bendix, in their classic *Social Mobility and Industrial Society* (1959), for example, defined social mobility as

> the process by which individuals move from one position to another in society – positions which by general consent have been given specific hierarchical values. When we study social mobility we analyze the movement of individuals from positions possessing a certain rank to positions either higher or lower in the social system.
>
> *(1991 [1959]: 1–2)*

This positional understanding of mobility still predominates in sociology, and studies of geographical mobility are limited to specific sub-fields such as migration studies or labor studies, and use very traditional methodological approaches that treat mobility as the movement from A to B (see Cresswell 2006).

Such structural approaches still influence the way sociology is taught today and the commonplace assumptions about what the term mobility means. However, there are other sociological traditions that do place more emphasis on *spatial* mobility, or what is sometimes called geographical mobility, especially the Chicago School of urban sociology. Sociologists in the 1920s addressed geographical mobility in several respects, including the residential mobility of groups migrating into cities, the daily mobility of urban dwellers and commuters, and the heightened stimuli of fast-paced "urban metabolism." American sociologists like Robert Park and Ernest Burgess were concerned with the potential negative effects of displacement and social destabilization linked to rapid urban expansion; but they nevertheless valued mobility as a vector for urban growth based on the fundamental capacity for human "locomotion." German sociologist Georg Simmel also influenced ideas of "urban metabolism" and the importance of circulation and mobility as crucial aspects of modern urban life, including the mobility not only of people, but also of capital. Mobilities researchers today are returning to some of these early sociological theorists to begin to re-think the sociology of mobilities.

Yet, as Kaufmann (2011) suggests, the field of urban sociology was early on hived off from specialist sub-fields such as the study of transportation, migration or communication. Sociology largely dropped its interest in spatial mobility, while those disciplines interested in spatial mobility developed highly specialized quantitative techniques of measurement and mapping. Mobilities theory was left outside the purview of mainstream US sociology due to the marginalization of early critical theorists and the fragmentation of sociology into policy-oriented sub-fields. The new transdisciplinary field of mobilities research effectively re-unites the specialist sub-fields that had been evicted from sociological research, including: the spatial mobility of humans, non-humans and objects; the circulation of information, images and capital, including critical theories of the affective and psycho-social implications of such mobility; as well as the study of the physical means for movement, such as infrastructures, vehicles, and software systems that enable travel and communication to take place. Thus it brings together some of the more purely "social" concerns of sociology (inequality, power, hierarchies) with the "spatial" concerns of geography (territory, borders, scale) and the "cultural" concerns of anthropology and media studies (discourses, representations, schemas), while inflecting each with a relational ontology of the co-constitution of subjects, spaces and meanings. Of course, it is precisely this anti-disciplinary hybridity that continues to situate the field as not-quite-sociology, even as it attracts students.

Despite the apparent obduracy of sociology in the US, the emergence of a new mobilities paradigm is nevertheless linked to a number of new academic institutions, networks and research initiatives that are attempting to re-position the sociology of mobilities. Amongst the leading institutions that include sociologists are the Centre for Mobilities Research (CeMoRe) at Lancaster University; the Center for Mobility and Urban Studies (C-MUS) at Aalborg University; the mobil.TUM Center at Technische Universität München; the Laboratory of Urban Sociology (LASUR) at Ecole Polytechnique Fédérale de Lausanne; and the Center for Mobilities Research and Policy (mCenter) at Drexel University. The main research networks, which sponsor conferences and research meetings, include the Cosmobilities Network and the Mediterranean Mobilities networks in Europe, and the Pan-American Mobilities Network, which is entering its fifth year of holding annual conferences in the USA and Canada, and includes members from Latin America. Key publications include the journal *Mobilities*, and the journal *Transfers: Interdisciplinary Journal of Mobility Studies*, as well as book series published by Routledge (Changing Mobilities) and by Ashgate. Out of this transnational, interdisciplinary nexus the field of mobilities research has gradually established a position that has a foot within sociology, but also reaches across many disciplinary boundaries.

Beyond the classical locus of urban sociology, and its important influence within human geography (Cresswell 2006; Adey 2009), mobilities research is also recognized as an important addition to the fields of transport research (Knowles *et al.* 2006), migration studies (Blunt 2007), tourism studies (Hannam and Knox 2010), and communication and media studies (De Souza e Silva and Gordon 2011). By focusing on the corporeal travel of people and the physical movement of objects, as well as dimensions such as imaginative travel, virtual travel and communicative travel (Urry 2007), it has stimulated transformative research agendas that reconvene the disparate fields of social science in a cross-cutting and dynamic configuration. Mobilities research holds the potential (and the threat) to reconfigure the boundaries, methodologies and theoretical lens of sociology. In what follows I aim to delineate in broad strokes some of the key areas in which mobilities research has perhaps been misunderstood by sociologists, and also where it can contribute to a renewed sociology. The first section is concerned with historicity, (im)mobility and power, arguing that mobilities research is not simply concerned with global flows or contemporary traveling elites, as it is sometimes misunderstood to be. The second section turns to some theoretical issues concerning micro and macro scales, and the relation between phenomenological and non-representational approaches within mobilities research and wider macro-approaches to structuration, systems and socio-technical change. The conclusion re-frames what mobilities research can offer contemporary sociology.

Historicity, (im)mobility and power

Although many theorists of postmodernity, late modernity and globalization began to describe a sense of societal motion, flow and liquidity in the 1990s (e.g. Bauman 2000), it is important to establish that the claim to a "new mobilities paradigm" is not simply an assertion of the novelty of mobility in the world today. Mobilities have long been a central aspect of both historical and contemporary existence, of urban and of non-urban locales, of Western and non-Western experience. Patterns of mobility are always shifting to support different modes of trade, interaction, urbanization and communication. While some (though certainly not all) groups of people *may* live more "mobile lives" today than in the past (Elliott and Urry 2010), geographical mobility and infrastructures of human, technological and informational mobility were as crucial to the existence of ancient imperial cities and seafaring empires of early modernity as they were to the nineteenth-century and early twentieth-century industrializing cities of Europe and America, and to the global trading ports, long-distance trade and pilgrimage routes, and modern global megacities of today.

To take one specific area of historical sociological research, a mobilities perspective can raise new questions around the emergence of the public sphere and its role in civil society – one of the classic problems of Habermasian-influenced sociology. Notions of public and private are fundamental to sociological analysis, yet are often oddly lacking a spatial perspective on how the mobilities of people and information shape the formation of publics and counterpublics, or how infrastructures and sorting systems might guide access to and movement between private and public spaces. New forms of mobility, new technologies of communication and novel convergences between travel, mobile communication and the infrastructures that support them have arguably reconfigured public and private life such that today there are new modes of public-in-private and private-in-public that disrupt commonly held spatial models of these as two separate 'spheres' (Sheller and Urry 2003). Publics are constituted not simply as abstract moments of communication, nor in the assumed form within sociological research as "public opinion" to be measured by surveys, but are part of deeply embedded social and machinic complexes involving the infrastructures that allow for the mobilities and coming together of people, objects, and information. Increasingly integrated modes of transportation, personal communication, and electronic work and entertainment have significant implications for the constitution of mobile publics, such as new forms of "net-locality" (De Souza e Silva and Sutko 2010).

Second, although the speed, intensity, and technical channeling of various mobile flows may be greater than ever before (for some people, in some places – though certainly not all), mobilities research emphasizes the relation of such mobilities to associated immobilities or moorings, and their ongoing reconfiguration in the past as well as in the present. The increase in cross-border transactions and of "capabilities for enormous geographical dispersal and mobility" go hand in hand with "pronounced territorial concentrations of resources necessary for the management and servicing of that dispersal and mobility" (Sassen 2002: 2). Such infrastructures and concentrations of mobile capital are linked to what David Harvey described as "spatial fixes" and later elaborated as "spatio-temporal fixes" (Jessop 2006). By bringing together studies of migration, transportation, infrastructure, transnationalism, mobile communications, imaginative travel and tourism, new approaches to mobility are especially able to highlight the relation between local and global "power-geometries" (Massey 1993). This brings into view the political projects inherent in the power relations informing processes of globalization (and associated claims to globality, fluidity or opening) that depend on various kinds of structured practices of mobilities and immobilities.

Third, with an emphasis on the relations between mobilities and immobilities, scapes and moorings, movement and stillness (Hannam *et al.* 2006: 3), the frictions and turbulence of differential mobilities are at the heart of recent mobilities research (Cresswell 2010). Thus it would be a great mistake to think that it is only concerned with the "hyper-mobile" elite of global capitalism. Differential capacities and potentials for mobility are analyzed via the concept of "motility," defined as "the manner in which an individual or group appropriates the field of possibilities relative to movement and uses them" (Kaufmann and Montulet 2008: 45). A person may have a high degree of motility without actually moving (for example, a well-connected professional who works from home), or they may be amongst the "mobility pioneers" who live highly spatially distributed lives yet seek sameness everywhere (Kesselring and Vogl 2008); while another may be involved in much physical displacement, but have low motility in terms of capacities, competencies and choices, especially if that movement is involuntary (for example, someone caught in the grips of a human trafficker). Issues of uneven motility and of mobility rights, ethics and justice have become crucial to the field of critical mobilities research (Cresswell 2006; Bergmann and Sager 2008; Uteng and Cresswell 2008), with attention to subaltern mobilities (and immobilities) as well as recognition of the importance of uprooting, dwelling, homing and grounding (Ahmed *et al.* 2003; Sheller 2003, 2004).

Here one can also begin to conceptualize "mobility capital" (Kaufmann *et al.* 2004) as the uneven distribution of these capacities and competencies, in relation to the surrounding physical, social and political affordances for movement (with the legal structures regulating who or what can and cannot move being crucial). Elliott and Urry (2010: 10–11) similarly describe "network capital" as a combination of capacities to be mobile, including appropriate documents, money and qualifications; access to networks at-a-distance; physical capacities for movement; location-free information and contact points; access to communication devices and secure meeting places; access to vehicles and infrastructures; and time and other resources for coordination. Uneven mobility capital is crucial to processes of globalization, effectively being created by particular forms of demobilizations and remobilizations (in the process of ongoing spatial fixes, temporal fixes and spatio-temporal fixes). Mobilities research is therefore highly engaged with debates over globalization, cosmopolitanism, postcolonialism, and emerging forms (and histories) of urbanism, surveillance and global governance of various kinds of differentiated or uneven mobility, all of which should be central concerns of contemporary sociology.

Theorizing mobilities at different scales

Mobilities theory departs from classic social theory in part because it builds on a wider range of philosophical perspectives to more radically re-think the relation between bodies, movement and space. In doing so, it treats scale in a different way than most sociology, because it is not limited by a micro vs. macro imagination of agency and structure. Through a relational approach to ontology, mobilities research enters as it were "between" scales, exploring connections across scales, and envisions a distributed agency that is both human and non-human and that circulates amongst people, objects, and environments. While in one sense this may alienate it from the more humanistic approaches of sociology, it also offers great opportunities for challenging the boundaries of "social" processes and where we locate action and social change (Sheller and Urry 2006a).

First, it draws on phenomenology to reconsider embodied practices and the production of being-in-motion as a relational affordance between the senses, objects, and kinaesthetic accomplishments. There are active corporeal engagements of human bodies with the sensed world, suggesting many different kinds of affordances between varied bodies, technologies (cars, phones, the internet, satellites), practices of movement (such as walking, biking, riding, driving or flying) and events of movement (such as commuting, migration, congestion, waiting, touring or pilgrimage) (Hannam *et al.* 2006). Merriman notes that writings on mobility have begun to trace "the more-than-representational, performative, expressive improvisations of bodies-in-movement-in-spaces" by describing "the production of complex entwined performativities, materialities, mobilities and affects of *both* human embodied subjects *and* the spaces/places/landscapes/environments which are inhabited, traversed, and perceived" (Merriman 2011: 99). Some recent work, for example, focuses on the micro-mobilities of the body in forms of dance or the bodily rhythms and motion involved in activities such as bicycling, rock climbing or walking (Fincham *et al.* 2010).

New methodologies are being developed to study these more ephemeral, embodied and affective dimensions of interlocking mobility and immobility, including attention not simply to fluidity or speed, but to slowness, stillness, waiting and pauses, which are all part of a wider sensuous geography of movement, affect and dwelling (Adey 2009; Bissell 2007, 2009; Bissell and Fuller 2009). Innovative mobile methods of video ethnography, mobile partici-pant observation, and being "mobile with" others are said to offer important insights into the accomplishment of various mobilities, and the affective economies surrounding move-ment and stillness. For example, Spinney's recent work on cycling emphasizes "the sensory, emotional, kinaesthetic and symbolic aspects of cycling" (Spinney 2011: 164); understanding "those fleeting, ephemeral, and often embodied and sensory aspects of movement," he argues, is vital for understanding how and why we move. Through these affective and atmospheric non-representational geographies of a wide range of embodied practices, we see a growing interest in cultures of "alternative mobility" (Vannini 2009) such as walking, biking, boating, climbing, riding ferries, etc. (Vannini 2011). We also gain an appreciation of the temporal pulse of transfer points and places of in-between-ness in which the circulation of people and objects are slowed or stopped, as well as facilitated and accelerated (Sheller and Urry 2006a; Hannam *et al.* 2006; Urry 2007).

Yet it is also crucial that we recognize that the field of mobilities research goes beyond a micro-sociology of practice. As the preceding section on histories of (im)mobilities sug-gested, it also draws on Foucauldian genealogies and governmentalities to address the mean-ings of (im)mobility, discourses and visual representations of speed and slowness, and the production of normalized mobile subjects. Mobilities research in its broadest sense concerns not only physical movement, but also potential movement, blocked movement, immobiliza-tion, and forms of dwelling and place-making (Büscher and Urry 2009), all of which are deeply enmeshed in relations of power and counter-power, disciplinary power and capillary power, strategies of control and tactics of resistance. Classic historical and comparative soci-ological questions of state formation, social movements and resistance can also be re-thought in terms of the state strategies for management of mobility, borders and the visibility of subjects within regimes of mobility, versus hidden mobility as a tactical escape from state power and anarchistic evasion of state governance (Scott 2009) that is still crucial to informal economies, piracy, and practices of offshoring.

Influenced by social studies of science and technology, in particular actor–network the-ory, mobilities theorists also pay close attention to the more-than-human infrastructures, technical objects, prostheses and practices that assist (or disable) mobility (Latour 1987, 1993; Büscher *et al.* 2010). This suggests "that contemporary landscapes are shot through with technological elements which enroll people, space, and the elements connecting people and spaces, into socio-technical assemblages – especially transportational technologies, such as roads, rail, subways and airports, but also the informational technologies such as signs, sched-ules, surveillance systems, radio signals, and mobile telephony" (Sheller and Urry 2006a: 9). In this sense, the classical emphasis of sociology on agency and structure, and on the individual and society, is displaced in favor of a more distributed, rhizomatic and post-humanist sense of what Deleuze called "agencement," translated as "assemblage." But the "agencement" of the world is not simply at the bodily level of personal interactions with spatial affordances, it is also very much concerned with larger scales of spatial production, urban form and infrastructural systems.

Having broken out of the straightjacket of society imagined as a national container with fixed boundaries at its borders, macro-level mobilities theory also draws on critical postcolonial theory and theories of political economy to re-think the performative politics of racial difference, secured borders and the governance of migration, sea-space and air-space. Crucial here are the in-between and liminal places at which movement is paused, slowed or stopped: borders, airports, toll roads, hotels, motels, detention centers, refugee camps, etc. (Mountz 2010). The study of mobilities at this scale too is also very much about waiting, stillness and non-movement. It is also very concerned with emotional geographies, and the ways in which affect circulates amongst that which moves and does not move, suffusing the speeds and still-nesses of (im)mobility with negative and positive polarities. Thus it offers a far more nuanced view of migration, border-crossing and various other kinds of travel, including tourism, and has been recognized in all of these sub-disciplines as an important contribution to how we might think about our field of study. Rather than assuming pre-constituted subjects who cross pre-existing borders, there is a move towards examining the co-constitution of mobile border-subjects or places-in-motion (Sheller and Urry 2004).

Through a kinaesthetic sense of bodily motion we apprehend time and space, orient ourselves toward the world, and create place through the frictions and rhythms of our movement. Movements have different rhythms, and those rhythms of movement flow through bodies, cities and landscapes, shaping their feel, sculpting their textures, and making places. Picking up on Henri Lefebvre's (2004) concept of rhythmanalysis, geographer Tim Edensor argues that "rhythmanalysis elucidates how places possess no essence but are ceaselessly (re)constituted out of their connections . . . Places are thus continually (re)produced through the mobile flows which course through and around them, bringing together ephemeral, contingent and relatively stable arrangements of people, energy and matter" (Edensor 2011: 190). Accordingly, he argues, the "organised braiding of multiple mobile rhythms produces distinct forms of spatio-temporal order, maintained through the orchestration of traffic management systems, the conventions of travel practice, the affordances of transport forms and the characteristics of the space moved through" (ibid.: 190). And this certainly echoes the feel of the work of Simmel on the stimulus of urban life and the rhythms of urban metabolism, yet places it into a contemporary framework that is relevant to understanding global urbanism today.

Conclusion

By revisiting a diverse range of historical and contemporary sociological issues, mobilities research re-casts some of the classical concerns of social stratification theory and urban ecology, expanding the notion of social mobility to wide-ranging spatio-temporal contexts and multiple scales. The journal *Transfers*, for example, in its first issue claims interests that "will range from analyses of the past and present experiences of vehicle drivers, passengers, pedestrians, migrants, and refugees, to accounts of the arrival and transformation of mobility in different nations and locales, to investigations of the kinetic processes of global capital, technology, chemical and biological substances, images, narratives, sounds, and ideas" (Mom *et al.* 2011). It would be a significant contribution to sociology were mobilities research recognized for its ability to bridge separate geographical and historical domains, to re-position the empirical content of sociology to be more inclusive, and to cross scales in analyzing the dynamics of structure and agency.

Mobilities research combines social and spatial theory in new ways, and in so doing bridges micro-interactional research on the phenomenology of embodiment, the cultural turn and hermeneutics, post-colonial and critical theory, macro-structural approaches to the state and political-economy, and elements of science and technology studies (STS) and new media studies. Büscher, Urry and Witchger argue that "Through investigations of movement, blocked movement, potential movement and immobility, dwelling and place-making, social scientists are showing how various kinds of 'moves' make social and material realities" (Büscher *et al.* 2010: 2). These moves, it must be noted, are not simply individual moves, but may be moves of infrastructure and spatio-temporal fixes, moves of meaning and representation, or moves of distributed power and evasive tactics. The mobilities turn, they continue, thus "open[s] up different ways of understanding the relationship between theory, observation and engagement. It engenders new kinds of researchable entities, a new or rediscovered realm of the empirical and new avenues for critique" (Büscher *et al.* 2010: 2).

The question is, where might this lead contemporary sociology? And are sociologists willing to make the moves that would be required to follow these new avenues and new forms of engagement with the empirical? Would such moves require the dissolution of sociology as we know it, and is the move towards what Urry called a "sociology beyond societies" too threatening to sociology as a discipline which has been built around an object called "society"? In some respects the field of mobilities research has already left sociology far behind, and constituted its own disciplinary matrix of highly productive research collaborations and conversations that span many other disciplines. If anything, it may be that this move, beyond sociology, is already part of the transition toward a new paradigm (implicit in the initial claims for the field), in which academic research will be more transformative, more innovative, and more mobile.

Bibliography

Adey, P (2009) *Mobility.* London and New York: Routledge.

Ahmed, S, Castañeda, C, Fortier, A and Sheller, M (2003) *Uprootings/Regroundings: Questions of Home and Migration.* Oxford: Berg.

Amin, A and Thrift, N (2002) *Cities. Reimagining the Urban.* Cambridge: Polity.

Bauman, Z (2000) *Liquid Modernity.* Cambridge: Polity.

Bergmann, S and Sager, T (eds) (2008) *The Ethics of Mobilities: Rethinking Place, Exclusion, Freedom and Environment.* Aldershot: Ashgate.

Bissell, D (2007) "Animating Suspension: Waiting for Mobilities." *Mobilities,* 2(2): 277–298.

Bissell, D (2009) "Moving with Others: The Sociality of the Railway Journey." In: Vannini P (ed.) *The Cultures of Alternative Mobilities: The Routes Less Travelled.* Farnham, UK and Burlington, VT: Ashgate, 55–70.

Bissell, D and Fuller, G (eds) (2009) "The Revenge of the Still." *M/C Journal,* 12(1). Available online at http://journal.media-culture.org.au/index.php/mcjournal/article/viewArticle/136/0 (accessed 16 August 2013).

Blunt, A (2007) "Cultural Geographies of Migration: Mobility, Transnationality and Diaspora." *Progress in Human Geography,* 31(5): 684–694.

Büscher, M and Urry, J (2009) "Mobile Methods and the Empirical." *European Journal of Social Theory,* 12(1): 99–116.

Büscher, M, Urry, J and Witchger, K (2010) *Mobile Methods.* London and New York: Routledge.

Cresswell, T (2006) *On the Move: Mobility in the Modern Western World.* London: Routledge.

Cresswell, T (2010) "Towards a Politics of Mobility." *Environment and Planning D: Society and Space*, 28(1): 17–31.

Cresswell, T and Merriman, P (eds) (2011) *Geographies of Mobilities: Practices, Spaces, Subjects*. Farnham and Burlington: Ashgate.

De Souza e Silva, A and Gordon, E (2011) *Net-Locality: Why Location Matters in a Networked World*. Malden and Oxford: Wiley-Blackwell.

De Souza e Silva, A and Sutko, D (eds) (2010) *Digital Cityscapes: Merging Digital and Urban Playspaces*. New York: Peter Lang.

Edensor, T (2011) "Commuter: Mobility, Rhythm, Commuting." In: Cresswell T and Merriman P (eds) *Geographies of Mobilities: Practices, Spaces, Subjects*. Farnham and Burlington: Ashgate, 189–204.

Elliott, A and Urry, J (2010) *Mobile Lives*. New York and London: Routledge.

Fincham, B, McGuinness, M and Murray, L (2010) *Mobile Methodologies*. Farnham: Ashgate.

Hannam, K and Knox, D (2010) *Understanding Tourism: A Critical Introduction*. London: Sage.

Hannam, K, Sheller, M and Urry, J (2006) "Mobilities, Immobilities, and Moorings." *Mobilities*, 1(1): 1–22.

Jessop, B (2006) "Spatial Fixes, Temporal Fixes and Spatio-Temporal Fixes." In: Castree N and Gregory D (eds) *David Harvey: A Critical Reader*. New York: Blackwell, 142–166.

Kaufmann, V (2011) *Rethinking the City: Urban Dynamics and Motility*. Lausanne: EPFL Press; Oxford and New York: Routledge.

Kaufmann, V, Bergman, M and Joye, D (2004) "Motility: Mobility as Capital." *International Journal of Urban and Regional Research*, 28(4) (December): 745–756.

Kaufmann, V and Montulet, B (2008) "Between Social and Spatial Mobilities: The Issue of Social Fluidity." In: Canzler, W, Kaufmann, V and Kesselring, S (eds) *Tracing Mobilities: Towards a Cosmopolitan Perspective*. Farnham and Burlington: Ashgate, 37–56.

Kesselring, S and Vogl, G (2008) "Networks, Scapes and Flows – Mobility Pioneers between First and Second Modernity." In: Canzler, W, Kaufmann, V and Kesselring, S (eds) *Tracing Mobilities: Towards a Cosmopolitan Perspective*. Farnham and Burlington: Ashgate, 163–180.

Knowles, R, Shaw, J and Axhausen, K (2006) *Transport Geographies: Mobilities, Flows, Spaces*. New York: Blackwell.

Latour, B (1987) *Science in Action: How to Follow Scientists and Engineers Through Society*. Milton Keynes: Open University Press.

Latour, B (1993) *We Have Never Been Modern*. Cambridge: Harvard University Press.

Lefebvre, H (2004) *Rhythmanalysis: Space, Time and Everyday Life*. New York: Continuum.

Lipset, S M and Bendix, R (1991 [195]) *Social Mobility and Industrial Society*. New Brunswick: Transaction Publishers.

Massey, D (1993) "Power-Geometry and a Progressive Sense of Place." In: Bird, J, Curtis, B, Putnam, T, Robertson, G and Tickner, L (eds) *Mapping the Futures: Local Cultures, Global Change*. Routledge: London.

Merriman, P (2011) "Roads: Lawrence Halprin, Modern Dance and the American Freeway Landscape." In: Cresswell, T and Merriman, P (eds) *Geographies of Mobilities: Practices, Spaces, Subjects*. Aldershot: Ashgate, 99–117.

Mom, G, Clarsen, G, Merriman, P, Seiler, C, Sheller, M and Weber, H (2011) "Editorial." *Transfers* 1(1): 3.

Mountz, A (2010) *Seeking Asylum: Human Smuggling and Bureaucracy at the Border*. Minneapolis: University of Minnesota Press.

Mountz, A (2011) "Refugees – Performing Distinction: Paradoxical Positionings of the Displaced." In: Cresswell, T and Merriman, P (eds) *Geographies of Mobilities: Practices, Spaces, Subjects*. Farnham and Burlington: Ashgate, 255–270.

Sassen, S (2002) "Locating Cities on Global Circuits." In: Sassen, S (ed.) *Global Networks, Linked Cities*. New York and London: Routledge.

Scott, J C (2009) *The Art of Not Being Governed: An Anarchist History of Upland Southeast Asia*. New Haven: Yale University Press.

Sheller, M (2003) *Consuming the Caribbean: From Arawaks to Zombies*. London and New York: Routledge.

Sheller, M (2004) "Automotive Emotions: Feeling the Car." *Theory, Culture & Society*, 21(4/5): 221–242.

Sheller, M (2012) "Cosmopolitanism and Mobilities". In: Nowicka, M and Rovisco, M (eds) *The Ashgate Research Companion to Cosmopolitanism*. Aldershot: Ashgate.

Sheller, M and Urry, J (2003) "Mobile Transformations of 'Public' and 'Private' Life." *Theory, Culture & Society*, 20(3): 107–125.

Sheller, M and Urry, J (eds) (2004) *Tourism Mobilities: Places to Play, Places in Play*. London and New York: Routledge.

Sheller, M and Urry, J (2006a) "The New Mobilities Paradigm." *Environment and Planning A*, 38: 207–226.

Sheller, M and Urry, J (2006b) "Mobile Cities, Urban Mobilities." In the introduction to Sheller, M and Urry, J (eds) *Mobile Technologies of the City*. London and New York: Routledge, 1–17.

Sorokin, P (1927) *Social Mobility*. New York: Harper and Brothers.

Spinney, J (2011) "A Chance to Catch a Breath: Using Mobile Video Ethnography in Cycling Research." *Mobilities*, 6(2) (May): 161–182.

Thrift, N (2008) *Non-Representational Theory: Space, Politics, Affect*. New York: Routledge.

Urry, J (2000) *Sociology Beyond Societies: Mobilities for the Twenty-first Century*. London: Routledge.

Urry, J (2007) *Mobilities*. Cambridge: Polity.

Urry, J (2010 [2001]) "Mobile Sociology." *The British Journal of Sociology – The BJS: Shaping Sociology Over 60 Years*, 61: 347–66.

Uteng, T P and Cresswell, T (eds) (2008) *Gendered Mobilities*. Aldershot: Ashgate.

Vannini, P (ed.) (2009) *The Cultures of Alternative Mobilities: The Routes Less Travelled*. Farnham, UK and Burlington, VT: Ashgate.

Vannini, P (2011) *Ferry Tales: Mobility, Place and Time on Canada's West Coast*. New York and Abingdon: Routledge.

4

Anthropology

Noel B. Salazar

It is not our feet that move us along – it is our minds.
(Ancient Chinese proverb)

Mobility captures the common impression that our lifeworld is in constant flux. It is also one of the preferred concept-metaphors for social descriptions of both Self and Other. Examples that are popular in anthropological theorizing include Walter Benjamin's "flâneur," Michel de Certeau's "pedestrian," Edward Said's "exile" (forced migrant), and Gilles Deleuze and Félix Guattari's "nomad." Anthropologists are mostly involved in unraveling the multiple meanings attached to various forms of movement, both for individuals and societies at large. The current interest in mobilities goes hand in hand with theoretical approaches that reject a "sedentarist metaphysics" (Malkki, 1992), questioning earlier taken-for-granted correspondences between peoples, places, and cultures, as well as critiquing "methodological nationalism" (Wimmer and Glick Schiller, 2003).

Anthropology's quest to dismantle concepts and theories that presume unitary cultures in fixed places has been important to both Marxian political economists (Wolf, 1982) and postmodernists (Gupta and Ferguson, 1997; Hannerz, 1996). Some scholars, however, have conflated the excitement of so-called "post-local" approaches and that of perceived new global developments, weakening the case for each. If older theoretical frameworks were unable to handle interconnection and mobility, this is a problem with the theories, not the mirror of an evolutionary global change. Anthropologists have also questioned the nature of mobility itself because "neglecting the practices that create the objects and processes of mobility leads analysts to miss alternative constructions that seriously challenge neat and teleological narratives of globalization" (Maurer, 2000, p. 688).

As the study of humanity (in all its diversity) remains the core business of the anthropologists, this chapter focuses on the wide range of anthropological scholarship on human mobilities. I briefly sketch the genealogy of conceptualizations of mobility and mobile methods in anthropology. Over the years, anthropologists have studied the most diverse forms of (im)mobility around the world and this is not an exhaustive review of all that work. Rather, I zoom in on key epistemological and methodological issues within social and cultural anthropology that have important repercussions for mobility studies as a whole.

A short history

Ideas of mobility have a long history in anthropology. They are already present in late nineteenth- and early twentieth-century transcultural diffusionism, which understood the movement of people, objects, and ideas as an essential aspect of cultural life. Franz Boas, diffusionist and one of the discipline's founding fathers in North America, conducted his first fieldwork in 1883–4 on migration as a cause of cultural change in the life of the Baffin Island Inuit in Canada. Around the same time in Europe, French structuralists developed notions of movement more fully in their theorizing of exchange. Marcel Mauss, for instance, related the seasonal mobility of Inuit (to stay with the example) to their moral and religious life. Bronisław Malinowski, a founding father in Europe, is credited for moving the discipline beyond armchair philosophizing and putting notions of migrancy at the heart of ethnographic practice (Wilding, 2007). Malinowski became famous for his 1915–16 field-work on the *kula* trading cycle of the Trobriand (now Kiriwina) Islands, which can be read as an early account of the interrelationships between diasporic people, objects, and mobility (Hage, 2005).

The mainstream study of colonized non-Western societies, however, was mostly based on models of homogeneity and continuity, reflecting colonial administrative policies and structures. Sedentarism, which stresses bounded places as the basis of human experience, was deeply embedded in British structural–functional anthropology (e.g. the work of Edward Evans-Pritchard and Alfred Radcliffe-Brown). The ethnographic descriptions of life in New Guinea by Margaret Mead in the late 1920s are also largely portraits of discrete and timeless cultures, unaffected by the outside world until the advent of the West (Brettell, 2003, p. ix). These and other classical monographs mostly confined their analyses of mobility to the areas of kinship (marriage mobility), politics (structure of nomadic peoples), and religion (pilgrimage).

As Tsing states, this classical type of anthropology constituted cultures "as essentially immobile or as possessing a mobility that is cyclical and repetitive . . . Those with culture are expected to have a regular, delimited occupation of territory. If they move, they must do so cyclically, like transhumant pastoralists or kula-ring sailors" (1993, p. 123). Indeed, mobility was too often limited to being a defining characteristic of groups such as hunter-gatherers or traveler-gypsies. It was used as a concept describing physical or abstract movement, not as something implying in and of itself social or cultural change (Farnell, 1999). As always, there were exceptions to the rule. For the Manchester School (and its Rhodes–Livingstone Institute in what is now Zambia), for example, labor migration was an important and recurring theme of research. Importantly, these scholars documented the long pre-colonial urban tradition in some African regions linked to trade and movement. Even here, though, the study of mobility remained subsumed under broad concepts such as class, social structure, kinship, or geographic space.

In the 1960s, Victor Turner started studying the symbolic aspects of mobility in life (particularly rites of passage). There is a remarkable parallel between his studies of pilgrimage and more recent concerns with the geography and sociality of mobility (Basu and Coleman, 2008). Marc Augé's (1995) "non-places," where people pass through while traveling, are strikingly similar to Turner's (1967, pp. 93–111) liminal "as if" stage in rituals, when people are "betwixt and between." This work left its mark on migration studies, where transnational migrants are frequently represented as liminal, and temporary migration in certain contexts has been interpreted as an almost mandatory rite of passage. In addition, the earlier (but related) anthropological work on threshold rites by Arnold van Gennep is being recycled these days to understand the dynamics of transnational borders. In the 1970s and 1980s, scholars such as Eric Wolf (1982) were instrumental in demonstrating that non-Europeans had always been deeply implicated in border-crossing mobilities (e.g. slave trades).

While classical anthropology tended to ignore or regard border-crossing movements as deviations from normative place-bound communities, cultural homogeneity, and social integration, discourses of globalization and cosmopolitanism (that became dominant after the end of the Cold War) shifted the pendulum in the opposite direction. In the 1990s, globalization – largely theorized in terms of trans-border "flows" – was often being promoted as normality, and too much place attachment a digression or resistance against globalizing forces. Mobility became predominantly a characteristic of the modern globalized world. This led to a new focus on transnational mobilities that deterritorialize identity. Arjun Appadurai's (1996) provoking notion of "ethnoscapes," for instance, privileges mobile groups and individuals, such as immigrants, exiles, tourists, and guest workers. As Aihwa Ong explains, "*Trans* denotes both moving through space or across lines, as well as changing the nature of something" (1999, p. 4).

By the turn of the millennium, there were already serious cracks in the master narrative of unfettered mobility, which accompanied the discourse of the benefits and necessity of (economic) globalization. According to Engseng Ho, who studied the movement of an old diaspora across the Indian Ocean over the past five hundred years, "the new anthropology of mobility has reintroduced a teleology of progress that had previously been derided and, so it seemed, discarded . . . Yet societies, cultures, and religions have been mobile for a long time" (2006, p. 10). The language of mobilities has inadvertently distracted attention from how the fluidity of markets shapes flexibility in modes of control. Especially since 9/11, barriers to border-crossing movements have increased dramatically, accompanied by the counter-narrative of securitization. In fact, critically engaged anthropologists were among the first to point out that modern forms of mobility need not signify privilege (Amit, 2007). Not all mobilities are valued equally positively and the very processes that produce global movements also result in immobility and exclusion (Cunningham and Heyman, 2004; Salazar and Smart, 2011).

Methodology and epistemology

From Malinowski's pioneering fieldwork onward, the notion of ethnographers as itinerant and "going somewhere" – traditionally from the West to non-Western cultures – has been reinforced and reproduced, as has been the notion of "being there" (in a fixed place), even if only for a short period of time (hereby reasserting the implicit connection between culture and place). Although the whole history of ethnography is intertwined with (technologies of) travel, Claude Lévi-Strauss (1961 (1955)) famously argued this has no place in the work of anthropologists; travel merely serves as a method to gather the necessary ethnographic material. James Clifford (1997), however, advocates traveling as a way of doing ethnography and argues that anthropologists need to leave behind their preoccupation with discovering the "roots" of socio-cultural forms and identities and instead trace the "routes" that (re)produce them. Malinowksi's work on the *kula* ring, for instance, illustrates how in Melanesia people move through the places (i.e. things) that they cause to travel (Strathern, 1991, p. 117).

I concur with Jo Vergunst that "ethnography is an excellent way to get at important aspects of human movement, especially in relating its experiential and sensory qualities to social and environmental contexts" (2011, p. 203). Observational and participative modes of fieldwork through places constitute insightful ways to investigate mobility. Focusing on movement as a way of understanding social spaces offers a means to get beyond biases inherent in the social science of space (Kirby, 2009). The development of field diaries and monographs, with subtle differences from the genre of travel writing, has been an interesting way to narrate physical as well as cultural mobility undertaken by anthropologists in search for otherness. Some ethnographies have even been written in a style "borrowed" from the cultural practices of the mobile people under study (e.g. Rethmann, 2001).

Ethnographers have always been concerned with the movements of their informants. As Marianne Lien (2003) points out, anthropologists' unease in relation to rapidly changing global connectivities clearly may be understood as a result of the way their discipline has traditionally delineated its object of study in time (synchronic studies, ethnographic present) and in space (a community, a small-scale society): a science which builds its epistemology on immersing oneself in a single place (over a period of a year or more) is hardly well-suited for dealing with transnational connectivities and flows. Epistemologies that treat society as a given, a contained entity, have problems explaining the increased interconnectedness of objects and subjects (Robbins and Bamford, 1997). David Coplan (2001), for example, focuses on rural (rather than urban) contexts of the cultures of mobility that accrue with migrancy in South Africa, using his empirical data to show that as much passes for custom and practice "on the road" than "in the village/homelands" (cf. Masquelier, 2002). There is also anthropological research on how (im)mobility impacts on people's identities (Mathers, 2010; Salazar, 2010a) or even creates new ones (D'Andrea, 2007).

The single-sited methodology, its sensibility, and epistemological presuppositions are felt by many to no longer be adequate for examining the realities of an increasingly mobile, shifting, and interconnected world (Ong, 1999). This explains the popularity of "multi-sited ethnography" (Marcus, 1998). According to George Marcus (1998), multi-sited ethnographies may focus on persons, things, metaphors, stories, allegories, or biographies. Tsing, for instance, abandons the fixed locale of the village to follow her informants, whose communities can be understood only "within the context of . . . mobility – from daily visits to annual field movements to long-term trajectories across the landscape" (1993, p. 124). However, as Matei Candea rightly points out, traditional ethnography also "gave rise in practice to works which were as mobile and, in some senses, 'multi-sited' as the *Argonauts of the Western Pacific* or those arising from the Manchester School's 'extended case method'" (2007, pp. 169–170).

Susan Frohlick (2006) has challenged notions of multi-sited methodology as a matter of systematically following the circulation of people, objects, or practices within globalized worlds. Rather than her simply following mobile informants, the latter follow (or bump into) her in contexts away from her conventional field, leading her to develop very new understandings of them. Lien (2003) suggests a complementary approach to the field based on multi-temporality. Instead of juxtaposing field-sites that differ in space, she juxtaposes the configurations of a single field-site as it differs over time. Indeed, mobility has spatial/geographic, temporal/local, and historical as well as symbolic features (Long, 2000). Michaela Benson (2011) revisits the centrality of mobility in fieldwork methodologies used to investigate mobile formations. She proposes a multi-faceted approach that embraces innovative thinking and flexible ways of building rapport with the subjects by engaging in mutual forms of everyday-life mobilities. Informed by the inductive tradition that constitutes the research canon in anthropology, Benson argues that alternative fieldwork strategies for mobilities studies, while sensitive to mobility, must not be determined or bound by it as an a priori category.

In his "anthropology of movement," Alain Tarrius (2000) proposes a "methodological paradigm of mobility" articulated around the space–time–identity triad, along with four distinct levels of space–time relations, indicating the circulatory process of migratory movements whereby spatial mobility is linked to other types of mobility (informational, cognitive, technological, and economic). What he describes as "circulatory territories" are new spaces of movement that "encompass the networks defined by the mobility of populations whose status derives from their circulation know-how" (Tarrius, 2000, p. 124). This notion indicates that geographical movement is always invested with social meaning. Discussing the concept of social navigation, Henrik Vigh nicely illustrates the analytical advantages of mobility-related concept-metaphors. As both process and practice, social navigation "joins two separate social scientific perspectives on movement, that is, the movement and change of social formations and societies, and the movement and practice of agents within social formations" (Vigh, 2009, p. 426). Such an approach reveals that social environments are not as solid as they are often presented as being and that this influences the way people move within them.

The use of mobile technologies, especially for recording, is well established in anthropology. In the 1950s, for instance, the portable film camera reshaped ethnography's ongoing investigation and recording of exotic peoples (e.g. the influential work of Jean Rouch). Film can approach the mobility of ordinary movement and provide a way of creating ethnographic data collaboratively. Anthropological methods in general have had a significant impact on mobility studies (D'Andrea, Ciolfi, and Gray, 2011). While direct participation in analyzing mobile practices is not at all new in anthropological research, what emerges in the more recent scholarship on mobilities is a concern with mobility as an assemblage of phenomena of its own kind, requiring specific methodologies and conceptual frameworks. Despite the long tradition, "the impact of movement (and motility) upon a researcher's own research remains largely unproblematized at the level of analytical representation" (D'Andrea, *et al.*, 2011, p. 154).

Anthropology has a long-established tradition of research on (semi-)nomadic people, and the latest research includes the use of GPS and other mobile technologies (Aporta and Higgs, 2005). Even this traditional field of study contributes to a more general understanding of mobility. Take, for example, the work of Joachim Habeck, who proposes to shift the perspective from the potential of movement (also called motility) to mobility "acted out" in order to "obtain more nuanced insights into how nomads and transhumant herders see the world that surrounds them and how they interact with the surroundings while doing their work" (Habeck, 2006, p. 138). There is some excellent ethnographic work on everyday mobile practices (Wolch and Rowe, 1992) and the actual processes of movement rather than the systems of mobility (Journal for the Anthropological Study of Human Movement (http://jashm.press.illinois.edu); Ingold and Vergunst, 2008). Tim Ingold, for instance, has not only written extensively on the comparative anthropology of hunter-gatherer and pastoral societies, but also offers a more grounded approach to human movement, sensitive to embodied skills of footwork (Ingold, 2004). Mobility infrastructure is more and more seen not as "non-places" (Augé, 1995), but as "the ideal place where an anthropologist can perceive, study, and even touch the various dynamic transnational and fluid sociocultural formations, literally in the making, from both below and above, and on the move" (Dalakoglou, 2010, p. 146).

Borders and boundaries

The movement of people may, and often does, create or reinforce difference and inequality, as well as blend or erase such differences (Salazar, 2010a). Despite the overly general celebration and romanticization, the ability to move is spread very unevenly within countries and across the planet. This presents a serious criticism to the overgeneralized discourse that assumes "without any research to support it that the whole world is on the move, or at least that never have so many people, things and so on been moving across international borders" (Friedman, 2002, p. 33). Border-crossing mobilities as a form of human experience are still the exception rather than the norm. Even the incessant socio–cultural mobility that is often seen these days as characteristic of contemporary life is only one part of the story (Geschiere and Nyamnjoh, 2000). For the very processes that produce movement and global linkages also promote immobility, exclusion, and disconnection. The boundaries people are faced with in mobility can also be related to social class, gender, age, lifestyle, ethnicity, national-ity, and disability (all of which have been addressed by anthropological research in some way or another).

In anthropology there is a persistent tension between structural, political-economy views and a postmodern attention to hybridity and cultural creativity along borders (Alvarez, 1995; Bruner, 2005). Although there often is a contradiction between the expectation of mobility and barriers in front of it (Nyíri, 2010), mobilities and borders are not antithetical. As Brenda Chalfin reminds us, "This is not a world without borders but a world in which all borders operate according to uniform terms that make mobility their priority" (2008, p. 525). Historically borders have been mobile and, as they move, people's previous daily connections suddenly become cross-border mobility. Actually, the first stages of the industrial revolution were marked by states trying to contain their labor within borders. As more people begin to move, states attempt to maintain authority over the interpretation of their movement (Nyíri, 2010).

Consideration of these themes focuses attention on the political-economic processes by which people are bounded, emplaced, and allowed or forced to move (Cunningham and Heyman, 2004; De Genova and Peutz, 2010). Such studies show how mobility is materially grounded. The physical movement of people entails not only a measure of economic, social, and cultural mobility, but also a corresponding evolution of institutions and well-determined "circuits of human mobility" (Lindquist, 2009, p. 7). Importantly, the substance of such cir-cuits is "the movement of people (and money, goods, and news, but primarily people) as well as the relative immobility of people who do not travel the circuit" (Rockefeller, 2010, p. 222). To assess the extent or nature of movement, or, indeed, even "observe" it sometimes, one needs to spend a lot of time studying things that stand still (or change at a much slower pace).

The future is mobile

Mobilities research directs new questions towards traditional anthropological topics. People are moving all the time, but not all movements are equally meaningful and life-shaping (for both those who move and those who stay put). Mobility gains meaning through its embed-dedness within societies, culture, politics, and histories (which are themselves, to a certain extent, mobile). Alongside gender, class, race, ethnicity, age, nationality, language, religion, lifestyle, disability, and geopolitical groupings, mobility has become a key difference- and otherness-producing machine, involving significant inequalities of speed, risk, rights, and status, with both mobile and immobile people being engaged in the construction of complex politics of location and movement (Salazar and Smart, 2011). The question is not so much about the overall rise or decline of mobility, but how various mobilities are formed, regulated, and distributed across the globe, and how the formation, regulation, and distribution of these mobilities are shaped and patterned by existing social, political, and economic structures.

Mobility studies urgently needs "methodological tools and paradigms which can respond to modern systems of mobility but do not in themselves necessarily reify such systems" (Vergunst, 2011, p. 204). Indeed, the cultural assumptions, meanings, and values attached to (im)mobility need to be empirically problematized rather than assumed (Lubkemann, 2008; Salazar, 2010b). Contemporary anthropology is well-equipped to challenge the (Western) assumptions embedded within much mobility studies. Anthropology's liminal positioning is well-attuned to the complex and rapidly changing world in which we live. Founding fathers such as Boas and Malinowski already showed how this in-betweenness, with constant methodological and theoretical boundary crossings, offers a fruitful level of grounded ethnographic analysis. Anthropologists should therefore engage more actively in the current debate by detailing how human (im)mobility is a contested ideological construct involving much more than mere physical movement.

References

Alvarez, R. R. (1995). "The Mexican–US border: The making of an anthropology of borderlands." *Annual Review of Anthropology*, 24, 447–470.

Amit, V. (ed.) (2007). *Going first class? New approaches to privileged travel and movement*. Oxford: Berghahn.

Aporta, C. and Higgs, E. (2005). "Satellite culture: Global positioning systems, Inuit wayfinding, and the need for a new account of technology." *Current Anthropology*, 46(5), 729–753.

Appadurai, A. (1996). *Modernity at large: Cultural dimensions of globalization*. Minneapolis: University of Minnesota Press.

Augé, M. (1995). *Non-places: Introduction to an anthropology of supermodernity* (J. Howe, trans.). London: Verso.

Basu, P. and Coleman, S. (2008). "Migrant worlds, material cultures." *Mobilities*, 3(3), 313–330.

Benson, M. (2011). "The movement beyond (lifestyle) migration: Mobile practices and the constitution of a better way of life." *Mobilities*, 6(2), 221–235.

Brettell, C. (2003). *Anthropology and migration: Essays on transnationalism, ethnicity, and identity*. Walnut Creek: AltaMira.

Bruner, E. M. (2005). *Culture on tour: Ethnographies of travel*. Chicago: University of Chicago Press.

Candea, M. (2007). "Arbitrary locations: In defence of the bounded field-site." *Journal of the Royal Anthropological Institute*, 13(1), 167–184.

Chalfin, B. (2008). "Sovereigns and citizens in close encounter: Airport anthropology and customs regimes in neoliberal Ghana." *American Ethnologist*, 35(4), 519–538.

Clifford, J. (1997). *Routes: Travel and translation in the late twentieth century*. Cambridge: Harvard University Press.

Coplan, D. B. (2001). "You have left me wandering about: Basotho women and the culture of mobility." In D. L. Hodgson and S. A. McCurdy (eds), *"Wicked" women and the reconfiguration of gender in Africa* (188–211). Exeter: Heinemann.

Cunningham, H. and Heyman, J. (2004). "Introduction: Mobilities and enclosures at borders." *Identities: Global Studies in Culture and Power*, 11(3), 289–302.

Dalakoglou, D. (2010). "The road: An ethnography of the Albanian–Greek cross-border motorway." *American Ethnologist*, 37(1), 132–149.

D'Andrea, A. (2007). *Global nomads: Techno and New Age as transnational countercultures in Ibiza and Goa*. London: Routledge.

D'Andrea, A., Ciolfi, L. and Gray, B. (2011). "Methodological challenges and innovations in mobilities research." *Mobilities*, 6(2), 149–160.

De Genova, N. and Peutz, N. M. (eds) (2010). *The deportation regime: Sovereignty, space, and the freedom of movement*. Durham: Duke University Press.

Farnell, B. (1999). "Moving bodies, acting selves." *Annual Review of Anthropology*, 28, 341–373.

Friedman, J. (2002). "From roots to routes: Tropes for trippers." *Anthropological Theory*, 2(1), 21–36.

Frohlick, S. (2006). "Rendering and gendering mobile subjects: Placing ourselves between local ethnography and global worlds." In S. Coleman and P. Collins (eds), *Locating the field: Space, place and context in anthropology* (87–104). Oxford: Berg.

Geschiere, P. and Nyamnjoh, F. (2000). "Capitalism and autochthony: The seesaw of mobility and belonging." *Public Culture*, 12(2), 423–452.

Gupta, A. and Ferguson, J. (eds) (1997). *Anthropological locations: Boundaries and grounds of a field science.* Berkeley: University of California Press.

Habeck, J. O. (2006). "Experience, movement and mobility: Komi reindeer herders' perception of the environment." *Nomadic Peoples*, 10(2), 123–141.

Hage, G. (2005). "A not so multi-sited ethnography of a not so imagined community." *Anthropological Theory*, 5(4), 463–475.

Hannerz, U. (1996). *Transnational connections: Culture, people, places.* New York: Routledge.

Ho, E. (2006). *The graves of Tarim: Genealogy and mobility across the Indian Ocean.* Berkeley: University of California Press.

Ingold, T. (2004). "Culture on the ground: The world perceived through the feet." *Journal of Material Culture*, 9(3), 315–340.

Ingold, T. and Vergunst, J. L. (eds) (2008). *Ways of walking: Ethnography and practice on foot.* Aldershot: Ashgate.

Kirby, P. W. (ed.) (2009). *Boundless worlds: An anthropological approach to movement.* New York: Berghahn Books.

Lévi-Strauss, C. (1961 (1955)). *Tristes tropiques* (J. Russell, trans.). New York: Criterion Books.

Lien, M. E. (2003). "Shifting boundaries of a coastal community: Tracing changes on the margin." In T. H. Eriksen (ed.), *Globalisation: Studies in anthropology* (vi, 236). London: Pluto Press.

Lindquist, J. A. (2009). *The anxieties of mobility: Migration and tourism in the Indonesian borderlands.* Honolulu: University of Hawaii Press.

Long, L. (2000). "Towards an anthropology of mobility." In E. Gozdziak and D. Shandy (eds), *Rethinking refugees and displacement: Selected papers on refugees and immigrants* (3, 322–342). Arlington: The American Anthropological Association.

Lubkemann, S. C. (2008). "Involuntary immobility: On a theoretical invisibility in forced migration studies." *Journal of Refugee Studies*, 21(4), 454–475.

Malkki, L. H. (1992). "National Geographic: The rooting of peoples and the territorialization of national identity among scholars and refugees." *Cultural Anthropology*, 7(1), 24–44.

Marcus, G. E. (1998). *Ethnography through thick and thin.* Princeton: Princeton University Press.

Masquelier, A. (2002). "Road mythographies: Space, mobility, and the historical imagination in post-colonial Niger." *American Ethnologist*, 29(4), 829–856.

Mathers, K. F. (2010). *Travel, humanitarianism, and becoming American in Africa.* New York: Palgrave Macmillan.

Maurer, B. (2000). "A fish story: Rethinking globalization on Virgin Gorda, British Virgin Islands." *American Ethnologist*, 27(3), 670–701.

Nyíri, P. (2010). *Mobility and cultural authority in contemporary China.* Seattle: University of Washington Press.

Ong, A. (1999). *Flexible citizenship: The cultural logics of transnationality.* Durham: Duke University Press.

Rethmann, P. (2001). *Tundra Passages: History and gender in the Russian Far East.* University Park: Pennsylvania State University Press.

Robbins, J. and Bamford, S. (eds) (1997). *Fieldwork revisited: Changing contexts of ethnographic practice in the era of globalization.* Theme issue, *Anthropology and Humanism*, 22(1).

Rockefeller, S. A. (2010). *Starting from Quirpini: The travels and places of a Bolivian people.* Bloomington: Indiana University Press.

Salazar, N. B. (2010a). *Envisioning Eden: Mobilizing imaginaries in tourism and beyond.* Oxford: Berghahn.

Salazar, N. B. (2010b). "Towards an anthropology of cultural mobilities." *Crossings: Journal of Migration and Culture*, 1(1), 53–68.

Salazar, N. B. and Smart, A. (eds) (2011). *Anthropological takes on (im)mobility.* Theme issue, *Identities: Global Studies in Culture and Power*, 18(6).

Strathern, M. (1991). *Partial connections.* Savage: Rowman & Littlefield.

Tarrius, A. (2000). *Les Nouveaux cosmopolitismes: Mobilités, identités, territoires.* Paris: Editions de l'Aube.

Tsing, A. L. (1993). *In the realm of the diamond queen: Marginality in an out-of-the-way place.* Princeton: Princeton University Press.

Turner, V. W. (1967). *The forest of symbols.* Ithaca: Cornell University Press.

Vergunst, J. (2011). "Technology and technique in a useful ethnography of movement." *Mobilities*, 6(2), 203–219.

Vigh, H. (2009). "Motion squared: A second look at the concept of social navigation." *Anthropological Theory*, 9(4), 419–438.

Wilding, R. (2007). "Transnational ethnographies and anthropological imaginings of migrancy." *Journal of Ethnic and Migration Studies*, 33(2), 331–348.

Wimmer, A. and Glick Schiller, N. (2003). "Methodological nationalism, the social sciences, and the study of migration: An essay in historical epistemology." *International Migration Review*, 37(7), 576–610.

Wolch, J. R. and Rowe, S. (1992). "On the streets: Mobility paths of the urban homeless." *City & Society*, 6(2), 115–140.

Wolf, E. R. (1982). *Europe and the people without history*. Berkeley: University of California Press.

5

Migration Studies

Anne-Marie Fortier

International migration constitutes one of the key defining features of the contemporary world, so much so that Stephen Castles and Mark Miller (2009) refer to the late twentieth- and early twenty-first-century era as the 'age of migration'. This is not to suggest that international migration is new, but that its scope, rate of increase and diverse character are unprecedented. The United Nations Population Division (UNPD) estimates that between 1960 and 2007 the number of international migrants more than doubled, from 76 million in 1960 to 200 million in 2000, 'or approximately three per cent of the world's 6.5 billion population' (Castles and Miller 2009: 5). Of these, approximately 10 million would be officially recognised refugees (Castles and Miller 2009: 7). The UNPD 'defines an international migrant as any person who changes his or her country of usual residence. An international migrant who changes his or her place of usual residence for at least one year is defined as a long-term migrant while a person who changes his or her place of usual residence for more than three months but less than one year is considered to be a short-term migrant' (United Nations 2011: 1). These estimates do not include those who undertake weekly or daily cross-border journeys, nor does it include undocumented migrants (for whom numbers are not easily available).[1]

There are different kinds of migrants who take different migration paths (see Section Five in this volume): asylum seekers, refugees, displaced and forced migrants, so called 'economic' migrants (which include migrant workers, skilled migrants, migrant investors, migrant professionals), spousal and family migrants, undocumented migrants, retirement migrants, 'return' migrants, 'trafficked' migrants, 'queer' migrants.[2] There are migrants who temporarily reside in the place of immigration, others who stay permanently, others who move between two or more places of residence.

The field of migration studies has a long history that precedes the emergence of mobility studies showcased in this handbook. An interdisciplinary field, it draws researchers from anthropology, sociology, politics, social policy, international relations, geography, history, linguistics, psychology, education, legal studies, media studies, literature and other areas. Research in migration can be roughly divided into three levels. First, migration itself as an object of study includes attention to macro-level types of structures and infrastructures of migration, such as institutional practices, policies and laws that regulate the movement of migrants as well as their settlement and 'integration', transnational movements or organisations. The second meso-level concerns technologies of travel and communication; strategies and conditions of migration and settlement; political and grassroots movements and various local, national, transnational or diaspora networks. Lastly, the micro-level focuses heavily on individual and collective experiences, strategies and aspirations, as well as household decision-making about migration, adjustment and mobility; it also includes cultural productions and representations of migrants and migrant lives.

It is not the purpose of this chapter to offer a comprehensive review of migration studies; what follows consists of a sketch of what is ultimately an incomplete landscape because it is always in flux.[3] It cross-cuts the themes that encompass the three levels named above and refers to recent developments in migration research, connecting them to other developments in social and cultural studies, such as 'methodological transnationalism', citizenship studies, affect, and the rise of neoliberalism in the restructuring of the self. The chapter is also incomplete as its geographic reference point is Europe and North America. Still, the questions raised and the arguments suggested here cast a wide net. The primary aim of this chapter is to ask: what can migration scholarship tell us about 'mobile worlds'? For if mobilities research forces us to think about migration in relation to the ways in which 'mobility' has been variously established (institutionally, legally, technologically, materially, idealistically) as a universal condition if not a universal 'right', migration studies force a reconsideration of the fluidity, accessibility and desirability of the assumed mobile world, as well as the conditions under which people are 'mobile' (or not). Crucial here is the relationship between mobility and immobility.

The discussion that follows is organised under three broad sub-headings: questions of methodology; citizenship and migration; imaginaries and affects. In each section, I offer a reflection on methodological and conceptual tools that could complement the rich array of research that already exists under the banner of 'migration studies'.

Questions of methodology

Two concepts have acquired prominence in migration studies over the last twenty years or so – diaspora and transnationalism (see Bauböck and Faist 2010) – which both serve to address various cross-border processes, flows and networks that are relevant to mobility studies. As Thomas Faist succinctly puts it, 'diaspora has been often used to denote religious or national groups living outside an (imagined) homeland, whereas transnationalism is often used more narrowly – to refer to migrants' durable ties across countries – and, more widely, to capture not only communities, but all sorts of social formations such as transnationally active networks, groups and organisations' (2010: 9). It is beyond the scope of this chapter to chart the various intellectual trajectories of, and debates about, each concept and their uses.[4] Suffice to say that 'studies of . . . diasporas and transnational citizenship [offer] trenchant critiques of the bounded and static categories of nation, ethnicity, community, place and state' (Hannam et al. 2006: 10). By refusing to assume a connection between territorial space (of migration, of residence, of 'origin') and social space (kinship, work, virtual and physical social networks, belonging), this strand of migration studies comes with a critique of 'container studies' in the social sciences (Faist 2010: 28) – 'methodological nationalism' (Wimmer and Glick Schiller 2003; also Glick Schiller 2010) and 'groupism' (Brubaker and Cooper 2001) – rather than favouring studies that can accentuate migrant networks, associations and groups across national and regional borders, or that can reveal the interrelatedness of state practices and laws regarding the management of migration (Bauböck 2010).

Both methodological nationalism and groupism are marked by the tendency to treat populations – 'migrants', 'ethnic minorities', 'nationals' – as stable social, historical and cultural units. Put simply, the assumption is that migrants arrive into (and disrupt) a unified national culture with their own unified cultural background – what I have referred to elsewhere, drawing on Anne McClintock and Edward Said, as the 'anachronistic space' of the imaginative geographies of immigration (Fortier 2008: 98).

The politics of what I shall call 'methodological transnationalism' aims at de-centring hegemonies of belonging and entitlement predicated on the 'groupist' alignment of territory-community-identity that lies at the basis of ethnicist, nativist or nationalist politics. However, methodological transnationalism does not mean doing away altogether with the critical analysis of nationalism, national politics, state practices and governing strategies. States remain significant actors within and across state borders. Likewise, nationalism remains a significant discourse through which states establish their authority, but also through which people establish a sense of collective coherence and belonging to an 'imagined community'. In this regard, transnational and diaspora studies often 'emphasise intense connections to national or local territories, especially in the case of migrants' (Faist 2010: 14). Attention to the nationalist practices, politics and discourses need not fall into the trap of methodological nationalism, but should rather be considered as part of a nexus where the global, national and local are mutually constitutive. As Peggy Levitt and Nina Glick Schiller point out,

> Finally, locating migrants within transnational social fields makes clear that incorporation in a new state and enduring transnational attachments are not binary opposites . . . Movement and attachment is not linear or sequential but capable of rotating back and forth and changing direction over time. The median point on this gauge is not full incorporation but rather simultaneity of connection. Persons change and swing one way or the other depending on the context, thus moving our expectation away from either full assimilation or transnational connection but some combination of both. The challenge, then, is to explain the variation in the way that migrants manage that pivot and how host country incorporation and homeland or other transnational ties mutually influence each other.
>
> *(2004: 1011)*

However, in privileging the migrant and mobile person, much of the migration and transnationalism scholarship, as well as much of mobilities research, has largely neglected those who stay put (pace Benhabib and Resnick 2009; Ahmed *et al.* 2003; Gray 2002; Levitt and Glick Schiller 2004). This dovetails into the wider question of the spatial politics of mobility and the relationship between mobility and immobility (see Adey 2006 on how mobility and immobility are two sides of the coin of mobility). Who moves freely and who doesn't? How does one's place of residence on the planet frame one's capacity to leave or travel, if she so desires? How does the movement of some rely on the immobility of others (Ahmed 2000; Kaplan 2003)? Who can travel and who can stay at home (Ahmed *et al.* 2003: 7)?

A first axis of analysis here concerns the relationship between mobility and immobility and the extent to which 'migration' and/or 'staying put' are entangled rather than mutually exclusive in the contemporary 'mobile world'. This has been foregrounded by Avtar Brah's concept of diaspora space, which she describes as '"inhabited" not only by diasporic subjects but equally by those who are constructed and represented as "indigenous"' (1996: 16). What is not clear in Brah's definition is whether the 'indigenous' are 'here' or 'there' (for example, those left behind; see Levitt and Glick Schiller 2004). However, the point I wish to emphasise here is that, in its predominant use, the concept of diaspora space refers to single diasporic populations who live outside a shared (imagined) homeland. Another use could be to analyse multi-ethnic spaces – an international movement, a multicultural country, a neighbourhood – as 'diaspora spaces', and to consider how they are imagined and lived as diasporic and/or indigenous by different actors, but also how they may be imagined or experienced as somewhere in-between.

The 'citizenship turn' in migration studies

Recent literature on citizenship and nationality in migration studies provides a good field in which to explore the two analytical axes of mobility–immobility and alien–native (e.g. Benhabib and Resnick 2009; Vink and de Groot 2010). This has developed in the context of the politicisation of migration and revaluation of national identity in several countries in North America and Europe (and elsewhere), leading to the re-introduction of policies for 'social cohesion', 'integration' and 'assimilation', which are cast against multiculturalism and the politics of recognition (Kostakopoulou 2010).

Turning the lens of migration research on citizenship brings a valuable contribution to theories of citizenship by highlighting the structures and conditions in which transnational individuals are simultaneously linked to more than one political entity (Bauböck 2010). Political and legal theories offer noteworthy insights about institutional regimes of attribution of citizenship (e.g. Bauböck 2006), immigrant incorporation as political members (e.g. Bloemraad 2006), or dual citizenship (Faist and Kivisto 2007; Faist 2007a; Nyers 2010). Grounded in normative theories that establish what citizenship ought to be, the aim of this scholarship is to expose the inequalities produced by the ways that governments implement some models of citizenship and to propose alternative models. Other comparative works show how citizenship policies change in response to migration flows (Bauböck 2010), or offer quantitative comparisons that condense legal provisions into indices.

An additional dimension that transnational migration research could shed light on relates to how and in what ways people are constituted as 'integrated', or as 'citizen', but also how, when and under what conditions the same people (as well as other people) might not be recognised as such. This forces the consideration not only that 'full citizenship' is never fully secured, but that the 'fully integrated subject' is also never fully secured. More broadly, a focus on citizenship attribution as a 'regime of practices' aims at 'grasping the conditions which make them acceptable at a given moment' (Foucault 1991: 75). For example, what makes new procedures for citizenship naturalisation – citizenship classes, tests, interviews – a practicable and thinkable solution to policing not only 'who comes into the country but who stays', in the words of the British Prime Minister David Cameron (2011).

Second, examining citizenship regimes of practice, or 'programmes of conduct' (Foucault 1991: 75), that explicitly target immigrants (for example, naturalisation) invites thinking of citizenship as not just a legal and political status, but also as social and cultural, charged with normative notions of what constitutes the acceptable attributes of not just 'good' citizenship but also of 'worthy mobility'. Thus practices designed with migrants in mind are more than simply about migrants. The analytic agenda here is to connect social and legal practices aimed at migrants, to wider social processes – for example, neoliberalism and its emphasis on the autonomous, entrepreneurial self, or on the 'affective citizen' (Fortier 2010) – that impact on migrants and non-migrants alike, and on how mobility and immobility are at times in tension with each other or deployed in contradictory ways. For instance, the 'citizen–non-citizen' status (for example the European blue card) entitles highly mobile people to certain rights and privileges in the eyes of the state. Within the frames of the neoliberal economic and governance strategies, the mobility of the investor and elite migrant (the 'highly skilled' migrant) is welcome and supported, while the mobility of the less-skilled or less-moneyed 'immigrant' is more closely monitored and regulated. Research that takes the diasporic or transnational subject as its unit of analysis (rather than the state), can offer evidence of multiple articulations, experiences and expressions of citizenship that together draw out the multifaceted character of citizenship and complicate the usual binaries established between 'formal' and 'social' or 'cultural' citizenship, on the one hand, and between national or trans-national/diasporic citizenship, on the other (binaries that map onto the immobility–mobility axis). For example, studies of migrant transnationalism have examined how expressions of citizenship are no longer confined to the nation-state (Basch *et al*. 1994; Laguerre 1999; Ong 1999). However, the prediction of some authors (e.g. Soysal 1994) that migrant transnation-alism will lead to an age of post-nationalism has not materialised; even though people are embedded within transnational networks and social fields, they are still bound by state reg-ulation. The tightening of naturalisation laws in North America and several European coun-tries testifies to what Sara Goodman (2010) and Dora Kostakopoulou (2010) calls the 'thickening of citizenship', for example by expecting 'new' citizens to have a 'deep' engage-ment with national values. Interestingly, this tendency exists alongside the rise in the number of states that tolerate dual or multiple citizenship (more than half of all states; Faist and Kivisto 2007). While this trend has been analysed as testifying to the breakdown of the opposition between citizens and foreigners (Nyers 2010), it also reveals dual citizenship as 'a test case for an ambivalent relationship: the growing liberalisation of citizenship laws on the one hand, and the increasing securitisation of citizenship, the erosion of popular sovereignty and the changing [though not disappearing] role of nationalism and nationhood for full membership on the other hand' (Faist 2007b: 2).

The examination of regimes of practices is not a replacement of analyses that reveal the differentiated and differentiating effects of citizenship which reproduce differences between citizens and non-citizens in terms of rights, or differences between migrants themselves, who arrive and 'settle' in a country under a range of different conditions that affect their access to and negotiation of a new citizenship status. But there is room for linking together in-depth analyses that focus on how citizenship produces inequalities and combining them to produce a close analysis of differentiating migration regimes. For example, Sarah van Walsum (2003) shows how family norms legalised and formalised in Dutch state family law diverge from the family norms deployed in immigration policies regarding family reunification. In this regard, the family is not simply a model of good kinship and a social institution, it is produced in the governing of populations and used by governments to legitimate increased restrictions on immigration (Luibhéid 2002). Furthermore, the family is a site where racist, gendered, het-erosexist and class norms are mobilised (and reproduced) in various ways, but remain con-cealed within national fantasies of intimacy and heterosexual romantic love, which are prerequisites of 'good citizenship'. There is valuable research on transnational families that shows how migration challenges conventional understandings of family formations and inti-macy (Bryceson and Vuorela 2002; Goulbourne *et al*. 2010). However, the point I wish to emphasise is that we need to look at how changing family forms are managed differently for different subjects. In turn, we could say that, although not necessarily transnational, the experience of several non-migrant families today include multi-locality and some meas-ure of mobility – children travelling between homes – that also challenge conventional understandings of the stable, nuclear family.

Imaginaries and affects

More than a set of practices, migration, as Didier Bigo suggests, has become a contentious image: 'Immigration is now problematized in Western countries in a way that is very different from the distinction between citizen and foreigner. It is not a legal status that is under discussion but a *social image*, concerning . . . the "social distribution of bad."' (2002: 71, my emphasis). This is about migration as social imaginary.

'Imaginaries', which shape and are shaped by regimes of practices, are deeply integrated in our everyday lives and inform our ways of seeing and understanding the world. Two questions can guide an analytical focus on the migration imaginary: how is migration imagined? And what is at stake, and for whom, in the deployment of the migration imaginary within the landscape of mobilities?

First, considering how migration is imagined includes studies of representations of migration, for example in film, literature, photography, art or other cultural productions. It can also include how migration and 'the migrant' are represented in social policy, political speeches, as well as migrant discourses themselves. For example, 'mass migration' signals the movement of large numbers of nameless bodies and objectifies migrants, with little specificities about their decisions, the conditions of migration, etc. Attending to representations is attending to the ways of seeing that various texts open up (or close down), and to the range of experiences, feelings and opinions that they simultaneously produce and occlude for those who are positioned as variously migrant or non-migrant subjects in a 'here' or 'there' world (Lewis 2006).

Imaginaries get attached to bodies and are figured in particular ways. For Didier Bigo, 'Migrant, as a term, is the way to designate someone as a threat to the core values of a country, a state, and has nothing to do with the legal terminology of foreigners' (Bigo 2002: 71).[5] The migration imaginary, as well as discourses, cultural representations or governance strategies, are routinely condensed in various 'figurations' of migrants, that is, 'a specific configuration of knowledge, practice and power' that 'also brings a particular [yet still contestable] version of the world into being' (Castañeda 2002: 4). I have elaborated elsewhere (2006) on how figurations of 'the migrant' are mobilised and circulated in ways that simultaneously embody the possibility of assimilation into, and destabilisation of, various 'groupisms'. Exploring the limits of 'group' containers through figurations takes us to the processes through which imperial and postcolonial, and national and international definitions of humanity and difference are naturalised and localised – in places, cultures and/or individual psyches. At times, figurations stand in for wider national or even global myths and characteristics – for example the good, quiet, white-enough 'mixed-race' child who embodies harmonious intercultural relatedness and integration that living in Europe makes possible. At other times, figurations are monstrous figures of deviance – the polygamous, the excessively patriarchal or submissive, the terrorist, the homosexual, the criminal, the angry rioter – that reveal the limits of civility by referring to the universalised principles that these figures violate – monogamy, heteronormativity, consent, tolerance, moderation, pride, respect for private property, good neighbourliness, democracy. Whether utopian or dystopian, it is important to reiterate that figurations, like imaginaries, work through particularisations that serve to discipline and normalise the population as a whole (not only migrants).

The migration imaginary shapes understandings of identity and difference, of borders and boundaries, of our relationship to others 'here' and 'elsewhere'. It is also a site where idea(l)s of integrity, integration, preservation, and recognition are embattled. Hence, more than a 'social fact' (Appadurai 1996) – although it is indubitably that – the imaginary 'refers to the organisation of cultural fantasies in ways that are part of the psychic production of subjects' (Stacey 2010: 10). As Jackie Stacey writes,

> Unlike the imagination, with its roots in philosophical and aesthetic conceptual tradition, the imaginary implies a set of structures for the production of subjectivities with the power to draw upon and reproduce unconscious attachments. While the imagination refers to patterns of emotional and artistic connectivity, the imaginary refers to the fears and desires organizing a particular repertoire of fantasies that have a deeper, often indirect, set of cultural investments and associations.
>
> *(2010: 10–11)*

Among other things, Stacey's psychoanalytic angle points to the role of anxieties and desires that structure and constitute the fabric of our imaginaries, and that together produce an ambivalent relationship to the object of attachment – say, 'migration' or 'the migrant'. Consider how, in many immigration debates, there is a constant oscillation between desires for the enrichment, integration and cosmopolitanism that immigration is seen to provide, on the one hand, and fears of it as a source invasion, loss, contamination and chaos, on the other. Rather than taking that opposition between the positive and negative effects of migration at face value – and consequently accepting the terms of the debate at face value – we could consider how they are not in opposition to each other but rather testify to the ambivalent relationship between desires and anxieties that structure the migration imaginary. Such structures of desire and anxiety, in turn, invest the desire to secure identities (national or 'ethnic', regional or religious, individual or communal, 'indigenous' or 'foreigner', etc.).

Similarly, migrants often negotiate mixed feelings about what is left behind, what is sacrificed, what is 'gained' through emigration–immigration. There is a small but growing interest in the relationship between affect and migration (Wise and Chapman 2005; Skrbis 2009; Gutiérrez-Rodríguez 2010), which is attentive to forms of affective attachments engendered by diasporic consciousness, that is the awareness of decentred attachments 'here', 'there' and 'elsewhere' that transnational migrants negotiate. This could be further complemented with considerations of political economies of feelings that migrants and non-migrants are caught up in. That is to say there are norms and rules regulating the production, circulation and distribution of legitimate feelings. Who can be fearful and who cannot? Who can be enraged and who cannot (Marciniak 2006)? Who can be hurt, and who cannot? The currency of feelings and their differential value delineates the codes of conduct of the 'good migrant'. And their exchange value is political: different feelings are attributed different values – or rather, they are differentially located within the 'national values' against which the 'value' of migrants is assessed.

What I suggest is that adding imaginaries and affect to the conceptual toolkit of migration research within mobility studies allows us to probe into the ways in which marginal and dominant, and mobile and sedentary subjects are embroiled in the inextricability of desire and politics through complex processes of internalisation, incorporation and (dis)identification.

Conclusion

What can migration scholarship tell us about 'mobile worlds'? Migration research forces us to interrogate the mobile world and its assumed fluidity, accessibility and desirability. It sheds light on experiences and practices of migration, and in turn, on how migration changes various practices, at the individual, familial, local, national or international levels. Migration studies, particularly transnational and diaspora studies, also propose a transnational methodology that contests 'groupist' definitions of collective social formations, such as ethnicist or nationalist understandings of communities as being homogeneous and unchanging.

Implicit in the discussion is a call for rethinking prevalent classificatory schemes (of race, ethnicity, gender, sexuality, class and generations) through practices, institutions, discourses and imaginaries, in an analysis that pays attention to the constant interplay of the micro, meso and macrophysics of power while it seeks to be 'more attuned to interwoven forces that merge and dissipate' temporal, spatial and bodily linearity, and coherence and permanency (Puar 2005: 127–128). Furthermore, if we are to take seriously the premise that the migration imaginary is a social imaginary that shapes and is shaped by 'public cultures of assumption, disposition, and action' (Gregory 2004: 28), we must consider that this implies a recognition of the array of sites through which the interplay of various forces operate and are deployed – from the home, workplace and urban, to the national, transnational, global, and from the artistic to the mediatic, legal, political, economic, scientific, technological and institutional, etc. At the same time, however, though these sites are not coterminous or homologous, they are part of wider polysemic cultural formations and, as such, are constitutive of, and constituted by, social imaginaries. In short, I would hope that an analysis such as the one outlined above might shed light on the varying post- and neo-colonial histories and politics of migration, representation, domination, desires and (dis)identifications that are constitutive of the complexities of the present.

Notes

1 One estimate is that there were 12 million people residing illegally in the US in 2006 (in a total population of 300 million [Passel in Castles and Miller 2009: 7].
2 It is worth noting that, despite the growing scholarship in queer migration (Fortier 2002; Gopinath 2005; Kuntsman 2009; Gormann-Murray 2007; Manalansan 2006; Luibhéid and Cantú 2005; Luibhéid 2008), migration studies still work predominantly within heterosexist frames of reference.
3 I am grateful to Sondra Cuban and Peter Merriman for their feedback on an early draft of this chapter.
4 In addition to Faist's (2010) useful overview of both concepts and how they relate to each other, for overviews of diaspora see Cohen 2008, Dufoix 2008, and Fortier 2005; for transnationalism, see Khagram and Levitt 2008, Vertovec 2009, and Rocco and García Selgas 2006.
5 Although I agree with Audrey Macklin's observation that 'revisions to the legal distinction between citizens and foreigner are precisely about the social distribution of "bad"' (2007: 62).

References

Adey, Peter (2006) 'If mobility is everything then it is nothing: towards a relational politics of (im)mobilities', *Mobilities* 1(1): 74–94.
Ahmed, Sara (2000) *Strange Encounters: Embodied Others in Postcoloniality*, London: Routledge.
Ahmed, Sara, C. Castañeda, A.-M. Fortier and M. Sheller (eds) (2003) *Uprootings/Regroundings: Questions of Home and Migration*, Oxford: Berg.
Appadurai, Arjun (1996) *Modernity at Large: Cultural Dimensions of Globalization*, Minneapolis: University of Minnesota Press.
Basch, Linda, Nina Glick Schiller and Cristina Szanton Blanc (1994) *Nations Unbound: Transnational Projects, Postcolonial and Deterritorialized Nation-States*, Amsterdam: Gordon & Breach Publishers.
Bauböck, Rainer (2006) *Migration and Citizenship: Legal Status, Rights and Political Participation*, Amsterdam: Amsterdam University Press.
Bauböck, Rainer (2010) 'Studying Citizenship Constellations', *Journal of Ethnic and Migration Studies* 36(5): 847–859.

Bauböck, Rainer and Thomas Faist (eds) (2010) *Diaspora and Transnationalism: Concepts, Theories and Methods*, Amsterdam: Amsterdam University Press.

Benhabib, Seyla and Judith Resnick (eds) (2009) *Migrations and Mobilities: Citizenship, Borders, and Gender*, New York and London: New York University Press.

Bigo, Didier (2002) 'Security and immigration: toward a critique of the governmentality of unease', *Alternatives* 27: 63–92.

Bloemraad, Irene (2006) *Becoming Citizen: Incorporating Immigrants and Refugees in the United States and Canada*, Berkeley, CA: University of California Press.

Brah, Avtar (1996) *Cartographies of Diaspora: Contesting Identities*, London: Routledge.

Brubaker, R. W. and Cooper F. (2001) 'Beyond "identity"', *Theory and Society* 29(1): 1–47.

Bryceson, Deborah and Ulla Vuorela (eds) (2002) *The Transnational Family: New European Frontiers and Global Networks*, Oxford: Berg.

Cameron, David (2011) 'Prime minister's address to Conservative party members on the government's immigration policy', available online at www.guardian.co.uk/politics/2011/apr/14/david-cameron-immigration-speech-full-text (accessed 14 April 2011).

Castañeda, Claudia (2002) *Figurations: Child, Bodies, Worlds*, Durham, NC and London: Duke University Press.

Castles, Stephen and Mark Miller (2009) *The Age of Migration*, 4th edition, Basingstoke: Palgrave Macmillan.

Cohen, Robin (2008) *Global Diasporas: An Introduction*, 2nd edition, London and New York: Routledge.

Dufoix, S. (2008) *Diasporas*, Berkeley: University of California Press.

Faist, Thomas (ed) (2007a) *Dual Citizenship in Europe*, Aldershot: Ashgate.

Faist, Thomas (2007b) 'Introduction: the shifting boundaries of the political', in T. Faist and P. Kivisto (eds) *Dual Citizenship in Global Perspective: Unitary to Multiple Citizenship*, Basingstoke and New York: Palgrave Macmillan, 1–23.

Faist, Thomas (2010) 'Diaspora and transnationalism: what kinds of dance partners?' in R. Bauböck and T. Faist *Diaspora and Transnationalism: Concepts, Theories, and Methods*, Amsterdam: University of Amsterdam Press, 9–34.

Faist, Thomas and Peter Kivisto (eds) (2007) *Dual Citizenship in Global Perspective: From Unitary to Multiple Citizenship*, New York and Basingstoke: Palgrave Macmillan.

Fortier, Anne-Marie (2002) 'Queer diasporas', in D. Richardson and S. Seidman (eds) *Handbook of Lesbian and Gay Studies*, London: Sage, 183–197.

Fortier, Anne-Marie (2005) 'Diaspora', in D. Sibley, P. Jackson, D. Atkinson and N. Washbourne (eds) *Cultural Geography: A Critical Dictionary in Key Concepts*, London: I. B. Tauris, 182–187.

Fortier, Anne-Marie. (2006) 'The politics of scaling, timing and embodying: rethinking the "New Europe"', *Mobilities* 1: 313–331.

Fortier, Anne-Marie (2008) *Multicultural Horizons: Diversity and the Limits of the Civil Nation*, London: Routledge.

Fortier, Anne-Marie (2010) 'Proximity by design? Affective citizenship and the management of unease', *Citizenship Studies* 14(1): 17–30.

Foucault, Michel (1991) 'Questions of Method', in G. Burchell, C. Gordon and P. Miller (eds) *The Foucault Effect: Studies in Governmentality*, Chicago: University of Chicago Press, 73–86.

Glick Schiller, N. (2010) 'A global perspective on transnational migration: theorising migration without methodological nationalism', in R. Baubock and T. Faist (eds) *Diaspora and Transnationalism: Concepts, Theories and Methods*, Amsterdam: Amsterdam University Press.

Goodman, Sara Wallace (2010) 'Integration requirements for integration's sake? Identifying, categorising and comparing civic integration policies', *Journal of Ethnic and Migration Studies* 36(5): 753–772.

Gopinath, Gaytri (2005) *Impossible Desires: Queer Diasporas and South Asian Public Cultures*, Durham (NC): Duke University Press.

Gormann-Murray, Andrew (2007) 'Rethinking queer migration through the body', *Social and Cultural Geography* 8: 105–121.

Goulbourne, Harry, Tracey Reynolds, John Solomos and Elisabetta Zontini (2010) *Transnational Families: Ethnicities, Identities, and Social Capital*, Abingdon and New York: Routledge.

Gray, Breda (2002) '"Breaking the silence" – Questions of staying and going in 1950s Ireland', *Irish Journal of Psychology* (Special issue on Diaspora), 23(3–4): 158–183.

Gutiérrez-Rodríguez, Encarnación (2010) *Migration, Domestic Work and Affect: A Decolonial Approach on Value and the Feminization of Labor*, New York and London: Routledge.

Hannam, Kevin, Mimi Sheller, and John Urry (2006) 'Editorial: Mobilities, immobilities and moorings', *Mobilities* 1(1): 1–22.

Kaplan, Caren (2003) 'Transporting the subject: technologies of mobility and location in an era of globalization', in S. Ahmed, C. Castañeda, A.-M. Fortier and M. Sheller (eds) *Uprootings/Regroundings: Questions of Home and Migration*, Oxford: Berg, 207–224.

Khagram, Sanjeev and Peggy Levitt (eds) (2008) *The Transnational Studies Reader: Interdisciplinary Intersections and Innovations*, London: Routledge.

Kostakopoulou, Dora (2010) 'Matters of control: integration tests, naturalisation reform and probationary citizenship in the United Kingdom', *Journal of Ethnic and Migration Studies* 36(5): 829–846.

Kuntsman, Adi (2009) *Figurations of Violence and Belonging: Queerness, Migranthood and Nationalism in Cyberspace and Beyond*, Oxford: Peter Lang.

Laguerre, Michael S. (1999) *Minoritized Space: An Inquiry into the Spatial Order of Things*, Berkley (CA): Institute of Government Studies Press.

Levitt, Peggy and Nina Glick Schiller (2004) 'Conceptualizing simultaneity: a transnational social field perspective on society', *International Migration Review* 38(3): 1002–1039.

Lewis, Gail (2006) 'Journeying toward the nation(al): cultural difference at the crossroads of old and new globalisations', *Mobilities* 1(3): 333–352.

Luibhéid, Eithne (2002) *Entry Denied: Controlling Sexuality at the Border*, Minneapolis and London: University of Minnesota Press.

Luibhéid, Eithne (ed.) (2008) 'Queer/Migration', thematic issue of *GLQ: Journal of Gay and Lesbian Studies* 14(2–3).

Luibhéid, Eithne and Lionel Cantú (eds) (2005) *Queer Migration: Sexuality, U.S. Citizenship, and Border Crossings*, Minnesota: University of Minnesota Press.

Macklin, Audrey (2007) 'The securitisation of dual citizenship', in T. Faist and P. Kivisto (eds) *Dual Citizenship in Global Perspective: From Unitary to Multiple Citizenship*, Basingstoke: Palgrave Macmillan, 42–66.

Manalansan, Martin F. (2006) 'Queer intersections: sexuality and gender in migration studies', *International Migration Review* 40(1): 224–249.

Marciniak, Katarzyna (2006) 'Immigrant rage: alienhood, "hygienic" identities, and the Second World', *Differences: A Journal of Feminist Cultural Studies* 17(2): 33–63.

Nyers, Peter (2010) 'Dueling designs: The politics of rescuing dual citizens', *Citizenship Studies* 14(1): 47–60.

Ong, Aihwa (1999) *Flexible Citizenship: The Cultural Logics of Transnationality*, Durham, NC and London: Duke University Press.

Puar, Jasbir (2005) 'Queer times, queer assemblages', *Social Text* 23: 121–140.

Rocco, Raymond and Fernando J. García Selgas (eds) (2006) *Transnationalism: Issues and Perspectives*, Madrid: Editorial Complutense.

Skrbis, Zlatko (2009) 'Transnational families: theorising migration, emotions and belonging', *Journal of Intercultural Studies* 29(3): 231–246.

Soysal, Yasemin (1994) *Limits of Citizenship: Migrants and Postnational Membership in Europe*, Chicago: University of Chicago Press.

Stacey, Jackie (2010) *The Cinematic Life of the Gene*, Durham, NC: Duke University Press.

United Nations (2011) International Migration Flows to and from Selected Countries: The 2010 Revision. CD-Rom Documentation. Department of Economic and Social Affairs, Population Division. Available online at www.un.org/esa/population/publications/CD_MF_2010/CD-ROM%20DOCUMENTATION_UN_Mig_Flow_2010.pdf (accessed 9 February 2012).

Van Walsum, S. (2003) 'Family norms and citizenship in the Netherlands', in C. Harzig and D. Juteau with I. Schmitt (eds) *The Social Construction of Diversity: Recasting the Master Narrative of Industrial Nations*, New York and Oxford: Berghahn.

Vertovec, Steve (2009) *Transnationalism*, London: Routledge.

Vink, Marteen P. and Gerard-René de Groot (eds) (2010) 'Citizenship Attribution in Western Europe: International Framework and Domestic Trends', thematic issue of *Journal of Ethnic and Migration Studies* 36(5).

Wimmer, A. and N. Glick Schiller (2003) 'Methodological nationalism and the study of migration', *International Migration Review* 37(3): 576–610.

Wise, Amanda and Adam Chapman (eds) (2005) 'Special Issue: Migration, Affect and the Senses', *Journal of Intercultural Studies* 26(1–2).

6

Tourist Studies

Adrian Franklin

Tourist studies is a relatively recent multi-disciplinary field of research which is largely dedicated to developing an understanding of the origins and development of tourism; the theoretical understandings of tourism as a form of social, economic, embodied and cultural practice; the wider social, cultural and economic impacts of tourism and the development of concepts and methodologies that enable clearer understandings of these processes. It dates back to an emergent sociology of leisure in the 1960s and 1970s, and particularly to the spectacular growth spurts of tourism in the 1980s, in the aftermath of de-industrialisation and the growth of service industries, and after the 1990s, following the de-regulation of the aviation industry and the opening up of wider circuits of global tourism, capital and taste. However, the way in which the spectacular growth of travel and tourism has been tied to its association with the mobile social elites of Europe and America and their direct influence on the development of new technologies of travel means that the actual study of tourism dates back a very long way.

The first literatures of the field include Thomas Coryat's book on the tour from London to Italy, *Coryat's Crudities* of 1611, and Richard Lassels's *The Voyage of Italy* of 1670. As with many seventeenth-century books, Lassels's influential best-seller was instructional and it identified four dimensions of the practice of travel (to Italy) that delivered self-improvement and advantage to the 'accomplished, consummate traveller': intellectual, social, ethical and political (Chaney 2000: 35). For this reason it was Lassels who gave a name, *The Grand Tour*, to this experience. Coryat and Lassels did much to increase the centrality of the Grand Tour in British aristocratic and artistic circles, but eventually these four by-products of tourism became the foundation for the valuation of travel itself; and, as a valuable end in itself as opposed to the value of particular destinations such as Italy, where the object had been to soak up and apply the combined fruits of classical civilisation and renaissance achievement.

Definitions, scale and breadth

In my book *Tourism* (2003a) I use a mobilities perspective to understand not only the changing nature of tourism as a social and cultural practice, but also to understand its principal orderings which changed quite dramatically during its historical development. I identified two principal eras of modern tourism mobilities, Mobilities I and Mobilities II, to denote two very different eras of travel and tourism for the periods 1850–1960 and 1960–present.

Tourism Mobilities I: 1850–1960

Mobilities I ranged from the mid-nineteenth century until the 1950s and was largely structured around a technical expansion of steam technologies, particularly the railways, which coincided with the consolidation and elaboration of nationally focussed modern societies. Although mostly privately funded and organised at the beginning, rail connectivity became increasingly regulated and controlled. The railway expansion during Mobilities I established strategic links between industrial regions and metropolitan market hubs, the growth of both often simultaneously dependent on the growth of rail connectivity. From the late nineteenth century, railways embarked on a second wave of investment by developing new branch lines that connected simultaneously with investments in seaside, mountain, city or resort development. This pattern of development was first innovated by Thomas Cook through his business model. He would first seek to establish a route into a new area, smoothing hitherto rustic and often non-passenger forms of railway conveyance by more comfortable and stratified classes of travel, together with other facilities that his travel company could provide (e.g. he mastered the process of transfers of people and luggage from railway to hotel – often where there was no culture of local provision – and he innovated the first ever credit cards). Then, once a regional tourism hub had been established in a town (including hotels, street maps, tourist guides that told of local customs, and sites and histories that had never previously been identified), Cooks sought to provide branch tours (both day trips and overnight tours) into the wider locality. In this mycelium-like manner tourism spread to include almost every place and landscape on earth, ordering it at the same time as spaces and cultures interpreted and translated for the consumption, pleasure and inclusion of other people and cultures.

With Thomas Cook we can see several very important features of tourism that came into view and developed during his tourism industry career (1841–1892). These include at least seven important elements. First, the pleasurability and excitement of travel and communitas (or special social bonds established among travelling parties) became an object itself of travel and tourism and an important arm in its marketing and definition. Second, tourism became more involved in 'placemaking' for the modern world (the need to reconstruct towns, cities, villages, regions, places and ecologies as places interpreted for, sympathetic to and legible to those from elsewhere). Third, it initiated the opening up of backwater and remote regions to globalising transport connections and their connection to worlds beyond the everyday. Fourth, the performance of ritualised patrols and inspections of new national territories, landmarks, places and historicised landscapes became the business of an increasing number of new and established nations (and an important part of nation formation) – many inaugurated a stream of new national holidays. Fifth, the branding of nations, cities and regions for the consumption of outsider visitors and the growth in the significance of tourist visitors to local and national economies created a more distributed and vital sense of a tourism industry. Sixth, the development of hotels, resorts and transport hubs as an important element in the built environment of cities and certain types of new touristic settlements such as spas, seasides, forest towns, mountain centres, historic monuments and industrial zones transformed the sombre nature of many industrial towns and introduced a more pleasureable everyday, one that more closely resembled the holiday. Finally, the advent and expansion of paid public holidays and the cross-subsidies of amenity and cultural exchange between visiting tourists and their host communities was an important element in the construction of what sociologists call leisure societies.

As already remarked, during Mobilities I domestic forms of tourism expanded exponentially as first companies and then nation states made provision for more holidays, paid leave and national public holidays. This formed the basis of annual holidays within or beyond regions and shorter 'day trips'. As the proportion of working-class holidaymakers and tourists grew, establishing 'mass' proportions by the 1930s, so a patchwork of socially differentiated tourism places developed, each with their own 'social tone' (Urry 2002). Cultures of the seaside changed from being winter-focussed health spas with pleasurable entertainment laid on as an added bonus to summer seasons where pleasure-seeking became an end itself; though health was still emphasised, it was now the bonus.

International tourism also expanded its scope hugely during this time through the development of steam liners (Miller 2011). Massive concentrations of wealth in Europe, the USA and the colonies ensured a very rapid technological development. The 1,200-ton paddle steamer *Britannia*, on which Charles Dickens travelled in 1842, took 10–12 days to cross from the UK to New York; this halved the time it took the best sailing ships to do the trip, but, as Dickens recalled, it was extremely uncomfortable, smelly and unpleasant. By the 1870s, competition between large companies delivered the new liners, 'floating hotels', combining ever more speed, luxury and scale. Said to be the most beautiful ship on the Atlantic, and with fittings alone costing £2 million, Inman Line's *City of Rome* (1881) was the first ship to be lit by electricity. By 1909 there was the superliner *Lusitania* (one of the 'Incomparables'), which weighed over 30,000 tons, carried 3,000 passengers and did Atlantic crossings in four days. While these machines, the biggest and most advanced ever built, enjoyed their glory days between 1929 and 1939, they were an object of pleasurable tourism only for a very small social elite (Miller 2011).

Tourism Mobilities II: 1960 to present

World War II terminated or curtailed luxuries such as pleasurable travel and civilian holidays, but afterwards tourism developed and expanded on a similarly steep trajectory. Mobilities II was significantly different for three main reasons. First, travel and tourism was no longer so heavily constrained by national and regional boundaries or organised by consumer taste for local or domestic travel and holidays. In the USA, for example, the war had broken long-standing practices of interior, mountain and lakes holidays by creating new tastes for the exotic locations and cultures across the Pacific and into Europe that were encountered by servicemen and women during the war. Tiki bars sprung up all across America that referenced a new enthusiasm for cultural tourism, tropical weather, less modernised resort locations, surfing, and intimate island encounters.

Second, travel across post-war Western Europe became both easier and cheaper. Travel itself became cheaper and more flexible with the advent of mass ownership of cars in the 1960s and the expansion of cheaper air travel through package tour companies in the 1970s (e.g. Laker Airways was established in 1966) and low-cost airlines from the 1980s and 1990s onwards (Ryanair arrived in 1985, but especially significant was the de-regulation of the aviation industry in 1997) (Franklin 2003a). In both the USA and Europe reliable sunny weather gradually became far more important in destination choices, and this created several 'pleasure peripheries' across southern Europe, the Pacific, the southern states of the USA and Mexico, the Caribbean, South East Asia and Australasia.

Global international tourist arrivals grew from 25.3 million in 1950 to 69.3 million in 1960, 166 million in 1970, 278 million in 1980, 440 million in 1990, 687 million in 2000 and to 940 million in 2010. In 2012 international tourist arrivals are predicted to top one billion. Massive increases in international air tourism since the 1990s has steadily democratised the so-called 'jet-set' habits of the social elite, who were once defined by their monopoly of international air travel. In Australia, for example, less than half the population (44 per cent) were making at least one international flight for tourism per year in 2001, but by 2011 this proportion had grown to 57 per cent. Over the same period, the average ratio of men to women departing for international short-stay trips, most of which were for tourism (only 10 per cent was for business), declined from 118 men to 100 women to 112:100 (Australian Bureau of Statistics 2011), and for some age groups the ratio was even. This supports Bauman's contention that mobility (particularly tourism, with its connotations for social status) makes 'the tourist' an apt metaphor for the acquisitive, inquisitive individualism of liquid modernity (Bauman 2000). Indeed Bauman has noted on several occasions (Bauman 1998; Franklin 2003b) the way in which tourism has become an important metaphor for contemporary social life itself, since to be a tourist (to be mobile, travelled, connected and without overriding ties and commitments to a locale) is how a successful life is now measured. Conversely, of course, to be mired in place, to be tied or fixed to a place, is often how poverty or failure is expressed, a factor Bauman (2011) mobilised in his explanation of the UK riots of 2011 and his figure of the 'vagabond' (Bauman 1998).

Third, Mobilities II not only democratised international tourism within the West and elsewhere, but began to identify almost everyone in the world as a tourist and every place as configured for tourism consumption. This means that the binaries that once defined tourism in Mobilities I, particularly home/destination; everyday/tourism spaces; familiarity/difference; stationary/mobile, began to break down as tourism became a more socially, economically, culturally and spatially distributed form of experience. As we will see below, it shifted ontological understandings of tourism away from clear, spatially focussed forms of ludic behaviour at sites separated from the everyday, to more significant and new *relational orderings* of culture, economy and society. In Mobilities II, therefore, tourism performed connections, assemblages and hybrids instead of the separate socio-spatial domains of difference in Mobilities I. Northern European tourism into Spain in the 1960s–90s period not only saw Scandinavians, Germans and British tourists visit Spain in the summer, but created colonies of permanent and semi-permanent European migrants in Spain; it created new tastes for Mediterranean foods and aesthetics in Northern Europe; and it created the demand for tapas bars and restaurants in every city, just as it laid the foundation for the massive Spanish agricultural investments to supply Northern Europe with year-round supplies of Mediterranean wines, vegetables and fruits (Franklin 2003a; Obrador *et al.* 2009). It introduced the idea that tourism created wider flows of ideas, materials, aesthetics and resources, that tourists bring something of themselves to the places they visit as well as taking something of these places back with them. In Tourism Mobilities II a deepening touristic knowledge of the world made it difficult to think of everyday home cultures as distinct and separate; increasingly they could only be thought of *in relation* to other places, as connected to other places; as ordered to varying degrees by other places and the connections established with them. Just as nationalism created the imperative and drive to become knowledgeable about and more intimate with the much wider spaces of citizenship in Tourism Mobilities I, so globalisation created an imperative and drive for understandings of and affective connections with much wider territories of relevance and belonging, particularly when the freedom to travel as tourists was extended to include work and migration.

At this point tourists could shop for biographical futures as well as souvenirs of biographical episodes.

The more that global spaces and places became places of touristic investment/enhancement and visitation, the more tourism began to cross-subsidise everyday spaces with amenity, interest and cosmopolitan worldliness, since local people were able to join travellers in the consumption of services and products laid on for them – often, for example, being introduced to hitherto uninterpreted elements of their own history, popular culture, nature and heritage. Tourist researchers have noticed how important this has been to the generation and strengthening of local identity and attachment, for example in Scotland (MacDonald 1997), northern England (Urry 2002), Nova Scotia (McKay and Bates 2010) and Austria (Graml 2004). In addition, tourism has brought to many places facilities, amenities, infrastructure and capacities they would otherwise lack. This is especially true in the West and developing countries, where dazzling cities of spectacle have been built on the visitor dollar (Hannigan 1998; Judd and Fainstein 1999), and least true in the many undeveloped areas of the world where tourism can do the opposite: make local people unwanted and powerless in their own homelands (the foundational story here is how the Ik of Uganda were evicted from their ancestral hunting lands in order that a safari game park could be established (see Turnbull 1972).

It is therefore instructive to take stock of how the share of global international tourism arrivals is currently distributed. Europe, the cradle of tourism, still accounted for over half of global arrivals in 2011 (503 million), whereas Asia accounted for around one-fifth (216 million), the USA one-tenth (100 million) and Africa one-twentieth (50 million). However, annual rates of growth in tourism arrivals for advanced economies were far weaker (1.8 per cent) than for emerging economies (5.6 per cent), indicating that a slow redistribution of tourism is under way. These data are a register for the continuing and expanding relevance of pilgrimages to Europe as the foundation of modern cultures as well as the seductive power of travel in Locke's reasoning.

Tourism Mobilities I and II stimulated their own specific forms of academic research that have shaped tourism studies in the period since 1960. The essentially novel form of modern tourism in its expanding, democratising and mass-market forms meant that tourism studies was a) relatively slow to grow a separate academic discipline; b) highly influenced by the intellectual leanings of its three formative disciplines: sociology, geography and social anthropology; and c) eventually organised mostly through its identity as a separate industry and thus attached to faculties of business and commerce. As a result, tourist studies has been beset with competing and often conflicting perspectives over very basic matters, such as its definition, ontological status and significance.

Disciplines and perspectives

Looming large in tourist studies is the idea that *the tourist* is the proper subject of study. This was established by the earliest works by Boorstin (1964) and MacCannell (1976), with the latter's influential structuralist book about tourism (an early application of Lévi-Straussian structuralist analysis of modern societies) being called *The Tourist*. Picken (2006) shows how the binary elements used to define tourism were always centred around the tourist: it is the tourist's home and the tourist's away that constitute the binary, as well as their everyday/ extraordinary. The notions of social centre and the social margin, work and play, authentic and inauthentic all wrap around the tourist at the centre of analysis, giving it a bias towards *tourist centricity* (Franklin 2007). This was compounded by the tendency for researchers to 'follow the tourist', to become tourists in their research practice. As Picken (2006: 162) argued, 'Hence tourism became (largely) the discourse of the tourist and this is reflected in most disciplinary orientations and notably of economics/business/commerce where so much attention has been *demand* focussed.'

Since the tourist was socially constituted by their site of tourism, tourist studies also became fixated on tourist localities (resorts, places, islands, landscapes, ecologies) rather than the emerging relations between them. Ironically, then, prior to mobilities perspectives, beginning perhaps in 2000 with the arrival of journals such as *Tourist Studies*, tourist studies was grounded in a view of travel and tourism as focussed specifically on *place* rather than *movement*. Only ten years earlier, John Urry's (1990) *Tourist Gaze* was orientated around places specifically constructed as visual registers of difference for visitor consumption. However, this pioneering book and its spatial focus chimed well with the disciplines of geography and social anthropology, which, for their own disciplinary reasons, compounded a view of tourism as spatially focussed.

In the wake of Rob Shields' *Places on the Margin* (1991), which theorised tourism around specific kinds of socio-spatial location, human geography began to see something quintessentially geographical about tourism, and it became responsible for a large and valuable archive of studies, with particular emphasis on the impact of tourism on localities, particularly its adverse impacts on culture and environment. However, as I have argued recently, 'geography might have had predispositions to tourism not only because it could be considered spatially constituted but also because geography was itself constituted touristically' (Franklin 2007: 133). Geography as a research practice was historically framed by the expedition, by intrepid travel and discovery in exotic locations. Through its dissemination in popular magazines and journals it had been influential in inculcating the travel and tourism impulse, as Ward and Hardy (1986) demonstrated in relation to the history of camping.

Social anthropology was predisposed towards site-focussed tourist studies through their principle methodology of immersive ethnographic fieldwork, but particularly because a new generation of researchers had found their historic interest in specific cultures breached by an increasing number of tourists and travellers. As with geography, their discipline had created a touristic market for human subjects and spaces that were hitherto 'their' domain of ethnography. As with human geography, social anthropology problematised tourism as a leading edge of ethnocide, cultural assimilation, exploitation, commodification and political marginalisation, beginning with its most famous collection of essays *Hosts and Guests*, edited by Valene Smith (1989). A second wave of research discovered a less passive, victimised host culture, resulting in more-nuanced forms of social transaction between local people and visitors, new concepts such as MacCannell's (2001) 'second gaze' and Bruner (2004) and Gillespie's (2006) 'reverse gaze', and even the reversal of previous fears that the performance of culture for tourists was in many circumstances sustaining cultures rather than threatening them (Ewins 2002; Abrams 1995).

Very close examinations of what tourists actually do at tourist sites (e.g. Edensor 1998, 2001a; Coleman and Crang 2002) resulted in a useful turn away from structuralist accounts of tourist behaviour at tourist sites, notably through phenomenological perspectives that focussed attention on performance, performativity and cultural exchange. Clearly, important exchanges were taking place, but from a mobilities perspective the transfers were not all site-specific, but included what tourists brought with them: 'cultural baggage'; their assumptions about host cultures and places; aspects of the tourists' cultures that *locals* found fascinating, etc. Equally, recent studies pick up the tension and interplay between the pedagogical aims of tourist sites such as museums and art galleries and the visceral affects they generate (e.g. Papastergiadis 2006; Crang and Tolia-Kelly 2010) among complex amalgams of visitors from different backgrounds.

As a discipline, sociology was the opposite of social anthropology and geography because its core mission and methodology focussed not on the cultural spaces of leisure and pleasure or 'the social margins/periphery' but on the world of work and the everyday of industrial Europe and America. As a discipline it was ordered by the twin concerns of the enlightenment (in the form of progress, reform and change) and counter-enlightenment thought (in the form of anxieties about loss of culture and community, and the weakening of social bonds). Its main research focussed on solving problems thrown up by this tension in the reorganisation and ordering of work, in poverty and inequality, and in maintaining social cohesion and social order in the city. The luxuries and liminal spaces of travel and tourism, along with the lifestyle and cultures of idle social elites were given less emphasis (Franklin 2009). Indeed it was not until the 1980s, when tourism began to revitalise sites and towns of deindustrialised Britain and more and more people were dependent on tourism (which was now an industry) for work, that it seemed fitting to research tourism (Urry in Franklin 2001: 115–117). In an interview he did with me back in 2001, John Urry said he was amazed that his *Tourist Gaze* (1990) became *almost* the only major overview of tourism issues, yet was actually based mostly on tourism of the industrial northwest of England. Indeed, the original research that stimulated this book was funded by the UK Social Science Research Council's programme 'Changing Urban and Regional Systems', which was actually intended to investigate the social and political consequences of economic change.

According to the French tourism sociologist Jean-Didier Urbain (Doquet and Evrard 2008), in France tourism was for a very long time widely considered to be an English cultural phenomenon. According to the French Dictionary *Larousse*, 'touriste' was an acceptable synonym for 'English' from around 1890 onwards. Not surprisingly, perhaps, with tourism strongly associated with Englishness (for which, read 'English dissoluteness') and the survival of its idle leisure classes (aristocrats and their bourgeois emulators), the French academy was even more hostile to the serious consideration of tourism. According to Urbain, this is still the case for mainstream French sociology.

Ironically, perhaps, *The Tourist Gaze* also owes its origin to the widespread reading of Foucault in the late 1980s, with its strong emphasis on visuality, framing and power alongside emergent postmodern themes of de-differentiation, the simulacra, heritage, theming and niche-marketing, flexibilisation and the growth of service industries. While these were used to understand the touristification of a former industrial landscape, the subject itself (tourism) continued to draw strongly on MacCannell's structuralist theory of 'the tourist'. The extraordinary success of *The Tourist Gaze* (1990) did much to consolidate and grow tourism studies as a discipline, although it can be said that its institutional growth was predominantly in business and commerce, rather than in sociology. This is one of the reasons why Franklin and Crang (2001) and other members of the 'New Turn' (see Tribe 2005 for a summary; Ateljevic *et al.* 2007) found that tourist studies had become repetitive and theoretically stale in the late 1990s. They called for a number of changes which resulted in many new areas of emphasis, including: i) a far wider sensual register of tourism ordering and engagement (sex, dance, touch, taste, etc.) (Jokinen and Veijola 1994); ii) an understanding of the wider social orderings of tourism, particularly through nationalism (Löfgren 1999; Franklin 2003a); iii) the avoidance of overly semiotic readings of tourism as representations by exploring tourism as 'theatres of enactment' (Edensor 2001b); iv) a widening of the spatial parameters of tourism enactment to include more spaces (and non-spaces) of tourism and *travel itself*, such as airports, aircraft cabins, trains, cars (Augé 1995; Law 2001; de Botton 2002; Merriman 2004; Urry 2004); and v) a concern with the relational materialism of tourism as networks, objects, assemblages and orderings drawing on ANT, the sociology of ordering and posthumanism, and the relationship of tourism to 'worldmaking' (Franklin 2004; Hollinshead 2007; Baerenholdt and Haldrup 2006; van der Duim *et al.* 2012).

Franklin (2004) and van der Duim *et al.* (2012) return to the challenge of a still-dominant structuralist foundation for an epistemology of tourism. Based as it was on strongly asserted universal structural antecedents, in its most 'elementary form' modern tourism was nothing more than the welling up of socio-spatial relationships between the everyday and the extraordinary, binaries that related back to archetypes such as the profane and the sacred, culture and nature, and the authentic and the artificial, where enactments such as tourism and travel comprised the liminal equivalence of other human transformative technologies such as pilgrimage and ritual.

Without seeking to challenge the usefulness of structuralism, I have challenged its lack of interest in history, contingency, discontinuities, presences and absences; the detailed innovations, narratives and social lives; and particularly the very obviously *distributed* forms of agency that extended beyond the human realm to include (or rather 'enrol') non-humans (Franklin 2004). I wanted to show how only through such considerations could we begin to glimpse tourism effects that were similarly socially and spatially distributed. Placing tourism spaces on the margin (spatially and socially), tourist studies were in danger of missing their really big story, their potentially 'big idea'.

Here, particularly, tourism could be related positively to other distributed social relations that had become detached from particular sites and the 'mycelium-like' orderings of large companies and nation states to become enrolled in the wider orderings of cosmopolitanisation, global consumerism, aestheticisation, and the liquefaction of many modern orderings – and to become implicated in all manner of subjectivities of mobility.

★　★　★

New work in this stream began the task of taking the agency of objects more seriously. This involved looking at technologies designed to smooth travel between places, and how objects performed/enacted translations between culture and places (Simoni 2012), how objects such as buildings and design awards enact mediations between tourism and everyday worlds (Picken 2011), and how tourism objects such as souvenirs, once 'unleashed', can develop second social lives as forms of memory, recognition and belonging (with consequences and concerns), a point that draws on Mol's (2002) insight about multiplicity as a key property of objects (Galliford 2011; Franklin 2010).

These approaches oppose structuralism in a number of ways. As Simoni (2012: 61) puts it, 'our research participants are fully acknowledged in their ability to create different "worlds" (ontologies) rather than just "world views" (epistemologies). The approach advocated . . . moves beyond taken-for-granted oppositions between representation and world, between discourse and "reality", and between concepts and things', and thus subject and object. This clearly breaches the humanism of all prior tourist studies since we have *both* humans and objects as our unit of analysis (and not the usual humanity for the humanities and non-humans/objects for science as separable entities). As Andrew Pickering (2008: 8) reminds us, 'production not only creates an object for a subject but also a subject for an object'. We find it blindingly obvious that mundane tourism objects such as buckets and spades, river rafts, beach shacks and walking shoes are made by specific human subjects, but we frequently forget that once unleashed on the world they have the capacity to create a subject community around the object – which would not exist otherwise – and a set of events and effects that can be followed ethnographically from children playing on beaches to risk assessors, shark attacks, and conservation biology and climate change conferences (Michael 2001). As Pickering (2008) argues, this leads us inevitably to the idea of a mutual becoming, co-production or co-evolution of people and things, and thus into the domain of posthumanism.

This is both a radical shift and simple idea. In essence it is thus a methodological innovation rather than a theoretical challenge. It poses the idea that there are no deep structural layers that need to be uncovered through abstract concepts and theories – merely connections, enactments, networks and assemblages that can be revealed through painstaking ethnographic fieldwork which seeks to recreate a body of knowledge based on the empirical case study. These case studies can take the form of orderings of smaller (e.g. Picken 2011; Peters 2012) and larger magnitudes (e.g. Franklin 2012; Huijbens and Gren 2012; van der Duim *et al.* 2012), and connectivities through materialities (e.g. Galliford 2011; Simoni 2012) and mobilities (e.g. Baerenholdt 2012; Farias 2012). The fast-developing community of researchers around these approaches has become something of a leading edge in tourist studies, with the first of many streams of work only just beginning to roll out (see *Tourist Studies* volume 10:2 and van der Duim *et al.* 2012).

References

Abrams, S. (1995) 'Performing for Tourists in Rural France' in S. Abrams, J. Waldren and D. V. L. Macleod (eds) *Tourist and Tourism: Identifying with People and Places*. Oxford: Berg.

Ateljevic, I., Morgan, N., and Pritchard, A. (eds) (2007) *The Critical Turn in Tourism Studies: Innovative Research Methodologies*. London: Elsevier.

Augé, M. (1995) *Non-Places: Introduction to an Anthropology of Supermodernity*. London: Verso.

Australian Bureau of Statistics (2011) '3401.0 – Overseas Arrivals and Departures, Australia, Dec 2011', available online at www.abs.gov.au/ausstats/abs@.nsf/lookup/3401.0Media%20Release1Dec%20 2011 (accessed 31 March 2012).

Baerenholdt, J. O. (2012) 'Enacting Destinations: The Politics of Absence and Presence' in R. van der Duim, C. Ren and G. T. Jóhannesson (eds) *Actor-Network Theory and Tourism: Ordering, Materiality and Multiplicity*. London: Routledge.

Baerenholdt, J. O. and Haldrup, M. (2006) 'Mobile Networks and Place Making in Tourism', *European Journal of Urban Studies* 13: 209–24.

Bauman, Z. (1998) *Globalisation*. Cambridge: Polity.

Bauman, Z. (2000) *Liquid Modernity*. Cambridge: Polity.

Bauman, Z. (2011) 'Interview – Zygmunt Bauman on the UK riots', *Social Europe Journal*, available online at www.social-europe.eu/2011/08/interview-zygmunt-bauman-on-the-uk-riots/ (accessed 5 June 2012).

Boorstin, D. (1964) *The Image: A Guide to Pseudo Events in America*. New York: Harper.

Bruner, E. (2004) *Culture on Tour*. Chicago: Chicago University Press.

Chaney, R. (2000) *The Evolution of the Grand Tour: Anglo-Italian Cultural Relations since the Renaissance* (1998; 2nd, paperback edition, 2000). London: Routledge.

Coleman, S. and Crang, M. (eds) (2002) *Tourism: Between Place and Performance*. Oxford: Berghahn.

Crang, M. and Tolia-Kelly, D. P. (2010) 'Nation, race, and affect: senses and sensibilities at national heritage sites', *Environment and Planning A* 42(10): 2315–2331.

de Botton, A. (2002) *The Art of Travel*. London: Hamish Hamilton.

Doquet, A. and Evrard, O. (2008) 'An interview with Jean-Didier Urbain', *Tourist Studies* 8(2): 175–192.

Edensor, T. (1998) *Tourists at the Taj: Performance and Meaning at a Symbolic Site*. London: Routledge.

Edensor, T. (2001a) 'Performing tourism, staging tourism: (re)producing tourist pace and practice', *Tourist Studies* 1(1): 59–81.

Edensor, T. (2001b) 'Walking in the British Countryside: Reflexivity, Embodied Practices and Ways to Escape', in P. Macnaghten and J. Urry (eds) *Bodies of Nature*. London: Sage.

Ewins, R. (2002) *Staying Fijian: Vatulele Island Barkcloth and Social Identity*. Hindmarsh, South Australia: Crawford House.

Farias, I. (2012) 'Destinations as Virtual Objects of Tourism Communication', in R. van der Duim, C. Ren and G. T. Jóhannesson (eds) *Actor-Network Theory and Tourism: Ordering, Materiality and Multiplicity*. London: Routledge.

Franklin, A. S. (2001) 'The tourist gaze and beyond: an interview with John Urry', *Tourist Studies* 1(2): 115–131.

Franklin, A. S. (2002) *Nature and Social Theory*. London: Sage.

Franklin, A. S. (2003a) *Tourism*. London: Sage.

Franklin, A. S. (2003b) 'The tourism syndrome: an interview with Zygmunt Bauman', *Tourist Studies* 3(2): 205–218.

Franklin, A. S. (2004) 'Towards a new ontology of tourism: tourism as an ordering', *Tourist Studies* 4(3): 277–301.

Franklin, A. S. (2007) 'The Problem with Tourism Theory', in I. Ateljevic, A. Pritchard and N. Morgan (eds) *The Critical Turn in Tourist Studies*. Oxford: Elsevier.

Franklin, A. S. (2009) 'The Sociology of Tourism', in T. Jamal and M. Robinson (eds) *Handbook of Tourism Studies*. London: Sage.

Franklin, A. S. (2010) *City Life*. London: Sage.

Franklin, A. S. (2012) 'The Choreography of a Mobile World: Tourism Orderings', in R. van der Duim, C. Ren and G. T. Jóhannesson (eds) *Actor-Network Theory and Tourism: Ordering, Materiality and Multiplicity*. London: Routledge.

Franklin, A. S. and Crang, M. (2001) 'The trouble with tourism and travel theory?' *Tourist Studies* 1(1): 5–22.

Galliford, M. (2011) 'Touring "country", sharing "home": Aboriginal tourism, Australian tourists and the possibilities for cultural transversality', *Tourist Studies* 10(3): 227–244.

Gillespie, A. (2006) 'Tourist photography and the reverse gaze', *Ethos* 34(3): 343–66.

Graml, G. (2004) '(Re)mapping the nation: Sound of Music tourism and national identity in Austria, ca 2000CE', *Tourist Studies* 4(2): 137–149.

Hannigan, J. (1998) *Fantasy City*. London: Routledge.

Hollinshead, K. (2007) 'Worldmaking and the Transformation of Place and Culture', in I. Ateljevic, A. Pritchard and N. Morgan (eds) *The Critical Turn in Tourist Studies*. Oxford: Elsevier.

Huijbens, E. and Gren, M. (2012) 'Tourism, ANT and the Earth', in R. Van der Duim, C. Ren and G. T. Jóhannesson (eds) *Actor-Network Theory and Tourism: Ordering, Materiality and Multiplicity*. London: Routledge, 146–163.

Jokinen, E. and Veijola, S. (1994) 'The Disorientated Tourist: The Figuration of the Tourist in Contemporary Cultural Critique', in C. Rojek and J. Urry (eds) *Touring Cultures*. London: Routledge.

Judd, D. R. and Fainstein, S. S. (eds) (1999) *The Tourist City*. New Haven: Yale University Press.

Lassels, R. (1670) *The Voyage of Italy, or A Compleat Journey Through Italy*. London: Starkey.

Law, J. (2001) *Machinic Pleasures and Interpellations*. Lancaster: Centre for Science Studies and the Department of Sociology, Lancaster University.

Löfgren, O. (1999) *On Holiday: A History of Vacationing*. Berkeley: University of California Press.

MacCannell, D. (1976) *The Tourist: A New Theory of the Leisure Class*. New York: Schocken.

MacCannell, D. (2001) 'Tourist agency', *Tourist Studies* 1(1): 23–38.

MacDonald, S. (1997) 'A People's Story: Heritage, Identity and Authenticity', in C. Rojek and J. Urry (eds) *Touring Cultures*. London: Routledge.

McKay, I. and Bates, R. (2010) *In the Province of History – The Making of the Public Past in Twentieth Century Nova Scotia*. Montreal: McGill–Queen's University Press.

Merriman, P. (2004) 'Driving places: Marc Augé, non-places and the geographies of England's M1 motorway', *Theory, Culture & Society* 21(4–5): 145–167.

Michael, M. (2001) 'These Boots Are Made for Walking', in P. Macnaghten and J. Urry (eds) *Bodies of Nature*. London: Sage.

Miller, W. (2011) *Floating Palaces: The Great Atlantic Liners*. London: Amberley.

Mol, A. (2002) *The Body Multiple*. Durham, NC: Duke University Press.

Obrador, P., Crang, M. and Travlou, P. (2009) *Cultures of Mass Tourism: Doing the Mediterranean in the Age of Banal Mobilities*. Farnham: Ashgate.

Papastergiadis, N. (2006) *Spatial Aesthetics: Art, Place and the Everyday*. London: Rivers Oram Press.

Peters, P. (2012) 'Walking Down the Boulevard: On Performing Cultural Tourism Mobilities', in R. van der Duim, C. Ren and G. T. Jóhannesson (eds) *Actor-Network Theory and Tourism: Ordering, Materiality and Multiplicity*. London: Routledge.

Picken, F. (2006) 'From tourist looking-glass to analytical carousels: navigating tourism through relations and context', *Current Issues in Tourism* 9(2): 158–170.

Picken, F. (2011) 'Tourism, design and controversy: calling on non-humans to explain ourselves', *Tourist Studies* 10(3): 245–264.

Pickering, A. (2008) 'New Ontologies', in A. Pickering and K. Guzik (eds) *The Mangle in Practice: Science, Society and Becoming*. Durham, NC: Duke University Press.

Shields, R. (1991) *Places on the Margin*. London: Routledge.

Simoni, V. (2012) 'Tourism Materialities: Enacting Cigars in Touristic Cuba', in R. Van der Duim, C. Ren and G. T. Jóhannesson (eds) *Actor-Network Theory and Tourism: Ordering, Materiality and Multiplicity*. London: Routledge, 59–79.

Smith, V. (ed.) (1989) *Hosts and Guests*. Philadelphia: University of Pennsylvania Press.

Tribe, J. (2005) 'New tourism research', *Tourism Recreation Research* 30(2): 5–8.

Turnbull, C. (1972) *The Mountain People*. New York: Simon & Schuster.

UNWTO (World Tourism Organisation) (2011) 'Tourism Highlights 2011 Edition', available online at http://mkt.unwto.org/sites/all/files/docpdf/unwtohighlights11enlr_3.pdf (accessed 31 March 2012).

Urry, J. (1990) *The Tourist Gaze*. London: Sage.

Urry, J. (2002) *The Tourist Gaze: Second Edition*. London: Sage.

Urry, J. (2004) 'The 'system' of automobility', *Theory, Culture & Society* 21: 25–39.

van der Duim, R., Ren, C. and Jóhannesson, G. T. (2012) 'Tourismscapes, Entrepreneurs, and Sutainability: Enacting ANT in Tourism Studies', in *Actor-Network Theory and Tourism: Ordering, Materiality and Multiplicity*. London: Routledge.

Veijola, S. and Jokinen, E. (1994) 'The body in tourism', *Theory, Culture & Society* 11: 125–151.

Ward, C. and Hardy, D. (1986) *Goodnight Campers! The History of the British Holiday Camp*. London: Mansell.

7

Queer Theory

Natalie Oswin

The mobilities literature, as recently developed across the social sciences and humanities, focuses analytic attention on the character and quality of movements and flows. This focus is not in itself novel. Rich bodies of work around such topics as transportation, diaspora, migration, globalization, and more have long brought scholarly attention to the importance of mobility to sociality and spatiality. What sets recent mobilities approaches apart is a particular take on the fact of movement. As Tim Cresswell, in an appraisal of mobilities scholarship, states: "Mobility here is as much about meaning as it is about mappable and calculable movement. It is an ethical and political issue as much as a utilitarian and practical one" (2010a, 552). Of course, this central focus is taken in multiple directions as mobilities scholars write from various perspectives, but for many, a mobilities approach emphasizes the social, cultural and political production of movements and flows and attends to the "fragile entanglement of physical movement, representations, and practices" (Cresswell 2010b, 18). Certainly, a strong strand of thinking within mobilities research "track[s] the power and politics of discourses and practices of mobility in creating both movement and stasis" (Hannam *et al.* 2006, 3–4) and emphasizes "the relation between human mobilities and immobilities, and the unequal power relations which unevenly distribute motility, the potential for mobility" (15). In other words, much mobilities work fundamentally attends to the differentiated politics of movement.

To understand the inequities of friction and flow, mobilities scholars grapple with the ways in which mobilities and immobilities are experienced as embodied. As Cresswell, again, states: "In the end, it is at the level of the body that human mobility is produced, reproduced, and, occasionally, transformed. Getting from A to B can be very different depending on how the body moves" (2010b, 20). Of course, 'how the body moves' depends in large part on whose body it is and on how that body is interpolated in social space. Schisms along lines of race, class, gender, sexuality, disability, nationality, age, and more play central roles in determining who moves, how, at what speed, and with what degree of autonomy. It is therefore surprising that queer theory, the subject on which I have been asked to write, has not been concertedly incorporated into mobilities approaches. Indeed, as a body of work, the mobilities literature has not highlighted sexuality – queer theory's main preoccupation – as a main topic of study.

This lack of engagement can perhaps be partially attributed to the fact that the best-known major works of queer theory do not consider mobility. Tomes by the likes of Judith Butler (1990), Michel Foucault (1978), and Eve Kosofsky Sedgwick (1990) have traveled far, informing debates across the social sciences and humanities for decades now. While these texts offer nuanced analyses of the ways in which sexual norms become rooted in place over time, they do not consider the circulations, movements, and flows that attend contingent sexual discourses and practices. Beyond these 'key texts,' however, much work within the broad, interdisciplinary field of queer studies does indeed centralize such concerns. This work has developed outside the mobilities literature per se. For the most part, it has neither been taken up by mobilities scholars nor been explicitly informed by mobilities scholarship. Nonetheless, in using the tools of queer theory to explain and critique the sexual politics of movement across various boundaries and scales, certain strands of work within queer studies have many synergies with the mobilities literature. Queer analyses of such phenomena as transnationalism, diaspora, migration, tourism, and urban cultural politics attend to the ways in which movement is differentiated by sexual norms, discourses, and practices. In the rest of this chapter, I turn first to a brief discussion of the term 'queer' in order to clarify the field of study. Then I survey a range of queer studies work on certain 'mobile' topics, demonstrating the need to account for 'queer' lives as lives in motion and arguing for further conversations between queer theory and mobilities scholarship in order to interrogate and counter the heteronormative limits of mobility.

Brief notes on 'queer'

The term 'queer' is a complex one. In popular parlance, it is used most widely as a simple descriptor for LGBT (lesbian, gay, bisexual, and transgender) communities and social movements. But its deployments in activist and scholarly circles have grown out of specific lineages and have particular meanings. In the early 1990s, 'queer' first began to be used as a label for a certain kind of activism by HIV/AIDS organizations in the US and UK. Groups like ACT UP and Queer Nation fought against the stigma of the widespread labeling of HIV/AIDS as a 'gay disease' by advancing a radical, sex-positive, and anti-assimilationist politics. These organizations re-appropriated the term 'queer,' rejecting its negative connotations and thereby challenging the definition of 'normal' sexuality. In this usage, a queer identity and politics "embraced literally anyone who refused to play by the rules of heteropatriarchy" (Bell and Valentine 1995, 21).

At around the same time, and mostly within the same locales, 'queer' entered the academy as a new mode of theorizing. Here too, the term took on a radical, politically confrontational tone. Queer theory, as it emerged within literary theory circles in the 1990s, offered a re-orientation of scholarly understandings of sexuality. Whereas the scholarship that came to be called 'gay and lesbian studies' in the 1970s and 1980s largely understood sexual identities to be natural, fixed, and biologically determined, queer theory asserts that sexual identities are social constructions that do not pre-exist their worldly (i.e. cultural and linguistic) deployments.[1] It maintains a focus on the plight of sexual minorities while fundamentally challenging the empirical validity and conceptual usefulness of identity categories. As Fran Martin states, "as 1990s feminist theory did with 'women' and postcolonial theory did with 'race' and 'culture,' queer theory was concerned to disrupt the assumed universality and internal coherence of previous categories of identification in 'gay and lesbian identity'" (2003, 25). The insight that sexualities are performed, that they are something we *do* rather than something we *have*, has formed the basis for the development of a significant interdisciplinary literature. Understanding both hegemonic heterosexuality and marginal non-heterosexualities as socially, historically, and geographically contingent, work within queer studies has taken on the critical tasks of understanding the ways in which sexual identities are performed and challenging the myriad processes through which sexual norms become naturalized in different times and places.

Thus, there are two central meanings of 'queer.' First, the term signifies a sexual identity, functioning as an umbrella term that is self-consciously embraced by many of those who fall outside the bounds of 'normal' sexuality. Second, it signifies a poststructuralist critique of the very notion of sexual identity. In this articulation, it is of course acknowledged that sexual identity categories come to take on social meaning and thus cannot be abandoned in political struggles over sexual citizenship and social justice. But, while urgently calling attention to and seeking to improve the lives of non-heterosexuals or 'queers,' queer theory pushes us to go beyond liberal frameworks of identity and difference. In this sense, queer is advanced as an analytic and diagnostic tool that facilitates the critical interrogation of the power of sexual norms and of the far-reaching effects of heteronormative cultural logics.

Having briefly discussed 'queer' in abstract terms, I now turn to the literature to demonstrate the promise, both empirically and conceptually, of a queer mobilities approach. In the survey of work on queer mobilities that follows, 'queer' features in both of the senses outlined above – as an identity and as an analytic. Much existing literature examines the flows, circulations and movements that animate LGBT lives and experiences, thus highlighting the need to address the tendency within the mobilities literature to presume a 'straight' mobile subject. At the same time, these 'queer' lives are understood as geographically and historically contingent, as wildly diverse, and as implicated within broad constellations of power. Further, much work goes beyond the 'queer' subject to offer a queer critique of the heteronormative limits of mobility for a wide range of sexual subjects.

Queer mobilities

As stated above, queer theory was originally a very geographically limited enterprise. But, beginning in the late 1990s, it began to look beyond Anglo-America as a 'transnational turn' swept through the field. Since that time, queer studies has truly gone global as studies of sexual lives, cultures, and politics have been extended to a variety of locales (for example, see: Alexander 2005; Bacchetta 2002; Boellstorff 2005; Cantu 2002; Currier 2010; Hoad 2007; Hochberg 2010; Jackson 2011; Kulpa 2011; Leung 2008; Swarr and Nagar 2003).[2] I suggest that this 'transnational turn' can also be seen retrospectively as a sort of 'mobility turn' for queer studies. For, as the field's geographical referents expanded, it became evident that queer theory could no longer remain a-mobile.

The effects of movement and flow on 'queerness' became a central concern for scholars seeking to understand sexual politics in a range of national contexts. In an early essay on the study of the globalization of gay and lesbian subcultures, Dennis Altman (1997) aims to make sense of what he observes as expressions of 'western-style' gayness outside the west. He launches an agenda for global queer studies as an undertaking that must carefully explore the workings of global/local, western/non-western, and traditional/modern binary relationships as 'gayness' globalizes. To do this, he asserts the importance of examining the ways in which homosexual identities are diffused at the global scale; and, for him, this diffusion goes from 'west' to 'rest.' He claims that "the images and rhetoric of a newly assertive gay world spread rapidly from the United States and other Western countries after 1969," the year in which the Stonewall protests took place in New York City (2001, 29). But Lisa Rofel, in her study of gay identities in China, is critical of Altman's assumptions of unidirectional flows. Instead, she argues that "the emergence of gay identities in China occurs in a complex cultural field representing neither a wholly global culture nor simply a radical difference from the West. Rather, Chinese gay identities materialize in the articulation of transcultural practices with intense desires for cultural belonging, or cultural citizenship, in China" (1999, 453). Many others offer similar findings. For instance, Peter Jackson states that gay and lesbian styles and terminology in Thailand are often "appropriated as strategies to resist local heteronormative strictures and carve out new local spaces. However, these appropriations have not reflected a wholesale recreation of Western sexual cultures in Asian contexts, but instead suggest a selective and strategic use of foreign forms to create new ways of being Asian *and* homosexual" (2001, 5, original emphasis). Further, it has also become apparent that a focus on 'west'–'non-west' relationships misses much. In her study of Taiwan's lesbian subcultures, Antonia Chao finds that Taiwan, "at least with respect to the traffic of sexual categories, may be 'closer' to Southeast Asia than East Asia or mainland China," and argues that "notions of globalization as a form of 'Americanization' or 'Westernization' are somewhat problematic" (2000, 379). Finally, even as we try to track flows of queer cultures across national boundaries, we must also pay attention to local gay and lesbian movements and subcultures as non–discrete and heterogeneous. In this vein, Bobby Benedicto examines "Manila's gay scene in the present of gay globality" and concludes that the embrace of 'gay modernity' has resulted in gender and class schisms within that city's gay culture (2008, 318).

It is worth mentioning that the urban scale features especially prominently within studies of queer globalizations as cities play a profoundly important role in facilitating the formation of gay and lesbian communities and movements around the world. More specifically, many scholars have devoted attention to the relationship between sexual diversity and the creative city strategies that travel around the globe through urban policy circuits. Richard Florida, who has been a very influential proponent of such policies, states, "creative people are attracted to, and high-tech industry takes root in, places that score high on our basic indicators of diversity – the Gay, Bohemian and other indexes . . . [because] members of the Creative Class in general prefer places that are open and diverse" (2002, 250). Queer scholars have put this argument under considerable scrutiny. For instance, David Bell and Jon Binnie (2004) note that Florida relies on census data on gays and lesbians in same-sex partnerships to make his linkage between the presence of 'gays' and 'creativity,' and that "the gay index is therefore an index of respectability, of nicely gentrified neighbourhoods" (1817). Further, they argue that the incorporation of 'sexual others' into entrepreneurial urban governance strategies of place promotion "has meant tightening regulation of the types of sexualized spaces in cities" (1818). They suggest, in other words, that "this 'sexual restructuring' of cities . . . is a powerful component of the 'new homonormativity'"; whereby homonormativity connotes a privatized, depoliticized gay and lesbian culture (1818; also see Manalansan 2005; Oswin 2012; and Rushbrook 2002).

This work on queer globalized lives and subcultures makes it impossible to ignore the fact that sexual subjectivities, even when seemingly rooted in place, are anything but sedentary. As Martin puts it, "If sexualities are the products of particular histories and cultures, and in globalization histories criss-cross one another while cultures become shifting organizations of knowledges of diverse provenance, then in this era, sexualities are inevitably constituted through cultural movement, conversation, and fragmentation" (2003, 7). The insights that gay and lesbian subcultures are the product of complex circulations, and that we cannot fix the terms gay, lesbian, or queer cross-culturally, are significant empirical findings. They also have important theoretical implications. In particular, this work on queer lives at the global scale reinforces queer theory's anti-identarian critique. As Rofel concludes, "moving from the global to the transcultural means moving from identity to identification, which means moving toward a politics of contingent alliances rather than toward simple essences or self-identical recognition" (1999, 470). Further, work on queer globalizations makes evident the necessity of bridging queer critique with postcolonial critique to challenge notions of teleological development. For instance, Arnaldo Cruz-Malave and Martin Manalansan challenge globalizing narratives predicated on a "developmental narrative in which a premodern, pre-political, non-Euro-American queerness must consciously assume the burdens of representing itself to itself and others as 'gay' in order to attain political consciousness, subjectivity, and global modernity" (2002, 6).

Though queer approaches to global flows were first developed in relation to LGBT issues, broader diagnoses of heterosexuality and heteronormativity have followed. This literature is smaller and less coherent. But I offer brief descriptions of three important texts to point to its critical promise and potential reach. First, Kate Bedford examines the ways in which reproductive heterosexuality is naturalized through circuits of international development policy and practice. She connects "discussions of heteronormativity to the policy documents, loans, and research activities of the World Bank" by examining this institution's "sexualized policy effects" (2009, xxii). The Bank's gender policy is the focus of her critique. As development experts have begun to recognize that women cannot be entirely responsible for social reproduction and attempts to bring men into its gender strategies, Bedford examines the ways in which the Bank attempts to restructure heterosexuality. As the Bank attempts to create 'loving couples,' she points out that many gender initiatives "rest on and reinforce a definition of good gender analysis as requiring sharing couplehood, and this profoundly privatizing conceptualization leads to privatizing policy solutions fixated on microadjustments in loving partnerships. In other words, it hails gender balance to intensify the privatization of social reproduction" (203). Bedford thus shines a light on international development policy as one way in which heteronormativity logics move.

Second, in *Terrorist Assemblages: Homonationalism in Queer Times*, Jasbir Puar puts queer theory to work in relation to "patriotism, war, torture, security, death, terror, terrorism, detention, and deportation, themes usually imagined as devoid of connection to sexual politics in general and queer politics in particular" (2007, xii). She aims to disrupt Euro-American claims to sexual exceptionalism that have been mobilized in the US-led 'war on terror.' To this end, she interrogates "the process of the management of queer life at the expense of sexually and racially perverse death in relation to the contemporary politics of securitization" (xiii). In a series of bold and creative readings, she juxtaposes the Garner and Lawrence Supreme Court decision on sodomy law with the US Patriot Act, rethinks turbaned bodies as queer assemblages, interrogates the coming together of Orientalism and sexual exceptionalism at Abu Ghraib, and problematizes the alignments of certain feminists and gay activists with patriotic nationalism.

Finally, J. K. Gibson-Graham's *The End of Capitalism (as we knew it)* argues that capitalism ought to be re-narrated since the predominant representations of capitalism as unitary, total, and monolithic prevent the emergence of a possible anticapitalist economic imaginary. One of the tools that they draw upon for this task is queer theory. They argue that capitalism's ability to spread and invade via globalization is commonly recounted as a non-reciprocal penetration that brings only loss to those people and institutions that it touches. Instead, Gibson-Graham asks how we might rescript this narrative so that globalization will "lose its erection – its ability to instill fear and thereby garner cooperation" (1996, 126–7). Their answer is to address the "homophobia that pervades economic theorizing" (137). Rather than acknowledging only the unidirectional penetrative nature of international financial markets, we are implored to begin to see them as "an *opening* in the body of capitalism, one that not only allows capital to seep out but that enables noncapitalism to invade" (138). For Gibson-Graham, then, queer theory facilitates the telling of a new story about capitalist globalization, a story that focuses on the infection of capitalism itself and allows us to declare that "we're here, we're not capitalist, get used to it!" (1999, 84).

Beyond queer work on globalization, the large literature on sexuality and migration can also be seen as a bridge between queer studies and mobilities scholarship; and, in this body of work, queer's dual valence is better exploited. Eithne Luibhéid describes queer migration scholarship as making a double movement. On the one hand, work focusing on LGBT migration "insists on recovering, theorizing, and valorizing histories and subjects that have been largely rendered invisible, unintelligible, and unspeakable in both queer and migration studies." On the other hand, she continues, "much of the scholarship also makes clear that 'queer migrants' in many ways comprise 'impossible subjects' with unrepresentable histories that exceed existing categories. This leads scholars to foreground and challenge regimes of power and knowledge that generate structures of impossibility where particular groups are concerned, and to examine how individuals negotiate them" (2008, 171). Thus queer migration scholarship foregrounds LGBT issues while also going further to look at the ways that migration regimes "normalize and naturalize heterosexuality and heterosexual practices including marriage, family, and biological reproduction by marginalizing persons, institutions, or practices that deviate from these norms" (Manalansan 2006, 225).

On the topic of gay and lesbian migrations, there has been a wealth of scholarship. Kath Weston's study of the 'great gay migration' to San Francisco was one of the first in this vein. While migration to major western cities with large and established gay and lesbian subcultures is often depicted as a necessary and unproblematic step in the 'coming out process,' Weston's research subjects reveal a much more complicated picture. She calls attention to problematic gender, race, and class dynamics in "the 'gay neighborhoods' of the Castro, the Village, and West Hollywood [that] fix the gay subject as wealthy, white, and male" (1995, 270) and points out that, "especially for those who did not fit the profile of the Castro clone, the journey to a big city that initially signified 'coming home' could end up raising more questions than it answered" (1995, 274). Many other studies report similar findings in relation to both rural to urban gay and lesbian migrations, while yet more work looks at the power dynamics of international migrations. For instance, in an ethnographic study of the experiences of Filipino gay male migrants to New York City, Manalansan demonstrates the ways in which these men challenge notions of modern gay identity by "charting hybrid and complex paths that deviate from a teleological and developmental route to gay modernity" (2003, x–xi). In addition, the notion that 'queer' migrations are urban migrations is contested. Gordon Waitt and Andrew Gorman-Murray (2011) disrupt notions of the rural as backward sexual spaces in their examination of gay and lesbian return migrations to Townsville, Australia. Further, governmental regulation of same-sex immigration has come under much scrutiny. Unfortunately, few countries have legalized same-sex couple migration. But even those immigration regimes that accept gay and lesbian family formations are not beyond reproach. Tracey Simmons (2008) examines the 'Unmarried Partners Rule,' a UK family reunion policy that applies to same-sex couples. She demonstrates that this apparently progressive policy does not apply to all same-sex couples equally, as the possession of 'attractive skills' and demonstration of financial dependency are important factors in the achievement of family reunion. Along similar lines, Audrey Yue finds that Australian same-sex migration policy "organizes sexuality around the heteronormative institutions of intimacy and the family, incorporating the queer migrant as a good citizen through self-cultivation and disciplinary regulation" (2008, 239–240).

Beyond this particular focus on gay and lesbian migration, queer migration scholars have also clarified that sexuality is a factor in all migration flows. While critical immigration scholarship has long interrogated the production of foreign others as 'undesirable,' a queer approach points out that we ought to take this characterization much more literally since notions of hegemonic heterosexuality are inseparable from, and work to shore up, national determinations of properly racialized, classed, and gendered citizens. After all, the social *reproduction* of the nation is the end game of immigration control. Luibhéid, in her study of the history of the regulation of US immigration, situates the exclusion of lesbian and gay migrants alongside analyses of immigration regulations aimed at keeping out Chinese prostitutes and Japanese picture brides. She finds that "lesbian and gay exclusion never functioned as an isolated system, but instead was part of a broader federal immigration control regime that sought to ensure a 'proper' sexual and gender order, reproduction of white racial privilege, and exploitation of the poor" (2002, xiv). Nayan Shah, in his historical examination of public health and Chinese immigration to San Francisco around the turn of the twentieth century, similarly finds that "the formation of respectable domesticity connected practices of individual health and sexuality to collective social well-being" (2001, 77). Given that not simply heterosexuals but white, middle-class, heterosexual couples with children were the societal standard, Shah states that "Chinese bachelor sexuality is represented as deviant because the presumed sexual relations of these men living in San Francisco were considered nonreproductive and nonconjugal" (2001, 78). Finally, I (Oswin 2012) analyze the heteronormative migration regime that underpins contemporary Singapore's global/creative city project. While 'foreign talent' are welcomed to join the city-state's national family, literally and figuratively, 'foreign workers' in the construction and domestic service sectors are stranded in a heterotemporality that is queered via regulatory mechanisms that render them permanently transient and outside normalization and naturalization. I argue that Singapore's migration policies set its alien surplus labor force on an alternative developmental path that precludes intimacy, love, and familial connection. Immigration regimes, as they sort acceptable and unacceptable migrants, render them normal or abnormal, productive or reproductive, and proper or queer.

Conclusion

As I stated at the outset, mobilities scholarship to date has not concertedly engaged with queer theory. Neither have what might be considered the major works of queer theory grappled with the facts of mobility and immobility. Nonetheless, much of the broad queer studies literature is relevant to mobilities scholarship. In this brief chapter, I have been able to provide just a small sample of this work. There is of course much more to be said about the rich literatures on globalization and migration on which I have focused. There is also more to write on queer approaches to such topics as diasporas, transnational activist networks, tourism, and sex work. Finally, while I have focused on studies of literal movements across space, there are other bodies of work that connects to mobilities scholarship's concern with embodied, performative, affective, and other more phenomenological aspects of mobility. In short, although queer theory has not been centrally integrated into mobilities approaches to date, there is most certainly a productive conversation to be had. Sexuality is an important axis of social differentiation, and one of many that produce the friction in which mobilities scholars have shown much interest. Mobility is indeed differentially accessed, in part according to sexual norms. So we need to both consider 'queer' lives as mobile lives and to critique the heteronormative limits of mobility.

Notes

1 This characterization of 'gay and lesbian' and 'queer' approaches is admittedly a caricature. Some scholars associated with gay and lesbian studies, such as John D'Emilio and Jeffrey Weeks were in fact among the first to advance social constructionist approaches to the study of sexuality. See Jagose (1996) for detailed discussion of these two approaches and their interrelations.
2 As this list of sources suggests, the geographical coverage of queer work on migration, tourism, diaspora, transnationalism, etc. is quite extensive. I thus wish to emphasize that the fact that the literature reviewed in this chapter emphasizes North America, Europe and Asia–Pacific is attributable to my own partial view on the literature.

Bibliography

Alexander, J. (2005) *Pedagogies of Crossing: Meditations on Feminism, Sexual Politics, Memory, and the Sacred*, Durham, NC: Duke University Press.

Altman, D. (1997) 'Global gaze/Global gays,' *GLQ*, 3: 417–436.

Altman, D. (2001) 'Rupture or continuity? The internationalization of gay identities,' in J. C. Hawley (ed.) *Postcolonial, Queer: Theoretical Intersections*, Albany: State University of New York Press.

Bacchetta, P. (2002) 'Rescaling transnational "queerdom": Lesbian and "lesbian" identitary-positionalities in Delhi in the 1980s,' *Antipode*, 34: 937–973.

Bedford, K. (2009) *Developing Partnerships: Gender, Sexuality, and the Reformed World Bank*, Minneapolis: University of Minnesota Press.

Bell, D. and Binnie, J. (2004) 'Authenticating queer space: Citizenship, urbanism and governance,' *Urban Studies*, 41: 1807–1820.

Bell, D. and Valentine, G. (1995) 'Introduction: Orientations,' in D. Bell and G. Valentine (eds) *Mapping Desire: Geographies of Sexualities*, London: Routledge, 1–27.

Benedicto, B. (2008) 'The haunting of gay Manila: Global space-time and the specter of *Kabaklaan*,' *GLQ*, 14: 317–338.

Boellstorff, T. (2005) *The Gay Archipelago: Sexuality and Nation in Indonesia*, Princeton, NJ: Princeton University Press.

Butler, J. (1990) *Gender Trouble: Feminism and the Subversion of Identity*, New York: Routledge.

Cantu, L. (2002) 'De ambiente: Queer tourism and the shifting boundaries of Mexican male sexualities,' *GLQ*, 8: 136–166.

Chao, A. (2000) 'Global metaphors and local strategies in the construction of Taiwan's lesbian identities,' *Culture, Health and Sexuality*, 2: 377–390.

Cresswell, T. (2010a) 'Mobilities I: Catching up,' *Progress in Human Geography*, 35: 550–558.

— (2010b) 'Towards a politics of mobility,' *Environment and Planning D: Society and Space*, 28: 17–31.

Cruz-Malave, A. and Manalansan, M. (2002) 'Dissident sexualities/alternative globalisms,' in A. Cruz-Malave and M. Manalansan (eds) *Queer Globalizations: Citizenship and the Afterlife of Colonialism*, New York: New York University Press.

Currier, A. (2010) 'Political homophobia in postcolonial Namibia,' *Gender & Society*, 24: 110–129.

Florida, R. (2002) *The Rise of the Creative Class: And How it's Transforming Work, Leisure, Community and Everyday Life*, New York: Basic Books.

Foucault, M. (1978) *The History of Sexuality: An Introduction, volume 1*, New York: Vintage Books.

Gibson-Graham, J. K. (1999) 'Queer(y)ing capitalism in and out of the classroom,' *Journal of Geography in Higher Education*, 23: 80–85.

Gibson-Graham, J. K. (1996) *The End of Capitalism (As We Knew It): A Feminist Critique of Political Economy*, Cambridge, MA: Blackwell.

Hannam, K., Sheller, M. and Urry, J. (2006) 'Editorial: Mobilities, immobilities and moorings,' *Mobilities*, 1: 1–22.

Hoad, N. (2007) *African Intimacies: Race, Homosexuality and Globalization*, Minneapolis: University of Minnesota Press.

Hochberg, G. (ed) (2010) 'Queer politics and the question of Palestine/Israel,' Special issue, *GLQ*, 16(4).

Jackson, P. (2011) *Queer Bangkok: 21st Century Markets, Media, and Rights*, Hong Kong: Hong Kong University Press.

— (2001) 'Pre-gay, post-queer: Thai perspectives on proliferating gender/sex diversity in Asia,' *Journal of Homosexuality*, 40: 1–24.

Jagose, A. (1996) *Queer Theory: An Introduction*, New York: New York University Press.

Kulpa, R. and Mizielinska, J. (eds) (2011) *De-centring Western Sexualities: Central and Eastern European Perspectives*, Burlington, VT: Ashgate.

Leung, H. H. (2008) *Undercurrents: Queer Culture and Postcolonial Hong Kong*, Vancouver: UBC Press.

Luibhéid, E. (2008) 'Queer/migration: an unruly body of scholarship,' *GLQ*, 14: 169–190.

Luibhéid, E. (2002) *Entry Denied: Controlling Sexuality at the Border*, Minneapolis: University of Minnesota Press.

Manalansan, M. (2006) 'Queer intersections: Sexuality and gender in migration studies,' *International Migration*, 40: 224–249.

Manalansan, M. (2005) 'Race, violence and neoliberal spatial politics in the global city,' *Social Text*, 23: 141–155.

Manalansan, M. (2003) *Global Divas: Filipino Gay Men in the Diaspora*, Durham, NC: Duke University Press.

Martin, F. (2003) *Situating Sexualities: Queer Representation in Taiwanese Fiction, Film and Public Culture*, Hong Kong: Hong Kong University Press.

Oswin, N. (2012) 'The queer time of creative urbanism: Family, futurity and global city Singapore,' *Environment and Planning A*, 44: 1624–1640.

Puar, J. K. (2007) *Terrorist Assemblages: Homonationalism in Queer Times*, Durham, NC: Duke University Press.

Rofel, L. (1999) 'Qualities of desire: Imagining gay identities in China,' *GLQ*, 5: 451–474.

Rushbrook, D. (2002) 'Cities, queer space, and the cosmopolitan tourist,' *GLQ*, 8: 183–206.

Sedgwick, E. (1990) *Epistemology of the Closet*, Berkeley: University of California Press.

Shah, N. (2001) *Contagious Divides: Epidemics and Race in San Francisco's Chinatown*, Berkeley: University of California Press.

Simmons, T. (2008) 'Sexuality and immigration: UK family reunion policy and the regulation of sexual citizens in the European Union,' *Political Geography*, 27: 213–230.

Swarr, A. L. and Nagar, R. (2003) 'Dismantling assumptions: Interrogating "lesbian" struggles for identity and survival in India and South Africa,' *Signs*, 29: 491–516.

Waitt, G. and Gorman-Murray, A. (2011) 'Journeys and returns: home, life narratives and remapping sexuality in a regional city,' *International Journal of Urban and Regional Research*, 35: 1239–1255.

Weston, K. (1995) 'Get thee to a big city: Sexual imaginary and the great gay migration,' *GLQ*, 2: 253–77.

Yue, A. (2008) 'Same-sex migration in Australia: from interdependency to intimacy,' *GLQ*, 14: 239–262.

8

Feminism and Gender

Georgine Clarsen

Feminist aspirations have been frequently articulated through the meanings, pleasures and potentialities of mobility. The very term 'feminist movement' suggests a valorisation of motion. The Enlightenment values of dynamism, progress, freedom and the escape from the confinement of irrational traditions have provided powerful motivating stories for many progressive collectivities across generations. For feminists, however, images of the transgressive movement of women beyond the limited spaces ascribed to femininity, often expressed in terms such as 'expanding women's horizons', have been especially pervasive and powerful.

The term 'feminist' is far from simple, and its meanings and associations have varied in time and place. It came into regular usage in Western Europe and Britain in the last decades of the nineteenth century, where it was largely associated with organised campaigns for women's political rights, critiques of masculinity, and aspirations for women to be included as active citizens in the new world that was heralded by the French revolution (Caine 1997). Feminism was a movement that sought to reduce the consequences of sexual difference by extending the newly conceived 'rights of man' to women. In the United States, 'woman movement' activists did not embrace the term until the second decade of the twentieth century as suffrage campaigns reached their peak. By the 1920s in the United States, 'feminism' referred to women's desires for personal emancipation and individual self-fulfilment in all spheres of life – in sexuality, at work, as well as in formal national processes (Cott 1987). What has been identified as a general feminist 'consciousness' or 'imagination', however, has been traced to at least the Middle Ages, well before the term was devised, and it continues into the present (Taylor 2003). 'Feminism' can be broadly characterised as the long history of overt actions and intellectual analyses that seek to further individual women's own and other women's status. Feminism always implies both an analysis of injustices between men and women and a claim to change them.

This discussion will examine the relationship between both of those aspects of feminism, within mobility research in general and the 'new mobilities paradigm' in particular. The two faces of feminism, the critical debates and academic disciplines that interrogate women's secondary status on the one hand and the activist campaigns devoted to precipitating change through emancipatory practices on the other have often been considered to be in tension. But feminists have increasingly refused their opposition, viewing campaigns to extend disparate mobilities to women and the intellectual projects that examine women and men's differential relationships to mobilities as inextricably intertwined. In this chapter I argue that the radical potential of the concept of gender has not been exhausted in mobilities scholarship and, conversely, a broad mobilities paradigm has not had a significant impact on feminist theorising, in spite of their commonalities in theoretical commitments and political aspirations.

Though the radical potential of feminist analysis has not been placed at the centre of mobilities scholarship, there have been strong connections between the two projects. Feminism's long engagement with women's mobilities is arguably one of the intellectual and political antecedents that shaped early formulations of the new mobilities paradigm and led to its emergence at a particular historical moment. Key foundational texts in mobility studies demonstrate that engagement with feminist politics, research projects and theoretical concerns. For example, *Sociology Beyond Societies*, John Urry's 'brave manifesto' (2000, 19) for his proposed 'new agenda' (1) for twentieth-century sociology puts forward an argument for a 'post-disciplinary reconfiguration' (3) that sounds rather familiar to feminist scholars who have always operated in counter-disciplinary and trans-disciplinary settings. Urry's discussion engages with a range of feminist writers and texts, as well as other foundational scholarship that has influenced feminist theory. He acknowledges that his key metaphors of movement and flow have been widely deployed by feminist theorists of the body, as well as in feminist debates surrounding nomadic subjectivities (26–27). Beyond that, and in common with feminism, Urry's vision of a revitalised sociology highlights the connections between embodiment and larger social processes, ascribing a central place to the corporeal and sensorial dimensions of individual and collective life (77 ff.). Throughout Urry's discussion, gender is named as a key axis of inequality, though he does not devote any detailed attention to it. Other early publications within the new paradigm (Sheller and Urry 2000) more explicitly consider gender as one of the key sites of differential mobilities. However, this has not translated to articles in the journal *Mobilities*. Since it was first published in 2006, only two articles have included 'gender' in the title, ten have included the term in the abstract, and only one article lists it as a keyword.

Urry couched the project in interdisciplinary terms and as increasing numbers of younger scholars began to adopt a mobilities perspective in the second half of the decade, it has proven to be less influential in sociology than in other disciplines (see Sheller in this collection). Notably, the resolutely modernist and masculinist field of transport studies has been influenced by the new mobilities paradigm. Transportation research has taken a distinct 'cultural turn', and gender is increasingly found as an important term of analysis. New scholars with a background in the humanities are entering the field, a greatly expanded range of research questions is emerging, and new professional bodies have been established (for example, the International Association for the History of Transport Traffic and Mobility, http://t2m.org). New publishing opportunities foster an interest in theoretical issues alongside the empiricism of traditional transport scholarship (for example, the annual *T2M Handbooks*, first published in 2009, and the new journal *Transfers: Interdisciplinary Journal of Mobility Studies*). Established journals in the field, notably the *Journal of Transport History*, have also responded with a distinct broadening of their offerings (the special Gender edition in 2002; Mom 2003; Millward 2008a).

Of all the academic disciplines, however, geographers have led the way in systematically developing the radical potential of mobilities formulations. Geography had long been concerned with movement of people and things across space, and during the 1980s and 1990s cultural geographers, including an influential generation of women, were engaged in a radical reconceptualisation of their discipline. Among other things, cultural geographers elaborated more dynamic conceptions of places as social productions, fluid and always in the processes of formation. Extending this project, geographers began to subject the concept of movement, until then a largely unexamined term, to critical analysis, teasing out the ways that movement (and its necessary other, stasis) were also socially produced (Cresswell 2001). Over the last decade, geographers of mobility have increasingly advocated a processual approach to mobilities, by emphasising the operations of power and mapping a differentiated politics of mobility. They have been at the forefront of new scholarship into gendered mobilities, which advances feminist debates and locates gendered differences as crucial to contextualising systemic inequalities. A group of British cultural geographers have stimulated research beyond their own discipline by suggesting productive schemas for analysing how movement is made meaningful within specific social contexts, for example in teasing out a gendered politics of mobility practices, experiences and representations (Cresswell 2006; Adey 2010; Cresswell 2010; Cresswell and Merriman 2011; Merriman 2012).

Feminist interest in what we now routinely call 'gendered mobilities' predates the new mobilities paradigm and it is important to briefly sketch a trajectory of some of those earlier debates and emancipatory ambitions. The ubiquitous relationship between sexual difference and mobility, across all modalities of human activities and experiences, and at scales from the personal to the global, has been well documented. Feminists have long asserted that mobility, as a social value and material practice, has been more available to men than to women. Men have been overwhelmingly associated with mobile activities such as warfare, the exploration of new worlds, pilgrimage, sports, adventure quests and *flâneurie*. They have been more closely engaged with the material technologies and infrastructures of mobilities such as bicycles, railways, steamships, automobiles and information systems. And pervading discourses assign positive values, such as dynamism, progress and entrepreneurship to masculine mobilities. Conversely, women have been routinely associated with stasis, confinement to a 'private sphere', the containment of bodily capacities, the surveillance of autonomous movement, and a less-than-authoritative relationship to modern technologies of mobility. Furthermore those qualities, particularly within Western traditions, have been ascribed a secondary status (Sheller 2008).

In response to that pervasive gendering of mobilities, countless women have produced narratives of their pleasure in transgressing such gendered norms, naming them as acts of defiance and personal growth. Many represented taking charge of their mobility in feminist terms – as 'seizing their own destiny'. Examples of such narratives of autonomous movement include Frances Willard's famous late-age embrace of the bicycle as a vehicle of pleasure and feminist politics (Willard 1895), the writings of women volunteers on the French front (Beauchamp 1919) or women who took to the skies in the interwar period (Batten 1938). It also includes women's aspirations to mobilise personal and political freedoms for themselves and others, such as Indonesian nationalist heroine and educator Raden Ajeg Kartini's desire to travel to Holland for a European education (Taylor 1992), or Shidzue Ishimoto's campaigns for birth control in Japan (Ishimoto 1935), or Indian dancer and actress Zohra Segal's travels across Europe and America (Erdman and Segal 1997).

Beyond these personal representations of women's diverse mobilities as transgressive actions, a great many feminist studies in a wide range of academic disciplines and across a variety of social contexts have documented men and women's differential mobilities and the discursive fields that surround them. Such research is increasingly being framed within, or broadly influenced by, a mobilities paradigm and it does not assume mobility to be intrinsically transgressive. The republishing of Victorian women travellers' texts by feminist presses in the 1980s led to flourishing scholarship on gendered travel narratives and their intersections with the discourses and practices of colonialism (Mills 1991; Pratt 1992; Blunt 1994; McEwan 2000; Woollacott 2001; Lahiri 2010). Feminist studies of Western urbanisation and modernity have traced how the growth of cities created spaces of liberation for women, offering new mobile practices and new spaces of work, pleasure, deviation and disruption (Wolff 1985; Wilson 1991; Nava 1996). Labour researchers and development scholars have revealed profoundly gendered patterns of men and women's workplace mobilities (Hanson and Pratt 1995) and the crucial role of mobilities in shaping women's livelihood opportunities (Mandel 2004). Migration researchers have highlighted structural inequalities using mobilities frameworks (Walton-Roberts and Pratt 2005; De Regt 2010). Feminist philosophers have investigated the phenomenological dimensions of gendered embodiment (Young 1980 and 1998; Bordo 1993), and this scholarship has been extended into many areas of gendered mobilities, such as women's engagements with sports (Scraton and Flintoff 2002), technologies (Millward 2008b; Clarsen 2008; DeLyser 2011) and in feminist politics (Cresswell 2005).

The wealth of research and debate is also indicated by the increasing number of collected volumes devoted to gendered mobilities of all kinds published by academic and activist presses. They attest to the continuing energy of the field (Constable 2005; Passerini et al. 2007; Cresswell and Uteng 2008; Ballantyne and Burton 2008; Metz–Göckel 2008; Resurreccion and Elmhirst 2009; Letherby and Reynolds 2009; Kusakabe 2012; Lund et al. 2013). While the full range of scholarship on gendered mobilities is too large and diverse to do more than gesture toward, the research cited here indicates how the concept of gender has proven productive for thinking through men and women's differential practices, experiences and representations of mobilities. The literature reveals a complex picture of the pervasive intertwining of mobilities and gender. Research suggests not only that women have been less able and less likely to move with the same degree of ease as men, but that even when their physical motion appears to be exactly the same as men's, the meanings ascribed to it are never quite the same – indeed, they are often very different. And it is not as if movement occurs through neutral physical space, but gendered bodies move through gendered social spaces, via material objects and technologies of travel and communication that themselves are often profoundly gendered. And finally, the research serves as a constant reminder that all of these gendered meanings, practices, potentialities, experiences, emotions, places, representations and objects have changed greatly over time and differ across diverse locations.

The publication of dedicated review essays surveying the gender and mobility literature confirms that a broad field is beginning to cohere and provide a platform for cross-disciplinary conversations (Law 1999; Silvey 2004; Yeoh 2005; Blunt 2007; Cattan 2008; Walsh 2009 and 2011; Clarsen 2009; Hanson 2010). Transport geographer Robin Law, in her widely cited early discussion, applauded the move away from traditional 'gender blind' transport research, but declared the time had come for scholarship that was based on a more systematic treatment of gender as a theoretical category (Law 1999, 568). Law argued that her field was constrained by the empiricist assumptions of conventional transportation research, such as its focus on the journey-to-work paradigm, and argued for a move away from the 'women and' approach into a more nuanced theorisation of gender and mobility that drew on wider intellectual traditions. She called on feminists in her field to continue to develop gender as a category of analysis that did not simply research the impact of gender on mobilities, but more crucially analysed how mobilities and gender are co-constituted in banal, everyday practices (Law 2002).

Law's call has been reiterated by similar literature surveys in the decade and a half since it was published, suggesting the need for constant reassessment of this apparently simple and intuitive concept in order to sustain its radical potential. Striking in many discussions of gender and mobility is that the meanings and usefulness of the term 'gender' are very often assumed rather than examined, as if we all already know what gender is. A close reading of the literature, however, suggests that its meanings are rather elastic and, as in everyday speech, 'gender' is often used as a descriptive category that is interchangeable with 'sexual difference', 'men and women', 'feminine and masculine' or sometimes just 'women'. My outline of the literature above exemplifies those shifting meanings, and this fuzziness of the analytical category deserves exploration.

Most discussions of gendered mobilities treat mobility as a concept that requires analysis or explication, but (with notable exceptions) they rarely provide a similar account of gender. Precisely because the concept has been so productive for feminist research, however, it is important to reassess the term forty years after it was so enthusiastically welcomed into the feminist toolbox. Teresa de Lauretis's injunction, offered at the moment when the term was becoming ubiquitous in feminist literature, that we need a notion of gender that is not so bound up with sexual difference as to be virtually coterminous with it, remains salient (de Lauretis 1987, 2). Gender itself is a mobile concept and how feminists have deployed the term has a history. In order to harness the critical power of the concept within mobilities studies it is important to consider how its various meanings have been useful for feminists at different strategic moments, and in particular social and geographical locations.

'Gender' was eagerly adopted in the 1960s by 'second wave', Western feminists as a key strategy to counter the widespread beliefs underpinning women's disadvantage: that differences between men and women were immutable because they were rooted in biology. The term, which had previously been used in English to indicate masculine and feminine forms in language, was then entering into the lexicon of psychologists, who used it to refer to trans-sexuals' expressions of masculinity and femininity. Feminists first embraced 'gender' not to critique the notion of the biological intractability of sex, but as a way of sidestepping that vexed issue. 'Gender' made room for change by asserting that it was social processes ('socialisation') that built variation onto those fixed biological differences between men and women. That perspective allowed both of the key but paradoxical assertions of feminism to be held at the same time: that there were crucial commonalities between women ('sister-hood') and also that those characteristics ('sex roles') could be transformed through political action (Nicholson 1994, 80–81). So, as prominent theorists later put it, it was the 'perceived dangers of biological reductionism' that compelled the repudiation of sex and the embrace of gender in feminist analytical discourse (Gatens 1996, 4). This linguistic tactic meant that gender could be 'quarantined from the infections of biological sex' (Haraway 1991, 134).

In this sense, the term 'gender' may be understood as a strategic response by western feminists, particularly in Anglophone contexts, to the prevailing conservative discourses and practices of biological determinism, at a particular historical moment and in specific social locations (Braidotti 2002; Moi 1999). The creation of the term marked a moment of histor-ical change, energising feminist research agendas and activist projects. Gender opened out new landscapes of opposition to the discourses, institutions and practices that constrained ('oppressed' was the term most often used) women. There was an outpouring of feminist research in the humanities and social sciences, and to a lesser extent in the sciences, that pro-duced a wealth of new knowledge about women's lives now and in the past. In retrospect, it is clear that the value of the term was not simply as a new descriptor for things that existed in the world (sexual difference open to change) but more crucially it was also a bid to break open a political and intellectual deadlock. And the term did indeed become a powerful agent of change, perhaps beyond the dreams of those who first formulated it. 'Gender' worked to reshape the contours of feminist debates and activism, in fact reshaping debates well beyond feminism.

Gender offered a productive solution to an historical impasse, but the term soon presented problems for feminist theory and practice. Both elements of the dualistic conception – fixed 'sex' and variable 'gender' – became the subject of increasing contestation by those who were marginalised or excluded by their terms. Over the following decades, 'first world' women of colour, 'third world' women, working-class women, lesbians, transsexuals and feminist men critiquing masculinity were among the groups who forged critical sites of enunciation out of those terms, refusing that simplistic characterisation of the sex/gender distinction and 'speaking back' to the limitations and normative assumptions built into them (Mikkola 2012). Such cumulative and intersecting critiques have been closely bound up with dramatic changes in feminist theory and activism: the undoing of the fantasy of a unitary feminist project, the insistence on the irreducibility of difference, the challenging of hierarchies of power within feminism, the construction of new identities, the installing of the centrality of the body to feminist politics, the highlighting of the relationality of gendered categories, and the development of an analytics of power from the intimate to the global. These processes of contestation over the meanings and usefulness of gender have generated the variety of ways that we see the term now used, which exceeds the unitary denotation intended at its inception.

What began as an important innovation in a positivist project to undo presumptions about women's historical lack of agency and their lives 'hidden from history', and to document instead the variety of ways that women held up 'half of the sky', had by the 1990s turned into a critique of positivism (Scott 1999, 3). The question became: could existing disciplinary paradigms be expanded to include women and other marginalised subjects, or did gendered research necessitate rethinking the foundational paradigms of those knowledges? For historian Joan Scott, one of the leading theorists of the category of gender (though rarely cited in the gender and mobilities literature), that accumulation of feminist scholarship did more than merely point out silences and fill in gaps in existing research. Even more fundamentally, it constituted and inspired a profound critical challenge to the knowledge claims of established disciplines. Critical feminist scholarship revealed how existing frameworks of knowledge, for all their assumptions of mastery, universality and objectivity, relied on the exclusion of women, producing and reproducing it, rather than accidentally omitting women from their terms. Disciplines were 'participants in the production of knowledge that legitimised the exclusion or subordination of women' (Scott 1999, 26). Her work was a powerful and provocative influence on the 'linguistic turn' in historiography and a marker of the discipline's (often reluctant) engagement with poststructuralism (Scott 1999, 9–10; Butler 2011, 19).

Though historians of gender rarely frame their research within a mobilities paradigm, Scott's historical perspective can do much to maintain a critical focus, and thereby enhance mobilities research. Her formulation places gender as much more than a descriptive category for the fixed subject positions of 'men' and 'women' whose meanings we already know in advance, or a qualifier to a field of research, such as 'gendered migration' or 'gendered automobility'. Scott's work opens out ways to think historically about how gender is integral to producing the analytic fields we investigate, and how we as researchers are inextricably complicit in that process (Butler 2011). While the growing work on gender and mobility serves to increase our knowledge about differential movements, it can do much more than simply indicate that men and women stand in different relation to mobilities. In fact, uncritical research that does not place gendered mobilities in their historical and discursive contexts can work to reinstall and naturalise those very power relations that feminists seek to understand and change (Subramanian 2008).

An historical perspective to gendered research continues to serve feminist ends when it seeks to make visible how the very concept of mobility, its practices and representations, has been built within complex and changing matrices of meanings that may sometimes appear to be unconnected to sexual difference. The ways and mechanisms through which mobility has historically come to organise our understandings of gender and what effects that has had in specific locations and at particular moments still needs much teasing out. Understanding precisely how and by what means shifting ideas of gender have come to structure the meanings of mobility in particular historical contexts is also an unfinished project. How have conceptions of gender naturalised the value of particular mobilities over others, and mobility over stasis? How do these processes operate within constellations of other categories of subjectivity? How have notions of gender served to structure fields of meaning for the movement of material things as much as for people? How are notions of gender bound into ideas such as justice, progress or sustainability? And finally, to recognise the agentic power of our research, how and by what means can the narratives of gendered mobilities that we produce serve as resources for articulating alternative visions and suggest ways to bring about change? Feminist historiography tells us that mobility research can further progressive ends when it nurtures gender's instability and critical potential as a contested process of meaning-making, and continues to resist routinised and essentialised approaches to gender that take it to be a static 'thing'.

References

Adey, Peter (2010) *Mobility*. London and New York: Routledge.
Ballantyne, Tony and Antoinette Burton (eds) (2008) *Moving Subjects: Gender, Mobility, and Intimacy in an Age of Global Empire*. Urbana and Chicago: University of Illinois Press.
Batten, Jean (1938) *My Life*. New York: George G. Harrap.
Beauchamp, Pat (1919) *FANY Goes to War*. London: John Murray.
Blunt, Alison (1994) *Travel, Gender and Imperialism: Mary Kingsley and West Africa*. New York and London: The Guilford Press.
Blunt, Alison (2007) 'Cultural geographies of migration: mobility, transnationality and diaspora', *Progress in Human Geography* 31 (5): 684–694.
Bordo, Susan (1993) *Unbearable Weight: Feminism, Western Culture and the Body*. Berkeley: University of California Press.
Braidotti, Rosi (2002) 'The Uses and Abuses of the Sex/Gender Distinction in European Feminist Practices', in Gabriele Griffin and Rosi Braidotti (eds) *Thinking Differently: A Reader in European Women's Studies*. London: Zed Books, 285–307.
Butler, Judith (2011) 'Speaking Up, Talking Back: Joan Scott's Critical Feminism', in Judith Butler and Elizabeth Weed (eds) *The Question of Gender: Joan W. Scott's Critical Feminism*. Bloomington: Indiana University Press.
Caine, Barbara (1997) *English Feminism: 1780–1980*. Oxford: Oxford University Press.
Cattan, Nadine (2008) 'Gendering Mobility: Insights into the Construction of Spatial Concepts', in Tanu Priya Uteng and Tim Cresswell (eds) *Gendered Mobilities*. Aldershot: Ashgate, 83–97.
Clarsen, Georgine (2008) *Eat My Dust: Early Women Motorists*. Baltimore, MA: Johns Hopkins University Press.
Clarsen, Georgine (2009) 'Gender and Mobility: Historicizing the Terms', in Gijs Mom, Gordon Pirie and Laurent Tissot (eds) *Mobility in History: The State of the Art in the History of Transport, Traffic and Mobility*. Neuchâtel: Éditions Alphil-Presses universitaires suisses, 235–241.
Constable, Nicole (ed.) (2005) *Cross-Border Marriages: Gender and Mobility in Transnational Asia*. Philadelphia: University of Philadelphia Press.
Cott, Nancy F. (1987) *The Grounding of Modern Feminism*. New Haven and London: Yale University Press.

Cresswell, Tim (2001) 'The production of mobilities', *New Formations* 43: 11–25.

Cresswell, Tim (2005) 'Mobilising the movement: the role of mobility in the suffrage politics of Florence Luscomb and Margaret Foley, 1911–1915', *Gender, Place and Culture* 12 (4): 447–461.

Cresswell, Tim (2006) *On the Move: Mobility in the Modern Western World*. New York and London: Routledge.

Cresswell, Tim (2010) 'Towards a politics of mobility', *Environment and Planning D: Society and Space* 28 (1): 17–31.

Cresswell, Tim and Peter Merriman (2011) *Geographies of Mobility: Practices, Spaces, Subjects*. London: Ashgate.

Cresswell Tim and Tanu Priya Uteng (2008) 'Gendered Mobilities: Towards an Holistic Understanding', in Tanu Priya Uteng and Tim Cresswell (eds) *Gendered Mobilities*. Aldershot: Ashgate, 1–12.

de Lauretis, Teresa (1987) *Technologies of Gender: Essays on Theory, Film and Fiction*. Bloomington and Indianapolis: Indiana University Press.

DeLyser, Dydia (2011) 'Flying: Feminisms and Mobilities – Crusading for Aviation in the 1920s', in Tim Cresswell and Peter Merriman (eds) *Geographies of Mobilities: Practices, Spaces, Subjects*. Burlington: Ashgate, 83–96.

De Regt, Marina (2010) 'Ethiopian domestic workers in Yemen ways to come, ways to leave: gender, mobility, and il/legality among Ethiopian domestic workers in Yemen', *Gender & Society* 24 (2): 237–260.

Erdman, Joan L. and Zohra Segal (1997) *Stages: The Art and Adventures of Zohra Segal*. New Delhi: Kali for Women.

Gatens, Moira (1996) *Imaginary Bodies: Ethics, Power and Corporeality*. London and New York: Routledge.

Hanson, Susan (2010) 'Gender and mobility: new approaches for informing sustainability', *Gender, Place and Culture* 17(1): 5–23.

Hanson, Susan and Geraldine Pratt (1995) *Gender, Work and Space*. New York: Routledge.

Haraway, Donna (1991) *Simians, Cyborgs and Women: The Reinvention of Nature*. London: Free Association Press.

Ishimoto, Shidzue (1935) *Facing Two Ways: The Story of My Life*. New York: Farrar & Rinehart. *Journal of Transport History* (2002) Special Edition on Gender, 23 (1).

Kusakabe, Kyoko (ed.) (2012) *Gender, Roads, and Mobility in Asia*. Rugby, UK: Practical Action Publishing.

Lahiri, Shompa (2010) *Indian Mobilities in the West, 1900–1947: Gender, Performance, Embodiment*. New York: Palgrave Macmillan.

Law, Robin (1999) 'Beyond "Women and Transport": towards new geographies of gender and daily mobility', *Progress in Human Geography* 23 (4): 567–588.

Law, Robin (2002) 'Gender and daily mobility in a New Zealand city, 1920–1960', *Social & Cultural Geography* 3 (4): 425–445.

Letherby, Gayle and Gillian Reynolds (eds) (2009) *Gendered Journeys, Mobile Emotions*. Aldershot: Ashgate.

Lund, Ragnhild, Kyoto Kusakabe, Smita Panda and Yunxian Wang (eds) (forthcoming 2013) *Gender, Mobilities and Livelihood Transformations: Comparing Indigenous People in China, India and Laos*. New York and London: Routledge.

Mandel, Jennifer (2004) 'Mobility matters: women's livelihood strategies in Porto Novo, Benin', *Gender, Place, and Culture* 11 (2): 257–287.

McEwan, Cheryl (2000) *Gender, Geography and Empire: Victorian Women Travellers in West Africa*. Bloomington: Indiana University Press.

Merriman, Peter (2012) *Mobility, Space and Culture*. London and New York: Routledge.

Metz-Göckel, Sigrid (ed.) (2008) *Migration and Mobility in an Enlarged Europe?: A Gender Perspective?* Leverkusen-Opladen: Barbara Budrich Publishers.

Mikkola, Mari (2012) 'Feminist Perspectives on Sex and Gender', in Edward N. Zalta (ed.) *The Stanford Encyclopedia of Philosophy (Fall 2012 Edition)*, available online at http://plato.stanford.edu/archives/fall2012/entries/feminism-gender/ (accessed 15 October 2012).

Mills, Sara (1991) *Discourses of Difference: An Analysis of Women's Travel Writing and Colonialism*. London and New York: Routledge.

Millward, Liz (2008a) 'The embodied aerial subject: gendered mobility in British inter-war air tours', *Journal of Transport History* 29 (1): 5–22.

Millward, Liz (2008b) *Women in British Imperial Airspace*. Montreal and London: McGill–Queens University Press.

Moi, Toril (1999) *What Is a Woman?* Oxford: Oxford University Press.

Mom, Gijs (2003) 'What kind of transport history did we get? Half a century of JTH and the future of the field', *Journal of Transport History* 24 (2): 121–138.

Nava, Mica (1996) 'Modernity's Disavowal: Women, the City and the Department Store', in Mica Nava and Alan O'Shea (eds) *Modern Times: Reflections on a Century of English Modernity*. London and New York: Routledge, 38–76.

Nicholson, Linda (1994) 'Interpreting gender', *Signs* 20: 79–105.

Passerini, Luisa, Dawn Lyon, Enrica Capussotti and Ioanna Laliotou (eds) (2007) *Women Migrants from East to West: Gender, Mobility and Belonging in Contemporary Europe*. New York: Berghan Books.

Pratt, Mary Louise (1992) *Imperial Eyes: Travel Writing and Transculturation*. London and New York: Routledge.

Resurreccion, Bernadette and Rebecca Elmhirst (eds) (2009) *Gender and Natural Resource Management: Livelihoods, Mobility and Interventions*. Singapore: Institute of Southeast Asian Studies.

Scott, Joan W (1999) [1988] *Gender and the Politics of History*. New York: Columbia University Press.

Scraton, Sheila and Anne Flintoff (eds) (2002) *Gender and Sport: A Reader*. London: Routledge.

Sheller, Mimi (2008) 'Gendered Mobilities: Epilogue', in Tanu Priya Uteng and Tim Cresswell (eds) *Gendered Mobilities*. Aldershot: Ashgate, 257–265.

Sheller, Mimi and John Urry (2000) 'The city and the car', *International Journal of Urban and Regional Research* 24 (4): 737–757.

Silvey, Rachel (2004) 'Power, difference and mobility: feminist advances in migration studies', *Progress in Human Geography* 28 (4): 490–506.

Subramanian, Sheela (2008) 'Embodying the Space Between: Unmapping Writing about Racialised and Gendered Mobilities', in Tanu Priya Uteng and Tim Cresswell (eds) *Gendered Mobilities*. Aldershot: Ashgate, 35–45.

Taylor, Barbara (2003) *Mary Wollstonecraft and the Feminist Imagination*. Cambridge: Cambridge University Press.

Taylor, Jean Gelman (1992) *Letters from Kartini: An Indonesian Feminist, 1900–1904*. Melbourne: Monash Asia Institute: Hyland House.

Urry, John (2000) *Sociology Beyond Societies: Mobilities for the Twenty-first Century*, London and New York: Routledge.

Walsh, Margaret (2009) 'Gender and Travel: Mobilizing New Perspectives on the Past', in Gail Letherby and Gillian Reynolds (eds) *Gendered Journeys: Mobile Emotions*. Aldershot: Ashgate, 5–18.

Walsh, Margaret (2011) 'Still a Long Way to Travel: Gender and Mobility History Revisited', in Gijs Mom, Peter Norton, Georgine Clarsen and Gordon Pirie (eds) *Mobility in History: Themes in Transport*. Neuchâtel: Éditions Alphil–Presses universitaires suisses, 255–264.

Walton-Roberts, Margaret and Geraldine Pratt (2005) 'Mobile modernities: a South Asian family negotiates immigration, gender and class in Canada', *Gender, Place & Culture* 12 (2): 173–195.

Willard, Frances (1895) *A Wheel Within a Wheel*. Bedford, MA: Applewood Books.

Wilson, Elizabeth (1991) *The Sphinx in the City: Urban Life, the Control of Disorder, and Women*. Berkeley and Los Angeles: University of California Press.

Wolff, Janet (1985) 'The invisible *Flaneuse*: women and the literature of modernity', *Theory, Culture & Society* 2 (3): 37–48.

Woollacott, Angela (2001) *Try Her Fortune in London: Australian Women, Colonialism, and Modernity*. New York: Oxford University Press.

Yeoh, Brenda (2005) 'Transnational Mobilities and Challenges', in Lise Nelson and Joni Seager (eds) *The Companion to Feminist Geography*. Oxford: Blackwell, 60–73.

Young, Iris Marion (1980) 'Throwing like a girl: a phenomenology of feminine body comportment, motility, and spaciality', *Human Studies* 3 (2): 137–156.

Young, Iris Marion (1998) '"Throwing Like a Girl": Twenty Years Later', in Donna Welton (ed.) *Body and Flesh: A Philosophical Reader*. Oxford: Blackwell, 284–290.

Section Two
Introduction: Qualities

Each chapter in this section takes seriously a quality of mobility. These are the characteristics of mobilities that will cross-cut many other of the chapters and sections within this handbook. A quality might be: a facet that constitutes the experience of mobility; an aspect of mobility that might frustrate analysis and prove tough to apprehend; a particular experience of time and distance; the curious pacing and qualitative rhythms mobilities seem to keep tempo to. Yet, despite the temptation for the overwhelming association of mobility with velocity or fastness that we introduced at the beginning of this handbook, chapters in this section slow down somewhat. In particular, they examine mobility's de-accelerations, its pauses and the corporeal experiences and practices that constitute it. If anything they determine that mobility is far more about the experience of slowness and frustration. Mobility is about clogging up, getting stuck, congestion and blockages. The novelist Ursula Le Guin has even called the airport terminal a constipation.

Helpfully, Tim Cresswell starts with Clausewitz's elaboration of friction in his examination of the battlefield. What is clear is that in mobility, as in war, something is always liable to go wrong, or break down. Confusion, chance and impediments to mobility can rule. Attending to friction can tell us not only why mobile things are so often slowed or stopped, but can help us to understand the constant efforts to manufacture systems, technologies and practices which try to evade those friction effects and to free things up. Friction is not a new topic for studies of mobility, ever appealing to the tyranny of distance and the resistances presented to mobile life, the things that get in the way of communications and social relations. Cresswell investigates a politics of friction which shows that some mobile persons are much more likely to experience friction than others. Friction is unequally distributed. Furthermore, friction is something that can be used to resist certain kinds of mobility. Friction may well be used as a weapon of the weak.

Phillip Vannini follows the same kind of curve as this. Except here friction is more than a weapon or something that frustrates. Instead, slowness is very much to be desired and achieved. Not always an easy accomplishment given the mobile pressures on people's everyday lives, slowness may be an actively pursued state of withdrawal from the freneticism of particularly fast or active mobilities. Vannini's focus is on the repertoire of performances that are designed to explicitly de-accelerate mobility, and therefore life, from the primacy of speed. Vannini explores the practices of off-gridders who have turned away from the formalized energy infrastructures and systems many of us take for granted. Off-gridders harness power from the elements and the rhythms of the seasons, which involves doing many things much more slowly. The chapter draws comparisons between other slow or off-grid lifestyles, such as the slow food movement, which articulates far less extensive and more local forms of food gathering, production and consumption. Or slow tourism, which is a direct rejection of the kinds of superficial social encounters anthropologist Marc Augé would describe as the key characteristics of a non-place or inauthentic setting. But judging slowness or identifying it is tricky. Without an absolute reference point how do we know when something is slow or not? How can we make these judgements outside of just quantitative measurement? Vannini suggests that we must look to slowing down as a phenomenological accomplishment.

Distance

What might constitute speed is the sense of distance overcome. While mobilities have been regularly understood as an activity to overcome, annihilate or foreshorten distance, chapters in this section rather investigate the social-spatial relations by which distance and closeness are produced through mobilities. By understanding distance as a relation of mobility, the chapters make two main moves. First, Larsen and de Souza e Silva and Gordon's chapters make the case that the proximities afforded by mobilities are both new and evolving. Moreover, for Larsen, the notion of distance has far more emotional freight than that of a cold and rational idea of geographic location. Larsen explores how new forms of social media and communication are permitting social relations to play out at a distance, looking at, for example, the social proximities required to sustain relationships such as mothering. Taking the example of Filipino transnational family lives, Larsen shows how mothering can be performed, to a certain extent, through email, extended telephone calls and social media. In this sense the intimate proximity mobility might enable becomes possible through other forms of networking. Even while the family ties of Filipino domestic labourers might be a relatively extreme example of this process, it highlights the importance of sustaining emotional proximity and 'strong ties', despite physical distance and irregular physical mobility. What de Souza e Silva and Gordon make clear, however, is that the maintenance of strong ties and social proximities with far-off peoples and places does not necessarily imply disconnection from local networks.

According to their chapter, new location-aware technologies mean far more intensive relationships with a place or locality, or what they term a 'net-locality', are now possible. Smartphones and other devices capable of GPS and handling social media technologies and games are enabling deeper and more grounded interactions between people and locations than networked communications approaches might have us believe. Their notion helps us to identify meaningful relations between geographically proximate people and places which are acquired through a range of social practices.

Finally, the discussion of distance and mobility would not be complete without a consideration of mobilities and its ethics. Mobilities research demands that we pay greater attention to our distance as researchers from our subjects, as well as the moral and ethical questions of responsibility that both we and our research participants hold. Freudendal-Pedersen holds this to be an issue of response. Or rather, she highlights the responsibility to respond to different mobile practices that might elicit an emotional or ethical counteraction. We learn how a mobile ethics is much more than individual choices, but involves a critical mass and crowd momentum. Furthermore, a mobility ethics is shown to be particularly future focused. For example, Bogotá becomes a place for the play and experimentation of *cultura ciudana* in the education and regulation of traffic. Such an ethics helped to reverse the usual understanding of traffic with road rage and incivility, by teaching people how to live and exist together in close proximity mediated by the car. Through this case study we discover how the ethics and responsibilities of mobility can be hardwired into the planning of cities such as Copenhagen.

Temporality

If mobility involves speed and distance then it certainly involves time. Mobilities are regulated by it and they might navigate it, while they part it, feel it, displace it and transform it. As a key quality of mobility the timing and time spent on the move is incredibly important to all manner of interests, but especially those responsible for the planning and design of contemporary transport systems. Eager to contest the established view that the time spent whilst travelling may not in fact be wasted, Glenn Lyons's chapter examines the way 'travel-time' is understood and questioned within transport policy, especially in debates over the planning of a new high-speed line between London and Birmingham in the UK. Lyons shows how 'travel-time' can be used productively for work, and is not simply time wasted or lost as a further friction of distance and the energy and investment of effort we use to surpass it. Mobility can provide productive time too, and not just in terms of the evaluation of productive labour.

In the context of planning transport systems this realization is an interesting one, and throws a particular spanner in the works of schemes which aim to raise productivity by shortening travel time. Lyons presents a nuanced and balanced argument which elucidates the total net balance of travel time. Lyons's ultimate argument is that not nearly enough evidence has been researched and presented on the qualitative experience of 'travel-time' in all modes of transport. Without this, how can evidence-based decisions be made in large-scale transport investment projects? Understanding people's travel habits, routines and particularly rhythms is essential to this project.

It is on such issues as rhythm, habits and corporeal experiences of mobility that Tim Edensor focuses his chapter to shed light on how rhythm makes up so much of the complex mobilities through which our world is composed. As Edensor argues, our public places are made up of complex rhythms, beats and tempos of walking, work and leisure, alongside a series of other mobile rhythms. Furthermore, they are inherently synchronous, having been regulated by timetables within public transport systems, technologies of traffic lights and the complex coordination of a city's transit network designed to perform in very uneven ways even during the space of a day or a working week.

Finally, the section ends with the notion of enthusiasm, which does not really satisfy the categories of speed, distance or time we have used to segment this section introduction. Injecting passion into the discussion, Alison Hui explores the idea of enthusiastic mobilities using the hobby and pursuit of bird watching, particularly for especially rare birds. This is not to say that the prior discussions on the qualities of mobility are absent of passions and emotion – rather that Hui's account explicitly crosses those categories to deliberate enthusiasm as a particularly strong affective relation. Her chapter positions enthusiasm in several ways: as a push, pull and enveloping relation to mobility. We see enthusiasm as some kind of driving force. Plato's magnetic attractor is mobility's pull that compels Hui's bird watchers to cross vast distances and endure long journeys. Enthusiasm makes these outward journeys intense and full of possibility, hope and expectation at the indeterminable presence of the birds at a given location and given time; whilst we see the journey home, if following a successful outing, can be immensely enjoyable, the road stretching out for reflection – the birder carried along by a wave of satisfaction.

9

Friction

Tim Cresswell

Introduction

> Suppose now a traveller, who towards evening expects to accomplish the two stages at the end of his day's journey, four or five leagues, with post-horses, on the high road – it is nothing. He arrives now at the last station but one, finds no horses, or very bad ones; then a hilly country, bad roads; it is a dark night, and he is glad when, after a great deal of trouble, he reaches the next station, and finds there some miserable accommodation. So in War, through the influence of an infinity of petty circumstances, which cannot properly be described on paper, things disappoint us, and we fall short of the mark.
>
> *(Clausewitz, 1832)*

Prussian military theorist (and soldier) Carl Philipp Gottfried von Clausewitz, in his treatise on the moral philosophy of war – *On War* (Clausewitz, 1832) – placed the idea of *friction* at the heart of his analysis. Clausewitz's treatise was based on his experience in the Napoleonic wars at the beginning of the nineteenth century, and was published after his death. His central argument was that war produced a continual "fog" of confusion, where perfect knowledge of the situation was always impossible. The details of war always got in the way of attempts at abstraction. It is these 'details' that he grouped under the heading of 'friction'.

Here Clausewitz uses a thought experiment of travel to illustrate the multitudinous impediments to the conduct of war. His concept of friction, like the one I develop below, borrows from physics but is resolutely social. The friction of physics is relatively simple. The social, as is always the case, is many times more complicated. At the heart of Clausewitz's friction is the stubborn stickiness of what is often called "the real world". Things just don't turn out the way they are planned – even for the powerful.

> This enormous friction, which is not concentrated, as in mechanics, at a few points, is therefore everywhere brought into contact with chance, and thus incidents take place upon which it was impossible to calculate, their chief origin being chance.
>
> *(Clausewitz, 1832)*

If we are to understand mobility (in war and elsewhere) then we have to include an understanding of friction. Friction, physics tells us, is a force which resists the relative motion of two materials sliding and rubbing against each other. Sometimes friction is sufficient to prevent motion, at other times it slows it down. It can occur between moving bodies or between moving and stationary bodies. But we are not in the realm of physics here so friction needs some translation into a social realm. Elsewhere I have described mobility as movement + meaning + power (Cresswell, 2006). Friction needs an equivalent translation as we are generally dealing with mobilities and not mere movements (or motions). Friction, like mobility, can apply in the world of meaning and can be the result of arrangements of power. Friction, here, is a social and cultural phenomenon that is lived and felt as you are stopped while driving through a city, or encounter suspicion at check-in at an international airport.

The significance of friction is in the way it draws our attention to the way in which people, things and ideas are slowed down or stopped. One reading of the mobility turn in the humanities and the social sciences is to see it as an analysis of a world of flow where friction has been reduced or (nearly) eliminated. This, for instance, is one reading of Manuel Castells's diagnostic of a Network Society in which a 'space of flows' has replaced a 'space of places' (Castells, 1996). Castells paints a picture of a world where the key actors in the process of globalization can travel easily in a self-contained and seemingly frictionless bubble. It is such a view that is resisted by Sallie Marston *et al.* in arguments against scalar ontologies.

> One strategy for countering scalar hierarchies is to replace their structuralist calculus with the language of flows and fluidity. According to this approach, the material world is subsumed under the concepts of movement and mobility, replacing old notions of fixity and categorization with absolute deterritorialization and openness. While we do not find ourselves at odds with the possibilities of flow-thinking *per se*, we are troubled by what we see as liberalist trajectories (absolute freedom of movement) driving such approaches, particularly when these develop alongside large-scale imaginaries such as the global and the transnational.
>
> *(Marston et al., 2005: 423)*

This would be a mistake. Foregrounding mobility in theory and methodology does not mean turning our attention away from friction but, instead, highlights it. Friction would not happen without at least the potential of movement (motility). Key to the development of mobility studies has been the recognition that mobilities need moorings – more-or-less stable points that facilitate movement (Hannam *et al.*, 2006). The obvious examples are infrastructural hubs such as airports but also include the relatively solid, more-or-less fixed structures of roads, pipelines and suchlike. Friction draws our attention to another way in which relative stillness, or slowness, becomes important in worlds of mobility (Bissell and Fuller, 2010). Marston *et al.* evocatively refer to such moments with metaphors of blockages and coagulation.

> We take issue, however with [the] reductive visualization of the world as simply awash in fluidities, ignoring the large variety of blockages, coagulations and assemblages (everything from material objects to doings and sayings) that congeal in space and social life.
>
> *(Marston et al., 2005: 423)*

While moorings refer to the necessary moments of relative stillness that enable mobilities, friction suggests an ambiguous, two-sided form of relative stillness that is both impeding mobility *and* enabling it.

Friction is not a singular category. We might think instead of a generative typology of frictions. Again, we can start by drawing analogies with the concept(s) of friction in physics. *Static* friction describes the friction that exists between two bodies that are not moving relative to each other. In this case the friction acts to hold the two bodies in place and produces no heat. *Rolling* friction is a kind of friction that exists where a rolling object is in contact with another surface. These surfaces are not slipping against each other at the point of contact so this is a form of static friction. *Kinetic* friction describes the form of friction which occurs when two surfaces are slipping against each other. This may be between a static and a moving surface or between two moving surfaces – in which case it is called *fluid* friction. Friction that happens within fluids leads to a relative thickening/slowing that is referred to as *viscosity*. Viscosity is but one step away from the coagulations that Marston *et al.* write about. All of these forms of friction are defined by the relative mobilities of the surfaces and whether or not a conversion of energy happens, which typically results in heat, light or sound. Kinetic forms do produce them and static forms do not. It is relatively straightforward to think of these forms in a social sense as social friction that holds things in place and social friction that is caused by the things, people, ideas, slipping against each other. We will return to the production of heat in the conclusions. For the most part, this short essay concerns social and cultural forms of kinetic friction.

Given the diversity of frictions at play in a mobile world, my aim here is not to formulate a singular approach to friction as it pertains to mobility studies. Rather I want to explore a number of ways in which friction might be mobilized as an empirical fact and as an analytical category at a variety of scales. All of these, however, are based on the recognition of friction as a force which works to slow or stop mobilities on the one hand, and make the very fact of mobility possible on the other.

The f(r)iction of distance

Geographers will have encountered friction most clearly in the practices of spatial science. In the isotropic worlds of spatial interaction theory, central place theory, gravity models and the like we encountered the 'friction of distance'. While these models were not identical they tended to assert that things further away exerted less influence than things nearby. This was neatly summed up by Waldo Tobler's 'first law of geography' which states that "everything is related to everything else, but near things are more related than distant things" (Tobler, 1970: 236). In these models, and under this law, simple contentless distance is the prime obstacle preventing someone or something getting from A to B (or to interact in other ways) due to the energy and effort needed to do so (Cliff *et al.*, 1974).

Such a simple equation necessarily disappears as soon as the premises of many such models are questioned. Once an isotropic plain is replaced by an actual landscape with peaks and valleys, for instance, it is obvious that distance (as the crow flies) is not the primary factor in getting quickly from A to B. If we then add conduits of movement from footpaths to highways the issues become more complicated as it may be faster to get from A to B by travelling further. Then we add the hierarchy of settlements by size and we realize that big settlements interact more than small settlements (often). By the time we get to the present day it is almost self-evident that there are more connections of certain kinds between Southall in South London (a place with a significant Anglo-Indian population) and India than there are between Southall and (for instance) Aberystwyth, on the west coast of Wales. All of these 'interferences' with the perfect workings of empty space can be modelled and quantified of course. But other kinds of kinks in abstract space produce other kinds of friction.

Derek Gregory provides one of the earliest systematic and evidence-based critiques of the 'friction of distance' in an exploration of post (mail) in nineteenth-century Britain. Here, of course, we would expect letters to take longer to get to places further away (from London in this case) and to be considerably more expensive. As soon as 'power' gets involved, things start to change. Alongside the 'General Post' in 1838 there was a system known as the 'Privileged Post':

> This was a statutory mechanism which provided for the free transmission of mail under the signature (or "frank") of designated public officials and Members of Parliament. Its purpose was, in effect, to secure the territorial cohesion of the state apparatus through the selective suppression of the friction of distance.
>
> *(Gregory, 1987: 140)*

The 'Privileged Post' was systematically abused by any number of bankers and merchants who used the 'official' users to frank their commercial correspondence. Access to this system was seen as an important and powerful advantage over competitors. In addition there was an array of unauthorized conveyors of mail undermining the system of charging dependent on distance that occurred before a flat rate of one penny (and with it the postage stamp) was introduced in 1839. Such was the level of clandestine activity, Gregory asserts, that the "*friction* of distance was, for many people in many places, the *fiction* of distance" (Gregory, 1987: 143). What Gregory's analysis of the postal system reveals is the importance of managing relative friction as part of the play of power. In this way the isotropic plain that forms the background for the friction of distance gets distorted. It is this politics of friction I want to turn to now.

The politics of friction

Elsewhere I have argued that a consideration of friction and the way that it works is a necessary part of a meso-theoretical construction of a politics of mobility (Cresswell, 2010). There is no necessary relationship between friction and power. To be sure, friction can be a tool in the production of power and can be used by the powerful to slow or stop the mobilities of the (relatively) weak. Examples of this are everywhere. Consider the way in which immigrations lines work in airports. As a British (and thus provisionally European) traveller I encounter the UK and EU passport line at Heathrow airport. At least I used to. I have had my iris scanned and, as a trusted traveller, I can now enter the UK without showing my passport but by placing my eyes in such a way that they can be scanned so that the automatic doors will open and let me through without so much as a "welcome home". There are two other visible ways of passing across the UK Border at Heathrow. One is the line for 'others' – the non-UK, non-EU citizens who have to stand in line the longest (usually). Finally there is the blue lane – the very fast lane for first-class and otherwise important travellers for whom country of citizenship is less of a burden. Here, at Heathrow, is a semi-permeable membrane – a form of friction that slows everyone but for different periods of time. The UK Border, like many borders, is a device for the production of variable friction. Similar processes can be seen across urban space. The use of CCTV and security devices in the city can be seen as a way of imposing higher levels of friction for some than for others as they traverse the city. Similarly the number of times that black people are stopped while driving by police in many western cities is much higher than it is for white people (Harris, 1997).

Perhaps the most spectacular example of the politics of variable friction comes from the hunting and killing of Osama Bin Laden. This process illustrates how the US and its allies were able to systematically ratchet up the level of friction for Bin Laden around the Afghanistan–Pakistan border while, at the same time, doing their best to erase friction as much as possible for their own drones which fly night and day, over vast ranges, essentially ignoring the existence of national borders below them. So while the US was able to operate semi-remotely (the drones are famously 'piloted' by personnel in the US) and at great distance, Bin Laden was eventually killed just a few hundred miles from the place he was last seen.[1] The practice of power is thus often about the management of friction – increasing it for some and erasing it for others.

Despite the 'success' of the US and its allies, however, they still come up against 'frictions of distance'. Derek Gregory has shown how the practice of logistics in neo-liberal, twenty-first century warfare still throws up surprising challenges. Even as the US military tries to pretend the world is, in fact, a featureless isotropic plain, events on the ground suggest otherwise. One example given by Gregory is the closing of the Pakistan–Afghanistan land border to NATO supply convoys as long as drones continue to illegally cross into Pakistani airspace overhead. Such events, Gregory argues, illustrate the continuing salience of Clausewitz's insistence on the importance of friction as a fact of war.

> The friction of distance constantly confounds the extended supply chain for the war in Afghanistan. This is no simple metric ('the coefficient of distance') or physical effect (though the difficult terrain undoubtedly plays a part). Rather, the business of supplying war produces volatile and violent spaces in which – and through which – the geopolitical and the geo-economic are still locked in a deadly embrace.
>
> *(Gregory, 2012)*

In many ways this is reassuring. While there are instances in which the relatively powerful attempt to eliminate friction for themselves, it appears that others are able to continuously use forms of friction as a weapon of the weak (Scott, 1985). In many forms, then, friction has been an aid to power. It is deliberately used to stop or slow down the mobilities of those who threaten established forms of power. This is the friction of the national border or the gate of the gated community. It is often territorial in form and protects the strategic interests of those who are invested in limiting the mobilities of the multitude (Hardt and Negri, 2000). There is a flip side to this however. Friction can also be the enemy of power. Clausewitz most famously expressed this formulation of friction in his account of the fog of war. However hard military strategists might try, he argues, events and chance will always produce friction. This view of ongoing friction-against-power contradicts the dystopian visions of Paul Virilio – the foremost contemporary philosopher of a frictionless world.

One of the most important ways in which mobility is being ordered in the contemporary world is through logistics. Paul Virilio has consistently been the prophet of a frictionless world. This lack of friction, to Virilio, is not a good thing. He suggests speed (and the conquest of friction) is a product of a military mode of logistical operation where the aim is for things to happen instantly – for nothing to get in the way.

> the goal sought by power was less the invasion of territories, their occupation, than a sort of *recapitulation of the world* obtained by the ubiquity, the suddenness of military

presence, a pure phenomenon of speed, a phenomenon on the way to the realization of its absolute essence.

(Virilio, 1991: 44)

Over a range of work Virilio has consistently argued that a military/logistical system is fast becoming the primary structuring principle in the production of space–time. Its aim is the removal of blockages and coagulations in order to produce a tyranny of the instant – a point where distance is no longer an issue. This abolition of distance is, to Virilio, not only a form of domination over people and territory but also an ecological disaster.

The abundance of natural resources goes down the more flows speed up. This will shortly reduce to nothing, or very nearly, the geographical expanse of the common world, just like the limits of the interval of time for political action, with *nano-chronologies* of the right moment now eating away at long historical periods.

(Virilio, 2010: 76)

Virilio paints a picture of a world in which both time and space have been produced by a logistical–military complex in such a way that geography (understood as a world in which distance matters and places are recognizably different) ceases to matter.

For the first time, history is going to unfold within a one-time-system: global time. Up to now, history has taken place within local times, local frames, regions and nations. But now, in a certain way, globalization and virtualization are inaugurating a global time that prefigures a new form of tyranny. If history is so rich, it is because it was local, it was thanks to the existence of spatially bounded times which overrode something that up to now occurred only in astronomy: universal time. But in the very near future, our history will happen in universal time, itself the outcome of instantaneity – and there only.

(Virilio, 1995)

The instantaneity of interactive video games, or the way in which a drone operator in the American desert can press a button and kill people in Pakistan or Yemen, are, to Virilio, examples of a new kind of tyranny. This tyranny is a result of the abolition of friction. What Gregory's account of the messiness of speed, distance and friction in Afghanistan/Pakistan shows us is that context, and the messiness on the ground, continues to confound any dreams of a frictionless world.

Friction as the "grip of worldly encounter"

Gregory's account of distance and intimacy in war confirms Marston *et al.*'s insistence on the continuing salience of blockages and coagulations in spaces of flow. This insistence is illustrated by the way in which seemingly global flows (often mistaken as smooth and frictionless) fail to have any impact without encountering the specificity of the particular site. This is the lesson of perhaps the most theoretically interesting account of friction given by the anthropologist Anna Tsing, in which she uses friction to describe the "grip of worldly encounter" (Tsing, 2005: 1). Tsing provides a detailed account of the kinds of coagulations and blockages that Marston *et al.* use as an antidote to the people they refer to as "flowsters". Her empirical work concerns the forestry industry in Indonesia and the way in which global flows of people, ideas, capital and politics are transformed as they enter the "sticky materiality of practical encounters" in the space of the rainforest (Tsing, 2005: 1). Space, as Martin Jones has observed, can be "sticky" (Jones, 2009). Indeed, there appears to be quite a body of work on the problem (or potential) of stickiness, which I read here as friction. While such things as national borders or literal roadblocks are certainly forms of stickiness and causes of friction, Tsing is suggesting a more profound and less-literal role for friction. She does not start with mobilities but, instead, with *universals* such as forms of truth, science or capital. Universals, she argues, are spread through connections and are, by definition, global and need to spread out in order to fulfil their existence *as* universal. She is interested in what happens when these mobile universals encounter place and particularity. Universals, she argues only materialize *in the particular*. It is when this translation occurs that friction happens – "the awkward, unequal, unstable, and creative qualities of interconnection across difference" (Tsing, 2005: 4).

> a study of global connections shows the grip of encounter: friction. A wheel turns because of its encounter with the surface of the road; spinning in the air it goes nowhere. Rubbing two sticks together produces heat and light; one stick alone is just a stick. As a metaphorical image, friction reminds us that heterogeneous and unequal encounters can lead to new arrangements of culture and power.
>
> *(Tsing, 2005: 5)*

Friction, in Tsing's work, militates against the idea of a world of unimpeded flow that Marston *et al.* and others critique. Here she shows how friction is double-edged. On the one hand we can think of friction as the "blockages" that Marston *et al.* insist on. In this case friction is a force that slows things down or stops them. On the other hand friction is necessary for things to move. If you try and run on ice in shoes with smooth soles you will simply fall over. If, however, you use rubber soles and walk on tarmac it is friction that creates the possibility of movement. In other words, friction hinders and enables mobilities. In Tsing's terms, the 'universals' that travel through global connections can only travel through their purchase on particular, and always different, situations. The dance of mobility and friction thus interferes with the dreams of unimpeded mobility. These dreams include the world of instantaneity that Virilio writes of and the world of capital, things and knowledge that gives shape to the fantasy worlds of neo-liberal globalization projects.

> By getting rid of national barriers and autocratic or protective state policies, everyone would have the freedom to travel everywhere. Indeed, motion itself would be experienced as self-actualization, and self-actualization without restraint would oil the machinery of the economy, science and society.
>
> *(Tsing, 2005: 5)*

Here we see Marston *et al.*'s "liberalist trajectories" working in concert with a global and transnational scale. Here is one utopian image of mobility as unfettered but tethered to the idea of 'self-actualization'. This is global mobility from above seeking to insinuate itself into every nook and cranny of every actually existing topos. But everywhere it goes, this mobility from above encounters the friction of context and the particular that give it shape and efficacy.

> Engaged universals travel across difference and are charged and changed by their travels. Through friction, universals become practically effective. Yet they can never fulfill their

promises of universality. Even in transcending localities, they don't take over the world. They are limited by the practical necessity of mobilizing adherents. Engaged universals must convince us to pay attention to them. *All* universals are engaged when considered as practical projects accomplished in an heterogeneous world.

(Tsing, 2005: 8)

Just as it would be impossible to walk without friction, so friction makes the actualization of mobile universals possible, but only at the expense of their status *as* universal. Universals, which have to be forms of mobility, can only experience *becoming* through the way in which they are made *particular* through friction and in *place*.

Conclusions

Critics of the mobility turn suggest that a focus on a world of flows turns our attention away from the stickiness of space and place. They argue that the world is full of blockages and coagulation. My argument here is that an approach to the world that foregrounds mobilities should, instead, provide a position that highlights friction. Friction, here, is defined as a social phenomenon with its own politics. Sometimes it slows and stops the mobility of people, things and ideas, and sometimes it enables them. Mobility is often impossible without friction. Friction makes things happen. In some contexts friction takes the form of quite literal blockages and coagulations that prevent the mobility of undesirables. At other times friction produces a fog of chance and turbulence that makes the logistical desire for smoothness a vain dream. There is no necessary politics to friction – it can be a force for domination, a tactic of resistance, or neither.

A by-product of friction in a physical sense is heat; fire even. The energy of mobility is converted into heat. If we think of heat metaphorically and socially it is possible to imagine social 'heat'. Such a notion has been around as long as social science has. In an effort to unify physical and social 'laws', the American economist Henry Carey wrote in his 1859 *Principles of Social Science* that: "In the inorganic world, every act of combination is an act of motion. So it is in the social one" (cited in Stark, 1962: 146). This led the Austrian economist Werner Stark to summise that:

> In the physical universe, heat is engendered by friction. Consequently the case must be the same in the social world. The 'particles' must rub together here, as they do there. The rubbing of the human molecules, which produces warmth, light and forward movement, is the interchange of goods, services, and ideas.
>
> *(Stark, 1962: 146)*

In the Carey/Stark world heat is evidence of lively society; a 'hot' society, where there is plenty of friction, is a modern, mobile society. Heat produces mobility. This can be inverted however to think about the way in which heat is produced by the friction that arises from differential mobilities. The grinding of mobilities against each other, or mobilities against relative stillnesses, produces hotspots – fiery points of contestation such as the border of Afghanistan and Pakistan, the 'kettles' enacted by the police in order to control marching protesters in London, or Saudi reactions to women attempting to drive. Friction, and the heat that it produces, has the potential to highlight the power geometries inherent to the politics of mobility (Massey, 1993). It can make what is often the smooth, hidden, workings of the space of flows suddenly visible (Cresswell and Martin, 2012). Friction can be both a symptom of mobile contestation and something that is itself contested: Where, when and how does friction occur? Who produces or ameliorates it? Who is affected by it?

Perhaps most importantly, friction provides the point where the mobilities of universals get purchase. Think of it this way: we have become used to thinking of place (or space, region, etc.) as relational and produced through connections and mobilities; perhaps it is time to consider this the other way around. Connections and mobilities are, in turn, produced through the management and distribution of friction as it is encountered in place.

Note

1 I am grateful to a talk Derek Gregory gave at Royal Holloway, University of London on 12th January 2012 for this insight. The talk was titled "The distance of death: from Vietnam to Afghanistan-Pakistan".

References

Bissell, D. and Fuller, G. (2010) *Stillness in a Mobile World*. New York: Routledge.

Castells, M. (1996) *The Rise of the Network Society*. Cambridge, MA: Blackwell Publishers.

Clausewitz, C. von (1832) *On War*. Translated by Colonel J. J. Graham, 1874. Available online at www.gutenberg.org/files/1946/1946-h/1946-h.htm#2HCH0007 (accessed 18 September 2012).

Cliff, A. D., Martin, R. L. and Ord, J. K. (1974) 'Evaluating the Friction of Distance Parametre in Gravity Models'. *Regional Studies* 8: 281–286.

Cresswell, T. (2006) *On the Move: Mobility in the Modern Western World*. New York: Routledge.

Cresswell, T. (2010) 'Towards a Politics of Mobility'. *Environment and Planning D: Society and Space* 28: 17–31.

Cresswell, T. and Martin, C. (2012) 'On Turbulence: Entanglements of Disorder and Order on a Devon Beach'. *Tijdschrift Voor Economische En Sociale Geografie* 103: 516–529.

Gregory, D. (1987) 'The Friction of Distance? Information Circulation and the Mails in Early Nineteenth-Century England'. *Journal of Historical Geography* 13: 130–154.

Gregory, D. (2012) 'Supplying War in Afghanistan: The Frictions of Distance'. *openDemocracy* n.p.

Hannam, K., Sheller, M. and Urry, J. (2006) 'Mobilities, Immobilities and Moorings'. *Mobilities* 1: 1–22.

Hardt, M. and Negri, A. (2000) *Empire*. Cambridge, MA: Harvard University Press.

Harris, D. A. (1997) 'Driving While Black and All Other Traffic Offenses: The Supreme Court and Pretextual Stops'. *Journal of Criminal Law & Criminology* 87: 544–582.

Jones, M. (2009) 'Phase Space: Geography, Relational Thinking, and Beyond'. *Progress in Human Geography* 33: 487–506.

Marston, S., Jones III, J. P. and Woodward, K. (2005) 'Human Geography without Scale'. *Transactions of the Institute of British Geographers* 30: 416–432.

Massey, D. (1993) 'Power-Geometry and Progressive Sense of Place'. In: Bird, J., Curtis, B., Putnam T. and Tickner, L. (eds) *Mapping the Futures: Local Cultures, Global Change*. London: Routledge, 59–69.

Scott, J. C. (1985) *Weapons of the Weak: Everyday Forms of Peasant Resistance*. New Haven and London: Yale University Press.

Stark, W. (1962) *The Fundamental Forms of Social Thought*. London: Routledge & K. Paul.

Tobler, W. (1970) 'A Computer Movie Simulating Urban Growth in the Detroit Region'. *Economic Geography* 46: 234–240.

Tsing, A. L. (2005) *Friction: An Ethnography of Global Connection*. Princeton, NJ: Princeton University Press.

Virilio, P. (1991) *The Aesthetics of Disappearance*. New York: Semiotext(e).

Virilio, P. (1995) 'Speed and Information: Cyberspace Alarm!' Available online at www.ctheory.net/articles.aspx?id=72 (accessed 18 September 2012).

Virilio, P. (2010) *The Futurism of the Instant: Stop-Eject*. Cambridge: Polity.

10

Slowness and Deceleration

Phillip Vannini

During a recent fieldwork visit to an off-grid community I asked an informant what "slow" meant. His answer was deceivingly simple: "It means that not everything can happen when you want it to; it means that you need to change your attitude and the way you act." Slowness was less of an essential quality for him, less of a state of affairs, and more a practical disposition, an orientation to action. Soon after saying this he excused himself and walked over to a small patch of grass behind his house – a cob structure, perched atop a rocky bluff, which he himself built around the natural curvature of a large arbutus tree and the shape of surrounding boulders. He bent down and picked up a sun oven – inside which was his slowly cooking dinner – and repositioned it facing southwest so it could lay more directly under the afternoon sun. "It should be ready in a few hours," he commented, "just in time for dinner." Taking inspiration from this brief ethnographic revelation, in this chapter I depart from slowness as essence and conceptualize "slow" instead as a verb. "To slow" thus implies a repertoire of performances oriented at transforming the temporal regime of everyday life.

In most of the contemporary Western world, and arguably much of the globe in its entirety, to slow down nowadays means to decelerate from an ever increasingly pervasive regime built around the logic of speed. Over the last few decades a panoply of social and cultural commentators have observed that consumer society is marked by a kind of spatiotemporal acceleration that results in a distinct time–space compression (Harvey 1991), a fetishism of speed as a form of social, political, and military power (Virilio 1986), and even the homogenization of place (Augé 1995), amongst many other effects. Thrift (1996) has argued that combined innovations in technologies of light, power, and speed have contributed to the formation of a machinic complex that has reshaped people's consciousness and perspective towards their everyday rhythms and speed. Similar to Schivelbusch's (1986) analysis of the effects of train travel's speed on the modern consciousness, Thrift's argument outlines how the assemblage of electricity, gas, rail, mail, telephone, and so forth has changed our temporal consciousness by pushing farther the sphere of consumer-driven capitalism and its live, on-demand character. Thus we have come to expect that our dinner should be ready in seconds with a microwave oven, and not in a whole day under raw sunlight exposure.

Much of the mobilities literature has followed these broad theoretical trends, taking painstaking care to examine fast mobilities – from instant mobile communications to intercontinental aeromobility. Yet slow mobilities continue to exist worldwide, and most of the world's seven billion passengers are more prone to experience, say, slow intercity bus travel than jet speed. And even amongst the kinetic elites slowness matters because to slow down, to decelerate, means to *affect* one's lifeworld in tactically notable ways, for desirable aims. To slow down, therefore, means to affect the way in which we dwell in the world, and in turn to be affected by it. To slow down is to act and move differently, to experience the social and ecological environment in ways that run counter to the logic of speed. To decelerate is also to conceptualize livelihood differently, therefore to represent time alternatively to the logic of speed – both to oneself and to others. In order to capture these three dimensions of slow – practice, experience, and representation – I employ the concept of mobility constellations (Cresswell 2010). According to Cresswell (2010: 17) mobility constellations are "historically and geographically specific formations" of movement which are comprised of particular patterns that make constellations different from one another. To maintain my focus on mobility studies I organize my writing in three sections: the slow movement of objects, slow tourism, and slow transport. I pivot my argument around the idea that to slow down is often (though not always) a tactical (de Certeau 1984) move – that is, an oppositional practice to the dominant culture of speed.

Slower-moving objects

The Canadian province in which I live, British Columbia, is rich with freshwater resources. Dams built on our province's rivers enable the generation of electricity that I – and simultaneously many other people in California, where much of our energy is sent and sold – need to live my day-to-day life. Most of us give very little thought to how the movement of river waters influences electrical currents on our continental grid and ultimately how power – intended as both electrical and social – is distributed in North America. But for a small number of people who have chosen to live off the electrical grid, power has acquired a great deal of existential significance. "Energy is work," an off-gridder recently told me; "when you generate energy by living off the grid you quickly realize that it demands a radical re-adjustment of your outlook on life; you can't be in a hurry anymore." The reasons why you cannot be in a hurry are multiple. The movements of the sun across the sky – both daily and seasonally – impose serious limits on the activities you are able to undertake. Similarly, the movements of air currents, which are entirely uncontrollable by humans, determine how much wind power you will have. And so do the seasonal flows of creeks – on which off-gridders often set up micro-hydro systems. "So if you want to vacuum or, if your kids want to play video games, you have to wait patiently for a sunny day, or maybe a windy day, or for the snow upstream to melt," I learned, "and in the meantime you just wait."

Not every off-gridder seeks to decelerate from the machinic complex of light, speed, and power that Thrift (1996) talks about (indeed for a few people living off-grid is nothing but the latest eco-chic thing to do), but for many people who live in communities entirely disconnected from dominant power infrastructures slowing down is quintessentially important for the way they dwell in the world. Their practices may therefore be understood as *tactics* challenging – though without dismantling – the hegemonic strategies of services and goods distribution on which consumer society depends. According to de Certeau (1984), tactics are oppositional everyday-life practices. Thus off-the-grid dwelling tactics are "infinitesimal transformations," "errant trajectories" constantly "jostling for position[ing]" (de Certeau

1984: xviii) and repositioning, which wind up "weaving" (Ingold 2000) alternative land-scapes of light, speed, and power. By delinking oneself from one or more grids an individual or a community makes a "technological choice" (Lemonnier 2002) for a different type of social relations, a different way of life, and a different collective "synchronicity" (Edensor 2006). These tactics do not unsettle the logic of power – social or technical – but exist beside it, thus resulting not in inverting dominant mobility constellations, but instead merely co-existing as alternative temporalities.

Light and power matter greatly in the practice, experience, and representation of everyday living, but so do material resources that directly enter our bodies, such as food and drink. In one of the most recent influential studies on slow living Parkins and Craig (2006) examine in detail the slow food movement, with a particular focus on central Italy, where it originated as a leftist, politically defiant response to fast food. Parkins and Craig build their observations about the impressive diffusion of the slow movement across the globe on the premise of the widely shared impression that busyness is increasing amongst people of different genders, race, classes, and cultures. For them "hurry sickness, as a response to the acceleration of just about everything, has become a recognizable late modern malaise" (2006: 1), and slow food distribution and consumption therefore represents a tactical response to this.

To slow down at the kitchen table means to invest everyday eating and the social relations that govern it with different value. Rather than consuming foods which may have been grown and/or processed thousands of miles away, members of the slow food movement aim to rediscover the local flavors of seasonal harvests, to re-appreciate long-standing food preparation rituals and collective local knowledge, and to rebuild ties with local farmers, growers, and chefs. In part these tactics answer the need to reduce the carbon footprint of our diets, but in addition to environmental concerns the slow food movement aims to destabilize the culture of fast eating and all it stands for – such as rationalization and uniformity. Slow food brings together eating and temporality in a "core philosophy where slowness is grounded in understandings of pleasure and taste, conviviality, and the value of local products and cultures" (Parkins and Craig 2006: 18). In light of this, slow eating represents a countercultural art and technology of the self, Parkins and Craig argue, and thus a form of life politics. As they write,

> Arts of the (slow) self are means, then, not only by which people cultivate a subjectivity based on the affirmation of values like attentiveness as daily pleasures, but they are also opportunities for "modest shifts" in broader articulations of social organization and public culture. Because such slow arts of the self are always situated and practiced within social networks and time cultures, they can throw into greater relief the ethical implications of an accelerated culture.
>
> *(Parkins and Craig 2006: 14)*

Often, slow eating does not occur in vacuum. As the research of Pink (2007, 2008) as well as Parkins and Craig (2006) has indicated, the success of the slow food movement has taken over the entire social organization of some communities, which have restructured themselves to accommodate for other kinds of slow arts and technologies of the self. The Slow Cities movement, or Città Slow movement, emerged in Greve in Chianti, Tuscany, in 1999 as an attempt to regulate (via municipal bylaws and policies) the mobilities of objects and people within a circumscribed legal jurisdiction. Amongst the more typical regulations are the banning of fast food outlets, the promotion of local farmers' markets, food co-ops, and community gardens, reductions in car traffic, stringent noise regulations, improvements in parks and common spaces, the organization of shared meals, carnivals, and festivals of various kinds, the restoration of historical buildings as a way of protecting collective memory, the training of people in culinary skills, and the banning of bright signs, car alarms, and even telecommunication towers (e.g. cellular phone towers). These measures have been implemented in many towns/cities of up to 50,000 inhabitants worldwide.

The motives of the Città Slow movement are now explicitly outlined on the website created by its association:

> Municipalities which join the association are motivated by curios [sic] people of a recovered time, where man [sic] is still protagonist of the slow and healthy succession of seasons, respectful of citizens' health, the authenticity of products and good food, rich of fascinating craft traditions of valuable works of art, squares, theaters, shops, cafés, restaurants, places of the spirit and unspoiled landscapes, characterized by spontaneity of religious rites, respect of traditions through the joy of a slow and quiet living.
>
> *(Cittaslow, n.d.)*

What is interesting about the way the movement represents itself is its relational, countercultural stance with regard to temporality. Città Slow situates itself as an oppositional movement, an expression of resistance from "dominant expressions and structures of modern living" (Parkins and Craig 2006: 82). Thus the mobility constellations of Città Slow are reshaped to allow for slower encounters; ordinary sites of interaction are repositioned from nodes of circulation to places of dwelling. In spite of the irony of enforcing an oppositional lifestyle by law, Città Slow defines its identity by homogenizing the rest of the world and taking distance from it – denigrating its speed-based logic, ethics, and aesthetics. Like the slow food movement and much of the off-grid lifestyle, the mobility constellation legislated by the Città Slow movement can therefore best be understood in relational terms – a topic to which I now turn in greater detail.

Slower-moving tourists

Echoing the philosophy of the Slow Food movement and Città Slow movement, Slow Tourism invites travelers worldwide to decelerate and smell the roses along their journeys. Slow Tourism is not a radically new affair – its roots are planted in earlier and better-known approaches to tourism and travel, such as rural tourism, responsible tourism, and eco-tourism. But in the words of the Slow Tourism Club, slow tourism goes a step further – or perhaps a step slower:

> Slow tourism . . . is a movement aiming at the promotion of a responsible and sustainable tourism, protection and safeguarding of valuable tourist destination, towards the training and information of the visitors and residents (tourist operators, local administration, citizens etc.) in order to preserve the ancient value and sense. [It] invites to a slow way of benefiting from tourist activities, to sightseeing a few places by entering in deep contact with them, live them, taste them, assimilate them and at the same time to protect them as invaluable human and social heritage belonging to all mankind and that need to be saved for the next generations too. [It] exhorts demanding curious, educated visitors to live intense emotions each corner of the territory, to discover also the unknown and remote places which also are part of the local culture, of the daily nature, worth to be discovered and appreciated in its real aspects. [It] fosters the social, i.e. responsible

tourism, which respects both natural and cultural diversities, requiring spirits of adaptability to new and unusual habits. It encourages residents and visitors to share the most peculiar features of the territory with positive and reciprocal curiosity. [It] invites, accompanies and assists rural and urban territory to promote an hospitality and reception policy to improve the attraction of a place in a perspective of social and environmental growth and sustainability. [It] promotes the concept of "Slow Life", representing a "return" to the abandoned, valuable model of lifestyle that is a base-value of a sustainable society.

(Slow Tourism Club, n.d.)

In their recent analysis of the phenomenon, Dickinson and Lumsdon (2010) argue that slow tourism's main concerns with locality, ecology, and quality of life originate in the growing social demand for less carbon-intensive travel, less commodified tourist experiences, and a greater emphasis on sociality as the key to authenticity in travel. For them the essence of slow tourism resides in a deeper engagement with local environments, a more protracted exploration of places, and a more meaningful sensual apprehension of difference. In this sense slow tourism is a counter-cultural phenomenon of sorts. It explicitly aims to resist speed, convenience, globalized homogeneity, rationalization, and all forms of commercial standardization (Dickinson and Lumsdon 2010). In sum slow-moving tourism "equates to quality time," it is practiced to "enjoy what is on offer," it is a "quality experience," it is about "meaning and engagement," and is "in tune with ecology and diversity" (Dickinson and Lumsdon 2010: 4).

Whether one "buys it" or not, however, is up for debate, and that is the important issue here. Tourists' demands for authenticity are well known. A massive amount of literature has spelled out rather clearly that authenticity is both a product and a service that is easily commodified. By extension of this argument, Slow Tourism might then seem like nothing but a crafty ideological veneer – an appealing commercial hook to sell destinations, like rural Tuscany, often depicted in popular movies and books (e.g. *Eat, Pray, Love; Under the Tuscan Sun*) as the epitome of slow places where tourists are able to establish seductively "meaningful" (but ultimately illusory) rapports with local individuals and the environment. But the obvious validity of this critical argument is so powerful that in the end it remains much too facile to apply. So, surely representations of the mobilities of slow tourism are motivated and partial. Surely it is impossible for tourists – no matter how slowly they move in their journeys – to truly become locals (provided that such is an agreed-upon measure of authenticity). And surely representations of tourist destinations such as rural Tuscany as slow places gloss over the obvious fact that these areas are governed by the same logic of speed that pervades the greater regional constellations within which they are embedded (indeed, as someone who was born in rural Tuscany and spent 23 fast-paced years there I find these romantic depictions utterly laughable). But in the end we would make an unforgivable mistake if we failed to appreciate both the fact that different constellations of mobility do exist, and the fact that these differences in the way mobilities are practiced, experienced, and represented are – however subtly and arguably exaggerated – important. Perhaps then, the key is to approach Slow Tourism differently.

There is nothing but conceptual trouble awaiting us if we understand slow/slowness as an ideal type or quality because there is no threshold or minimum limit to slowness or deceleration that we can use to judge particular instances against. Indeed if we assess slow as if there were such a threshold, as if we had a clear understanding of what constitutes mobilities that are a bit too fast to be considered truly slow, then judgments inevitably become subject to the specious logic of exception. By that logic then, a two-month-long stay in the Chianti region, fueled by bicycle power, red wine, and local produce might initially qualify as slow tourism. But when compared with a one-year stay in an off-grid cob home on a remote island off the British Columbia coast, suddenly Tuscany feels like Hollywood. And it is not difficult to think of places in South America or in Africa where the kind of slow holiday-making one can do might make the British Columbia off-grid home's claim to slowness simply vacuous.

If we want to avoid fetishizing ideal thresholds of slowness, and therefore entirely bypass the vitiated logic of slowness degree zero – that is, the kind of authentically slow that makes all other speeds and rhythms seem fast in comparison – then the solution is to view slowness relationally. Adey (2009) argues that any type of mobility is always positioned in relation to something or somebody else. For him mobilities and immobilities, and by the same token acts of speeding up and decelerating, are the "'special effects' of a relation; they are an out-come or an accomplishment" (2009: 17–18), and for Bissell (2007, 2008) this relationality pre-empts arguments centered on oppositions, such as speeding up as activity and slowing down as passivity. To understand slowness, therefore, we need to take into account the position from which the effort to slow down is practiced, experienced, and represented. And, relatedly, we need to understand what that effort judges itself against. Thus, off-gridders and slow food enthusiasts do indeed slow down the circulation of resources in comparison to that in a world dominated by the logic of light, speed, and power, and perhaps a McDonaldized (Ritzer 1993) world too. And by the same token, slow tourists, slow tourism operators, and Città Slow residents and visitors slow down in relation to apocryphally faster – more or less real – counterparts, such as frenzied, traffic-rich cosmopolitan centers. A relational approach to mobility constellations allows us to understand slow not as an essential quality but as a process, and therefore a verb: a pattern of practices, experiences, and representations focused on the objective of moving slower *than* a significant or generalized other.

Slower-moving riders

If we agree that it is more fruitful to understand how some constellations of mobility are slower than other constellations – rather than classify some as slow and others as fast – then a useful way of tackling these different temporalities is by appreciating their different affects. The concept of affect refers to social and material relations unfolding amidst bodies and places, fostering "variations in relative movements and speeds" (Woodward and Lea 2009: x) that correspond to a series of "affections of the body by which the body's power of acting is increased or diminished, helped or hindered" (Spinoza 2000: 164). An example should serve the purpose of explaining this complex idea. For that I turn to my own research on ferry mobilities on the British Columbia coast (Vannini 2012a).

Every year, full-time residents of Hornby Island patiently await Labour Day. On that September day an important event punctually unfolds: the tourist season ends. As the hours tick by more and more tourists depart by ferry (the only way in and out of the island), until the very last ferry of the evening arrives from nearby Denman Island to drag away the remaining few. Hornby residents – as the ritual goes – drive down to the pub located nearby the ferry terminal and begin the party. They toss back a few drinks, dance, light up fire-works, and as the last ferry finally leaves they mark the end of the tourist season by streaking in front of the ferry, by jokingly chasing it on their boats, and by having a merry ole' time. Often the ferry's captain even takes the ferry for a celebratory spin – carving a doughnut on the water. The point of the whole evening is that full-time residents get their island back to themselves. "We don't mind tourists that much," an islander explains, "but they make our beautiful island feel hectic. It always seems too busy in the summer, so frenzied." The irony of it all – and simultaneously the key empirical lesson behind all this – is that visitors come to Hornby Island precisely to slow down. From Vancouver it takes three ferries to get here, each one smaller and slower than the previous one. What the visitors experience as a slow island to get away to, the locals can hardly wait to get away from.

But it does not end there. Ferry routes, the speed and duration of crossings, and sailing frequencies continue to affect both full-time islanders and part-time residents year-round. Full-timers, for example, might need to actually work hard at slowing down when job demands, commutes to school, or the need to generate an income on- or off-island during the rainy months pull them away from their desired rhythms. And part-timers might have to work equally hard at reintegrating themselves into the local temporal order as the occasion of a long weekend or holiday stay present themselves again. The point of all this is that slow is something that requires bodily attention and care, something that requires work intended to affect variation in the way people relate to place, to themselves, and to others.

A profitable way to understand slowing down as an effort, as an accomplishment, is not only by understanding it relationally, but also by understanding it contextually and phenomenologically. Moving slower or moving faster is something that must be apprehended as an embodied sensation and performance. Consequently, "powers of acting and capacities for being affected are partly determined by the circumstances in which a being finds itself" (Gatens and Lloyd 1999: 101). Going slower or faster than an idealized other, or simply going slower or faster than one would in another place, and/or at another time, are actions that affect the body in meaningful ways, giving rise to affective sensations subject to meaningful reflection. Whether linguistic or pre-objective, such reflections over the speed, rhythm, and duration of one's movement attract and repel, bind and separate, and engender increases or decreases in one's capacity to act, orienting thought and practice, shaping and reshaping the sociality and materiality of the lifeworld (Woodward and Lea 2009).

By this token we have all sorts of mobility studies which point to how slowing down affects riders and passengers. We have the sedentary affects of seating (Bissell 2008), the mellow floating communities of round-the-world yachties (Kleinert 2009), the easy-go-lucky adventures of alternative coach travelers (Neumann 1993), the animated suspension of people placidly waiting for their departures (Bissell 2007; Vannini 2012b), the slowing down enacted by commuters who make the time to experience the details of alleged non-places like motorways (Edensor 2003) or to craft meaningful commuter spaces like the train coach (Watts 2008). And we also have access to slow-as-affect in the form of mobility practices and experiences that directly show the physical work, the struggle, and the fatigue of movement – such as that experienced by mountaineers (Lorimer and Lund 2003), cyclists endeavoring to climb steep peaks (Spinney 2006), and of course walkers (Vergunst and Ingold 2009). And problematizing the very idea of slowing down as a countercultural *choice* – but still an oppositional practice – we have evidence of slower individuals and groups struggling with exclusion and limited access (Hine 2007), and surveillance regimes limiting free cross-border mobility (Harker 2009), amongst other forces.

In conclusion, understanding slowing down relationally and as affect can show us at the very least three things. First, it can show us that the body's capacity to move at a desired speed is reduced by affective political regimes that put a differential and stratified premium on velocity – encouraging and enabling the speed of some, while simultaneously slowing down others by increasing the amount of frictions in their movements or their costs (e.g. see Vannini 2012a). Second, it can show us that slowing down can be a way of increasing the body's capacity to cultivate reflexive awareness of self, movement, and sense of place (e.g. see Edensor 2000). Third, and finally, it can show us that slowing down might even at times be less of an intentional and fully conscious tactic than it seems. Indeed it could very well be that slowing down occasionally unfolds as "a sequence of emergencies, affinities, and distanciations" through encounters with self, others, temporarilities, materialities, and spatialities "with which we act and sense" (Wylie 2005: 246), and with which we generate slowness as the inevitable counterpart, and indeed the specter, of speed.

References

Adey, P. (2009) *Mobility*, London: Routledge.

Augé, M. (1995) *Non-Places*, London: Verso.

Bissell, D. (2007) 'Animating suspension: waiting for mobilities,' *Mobilities*, 2: 277–298.

Bissell, D. (2008) 'Comfortable bodies, sedentary affects,' *Environment and Planning A*, 40: 1697–1712.

Cresswell, T. (2010) 'Towards a politics of mobility,' *Environment and Planning D*, 28: 17–31.

Cittaslow (n.d.) *About Cittaslow Organization*, available online at www.cittaslow.org/section/association (accessed January 2012).

de Certeau, M. (1984) *The Practice of Everyday Life*, Berkeley: University of California Press.

Dickinson, J. and Lumsdon, L. (2010) *Slow Travel and Tourism*, London: Earthscan.

Edensor, T. (2000) 'Walking in the British countryside: reflexivity, embodied practices, and ways to escape,' *Body & Society*, 6: 81–106.

Edensor, T. (2003) 'M-6 Junction 19–16: defamiliarizing the mundane roadscape,' *Space and Culture*, 6: 151–168.

Edensor, T. (2006) 'Reconsidering national temporalities: institutional times, everyday routines, serial spaces, and synchronicities,' *European Journal of Social Theory*, 9: 525–545.

Gatens, M. and Lloyd, G. (1999) *Collective Imaginings: Spinoza, Past and Present*, New York: Routledge.

Harker, C. (2009) 'Student im/mobility in Birzeit, Palestine,' *Mobilities*, 4: 11–35.

Harvey, R. D. (1991) *The Condition of Postmodernity: An Enquiry into the Origin of Cultural Change*, London: Blackwell.

Hine, J. (2007) 'Travel demand management and social exclusion,' *Mobilities*, 2: 109–120.

Ingold, T. (2000) *The Perception of the Environment*, London: Routledge.

Kleinert, M. (2009) 'Solitude at sea or social sailing? The constitution and perception of the cruising community,' in P. Vannini (ed.) *The Cultures of Alternative Mobilities: Routes Less Travelled*, Surrey: Ashgate, 159–176.

Lemonnier, P. (ed.) (2002) *Technological Choices: Transformations in Material Culture Since the Neolithic*, New York: Routledge.

Lorimer, H. and Lund, K. (2003) 'Performing facts: Finding a way over Scotland's mountains,' in B. Szerszynski, W. Heim, and C. Waterton (eds) *Nature Performed: Environment, Culture, Performance*, London: Blackwell, 130–144.

Neumann, M. (1993) 'Living on "Tortoise Time": alternative travel as the pursuit of lifestyle,' *Symbolic Interaction*, 16: 201–235.

Parkins, W. and Craig, G. (2006) *Slow Living*, London: Berg.

Pink, S. (2007) 'Sensing Cittàslow: Slow living and the constitution of the sensory city,' *The Senses & Society*, 2: 59–77.

Pink, S. (2008) 'Re-thinking contemporary activism: From community to emplaced sociality,' *Ethnos*, 73: 163–188.

Ritzer, G. (1993) *The McDonaldization of Society*, New York: Polity.

Schivelbush, W. (1986) *The Railway Journey*, New York: Blackwell.

Slow Tourism Club (n.d.) Available online at www.poduzetnicki-centar.hr/show.jsp?page=269914 (accessed 2 February 2012).

Spinney, J. (2006) 'A place of sense: A kinaesthetic ethnography of cyclists on Mont Ventoux,' *Environment and Planning D: Society and Space*, 24: 709–732.

Spinoza, B. (2000) *Ethics*, New York: OUP.

Thrift, N. (1996) *Spatial Formations*, Thousand Oaks, CA: SAGE.

Vannini, P. (2012a) *Ferry Tales: Mobility, Place, and Time on Canada's West Coast*, New York: Routledge.

Phillip Vannini

Vannini, P. (2012b) 'In time, out of time: Rhythmanalyzing ferry mobilities,' *Time & Society*, 21(2): 241–269.

Vergunst, J. L. and Ingold, T. (eds) (2009) *Ways of Walking*, Farnham: Ashgate.

Virilio, P. (1986) *Speed and Politics*, New York: Semiotext(e).

Watts, L. (2008) 'The art and craft of train travel,' *Social & Cultural Geography*, 9: 711–726.

Woodward, K. and Lea, J. (2009) 'Geographies of affect,' in S. Smith, R. Pain, S. Marston, and J. P. Jones (eds) *The SAGE Handbook of Social Geographies*, London: SAGE, 154–175.

Wylie, J. (2005) 'A single day's walking: narrating self and landscape on the South West Coast path,' *Transactions of the Institute of British Geographers*, 30: 234–247.

11

Distance and Proximity

Jonas Larsen

Introduction

This chapter discusses how various forms of mobility have reconfigured everyday experiences of distance and proximity, as well as the spatial orderings of social networks. It treats physical distances, transport and new media technologies, and the complex mix of presence and absence that they entail, as hugely important for understanding historical, contemporary and future spatialities of social life and networks. Social life is increasingly lived 'at-a-distance.' It is conducted through occasional trips to meet or visit significant others and frequent messages, calls and chats enacted by a plethora of internet and mobile phone platforms that swarm much of the world today. This also means that ordinary people are fully dependent upon, or locked into, such technologies and resources such as electricity, and especially oil. We may say that distances have never meant so little *and* so much, with the world getting smaller *and* larger at the very same time. While innovations in transport and communications constantly compress distances, people have to deal with spatially dispersed friends and family members, traveling and socializing on screens 'at-a-distance,' as their social lives, we might say, 'sprawl' over great distances and become 'translocal.' They connect and separate at the same moment; communications and mobility are both the curse *and* the medicine. This chapter demonstrates that social life has become increasingly distanciated over time, and it outlines the roles that transport and media have had in this process and are likely to have in the future. The chapter is equally concerned with giving qualitative examples of how distanciated and networked life is accomplished in practice as part of people's everyday life.

In this chapter I follow Urry, who has argued that it is necessary to understand distance and proximity (and what he terms 'meetingness') in order to understand the need for physical mobility. Travel is required for attending meetings, since many ties are not around the corner but 'at-a-distance.' For Urry, much travel results from a powerful 'compulsion to proximity' that makes it 'obligatory, appropriate or desirable' (Urry 2003: 164–5). Urry echoes Boden and Molotch's idea that 'the robust nature and enduring necessity of traditional human communication procedures have been underappreciated in writing on media and globalisation' (1994: 258). This is surely correct. But my point will be that the 'mobilities turn' has somewhat exaggerated the significance of corporeal meetings and travel, and, more importantly, underappreciated mediated communication despite the fact that this is the *everyday* lifeline of mobile people, as this chapter will show. Face-to-face interaction is not always desirable or the best way to be close or sincere to somebody. People may not be able to express their feelings because of their proximity; they might be intimidated by the other person's presence and their affective and emotional reactions. Issues will be hidden and remain untold. There will always be some distance in any meeting.

I begin by briefly showing how much of life in the early twentieth century was localized within proximate neighborhood networks typified by little movement 'elsewhere' or long-distance travel. Then I examine in more detail how many networks within the last decades have moved 'beyond neighborhoods' and become increasingly distanciated or 'trans-local' (Conradson and McKay 2007), with many people living what Elliott and Urry aptly call 'mobile lives' (2010). Inspired by Urry's (2011) recent writing about mobile scenarios in the face of oil shortage and climate change, I conclude by speculating about future network distances and proximities.

Neighborhood life

Much social life in at least parts of Europe and North America in the first half of the twentieth century was lived within a 'little box,' based upon geographical propinquity, or what Wellman terms door-to-door connectivity (2001: 231; see classical studies by Young and Willmott 1962; Gans 1962). Richard Hoggart, in writing about a 1930s urban setting, argued: 'The core of working class attitudes . . . is a sense of the personal, the concrete, the local . . . first the family and second the neighbourhood.' Later he argued that within 'the massed proletarian areas' there are 'small worlds, each as homogenous and well-defined as a village where one knows practically everybody, an extremely local life, in which everything is remarkably near' (cited in Albrow 1997: 40). Family life, work and friendships were synchronized within such tight-knit communities that had localized structures of support, friendship, kinship, attachment and 'taste.' Social networks were based upon close geographical propinquity within one's own and nearby neighborhoods. Many lived their whole lives in a particular town/city and even neighborhood. Significant others were encountered through walking and bumping into them on the street. Cars were a scarcity, many consumer goods, media and services were 'local,' and holidays were few and took place in nearby resorts (as with Blackpool in North West England, see Urry and Larsen 2011). While the phone connected households to distant households, distant calls were expensive and something rationed within most families.

Yet not all network ties were local and some people moved 'elsewhere' in search of a better life. But the emotional price was high because it disconnected networks. There are many migrant stories of the pain and guilt of leaving people behind and separating families. Given that money was scarce, long-distance travel costly, and long-distance communication either slow or expensive, many close contacts were lost because of the physical distances separating them, and this caused much 'homesickness' (Hammerton 2004: 274).

It was also the case that networks and social life were not entirely localized and that not everybody knew each other. People in the modern metropolis increasingly found themselves amongst strangers and they therefore had to learn the social skill of distancing themselves from the mobile crowd. Simmel adopted the figure of the stranger to illustrate the modern metropolis's unique geographies of proximity and distance: here people are close in a spatial sense, yet remote in a social sense. Simmel thus suggests that strangers are nearby, while 'close ones' are likely to be distant (see Allen 2000: 57; Harvey 1989). And indeed throughout the twentieth century new forms of mobile 'high-carbon lives' dislocated networks and consumer practices from neighborhoods (Urry 2011).

Beyond neighborhoods

The last decades have seen a shift to complex networks where connections are spatially dispersed and desynchronized, interaction is highly mediated, and the consumption of places, services and goods are globalized (Larsen *et al.* 2006; Urry 2011). Various interlocking structures are shaping this 'distanciation.' It is partly the result of various transport and communication innovations that have habituated people to living highly mobile and networked translocal and even transnational lives where staying put, being slowed down and disconnected is neither possible nor desirable. According to Bauman the good life has come to be thought of as akin to a 'continuous holiday' (1993: 243), crucially, we may add, with a laptop, smart phone and iPad at hand. They have afforded high levels of movement for jobs, business, education, holidays and international migration, as well as the movement of objects, resources and information from all over the world. And they have largely done so within a framework where travel and communications (relatively speaking) have become increasingly affordable and widespread (see Larsen *et al.* 2006).

The twentieth century has been the 'century of the car' (Urry 2007), and from the 1960s onwards cars (and motorways) spread social networks and consumption practices through urban sprawl, everyday commuting between home and work, and the occasional touring and consuming of new places. The 'tourist gaze' traveled abroad when, especially as a result of package tours, air travel became cheap and easy. And within the last decade budget airlines such as easyJet and Ryanair have made traveling to Europe's major cities incredibly cheap and therefore widespread. Berlin, Paris, Barcelona and London have become weekend playgrounds to what we might call the easyJet-generation (Urry and Larsen 2011). Overall, travel time and cost has reduced within the past decade, so frictions of distance and the cost of travel only matter partly in relation to physical travel; so many places are within reach quickly and cheaply. And as a consequence many people have become habituated to mobile leisure lifestyles and a touristic cosmopolitan outlook that presupposes travel by cars and planes. And as various consumer objects have become mobile too, neighborhoods, and even nations, are much less significant in structuring what we eat, wear and whom we 'support' (e.g. music groups and football teams). Such high-carbon lives involve much and regular long-distance travel to attend football matches, concerts, festivals, hen nights, stag nights, weddings, reunions and so on.

Ordinary people in 'rich' societies are not only traveling more but also communicating more to connect with and synchronize their individualized time–space trajectories with absent others. The first innovation that habituated networked lives was the telephone, which connected distanciated households in 'place-to-place' connectivity. Recently, 'networked computers' and 'mobile telephony' have been crucial in producing a network society of 'person-to-person' connectivity (Wellman 2001). This 'wires' households and mobile individuals into other households and individuals across great distances through satellite TV, e-mails, blogs, social networking sites (e.g. Facebook), text messages, Webcam, Skype and much more. Much of this communication is liberated from the house and takes place 'on the move' and in public. Phones and computers have become light, bodily fitted mobile devices with wireless connectivity. And they have become 'smart': internet and multimedia-enabled wireless smartphones to record video, take photographs, send texts and emails, receive visual voicemail, play music and video, browse the web and navigate one through a city. So there is a widespread adoption of such 'miniaturized mobilities' that affords the mobilization and coordination of social networks, with the making and sustaining of connections 'at-a-distance' (Elliott and Urry 2010: 28).

As discussed by Madianou and Miller (2011), the last couple of years have seen the emergence of what they term 'polymedia.' This refers to the current situation where most mobile people – including many poorer migrants (as discussed below) – have access to an unprecedented plurality of the new media and communication possibilities mentioned. It also refers to the fact that more and more people have the media literacy to take advantage of these technologies. And, finally, it refers to the situation where the main costs are related to the hardware, such as the web-camera, computer and the internet connection, while the actual communication is more or less cost-free (such as Facebooking, Skyping, IM). The implication of this, according to Madianou and Miller (2011), is that long-distance communication is much more common and fulfilling as people can choose the media that best allows them to express their state of mind.

This is in part because they can be said to reconfigure humans as physically moving bodies and as bits of mobile information and image. So they transform the sense of who is near or far, present or absent, affording networking 'at-a-distance.' In this sense, co-presence becomes both a location and a relation (Callon and Law 2004: 9). They can create small worlds of perpetual catching-up and small-talk, blurring distinctions between presence and absence. They afford networked talk and chat 'anytime, anyplace, anywhere,' of living in 'connected presence' with one's more or less dispersed social networks (Licoppe 2004). Family photographs can also bridge distances and forge proximity. They are often set in motion to bridge distance, emotionally reaching out for close ones at a distance: 'the more distant people are, the more important photographing becomes . . . A major reason for sending family photographs to relations and friends is that they do not see the children of the family frequently enough' (Rose 2003: 11). Rose continues: 'family snaps are seen as a trace of a person's presence; but they are also taken, displayed and circulated in awareness of the pervasiveness of absence and distance. Hence the spatial stretching of domestic space beyond the home. Photos bring near those far away' (ibid.: 13; see also McKay 2010).

So this rich world of polymedia connects remote places and produces emotional attachment between those living far apart. Such objects and technologies 'bridge' places and compensate for the decline of neighborhoods, making it possible to live a translocal life. This helps people to come to terms with living in distanciated networks, where people physically bump into each other less often. Even when people are absent they can remain in communicative propinquity to their social networks, which in this sense constitutes proximity between distant others. Yet of course they can also create 'distance' if, for example, they wish to pass on unpleasant news rather than meet face-to-face. Thus, 'geographical proximity or distance do not correlate simply with how emotionally close relatives feel to one another, nor indeed how far relatives will provide support or care for each other' (Mason 2004: 421). We need to redefine conventional notions of what it means to be close as networks of care, support and affection travel large geographical distances (Chamberlain 1995), and this is especially so in societies with extensive travel and mobile communication facilities.

One empirical indication of this is Larsen et al.'s (2006) 'mapping' of the social networks of youngish architects, employees in fitness centers and security staff in the north-west of England. They examine how *strong* ties are spatially distributed: how people network at-a-distance and live translocal lives within and beyond the UK. On average each respondent has moved to a different town or city a couple of times in the past 15 years and the majority has lived some time beyond the north-west of England. This is in part why they live on average almost 500 km from each of their identified strong ties, with one-third having strong ties abroad. So we may say that people often live closely with strangers, while their significant others are far away. Those with the highest average distances tend to have studied, worked and lived in more than one place and have friends and family members that have been 'on the move' too. So network geographies are relational and indeed some less-mobile people have distanciated networks too, if their ties have moved elsewhere.

This study indicates that close ties do not need to be close by and that mobility and distance do not necessarily disconnect strong ties, as was so often the case in the past. We cannot equate emotional closeness with residential closeness and daily, or weekly, co-present visits. However, not all ties are 'beyond neighborhoods.' All the respondents have nearby strong ties too, more or less within their neighborhoods. People need close-by strong ties so that they can regularly and spontaneously meet for a coffee or beer, or watch a film. When networks are distanciated it is obviously harder to meet *physically*. Indeed the study shows that it is not 'cost free' in terms of proximity to have distanciated networks, as increasing distance between ties means much less frequent face-to-face contact (yet meetings tend to become of longer duration as distances grow) (see also Putnam 2000; McGlone *et al.* 1999). For mobile people, new 'weak ties' can quickly become 'strong ties' if they live locally because of the need for proximity, but they are likely to turn weak again if one of them moves. Distance and proximity matters greatly in relation to *new* ties but apparently less so with old ties that are more rooted and have more foundation to exist 'at-a-distance.'

As many ties are distributed 'far and wide,' communications and travel are essential for maintaining a rewarding family and social life. In-between physical meetings, people overcome the 'frictions of distance' and manage dispersed networks with communication technologies. Distanciated networking involves complex combinations of occasional travel to meet up with friends and family members face-to-face, at-a-distance, and face-to-*inter*face interaction. While the respondents stress the significance of such mediated communication, they equally stress that face-to-face proximity makes networks come intermittently to life. They believe that friends have to come together from time to time, in various places. Distances matter because they are barriers to face-to-face interaction. Communications will often be too one-dimensional to fulfill significant social obligations. Tourist traveling has become a habitual practice through which young adults not only consume exciting places but also socialize with their more or less distant friends. It is not only seen as desirable but sometimes also as necessary. They spend many evenings and especially weekends traveling in cars, trains and planes to meet up with and be proximate with their strong ties, at their private homes and interesting tourist places.

For these respondents – and by implication many others – the good life presupposes being able to visit and entertain far-flung friends and attend their network's obligatory events, such as weddings, birthdays and reunions, wherever they happen to take place. So for this generation, tourist travel should not be seen as marginal – rather travelling, visiting *and* hosting are necessary to much social life conducted at a distance. Tourist travel sometimes involves connections with, rather than escape from, social relations, and the multiple obligations of a distanciated social life. Tourist travel is also very central to the transnational life of richer immigrants, with diasporas having their own travel agents, tour operators and airlines (Ali and Holden 2006: 233). They travel 'home' to keep their national and local sense of belonging and family networks alive.

Our study was conducted at a time before the breakthrough of 'polymedia,' and notably the popularization of Skype and social networking sites, especially Facebook, that have swept through much of the world's mediascape (see Miller 2011). The majority of our respondents are most certainly using Facebook and some will have rediscovered old friendships and strengthened others through messages, status updates, links, photographs and by participating in 'communities.' Miller argues that Facebook is a powerful substitute for neighborhood communities and that it might be as emotionally rewarding and effective as face-to-face meetings:

> Thanks to Facebook, one can maintain a friendship with less expenditure of time or dependency upon transport. It is possible to argue that driving two hours to see someone is a sign of deep friendship. But it is equally possible to argue that using two hours in direct IM communication, discussing, for example, the breakup of someone else's relationship or reciprocally viewing our activities, makes for a deeper friendship than sitting in traffic just so we can meet face-to-face.
>
> *(Miller 2011: 167)*

IM (instant messaging) communication and Skyping have some of the same affordances as face-to-face meetings: they are instantaneous and relatively rich with regard to visual cues such as facial expressions. I will now examine one aspect of such distant communication by discussing the phenomenon of 'distant mothering.'

Distant mothering

Elliott and Urry examine how highly mobile and network-capital-rich professionals use various 'miniaturized mobilities' to meet obligations to their partners and children while away on business trips. Consider Sandra:

> But, for Sandra, her beauty of the digital lifestyle is that she gets to bring her family (or, more accurately, her emotional connection with her family) along on these virtual networks. For though she might be physically separated from family life for much of the week, the digital lifestyle of mobile communications means she is never far away from them – or so it seems to Sandra.
>
> *(Elliott and Urry 2010: 26)*

Others examine transnational migrant mothers with considerably less 'network capital.' Vast numbers of especially Filipino mothers are 'au pairing' for rich and busy families like Sandra's. 27 percent of Filipino youths grow up with a parent abroad (predominately the mother). The mothers leave behind their own children to care for other children and 'the opportunities for cheap and instant communication feature strongly in migrant mothers' justifications regarding their decisions to migrate and settle' (Madianou and Miller 2011: 2). Such families suffer from a lack of physical co-presence. The average au pair in Parreñas's study will have only spent some 24 weeks with their children during the last 11 years (Miller 2007: 541). So 'the joys of physical contact, the emotional security of physical presence, and the familiarity allowed by physical proximity are denied to many transnational family members' (Parreñas 2005: 333). The distances between them and the cost of long-distance travel are barriers to face-to-face interaction that in the rich north is regarded as necessary for sustaining relationships and talking through issues (Urry 2007). There is *not* a death of distance for such mothers and their left-behind children; they have to live by communications. Instead, everyday communication is part and parcel of *everyday* life in transnational families (Parreñas 2005: 317). Mobile phones and pre-paid phonecards are the lifeline of migrants and their translocal subjectivities (Vertovec 2004; Parreñas 2005). Mobiles are crucial to the way in which a great many absent Filipino mothers 'mother' 'at-a-distance.' They are attempting to be 'there' through routinized communication, which may include almost *daily* text messages:

> Migrant mothers . . . rely on sending an SMS to communicate with their children on a daily basis. Some children even told me that they wake up to biblical messages from their migrant mothers every morning . . . Sending text messages is one system mothers use to make sure that their children are ready for school in the mornings.
>
> *(Parreñas 2005: 328)*

Such transnational family lives are also characterized by, and enacted through, longer telephone *conversations*, normally taking place once a week, at a particular time and day (especially Sundays) (see Wilding 2006). Such lengthy turn-taking telephone meetings, where news is exchanged, troubles are talked through, and solidarity expressed, are crucial for maintaining the bond between migrant mothers and their children at home, as well as for forming their common translocal place (Conradson and Mckay 2007). As a consequence, migrant mothers spend a considerable part of their income on phone bills. And, more recently, such phone calls resemble face-to-face meetings even more. Various forms of VOIP (e.g. Yahoo Messenger and Skype) afford a richness of facial and spatial cues. And since there is no cost involved, conversations will be longer and not rationed, as was the case especially with long-distance telephone calls in the past. 'Seeing the face' has meant that it is much easier for mothers and children to be in touch and recognize each other's faces (recall that they hardly ever see each other). So such technologies have allowed mothers to continue to be mothers despite the vast distances separating them. While this has surely empowered such families, a family life on the screen is not emotionally fulfilling, cost-free or desirable. Migrant mothers and their children will constantly feel the weight of the distance when connected virtually. Every so often they are given an illusion of proximity, where loved ones are there, but yet they are out of touch (Madianou and Miller 2011: 2).

Conclusion

Many people have become habituated to living in distanciated networks, having many of their strong ties 'at-a-distance' and living mobile social lives. While I have highlighted some of the apparent costs of such a life, it is, generally speaking, regarded by most – especially by those with high network capital – as rewarding, exciting and pleasurable, especially in comparison to immobile 'neighborhood lives.' Once people have become used to travel and have connections 'at-a-distance,' it is virtually impossible to imagine a pleasurable life that involves staying put and being confined by 'neighborhoods.' If 'business were as normal' then we would expect that most networks would continue to be 'at-a-distance' and places and networks be physically traveled to for a long while yet. Yet, as Urry argues in his latest book (2011), business is not as usual, and this scenario is not a given. As Urry reminds us, the kinds of mobile practices discussed in this chapter are utterly dependent upon electricity and especially oil; the latter is running out and travel is causing severe climate change. So in the future it seems probable that travel is likely to become increasingly expensive, which makes the long-term growth in travel and tourism less likely. Unless some sort of unexpected technological fix occurs, Urry envisages that there will be a de-mobilization of much social life, except perhaps for the super-rich with abundant network capital. Moreover, shortage of oil and climate changes may necessitate various policies and taxes aiming at making travel more sustainable but also more expensive and restrictive. Such incentives are likely to cause widespread contestation by generations habituated to mobile lives and distanciated networks. If I am right about the distributed geographies of many networks, the need and desirability for face-to-face meetings, and the lure of foreign places, then reducing travel is much of a challenge. It will impact negatively upon the social capital of many mobile people for whom travel is essential for performing their social relations.

The necessary transition to more 'low-carbon lives' seems to require a long-term reversal of the advances regarding network distances and face-to-face proximities described in this chapter. It requires that we change habits and outlooks. One of Urry's scenarios, termed 'local sustainability,' involves a dramatic global shift towards networks and lifestyles more local and smaller in scale: 'Friends would have to be chosen from neighboring streets, families would not move away at times of new household composition, work would be found nearby, walking, cycling and public transport replace cars and planes, education would be sought only in local schools and colleges, the seasons would determine which and when foodstuffs were produced and consumed, most goods and services would be simpler and produced nearby . . . This scenario depends upon new kinds of "friendship," on choosing to know mostly those who live close by and can be walked or cycled to' (2011: 146). So almost all travel would be localized with very little long-distance tourist travel as such, with the exception of public transport. Long-distance travel will be a mark of low status. This scenario requires that people contest travel and the environmental ills that it generates, as well as articulate discourses that promote the *positive* outcomes of returning to some sort of neighborhood life. This is not an easy transition as many people were more than happy to escape such bonded life, and it will be even more difficult for today's mobile people to be at ease with such confinement.

Another scenario discussed by Urry is that of 'low carbon, digital networks.' One aspect of this scenario is that 'much travel would be replaced by virtual travel' (Urry 2011: 151). So far, phones and various types of screens have been poor substitutes for the sensuous richness of face-to-face sociality. Today, virtual communications are often about coordinating physical travel and enabling talking between visits and meetings rather than substituting for corporeal travel. This scenario implies a world where most networking with distant ties is performed on the internet and mediated by various screens, and where physical proximity is therefore not necessary for sustaining intimate social relations. This scenario requires the further innovation of communications that affectively stimulate the richness of face-to-face interaction and discourses that promote the joys of virtual interactions. Yet, interestingly, this is how poor migrants – like the Filipino mothers discussed earlier in this chapter – already conduct their mobile life today. Perhaps the mobile middle-classes in the rich north will also be denied the richness of bodily proximity and have to network mainly by virtual communication. This might be the likely solution if people continue to live far away from their friends and family members.

Acknowledgement

Parts of this chapter are based on work published elsewhere with John Urry and Kay Axhausen. I have made references to this work throughout the chapter.

References

Albrow, M. (1997) 'Travelling beyond Local Cultures: Socioscapes in a Global City,' in J. Eade (ed.) *Living the Global City: Globalization as Local Process*, London: Routledge, pp. 37–55.
Ali, N. and Holden, A. (2006) 'Post-colonial Pakistani Mobilities: The Embodiment of the Myth of Return in Tourism,' *Mobilities*, 1(2): 217–242.

Allen, J. (2000) 'On George Simmel: Proximity, Distance and Movement,' in M. Crang and N. Thrift (eds) *Thinking Space*, London: Routledge.

Bauman, Z. (1993) *Postmodern Ethics*, London: Routledge.

Boden, D. and Molotch, H. (1994) 'The Compulsion of Proximity,' in R. Friedland and D. Boden (eds) *Nowhere: Space, Time and Modernity*, Berkeley, CA: University of California Press.

Callon, M. and Law, J. (2004) 'Guest Ediorial,' *Environment and Planning D: Society and Space*, 22: 3–11.

Chamberlain, M. (1995) 'Family Narratives and Migration Dynamics,' *Immigrants and Minorities*, 14(2): 153–169.

Conradson, D. and McKay, D. (2007) 'Translocal Subjectivities: Mobility, Connection and Emotion,' *Mobilities*, 2(2): 167–174.

Elliott, A. and Urry, J. (2010) *Mobile Lives*, London: Routledge.

Gan, H. (1962) *The Urban Villagers: Group and Class in the Life of Italian-Americans*, New York: Free Press of Glencoe.

Hammerton, J. (2004) 'The Quest for Family and the Mobility of Modernity in Narratives of Postwar British Emigration,' *Global Networks*, 4(4): 271–284.

Harvey, D. (1989) *The Condition of Postmodernity*, Oxford: Blackwell.

Larsen, J., Urry, J. and Axhausen, K. (2006) *Mobilities, Networks, Geographies*, Aldershot: Ashgate.

Licoppe, C. (2004) '"Connected Presence": The Emergence of a New Repertoire for Managing Social Relationships in a Changing Communication Technoscape,' *Environment and Planning D: Society and Space*, 22: 135–156.

McGlone, F., Park, A. and Roberts, C. (1999) 'Kinship and Friendship: Attitudes and Behaviour in Britain 1986–1995,' in S. McRae (ed.) *Changing Britain: Families and Households in the 1990s*, Oxford: Oxford University Press.

McKay, D. (2010) 'On the Face of Facebook: Historical Images and Personhood in Filipino Social Networking,' *History and Anthropology*, 21(4): 479–498.

Madianou, M. and Miller, D. (2011) 'Mobile Phone Parenting: Reconfiguring Relationships between Filipina Migrant Mothers and Left-behind Children,' *New Media & Society*, 13(3): 457–470.

Mason, J. (2004) '"Managing Kinship over Long Distances": The Significance of "The Visit",' *Social Policy & Society*, 3(4): 421–429.

Miller, D. (2007) 'What Is a Relationship? Is Kinship Negotiated Experience?,' *Ethnos*, 72(4): 535–554.

Miller, D. (2011) *Tales from Facebook*, Cambridge: Polity.

Parreñas, R. (2005) 'Long Distance Intimacy: Class, Gender and Intergenerational Relations between Mothers and Children in Filipino Transnational Families,' *Global Networks*, 5(4): 317–336.

Putnam, D. R. (2000) *Bowling Alone: The Collapse and Revival of American Community*, New York: Simon & Schuster.

Rose, G. (2003) 'Family Photographs and Domestic Spacings: A Case Study,' *Transactions of the Institute of British Geographers*, 28(1): 5–18.

Urry, J. (2003) 'Social Networks, Travel and Talk', *British Journal of Sociology*, 54(2): 155–175.

Urry, J. (2007) *Mobilities*, Cambridge: Polity.

Urry, J. (2011) *Climate Change & Society*, Cambridge: Polity.

Urry, J. and Larsen, J. (2011) *The Tourist Gaze 3.0*, London: Sage.

Vertovec, S. (2004) 'Cheap Calls: The Social Glue of Migrant Transnationalism,' *Global Networks*, 4: 219–224.

Wellman, B. (2001) 'Physical Place and Cyberplace: The Rise of Personalised Networking,' *International Journal of Urban and Regional Research*, 25(2): 227–252.

Wilding, R. (2006) '"Virtual" Intimacies? Families Communicating Across Transnational Contexts,' *Global Networks*, 6(2): 125–142.

Young, M. and Willmott, P. (1962) *Family and Kinship in East London*, Harmondsworth: Penguin Books.

12

Net Locality

Adriana de Souza e Silva and Eric Gordon

The pervasiveness of mobile location-aware technology has made it possible to consistently and persistently *locate* ourselves and be networked while moving through physical space. As location-aware mobile devices become commonplace, we experience a shift in the way we connect to the Internet. We call this shift *net locality* (Gordon and de Souza e Silva 2011). In net locality, location becomes the organizational logic of social and networked interactions. Contrary to what was often forecasted in the early days of the Internet, being networked actually increases our awareness of the local, and our connection to physical spaces. Net locality suggests that access to the Internet is dependent on users' locations, local communities, cultures and contexts.

In this chapter, we define net locality as a new approach for understanding the social practices that shape digital networks and mobility in urban spaces. The idea of net locality is based on two general frameworks: the network society (Castells 2000) and the mobilities paradigm (Sheller and Urry 2006). For years, scholars focused on the growing influence of global networks on local contexts (Castells 2000; Meyrowitz 2005; Friedman 2007). However, what we can observe now, in perhaps comparable intensity, is the influence of local knowledge and local information in shaping global networks and nearby interactions (Gordon 2009; Gordon and de Souza e Silva 2011).

We begin by describing what we call the network model. We focus on two of its characteristics: the 'death of geography,' and the birth of the global city as a convergence point of information flows. We then turn to the mobilities paradigm. We analyze how mobility studies has emphasized the importance of physical spaces for physical travel. However, within the mobilities paradigm the structure of social experience and the value of the global city are still grounded on ideas of speed and information flows, which are translated into movement and circulation. We then look at how early studies on mobile communication largely ignored the connection of people with their nearby environment, focusing instead on remote connections with remote people (Katz and Aakhus 2002; Moores 2004). In the final section, we define the concept of net locality in relation to the ideas of the network society and the mobilities paradigm.

The network society

Castells (2000) popularized the concept of the network society, an idea which was adopted as an important metaphor for describing spaces of sociability online, such as virtual worlds and chat rooms. Although Castells's model was an all-encompassing one, focusing on the broad interrelations between economics, politics, society and technology, many scholars, sci-fi writers and journalists were concerned by the idea that digital (networked) spaces could be independent of physical spaces (Mitchell 1995; Negroponte 1995; Donath 1997; Benedikt 2000). For example, there were fears that because people could socialize online, public spaces of gathering such as parks and plazas would be endangered. Or that because people could shop online, retail shops would disappear (Townsend 2004). And because people could work remotely, they would no longer feel the need to leave their houses (Castells 2000).

Much of this rhetoric around the Internet was premised on the idea that when everything is accessible from anywhere, and the whole world is connected, digital networks would render physical distances and space irrelevant. This is what we call the network model: it is the logic of the network society that suggests that speed and efficiency chips away at the importance of physical distances.[1] As such, communication and social interaction could become independent of our physical bodies and their locations. These fears were often included under the apocalyptic framework of the 'death of geography' (Morgan 2001).

However, as Couclelis (2007) rightly observes, this is an oversimplification of these arguments, and not all scholars feared that the popularization of online social spaces would actually lead to the end of geography. Many indeed emphasized the relevance of urban spaces and urban infrastructures as supports of the increasingly globalized world (Graham and Marvin 2001). And although conflicting perspectives on the relationship between the Internet and physical spaces still exist, the idea that digital networks efficiently and quickly transmit information from node to node, therefore decreasing the relevance of the paths, has been a cultural dominant (Jameson 1991) since the popularization of the Internet in the 1990s.

This perspective is foregrounded in the work of globalization scholars. While they acknowledge the physical growth of cities and the increasing concentration of people, goods and networked connections (Sassen 2001; Canclini 2001; Castells and Cardoso 2006), they simultaneously emphasize the centrality of digital networks in the formation of global cities. Cities such as New York, Tokyo and São Paulo gained importance because of their position within the global network and capacity to exchange information with other nodes, rather than because of their local characteristics or physical location. Castells characterized this shift in values as the prioritization of the 'space of flows' over what he calls the 'space of places' (Castells 2000). According to the logic of the space of flows, centrality in the network depends on the number of connections a place can sustain, rather than its geographical location.

While these scholars addressed the correlation between society and cities, acknowledging the relevance of urban spaces in contemporary society, they also tended to focus on globalization and information flows, demonstrating either how digital networks were replacing the functionality of city spaces or how city spaces were becoming mere access points to digital networks. In this model, networked connections overwhelm physical distances. While we argue against these assumptions, there are two aspects of the *network model* that are helpful in framing our concept of net locality: (1) the awareness that connectivity and social interaction expand beyond physical co-presence; and (2) the idea that digital networks can provide support for social interactions.

The mobilities paradigm

With the popularization of mobile communication devices in the beginning of this century, another cultural dominant emerged for understanding the relationships between the Internet, spaces and society: mobilities. As Cresswell (2010) pointed out, mobilities is not new, since other scholars have acknowledged the importance of global travel, micro-movements of the body, and nomadism. But new studies emphasize the lack of an integrated interdisciplinary perspective and methodology to understand mobilities and flows.

The new mobilities paradigm (Sheller and Urry 2006) emerged partly as a reaction to the prevailing logic of networks that ignored physical space as traveled space. It focuses on flows of mobility that happen in-between locations, and on the importance of physical space as support for networks. Mobility scholars argue that mobility has always been critical for the creation of social networks and to the development of connections to places (Larsen *et al.* 2006). This perspective challenged traditional scholarship that often ignored the social dimensions of mobility, overlooking how travel and transportation networks help to constitute modern societies and communities.

As such, the mobilities paradigm also assigned meaning to the act of moving through space. Mobility, rather than being just a means of going from A to B, became embedded with social activities (Sheller and Urry 2006). With the development of mobile communication technologies, these social interactions also include people who are not co-present. In contrast to a popular perspective from the network society, according to which connection to the Internet required being static in front of a screen (Donath 1997), Lyons and Urry (2005) suggest that with the popularization of digital mobile technologies, travel time becomes activity time, because people can be moving from place to place while working on their laptops, or socializing on their mobile phones. As a result, traveled time is no longer considered 'dead time,' and connectivity is no longer associated with lack of mobility.

The problem with this perspective is that mobile, networked interactions are too often correlated with the process of establishing remote connections with people. This is clear in the comparison between physical and virtual mobilities. While physical mobilities include the physical travel of people, and physical movement of objects, virtual mobilities refer to imaginative travel, virtual travel on the Internet, and communicative travel (Larsen *et al.* 2006). Because virtual mobilities is primarily related to the ability of connecting to what is physically distant, Kellerman (2006) suggests that virtual mobilities effectively eliminates the physical space (and physical movement) between nodes. As such, the idea of virtual mobilities finds a parallel in the network model.

The concept of virtual mobilities was also strongly embraced by mobile communication scholars. Mobile technologies have been characterized as allowing people to move 'virtually' by connecting to others remotely, while simultaneously disconnecting them from their surrounding local spaces.[2] For example, Rheingold (2002) observed that on trains and buses in Japan passengers preferred to talk to somebody who was physically absent than with people who were in the same vehicle. This absent presence (Gergen 2002) had the power to transform physical space into non-place (Auge 1995), deprived of meaning and social interactions, for people no longer connected with anyone in their vicinity.

As with the network model, not all mobile communication scholars emphasized users' disconnections from their surroundings. A number of mobile communication studies acknowledged that forging remote connections did not necessarily eliminate or substitute communication with people nearby (Matsuda 2005; Hampton and Wellman 2001; Ling 2004). As Wellman (2001) puts it, 'computer mediated communication supplements, arranges and amplifies in-person and telephone communication rather than replaces them.' However, while mobile communication scholars recognize the complementarity between local connections and remote ones, this recognition is generally in service to the argument that people's experiences are now global, rather than local. Furthermore, local connections are considered to be synonymous with face-to-face interactions.

An exception to this assumption is found in the work of early locative media artists who realized the potential of location-based technologies to connect people to nearby locations, by accessing location-specific information through their mobile devices (Hight 2006; Galloway 2006; Silverstone and Sujon 2005; Hemment 2006; Tuters and Varnelis 2006). Through digital mapping, mobile annotation, and hybrid reality games such as *Can You See Me Now?* (Blast-Theory and The-Mixed-Reality-Lab 2001), *Urban Tapestries* (Proboscis 2002–2004), and *34 North 118 West* (Knowlton *et al.* 2002), locative media artists showed that access to location-based information through mobile technologies transforms how people interact with their surrounding space and how they develop social connections to people nearby (de Souza e Silva 2004; de Souza e Silva and Sutko 2008). For example, in *34 North 118 West* users could walk around Los Angeles and listen to historical details about their location. Similarly, *Urban Tapestries* allowed users to share location-based information, such as personal narratives and restaurant reviews. Locative media artists were the first to acknowledge the importance of location in our networked interactions, as a result of the Internet being available in physical spaces.

These innovative approaches to the meaning of location are part of what we call net locality. Net locality is a shift in the way we understand our networked connections (to the Internet, to other people around us), highlighting the fact that digital networks are increasingly composed of local information and that the organizational logic of networked interactions depends also on what is nearby, and not only on what is far away. This idea has profound implications for our current perceptions of privacy, interactions with public spaces, and development of sociability.

Net locality

Net locality is built on some key ideas of the network model and the mobilities paradigm, such as the networked support for social interactions, the importance of physical spaces, and the awareness that digital information can be accessed while on the move. However, we face today another shift in how we understand the relationship between the Internet and physical spaces, which foregrounds a new character of location. The notion of location has received scarce attention among place and space scholars. It has often been contrasted to places, but conceptualized as a place deprived of meaning (Agnew 1987; Harvey 1996; Cresswell 2004). As David Harvey noted, places have 'a discursive/symbolic meaning well beyond that of mere location, so that events that occur there have a particular significance' (Harvey 1996). Locations are different from places in that they have 'fixed objective co-ordinates on the Earth's surface' (Cresswell 2004). Although places can also be located, as Cresswell shows, they are not always stationary. He uses the example of a ship to point out a type of mobile place for people who are on a journey. A ship is a place, 'even though its location is constantly changing' (Cresswell 2004). However, with the popularization of location-aware mobile technologies we witness a shift in the character of location: they still include fixed geographical coordinates, but they now become dynamic due to the constantly changing location-based digital information that is 'attached' to them (de Souza e Silva and Frith 2012). Now, the meaning of location is intrinsically linked to the presence of networked location-based information.

Net locality is based on the recognition that we are networked, but still connected to localities, and that belonging to a global network strengthens local connections. In fact, people do not experience physical *or* virtual spaces, but instead experience hybrid spaces (de Souza e Silva 2006). According to this logic, networked connections influence not only our remote interactions, but also how we interact with our surrounding spaces and co-present people. Consider the case where somebody opens the location-based social network *Foursquare* in order to 'check in' to a café. The act of 'checking in' already establishes a connection to that location, which is broadcast to other people in their social network. Net locality also has the potential to generate new patterns of mobility in the city. For example, while 'checking in' in *Foursquare* a user 'sees' on their mobile screen that another friend is in a bar a block away. The user then decides to walk to the nearby bar to say 'Hi' to the friend. The application, in this case, draws the user's attention to nearby people and the local environment, influencing how people move in networked spaces. An interesting example of how location-based mobile games influence urban mobility is the game *Mogi* in Japan. Licoppe and Inada (2006) describe the case where users get together to form 'expeditions' to collectively go to a specific part of the city to find virtual objects (such as fruits and animals) to complete their game collection. Humphreys (2007) also described how users of the mobile social network *Dodgeball* used the application to coordinate where to meet and where to go out in the city, moving from bar to bar.

Net locality, however, is not a set of technologies, but a set of social practices associated with the increasing use of location-based technology in public spaces. Some of these technologies are 'smartphones' that run applications ('apps') such as *WikiMe*, with which users can access location-specific Wikipedia articles, and *Foursquare* and *Loopt*, which allow people to see the locations of other people on a map on their mobile phone screen. While location-based services and social networks have previously been developed by locative media artists and researchers, only with the increased popularity of smartphones such as the iPhone and the Android system have they become accessible to the general public. As a consequence, what we witness today is comparable to what happened in the early 1990s: the world wide web made the Internet available and easily accessible to the common user. Although aspects of net locality did exist before within research and artistic circles, its impact on mobility, privacy, sociability and public spaces are just now starting to show up.

Locational privacy is among the major concerns related to the use of mobile location-based technologies (Gordon and de Souza e Silva 2011; de Souza e Silva and Frith 2012). In order to take advantage of location-based information, people must disclose their location to mobile phone providers, and sometimes to other people. In January 2010 Google and Google Maps began integrating location data into all searches – either the location of an IP address of a desktop computer or the GPS coordinates of a phone now factors into search results. An increasing number of applications in smartphones query users about their location before they launch. Online social networks become location-based, with applications such as *Foursquare*, *Loopt* and *Google Latitude* allowing users to broadcast their location to their network of friends. Other types of location-based services help users to find the nearest gas station, best restaurant or the next bus. Most location-based 'apps' include opt-in features, allowing users to choose with whom to share their location information. However, these apps' privacy policies are not always clear, and often location information is shared with other commercial partners without users' awareness. As a result, people are frequently targeted with unrequested location-based advertisements, which is the fastest growing segment of location-based services (ABI 2009).

Other frequent concerns about locational privacy include disclosing location to unknown others, or collateral surveillance (de Souza e Silva and Frith 2012). Collateral surveillance can be understood not only in terms of locational privacy, but also in terms of power asymmetries. While studying player interactions in the location-based game *Mogi*, Licoppe and Inada (2009) found out that interaction between players is perceived as creepy or a case of stalking when one player claimed to be close enough to the other in order to literally see them, but the player being watched either could not see the other players or did not know if the claim was true. Power asymmetries happen outside games as well. Devices that allow people to enact collateral surveillance are becoming increasingly popular. From the anklet GPS used to track parolees in California (Shklovski *et al.* 2009) to airport tracking technologies (Hansen *et al.* 2009), these systems are based on differential power relationships that allow one person to track, and another to be tracked. Momentarily, people give up control over their location information, even if they consent to this external control, as is the case with location-based social networks and airport tracking systems. Location-sharing systems highlight already existing power relationships, but also support the creation of new power differentials, based on the control over location information.

The control over location information is not only evidenced in interpersonal relationships mediated through location-based technologies, but it is also present in the relationship between users and space. With location-based services, people are able to select from their surrounding space the information that they are willing to see. For example, a *Foursquare* player is able to see other *Foursquare* players nearby, and can contribute to the information ecology of their current location by uploading, for instance, a tip about the local museum. Another *Foursquare* user visiting the museum will be able to access that location-based information 'attached' to that location. In contrast, she might not be aware of other reviews in other apps or in the local paper. Public space, then, becomes more filtered (de Souza e Silva and Frith 2012).

A question to ask is whether net locality leads to homogenous spaces, filtered to individualized needs. For example, if an American *Foursquare* player goes to China and chooses to visit only places where he can see other Americans 'checked in,' he might be missing out on non-tourist spaces, where he could interact with the local culture and local people. According to this logic, some might claim that people will increasingly connect with those similar to them and ignore those who are different. But there is also an equally compelling counter argument, which is that sameness pulls one into difference. If a *Foursquare* player 'sees' that many of her friends are checked in at a new art gallery in an unfamiliar part of Copenhagen, she might be compelled to go there because their presence implicitly endorses the place. And this works both ways. Not only do people endorse places, but places endorse people: if a user opens her location-based app and sees that a place nearby has many good reviews, she might desire to meet those people. As a result, locations acquire new meanings through the digital information embedded in them.

Net locality is also becoming an important framework for community formation and political participation (Gordon and de Souza e Silva 2011). Location-based apps such as *iTransitBuddy* contextualize city transportation data to the location of the user by supplying GPS locations for city buses. Similarly, apps such as *FixMyStreet* and *SeeClickFix* help users report problems like potholes or graffiti to the local government. While governments and local community organizations in South Korea, Japan, the United States and countries in Europe are rapidly adapting to the new framework of net locality, the same can be observed in other parts of the world as well. As smartphones become available in developing nations, they are often responsible for people's first connection to the Internet (Donner and Gitau 2009; Ling and Horst 2011). As such, the perception that the Internet renders locations irrelevant will never be part of their daily experience of what it is to be networked.

Adriana de Souza e Silva and Eric Gordon

Conclusions

The network model is based on the assumption that social, economic and cultural relations are shaped as networks, and that the Internet is the support for these relations. However, many Internet scholars, when applying the network model to the Internet, focused on how instant communication would lead to the irrelevance of physical spaces, a phenomenon known as the 'death of geography.' As a result, many were led to believe that social connections could be forged independently of physical distances. As globalization scholars often privileged the global over the local, the global city was described as part of the space of flows, and localities were still regarded as subordinate to the global. Net locality, however, provides a context from which to understand how local spaces are also transformative of global networks.

The mobilities paradigm emphasized the relevance of using the paths of the network (physical space) when traveling from place to place. However, mobility scholars also focused on the potential for virtual mobilities – that is, to connect to those remote, rather than co-present people. Net locality does not oppose virtual travel to face-to-face interactions, nor does it oppose physical mobility to virtual mobility. Consequently, if the space of flows was the dominant spatial logic of the network society, hybrid spaces are the dominant spatial logic of net locality. Within net locality, location-aware technologies connect us to local spaces, and therefore influence how we interact with localities, and generate new patterns of mobility. Future studies on the interrelationships between the Internet, public spaces and mobility should take the net locality framework into consideration as a way of analyzing the social, political and spatial implications of mobile and location-based technologies and practices.

Notes

1 Not all conceptualizations of networks focus on the speed and efficiency of connection among nodes and ignore the paths. Indeed, many authors besides Castells focused on the social, political and cultural implications of the network society (Galloway and Thacker 2007; Canclini 2001; Sassen 2001). However, the idea of the network society was often appropriated to support a perspective that emphasized connection between remote nodes, rather than local interactions.
2 For a more detailed argument see de Souza e Silva and Frith (2012), Chapter 3.

References

ABI 2009. 'Mobile location based services: Applications, platforms, positioning technologies, handset evolution, and business model migration,' available online at www.abiresearch.com/research/pro-duct/1005243-location-based-services-lbs-markets-carrie/ (accessed 8 April 2012).
Agnew, J. A. 1987. *Place and Politics: The Geographical Mediation of State and Society*, Boston and London: Allen & Unwin.
Auge, M. 1995. *Non-places: Introduction to an Anthropology of Supermodernity*, London and New York: Verso Books.
Benedikt, M. 2000. 'Cyberspace: The First Steps' in: Bell, D. and Kennedy, B. M. (eds) *The Cybercultures Reader*, New York: Routledge.
Blast-Theory and The-Mixed-Reality-Lab 2001. 'Can You See Me Now? Sheffield, Rotterdam, Tokyo, Barcelona,' available online at www.blasttheory.co.uk/bt/work_cysmn.html (accessed 8 April 2012).
Canclini, N. G. 2001. *Consumers and Citizens: Globalization and Multicultural Conflicts*, Minneapolis: University of Minnesota Press.

Castells, M. 2000. *The Rise of the Network Society*, Oxford: Blackwell.

Castells, M. and Cardoso, G. 2006. *The Network Society: From Knowledge to Policy*, Washington DC: Johns Hopkins Center for Transatlantic Relations.

Couclelis, H. 2007. 'Misses, Near-misses and Surprises in Forecasting the Informational City' in: Miller, H. J. (ed.) *Societies and Cities in the Age of Instant Access*, Dordrecht, The Netherlands: Springer.

Cresswell, T. 2004. *Place: A Short Introduction*, Malden, MA: Blackwell.

Cresswell, T. 2010. 'Towards a politics of mobility,' *Environment and Planning D: Society and Space*, 28, 17–31.

De Souza e Silva, A. 2004. 'Mobile networks and public spaces: Bringing multiuser environments into the physical space,' *Convergence*, 10, 15–27.

De Souza e Silva, A. 2006. 'From cyber to hybrid: Mobile technologies as interfaces of hybrid spaces,' *Space and Culture*, 3, 261–278.

De Souza e Silva, A. and Sutko, D. M. 2008. 'Playing life and living play: How hybrid reality games reframe space, play, and the ordinary,' *Critical Studies in Media Communication*, 25, 447–465.

De Souza e Silva, A. and Frith, J. 2012. *Mobile Interfaces in Public Spaces: Locational Privacy, Control and Urban Sociability*, New York: Routledge.

Donath, J. 1997. *Inhabiting the Virtual City: The Design of Social Environments for Electronic Communities*, Cambridge, MA: The MIT Press.

Donner, J. and Gitau, S. 2009. 'New paths: Exploring mobile-centric internet use in South Africa,' Int. Comm. Assoc. Conf., Chicago, IL, available online at http://research.microsoft.com/apps/pubs/default.aspx?id=102002 (accessed 8 April 2012).

Friedman, T. L. 2007. *The World Is Flat 3.0: A Brief History of the 21st Century*, New York: Picador.

Galloway, A. 2006. 'Locative media as socialising and spatialising practices: Learning from archaeology,' *Leonardo Electronic Almanac*, 14, 12.

Galloway, A. R. and Thacker, E. 2007. *The Exploit: A Theory of Networks*, Minneapolis: University of Minnesota Press.

Gergen, K. 2002. 'The Challenge of Absent Presence' in: Katz, J. and Aakhus, M. (eds) *Perpetual Contact: Mobile Communication, Private Talk, Public Performance*, New York: Cambridge University Press.

Gordon, E. 2009. 'Redefining the Local: The Distinction between Located Information and Local Knowledge in Location-based Games' in: De Souza E Silva, A. and Sutko, D. M. (eds) *Digital Cityscapes: Merging Digital and Urban Playspaces*, New York: Peter Lang.

Gordon, E. and de Souza e Silva, A. 2011. *Net Locality: Why Location Matters in a Networked World*, Boston: Blackwell Publishers.

Graham, S. and Marvin, S. 2001. *Splintering Urbanism: Networked Infrastructures, Technological Mobilities and the Urban Condition*, New York: Routledge.

Hampton, K. and Wellman, B. 2001. 'Long distance community in the network society,' *American Behavioral Scientist*, 45, 476.

Hansen, J., Alapetite, A., Andersen, H., Malmborg, L. and Thommesen, J. 2009. 'Location-based Services and Privacy in Airports' in: Gross, T., Gulliksen, J., Kotzé, P., Oestreicher, L., Palanque, P., Prates, R. and Winckler, M. (eds) *Human–Computer Interaction – interact 2009*, Berlin/Heidelberg: Springer.

Harvey, D. 1996. *Justice, Nature and the Geography of Difference*, Cambridge, MA: Blackwell Publishers.

Hemment, D. 2006. 'Locative arts,' *Leonardo*, 39, 348.

Hight, J. 2006. 'Views from above: Locative narrative and the landscape,' *Leonardo Electronic Almanac*, 14, 9.

Humphreys, L. 2007. 'Mobile social networks and social practice: A case study of Dodgeball,' *Journal of Computer-Mediated Communication*, 13, article 17.

Jameson, F. 1991. *Postmodernism; or the Cultural Logic of Late Capitalism*, Durham: Duke University Press.

Katz, J. and Aakhus, M. (eds) 2002. *Perpetual Contact: Mobile Communication, Private Talk, Public Performance*, Cambridge: Cambridge University Press.

Kellerman, A. 2006. *Personal Mobilities*, London: Routledge.

Knowlton, J., Spellman, N. and Hight, J. (2002) *34 North 118 West*. Los Angeles, available online at http://34n118w.net (accessed 8 April 2012).

Larsen, J., Urry, J. and Axhausen, K. W. 2006. *Mobilities, Networks, Geographies*, Farnham, UK: Ashgate.

Licoppe, C. and Inada, Y. 2006. 'Emergent uses of a multiplayer location–aware mobile game: The interactional consequences of mediated encounters,' *Mobilities*, 1, 39–61.

Licoppe, C. and Inada, Y. 2009. 'Mediated co-proximity and its dangers in a location-aware community: A case of stalking' in: de Souza e Silva, A. and Sutko, D. M. (eds) *Digital Cityscapes: Merging Digital and Urban Playspaces*, New York: Peter Lang.

Ling, R. 2004. *The Mobile Connection: The Cell Phone's Impact on Society*, San Francisco: Morgan Kaufman.

Ling, R. and Horst, H. A. 2011. 'Mobile communication in the global south,' *New Media & Society*, 13, 363–374.

Lyons, G. and Urry, J. 2005. 'Travel time use in the information age,' *Transportation Research Part A*, 39, 257–276.

Matsuda, M. 2005. 'Mobile Communication and Selective Sociality' in: Ito, M., Okabe, D. and Matsuda, M. (eds) *Personal, Portable, Pedestrian: Mobile Phones in Japanese Life*, Cambridge: The MIT Press.

Meyrowitz, J. 2005. 'The Rise of Glocality: New Senses of Place and Identity in the Global Village' in: Nyíri, K. (ed.) *A Sense of Place: The Global and the Local in Mobile Communication*, Vienna: Passagen Verlag.

Mitchell, W. 1995. *City of Bits: Space, Place and the Infobahn*, Cambridge/London: The MIT Press.

Moores, S. 2004. 'The Doubling of Place: Electronic Media, Time–Space Arrangements and Social Relationships' in: Couldry, B. and Mccarthy, A. (eds) *Media/Space: Place, Scale and Culture in a Media Age*, London: Routledge Comedia Series.

Morgan, K. 2001. 'The exaggerated death of geography: Localised learning, innovation and uneven development,' The Future of Innovation Studies Conference, September, 2001, The Eindhoven Centre for Innovation Studies, Eindhoven University of Technology, 20.

Negroponte, N. 1995. *Being Digital*, New York: Vintage Books.

Proboscis 2002–2004. *Urban Tapestries*, available online at http://research.urbantapestries.net (accessed 8 April 2012).

Rheingold, H. 2002. *Smart Mobs: The Next Social Revolution*, Cambridge, MA: Perseus Publishing.

Sassen, S. 2001. *The Global City*, New York, London, Tokyo, Princeton, NJ: Princeton University Press.

Sheller, M. and Urry, J. 2006. 'The new mobilities paradigm,' *Environment and Planning A*, 38, 207–226.

Shklovski, I., Vertesi, J., Troshynski, E. and Dourish, P. 2009. 'The commodification of location: Dynamics of power in location-based systems,' *Proceedings of the 11th International Conference on Ubiquitous Computing*, Orlando, Florida, USA: ACM.

Silverstone, R. and Sujon, Z. 2005. 'Urban tapestries: Experimental ethnography, technological identities and place,' available online at www.lse.ac.uk/collections/media@lse/pdf/EWP7.pdf (accessed 2 January 2010).

Townsend, A. 2004. 'Digitally mediated urban space: New lessons for design,' *Praxis*, 6, 100.

Tuters, M. and Varnelis, K. 2006. 'Beyond locative media: Giving shape to the Internet of things,' *Leonardo*, 39, 357–363.

Wellman, B. 2001. 'Physical place and cyberplace: The rise of personalized networking,' *International Journal of Urban and Regional Research*, 25, 227.

13

Ethics and Responsibilities

Malene Freudendal-Pedersen

> We are ethical beings, not in the sense that we necessarily always behave ethically, but that as we grow up we come to evaluate behavior according to some ideas of what is good or acceptable.
>
> *(Sayer 2011: 143)*

The willingness to address and accept these ethics, and the subsequent responsibility called for – not least in relation to sustainability and climate change – seems to be a general concern for many mobility researchers (Cresswell 2006; Canzler *et al.* 2008; Dennis and Urry 2009; Urry 2011; Cresswell and Merriman 2011). Much contemporary research on mobilities, in varying degrees, takes sustainability and/or climate change as its starting point, background or vision for the future. The responses to these issues vary from the very dystopian to the very utopian narratives of what future mobilities might bring. Either way, there is a clear sense of an ethical foundation and a need to respond to these pressing issues within mobilities research.

As Sayer (2005) stated, we are all, one way or the other, ethical beings and this is an important starting point when writing about the ethics and responsibilities of mobility. Writing this piece has led me in a multitude of directions, energized by ideas and a belief in the importance of this issue and then paralyzed by the fact that it seems an impossible topic to cover in a respectful and precise way. When Sayer (2005) reminds us that we are all ethical beings, it is a project aimed at social scientists, challenging us to acknowledge our own ethics, as well as the ethics of the people inhabiting the world we analyze, try to understand and maybe also change. Thus, the centre of attention, or the paths I have chosen to follow in this chapter, must be focused on mobilities research on the mobilities of everyday life and city planning, since this is the centre point for my academic and personal, internal and external, discussions on ethics and responsibilities. This encloses discussions of normativity and morality, as well as visions and utopias. I start out by discussing how ethics is closely related to morality and normativity and, thus, responsibility, not the least in relation to mobile methods. In the following, I discuss what responsibility actually is and how it is linked to individualization and freedom. This brings me to the example of Bogotá, demonstrating the significance of acknowledging and working with the ethics of the mobilities of everyday life.

And, finally, I discuss how we, as mobility researchers, have a responsibility for the future we are co-creating.

Ethics, morality and normativity

Within the mobilities research community I suppose it is safe to say that most people regard some mobilities to be better than others; for example: sustainable mobility is better than unsustainable mobilities. The differences appear in relation to what should be sacrificed; for instance, which freedoms everybody should be entitled to. This illuminates our personal ideas of right or wrong, our moral standards on how the world 'should' be, or, in other words, our own ethically based normativity. As Sayer writes:

> Social scientists are taught to adopt and prioritize the positive point of view and, unless they also read philosophy, to suppress normative reasoning. The gradual separation of positive and normative thought that has occurred over the last 200 years in social science has involved not only an attempted (though incomplete) expulsion of values from science, but an expulsion of science or reason from values, so that values appear to be mere primitive, a-rational subjective beliefs, lying beyond the scope of reason.
>
> *Sayer (2005: 5–6)*

Normativity is not a barrier for mobility researchers' knowledge production. However, it needs to be accompanied by respect for, and understanding of, others' social realities, wishes and preferences. This respect and open-mindedness is only attained by a clear and conscious approach to one's own ethics and one's own scientific ontology. Being conscious about normativity has significant impact on empirical work, and believing that one, through the empirical, can access an objective social reality, independent of the researcher, is according to Kvale (1996/1997)[1] evidence of a "naive empiricism."

The empirical plays a significant role within mobilities research, calling for development within traditional methodological approaches. Thus, mobile methods developed in the wake of the evolving mobilities paradigm are described by Büscher and Urry as giving an opportunity to develop new critical engagements with the future:

> the mobilities paradigm, particularly through its immersive and at the same time analytical momentum, enables researchers to critically engage with the people and the matters they study in novel and highly effective ways, and to orient critically towards the future, not only the past.
>
> *Büscher and Urry (2009: 111)*

Thus, by trying out new methods, and combining them with already familiar ones, new understandings and ideas concerning future developments evolve. Mobilities research is transdisciplinary, and when at its best it bridges disciplines in a mode 2 science. Mode 2 science is context-sensitive and develops alongside that which it aims to understand and analyze. It is a break away from the traditional understanding of science as that which, from a distance, analyzes and evaluates society. A mode 2 science understands science and society as commingling and developing transgressive arenas (Nowotny *et al.* 2001; Kemp and Martens 2007). In the same way, mobile methods can be characterized as mode 2 methods. When mobile methods bridge different disciplines they disclose taken-for-granted knowledge about which methods to use. This offers new perspectives and understandings about how mobilities transform the world we live in – at all scales. At the same time, new ethical questions also emerge. Filming and taking photographs stimulates new discussions about privacy issues when moving around with respondents in public space or in private homes (see for example Haldrup and Larsen 2009; Spinney 2011). And research on emerging online communities (see for example Licoppe and Inada 2006; de Souza e Silva and Sutko 2009), or following business travelers' time use and virtual encounters while on the move[2] results in discussions about privacy in relation to virtual communication. Is following people online the same as reading their private mail and so forth? All of these issues force mobilities researchers to be clear and reflexive about a whole new series of questions concerning the ethics of research.

This refers back to discussions on ethics and responsibilities. Is there an epistemological difference between ethics and responsibility, or is it ontological? One can have underlying ethics without responding to it, bringing us back to the ancient conflict between action and attitude. How do we find a way to act upon our ethics or attitudes and, especially, how do we bridge the gap between these in relation to (more sustainable) mobility behavior? In line with Sayer (2005), I would argue that "lay ethical practices – are concrete and governed by practical reason as well as by rules; it is messy, concrete and practical rather than tidy and concise" (146). This often conflicts with the researcher's requirements to present mobility practices as tidy and concise in order to create resonance and understanding for a wider audience. So, based on the ethics of research practice this means there is a responsibility in remembering that mobility preferences, everyday life, politics and planning are messy, concrete and practical. Thus, the responsibility within mobility research is to be careful and reflexive in relation to the empirical analysis. When, for instance, mobility research is presented in a tidy and concise manner in order for it to convince colleges or future funding partners, it is a fine line between being true to the messy, concrete and practical while still trying to make it palatable for those still unsure why mobility research is essential in understanding modern lives.

Sayer (2005, 2011) called for reintroducing the ethics and morals of human beings as significant to social science and thus to "help social science do justice to this relation of concern, to lay normativity, and to the fact that we are sentient beings who can flourish and suffer" (2005: 7). If we are pure realists, and we only relate to the world from the visible and facts, we lose the moral compass and the values we wish to preserve or create (Lefebvre 1970/2003; Pinder 2005; Sayer 2005, 2011). The discussion about the epistemological difference between ethics and responsibilities is, as stated, about the discrepancy between attitude and action; the action is where the responsibility is epistemological.

Individualized responsibility

Zeitler (2008: 233) handles the issue of responsibility by saying, "proper responses depend on our ability to respond, our 'response-ability.'" This 'response-ability' he proposes as a keyword in ethical theory as well as in mobility and planning. For Zeitler, ethics is ontology coming from our sense of right and wrong, our built-in normativity. Sayer (2005: 5) addresses this normativity, arguing for the responsibility of social science researchers to acknowledge and take seriously the lay normativity of both researchers and their fields of study: "[t]his project therefore requires us to take lay normativity seriously, particularly regarding the ethics of everyday life, and attend to its content and internal rationales." According to Sayer there is a tendency in social science to ignore or reject ethical and thus normative considerations about the world, from small situations to overarching situations of the world:

> Emotional responses to the inequalities and struggles of the social field and how people negotiate them are to be taken seriously both because they matter to people, and because they generally reveal something about their situation and welfare; indeed, if the latter were not true the former would not be either.
>
> *Sayer (2005: 37)*

Based on my own empirical research on everyday mobilities I would, in line with Zeitler, argue that most individuals have an inherent 'response-ability.' An ability to respond to issues of ethics permeates responses to everyday mobility practices. And yet, in relation to, for instance, sustainable mobility there seems to be a big gap between the ethic and the ability to respond to the pressing challenges of the future, such as changing mobility behavior. Why this discrepancy in attitude and action? The word in question is ability. The ability to respond to a common good in a world where individualization is a main driver seems from an everyday-life perspective to be increasingly challenged (Beck 1992; Kesselring 2008; Freudendal-Pedersen 2009). This should not be mistaken for egoism, nor lack of ethics, nor common responsibility. Instead a permeating paralysis hinders individuals' ability to respond to that which their ethics tells them needs a response. This is also a question of scale. The path dependency, very visible in relation to automobility, supports the reification of which elements of everyday life and society as a whole can be influenced (Graham and Marvin 2001; Urry 2007; Dennis and Urry 2009; Furness 2010).

Thus, the philosophical idea of response-ability does not make a clear epistemological distinction between ethics and responsibility. Individuals can feel responsible but without feeling they have an ability to respond. As Sayer (2005) pointed out, lay normativity and morality also entail good heartedness, benevolence, compassion, gratitude and so forth. But mobile everyday lives demand flexibility and reflexivity that is a challenge for individuals to handle, and at first sight seems as a barrier for creating the good life for themselves and their families. This is where reification sets in (Berger and Luckmann 1966), and also why structural stories (Freudendal-Pedersen 2009) become an important part of handling everyday life because of the feeling of scarce response-ability. The reification and the structural stories are ways of handling the ambivalence of modern mobile lives.

In contrast to Sayer (2005), Bauman (1995) argues that there is a need to re-establish the individual as a moral actor. This is a consequence of the common understanding that it is impossible to get one specific certain order of knowledge, and therefore morals, on social life. Thereby, it becomes difficult to maintain one, collective societal ethics with rules for correct behaviour. This means that the responsibility for action and choosing what is morally correct falls back on the individual. The question here is whether mobilities dominating modern lives really erode common morals and ethics. At the end of the old and the beginning of the new millennium, the prevailing idea was that mobilities meant that communities were eroding because of the ability to transgress time/space (Putnam 2000; Bauman 2001). Ten years later, it seems there is a different understanding, according to which communities might be different in different (virtual) spaces and different flexible forms, but are not eroding. Likewise, morality might be a common factor in other and different time/space configurations than local communities or within nation states. Individuals are still forced to relate to the moral issues emerging in everyday life, where most actions are conducted by routine (Giddens 1991; Bauman 1995), an everyday life which, to a higher degree, is influenced by knowledge, conflict, and actions at many scales. And, maybe, the moral questions are even more present in a mobile life – not necessarily handled, but nevertheless present.

Bauman (1995) addressed two kinds of morality. First, conformity-morality, where individuals are responsible according to expressed conventions or institutional rules (the structural stories on mobility are based on a conformity-morality) and, second, responsibility-morality, where individuals are responsible to someone or something based on a personal commitment (emerging online communities also create such personal commitments). Bauman (1995) claimed that the modern project of ethics seeks to ground moral choices in universally, rationally accessible principles and, by doing so, to relieve the individual of the ambivalence – the ambivalence of freedom. But this ambivalence is ever-present in mobile everyday lives, where the freedom is closely related to mobilities. The close relation between mobility and freedom, which may mean ethically staying put or dwelling without any ambition to move, needs to be a conscious choice with a formulated argumentation attached to it. The expectation on individuals in modern lives to be flexible and ready to change, to move, is as much a burden as freedom (Urry 2007; Sheller 2008; Freudendal-Pedersen 2009).

Freedom, responsibility and communities

As praised and valued as freedom is, it also entails problems and in modern mobile lives a major problem is that it places responsibility solely on the individual, where it constitutes a paralyzing burden (Beck 1992), thus creating more insecurity, ambivalence and lack of action often mistaken for egoism by some social scientists. Indeed, freedom often becomes an un-freedom when it leaves the individual alone with the long-term consequences and responsibility of his or her own actions (Bauman 1988; Freudendal-Pedersen 2009).

Still, there is also the option to respond to these ambivalences when they also entail the possibility for social learning (Becker-Schmidt 1999). Becker-Schmidt (1999) described two ways of ambivalence-praxis: 'ambivalence-tolerance' and 'ambivalence-defend.' Some of the ambivalences individuals are able to learn to live with and navigate, while others are ignored or evaded. Social learning is about recognizing ambivalences and their causes. It is a way of handling the ambivalences, assuming that things can get better, not understood as contradictions that can be dissolved, but that the individual can handle ambivalences better when recognizing them (Becker-Schmidt 1999). The ability to respond is strengthened and supported by communities of social learning (Freudendal-Pedersen and Hartmann-Petersen 2006). This goes on in different forums but, in relation to mobility, critical mass would be the most pressing example and, in smaller terms, shared cars communities, walk-buses and other smaller communities of mobilities without the car as the main mode of transport would be relevant examples of these kinds of communities (see, for example, Furness 2010; Golub and Henderson 2011).

In this context, jointly with Lise Drewes Nielsen and Aslak Kjærulf, I am working on a project, Formula M, combining different methodological approaches in order to create forums for social learning (see Freudendal-Pedersen et al. 2010 on the methodological approach). Inspired by action research, we have been working on creating spaces for visions and utopias and thus established new communities for municipalities working towards creating more sustainable mobility behavior in their cities. Overall, the project seems to be successful in restoring communities' significance when moving toward sustainable mobility behavior. It seems we are helping planners to find ways to respond to the pressing issues of mobilities in cities. In order to have the ability to respond to ethics, individuals thus need to share the responsibilities for everyday mobilities.

147

The freedom of mobilities has transformed some local communities into modern-day utopias – often described with a longing for community as we knew it 40 years ago. Discussions about 'community' have a long tradition (Tönnies 1996; Bauman 2001), and, to a large extent, accuse mobility of being an important factor in the erosion of communities. In this line, in his call for a 'better' future, Putnam wished for more dwelling and less mobility:

> Let us act to ensure that by 2010 Americans will spend less time travelling and more time connecting with our neighbours than we do today, that we will live in more integrated and pedestrian-friendly areas, and that the design of our communities and the availability of public space will encourage more casual socializing with friends and neighbours.
>
> *Putnam (2000: 408)*

Traditionally, both freedom and community have been understood as a 'moral good,' but it seems that they are being transformed by mobilities, leaving an ambivalence confronting ethics and responsibilities. This transformation – the fragmentation of late-modern lives and the processes that make all, both individuals and artefacts, into objects of consumption – might be why Bauman's (2005) discussion on utopianism in his book *Liquid Life* treated utopias as weak signifiers. He claimed that modern life is more than ever about consuming, while individualization and its invertible ambivalence towards risks and responsibility, are put solely on the individual to handle. "Liquid life means constant self-scrutiny, self-critique and self-censure. Liquid life feeds on the self's dissatisfaction with itself" (Bauman 2005: 10–11). An understanding of modern life creating dissatisfaction leaves no room for common utopias but only paralysis, with no possibilities of social learning. This also, almost predictably, brings forward the claim that "the advent of liquid modern society spelled the demise of utopias centred on society and more generally of the idea of the 'good society'" (Bauman 2005: 11). Mobilities research has the opportunity, and maybe also a responsibility, to counter this understanding of modernity through its ability to understand how new types of communities, challenging ethics and local/global responsibilities, are also a part of mobile lives that can be transformed into positive future utopias.

Responsibilities in urban mobility planning

The 'good' society lives in a framework created by architects and city planners. Taking into account ethics and responsibility is a challenge that needs to be met where lives are being lived. One of the most interesting examples of a morally conscientious starting point in relation to mobilities is Bogotá, in Colombia. Throughout the 1980s and early 1990s Bogotá had serious problems with violence and drugs, and one of the highest murder and kidnapping rates in the world. As Ardila-Gómez describes:

> By 1993, Bogotá had become totally chaotic. The quality of life deteriorated, with few city services. One could say that the city mistreated its inhabitants, and the citizens reacted in kind. People often tossed their garbage on the street. Drivers careened their cars at pedestrians, actually speeding up as people attempted to cross the street. No one stopped for red lights.
>
> *(Ardila-Gómez in Berney 2008: 12)*

Bogotá was marked by armed conflict between government forces, guerrilla movements and paramilitary groups. Kidnapping, drugs and arms smuggling, and other criminal acts were (and still are) lucrative businesses and financed the violent acts on all fronts. The political system was corrupt, influencing the mood of disillusionment, anarchy and total disrespect for authority. The life of Bogotá's inhabitants was marked by an absence of state authority, violence and an unreliable economy, resulting in low confidence in the state, the public system and the common societal project (Berney 2008: 11; Coghlan 2004). On a city-planning level this meant chaotic urbanization and unmanaged urban planning, resulting in an extremely segregated city (Berney 2008; Coghlan 2004; Mahecha and Arestibal 2009). Around 70 percent of the population lived below the poverty line, in areas without electricity, sanitation or clean water (Berney 2008: 44), while approximately five percent were very rich and lived sheltered lives in gated communities.

The challenges of Bogotá were most prominently confronted by two mayors, guided by explicit ethics, namely those of Antanas Mockus (1995–1997 and 2001–2003) and Enrique Peñalosa (1998–2000). Their project became possible through Mayor Jaime Castro, who implemented greater transparency in politics and personal preferences as well as financial reforms and a modernized tax system, doubling the tax income in the years 1993–94 (Mahecha and Arestibal 2009; Berney 2008). Mockus was guided by a visionary and normative project to reintroduce coexistence and what he called *cultura ciudana* – a form of citizenship-culture about creating "a non-violent shared life among individuals . . . strangers . . . and diverse social groups" (Mockus 2002: 20). By using metaphors, symbols and humor Mockus created situations and campaigns with a strong visual and psychological impact in order to get people to reflect on their lives and dealings with others, and thereby alter coexistence. Many of these campaigns were related to behavior in traffic, teaching people to coexist instead of fight in their different modes of mobility. Instead of hiring traffic police, mimes were put in the streets showing people how to coexist. The mimes mingled with people in the street and 'showed' how to cross the street and show consideration towards other fellow pedestrians. They stopped busses and cars that were not respecting the stoplights in the crossways. By their way of dressing and behavior, the mimes stood out clearly and became a very visible example of how to behave and be tolerant to fellow road users. Mockus was quite successful with this project and this cleared the way for Peñalosa's focus on the physical design of mobility infrastructures. Peñalosa's ambition was to create a city with equal access to mobility, green areas and public spaces. He created a coherent cycle path network of about 300 km and improved conditions for pedestrians, created El TransMilenio – a rapid bus-transit system – and placed restrictions on driving in the city. He saw transport not as a technical, but a political issue. "Pavements, bicycle lanes, plazas, parks, promenades, waterfronts and public sport facilities show respect for human dignity and begin at least to compensate for the inequalities in other realms" (Peñalosa 2007: 311).

Allowing cars on sidewalks and bike paths was in Peñelosa's view an expression of disrespect for people who are not able, or did not want, to own a car. For him, physical planning was about recognizing the presence of others across cultural, social and economic conditions (Peñalosa 2007). To Mockus and Peñalosa, planning was a project to foster respect for human dignity and quality of life, and it was as much a technical and economic issue as it was about basic human needs and emotions. They responded to an ethical starting point that city planning creates the conditions of everyday coexistence, constituting the arena for encounters between people, public transportation, public spaces, public institutions and neighborhood partnerships. Efforts to transform society also need to take place where the meeting occurs, not only behind desks and on the lectern, and with attention to human morality and norms of behavior (Mockus 2002; Sayer 2005).

The systemic change required to create sustainable mobilities needs to be grounded in the ethics of everyday life. From here, taken-for-granted knowledge, reification and path dependency is reinforced and diffused into all spheres of society. In their narratives about future cities, much contemporary architecture and city planning is very attentive to sustainability as an important part of future plans. Often, narratives impossible to contradict are created, encompassing green and social spaces and introducing ideas of hedonistic sustainability (meaning no loss of opportunities or lack of enjoyment) (Jensen and Freudendal-Pedersen 2012). But, in order to 'sell' these ideas, mobilities are often only described in a frictionless and flexible flow, without any unintended consequences, resulting in a reproduction of mobilities' path dependency masked by positive green, and social visions of future cities based on a prediction and provided mindset. The consequence of this is that the high-mobility requirements entailed in the plans made for new city areas are not questioned. The speedy, frictionless neighborhood is presented as a sustainable community, with sustainable solutions for water and waste management but without restrictions on car traffic. The space-consuming, polluting, congestion and risk factors that all these highly mobile individuals bring along is happily ignored. The courage to regulate or question how sustainability and a high degree of private car mobility interact is most often absent in these new projects.

Looking briefly at Copenhagen's two newest development projects, Carlsberg and Nordhavn, the difficulties in regulating car driving are very obvious. Both developments are placed in the inner city and the overall plan for mobilities is that only necessary car driving in the residential areas is allowed. But nobody has the courage to define what 'necessary' is. The ethics and responsibility of this are difficult: who has the courage (or the moral superiority) to judge what is necessary? Maybe the climate issues and environmental effects from mobilities place mobilities researchers in a position where the empirical field makes it necessary to have this kind of courage.

Conclusion: is there the ability for researchers and academics to respond?

This necessity is formulated in Mike Davis's article, 'Who will build the ark?,' about climate change, pessimism and utopia. In this article he calls for researchers and academics not to fall into pessimism, but to take the responsibility upon them to find pathways to optimism. He writes,

> One of the most encouraging developments in that emergent intellectual space where researchers and activists discuss the impacts of global warming on development has been a new willingness to advocate the Necessary rather than the merely Practical.
>
> *(Davis 2010: 45)*

When Davis addresses the "Necessary" instead of the merely "Practical," he points out that researchers needs to take upon themselves the responsibility of not only being researchers, but also intellectuals who promote ideas of how to create a better and more sustainable future. This leads directly to the point of transdisciplinarity, which is about acknowledging one's own disciplinary limitations and the need for others both professionally as well as personally. Transdisciplinarity does not mean covering everything; to my knowledge no good research about everything has yet been done. It is instead about being aware of one's own strengths as well as limitations, and using this knowledge in collaboration with others.

Transdisciplinarity is also about mobile methods, and the responsibility here is also about returning to the field. Ways of doing this are demonstrated through evolving and very inspiring collaborations with artists who, through their often much more visual approach, have a completely different reach (Witzgall *et al.* 2012). Working with futures workshops is another option, where the creation and strengthening of future scenarios is in focus (Freudendal-Pedersen *et al.* 2010). These methods offer the possibility to involve, for example, politicians, planners and citizens in the process of creating new ideas or further evolving methods and assessment tools. Thus, interdisciplinarity is not only within research communities, but also in the field of practice, in the places where frames for possible everyday practice are formed and shaped.

It is not difficult to understand why the dystopian future scenario Davis addressed is so predominant today. In a neoliberal society, with a continuing growth strategy following familiar patterns, hindering our ability to respond because of an extremely strong path dependency, positive visions of future mobilities are hard to believe in. Bogotá, despite all its ongoing problems, demonstrates how discussion, dissemination and work with morality and democracy, in relation to mobilities and city planning, actually matter. The responsibility of mobilities is about creating new hope and vision for the future in order to give people something to respond to. The paralyzing tendencies of the risk society, making people feel they have no ability to respond or make a difference, needs to have an alternative vision. Harvey (2000: 154–156) asked the question, in the context of Margaret Thatcher's 'there is no alternative' argument for the free market: how can we have such lack of imagination that we believe there is no alternative?

Harvey continued in his book *Spaces of Hope* (2000) to discuss the need for a spatio-temporal utopianism, along with the responsibility that this entails. He invites us to think about and fight for concrete utopias, to create or find them in ourselves, maybe by looking inside ourselves and taking steps to strive for what we desire. The responsibility in utopias relates to the fact that the materialization of anything needs 'closure.' This 'closure' is a dialectical process entailing an either/or and cannot be a both/and. This is not easy when the consequences of closure (some mobilities are left out, some freedoms are prioritized) mean that the necessary is a moral choice to make, a choice which is guided by our ethics and our wish to respond to them. In responding to our ethics, in moving towards the necessary, utopias are essential, both to ourselves in our work but to those whose mobilities (lives) we wish to transform. As Harvey (2000: 189) beautifully puts it, "for many contemporary theorists (the concept of utopia) should remain a pure signifier of hope destined never to acquire a material referent. But the problem is that without a vision of utopia there is no way to define that port to which we might want to sail."

Through researching and disseminating ethics, morals and emotions and their interconnectedness with mobilities and materialities in everyday life, there is an important part to play in showing the hope, the goodheartedness, the generosity, the need for communities and the hopeful futures also present in people's lives. This is only a small part of the puzzle, but it can be a contribution to sustainable mobilities of the future. A future that can only be understood and changed through an assemblage, through the communities.

Notes

1 This statement is added in Kvale's Danish version of the book from 1997, together with some other quite critical statements.

2 To my knowledge no research on this has been done yet, but the issues were discussed in a workshop on business mobilities in Lancaster in 2011, facilitated by James Faulconbridge and John Urry.

References

Bauman, Z. (1988) *Freedom* (Milton Keynes: Open University Press).
Bauman, Z. (1995) *Life in Fragments – Essays in Postmodern Morality* (Oxford: Blackwell).
Bauman, Z. (2001) *Community: Seeking Safety in an Insecure World* (Cambridge: Polity Press).
Bauman, Z. (2005) *Liquid Life* (Cambridge: Polity Press).
Beck, U. (1992) *Risk Society: Towards a New Modernity* (London: Sage).
Becker-Schmidt, R. (1999) In Illeris, K. (ed.) 'Widersprüchliche Realität und ambivalenz: Arbeitser-fahrungen von Frauen in Fabrik und Famille' ('Contradiction in reality and ambivelance: Work experiences of women in factory and family') *Læring – aktuellæringsteori I spændingsfeltetmellem Piaget, Freud og Marx* [*Learning – Current Theory of Learning in the Tension Field between Piaget, Freud and Marx*] (Roskilde: Roskilde University Press).
Berger, P. L. and Luckmann, T. (1966) *The Social Construction of Reality: A Treatise in the Sociology of Knowledge* (Harmondsworth: Penguin).
Berney, R. E. (2008) 'The pedagogical city – How Bogatá, Colombia, is reshaping the role of public space.' PhD dissertation, University of California.
Büscher, M. and Urry, J. (2009) 'Mobile methods and the empirical' *European Journal of Social Theory* 12(1): 99–116.
Canzler, W., Kaufman, V. and Kesselring, S. (2008) *Tracing Mobilities – Towards a Cosmopolitan Perspective* (Aldershot: Ashgate).
Coghlan, N. (2004) *The Saddest Country – On Assignment in Colombia* (Montreal: McGill-Queens University Press).
Cresswell, T. (2006) *On The Move – Mobility in the Modern Western World* (London: Routledge).
Cresswell, T. and Merriman, P. (eds) (2011) *Geographies of Mobilities: Pratices, Spaces, Subjects* (Farnham: Ashgate).
Davis, M. (2010) 'Who will build the ark?' *New Left Review* 61: 29–46.
Dennis, K. and Urry, J. (2009) *After the Car* (Cambridge: Polity).
de Souza e Silva, A. and Sutko, D. M. (eds) (2009) *Digital Cityscapes – Merging Digital and Urban Playspaces* (New York: Peter Lang).
Freudendal-Pedersen, M. and Hartmann-Petersen, K. (2006) 'Fællesskabersomudgangspunkt? – Refleksivmobilitetog Human Security imobilitetsforskningen' [Community as point of departure? Reflexive mobility and Human Security within mobility research) *Nordisk SamhällsgeografiskTidsskrift* 41(42): 175–195.
Freudendal-Pedersen, M. (2009) *Mobility in Daily Life – Between Freedom and Unfreedom* (Farnham: Ashgate).
Freudendal-Pedersen, M., et al. (2010) 'Mixing Methods in the Search for Mobile Complexity' in Fincham, B., McGuinness, M. and Murray, L. (eds) *Mobile Methodologies* (Palgrave: Macmillian).
Furness, Z. (2010) *One Less Car: Bicycling and the Politics of Automobility* (Philadelphia: Temple University Press).
Giddens, A. (1991) *Modernity and Self-Identity* (Cambridge: Polity Press).
Golub, A. and Henderson, J. (2011) 'The Greening of Mobility in San Francisco' in Slavin, M. (ed) *Sustainability in America's Cities – Creating the Green Metropolis* (Washington DC: Island Press).
Graham, S. and Marvin, S. (2001) *Splintering Urbanism: Networked Infrastructures, Technological Mobilities and the Urban Condition* (London: Routledge).
Haldrup, M. and Larsen, J. (2009) *Tourism, Performance and the Everyday – Consuming the Orient* (London: Routledge).
Harvey, D. (2000) *Spaces of Hope* (Berkeley, LA: University of California Press).
Jensen, O. and Freudendal-Pedersen, M. (2012) 'Utopias of Mobilities' in Hviid Jacobsen, M. and Tester, K. (eds) *Utopia: Social Theory and the Future* (Farnham: Ashgate).
Kemp, R. and Martens, P. (2007) 'Sustainable development: How to manage something that is subjective and can never be achieved' *Sustainability, Science, Pratice & Policy* 3(2): 5–14.

Kesselring, S. (2008) 'The Mobile Risk Society' in Canzler, W., Kaufmann, V. and Kesselring, S. (eds) *Tracing Mobilities: Towards a Cosmopolitan Perspective* (Aldershot: Ashgate).

Kvale, S. (1996) *Interview – An Introduction to Qualitative Research Interviewing* (London: Sage).

Lefebvre, H. (1970/2003) *The Urban Revolution* (Minnesota: University of Minnesota Press).

Licoppe, C. and Inada, Y. (2006) 'Emergent uses of a multiplayer location–aware mobile game: the interactional consequences of mediated encounters' *Mobilities* 1(1): 39–61.

Mahecha, E. and Arestibal, N. (2009) 'Bogotá, Colombia' in Carmona, M., Burgess, R. and Badenhorst, M. S. (eds) *Planning Through Projects – Moving from Master Planning to Strategic Planning* (Amsterdam: Techne Press).

Mockus, A. (2002) 'Co-existence as harmonization of law, morality and culture' *Prospects* 32(1): 19–37.

Nowotny, H., Scott, P. and Gibbons, M. (2001) *Re-Thinking Science – Knowledge and the Public in an Age of Uncertainty* (Cambridge: Polity).

Peñalosa, E. (2007) 'Politics, Power, Cities' in Burdett, R. and Sudjic, D. (eds) *The Endless City* (London: Phaidon).

Pinder, D. (2005) *Visions of the City* (Edinburgh: Edinburgh University Press).

Putnam, R. D. (2000) *Bowling Alone: The Collapse and Revival of American Community* (New York: Simon & Schuster).

Sayer, A. (2005) *The Moral Significance of Class* (Cambridge: Cambridge University Press).

Sayer, A. (2011) *Why Things Matter to People – Social Science, Values and Ethical Life* (Cambridge: Cambridge University Press).

Sheller, M. (2008) 'Mobility, Freedom and Public Space' in Bergman, S. and Sager, T. (eds) *The Ethics of Mobility – Rethinking Place, Exclusion, Freedom and Environment* (Aldershot: Ashgate).

Spinney, J. (2011) 'A chance to catch a breath: using mobile video ethnography in cycling research' *Mobilities* 6(2): 161–182.

Tönnies, F. (1996) *Community and Society* (New Brunswick: Transaction Books).

Urry, J. (2007) *Mobilities* (Cambridge: Polity Press).

Urry, J. (2011) *Climate Change and Society* (Cambridge: Polity Press).

Witzgall, S., Vogl, G. and Kesselring, S. (eds) (2012) *New Mobilities Regimes: The Analytical Power of the Social Sciences and Arts* (Burlington VT: Ashgate).

Zeitler, U. (2008) 'The Ontology of Mobility, Morality and Transport Planning' in Bergman, S. and Sager, T. (eds) *The Ethics of Mobilities – Rethinking Place, Exclusion, Freedom and Environment* (Aldershot: Ashgate).

14

Times

Glenn Lyons

Time is a defining parameter of people's mobility. As individuals we must make time in order to travel and in turn we make choices about how such travel time is consumed in the enactment of travel. In this chapter, the meaning and consumption of travel time is explored. This is done in such a way that brings the field of transport studies and the more recent field of mobilities research together. The terms 'transport' and 'mobility' will be used interchangeably within the chapter with both referring to the physical movement of an individual between different spatial locations.

There has been a growing interest in recent years, within the fields of transport studies and mobilities research, in the study of how people spend their time when on the move. The significance to the shaping of transport and society of how we interpret travel time use and its value is underlined by the UK Government's announcement on 10 January 2012 of its decision to proceed with a £33 billion investment in high-speed rail (DfT, 2012). If this investment goes ahead it will undoubtedly reshape patterns of travel, economic activity and land use – in short it will play a part in reshaping UK society. "Travelling at speeds of up to 250mph, passengers will be able to commute from Birmingham to London in 49 minutes, reducing the journey time by almost half from one hour and 24 minutes" (BBC News, 2012). The Department for Transport's economic case for what is called High Speed 2 (HS2) (DfT, 2011a) sets out the estimated costs and benefits of this investment. The value of savings in travel time accounts for around half of the total monetary benefits. In essence, the economic case is strongly (though not exclusively) founded upon an apparent *assumption* that travel time is wasted, and by making journeys quicker such unproductive time is recovered and put to productive use elsewhere, which has economic and hence monetary value. From the first high-speed train launched in Japan in 1964 (Givoni, 2006), high-speed rail is now in operation around the world "providing high-speed services to passengers willing to pay for shorter travel time" (Campos and de Rus, 2009: 19).

This chapter explains how travel time has traditionally been interpreted in transport studies and in particular in the economic appraisal of transport investment. It then presents new, richer perspectives on travel time use that emanate from the paradigm of mobilities research. It goes on to explore how such perspectives may challenge the orthodox interpretations that continue to endure. The chapter concludes by underlining the important part travel time plays in society and why it is deserving of continued research efforts on the part of both the mobilities domain of social science and the travel behaviour and economics expertise within transport studies.

Orthodox interpretation of travel time in transport studies

Within transport studies, the mobility of individuals – the trips they make – has principally been taken to be a derived demand. Mobility is derived from people's need or desire to participate in activities at alternative locations. In this context, mobility represents a disutility for the individual. It is the 'cost' incurred in order to realise the positive utility from the destination activities. There is, for motorised trips at least, a monetary cost to the trip being made. There is also a time cost – time spent travelling prevents that time being available for other (better) uses. It follows that if travel time can be saved (i.e. if journeys can be made quicker) then it can be reinvested. In essence it is taken that time is a scarce resource and that time spent travelling represents an opportunity cost. Since the 1960s transport economists worldwide have sought to attribute value to the saving of travel time (Beesley, 1965; Oort, 1969; Cherlow, 1981; Mackie et al., 2003). As Mackie et al. note, "[h]undreds, if not thousands, of studies have been undertaken from which behavioural values of time can be deduced" (Mackie et al., 2001: 91–92).

Our interpretation of this time cost has been fundamental to the shaping of transport and society. Politicians' decisions about major transport investment schemes are informed by economic appraisals of such schemes – in short, an analysis of the monetised costs and benefits. A scheme having a benefit to cost ratio well in excess of 1 is typically a prerequisite for investment to be made. "Travel time savings are the single most important component in the measured transport benefits/disbenefits of most schemes and policies. Hence the methods of valuing them critically affect the measurement of the economic impacts of schemes" (SACTRA, 1999: 183). I focus below on the case of the UK, but economic appraisal of transport schemes worldwide has time and its saving as a key consideration (Grant-Muller et al., 2001).

How then are travel time savings interpreted in (UK) economic appraisal (Mackie et al., 2003)? Assumptions are first made about the ownership of time. If an individual is travelling during the course of work then it is assumed that their employer owns their time. If they are travelling outside the course of work (including commuting) then the individual owns their time. For this non-work travel a 'willingness to pay' approach is employed to value savings in travel time. Stated preference experiments are used to present individuals with different travel scenarios involving different travel times and monetary costs, and individuals are asked to choose their preferred scenarios within different pairs (e.g. Calfee and Winston, 1998). In essence, by being confronted by a cheaper, slower journey and a more expensive, quicker journey the individual's choice-making begins to indicate how much they value saving time. There are resulting established national values of unit time saving for non-work travel that are used in economic appraisal.

For travel during the course of work, what is known as the *wage rate approach* is adopted to establish values of time. "Time spent travelling during the working day is a cost to the employer's business. It is assumed that savings in travel time convert non-productive time to productive use and that, in a free labour market, the value of an individual's working time to the economy is reflected in the wage rate paid" (DfT, 2011b: 2). Again there are established national values of travel time, which are calculated per mode on the basis of the average wage of travellers on that mode. For example, the value of one hour of travel time for someone travelling by rail during the course of work is currently assumed to be £37 (at 2002 prices). This compares to a value of £5 for commuting (by any mode).

Transport modelling is undertaken for a proposed scheme which aims to determine how the scheme will affect overall travel – the destinations people travel to, the modes and routes they use and the time they take. Appraisal of a transport scheme examines such effects over a sixty-year period from scheme implementation. Assumptions are involved here as well about travel time in terms of how it affects trip choices. Such modelling is used to calculate, for the transport system as a whole under consideration, how the travel time across all trips and over the sixty-year period is affected by the scheme. By using the monetary values mentioned above, savings in travel time attributable to the scheme introduction are then calculable.

For nearly half a century (Mackie *et al.*, 2003) the above approach has informed the decisions that have shaped our transport system with investment made on the basis that speeding up travel has economic value – and this includes the recent decision by the UK Government to invest in high-speed rail. One can argue that this approach has been driven by a 'transport is here to serve' mentality on the part of our transport analysts and policymakers (Lyons, 2004). However, as the transport system changes, it influences our mobility and our patterns of activity and social engagement – thus, as we shape our transport system we are playing a part in shaping society.

An apparent challenge to the orthodoxy – positive utility of travel time

There is a reductionist and pragmatic logic to the approach above. However, what leaps out as an *apparent* fundamental flaw in the logic is the inference, if not explicit indication, that time spent in the course of travel is wasted. Most clearly for travel during the course of work, this seems to indicate that individuals do nothing of any value whilst travelling. Yet anyone who has travelled by train during the course of work will appreciate that people do things with that travel time. Does this mean that transport appraisal and in turn the decisions on transport investment made by our politicians are misguided? Are we inappropriately shaping transport and society? Such questions have been the stimulation for me wishing to examine what people do with their travel time and whether or not it is (perceived as) wasted (Lyons and Urry, 2005). This part of the chapter sets out what insights have emerged from ensuing research pursuits and those of other colleagues motivated to examine travel time use. After this, we will return to the question of whether or not the orthodoxy above is flawed. This will be done with a particular focus upon rail travel because this has a notable political salience in the UK at present, with a government announcement in January 2012 that it intends to go ahead with a £33 billion investment in developing high-speed rail.

An important opportunity to empirically examine travel time use has come in the form of the National Passengers Survey for British rail travel. The survey elicits feedback from some 50,000 passengers each year. In the autumn 2004 and autumn 2010 waves of the survey (each with usable sample sizes of around 20,000), myself and colleagues were given the opportunity to include questions on what people had done with their time on particular train journeys, how worthwhile they had considered their time to be, what artefacts they had carried and used on their journeys and to what extent they had planned their time use in advance.

The results are revealing (Lyons *et al.*, 2007; Lyons *et al.*, 2012). In terms of the activity people indicate they spend most of their time on for a given journey, three activities account for over 70 per cent of all responses: reading for leisure; window gazing/people watching;

and working/studying. This has remained stable over a six-year period. However, are people 'killing time' or deriving value from it? Only two per cent of passengers indicated in 2010 that they spent most of their time being bored; only 10 per cent spent *any* time being bored on the train. When asked whether time use on the train had been very worthwhile, of some use or wasted, 30 per cent of travellers overall in 2010 indicated 'very worthwhile', compared with 13 per cent who found it wasted. There is change over time here: for passengers collectively, rail travel time use appears to be *increasingly* worthwhile. Between 2004 and 2010 the proportion of travellers considering their time use very worthwhile grew by a quarter (30 per cent up from 24 per cent) and the proportion considering it wasted went down by nearly a third (13 per cent down from 19 per cent).

Information and communications technologies (ICTs) are an increasing feature of life on the move. Seventeen per cent of passengers spent some of their train journey checking emails in 2010, with 1 in 10 browsing the internet. One in five people are now listening to music/radio/podcasts during their journeys – twice the level in 2004. There has been a 60 per cent increase in the proportion of rail travellers with laptops. Two per cent in 2010 had an ebook/iPad. It seems no coincidence that travel time worth is increasing in the face of increasing prevalence of ICTs and their use.

What of planning in advance for how to use time on the train? Twenty-three per cent planned a little and eight per cent a lot in 2010. Nearly two-fifths of passengers indicate planning very little in advance because they always use their journey time in the same way. Those who planned a lot were three times as likely to find their time use very worthwhile as those who did not plan at all and twice as likely as those who planned very little.

This might suggest that there remains considerable scope over time, through people rethinking their travel time use and having, arguably, a greater diversity and flexibility of time use facilitated through ICTs, for the overall worth of travel time use to increase. The survey evidence also reveals that ownership of time is 'suspect' – over 1 in 10 commuters (and some five per cent of leisure travellers) are spending most of their (own) time working/studying. Nearly a quarter of outbound business travellers are spending most of their (employer's) time reading for leisure.

Such empirical evidence tells us what people are doing but is limited in being able to capture the more subtle meanings to people of travel time use. However, other qualitative research methods – interviews, focus groups and travel ethnography – have allowed this to be explored further (Jain and Lyons, 2008; Watts, 2008; Watts and Urry, 2008). Travel time, it emerges, can be conceived of as a gift. It can be a gift to others – a social capital investment – in the sense of the time we are prepared to give in order to be co-present. It is also a gift to oneself. It can constitute *transition time* – time to adjust between different life roles: for the opportunity to experience distance and to gear up to the destination's demands. Jain and Lyons (2008) refer to people's comments about 'time to wake up', 'mentally tuning up', 'preparing'; and conversely 'de-stressing time' and 'time to unwind'. It can also constitute *time out* – time to escape from the obligations in different life roles: an opportunity for 'back-stage' time to be oneself and to use that time selfishly or indulgently. This can include something Mokhtarian *et al.* (2001) refer to as anti-activity – for example resting or daydreaming, or the window-gazing referred to above. Jain and Lyons (2008) point to people's examples of seeing travel as the only time to be on their own, to chill out or do nothing, or of valuing it as quality time for concentrated thinking that is hard to find elsewhere. Ross points to the commute as becoming "a respite, a retreat" (Ross, 1995: 55). With the advent of mobile and now smart phones and mobile internet comes the notion of *connected time*; formerly unable to interact with others that are not co-present while travelling, individuals can now remain 'connected' while travelling. However, this apparent opportunity may also be experienced as a burden with the notion of *infected time* – the isolation and time out that travel can provide can now be invaded by communications from others or obligations to communicate with others through technology. Travel time use reminds us that there is a distinction between *clock time* and *experienced time*. Compared with clock time, experienced time can be *stretched* or *compressed*. Perhaps an ultimate compression is falling asleep – a sensation of instantaneous travel or teleportation. Travellers themselves exist in two forms – *packed* and *unpacked* – with the latter typically having a larger footprint but better lending itself to flexible and worthwhile time use.

Such insights very much underline that far from being a mere 'cost' to transcending space, travel time has meaning to individuals and it is constituted, shaped and interpreted in many different ways. On average (though one should always be wary of averages implying homogeneity) there has been a remarkable constancy in terms of the amount of travel in society. UK national travel survey data over a period of some 30 years has shown that it remains at about one hour per person per day (Metz, 2008). Indeed there is wider examination to suggest that this is a global phenomenon (Schafer and Victor, 2000). This suggests that there is something fundamental about a human capacity or indeed need to encapsulate a certain amount of travel within the pursuit of their social practices. Even if the utilitarian need for travel time could be reduced to zero by the ultimate transport scheme of teleportation, it seems unlikely that this would remove society's desire for movement. Indeed, in relation to the commute it appears that people's ideal commute time (on average) could be around 15–20 minutes, as opposed to zero (Mokhtarian and Salomon, 2001).

Is the orthodoxy flawed?

Can the evidence above – that travel time has positive meaning and value to (some) individuals – be reconciled with the orthodoxy of economic appraisal in transport policy?

Two points have been made to me in defence of the orthodoxy: (i) economic appraisal is concerned with the value of travel time *saved*, not the value of travel time; and (ii) economic appraisal is concerned with the aggregate or average situation.

The first point is coupled by an acknowledgement that while some time during a journey may indeed be productively used, it would logically be the case that any time not used productively would be that which would be saved if a journey were made quicker. This is depicted in Figure 14.1. If an individual (travelling during the course of work) productively uses 40 minutes of a 60-minute journey and a proposed transport scheme would reduce the journey time by 20 minutes, then it will be the unproductive 20 minutes that will be saved – converting wasted time to into some other (more) productive use.

Yet this argument seems no more valid than other ways of conceiving of travel time use in practice (also shown in Figure 14.1). What if an individual could be partially using time productively throughout the journey? What if unpacking and packing up at the start and end of the journey are classed as unproductive blocks of time with all other time in-between used productively? Any journey time reduction would then eat into this productive time. What if an individual used all the journey time productively throughout the journey but used some of the time for work-related purposes and some for personal purposes?

The second point above (appraisal is concerned not with individuals but with the average) implies that being able to cite examples of productive time use may not alter the prevailing aggregate picture. In relation to this, consider Figure 14.2, which depicts conceptually how all travel may be distributed in terms of the productivity of travel time. In the figure,

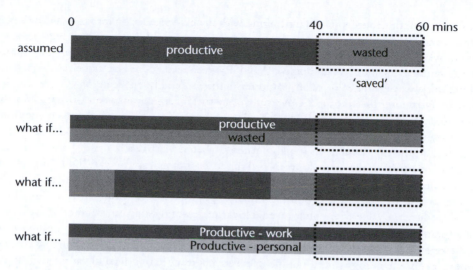

Figure 14.1   Different possibilities of saved travel time

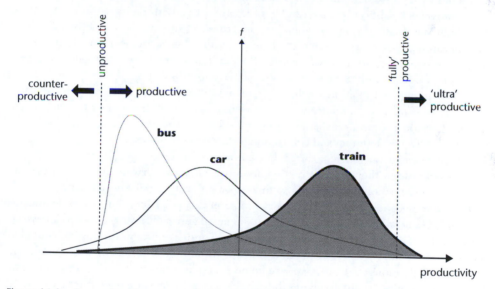

Figure 14.2   Conceptual frequency distributions of journeys by given modes according to productivity of travel time (Lyons and Urry, 2005: 270)

'counterproductive' refers to the prospect that a journey experience is so unsavoury that it adversely affects productivity of time use at the destination. Meanwhile 'ultra' productive is used to suggest that the travel environment is such that it lends itself to activity and achievement that are in excess of what would be achieved were the time to have been used outside of the journey. The extent (and nature) of 'productivity' will be affected by the mode of travel (a car driver cannot (easily or safely) type, write, read, sleep in the way a rail passenger can), the duration of the journey (e.g. too short and unpacking and packing up may not be practicable), the travel conditions (crowding and whether or not one has a seat; unexpected congestion that can cause distraction or stress), state of the traveller (energised or tired) and so on. Taking this conceptual diagram along with the evidence above for rail travel, it seems almost certainly the case that travel time use *does* affect the average or the aggregate and in such a way that, overall, travel time use has some positive value – it is not simply unproductive (even if it might be less productive than if it were saved and reinvested elsewhere). This being the case, the unit value of any saved travel time should be reduced.

It is intriguing that the UK Government, as part of its consultation on proposals for investment in high-speed rail, set out and addressed a number of frequently asked questions on its website, one of which was as follows: "I've heard that the business case is based on the idea that all the time passengers spend on train is wasted. Isn't that stupid?" I am, then, not alone in questioning the orthodoxy. In making its economic case for rail (DfT, 2011a), the Government was at pains to confront this question. In essence it conceded that no doubt (some) people were able to use (some of) their time productively while on the train, which would reduce the value of any time saved. However, it was reasoned that if productive use of time on the move was recognised and accounted for then it would also be necessary to account for two other consequences: mode shift and crowding. The reasoning was that where, as a result of high-speed rail, people were choosing rail instead of car for their journeys, there would be economic gains in terms of use of travel time – people in cars cannot be as productive as people on trains (it was asserted). In relation to crowding it was reasoned that in less-crowded conditions people can be more productive with their time on a train, and since high-speed rail investment would reduce crowding this would accrue benefits from the improved productivity of time used on the train. Taking these points together the Government, in its report, reached a conclusion that in fact accounting for productive use of travel time would actually *increase* the economic benefits of investing in high-speed rail.

For my own part I continue to have serious reservations here. The reasoning above is credible; however, it is not founded on a sufficient empirical understanding of what people do with their travel time and what meaning and value this time has in their lives and in the social and economic activities and contributions they make to society.

Until it is empirically tested, we do not know to what extent people are also deriving positive utility from their time in cars (either as passengers or drivers). Laurier's work has been a rare example of examining how time is used during car travel (Laurier and Philo, 1998; Laurier 2004). Granted, a car driver cannot sleep, watch films or annotate documents in the way that a rail passenger may be able to (as noted above). However, car driving where the cognitive demands of the driving task are low (familiar journeys such as the commute being a good example) can offer valuable time for thinking and reflection – for pondering over difficult decisions relating to work or home – for getting a sense of perspective. Indeed, mobile technologies are also allowing the driver to multi-task – notably with the option to talk (hands-free) on the phone to people outside of the travelling environment.

Crowding certainly introduces restrictions to the space an individual has on a train. However, mobile technologies and the way we communicate are increasing our potential to do things with our times even in sub-optimal travelling conditions – one could argue that the adverse effects of crowding are diminished.

Conclusion

The jury remains out on whether the orthodoxy is flawed, although major investment decisions continue to be made on the assumption that it is fit for purpose. What I have sought to expose in this chapter is that by simply looking at travel time through the traditional lens of transport studies we only take a partial view – the richness of meaning and consequences are potentially obscured and the parts we cannot see may be significant. Through the 'mobilities' lens, with a greater receptiveness to the importance of social meaning and deeper understandings of how and why time is consumed in the way that it is, the obscuration of our view is reduced. Whether or not a more complete view is illuminating remains to be seen.

Recognising the opportunities for travel time use to be worthwhile and for its 'worth' to be improved, the suggestion arises that the same effect as saving 'wasted' travel time by investing in transport schemes could be achieved by investing in ways to make travel time itself more worthwhile. Perhaps appraisal should be taking steps to value travel time *used* as well as or instead of valuing travel time *saved*. However, a dilemma may arise in moves to improve the experience of travel time; this could facilitate or even encourage greater amounts of travel as we engage in activities on the move – travel time being an end in itself as well as a means to an end. Therefore the challenge may be to improve journey experiences while, from a transport system and sustainability perspective, taking steps to 'lock in the benefits'. We could also see a growing degree of infection of travel time (as referred to earlier) such that 'time out' and 'time for' is compromised and the reprieve of the interspace of travel in people's busy lives may come under threat.

Travel time is a persistent feature of most people's everyday lives. It is an area that continues to need more attention from transport studies and mobilities researchers alike if we are to increase our understanding and identify and come to terms with the ramifications of such an understanding for how we treat travel time as a phenomenon that undoubtedly plays a significant part in the shaping and functioning of society.

References

BBC News (2012) *HS2: High-speed rail network gets go-ahead*. BBC News website. Available online at www.bbc.co.uk/news/uk-16478954 (accessed 9 September 2013).

Beesley, M. E. (1965) 'The value of time spent travelling: some new evidence', *Economica*, 32, 172–185.

Calfee, J. and Winston, C. (1998) 'The value of automobile travel time: implications for congestion policy', *Journal of Public Economics*, 69, 83–102.

Campos, J. and de Rus, G. (2009) 'Some stylized facts about high-speed rail: A review of HSR experiences around the world', *Transport Policy*, 16, 19–28.

Cherlow, J. T. (1981) 'Measuring values of travel time savings', *Journal of Consumer Research*, 7(4) – Special Issue on Consumption of Time, 360–371.

DfT (2011a) *Economic Case for HS2: The Y Network and London–West Midlands*, Department for Transport, February, London.

DfT (2011b) *Values of Time and Operating Costs. Transport Analysis Guidance (TAG) Unit 3.5.6*, Department for Transport, April, London.

DfT (2012) *High Speed Rail: Investing in Britain's Future – The Government's Decisions*, Department for Transport, January, London. Available online at www.gov.uk/government/uploads/system/uploads/attachment-data/File/14597/hs2-government-decisions.pdf (accessed 9 September 2013).

Givoni, M. (2006) 'Development and impact of the modern high-speed train: A review', *Transport Reviews*, 26(5), 593–611.

Grant-Muller, S. M., MacKie, P., Nellthorp, J. and Pearman, A. (2001) 'Economic appraisal of European transport projects: The state-of-the art revisited', *Transport Reviews*, 21(2), 237–261.

Jain, J. and Lyons, G. (2008) 'The gift of travel time', *Journal of Transport Geography*, 16, 81–89.

Laurier, E. (2004) 'Doing office work on the motorway', *Theory, Culture & Society*, 21(4/5), 261–277.

Laurier, E. and Philo, C. (1998) *Meet You at Junction 17: A Socio-technical and Spatial Study of the Mobile Office*, Dept. of Geography, University of Glasgow: Glasgow; ESRC: Swindon.

Lyons, G. (2004) 'Transport and society', *Transport Reviews*, 24(4), 485–509.

Lyons, G. and Urry, J. (2005) 'Travel time use in the information age', *Transportation Research*, 39(A), 257–276.

Lyons, G., Jain, J. and Holley, D. (2007) 'The use of travel time by rail passengers in Great Britain', *Transportation Research*, 41(A), 107–120.

Lyons, G., Jain, J., Susilo, Y. and Atkins, S. (2012) 'Comparing rail passengers' travel time use in Great Britain between 2004 and 2010', *Mobilities*.

Mackie, P., Jara-Dias, S. and Fowkes, A. S. (2001) 'The value of travel time savings in evaluation', *Transportation Research Part E*, 37, 91–106.

Mackie, P. J., Wardman, M., Fowkes, A. S., Whelan, G., Nellthorp, J. and Bates, J. (2003) *Value of Travel Time Savings in the UK*, Report to the Department for Transport, January, London.

Metz, D. (2008) 'The myth of travel times saving', *Transport Reviews*, 28(30), 321–336.

Mokhtarian, P. L. and Salomon, I. (2001) 'How derived is the demand for travel? Some conceptual and measurement considerations', *Transportation Research A*, 35, 695–719.

Mokhtarian, P. L., Salomon, I. and Redmond, L. S. (2001) 'Understanding the demand for travel: It's not purely "derived"', *Innovation* 14, 355–380.

Oort, C. J. (1969) 'The evaluation of travelling time', *Journal of Transport Economics and Policy*, 3, 279–286.

Ross, K. (1995) *Fast Cars, Clean Bodies: Decolonization and the Reordering of French Culture*, Cambridge, MA: MIT Press.

SACTRA (1999) *Transport and the Economy*, The Standing Advisory Committee on Trunk Road Assessment, October, TSO, London.

Schafer, A. and Victor, D. G. (2000) 'The future mobility of world population', *Transportation Research A*, 34, 171–205.

Watts, L. (2008) 'The art and craft of train travel', *Journal of Social and Cultural Geography*, 9(6), 711–726.

Watts, L. and Urry, J. (2008) 'Moving methods, travelling times', *Environment and Planning D: Society and Space*, 26(5) 860–874.

15

Rhythm and Arrhythmia

Tim Edensor

In this chapter, I explore the relationship of rhythm to mobility. Rhythm provides a valuable focus in exploring the multiple temporalities of places and forms of mobility, the processes that flow through and reproduce and reconstitute place, the regulation and synchronisation of mobilities, the ways in which mobilities may be sensually experienced, as well as the contestations and multiple mobilities that interweave in and through place.

Henri Lefebvre claims that '[E]verywhere where there is interaction between a place, a time, and an expenditure of energy, there is *rhythm*' (2004: 15), thus contributing to refuting reified notions of place as static or contained within a bordered spatial envelope, and highlighting how places possess no essence but are ceaselessly (re)constituted out of the processes which flow to, through and across them. Yet though dynamic rhythms foreground the fluidity of place, they also provide certain consistencies, a 'polyrhythmic ensemble' (Crang, 2001) of processes that continuously reproduce place, including the rhythmic mobile flows which generate ephemeral, contingent and relatively stable arrangements of people, energy and matter. Accordingly, one way of understanding place is to distinguish the particular ensemble of rhythms of varying regularity, the multiple '*bundles, bouquets, garlands* of rhythms' (Lefebvre, 2004: 20), whether 'slow or fast, syncopated or continuous, interfering or distinct' (ibid.: 69), that produce spatial and temporal fluidity but also the 'repetitions and regularities that become the tracks to negotiate urban life' (Amin and Thrift, 2002: 17).

These rhythmic regularities are produced by repeated individual encounters and movements in familiar space, reiterated temporal patterns of engagement that, crucially, converge with those of others to constitute what David Seamon (1980) refers to as 'place ballets': the habitual manoeuvres that people make in and around place as part of their daily routines. Individuals thus repeatedly synchronise their consumption practices, work habits and leisure pursuits, (re)making regular paths and points of spatial and temporal intersection which routinise action and constitute the patterns through which stasis and mobility are organised at various spatial and temporal levels (for instance daily, weekly and annually).

The mobile rhythms of place

At a daily level, mobile rhythms provide a backdrop to everyday life as mundane practices are reproduced and improvised, (re)producing 'a stable but also eventual everyday temporality' replete with 'different durations with concomitant durabilities' (Simpson, 2008: 810). One way to grasp mobile rhythms is to consider the daily walking practices of urbanites: the timetabled journeys of throngs of children walking along routes that converge on schools, crossing roads as lollipop men and women arrest the flow of vehicles, often themselves conveying children to school, intersect with the route marches of early shoppers (Kärrholm, 2009) and strolling workers en route to places of employment. These rhythmic walking routines, characterised by particular duration, route, tempo and pace, may also traverse the early morning amblings of the unemployed or flaneurs of various kinds. Contrast these mobile morning rhythms of walking with those of the evening, as shoppers and commuters have already drifted back home, and hedonistic crowds of evening clubbers, drinkers and cinema-goers animate the streets of the city with purposive and more exuberant styles of walking. These rhythms contrast, in turn, with those that occur throughout the afternoon, along with the slow wanderings of the homeless (Hall, 2010) and scheduled guided tourist excursions. And these walking rhythms co-exist and intersect with a host of other mobile rhythms: the regular timetabled bus, train and tram travel, the pulse of cyclists, cars and motorcycles, and the non-human pulse of electricity, water, gas and telephony. These multiple mobile rhythms of place further supplement seasonal, climatic and tidal rhythms (Jones, 2010), and rhythms of plant growth, bird nesting and river flow. Since places are always becoming, walking humans are one rhythmic constituent in a seething space pulsing with intersecting trajectories and temporalities.

The walking rhythms of place typically crisscross with other rhythmic mobilities of work and play at squares, junctions, bus and railway stations, supermarkets, post offices and a host of smaller spaces, and they are conditioned by institutional and normative procedures that inhere in postal deliveries (Labelle, 2008: 192) and traffic control, shop and pub opening hours, and work schedules. These successively enacted practices become sedimented in bodies, and an unreflexive practical and sensual apprehension of place emerges as individuals become habituated to scenes, textures, smells, sounds and a host of affordances, stopping points, bodily manoeuvres and social interactions.

In cities and other sites of multiple pathways and convergence, the systemic management and production of synchronic mobilities is necessary. Thus schedules and timetables, traffic systems involving the organisation of flow through traffic lights and filter lanes, and procedures for channelling and policing pedestrian movement and public transport systems combine with other rhythmically ordered flows of electricity, sewage, water, money, information and commodities. And because there are sites at which the coordination of traffic necessitates the stopping of vehicular movement, other actors take advantage of the regularities of this predictable rhythmic passage: itinerant peddlers and beggars weave through stationary traffic on roads in large Indian cities, seeking out business and donations, and advertising companies ensure that large advertising hoardings are situated on roadsides adjacent to sites where vehicles pause (Cronin, 2006). Thus a series of different-paced and orchestrated mobile rhythms produces a collectively constituted choreography that gives temporal shape to place.

The effort to maintain the smooth running of these mobile rhythms requires the performance of further rhythmic procedures – without repair and maintenance, technical infrastructures would wear out and rapidly lead to arrhythmia (Graham and Thrift, 2008; Edensor, 2011a). Yet systems inevitably do break down, or the sheer number of vehicles may culminate in traffic jams, and, subsequently, systems may need to be redesigned or overhauled to facilitate the advent of smoother rhythms. For instance, the lack of foresight among road designers that British motorways would become congested due to the explosive increase in car ownership has led to widening schemes, the building of supplementary roads and more intensive programmes of instantiating new and more variegated rhythms.

Certain sites and interconnected spaces are venues for particular kinds of mobile rhythms. For instance, a complicated array of schedules and timetables constitutes contemporary package tours, organised to reinforce rhythmic regularity and reduce the potential for arrhythmic experience. Integrated systems involving a variety of facilitators and technologies arrange the rhythmic flow of bodies from airport to hotel to guided tour, seeking to minimise external intrusions and cultivate relaxing atmospheres, particularly in the space of the 'other', where life may move to a different beat. Timetabled activities, selective routes and sights, and the reiteration of potted narratives strain toward rhythmic repetition and predictability, instantiating an ersatz homely, daily routine. There are, of course, other kinds of mobile rhythms in tourism, for instance the British working-class holiday-makers who collectively synchronised their trips to seaside resorts such as Blackpool, Scarborough and Margate in the era of mass tourism, and the more contingent rhythms of independent travellers and backpackers who follow more individualised and specialised itineraries, though they are often no less rhythmically predictable in their daily eating, socialising and communicating practices.

Rhythm and a mobile sense of place

Although I have emphasised that mobile rhythms contribute to the dynamic and stable qualities of place in and over time, the repeated inscription of rhythmic practice and experience may also shape a more stretched out, mobile sense of place. Daily mobile practices such as commuting to work (Edensor, 2011b) can produce an extended sense of place, whether carried out via train or car, or by foot (Middleton, 2009). The various speeds, paces and periodicities of habitual journeys produce a linear, rhythmic apprehension of place shaped by the form of a road, railway or footpath. During these oft-repeated journeys, familiar features are persistently confronted, installing a sense of spatial belonging. The buildings, gardens and infrastructure bypassed, the street furniture, the parts of the journey where travel slows or speeds up, and the familiar stopping points where tickets, food and newspapers are purchased and travelling companions join the journey enfold spatial and social relations into the daily ritual (Edensor, 2003). In vehicular travel, familiar rhythmic experience is further underpinned by the pulse of the engine and the sonic effects of mobility, for instance the metronomic swish of regularly spaced telegraph poles as they are passed, as well as their contribution to the visual apprehension of recurrent visual fixtures. Such daily apprehension of routine features may provide a comforting rhythmic reliability and mobile homeliness, as with the commuters on Santiago's Metro system depicted by Jiron (2010), who enjoy recurrent passage through familiar tube stations and scenic views as part of a distinct embodied, material and sociable 'dwelling-in-motion' (Sheller and Urry, 2006).

This underappreciated rhythmic familiarity that allows a nuanced sense of place to emerge through mobility also fosters an awareness of change. The sudden road accident, newly painted house, unusual bird or animal, peculiar vehicle or passer-by stand out in relief to the usual. Moreover, change can also be witnessed over a more extended period: leaves turn colour as autumn approaches, a new housing estate next to the route emerges from waste land to completion. This rhythmic sense of belonging may therefore incorporate sensations of transience as well as 'prolonged or repeated movements, fixities, relations and dwellings' (Merriman, 2004: 146), refuting conceptions that 'places marked by an abundance of mobility become *placeless*' realms of detachment (Cresswell, 2006: 31),

The regular rhythms of mobility also facilitate automatic, unreflexive activities, where commuters are on 'auto-pilot, free and absorbed in the moment' (Ford and Brown, 2006: 159). Habitual modes of negotiating mobile space become sedimented in the body – procedures that usually require little or intermittent attention, a rhythmic consistency that opens up the potential for relaxation, productivity, creativity or play, as Lyons *et al.* (2007) reveal in their survey of rail passengers in which few respondents found travelling boring or a waste of time. This is particularly recognisable in how passengers surrender to the imposed rhythms of air travel, taking the opportunity to read, write, watch a movie, listen to music, eat, drink, chat or sleep, a series of activities that individuals negotiate and improvise within a rigid schedule, abandoning themselves to a different rhythm and temporal structuring.

Mobile embodiment, dressage, eurhythmy and arrhythmia

Bodily habituation to regular mobile rhythms highlights the concord between machinic and somatic rhythms, whereby the pulse of the engine produces a eurhythmic consistency, a comfortable, homely and relaxing setting within which the body is enfolded and lulled into a state of kinaesthetic and tactile relaxation. However, revealing the tensions between the enabling and constraining potential of rhythm management, such accommodation may also be conceived as produced by techniques and strategies to ensure that bodies accord with and conform to dominant rhythms, a process Lefebvre terms 'dressage'. The regulation of moving bodies includes strictures that organise arrival and departure from work at specific times, the Taylorism of managing workers' movement on production lines, as well as the obvious drills and marches imposed by disciplinary military procedures. Lefebvre discusses how the breaking-in of individuals by enmeshing the body within an assemblage of instructions, spaces, uniforms, architectures, classifications and mechanical apparatuses may (re)produce 'an automatism of repetitions' (2004: 40) that enlist docile bodies into required manoeuvres. Yet Evans and Franklin also conceive dressage as enabling in their investigation of actual equestrian dressage, in which riders train themselves and their horses with intensive discipline and dedication in order to perform a number of detailed, pre-arranged manoeuvres of movements that should appear effortless. Without a forbidding level of commitment, horse and rider would not be able to achieve eurhythmy, for bodies 'disciplined in the nuances of stride, comportment and whole-body movement perform their rhythmical harmony in such a way that the training disappears, subsumed in the kinaesthetic union characterised by synchrony and synthesis' (2010: 174).

In addition, though the training of bodies in mobility undoubtedly has an impact in inscribing the conventions of movement in and through space, in order to avoid reductive, causational understandings of the relationship between imposed and individual rhythms it is essential to return to Lefebvre's insistence that while there is no 'rhythm without repetition in time and space, without reprises, without returns, in short, without measure . . . there is no identical absolute repetition indefinitely . . . there is always something new and unforeseen that introduces itself into the repetitive' (2004: 6). More specifically, Lefebvre foregrounds bodily rhythms, with their 'respirations, pulses, circulations, assimilations' (2004: 5), arguing that the regulated 'rational' rhythms of industrial and bureaucratic life are constantly in contact with 'what is least rational in human being: the lived, the carnal, the body' (ibid.: 9). For instance, on a typical tourist coach excursion – a four-hour, 80-mile tour around the Ring of Kerry, in Southern Ireland – much of the journey is experienced through the rhythms induced by cushioned, gentle motion, productive of a relaxed, somnolent state as the vehicle smoothly glides over straight, well-surfaced roads, with regular pulses of acceleration and mild braking. At other times, however, rougher roads jar passengers out of a relaxed state, and travelling bodies become uncomfortable, feel hungry, desire physical exercise or need to stretch or urinate, adding to arrhythmic potentialities (Edensor and Holloway, 2008). Similarly, Emily Falconer (2011) discusses how Western female backpackers must deal with an array of frustrating embodied risks and emotions that threaten their quest for independence and adaptability, managing these arrhythmic and rhythmic social and somatic effects in order to attain the cultural capital and sense of achievement for which they aim.

In addition to somatic intrusions, mobile eurhythmia is threatened by the affordances and contingencies of travel – on roads, for instance, with the disruptions provided by roadworks, bad driving, uneven roads and sharp braking to avoid dangers. Traffic jams and accidents further produce arrhythmia, as bodies grow tense and stiff, marooned in vehicles. Robertson describes how she leaves her car, in which she had been an 'insulated observer', to change a tyre on the Westway in London (2007) and is hurled into a radically different rhythmic environment in which other vehicles move past her at speed. An evident rhythmic realignment caused by extensive mobility comes when long-distance travel produces jet-lag, in which the usual rhythms of sleep and eating are disrupted and we feel 'out of synch', and, subsequently, must adapt to different rhythms. Yet adaptation to arrhythmia and unfamiliar rhythms is integral to any consideration of rhythms. For instance, Delyser (2010) shows how pioneering female pilots responded to the suspension of regular rhythms of flight, to the perilous advent of arrhythmia, with improvisatory reactions that had been instilled by training and repetition.

Rebecca Solnit contends that, ideally, walking is 'a state in which the mind, the body, and the world are aligned, as though they were three characters finally in conversation together, three notes making a chord' (2001: 5). Yet this eurhythmy is an idealised aim and the reveries and desires that do emerge are interspersed by attentiveness to surroundings and one's own bodily effects. Accordingly, the walking body can rarely move seamlessly through space, for the aforementioned contingencies of the body and the qualities of space ensure that walking rhythms are continuously adapting to circumstances, changing over the walk's duration. At the start of a long walk, a sprightly gait may produce a pleasing and bouncy rhythm, allowing for an alert relationship to surroundings and a sense of well-being. However, towards the journey's end exhaustion and aching feet and legs cause the body to stop, rest and plod ahead to the end, and hunger, sore muscles and blisters may preoccupy the walker. Moreover, terrain forces the body to intermittently leap, climb and balance as the varied affordances of rocky ground, springy forest floor, marsh, heathery moorland, long grass, smooth pasture, tarmac and autumnal leafy carpets produce varied walking rhythms (Edensor, 2000b, 2010). Vergunst (2008) reveals this improvisational rhythmicity, drawing attention to the ways in which walkers continuously become attuned to changing gradients, surfaces and textures on Aberdeen's granite pavements.

Attempts to inculcate good mobile habits persist. Schivelbusch (1979) highlights how the unfamiliar rhythms of train travel initially disordered the senses, with the disorienting experience of speedier movement, and its effects on the apprehension of the outside world framed through the window. Such mobile experience gradually became unremarkable and banal. At other times, mobile systems of traffic flow require that pedestrian mobilities be reorganised to conform to the needs of vehicular travel. Richard Hornsey shows how British interwar traffic management policies were devised to encourage pedestrians to adapt to the quicker rhythms of the growing number of cars on London's roads, to 'recodify their practices as a disciplined set of habituated responses' (2010: 111). However, pedestrians tended to take short cuts, cross busy roads despite laws and advice, and adopt other improvisatory

practices, highlighting the ongoing tensions between the regulation of mobility and resistance to it, and between eurhythmy and arrhythmia.

Contesting mobile rhythms

These tensions and contrasts are further evident in the ways in which the rhythms of mobility are contested, according to varying 'norms, habits and conventions' about temporality
and questions about 'when, how often, how long, in what order and at what speed' (Adam,
1995: 66). While spaces, timings, materialities and mobilities are orchestrated to provide
'relatively smooth "corridors" for some' (Sheller and Urry, 2006: 213), for others, travelling
rhythms are far from smooth and there may be 'disconnection, social exclusion, and inaudi-
bility' (ibid.: 210). Consider, for instance, the poor rail commuters that pack trains to and
from Bombay, on which over 4,500 passengers may occupy travelling space reserved for
1,700 at peak times, to produce what has been termed a *Super-Dense Crush Load* of 14 to 16
standing passengers per square metre of floor. As a consequence, many are unable to purchase
a position inside, clinging on to the train's exterior, with resultant injuries and fatalities. And
homeless bodies may engage in 'perpetual movement' precisely because they have nowhere
to go (Kawash, 1998), rhythms that Tom Hall suggests are labelled 'unproductive' by city
managers and business. More dramatic are the conditions of immobility imposed on asylum
seekers (Conlon, 2010) and prisoners.

Contemporary processes of globalisation have prompted hyperbolic academic and everyday assumptions that we now live in a speeded-up world (Tomlinson, 2007). However, as
reference to the arrhythmias produced by flight delays, traffic jams and systems breakdown
testifies, much contemporary mobility 'involves speeding up, stopping, slowing down, hur-
rying and waiting' (Germann Molz, 2009: 272). The contrasts and contestations between fast
and slow mobile rhythms are becoming particularly evident in mobilities organised around
tourism, modalities around which 'certain values come to be associated with stillness, slowness or speed' (ibid.: 271). In contrast to the aforementioned organised rhythms of often rapid
transit in package tourism, other practices emphasise slower tourist mobilities, typically in
rural and non-Western destinations, where visitors may 'wind down'. In such realms, the
rhythms of the day are typically represented as slower – an urge for more deliberate rhythms
that reaches its zenith in the Slow Travel movement, which recommends that would-
be-tourists reside in rural cottages and country hotels and immerse themselves in the local
culture, avoiding the rush to 'must-see' attractions. Walking, cycling and canal cruising are
all championed in aiding this quest for a slower rhythm (Edensor, 2011c).

Some tourists seek a mixture of experiences, combining the fast rhythms of cities with the
slow pace of beach resorts and rural settings. Others search for a greater contrast from familiar rhythms through activities that foreground an enlivened embodied experience. Most
obviously, 'adventure' tourists seek sensory immersion in boiling torrents on white water
rafting voyages in New Zealand, toiling seas in sea kayaks off the West coast of Scotland,
rough terrain on mountain or quad bikes in the French Alps or Canada, and turbulent air
whilst hang gliding in California, experiencing rhythms of alterity.

Similarly, independent tourists may confront equally unfamiliar rhythms that may be
experienced as frighteningly disorientating or thrilling. For instance, a tourist walking down
a street in an urban Indian bazaar (Edensor, 2000a) must weave a path, negotiating obstacles
and maintaining an awareness of traffic because of the not-only-linear, cross-cutting mobilities of numerous forms of transport, people and animals that move alongside and across their
path at a variety of speeds. Further distracted by heterogeneous activities and sights that cause

the gaze to continuously shift, walking must be improvisational, guided by sensation, happenstance, intuition and whim, and cannot follow a regular rhythmic gait because of the variability of the surface underfoot and the cluttered fixtures that block progress along a seamless path. Such an example reveals how many forms of unregulated touring mobilities must confront a 'polyrhythmic ensemble of competing and overlapping rhythms' (Highmore, 2005: 322).

Indeed, the multiplicity of co-existing mobile rhythms of place, with their various pacings, speeds and tempos, extends far beyond tourism, and inheres in particular modes of mobility. Consider the different rhythms of car driving. There is the short but repetitive daily journey to work or taking children to school, the leisurely weekend 'tootle', the travelling salesperson's instrumental drive from A to B, and the more lengthy, improvisational road-trip holiday. And commuters who travel on the Paris Metro, the Tokyo bullet train or by car in Calcutta are enmeshed in distinctly different mobile rhythmic experiences. As Spinney (2010) has shown, cyclists may move through the city producing staccato, fluid or wildly variable rhythms, and Wunderlich compares 'purposive walking' at constant rhythmical and rapid pace with the more varied rhythm of spontaneous 'discursive walking', as well as with the 'conceptual', critical walking mobilised by situationists and psychogeographers (2007: 37–8). More strategically, in particular cities the *cittàslow* movement attempts to organise everyday life at a slower pace in order to achieve more communal, local forms of living, working, consuming, eating and moving (Pink, 2007).

Rhythmic multiplicity and contestation is increasingly exacerbated by growing flows of people, opening up the coinciding, competing and melding of a host of different rhythms, and again tourism is exemplary in highlighting this temporal clashing and harmonising. The playing-out of diverse tourist rhythms is expanding as Asian, African and South American tourists who perform and expect culturally specific temporal and rhythmic experience are increasingly participating in global adventures, and these may synchronise, collide and contrast at particular tourist sites, producing arrhythmia, asynchronicity and synchronicity. Accelerating globalisation promises to intensify these mobile rhythmic contestations.

Lefebvre's account of rhythmanalysis is richly suggestive rather than a substantive depiction of the multiple rhythms of place, body, nature and mobility. In this sense, studies of the rhythms and other temporalities of mobility are in their infancy at present. Future study could explore in greater detail these multiple and contesting mobile rhythms and the values and practices that surround them. It may also be profitable to assess the entangling of somatic, mechanical and spatial rhythms in terms of their production of eurhythmy and arrhythmia, and understand the productive and destructive effects of the various mobile rhythms that flow through and constitute place. Investigating mobile rhythms would further produce more convincing, less reified accounts of place temporality, and identify the enhanced, expansive sense of place that can accumulate through regular travelling practices. Finally, given that more ecocentric mobilities may emerge following the demise of the era of peak oil, it is likely that the virtues of slower mobile rhythms will come to be considered more seriously.

Bibliography

Adam, B. (1995) *Timewatch: The Social Analysis of Time*, Cambridge: Polity.
Amin, A. and Thrift, N. (2002) *Cities: Reimagining the Urban*, Cambridge: Polity.
Conlon, D. (2010) 'Fascinatin' rhythm(s): polyrhythmia and the syncopated echoes of the everyday', in T. Edensor (ed.) *Geographies of Rhythm: Nature, Place, Mobilities and Bodies*, Aldershot: Ashgate.

Crang, M. (2001) 'Rhythms of the city: temporalised space and motion', in J. May and N. Thrift (eds) *Timespace: Geographies of Temporality*, London: Routledge.

Cresswell, T. (2006) *On the Move: Mobility in the Modern Western World*, London: Routlege.

Cronin, A. (2006) 'Advertising and the metabolism of the city: urban space, commodity rhythms', in *Environment and Planning D: Society and Space* 24: 615–63.

Delyser, D. (2010) '"The engine sang an even song": rhythm and mobilities among early women aviators', in T. Edensor (ed.) *Geographies of Rhythm*, Aldershot: Ashgate.

Edensor, T. (2000a) 'Moving through the city', in D. Bell and A. Haddour (eds) *City Visions*, London: Prentice Hall.

Edensor, T. (2000b) 'Walking in the British countryside: reflexivity, embodied practices and ways to escape', in *Body and Society*, 6(3–4): 81–106.

Edensor, T. (2003) 'M6: Junction 19–16: defamiliarising the mundane roadscape', in *Space and Culture*, 6(2), 151–168.

Edensor, T. (2010) 'Walking in rhythms: place, regulation, style and the flow of experience', in *Visual Studies*, 25(1): 69–79.

Edensor, T. (2011a) 'Entangled agencies, material networks and repair in a building assemblage: The mutable stone of St Ann's Church, Manchester', in *Transactions of the Institute of British Geographers*, 36(2): 238–252.

Edensor, T. (2011b) 'The rhythms of commuting', in T. Cresswell and P. Merriman (eds) *Mobilities: Practices, Spaces, Subjects*, Aldershot: Ashgate.

Edensor, T. (2011c) 'The rhythms of tourism', in C. Minca and T. Oakes (eds) *Real Tourism: Practice, Care and Politics in Contemporary Travel Culture*, London: Routledge.

Edensor, T. and Holloway, J. (2008) 'Rhythmanalysing the coach tour: the Ring of Kerry, Ireland', in *Transactions of the Institute of British Geographers*, 33(4): 483–502.

Evans, R. and Franklin, A. (2010) 'Equine beats: unique rhythms (and floating harmony) of horses and their riders', in T. Edensor (ed.) *Geographies of Rhythm*, Aldershot: Ashgate.

Falconer, E. (2011) 'Risk, excitement and emotional conflict in women's travel narratives', in *Recreation and Society in Africa, Asia and Latin America*, 1(2): 65–89.

Ford, N. and Brown, D. (2006) *Surfing and Social Theory: Experience, Narrative and Experience of the Dream Glide*, London: Routledge.

Germann Molz, J. (2009) 'Representing pace in tourism mobilities: staycations, Slow Travel and *The Amazing Race*', in *Journal of Tourism and Cultural Change*, 7(4): 270–286.

Graham, S. and Thrift, N. (2008) 'Out of order: understanding repair and maintenance', in *Theory, Culture & Society*, 24(3): 1–25.

Hall, T. (2010) 'Urban outreach and the polyrhythmic city', in T. Edensor (ed.) *Geographies of Rhythm*, Aldershot: Ashgate.

Highmore, B. (2005) *Cityscapes: Cultural Readings in the Material and Symbolic City*, Basingstoke: Palgrave.

Hornsey, R. (2010) '"He Who Thinks, in Modern Traffic, is Lost": automation and the pedestrian rhythms of interwar London', in T. Edensor (ed.) *Geographies of Rhythm*, Aldershot: Ashgate.

Jiron, P. (2010) 'Repetition and difference: rhythms and mobile place-making in Santiago de Chile', in T. Edensor (ed.) *Geographies of Rhythm*, Aldershot: Ashgate.

Jones, O. (2010) '"The Breath of the Moon": the rhythmic and affective time-spaces of UK tides', in T. Edensor (ed.) *Geographies of Rhythm*, Aldershot: Ashgate.

Kärrholm, M. (2009) 'To the rhythm of shopping: on synchronisation in urban landscapes of consumption', in *Social and Cultural Geography*, 10(4): 421–440.

Kawash, S. (1998) 'The homeless body', in *Public Culture*, 10(2): 319–339.

Labelle, B. (2008) 'Pump up the bass: rhythm, cars and auditory scaffolding', in *Senses and Society*, 3(2): 187–204.

Lefebvre, H. (2004) *Rhythmanalysis: Space, Time and Everyday Life*, trans. Stuart Elden and Gerald Moore, London: Continuum.

Lyons, G., Jain, J. and Holley, D. (2007) 'The use of travel time by rail passengers in Great Britain', in *Transportation Research Part A*, 41: 107–120.

Merriman, P. (2004) 'Driving places: Marc Augé, non-places and the geographies of England's M1 motorway', in *Theory, Culture & Society*, 21(4/5): 145–167.

Middleton, J. (2009) '"Stepping in time": walking, time, and space in the city', in *Environment and Planning A*, 41: 1943–1961.

Pink, S. (2007) 'Sensing cittàslow: slow living and the constitution of the sensory city', in *Senses and Society*, 2(1): 59–78.

Robertson, S. (2007) 'Visions of urban mobility: the Westway, London, England', in *Cultural Geographies*, 14: 74–91.

Schivelbusch, W. (1979) *The Railway Journeys: Trains and Travel in the 19th Century*, Oxford: Blackwell.

Seamon, D. (1980) 'Body-subject, time-space routines, and place-ballets', in A. Buttimer and D. Seamon (eds) *The Human Experience of Space and Place*, London: Croom Helm.

Sheller, M. and Urry, J. (2006) 'The new mobilities paradigm', in *Evironment and Planning A*, 38: 207–226.

Simpson, P. (2008) 'Chronic everyday life: rhythmanalysing street performance', in *Social and Cultural Geography*, 9(7): 807–829.

Solnit, R. (2001) *Wanderlust: A History of Walking*, London: Verso.

Spinney, J. (2010) 'Improvising rhythms: re-reading urban time and space through everyday practices of cycling', in T. Edensor (ed.) *Geographies of Rhythm*, Aldershot: Ashgate.

Tomlinson, J. (2007) *The Culture of Speed: The Coming of Immediacy*, London: Sage.

Vergunst, J. (2008) 'Taking a trip and taking care in everyday life', in T. Ingold and J. Vergunst (eds) *Ways of Walking: Ethnography and Practice on Foot*, Aldershot: Ashgate.

Wunderlich, F. (2007) 'Walking and rhythmicity: sensing urban space', in *Journal of Urban Design*, 13(1): 31–44.

16

Enthusiasm

Allison Hui

> Nothing great was ever achieved without enthusiasm. The way of life is wonderful.
> It is by abandonment.
>
> *(Emerson, 1951: 227)*

While researchers attribute many characteristics to contemporary mobilities, enthusiasm is rarely among the list. Descriptors of speed, distance and temporality are familiar standards, while the possibilities of many other imaginative attributes remain unexplored. This chapter therefore examines enthusiasm as a key characteristic shaping the relationships, momentum, and possibilities of contemporary mobilities.

Enthusiasm has long been connected to understandings of mobilities. Plato described enthusiasm in terms of inspiration, comparing it to a magnetic stone that attracts iron rings and gives them the ability to likewise attract others (1953: 107–8). This image of attraction made an early connection between enthusiasm and ideas of "communicability, circulation and transmission" (Herd, 2007: 5). While these enthusiastic mobilities could be positive and inspiring, they also came to be feared. During the seventeenth and eighteenth centuries, the potential of enthusiasm to aid the circulation of unorthodox religious or philosophical ideas was deemed dangerous, and led people to associate enthusiasm with madness and mental illness (Heyd, 1995: 45). Enthusiasm, and its potentially damaging and uncontrollable mobilities of ideas, were medicalized and "counterposed to reason" (Herd, 2007: 5). Evaluations of enthusiasm's capacity to move, however, transformed over time, and the "tradition of enthusiasm" became an esteemed hallmark of Modern American literature (Herd, 2007: 22). The mobilities of enthusiasm, which were once feared and fought, later fostered cultural heritage to be prized and passed on.

As these examples make clear, enthusiasm is not just a subjective emotion. It is not merely one person's excitement or intense interest. Rather, the "rapturous intensity of feeling" and "passionate eagerness" of enthusiasm (OED, 1989) needs to be situated within relations – as an affect. Whereas emotions belong to subjects, affect "is not bound to particular individual bodies" (Bissell, 2010: 271). Instead, affects are located in-between objects and bodies as a "capacity to relate" (Adey, 2008: 439) or a capacity to act (Hynes, 2011: 66). Affect "depends on a sense of push in the world" that exists between things (Thrift, 2004: 64). It can also be seen to pull, as "relations that inspire the world" (Dewsbury *et al.*, 2002: 439). Therefore while emotions are understood to be subjective states where the body is an object of emotion, affects are pre-personal relations, existing in-between people and things as potentials (Hynes, 2011: 66). Seeing enthusiasm as an affect foregrounds "the motion of emotion" in relations (Thien, 2005: 451).

Exploring enthusiastic mobilities is therefore not about identifying people who move during emotional states of passion. It is about interrogating relationships where passion and inspiration are manifest in mobilities. As this chapter illustrates, enthusiasm inspires the body to be pushed and pulled through space. Enthusiastic relationships between people, things, and ideas shift the capacity and potential for mobilities. Just as Kant notes how enthusiasm imparts impetus and momentum to ideas in the mind (1952: 124), it can likewise be seen to propel corporeal and object mobilities. Enthusiastic mobilities are therefore not driven by people alone – that is, travel is not enacted as autonomous choices. Rather, enthusiastic mobilities emerge as moments within enthusiastic relations. Connections between people, objects, spaces, and ideas reveal and inspire potential movements.

The following sections therefore explore three ways that enthusiasm characterizes mobilities: as an atmosphere for mobilities *within* spaces, as a force *pushing* people *through* spaces, and as a lure *pulling* people *to* spaces. In each case, enthusiasm exists as a relation between different things. The first approach puts a spatial boundary on enthusiastic relationships, considering how bodies relate to built spaces. It examines how architects and designers try to engineer the "affective atmospheres" (Bissell, 2010) that emerge in relations between built environments, people, and objects. The second section isolates instances where enthusiasm *pushes* people through spaces, emphasizing relationships between people and specific ways of moving. In leisure activities such as parkour, enthusiasm relates to the skills and objects used in motion between point A and point B. Here enthusiasm pushes people to trace more and more journeys, generating new mobilities. Finally, the journey is less important than arrival in the third section, where enthusiasm *pulls* people to spaces. Drawing upon my qualitative study of bird watching, I demonstrate how the enthusiasm that exists between distant objects and people can prompt mobilities.[1]

While these three dynamics and the cases used to illustrate them are not mutually exclusive, presenting each in turn highlights different ways that mobilities might be deemed enthusiastic. Distinguishing between enthusiastic relations that are spatially bounded, those that involve a push to travel, and those that pull people to destinations, is an analytic strategy for unpicking some of the complex links between affects of enthusiasm and mobilities. In addition, while this chapter focuses largely upon how enthusiasm shapes people's mobilities, it also acknowledges the multiple mobilities[2] that exist, including those of objects and information. Interrogating multiple mobilities in future research will help to reveal additional aspects of enthusiastic relations. The next section, however, makes an initial step towards understanding enthusiastic mobilities by considering how enthusiasm might be engineered within spaces.

Engineering enthusiasm within mobile spaces

One way of understanding enthusiasm as a characteristic of mobilities is to locate it within spaces that are inherently mobile. Tourist places such as beaches, for instance, are performed through "a multiplicity of intersecting mobilities" (Bærenholt *et al.*, 2004: 2). Even built spaces such as houses can be seen as permeated by routes, conduits, and mobilities rather than as stable and static containers (Lefebvre, 1991: 93; Urry, 2000: 20).

In addition to being mobile, social spaces are affective spaces. As Bissell notes, spaces such as trains enable distinct "affective atmospheres" that form a backdrop to everyday mobilities (2010: 272). People bring laptops and mobile phones onto trains, which in conjunction with a quiet carriage and the work practices of other people allow an affective atmosphere conducive to work to emerge (2010: 274). At other times, trains become "therapeutic spaces" with a prevailing atmosphere of grief or joy, as commuters confide in one another during recurrent trips (Jensen, 2011: 5). The shifting of routines and passengers over the course of a week transforms the affective atmosphere of trains, with the enthusiasm of weekend crowds meeting the exhaustion of Friday commuters (Bissell, 2010: 275). Enthusiasm is therefore only one of many affective atmospheres within spaces. Depending on the performances that occur – which depend on who and what is involved – affective atmospheres shift and evolve, enthusiasm perhaps giving way to boredom. In this way, a complex ecology of affects exists – of enthusiasm, hope, fear, desire (Davidson et al., 2011). These ecologies are not fixed systems, but consist of relationships that are in flux and spark unpredictable emergence (Park et al., 2011: 6). At some times, enthusiasm may dominate, while at others it is one of many atmospheres flourishing in different niches. The affective atmospheres of mobile locations emerge and disappear alongside the mobilities that constitute them.

How then can affective atmospheres and the wider ecologies they create be shaped, changed, and even engineered? The things people do in spaces undoubtedly play a role in shaping enthusiastic spaces. Train stations, for example, can be filled with enthusiasm due to passengers' impending vacations, long-awaited reunifications, or the sheer love of trains. When they were first constructed, however, they were sites of nervousness, with shifts between "anxiety and exhilaration, longing and dread" (Löfgren, 2008: 348). In part, changing these affective atmospheres involved promoting new skills of social interaction. Passengers learned how to keep distances, how to approach new people, and how to mark out territory, and today these skills are so widespread that they form a banal part of train commuting (Löfgren, 2008: 342, 31; Watts, 2008). By doing different things in spaces, people transform affects.

Changing affective atmospheres, however, also involves changing built spaces. Architects play a key role in the formation of affective ecologies because enthusiasm, nervousness, and boredom exist in relation to material spaces. Attempts can therefore be made to exert "affective control" by engineering spaces that promote and facilitate specific affects (Adey, 2008: 445). In the early twentieth century, the architect for Copenhagen's Grand Central Station aimed to minimize nervousness and anxiety in his design (Löfgren, 2008: 338). Similarly, contemporary airport architects anticipate and attempt to facilitate desirable patterns of affective mobility, such as the flow of people past retail outlets (Adey, 2008: 444).

How then might enthusiastic atmospheres be engineered within mobile spaces? A consideration of tourism offers one set of possibilities. From the production of themed environments such as the playscapes of Dubai's man-made islands (Junemo, 2004) to proposals for "creative enclaves" that engage people's creative potentials (Richards and Wilson, 2006), tourism has long involved spaces in which passions and inspirations can flourish. While such spaces involve a degree of control, notably in terms of the capital required for entrance (Junemo, 2004: 190), they also facilitate freedom. Having space in which to direct their own activities, whether at rented summer homes or sports entertainment zones, leads people to experience significant "enthusiasm, energy, and action" (Haldrup, 2004; Sherry et al., 2007: 30). The open-ended nature of built spaces is therefore important because it opens up opportunities for unpredictable relationships, mobilities, and performances.

Engineering enthusiasm then is less about affective control and more about affective opportunities. While airport architects try to create "an automatic response" from people by building obstacles and "limiting the possible movements" (Adey, 2008: 444), this approach engineers atmospheres of efficiency and commercialism rather than enthusiasm. Fentress Architects, who designed the Seoul Incheon Airport, conversely suggest: "timeless design is built on intangible factors such as dreams and inspiration" (Fentress Architects, 2012). On arrival in Seoul, guests can visit the Korean Culture Museum or one of the Traditional Korean Cultural Experience Zones, where they can watch performances or learn to make traditional handicrafts for free (Incheon International Airport Corporation, 2011). Rather than herding passengers through the airport, these areas provide opportunities to stop and engage – to become infected by a creative urge and an enthusiasm for Korean culture. Engineering enthusiasm is in this way about creating opportunities for affective contagion – creating opportunities for inspiration to be encountered and communicated.

There is a different architectural approach then to affective control than to engineering enthusiasm. The former corresponds with a tradition of making "predictable and boring boxes," while the latter is exemplified by Danish architects BIG's aim to produce "pragmatic utopian architecture" and embrace the slogan "yes is more" (BIG, 2009: 12). The former tries to limit and homogenize affective ecologies while the latter encourages inspirational and potentially unpredictable enthusiastic atmospheres. While lofty architectural ideals drive marketing as much as design, the possibilities of utopian mobilities need to be taken seriously (Jensen and Freudendal-Pedersen, 2012). Letting the imagination run free, giving in to enthusiasm's "taste for the infinite" (Hynes, 2011: 65; Kant, 1952), might therefore be an appropriate strategy for encouraging and engineering enthusiasm within mobile spaces.

While enthusiasm can emerge within the affective ecologies of mobile spaces, there is also an extent to which mobilities exceed these spaces. As even architects acknowledge, people find ways around the affective intentions of built spaces (Adey, 2008: 445). In addition to exceeding the expectations of designers, mobilities also extend beyond bounded spaces, etching paths that cross many spaces. The next section therefore considers how an enthusiasm for movement can generate new pathways that in some cases ignore planners' intentions.

An enthusiastic push

Sometimes enthusiastic relations are not about being in a space, but about moving through spaces. Passion and inspiration becomes a proverbial wind at one's back, pushing the body to travel through spaces in a particular way. Here enthusiasm is not about atmospheres in space, but about generating new pathways and exploring new ways of moving.

Matthew Tiessen, for example, is a self-avowed enthusiast of mountain biking. As he notes, mountain bikers:

> seek out challenging trails that enable them to achieve maximum 'flow,' that enable them to respond and interact with the earth's offerings. They thereby become a sort of bio-techno-human-hybrid – the Mountain Biker – that generates euphoria, thrills, and adrenaline.
>
> *(Tiessen, 2011: 129)*

Though this interaction involves space, it is not about being in specific spaces. Rather, an enthusiasm for mountain biking – for reproducing these relationships between body and bike and earth – pushes body-machine hybrids into new spaces, generating new mobilities.

This creative energy re-writes spaces and exceeds common expectations. Mountain bikers create what Tiessen calls "desire lines." The term, which is used by architects to refer to the footpaths people create when wandering off sidewalks and other planned routes, often carries a negative connotation – one of deviance and a need for standardization (Tiessen, 2011: 129). Tiessen, however, suggests these traces of mobility are interactions – interactions between spaces that present possible trajectories and people who respond in expressions of efficiency, playfulness, or, I might add, even enthusiasm (2007). The push and pull relationship of affect therefore becomes central to the mountain biker's movements: "The desire path ... is a product of a relationship, a reciprocal relationship of offering (by the topographical context) and acceptance (by you or me)" (Tiessen, 2011: 129). Working together, the space, the bike, and its capable rider enact enthusiastic mobilities, cleaving out paths that didn't exist before.

An enthusiasm for moving similarly pushes people to generate new paths in parkour. Also known as freerunning, parkour involves jumping, climbing, and running as efficiently as possible over built structures in the urban landscape. While walls and railings are for most people barriers that must be walked around, in parkour they are invitations to enact new desire lines. This language of invitation fits the practice well because, as Saville notes, parkour "does not give any particular clear or finished blueprint for action ... but constantly seeks new ways to move playfully *with* places" (2008: 892). A passion for parkour, for learning to move differently through the city, therefore pushes people to generate new mobilities, considering new routes and opportunities to creatively extend the boundaries of how bodies interact with urban forms.

Though enthusiasm may push people to carve out new paths, it does not ensure the process will be easy. Saville tells the story of parkour founder David Belle, who fell, in front of people and video cameras, during a 2006 attempt to pull himself over a solid wall (2008: 891). While falling is routinely associated with disappointment and shame in Western cultures, and the public nature of this demonstration would normally enhance these affects, Saville notes that Belle "was pleased and excited. After the 'fakeness' of Californian media-appeasing performances, the Frenchman said he felt more 'real'" (2008: 891). Belle's enthusiasm for parkour, as a way of moving about the city, was fed and urged on by his failure. This is because responding to the push of enthusiasm and creatively carving out new desire lines is more important as a practitioner than seamlessly flowing along any one path. Trying new mobilities is more important than perfecting them. As a result, affects such as risk and fear have a complex role within this practice. While fear can counteract the push of enthusiasm and stop people from attempting new movements, it can also push them to revisit and obsess over spaces and certain ways of moving (Saville, 2008: 901–3). The push of enthusiasm becomes intermingled with fear, excitement, anger, and enjoyment as practitioners repeatedly move.

In mountain biking and parkour, an intense interest and passion for specific ways of moving generates new mobilities. The same could be said for automobile enthusiasts such as hot rodders (Moorhouse, 1991), or even everyday drivers who find cars "too comfortable, enjoyable, exciting, even enthralling" to give them up (Sheller, 2004: 236). In each instance, affects like fear can redirect or reinvigorate paths, while enthusiasm pushes people through space, attached to different technologies, seeking out different spaces for performing creative desire lines.

While in these cases the process of moving is itself inspiring and the subject of passion, sometimes enthusiasm isn't apparent during the journey. Travelling sometimes seems a prelude to passion – a way of facilitating enthusiastic performances. The next section therefore considers how enthusiasm can pull people to destinations that are the focus of inspiration.

The pull of enthusiastic performances

> I don't really *enjoy* the long drives, but I enjoy the drive back if we've been successful.
>
> *(Mike, birder)*

The ambivalence Mike demonstrates for car travel seems miles away from the notion of enthusiasm as passion. Yet each year Mike travels 30,000–40,000 miles to pursue his passion for bird watching. Several times each day Mike checks his bird pager and several specialized bird websites, which report rare birds that have been spotted across the UK. Then, if he notices a bird he wants to see, perhaps one he hasn't seen yet this year, Mike quickly arranges transportation in the hopes of being able to reach and see the bird before it departs.[3] An unenjoyable ride to the destination will, if he manages to spot the bird, be rewarded with a satisfying return voyage.

Could this mobility be deemed enthusiastic? If one were concentrating on particular spaces then the answer would be a qualified no. After all, the spatial pattern of Mike's trips is widely varying – birds show up all over the place, and so Mike ends up travelling all over the place. Though he is part of temporary atmospheres of enthusiasm in the locations he visits, his enthusiasm is not for these spaces, and he makes few return trips to them. To concentrate instead upon Mike's way of moving doesn't help either. His enthusiasm is not linked to the journeys he takes, and he is not interested in responding to spaces by carving desire lines. Instead, he wants to get to the *right* space – the one in which the bird resides.

Though Mike's long car rides are not enthusiastic in these ways, they do demonstrate considerable enthusiasm for birds and bird watching. Indeed, this enthusiasm is enhanced, rather than diminished, by his ambivalence for the journeys. Enduring long, unsatisfying rides demonstrates Mike's intense interest in watching birds. It also separates him from people like Jon, who doesn't want "to spend four hours sat in a car to get out for twenty minutes to see a bird . . . when I could actually spend *eight* hours out and about [watching birds]." Mike's enthusiastic mobilities must therefore be understood differently.

For Mike, enthusiasm exists in his relationship to the unpredictable and widely dispersed distribution of birds. Having seen many rare birds, he is inspired to see many more – to be witness to the unexpected presence of birds that are normally found elsewhere. Enthusiasm pulls Mike towards these rare birds, entices him to travel long distances in order to be near them. The birds, like Plato's stone, have a kind of magnetic attraction.

Before Mike can give in to this attraction, however, he needs to discover and locate the birds. He is not willing to travel across the country to see a common garden bird, and therefore searching and finding information about *rare* birds plays an important role in feeding and directing his enthusiasm. One of his sources of information is the BirdGuides website (2012). This website features a constantly updated "BirdMap" of the UK, with squares indicating the location of bird reports. The relative importance of reports is indicated by squares of different sizes – the most common birds being marked by very small ones and extremely uncommon "Mega" finds by large ones. While small squares are unlikely to have a strong enough pull to draw Mike's attention, the large squares indicate both rarity and, within the community of rare-bird twitchers, an enthusiasm to travel. In order to see rare birds, Mike is impelled along certain trajectories, pulled by the promise of birds he knows to be irregularities.

To speak of his being *pulled by enthusiasm* towards destinations is not to reject the materiality of his body. It is not, as Solnit suggests, to take a postmodern perspective on frictionless flows where: "the body is nothing more than a parcel in transit, a chess piece dropped on another square, it does not move but is moved" (2001: 28). As an affect, enthusiasm speaks to the capacities of Mike's body. In order to respond to this pull, his body must be engaged, even if only in enduring the embodied constraints of long hours as a passenger in cars or planes. Depending on the state of his body, and competing forces in his life, Mike may not be able to give in to the allure of birds, his embodied enthusiasm giving way to longing or regret.

The key is that Mike's travel cannot be separated from his rare bird watching. The capacity to move to these spaces is contingent on enthusiastic relations between his body and the birds, his knowledge of bird behaviors, and the information that travels to him through websites and pagers. Travelling long distances is not a free choice – indeed, he doesn't particularly like the long drives. But he is enthusiastic about seeing rare birds, and in order to do so, he is pulled to enact new mobilities.

Just as the religious enthusiasm of the seventeenth and eighteenth centuries was positioned in opposition to reason, there is something about this enthusiastic mobility that goes beyond notions of choice. Mike's travel patterns are not about distinct choices made in relation to minimizing travel time or cost. Rather, his travel results from the interaction of personal circumstances and collectively reproduced mobilities. Mike's mobilities are not only about his body, or his desires. They also draw upon collectively reproduced mobilities. The circulation of objects such as rare-bird pagers helps to reinforce a widely shared motivation to see rare birds, and also facilitates travel by connecting this motivation to particular destinations. The evolving virtual mobilities of the BirdMap website connect past bird sightings and future ones, giving specific destinations to the pull of enthusiasm. Together, these overlapping mobilities reproduce a pre-personal enthusiasm that establishes patterns of travel. With their help, mobilities that would seem abnormal to many thus become quite normal:

> Convention dictates to any teenager, in fact, to most normal people that you don't simply set off to drive through the night for 550 miles . . . Twitching shatters those restraints. It tells you that you can actually go anywhere at any time. More important, perhaps, is the fact that, on most occasions, when you get there you'll meet scores of others who have made exactly the same journey, reinforcing a communal notion that it's all perfectly normal.
>
> *(Cocker, 2001: 60)*

The enthusiastic mobilities of objects, information, and people all work together to direct corporeal travel and make seeing rare birds possible and, moreover, normal.

This case highlights that enthusiasm is not just a quality of human mobilities. Rather, as Mike's bird watching illustrates, the enthusiasm inherent in flows of rare bird information precede and in some sense pull Mike to enact his own corporeal mobilities – mobilities undertaken in order to meet up with moving birds that are themselves pulled along by winds and migration patterns. Enthusiasm is not often something Mike experiences for travelling itself, but it is intimately connected to where and why he travels.

Conclusion

As this brief discussion has shown, there are many ways in which enthusiasm can be deemed a quality of mobilities. Though enthusiasm has seldom been a central unit of study, it offers opportunities to reconsider the relationships and momentum behind patterns of contemporary mobility. As Letherby and Reynolds suggest, "it is not just that travel/mobility shapes emotions but also that the emotions shape mobilities" (2009: 3). The same can be said of affect, and starting from a consideration of affect offers new ways of understanding how mobilities take various forms.

As this chapter has illustrated, different frames can be used for understanding how the passion of enthusiasm sparks mobilities. Enthusiastic mobilities can be engineered in mobile spaces, and enthusiasm can also be seen to push and pull people and objects through and to spaces. Highlighting these different dimensions of affective relationships provides insight into the ecologies of affect that emerge and evolve, as well as how multiple mobilities work together to lure bodies into movement. Recognizing the enthusiastic nature of mobilities also requires acknowledging that personal choice is not the main driver of people's travel. Built spaces contribute to affects and mobilities, as do the affordances and travel of ideas and objects. Mobilities, like the enthusiasm that characterizes them, are not merely subject-centered – they emerge out of relations.

This discussion has also revealed the productive and creative tendency of enthusiasm. Rather than closing down or controlling mobilities and performances, the passion, possession, and inspiration of enthusiasm has been shown to push and pull people onwards – to explore unexpected opportunities in spaces, to generate more ways of moving through the city, to visit more birds. While it is important to recognize the barriers, closures, and power articulated during attempts to affectively control built spaces, investigating enthusiasm has pointed towards the importance of also considering openings and excited explorations. As the cases in this chapter have demonstrated, enthusiasm has a propensity to overflow, instigating new mobilities of ideas, objects, and people. This creative extending of enthusiasm into new spaces is of significant interest when trying to understand the opportunities and limitations of established and future mobility systems.

To recognize enthusiasm's communicable and creative impulse, however, is not to dismiss its potentially dangerous and destructive side. Just as natural ecologies fare poorly when dominated by one species, letting enthusiasm run wild could be similarly disastrous. Mike, for instance, continues to travel widely in order to see rare birds, despite his admission that this travel has a significant environmental cost. This mismatch between the momentum of enthusiastic mobilities and wider social concerns about the environment highlights the potential for enthusiasm to once again become dangerous, as it was in the seventeenth and eighteenth centuries. Though, as Emerson suggests, great things can be done with enthusiasm, abandoning oneself to enthusiasm can also be costly. Studying how the push and pull of enthusiasm shapes mobilities therefore remains a crucial topic for future research.

Acknowledgments

This chapter draws upon research that was gratefully supported by a PhD scholarship from the Commonwealth Scholarship Commission of the UK. Many thanks to David Bissell, Misela Mavric, and Tonya Davidson for their helpful comments on previous drafts.

Notes

1 Participant observation and semi-structured interviews with ten bird watchers were undertaken as part of a wider study of leisure mobilities.
2 As Sheller and Urry argue, mobilities are not about people alone, and also include movements of people and ideas (2006). Urry, for instance, discusses five types of travel: people's corporeal travel, the travel of objects, imaginative travel, virtual travel, and communicative travel (2000: 49; 2007: 47).
3 This type of travel, covering extreme distances to see rare birds, which appear for short periods of time, is known, often pejoratively, as twitching.

Bibliography

Adey, P. (2008) "Airports, mobility and the calculative architecture of affective control," *Geoforum*, 39: 438–51.

Bærenholdt, J. O., Haldrup, M., Larsen, J. and Urry, J. (2004) *Performing tourist places*, Aldershot: Ashgate.

BIG (2009) *Yes is more. An archicomic on architectural evolution*, Copenhagen: BIG ApS.

BirdGuides Ltd. (2012) "BirdGuides." Available online at www.birdguides.com (accessed 8 March 2012).

Bissell, D. (2010) "Passenger mobilities: affective atmospheres and the sociality of public transport," *Environment and Planning D: Society and Space*, 28: 270–89.

Cocker, M. (2001) *Birders: tales of a tribe*, London: Vintage.

Davidson, T. K., Park, O. and Shields, R. (eds) (2011) *Ecologies of affect: placing nostalgia, desire, and hope*, Waterloo: Wilfrid Laurier University Press.

Dewsbury, J.-D., Harrison, P., Rose, M. and Wylie, J. (2002) "Introduction: enacting geographies," *Geoforum*, 33: 437–40.

Emerson, R. W. (1951) *Essays by Ralph Waldo Emerson: first and second series complete in one volume*, San Bernardino, CA: The Borgo Press.

Fentress Architects (2012) "Design for people." Available online at www.fentressarchitects.com/theartinside.htm (accessed 8 March 2012).

Haldrup, M. (2004) "Laid-back mobilities: second-home holidays in time and space," *Tourism Geographies*, 6(4): 434–54.

Herd, D. (2007) *Enthusiast! Essays on modern American literature*, Manchester: Manchester University Press.

Heyd, M. (1995) *'Be sober and reasonable': The critique of enthusiasm in the seventeenth and early eighteenth centuries*, Leiden, The Netherlands: E. J. Brill.

Hynes, M. (2011) "Surpassing ecstasy, infinite enthusiasm," *Parallax*, 17(2): 59–70.

Incheon International Airport Corporation (2011) "Incheon (ICN) International Airport: Traditional culture experience." Available online at www.airport.kr/iiacms/pageWork.iia?_scode=C2605010200 (accessed 8 March 2012).

Jensen, H. L. (2011) "Emotions on the move: mobile emotions among train commuters in the South East of Denmark," *Emotion, Space and Society*. Available online at http://dx.doi.org/10.1016/j.emospa.2011.07.002 (accessed 9 March 2012).

Jensen, O. B. and Freudendal-Pedersen, M. (2012) "Utopias of mobilities," in M. H. Jacobsen and K. Tester (eds) *Utopia: social theory and the future*, Aldershot: Ashgate, pp. 197–217.

Junemo, M. (2004) "'Let's build a palm island!': playfulness in complex times," in M. Sheller and J. Urry (eds) *Tourism mobilities: places to play, places in play*, New York: Routledge, pp. 181–91.

Kant, I. (1952) *The critique of judgement*, trans. J. C. Meredith, Oxford: Clarendon Press.

Lefebvre, H. (1991) *The production of space*, trans. D. Nicholson-Smith, Oxford: Blackwell.

Letherby, G. and Reynolds, G. (2009) "Introduction: planning the journey – theoretical background," in G. Letherby and G. Reynolds (eds) *Gendered journeys, mobile emotions*, Aldershot: Ashgate, pp. 1–4.

Löfgren, O. (2008) "Motion and emotion: learning to be a railway traveller," *Mobilities*, 3(3): 331–51.

Moorhouse, H. F. (1991) *Driving ambitions: an analysis of the American hot rod enthusiasm*, Manchester: Manchester University Press.

OED (1989) "Enthusiasm," in J. A. Simpson and E. S. C. Weiner (eds) *The Oxford English Dictionary* (2nd ed., vol. 5), Oxford: Oxford University Press, p. 296.

Park, O., Davidson, T. K. and Shields, R. (2011) "Introduction," in T. K. Davidson, O. Park and R. Shields (eds) *Ecologies of affect: placing nostalgia, desire, and hope*, Waterloo: Wilfrid Laurier University Press, pp. 1–15.

Plato (1953) *The dialogues of Plato*, trans. B. Jowett, Oxford: Clarendon Press.

Richards, G. and Wilson, J. (2006) "Developing creativity in tourist experiences: a solution to the serial reproduction of culture?" *Tourism Management*, 27: 1209–23.

Saville, S. J. (2008) "Playing with fear: parkour and the mobility of emotion," *Social & Cultural Geography*, 9(8): 891–914.

Sheller, M. (2004) "Automotive emotions: feeling the car," *Theory, Culture & Society*, 21(4–5): 221–42.

Sheller, M. and Urry, J. (2006) "The new mobilities paradigm," *Environment and Planning A*, 38: 207–26.

Sherry, J. F., Kozinets, R. V. and Borghini, S. (2007) "Agents in paradise: experiential co-creation through emplacement, ritualization, and community," in A. Carù and B. Cova (eds) *Consuming experience*, London: Routledge, pp. 17–33.

Solnit, R. (2001) *Wanderlust: a history of walking*, London: Verso.

Thien, D. (2005) "After or beyond feeling? A consideration of affect and emotion in geography," *Area*, 37(4): 450–6.

Thrift, N. (2004) "Intensities of feeling: towards a spatial politics of affect," *Geografiska Annaler*, 86 B(1): 57–78.

Tiessen, M. (2007) "Accepting invitations: desire lines as earthly offerings," *Rhizomes: Cultural Studies in Emerging Knowledge*, 15. Available online at www.rhizomes.net/issue15/tiessen.html (accessed 13 March 2012).

Tiessen, M. (2011) "(In)human desiring and extended agency," in T. K. Davidson, O. Park and R. Shields (eds) *Ecologies of affect: placing nostalgia, desire, and hope*, Waterloo: Wilfred Laurier University Press, pp. 127–42.

Urry, J. (2000) *Sociology beyond societies: mobilities for the twenty-first century*, London: Routledge.

Urry, J. (2007) *Mobilities*, Cambridge: Polity Press.

Watts, L. (2008) "The art and craft of train travel," *Social & Cultural Geography*, 9(6): 711–26.

Section Three

Introduction: Spaces, systems, infrastructures

While much early interest in mobilities has focused on that which moves, i.e. the people, vehicles, information, or objects in motion, there is also a growing concern with the infrastructures that enable mobility. Mobilities are always supported by a wide range of systems and infrastructures that create particular kinds of mobility spaces, and such spaces produce power differentials in the capability for mobility. As explored in the chapters in this section, these may be physical infrastructures for moving things, such as roads (Merriman), railways (Thomas), data centers (Farman), or pipes and cables (McCormack); or they may be protocols that enable particular kinds of mobility, such as logistics systems (Cowen), mobile communications systems (Parks), or various systems for queuing (Fuller).

Spaces, systems and infrastructures are often imagined as formal, fixed, inert or locked-in to some extent, but they may also be informal, as McFarlane and Vasudevan remind us, or unstable and constantly morphing into new shapes, as Merriman describes roads. Indeed, recent mobilities theory has moved away from dualistic models of a dichotomy between a fast-moving and abstract "space of flows" versus a more territorialized and physically located "space of places," as Manuel Castells imagined in the 1990s, instead exploring the interesting ways in which (im)mobilities coproduce and interpenetrate one another. Thus the chapters in this section overlap with both an interest in materialities, as explored in the next section, and in events and temporalities, the rhythms and pauses of stopping and going.

Geographers such as Stephen Graham and Nigel Thrift (2007) have shown how the world appears to us "ready-to-hand" because of the behind-the-scenes yet often labor-intensive activities of maintenance and repair of urban infrastructures, from roads and electricity to water and sanitation. Logistics is perhaps the ultimate system of systems that makes things appear ready-to-hand, even as it falls into the invisible background. Cowen argues that logistics ("the management of the movement of *stuff*") has undergone profound changes since World War II, becoming a driving force of military strategy and tactics, as well as in corporate practices for the global organization of trade. With the rise of the shipping container, the computer, and satellite communications to manage logistics, new forms of systems thinking have come to the fore, re-shaping labor relations, landscapes and forms of security. Understanding logistics concerns both the infrastructure of the global movement of goods and people and the imaginaries and symbolic meanings that drive such organizations of space and time.

Roads are perhaps the most obvious infrastructure for mobility, yet in many ways the least commented upon. Merriman draws our attention to the history and materiality of roadways, from the ancient Roman road to the emergence of an alienating "machine space" of the modern highway. Yet he notes that people also inhabit and dwell upon the road, ascribing many different kinds of meanings to them, from nostalgic memories of driving through particular landscapes, to vehement protests against the building of new roads. Thus they are not just functional spaces, but may be full of lively practices, affects, rhythms and materials. And roads, of course, may be associated with stoppages, closure or stillness.

When we are too focused on mobility as movement, we sometimes forget that it also may involve a great deal of waiting, and that such intervals of waiting are also systemically organized. One form waiting may take is the queue, or line-up. The queue is a kind of "everyday infrastructure," according to Fuller, in which we all participate almost without thinking. It may be a physical formation "at ATMs, ticket machines, in supermarkets, motor registries, and hospitals, at any place where traffic, in the broadest sense of the term, congregates." Or it may be an electronic wait to download data or have a phone call answered. Fuller describes queues as a "control architecture," which becomes an ethical concern when perceived "queue jumping" arises. Fuller's study of queues draws us both to the patterns in rhythms of stop-and-go mobility, and to the power relations inherent in the organization of waiting.

Thomas brings into focus another slow kind of temporality, that of waiting for new infrastructures to be built. Railways in particular take a very long time to be built, even as they transform landscapes, bodily experiences and social relations. Both material and symbolic in their impacts, they helped to create new forms of urban life, from daily commuting to the governing of colonial empires. Nor should we imagine the infrastructure of the railway as simply constituted by the big systems like tracks and stations, for railways are also socio-technical systems involving signaling equipment, practical know-how, ticketing systems, maintenance, etc., as well as imaginaries of what Julie Cidell calls "trainspace." Thomas pushes us to think beyond the physical materiality of the line, opening up these spaces of infrastructure to literary, cultural and personal meaning, including the "imminent" expectancy and hopeful attachments that are invested in the plans for yet-to-be-built railway lines, or the disenchantment in their forever deferred future promise.

Also taking a historical perspective, McCormack reminds us of an even wider range of tubular systems for mobility, from the pneumatic tubes for delivering messages to the pipes for distributing water, oil or gas, and the wires that deliver electricity: "it is precisely the capacity to render materials and substances mobile in controllable and manageable ways that marks the emergence of inhabitable assemblages." If urban imagery includes the elegant suspension cables of the Brooklyn Bridge, it should also not forget the vertical rigging of elevators (lifts), funiculars, cable railways and aerial tramways. Steel cables are one of the crucial support structures of mobility, as well as a possible means for its disastrous failure. Cables and pipes not only support the external infrastructure of mobility, but might also be internal to vehicles, as in the hydraulic and later fly-by-wire systems that guide airplanes. Whether moving goods and freight, or transmitting signals and information, the anxieties or hopes invested in such infrastructures may exceed their capacity to carry them.

While the building of a new road or railway is a highly visible act of infrastructural extension, communications infrastructures may take a more hidden form, though are equally significant in shaping the landscape of everyday life. In his analysis of the infrastructure of data centers, antennas, fiber optic lines and other kinds of physical relays that support mobile locative communications, Farman observes that such technologies are not only based on person-to-person connectivity, but also involve a vast amount of human-to-technology connectivity and often invisible (or at least hidden to most users) technology-to-technology connectivity. All the time there is "data talking to data, machines talking to machines, signals talking to infrastructure." As he updates his Foursquare location while standing in a Washington, DC, area data center, Farman interrogates the power relations of visibility and invisibility underpinning our awareness of infrastructures and communication devices as ready-to-hand yet largely invisible background.

Building further in the same direction, Parks argues that mobile phone infrastructures should be "studied in relation to particular socio-historical, geophysical, political, economic, and cultural conditions." She takes us to the opposite side of the world, to Ulaanbaatar in Mongolia, where she conducts a "footprint analysis" of the "dispersed hardware, physical installations, spectrum, footprints, and interfaces that enable mobile telephone services as well as the human labor and activity that supports such arrangement and use." Rather than bringing to light a homogenous and universal socio-technical system, her research reveals how infrastructural assemblages may be flexibly produced and scaled to local contexts, in this case resulting in a public mobile telephony that reinterprets Mongolian nomadic practices and collectivist ethos in a new digital urban space.

Finally, McFarlane and Vasudevan also immerse us in the highly local contexts and material practices of the informal infrastructures created by those who live "between schemes and institutions," in the precarious interstices of burgeoning urbanism. Envisioning "urban informality as a *mobile* process," they reveal practices of deregulation and irregularity that extend across different forms of makeshift urban life, both elite and subaltern. Ranging from the autonomous and collective practices of community-based sanitation movements in Mumbai to the DIY culture of squatting in Berlin in the 1980s–90s, McFarlane and Vasudevan suggest that mobile informal architectures recreate a politics "predicated on the materialization of different urban flows." In drawing together mixed sets of resources and translocal constituencies, they find urban groups are able "to build open-ended and ongoing forms of radical incrementalism" which constitute an unexpected kind of urban politics, a "politics of mobile informal infrastructures."

Ultimately this section collectively takes us far beyond the empty train car on the cover of this book, as discussed in the Introduction. It plunges us into the infrastructural background, revealing the social, technical and material assemblages that make mobility work, as well as the local contexts, affects and atmospheres that enliven and animate mobility spaces and a politics of systems.

17

Logistics

Deborah E. Cowen

Moving matter, mobile meanings

'Logistics' is a word that casually enters the popular lexicon, yet few are familiar with its professional meanings or the pivotal role it has played in reorganizing the practice of warfare and global social and economic life. At its core, logistics is the seemingly banal management of the movement of *stuff*. Little more can be said about the field without engaging its shifting meaning and practice. Above all else, it is a series of astounding transformations that characterizes the life of logistics. Profound change has been underway in logistics' infrastructures, technologies, landscapes, forms of labour, and expertise, but also and perhaps most importantly, in the very meaning of the term. Only a century ago, 'logistics' identified a military art that concerned the movement of supplies to the battlefront. Logisticians were a lowly lot who stocked specialized shelves, fuelling 'men and machines' for battle (Van Creveld 2004). Logistics remained firmly in the shadows of the prized art of strategy. Since that time, logistics has grown far more important for battle – it has become the driving force for strategy and tactics (Jomini 1836; DeLanda 1991). Yet, over the past four decades, logistics has made an even more stunning transformation – it has reconfigured the corporate boardroom (Allen 1997; Cowen 2010). It is now at the centre of corporate practice, both underpinning and managing the global organization of trade (Bonacich and Wilson 2008; Reifer 2004). In the early years of the twenty-first century, logistics was associated with corporate giants like Amazon and Wal-Mart and had become the profession governing the circulation of stuff across production, consumption and destruction. Logistics has taken on a whole new civilian life without shedding its military identity and authority.

This chapter outlines the shifting life of logistics. It tracks transformations in the field: its long role in warfare, its rising importance in post-WWII business management, its globalized and standardized geographies, and its material and political technologies. Amidst all this change, the discussion highlights the persistence of imperial imaginaries and logics that are often hidden in plain view, as it also traces the increasing ubiquity of logistics in complex systems management beyond militaries and corporations. The discussion that follows centres explicitly on the United States, prompted by the practical need to locate the analysis of a globalized system in place, and because of the pivotal role that the US military and corporations have played in the transformation of the field, within the broad skein of US imperial power.

The logistics of war

The etymology of logistics is often traced to the Greek, 'logistikos', meaning 'skilled in calculating'. The Greeks were not the first to be concerned with provisioning the battlefield, and a whole history of 'logistics', before it was so named, remains to be written. Wilson (2008: 362) notes that Sun Tzu's writing helped to define a deliberate art of war and a 'professional' cadre of military officers concerned centrally with technical questions of supply and provisioning, which displaced the longstanding emphasis on charismatic leadership. Yet, it is not surprising that logistics was named first by the Greeks; military leaders of the time were deeply concerned with questions of supply in the broader organization of war. The sheer volume of cargo transported for military campaigns became a target of reform for Alexander the Great. Engels (1980) estimates the dramatic work of supplying military campaigns, noting that 1,000 horses were needed simply to transport the fodder for cavalry horses and baggage animals. This heavy burden explains why supply became "the basis for Alexander's strategy" (Engels 1980: 119, see also McConnell and Hardemon 2010). Roth (1999) makes similar arguments about the Romans, suggesting that underpinning the strategies and tactics that became celebrated in military history are the banal but definitive questions of supply. In his estimation, logistics was for the Romans "both as a strategic and a tactical weapon", and failure in this area – in feeding soldiers – accounts centrally for the fall of the Empire (1999: 279, see also Thomas 2004).

It is the modern life of logistics however where a dramatic expansion of its power and authority unfolded. In the era of European nation-state building and colonization, logistics became marked as one of the three arts of war, along with strategy and tactics. On both sides of the Napoleonic wars, logistics was a focal point: Clausewitz and Jomini both became increasingly concerned with questions of provisioning and supply. In his classic text 'On War', Clausewitz was deeply concerned with 'friction' – problems of circulation which were inherently in the domain of logistics (Cowen, forthcoming). Jomini (1836) explicitly articulated the changing role of logistics vis-à-vis strategy and tactics, insisting that the hierarchal relations between these arts were in motion and that logistics was assuming a leading role (Jomini 1836). However, as Van Creveld argues, the most significant shift in the field took place not with Alexander or Napoleon but with the rise of industrial warfare fuelled by petrol, oil and lubricants (POL), when "strategy becomes an appendix to logistics". POL transformed the battlefield: it boosted the killing power on the battlefield, but also kept military forces more tightly, physically, tethered to supply lines. As a result, supply became more and more definitive in the success of campaigns, and logistics ascended from a residual to a commanding role in military strategy. WWI was the first large-scale experiment with POL warfare, yet as Rainey *et al.* (1999: 55) suggest, the major logistical problems of the First World War remained those associated with livestock and fodder. Without a doubt, WWII was an industrial war organized largely around the logistics of petroleum and petroleum-dependent machines. As Fleet Admiral Ernest King would stress in his 1946 report to the Secretary of the US Navy, the Second World War was "variously termed a war of production and a war of machines", but "whatever else it is . . . it is a war of logistics".

The revolution in logistics and the rise of a corporate science

If the rise of POL and the event of World War II propelled logistics to the fore of military power, the postwar period saw increased interest in its application in the business world. Building on military practice during WWII and RAND's operations research, logistics was gradually transformed from military art into business science in the two decades that followed. What could logistics bring to the world of business and why did it draw attention from leaders in business management at this time? Military logistics during WWII had demonstrated extraordinary capacities for coordinating the movement and circulation of vast quantities of goods and people. In the context of postwar recession, management profession-als saw logistics as a solution to complex problems. Deliberate collaborations between military and business leaders ushered in a 'revolution' in the field (Cowen 2011).

From the late 1950s there was persistent expansion of professional organizing: new con-ferences, journals, degree programmes and professional organizations were built. But it was not simply the expansion of interest in the field that was important in this period, but radical shifts in how logistics, and the civilian science then known as 'physical distribution', were re-conceptualized. These shifts had everything to do with the rise of systems thinking (Smykay and LaLonde 1967; LaLonde *et al.* 1970). Until this time, the civilian field of 'phys-ical distribution' held authority over the transportation of finished goods to the consumer *after production*. Reducing the cost of transportation from production to the point of sale was the overarching mandate of distribution specialists, and it was thus accorded a minor role in the overall operation of the firm. Systems thinking invited managers to reconsider distribu-tion as an element of the overall 'system' of production rather than a discrete act that followed (Ackoff 1971), making it a much more critical corporate calculation and dramatically elevat-ing its place within the firm. Calculating the cost of transportation – something that had been a straightforward matter of distance multiplied by the cost of the mode of transport in question per ton–mile, became the topic of serious scrutiny. A whole new kind of calculation was brought to life. 'Total cost' changed the game. Derived from RAND research in air force procurement, total cost aimed to account for the actual costs of distributing products through the entire business system. All movement of materials – in production, in warehousing and so forth – would be accounted for, rather than the much more limited cost of the transporta-tion of finished products to consumers. As Drucker argued in 1969, "the largest single phys-ical distribution cost happens to exist under the roof of the manufacturing plant", thus "it is not enough to do what a good many other people in this field are doing – that is, to start at the loading ramp".

The implications of this shift were profound; it introduced a whole new logic to the rela-tionship between space and economy. With systems thinking and the calculations of total cost, managers found that *greater distance* between production and consumption could actually add value across the 'system' of production and distribution (LeKashman and Stolle 1965). In other words, extending distance could increase profit. Systems approaches and total cost cal-culations transformed the field precisely by bringing the border between production and distribution under conceptual attack. 'Physical distribution' was redefined as 'business logis-tics' and professional focus shifted from the cost of distribution (following production), to value-added across circulatory systems that span production and distribution.

The legacies of the revolution in logistics are multiple. Crucial was the way in which the 'interdisciplinary' analysis of total cost required coordination of top management. This propelled logistics to a much higher level of authority in the firm – a kind of 'umbrella' science of business management (Allen 1997). Related to this rising importance of logistics within the firm is the tremendous expansion of global logistics systems; the connection of the revolution in logistics to the globalization of trade and production systems is direct. In the wake of the revolutionary 1960s, a boom in global cargo circulation occurred and the volumes have since continued to rise. The revolution in logistics might tempt a tale of the 'civilianization' of the field over the past six decades. Yet its ongoing importance in warfare (cf. Pagonis 1992) suggests that the revolution launched a different, even deepened entanglement between military and market methods. Today, in an important reversal it is the military that largely takes its cue from corporate practice, and military logistics is extensively outsourced to private security companies even as it remains vital to contemporary warfare.

Logistics technologies

Logistics is a profoundly socio-technical tale; it has long been a field that mobilizes technologies, from the domesticated horse as a mode of transport to the petroleum engine that replaced it. In addition to the calculative technologies highlighted above, the possibility for radically reforming logistics into a business science was contingent on the shipping container, the computer and, eventually, a wide range of information technologies, all of which had important early lives in the military.

A range of social and industrial technologies that were designed to support the American battlefield during and after World War Two became essential to corporate logistics systems. The US military played a key role in the development of Just-In-Time techniques, first through the training of workers in occupied Japan in the post-WWII period to meet US procurement needs, and then by diffusing these techniques through contracting for Korean War supplies (Reifer 2004: 24; Spencer 1967: 33). The standard shipping container, another US military innovation, has been repeatedly dubbed the single most important technological innovation underpinning the globalization of trade (Levinson 2006; Economist 2002). While shipping containers have a long history of experimentation, the standardization of an intermodal container that could be transferred across different modes of transport was first experimented with during WWII as a means to reduce the time and labour involved in transporting military supplies to the front. It was not until the Vietnam War that the military use of the shipping container entrenched its standardized global form (Levinson 2006: 8, 178). Likewise, the satellite and telecommunications networks that made the information flows that underpin the global coordination of logistics systems possible were developed by the Pentagon's system of industrial planning.

It is easy to underestimate the importance of the computer for contemporary logistics. The revolution in logistics could have never taken place without it; the calculations of 'total cost' would have otherwise remained impossibly labour-intensive (Magee 1960: 95). The first general-purpose electronic digital computer, the Electronic Numerical Integrator and Computer (ENIAC) was developed by the United States Army in 1946 (US Army 1946). More broadly, as Gourdin (2006: 13) argues, "information systems are the glue that hold the logistics system together".

In recent years, logistics has become highly automated, and many transshipment facilities operate with a minimum of human labour. Seaports and inland ports alike are relying ever more on automated container transport systems. Leaders in the field like Wal-Mart introduced Electronic Data Interchange, whereby orders are automatically sent to producers when inventory levels drop below a set level, which has been crucial to the rise of a "pull" system of production and distribution (Amin 1994; Aoyama and Ratick 2007). Radio Frequency Identification (RFID) tags emit low-range radio frequency with information about container contents, and have been in use for some time. More recently, they have become standard issue for transport workers in the United States and elsewhere, who, in the post-2001 era of securitization, must carry identity cards that hold biometric data (Cowen 2010). Distribution centres rely on a whole range of communications technologies to manage inventory and its circulation. Mobile robotics systems developed by US military research for defence purposes now organize and assemble shipments in automated corporate facilities (Everett and

Gage 1999). Human labour and the human body are themselves automated; labour–intensive work like picking and packing is now guided by computer-managed voice software that directs the minute movements of warehouse workers via headsets connected to small portable computers. Technology is often a means of replacing or augmenting human labour in the interests of profit maximization, but it also intersects directly with labour in contemporary logistics in the realm of discipline, surveillance and 'security' (Kanngieser 2012).

The labour of logistics

Transportation has long been understood as a source of value. In Chapter 6 of *Capital*, Volume 2, Marx outlines how use-value, realized in the consumption of commodities, may require a "change in location" and thus an "additional process of production, in the transport industry". The rise of corporate logistics relied centrally on extracting more value from transport workers and reorganizing longstanding regulation in the sector to cultivate competition. Indeed, the revolution in logistics required a significant refiguring of the rights of workers in the US transport sector, and has involved sustained suppression of labour ever since (Bonacich and Wilson 2008).

Deregulation of the transport sector was critical to the revolution in logistics and the birth of intermodalism in the US. Lobbying for deregulation began in the 1950s and bi-partisan support followed under Eisenhower, Kennedy and Johnson. Following the oil crisis of the 1970s, the efforts were stepped up. Nixon, Ford and Carter all took up the cause of deregulation (Allen 1997: 108). Deregulation took shape differently in various sectors of the transportation industry (Peoples 1998: 128). Yet the different approaches and effects of deregulation in trucking, rail, air and telecommunications stand alongside common trajectories; deregulation undermined the strength and scale of organized labour in transport, led to a decline in conditions of work, deepened racialized wage gaps, opened the field to intermediary operators, and oriented the industry towards the transnational rather than national shipment of goods (LaLonde *et al.* 1970; Peoples 1998; Bonacich and Wilson 2008; Rodrigue and Notteboom 2008).

The invention of the global supply chain stretched the factory around the world such that commodities are increasingly manufactured across states precisely to incorporate radically uneven modalities of labour into the production process. This has entailed the de-industrialization of many old industrial regions and the offshoring of production to lower-wage regions of the world. It has also meant downward pressures on conditions of work in the global north (where many precarious workers are migrants from the global south) in relation to the hyperexploitation of workers in the global south but within the same disaggregated production process (see Cowen 2009).

After decades of pressure on US transport labour, the industry is left largely low-wage, precarious and highly racialized (Bonacich and Wilson 2008). Logistics workers in the US also have extraordinarily high rates of workplace injury – second only to construction (Lydersen 2011). Wal-Mart, the world's largest corporation, notorious for its low wages, poor benefits and highly gendered and racialized labour force, has been setting the path for the industry – both in its own employment and contracting practices, but also in the transport sector more broadly through its key role in lobbying government through industry groups like California's West Coast Waterfront Coalition (Bonacich and Wilson 2008).

The revolution and globalization of logistics has been a hard story for workers in the supply chain thus far, but things may nevertheless be changing. Bonacich (2005) suggests "Logistics workers are crucial local factors in global production and delivery systems . . . they cannot 'be moved offshore.'" Reifer (2004: 10) argues that the logistics revolution "arguably increased the power of workers in the global supply chain", suggesting that if "coalitions are able to capitalize on their strategic strengths as key nodal points in global trade and production and actively work on international solidarity across borders, the stage could be set for a radical revamping of the global system".

The landscapes of logistics

Logistics has been actively making landscapes since its earliest practice as both military art and business science. Some of the most striking and lasting logistics landscapes such as the Suez and Panama Canals mark the entangled histories of imperial trade and violence (Carter and Harlow 2003; Wallach 2005). Both canals were built to extend trading influence in the context of colonial rule and are landscapes that continue to define global maritime circulation today. Another stark example of a logistics landscape that holds entwined military and market history is the US National System of Interstate and Defense Highways, built by Eisenhower and directly inspired by the German autobahn – the world's first national high-speed road network, built largely under Hitler's rule with explicitly national militarist aims of facilitating troop movement. Canals and highways are landscapes themselves, but as spaces of circulation they also play a profound role in reshaping the production of landscape itself. For instance, the construction of the US highway system is inextricably linked to mass suburbanization (Easterling 1999). Suburbanization, and in particular suburban consumerism, had recursive effects for logistics, throwing up new challenges in inventory and distribution that helped provoke early experimentation of the logistics revolution (Allen 1997: 108).

Today, logistics is often associated with some of its hallmark civilian landscapes – highways, big-box stores, distribution centres and ports. The sprawling, suburban landscapes of global logistics are a feature of the increasing standardization of human environments devoted to efficient circulation. The growing standardization of the logistics landscape is geared towards smooth circulation. In other words, logistics landscapes cannot be understood only as the production of *places* but also the production of spaces and circuits of flow. Intermodality – the capacity to keep stuff moving with a minimum of disruption and human labour across multiple terrains and infrastructures – is at the core of the logistics revolution. The kernel logic of intermodality is standardization, as illustrated above with the rise of the container, or in the production of banal corporate distribution and retailing landscapes. Indeed, the 'retail revolution' that has drawn significant recent attention (see Bonacich 2005; Wrigley and Lowe 2002), relied on the revolution in logistics. Wal-Mart may be widely known as a mammoth retailer, but in the world of business management it is known as a logistics company. Wal-Mart has the largest civilian satellite network, second only to the US Department of Defense. And it is through complex systems of pull production that rely deeply on real-time IT connection between seller and producer that the corporation distinguished itself. Given the immense corporate power of Wal-Mart, any analysis of the production of logistics landscapes demands an engagement with Wal-mart's business strategy (Turner 2003; Hernandez and Simmons 2006: 477).

Supply chains and security

At the beginning of the twenty-first century, a new form of security concerned entirely with logistics systems and infrastructures emerged (Cowen 2010). 'Supply Chain Security' responds to longstanding tensions between logistics and geopolitics, and specifically the conflicting imperatives between the fast flow of goods and the security of national borders in the context of deepening globalization and securitization.

Concerns for protecting commodity circulation have intensified gradually alongside the globalization of trade; Just–In–Time logistics systems are vulnerable and sensitive to disruption. Yet, an account of more acute events is essential in any genealogy of supply chain security. Implementation of the first-ever global architecture for supply chain security began in 2001, following the disruption to international trade that followed the attacks of September 11. Since then, the US has implemented eleven plans to address supply chain security, in addition to a series of programmes that target particular sites within transport and trade networks. These national initiatives were followed by mandatory global standards for supply chain security, issued by the International Maritime Organization, the International Standards Organization and the World Customs Organization, though at the direct behest of the US government.

Supply chain security is already reconfiguring border space. New security programmes seek to govern integrated global economic space, while at the same time retain politically differentiated sovereign territories (Cowen 2010). Efforts to recalibrate security around 'pipelines' or corridors of trade – the networked space of supranational supply chains – challenge longstanding territorial notions of state sovereignty. They extend the zone of border management 'outwards' into the ports of foreign states, 'inwards' along domestic transport networks and into the space of 'logistic cities' (Cowen 2009), and through the creation of exceptional zones – 'secure areas' – around ports where normal laws and rights are either mediated or suspended (Cowen 2007). Supply chain security takes the protection of commodity flows, and the transportation and communication infrastructure that support them, as its central concern. What began as piecemeal efforts of different strategies at various sites by a wide range of actors, is becoming an integrated national and international system of risk-based, layered and networked security, focusing particularly on container movement. Yet, supply chain security also relies on military interventions; naval forces are actively patrolling critical shipping corridors such as the Gulf of Aden.

The ubiquity of logistics

From the protection of national states and territories, to the protection of transportation networks, corridors and nodes, the geographies of logistics have changed dramatically over the past two and a half centuries, throwing its very meaning into question. If the art of logistics came to drive geopolitical military strategy and tactics in the early twentieth century, today, market models of economic space have increasingly come to drive the science of logistics across the blurring bounds of military and civilian domains. These transformations propel logistics from a discrete and specialized military art to a ubiquitous science of the government of circulation.

Logistics clearly has a long history as a military art and business science, and both market and military forces have been critical in transforming the field. And yet, these actors do not exhaust the terrain. Recently, logistics has become important to the management of many forms of complex systems and operations to a wider range of actors – most notably emergency response, humanitarian aid, organized labour and even protest movements. Logistics management is so frequently mobilized for humanitarian aid that there are now a number of institutes, textbooks and, since 2011, even a professional journal devoted entirely to the subject. The labour movement has initiated its own logistics think tank in California in collaboration with scholars in order to rethink the socially just supply chain. And in activist worlds such as those protesting G8 and G20 meetings, and, more recently, the 'Occupy' movement, logistics have become a crucial resource.

Logistics is haunted by its military, imperial and more recent corporate past. In training programmes, professional circuits, institutional expertise and in its primary sites of deployment, corporate and military men and methods dominate. Logistics also drives neoliberal forms of anti-political calculation where cost–benefit analysis and assumptions of market efficiency are embedded into its basic techniques (Cowen 2010). Nevertheless, emerging in other sites is a claim on logistics as a technique for organizing around the 'how' problems of material life where both ends and means matter.

Bibliography

Ackoff, R. (1971) *Towards a System of Systems Concepts*. Institute of Management Sciences.

Allen, B. (1997) 'The Logistics Revolution and Transportation.' *Annals of the American Academy of Political and Social Science*, 553.

Amin, A. (1994) 'Post-Fordism: Models, Fantasies and Phantoms of Transition,' in Amin, A. *Post-Fordism: A Reader*. Oxford: Blackwell Publishers.

Aoyama, Y. and Ratick, S. (2007) 'Trust, Transactions, and Information Technologies in the U.S. Logistics Industry.' *Economic Geography*, 83: 159–180.

Ballantine, D. S. (1947) *US Naval Logistics in the Second World War*. Princeton: Princeton University Press.

Ballou, R. N. (2006) 'The Evolution and Future of Logistics and Supply Chain Management.' *Produção*, (16)3: 375–386.

Belzer, Michael (2000) *Sweatshops on Wheels: Winners & Losers in Trucking Deregulation*. Oxford University Press.

Bonacich, E. (2005) *Labor and the Global Logistics Revolution. Critical Globalization Studies*. New York: Routledge: pp. 359–368.

Bonacich, E. and Wilson, J. B. (2008) *Getting the Goods: Ports, Labor and the Logistics Revolution*. Cornell University Press.

Bowersox, D. (1966) 'Physical Distribution in Semi-Maturity.' *Air Transportation*, January 1966.

Carter, M. and Harlow, B. (2003) *Archives of Empire: From the East India Company to the Suez Canal*. Duke University Press.

Cowen, D. (2007) 'Struggling with "Security": National Security and Labour in the Ports.' *Just Labour*, 10: 30–44.

Cowen, D. (2009) 'Containing Insecurity: US Port Cities and the "War on Terror",' in Graham, Steve (ed.) *Disrupted Cities: When Infrastructure Fails*. New York and London: Routledge: pp. 69–84.

Cowen, D. (2010) 'A Geography of Logistics: Market Authority and the Security of Supply Chains.' *The Annals for the Association of American Geographers*, 100(3): 1–21.

Cowen, D. (2011) '"Logistics Liabilities," Anthropological Research on the Contemporary.' Available online at http://anthropos-lab.net/studio/logistics'-liabilities.

Cowen, D. (forthcoming) *Rough Trade: Logistics Space and the Citizenship of Stuff*. University of Minnesota Press.

Davis, G. M. and Brown, S. W. (1974) *Logistics Management*. Lexington, MA: D. C. Heath and Company.

Dawson, J. (2000) 'Retailing at Century End: Some Challenges for Management and Research.' *The International Review of Retail, Distribution and Consumer Research*, 10.2: 119–148.

DeLanda, M. (1991) *War in the Age of Intelligent Machines*. New York: Zone Books.

Drucker, P. (1969) 'Physical Distribution: The Frontier of Modern Management,' in Bowersox, D. J., Lalonde, B. J. and Smykay, E. *Readings in Physical Distribution Management*. MacMillan Co.

Easterling, K. (1999) *Organization Space*. MIT Press.

The Economist (2002) 'When Trade and Security Clash.' April 4.

Engels, D. C. (1980) *Alexander the Great and the Logistics of the Macedonian Army*. Berkeley: University of California Press.

Everett, H. R. and Gage, D. W. (1999) 'From Laboratory to Warehouse: Security Robots Meet the Real World.' *The International Journal of Robotics Research*, July 1999 18: 760–768.

Gourdin, K. (2006) *Global Logistics Management*. Blackwell.

Hamilton, Gary G. and Gereffi, G. (2009) 'Global Commodity Chains, Market Makers, & the Rise of Demand-Responsive Economies,' in Bair, Jennifer (ed.) *Frontiers of Commodity Chain Research*. Stanford University Press: pp. 136–162.

Harlow, Barbara and Carter, Mia (2003) *Archives of Empire 1: From the East India Company to the Suez Canal.* Duke University Press.

Hernandez, T. and Simmons, J. (2006) 'Evolving Retail Landscapes: Power Retail in Canada.' *Canadian Geographer*, 50.4: 465–486.

Jomini, B. 2009 [1836] *The Art of War.* Kingston, ON: Legacy Books Press Classics.

Kanngieser, A. (2012) 'Tracking and Tracing Bodies.' *Transit Labour: Circuits, Regions, Borders.* Available online at http://transitlabour.asia/blogs/author/anjakanngieser.

LaLonde, B. (1994) 'Perspectives on Logistics Management,' in Robeson, J. F. and Copacino, W. C. (eds) *The Logistics Handbook.* New York: The Free Press.

LaLonde, B., Grabner, J. and Robeson, J. (1970) 'Integrated Distribution Management: A Management Perspective.' *International Journal of Physical Distribution*, 1, October.

LeKashman, R. and Stolle, J. F. (1965) 'The Total Cost Approach to Distribution.' *Business Horizons*, Winter: 33–46.

Levinson, M. (2006) *The Box: How the Shipping Container Made the World Smaller and the World Economy Bigger.* Princeton: Princeton University Press.

Lydersen, K. (2011) 'From Racism to Lung Cancer, Workers Cope with Life in the Logistics Industry.' *In These Times*, May 2.

Magee, J. F. (1960) 'The Logistics of Distribution.' *Harvard Business Review*, 40: 89–101.

Marx, K. (1992) *Capital: A Critique of Political Economy.* Vol. 2. Penguin.

McConnell, D. and Hardemon, R. A. (2010) 'The Logistics Constant Throughout the Ages.' *Air Force Journal of Logistics*, (34) 3: 82–88.

Pagonis, W. G. (1992) *Moving Mountains: Lessons in Leadership and Logistics from the Gulf War.* Harvard Business School Press.

Peoples, J. C. (1998) 'Deregulation and the Labor Market.' *The Journal of Economic Perspectives*, (12) 3: 111–130.

Rainey, J. C., Scott, Beth F. and Reichard, Jeanette O. (1999) *Global Thinking, Global Logistics.* Air Force Logistics Management Agency.

Reifer, T. (2004) 'Labor, Race & Empire: Transport Workers & Transnational Empires of Trade, Production, and Finance,' in Gonzalez, G. and Fernandez, R. (eds) *Labor Versus Empire: Race, Gender, and Migration.* London and New York: Routledge: pp. 17–36.

Rodrigue, J.-P. and Notteboom, T. (2008) 'The Geography of Containerization: Half a Century of Revolution, Adaptation and Diffusion.' GeoJournal. Accessed October 28, 2012. Available online at http://people.hofstra.edu/jean-paul-rodrigue/downloads/Future_Containerization_TN_JPR_pre-introduction.pdf

Rodrigue, J.-P., Comtois, C. and Slack, B. (2009) *The Geography of Transport Systems.* Second Edition, New York: Routledge.

Roth, J. P. (1999) *The Logistics of the Roman Army at War.* New York: Columbia University Press.

Smykay, E. W. and LaLonde, B. J. (1967) *Physical Distribution: The New and Profitable Science of Business Logistics.* Chicago and London: Dartnell Press.

Spector, R. (2005) *Category Killers: The Retail Revolution and its Impact on Consumer Culture.* Boston: Harvard Business School Press.

Spencer D. L. (1967) 'Military Transfer: International Techno Economic Transfers via Military By-Products and Initiatives Based on Cases from Japan and Other Pacific Countries.' Defense Technical Information Center, Defense Logistics Agency, Washington DC AD660537, March

Thomas, C. (2004) 'Logistical Limitations of Roman Imperialism in the West.' Doctoral Dissertation. University of Auckland.

Turner, M. (2003) *Kmart's Ten Deadly Sins: How Incompetence Tainted an American Icon.* New Jersey: John Wiley & Sons Inc.

United States Army (1946) 'Report on the ENIAC (Electronic Numerical Integrator and Computer' Technical Report #1. Available online at http://ftp.arl.mil/~mike/comphist/46eniac-report/index.html.

Van Creveld, M. (2004) [1977] *Supplying War: Logistics from Wallerstein to Patton.* Cambridge University Press.

Vias, A. (2004) 'Bigger Stores, More Stores, or No Stores: Retail Restructuring in Rural America.' *Journal of Rural Studies*, 20: 303–318.

Wallach, B. (2005) *Understanding the Cultural Landscape.* Guilford Press.

Wilson, A. R. (2008) 'War and the East.' *Orbis*, 52 (2): 358–371.

Wrigley, N. and Lowe, M. (2002) *Reading Retail: A Geographical Perspective on Retailing and Consumption Spaces.* London: Arnold.

18

Roads

Peter Merriman

Mud, grit, stone, ice, wood, sand, concrete, tarmac. Roads can be and have been formed of many substances, and they have emerged and been created for many reasons. Roads *matter* in different ways. They may be fairly permanent and durable, or they may be seasonal and become impassable – being liable to flood, collapse or melt (Merriman 2011). What's more, people inhabit roads in different ways in different cultural contexts, giving rise to very different cultural attitudes to the socio-material assemblage of 'the road' and to differences in customs and laws relating to such things as speed, conduct, roadside activity and the types of vehicle and user permitted (Miller 2001; Edensor 2004; Merriman 2009a; Dalakoglou and Harvey 2012). Roads, then, are not simply material artefacts or landscape features which are of interest to engineers, planners and politicians. Roads are key infrastructures facilitating cultural and economic flows of people, goods and information. Roads facilitate the networking of communities, but they have only received a limited amount of attention from social science and humanities scholars, playing second-fiddle to mobile vehicles and mobile subjects in many recent literatures on road-based mobilities.

The practices of automobility and spaces of the car have received widespread attention from anthropologists, sociologists, geographers and cultural historians (e.g. O'Connell 1998; Sheller and Urry 2000; Featherstone *et al.* 2005; Böhm *et al.* 2006; Paterson 2007; Redshaw 2008; Merriman 2012), but the infrastructures of the road have received far less attention, and there has arguably been much more interest from scholars working beyond the so-called 'new mobilities paradigm', whether in humanities disciplines such as architecture and history, or the history of science, transport or landscape (e.g. Merriman 2007; Mom and Tissot 2007; Zeller 2007; Mauch and Zeller 2008; Hvattum *et al.* 2011; Guldi 2012). There are exceptions. In their article on 'The city and the car', Sheller and Urry (2000) argued that there was a need for research on the various 'scapes' which partly constituted the hybrid networks of automobility, but far more work has been undertaken by scholars in disciplines such as archaeology and anthropology on the diverse ways in which people have shaped and inhabited the spaces of the road, than in disciplines such as sociology or cultural studies (see Snead *et al.* 2009; Dalakoglou and Harvey 2012; Merriman, in press).

In this chapter I outline some of the different ways in which the spaces of the road have shown up in the social sciences and humanities over the past century or so. I start by examining the role of roads in the regional descriptions of geographers and historians, before tracing how roads were abstracted and represented as lines by regional scientists and spatial scientists in the 1950s and 1960s. In the third section I examine how humanistic geographers and planning activists reacted to the increasing impact of motor vehicles and highway construction projects on communities, characterising them as erosive and destructive forces; and then in the final section I outline the work of thinkers who have highlighted the diverse ways in which people inhabit and ascribe meanings to roads in different cultural contexts, from the motorways of Britain to tarmac roads in Niger.

Roads, regions, landscapes

Ships slide through the water, the cleft waves roll together, and all trace of the passage is blotted out. But land preserves traces of the routes early travelled by mankind. The road is branded on the soil.

(Vidal de la Blache 1926, p.370)

In his posthumously published collection *Principles of Human Geography*, the French geographer Paul Vidal de la Blache reflects upon the importance of roads, transportation and circulation to *la géographie humaine*. Roads are categorised into various types, from 'natural highways' traversed on foot, to 'artificial highways' such as Roman roads or modern motor roads organised 'into a system, a network, whose various parts feed into one another' (Vidal de la Blache 1926, p.378). Roads are seen to be influenced *by* topography, but also to have a clear influence *on* geography, ranging from their use in 'European colonisation' to their influence on settlement, politics, the economy and social relations (p.383). Vidal's human geography is one in which 'the natural environment offers *possible* avenues for human development' (Cloke *et al.* 1991, p.65), but while his regional geography discussed various habits and patterns of roads found in different places, we are provided with a rather descriptive regional geography and a rather weakly humanistic geography where there is little sense of human agency.

Roads and other transport and communications infrastructures were to become a key aspect of regional-historical geographies and regional and local histories concerned with tracing the impact of 'mankind' on the physical landscape. In his 1951 New Naturalist volume *A Natural History of Man in Britain* the anthropologist and geographer H. J. Fleure included a chapter on the history of 'communications and transport', tracing the evolution of these infrastructures, from ancient tracks to railways and canals (Fleure 1951). Writing a few years later in his landmark study *The Making of the English Landscape*, historian W. G. Hoskins focussed on the roads built in different ages which featured on just one Ordnance Survey map, sheet 145, covering areas of North Oxfordshire and Northamptonshire. For Hoskins, the map and the landscape itself provided clues to a past history, of ancient roads and old tracks and lanes, although much of this past beauty was seen to be under threat from modern development, including modern traffic and the ubiquitous 'by-pass' road, which:

are entirely without beauty. Is there anything uglier in the whole landscape than an arterial by-pass road, except an airfield? Old roads have been straightened, and have lost all their character, historic and otherwise.

(Hoskins 1955, p.247)

The straight modern road is placed into an entirely different category to the straight Roman road. Modern roads and their traffic are seen as 'ghastly infliction[s] on the English landscape' (Hoskins 1973, p.95), while ancient or medieval tracks and roads are framed as naturalised features which have evolved *with* and melded into the landscape over centuries. For regional geographers and landscape historians, roads and tracks were identified as one among many landscape features, but other scholars lamented the rather peripheral status of communications and transport in many regional descriptions and in geographical scholarship more generally. As the geographer and landscape historian Jay H. Appleton put it in his 1962 book on *The Geography of Communications in Great Britain*:

> Communications seem to be the Cinderella of geographers. They are always accorded lip-service in theoretical discussion and their importance is invariably acknowledged in regional descriptions. But few geographers have set themselves the task of examining communications for their own sake.
>
> *(Appleton 1962, p.xvii)*

In reply, Appleton focussed his attention on the economic and regional geographies of communications and transport infrastructures in Great Britain, discussing the impact of topography on routes, tracing the 'form and functions of communications', and delineating the emergence of 'nodes and junctions' in the landscape (Appleton 1962, p.ix). Communications are skilfully and richly interpreted through the traditional lens of topographic description, but the numerous maps and line diagrams which populate Appleton's text do still, at times, render these infrastructures as rather linear features on a paper/earth surface. Roads could be approached in terms of their linear and nodal geographies, and it was not just traditions of regional description and landscape history which approached communications and transport in these terms.

Routes, lines and optimal paths

During the 1950s, regional geographers and regional historians were enthusiastically tracing the historical development of transport networks in the landscape, but other academics were beginning to approach the geographies of roads in an altogether different manner. Inspired by the writings of regional theorists, geographers, economists and pioneers of social physics (notably Von Thünen, August Lösch, Walter Christaller, John Q. Stewart and George Zipf), a small but ever-increasing number of geographers started to turn to scientific methodology, quantitative methods, economic theory, and even fluid dynamics to advance new forms of spatial analysis and regional theory in the 1950s and 1960s. At the heart of much of this new work was an attempt to develop general or universal theories and models of geographic patterns and processes. Geographic patterns could be broken down into constituent geometric forms such as lines, planes, surfaces, points, and related measurements of distance and connectivity (Nystuen 1963), and roads and railways were upheld as key examples of routes or lines linking particular points or places.

Writing in *Locational Analysis in Human Geography*, Peter Haggett (1965) drew upon Zipf's 'principle of least effort' and Lösch's 'law of minimum effort' to explain how, in theory, movements tended to occur along the shortest or optimal path, but in actual situations 'paths are likely to diverge from the optimal paths (in distance terms) for a wide range of rational and irrational reasons' (Haggett 1965, p.33). Rational theories from economics, and physical theories from mathematics and physics, might suggest that flows occur in straight lines or that roads will be straight, but Haggett demonstrates how empirical applications of 'route theory' and 'network geometry' (particularly 'graph theory') rarely correspond to the simple propositions of location theory (Haggett 1965, pp.61–62). As anthropologists, sociologists, human geographers and historians are all-too aware, and as everyday experiences and encounters may reveal, mobile subjects are far from being entirely rational actors, or indeed from behaving or moving like fluids in a hydrological system or like matter under force of gravity. Nevertheless, road networks, flows and patterns were increasingly approached using the quantitative methods and techniques of an emerging spatial science, spurred on in the USA by a government imperative 'to assemble information on user and nonuser benefits from [the] highway improvements' which followed the enactment of the Highway Revenue Act of 1956 – the legislation which enabled the construction of the US interstate system (Hennes 1959, p.v).

At the University of Washington, leading spatial scientists – including William Garrison, Brian Berry, Duane Marble, John Nystuen and Richard Morrill – worked on a series of projects funded by the Washington State Highway Commission and the US Bureau of Public Roads: examining the impact of highways on central business districts, residential location, retailing, and the provision of services such as medical care (Garrison *et al.* 1959). As Trevor Barnes has shown, the Washington highways study provided extensive funds by which Garrison could build and sustain his research team – supporting students such as Brian Berry and Duane Marble; and these opportunities initially arose from Garrison's dialogues with researchers in the engineering and economics departments at the University of Washington, notably Robert G. Hennes, Professor of Engineering and one-time Chairman of the Washington State Commission for Highway Research (Garrison *et al.* 1959; Barnes 2001, pp.419–420). Hennes penned the foreword to Garrison, Berry, Marble, Nystuen and Morrill's landmark *Studies of Highway Development and Geographic Change*: a 291-page volume summarising their positivist research on the relations between highway location, land use and economic development.

Following Barnes's writings on the social and material networks underpinning the emergence of spatial science, we might suggest that it was not just personal biographies and philosophies, money, and computational machines which came together at this one key site of the quantitative revolution in human geography. US roads – particularly the new roads proposed for Washington state as part of the interstate highway system – were central to the knowledge networks of the University of Washington's spatial scientists. Of course, highways were a key *subject* of study, but it was, in part, the imperative to construct roads to aid the national economy and national defence, which resulted in funds being released for their research. Equipped with large – though not, by today's standards, powerful – IBM computers, spatial scientists approached roads as calculable spaces in terms of their location, distance from populations, and the flows of vehicles along them. But they were not the only professionals who approached roads as spaces for the calculation of actual and potential movement.

The late 1950s and 1960s was a period when many western highway engineers and civil servants turned to computers in an attempt to calculate future traffic flows and justify planning decisions. In Britain, this new method of future forecasting and highway planning became known as 'predict and provide', and the calculating power of computer technologies was harnessed to reinforce the authority of planners and highway engineers (Starkie 1982; *Traffic* 1999). As a highway planner from the 1960s might have argued: 'The computer and its statistical calculations show that traffic levels will increase, so we must provide a new road to fulfil this demand and ease congestion.' While many of these urban motorways and expressways had been envisioned by modern architects, planners and politicians in the 1930s and 1940s, economic depression and war-time necessities meant that these plans often remained on the drawing board until the late 1950s and 1960s (Merriman 2007). As traffic levels increased and motor vehicles and new roads started to have increasingly negative effects on urban life, so critical planners, architects, geographers and others struck back at prevailing attitudes to road construction and urban planning.

Erosive and placeless forces

While many spatial scientists and planners approached roads as linear features connecting places (paying little regard to the impact of these roads on local landscapes or the experiences of travellers), other planners, architects and indeed geographers emphasised the negative impact that new roads could and would have on different environments, ecologies and places. The US planning activist Jane Jacobs included a chapter entitled 'Erosion of cities or attrition of automobiles' in her 1961 book *The Death and Life of Great American Cities: The Future of Town Planning*, explaining how 'traffic arteries, along with parking lots, filling stations, and drive-in movies, are powerful and insistent instruments of city destruction' (Jacobs 1961, p.352). Likewise, the US geographer Ronald Horvath traced the expansion of 'automobile territory' in North American cities, focussing on the examples of East Lansing and Detroit in Michigan (Horvath 1974, p.168). Horvath took his lead from Jane Jacobs, but in mapping 'automobile territory', i.e. 'any area that is devoted to the movement, storage, or servicing of automobiles', he provided a powerful visualisation of the amount of space occupied by motor vehicles, with up to 65 per cent of downtown Detroit being classified as 'machine space' (Horvath 1974, pp.169–171). Machine space, and particularly automobile territory, was seen to be spreading under the influence of powerful 'political and economic institutions', with the average American having very little power to control such spaces and forces – leading Horvath to conclude that 'machine space is alienated territory' (1974, p.181).

Modern, enclosed high-speed vehicles are seen to take over places, separating passengers from their surroundings; and in later humanistic writings by geographers such as Edward Relph, modern roads are framed as communications infrastructures which are detached from the landscape, eroding local senses of place:

> Roads, railways, airports, cutting across or imposed on the landscape rather than developing with it, are not only features of placelessness in their own right, but, by making possible the mass movement of people with all their fashions and habits, have encouraged the spread of placelessness well beyond their immediate impacts.
>
> *(Relph 1976, p.90)*

This is not an uncommon view. For Relph, and later thinkers such as the French anthropologist Marc Augé, motorways and modern roads are key agents of placelessness; they are 'non-places' which reflect the globalisation of western technologies, commodities, architectural styles and lifestyles (Augé 1995; cf. Merriman 2004, 2009b, 2012). While many readers may sympathise with such a view, there is a danger that such sweeping interpretations overlook the diverse ways in which people inhabit these spaces and landscapes. People inhabit and dwell on and around roads in all manner of different ways, and as the next section shows it is these diverse practices of inhabitation and consumption which have pre-occupied many social science and humanities scholars over the past decade or so.

Inhabiting the road

In recent years, cultural geographers, anthropologists, historians and cultural theorists have started to pay increasing attention to the complex ways in which people travel along, occupy, inhabit or ascribe meanings to roads of different kinds. Road building and road improvement have long been seen to be key strategies of modernisation, whether in western states, colonial territories or in developing nations. Writing in 1947, the prominent British politician, writer and colonial administrator Lord Hailey suggested that 'the expansion of road communications is the pre-condition of development in most of our colonies' (Hailey 1947, p.viii). In the 1950s and 1960s motorways were positioned as vital to the reconstruction of post-war Britain and other western nations (Merriman 2007), while in recent times the modernity of motorways has been celebrated in rapidly developing countries such as China and Malaysia (Williamson 2003; Seiler 2012). Here, new roads and motorways are presented as key catalysts to economic development and prosperity, and for many regional geographers roads and transport corridors are still approached in terms of their economic importance as corridors of growth and development (Hebbert 2000; Merriman 2011). However, roads and motorways are not simply products of political decision-making, planning or engineering, for a large number of actors are required to bring about such socio-technical achievements: from human actors such as planners, politicians, engineers, lobbyists, labourers and landscape architects, to distinctive arrangements of concrete, tarmac and steel (Merriman 2005, 2007; also Graham and Marvin 2001). What's more, 'completed' roads also require a considerable amount of ongoing maintenance and repair (Graham and Thrift 2007).

It would be all-too easy to approach roads as purely functional spaces designed (or at least used) for purposes of travel and transport, but many road spaces are much more than this: serving as spaces of commerce or pleasure; connecting or separating communities; networking and binding together nations; and in some cases being designed either to fit into the landscape or to enable drivers to experience and view the landscape in pleasurable ways (Crowe 1960). Motoring is frequently framed as a distinctive and important way of engaging with, viewing and being in the landscape, being underpinned by a series of dynamic embodied practices which lead to a reconfiguration of aesthetics and modes of landscape appreciation (Merriman 2006). For the Brutalist architect Alison Smithson, 'the car-moved-seeing' produced 'a new sensibility' – a new way of being in, seeing and moving through the landscape (Smithson 1983, pp.15–16). Likewise, the acclaimed British sculptor Barbara Hepworth remarked in her autobiography on how early car journeys with her father defined her relationship to the forms, textures and shapes of landscape and sculptures:

> All my early memories are of forms and shapes and textures. Moving through and over the West Riding landscape with my father in his car, the hills were sculptures; the roads defined the form. Above all, there was the sensation of moving physically over the contours of fulnesses and concavities, through hollows and over peaks – feeling, touching, seeing, through mind and hand and eye. The sensation has never left me. I, the sculptor, *am* the landscape. I am the form and I am the hollow, the thrust and the contour.
>
> *(Hepworth 1993, p.11)*

Road, car and driver set the speed and rhythm with which the passenger moves through and embodies the landscape. Landscape, movement and sensation become entwined.

Roads are frequently celebrated as positive additions to the infrastructural landscape, but this is not always the case. Protests have emerged in western and non-western countries over both urban and rural road construction projects. In many developed countries campaigners have criticised the impact of new roads on local landscapes, heritage sites, valuable ecosystems and the global environment (e.g. Wall 1999), but in non-western countries new roads have sometimes attracted a very different set of criticisms and meanings. For example, as the anthropologist Adeline Masquelier has shown, the Mawri peoples of post-colonial Niger are often fearful of new tarmac roads, feeling that 'wrecks and calamities occurring on the road are never merely accidental', rather those killed are 'thought to be victims of bloodthirsty spirits who roam the highway in search of human prey' – spirits who are often deemed to be disturbed during the construction of roads (particularly with the felling of trees) (Masquelier 2002, pp.838–839). Modern tarmac roads are seen to interfere with spirit forces, capturing the souls of the spirits, which take their revenge on travellers.

Driving and the spaces of the road become associated with a diverse array of practices, affects, atmospheres, and cultural meanings and values. Driving can be framed as a means of escape or of achieving freedom, a rite of passage, an economic or social necessity, a modern pastime, a westernised activity, a thrilling leisure-practice, or a risky or dangerous pursuit. Roads may be framed as functional transport corridors, ancient or modern routes, symbols of empire or nation-building, environmentally destructive infrastructures, exciting race tracks, or as sites of death and memory. In previous research I have undertaken on the history of England's M1 motorway, I have shown how the first sections of this modern dual-carriageway road – opened in November 1959 – were celebrated as a distinctively modern and somewhat foreign presence cutting through the rural landscapes of South-East England. The motorway was envisioned as an experimental space for the testing of new materials, designs of bridge, sign, lighting, and rules and regulations, and the novelty of the road, lack of speed limit, and bright modern service areas lent the motorway an exotic air (Merriman 2007). In the months following its opening, the motorway became something of a tourist attraction, capturing the public's imagination. Motorists made special trips to see and travel along the motorway, standing on its bridges to watch the traffic, taking Sunday drives along its carriageways, and booking bus trips organised by London Transport (*The Times* 1959). The motorway was an exciting, exotic and modern space, and it was frequently depicted in a range of cultural forms, from a pop song, play and several children's books, to the covers of toy sets, in advertisements, and on television and radio programmes (Merriman 2007). These cultural texts and the road's physical infrastructures brought the motorway 'close' to a variety of consumers, from local residents and long-distance drivers, to radio listeners and excited children playing with toys and reading books. Motorways, then, are not simply physical and strikingly linear infrastructures in the landscape. Rather, they are continually practised, placed and ordered through the incessant enfolding of different atmospheres, subjects, materials, rhythms, texts and practices into a non-linear, topological and 'scrumpled geography' (Doel 1996, p.421; also Merriman 2011).

Conclusions

Roads are a persistent – if rather banal – presence in many people's everyday lives, providing more-or-less clear demarcations of routes through variable topographies and/or landscapes carved up by property owners. Roads may have developed over thousands of years or be purposefully routed and designed features in the landscape. Either way, roads are often presented as firmly located features which can be easily mapped, but I want to argue that roads are not simply engineered objects which are located in a physical landscape. Roads are also a key technology that mediates people's experiences of and engagements with landscapes (alongside various vehicular technologies). They shape and guide our experiences, and they have gathered countless meanings over thousands of years, from traveller's tales, to the representations of today's road movies. Indeed, it was the Russian literary theorist Mikhail Bakhtin who famously argued that 'the road' was 'a unique novelistic chronotope' which provided 'an enormous role in the history of the genre' of the novel (Bakhtin 1981, p.120). The road as 'chronotope'. The road as 'time space'; 'a path of life' upon which narratives are plotted (p.120). Roads are seen to conjure up images and sensations of movement, rhythm, direction, and temporal and spatial progression. But roads can also be associated with stillness, stopping, break-downs and blockages. Movement may be the goal, but it may not be achieved, possible or desirable. A quiet lane might appear to be interrupted by movement, traffic and noise. A busy road might be stilled by a closure, a crash, road works or an unusual event.

Acknowledgments

I would like to acknowledge the financial support of the AHRC under their 'Connected Communities' research programme, award reference AH/J011207/1. Thanks to James Kneale for pointing me towards the Bakhtin material some years ago.

References

Appleton, J. H. (1962) *The Geography of Communications in Great Britain*. London: Oxford University Press.

Augé, M. (1995) *Non-Places: Introduction to an Anthropology of Supermodernity*. London: Verso.

Bakhtin, M. M. (1981) *The Dialogic Imagination*. Austin, TX: University of Texas Press.

Barnes, T. J. (2001) 'Lives lived and lives told: biographies of geography's quantitative revolution', *Environment and Planning D: Society and Space* 19(4), pp.409–429.

Böhm, S., Jones, C., Land, C. and Paterson, M. (eds) (2006) *Against Automobility*. Oxford: Blackwell Publishing.

Cloke, P., Philo, C. and Sadler, D. (1991) *Approaching Human Geography*. London: PCP.

Crowe, S. (1960) *The Landscape of Roads*. London: The Architectural Press.

Dalakoglou, D. and Harvey, P. (2012) 'Roads and anthropology: ethnographic perspectives on space, time and (im)mobility', *Mobilities*, 7(4), pp.459–465.

Doel, M. (1996) 'A hundred thousand lines of flight: a machinic introduction to the nomad thought and scrumpled geography of Gilles Deleuze and Félix Guattari', *Environment and Planning D: Society and Space* 14(4), pp.421–439.

Edensor, T. (2004) 'Automobility and national identity: representation, geography and driving practice', *Theory, Culture & Society* 21(4–5), pp.101–120.

Featherstone, M., Thrift, N. and Urry, J. (eds) (2005) *Automobilities*. London: Sage.

Fleure, H. J. (1951) *A Natural History of Man in Britain*. London: Collins.

Garrison, W., Berry, B., Marble, D., Nystuen, J. and Morrill, R. (1959) *Studies of Highway Development and Geographic Change*. Seattle: University of Washington Press.

Graham, S. and Marvin, S. (2001) *Splintering Urbanism: Networked Infrastructures, Technological Mobilities and the Urban Condition*. London: Routledge.

Graham, S. and Thrift, N. (2007) 'Out of order: understanding repair and maintenance'. *Theory, Culture & Society* 24(3), pp.1–25.

Guldi, J. (2012) *Roads to Power: Britain Invents the Infrastructure State*. London: Harvard University Press.

Haggett, P. (1965) *Locational Analysis in Human Geography*. London: Edward Arnold.

Hailey, Lord (1947) 'An appreciation', in T. Salkield, *Road Making and Road Using (Third Edition)*. London: Sir Isaac Pitman and Sons, pp.vii–viii.

Hebbert, M. (2000) 'Transpennine: imaginative geographies of an interregional corridor', *Transactions of the Institute of British Geographers*, 25, pp.379–392.

Hennes, R. G. (1959) 'Foreword', in W. Garrison, B. Berry, D. Marble, J. Nystuen and R. Morrill, *Studies of Highway Development and Geographic Change*. Seattle: University of Washington Press, pp.v–vi.

Hepworth, B. (1993) *Barbara Hepworth: A Pictorial Autobiography*. London: The Tate Gallery.

Horvath, R. J. (1974) 'Machine space', *The Geographical Review* 64(2), pp.167–188.

Hoskins, W. G. (1955 [1983]) *The Making of the English Landscape*. Harmondsworth: Penguin.

Hoskins, W. G. (1973) *English Landscapes*. London: British Broadcasting Corporation.

Hvattum, M., Brenna, B., Elvebakk, B. and Kampevold Larsen, J. (eds) (2011) *Routes, Roads and Landscapes*. Farnham: Ashgate.

Jacobs, J. (1961 [1965]) *The Death and Life of Great American Cities: The Future of Town Planning*. Harmondsworth: Pelican.

Masquelier, A. (2002) 'Road mythographies: space, mobility, and the historical imagination in postcolonial Niger', *American Ethnologist* 29(4), pp.829–856.

Mauch, C. and Zeller, T. (eds) (2008) *The World Beyond the Windshield: Roads and Landscapes in the United States and Europe*. Athens, OH: Ohio University Press.

Merriman, P. (2004) 'Driving places: Marc Augé, non-places and the geographies of England's M1 motorway', *Theory, Culture & Society* 21(4–5), pp.145–167.

Merriman, P. (2005) '"Operation motorway": landscapes of construction on England's M1 motorway', *Journal of Historical Geography* 31(1), pp.113–133.

Merriman, P. (2006) '"A new look at the English landscape": landscape architecture, movement and the aesthetics of motorways in early post-war Britain', *Cultural Geographies* 13(1), pp.78–105.

Merriman, P. (2007) *Driving Spaces: A Cultural-Historical Geography of England's M1 Motorway*. Oxford: Blackwell.

Merriman, P. (2009a) 'Automobility and the geographies of the car', *Geography Compass* 3(2), pp.586–599.

Merriman, P. (2009b) 'Marc Augé on space, place and non-places', *Irish Journal of French Studies* 9, pp.9–29.

Merriman, P. (2011) 'Enfolding and gathering the landscape: the geographies of England's M1 motorway corridor', in M. Hvattum, B. Brenna, B. Elvebakk and J. Kampevold Larsen (eds), *Routes, Roads and Landscapes*. Farnham: Ashgate, pp.213–226.

Merriman, P. (2012) *Mobility, Space and Culture*. London: Routledge.

Merriman, P. (in press) 'Archaeologies of automobility', in P. Graves-Brown, R. Harrison and A. Piccini (eds), *The Oxford Handbook of the Archaeology of the Contemporary World*. Oxford: Oxford University Press.

Miller, D. (ed.) (2001) *Car Cultures*. Oxford: Berg.

Mom, G. and Tissot, L. (eds) (2007) *Road History: Planning, Building and Use*. Neuchâtel: Éditions Alphil.

Nystuen, J. D. (1963) 'Identification of some fundamental spatial concepts', *Papers of the Michigan Academy of Science, Arts and Letters* 48, pp.373–384.

O'Connell, S. (1998) *The Car and British Society: Class, Gender and Motoring, 1896–1939*. Manchester: Manchester University Press.

Paterson, M. (2007) *Automobile Politics: Ecology and Cultural Political Economy*. Cambridge: Cambridge University Press.

Redshaw, S. (2008) *In the Company of Cars: Driving as a Social and Cultural Practice*. Farnham: Ashgate.

Relph, E. (1976) *Place and Placelessness*. London: Pion.

Seiler, C. (2012) 'Welcoming China to modernity: US fantasies of Chinese automobility', *Public Culture* 24(2), pp.357–384.

Sheller, M. and Urry, J. (2000) 'The city and the car'. *International Journal of Urban and Regional Research* 24(4), pp.727–757.

Smithson, A. (1983) *AS in DS: An Eye on the Road*. Delft: Delft University Press.

Snead, J. E., Erickson, C. L. and Darling, J. A. (2009) *Landscapes of Movement: Trails, Paths and Roads in Anthropological Perspective*. Philadelphia, PA: Pennsylvania University Press.

Starkie, D. (1982) *The Motorway Age*. Oxford: Pergamon.

The Times (1959) 'Trips to see motorway'. 6 November, p.6.

Traffic (1999) 'Episode 2: Motorways', Produced by Lion Television, Broadcast on BBC 2, 1999.

Vidal de la Blache, P. (1926) *Principles of Human Geography*. London: Constable.

Wall, D. (1999) *Earth First! And the Anti-Roads Movement*. London: Routledge.

Williamson, T. (2003) 'The fluid state: Malaysia's national expressway', *Space and Culture* 6(2), pp.110–131.

Zeller, T. (2007) *Driving Germany: The Landscape of the German Autobahn, 1930–1970*. Oxford: Berghahn Books.

19

Queue

Gillian Fuller

> We treat each [of them] as a thing rather than as a progress, forgetting that the very permanence of their form is only the outline of a movement.
>
> (*Henri Bergson, Creative Evolution*)

Consider a typical urban scene – say, Town Hall Station, Sydney, 3.45 pm on a Tuesday. It is the beginning of the afternoon peak hour and the foot traffic along the concourse begins to build. The movement of bodies is mainly bidirectional – the bulk of the traffic moves towards the entry turnstiles but a small stream of people also move against this purposeful flow, away from the trains and towards the station exits that lead to sunlight, shopping and the business district above. Occasionally clusters form and then dissolve. Someone stops midstream, perhaps to regain orientation in the seemingly mindless flow now bifurcating around them, creating an eddy. Sometimes the cluster appears to harden and begins forming a tail: it becomes a queue.

The queue may appear unified – resolute in its collective stillness, steadfastly holding position amongst the milling, moving crowds. Observe a little longer and one may note that each person in the queue appears a little blasé, preoccupied with their own tasks of text messaging, hunting for change in their bags, reading the paper or just staring into space. Unknown to each other, they appear indifferent, insular in their thoughts and activities and yet their bodies are synched. If someone in the queue takes a lateral step, some kind of collectively known and viscerally sensed displacement occurs. The queue responds, realigning itself so the aberrant kink is reincorporated and smoothed back into alignment. These bodies seem to be responding to unseen commands, initiated by the viscerally felt interactions of the bodies themselves. A form of collective proprioception occurs. Somehow, although not unified, this tail registers displacements within itself self-referentially. Preoccupied with their own tasks, but alert to each other's positions and movements. The closer one gets to the head of the queue, the more closely the bodies press together. The taboo of anonymous touch dissolves – the queue appears to take on the characteristics of Canetti's crowds, they no longer 'fear the touch of the unknown'. But this is not a crowd; its potential for becoming something else is redirected into the serial linearity of a queue.

Queuing is the slow dance of the everyday. Most people queue every day without thinking about it. We queue at ATMs, ticket machines, in supermarkets, motor registries and hospitals, at any place where traffic, in the broadest sense of the term, congregates. We also queue when we ring call centres, or when we download data from the internet. There seems to be an unspoken and largely unquestioned respect for queues. People tend to accept their existence as a type of moral and fair mode of organisation. The base syntax of a queue is $x \wedge x$, or one then one. It seems so simple and fair. A neat, linear structure that seems to transparently echo a tidy discursive line that says something like 'good things come to those who wait'. While queues may be part of the rhetorico-practical regime of distribution economies, they are also embedded within an informational communicational economy. They are a type of control architecture where a temporal/spatial position seems to override a social position. Politics appear to dissolve into the distributive architectures of networks, transforming into a series of local and logical, rather than total and moral, modulations. Queues are not merely technical; they cut across all dimensions and in every direction, moving seamlessly from management to morality and back again. Queues are a type of strange attractor, a singularity that captures the motion of a multitude and directs it into a sequence.

But before I proceed another strand needs to be woven into this tail. One which brings into focus just how powerfully the queue operates as a diagram of a complex socio-technical infrastructure.

Queue-jumpers!

I mean we've always taken refugees and we always will. But what they are doing is queue jumping. I don't care what anybody says and they are not being held unreasonably. I mean I've heard some people describe the conditions in which they're held as concentration camps. That is insulting and demeaning to people who were held in concentration camps during World War II and it's a ridiculous and extravagant and outrageous criticism.

(John Howard, Prime Minister of Australia in a radio talkback interview, 2001)

Howard again, in 2004:

Look, I took a strong position on – on border protection. And I make no apology for that. But the proof of the pudding's in the eating. The – the illegal immigration has stopped.

I mean, it worked. It was right. It protected our borders. It stopped people queue jumping.

(Howard 2004)

Since the arrival of Vietnamese 'boat people' in the late 70s (Smit 2010) the term 'queue-jumper' has become a significant trope in the wedge politics that cyclically dominate Australian public life. The election of the neo-liberal government of John Howard in 1996 powerfully inaugurated another cycle. Despite a change of government in 2008, the refrain of the queue-jumper has now become a 'go to' sound bite – from the government and opposition, talk back radio, letters to the editor.

if you arrive in Australian waters and are taken to Malaysia, you will go to the back of the queue.

(Prime Minister Julia Gillard 2011)

In Australia (and elsewhere but not everywhere) queues have a decided moral dimension, where 'to jump the queue' is indexical with impoverished moral values and antisocial civil disobedience. To call someone (typically an asylum seeker from the developing world, who arrives in Australia by boat) a 'queue-jumper' is a form of vilification, justifying all kinds of cruel nonsense from internment in offshore detention centres to temporary visas. And, in a broader social context, we see a rising form of aggression being labelled 'queue rage'. We might think then that queues not only represent a technical structure but might also be seen as one of the dominant ethical indexes of contemporary life. Move but keep your place, move but stay in line. We may move more, but this movement is modulated through the technical/architectural ethos of the queue.

We live in a time in which threshold control and security (from national borders to network firewalls) coalesce to understand, harness and commoditise the necessities of mass movement. A refrain emerges that justifies further control: someone has 'jumped the queue' – they have committed a seemingly sacrilegious, immoral and unethical act: they have moved 'out of turn'.

At this point a couple of question are begging to be asked: what's so ethical about a queue? Moreover, how can such putative ethical concerns shade into the area of morals and what are the cultural implications of queues as a mode of organisation and control?

The power of sequence

A queue is a structure in which biology, sociology and architecture interpenetrate, forming in the process a temporal/spatial mode that coheres through serialised events. The term 'queue' derives from the Latin *cauda* (meaning tail) and came into the English language and practice (it seems) from French (*former la queue*). Up until the mid-eighteenth century the dominant meanings of the word related to tails or individual appendages that looked like tails, such as plaits and pigtails. In the mid-eighteenth century, according to my *Oxford English Dictionary*, the term evolved, as the times demanded, to cover a more abstracted idea of a tail – 'a line of people, vehicles etc, awaiting *their turn* to proceed, to be attended to'. However, the term 'queue' (as in form a line) didn't really gain public currency until a century after, if the archive of *The London Times* is to be trusted on these matters. In 1839 one finds the first mention of queues as waiting lines, but it is always made with reference to French idiom (*former la queue*, or *de faire la queue*). However, by the beginning of the twentieth century the English seem well-acquainted with the concept, and articles discussing the problems of beggars approaching captive queuers in theatre lines, the 'usual lengthy waits' at women's toilets, problems with trams arriving 'en queue' at the terminus in Blackfriars and the like proliferate. The queue may have solved the problem of crushes (where ladies would be stomped and their dresses torn) and the unruly behaviour of crowds, but it presented new ones: endless bureaucracy and an even tighter disjuncture between the civil behaviours of queuers and the suspicious activity of the mob who would bypass the order of the line, or even worse use the inherent vulnerability of motionlessness and rigid territoriality for begging, pickpocketing and the like.

But queues are not just visible tails that appear when crowds form around thresholds – they are also fundamental to the architecture of information society. The concept of queuing theory appears in the field of telephony in work by A. K. Erlang in the early twentieth century (Erlang 1909). Queue theory, in this context, is a mathematical theory that models the stochastic processes inherent in waiting lines (probable rates of arrival, number of servers available, rates of service, priority of service, size of system, size of potential customers/queuers, rates of drop out, etc.). In other words, queuing theory co-evolves with the flows of traffic associated with networks, modelling randomness as probable patterns of movement.

Queuing theory is thus about reducing queues, probabilising the potential and possible chaos of traffic.

Queues theorised in early telephony, which dealt with switching circuits (in which telephone operators created a circuit between A to B through the manual insertion of plugs in a switchboard), differ quite markedly from those that enable data to traverse the internet. Traditional telephony works along circuits – a continuous dedicated line between two points. Early attempts to use circuit systems as a mode of opening-up lines of communication between computers were found to be inadequate.[1] As Leonard Kleinrock, who, along with Paul Baran from the Rand Corporation, is credited with developing packet switching, notes:

> "Computers burst data, they transmit then they stop a while, while they're thinking or processing or whatever. And in those days data communication lines were really expensive", he said. "The idea was, don't dedicate a resource to somebody – when I was sitting there, scratching my head, that machine was idle, I'm not using it. You want to do it in dynamic fashion: whoever needs it gets it now. If you're not using it, let somebody else in."
>
> *(Kleinrock in Welch 2000)*

Thus, processing needed to be distributed and the notion of packet switching (breaking data into finite chunks rather than one synchronous circuit) was developed, based on the idea that a single data communication line could process multiple blocks of data from multiple sources on (originally) a first-in, first-out basis (FIFO). Packet-switching allowed for information to disperse and yet still retain coherence by breaking up data into digital packets and tagging each with a set of identifying labels and instructions so they could be located, directed, identified and reassembled after processing. The point here is that packeting and queues enable a resource to be shared efficiently in traffic flows (enabled by routers which identify quickest routes and traffic jams in the systems).

The way in which store and forward systems operate, particularly in the way that data queues configure movement as a series of events, and where duration is experienced as delay, points to the productivity of thinking about queues as informationalised and diagrammatic rather than just merely ideological or technical apparatuses (although they are these as well). Queues store events, realised through the forwarding processes of packet switching. Data does not 'move down the line' any more than a person moves down the line of a queue. The queue's form may look like something – a line or a tail – but the queue is a metastable form: stable in its continual variance, complex in its internal and constantly changing dynamics. The processes of 'storing and forwarding' do differ between data and bodies and it may be too much to say that the relationship is analogous; however, certain productive insights can be gained by considering these systemic behaviours topologically.

> If there is an informational quality to contemporary culture, then it might be not so much because we exchange more information than before, or even because we buy, sell, or copy informational commodities, but because cultural processes are taking on the attributes of information – they are increasingly grasped and conceived in terms of their informational dynamics.
>
> *(Terranova 2004: 7)*

Following Terranova's techno-cultural recuperation of Shannon's work in information theory, in which information is not reduced to 'content' but is rather a statistical measure of uncertainty in a system, one is able to be 'abstract enough' to reconsider an informational milieu that encompasses a range of both hard and soft communicative techniques. From this perspective one can consider the relations of communication and control as both modalising (signifying systems of semiotics) and modulating systems (a–signifying semiotic systems, such as invocatory commands, programming and coding architecture). The queue is not just a symptom of mass distribution, it is also a diagram of how bodies and bits, people and structures move relationally in a world where total sensorium is increasingly integrated into logistics and its motivated methods.

Queues are a form of control. They are material abstractions that structure relations between the one and the many. They are 'stateless', inasmuch as they can form anywhere and each server request is considered independently (this is certainly true technically for TCP/IP, the store/forward protocols of the internet, but also 'in principle' true for embodied lines) – although queues in both contexts are not without affective residues, the most visible being server burnout and queue-rage. But they are also 'state' structures in the way they produce 'territory', marking out the borders between the orderly queue and the unpredictable mob, and in the way they reproduce across all levels of social interaction – limiting potential into algorithms of probability. Despite the fact that queues seem to be proliferating, from food lines at UN facilities to telequeues for call centres distributed across the world, to talk about queues is in no way to talk about 'the future' in the sense of potentials of technocultural interaction. Rather it is to think of the future as a risk (or potential uncertainties around distribution systems that are commodified into risk) to be managed and controlled. In a world of speed, queues configure time as space and make delay and stillness a political issue. As Erin Manning notes:

> Controlling space is a way of creating a *locus operandi* for a pact of Reason. This is one of the functions of the state. Reason must maintain its borders. Bodies without Organs are not eminently reasonable. For that there is too much leakage. Hence, they must be policed, ordered, categorized, transformed into the national body-politic, into the definition of an imaginary that represents the sublation of identity and territory promised by the myth of the sovereign state.
>
> *(Manning 2004: n.p.)*

In other words, queues attempt to make bodies (which can be dividuated and managed) out of the dynamic interconnectivities of disparate elements not tied to any one system and thus without organs.[2] Queues reterritorialise the smooth displacements of movement itself into direction and sequence.

★   ★   ★

The queue braids together many complex systems through its intrinsic ability to reconfigure and rearrange bodies and bits. It does this by abstracting distribution architecture in the mode in which much contemporary media operates. One obvious way that queues informationalise is in their packeting, tagging and serialising.

Looking at a queue with figures standing, texting, chatting and the like, one might think of Sartre's holding forth of the queue as exemplary of a *plurality of isolations* (Sartre 2004: 256), which for Sartre and so many others is an indicative by-product of the city. The queue concept both abstracts and concomitantly individualises. The tail ceases being the appendage of an individual human and becomes a form that manifests through gatherings of people in relational motion. But if we want to return to Terranova's assertion about informational dynamics, we may want to broaden our terms a bit here and say: queues serialise relations so that many become one, and this many could be people, planes or information – bodies and bits in the broadest sense possible.

On an organisational level queues produce a singular yet collective subjectivity based on serialisation. On a micro level multiplicities emerge, cohere and dissolve. The many that become one become so through a serialised and event-based temporality. Describing the hyper-controlled bus queuing system in France, where one takes a ticket when arriving at a bus stop to secure one's position in the queue, Sartre writes:

> to the extent that the bus designates the present commuters, it constitutes them in their *interchangeability*: each of them is effectively produced by the social ensemble as united with his neighbours, in so far that he is strictly identical with them. In other words, their being-outside (that is to say, their interest as regular users of this bus service) is unified, in that it is a pure and indivisible abstraction, rather than a rich, differentiated synthesis; it is a simple identity.
>
> *(Sartre 2004: 259)*

So queues establish one (identity) in relation to another one (identity), i.e. one is third not tenth, etc. Such interchangeability establishes, as Sartre later notes, the impossibility of deciding. This is what he calls a serial unity – a 'homogenous medium of repetition', which determines one's fate as 'Other by every other as other' (Sartre 2004: 261).

A daily dance

What drives this next to next to next? There is no clear protagonist – not the queuer or the bus – or a distribution of scarcity, or a government responsible for infrastructure, they all emerge in this daily event. An event so regular across so many zones of activity and states of mind that it forms into a habit. It is, or becomes, sensory. It doesn't require 'thought' – it is registered into the body. Sequenced movement is so ingrained in compulsory mobility – it comes from both outside and inside.

★   ★   ★

The queue is exemplary of how grace is leached from the 'dance' of relational movement by displacing the displacement of movement into a lockstep governed by serial sequence.

> Creating movement is initiating a dance. This dance. This dance demands grace. A grace that is not succumbing to an outside, but a feeling of the inside, inside-out. "Grace is like the paradigm of intensity that escapes all qualitative reduction of movement". (Bergson 1959/1970: 12–13) Grace is never felt solely through a step. Grace is the becoming-dance of the step, when walking flows in the between of direction where holes become emergent openings rather than missed opportunities.
>
> *(Manning 2009: 30)*

In the queue the force of movement is reshaped into a line. This is not to say that the queue doesn't have its moments of grace. Often when I talk to people about my queue project, many will discuss what for them is the 'docility' of the queue – a presumed 'time out' from struggle and interaction as the queuer waits – or the random and often surprising (in a good way) interactions with fellow queuers. However, as Terranova points out,

> Information is not about brainwashing as a form of *media effect*, but it does involve a level of *distracted* perception; it thus informs habits and percepts and regulates the speed of a body by plugging it into a field of action. In this sense, the informational dimension of communication is not just about the successful delivery of a coded signal but also about contact and tactility, about architecture and design implying a dynamic modulation of material and social energies.
>
> *(Terranova 2004: 19)*

For instance, when we are in a call centre telequeue we are in a *Zu Befehl* state – we are 'like good soldiers . . . always in a state of conscious expectation of commands' (Canetti 1984: 312). For Canetti 'a soldier is like a prisoner who has adapted himself to the walls enclosing him, one who does not mind being a prisoner and fights against his confinement so little that the prison walls actually affect his shape' (1984: 312). This discipline shapes both system and user through a shared architecture of inputs, menus and commands that are so mutually implicative they are no longer generated by the outside (an *Ur* principle of commands for Canetti) – rather they take on the more intimate relations of prompts.

Still in the telequeue, the command prompt [press 1 for credit cards, etc.] signals the computer's need for input for the informational exchange to continue. Commands and the syntax for entering them constitute the interface – a cyborg convergence of 'natural semantics' and computer language in which self/other or inside/outside dissolve in an informational multitude. One is one in a sequence in which the only way out is to get off the network entirely or find some way to 'jump the queue'. Businesses have always seen the potential in selling speed and this now extends to the commodified queues, in which money trumps FIFO for priority services.

Dis-place-ment

Queues work within paradigms of scarcity, control and risk management. Their very existence invokes a shortage of resources, even if this scarcity is, for various reasons, state manufactured. Against the seemingly limitless expansion of capital, queues are control architecture for the many who can no longer be considered a people, but should, following Virno (2004) be considered a multitude.

A queue, unlike a crowd, unlike the people, does not synthesise the many into a One. Queues are public infrastructures that are mobile, ephemeral and metastable. They grasp the field of the many and direct them to the sequenced dividuations of the queue. They also make the complex architecture of network structures more manageable both technically and rhetorically. In a recent M/C article, Mark Nunes argues that 'apparatuses of capture modulate flows by eliminating the interstitial and regulating transmission as a mode of order' (Nunes 2005). Queues as apparatuses of motion capture work within the same topology. This is the condition of movement – of the dissolution of the 'people' to the algorithms of the multitude. We live in non-places – never at home – 'no longer having at our disposal any "special" or sectorial ethical-communicative codes' (Virno 2004: 37). The queue is a series of spatially arranged *dis*placements where proximate social relations are negotiated anonymously, and procedurally.

They constitute a mode that is neither here nor there, neither stops nor goes, but is restrained agitation toward movement. A place to consider how many become one, how crowds becomes queues, and units become unities as the spatiotemporal coordinates of store-forward reinvoke the spectres of scarcity and the promises of abundance and a life suspended through anticipation – of those who wait. The juxtaposition, made by Serres and others, of glittering towers and shanty towns, airports and refugee camps can be seen in the informational form in the topologies of waiting that occur at checkpoint, airport or on dial-up connection. If speed and movement is a commodity then delay is the control.

Queues are one of the fundamental architectural principles of all networks. They are infinite and stochastic and yet utterly controllable. Queues are a distribution technology: they are a resource for sharing, smoothing the striations that form at thresholds and producing a particularly linear and commodified form of justice that is proliferating and self-generating into multiple forms – for some, with smart technologies and good salaries, queues can be jumped, for others they are unavoidable. Queues diagram a relationscape of mobile life in which displacement is governed by a commonness of habits, in which the intervals of movement – the nextness of movement – are a form of 'distracted waiting' for the next input to initiate action in a sequence.

Notes

1 In 1965 Thomas Merrill and Lawrence Roberts connected the TX-2 computer in Massachusetts to the Q-32 in California with a low speed dial-up telephone line, creating the first (however small) wide-area computer network ever built. The result of this experiment was the realisation that the time-shared computers could work well together, running programs and retrieving data as necessary on the remote machine, but that the circuit-switched telephone system was totally inadequate for the job. Leiner M. *A Brief History of the Internet.* Available online at www.internetsociety.org/internet/ internet-51/history-internet/brief-history-internet (accessed 30 May 2012).
2 The Body without Organs (sometimes referred to as BwO) that Manning refers to here is developed by Deleuze and Guattari, following on from Antonin Artaud. The BwO is an assemblage or body with no underlying organisational principles, and hence no organs within it. The Body without Organs is not an organism (like a Body with Organs), it is a 'plane of consistency', by which movement can occur. Or put another way a BwO consolidates heterogenous elements into consistency rather than a system of organisation. The queue therefore works to striate the smooth space of a BwO into the *organ*ised space of a Body (my italics to emphasise the relationship of organ and organisation).

References

Augé, M. (1995) *Non-places: An Introduction to an Anthropology of Supermodernity*, trans. J. Howe, London: Verso.
Bergson, H. (1911/1984) *Creative Evolution*, trans. A. Mitchell, New York: Henry Holt and Company.
— (1959/1970) 'Essai sur les données immédiates de la conscience', in OEuvres/Henri Bergson edited by Andre Rubinet. Paris: Presses universitaires de France.
Canetti, E. (1984) *Crowds and Power*, New York: Farrar, Straus and Giroux.
De Landa, M. (2002) *Intensive Science and Virtual Philosophy*, New York: Continuum.
Deleuze, G. and Guattari, F. (1987) *A Thousand Plateaus: Capitalism and Schizophrenia*, trans. B. Massumi, London: Athlone Press.
Erlang, A. K. (1909) 'The theory of probability and telephone conversations' in E. Brockmeyer, H. L. Halstrom and A. Jensen (eds) (1948) *The Life and Works of A. K. Erlang, Volume 2*, Copenhagen: Danish Academy of Sciences.
Gillard, J. and Bowen, C. (2011) 'The regional cooperation framework', Joint media release with Julia Gillard – Prime Minister of Australia, and Chris Bowen – Minister for Immigration and Citizenship. Released 7 May 2011. Available online at www.minister.immi.gov.au/media/cb/2011/ cb165079.htm.

Howard, J. (2001) Interview with Neil Mitchell Program, Radio 3AW: Melbourne. Full transcript available online at http://sievx.com/articles/psdp/20010817HowardInterview.html.

— (2004) Interview (15 August 2004) with Laurie Oakes, *Sunday*, Channel Nine: Australia.

Le Bon, G. (2002/1896) *The Crowd: A Study of the Popular Mind*, New York: Dover Publications.

Manning, E. (2004) 'Sensing Beyond Security: What a Body Can Do', paper presented at Security Bytes, University of Lancaster, July 2004.

— (2009) *Relationscapes: Movement, Art, Philosophy*, Cambridge, MA: MIT Press.

Marr, D. (2001) 'Both sides singing the same old song on boat people', *The Age*, 21 Aug 2011. Available online at www.theage.com.au/national/both-sides-singing-the-same-old-song-on-boat-people-20110821-1j4u5.html.

Nunes, M. (2005) 'Distributed terror and the ordering of networked social space', *M/C Journal* 7, 6. Available online at http://journal.media-culture.org.au/0501/01-nunes.php.

Office of the Chief of Naval Operations, US Navy at War (1941–1945) 'Official Reports to the Secretary of the Navy by Fleet Admiral Ernest J. King, Commander in Chief U.S. Fleet and Chief of Naval Operations', Washington, DC: US Navy, Department, 1946, 36.

Sartre, J.-P. (2004) *Critique of Dialectical Reason vol. 1*, trans. A. Sheridan Smith, London: Verso.

Smit J. H. (2010) 'Malcolm Fraser's response to "commercial" refugee voyages', *Journal of International Relations* 8(2): 97–103.

Terranova, T. (2004) *Network Culture: Politics for the Information Age*, London: Pluto Press.

Virno, P. (2004) *The Grammar of the Multitude*, Semiotext(e): New York.

Welch, M. (2000) 'BIRTH OF A BLUEPRINT: Profile Internet Father, Leonard Kleinrock', *The Zone News*, January 2000.

20

Railways

Peter Thomas

In a recent interview, John Urry suggested that public or collective transport in its current form will become less significant in the future (Adey and Bissell 2010). The lock-in of steel and petroleum automobility over the course of the twentieth century and the greater flexibility that cars afford has, according to Urry, guaranteed automobility's status as an 'entire culture', and one which makes it difficult to imagine a return to collective forms of transport for most people. However, as a consequence of the dominance of the car, our current systems of automobility are, in many places, becoming socially, economically and environmentally unsustainable. The gridlocked streets and long traffic jams that characterise the experience of automobility for many world cities is a stark reminder of how the infrastructures that underpin this system of individualised personal mobility are at breaking point. Significantly, the hegemonic solution of merely increasing infrastructural capacity to resolve these issues has been challenged by many who argue that increasing capacity only serves to exacerbate congestion and, thus, the associated economic, social and environmental problems (Shaw and Docherty 2008; Goodwin *et al.* 1991). Indeed the benefits that the flexibilities permitted by automobility bring are, in many places, being severely compromised by the stresses and strains induced by congestion, a problem intensified by the increasing costs associated with running a car.

In response, for many cities, the social, economic and environmental problems induced by systems of automobility have generated a renewed enthusiasm for developing alternative forms of mobility, and in particular, for railways. Many cities are investing heavily in new and upgraded railway infrastructures to respond to the growing commuter demand. London's Crossrail is an exemplary project in this regard, demonstrating a significant investment in collective public mobility. Furthermore, this expansion of urban railways parallels a renewed enthusiasm for long-distance high-speed rail between major urban centres, particularly in the UK, Europe and the United States. However, whilst it is clear that new urban railways offer multiple social, economic and environmental benefits for city dwellers, the enthusiasm for such infrastructure projects is often not realised in actual construction projects for many reasons. After summarising the existent mobilities research on railways, this chapter turns the spotlight on Sydney. For politicians and commuters alike, new urban railways offer an ideal solution to Sydney's congestion problems. Yet such infrastructures are painfully slow to materialise. As such, this chapter explores just why infrastructure projects often take such a long time to be realised, relative to the immediacy of the problems that they promise to alleviate. This opens up new questions for mobilities research concerning the relationship between the expectancies that infrastructure projects generate and the lived experience of urban mobilities.

Railway mobilities

Railways have been at the heart of change since their inception in the 1830s, both driving and reflecting broader changes in the social, cultural and economic landscape within which they are situated. For Schivelbusch (1986) the emergence of the railway was quite simply a revolution for mobility: a unified 'machinic assemblage' that stood in stark contrast to the fragmentation that characterised previous forms of transportation. This great machine not only radically transformed perceptions of distance and time, but it had significant effects on the character of the places which were brought into closer proximity. Whilst the railway gave rise to new commuting cultures and new leisure practices, these new flows of people together with the time–space compression that they effected were also accused of contributing to the spread of 'placelessness' through the weakening of attachments to discrete places (Relph 1976), as well as being a threat to the beauty of rural areas.

Railways created new socialities and transformed people's senses of self. They gave rise to new modes of spectatorship (Kirby 1997) and in doing so rewired how bodies sensed and perceived the landscapes that they moved through (Nye 1997), now witnessed as a swiftly passing panorama. At the same time, this 'parcelling' of passengers hurled through the landscape at great speed generated all kinds of social and somatic anxieties, revealed most acutely in accounts that underscore fears for personal safety and anxiety of criminal activity and 'railway spine' (Harrington 2003). The railway gave rise to new, mobile publics, requiring the development of new skills to negotiate crowds, handle strangers (Löfgren 2008), and ensure that the necessary preparation was done to accomplish journeys successfully (Anon 1971), together with new literary and musical genres. Indeed the space of the train carriage remains a place where social relations amongst unacquainted people are negotiated and redrawn. Marc Augé's (2002) evocative account of the Paris métro reminds us of how different cultures move and press up against each other in the space of the train – relations that are as much affective as they are ideological, and revealed through torsions of uplift and frustration (Bissell 2010). Alternatively, railways might be constructed as much with a mind to screen passengers from 'undesirable' forms of difference (Graham 2002).

Railways have transformed the nature of urban life, not just by increasing the size of the hinterland that city workers can commute from, but also through the parallel emergence of new urban spaces. In the nineteenth century, large, urban railway stations were the cathedrals of their age, complete with imposing façades and intricate iconography. Today, many of these large railway stations are magnets for processes of gentrification through the redevelopment of railway quarters (Bertolini and Spit 1998) and as such have become destinations in their own right – designed in ways that seek to maximise positive affects, although they are often felt rather differently (Bissell 2009). Parallel to this, as quasi-public–private spaces, railway stations are becoming subject to new, intensified regimes of surveillance and control (Müller and Boos 2004).

More broadly, railways have always been intricately bound up with broader processes of global change and transformation. Whilst they were vital drivers of nineteenth-century industrialisation, enabling both people and goods to be moved over vast distances relatively quickly, they were also an integral part of the processes of European colonialism and empire-building, particularly in Africa and South East Asia. Furthermore, their role in governing territory was integral to the processes of colonisation in countries such as Australia and the United States. In terms of large-scale population movements, whilst mobilities researchers have illustrated the pivotal role of ships and planes in processes of migration, railways have also played a key part of the mass movement of people over the long distances implicated in both documented and undocumented migration (Martin 2011) and mass-movements of 'floating populations' such as during China's Spring Festival (Crang and Zhang 2012).

Railways facilitate both material and symbolic flows. As symbols of cooperation between nation states, transnational railway projects are conduits for people, objects, ideas and trust. The more sinister side of railway mobilities, however, is revealed in their co-option into military conflicts to transport troops and munitions. Whilst they played a pivotal role in the evacuation of British children during the aerial bombardment of UK cities, they were also responsible for transporting millions of innocent people to their deaths at concentration camps. As infamously, railway construction in Burma used forced labourers and prisoners of war to create an infrastructure to expand the Japanese empire.

Yet these railway infrastructures are more than the most visible aspects of trains, tracks and stations. They are a complex assemblage of tightly meshed socio-technical systems, involving different forms of knowledge and practical know-how (Law and Mol 2002), where signals, signalling equipment, staff rosters, ticketing systems, rules and regulations, and maintenance regimes, amongst many other components, must all work together for the mobility system to operate smoothly. Indeed small fractures to any of these components can have potentially catastrophic system-wide effects (Law and Mol 2002). Through these infrastructures are threaded the smaller-scale 'personal infrastructures' that are required to be a passenger, such as luggage and tickets (Watts 2008). Furthermore, the diversity of trains running along tracks adds to this complexity. High-frequency urban commuter trains are principally involved in the transportation of commuters from suburbs and satellite communities to their workplaces in cities on a routine, everyday basis, whereas longer-distance trains whose passengers are likely to travel less frequently have a greater proportion of people travelling for leisure. This contrasts with freight trains, crucial to both the transportation of raw materials and distribution of goods for sale.

Julie Cidell's (2011) concept of 'trainspace' reminds us that the sphere of influence that railways have for our understanding of place goes far beyond the physical infrastructure of the railway itself. Indeed railways have had a profound effect on popular culture, permeating many diverse spheres. Today, the aesthetic draw of 'romance of the rails' can be witnessed in the evocative lure of the luxury elite mobilities epitomised by the Orient Express, Blue Train, and Indian Pacific, often tinged with the halcyon days overtones that characterise nostalgia-infused preserved railway lines. Model railway enthusiasts recreate railways systems in miniature form (Yarwood and Shaw 2010), whilst armchair travellers browse timetables to construct imaginative mobilities (Jain 2006).

Australian trainspace

There is, of course, a geographical specificity to 'trainspace'. Whilst much attention within the historical mobilities literature has focused on the development of railways in the United Kingdom (Freeman 1999), much less attention has been given to developments in Australia which mesh onto specific moments and events in the history of colonisation and of the development of the federation, revealing a rather different set of concerns. The development of railway infrastructures within Australia, and specifically in New South Wales, needs to be understood within the geopolitical context of settler expansion from the mid-nineteenth century. The focus of railway construction during the initial period of railway expansion in the nineteenth century was on building railway lines that would 'open up the interior' and assist in the transportation of freight, particularly crops and cattle, from farmlands to ports (Collins 1983). This imbrication of the railway in the process of nation-building paralleled similar imperatives in the United States (Verstraete 2002). However, this focus on engineering rural railways in New South Wales came at the expense of constructing a more comprehensive urban railway network in Sydney, a problem that would later haunt the city – as will be seen in the second section of this chapter.

Today, railways in Australia still play a vital role in the transportation of goods and people. Freight trains that extend for multiple kilometres testify to the vital role of the railway in the mineral-dominated economy of contemporary Australia, whilst passenger railways predominantly serve commuters in the large urban centres. Longer-distance passenger trains play a much less significant role in transporting people between cities, owing in part to a lack of investment and the vast distances between urban centres which are more competitively served by air. Many persistent anxieties about Australian national identity are still playing out in trainspace, revealed most acutely in the completion of the Adelaide to Darwin railway in 2000, where sensitive indigenous land-rights issues came head to head with a more brazen 'technological nationalism' (Bishop 2002). A rather different set of trainspace anxieties are currently playing out in Sydney, as explored below.

Rail futures in north-western Sydney

In 2011, Sydney's mobility problems came to a head. The discontentment associated with moving around the city, which had grown to be such an endemic part of the city's everyday discursive and affective landscape, were confirmed in a report indicating that Sydney is the tenth worst city in the world for commuter pain, and the worst in Australia (IBM 2011). Between 1991 and 2010 Sydney's population grew from 3.7 million to 4.6 million (Australian Bureau of Statistics 1997, 2011). This growth manifested itself through significant outward expansion of the city limits, together with an increased density of people living within the inner-city areas of the city, both of which necessitated new infrastructural provision to keep pace with the city's growing mobility requirements. However, investment in transport infrastructure has not kept pace with the expanding population and, as a result, the city now suffers from some of the most severe congestion problems in Australia.

The stresses and strains of moving around Sydney dominated the 2011 New South Wales state election, the body responsible for the city's transport system. The perceived absence of action of the then-government to deliver on promised solutions helped to deliver election victory to the opposition Coalition parties after 17 years of being out of government. The newly elected Premier of New South Wales, Barry O'Farrell, committed to making transport a top priority (Robins 2011) and committed the government's support to a north-west rail link (see Figure 20.1) shortly after being elected (O'Farrell 2011). Yet, significantly, the mobility solutions so vital to attend to this population growth *have* been a significant part of the city's political landscape for many years. Indeed thirteen years before the 2011 election, the effects of congestion on the city's socioeconomic well-being were documented in the state government's 'NSW Action for Transport 2010 plan' (Department of Transport 1998).

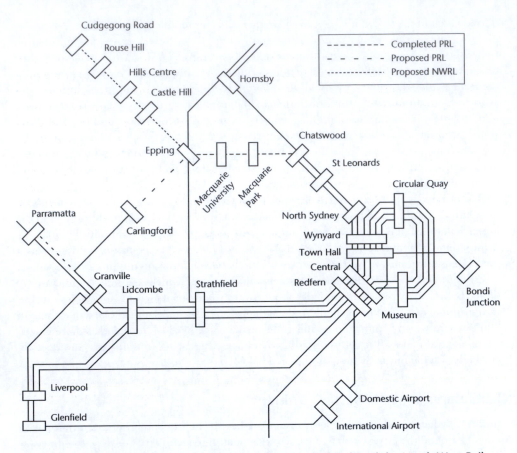

Figure 20.1 Simplified map of the proposed Parramatta Rail Link and the North West Rail Link alongside the existing urban railways in Sydney (Adapted from RailCorp 2012 by Andrew Gregory)

The growth of the city and the increasing number of people living and working beyond the existing transport network was identified in the plan as an impending problem for the city that required urgent action. Significantly, the western and north-western areas of Sydney were identified as being particularly poorly served by public transport. The plan stated that to help meet the future residential and employment growth of the city, vital public transport infrastructure improvements were required to reduce the road–dependency that had come to characterise Sydney's mobility. As part of the public transport initiatives required to accommodate the city's growth, the 1998 plan proposed the construction of eight new urban railway lines to be completed by 2010. However, over the 12 years of this period, only one of those planned railways was completed, and part of a second was begun. In a strikingly similar vein to transport policy in the United Kingdom (see Shaw and Docherty 2008), transport problems were identified, continuous road-building was rejected as a solution, and progressive commitments to deliver a more sustainable transport solution through public transport were advocated. This mismatch between promise and delivery has left many parts of Sydney, particular those in the high-growth north-west corridor, severely congested and over-reliant on individualised road transport.

Obdurate imminent mobilities

Infrastructure plans and the promises they make to deliver mobility systems enact power. Here I use the term 'imminent mobilities' to refer to how infrastructure plans generate their own flows and attachments. Their *virtual* existence is felt in the urban landscapes through the places they are to pass. Revealing a similar affectual landscape to those documented in periods of early railway construction, these plans enact similar torsions of excitement and anxiety, celebration and repulsion. Whilst potentially more-comfortable journeys to work excite people whose current commuting practices are dogged with the stresses and strains associated with congestion, the potential visual impact and increased noise concern others, worried about how a new railway line will irrevocably transform the character of the urban landscape. Put simply, the virtual powers of the plans have very real effects. Even though the infrastructures in the plans are not (yet) physically constructed in the city's landscape, they manifest themselves symbolically and affectively in powerful ways.

In particular, the maps and route diagrams for the new lines, that form a significant part of the plans themselves, create new visions of the city, generating significant mobility potential (Kaufmann 2002) for those within its orbit. Their circulation through different media channels to fire the public's imagination actualises a possible urban future, bringing it into the present, and rendering it tangible. These mobility diagrams are powerful technologies through the ways in which they sculpt how the city is perceived and navigated (Vertesi 2008), revealing tangible possibilities for future ways of moving about the city, linking previously distanced places and making new flows possible. Even in the absence of construction, the plans themselves can manifest themselves in powerful ways in the physical transformation of urban landscapes. They are used to pinpoint new areas for residential and industrial development, which affects the morphology of urban growth before the railway even appears. Indeed these 'imminent' mobilities are charged with important political capital that can be wielded by politicians with their electorates. Furthermore, at the national scale, these imminent mobilities satisfy broader concerns about enhancing the city's image on the world stage (Butcher 2011).

★　★　★

Whilst the majority of the railways proposed in the 1998 transport plan have not been constructed, the imminent mobilities that they generated continue to live and their effects are still present. The announcements that were made, the documents and diagrams that were produced setting forth mobility solutions, and the ambitious plans to construct new railways to generate a series of new mobile flows within the city continue to live a powerful virtual existence. Although absent from the landscape, they remain stubbornly present, manifesting themselves in complex and subtle ways which have significant political effects. These imminent mobilities exist as unfulfilled paths of connection within the city, revealing their power through the frustrations that are experienced when the existing mobility system fails; when places and key landmarks earmarked for development are passed through; and when public debate once again highlights the potential mobilities that they afford. Indeed for Sydney, this landscape over-brimming with the imminent mobilities formed of plans, commitments and promises is in tension with the relative absence of actual railway construction. These imminent mobilities fizz with potential in the way that they both offer relief from the problems that they promise to resolve, but also at the same time exacerbate frustration through their absence of translation into the built form of the city.

Fluctuating imminent mobilities

The ingrained effects of these imminent mobilities, however, stand in contrast to their fluc-tuating character, which changed significantly over the 13 years since the publication of the 1998 report. Since 1998 only one of the planned railway lines has been completed in full and one other has been partially completed. Unpacking the development of this partially com-pleted railway line, the Epping to Chatswood rail link, reveals these oscillations in full force, providing a lens through which the socio-political complexities of future railway mobilities can be unpacked.

As part of the 1998 'Action for Transport 2010' plan the 'Parramatta Rail Link' (PRL) was proposed, linking the city's expanding west in Parramatta with the significantly growing areas of Epping and Chatswood to the north of the CBD. In addition, a North West Rail Link (NWRL) was also proposed, which would extend the existing rail network by running from Epping through to the north-west suburbs as far as Castle Hill. However, soon after the publication of the report, doubts started to emerge over the project's financial viability and the commitment of the government to deliver the project. In 2002, the Transport Minister announced a preferred, extended route for the NWRL, going as far as Rouse Hill, but the government would not give an indication of when construction of the project would begin or when the line might open (Scully 2002). Instead reference was made to extensive consul-tation with the public, and that such projects normally take 10–15 years to complete (Scully 2002). Furthermore, it was announced that construction on the NWRL would likely not follow until the PRL had been completed in 2010 (Scully 2002).

By October of 2002, a feasibility study reported that the NWRL could be extended to meet the existing Richmond line. Planning approval was granted for the PRL in February 2002 and construction started on the section between Epping and Chatswood (Ministry of Transport 2003). Then, in June of 2003 the Transport Minister requested a review of the Parramatta to Epping section of the route. The review looked at different route options and recommended a modified version of the approved route (Ministry of Transport 2003). But the government did not take this recommendation forward and instead announced that the Epping to Parramatta section of the PRL would be postponed indefinitely (Kerr 2003).

The government's intentions to build the new railways promised in the 'Action for Trans-port' were becoming unstuck and, with the exception of the completed airport railway, progress was not being made on any of the other proposed lines. So in 2005, the State Premier announced a revival of Sydney's railway expansion plans through the new 'Metropolitan Rail Expansion Plan', which contained a promise to build three new railways: a South West Rail Link, a new CBD rail line between Chatswood and Redfern, and re-committal to the NWRL, but in a further modified form from Cheltenham to Rouse Hill (Department of Planning 2005). A year later, a 'Project application and preliminary environmental assess-ment report' was published to assist in the planning of the NWRL (Transport Infrastructure Development Corporation 2006). However, a change in State Premier in March 2008 and delays in starting construction on the line led to a further change: the NWRL was to become a 'metro' style railway (NWMetro) rather than a traditional 'heavy rail' line (New South Wales Government 2008). But then, by October of that year, new plans were afoot: the plans for a CBD railway line were also changed to a metro line, and the NWMetro was to be sig-nificantly shortened. Only a few weeks later, the entire NWMetro program was deferred indefinitely due to budgetary cuts (ABC News 2008). The only part of the PRL/NWRL plan to be constructed, the link from Chatswood to Epping, opened in February 2009.

By 2010 there was no sign of plans to start work on the missing Epping to Parramatta part of the PRL, and no sign of taking the line further north-west for the NWRL. Another new Premier was sworn in, and immediately a transport plan was devised – the 'Metropolitan Transport Plan' (Department of Planning 2010) – and then released in February 2010, which effectively cancelled the CBD metro as it was missing from the new transport plan. This was despite project planning approval being granted a month previously, and the award for major construction contracts and construction itself scheduled for 2010. Work already in progress to the value of A$176 million had to be written off, and compensation of A$93.5 million paid by the government for cancelled contracts and tenders it was no longer proceeding with (Sydney Metro 2010). The new plan revived the government's commitment to construct an NWRL, which was to be built over the plan's ten-year period. In August 2010, an application for funding by the state government to the federal government through Infrastructure Australia to bring forward the construction of the NWRL was turned down. The future construction of both the NWRL and the PRL railways in Sydney remains uncertain. The new Premier Barry O'Farrell has committed to start construction on the NWRL before the next state election in 2016. Consultations with the public are currently underway, but construction has not yet begun.

Waiting for infrastructures

Since the 1998 'Action for Transport 2010' plan, the nature of the challenge remains broadly the same, with Sydney expanding further outwards and its population growing, particularly in the north-west of the city. Yet this key growth area remains largely excluded from Sydney's rail network to this day, in part a symptom of the changeability of imminent mobility of the three transport plans and intervening changes made to these plans. So why have these oscillations taken place? In this final section, whilst space does not permit a fuller discussion that would be more sensitive to the complexity of the issues at play, four key tensions will be highlighted so as to begin to understand this on-going deferral of translation from the imminent mobility of plans to the physical infrastructure that Sydney so desperately requires.

First, the proposed building of both the NWRL and PRL was deferred owing to tensions between different tiers of government, and these tensions have, at times, pulled the proposed new railways in different directions. Since 1998 there were times when the different layers of government had divergent agendas and allegiances, working towards different imperatives to solve their own vested concerns. The federal government prioritised completing the missing section of the PRL over the state government's most recently preferred option of embarking on the NWRL, a prioritisation made within a political election campaign within marginal electorates set to benefit from such an outcome. Tensions between local and state government have emerged as the lack of development on the NWRL led to one local council to refuse to permit further expansion within an economic growth zone until the state government delivered on their commitments. This tension resulted in the state government threatening to remove the local council's responsibility for planning within the area. These tensions threaten to pull the complex assemblage required to bring such changes in both transport infrastructure and urban development in different directions, and lead to a stasis in progress.

Second, tensions existed not only between the different tiers of government but also within them. For the state government, as time passed other priorities emerged that took precedence over what had previously been identified as *the* key problem for the city. With the costs of the proposed projects increasing beyond their initial estimates, and with finite state resources, the state government's treasury saw maintaining a positive credit rating with leading credit rating agencies as a greater and more immediate problem to resolve than that of embarking on a long-term project. The benefits of delivery seemed both distant, and also partial, in terms of the numbers of people, and more importantly voters, that would actually make use of the lines. The synonymous historical relationship between railway construction, cost over-runs and the inability of such forms of transport to repay their direct capital costs can lead to unease for those charged with making the financial decision for go-ahead. The longer-term social, environmental, and economic benefits brought about by railway infrastructures cannot be easily accounted for.

Third, some of the changes witnessed in the infrastructural plans emerged through symbolic-aesthetic tensions that reflected changing dispositions to different modes of public transport. Whilst the 1998 plan favoured the extension of the current heavy rail network, the switch in preference of a light rail metro system in 2008 in part reflects changing attitudes to what constitutes comfortable and convenient public transport in a contemporary world city. After ten years of waiting for construction to commence on this proposed route, rather than re-promise the same undelivered mobility solution, a new solution in the form of a metro was instead promised. Delivering this new metro would satiate Sydney's desire to be a truly world-class city, giving it high-quality, modern public transport in common with other cities of this stature.

Fourth, building new railway lines is a significant undertaking, taking a considerable amount of time and capital but also requiring commitment, belief and enthusiasm, those immaterialities that are equally vital to driving infrastructure projects. The disjuncture between the temporalities of experiencing the benefits of building the NWRL and those of building the PRL stand in stark contrast to the temporalities of political cycles which the key people responsible for seeing through such commitments inhabit. Promising new railways offers quick and short-term relief from the constrained mobilities currently felt within the city. Undertaking feasibility studies, planning possible route alignments, and proclaiming the benefits of such schemes in the future all give the appearance that 'something is being done', and that these imminent mobilities will eventually translate into actual mobilities.

Conclusion: disrupted imminent mobilities

In contrast to Urry's contention that public transport will play a relatively minor role in mobility futures (Adey and Bissell 2010), railways have been positioned as a key solution to Sydney's chronic mobility problems through successive urban transport plans. Referring to infrastructural assemblages, Law and Mol (2002) remind us how manifesting 'the good' requires close coordination between different parts of decision-making assemblages. However, through each of these tensions outlined above, we can start to understand how the priority identified by 'the good' changes over time, and becomes fractured, disputed and highly contentious. Indeed for Sydney, the oscillations generated by these tensions have resulted in the perpetual stalling of the practical action so desperately required to resolve one of the city's most endemic and challenging problems. At the same time, the imminent mobilities enacted through the plans and announcements since 1998 each set up new anticipations, new atmospheres of expectancy and new visions of the city's future. However, these new plans and announcements do not occur in a temporal vacuum but slice through an urban landscape that is already overflowing with the affective charge of previous plans and announcements. The reception of new plans and announcements is always already conditioned by the hopes and frustrations of previous promises.

While events of mobility disruption have usually been conceptualised through disruptions to existing infrastructures (Graham 2009), this chapter has illustrated how ruptures and disruption are equally a part of the imminent mobilities of future urban transport plans. Whilst the effects might be less immediately catastrophic, they are no-less significant to the social, economic and political fabric of cities. Disruption to these imminent mobilities significantly impacts on the immaterialities of belief and will: those intangible, affective drivers that are so important to getting infrastructure built. The effect of perceived 'broken promises' and their manifestation in negative affects for city inhabitants, such as cynicism and disenchantment, goes far beyond mere malaise with decision-makers but crucially conditions and feeds back into the shape of future decisions. That the planning and decision-making apparatuses are a hugely significant dimension of the mobility assemblage is something that transport studies have taught mobility researchers well. But more research is required to understand precisely how these topologies of expectancy and disenchantment generated by the oscillatory nature of imminent mobilities of plans and announcements feed into the everyday, lived experience of mobile life in the city.

References

ABC News (2008) *Rees Scraps North-West Metro*. Available online at www.abc.net.au/news/2008-10-31/rees-scraps-north-west-metro/189166 (accessed 23 October 2011).

Adey, P. and Bissell, D. (2010) 'The mobility of thought: an interview with John Urry', *Environment and Planning D: Society and Space* 27: 1–16.

Anon. (1863/1971) *Railway Traveller's Handy Book*, J. Simmons (ed.). London: Adams and Dart.

Augé, M. (2002) *In the Metro*, trans. T. Conley. Minneapolis: University of Minnesota Press.

Australian Bureau of Statistics (1997) *Regional Population Growth, Australia, 1991–96*. Commonwealth of Australia: Canberra.

Australian Bureau of Statistics (2011) *Regional Population Growth, Australia, 2009–10*. Available online at www.abs.gov.au/ausstats/abs@.nsf/Products/3218.0~2009-10~Main+Features~New+South+Wales?OpenDocument (accessed 5 January 2012).

Bertolini, L. and Spit, T. (1998) *Cities on Rails: the redevelopment of railway station areas*. London: Routledge.

Bishop, P. (2002) 'Gathering the land: the Alice Springs to Darwin rail corridor', *Environment and Planning D: Society and Space* 20: 295–317.

Bissell, D. (2009) 'Conceptualising differently-mobile passengers: geographies of everyday encumbrance in the railway station', *Social and Cultural Geography* 10: 173–95.

Bissell, D. (2010) 'Passenger mobilities: affective atmospheres and the sociality of public transport', *Environment and Planning D: Society and Space* 28: 270–89.

Butcher, M. (2011) 'Cultures of commuting: the mobile negotiation of space and subjectivity on Delhi's Metro', *Mobilities* 6: 237–54.

Cidell, J. (2011) 'Fear of a foreign railroad: transnationalism, trainspace, and (im)mobility in the Chicago suburbs', *Transactions of the Institute of British Geographers*, online first, doi: 10.1111/j.1475-5661.2011.00491.x.

Collins, I. (1983) 'The "country interest" and the eastern suburbs railway 1875–1932', in G. Wotherspoon (ed.) *Sydney's Transport*. Sydney: Hale & Iremonger.

Crang, M. and Zhang, J. (2012) 'Transient dwelling: trains as places of identification for the floating population of China', *Social and Cultural Geography* 13: 895–914.

Department of Planning (2005) 'Transport Strategy for Sydney', *City of Cities: A Plan for Sydney's Future*. Sydney: Department of Planning.

Department of Planning (2010) *Metropolitan Plan for Sydney 2036*. Sydney, NSW: Department of Planning.

Department of Transport (1998) *Action for Transport 2010: an integrated transport plan for Sydney*. Sydney: Department of Transport.

Freeman, M. (1999) *Railways and the Victorian Imagination*. London and New Haven: Yale University Press.

Goodwin, P. B., Hallett, S., Kenny, F. and Stokes, G. (1991) *Transport: The New Realism. Report 624.* University of Oxford: Transport Studies Unit.

Graham, S. (2002) 'FlowCity: networked mobilities and the contemporary metropolis', *Journal of Urban Technology* 9: 1–20.

Graham, S. (ed.) (2009) *Disrupted Cities.* London: Routledge.

Harrington, R. (2003) 'On the tracks of trauma: railway spine reconsidered', *Social History of Medicine* 16: 209–23.

IBM (2011) 'Australian cities not keeping up with commuter needs: IBM Commuter Pain Study', press release, 17 February 2011. Available online at www.03.ibm.com/press/au/en/pressrelease/33560. wss (accessed 5 January 2012).

Jain, J. (2006) 'Bypassing and WAPing: reconfiguring timetables for "real-time" mobility', in M. Sheller and J. Urry (eds) *Mobile Technologies of the City.* London: Routledge.

Kaufmann, V. (2002) *Re-thinking Mobility and Contemporary Sociology.* Aldershot: Ashgate.

Kerr, J. (2003) 'Big-ticket items go as Costa redrafts transport blueprint', *Sydney Morning Herald,* 22 August 2003. Available online at www.smh.com.au/articles/2003/08/21/1061434990699.html (accessed 20 January 2012).

Kirby, L. (1997) *Parallel Tracks: The Railroad and Silent Cinema.* Durham: Duke University Press.

Law, J. and Mol, A. (2002) 'Local entanglements or utopian moves: an inquiry into train accidents', in M. Parker (ed.) *Utopia and Organization.* Oxford: Blackwell.

Löfgren, O. (2008) 'Motion and emotion: learning to be a railway traveller', *Mobilities* 3: 331–51.

Martin, C. (2011) 'Desperate passage: violent mobilities and the politics of discomfort', *Journal of Transport Geography* 19: 1046–52.

Ministry of Transport (2003) *Parramatta Rail Link: PRL West options Project Director's report.* Parramatta: Parramatta Rail Link Company.

Müller, C. and Boos, D. (2004) 'Zurich main railway station: a typology of public CCTV systems', *Surveillance and Society* 2: 161–76.

New South Wales Government (2008) *Sydney Link: The Future of Sydney's Transport.* Sydney: New South Wales Government.

Nye, D. E. (1997) *Narratives and Spaces: Technology and the Construction of American Culture.* New York: Columbia University Press.

O'Farrell, B. (2011) *Fast Track of North West Rail Link Underway,* New South Wales Government media release. Available online at www.premier.nsw.gov.au/sites/default/files/110406-NWRAIL.pdf (accessed 10 October 2011).

RailCorp (2012) 'CityRail Network'. Available online at www.cityrail.info/stations/pdf/CityRail_network_map.pdf (accessed 22 January 2012).

Relph, E. (1976) *Place and Placelessness.* London: Pion.

Robins, B. (2011) 'Transport and roads to be focus of first 100 days', *Sydney Morning Herald,* 28 March 2011. Available online at www.smh.com.au/nsw/state-election-2011/transport-and-roads-to-be-focus-of-first-100-days-20110327-1cc10.html (accessed 12 October 2011).

Schivelbusch, W. (1986) *The Railway Journey: The Industralization of Time and Space in the 19th Century.* Berkeley: University of California Press.

Scully, C. (2002) *Release of the Preferred Route for the Proposed Rail Link for Sydney's North West.* Ministry of Transport media release. Available online at http://pandora.nla.gov.au/pan/49629/20050503-0000/www.transport.nsw.gov.au/news/media-nwrl-min.html (accessed 10 December 2011).

Shaw, J. and Docherty, I. (2008) 'New deal or no new deal? A decade of "sustainable" transport in the UK', in I. Docherty and J. Shaw (eds) *Traffic Jam: Ten years of 'Sustainable' Transport in the UK.* Bristol: The Policy Press.

Sydney Metro (2010) *2010 Annual Report.* Sydney, NSW: New South Wales Government.

Transport Infrastructure Development Corporation (2006) *North West Rail Link Project Application and Preliminary Environmental Assessment.* SKM: Sydney.

Verstraete, G. (2002) 'Railroading America: towards a material study of the nation', *Theory, Culture & Society* 19: 145–59.

Vertesi, J. (2008) 'Mind the gap: the London underground map and users' representations of urban space', *Social Studies of Science* 38: 7–33.

Watts, L. (2008) 'The art and craft of train travel', *Social and Cultural Geography* 9: 711–26.

Yarwood, R. and Shaw, J. (2010) '"N-gaugin" geographies: craft consumption, indoor leisure and model railways', *Area* 42: 425–33.

21
Pipes and Cables

Derek P. McCormack

In a world where we expect more and more mobile devices and experiences to be wireless, it is easy, perhaps, to forget that physical connections of various kinds are critical elements of the organizational infrastructures of mobile forms of life. Wires, pipes, tubes, and cables are all central to the engineering of structures and networks that act as conduits and route-ways for different technologies of transport, forms of mobility, and moving materials. In the context of efforts to think of materialities in terms of movement, flow, and circulation, it is tempting to depict these infrastructures as fixed, inert, and immobile. In what follows I hope to show that this is not the case. Indeed, understanding the design and distribution of such technologies of connectivity is an important part of mapping the broader field of mobilities across a range of domains of life and expertise. Equally, it is also important to remember that these technologies are woven into, and are in some sense productive of, distinctive modes of experience associated, for instance, with the construction of infrastructures of mobility, with their everyday use, and with the forms of aesthetic and affective attachment generated in the process. What emerges through thinking about such mundane things as pipes and cables is a sense of the rigging and routing of assemblages of mobility composed of multiple devices, materials, and agencies, organized in various ways and con-tinuously generating – albeit at different speeds – the infrastructural conditions for different experiences.

Suspension

In July 1876, the second of the twin towers of the Brooklyn Bridge was completed on the Manhattan side of the East River. At the time, along with the tower on the Brooklyn side of the river, it was the highest free-standing structure in North America, its solid granite mass dwarfing the buildings on Manhattan. Shortly afterwards, work commenced on spinning the four cables from which the road, rail, and pedestrian crossings would be suspended. Each cable was 15¾ inches thick, and was spun from over 5000 individual steel wires bundled into 19 strands. When joined together, the wires in each strand – or skein – formed a continuous length of about 200 miles, passing across and back between the anchor points on either side of the bridge 278 times (Conant, 1883). The wire for the cables were spun *in situ* over an

18-month period by men shuttling back and forth in mobile buggies, or carriers, suspended high over the East River.

The success of the entire project depended upon the proper positioning and tensioning of the wires in order to produce a carefully calculated catenary curve between the massive towers. The weight of the cable was borne by the towers, serving in turn to stabilize them further. Spinning the cable was a process requiring not just detailed knowledge of engineering and the physics of forces: it also involved skilled movement of metal and bodies, and in particular demanded practical and careful handling of the wires as they travelled high above the river. In this sense, it was remarkably similar to the process of rigging a ship, and the men who worked at height on the bridge required similar skills to sailors who worked between the masts above deck. Like its maritime counterpart, the whole process of running the wires for the Brooklyn Bridge could be understood as a kind of elaborate choreography of bodies and wires in order to produce a structure of opposing forces in dynamic tension. The historian David McCullough describes part of the process thus:

> With everything working right, it took the carrier about ten minutes to make the full trip from anchorage to anchorage. Along the way men were stationed on the towers and cradles to watch the progress of the traveling wire and to see that each wire was positioned with the proper sag and tension. As the running wire went over the tower, pulled by the carrier, a man would lightly guide it with his hand to keep it from chafing against the timbers of masonry.
>
> *(1972: 380)*

While a suspension bridge depends upon the careful choreography of forces through the movement of bodies and cable, its strength also relies upon the very material qualities of the cables and the necessary understanding of these qualities. Thus, while by no means the first suspension bridge, the Brooklyn Bridge was one of the first major bridges in the world to employ steel suspension cables. Its designer, John A. Roebling, was a German immigrant who had made a fortune as the first manufacturer of wire rope in America, and was at the forefront of innovation in cable design. Roebling did not live to see the completion of his design, however: he died of tetanus following an accident during initial surveying for the bridge. Roebling's son, Washington, then took overall charge of the project, before he was incapacitated in 1872 after spending too much time within the compressed air of the caissons used to construct the towers.

This biographical detail is not incidental: one of the most important aspects of the construction of the Brooklyn Bridge is the fact that its construction opened up for scrutiny the gendered relation between materials, engineering, and politics. Following her husband's incapacitation, Emily Roebling became thoroughly involved in the construction project, acquiring extensive knowledge of and expertise in "higher mathematics, strength of materials, stress analysis, the calculation of catenary curves, bridge specifications, and the intricacies of cable construction" (Tietjen and Reynolds, 1999: 207). Despite the crucial role she played, Emily Roebling's status in the project has often tended to be erroneously reduced to that of a kind of unstinting messenger or spokesperson for the engineering vision formed in the mind of her husband. The different ways in which she was depicted at the time reflected public assumptions about how involved a woman should be in such a project and, in turn, what such a degree of involvement might do for confidence in what was already a public structure – one whose use would demand absolute faith in technological and material innovation (Stuart, 1998).

The construction of the Brooklyn Bridge was politicized in other, related ways, not least in relation to its key material – the steel wires from which its cables were formed – which became subject to various controversies. Thus, while the Roebling firm could well have supplied the steel wire with which to complete the bridge, the decision about who should be awarded the contract became an intensely political one. Eventually the contract was awarded to a Brooklyn firm who, it was subsequently found, supplied under-strength wire, much of which had already been spun into the cable and could not be removed. In terms of the strength of the completed bridge this did not prove to be a problem because the amount of cable had been deliberately overestimated by Roebling. But the scandal did temporarily undermine public confidence in the project. Indeed, 12 people were trampled to death on the bridge a week after it opened due to panic generated by fear of collapse (see McCullough, 1972).

Such affectively charged events serve as a reminder that many of the structures that facilitate modern mobility are more than physical objects. They are always bound up in webs of meaning and affect excessive of, but not entirely opposed to, their physical engineering and construction. However there is something about the structure of a suspension bridge which captures the tension between movement and stasis characteristic of modernity (see Haw, 2005). It is certainly possible to imagine that the designer of the bridge, John A. Roebling, grasped the fact that engineering structures expressed relations and processes that were never merely technical, and that the qualities of these could also be grasped in philosophical or aesthetic terms. While a student in Berlin, Roebling had taken lectures in philosophy from Georg Hegel. As Joseph Arpad remarks, it is not too fanciful to think of the suspension bridge itself as having a kind of Hegelian quality, insofar as it is a "perfect synthesis of antithetical elements, of opposing forces, the chains in tension, the towers of compression, uniting to form a coherent structure of surprising strength" (Arpad, 1967: 78). In this sense the bridge itself is stable without being static, designed precisely to accommodate different forces and movements. Roebling used diagonal cables to dampen vertical oscillation of the bridge that might be caused by gusting winds – this means that the bridge has much greater stability than other similar structures, and is one of the reasons it still stands while others do not.

It is precisely the interplay between the diagonal, vertical, and suspension cables that others found so aesthetically wonderful (see Billington and Mark, 1984). For instance, writing in the 1920s, Lewis Mumford claimed that "the stone plays against the steel: the heavy granite in compression, the spidery steel in tension. In this structure, the architecture of the past, massive and protective, meets the architecture of the future, light, aerial, open to sunlight, an architecture of voids rather than solids" (cited in McCullough, 1972: 550). The poet Hart Crane was similarly impressed, capturing in the long poem *The Bridge* his own sense of the continuous dynamic interplay between the active and passive, the moving and the still, held together in tension by the structure. As Jaffe observes, "cables and wires in Crane's poem are like veins and arteries carrying the sap of life through the body of the image" (1969: 107). The cables and wires of the Brooklyn Bridge might therefore be seen to exemplify the generative interplay between bodies, movement, and materials, of which the infrastructures of mobilities are composed.

Lift, pull, and cut

At the time of the construction of the Brooklyn Bridge, New York was a city expanding primarily in a horizontal rather than a vertical direction. Indeed, in some ways the Bridge facilitated this directional expansion, offering a conduit for eastward development beyond the confines of Manhattan Island. In time, it would also serve as a kind of escape route, and the site of political protest. And yet the technology to allow vertical expansion in cities such as New York was already emerging in the form of passenger elevators, the first example of which in that city was installed in 1857. Mechanical elevation systems had already existed for some time prior to that, particularly in industrial and manufacturing contexts. However, no reliable system for passenger transport existed until the early 1850s (Goetz, 2003). Confidence in elevators depends upon the cables that support them, and, more importantly, upon the effectiveness of the braking mechanism employed should the cable be severed. Thus, while not the first to design and build an elevator, Elisha Otis made possible the vertical expansion of cities including New York: at the 1853–1854 New York World Fair, Otis demonstrated that, should its cable be cut, the fall of an elevator could be successfully and safely arrested. In many ways then, inhabiting extremely high structures became possible once the mechanics of elevators could be backgrounded and effectively forgotten by those who travelled in them. Sometimes, of course, elevators, particularly in more recent buildings, deliberately have their workings and cables exposed for aesthetic effect, in ways that work to "alternately . . . celebrate and disguise the awe and terror of vertical ascent, the miracle of levitation" (Hall, 2003: 71). More broadly, the development of trustable cable and brake technology for elevators does more than simply allow cities to expand vertically through the construction of progressively taller buildings – it also generates new experiential space–times in which people dwell – literally, affectively, and imaginatively – in a myriad of ways (for a review see Thain, 2009).

Elevator journeys are, of course, an incredibly common form of mobile experience in many contemporary cities. For instance, it is estimated that in New York 58,000 elevators generate 11 billion passenger trips a year (Paumgarten, 2008: 107). And yet elevators are by no means the only devices for which cables facilitate vertical mobility. Funiculars, cable railways, and aerial tramways are some of the other technologies of travel made possible by cables. In each case the system relies upon the movement of a cable; what differs is how the vehicle in question – a carriage, car, or gondola – is attached to the cable. Thus, funiculars are cars that ascend and descend steep slopes while attached permanently to a cable. Cable railways, or street cable cars, in contrast, can disengage and reengage with a moving cable that runs under the street and which is driven by an engine located in a cable house. Perhaps the most famous example of this technology is the San Francisco streetcar system. Like the Brooklyn Bridge, it is a National Historical landmark, albeit one that is more obviously mobile. And like the construction of the former, the operation of the San Francisco streetcar involves a particular way of working with moving cable. Streetcars were and continue to be operated by "gripmen", who require significant upper-body strength to operate the cable grip, or brake, that grasps or releases the moving cable running under the street.

Perhaps the technology of transport most often associated with the term "cable car" today is the aerial tramway. This uses gondolas suspended below a cable to facilitate movement up and down slopes or mountainsides. As such, one of the most obvious aspects of travelling in this way is the opportunity it affords for certain kinds of mobile visions and visualities. Indeed, and more generally, travelling in lifts, streetcars, funiculars, or aerial tramways offers different possibilities for being and becoming a passenger through various arrangements of materials and visualities, and through the affective atmospheres that characterize each technology of travel (see Bissell, 2009, 2010). Beyond this, and in addition to the cable, one thing that links the experience of travelling in each of the above is the potential for a particular affect. Most of the time this affect lurks in the background, but occasionally it becomes palpable as a vague sense of disquiet generated by the prospect that somehow the cable could break and everything might fall to the ground. This affect is amplified by stories and images of such events, even if actual episodes of the free-fall of cable-operated technologies of mobility are extremely rare. Strangely, when they have happened, it has often been due to aircraft. For instance, on July 28, 1945, a Boeing B-25 crashed into the Empire State Building after getting lost in fog while trying to land at La Guardia airport. An elevator operator was injured in the incident as he was being lowered in an elevator from the 75th floor. The cables were probably damaged during the incident, and the elevator plunged to the ground. The woman survived. The next incident of a free-falling elevator occurred when the twin towers of the World Trade Center were struck by jet airliners on the morning of September 11, 2011. Among the many fatalities it is estimated that a large number of people were killed in falling elevators (see Paumgarten, 2008).

Arrest, control, and circulation

In 1998 a US Marine Corps EA-6B Grumman Prowler, flying above the Italian ski-resort of Cavalese, severed a cable supporting a gondola in which 20 people were descending. All 20 were killed, although the crew of the Prowler survived. An aircraft such as the Grumman Prowler is capable of carrier-borne operations. For these it employs an arrestor-hook to snag one of a series of cables stretched across the flight-deck of an aircraft carrier. Each cable is linked to a mechanism (often hydraulic) that absorbs the kinetic energy of the landing aircraft. This is only one way, however, in which cables are implicated in the organization and facilitation of forms of "aerial life" (Adey, 2010). Early balloons and airships relied upon cables and ropes to attach gondolas to envelopes. And the large tethered balloons that were such a prominent feature of world exhibitions and expositions during the late nineteenth and early twentieth centuries also depended upon cables.

More broadly, and more recently, the story of heavier-than-air aviation can be told in terms of how aircraft were rendered dirigible and stable through an articulated system that linked bodily capacities with control surfaces (rudder, elevator, and ailerons). Aircraft, in this sense, are distributed, hybrid systems in which human capacities and technological processes are engineered together. The control surfaces of aircraft in the early decades of air travel were manipulated via a system of cables and rods that transmitted the physical effort of the pilot directly to the surfaces. However, as the speed of aircraft and the size of their control surfaces increased, the sheer physical effort required to move those surfaces became too great for pilots. Cables and rods were replaced with hydraulic systems consisting of narrow pipes containing fluid whose pressure could move the control surfaces. Until the 1990s, hydraulic systems were the primary means by which physiological effort was transferred to control surfaces. When these systems failed, aircraft became uncontrollable, with fatal consequences. In 1985, 520 people were killed when a JAL 747 flying from Tokyo to Osaka crashed into a mountainside after having lost hydraulic power to the control surfaces. In 1989, a McDonnell-Douglas DC-10 flying from Denver to Chicago lost all its flight control systems when its hydraulic fluid lines were damaged by shrapnel from an explosion in the rear engine. 111 people were killed in the resultant crash. During the 1980s, hydro-mechanical systems in large jetliners were replaced with computer-based flight control, or fly-by-wire, systems. Here again, electronic cables replaced pipes as part of the on-going re-composition of assemblages of mobility.

The centrality of pipes and cables in the design and control of aircraft points to the importance of tubular forms in the design and organization of assemblages of mobility (see Virilio, 1991). The importance of these tubular forms is on one level about facilitating the movement of vehicles in the air. But it can also be about the use of air as part of technologies of propulsion and circulation. We can think here of pneumatic technologies, exemplified in various experiments with propulsion systems that never achieved popularity – failed innovations such as "atmospheric railways", for instance, the first example of which was constructed in Dalkey, Dublin. For a brief period during the middle of the nineteenth century, atmospheric railways appeared to offer a viable competitor to steam propulsion technologies (see Hadfield, 1967; Buchanan, 1992). Pneumatic transportation systems have also, of course, been employed to move smaller objects as part of communication networks in cities and organizations. In 1853 a 220-yard pneumatic tube was constructed between the London Stock Exchange and the Lothbury Telegraph Office in order to speed up communication with the exchange. Similar and increasingly extensive pneumatic systems were installed in cities during the latter part of the nineteenth century, the most notable of which was in Paris. Cylinders containing mail items were propelled throughout the network by differential air pressure behind or ahead of the cylinder (see Hayhurst, 1974). The system operated until the early 1990s, and features in François Truffaut's 1968 film *Baisers Volés* (*Stolen Kisses*). One of the characters in the film drops a letter into the system, through which it passes in a sealed pneumatic cylinder. The journey of the cylinder is signalled in the scene by the rattling of underground tubes that correspond to various over-ground locations. While city-wide systems like this no longer exist, they remain widely used in hospitals and banks for the distribution of documents.

But tubular mobility in pipes of different kinds is also about infrastructural networks that act as conduits for all sorts of forces, materials, and substances rather than discrete objects – we might think here of electricity, electromagnetic energy, water, oil, and gas. Much has been written, for instance, about the flow of water throughout cities, and indeed, the centrality of water distribution systems above and below ground to the emergence of the modern city as a series of assemblages that extend the body into the city and the city into the body through forms of cyborg urbanism (Kaika, 2005; Gandy, 1999, 2004, 2005). Others have written about oil and gas in broadly similar ways, often with an emphasis on the controversial materiality of distribution infrastructures (see Barry, 2005). Equally, we might also think about the importance of the distribution, circulation, and recirculation of air and water around cities and buildings as part of heating, ventilation, and air conditioning systems that make environments inhabitable by producing and regulating distinctive atmospheres (Cooper, 1998; Collier, 2004; Hitchings and Lee, 2008). The point here is that it is precisely the capacity to render materials and substances mobile in controllable and manageable ways that marks the emergence of inhabitable assemblages. Thus it is not just lifts that make extremely tall buildings possible, but also the design and installation of a system for the circulation of air via ducts through which the thermal properties and moisture levels of a building's atmosphere can be controlled.

Tensed

The twin towers of the World Trade Center were officially opened in April 1973. For a time, they were the tallest buildings in the world and were equipped with extremely complex elevator and HVAC systems. On August 7, 1973, the French high-wire walker Philippe Petit, aided by a number of friends and assistants, rigged a cable between the twin towers. At about 7:15 am, Petit began to edge out onto the cable. People far below began to notice, looking up. He eventually spent 45 minutes on the cable, crossing between the buildings eight times before being arrested and returned to the ground (see Marsh, 2007). As a high-wire walker, Petit was thoroughly familiar with the dynamics and movement of cables, with their capacity to twist, flex, sag, and tighten. In a fictionalized account of the walk, novelist Colum

McCann writes that for a walker like Petit there could be no "surprises. The cable had its own moods. The worst of all was internal torque, where the cable turned inside itself, like a snake moving through a skin" (McCann, 2009: 163).

Petit, of course, is the latest in a long tradition of performers who have used cables and wires to become aerial through different styles and spaces of performance. There may well be a link here between traditions of working with rope and cable in certain occupations and a cultural disposition towards and interest in wire-based aerial performance. As Steven Connor writes, "for seafaring nations like the British and the French, the two nations in which tightrope walking has been most popular and most perfected, walking up and down ropes and cables has un-ignorable maritime associations; as in the space of the theatre, this kind of rigging turns terrestrial places into vertiginously mobile vessels" (2008: no pagination). The circus is one such mobile place, anchored temporarily by ropes, rigging, and cables, and associated with its own form of wire-based aerialism. As Peta Tait (2005: 4) has argued, aerial performance in the circus was radically transformed through the "advent of the trapeze" in 1860. For Tait, the performance of the circus aerialist emerged as a culturally layered assemblage of technology and technique, in which confidence in both cable and an exuberantly skilful body was always balanced with fear of falling or loss of balance. Equally, aerial performance in this context provided opportunities for pushing the bodies that swung and flew from wires to transcend certain culturally inscribed senses of embodiment: female aerialists could be muscular, while their male counterparts could be graceful. The Australian-born Ella Zuila, for instance, was one of the most famous aerialists performing in the US during the later nineteenth century. Like Charles Blondin, Zuila was an expert wire-walker, for whom the wire was not just a means for traversing between two points, but was a line that opened up a performance space of possibility.

In this sense, high-wire walking has little to do with mastering space. To undertake this kind of activity is not about the "view from above", or about lifting oneself out of the city in a way that conquers verticality in the manner outlined by De Certeau (1984; see also Dorrian, 2007). Instead, wire-walking is an extreme and aesthetic version of myriad practices of becoming aerial through working with wires and cables. The wire, in effect, becomes a space–time for a particular form of practised mobility. To quote Steven Connor again: "the wire-walker aims to occupy rather than merely to penetrate space, to tangle up the line into a maze, to thicken the infinitesimally thin itinerary of the wire into a habitat" (2008, no pagination). However rarefied or *avant-garde*, such practices remind us of a more general and mundane point that emerges from this brief discussion: cables, wires, tubes, and pipes are woven into mobile assemblages through multiple forms of knowledge and knowing, through styles of thinking and moving, and through forms of attachment, each of which make mobile worlds liveable in different ways.

References

Adey, P. (2010) *Aerial Life*. Oxford: Wiley-Blackwell.

Arpad, J. (1967) 'Hart Crane's Platonic Myth: The Brooklyn Bridge', *American Literature* 39(1): 75–86.

Barry, A. (2005) 'The British–Georgian Case: the Baku-Tbilisi-Ceyhan Pipeline', in Latour, B. and C. Gramaglia (eds) *Territoires, environnement et nouveaux modes de gestion: la gouvernance en question*, Paris: CNRS. pp. 105–118.

Billington, D. and Mark, R. (1984) 'The Cathedral and the Bridge: Structure and Symbol', *Technology and Culture* 25(1): 37–52.

Bissell, D. (2009) 'Visualising Everyday Geographies: Practices of Vision through Travel-time', *Transactions of the Institute of British Geographers* 34(1): 42–60.

Bissell, D. (2010) 'Passenger Mobilities: Affective Atmospheres and the Sociality of Public Transport', *Environment and Planning D: Society and Space* 28(2): 270–289.

Buchanan, R. (1992) 'The Atmospheric Railway of I.K. Railway', *Social Studies of Science* 22: 231–243.

Collier, S. (2004) 'Pipes', in Harrison, S., Pile, S., and Thrift, N. (eds) *Patterned Ground: Entanglements of Nature and Culture*, London: Reaktion Books. pp. 50–52.

Conant, W. C. (1883) 'The Brooklyn Bridge', *Harper's New Monthly Magazine* 66: 944.

Connor, S. (2008) 'Man is a Rope'. Available online at www.stevenconnor.com/rope/ (accessed 17 August 2013).

Cooper, G. (1998) *Air-conditioning America: Engineers and the Controlled Environment, 1900–1960*, Baltimore, MD: John Hopkins University Press.

De Certeau, M. [1984] 1988 'Walking in the City', in *The Practice of Everyday Life*, Berkeley: University of California Press. pp. 91–110.

Dorrian, M. (2007) 'The Aerial View: Notes for a Cultural History', *Strates*, 13, no pagination. Available online at http://strates.revues.org/5573 (accessed 22 August 2012).

Gandy, M. (1999) 'The Paris Sewers and the Rationalization of Urban Space', *Transactions of the Institute of British Geographers* 24(1): 23–44.

Gandy, M. (2004) 'Rethinking Urban Metabolism: Water, Space and the Modern City', *City 8* (3): 371–387.

Gandy, M. (2005) 'Cyborg Urbanization: Complexity and Monstrosity in the Contemporary City', *International Journal of Urban and Regional Research* 29(1): 26–49.

Goetz, A. (2003) *Up, Down, Across: Elevators, Escalators and Moving Sidewalks*, Washington, DC: National Building Museum; London: Merrell.

Hadfield, C. (1967) *Atmospheric Railways: A Victorian Venture in Silent Speed*. Newton Abbot: David and Charles.

Hall, P. (2003) 'Designing Non-space: The Evolution of the Elevator Interior', in Goetz, A. (ed.) *Up, Down, Across: Elevators, Escalators and Moving Sidewalks*, Washington,DC: National Building Museum; London: Merrell. pp. 59–78.

Haw, R. (2005) *The Brooklyn Bridge: A Cultural History*, New Brunswick, NJ: Rutgers University Press.

Hayhurst, J. D. (1974) 'The Pneumatic Post of Paris'. Available online at www.cix.co.uk/~mhayhurst/jdhayhurst/pneumatic/book1.html (accessed 17 August 2013).

Hitchings, R. and Lee, S. J. (2008) 'Air Conditioning and the Material Culture of Routine Human Encasement', *Journal of Material Culture* 13(3): 251–265.

Jaffe, I. (1969) 'Joseph Stella and Hart Crane: The Brooklyn Bridge', *American Art Journal* 1(2): 98–107.

Kaika, M. (2005) *City of Flows*, London: Routledge.

Marsh, J. (2007) *Man on Wire*, DVD, Icon.

McCann, C. (2009) *Let the Great World Spin*, London: Bloomsbury.

McCullough, D. (1972) *The Great Bridge: The Story of the Building of the Brooklyn Bridge*, New York: Simon and Schuster.

Paumgarten, N. (2008) 'Up and then Down: The Lives of Elevators', *The New Yorker*, New York 84(10): 106–115.

Stuart, J. (1998) 'Gender Reconfigured: Emily Roebling and the Construction of Brooklyn Bridge', *Architectural Theory Review* 3(1): 23–34.

Tait, P. (2005) *Circus Bodies: Cultural Identities in Aerial Performance*, London: Routledge.

Thain, A. (2009) 'Insecurity Cameras: Cinematic Elevators, Infidelity and the Crime of Time', *Intermediality* 14: 51–66.

Tietjen, J. and Reynolds, B. (1999) 'Women Engineers Bridging the Gender Gap', *Technology and Society, Conference Proceedings: Women and Technology: Historical, Societal, and Professional Perspectives*, 206–210.

Trachtenberg, A. (1965) *Brooklyn Bridge: Fact and Symbol*, New York: Oxford University Press.

Virilio, P. (1991) *The Lost Dimension*, translated by D. Moshenberg, New York: Semiotext(e).

22

Locative Media

Jason Farman

For several years now, I have been using locative media to "check in" to locations I visit. When I arrive to a location, I will turn on my phone, load the Foursquare app, click the "Check In" button, wait until the phone returns a list of possible locations that are near my GPS coordinates, and check in. For my own purposes, I find this practice to be a useful tool for journaling. Returning to the locations I checked in to over the past year unveils the intimate connection between space and practice, between the place and the meaning of the place, and between a location and the embodied production of that location.

One recent check in on Foursquare stands out for me because it dramatically transformed the way that I think about locative media. On October 27, 2011, I visited a major site for the internet on the outskirts of Washington, DC: the Equinix Data Center. This "internet peering point" serves as one of the key places for internet traffic on the East Coast of the United States, since most of the data that moves in and out of this part of the country goes through this facility at some point. Along with most other major companies that do business in the United States, Foursquare houses its database here (run through Amazon's Cloud servers). I was able to tour the facility with my graduate students. We touched base with our tour guide on the phone that day and were asked to meet him at a non-descript door. "Since there are no signs for the facility – for security reasons – you'll drive to the end of the warehouse area and look for the only door with a handle," he said. That door led to a room that was only as big as a medium-sized elevator. Brian, our tour guide, placed his hand on a biometric scanner and punched in his passcode in order to open the doors into the next room. This led us to the security area, where we showed our identification and were given visitor badges. Brian scanned his hand on another biometric scanner, punched in his passcode, and led us to the waiting area that had a conference room, where we were told about the history and current practices of this Equinix facility. Brian led us to the next set of doors that was the entrance to the data center. Once he had scanned his hand and entered his passcode one last time, we walked into a frigid, dark, and extremely loud environment. Here, there were long stretches of aisles in all directions, bounded by black steel cages housing servers stacked to the ceiling (see Figure 22.1). These servers run non-stop, 24-hours a day, and produce so much heat that one of the primary concerns for these facilities is keeping the electricity running to the air conditioning system that keeps everything cool. Thus, upon entering the data center, I could barely hear Brian talk above the noise of cold air blasting down onto the front faces of the server racks. Above my head, running down the center of each aisle, was a yellow tray that held the fiber-optic cables running to and from each server. Along these cables, data was flowing around the world at speeds so incredibly fast that it was difficult for me to comprehend.

It was here that I pulled out my mobile phone, loaded up Foursquare, and checked into the Equinix data center over a 3G network. Knowing that Foursquare's databases were housed somewhere at this facility – located on servers behind one of these cages – I began to wonder about the flows that my information took. What information pathways were necessary in order for me to be "located" and to broadcast my location to my network of friends on Foursquare? What does the infrastructure behind locative media and mobility actually look like?

Tracing the flows of my locative data turned out to be an enlightening endeavor. Combining research on the ways that the mobile internet works with physically walking around and locating cell towers and antennas, I discovered that as my mobile device sent out its signal from the Equinix building, it connected with my carrier's nearest cell antenna. However, this antenna was not hard-wired into the internet infrastructure. It served, instead, as a node in what is termed a "mesh network" of antennas. Since the signal from a mobile phone works on a line-of-sight connection, not all connections can be made directly to cell towers that are linked in with the fiber-optic or copper cables that connect to the internet. Thus, a mobile device initially connects to a node in the mesh network and gets bounced over to this main cell tower (called a "backhaul"). As soon as my signal connected with this cell tower, the rest of the pathway was not wireless; instead, the journey to Foursquare's database took place

Figure 22.1 The inside of the Equinix Internet Peering Point in Ashburn, Virginia. Behind the cages are the servers that are run by major companies like Amazon, EA Games, Verizon, and Google. The yellow trays along the aisles hold the fiber-optic cables running between these server cages. © 2011 Equinix, Inc. All rights reserved. The Equinix logo is a trademark of Equinix, Inc.

entirely through the material, hard-wired, tangible infrastructure of the mobile internet. The signal ran down the wires of the cell tower, connected into the fiber optics of the internet infrastructure, and came shooting straight back to my location – the Equinix data center – in order to access Foursquare's database. It is quite possible that the request made by my mobile device traveled on the fiber-optic cables directly over my head in the data center where I was standing as this request went down into one of the cages and pulled the relevant data from the server. Here, using the GPS coordinates delivered to the server by my mobile device, Foursquare was able to pull up a list of nearby locations. It then sent that information back along the fiber-optic cables, up the cell tower lines, and back out to the mesh network of antennas, eventually landing right back on my mobile device.

When tracing the flow of my data, it struck me how circuitous the pathway was to send and receive information. Even more striking was the fact that much of the journey of my data took place across a very static infrastructure. In fact, much of what we consider to be "mobile" media is generated through very non-mobile technologies such as the cell tower and fiber-optic cable.

The largest take-away for me gained by tracing the flows of my mobile and locative data – with which this chapter will be most concerned – is that most of these interactions took place at a level that was far beyond my awareness. I tend to imagine that locative media begin and end at the level of the interface; however, this sentiment couldn't be further from the truth. The vast majority of locative media takes place well beneath the level of the interface, with technologies communicating with technologies in ways that exceed my own sense perceptions. Therefore, as we continue to theorize location-aware technologies, especially as they impact the practices of embodied space, social interaction, and site-specificity, we need to look beyond the human-to-human connectivity to take into consideration both the human-to-technology and the vital technology-to-technology interactions that take place beyond the realm of the perceptible. Ultimately, what is gained from such an inquiry is a necessary insertion of objects into our understanding of the production of space and of the ability for embodied people to truly engage a political practice of difference. My sense of embodied identity is not simply gained through social interactions with other humans; instead, it is continually constituted by what I term a "sensory-inscribed" engagement with people, objects, social and cultural structures, protocols, and the spaces produced through the interactions among these things.

Ultimately, to argue for this mode of embodiment, it becomes apparent that many of these interactions are not visible to us. They tend to recede into the background of our practices with locative technologies. In fact, many of these technologies are designed to withdraw from view (if they are designed well, according to the designers). Thus, as I try to unveil the role that objects play in the practice of location-aware technologies, my hope is to push on the categories of "visible" and "invisible" to trouble the ways that these concepts are implemented in the design and everyday practices of mobile and locative media.

The audience of locative media

When I checked in to the Equinix facility, I attached a brief note to my check-in saying, "Here to 'see the internet' with my grad students." This note, along with my location, was broadcast to those in my network on Foursquare. So, if any of my 78 friends and colleagues happened to load Foursquare that evening – or if any of them had push notifications enabled on their devices that would automatically send my message to the screens of their mobile devices – they would have known that I was visiting this site with my small group of graduate students from the University of Maryland. This seems to be the most obvious audience for locative media and, in fact, most scholarship on locative media tends to focus on it as an extension of social media sites like Facebook by bringing it out onto the streets and into the everyday movements of these networks of people. For me, as I mentioned at the beginning of this chapter, my primary use of Foursquare is as a kind of spatial journal to log my movements throughout a given day. So, my network was not my primary audience; instead, I thought of myself as the audience of this message, which I received exactly one year later on email in a message that read: "Your check-ins from one year ago today." This service, now called Timehop (though once cleverly called 4SquareAndSevenYearsAgo), sends reminders to Foursquare users of what they were doing a year ago on this day.

Yet, my check-in to Equinix forced me to ask: who is the primary audience of locative media? Could it possibly be the objects that are interacting and exchanging information with each other beyond the realm of my human awareness? When I loaded my phone to check in, I was searching for a 3G signal and searching for my location from Foursquare's database. Simultaneously, my phone was searching for the nearest antenna, which searched for the nearest backhaul, which searched for the correct IP address in order to connect to the right fiber-optic line leading down the long yellow tray that ran above my head and down into a cage in the data center, connecting to the exact server that held the information that corresponded to my GPS coordinates. Here, machines are talking to machines. There is an entire network of connectivity that encircles this one act of "checking in," and I am just one node in that network. And while I might have been the initiator of this particular request ("Foursquare, please locate me and log my visit to this location"), my phone was already engaging this network of technological objects long before I made the request. My phone is able to navigate handoffs between various network "cells" – hopping from antenna to antenna to maintain a seamless connection so I never have to drop a call or receive an error message on a website I'm browsing. My phone is also tracking my movements, often without me giving it permission to do so (a process which has, in recent years, caused major controversies). It connects with GPS satellites – those celestial objects constantly orbiting the earth and only visible to me at night when they look like extremely slow shooting stars – three at a time in order to triangulate my position. My phone runs constant checks on my email, on my text messages, my voicemails, messages to me on Twitter, and a host of other services I have set up to run in the background while I go about my day. This is all happening right now as my phone sits at the bottom of my pocket.

When this begins to truly sink in, I realize how small my Foursquare request was and that I am not the primary audience for locative media. I am only *one* audience member among many, including my phone, the cell antennas, the cell tower, the fiber-optic cables, the servers, data talking to data, machines talking to machines, signals communicating to infrastructure. There are a whole host of communicative objects that are connecting and serve as the "audience" of locative data. This shifts the entire focus of locative media in fairly radical ways. Instead of being this solipsistic interface for the oversharing of banal information (e.g. "To all of my friends: I am currently at the corner gas station filling up my car"), locative media highlight the site-specific interactions among human agents and the informational objects that are weaving themselves into the fabric of our everyday lives.

Mobile media and object-oriented phenomenologies

The role these informational objects play in the practice of locative media initially rubbed against the grain of my theorizations of embodied space in a mobile media age. As I worked to define "interface" in an early draft of my book *Mobile Interface Theory: Embodied Space and Locative Media*, I wrote that the interface is "constituted as a larger set of social relations" and is the nexus of these relationships. Therefore, the mobile phone, in and of itself, is not an interface (I still hold this to be true). Only when the mobile phone serves as the nexus of relationships and interactions does it become an interface. I draw here largely from Johanna Drucker's arguments when she writes, "What is an interface? If we think of interface as a *thing*, an entity, a fixed or determined structure that supports certain activities, it tends to reify in the same way a book does in traditional description. But we know that a codex book is not a *thing* but a structured set of codes that support or provoke an interpretation that is itself performative."[1] However, my attempts to think beyond the "thingness" of the mobile-phone-as-interface (and instead think of the interface as the nexus of relationships) led me down an ill-reasoned path. In this early draft of my book, I went on to say, "The mobile device, on its own, is nothing but a beautifully designed paperweight." For me, as I worked to theorize embodied space as something that is produced through *practice*, the mobile phone sitting on my desk seemed to not engage these practices because I was not directly interacting with it. Once I began to see beyond this narrow box of human–computer interaction and practice, the device's engagement with its own practices and its own audiences, its own content opened up an entire realm vital to my theorizations of the production of space.

My theorization of embodiment is founded on the ideas in phenomenology, especially the work of Maurice Merleau-Ponty. This mode of inquiry prioritizes an experience of the world gained through the body and through the senses. It takes up experiences, sense perception, the body's role in knowledge production, and the philosophies of being as its main objects of study. It is focused on subjectivity and embraces the limited perspectives of human perception as the main window through which we understand the world. By inserting mobile objects – the materiality that serves as the foundation of locative media – into a phenomenological approach to understanding embodied interaction, we begin to see some of the possible limits to phenomenology (limits, I will argue, that don't accurately characterize the phenomenological approach of those like Merleau-Ponty and Martin Heidegger).

In a 1946 presentation of his work to the *Société française de philosophie*, Merleau-Ponty was challenged to defend his work against the idea that phenomenology was solipsistic and always must come back to the individual's perspective on the world. During the question and answer session of his presentation, another philosopher of the time, Emile Bréhier, lobbed a complaint against Merleau-Ponty and his phenomenological approach. His complaint is one that would thereafter be echoed multiple times since by detractors of phenomenology: "When you speak of the perception of the other, this other does not even exist, according to you, except in relation to us and in his relations with us. This is not the other as I perceive him immediately; it certainly is not an ethical other; it is not this person who suffices to himself. It is someone I posit outside myself at the same time I posit objects."[2]

Indeed, phenomenology, as with the main object of study for this chapter – locative media – can be seen (and misunderstood) as giving an overemphasis to the individual rather than the community or others that are able to exist beyond our realm of understanding. This kind of "immanence" of the individual comes at the cost for any existence of "transcendence" of the other. As Jack Reynolds puts it, referencing Emmanuel Levinas's concern with this approach to being-in-the-world, "phenomenology hence ensures that the other can be considered only on the condition of surrendering his or her difference."[3]

Michael Yeo phrases the problem of immanence and transcendence by asking, "How is it possible to experience the other as other – as really transcendent – given that I cannot but experience her in relation to my own immanent frame of reference?"[4] However, any theorization of difference requires the ability for us to engage transcendence, for a recognition that not all things exist on the plane of immanence, but instead can exist beyond our understanding and realm of experience. People need to be able to exceed their individual understandings and frames of reference in order for there to be any sense of knowledge, surprise, and cross-cultural exchange. As Reynolds argues, "Not only can interactions with the other involve us in a renewed appreciation of their alterity (i.e. the ways in which they elude us), but the other is equally importantly that which allows us to surprise ourselves, and move beyond the various horizons and expectations that govern our daily lives."[5] Within this framework of alterity, we *must* include objects. Objects have to be considered as often exceeding our realm of understanding (and thus existing on the horizon of transcendence).

The flow of my mobile data demonstrates an important example of this: most people, including myself prior to this investigation, typically engage the mobile internet without any sense of awareness about the larger network of objects that make such connectivity possible. Though these objects and their interactions with one another often exceed our realm of human perception, they nonetheless shape the sense of self via location-aware technologies. We still deeply understand our sense of space even though we may not be aware of the informational objects that help produce that sense of space. For a "sensory-inscribed" phenomenology of embodiment, which stakes a claim in the continued value of phenomenology for analyzing our sense of being-in-the-world, transcendence is always at the forefront of what it means to be human in a technological world. This transcendence, however, takes place on many phenomenological levels. The phenomenology of sensory-inscription, as produced simultaneously through the senses and through various cultural inscriptions, takes into account the distinction that cognitive scientists have made between "cognitive awareness" and the "cognitive unconscious."[6] There are things that we gather through human sense perception that we're aware of: I turn on my phone, load Foursquare, compare its results to where I think I am, check in, and finally compare my position in the world with my friends and colleagues. These are actions of which I am conscious. My awareness of these various levels of mediation involved in the ways space is produced ultimately results in an embodied sense of proprioception (i.e. of knowing where my body fits as it moves out into the world, of knowing the spatial relationships that constitute my place in this locale). However, there is much beneath the surface of human perception that is still vital to this sensory-inscribed experience of space. This takes place at the level of the "cognitive unconscious." Many of the aspects of life and the uses of our emerging technologies require our ability to either filter out excess information in order to focus, or, alternatively, to simply not be aware of certain aspects of our lives and surroundings (both biologically, such as not knowing how many times you've blinked in the last five minutes, and socially, such as not knowing the name of the person at the Foxconn factory who put the screen on your iPhone).

While much of our experience of location-awareness through our technologies does engage the cognitive unconscious, it is often *designed to do so*. For many designers of mobile devices and mobile applications, a good design is one that is not noticeable. If done well, it should recede into the background of your everyday life. Designers dating back to at least Mark Weiser's work on ubiquitous computing have sought to design for invisibility or what Jay David Bolter and Richard Grusin have called the immediacy of the interfaceless-interface.[7] As Weiser argues, "The most profound technologies are those that disappear. They weave themselves into the fabric of everyday life until they are indistinguishable from it."[8] This is what Heidegger calls "readiness-to-hand," and what philosophers in the field of Object-Oriented Ontology (OOO) like Graham Harman term "tool-being."[9] The tool, in its essence as a tool (its tool-being), is invisible to us. Only when the tool stops working (and, for Harman, no longer exists in its essence as the tool it once was) do we actually notice the tool. This move from ready-to-hand to present-at-hand is the move from invisibility to visibility.

Moving mobile media from the realm of the invisible to the visible

The categories of "ready-to-hand" and "present-at-hand" are rarely clear-cut and distinct from one another. Emerging mobile devices are representative of the bleed-over between these categories. While designers and theorists of ubiquitous computing, like Weiser, hope to achieve a design that so intimately weaves itself into the fabric of our everyday lives that we rarely notice it as a distinct interface from "the interface of everyday life,"[10] there is also a cultural desire for our devices to engage this kind of seamless integration *and* be a visible object of significance. For many designers and consumers, the device's immediacy should be obtained while allowing for the device to still function as a status symbol, a technological fetish object, and a signifier of a person's brand loyalties. The fluctuation between these levels of invisibility and visibility are a result of the power structures (such as capitalism) that are invested in maintaining various levels of visibility and invisibility and the cultural desires that are founded on such structures.

For mobile and locative media, an analysis of the relationship between visibility and invisibility is a productive one, and one of the best examples is seen in the attempts to camouflage cell phone towers (and their resulting hyper-visibility). I see this daily as I drive to work, making the 35-minute commute to College Park, Maryland. As I drive through the northern part of the town of Silver Spring, at the corner of Bonifant Road and Layhill Road, there is a brick building with cell antennas perched on the top. These antennas are covered with a faux-brick veneer in order to make them blend in with the building. Driving another few minutes east on Bonifant, there is an extremely large tree standing in a field, twice as large as any other tree in the area. Even from a distance, it is apparent that this is a cell tower disguised to look like an evergreen tree (Figure 22.2).[11] As I turn south onto New Hampshire, I see an interesting contrast between a huge cell tower on the busy intersection of Randolf Road and New Hampshire, standing high above the ground without any attempt to disguise it, and, further down New Hampshire, a cell antenna that blends into a church steeple near Adelphi Road.

This attempt to make the infrastructure of mobile technologies invisible is, in large part, one of the only recourses a community has as a response to the excessive visibility of these towers. As Ted Kane and Rick Miller note, the Telecommunications Act of 1996 essentially removed local oversight about where cell towers could be placed, thus "local governments are limited to regulation based on community planning standards, largely imposing some form of *visual control*."[12]

These methods of visual control, however, almost always make the infrastructure more pronounced and *more visible*. The attempts at disguise only draw our eye to the towers rather than allowing them to blend in. In thinking of an object-oriented approach to the study of these towers, this invisibility-made-visible led me to ask, "Who do these attempts at invisibility address?" Since mobile technologies work on line of sight (the signal from your mobile phone must connect with an antenna based on a direct, visible connection), the height of the evergreen cell tower in Silver Spring, Maryland, is designed to be visible to mobile devices in the area. The technologies work because they are visible to one another. However, the invisibility of the tower – the attempt to camouflage it as a tree – is done for the human users and inhabitants of this region.

Figure 22.2 A cell tower disguised as an evergreen tree in Silver Spring, Maryland, © 2012
Jason Farman

It might seem obvious who the visible/invisible divide addresses; however, the political consequences are significant. As Lisa Parks notes, the attempts to make our technologies invisible, as profoundly seen in the attempts at disguising cell towers, highlight a cultural desire to remove particular technological objects from view and, thus, to remove the political consequences of having those objects play a vital role in the ways that we practice space, identity, and community creation.[13] The move to make our mobile objects and infrastructures invisible is to deny the "vibrant matter" of things and the essential part they play in the ways that we think about being human in this pervasive computing age. This resonates with Jane Bennett's concerns when she writes, "How would political responses to public problems change were we to take seriously the vitality of (nonhuman) bodies? By 'vitality' I mean the capacity of things – edibles, commodities, storms, metals – not only to impede or block the will and designs of humans but also to act as quasi agents or forces with trajectories, propensities, or tendencies of their own."[14] She goes on to argue that things like patterns of consumption would change "if we faced not litter, rubbish, trash, or 'the recycling,' but an accumulating pile of lively and potentially dangerous matter."[15]

What would be the consequences of approaching mobile infrastructure in a similar way? Would advocating for a "vibrant materiality" of our mobile devices and infrastructures have an impact on things like consumption and purchasing patterns? On the ways we understand and legislate labor in the digital age? By inserting these vibrant objects into our understanding of locative experiences through mobile media, our phenomenological engagement with the world requires us to address the need for otherness and alterity: not only is locative media about connecting with one another, but it is about connecting with the various information objects around us, the spaces in which those objects exist, the labor that produces these devices and infrastructures, and, ultimately, about objects connecting with objects. Objects like the cell tower and the data center are extreme versions of otherness, communicating and interacting with each other in ways that far exceed my realm of understanding. Yet, the ways we make these things invisible very likely are derived from a stance not of seeking the transcendence of others, but instead a stance that seeks immanence of the self, that seeks to place the individual far above any of the networked social connections that are responsible for the constitution of the self.

Conclusion: toward visibility

Realizing the various objects that make something as simple as a locative application like Foursquare work has been illuminating for me. I see my mobile phone differently. I see the landscape around me differently, constantly noticing cell towers, antennas, and networked infrastructures of all kinds. And while most of these things still remain outside of the realm of full visibility – for some things, like data transfer speeds across a fiber-optic cable or the signal emitting from my mobile device, I will never be able to fully grasp on a sensory level – I believe the push toward increased levels of visibility with our mobile tools and infrastructure is ultimately vital to our understanding of identity and difference broadly. The push to make our objects disappear ends up mirroring our push to make otherness disappear. And, ultimately, as we continue to engage in cultural analysis and theory, this kind of difference plays a central role. As those modes of inquiry continue to grow, they will need to include objects as a central object of study. For through the study of objects like emerging locative and pervasive computing tools, we can begin to locate the essential relationship between humans and objects, and between visibility and alterity.

Notes

1 Johanna Drucker, "Humanities Approaches to Interface Theory," *Culture Machine 12* (2011): 8.
2 In Maurice Merleau-Ponty, *The Primacy of Perception* (Evanston, IL: Northwestern University Press, 1964), 28.
3 Jack Reynolds, *Merleau-Ponty and Derrida: Intertwining Embodiment and Alterity* (Athens, OH: Ohio University Press, 2004), 125.
4 Michael Yeo, "Perceiving/Reading the Other: Ethical Dimensions," in *Merleau-Ponty, Hermeneutics, and Postmodernism*, ed. Thomas W. Busch and Shaun Gallagher (Albany, NY: State University of New York Press, 1992), 38.
5 Jack Reynolds, *Merleau-Ponty and Derrida*, 128.
6 See John F. Kihlstrom, "The Cognitive Unconscious," *Science 237* (1987): 1445–1453.
7 Jay David Bolter and Richard Grusin, *Remediation* (Cambridge, MA: The MIT Press, 1999), 23.
8 Mark Weiser, "The Computer for the 21st Century," www.ubiq.com/hypertext/weiser/SciAmDraft3.html.
9 See Graham Harman, *Tool-Being: Heidegger and the Metaphysics of Objects* (Chicago: Open Court, 2002). Harman, as well as Ian Bogost in his book *Alien Phenomenology, Or, What it's Like to be a Thing* (Minneapolis: University of Minnesota Press, 2012) argue for an "object-oriented ontology" that extends the theorizations of those like Bruno Latour and actor-network theory by arguing for "things" that can be theorized even outside of the network. Bogost's approach finds limitations in actor-network theory since "entities are de-emphasized in favor of their couplings and decouplings."
10 Jason Farman, *Mobile Interface Theory: Embodied Space and Locative Media* (New York: Routledge, 2012), 86–87.
11 Interestingly, since it is "evergreen" and surrounded by mostly deciduous trees, there are a remarkable number of birds living in this cell-tower-made-tree because it offers year-round shelter.

Jason Farman

12 Ted Kane and Rick Miller, "Cell Structure: Mobile Phones," in *The Infrastructural City: Networked Ecologies in Los Angeles*, ed. Kazys Varnelis (New York: Actar, 2008), 152. Emphasis mine.
13 Lisa Parks, "Around the Antenna Tree: The Politics of Infrastructural Visibility," *Flow 9*, no. 8. Available online at http://flowtv.org/2009/03/around-the-antenna-tree-the-politics-of-infrastructural-visibilitylisa-parks-uc-santa-barbara/ (accessed 23 August 2013).
14 Jane Bennett, *Vibrant Matter: A Political Ecology of Things* (Durham: Duke University Press, 2010), viii.
15 Ibid.

23
Walking Phone Workers

Lisa Parks

As mobile telephones have emerged around the world over the past two decades they have altered people's daily lives, making new practices of mediated conversation, messaging, photo-sharing, and game-playing, among other things, possible across public and private, indoor and outdoor, and moving and fixed locations. In the process they have also brought about new structures of attention and distraction, positioning and disorientation, connection and disconnection. Though billions of people in the world are now familiar with mobile devices, they tend to be less interested in the infrastructures that support them – the towers, transponders, transmitters, footprints, and workers that are involved in the trafficking of mobile telephone signals from one site to another. Ironically, most people only notice mobile phone infrastructures when they are conspicuously camouflaged as freakish-looking pine or palm trees, or when they appear in unseemly sites such as national parks or affluent neighborhoods (Parks, 2009a). As such examples imply, mobile phone infrastructures are not uniform; they vary from node to node and from country to country. Because of this, they should be conceptualized as sites of variation and studied in relation to particular socio-historical, geophysical, political, economic, and cultural conditions (Graham & Marvin, 2001; Horst & Miller, 2006; Larkin, 2008).

Much early social science research on mobile telephony has focused on urban, post-industrial settings (Katz & Aakhus, 2002; Goggin, 2006), but during the past decade researchers have explored the organization and use of mobile telephony across various developing contexts as well. This research has tended to focus on issues and impacts of diffusion and adoption (Baliamoune-Lutz, 2003; Yeow, *et al.*, 2008; Wallis, 2011) and "m-development" (Duncombe, 2011) – the use of mobile telephony to support development-related projects such as education (Gronlund and Islam, 2010), agriculture (Islam and Gronlund, 2011), financial services (Duncombe & Boateng, 2009), or health care (Kaplan, 2006; Idowu, *et al.*, 2006; Lester, 2010; Kahn, *et al.*, 2010). Other research has examined changing attitudes toward mobile phone technology (Kaba, *et al.*, 2009) or regulatory questions involving universal service obligations (Hamilton, 2003; Burkhart, 2007). As Jonathan Donner observes, "Though the number of studies focused on mobiles in the developing world is growing steadily, these studies have appeared in relative isolation from each other, separated by regions, and by disciplines" (Donner, 2008: 140). In addition, this research often approaches mobile telephone infrastructure as a given rather than as a historically situated and variable techno-social formation. Few, for instance, have explored the issue of technological innovation in developing contexts – that is, the local "reinvention" (Michaels, 1994) of mobile telephone systems designed and imported from elsewhere. Furthermore, few have delineated the multiple kinds of mobilities (whether physical, social, economic, cultural) that such "reinvented" systems both emerge from and afford.

In this essay I examine mobile telephone infrastructure in Mongolia from a critical humanistic perspective, situating the technology's emergence within a socio-historical context. By mobile telephone infrastructure I am referring to the dynamic and coordinated arrangement and use of dispersed hardware, physical installations, spectrum, footprints, and interfaces that enable mobile telephone services as well as the human labor and activity that support such arrangement and use. Building on my previous research on satellite and wireless technologies in Aboriginal Australia and post-war Yugoslavia (Parks, 2005a, 2005b), I became interested in Mongolia for several reasons. First, in 1970 Mongolia built one of the Intersputnik satellite earth stations used to interlink communist countries, and as such was an early (though little-known) participant in one of the world's first global satellite systems. Second, since Mongolia is situated between Russia and China it has an important geopolitical position and, not unlike Aboriginal Australia, historically has had to contend with and (re)negotiate its relation to colonizing forces and influences. Third, when the Soviet Union collapsed in 1989 Mongolia gained its political and economic independence and, like the new states of the former Yugoslavia, the post-communist nation augured in a series of reforms, including the privatization of telecommunication and media sectors. Finally, Mongolia has a long tradition of pastoral nomadism that has persisted in the context of the nation's modernization and as such serves as a unique setting for the study of technologized mobilities.

What follows, then, is a highly abridged version of a study of mobile telephone infrastructure in the capital city of Ulaanbaatar. This study involved ethnographic research at more than 100 mobile telephone access points scattered across and beyond the city, during two separate visits to Mongolia in 2004 and 2007. I argue that while Mongolians have imported and installed mobile telephone hardware like many other countries, they have reinvented its infrastructure by creating a publicly accessible and flexible system that is adapted and scaled to local capacities, needs, interests, and desires. To substantiate this claim, I use the critical practice of *footprint analysis*, which begins with maps of wireless coverage zones (or footprints) and proceeds by moving through and describing localized conditions within them (Parks, 2009b). This geo-annotative practice moves between cartography and ethnography, the spectrum and ground, in an effort to explore mobile telephone technologies as part of systems of distribution, patterns of everyday life, and cultural atmospherics. Footprint analysis complicates the seamless claim to territory by wireless corporations by setting their maps into play with discussions of infrastructure sites and the socio-economic conditions that surround them. Only by supplementing the footprint maps of Mongolian wireless service providers with such discussions would we know that a system of *public mobile telephony* emerged that employs a new class of workers, combines the collectivist ethos of communism with aspects of digital capitalism, and reinvents nomadic practices in urban space.

The emergence of walking phone workers

During the 1930s Owen Lattimore, a scholar of Central Asian politics, described Mongolia as a "geo-strategic 'pivot' whose control would serve as a basis for continental domination" (cited in Kotkin & Elleman, 1999: 11–12). Intrigued by its status as the Soviet's first political satellite, Lattimore used Mongolia as a prototype to define a "satellite politics" as distinct from colonial or puppet regimes, insisting that Mongolians had managed to maintain political autonomy in relation to the Soviets since the 1920s (Lattimore, 1956). In 1946, after explaining how the leftist/Marxist tradition in Mongolia differed from that of the Soviets, he concluded, "Outer Mongolia indicates the possibility of political, economic and social complexes eclectic in origin and novel in structure and function, but with a stability of their own and with real survival value" (Lattimore, 1946: 660). Of course, much has happened since Lattimore published this work, but his insights about the geopolitics of what he called the "inner Asian frontier" remain relevant to the discussion of Mongolia's recent democratization and privatization initiatives and the ongoing emergence of new communication infrastructures in the region.

A communist state since 1924, Mongolia restructured its political and economic system after the Soviet collapse in 1989, redefining itself as a democratic state and initiating a market economy. In the midst of grave financial conditions, the Mongolian parliament adopted a series of measures throughout the 1990s designed to privatize its telecom and media sectors, which it saw as key to democratic reform. A master plan for Mongolian telecommunications was prepared in 1994 with the assistance of the International Telecommunications Union and in 1995 a law on telecommunications was adopted by the Mongolian parliament that provided for investment in and regulation of the sector. In 1998 a telecom sector policy statement called for the privatization of all government-owned communication networks and infrastructure, excluding long-distance transmission networks, international switches, and national radio and television broadcasting infrastructure, which would be retained by the government. And in 2002 a Communications Regulatory Commission was formed to oversee new telecom regulations.

When I first visited Mongolia in 2004, cable and satellite television, mobile phones, and Internet cafes were in use throughout the capital of Ulaanbaatar and in parts of the countryside as well. The most striking scene appeared on the outskirts of the city, however, where I saw several men riding horses while talking on cell phones. This probably should not have surprised me. Mongolia has a long history of horse-carried communication as pre-modern Mongol society was organized around long-distance trade, travel, and communication (Bruun and Narangoa, 2006: 3). In 1234, Ögedei Khan (who succeeded his father, Genghis Khan, as ruler of the Mangol empire) established the world's first long-distance postal system, known as "Morin urtuu" (Horse relay station). A letter could travel from the empire's headquarters in Kharakhorum to the Caspian Sea in one week. This system remained in place until the 1930s, when the first international telephone exchange was established in Mongolia (Communication and Information Technology in Mongolia, 2003). While horses formed the crucial backbone of early communication systems in Mongolia, the landscape has changed and this territory is now a patchwork of wireless footprints.

In *Perpetual Contact*, Katz and Aakhus proclaim, "The physical landscape is . . . changing. Billboards abound, encouraging people to subscribe to a mobile phone service. Ungainly signal transmission towers are prominent features of one's view of the panoramic landscape. Public space and public buildings are being modified to accommodate the use of mobile devices" (2002: 302). And yet, as the instance of the horse-riding cell phone user makes clear, such processes are emerging in different ways in different parts of the world. Despite Thomas Friedman's contention that digital technologies have equalized or "flattened" differences in the world (2005), I am convinced that enormous variations and disparities remain to be described and analyzed. For one, media infrastructures are certainly not the same all over the world: they are amalgams of old and new systems, relics of various stages of capitalism and/or socialism, involve both bodies and machines, and have different histories and uses. They are embedded in different patches of earth, operate at various scales and speeds, and serve different populations. I am more swayed by Siegfried Zielinski's insistence upon the "variantology of the media" and his suggestion that we engage with "dynamic moments in the media-archaeological record that abound and revel in heterogeneity" (2006: 7, 11).

The footprints of four wireless service providers, Mongol Telecom, Mobicom, Skytel, and Unitel, cover the capital city of Ulaanbaatar, which had a population of 800,000 in 2004, which jumped to one million in 2007. Mobicom, a Japanese–Mongolian joint venture, formed in 1996 to become the first wireless provider in Mongolia, and worked with the French company Alcatel to establish a GSM infrastructure throughout populated parts of the vast country. By 2006 Mobicom provided service to 106 of Mongolia's province centers and towns throughout 21 of the official provinces, and had 466,000 subscribers (Mobicom, 2006a). The second major provider, Skytel, a joint venture between Mongolian (40 percent) and Korean (60 percent) firms, began offering CDMA services in 1999. By the end of 2006, Skytel had 135,000 subscribers (Skytel, 2007). Unitel is a third provider, initiating GSM services in 2005, and has become a strong competitor with its "Dream life" campaign, and, finally, G Mobile launched services in rural communities in 2007. All corporations have set up service centers throughout Ulaanbaatar and other urban areas and have leased space on billboards throughout the capital city. By 2005, 156,000 Mongolians had landlines and 557,000 had cell phones, suggesting that wireless has become the primary mode of telephony in the country, which has a relatively small population of 2.7 million (Central Intelligence

Figure 23.1   Wireless towers are installed in the "Ger-burbs" of Ulaanbaatar (Source: Author)

Agency, 2007). Emphasizing Mongolia's technical advances, a 2006 investment forum report boasted, "The telecommunications network of the country was renovated and installed according to international standards by Alcatel of France, EWSD of Germany and KDD of Japan" (Mongolia Investors Forum, 2006).

During the first decade of the 2000s, Mobicom, Skytel, and Unitel, as well as Hitachi, Nokia, Panasonic, and others, inscribed their brands within the footprint, and billboards for cell phones and wireless services crisscrossed major intersections throughout Ulaanbaatar. This branding has occurred with the emergence of wireless telephony in cities around the world, where billboards function as corporate transponders that publicize and give material form to wireless infrastructures that are described as "anywhere and everywhere" yet cannot be perceived themselves. Billboards localize dispersed wireless infrastructures in the frame of commercial culture and encourage affective associations with various themes, colors, characters, and services. Since they occupy a place somewhere between the ground and sky, between urban space and the electromagnetic spectrum, they demarcate a vertical field of mediated culture and help to shape a kind of cultural atmospherics. By this I mean a field of activity that includes everything from imperceptible bandwidth and signal traffic to material-semiotic conditions on earth. To be more specific, Mobicom and Skytel footprints are filled with communist-style apartment buildings, renovated Buddhist temples, and ger-settlements. Old men who once worked in communist factories or as herders in the countryside now live without pensions and sit on sidewalks with rusty scales, charging

Figure 23.2 A billboard promoting Unitel's "Dream Life" mobile phone package appears on the side of a building in Ulaanbaatar (Source: Author)

Figure 23.3 Vibrant MobiCom billboards showcasing a new generation of Mongolian mobile telephone users pop out of the cityscape (Source: Author)

passersby less than a penny to weigh themselves. In zones where mobile phone signals circulate, people live in cargo containers. Taxis, buses, and horses move through the same streets. Sony game centers are crammed into basements of buildings that experience regular electrical outages. And during winter orphan kids live underground in sewer pipes where warm water circulates.

Despite aggressive outdoor advertisement not all Mongolians can afford to buy a cell phone and service, as more than one-third of the country's citizens live in poverty (World Bank, 2004). Thus a system of *public mobile telephony* emerged. In 1999 Mobicom began offering a service known as MobiFone – "a wireless communications service designed for those families and small business enterprises that have no access to a fixed line due to geographical factors" (Mobicom, 2006b). With a MobiFone users can make calls within Ulaanbaatar, and to other cities and countries. The network is a wireless local loop (WLL) system that uses the CDMA (code division multiple access) standard. The phones, manufactured by LG Electronics, could be purchased for 395,000 MNT or leased for 100,000 MNT (US$90.00) for three years. In addition, users pay per-minute fees of 12 MNT (US$0.01) to a landline and 26 MNT (US$0.024) to mobile phones (Mobicom, 2006c). Although originally intended for families and businesses beyond the fixed-line telephony infrastructure, many Mongolians ended up buying or leasing the phones, and then sitting on the street and charging passersby a fee of 100 MNT per minute to call landlines, which is about 0.09 MNT per minute. Their profit, 0.09 − 0.01 = 0.08 MNT per minute.

In the midst of a transitional economy, walking phone work became a viable new form of labor. In 2007 I interviewed a former herder, a former tractor operator, a former construction worker, and a former cafe owner, all of whom had migrated to Ulaanbaatar looking for work and, after being displaced from their previous jobs, found walking phone work to provide a steady form of income. Several people I spoke with indicated that families and friends often share the responsibility of performing walking phone work, taking turns doing shifts, working in different parts of the city, and tending to others' phone stands if someone is sick. Some families have managed to obtain more than one white phone and have been able to pool the revenue they generate to provide financial support to all members of the family, some of whom are disabled or elderly and are unable to work. Walking phone operators earn approximately 200,000–500,000 MNT or US$180–450 per month, which is considered a very good income in Mongolia, given that government employees earn much less at US$70–200 per month and the average per capita income in Mongolia in 2005 was US$690 per year (World Bank, 2006). About 80 percent of the Ulaanbaatar population uses these white phones because they are widely accessible and cheaper than mobile phone subscriptions (Mobicom sales representative, 2007).

In Mongolia in 2006 there were 195,000 fixed landlines and 721,000 mobile subscribers in the entire country (for a mobile saturation rate of 30 percent) (BuddeComm, 2012), and approximately 17,000 white phone workers (Skytel marketing director, 2007; Mobicom sales representative, 2007). During the first decade of the 2000s public mobile phones, or "walking phones" as they are locally known, became the predominant model of telephony in Ulaanbaatar. One could look in almost any direction, particularly in busy, well-trafficked

Figure 23.4 A walking mobile phone operator crosses the street amidst urban traffic in Ulaanbaatar (Source: Author)

areas of the city, and see at least two or three. Walking phone workers have intimate knowledge of the densities and schedules of traffic flow in Ulaanbaatar and move around accordingly. Some of them establish makeshift stations with cardboard boxes or folding tables next to depots where vans transport people to and from the outskirts of the city. Others are situated next to the post office or state department store throughout the day. Still others can be found standing or sitting on the sides of busy streets and approach drivers who pull over to use the phone. They work day and night, summer and winter. In the winter, animal furs or other coverings are placed over the phone to keep it warm and preserve battery power.

Some of the white phone workers wear surgical masks, which began during the SARS scare of 2004 and continued thereafter to limit exposure to other communicable diseases. Since they work on the street for long hours these masks block out toxic fumes and other potential contagions from different clients placing their hands and mouths on the phone. Because walking phone workers operate somewhat informally and in the midst of urban

Figure 23.5 A walking mobile phone operator awaits a customer near a Coca-Cola-branded newspaper kiosk in Ulaanbaatar (Source: Author)

distractions, the masks serve as a way of marking and identifying them. Another possible effect of the surgical mask is to provide the semblance of privacy for the caller by concealing the phone operator's face. Much has been written about mobile telephony's reorganization of public/private boundaries. As Jukka-Pekka Puro explains, "One of the most distinctive characteristics of a mobile phone is that it privatizes public places. That is, as someone talks on the phone, one is in her or his own private space . . . The speaker may be physically present, but his or her mental orientation is towards someone who is unseen" (2002: 23). Kenneth Gergen refers to this as "absent presence" and describes it as one of the social drawbacks of mobile telephony because it normalizes a condition where people speaking on the phone are in a particular time–space but are paying more attention to a person that is elsewhere (2002: 227). The case of Mongolian public mobile telephony complicates this assumption by adding a third party to the transaction. Since the mask conceals the face of the operator he/she becomes the "absent presence," temporarily blending in with the system to produce a privacy effect for the caller. Here privacy may be incidental rather than intentional. Totally private wireless conversation may come at a cost that most Mongolians cannot afford and may not even find necessary or desirable.

Figure 23.6 Some walking phone operators worked as animal herders in the countryside before moving to the city and participating in this new line of work (Source: Author)

Walking phone workers are implicated in a flexible economy in which they conspicuously declare their presence on the streets at times and blend in with the system at others, generating a structure of modulated presence. In this sense, their position resonates with Gregory Downey's historical accounts of telegraphy infrastructure and messenger boys. As he writes, "The technological network of the telegraph was more than just a combination of electromechanical systems; it was also a combination of systems of labor, in which messenger boys served different functions at different moments – sometimes working as technological components themselves, sometimes being sold as commodities along with the telegrams they carried, and sometimes acting as agents of change within the technological network itself" (Downey, 2002: 7). By moving about the city and facilitating access to mobile telephony, walking phone workers function in a similar fashion – sometimes operating as network access points, sometimes commodifying their own knowledge of urban space and traffic, and sometimes altering the configuration of the infrastructure itself.

What we are able to perceive and sense at walking phone stands is the externalization of infrastructural processes that are typically internalized and imperceptible in the age of global digital capitalism. Not only are mobile phones visible on the sidewalk instead of buried in the pocket, but money is passed from hand to hand instead of through wires, access points are spatially demarcated whether by masks or stands, and an operator's/worker's body is present, even if in modulated ways. It is as if digital capitalism pauses at these stands to allow us to perceive and contemplate processes that now occur internally in 1s and 0s and at the speed of light. Mobile telephone infrastructure not only becomes more intelligible at these access points, it is also reinvented as local practices of movement, valuation, and exchange dynamically modify the ways the system ultimately takes form and is used. Walking phone workers thus challenge us to understand mobile telephony not as a uniform infrastructure that is plopped down on the earth (as footprint maps as some researchers imply), but rather as a technologized system of distribution that takes a unique shape and form in relation to the historical and socio-economic conditions that surround it.

Conclusion

Consumers around the world are bombarded with advertisements and social patterns that push private ownership of mobile phones, but there is a lot of dead time in the pocket. The case of the Mongolian walking phone workers exemplifies that a mobile telephone infrastructure can be adapted to a transitional economy where citizens' access and employment may be valued over and balanced against global trends toward private mobilization. While the system's value upon access and work may articulate the prerogatives of a formerly communist state, it also affords an entrepreneurial logic as individuals can choose to purchase or lease a phone and sell time according to their own schedules, needs, and interests. In addition, there may be unanticipated refigurations of pastoral nomadism in walking phone work as well. As Alicia Campi suggests, "Foreign and domestic economic policymakers must comprehend the nomadic character of Mongolian economic life, its resilience, and persistent influence" (2006: 90). Whether walking phone work might "transition" people with a nomadic background into a labor market for the digital age is a complex topic that I cannot explore in depth here. Suffice it to say, this kind of work, which requires no specialized training, may have been amenable to herders who were forced to abruptly migrate to Ulaanbaatar after a series of harsh winters killed millions of animals and destroyed their livelihoods as well.

Finally, it is important to situate these mobile telephone practices in a broader global context. In recent years Mongolia has become a favored Central Asian nation of the US and Western Europe because of the relative success of its democratization and liberalization initiatives. George W. Bush became the first US president ever to visit Mongolia in 2005 and in a public address in Ulaanbaatar, after comparing the country to Texas, he declared the US was proud to be its "third neighbor" behind Russia and China (White House press release, 2005). Patting Mongolians on the back, he proclaimed, "You've established a vibrant democracy and opened up your economy. You're an example of success for this region and for the world," and went on to emphasize Mongolian soldiers' service in the wars in Iraq and Afghanistan (White House press release, 2005). Since Mongolia has untapped natural resources (copper, petroleum, gold) and is situated at the back door of emerging markets in former Soviet republics and China, the country, as Lattimore predicted long ago, remains of high strategic importance. Rather than look to Mongolia as a site for natural resource extraction or as another recruit for the "coalition of the willing," the US and West should recognize Mongolia's practice of public mobile telephony as an important technological and social innovation. While its mobile telephone infrastructure has been organized to serve local needs, it could also become a model exported to other financially strained countries or regions.

In the global scheme of things, Mongolian walking phone workers serve as an intriguing counterpoint to Indian telemarketers. Rather than work in highly controlled artificial environments crafted by large US conglomerates and adapt to a schedule, dialect, and economy from elsewhere, walking phone operators work on urban streets (yes, among fumes, contagions, and sometimes in harsh weather) according to their own schedules, and facilitate phone access and the circulation of Mongolian language and signal traffic within an infrastructure partly owned by Mongolian companies. It may be that in so-called "transitional" societies the systems that emerge in times of transition are highly viable themselves and should not necessarily be discarded in favor of more "advanced" or "developed" systems. The idea that everyone needs to own a mobile phone (if not two or three) is a pipe dream promoted by manufacturers like Nokia, Siemens, Motorola, Samsung, and Apple. As the walking phone workers demonstrate, there are other ways of arranging mobile telephony systems. And yet it is also important to point out that this system does not serve capital to its full potential, and, precisely because of that, it might not last!

Acknowledgements

I thank Naran Zorigt, Zaya, and Enkhbayar Dagvladorj for research assistance and translation services. I worked on this project while I was a research fellow at the Wissenschaftskolleg (Institute for Advanced Study) in Berlin, and thank the institute and its staff for their support. My photographs related to this research have been exhibited as a multimedia art project entitled "Roaming" in Berlin and Zurich.

Bibliography

Baliamoune-Lutz, Mina (2003) "An Analysis of the Determinants and Effects of ICT Diffusion in Developing Countries," *Information Technology for Development*, vol. 10, 151–169.
Bruun, Ole and Li Narangoa (eds) (2006) *Mongols from Country to City: Floating Boundaries, Pastoralism and City Life in the Mongol Lands*, Copenhagen: Nordic Institute of Asian Studies Press.
BuddeComm (2012) "Mongolia – Telecoms, Mobile and the Internet Executive Summary," Budde Communication Research, available online at www.budde.com.au/Research/Mongolia-Telecoms-Mobile-and-Internet.html, accessed March 29, 2012.

Burkhart, Patrick (2007) "Moving Targets: Introducing Mobility into Universal Service Obligations," *Telecommunications Policy*, vol. 31, 164–178.

Campi, Alicia (2006) "The Rise of Cities in Nomadic Mongolia," in *Mongols from Country to City: Floating Boundaries, Pastoralism and City Life in the Mongol Lands*, Bruun, Ole and Li Narangoa (eds), Copenhagen: Nordic Institute of Asian Studies Press, 22–55.

Central Intelligence Agency (2007) "Mongolia: Communications," *CIA World Fact Book*, available online at www.cia.gov/cia/publications/factbook/geos/mg.html, accessed March 6, 2007.

Communication and Information Technology in Mongolia (2003) "Mongolia Information Guide," available online at www.ub-mongolia.mn, accessed October 25, 2006.

Donner, Jonathan (2008) "Research Approaches to Mobile Use in the Developing World: A Review of the Literature," *The Information Society*, vol. 24, 140–259.

Downey, Gregory (2002) *Telegraph Messenger Boys: Labor, Technology, and Geography, 1850–1950*, New York: Routledge.

Duncombe, Richard (2011) "Researching Impact of Mobile Phones for Development: Concepts, Methods and Lessons for Practice," *Information Technology for Development*, vol. 17:4, 268–288.

Duncombe, Richard and Richard Boateng (2009) "Mobile Phones and Financial Services in Developing Countries: A Review of Concepts, Methods, Issues, Evidence and Future Research Directions," *Third World Quarterly*, vol. 30:7, 1237–1258.

Friedman, Thomas (2005) *The World Is Flat: A Brief History of the Twentieth Century*, London: Allen Lane.

Gergen, Kenneth (2002) "The Challenge of Absent Presence," in *Perpetual Contact: Mobile Communication, Private Talk, Public Performance*, James Katz and Mark Aakhus (eds), Cambridge: Cambridge University Press, 227–241.

Goggin, Gerard (2006) *Cell Phone Culture: Mobile Technology in Everyday Life*, London: Routledge.

Graham, Stephen and Simon Marvin (2001) *Splintering Urbanism: Networked Infrastructures and the Urban Condition*, London: Routledge.

Gronlund, Ake and Yousuf Islam (2010) "A Mobile E-learning Environment for Developing Countries: The Bangladesh Virtual Interactive Classroom," *Information Technology and Development*, vol. 16:4, 244–259.

Hamilton, Jacqueline (2003) "Are Main Lines and Mobile Phones Substitutes or Complements? Evidence from Africa," *Telecommunications Policy*, vol. 27, 209–133.

Horst, Heather and Daniel Miller (2006) *The Cell Phone: An Anthropology of Communication*, Oxford: Berg Publishers.

Idowu, Bayo, Rotimi Adagunodo and Rufus Adeoyin (2006) "Information Technology Infusion Model for Health Sector in a Developing Country: Nigeria as a Case," *Technology and Health Care*, vol. 14, 69–77.

Islam, M. Sirajul and Ake Gronlund (2011) "Bangledesh Calling: Farmers' Technology Use Practices as a Driver for Development," *Information Technology for Development*, vol. 17:2, 95–111.

Kaba, Bangaly, Koffi N'Da, Peter Meso and Victor Wacham Mbarika (2009) "Micro Factors Influencing the Attitudes toward and the Use of a Mobile Technology: A Model of Cell-Phone Use in Guinea," *IEEE Transactions on Professional Communication*, vol. 52:3, 272–290.

Kahn, James G., Joshua Yang and James S. Kahn (2010) "'Mobile' Health Needs and Opportunities in Developing Countries," *Health Affairs*, vol. 29:2, 254–261.

Kaplan, Warren (2006) "Can the Ubiquitous Power of Mobile Phones Be Used to Improve Health Outcomes in Developing Countries?" *Globalization and Health*, vol. 2:9, 1–14.

Katz, James and Mark Aakhus (2002) "Conclusion: Making Meaning of Mobiles – A Theory of *Apparatgeist*," in *Perpetual Contact: Mobile Communication, Private Talk, Public Performance*, James Katz and Mark Aakhus (eds), Cambridge: Cambridge University Press, 301–320.

Kotkin, Stephen and Bruce Elleman (1999) *Mongolia in the Twentieth Century: Landlocked Cosmopolitanism*, Armonk, NY: M. E. Sharpe.

Larkin, Brian (2008) *Signal and Noise: Media, Infrastructure, and Urban Culture in Nigeria*, Durham: Duke University Press.

Lattimore, Owen (1946) "The Outer Mongolian Horizon," *Foreign Affairs*, vol. 24:4, 648–660.

Lattimore, Owen (1956) "Satellite Politics: The Mongolian Prototype," *The Western Political Quarterly*, vol. 1:9, 36–43.

Lester, Feder (2010) "Cell-Phone Medicine Brings Care to Patients," *Health Affairs*, vol. 29:2, 259–263.

Michaels, Eric (1994) *Bad Aboriginal Art: Tradition, Media and Technological Horizons*, Minneapolis: University of Minnesota Press.

Mobicom (2006a) "Greetings from the CEO," Mobicom website, available at www.mobicom.mn/index.php?selLang=ENG, accessed October 16, 2006.

Mobicom (2006b) "Mobifone Service Overview," Mobicom website, available at www.mobicom.mn/index.php?con=vw&id=2814, accessed October 21, 2006.

Mobicom (2006c) "Service Fees and Charges," MobiCom website, available at www.mobicom.mn/index.php?con=vw&id=281412, accessed October 21, 2006.

Mobicom sales representative (2007) Interview at Mobicom corporate headquarters, Ulaanbaatar, June.

Mongolia Investors Forum (2006) "Information and Communication Technology Sector," available online at www.investmongolia.com/forum/t4c.htm, accessed March 28, 2012.

Parks, Lisa (2005a) *Cultures in Orbit: Satellites and the Televisual*, Durham: Duke University Press.

— (2005b) "Postwar Footprints: Satellite and Wireless Stories in Slovenia and Croatia," in *B-Zone: Becoming Europe and Beyond*, Anselm Franke (ed.), Barcelona: ACTAR Press, 306–347.

— (2009a) "Around the Antenna Tree: The Politics of Infrastructural Visibility," *Flow*, available online at http://flowtv.org/?p=2507, accessed March 20, 2012.

— (2009b) "Signals and Oil: Satellite Footprints and Post-Communist Territories in Central Asia," *European Journal of Cultural Studies*, vol. 12(2), 137–156.

Puro, Jukka-Pekka (2002) "Finland: A Mobile Culture," in *Perpetual Contact: Mobile Communication, Private Talk, Public Performance*, James Katz and Mark Aakhus (eds), Cambridge: Cambridge University Press, 19–29.

Skytel (2007) "About Us," Skytel website, available at www.skytel.mn, accessed February 12, 2007.

Skytel marketing director (2007) Interview at Skytel corporate headquarters, Ulaanbaatar, June.

Wallis, Cara (2011) "Mobile Phones without Guarantees: The Promises of Technology and the Contingencies of Culture," *New Media & Society*, vol. 13:3, 471–485.

White House Press Release (2005) "Interview of President by Eagle Television," Nov. 8, available online at www.whitehouse.gov/news/releases/2005/11/print/20051108-6.html, accessed October 21, 2006.

World Bank (2004) "More Than Third of Mongolians Live in Poverty," Launch of the Main Report of "Household Income and Expenditure Survey/Living Standards Measurement Survey," East Asia and Pacific, Dec. 9, available online at http://web.worldbank.org/WBSITE/EXTERNAL/COUNTRIES/EASTASIAPACIFICEXT/0,,contentMDK:20291925~menuPK:2098868~pagePK:64002643~piPK:64002619~theSitePK:226301,00.html, accessed March 29, 2012.

World Bank (2006) "GNI Per Capita," World Development Indicators Database, July 1, available online at http://siteresources.worldbank.org/DATASTATISTICS/Resources/GNIPC.pdf, accessed March 6, 2007.

Yeow, Paul H. P., Yee Hen Yuen and Regina Connolly (2008) "Mobile Phone Use in a Developing Country," *Journal of Urban Technology*, vol. 15:1, 85–116.

Zielinski, Siegfried (2006) *The Deep Time of the Media*, Cambridge: MIT Press.

24

Informal Infrastructures

Colin McFarlane and Alex Vasudevan

In a recent collection of essays, the Indian author and activist Arundhati Roy takes us to the scene of a protest at Jantar Mantar on Parliament Street in New Dehli. An old observatory built in the eighteenth century by the Maharaja Sawai Jai Singh II of Jaipur, Jantar Mantar is the only remaining site in Dehli where Section 144 – the revived nineteenth-century law that bans the gathering of more than five people – is not enforced. In the spring of 2010, over a thousand pavement dwellers descended on the site to demand "the right to shelter, to food (ration cards) and to life (protection from police brutality and criminal extortion by municipal officers)" (Roy, 2011: 152). Who, Roy asks, are these protesters and where have they come from? They are, she writes, the "representatives of the estimated sixty million people who have been displaced by rural destitution, by slow starvation, by floods and drought (many of them man-made), by mines, steel factories, and aluminum smelters, by highways and expressways, by the 3300 big dams built since Independence, and now by special economic zones (SEZs)". They are, Roy continues, the "millions who make up the chain gangs that are transported from city to city to build the New India". They are, in other words, the "*shadow people who live in the cracks that run between schemes and institutions*. They sleep on the streets, eat on the streets, make love on the streets, give birth on the streets, are raped on the streets, cut their vegetables, wash their clothes, raise their children, live and die on the streets" (Roy, 2011: 154, 153; emphasis added).

While Roy's powerful description allows us to zoom in on the logics of dispossession and displacement that have repeatedly condemned significant numbers of people in the global South to misery and prompted many to seek alternative forms of housing and shelter, she does not develop what it might mean to live informally 'between schemes and institutions'. In this chapter we therefore ask how one might begin to attend – theoretically and practically – to the informal *assembly* of the city and the diverse capacities of urban residents to cope with "incessant insufficiency". Is it possible, and contra Roy, to re-think informality less as a territorial habitus of the dispossessed and more as a set of *mobile planning practices* generative of another urbanism? In what way do these practices seek to re-articulate the city as a "flexible resource" for other forms of political, social, and economic organization (Simone, 2008: 200)?

In order to answer these framing questions, this chapter examines the intertwinement of infrastructure, informality, and mobility as a way of opening up an alternative realm of neglected urban politics. We seek to draw attention to the complex *material geographies* through which cities are differentially composed and re-assembled (see McFarlane, 2011; Vasudevan, 2011). To do so requires a conception of the city as a dwelling process that aligns multiple space-times of knowledge, ideas, materials, resources, and people. Urbanism, we believe, is a process that is increasingly dwelt through multiple mobilities shaped by uneven relations of power, resource, and knowledge. As AbdouMaliq Simone (2011: 356) has so eloquently put it, "urbanization is not simply a context for the support or appropriation of specific lives as it is the plane upon which people circling, touching, avoiding, attaching – come together, sometimes kicking and screaming, as an infrastructure". This is an understanding of the urban, we argue, that is incessantly mobile – "a textured surface that speeds things up and slows them down, where the interruptions enable points of view, attentions, memories, condensations and dissipations of effort and association, framing devices, different vertically layered strata of articulation, and different ways of paying attention and of being implicated in what is going on" (Simone, 2011: 356). For Simone, cities are places "always on their way somewhere, with different reach and possibilities, and always transformed by what people, materials, technical and discursive instruments do in the passing" (ibid.).

In this chapter we set out to rethink urban informality as a *mobile* process through which often precarious lifeworlds are assembled. The argument moves in two stages. First, we re-examine the notion of informality as a mode of urban constitution. Second, we show how the assembling of informal infrastructures can reveal important issues around the making of a radical urban politics through reference to our own work in Mumbai and Berlin. The paper concludes by setting out the case for the development of a critical urbanism as a product of mobile informal architectures. Such a view, we believe, opens up the possibility for the articulation of a neglected urban politics.

Re-thinking informality and infrastructure

Cities are made, in part, through a diverse combination of different formal and informal practices, but attention is usually focused on the realm of the seemingly formal – planning, policy, regulation, law, finance, and so on – over the informal, the below-the-radar practices of everyday life and culture that not only grease the wheels of these apparently formal realms, but which may indeed be more important than the formal domain. As Ananya Roy (2009a, 2009b) has argued in relation to urban planning in India and elsewhere, informality might be considered less an exception, and more as a central idiom of urbanization. We might consider here how political, economic, and legal elites use or suspend the law to enable violation of, for example, planning or building controls or order to allow new developments. Informality, in this perspective, becomes central to urban planning regimes: "By informality I mean a state of deregulation, one where the ownership, use, and purpose of land cannot be fixed and mapped according to any prescribed set of regulations or the law. Indeed, here the law itself is rendered open-ended and subject to multiple interpretations and interests, the 'law as social process' is as idiosyncratic and arbitrary as that which is illegal" (Roy, 2009b: 80). "The Indian city", writes Roy (2009b: 81), "is made possible through an idiom of planning whose key feature is informality".

What this opens up is a reading of informality not as a territorial category (e.g. the slum) or as a category of labour, but as a set of practices that *extend* across different forms of urban life and which make crucial contributions to how cities are made and lived in. Informality here is a domain of urban constitution, but it is also an infrastructure of makeshift urbanism. Indeed, the claim so often made by urban states that the makeshift infrastructures of the poor – especially the infrastructures of water, sanitation, and power, upon which many 'slum' neighbourhoods depend – are illegal and therefore worthy of often violent removal, can also be applied to many so-called 'formal' infrastructures developed by the state working with the private sector (e.g. see Ghertner, 2010, on 'rule by aesthetics' in Delhi; and Goldman, 2011, on 'speculative urbanism' in Bangalore). If the makeshift infrastructures of the state are deemed 'formal' and thereby legitimate – often because, as Ghertner (2010) shows, they *look* 'formal' – the poor's makeshift urbanism is so often that which is deemed 'informal' and undesirable. As MacLeod and Jones (2011: 2452) put it: "The fundamental analytical, and indeed political, question is why some instances of informality are designated as illegal and their inhabitants criminalised while other land transformations appear to be protected and formalised to enjoy state sanction or even endorsed as practices of the state".

We are interested in instances of makeshift informal infrastructures developed by marginalized and alternative urban groups. We see the making of informal infrastructures as one of continuous effort, as is evidenced by the practices that constitute much of the daily life for people within marginalized neighbourhoods. This is particularly the case for women, who tend to take on the majority of household construction and maintenance. In the words of the journalist Robert Neuwirth (2006: 21–22), "with makeshift materials, they are building a future in a society that has always viewed them as people without a future. In this very concrete way, they are asserting their own being". Writing in turn about cities as "platforms for trajectories of incrementalism", Simone (2008: 28) describes diverse practices of urbanism that are "added onto bit by bit", including the mobilization of family labour that buys time for a small business to grow, or mobile work crews "formed to dig wells, help with construction, or deliver goods until they make enough contacts to specialize on one particular activity", or the construction of temporary or more long-term social and material infrastructures that bring some predictability to urban life.

These forms of informal work are themselves mobile: materials being translated into different uses, migrants shifting around and between cities in search of casual work, particular urban spaces being used for different functions over time, state bureaucrats displacing formal regulations in order to facilitate a new shopping mall or high-end residential complex, and so on. They are social and material infrastructures made through acts of displacement and translation, of shifting between different uses, contexts, and possibilities. As Graham and Thrift (2007) have argued in relation to urban infrastructures – from roads and electricity to water and sanitation – it is through often labour-intensive sociotechnical processes of maintenance and repair that the urban world appears to us 'ready-to-hand'. Infrastructures may sometimes appear obdurate or pre-formed, but in practice they are *articulations* that require the management of different mobilities, including changing intensities of labour, resource, and learning.

What interests us in particular is how informal infrastructures constitute urban politics. There are few attempts to grapple not only with the forms of informal adaption, improvisation, and repair that assemble a sense of 'cityness', but also the ways in which they are *constitutively political*. For Edgar Pieterse (2008: 6), incremental processes of "stumbling across what works and what does not" can encode a politics that he calls 'radical incrementalism'. Radical incrementalism is a "sensibility that believes in deliberate actions of social transformation but through a multiplicity of processes and imaginations, none of which assumes or asserts a primary significance over other struggles" (ibid.). These are "surreptitious, sometimes overt, and multiple small revolutions that at unanticipated and unexpected moments galvanize into deeper ruptures that accelerate tectonic shifts of the underlying logics of domination and what is considered possible" (ibid.). For Pieterse, this process of galvanizing depends on the work of civil society organizations built around not patriarchal or authoritarian structures but strong internal democratic practices and reflexivity. This is also a politics of mobility: galvanizing depends on working through mobilities of different sorts, including an alertness to the work of other urban "progressive networks and epistemic communities" (Pieterse, 2008: 172) in acts of coalition building, as well as to the "numerous and ever-changing rhythms of the city" which generate cultural novelty and potential resources for renewing political strategies (ibid. 174). For Pieterse, these practices are closely linked to processes of empowerment, but only in cities where governance structures and cultures allow for genuinely participatory collaboration. Without those conditions, as is the case in many cities, politics requires "militant direct action that can lead to the institutionalization of participatory democratic systems" (ibid. 143).

We are interested, then, in how urban groups draw together different social, material, and epistemic resources to build open-ended and ongoing forms of radical incrementalism that themselves can be put to work as mobile political practices. Our contention is that attending to *how* informal infrastructures are assembled can contribute to the constitution of a different critical urbanism. In the next section, drawing on our respective work in Mumbai and Berlin, we provide some illustrative examples.

Making political infrastructures

A key starting point for considering the politics of mobile informal infrastructures is to turn to translocal urban movements for basic infrastructures and services. For example, the influential movement Slum/Shack Dwellers International (SDI) is premised on a politics of working at informal infrastructures. Drawing on the experiential knowledge people have in building and rebuilding homes and infrastructures, SDI pulls residents and activists together in a process of informal discussion and experimentation to, amongst other strategies, build model houses and toilets. This act of building small and full-size models is not an incidental materialization of SDI's politics. Instead, these practices perform, make visible, and provide a context through which to breathe life into SDI's politics. It is in these acts of making houses that the depiction of slum residents as passive is subverted by an image of the resident as a skilled, active subject. Model housing and toilets often provide a staging for encounters between residents and political figures, and here SDI activists point to models as examples of how community organizations can take responsibility for their own development if only the state treated them as partners and provided the land. This is a mobile material politics that performs, then, a particular kind of entrepreneurial urbanism, and in this sense is at one with ideologies of state withdrawal and the shifting of responsibility to the poor.

These working through informal infrastructures fit with a broader governance context of institutional pluralism, where the state facilitates urban development in 'partnership' with civil society and the private sector. But more importantly, they perform and demarcate the scope of radical incrementalism by fronting an entrepreneurial conception of social change that starkly delimits the role of the state. This strategy of building models is also a mobile informal infrastructure: it has travelled to partner organizations in the SDI movement internationally, and in the process has generated often heated debate around not just housing and infrastructure forms, but about the expectations and responsibilities of the state to poor communities (Peiterse, 2008; McFarlane, 2011). The ways in which mobile informal infrastructures in SDI are made and represented both encode the movement's politics, and constitute a contested arena both within and outside the movement as people grapple with what the role of the state versus poor communities should be, or question the very strategy of expensive processes of exchange and infrastructural experimentation (Podlashuc, 2011).

Indeed, the sorts of informal infrastructures that become mobile, and specifically that travel amongst political elites from local states to international donors and think tanks, are often the kinds that fit with dominant scripts for urban development. SDI is one of the most successful urban movements in the world in gaining funding and recognition from the World Bank, the UN, bilaterals, organizations like the Gates or Clinton Foundations, and think tanks. But we also see this in the sorts of informal infrastructures that travel through elite groups and which are heralded as good practice. For example, in 2007 the prestigious Deutsche Bank Urban Age (DBUA) Award was awarded to a toilet block built by a community organization working with particular state officials in Khotwadi, a well-established informal settlement in west Mumbai. The award was established to encourage citizens to take initiatives to improve their cities, and runs alongside the Urban Age Project, a joint initiative of the London School of Economics and Deutsche Bank's Alfred Herrhausen Society. Describing why the award was given for this toilet block, Deutsche Bank wrote that the project "is a striking example of the poor helping themselves, and gives the lie to the stereotypical depiction of slum dwellers as helpless or indolent victims" (Deutsche Bank, 2007: no pagination). The award offers far more than just prestige: US$100,000 was given to the community-based organization that runs the block, Triratana Prerana Mandal (TPM), that have subsequently used the award to help fund the construction of a large community sports centre along the road from the toilet block ('triratana' means three jewels, and for the activists refers to education, sports, and culture).

This is an award for a form of citizen entrepreneurialism that refuses to wait for the state but instead takes matters – in this case the most basic and fundamental of matters – into its own management. Suketu Mehta (2011: 155), author of the celebrated 2004 book on Mumbai, *Maximum City*, and one of the Urban Age judges, described the toilet project as "an ingenious as well as indigenous solution that needed very little investment and could be replicated in slum colonies around the world". The award was given not just because TPM has built a well-run, well-maintained, and clean toilet block in the neighbourhood, but because the toilet block has become an unlikely focal point for a range of additional social activities. For example, 200 students from around the local area attend basic computer classes at the block (upstairs from the toilets), paying around Rs.750 for a three-month class. There are women's groups involved in community savings. More recently it has attained solar hot water, set up a biogas plant, started rainwater harvesting, and begun collecting ground water through boring – all through new city and state environmental funding schemes. They have won international funds for equipment, women's empowerment, and sustainable development. Khotwadi is a flood-prone area of western Mumbai – many houses were badly damaged, for instance, in the 2005 monsoon flood, leaving residents to manually clear houses, unblock drains, and shift piles of garbage. TPM is involved in solid waste management, sorting waste into wet and dry garbage and turning it into value through recycling, for instance through children recycling plastic bottles and bags into new objects for sale. The decentralized mobility of waste maps onto the decentralized nature of community activism through TPM. This is mirrored by the fact that Khotwadi does not have municipal sewerage connections, so the mobilities of waste in TPM's work involve both decentralized waste infrastructures and decentralized social processes of arranging for septic tanks to be cleared and maintained. For all the cheap and stereotypical caricatures of slums as pariah spaces of despair and refuse, here is an example of turning waste into an indicator of progress, possibility, and value (see Appadurai, 2002, on toilet activism in Mumbai; Gidwani and Reddy,

2011). While the award itself is an entirely laudable effort to raise the profile of slum sanitation and to support an undoubtedly creative and committed group of community activists, it is also a reminder of the sorts of stories and politics elite groups wish to hear about concerning sanitation, and which thereby become mobile through these kinds of routes – not the messy, excremental politics of daily grind, but the shining and seemingly harmless success stories that fit with elite aspirations to build more entrepreneurial cities.

From radical incrementalism to insurgent urbanism

If, as we argue, the assembling of informal infrastructures is a mobile translocal process that depends on a contingent set of relations between bodies, spaces, and materials, it has also been accompanied by the flourishing of new *insurgent* modes of association and action (see Vasudevan, 2011). Recent scholarship has zoomed in, for example, on the relationship between urban informality, radical politics, and social justice. Particular attention has been paid to the emergence of new "insurgent" forms of citizenship and identity. The work of the anthropologist James Holston has, in this context, highlighted the important role that differentiated legal processes have come to play in shaping informal planning and construction in urban Brazil (see Holston, 2008). While Holston's main focus is on São Paulo and the gradual and uneven formalization of the city's squatted, auto-constructed peripheries, he demonstrates how struggles over territorial rights and political recognition were both mutable and mobile. For Holston, the law became a *formalizing* tool that brought the experiences of the urban poor into the mainstream and served as a solid platform for Brazil's "right to the city" movement. If the development of informal infrastructures was thus predicated on the transformation of legal struggles into political practices capable of securing social and legal legitimacy, it also continued to provide resources for contesting the increasingly iniquitous geographies of contemporary urbanization. In the words of Holston, "[this] is an insurgence that begins with the struggle for rights to have a daily life in the city worthy of a citizen's dignity" (2008: 204, 313).

The work of Holston and others demonstrates how informal infrastructures are increasingly assembled through a variety of sites, people, objects, and processes while operating at a number of scales. Indeed, the recent historical geography of squatting and informal settlement in both the global North and South has depended on broader transnational networks that have facilitated the forging of new identities and the rebuilding of solidarities across time and space. At stake here, as a number of studies have shown, is the defining role played by informal infrastructures in the production of what Jenny Pickerill and Paul Chatterton have elsewhere described as *autonomous geographies* – "those spaces where people desire to constitute non-capitalist, egalitarian, and solidaristic forms of political, social, and economic organization through a combination of resistance and creation" (2006: 730). For Pickerill and Chatterton, the production of autonomous geographies is a multi-scalar process that weaves "together spaces and times" and that may be variously understood "as a form of interstitial politics; as a process of resistance and creation; and as a coherent attempt at praxis with its strong sense of prefigurative politics and commitment to the revolution of the everyday" (2006: 732). To the extent that this is a process that is contextually and relationally grounded in social struggles that stretch across different times and spaces, it also depends, we argue, on informal practices of maintenance and repair that are themselves mobile.

As the history of the squatting movement in Berlin, for example, shows, the practice of 'occupation' represented an act of collective *world-making* – a radical DIY empiricism – through which an alternative informal sense of 'cityness' was continuously composed and recomposed (Vasudevan, 2011). For many activists in the scene, this was predicated, in the first instance, on *queering* the idea of the home as a site of domesticity and social reproduction and where the everyday micro-politics of making a 'home' countered not only traditional performances of housekeeping and kinship but also unsettled conventional distinctions between publicity and privacy and, in so doing, altered the possibilities for dwelling in the city (Amantine, 2011). For others still, this involved a more basic attempt to carve out autonomous spaces that not only responded to the hardships of creative destruction and accumulation by dispossession but also served as emancipatory sites that would come to challenge the unyielding predetermination of lives and livelihoods (Bodenschatz *et al.*, 1983; Vasudevan, 2011). In practical terms, this depended in no small part on a modest *ontology of mending and repair*. Squatters in Berlin often confronted abandoned spaces that required significant renovation. While DIY maintenance focused on the re-connection of utilities including water and electricity, squatters also responded to normative assumptions about living and the 'home' through the re-assembling of its more basic spatialities. In many cases, the permeability of a building was increased and re-worked to match the changing needs and wishes of the squatters. Walls were removed in order to increase the size of collective spaces, while stairwells were created to produce a new geography of experimentation and movement (see Sheridan, 2007). These experiments with the built form thus became a key process for exploring a new micropolitics of alignment, interdependency, and connection (Simone, 2004: 12). But they also circulated beyond a local ecology of informal practices and knowledges. Squatters in Berlin and elsewhere became increasingly dependent on a host of *transversal geographies* that linked activists across Northern and Southern Europe and that played a crucial role in the circulation and assembling of an alternative makeshift urbanism.

And yet, if squatters across Europe disseminated and shared informal practices of DIY maintenance and repair, these were practices that also *moved* into and *circulated* within formal policy networks. In Berlin, squatted houses in the 1980s and 1990s were often contractually "pacified" through legalization and the promise of public funding (Holm and Kuhn, 2010). What began as an insurgent form of 'self-help' thus became a major mechanism in the commodification of urban space, as tactics of informal urban living were quickly transformed into new strategies for neo-liberal urban renewal (Balaban, 2011). At the same time, the dissolution of one set of autonomous spaces was more often than not accompanied by the intensification and multiplication of *other* autonomous geographies both in time and in space. Informal infrastructures were, in other words, continuously mobile, producing new sites of autonomy and emancipation. It is this processual conception of dwelling that is, in our view, central to the constitution of a different kind of urban politics.

Conclusion

Thinking about mobile informal architectures opens up a neglected urban politics, where the nature of politics itself is predicated on the materialization of different urban flows and the making-mobile of particular urban forms. While we would agree that tracking the politics of contemporary technosocialities, from smart phones and social networking to the embedding of digital code in a vast texture of urban life, is an urgent critical task (e.g. see Kitchen and Dodge, 2011), we cannot lose sight of an enduring and basic politics of inhabitation, where the struggles are for housing, toilets, water, and resource. These more fundamental metabolic struggles do, of course, travel across digital networks and into translocal information spaces (blogs, news items, tweets, and so on), which in turn attracts additional mobilities of funding, researchers, journalists, and activists. Indeed, the wall upstairs from the TPM block is replete with information about visitors from across the world, and the TPM visitor book is an interesting archive of global and national mobilities in its own right. Investigating these sometimes entangled, sometimes divergent assemblages is a key challenge for research on urban mobilities, but here our focus has been on how material mobilities take shape politically through place-based struggles. How are informal infrastructures used to entrain different mobilities in the pursuit of different urban political projects, whether radical incrementalism or insurgent urbanism, or some other political rubric? How do urban forms and processes – streets, buildings, migrant labour camps, squatter neighbourhoods, infrastructures, and meeting points like Jantar Mantar – both enact and translate the articulation of mobile informal infrastructures, and operate to limit their political scope? How do different rhythms and speeds – of materials, resources, group dynamics, and events – enter into the making and unmaking of informal infrastructures? What kind of theoretical and methodological resources might we need to develop in order to track them?

If we do not have all the answers to these questions, we hope to have opened up a critical space for re-conceptualizing the ways in which informal urban lifeworlds are pieced together. Our aim has been to disclose an alternative set of orientations for rethinking the relationship between informal infrastructure and the logics of urban dwelling. To do so is to offer the promise of a different rendering of critical urbanism that is ultimately more alive and attentive to the politics and mobilities through which everyday life is secured, contested, and perhaps even remade.

References

Amantine (2011) *Gender und Häuserkampf*. Münster: Unrast Verlag.

Appadurai, A. (2002) 'Deep democracy: urban governmentality and the horizon of politics'. *Public Culture* 14: 21–47.

Balaban, U. (2011) 'The enclosure or urban space and consolidation of the capitalist land regime'. *Urban Studies* 48: 2162–2179.

Bodenschatz, H., Heise, V. and Korfmacher, J. (1983) *Schluss mit der Zerstörung? Stadterneuerung und städtische Opposition in Amsterdam, London und West-Berlin*. Giessen: Anabas.

Deutsche Bank (2007) 'Deutsche Bank Urban Age Award given to two city projects which transform the lives of Mumbai's citizens'. *The Deutsche Bank Urban Age Award*. Available online at http://urban-age.net/0_downloads/PressRelease-DBUA-Award_311007.pdf (accessed July 2013).

Ghertner, D. A. (2010) 'Calculating without numbers: Aesthetic governmentality in Delhi's slums'. *Economy and Society* 39(2): 185–217.

Gidwani, V. and Reddy, R. N. (2011) 'The afterlives of "waste": notes from India for a minor history of capitalist surplus'. *Antipode* 43(4): 1625–1658.

Goldman, M. (2011) 'Speculative urbanism and the making of the world city'. *International Journal of Urban and Regional Research* 35(3): 555–581.

Graham, N. and Thrift, N. (2007) 'Out of order. understanding repair and maintenance'. *Theory, Culture & Society* 24: 1–25.

Holm, A. and Kuhn, A. (2010) 'Squatting and urban renewal: The interaction of squatter movements and strategies of urban restructuring in Berlin'. *International Journal of Urban and Regional Research* 35: 644–658.

Holston, J. (2008) *Insurgent Citizenship: Disjunctions of Democracy and Modernity in Brazil*. Princeton, NJ: Princeton University Press.

Kitchen, R. and Dodge, M. (2011) *Code/Space: Software and Everyday Life*. Cambridge, MA: The MIT Press.

MacLeod, G. and Jones, M. (2011) 'Renewing urban politics'. *Urban Studies* 48(12): 2443–2472.

McFarlane, C. (2011) 'The city as assemblage: dwelling and urban space. *Environment and Planning D: Society and Space* 29: 649–671.

Mehta, S. (2011) 'Maximum cities: Mumbai, New York'. In Krull, W. (ed) *Research and Responsibility: Reflections on Our Common Future*. Leipzig: Europaische Verlagsanstalt, 149–166.

Neuwirth, R. (2006) *Shadow Cities: a Billion Squatters, a New Urban World*. London: Routledge.

Pickerill, J. and Chatterton, P. (2006) 'Notes towards autonomous geographies: creation, resistance and self-management as survival tactics'. *Progress in Human Geography* 30: 730–746.

Pieterse, E. (2008) *City Futures: Confronting the Crisis of Urban Development*. London: Zed Books.

Podlashuc, L. (2011) 'The South African Homeless People's Federation: interrogating the myth of participation'. Working Paper 2: African Centre for Citizenship and Democracy, School of Government, University of the Western Cape.

Roy, A. (2009a) 'Strangely familiar: planning and the worlds of insurgence and informality'. *Planning Theory* 8(1): 7–11.

Roy, A. (2009b) 'Why India cannot plan its cities: informality, insurgence and the idiom of urbanization'. *Planning Theory* 8(1): 76–87.

Roy, A. (2011) *Broken Republic: Three Essays*. London: Hamish Hamilton.

Sheridan, D. (2007) 'The space of subculture in the city: getting specific about Berlin's indeterminate territories'. *Field Journal* 1: 97–119.

Simone, A. (2004) *For the City Yet to Come: Changing African Life in Four Cities*. Durham, NC: Duke University Press.

Simone, A. (2008) 'The politics of the possible: making urban life in Phnom Pehn'. *Singapore Journal of Tropical Geography* 29: 186–204.

Simone, A. (2011) 'The surfacing of Urban Life: A response to Colin McFarlane and Neil Brenner, David Madden and David Wachsmuth'. *City* 15: 355–364.

Vasudevan, A. (2011) 'Dramaturgies of dissent: the spatial politics of squatting in Berlin, 1968'. *Social and Cultural Geography* 12: 283–303.

Section Four
Introduction: Materialities

Mobilities research is at the forefront of developing new ways of thinking about the politics of matter. Whilst people are mobile, the equally differentiated mobilities of information, capital, goods and services that are essential for contemporary life are a sustained feature of mobilities research. Indeed one of the defining characteristics of mobilities research is its attention to the mobilities of multiple materialities, both human and non-human. While the previous section of the handbook focused on the spaces, systems and infrastructures that these multiple materialities are entrained within, this section drills down to interrogate the actual stuff that is in motion. This is significant because, for many, the networked and globalizing quality of the contemporary world means that mobile practices bound up with everyday work, leisure, personal and family life are often contingent on specific things needing to be in the right place at the right time. More significantly, though, getting to grips with the diversity of materialities in motion is vital for helping to better understand some of the significant contemporary challenges posed by global climatic change, fresh water provision, and food security. Each of the chapters in this section illustrates how mobile lives are composed of complex, differentiated materialities: materialities that have different qualities, different properties, different capacities, and are formed of different relations. Foregrounding a broadly post-human ethos, each chapter underscores the significance of taking seriously the way that different materialities perform in the world, generate different forms of encounter, and sculpt new political configurations and attachments. This introduction outlines some of the key themes that this section addresses around sustenance, disruption, transformation, prostheses, and immateriality.

The sustenance of populations is reliant on the mobility of a crucial suite of drinkable and edible materialities. As processes of urbanization continue apace in the twenty-first century, the health and vitality of city populations is reliant on secure and safe water supplies. Pushing important debates on water scarcity in new directions, Rowan Ellis's chapter reminds us that the politics of water play out in geopolitically specific ways. Drawing attention to cities in the global south, Ellis describes how struggles for social and spatial justice are bound up with who controls the flow of access to water. Through the trope of urban metabolisms, we learn too that water is not only vital to the heath of urban populations for consumption, but it is also a materiality that is intimately linked with social and spatial mobility, powerfully

exemplified by the centrality of 'hydro-spectacular' landscapes to new commercial developments. The materiality of water parallels the mobile materialities of food, which raises equally
thorny ethico-political questions around its circulation and transportation, particularly in
relation to the carbon footprint of these commodity chains. Sebastian Abrahamsson and
Annemarie Mol's chapter takes the humble Pizza Hawaii as a signature of truly globalized
food mobility, but one whose provenance exhibits real topological complexity. Abrahamsson
and Mol show that the properties and qualities of the ingredients that go into Pizza Hawaii
require very specific forms of movement, some of which are caught up with myriad ethical
challenges such as the transportation of live animals. They remind us that these materialities
have specific histories and are caught up in multiple intersecting temporalities of growing
cycles, corporate capital and tourist itineraries.

Certain mobile materialities can be incredibly disruptive. Dan Swanton's chapter
underscores the significance of dust generated by the production of steel as a flighty, volatile
materiality that leads to all kinds of health hazards. Swanton's chapter illustrates how such
volatile mobilities have led to the development of all kinds of strategies of containment and
boundary-making in order to immobilize and close down the capacity of waste to act. But
the mixed success of these strategies is demonstrated by the capacity of waste materialities to
remain mobile, for example through the slow-creep of contaminants through the rock, water
and soil at former industrial sites, often presenting themselves unexpectedly. Part of the problem here is that of not knowing exactly what is on the move, something that is strikingly
revealed in the fugitive movements of the H5N1 virus that Stephanie Lavau's chapter examines. Lavau demonstrates how such volatile materialities have prompted the development of
new technologies of monitoring and surveillance. These technologies have multiplied the
ways that mobile materialities are sensed, surveyed and discerned. New techniques of measurement and accountancy are also revealed in Matthew Paterson's chapter, where the intan-
gibility of carbon becomes known through the construction of new property rights, and
technologies that re-mobilize carbon in the form of credits and other financial instruments.
In the context of viruses, a set of political techniques around pre-emption and anticipation
have become new methods for identifying and regulating these disruptive mobile materialities that so often evade capture and whose trajectories are difficult to predict. The difficulties of engineering and mitigating the effects of such volatile materialities are illustrated
in a rather different context by Esther Milne. Milne's description of postcard mail-art in
particular demonstrates the potency of this unassuming materiality in generating its own
affective disruptions.

What each chapter in this section powerfully illustrates is that mobile materialities are not
inert and unchanging. Whilst mobilities research has for some time now emphasized that to
maintain something in the same state requires considerable energy and labor, illustrated for
example in Abrahamsson and Mol's chapter on the movement of food, many of these chapters
underscore the transformative aspects of mobile materialities. Sometimes these transformations are unpredictable, thereby generating considerable anxiety. For example, Lavau's chapter persuasively demonstrates that central to the mobility of viruses are the forms of
molecular transformation that emerge over time and that change the viruses' capacities not
only to travel, but crucially, to infect and debilitate. Indeed, as Swanton demonstrates through
a discussion of the decommissioning processes of heavy industry, it is the transformative
capacities of these unpredictable mobile materialities that often capture public attention,
mobilizing pressure to contain and constrain. However, sometimes these material transformations are more intentionally engineered, as Zack Furness describes in the context of
DIY bike culture. Furness describes how the purposive modification of bicycles is not

instrumental or necessarily task-oriented with the aim of getting somewhere more easily or quickly. Neither is it directly conscripted into moral debates on environmental sustainability. Adaption and modification in the context of bike culture is about experimenting with ways of redrawing the webs of meaning and signification that the bike dwells within, clearly demonstrating how material transformations are equally discursive and symbolic. This is something that Paterson illustrates too in the context of carbon, where in order to be put to work, for example in financial instruments, carbon must become remobilized as a discursive and symbolic referent.

A focus on mobile materialities problematizes simplistic distinctions between humans and non-humans and instead retunes attention towards the assemblages of matter that move. The transformation of viruses described in Lavau's chapter and their capacity to infect different organisms, for example, refocuses attention on the molecular relationships that transcend different species through processes of infection and transmission. Conceptualizing viruses as 'companion species' therefore not only invites us to consider how different materialities move together to create different effects, but it also invites us to multiply the ways in which the figure of the 'passenger' can be conceptualized in mobilities research. While people and birds become the prostheses of viruses, other forms of prosthetic assemblages are evidenced at the border. Echoing how we travel with our 'data doubles' as fellow passengers in spaces of transit, Lily Cho examines the passport as a key biopolitical document to demonstrate how international passage is usually contingent on the production of this portable materiality. However, far from according rights of passage universally, Cho poignantly illustrates how the persistence of information regarding place of birth generates highly differentiated forms of citizenship. In being tethered by her passport to a particular provenance, the holder is enrolled into all kinds of freedoms and constraints, demonstrating a 'sedentary metaphysics' that prioritizes one's roots as a marker of relative credibility and trust. This 'raced' feature of this mobile materiality is incredibly powerful in underscoring not only how it continues to be used as a punitive document for citizens born abroad, but more broadly that citizenship is culturally invested precisely through such mobile materialities.

Finally, the chapters in this section emphasize the importance of taking seriously the immaterialities that underscore mobile worlds. These are materialities that have a rather different manifestation in that they are less tangible but no less powerful in terms of the effects that they exert. The significance of immaterialities come to the fore in Abrahamsson and Mol's chapter that describes the importance of knowledge and know-how central to the production and movement of Pizza Hawaii. Whilst these immaterialities might have a presence, for example in books and manuals, techniques and ideas are manifested and transmitted in much more bodily ways, through forms of tacit and haptic knowledge. Such immaterialities are also discernible in work on the mobility of policy and governance. But these are not the only significant immaterialities. Milne's chapter is a powerful demonstration of the immateriality of affect as a significant aspect of mobile materialities. Thus, whilst the material form of the postcard is a relatively benign rectangle of card, its power to move a body affectively is constituted by its immaterial charge. In the context of mail-art, this is typically generated by affectively charged writing – a charge intensified by its articulation of intimacy and privacy. The excessive quality of these affective immaterialities is also powerfully demonstrated in Swanton's discussion of the afterlife of industrial sites, whose presence continues to haunt long after any material trace has gone. Echoing the way that Milne's postcards challenge commonplace understandings of presence and absence, Swanton hints at the spectral effects of pasts and futures that crowd the lived experience of dwelling at former industrial sites: effects that generate their own disquieting kinds of disruption.

25

Water

Rowan Ellis

It may be stating the obvious to say that water is mobile. As primordial H_2O, water flows under the forces of gravity and at the behest of the earth's geomorphology. This immutable mobility has come to symbolize all that is on the move about modern life: (post)modernity is "liquid" (Bauman, 2000). But despite possessing this 'lively materiality' of its own, water cannot be separated from the processes which are shaping and reshaping the dynamics, frequency, speed, and consequences of how people, ideas, and things move. Water is intimately bound up with our social relations, not just as a necessity for sustaining biological life, but because the ways we come to interact with, use, and 'know' water are structured by and productive of these relations. In this sense, water is hybridized with the social – it's a socio-natural thing, the movement of which is bound up with various forms of social and spatial mobility. Accordingly, the movement of water also confers terribly unequal benefits and burdens. The absurdity of irrigated lawns and swimming pools amidst life-threatening water scarcity in cities as diverse as Los Angeles and Tripoli, or the spectacle of tanker trucks selling drinking water to slum residents whose homes are flooded by monsoon rains, testify to water's highly uneven social and material geographies. It is clear that the experiences of water as flow or impasse, purification or contamination, deluge or trickle are highly socially differentiated.

Perhaps nowhere are the permutations of the social and the natural through the medium of water more evident than in urban areas. This is because for water to 'work' in the city – that is, to enter people's homes as tapped water and exit as waste, irrigate lawns and cool machinery, run off roofs and drain from streets, to be enjoyed at parks and public baths – requires water to be transformed in a myriad of ways. Water is rarely, if ever, left to its own devices in cities because water is an essential element of the modern city. It is integral to the economic, environmental, political, and cultural life of cities. It would stand to reason, then, that as people, goods, money, and ideas become more or differently mobile, the ways in which water moves around the city, and the implications of this movement, are being transformed. Urban water, therefore, is a productive place to start thinking critically about the mobility of water. This focus on urban water is in no way meant to gloss over all there is to say about how water structures the relationship between urban and rural spaces. It is impossible to disentangle rural and urban water, not least because the huge volumes of water necessary for sustaining urban life are so often drawn from sources outside the city. Equally significant are the relationships between rural water scarcity, displacement, and migration to urban areas. The effects of water's circulation in urban areas are experienced well beyond the official or lived boundaries of the city. By limiting this analysis to urban water, I only hope to offer a grounded, albeit partial, account of the social, political, and economic processes that produce, accentuate, and give meaning to water as a mobile materiality.

In this chapter I will draw upon some key insights from urban political ecologists who have shown how the metabolization of water in cities is revealing of wider social, economic, and political relations (Swyngedouw, 2004). Of particular interest here are the ways that the circulations of water are articulated with, or 'map' to, flows of capital, the movement of people, and shifting landscapes of political power. Taking this premise forward, I will point to some recent work that draws productive links between water and other forms of social and spatial mobility. I find these processes particularly salient within research on the politics of water in cities of the South, where, increasingly, struggles for social and spatial justice invoke questions of who controls the flow of and access to water. I then move into a discussion of some new sites where social and spatial mobility are being transformed through the production of what I describe as hydro-spectacular landscapes.

Urban metabolism: a framework for examining the mobile materialities of urban water

Efforts to facilitate the movement of water in newly industrial cities led to some early attempts at theorizing water's mobile materiality. A growing awareness of the link between public health and the urban environment inspired organicist metaphors that likened the circulatory exchanges of water, energy, and waste in the city to the circulatory systems of the body (Gandy, 2004; Swyngedouw, 2006). Water was seen as part of the metabolic structure of the city, and the health of the city depended on the constant circulation and exchange of water. These organicist metaphors were functionally translated into a techno-scientific and managerial assemblage that produced what Matthew Gandy (2004, 2006) describes as the "bacteriological" or "hygienist city." The hygienist city was organized around a particular relationship between the social body and urban water – a hydro-social order, the mainte- nance of which became the raison d'être for municipal governance.[1] For much of the twentieth century, the primary role of municipal governments was to provision urban infra- structure and facilitate the circulations upon which the modern city so relied. It was the management of water's cleansing, but also potentially problematic, mobile materiality that produced the modern city as a particular, and at least temporarily static, assemblage of tech- nology, nature, and social relations. However, by about the mid-twentieth century, the water infrastructure that once stood as a symbol of urban modernity had gone underground, both metaphorically and literally. In the advanced industrial cities of the North, advancements in urban water infrastructure allowed water provision to become taken for granted as an invis- ible, immutable, piped system. In so doing, the metabolic socio-natural relationships within which water is entangled have become increasingly obscured, making water appear as part of the 'fixed' or hard-wired infrastructure of the city (Kaika and Swyngedouw, 2000).

In the twenty-first century, that most inherently mobile materiality, water, appears rela- tively immobile. As new advances in telecommunications and travel problematize static notions of urban space, because of its weighty, stubborn, life-giving materiality, water remains an immutable part of the material constitution of the city. While new insights about the mobility of social relations explode bounded conceptions of the city, the persistent and growing demands for water and all the infrastructure that goes along with providing water stands as a potent example of the ways mobile lives rely on relatively immobile systems (Graham and Marvin, 2001; Hannam *et al.*, 2006). Yet even though water infrastructure is relatively immobile, it is often incapable of meeting increased demands that growing cities place on it. Particularly in the rapidly expanding cities of the South, where the modernist ideal of seamlessly networked and invisible infrastructure has never been fully realized (see Gandy, 2004), water provision takes heterogeneous forms. Unmet material requirements for water in the city necessitate creative means of bypassing, supplementing, and pirating relatively immobile water infrastructures. At the same time, urban water is increasingly plugged into circuits of globally mobile capital and commodities as a source of profit, a luxury consumable (Hawkins, 2009), a contested territorial resource, and a spectacle (or specter). Despite its weighty materiality, the articulations between water and the social, economic, and political geography of these cities are undoubtedly in motion. How, then, do we think through water's differently mobile materialities? How do we account for the fact that urban water is at once hyper-mobile and fluid, but also part of the 'locked-in' infrastructure of the city?

The last decade has seen scholars embracing the concept of urban metabolism to exhume the city as a socio–natural 'thing,' that is, as a hybrid configuration emerging out of the historical and ongoing urbanization of nature (Swyngedouw, 2006). A revamped[2] understanding of urban metabolism allows for an appreciation of not only the hybridity of social and natural relations, but of the liveliness of this relationship, of the pulsing movement, flow, and circulation that make the city a palimpsest of constantly changing socio–ecological relations. Thus the city as a socio–ecological thing is also fundamentally mobile. The reanimation of these concepts contributes to an emerging urban political ecology (UPE), which takes much inspiration from neo-Marxian theories about the production of nature (Keil, 2005). A central premise in Marx's writing is that capitalist growth is predicated upon the metabolic production and urbanization of nature (Harvey, 1996; Smith, 1996). The capitalist production of nature relies on an externalization of nature, an ideological separation between forms of socio-economic domination and the exploitation of nature. Through this separation we get an a-historic concept of nature as neutral, passive, and external to social relations (also Smith, 1984). It is this ideological separation that obscures the socio–ecological relations that produce space, making such spatial forms as the city appear unnatural. Perhaps nowhere is this ideological separation more complete than when we consider the disappearance of urban water infrastructure and the mystification of urban water provision (Kaika, 2005; see also Graham and Marvin, 2001).

A crucial first step in thinking critically about the materiality of urban water, then, is to open up the 'black boxes' of water infrastructure that have obscured the socio–ecological relations underpinning the production of urban space. By opening up water infrastructure in this way, a Marxist-informed UPE also seeks to repoliticize the socio–ecological relations that underpin urban water (Heynen *et al.*, 2006). Such repoliticization requires that we question who benefits from particular socio-natural assemblages, by whom and for who these assemblages are produced, and what a more just socio-natural world might look like. In line with these objectives, there are several key pieces of work that in recent years have sought to demystify the workings of urban water, reveal the hydro-social power relations that constitute the city, and shed light on the social and spatial consequences of these relations in diverse geographical and historical sites (see Bakker, 2005; Gandy, 2008; Kaika, 2005; Loftus, 2007; Swyngedeouw, 2004; Swyngedouw *et al.*, 2002). Other work has considered contested meanings of water and how these have evolved along with particular social, economic, and political shifts in water management (Strang, 2004; Linton, 2010; Tvedt and Jakobsson, 2006). A new book edited by Farhana Sultana and Alex Loftus (2011) considers how 'rights-based' discourses about water are articulated with particular geographical and historical hydro-social conditions. Radical insights about the materiality of water are also emerging from work that examines the 'micro-political' processes that mediate water access and carve out new forms of "hydraulic citizenship" (Anand, 2011; Bawa, 2011; Coelho, 2006; and for a feminist analysis of the political ecology of urban water see Truelove, 2011). This work reveals the multitude ways in which water moves around the city when infrastructure falls short. Shortfalls in water connectivity lead to the proliferation of systems of informal water delivery, systems which constitute something of a shadow network of water infrastructure (Bakker, 2003). These informal mechanisms for water delivery take many forms. Those who can afford it rely more on purified water delivered to the home, commercially produced and sold bottled water, or on large tankers that fill private cisterns during periods of drought or shortage (see Hawkins, 2009). The urban poor are often also forced to purchase water from various small and large water vendors operating out of push-carts that sell bucket-quantities of water from privately owned boreholes, or to buy home-boiled water sold in plastic satchels out of street stalls or delivered to homes by bicycle courier. Many also travel great distances to stationary water kiosks to collect water and transport it back home. What comes into view when we consider the reality of these forms of everyday water provision is a whole other set of mobile social relations.

Though few of their arguments are articulated as such, recent discussions of the micro-politics of urban water seem increasingly rooted in an understanding of the dialectic, "metabolic" relationship between urban water and other forms of social and spatial mobility. In the section that follows I consider yet another set of hydro-social relations that have so far not captured the attention of urban political ecologists, but which shed light on both the metabolic processes out of which urban space is produced and how these are linked with some of the other forms of mobility discussed elsewhere in this volume. The following section considers the materiality of urban water through what I am calling hydro-spectacular urban spaces, that is, manufactured water-oriented landscapes like river-walks, eco-parks, and quays, which function simultaneously as sites of investment and accumulation, consumption and class (re)production, and as spaces of intense social exclusion. They are spectacular not only because they often mete out dramatic changes to the physical structure of the city, but also because they attempt the rather ambitious feat of re-scripting the social relations of urban nature, to alter the way people interact with urban water in line with capitalist urbanization. These hydro-spectacles in many ways represent the symbiosis of multiple mobilities. They are places where water is managed, harnessed, and remade in relation to mobile capital, but which also carve out other forms of social and spatial mobility.

Hydro-spectacular urban environments

There seems to exist a shared and common-sense understanding that highly mobile, transnational capital prefers redeveloped waterfronts, eco-parks, river walks, and canal-side shopping. A survey of recent high-profile, globally orientated projects confirms that water is often the star player in the competitive strategies of cities (Chang and Huang, 2011; Desfor et al., 2011; Dovey, 2005; Kang and Cervero, 2009; Oakley, 2007; Zitoun, 2010). In numerous and geographically diverse urban settings the landscape is being remade around high-priced, 'carnivalesque' water-orientated leisure and consumption amenities, which suggest that a shift is occurring in the way urban water is valued. Over the past decade cities from Algiers to Durban, Singapore to Seoul, have embarked on initiatives to transform urban waterways into sites of accumulation. Driven in part by the expansion of municipal bond markets, and in part by a generalization of gentrification as a global urban strategy (Smith, 2002), cities in the South appear to be operating under the belief that the 'ecological value' of water in the landscape can and should overlap with the commercial value of urban land (Coelho and Raman, 2010). The driving principle behind hydro-spectacular developments is a belief that waterfronts "facilitate flows of capital and desire" (Dovey, 2005), and that the successful fusion of commercial, cultural-consumptive, and residential functions in these spaces is a measurement of a city's attainment of world-class status (Chang and Huang, 2011).

Chennai, in the South Indian state of Tamil Nadu, recently inaugurated what was billed as a 'world-class ecological park' along the estuarine mouth of the Adyar River. The Adyar Poonga Eco-Park promises to serve as a model, or exemplar, of best practice in urban wetland and river restoration, and to function as a "fulcrum of environmental awareness" (Adyar Poonga Trust, 2007). But behind the jargon of a public relations campaign, the evolution of the Adyar Poonga and its associated eco-restoration on the Adyar River reveals the shifting geographies of urban water in the context of heightened capital mobility and changing social geographies of the city.

Since the 1990s, the area surrounding the Poonga site has been transformed by a real-estate development boom in Chennai, spurred by speculative investment and rising demands for luxury housing and light commercial property. Today, the Adyar Poonga is situated within a part of the city that boasts some of the highest-value urban land. A growing urban middle class has stimulated the development of new, high-end, exclusive residential space in the city. Heightened levels of civic activism among the middle and upper classes maintain the exclusivity of Chennai's emerging residential geography. In multiple Indian cities, urban elites organized as resident welfare associations, concerned citizen forums, and non-governmental organizations have successfully hijacked democratic processes and aggressively laid claims to city space (see Anjaria, 2009; Arabindoo, 2005; Bhan, 2009; Ellis, 2011a; Fernandes, 2004; Harris, 2006; Zerah, 2007). In not just Chennai, but a startling diversity of contexts, urban natural environments have been at the frontline of elite efforts to reterritorialize urban space, with campaigns that seek to produce clean, ordered, and hygienic city space coalescing into what Amita Baviskar (2003) describes as a "bourgeois environmentalism" (see also Mawdsley, 2009). Key to these forms of bourgeois environmentalism is a discourse that paints the urban poor as ecological villains, a sentiment which enables environmentalism to be translated into slum clearance and "eco-gentrification" (Dooling, 2008; Quastel, 2009).

The Adyar Poonga project has transformed what was once a slow-moving backwater, its banks dotted with informal settlements and a favored site for the illegal disposal of construction and household waste, into a highly manufactured landscape of lagoons, bridges, habitat for wading birds, and interactive exhibits for visitors. Indeed, in the various controversies and court challenges to the project, environmental activists argued that the Poonga would not restore the ecological health of the Adyar River, and that it functioned more as a simulacrum of wetland nature, or an environmental theme park, rather than a conservation project. The shaky restorative claims of the project notwithstanding, the Poonga is about much more than cleaning up a polluted waterway. The public–private partnership charged with commissioning the design and construction of the project, the Adyar Poonga Trust, sees the Poonga as an important component of the city's competitive, world-class ambitions. Representatives from the Trust argue that the Poonga will stimulate investment in the area and attract new business to Chennai. Since the decision was taken to build the Poonga, other developments are being envisioned for the area, including elevated transportation corridors, a new Anna University campus, several broad pedestrian walkways, and a river promenade.

★   ★   ★

The forms of ideal-type mobility that such investments and upgrades symbolize are directly linked to, even predicated upon, the exclusion of certain groups from revalued urban space. Already, the construction of the Poonga required the forced eviction of those 'encroachers' living in the approximately 500 homes that fell within the Poonga's 58-acre plot. These families were relocated some 20 kilometers south of the city, many forced to commute back into the city for work at great expense (Ellis, 2011b). The large neighboring settlement at Srinivasapuram now faces the threat of evictions as the city's world-class ambitions for the Adyar River spill the banks of the Poonga site. The new desired occupants, those middle-class residents who will populate the river promenade and pay for entry to the Adyar Poonga, are also seen as crucial bodies in the landscape, bodies that will mitigate against the return of displaced 'encroachers' (Adyar Poonga Trust, 2007). The continued circulation of people and investment into the area surrounding the Adyar River is seen as essential to the success of the project, so it is perhaps not so surprising that metaphors of stagnation and circulation, blockage and flow are rife within the planning documents for the area. The Adyar Poonga Master Plan several times describes the pre-restoration condition of the river as "languid," and the riverbank as being "dotted with hutments" that create "sludge" following a "meandering course" (ibid.). The Poonga promises to restore the river's flow and tidal exchange, facilitate the return of migratory species, and reconnect humans to 'natural systems,' particularly in the face of an ecologically disruptive urbanism.

The Adyar Poonga is but one example of the numerous and various ways in which city governments and urban elites attempt to change the material meaning of water in relation to the new or intensified movement of capital and people. This transformation is about the production of landscapes that facilitate capital circulation and reproduction through new real-estate commodities, the enhancement of residential property values, and through the creation of new opportunities for retail profits. In this sense, forms of ecological restoration like the Adyar Poonga are part of the generalization of "gentrification, as a global urban strategy," the manifest outcome of the way mobile capital has internationalized into urban real-estate markets (Smith, 2002). On the coattails of this highly mobile investment capital are cosmopolitan trends in urban design, with waterfront redevelopments in Singapore borrowing aesthetic and design elements from Miami's Coco Walk (Chang and Huang, 2011), or as evidenced in the "Dubai-ification" of Algiers.

Yet crucially, the accumulative potential of these new projects rests on their ability to reorient the relationship between social (re)production, consumption, and nature. Once built, these hydro-spectacles promise to become sites of social mobility and class reproduction as urbanites are invited to dine, shop, and play – disposable income permitting. In this sense, such developments re-script the relationship between social production and urban nature around leisure and consumption. This leisure-orientated socio-nature belies a whole host of other, related hydro-social relations, particularly ones that result in socio-spatial exclusion and material injustice. Such dramatic transformations of urban physical space not only facilitate preferred forms of mobility, they also create forms of adverse mobility through forced displacement, long commutes, and general downward social mobility for those groups excluded from remade urban environments. The hydro-spectacular development is as much about 'hooking in' to the circuits of globally mobile capital and facilitating a classed transformation of urban space, as it is about externalizing rarified nature so as to make such transformations appear neutral, outside of politics and power relations, and outside of the experience of water scarcity and conflict which characterizes life for the urban poor.

Conclusion

Water is ubiquitous in cities, as piped and potable water, as waterways and water bodies, and as unruly water that floods, stagnates, contaminates, and is otherwise problematized in the urban landscape. It is this very ubiquity that makes it challenging to disentangle the multitude and layered mobilities that attend urban water. This chapter responds to the calls from an emerging new mobilities paradigm to "open up all sites, places, and materialities" to the mobilities that are already coursing through them (Sheller and Urry, 2006: 209). When we open up urban water to such an inquiry, what we find are forms of graduated mobility and immobility that betray a romantic or 'nomadicist' imaginary of an unfettered liquid modernity.

The blatantly unequal geographies of water excess and scarcity, specter and spectacle in cities of the South are potent examples of how water's movement is structured by and also constitutive of social relations. This should not comes as a surprise because, when looking to the historical development of urban water systems, it becomes clear that the ability to control movement and flow has always been linked with forms of social power and the production of urban space. The link between the material mobility of water and urban social space was recognized by the engineers of nineteenth-century urban water systems who imagined the city as an organism, where the circulation of water was a prerequisite for all other forms of social and economic vitality: the 'lifeblood' of the city. Such 'organicist' metaphors persist into contemporary urban discourse, which imagines the city as a space of flows and connectivity. Scholars like Eric Swyngedeouw (2006) have been keen to highlight the correspondence between long-standing imaginaries of the city as a terrain through which water must perpetually circulate and more contemporary depictions of the city as a node for fast-circulating money. But drawing parallels between mobile metaphors alone is not enough.

Here is where work organized around an urban political ecology analytic, particularly work that utilizes a neo-Marxian theory of urban metabolism, can be brought together with the new mobilities paradigm to examine the consequences of shifting forms of mobility for different people and different places. A critical theory of water's mobile materiality must not only excavate the sites and spaces where the movement of water intersects with other forms of mobility, but also question whose interests are served when certain forms of circulation are privileged over others. It is only by politicizing the mobility of urban water in this way that we can begin to imagine and convene alternative futures.

Notes

1 For much more in-depth discussion of the role of water management systems and hydraulic infrastructure in the development of the modern city and urban governance, see Graham and Marvin (2001); Marvin and Medd (2009); Melosi (2000).
2 Scholars who advocate the neo-Marxian use of urban metabolism deliberately distinguish this framework from teleological or Malthusian understandings of urban ecology that informed the bacteriological city and have been recently revived in debates about urban sustainability and carrying capacity.

Bibliography

Adyar Poonga Trust (2007) "Draft Concept Plan" Chennai Metropolitan Development Corporation. Available online at www.scribd.com/doc/45884189/The-Adyar-Poonga-Project (accessed 27 November 2011).

Anand, Nikhil (2011) "Pressure: The PoliTechnics of Water Supply in Mumbai" *Cultural Anthropology*, 26: 542–564.

Anjaria, Jonathan Shapiro (2009) "Guardians of the Bourgeois City: Citizenship, Public Space, and Middle-Class Activism in Mumbai" *City and Community*, 8: 391–406.

Arabindoo, Pushpa (2005) "A Class Act: The Bourgeois Ordering of Public Spaces in Chennai," paper presented at the BASAS Annual Conference, Edinburgh, 2005.

Bakker, Karen (2005) "Neoliberalizing Nature? Market Environmentalism in Water Supply in England and Wales" *Annals of the Association of American Geographers* 95: 542–565.

— (2003) "Archipelagos and Networks: Urbanization and Water Privatization in the South" *The Geographical Journal*, 169: 328–341.

Bauman, Zygmunt (2000) *Liquid Modernity*, Cambridge: Polity Press.

Baviskar, Amita (2003) "Between Violence and Desire: Space, Power, and Identity in the Making of Metropolitan Delhi" *International Social Science Journal*, 55: 89–98.

Bawa, Zainab (2011) "Where is the State? How is the State? Accessing Water and the State in Mumbai and Johannesburg" *Journal of Asian and African Studies*, 46: 491–503.

Bhan, Gautam (2009) "'This is No Longer the City I Once Knew': Evictions, the Urban Poor, and the Right to the City in Millennial Delhi" *Environment and Urbanization*, 21(1): 127–142.

Chang, T. C. and Shirlena Huang (2011) "Reclaiming the City: Waterfront Development in Singapore" *Urban Studies*, 48: 2085–2100.

Coelho, Karen (2006) "Tapping In: Leaky Sovereignties and Engineered Dis(Order) in an Urban Water System." In Monica Narula, Shuddhabrata Sengupta, Ravi Sundaram, Jeebesh Bagchi, Awadhendra Sharan, Geert Lovink (eds) *Sarai Reader 06: Turbulence*, Delhi: Sarai Media Lab, 497–509.

Coelho, Karen and Nithya V. Raman (2010) "Salvaging and Scapegoating: Slum Evictions on Chennai's Waterways" *Economic and Political Weekly*, 45(21): 19–23.

Desfor, Gene, Jennfier Laidley, Quentin Stevens, and Dirk Schubert (2011) *Transforming Urban Waterfronts: Fixity and Flow*, New York: Routledge.

Dooling, Sarah (2008) "Ecological Gentrification: Re-negotiating Justice in the City" *Critical Planning*, 15: 40–57.

Dovey, Kim (2005) *Fluid City: Transforming Melbourne's Urban Waterfront*, London: Routledge.

Ellis, Rowan (2011a) "'A World Class City of your Own!': Civic Governmentality in Chennai, India" *Antipode*, doi: 10.1111/j.1467-8330.2011.00958.x.

— (2011b) "'Whose Participation, Whose Sustainability?': A Critical Analysis of Initiatives for Urban Sustainability in India" *Scottish Geographical Journal*, 3: 193–208.

Fernandes, Leela (2004) "The Politics of Forgetting: Class Politics, State Power and the Restructuring of Urban Space in India" *Urban Studies*, 41(12): 2415–2430.

Gandy, Matthew (2008) "Landscapes of Disaster Water, Modernity, and Urban Fragmentation in Mumbai, *Environment and Planning A* 40: 108–130.

— (2006) "Chapter 15: Water, Modernity, and the Demise of the Bacteriological City." In Terje Tvedt, Richard Coopey, Terje Oestigaard (eds) *Water Control and River Biographies*. Vol. 1 in *A History of Water*, London: I. B. Tauris.

— (2004) "Rethinking Urban Metabolism: Water, Space and the Modern City" *City: Analysis of Urban Trends, Culture, Theory, Policy, Action*, 8(3): 363–379.

Graham, Stephen and Simon Marvin (2001) *Splintering Urbanism*, London: Routledge.

Hannam, Kevin, Mimi Sheller, and John Urry (2006) "Editorial: Mobilities, Immobilities, and Moorings" *Mobilities*, 1(1): 1–22.

Harris, John (2006) "Middle Class Activism and Poor People's Politics: A Perspective on Class Relations and Civil Society in Indian Cities" *Critical Asian Studies*, 38(4): 445–465.

Harvey, David (1996) *Justice, Nature, and the Geography of Difference*, Oxford: Blackwell Publishers.

Hawkins, Gay (2009) "The Politics of Bottled Water: Assembling Bottled Water as Brand, Waste, and Oil" *Journal of Cultural Economy*, 2(1–2): 183–195.

Heynen, Nik, Maria Kaika, and Erik Swyngedouw (2006) *In the Nature of Cities: Urban Political Ecology and the Politics of Urban Metabolism*, London and New York: Routledge.

Kaika, Maria (2005) *City of Flows. Modernity, Nature and the City*, London: Routledge.

Kaika, Maria and Erik Swyngedouw (2000) "Fetishizing the Modern City: The Phantasmagoria of Urban Technological Networks" *International Journal of Urban and Regional Research*, 24: 120–138.

Kang, Chang Deok and Robert Cervero (2009) "From Elevated Freeway to Urban Greenway: Land Value Impacts of the CGC Project in Seoul, Korea" *Urban Studies*, 46: 2771–2794.

Keil, Roger (2005) "Progress Report – Urban Political Ecology" *Urban Geography*, 26(7): 640–651.

Linton, Jaime (2010) *What is Water? The History of a Modern Abstraction*, Vancouver: University of British Columbia Press.

Loftus, Alex (2007) "Working the Socio-Natural Relations of the Urban Waterscape in South Africa" *International Journal of Urban and Regional Research*, 31: 41–59.

Marvin, Simon and Will Medd (2009) "Making Water Work: Intermediating between Regional Strategy and Local Practice" *Environment and Planning D: Society and Space*, 26: 280–299.

Mawdsley, Emma (2009) "Environmentality in the Neoliberal City: Attitudes, Governance, and Social Justice." In H. Lange and L. Meier (eds) *The New Middle Classes*, London: Springer.

Melosi, M. V. (2000) *The Sanitary City, Urban Infrastructure in America from Colonial Times to the Present*, Baltimore: Johns Hopkins University Press.

Oakely, Susan (2007) "The Role of Urban Governance in Re-constructing Space, Economic Function, Social Relations, in Urban Waterfront Regeneration: The Case of Port Adelaide, South Australia" *Space and Polity*, 11(3): 279–295.

Quastel, Noah (2009) "Political Ecologies of Gentrification" *Urban Geography*, 30(7): 694–725.

Sheller, Mimi and John Urry (2006) "The New Mobilities Paradigm" *Environment and Planning A* 38: 207–226.

Smith, Neil (2002) "New Globalism, New Urbanism: Gentrification as Global Urban Strategy" *Antipode*, 34: 427–450.

— (1996) "The Production of Nature." In G. Robertson, M. Mash, L. Tickner, J. Bird, B. Curtis, T. Putnam (eds) *Future-Natural–Nature/Science/Culture*, London: Routledge, 35–54.

— (1984) *Uneven Development: Nature, Capital and the Production of Space*, Oxford: Basil Blackwell.

Strang, Veronica (2004) *The Meaning of Water*, Oxford: Berg.

Sultana, Farhana and Alex Loftus (2011) *The Right to Water: Politics, Governance, and Social Struggles*, London: Routledge.

Swyngedouw, Erik (2006) "Circulations and Metabolisms: (Hybrid) Natures and (Cyborg) Cities" *Science as Culture*, 15(2): 105–121.

— (2004) *Social Power and the Urbanization of Water: Flows of Power*, Oxford: Oxford University Press.

Swyngedouw, Erik, M. Kaika, and E. Castro (2002) "Urban Water: A Political-ecology Perspective" *Built Environment*, 28: 124–137.

Truelove, Yaffa (2011) "(Re-)conceptualizing Water Inequality in Delhi, India through a Feminist Political Ecology Framework" *Geoforum*, 42(2): 143–152.

Tvedt, Terje and Eva Jakobsson (2006) "Introduction: Water History is World History." In Terje Tvedt, Richard Coopey, Terje Oestigaard (eds) *Water Control and River Biographies*. Vol. 1 in *A History of Water*, London: I. B. Tauris.

Zerah, Marie Helene (2007) "Middle Class Neighbourhood Associations as Political Players in Mumbai" *Economic and Political Weekly*, 42: 61–68.

Zitoun, Madani Safar (2010) "The Development of the Bay of Algiers: Rethinking the City through Contemporary Paradigms" *Built Environment*, 36(2): 206–215.

26

Foods

Sebastian Abrahamsson and Annemarie Mol

In a book that explores global transportations and mobilities, food definitely deserves to be included.[1] Over the last few decades, the total mileage that food travels across the globe – difficult to imagine, let alone calculate – has not just risen, but also become increasingly contested (Jackson *et al.*, 2006). Many decry that all in all food travels far too far. But how does it do so? How does it move across the globe? The answer is: in many different ways. It moves out and it moves in. It moves fresh and it moves cooked. It moves as ingredients and as a recipe. The implication is that, more often than not, on any single plate many places come together. Here, we will illustrate the topological complexity of ordinary meals by presenting a mundane but intricate case: that of Pizza Hawaii.

There it is, on the photograph. A well-baked crusty dough, topped with tomato sauce, cheese, ham and pineapple. Preferably some oregano on top. It can be eaten with fork and knife, but, once cut into slices, it is also possible to pick it up with bare hands. It is not, or only rarely, a dish that people make from scratch at home, but it is, at present, available in restaurants all over the world. Where does it come from? What are the achievements, movements and transportations that have brought it to the plate depicted here, and to many others? As we present an answer to these questions, we will disassemble 'Pizza Hawaii'. Historically speaking the various ingredients and the recipe of the dish that now travels so widely have different geographical provenances. And, at this particular moment in time, the very ingredients and recipe of this apparently singular pizza all have their own spatial and mobile specificities too. The implication is that many (often far away) places are crucial to any single pizza. They may not immediately catch the eye and they cannot necessarily be tasted, but, while inconspicuous, they are crucial. Which is to say that, in every Pizza Hawaii, a lot of the rest of the world is *absent-present*. The fact that pizza, as it travels everywhere, simultaneously carries many other sites and situations within it, makes us speak of the pizza's 'topological complexity'. It is this topological complexity that here we set out to explore.[2]

Ingredients, long term

Natural histories attend to how winds, sea currents and animals have transposed and transplanted seeds, thus contributing to the spread of edible plant life (Stiles, 1992). Agricultural

278

Figure 26.1   Pizza Hawaii (Source: Annemarie Mol)

histories tell of how human beings learned to actively grow local wild plants that were good to eat, to then, gradually, carry the seeds and growing techniques with them over long distances. Animals, too, once they had been domesticated in a single spot, were taken along to other places by traders and adventurers (Jones, 2007). And then there are histories (of later periods) that tell how the quest for spices fuelled colonial explorations and exploitations. In this way, spices, and later tea and coffee, grown elsewhere, travelled to Europe and shaped imperialism (Krondl, 2007). At the same time, Europeans settling in places far from home brought their favourite crops and animals along with them, fostering these to the detriment of local creatures and ecosystems (Crosby, 1986).

It is against this background that we would like to talk about the most important ingredient of a pizza's crust: wheat. Where does it come from? It is one of the grains of early agriculture. In China, people ate, and then started to cultivate, rice. It was in the Fertile Crescent, close to Euphrates and Tigris, that wheat made the shift from food gathered to food cultivated. The history of the early wheat cultivators used to be written as if human beings were in total control of the process. These days archaeologists tell more symmetrical stories: 'although humans domesticated wheat, one may argue that dependence on wheat also domesticated humans' (McCorriston, 2000: 159). This is because it took a considerable amount of time to grow and harvest wheat. Patience and a sedentary way of living were essential. While gatherers need to move from one place to another in search for food, cultivators cannot move so speedily. Wheat, after all, thrives on attention and care between the moment of sowing and that of harvesting. By eradicating competing plants, labelling them 'weeds' in the process, early farmers were able to improve their harvest. Building a granary allowed them to store that harvest, eat from it for months, and then use some of the seeds for a next round of sowing: further incentives to be sedentary. But granaries attracted mice, pleased that humans did agricultural work for them. The mice, in their turn, attracted wild cats, who fed on them. Humans preferred mice-eating cats over wheat-eating mice and welcomed the cats into their households (Diamond, 1998). All of which is to say that, while now popular almost everywhere, historically speaking, wheat is tied up with the mutual domestication of crops, humans, mice and cats in the Middle East.

Not so tomatoes, essential pizza ingredient number two. Since tomatoes are fragile and rapidly perish, they have left no archaeological traces. Archaeologists speculate that winds, water or birds may originally have carried tomato seeds from the Andean region to Meso-america. Alternatively, human carriers may have been responsible for the journey. Either way, both Aztecs and Mayas in Mexico, or so the records tell, grew and ate *tomatl* – 'something round and plump' (Barndt, 2008: 11). The Spaniards who conquered and plundered Mexico must have liked *tomatl* because they took seeds and plants with them when they returned. Still, tomatoes were not instantly popular in the Mediterranean, remaining, in the sixteenth and seventeenth centuries, exotic specimens of interest only to botanists. Prospective eaters were not too eager, fearing that tomatoes might be poisonous. It was only in the eighteenth century, when there was a food shortage across the Mediterranean, that tomatoes became an agricultural success. The plants were easy to grow in the moderate climate and loose soil, and the fruits proved to be a versatile ingredient. The incorporation of the tomato, along with other American plants, into the Mediterranean diet may well have helped to strengthen and increase the otherwise declining population (Long, 2000).

So what do we learn? Just the first two pizza ingredients that we attend to, wheat and tomatoes, appear to already fold crucial global sites into this modest dish. There they are. For one, there is the wheat that was domesticated in the Middle East, thus helping to domesticate humans in the Eastern hemisphere. And then, second, there is the tomato of the Western hemisphere, transported from Mesoamerica to the Mediterranean thanks to colonialists who had not set out to find tomatoes, but the spices of India – or, less edible, silver and gold (Todorov, 1992).

The pizza recipe

Pizza originally comes from Italy. Doesn't it? Well, maybe it is better to say that it originated in the various cities that joined to form Italy in the late nineteenth century. Pizza, in other words, predates the nation. Traditionally, each city had its own particular pizza favourites. Take Napoletana: this pizza does not so much come from Italy as from Naples. These days provenances are a matter of cultural pride and commercial vigilance. In line with this, the EU, willing to foster (and support the invention of) food traditions, has awarded Pizza Napoletana with the status 'traditional speciality guaranteed'. This implies that any restaurant that claims to sell a 'real' Napoletana has to follow a meticulously spelled-out, *traditional* recipe – from Naples (DeSoucey, 2010). But the restaurant does not have to be in Naples. From the cities of Italy pizza has travelled, and one of the places in which it did well was New York, the city where the first pizzeria in the United States was opened in 1905 by Genarro Lombardi. That is, if we believe *PMQ Magazine*, the *New York Pizza Show*, and the proud present-day owner, who attracts a lot of customers by declaring his restaurant a heritage site.

The date, however, is contested. There might have been a pizzeria ten years earlier. 'After the end of the Second World War, the allies brought pizza with them to the US. But there people knew about pizza already. In New York the first pizzeria was opened in 1895. After the First World War one pizzeria after the other was opened in Manhattan, Brooklyn and the Bronx.' (*New York Pizza Cookbook*, 2008) This quote is from a cookbook published by a pizzeria chain in the Netherlands by the name of *New York Pizza*. Here, Naples is being sidelined. So, too, are Rome, Verona, Milano and Bologna. We quote again: 'It was in New York that the pizza became a real pizza. The New York style pizza distinguishes itself from the Italian through its crust which is thicker than the Italian one, and crispy on the outside but soft on the inside' (ibid). So *real* pizza does not come from Italy at all, it comes from New York. Doesn't it?

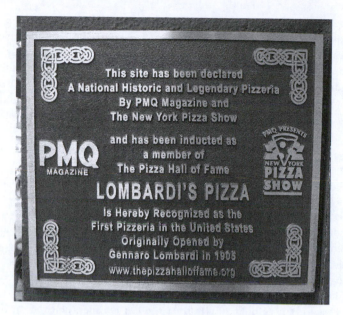

Figure 26.2   Lombardi's Pizza (Source: Leonard J. DeFrancisci)

In the US, pizza became popular in the mid-twentieth century. It incorporated local ingredients and styles and reflected the relative abundance of food in the country at the time (Diner, 2001). Still, there are other histories to tell and these complicate the issue of where pizza came from. Look again at Figure 26.1, the Pizza Hawaii. It shows a flatbread with topping on it. There is an interesting predecessor to this dish. Historically, flatbreads have been variously used as edible plates. Such a plate could be carried around, shared or distributed as a gift. There are historical records of bread with highly varied local ingredients added on top. Basically, the edible plate was convenient, tasty and nutritionally satisfying. Here, food historians teach us that '[t]he universality of the flatbread-as-plate suggests that convenience, perhaps for the sake of mobility or out of economic necessity, shaped ancient eating habits. Using bread as a plate made sense to those who couldn't afford plates and it also made sense to those who had to remain mobile . . . topped with herbs or mushrooms, or a sauce, they constituted an entire meal' (Helstosky, 2008: 18).

The dish was versatile and may be traced though different languages. The word pizza is etymologically related with the word *pita* – a pocket bread inside which filling can be put (Jakle and Sculle, 1999: 242). There are also mobile and edible breads in other kitchens. Some of these are prepared without wheat. Some are not baked in the oven but on a flat stone or in a pan. The Ethiopian *injera* is made with teff, and the dough is fermented before baking so that it is spongy and flexible rather than crunchy and stiff like the pizza. The Mexican *tortilla* is made with maize and is soft too, thus limiting the amount of topping or filling. The Dutch *pancake*, originally made with buckwheat (more tolerant of poor soils and therefore cheaper than wheat) was, when possible, made interesting with savoury bacon or sweet apple. And, finally, there is the Turkish *lahmacun* which comes close to 'real' pizza – but it is thinner. Some *lahmacuns* are topped with meat, others with cheese and meat. Some are stuffed, others flat. Recently, Italian pizzerias have become successful in Turkey, as they have everywhere else. But here, to keep themselves in business, most pizza bakers incorporate a variant of *lahmacun* in their menu (Halici, 2001).

So what do we learn? Just as ingredients travel, so do recipes and preparation techniques for dishes. At the same time, a recipe or a preparation technique may have not just one, but various origins. In the case of pizza this is particularly striking. For whether made with wheat or not, spread with tomato sauce or not, whether thin or thick, crusty or soft, a flatbread conveniently carrying what is on top of it has many places of origin. Crucial to the Pizza Hawaii, however, is the successful ocean crossing of an 'Italian' dish to New York.

Ingredients, short term

Inquiries into present-day movements of food highlight the many ways in which the travels of 'food stuff' intertwine with other issues. The bananas that manage to reach North America and Japan all the way from Mesoamerica and the Philippines come with big companies attached. These gained both enormous financial and political power as they sought to control the trade in this fragile, easy to eat fruit (Sheller, 2005). Papayas, travelling from farms in Jamaica to supermarkets in the UK, may remain recognisable as fruit, but are often consumed concealed in chewing gum, toothpaste, canned meats and vegetarian cheese. They even end up in leather goods. Indeed, 'papayas are impossible to avoid. Perhaps. Even if you've never eaten one' (Cook, 2004). Over the last decades, cheered on by economists who see exports as crucial to development, beans have got to travel from Kenya (where people increasingly eat fewer vegetables) to the Netherlands (where beans are no longer seasonal, but available all year round) (Albala, 2007). All these foods travel fast, at huge energy costs. They often move to places where their growers would never be allowed to go, for many borders that are open to goods are firmly closed to people, especially poor people who seek an income and care to make a living wherever they might find a job (Massey, 2005). The borders are also closed to travelling viruses and food-borne diseases. Or they are supposed to be, but sometimes trespassing occurs (Law and Mol, 2008). Thus, travelling food is dense with politics of all kinds. This is not obvious in daily life, as food is made to travel 'in such a way as to conceal almost perfectly any trace of origin, or the labor processes that produced them, or of the social relations implicated in their production' (Harvey, 1990: 300).

What does this imply in the case of Pizza Hawaii? This we will illustrate not by attending to present-day wheat and tomatoes, but by foregrounding, this time, pineapple and ham. Where do these come from? Let's begin with the pineapples. Their conquest of the globe is recent. In the nineteenth century, pineapples travelled from the northern coasts of South America to France, and from there to England, where they only grew in the greenhouses of botanical gardens. Via this detour they reached Hawaii, where they were later cultivated on a massive scale. Even so, Western Europe pineapples remained a rarity, an exotic and expensive fruit. This is not strange, given that they were mainly shipped in from Hawaii. In the 1970s this provenance, suitably alluring, was used in the names of dishes to which pineapple was added. Yet, as soon as this name was established, the growing numbers of pineapples on the European market no longer came from Hawaii: in the early 1980s leading companies such as *Dole* and *Del Monte* relocated production to Southeast Asia, where labour was cheaper and the climate more favourable (Burch and Goss, 1999).

With increased production and a drop in price, pineapples became less exclusive. Their rapid spread was aided by canning and peeling techniques invented in the early twentieth century and possibilities of refrigerated sea transportation, developed in the 1950s. Today pineapples still travel both as fresh fruits and as slices or chunks in cans, the latter ending up

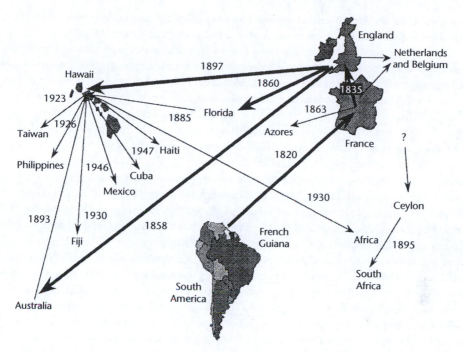

Figure 26.3 Distribution of the Smooth Cayenne cultivar (after Collins, 1951) (Bartholomew *et al.*, 2003)

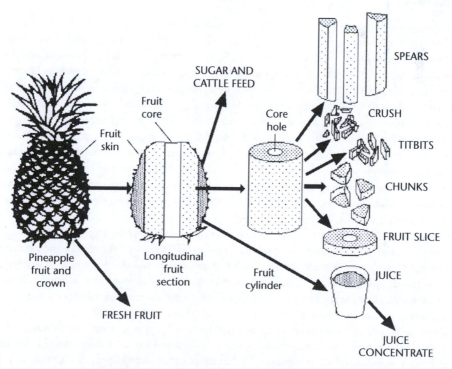

Figure 26.4 Pineapple products (Bartholomew *et al.*, 2003)

on your average Pizza Hawaii. Meanwhile, the heartland of pineapple production has once again been relocated, with most of the fresh fruit now coming from Costa Rica.

Like the pineapple, the ham added to a Pizza Hawaii may travel in cans, this time filled with preservatives to protect the meat from bacteria, insects and decay. But can-travel is not the only kind of transport ham is involved in. While traditionally pigs lived within individual households, mainly fed with the kitchen waste of, at most, a few families (Stuart, 2009), these days they are reared on an industrial scale. In 2007 it was estimated that at any given moment there were 159,724 million pigs living in Europe. The highest pig density is in Denmark, a relatively small country in terms of both territory and population. In 2006, with less than 5.5 million people, Denmark had 22 million pigs. Of the pork, ham and bacon that resulted from these, 85 per cent was exported, entering the world market via established food transportation routes (Hamann, 2006). And ham is not just carried around after being cured: live and kicking, pigs are made to travel across the continent. Animal rights activists insist that meat producers should take the animals' welfare into account, making it more 'humane' (Roe *et al.*, 2011; Stassart and Whatmore, 2003). Besides welfare concerns, transporting living pigs also raises logistical issues to do with cages, travel distances, weather conditions and the importance of delivering on time. On top of which there is the question of the quality of the meat. When animals are stressed the glycogen in their muscles may break down, leading to meat that is pale and of a pronounced acidity. Minimising the stress and potential pre-slaughtering injuries that transport may induce is – or such is the concern in the industry – not just crucial to ensuring an 'ethically viable and durable product' but also for 'quality taste' (Chambers *et al.*, 2001).

Pizza Hawaii

Globally, pizza is strikingly successful. It is, even more than the hamburger, the most striking example of the globalisation of foods (Ritzer, 2010). Still, though available in Bangkok (Thailand), Stockholm (Sweden), Moscow (Russia), as well as Accra (Ghana) and Seoul (Korea), in these varied sites not many people have taken to baking pizza at home. The recipe is not particularly difficult but, like bread dough, pizza dough contains yeast, which needs time to produce carbon dioxide and thus the bubbles upon which the airiness of the crust depends. Besides, pizzas need to be baked in a hot oven. That is expensive and many households do not own one. In large areas of the world, for instance in most of Asia, the local cuisine thrives perfectly well without ovens. Hence, in most places where it travels, pizza is not homemade. It is pre-packed and deep-frozen, to be heated up at home. It is sold in slices to eat in the street. You may sit down for it in a restaurant, or buy one to take away. In many cities around the world you can have a pizza delivered to wherever – house, hotel room, park – you order it from.

How is it that this particular dish has travelled so successfully? In many ways and in many sites, eating local food, prepared according to 'traditional' recipes, is crucial to the experience of home (Mintz, 1996; Sutton, 2001). And yet some dishes travel. Often they have done so along with travelling migrants. Dishes from (different culinary traditions within) China are a case in point. They travelled with restaurants that first catered for Chinese migrants and then quickly found modes of adapting to local tastes (Cheung and Wu, 2002). Something similar may be going on for pizza in some sites, such as Germany, where Italians settled and created a niche for themselves by opening pizzerias as relatively affordable restaurants. Elsewhere pizzas have travelled differently. In Thailand pizzas were, for quite a while, mainly sold in backpacker restaurants. The tourists involved enjoyed their pizzas as a welcome taste of home-away-from-home. To savour a Pizza Hawaii in Bangkok, as if it were New York, was just wonderful. But while the tourist trail has helped pizza to travel, these days pizza restaurants (be it in Bangkok or Beijing) are mainly filled with locals, for whom pizza holds a promising taste of elsewhere (cf. Germann Molz, 2005). In the form of pizza, *elsewhere* is *en vogue*. Within limits. For the ham, crucial to the success of Pizza Hawaii as it provides a salty contrast to the sweet pineapple, may work wonders in New York and Thailand, but impedes the dish from travelling to Indonesia, where eating pork is forbidden by Islam. It is impure. At the same time, Pizza Hawaii hasn't travelled particularly well to France either, as there the combination of salty ham and sweet pineapple is deemed 'vulgar, indeed even laughable' (Pitte and Gladding, 2002: 96).

Which leaves us with the conclusion that Pizza Hawaii travels around the world, but not quite everywhere. That is topological complexity number one, conjuring up a globe where travelling is sometimes easy, while elsewhere there are boundaries that are hard or even impossible to cross. The second topological complexity that Pizza Hawaii presents is that of ingredients that, coming from many places, hold together on a single plate. This is a fold: a monad in which 'the whole world' comes together in a single site. Which begs the question: where does Pizza *Hawaii* originate – not pizza in general, but this specific variant? The *New York Pizza* in Amsterdam proudly declares: 'Pineapple is one of the few fruits that we put on our pizzas. The popular Pizza Hawaii, which can also be found on the menu in New York, contains this delicious fruit which is full to the brim of vitamins. This pizza was introduced in the Netherlands in the 1970s when it became popular to add pineapple to all sorts of traditional dishes.' (*New York Pizza Cookbook*, 2008) Then, however, follows the warning, the sign of a broken authenticity: 'But in Italy you will not find the Pizza Hawaii!' (ibid) So Pizza Hawaii does not come from Italy. A journalist from *The New York Times* was painfully confronted with this when he flew all the way to Naples. When he asked the local pizza baker Alfonso Cucciniello whether he liked Pizza Hawaii, Cucciniello had no idea what the journalist was talking about. Once the dish was explained to him, he replied, 'Pizza with pineapples? That's a cake' (NY Times, 9 September 2004).[3] Thus, in Italy, where 'pizza' comes from, Pizza Hawaii is not even a pizza at all. This, then, is topological complexity number three. That some things become so folded, so 'meshed up', that they have no *originality* at all.

Notes

1 Since we study *The Eating body in Western practice and theory* thanks to an ERC Advanced grant (gratefully acknowledged), we are inclined to see the relevance of food for all issues and notice eating everywhere. We would like to thank the editors for inviting us to contribute to this volume. For inspiration and comments thanks to *the team*: Filippo Bertoni, Anna Mann, Emily Yates-Doerr, Michalis Kontopodis and Rebeca Ibáñez Martín. For his investments in topology thanks to John Law. And for his energetic ability to notice where it is possible to buy Pizza Hawaii 'all over the world', or almost, thanks to Johannes van Lieshout (one of his pizzas serves as our crucial illustration).

2 Though we draw on our experiences with pizza (while travelling and in the variously located homes that each of us lived in), this text is not particularly based on new empirical research. Instead, we gratefully draw on the literature, and thus the empirical studies of others. Our contribution is in bringing these together in an original way. Not entirely original (of course). The kind of topological complexity that we explore here was articulated a long time ago in Soja (1989). For the notion *absent-present* that we use, see Law 2002. And for topological configurations in techno–science, see Law and Mol (2001).

3 Alfonso Cucciniello, local pizza baker in Naples, quoted in 'For the Pizza Makers of Naples, A Tempest in a Pie Dish', *New York Times* (9 June 2004), p. 2.

References

Albala, K. (2007) *Beans: a history*, Oxford, Berg.

Barndt, D. (2008) *Tangled routes: women, work, and globalization on the tomato trail*, Lanham, MD, Rowman & Littlefield Publishers.

Bartholomew, D. P., Paull, R. E. and Rohrbach, K. G. (eds) (2003) *The pineapple: botany, production and uses*, Wallingford, CABI Pub.

Burch, D. and Goss, J. (1999) 'Global sourcing and retail chains: shifting relationships of production in Australian agri-foods'. *Rural Sociology*, 64, 334–350.

Chambers, P., Grandin, T., Heinz, G. and Srisuvan, T. (2001) *Guidelines for human handling, transport and slaughter of livestock*, Rome, FAO.

Cheung, S. C. H. and Wu, D. Y. H. (2002) *The globalization of Chinese food*, London, Routledge.

Collins, J. L. (1951) 'Notes on the origin, history, and genetic nature of the Cayenne pineapple'. *Pacific Science* 5(1), 3–17.

Cook, I. (2004) 'Follow the thing: papaya'. *Antipode*, 36, 642–664.

Crosby, A. W. (1986) *Ecological imperialism: the biological expansion of Europe, 900–1900*, Cambridge [Cambridgeshire]; New York, Cambridge University Press.

DeSoucey, M. (2010) 'Gastronationalism'. *American Sociological Review*, 75, 432–455.

Diamond, J. M. (1998) *Guns, germs, and steel: the fates of human societies*, New York, W. W. Norton & Co.

Diner, H. R. (2001) *Hungering for America: Italian, Irish, and Jewish foodways in the age of migration*, Cambridge, MA, Harvard University Press.

Germann Molz, J. (2005) 'Guilty pleasures of the golden arches: mapping McDonald's in narratives of round-the-world travel'. In J. Davidson, M. Smith and L. Bondi (eds) *Emotional geographies*, Aldershot, UK: Ashgate. pp. 63–83.

Halici, N. (2001) 'Turkish delights'. *Gastronomica: The Journal of Food and Culture*, 1, 92–93.

Hamann, K. (2006) 'An overview of Danish pork industry integration and structure'. *Advances in Pork Production*, 17, 93–97.

Harvey, D. (1990) *The condition of postmodernity: an enquiry into the origins of cultural change*, Oxford, Blackwell.

Helstosky, C. (2008) *Pizza: a global history*, London, Reaktion.

Jackson, P., Ward, N. and Russell, P. (2006) 'Mobilising the commodity chain concept in the politics of food and farming'. *Journal of Rural Studies*, 22, 129–141.

Jakle, J. A. and Sculle, K. A. (1999) *Fast food: roadside restaurants in the automobile age*, Baltimore, MD, Johns Hopkins University Press.

Jones, M. (2007) *Feast: why humans share food*, Oxford; New York, Oxford University Press.

Krondl, M. (2007) *The taste of conquest: the rise and fall of the three great cities of spice*, New York, Ballantine Books.

Law, J. (2002) *Aircraft stories: decentering the object in technoscience*, Durham, NC, Duke University Press.

Law, J. and Mol, A. (2001) 'Situating technoscience: an inquiry into spatialities'. *Environment and Planning D: Society and Space*, 19, 609–621.

Law, J. and Mol, A. (2008) 'Globalisation in practice: on the politics of boiling pigswill'. *Geoforum*, 39, 133–143.

Long, J. (2000) 'Tomatoes'. In *The Cambridge world history of food 1*, Cambridge, Cambridge University Press.

Massey, D. B. (2005) *For space*, London; Thousand Oaks, CA, SAGE.

McCorriston, J. (2000) 'Wheat'. In *The Cambridge world history of food 1*, Cambridge, Cambridge University Press.

Mintz, S. W. (1996) *Tasting food, tasting freedom: excursions into eating, culture, and the past*, Boston, Beacon Press.

New York Pizza Cookbook (2008) Amstelveen, New York Pizza.

Pitte, J.-R. and Gladding, J. (2002) *French gastronomy: the history and geography of a passion*, New York, Columbia University Press.

Ritzer, G. (2010) *The McDonaldization of society*, Thousand Oaks, CA, Pine Forge.

Roe, E., Buller, H. and Bull, J. (2011) 'The performance of farm animal assessment'. *Animal Welfare*, 20, 69–78.

Sheller, M. (2005) 'The ethical banana: markets, migrants and the globalisation of a fruit'. *STS Visiting Speakers Series: Globalization in Practice: Science and Technology Studies (STS) perspectives on the every day life of globalization*, Said Business School, University of Oxford.

Soja, E. W. (1989) *Postmodern geographies: the reassertion of space in critical social theory*, London; New York, Verso.

Stassart, P. and Whatmore, S. J. (2003) 'Metabolising risk: food scares and the un/re-making of Belgian beef'. *Environment and Planning A*, 35, 449–462.

Stiles, E. (1992) 'Animals as seed dispersers'. In Fenner, M. (ed.) *Seeds: the ecology of regeneration in plant communities*, Wallingford, Oxon, CAB International.

Stuart, T. (2009) *Waste: uncovering the global food scandal*, London, Penguin.

Sutton, D. E. (2001) *Remembrance of repasts: an anthropology of food and memory*, Oxford, Berg.

Todorov, T. (1992) *The conquest of America the question of the other*, New York, NY, HarperPerennial.

27

Waste

Dan Swanton

> If we can abstract pathogenicity and hygiene from our notion of dirt, we are left with the old definition of dirt as matter out of place. This is a very suggestive approach. It implies two conditions: a sort of ordered relations and a contravention of that order. Dirt then, is never a unique, isolated event. Where there is dirt there is a system.
>
> (*Douglas 2003: 44*)

This chapter explores the multiple and complex mobilities of waste. Anna Davies (2012: 192–3) has recently drawn up a typology of waste mobilities that marshals diverse and unruly work on how waste and end-of-life things move (and are moved) into four themes: 1) mapping flows that are concerned with the 'physical and political trajectories of end-of-life matter, highlighting the interrelationship between trade, regulation and environmental justice'; 2) following things that trace the unmaking of end-of-life things to expose processes of material transformation and valuing; 3) illegal mobilities that explore both failures in regulatory regimes and the 'illicit movement of materials'; 4) and the immobility of some wastes that stubbornly stay in place for varying durations. Here, I cover similar ground, but take a very different approach. I introduce three stories of differing mobilities of waste related to the steel industry to open up a set of questions about the entanglement of mobility with processes of *wasting* and *valuing*, that are also caught up with a host of matters of concern that include making boundaries and distinctions, environmental damage, performing risky work, and human health. These stories overlap with a number of the themes Davies identifies. But I am particularly interested in thinking through the mobilities of waste to explore Mary Douglas's (2003) richly suggestive conception of waste as 'matter out of place' and to build on recent work that engages more fully with the materiality of waste (Hawkins 2006, 2009; Gregson *et al.* 2010c; Gregson and Crang 2010a).

Mary Douglas's notion of waste as matter out of place is perhaps most commonly associated with psychoanalytic approaches that emphasise the symbolism of waste's polluting effects and how social distinctions and orderings are enacted through practices of separating, demarcating, purifying, abjecting and expelling (see also Gregson and Crang 2010a: 1027). The indeterminacy, ambiguity and transgressive presence of waste threaten to defile that which is clean, pure and whole. This indeterminacy impels action to expel and distance waste matter.

But as Gregson and Crang (2010a: 1026) note, much of this work remains immaterial, it tends to be 'shy of the *stuff* of waste'. Here, I join recent writing that takes the materiality of waste seriously in ways that consider social and the material together (Hawkins 2006, 2009; Gregson *et al.* 2010c; Bennett 2004, 2010). In this work, waste matter – whether it is plastic bottles, piles of trash, end-of-life ships, asbestos, or excrement – becomes the 'stuff of politics' in a 'more fully materialist theory of politics, one that allows a place for the force of things and opens new possibilities for imagining the relationship between scientific and political practices and orderings' (Braun and Whatmore 2010: x). Here waste is not cast as an *object* of politics. Instead this materialist politics is interested in how wastes get caught up in, and reproduce, material orderings of the world (see Law and Mol 2008). Focussing on the materiality of waste brings to the fore the force of wasted things, and this materiality becomes significant in the social relations, political alliances and material practices that are enacted in attempts to deal with waste matter (Gregson and Crang 2010a).

The mobility of waste matter offers an instructive lens for exploring the politics of wasted stuff. Often the dovetailing of mobility and waste involves the tracking of the problematic movement and/or immobility of wasted things, in research that documents a politics of local protest in the face of transnational flows of waste (for example Khoo and Rau 2009). But here I am interested in using mobility to push our understanding of waste and materiality in some different directions. Drawing on Adey's (2010) description of mobility as a lived relation and orientation, I use three stories that focus on the complex and multiple mobilities of metallic wastes to expose the politics of stuff. These stories of waste mobility draw on different aspects of research on the steel industry as part of The Waste of the World project (Gregson and Crang 2010a, 2012; Crang 2010; Hudson and Swanton 2012; Swanton 2012, 2013) and seek to dramatise different aspects of a politics of stuff.[1] The first story, 'containment', focuses on the material practices and technologies that seek to contend with the unruly mobility of flighty waste materials like dust. The second story, 'circulation – following scrap', introduces the mobile method of following the things in ways that trouble the conceptualisation of waste as an end point (Gregson *et al.* 2010b; Lepawsky and Mather 2012). Introducing research on the ship-breaking beaches of Chittagong, Bangladesh (Gregson *et al.* 2010b, 2012), this story exposes wastes in their transformative states, where things are better understood not as stable things, but in terms of what they might become through their unmaking. The final story, 'immobile wastes?', takes us to landscapes of de-industrialisation in Dortmund, Germany. Here we witness how the stuff that gets left behind after industry closes does not remain immobile in what Jennifer Gabrys (2009) has called 'sinks'. Just as mobilities work has opened up the movements of human bodies as a site of meaning, here I track some of the mobilities of metallic waste matter to show how movements are not dead time en route to an end point, but these mobilities are full of life, exposing social relations, material orderings, power relations and material transformations.

Containment

The economic activity of making steel depends on a set of material transformations. Steel making might be productively considered in terms of day-to-day struggles with the material world and the labour of holding together production processes that consist of a more or less stable lash-up of technologies (Swanton 2012). But steel plants don't only produce finished steel in blooms, billets and slabs. The material transformations required to make steel, and the various technologies that contain these transformations, produce many other materials – huge quantities of off-gases, slags, oily sludges, filtercakes, dusts, concentrations of heavy metals and carcinogens, used packaging, old computer equipment, etc. These other materials are routinely assigned to the (often fluid and fuzzy) categories of by-products (where value can be extracted) or waste (where the materials have little or no re-use value). In this section I want to focus on just one lowly waste – dust. Steel makers have to contend with waste matter that is more expensive and problematic. For example, CO_2 emissions have become more expensive in the EU with the advent of emissions trading that puts a financial cost on the use of the atmosphere as a repository for waste gases linked to climate change or various hazardous materials (heavy metals, radioactive elements, carcinogens) that accumulate and concentrate through material transformations and threaten human life and contaminate land. But the story of dust is instructive, opening up a series of stories that provide insights into the operations of a material politics.

Dust

The material transformations involved in steel making produce vast quantities of dust – fine particles scattered during the handling and storing of iron ore and coking coal; metallic elements that escape as the slag that is produced to remove impurities from molten metal cools; or the large quantities of dust-rich flue gases emitted in steel making. The material properties of these dusts afford them unruly and disruptive mobilities. These dusts are difficult to contain, and their flightiness causes problems – the excessive mobilities of these particles fail to respect boundaries, and these fugitive particulates (PM_{10}s, $PM_{2.5}$s) pose a health hazard (dusts have been related to elevated incidences of respiratory diseases and lung cancer), reduce air quality leading to the violation of environmental permits, and cause an environmental nuisance as dusts settle on local golf courses, on washing hanging on lines, and on windows and cars after rain showers.

At steel plants in northern Europe I encountered a host of material practices and technologies enrolled to contain, hide and expel these waste materials. For example, dust suppression sprayers are being installed at coal- and ore-handling and storage facilities and in slag pits. These suppression sprayers produce a highly atomised mist of microscopic water droplets that attack the dust particles at a molecular level in an attempt to immobilise them. In other parts of a steel works, dust abatement has required investment in expensive technologies. For example, primary and secondary de-dusting units have been retrofitted in some plants to extract the dust-rich flues expelled by basic oxygen converters that transform molten iron into liquid steel. The primary de-dusting unit scrubs flue gases with water, while the secondary de-dusting unit uses an 'aerodynamic exhaust hood, with an extraction rate of 2.4 million m³ an hour' and channels the flues through a collector piper and a 'battery of 7,200 filter sleeves' (World Steel Association 2010). In other places workers improvise to contain the excessive mobilities of dust. During one escorted tour of a steel plant, I was shown how traffic lights and a weather vane had been lashed up to a slag crane. This crane handles slag produced during the de-sulphurisation of molten iron. As this slag cools it forms a fine dust that is dispersed by the slightest breeze or movement. To prevent the dust becoming airborne, the slag must not be moved for 12 hours or until it cools to below 80°C. But treating each ladle of hot metal produces 6–7 tonnes of slag and the slag pots have to be moved before the slag has had sufficient time to cool. And so an accommodation with this unruly matter has been reached. A red light indicates the prevailing wind is heading towards the town, while a green light signals that the wind is blowing out to sea. The slag is only moved and tipped into to the slag pits when the unruly particles of dust will travel out to sea.

Here, I want to suggest that we are witnessing what Law and Mol (2008) call material politics. Law and Mol are looking to trouble how conventional politics privileges the 'life of the mind over the stubborn obduracy of the material' or reduces the material to a single order (their example is a sleeping policeman), where no space is allowed for opposition or otherness (Law and Mol 2008: 134). Material politics is a version of politics that foregrounds materiality and difference. It is interested in how 'politics gets caught up in and reproduced in material arrangements' (ibid.). Using the example of boiling pigswill in the context of an outbreak of foot and mouth in Britain, Law and Mol read boiling pigswill as a political technology that makes boundaries and produces differences (between rich and poor countries, between disease-free and diseased). Their broader point is that focussing on things and their mobility brings a particular kind of politics into sight. Politics is shaped through the work of contending with the material properties of things, and enacted through the labour of making boundaries in ways that order the world, and link distant places in complex ways.

The practices and technologies enrolled to contend with the unruly mobility of particles on a steel plant offer similar insights into the labour of ordering. The practices and technologies for immobilising or controlling the mobility of dust are all attempts to make and enforce boundaries. On one level dust abatement is about being a 'good neighbour' and minimising environmental nuisance. But more significantly, the mobility and force of dust particulates also produces an assemblage of surveillance and monitoring technologies designed to monitor ambient air quality and address public health concerns relating to the ingestion of dusts. For example, in Europe, environmental legislation and regulation enact boundaries in an attempt to limit the harm done to the environment and human health by industrial processes. Environmental protection agencies use continuous ambient air quality monitoring systems to measure, among other things, concentrations of particulates. The mobility of dust is measured as particulates moving through these monitoring systems and the amount of particulates is regulated through environmental permits and licences; excessive emissions are punished through enforcement notices, the removal of permits, fines and prosecution. And so we witness how the propensities of material things (in this case the flightiness of dust and its capacity for causing harm to human health when ingested), alongside technologies of monitoring and enforcement, are constitutive of a politics of public health and environmental protection. The material politics extends beyond the political techniques and technologies deployed by environmental protection agencies and public health agencies. Steel companies also draw on dust abatement and their adherence to environmental regulations to make distinctions between 'clean' steel making and environmental steel making and 'dirty' unregulated, or under-regulated, steel making elsewhere; between responsible, environmentally sustainable industrial production and cheaper, but supposedly less environmentally sound, production in other parts of the world. And so the material practices involved in containing the mobility of lowly dust particles is also about improving the environmental performance and reputation of steel makers in Europe and the US, while also drawing boundaries between 'clean production' and industrial processes elsewhere where environmental controls are less stringent or rigorously enforced – for example China, which has well-documented problems with industrial dusts (*New York Times* 2007).

Circulation – following scrap

Disposal, I contend, is not primarily about waste but about placing. It is as much a spatial as a temporal category. Terms like 'waste disposal' and waste management' are misnomers. Rather disposal is about placing absences and this has consequences for how we think about 'social relations'.

(Hetherington 2004: 159)

My second story opens up what are perhaps some more obvious connections between mobility and waste, namely the transnational flows of waste matter. Waste has figured in the early imagination of the 'new mobilities paradigm', featuring, for example, in John Urry's (2000: 1) list of mobile things that offer points of departure into a 'sociology beyond societies'.[2] What comes to mind immediately are problematic flows of hazardous wastes – both legal and clandestine – from 'rich' to 'poorer' countries, and the failures of attempts like the Basel Convention and its amendments to regulate trans-border shipments of hazardous waste (Davies 2012; Lepawsky and McNabb 2010). These material flows of waste expose a hidden underside of globalisation. Particular wasted things and certain sites have become emblematic of the environmental injustices of these flows – notable examples include e-waste dumping in Guiyu (China) and Lagos (Nigeria), and ship-breaking on the beaches of Chittagong (Bangladesh) and Alang (India). The circulation of visual materials through international media and campaigns led by environmental non-governmental organisations (like Basel Action Network and Greenpeace) expose these abject flows of matter and the unseen worlds upon which our comfortable lives depend. For example, Mike Crang (2010) has written about ship-breaking in Chittagong and how the visual documentation of appalling and exploitative working conditions and monumental environmental harm demand an ethical and political response. Photography and film document and communicate the overwhelming of local regulations by transnational flows, exploitation of a precarious and disposable work force and the enormous environmental harm done through ship-breaking (Crang 2010).

But in this story I want to shift our gaze away from mapping flows of waste matter, and focus on following wasted things. Following things of waste or failed value reveals how waste can be a misleading category that obscures the potential for waste matter to be transformed and its value rekindled. Following 'the thing' has emerged as a powerful mobile method that traces the biographies of things in ways that 'get with the fetish' (Taussig 1992: 122; Cook 2004; Cook *et al.* 2005). However, as Gregson *et al.* (2010b) argue, much of this following work has focused on consumer products (from papayas to cut flowers), dwelling on movement up value chains to the final consumption of products in the west. Recent research has started to follow wastes and end-of-life things (Gregson *et al.* 2010b; Lepawsky and Mather 2010; Beisel and Schneider 2012) and has produced some remarkable insights. Most notably, studying the travels of wasted things begins to unravel the category of 'waste'. Lepawsky and Mather's (2010: 242) account of following e-waste in Bangladesh is particularly instructive:

> We flew to Dhaka, spent 4 months tracking what we thought was e-waste, but we couldn't find any. We found used printers. Old monitors (tons and tons of them). Hard-drives from the US embassy and Exxon. Old silicon chips, motherboards and piles of circuitry. Amidst all this stuff we could hardly find any waste. Almost everything had value.

As Lepawsky and Mather suggest, waste is not an end point, it is – to cite Thompson's (1979) celebrated phrase – a 'fulcrum'. Following the transnational journeys of wasted things reveals how becoming rubbish can mark a point of transformation where things, or the materials that comprise these things, become re-valued. Waste is a category that things move in and out of. And following wasted things exposes processes of categorisation and re-valuing where things that are discarded in one place turn up elsewhere as valuable.

So following the journeys of end-of-life things disrupts linear values chains that assume progressions from production to consumption and disposal (Lepawsky and Mather 2010). It does not lead to some final resting place, but takes us to the middle of things. Following the mobility of end-of-life things – whether it is a mobile phone or a ship – quickly becomes a story about the unmaking of things (Gregson 2010c). Rather than stable objects, end-of-life things are better understood as assemblages of heterogeneous materials. While the thing may no longer have use-value as a thing, it does have value for what it might become. Following the material flows of things to workshops in Guiyu or the beaches of Bangladesh illustrates this powerfully. Following things becomes about stories of 'wasting and valuing' (Lepawsky and Mather 2010), as things are broken down into constituent materials, sorted, sifted and cleaned to become the raw materials for new rounds of production and new forms of value. Following scrap through the destructive work of ship-breaking on the beaches of Bangladesh offers an extreme, but telling, example.

On Sitakunda beach, near Chittagong, Bangladesh, some of the largest decommissioned tankers in the world are broken. Recent research as part of The Waste of the World project (Gregson 2010c, 2012; Crang 2010) has examined ship-breaking on this beach, following end-of-life ships and highlighting how the beach operates as a vast – and environmentally devastating – complex for sorting and sifting materials (Gregson 2010c). The Basel Convention prohibits the export of hazardous waste from 'richer' to 'poorer' countries – and each of these ships contain tonnes of hazardous wastes. However, various legal loopholes and slippery categorisations allow ship brokers and breakers to circumnavigate international law (Crang 2010). The financial logics underpinning breaking on this beach are clear. These ships no longer have use-value as ships, and owners would have to pay to have them broken in the US or Europe. But in Bangladesh – which breaks one-third of the ships broken globally – these ships have value as 'assemblages of heterogeneous materials' (Gregson 2010c). The ships are bought for their weight in scrap steel and the steel salvaged by ship-breaking supplies a staggering 90 percent of the steel consumed in Bangladesh; the steel is largely re-rolled into steel bars that are used to reinforce concrete in construction (Gregson 2010c). But it is not only the steel that is salvaged. As Gregson (2010c) show, everything from electricity generators to western toilets, chandlery to chip board are stripped and sold from these ships. And so, following the ships' rubbish value exposes the mutability of things and disrupts taken-for-granted accounts of waste as an end point. The destructive work on this beach exploits the mutability of things through salvaging, sorting, reconditioning and re-fabricating to produce 'a range of objects and differentiated streams of material which form the basis of secondary manufacturing, craft and retail activities in Bhatiary' (Gregson 2010b: 847). Ship-breaking on the beaches of Bangladesh offers an admittedly extreme example of the mobility of scrap steel and the circulations of waste materials. But following other flows of scrap metal exposes similar material practices of breaking down and sorting in 'human-powered recycling centres' – albeit in different places and at different scales – as reusable metals are harvested from scrapped cars, old engines and discarded white goods (Minter 2011).

The Waste of the World research following end-of-life ships illustrates powerfully that waste is not an end point; rather it marks a moment in the circulation of scrap and other things through processes of wasting and valuing. But following wasted things is about more than making a conceptual point about categories. Following end-of-life ships troubles representations of ship-breaking on beaches in Bangladesh as dumping, or an example of the pollution haven hypothesis in action (for a parallel argument about e-waste see Lepawsky and McNabb 2010). What emerges from following these ships and their unmaking is a more complicated story of recycling and revaluing, and an economy that is dependent on the materials produced through destructive work. It also opens up spaces for different kinds of political intervention, like making health and safety equipment available or transferring more environmentally sound technologies and practices (Gregson 2011). Here, interventions are concerned with mitigating the devastation of the littoral environment and exploitation of vulnerable workers, in the recognition that further environmental legislation is unlikely to stall the destruction work on this beach (Gregson 2011).

Immobile wastes?

The third story begins in 2001, during a slump in the global steel market. The German steel giant ThyssenKrupp announced the closure of a recently acquired steel plant in Dortmund. This integrated steel works was spread over four vast sites that together totalled over 550 hectares and were connected by a tangled network of pipes and railways that traversed the city. Within a month of the closure, ThyssenKrupp announced that they had sold the steel plant to a steel maker in China. By 2005 Shagang Iron and Steel Company had shipped the steel plant in its entirety to China. The scale, complexity and logistical demands of transplanting this steel works are breathtaking. By 2005 more than 250,000 tonnes of steel plant – pipes, computers, blast furnaces, rolling stands, coke ovens, oxygen converters and so on – had been dismantled and shipped piece-by-piece 5,600 miles, first by canal and then sea from Dortmund to Shagang's steel plant on the alluvial plains of the Yangtze, north-west of Shanghai. Just the technical drawings needed to rebuild the deconstructed industrial complex filled two shipping containers and weighed 40 tonnes. It took around 1,000 Chinese workers a year to disassemble the plant in Dortmund, and over 2,000 workers just two years to rebuild the plant in Shagang (Kynge 2006).

The logics underpinning this extraordinary story of the mobility of the supposedly fixed capital of industrial technologies are explored elsewhere (Hudson and Swanton 2012). But here my interest is in what is left behind. Dortmund's landscapes of de-industrialisation are littered with disused railway lines, defunct pipework, contaminated soils, industrial heritage museums, empty industrial sheds, tracts of wastelands populated by concrete pans, piles of rubble and colonising wildlife. Parts of the urban landscape have become repositories for waste matter. It is tempting to see these material remnants as immobilised in the urban landscape. They are problematic through their persistence and failure to move on. But on closer inspection we can begin to trace all kinds of movement and mobility in this landscape of de-industrialisation. Decay, entropy and the invasion of plants and animals introduce particular kinds of mobility. What might appear to be dead, abandoned spaces are often full of movement and life. And as Tim Edensor (2005: 318) has shown, decay transforms 'the form and textures of objects, eroding their assigned functions and meanings, and blurring the boundaries between things'. The presence of biological and chemical life means that industrial ruins and wastelands are far from stable landscapes – instead their falling apart and decay alert us again to the mutability of matter and revitalisation (albeit in less productive ways than the beach in Bangladesh). But here I want to focus on the mobility of waste matter at a particular site.

This photograph introduces a striking example of how waste matter can remain mobile in a landscape. The site has a history of contamination and failed remediation. Until the late 1970s, a coke oven by-product plant stood on this ground, releasing – over decades – unknown quantities of heavy metals and carcinogens. The soil became what Jennifer Gabrys (2009) calls a sink: a site for storing, filtering and transforming inorganic compounds produced by the industrial processes that once stood on this ground. And so sinks harbour

Figure 27.1   Sink

matter out of place, but they do not immobilise wastes. Gabrys (2009) is keen to emphasise the indeterminacy and disruptive geographies of sinks – waste matter has a tendency to migrate, seep, spill over and recirculate in unexpected ways. On this land the mobility of waste matter and the disruptive geographies of the sink had lethal consequences. After the coke oven closed, the land was inadequately remediated and then redeveloped as housing. A cancer cluster emerged within the first decade of the redevelopment. Inorganic compounds seeped and migrated; they conjoined with organic bodies. The bodies of local residents had been exposed to the deadly vitality of matter. The liveliness and mobility of matter commanded human attention, but through registers of fear and respect, not enchantment and generosity (Gregson *et al.* 2010b; cf. Bennett 2004). In the end the housing was razed and an impermeable skin – designed to immobilise hazardous matter and prevent it from migrating and penetrating human bodies – was put down. Again, we see how the mobility and capacities of matter are constitutive of a kind of material politics, a reordering of the world. A photograph of a climbing wall in a park, only remarkable at first glance due to the apparent absence of life, tells a very different story about vital materialism and the liveliness and mobility of some waste materials.

Conclusion

These three stories about the mobility (and immobilisation) of metallic waste matter have offered three avenues into thinking about the materiality of waste and material politics.

Reworking Mary Douglas's fertile conceptualisation of waste as 'matter out of place' through recent writing on vital materialism has offered a series of moments to take seriously the mobility of waste matter. Each story points, in different ways, to the 'constitutive nature of material processes and entities in social and political life' (Braun and Whatmore 2010: x). They disrupt some entrenched assumptions about what waste is, what waste means, and what waste can do. Much of the academic focus on waste and mobility to date has been dedicated to tracking and mapping problematic movements of wasted things. This work tends to cast waste as an *object* of politics. But my stories have cultivated a different orientation to waste. They have charted how wastes get caught up in, and reproduce, material orderings of the world. They have also drawn on arguments for a performative cultural economy that use narrative to foreground material encounters (Gregson 2009). Together, the 'politics of stuff' and performative cultural economy open up some exciting avenues for new research. They show how movements of waste are rarely dead time en route to some end point. Instead, the mobilities of waste are both lively and instructive. Movements of waste are entangled in all kinds of social relations, material orderings, power relations, material transformations and injustices.

Notes

1 The first and third stories draw on ethnographic observations made during escorted tours of steel plants in Europe, as well as fieldwork on the landscapes of deindustrialisation in Dortmund. The second story, 'circulation', introduces other research from The Waste of the World project that focused on end-of-life ships and following things of rubbish value.
2 Urry (2000: 1) argues for a 'new mobilities paradigm' concerned with the 'diverse mobilities of peoples, objects, images, information and wastes, and complex interdependencies between and social consequence of, these diverse mobilities'.

Bibliography

Adey, P. (2010) *Mobility*, London: Routledge.
Beisel, U. and Schneider, T. (2012) 'Provincialising waste: the transformation of ambulance car 7/83–2 to tro-tro Dr.JESUS', *Environment and Planning D: Society and Space*, 30: 639–654.
Bennett, J. (2004) 'The force of things: steps towards an ecology of matter', *Political Theory*, 32: 347–372.
Bennett, J. (2010) *Vibrant Matter: A Political Ecology of Things*, Durham, NC: Duke University Press.
Braun, B. and Whatmore, S. (2010) *Political Matter: Technoscience, Democracy and Public Life*, Minneapolis: University of Minnesota Press.
Cook, I. (2004) 'Follow the thing: papaya', *Antipode*, 36(4): 642–664.
Cook, I. *et al.* (2005) 'Geographies of food: following', *Progress in Human Geography*, 30(5): 655–666.
Crang, M. (2010) 'The death of great ship: photograph, politics, and waste in the global imaginary', *Environment and Planning A*, 42: 1084–1102.
Davies, A. (2012) 'Geography and the matter of waste mobilities', *Transactions of the Institute of British Geographers*, 37: 191–6.
Douglas, M. (2003) *Purity and Danger*, London: Routledge.
Edensor, T. (2005) 'Waste matter – the debris of industrial ruins and the disordering of the material world', *Journal of Material Culture*, 10(3): 311–332.
Gabrys, J. (2009) 'Sink: the dirt of systems', *Environment and Planning D: Society and Space*, 27: 666–681.
Gregson, N. (2009) 'Material, literary narrative and cultural economy: Primo Levi and the industrial short story', *Journal of Cultural Economy*, 2: 285–300.
Gregson, N. (2011) 'Performativity, corporeality and the politics of ship disposal', *Journal of Cultural Economy*, 4: 137–156.
Gregson, N. and Crang, M. (2010a) 'Materiality and waste: inorganic vitality in a networked world', *Environment and Planning A*, 42: 1026–1032.

Gregson, N., Crang, M., Ahamed, F., Akhter, N. and Ferdous, R. (2010b) 'Following things of rubbish value: end-of-life ships, "chock-chocky" furniture and the Bangladeshi middle class consumer', *Geoforum*, 41: 846–854.

Gregson, N., Watkins, H. and Calestani, M. (2010c) 'Inextinguishable fibres: demolition and the vital materialisms of asbestos', *Environment and Planning A*, 42: 1065–1083.

Gregson, N., Crang, M., Ahamed, F., Akter, N., Ferdous, R., Foisal, S. and Hudson, R. (2012) 'Territorial agglomeration and industrial symbiosis: Sitakunda-Bhatiary, Bangladesh, as a secondary processing complex', *Economic Geography*, 88: 37–58.

Hawkins, G. (2006) *The Ethics of Waste*, Lanham, MD: Rowman and Littlefield Publishers.

Hawkins, G. (2009) 'The politics of bottled water: assembling bottled water as brand, waster and oil', *Journal of Cultural Economy*, 2: 183–195.

Hetherington, K. (2004) 'Secondhandedness: consumption, disposal, and absent presence', *Environment and Planning D: Society and Space*, 22(1): 157–173.

Hudson, R. and Swanton, D. (2012) 'Global shifts in contemporary times: the changing trajectories of steeltowns in China, Germany and the United Kingdom', *European Urban and Regional Studies*, 19(1): 6–19.

Khoo, S.-M. and Rau, H. (2009) 'Movements, mobilities and the politics of hazardous waste', *Environmental Politics*, 18(6): 960–980.

Kygne, J. (2006) *China Shakes the World*, London: Phoenix.

Law, J. and Mol, A. (2008) 'Globalisation in practice: on the politics of boiling pigswill', *Geoforum*, 39: 144–143.

Lepawsky, J. (2012) 'Legal geographies of e-waste legislation in Canada and the US: jurisdiction, responsibility and the taboo of production', *Geoforum*, 43(6): 1194–1206.

Lepawsky, J. and Mather, C. (2010) 'From beginnings and endings to boundaries and edges: rethinking circulation and exchange through electronic waste', *Area*, 43(3): 242–249.

Lepawsky, J. and McNabb, C. (2010) 'Mapping international flows of electronic waste', *Canadian Geographer*, 54(2): 177–195.

Minter, A. (2011) 'China's scrap metal workers are human recycling machines', *The Atlantic*. Available online at http://grist.org.article/2011-03-04-chinas-scrap-metal-workers-are-human-recycling-machines/ (accessed 26 August 2012).

New York Times (2007) 'As China roars, pollution reaches deadly extremes'. Available online at www.nytimes.com/2007/08/26/world/asia/26china.html?pagewanted=all&_moc.semityn.www (accessed 27 September 2012).

Swanton, D. (2012) 'Afterimages of steel: Dortmund', *Space and Culture*, 15(4): 264–282.

Swanton, D. (2013) 'The steel plant as assemblage', *Geoforum*, 44(1): 282–291.

Taussig, M. (1992) *The Nervous System*, London: Routledge.

Thompson, M. (1979) *Rubbish Theory: The Creation and Destruction of Value*, Oxford: Oxford University Press.

Urry, J. (2000) *Sociology beyond Societies: Mobilities for the Twenty-First Century*, London: Routledge.

World Steel Association (2010) 'ArcelorMittal: Dust control in Belgium'. Available online at www.worldsteel.org/steel-by-topic/sustainable-steel/company-case-studies/limiting-steel-dust-ArcelorMittal.html (accessed 28 August 2012).

28

Viruses

Stephanie Lavau

In January 2012, an international consortium of scientists made a rather surprising announce-ment in a letter hastily published in the eminent journals *Nature* and *Science*. They announced not an exciting new discovery, method or fact, but instead a self-imposed moratorium on their laboratory research, an action that was without precedence in the biomedical sciences. What were they working on that was so potentially dangerous and controversial so as to prompt such a drastic measure? It was a virus, more specifically, the star of Soderbergh's 2011 blockbuster disaster movie *Contagion*: avian influenza. In their public statement, researchers from 39 laboratories declared, "we have agreed on a voluntary pause of 60 days on any research involving highly pathogenic avian influenza H5N1 viruses leading to the generation of viruses that are more transmissible in mammals" (Fouchier *et al.* 2012). From scientific publications to newspapers, to blogs and tweets: the announcement rapidly propagated through media around the world, with the virus at the centre of all this fuss attracting hyper-bolic headlines as the "Armageddon flu" (Anon. 2012) and the "Doomsday flu" (MacKenzie 2012). Why so much concern for this virus and this research?

In this chapter, I attend to intersections between "our mobile ways of life" (Adey *et al.* 2012: 1), and those of birds and viruses. If mobility can be said to be "central to what it is to be human" (Cresswell 2006: 1), the same may indeed be argued of what it is to be viral. The moratorium on transmissibility studies of H5N1 viruses was a moment in which concerns with certain types and patterns of movement, circulation and exchange – past, present and future – came rushing to the fore. These include those of viruses (e.g. from south-east Asia to Europe; between birds, pigs and people; out of laboratories), of people (e.g. from farm to farm; through livestock markets), of wild and domestic birds (e.g. along migratory flyways; through farms, markets and trade), and of data (e.g. from virologists to public health research-ers, or perhaps to terrorists).

At the heart of concerns for H5N1 is the potential for certain intersections between what I identify as two modes of mobility, that of viral *movement* and that of *mutability*. Whereas movement has been the core interest of mobility studies to date, mutability may represent a new category to be added to Urry's (2007) inventory of mobilities. Drawing on a "multispe-cies ethnography" (Kirksey and Helmreich 2010) of the surveillance of wild birds for avian influenza, I present two styles of practising disease that produce different versions of the mobile virus. First, the Great Britain Avian Influenza Wild Bird Survey practises H5N1 as an undesirable, unintended and perhaps unsuspected *travel companion* of wild birds, a virus that is *moved from place to place*. Second, preliminary efforts to understand the disease ecology of an outbreak in wild swans in 2008 practises H5N1 as genetic flux, as a virus that is *constantly mutating and being reconstituted* through interactions with host immune systems and other influenza viruses. I suggest that this second style of practising disease encourages us to attend to the mobile virus as *companion species*, as "constituted in intra- and interaction . . . consequent on a subject- and object-shaping dance of encounters" (Haraway 2008: 4). In other words, the virus is also *ontologically* mobile: a shifting set of relations rather than a fixed, well-bounded form (Law and Singleton 2005). Bringing these two forms of mobility together, I suggest that the virus may provide a useful figure for the constitutive relations or "intra-action" (Barad 2007) of those people/things that travel and those people/things that transport, contributing to a renewal of the figure of the passenger (Adey *et al.* 2012).

Virus as travel companion

> Mobility. 1a. *the ability to move or be moved; capacity for movement or change of place; movableness, portability.*
>
> (*Oxford English Dictionary Online 2012*)

As mobility studies attest, the twenty-first century is seemingly one of more and more movement, first in the sense of more people, technologies, services, capital, information and goods on the move, but also in the sense of an intensification of movement, moving faster and further, if not more frequently (Urry 2007). Viruses themselves are not motile, having no means of self-locomotion, and yet they are far from still. As evidenced by the spread of H5N1 in 2005, viruses can travel widely and quickly around the globe, hijacking other circulations of people, animals and materials. "An epidemic can only be an epidemic – and not simply 'endemic'," writes Thacker (2009: 149), drawing on Foucault (2007), "if the networks of trade and travel are correctly functioning".

Highly pathogenic avian influenzas (HPAI) have been reported in poultry for over a century, but were virtually unknown in wild birds until the arrival of H5N1 (Alexander and Brown 2009). First isolated from a farmed goose in China in 1996, H5N1 rapidly became an endemic disease of poultry in south-east Asia. The high mortality rate amongst those birds infected has been matched with mass "prophylatic" culling of survivors to prevent further spread of this highly contagious virus. Avian influenza viruses do not normally infect humans (Crawford 2002), so the disease gained further notoriety in 1997 with the first reported human cases in Hong Kong, 6 of the 18 cases being fatal. In 2005, H5N1 became a more global animal and public health concern as it spread into central Asia, the Black Sea region, and then Europe. In April of that year, several thousand wild birds died over several weeks on Qinghai Lake in central China, only the second reported instance of a HPAI causing mass death of wild birds (Artois *et al.* 2009). By now, migratory wild birds were being implicated in the spread of the virus, as was trade in poultry and captive wild birds, in the rush to identify "pathways" of viral movement (Sabirovic *et al.* 2006).

Given the impossibility of governing wild birds by exclusion or control, the strategy for dealing with this viral pathway has been one of security in the Foucauldian (2007) sense, that is of regulating and watching over circulations (Hinchliffe and Lavau 2013). In 2005, the surveillance of dead and live wild birds for certain avian influenza viruses became compulsory for member states of the European Union, as an "early detection and monitoring system for the presence of H5N1 HPAI and other AI viruses" (VLA 2010: 2). In a sense, this was a contemporary version of augury, of looking to bird ecologies and bodies to portend the present and foreshadow the future. It was also an investment in biosecurity as the regulation of a healthy inside (the nation state) and a diseased outside, with the threat of an H5N1 outbreak being one of incursion (Leach *et al.* 2010; Hinchliffe *et al.* 2012). In Great Britain, the requirement for wild bird surveillance produced the Avian Influenza Wild Bird Survey (AIWBS).

On a cold winter's morning, behind the raised bank of a wetland in East Anglia, there's an orderly collection of birds awaiting processing: ducks in plastic crates, and swans in pens, sorted by species. Despite the early hour and the frantic waving and wading required to capture the birds, this gathering of reserve managers, ornithologists, wildlife health officers and volunteers is also somewhat orderly – all kitted-out in wellington boots, waterproof trousers and jackets, white respiratory masks and blue rubber gloves. The birds, trapped during a routine morning feed, are not an altogether random sample. In 2006, ornithologists and wildlife health experts compared information on 573 wild bird species found in Britain – their migratory flyways, grouping behaviours, habitat preferences, biology, and likely pathogens – to produce an "Avian Influenza Incursion Analysis (through wild birds)" (Crick *et al.* 2006). Twenty-four bird species were categorized as at high risk of carrying AIs into Britain (particularly long-distance migratory species such as these swans and ducks), and particular places were deemed as at high risk of incursion (including this area in the east of England, with its high concentration of poultry holdings). These birds and places became targets for surveillance.

As the survey proceeds, each bird is carried by a volunteer handler from workstation to workstation, where it is identified by species, age and sex, then ringed around the ankle (if not already), weighed and measured, and finally swabbed. At the final table, Rachel, a wildlife health officer, takes buccal and cloacal samples from each bird. "Pochard. Ring number, GC37694. Age, four. Sex, male", intones Vicki, arriving at the table with a small, red, black and grey duck grasped firmly with both hands. Her words become data in the sheet marked "Avian influenza live healthy bird survey". As Vicki holds the duck belly-up, Rachel fiddles around its back end, inserting and twisting a cotton swab to collect faecal material. The swab goes back into a plastic vial, and a sticky barcode from the vial is transferred onto the survey sheet, in the space marked C for cloaca. Another vial, another swab, and this time Rachel holds open the small beak, reaches with the swab to the back of the throat, and then swipes along the tongue. The barcode from this swab goes in the space marked B for buccal. The handler and the bird move on, making way for the next handler and the next bird, and the next row on the survey sheet. And so it continues, pochards, Whooper swans, and Bewick's swans, as 157 birds pass along this production line, filling vial after vial with swabs containing bird secretions and pathological companions, viral or otherwise.

The birds are released back onto the wetlands, where they may over-winter amongst other avian visitors and residents, or continue their migratory journey elsewhere. The samples travel to a veterinary research institute near London. "[The AIWBS] has a precise objective of early warning of H5N1, of high pathogenic AI," says Ray, a virologist at the institute. "All we can say is, 'We found a virus in a bird at a particular time and location.'" Ray and his colleagues make an important distinction between birds as "hosts" and "carriers" of viruses. Some wild birds provide passage for H5N1 as carriers, that is asymptomatically, whereas others do so as hosts, as clinically diseased bodies that twitch, stumble, die.

The reception lab at the veterinary research institute resembles yet another production line. Workers in identical white lab coats sit side by side, registering and preparing incoming samples of various animals and their diseases. Today some visceral tissue samples from wild birds, taken at post-mortem, are to travel through a standardized screening process for the matrix gene, an indicator of influenza A, the sub-group to which avian influenzas belong. Moving through a series of laboratories, machines, tubes and media, these visceral tissues and any attendant pathological agents are progressively transformed, first into a suspension of inactivated cells and pathogenic particles, then into a cocktail of extracted RNA, into amplified viral DNA, and finally into a score that tells of the presence/absence of the matrix gene (and thus an influenza A virus). Like most days, there are no suspected positive samples today. These would then be subjected to confirmatory screening, testing for the H5 and N1 genes, and further characterisation.

Through the surveillant practices of the AIWBS, each bird sampled is confirmed or not as a host or carrier of highly pathogenic H5N1. Each detection provides early warning of a potential HPAI outbreak in a particular place, but they are also collectively plotted on distribution maps – those of Europe produced by the Community Reference Laboratory for Avian Influenza (VLA 2010), or worldwide maps produced by the World Organisation for Animal Health. Collectively assembled, these detections speak of a shifting frontline of viral movement, and can be used to identify certain bird species and their migratory flyways as more or less risky pathways for H5N1 incursion (Sabirovic and Clarke 2008). This style of surveillance is primarily concerned with presence/absence and the extensive distribution of H5N1 (e.g. is the virus present amongst migratory birds over-wintering in the wetlands of East Anglia, or does the area remain disease-free?), as well as the means through which the virus travels from place to place (e.g. in which bird species is the virus found, and by which pathway did the virus arrive in this place?).

So what kind of mobile virus is figured in these particular practices of knowing and managing avian influenza? H5N1 is a traveller, a pathological companion to migratory birds as they make their journeys across national borders. Whilst the bird may find itself at the mercy of the virus, the virus is also at the mercy of its carrier or its host, relying on the arrow of movement that is the "vector" in order to get around. There is a presumed "submission to the powers of the passage" (Adey *et al.* 2012: 18), in this case to the migratory behaviours of the host species, the individual bird's migratory history and preferences, the weather conditions. Through the sampling and screening practices of this survey, any active AI virus is isolated from bird bodies, tissues and genetic material, and even from other pathogenic agents that may be present. As a result, the virus seemingly travels solo, self-contained, a "monadic microbe, isolated and alone" (Attenborough 2011: 91). Through a spatial logic of regions (Mol and Law 1994; Law and Singleton 2005), this mode of surveillance produces a well-bounded virus that moves from body to body, and place to place. The threat that this mobile H5N1 virus represents is one of incursion, of moving into places and bodies it should not, such as disease-free zones or poultry. In the public debates that surrounded the moratorium in early 2012, these fears of incursion extended in other directions, to an unintended movement beyond the containment of civil laboratories, or into the clutches of bioterrorists, or even perhaps from ferrets into humans.

Virus as companion species

> Mobility. 2a. the ability or tendency to change easily or quickly; changeableness, instability; fickleness. Now chiefly literary.
>
> (Oxford English Dictionary Online 2012)

When the moratorium was declared, there had been 582 human cases of H5N1 reported to the World Health Organization since 2003, 343 being fatal (WHO 2012). With no evidence of human-to-human transmission to date, the big question is whether H5N1 can mutate to become more easily transmissible between humans, whilst retaining its high mortality rate (Fouchier *et al.* 2012; MacKenzie 2012). It was the imminent publication of two recent studies on improved transmissibility of laboratory-manipulated H5N1 in ferrets (considered a good model for humans) that prompted the moratorium. Fearing the use of this data for bioterrorism, there were calls for the results to be censored. Experts at a meeting convened by the WHO in February 2012 agreed that this risk was outweighed by the public health benefit of sharing information about the potential threat of naturally occurring mutations in H5N1. Whilst it was decided that the results should eventually be published in full (which they were later that year), the moratorium was nevertheless continued to allow public debate about the risks of the virus escaping the laboratory or being modified as a biological weapon.

Amidst these fears of an H5N1 outbreak, we encounter a second mobility of AI viruses, that of their mutability, which intersects concerns for the virus moving into particular places and bodies. This mutability takes two forms. First, influenza viruses have a high rate of genetic mutation, producing antigenic drift: a slow drift away from the virus's previous forms and away from a host's acquired immunity (Crawford 2002). A host's antibodies work by recognizing and blocking the virus's surface proteins or antigens (those eponymous, enumerated Hs and Ns) from hooking onto host cells. Cumulative changes to these antigens may allow the virus to evade a host's previously acquired immunity. So there is a constant, competitive dance going on between host antibodies and viral antigens, each under pressure to out-manoeuvre the other. In addition, and unique to influenza A viruses, is antigenic shift: a more abrupt change in genetic material, and thus protein structure, resulting from the reassortment of genes between different viruses infecting the same cell simultaneously. Reassortment may happen in co-infected bird cells, but perhaps more worryingly in those of pigs, which can be infected by both human and avian influenza viruses. Such was the origin of the infamous 1918 Spanish flu. So species meet, viruses and hosts, and in this "dance of encounters" (Haraway 2008: 4) or "intra-action" (Barad 2007), they are constantly made and remade.

Given this ongoing interplay and patterning, tidy taxonomic groupings such as "species" don't work well for viruses, neither do notions of arboreal descent (Hinchliffe 2004; Hird 2010). AI viruses are more loosely described as "clouds", or "clusters of genomes with unstable group boundaries" (Lowe 2010: 625), or, according to a virologist at the veterinary research institute, "AI soup". This mutability is figured in a second style of practising disease, one that attends to viral ecologies, the exchanges between viruses and with hosts, and the mutations and reassortments that may give rise to more highly pathogenic viral strains. This includes transmissibility studies of mutated AI viruses, but also another form of survey, that of the "AI soup" that circulates within an avian population. "The fundamentals of disease ecology are still unknown," admitted an epidemiologist at the veterinary research institute. "We're still not really clear whether wild birds are a proper reservoir for high path[ogenic viruses] . . . And how does prior exposure affect infection?"

There is a feeling amongst these researchers of a missed epidemiological opportunity following the Abbotsbury outbreak in 2008. Abbotsbury swannery, a rare example of a mute swan colony, is managed as a tourist attraction on the south-west coast of England. Amidst the reed beds and coastal woodlands, nests have been provided for the swans, sometimes within arm's reach of the path, but always within view. The swannery is renowned for opportunities for feeding swans and for close encounters with fluffy grey cygnets. However Abbotsbury is also now known for the H5N1 outbreak that resulted in the death of 11 infected birds, and the subsequent temporary lock-down and surveillance of wild birds and poultry within designated control and monitoring areas (NEEG 2008). There are still traces of this incident inscribed on the reserve, from the boot scrubber at the entrance, to the prominent display of antimicrobial hand gel in the feeding area.

These 11 birds are listed amongst the statistics of the AIWBS: 10 mute swans and 1 Canada goose, positive for HPAI H5N1. "The first bird [that tested positive] had a smashed leg," a reserve manager tells me. "Otherwise it looked fit. I was shocked that it was positive." At the time of the outbreak, there was hope that these birds might also figure in another AI survey, one that would look at the viral ecology within the swan colony. Indeed, a limited number of blood samples were taken from the swan population for serological testing, which provides a record of each bird's antibody production and thus viral encounters (albeit without being able to distinguish active from past infections). The lab processes are largely the same as those of the AIWBS, but deal with avian blood rather than tissues and secretions, and viral mixtures rather than isolated viruses. The sampling design differs, requiring large numbers of birds to account for heterogeneity within the population, thus being resource intensive. "I've wondered why there wasn't greater mortality [during the Abbotsbury outbreak]. H5N2 antibodies were found. Did this give resistance to H5N1?" wonders the reserve manager. What other viruses were circulating unseen in these animal bodies at the time? What exchanges may have been occurring or had occurred between birds and viruses, and between viruses? These are the questions the epidemiologist, reserve manager and others wished to have answered with a more comprehensive serological profiling of the Abbotsbury swans.

From transmissibility studies to serological surveys: these practices of knowing and managing avian influenza figure a differently mobile virus, a mutable virus, a shuffling, shifting virus. Operating through a spatial logic of fluidity (Mol and Law 1994; Law and Singleton 2005), these scientific practices produce an ontologically mobile virus. It is not just animal and human bodies that are "thrown into a chaotic and unpredictable molecular world filled with emergent yet unspecifiable risks" (Braun 2007: 7); so too are viruses. Disease ecology attends to viruses as unbounded, porous entities, drifting and shifting within a volatile world of molecular trade and circulation, with host antibodies, with other influenza viruses. AI viruses are gregarious, "nomadic" (Attenborough 2011), always moving and mutating, in the company of others. They are promiscuous, forming intimate couplings with other viruses, and being intimately touched by hosts. These are companion species (Haraway 2008), beings constantly made and remade in encounter, a becoming-with. "There is contagion at work in Haraway's species-meeting", Hird (2010: 36) notes. In the epidemiological imaginary, the threat represented by the mutable virus is one of incubation, the brewing of new viruses, whether in the laboratory or the bodies of animals – new viruses that are potentially more lethal to and transmissible amongst humans.

Going viral: a mobile metaphor?

I have argued that the 2012 moratorium on H5N1 transmissibility studies marked a moment of public attentiveness to the potential convergence of two forms of viral mobility: movement and mutability. Whether it takes the form of a virus mutating through the medium of birds, pigs, or ferrets, in the wild or in the laboratory, civil or otherwise; whether the virus is moved in the migration of birds, the illegal or illicit trade of birds and poultry, or by publication: these intersections between mobility and mutability are generally feared as destructive to human and animal lives. I have explored the moveable virus (travel companion to birds) and the mutable virus (companion species to birds, viruses and others) through two examples of knowing and managing disease in wild birds. The Avian Influenza Wild Bird

Survey is on the lookout for specific viruses on the move, and the risk of incursion. The preliminary disease ecology survey of Abbotsbury swans was on the lookout for viral mixtures and mutability, and the risks (and perhaps immunological benefits) of incubation. Its version of avian influenza is suggestive of a more "fluid" object, a "mutable mobile" that is produced through shifting sets of relations between viruses, bodies, samples and many other entities (de Laet and Mol 2000; Law and Singleton 2005). Rather than making a case for one style of practising disease over the other, my interest is in their encounters, and what they may produce.

So what might it be to think mobility through a virus, and might we generate a productive interference between viral movement and mutability, between travel companion and companion species? In this, we may take our lead from Merriman (Adey *et al.* 2012), who reminds us of the etymological journey of the "passenger". In the fifteenth and sixteenth centuries, "passenger" marked both a person that travelled *and* a person or thing that provided passage. The virus may provide a helpful metaphor in rethinking the figure of the passenger as "an emergent torsion of the active and the passive; the deliberative and the acquiescent" (Adey *et al.* 2012: 18). To "go viral" already signifies an ever intensifying movement and proliferation by parasitizing existing modes of circulation. But viruses mutate as they move; they are carried by animal bodies and carry genetic traces of these bodies and viral exchanges. They are simultaneously transported and transporter, borne and born. Might this ontological mobility, this "intra-action" (Barad 2007), also be held within the phrase "going viral"?

Acknowledgements

This research was supported by an ESRC research award 'Biosecurity Borderlands' RES-062-23-1882, as well as the generosity of those people and institutions who gave access to their work places and practices.

Bibliography

Adey, P., Bissell, D., McCormack, D., and Merriman, P. (2012) "Profiling the passenger: mobilities, identities, embodiments", *Cultural Geographies*, 19: 1–25.

Alexander, D. J. and Brown, I. H. (2009) "History of highly pathogenic avian influenza", *Scientific and Technical Review of the International Office of Epizootics*, 28: 19–38.

Anon. (2012) "Scientists behind Armageddon flu virus suspend their research because it 'could put world at risk of catastrophic pandemic'", *Daily Mail*, 23 January 2012. Available online at www.dailymail.co.uk/news/worldnews/article-2089941/Scientists-Armageddon-flu-virus-suspend-research-world-risk-catastrophic-pandemic.html#ixzz1pC0KyNS5 (accessed 12 February 2012).

Artois, M., Bicout, D., *et al.* (2009) "Outbreaks of highly pathogenic avian influenza in Europe: the risks associated with wild birds", *Scientific and Technical Review of the International Office of Epizootics*, 28(1): 69–92.

Attenborough, F. (2011) "The monad and the nomad: medical microbiology and the politics and possibilities of the mobile microbe", *Cultural Geographies*, 18: 91–114.

Barad, K. (2007) *Meeting the Universe Halfway: Quantum Physics and the Entanglement of Matter and Meaning*, Durham: Duke University Press.

Braun, B. (2007) "Biopolitics and the molecularization of life", *Cultural Geographies*, 14: 6–28.

Crawford, D. (2002) *Invisible Enemies: A Natural History of Viruses*, Oxford: Oxford University Press.

Cresswell, T. (2006) *On the Move: Mobility in the Modern Western World*, London: Routledge.

Crick, H. Q. P., Atkinson, P. W., *et al.* (2006) *Avian Influenza Incursion Analysis (Through Wild Birds)*, a report of the British Trust for Ornithology, Wildfowl & Wetlands Trust and Veterinary Laboratories Agency to the Department for Environment, Food and Rural Affairs, Thetford, Norfolk: British

Trust for Ornithology. Available online at www.bto.org/sites/default/files/u196/downloads/rr448. pdf (accessed 3 March 2010).

de Laet, M. and Mol, A. (2000) "The Zimbabwe bush pump: mechanics of a fluid technology", *Social Studies of Science*, 30: 225–63.

Foucault, M. (2007) *Security, Territory, Population. Lectures at the Collège de France 1977–1978*, Basingstoke: Palgrave Macmillan.

Fouchier, R. A. M., Garcia-Sastre, A., *et al.* (2012) "Pause on avian flu transmission research", *Science Express*, 20 January 2012. Available online at www.sciencemag.org/content/early/2012/01/20/science.1219412.abstract (accessed 12 February 2012).

Haraway, D. J. (2008) *When Species Meet*, Minneapolis: University of Minnesota Press.

Hinchliffe, S. (2004) "Viruses", in S. Harrison, S. Pile and N. Thrift (eds) *Patterned Ground: Entanglements of Nature and Culture*, London: Reaktion Books.

Hinchliffe, S., Allen, J., Lavau, S., Bingham, N. and Carter, S. (2013) "Biosecurity and the topologies of infected life: from borderlines to borderlands", *Transactions of the Institute of British Geographers*, 38(4): 531–43.

Hinchliffe, S. and Lavau, S. (2013) "(Non) integrated circuits: the ecologies of knowing and securing life", *Environment and Planning D: Society and Space*, 31(2): 259–74.

Hird, M. (2010) "Meeting with the microcosmos", *Environment and Planning D: Society and Space*, 28: 36–9.

Kirksey, S. E. and Helmreich, S. (2010) "The emergence of multispecies ethnography", *Cultural Anthropology*, 25: 545–76.

Law, J. and Singleton, V. (2005) "Object lessons", *Organization*, 12(3): 331–55.

Leach, M., Scoones, I. and Stirling, A. (2010) "Governing epidemics in an age of complexity: narratives, politics and pathways to sustainability", *Global Environmental Change*, 20: 369–77.

Lowe, C. (2010) "Viral clouds: becoming H5N1 in Indonesia", *Cultural Anthropology*, 25: 625–49.

MacKenzie, D. (2012) "Doomsday flu decision time: the story so far", *New Scientist*, 6 February 2012. Available online at www.newscientist.com/article/dn21432-doomsday-flu-decision-time-the-story-so-far.html (accessed 12 February 2012).

Mol, A. and Law, J. (1994) "Regions, networks and fluids: anaemia and social topology", *Social Studies of Science*, 24: 641–71.

National Emergency Epidemiology Group (2008) *Highly Pathogenic Avian Influenza II5N1 in Wild Swans in Dorset*, Animal Health, Department for Environment, Food and Rural Affairs, and Veterinary Laboratories Agency. Available online at http://archive.defra.gov.uk/foodfarm/farmanimal/diseases/atoz/ai/documents/epireport-080212.pdf (accessed 20 July 2011).

Oxford English Dictionary Online (2012) "Mobility, n.1". Available online at www.oed.com/view/Entry/120494?rskey=Ho7FVa&result=1&isAdvanced=false#eid (accessed 25 February 2012).

Sabirovic, M. and Clarke, G. (2008) *Highly Pathogenic Avian Influenza – H5N1: Recent Developments in the EU and the Likelihood of the Introduction into Great Britain by Wild Birds*, Department for Environment, Food and Rural Affairs: London. Available online at http://archive.defra.gov.uk/foodfarm/farmanimal/diseases/monitoring/documents/qra-h5n1-wildbirds081029.pdf (accessed 20 November 2011).

Sabirovic, M., Hall, S., Wilesmith, J., Coulson, N. and Landeg, F. (2006) *HPAI H5N1 Situation in Europe and Potential Risk Factors for the Introduction of the Virus to the United Kingdom*, Department for Environment, Food and Rural Affairs: London. Available online at www.elika.net/datos/articulos/Archivo247/DEFRA_IAAP_ER06.pdf (accessed 13 December 2011).

Thacker, E. (2009) "The shadows of atheology: epidemics, power and life after Foucault", *Theory, Culture & Society*, 26: 134–52.

Urry, J. (2007) *Mobilities*, Polity Press: Cambridge.

Veterinary Laboratory Agency (2010) *Annual Report on Surveillance for Avian Influenza in Wild Birds in the EU in 2008*, European Commission, Directorate-General for Health & Consumers, Veterinary Laboratories Agency. Available online at http://ec.europa.eu/food/animal/diseases/controlmeasures/avian/res_surv_ai_wb_annual_08_en.pdf (accessed 14 December 2011).

World Health Organization (2012) "Cumulative number of confirmed human cases for avian influenza A (H5N1) reported to WHO 2003–2012", 20 January 2012. Available online at www.who.int/influenza/human_animal_interface/EN_GIP_20120120CumulativeNumberH5N1cases.pdf (accessed 24 February 2012).

29

Postcards

Esther Milne

The crucial function played by mobility in the efficient distribution of information has long been recognised by the users of postal networks. Writing in 1788, Hannah More (1745–1833) complains to a friend that the recently invented British Mail Coach fails to connect her with the news of contemporary political and cultural life:

> Letters and newspapers, now that they travel in coaches like gentlemen and ladies, come not within ten miles of my hermitage. And while other fortunate provincials are studying the *World* [a daily newspaper] and its ways ... I am obliged to be contented with village vices, petty iniquities and vulgar sins.
>
> *(in Lewis et al. 1961: 264)*

Metaphors of transportation and travel, of arrival and departure, of traversing distance and imagining presence define the epistolary register. 'More than kisses, letters mingle souls for thus, friends absent speak' as John Donne put it (1633: 180). Indeed, the letter as a vehicle is itself a richly historical conceit of representation: letters carry meaning, convey news, circulate and are delivered. It is this generic affordance that makes the letter such a poignant choice for literary fiction, as Janet Altman explains: 'an entire plot tradition, the novel of seduction through letters, is built around the letter's power to suggest both presence and absence, to decrease and increase distance' (1982: 15).

In this context one could refer to the eighteenth-century epistolary novel *Les Liaisons Dangereuses*, since the distributive power of the network is a generative force of desire, treachery and loss. Of his correspondence with his lover, Madame de Tourvel, Valmont observes that 'my letters themselves are a little *casus belli*: not content with leaving them unanswered, she refuses to receive them' (Laclos 1782: 81). The flows of the postal system have also been explored in literary works not considered strictly to conform to conventions of the epistolary genre. *Dracula*, for example, traces the rapid circulation of information across a multiplicity of socio-technical platforms such as telegrams, letters, diaries and the phonograph to map the traffic of data and bodies (Stoker 1897). Similarly, in *The Crying of Lot 49* Pynchon demonstrates how postal codes function figuratively and materially in the construction of a national communication infrastructure (1966).

But perhaps of all postal media it is the postcard that clearly draws attention to the conditions of mobility through both material and symbolic practices. In particular, mobility studies have focused on the function of the postcard as a tourism object. Celia Lury, for example, deploys the postcard as a means to engage with emerging debates about 'portable cultures', a rejoinder to tourism configured as the 'unity of place and culture' (1997: 75). Instead, Lury urges researchers to understand objects such as souvenirs and postcards as more than 'the traveller's extended baggage' (76) since these material artefacts take on a life of their own, often circulating independently of the tourist. Similarly, Crispin Thurlow, Adam Jaworski and Virpi Ylänne question the reification of place in critical tourism by situating their postcard survey within the 'new mobilities paradigm' (2010: 92) (see also Wilken 2011). For these authors, the material and symbolic registers of postcard communication coalesce at the level of performativity. In other words, through the acts of selecting, composing and sending a postcard, tourists are 'rehearsing "being a tourist"' (2010: 113). The literature of tourism itself is, of course, keenly aware of how the postcard distributes images across borders and cultures (e.g. Edwards 1996; Robinson and Ploner, forthcoming).

In general, however, such research examines the postcard as an isolated media technology. Operating as a singular and distinct event of autonomous affect, the postcard appears severed from historical media flows. This chapter, therefore, extends current debates by locating the mobility of postcard communication within the trajectories of postal history. Specifically, it examines historical and contemporary settings of postcard circulation across three key modes of distribution: public privacy, mail art, and postal fiction. In so doing, the analysis is underpinned by an interest in technologies of presence and intimacy (Gumbrecht 2004; Hjorth and Richardson 2009; Milne 2010) and I use the phrase 'affective geographies' to capture the complexity and agility of affect as a terrain of academic debate where, to provide an iconic example, the category of emotion becomes a problematic point of departure (Terada 2001; Parikka 2012). Geographies operate simultaneously as matter and signification; territory and map, so the phrase, therefore, gestures to the ways in which affect is articulated though the content and distribution of postcard media.

Public privacy and the invention of the postcard

When new technologies of communication are introduced, the cultural response is often one of fear and incredulity (Marvin 1988; Sconce 2000; Gitelman 2006). During the period following the invention of the postcard, disquiet was expressed about the transformation this new media would bring to public and private life. What seemed particularly troubling to correspondents was the fact that postcards circulated without the cover of an envelope. This socio-material fact led commentators to worry that postal clerks or servants might read the postcard before its intended recipient. An etiquette manual of the day advises that 'a private communication on an open card is almost insulting to your correspondent' (Anon. 1890: 80). And an 1870 newspaper warned of the 'absurdity of writing private information on an open piece of card-board, that might be read by half a dozen persons before it reached its destination' (in Carline 1971: 55). For the inventor of the postcard, Heinrich von Stephan, it was precisely the public nature of this new form of communication that deemed it worthy of acceptance. In 1865, as Postmaster General of the German Empire, von Stephan addressed delegates at the Austro-German Postal Conference and presented his idea for epistolary reform. The postcard or 'open post-sheet' (*offenes Postblatt*), he argued, would help to foster a particular kind of 'open' communication that, in the 1860s, was not provided to the public sphere by the existing mail technologies. As he put it:

> The present form of the letter does not . . . allow of sufficient simplicity and brevity for a large class of communications. It is not simple enough, because note-paper has to be selected and folded, envelopes obtained and closed, and stamps affixed. It is not brief enough, because, if a letter be written, convention necessitates something more than the bare communication. This is irksome both to the sender and the receiver.
>
> *(in Staff 1979: 44)*

Due, in part, to fears expressed about the loss of epistolary privacy, it was not until 1869 that the Postcard was introduced by the Austrian Postal Department and, even then, it was thought the public required careful instructions when using this new technological form. Announcing the introduction of postcards, the 1869 Post Office Regulation warned that:

> The post Department will not be responsible for the contents of the message. Neverthe-less the post offices are instructed, similar to an order existing for letters that carry offensive remarks in the address . . . to exclude postcards likewise from transportation and delivery, if obscenities, libellous remarks or other punishable acts are found on the cards.
>
> *(in Staff 1979: 84)*

The Austrian Postal Department was indeed prescient in its advice to correspondents about the legal consequences of using this highly mobile media for sending certain messages through the post. In the United Kingdom, where the postcard was introduced in 1870, courts were regularly asked to decide libel cases on the basis of this mode of communication. In general, for a cause of action to be brought under libel or defamation law, the relevant content must be accessible to a third party other than that supposedly libelled in the material under question. Although this situation is possible in epistolary communication where a letter may be read by a number of people, the potential audience for a postcard is, by definition, significantly broader. This would seem to be the motivation for an advertisement that appeared in *The Times* newspaper in 1870, which read:

> Anonymous Postal Cards FIFTY POUNDS REWARD – Whereas several leading West-End firms complain to me respecting certain postal cards received by them, containing malicious innuendoes and purporting to emanate from my office – The above reward will be paid by me for such INFORMATION as shall lead to the conviction of the writer of said spurious and infamous productions.
>
> *(in Langbridge 1974: 13)*

While this notice is directed at possible libel in relation to the commercial sector, a number of the cases were brought on personal grounds. In 1871, for example, a jury awarded damages of thirty pounds against a man for libelling his brother-in-law on a postcard. The defendant addressed the card by use of the term 'Blue Beard' (the plaintiff had been married before) and adding 'Your unmanly conduct to my sister is known to me. It shall be known to the world at large if you do not reform you coward' (*Manchester Evening News*, 1871: 4). A similar case concerned an estranged couple in which the husband, Walter Smith, sent libellous postcards to his wife's mother and father accusing them of causing the breakdown of the marriage through their treachery. In these postcards he called the behaviour of their daughter, his wife, 'disgraceful' and described the family as liars. Nevertheless, he defended his action by asserting he had written the cards only to effect a reconciliation with his estranged wife. In finding for the plaintiffs, the Judge drew attention to the manner by which the postcards circulated, publicly remarking that if it really was Mr Smith's aim 'to win back his wife's love' then it was 'curious' he chose to write what he did 'on postcards to be sent to a little village where everyone was only too willing to listen to scandal, and where every postcard that passed through the local post office seemed to become known to every one in the village' (*The Register*, December 13, 1923: NP).

Perhaps the judiciary should have heeded warnings in the press about the capacity afforded by postcard communication for the rapacious and public dissemination of data. An editorial in the *Preston Chronicle* of 1870 called on the British Government to legislate against the introduction of the postcard for personal communication because of its 'capabilities for mischief' through 'slanderous, indecent and awkward communications'. Specifically, the column argues that the new cards should permit only printed matter to travel by postcard because, presumably, this would limit the dangers of libel. Personal, handwritten messages on postcards represented greater scope for defamation because this could be committed through the use of strategically worded code:

> The most destructive slanders and the most abominable aggravations may be couched in terms which only a few persons would understand, and for those few to be communicated with through the medium of the card may suit the purposes of an anonymous libeller.
>
> (*The Preston Chronicle* 1870: 5)

Rather than to destroy privacy, as commentators fear, evidence such as this suggests that users of postcards find inventive ways to communicate highly personal or intimate messages across these public signifying systems. As Tom Phillips demonstrates, one of the most popular cultural uses of postcards has been for courtship, and couples – who are keen to avoid the prying eyes of parents, siblings or servants – discovered 'the final mode of obtaining privacy was a code'. Such strategies of secrecy, he explains, include mirror writing and use of shorthand or acronyms (2000: 13–14). Similarly, as Paul Fussell has found, wartime correspondents developed novel ways of communicating without attracting the censor's attention (1979). In this way, then, the postcard plays a crucial step in the emergence of what has been called 'Public Privacy' (Kitzmann 2004; Senft 2008; Berlant 2008; Boyd 2010; Hjorth 2011; Lovink 2011; Milne 2011). In her work on social media, Danah Boyd, for example, coins the term 'social steganography' to explain how Facebook and Twitter participants 'hide in plain sight' through the use of coded song lyrics to communicate particular messages to a select audience, while their posts remain incomprehensible or, at least, innocuous to others. For Lauren Berlant the 'intimate public' is a commodified sphere of feminine confession, an intricate platform for articulating what she calls 'the unfinished business of sentimentality' (2008: 2). And Geert Lovink argues such 'everyday disclosures' construct the 'private in the public' through self-surveillance (2011: INC).

Having provided a historical context for the affective geographies of postcard communication, the next section explores some contemporary aesthetic responses to questions of public privacy and mobility.

Mail art

As Jacques Derrida has illustrated, a compelling feature of postcard communication is the enigmatic identity of the addressee. In his 'epistolary simulacrum' Derrida sends a series of postcards to an unknown recipient, all the while using the second person overtly and with palpable cryptic relish 'and when I call you my love, my love, is it you I am calling or my love? You, my love, is it you I thereby name, is it to you that I address myself?' (Derrida 1987: 8). In critical theory, it is, of course, axiomatic to state that the recipient of the poststructuralist postal system is 'indeterminate'. But this perhaps elides too glibly the semantic and affective power of that form of address. Without the desire to discover the identity of 'you', epistolary discourse, mail art, and arguably, most of Twitter, would not function. Certainly the now quite famous mail art project *PostSecret* is underpinned by a desire, simultaneously, to share and protect the identity of both sender and recipient of the distributed secrets. Before outlining the genesis and practices of *PostSecret*, it is worth mentioning briefly some key sites and moments within mail-art history.

As an aesthetic and activist movement, mail art has a complex trajectory. In relation to the image, for example, one could include in the genre the development of pictorial envelopes during the 1840s and the introduction of the picture postcard in the late nineteenth century. So too could one mention Marcel Duchamp, who used postcards as 'readymades, distributing his ideas through the postal service' (Bell 1981); or the date painting and postcards sent through the mail by Japanese conceptual artist On Kawara (Denizot 1991). But in general the key figure is usually identified as Ray Johnson and his connection with the emergence of the New York Correspondence School in 1962. During 1970 Johnson curated a mail-art 'Correspondance' exhibition at the Whitney Museum of Art. Johnson called for entries – 'letters, postcards, drawings and objects' – to be sent, promising that everything received by the Whitney would be exhibited (Held 2005: 96). The show received mixed reviews, in part because of assumptions about the critical tensions that were revealed between exhibiting in a fixed gallery space and utilising the mobility of a postal network. Writing in *Artforum*, for example, one critic remarked there was an inherent problem with exhibiting 'a living thing in flight' while endeavouring 'to pin it down and make a museum display of it' (in Held 2005: 96–97).

The tensions identified by this critic point to some of the underlying historical and contemporary debates about the definitions and lineage of mail art. Johnson's original stipulation, that all contributions sent through the mail must be exhibited was, for some practitioners, a 'sacrosanct mail art concept'. This criterion, however, became a controversial turning point in mail-art history, as John Held, a key figure in the archival research on mail art, has documented. In 1984 The Franklin Furnace art network in New York mounted an exhibition called 'Mail Art Then and Now'. One of the contributors complained when he realised his work had not been included, writing an open letter to the curator, Ronny Cohen, pointing out that the 'primary aspect of mail art exhibitions' is that everything received is exhibited:

> **No rejections** is synonymous with mail-art, especially as the work is given and not returned, and you have arbitrarily decided to reject and edit. That you have decided to disregard this concept marks you as no friend to mail art or to mail artists and denies perhaps the most unique and appealing feature of this universal movement.
>
> *(in Held 2005: 103; emphasis in original)*

During the course of the following decades, debates about the definitions, scope and remit of mail art have continued apace alongside regular exhibitions and calls for participation. In 2009, for example, well-known mail-artist Ed Varney curated a large-scale international exhibition entitled 'Mail Art Olympix'. Exhibitors were invited to submit pieces by post that met the criteria in one of three aesthetic categories: 'self portrait', 'artiststamps' and 'mani-festo'. The resulting exhibitions displayed work by 340 artists from 41 different countries. For Varney, receipt of the piece and the materiality of the envelope were key aspects of the exhibition. He comments that 'the best part of this project was opening the envelopes [and the] imagination, cleverness, skill, quality, and generosity of Mail Artists'. For Varney, 'it was incredibly exciting to receive so many wonderful art works, often in colourful decorated envelopes' (Varney 2009).

A similar preoccupation with definitions framed the mail art exhibition of the New York art collective Hyperallergic. Entitled 'Presents: Three Months of Mail Art' and co-curated by Kate Wadkins and Hrag Vartanian, the show invited participants to send mail-art contributions in diverse media forms including sculpture, installation, video and works on paper. The exhibition ran in June 2011 and produced a zine catalogue which was not available for personal collection but in the spirit of the show was only to be mailed to contributors. Emphasising how materiality and public privacy underpin postcard communication, Hrag Vartanian noted of the submissions that

> Strangely, the beauty of postcards is their open anonymity . . . you're not expected to provide a return address – though many of the postcard artists curiously did – and at the same time you know full well that the mail carrier or anyone else will be able to read them during the course of their journey. There are no secrets in postcards, not big ones anyway, yet they can still feel very personal.
>
> *(Wadkins and Vartanian 2011)*

Secrets – their suppression, conveyance and transgression – are, of course, the conceptual motivation behind Frank Warren's *PostSecret* project. This work began in November 2004, when Warren distributed 3,000 postcards by handing them out at subway stations and art galleries, as well as by inserting them into library books. Warren asked people to participate anonymously by inscribing a postcard with a secret and mailing it to him at an address in Maryland, USA. 'Your secret', stated his instructions, 'might be a regret, fear, betrayal, desire, confession, or childhood humiliation'. Participants were invited to 'reveal *anything* – as long as it is true and you have never shared it with anyone before' and instructed to 'be brief. Be legible. Be creative' (Warren 2005: 1). This invitation elicited contributions internationally sent to him on a diverse range of homemade postcard media such as photographs, wedding invitations and old shopping lists. During its eight-year history *Post-Secret* has produced an estimated 500,000 secret messages which have been displayed and distributed across art exhibitions; four printed edited book collections; lecture tours; a website network; and an iPhone application. Launched in mid-2011, this service provided another avenue for the submission of secrets and became one of the highest selling applications through the Apple Store. Its focus on 'absolute anonymity' was, explains Warren, the reason for its relatively short life. In January 2012 it ceased operation due to complaints made to Apple and the FBI about offensive and 'gruesome' content being uploaded (Warren).

Illustrative examples of secrets sent to *PostSecret* include the following:

> I don't eat dinner at your parents because their house is filthy (accompanied by an image of a table setting in which a dead fly lies upon the plate).
>
> *(Warren 2005: 75)*

I show pictures of my feet to a man online so he'll buy me stuff (the text is accompanied by photographs of feet, one pair bare; one pair wearing high heel shoes).

(Warren 2005: 147)

I'm terrified of not existing (inscription appears on a plain, grey postcard).

(Warren 2005: 41)

In mail art, then, the postcard functions as a highly mobile site for the affective register. We now consider a related, yet distinct, socio-aesthetic category of postcard communication that draws together a number of the formal and discursive properties so far discussed.

Postal fiction: 'A Post Card Novelette'

During the Franco-Prussian War (1870–1871) postcards and letters were transported by balloon out of France. Because Prussia had isolated Paris, there were few viable modes of communication in operation between Paris and the rest of France, or between France and the outside world. The balloon offered a way of conveying both information and bodies, having previously been used successfully to transport passengers on a number of occasions (Staff 1979: 50). Across the Channel the carriage of postcards by balloon was the pretext for an article published in *Vanity Fair* dated December 1870 and titled 'A Post Card Novelette', in which the author discusses communication by balloon, postcard composition and, interestingly, imagines a new form of epistolary fiction.

'A Post Card Novelette' is divided into three parts. The first part, 'Postcard to the Editor', an extract from which appears below, functions in a similar manner to the 'preface' that usually introduces and frames a published collection of letters:

> Having received a 'complete pack' of postal cards from a Parisian acquaintance of mine who has arrived in his country from Paris part of the journey having been accomplished by balloon, I venture to submit the contents of the 'card' duly numbered to the Editor of *Vanity Fair*, who may discover in this curious narrative, so succinctly and microscopically penned, the elements, at least, of a modern novel of interest. . . . A greedy devourer of romance may in this way carry several sets of the newest novels of the season in his breast pocket . . . there is no assignable limit to the advantages that may result from this mode of supplying the public with fiction, for which I therefore bet to claim credit as the greatest literary discovery of the period. As I do not myself write in a microscopic hand, my card is full.
>
> (Vanity Fair, 24 December 1870: 257)

Following the 'preface' are two sections that transcribe the text 'found' on the postcards. For this reason they assume the voice of the fictional correspondent, the 'Parisian acquaintance'. 'A Post Card Novelette' also draws on what has been called the 'editor-publisher figure' of epistolary fiction, often used to provide a detailed explanation of how this document came to be published. As Altman comments, 'the editor-publisher figure, by having one foot planted in the world of the correspondents and one in the world of the reader, seemingly guarantees the authenticity as well as the original privacy of the transmitted text' (1982: 202). In epistolary fiction, effects such as these are often complemented by footnotes or other 'asides' which issue from an authoritative voice who comments, extra-diegetically, on the letters. At one point in this 'Post Card Novelette', for example, the editor-publisher figure intervenes by way of a footnote to discuss certain characteristics of the correspondent's handwriting.

Nevertheless, despite these similarities between epistolary fiction and this instance of postcard fiction, the author identifies several key differences between letters and postcards. In the first place, the author notes that the small writing surface of the postcard encourages 'microscopic' handwriting. As postal historians have observed, the narrow confines of the postcard can sometimes contain *more* rather than less writing. There is the story, for example, of the American correspondent who managed to transcribe a Presidential address – all 15,000 words – onto one side of a postcard. This author's next effort was to squeeze 18 columns of *The Boston Post* newspaper onto a postcard. Other postal feats include an 1890 exhibition at Düsseldorf where a postcard was displayed carrying the transcript of the first three books of the *Odyssey*. As Carline notes:

> for some reason, hard to fathom, many people had this urge to accept the postcard's chal-
> lenge and turn its apparent victory over wordiness into a defeat. Far from encouraging
> brevity, they vied with one another to see how much could be crammed on to a postcard.
>
> *(1971: 60)*

Although a degree of loquacity might be sustained in postcard communication, according to the author of the *Vanity Fair* 'novelette', this is achieved at some cost. The editor assumes the correspondent to be a woman but admits that this assessment may be inaccurate for 'one disadvantage of this microscopic style of writing is that it destroys all character in the callig-raphy' (*Vanity Fair*, 24 December 1870: 257). This evaluation is based on the assumption that character, individuality and identity are qualities that can be expressed by handwriting. As Friedrich Kittler has shown, such a belief is historically and technologically contingent, dependent on (amongst other factors) a reading practice in which certain textual forms are taken as signs for the individual (1990).

The microscopic hand of the correspondent does not render the message unreadable. The difficulty of confidently determining character from the calligraphy does not hide all connec-tions between the text and its author. Indeed, far from being obscure, these 'postcards' carry an eminently readable yet complex narrative, 'succinctly and microscopically penned', of bal-loon travels, the Parisian siege and England's colonial fiat. Nevertheless, this postcard fiction suggests that there is a point at which handwriting loses its status as an authentic link to nature and identity – as 'the essence of man', in Heidegger's words (in Kittler 1990: 198). That 'point', in this example at least, seems to occur when the handwriting becomes uniform and standard and the flourishes of 'penmanship' are no longer discernible. These observations provide evi-dence for the view that the postcard standardises communication in an unprecedented fashion (Siegert 1997). This view, however, is challenged by, among others, epistolary scholars Julia Gillen and Nigel Hall. In their ethnographic study of the 'vernacular literacies' (2010: 23) of postcard collectors, Hall and Gillen demonstrate how the distribution of intimacy is made possible though the material affordances of the media. As we have seen during this chapter, the authors of postcard correspondence often work against the constraints of uniformity and standardisation, producing material and symbolic intensities of affect.

Conclusion

The postcard functions as a liminal object; traversing the public sphere, it articulates moments of intimacy and privacy. Although ostensibly a banal media form, its history reveals it as a site for expressions of gravitas and anger, demonstrated by the legislative and legal attention it receives. Moreover, the postcard has proved a particularly resilient technology appearing within diverse aesthetic and symbolic registers. Networked postcard communication, for example, reconfigures mail art distributed across platforms of social media. Contrary to socio-technical fears, the invention of the postcard does not destroy privacy but, importantly, nor does it render invalid the desire for secrecy and intimacy. Indeed, as this chapter has argued, postcards are the material trace of affective geographies.

References

Altman, J. (1982) *Epistolarity: Approaches to a Form*, Columbus: Ohio State University Press.

Anon. (1982, 1890) *Don't: A Manual of Mistakes and Improprieties*, Kent: Pryor Publications.

Bell, D. (1981) *Contemporary Art Trends 1960–1980: A Guide to Sources*, Metuchen, NJ: Scarecrow Press.

Berlant, L. (2008) *The Female Complaint: The Unfinished Business of Sentimentality in American Culture*, Durham: Duke University Press.

Boyd, D. (2010) 'Social Steganography: Learning to Hide in Plain Sight', available online at http://bit.ly/iBQwam (accessed 19 August 2013).

Carline, R. (1971) *Pictures in the Post: The Story of the Picture Postcard and its Place in the History of Popular Art*, Folsom, PA: Deltiologists of America.

Chansanchai, A. (2012) 'PostSecret iphone App Closed', available online at www.today.com/tech/postsecret-iphone-app-closed-due-threatening-pornographic-content-118203 (accessed 19 August 2013).

de Laclos, Choderlos (1782, 1961) *Les Liaisons dangereuses*, trans. P. W. K. Stone, London: Penguin.

Denizot, R. (1991) *On Kawara Catalog*, Frankfurt: Museum für moderne Kunst.

Derrida, J. (1987) *The Post Card: From Socrates to Freud and Beyond*, trans. A. Bass, Chicago: University of Chicago Press.

Donne, John (1633, 1968) 'To Sir Henry Wotton' in H. J. C. Grierson (ed.) *The Poems of John Donne*, London: Oxford University Press.

Edwards, E. (1996) 'Postcards – Greetings from Another World' in Tom Selwyn (ed.) *The Tourist Image: Myths and Myth Making in Tourism*, New York: John Wiley, 197–221.

Fussell, Paul (1979) *The Great War and Modern Memory*, London: Oxford University Press.

Gillen, J. and Hall, N. (2010) 'Any Mermaids? Tracing Early Postcard Mobilities' in Monika Büscher, John Urry and Katian Witchger (eds) *Mobile Methods*. New York: Routledge, 20–35.

Gitelman, L. (2006) *Always Already New: Media, History and the Data of Culture*, Cambridge, MA: The MIT Press.

Gumbrecht, H. U. (2004) *Production of Presence: What Meaning Cannot Convey*, Stanford: Stanford University Press.

Held, J. (2005) 'The Mail Art Exhibition: Personal Worlds to Cultural Strategies' in Annmarie Chandler and Norie Neumark (eds) *At a distance: precursors to art and activism on the Internet*, Cambridge, MA: The MIT Press, 89–114.

Hjorth, L. and Richardson, I. (2009) 'The Waiting Game: Complicating Notions of (Tele) Presence and Gendered Distraction in Casual Mobile Gaming', *Australian Journal of Communication*, volume: 35, issue: 7, 23–35.

Hjorth, Larissa *et al.* (2011) Video and photography exhibition, available online at http://bit.ly/tspPXc (accessed 29 February 2012).

Kittler, F. (1990) *Discourse Networks 1800/1900*, trans. Michael Metteer, Stanford: Stanford University Press.

Kitzmann, A. (2004) *Saved From Oblivion: Documenting the Daily from Diaries to Web Cams*, New York: Peter Lang.

Langbridge, R. H. (1974) *Life in the 1870s: Seen through Advertisements in 'The Times'*, London: Times Books.

Lewis, W. S., Smith, R. A. and Bennett, C. H. (eds) (1961) *Horace Walpole's Correspondence*, vol. 31, New Haven: Yale University Press, 264.

Lovink, Geert (2011) 'Unlike Us: Understanding Social Media Monopolies and their Alternatives', Research Project, Institute of Network Cultures, available online at http://bit.ly/qyoGVd (accessed 29 February 2012).

Lury, C. (1997) 'The Objects of Travel' in C. Rojek and J. Urry (eds) *Touring Cultures: Transformations of Travel and Theory*, London: Routledge, 75–95.

Marvin, C. (1988) *When Old Technologies Were New: Thinking about Electric Communication in the Late Nineteenth Century*, New York: Oxford University Press.

Milne, E. (2010) *Letters, Postcards, Email: Technologies of Presence*, London: Routledge.

—— (2011) 'Historical Provocations: Postal Presence, Intimate Absence and Public Privacy', *Proceedings of the International Society for Presence Research Annual Conference*, Edinburgh Napier University, available online at http://bit.ly/wByAFi (accessed 29 February 2012).

Parikka, Jussi (2012) *What is Media Archaeology?* Cambridge: Polity.

Phillips, T. (2000) *The Postcard Century: Cards and their Messages*, New York: Thames & Hudson.

Pynchon, T. (1966) *The Crying of Lot 49*, Philadelphia: Lippincott.

Robinson M. and Ploner J. (eds) (forthcoming) *Cultures through the Post. Selected Essays on the Tourist Postcard*, Clevedon: Channel View Publications.

Sconce, J. (2000) *Haunted Media: Electronic Presence from Telegraphy to Television*, Durham, NC: Duke University Press.

Senft, Theresa M. (2008) *Camgirls: Celebrity & Community in the Age of Social Networks*, New York: Peter Lang.

Siegert, B. (1997) *Relays: Literature as an Epoch of the Postal System*, trans. Kevin Repp, Stanford: Stanford University Press.

Staff, Frank (1979) *The Picture Postcard and its Origins*, London: Lutterworth.

Stoker, Bram (1897, 1979) *Dracula*, London: Penguin.

Terada, R. (2001) *Feeling in Theory: Emotion after the 'Death of the Subject'*, Cambridge: Harvard University Press.

Thurlow, C., Jaworski, A. and Ylänne, V. (2010) 'Transient Identities, New Mobilities: Holiday Postcards' in Thurlow and Jaworski *Tourism Discourse Language and Global Mobility*, New York: Palgrave Macmillan, 91–125.

Varney (2009) 'Artolympix', website available online at http://artolympix.com (accessed 8 October 2013).

Vartanian, Hrag (2011) 'Mail Art Bulletin: Postcards', 7 May, available online at www.hyperallergic.com/24026/postcards/ (accessed 8 October 2013).

Wadkins, Kate and Vartanian, Hrag (2011) 'Presents: Three Months of Mail Art for Hyperallergic HQ', available online at www.hyperallergic.com/24026/postcards/ (accessed 29 February 2013).

Warren, Frank (2005) *PostSecret: Extraordinary Confessions from Ordinary Lives*, New York: Harper Collins.

Wilken, R. (2011) *Teletechnologies, Place, and Community*, New York: Routledge.

30

Bicycles

Zack Furness

Introduction

On February 23, 2006, employees at each of Brooklyn Industries' four designer clothing stores in New York City arrived at work to find a message inscribed in etching fluid across their front display windows: "BIKE CULTURE NOT 4 SALE." The juxtaposition of the drippy phrase with the "tall bikes" featured prominently in the display cases must have seemed quite odd, if not totally confusing, to people passing by. In the weeks before the New York City alternative weekly newspaper, *Village Voice*, widely publicized the incident (Tucker, 2006), bike enthusiasts and critics were already immersed in online forums debating how and why the store's display of bicycles – handmade machines welded two-frames high, hence "tall" – sparked such a strong reaction. Suspicions were immediately cast on members of New York City's various bicycle gangs: groups known for transforming junked bicycles and scavenged parts into hand-welded mobile masterpieces known variously as "mutant bikes" or "freak bikes." People familiar with the inner workings of bike gangs like Chunk 666 or the Black Label Bicycle Club brought some interesting perspectives to bear on the Brooklyn Industries debacle. In particular, a handful of cyclists posting on blogs touched on the issue of cultural commodification, highlighting the manner in which Brooklyn Industries essentially co-opted an icon of anti-consumerism as a cheap marketing ploy (Seelie, 2006). Some commentators disagreed entirely and condemned the response as an act of subcultural elitism and misplaced aggression. Others were clearly just trying to get an answer to the question that non-bike-riders were undoubtedly asking themselves: just what the hell is *bike culture* and what does it have to do with these weird-looking machines?

While the graffiti and the ensuing media squabbles may not provide any definitive answer to the latter question, they undoubtedly hint at some of the ways in which the representation of bicycling and the uses of bicycles themselves are increasingly seen as issues worth debating and struggling over. Indeed, the junk-welding architects spotlighted by the Brooklyn Industries incident are just one part of a variegated network of bicycling enthusiasts that have been formulating new cultural practices and identities around urban cycling, and actively forging passionate counternarratives of mobility that seek to re-define the meaning of bicycle transportation. Among this group are sizeable numbers of punk rockers who, in recent decades, generated grassroots support for bike riding that substantively influenced cycling trends and aesthetics in the US. In this chapter I call specific attention to the relationship between biking and punk culture because, as a constellation of geographically localized scenes, subcultural enclaves, ethics, and media texts, punk does some interesting and rather unique work in terms of orienting people toward a critical and often politicized engagement with both the bicycle and the norms of automobility. Along with a notable number of punks and ex-punks who have since become bicycling advocates, educators, builders, mechanics, and industry professionals, the set of practices and dispositions fostered through DIY punk have at times been explicitly pronounced across a range of urban cycling cultures. In what follows, I highlight some of the prominent narratives and practices that punks (and fellow DIY travellers) connected to bicycle transportation in the late 1990s and early 2000s in order to consider one of the ways in which cycling is made meaningful as a cultural practice. However, I want to begin by more clearly situating this essay within a theoretical framework informed by recent scholarship on bicycling and mobilities.

Bicycling and mobilities research

In addition to its function as a transportation technology, the bicycle – like the automobile – is an object that becomes meaningful through its relationships to an entire field of cultural practices, discourses, and social forces. These linkages, or what some cultural theorists call *articulations*, are not naturally occurring, nor are they due to the essence of the bicycle itself. Rather, people actively construct and modify these connections. Along with the act of cycling, communication is central to the process of making and unmaking of meaning around, and through, the bicycle. First and foremost, the bicycle itself can rightly be seen as a communications technology; it has historically served as a material link in a communications networks as well as a vehicle with which a cyclist can send the most basic 'message' of his or her own body. But more than that, cycling enthusiasts, bicycle manufacturers, and political activists are among those who have long imbued bicycles with symbolic meaning, whether as icons of women's liberation, symbols of environmentalism and radical politics, or even markers of one's cache as an urban 'hipster.' In conjunction with trade publications devoted to cycling, scholars have started to play a distinct role in this process by drawing attention to the ways in which cycling affects people's experience of space and place, their identities, their daily rhythms, and quite often, their political opinions about transportation and urban planning.

Through this emerging discourse bicycling is rendered visible as a practice that can be used to radically rethink not only the ensemble of materialities, temporalities, socialities, and geographies that co-constitute 'car culture,' but also the prevailing cultural common sense that sees automobility as either unproblematic, inherently desirable, or more often than not, as an incontrovertible fact of life: an almost 'natural' phenomenon. As Dave Horton writes, "the bicycle is not a mere appendage to 'business as usual,' but a vehicle which helps to re-evaluate, restructure and reorganize everyday life in contemporary societies" (2006: 51). In this same vein, Ben Fincham suggests that bicycling is a "potential resolution" to the tension between the idea of automobility (e.g. independence, freedom of movement) and "the impossibilities of the car system" that often inhibit the very autonomy and efficient mobility thought to be guaranteed by and through the act of driving (2006: 209–210). The notion that bicycling can, in fact, play some role in delivering on the "broken promises of the automobile" (Hagman, 2006) has long animated the project of bike advocacy and infiltrated the common sense of bicycle workers and commuters alike. But in recent years this idea has become more apparent to a wider range of urban planning scholars, transportation historians, and researchers situated in the interdisciplinary field of mobilities (Sheller, 2011). Indeed, as both an extension of and complement to the range of critical work on automobility and driving (Böhm, *et al.*, 2006), the burgeoning body of scholarship devoted to *vélomobility* speaks to some of the profound personal, sociocultural, and political dimensions of riding a bicycle, whether for everyday transportation or leisure (Vivanco, 2013; Furness, 2010; Horton *et al.*, 2007).

Mobilities researchers have rightfully rejected the notion of bicycling as an exclusively "rationalized and instrumental practice" (Spinney, 2009: 818), and have sought instead to interrogate the psychological, affective, and embodied aspects of cycling that, among other things, play a role in the formation of cycling subcultures and identities (Fincham, 2007). With the acknowledgement that bicyclists do not have a uniform set of needs that are "determined by the shared objective reality of being 'cyclists'" (Cox, 2005: 2), critical scholars recognize the importance of understanding some of the nuanced ways in which bike riders conceptualize their practice, articulate their desires, and make sense of the social and cultural dimensions of mobility. Ethnography has been an effective tool for producing such knowledge, but it has thus far been limited in its capacity to reflect upon the diverse and otherwise constitutive roles that communication actually plays in framing the image of the bicycle in both popular culture and in the everyday lives of bike riders. Without diminishing its value as a necessary research tool, I would simply argue that the discourses of cyclists and bike advocates need to be brought to the fore because they are as crucial to the project of envisioning a more sustainable future as they are invaluable to those of us interested in understanding how bicycling can also be a means for imagining "potential *presents*" (Aldred and Jungnickel, 2012: 536). Yet, with few notable exceptions (Furness, 2010; Pesses, 2010), there is little substantive engagement with the ever-growing archive of contemporary media produced by, for, and about cyclists.

By not taking seriously forms of communication that extend beyond select cycle advocacy campaigns, corporate news coverage of bicycling, and statements limited to those recorded by ethnographers, scholars end up implicitly (though perhaps unwittingly) trivializing the role that cultural production plays in the production of culture and cultural identity. That is to say, they not only ignore the pantheon of media through which cyclists creatively and meaningfully express ideas about cycling; they also, by default, promote a deceivingly uncomplicated view of the process of representation itself. In direct contrast, I would argue that whether one seeks to theorize the social role of vélomobility or is focused on changing its image, it is imperative to critically analyze such processes, as well as the specific instances in which this cultural work is done.

Up the bikes

"Riding your bike is punk," writes Kim Nolan in the debut issue of the now defunct publication *Punk Planet* (1994: 13). Her proclamation in the mid-1990s now reads somewhat prophetically, since bicycling emerged in the US as the punk mode of transportation de rigueur by 2001–2002, or at the very least, the preferred mode of urban mobility within the loose-knit Do-it-Yourself (DIY) punk scene: the vestige of punk's counterculture that could best be characterized by its scrappy aesthetics, anti-corporate politics, anarchist leanings, and passionate support for independent media production and participatory institutions. Bikes are popular amongst this crowd in part because they are cheap, easy to fix, fun to ride, and allow for a great deal of autonomy: they are the DIY solution to everyday transportation. Yet bicycling also resonates with the ethics, feelings, lifestyle choices, and politics that inform not only people's identities as punks but also the music, writing, art, and indeed the entire set of practices that co-constitute punk as a cultural formation. At the risk of over-generalizing, people who ride bikes and identify as punks tend to see distinct analogies between alternative transportation, alternative media production, and modes of cultural resistance rooted in the rejection of dominant social norms and consumerist values. The Dutch Provo, who aligned themselves with anarchists, antiwar activists, beatniks, freaks, and the like, actually articulated this 'punk' disposition as far back as the 1960s when describing their allies as a worldwide "Provotariat," who dwell in "carbon-monoxide-poisoned asphalt jungles": they are the people who "don't want a career, who lead irregular lives, *who feel like cyclists on a motorway*" (1966). While an apt metaphor, this sentiment is also a truism for many contemporary dissidents who, like the Provo, actually *are* the cyclists on the motorway. Thus, it is hardly surprising that the DIY punk underground has spawned an array of politicized (if not politically disorganized) cyclists who are passionate about car-free living, technical skill sharing, and the idea of gaining some independence from both the auto and oil industries. Indeed, within certain punk scenes, bikes are as integral to punk culture as seven-inch records, tattoos, and weird haircuts.

DIY punk has a long history of advocating alternatives to the dominant norms of consumer culture, whether in the form of protest and direct action, or more often, through practices that could be best described as politically motivated or aspirational. That is to say, while the object of radical transformation may be structural in nature, punk politics are often focused first and foremost on the transformation of oneself, in terms of grappling with one's position as a political subject and a social actor. In this context, biking is a comfortable fit with a disposition that sees 'the personal' and 'the political' as a dialectic that begins at the corporeal level. "The body," artist Jimmy Baker notes, "has always been central to punk culture," and he describes the pro-bicycle stance of his former band, The Awakening, as a way of "creating a resistant energy against the fog of subscribing to a petroleum answer" (2008). One can similarly see this personal-as-political-as-bodily sentiment in songs composed by other pro-bicycle punk bands, such as the UK's Red Monkey: "It could be so much better on our wheels, on our axles/Our fuel . . . so renewable/Our muscles . . . so sustainable!" (1999). Biking, in this sense, is seen as an extension of the DIY ethos – a way of asserting oneself by making one less reliant on "bosses, mechanics, and oil companies" (Boerer, 2007).

While punk politics tend to stress the role of individual autonomy, it is part of a paradigm that, despite its contradictions and limitations, is intricately tied up with both an egalitarian sensibility and a broader desire for social change. Indeed, in roughly fifty interviews I conducted with bike-riding punks between 2003 and 2008, the vast majority connected bicycling to both the politics espoused within DIY punk culture and to a broader set of political issues including environmental pollution, US oil wars (at the time, in Iraq), and capitalism itself. Whether biking became or is now an authentically 'punk' or 'subcultural' activity is hardly my concern, but what *is* interesting is that an 'eco-friendly' mode of transportation somehow became normalized in pockets of a van-propelled subculture once steeped in anti-hippie rhetoric and an alienated sense of 'No Future.'

Bikes in punk music and zines

Beginning in the late 1990s, bike riding and bicycles became prevalent themes in the lyrics and imagery of dozens of DIY punk bands in the US, such as Fifteen, RAMBO, Dead Things, Latterman, Japanther, and This Bike is a Pipe Bomb – a band whose stickers still adorn many bicycles throughout the country and occasionally prompt irrational, if not amusing, responses from police departments and bomb squads. Self-styled "bike punks" in the US, the UK, and beyond were not the first to pay homage to bicycles in song, but their melodies and lyrics have a markedly different tone than Queen's operatic "Bicycle Race" or Syd Barrett's psychedelic musings on Pink Floyd's "Bike." For example, Divide & Conquer was one of the many hardcore (punk) bands to convey a radical environmentalist critique of automobility that, while slightly tongue-in-cheek, is a sincere response to the everyday frustrations of being a bike rider in a car culture, both literally and metaphorically:

> Trash the El Camino because the kids are ready to ride
> Go two-wheeled disaster! Shout it out: Bike Pride!
> Pissing every car off, we'll call them nasty names
> Extend the middle finger and ride in every lane
> Bike Punx!
> With freedom on our minds and wrenches in our hands
> Fuck highway construction, let's go take the land
> We'll pedal through the cities, this war cry we will send
> When internal combustion meets the bitter end
> Bike Punx!
>
> *(1996)*

Whether in earnest or as part of symbolic fantasies that see bike riders navigating post-apocalyptic/post-automobile landscapes (The Awakening, 2003; RAMBO, 2002), smelting millions of cars into bicycles (Fifteen, 1996), or calling for the head of Henry Ford (Divide & Conquer, 1999), the articulation of bicycling to a resistance identity – a punk ethos – is one of the means by which cyclists validate their personal experiences and opinions by "authorizing themselves to speak" and by "making public" their voices (Atton, 2002: 67–68). As Chris Atton notes, political dissidents frequently utilize independent, 'alternative' media to construct a resistance identity for themselves, but in most of the bike-centric media produced within the DIY punk scene the emphasis is placed more squarely on how the practice of cycling, rather than bicyclists' singular identities, is that which is "marginalized, devalued or stigmatized by dominant forces" (2002: 68). Like Divide & Conquer, the Philadelphia hardcore band RAMBO similarly articulated a resistance identity – a punk ethos – to anarchist politics and bicycle transportation. One of their self-described odes to bike militancy is a song called "U-Lock Justice" that includes the lines "For every time I hear them say/'Get the fuck out of the way,'/I will defend my right of way/That heap of steel I'm gonna slay" (2000).

Punk music can clearly serve as an outlet for venting pent-up aggression, as well as a forum for expressing radical perspectives on biking and car culture, albeit in brief stanzas, short bursts of energy, and with more than a little irony. But bands professing an interest in bikes also vary significantly in terms of their musical styles, the kind of songs they write, and the aspects of DIY punk culture to which they explicitly or tacitly connect cycling. That is to say, while a dissonant hardcore band like Zegota makes a political plea for humanity to "pedal away from global decay" (1999), other punks have penned upbeat songs about bike lanes (Dead Things, 2002), vagabond bicycle treks with friends (The Blank Fight, 2002), and the unique and sometimes contradictory perspectives that cycling lends to the experience of a city. Aaron Elliot, a veteran punk drummer, conveys this sensibility in his lyrics to "West Side Highway":

> As I ride, I can feel the street
> Like a river, it flows rapidly

Through the city, it propels
Me towards a tragic, bloody crash, oh well
An inch from death seems to be
The only place to find some peace
The only place to ride a bike and
Feel alive and find a sense of pride
And dignity.

(Pinhead Gunpowder, 2008)

Like Elliot, who is probably most well-known as the self-published author of *Cometbus*, many of the people involved in DIY punk similarly express themselves through (and are also the audiences for) fanzines, or 'zines': homemade, photocopy-produced publications that are either sold for a small fee, given away, or traded between zine writers. Prior to the development of both interactive online publishing and social media, zines were – and in many cases still are – a means of communication for bicyclists who lack either the resources, ability, or desire to publish articles through mass media outlets. Unlike the truncated format of song lyrics, bike zines published throughout the last two decades provide a venue in which to construct a more complex narrative about both the individual and cultural aspects of bicycling. Specifically, riders often explore entirely different dimensions of bicycling and car culture than one would typically find in US media, most notably that of adults using bicycles for creative, fun, utilitarian and/or humanitarian purposes. Whether as venues for documenting advocacy (Biel, 2008) or spaces for analyzing the gendered dynamics of bike culture (Blue, 2010; Jackson, 2007), zines fill an important void for adults who ride bicycles but may not identify as 'cyclists' in the conventional sense. At the same time, the subjective, personalized qualities of zines – much like the plethora of bike blogs that now dot the Internet – highlight the benefits of bicycle transportation in ways that bring it squarely within the framework of everyday life. These mediated spaces serve a distinctly pedagogical function and they can also open up channels of communication through which new communities of cyclists are constituted (Carlsson, 2008: 117–118).

Re-writing/riding the city

Despite the variety of ways in which bicycling has been and continues to be connected with countercultural ethics and politics, one of the strongest thematic commonalities between punk songs, zines, and a range of media produced in DIY bike culture (e.g. blogs, cartoons, poster art, and documentary films) is the emphasis on bicycling as a tool for rethinking urban mobility, space, and place. Alternative media prove a fertile ground for mapping the emotional and cognitive geographies of bicycling; one can look to these texts to better understand the how bicycling – especially using a bike for everyday transportation – produces a unique urban subjectivity and facilitates a heightened awareness of one's habitat. For the everyday rider, one's world often becomes re-articulated around and through one's bicycle as spaces become instinctively mapped in terms of their bikeability:

Anywhere you want to go in Gainesville, you can probably get there from the intersection of university and main on bike in 20 minutes. From my house it's fifteen minutes to Ward's grocery, fifteen to No Idea, eight to Wayward Council Records, ten to school, twelve to my friends at the ranch.

(Scenery and Fristoe, 2001: 82–83)

DIY media constitute a small but productive symbolic space in which cyclists reflect upon, and make meaning of, their own relationships to the city. Significantly, these narratives construct "shadow maps" (Duncombe, 1997: 59) of cities that document the amalgam of routes, flows, and spaces performed by cyclists both within, and outside of, the purview of automobility. This dialectic of bicycling and representation engenders an acute experience of place, inasmuch as it fosters localized knowledge(s) and personal connections to specific neighborhoods, and at times, entire cities. Erik Ruin, a printmaker and author of the *Trouble in Mind* zine, writes:

> There's a way of knowing a city that's very particular to biking through it. The slowness allows you to really see things, even to stop and look. The speed gives you some safety and a distance that's really conducive to fluid thought.
>
> *(n.d.:)*

In their song "Bikes and Bridges," the band Defiance, Ohio speaks to the emotional/affective aspects of this dynamic:

> Even Columbus looks better on the back seat of a bike
> All my fears get washed away in a stream of blinking lights
> And the concrete strip below seems less like a noose
> And more like a tie that binds or at least a tourniquet.
>
> *(2004)*

One could argue that the process of re-thinking the city through the bicycle is as much discursive as it is physically performative: it takes place through the production and dissemination of songs, films, online communiqués, zines, and artwork in which people reflect on the ways in which bicycling shapes their experience of urban life. Lee Williams gestures toward this bicycle–city reciprocity in *Cranked*, a zine devoted to bike culture in the Northwest:

> As urban cyclists we are intimately engaged with our city's neighborhoods in a way automobile commuters may never experience . . . For the cyclist, these myriad aspects of the city are immediate and tactile, not concealed behind steel and glass.
>
> *(n.d.: 46)*

While admittedly a highly romanticized view of bicycling, Williams expresses the sentiments of cyclists who see biking not simply as a transportation choice but a way to radically realign perception and one's entire way of seeing. Bicycling, in the simplest terms, transforms 'out there' to 'right here,' inasmuch as it disarticulates autonomous mobility from the privatized experience of the automobile and rearticulates it to a more visceral experience of the urban. This process does not always foster a more 'authentic' engagement with the city, as so many cyclists would have it, but it necessarily forces a different kind of engagement. In this sense, bicycling is also a social experiment that can cultivate not only a keen awareness of one's 'right to the city' but also one's right to *experience* the city:

> I feel about this city [New Orleans] the way one dreams of feeling about the perfect love affair. I feel connected, forgiving, in full admiration and acceptance for its beauty and its shortcomings. I never thought I could feel this way about a place . . . it struck me that the things I love about this city are things I may not have noticed or appreciated enough if it weren't for my mode of transportation, my lovely bicycle.
>
> *(Jackson, 2007: 1)*

Unlike some of the well-documented frustrations that cyclists endure while adjusting to the rhythms and flows of auto traffic, the larger process of conforming one's mobility, as well as one's cognitive map to the contours of the urban landscape can be a fascinating experience. Somewhere within this process of *performing the city* (Jones, 2005) bike riders find their own rhythms and flows, and create news ways to both explore and celebrate the ludic qualities of cycling as well.

Conclusion

While there is much more one could say about the urban narratives and perspectives on space and place documented in alternative cycling media, I draw attention to this specific theme because it brings into focus several points that I want to make about the significance of bicycling and DIY punk culture more broadly. First, as I argued from the outset of this essay, scholars interested in analyzing bicycling as a sociocultural form of mobility need to start taking seriously the discourses and media produced by cyclists, and to try and better understand how they are interconnected to/with cycling practices in specific cultural contexts. In this regard, the excerpted zines and lyrics in the last section provide some distinct observations that bike riders make about urban mobility, whether in describing how they see and interpret cities from a different vantage point than drivers – through the "wrong lens," as Spinney puts it (2007: 30) – or by revealing some of the nuanced ways in which bicycling functions as a form of negotiation where "social norms, cultures of interaction, and identity" (Jensen, 2010: 401) are produced through people's engagement with their environments. That is to say, even within this small sample of narratives one finds insights about the importance of urban space/place in subcultural cycling discourses that are not only valuable unto themselves, but also significantly engaged with some of the same issues that researchers take pains to highlight when analyzing the cultural dimensions of mobilities (Furness, 2007).

But more specifically, one does not have to look very hard to find abundant examples of punk bands and zine writers that give voice to the affective dimensions of cycling that are, to date, under-appreciated and under-examined. In the examples above, I wanted to briefly show how within DIY punk culture bicycling becomes meaningful as part of a "network of empowerment," or what Lawrence Grossberg calls an *affective alliance*: "an organization of concrete material practices and events, cultural forms and social experience which both opens up and structures the space of our affective investments in the world" (1984: 227). DIY punk culture, as I have tried to illustrate here, creates the conditions of possibility in which biking not only 'makes sense' (politically, socially, financially) to punks, but more importantly, is seen as a desirable and exciting practice that strongly resonates with DIY ethics, attitudes, and orientations; for example, punk's celebration of localism, place, and the 'nitty gritty' details that make cities feel like home.

The articulation of bicycle transportation to DIY punk ethics is significant not only for how it positions biking as a way of "Doing Mobility Yourself" but also for the way it offers an alternative to the dominant representational strategies of formal bike advocacy, both in terms of production and distribution (grassroots circulation vs. strategic marketing campaigns). Furthermore, punks' appropriation of bicycling offers a useful example for understanding some of the ways in which cultural narratives and practices not only shape transportation habits and identities, but can also point people toward more substantive engagements with issues that are by no means reducible to transportation alone. One can certainly debate the impact of such efforts, but one of the main points is that it is impossible to draw such conclusions without considering how and in what ways bicycling is represented and made meaningful. Critical researchers must attend to these discourses dialectically in order to understand the ways in which they fit into a web of articulations and affective alliances that provide foundations upon which cycling identities, knowledges, and practices are constructed and transformed in everyday life.

Bibliography

Aldred, R. and Jungnickel, K. (2012) 'Constructing mobile places between "leisure" and "transport": a case study of two group cycle rides,' *Sociology*, 46: 523–539.

Atton, C. (2002) *Alternative Media*, London: Sage.

Baker, J. (2008) Personal correspondence, 6 July.

Biel, J. (2008) *Bipedal, By Pedal! #1*, Portland, OR: Microcosm Publishing.

Blue, E. (2010) *Taking the Lane, Vol 2*, Portland, OR: Cantankerous Titles.

Boerer, E. (2007) Personal correspondence, 15 January.

Böhm, S., Jones, C., Land, C. and Paterson, M. (eds) (2006) *Against Automobility*, Malden, MA: Blackwell/Sociological Review.

Carlsson, C. (2008) *Nowtopia*, Oakland, CA: AK Press.

Cox, P. (2005) 'Conflicting agendas in selling cycling,' paper presented at Velo-City Conference, Dublin, June 2005.

Dead Things (2002) 'Bike lane,' *Because Sometimes You Just Want to Ride Your Bike to the Show*, Slave Audio, CD.

Defiance, Ohio (2004) 'Bikes and Bridges,' *Share What Ya Got*, Friends and Relatives Records, LP.

Divide & Conquer (1999) 'Bike militia,' *The Need to Amputate*, Ginger Liberation/MalokaRecords, EP.

— (1996) 'Bike punx,' *Sanjam Split International Compilation*, Sanjam Records, 7" record.

Duncombe, S. (1997) *Notes from Underground: Zines and the Politics of Alternative Culture*, London: Verso.

Fifteen (1996) 'Helter smelter,' *Buzz*, Grass Records, LP.

Fincham, B. (2007) 'Bicycle messengers: image, identity and community,' in D. Horton, P. Rosen and P. Cox (eds) *Cycling and Society*, Aldershot, UK: Ashgate, pp. 179–195.

— (2006) 'Bicycle messengers and the road to freedom,' *Sociological Review*, 54: 208–222.

Furness, Z. (2010) *One Less Car: Bicycling and the Politics of Automobility*, Philadelphia: Temple University Press.

— (2007) 'Critical mass, urban space and vélomobility,' *Mobilities*, 2: 299–319.

Grossberg, L. (1984) 'Another boring day in paradise: rock and roll and the empowerment of everyday life,' *Popular Music*, 4: 225–258.

Hagman, O. (2006) 'Morning queues and parking problems: on the broken promises of the automobile,' *Mobilities*, 1: 63–74.

Horton, D. (2006) 'Environmentalism and the bicycle,' *Environmental Politics*, 15: 41–59.

Horton, D., Rosen, P. and Cox, P. (eds) (2007) *Cycling and Society*, Aldershot, UK: Ashgate.

Jackson, S. (ed.) (2007) *Chainbreaker #4*, New Orleans: Self-published.

Jensen, O. B. (2010) 'Negotiation in motion: unpacking a geography of mobility,' *Space and Culture*, 13: 389–402.

Jones, P. (2005) 'Performing the city: a body and a bicycle take on Birmingham, UK,' *Social & Cultural Geography*, 6: 813–830.

Nolan, K. (1994) 'Debut column,' *Punk Planet*, 1: 12–13.

Pesses, M. (2010) 'Automobility, vélomobility, American mobility: an exploration of the bicycle tour,' *Mobilities*, 5: 1–24.

Pinhead Gunpowder (2008) 'West Side Highway,' Recess Records, 7" record.

Provo (1966) 'Appeal to the international provotariat,' *Provo*, 11, Amsterdam: Self-published.

RAMBO (2002) 'Apocalypse riders,' *Rambo/Crucial Unit*, Ed Walters Records, 7" record.

— (2000) 'U-Lock justice,' *Wall of Death the System*, 625 Records, LP.

Red Monkey (1999) 'Bike song,' *Difficult is Easy*, Troubleman Unlimited, LP.

Ruin, E. (n.d.) 'Real Time Detroit,' *Trouble in Mind*, Detroit, MI: Self-published.

Scenery, M. and Fristoe, T. (2001) 'Biking,' in J. Angel and J. Kucsma (eds) *The Zine Yearbook, Vol 5*, Bowling Green: Become the Media, pp. 81–83.

Seelie, T. (2006) 'Brooklyn vs. brokelyn,' *Suckapants*, 23 February. Available online at http://suckapants.com/2006/02/brooklyn-vs-brokelyn.html (accessed 1 March 2006).

Sheller, M. (2011) 'Mobility,' *Sociopedia.isa*. Available online at www.sagepub.net/isa/resources/pdf/Mobility.pdf (accessed 15 September 2012).

Spinney, J. (2009) 'Cycling the city: movement, meaning and method,' *Geography Compass*, 3: 817–835.

— (2007) 'Cycling the city: non-place and the sensory construction of meaning in a mobile practice,' in D. Horton, P. Rosen and P. Cox (eds) *Cycling and Society*, Aldershot, UK: Ashgate, pp. 25–46.

The Awakening (2003) 'Front wheel' and 'Back wheel,' *The Awakening/Virginia Black Lung*, Ed Walters Records, CD.

The Blank Fight (2002) 'This bike and this guitar,' *House Band Feud*, Plan-it-X Records, CD.

Tucker, K. I. (2006) 'Mutant bike gangs of New York,' *Village Voice*, 14 March.

Vivanco, L. (2013) *Reconsidering the Bicycle: An Anthropological Perspective on a New (Old) Thing*, New York: Routledge.

Williams, L. (n.d.) 'Community,' *Cranked #4*, Seattle: Self-published.

Zegota (1999) 'Bike song,' *Movement in the Music*, Crimethinc, LP.

31

Carbon

Matthew Paterson

Carbon has become increasingly pervasive as a signifier for the socio-ecological dimensions of mobilities. It could be argued it has attained the status of an empty signifier – standing in for long chains of equivalence, subsuming food, transport, housing, cooking, forests, oceans, and so on in a single fetishized frame of reference. As a concept, it has itself become mobile, ceasing to be a simple reference for a specific chemical element, becoming instead a signifier of personal virtue and vice, novel financial markets, innovative industrial practices, and a whole host of other things. Conversely, this discursive reframing has enabled the construction of new property rights that directly re-mobilize 'actual' carbon, in the form of 'carbon credits' and other carbonified financial instruments, as well as in practices like 'carbon capture and storage.' Perhaps surprisingly however, it has received little attention within the turn to mobilities in recent research (for a notable exception, see Urry 2011, especially ch. 5). This chapter seeks to fill this gap and explores how carbon has come to be so mobile, and interrogates the consequences of its unleashing.

Carbon for mobilities

First, however, it is worth outlining how 'carbon' itself operates as a material underpinning for all of the other aspects of mobility that have animated the interest of what has become called the 'new mobilities' literature (e.g. Hannam *et al.* 2006; Sheller and Urry 2006). This is not to be understood as somehow 'pre-discursive' – all of the well-known practices and histories I elaborate below have themselves become re-framed by the relatively recent carbonification (Stephan 2012) of our conceptual universe. It is of course not only carbon in its narrow chemical sense that does this work. Principally it entails a variety of processes of transforming energy (for the most part either metabolic or combustive) that entail varying combinations of carbon, hydrogen, and oxygen. These are transformed in ways that release energy for growth, walking, running, jumping, or later for heating water and air, or moving many sorts of machines. Indeed it is possible to claim that we have in some senses seen a re-writing of human history via a history of our mobilization of and by carbon.

Re-framed this way, human history can be written as a series of mobilizations of the energy in carbon molecules (specifically, hydrocarbons and carbohydrates). Perhaps the initial forms of this are in eating and cooking. The metabolic process is effectively one of transforming the chemical bonds in food (mostly in the form of carbohydrates – sugars and so on) to release energy.[1] This mobilization of energy then enables our own mobilizations – growth, walking, running, and so on. Cooking then also entails mobilizing the energy contained in the various combinations of carbon, hydrogen, and oxygen molecules in wood, peat, or manure (and later of course, coal, oil, and gas) that enable food to be heated and transformed either for pleasure or simply to make it digestible.

While these mobilizations have been central to human activity for its entire history, written from this point of view, the crucial shift that occurs in Europe in the eighteenth century is the shift from the dominance of wood as an energy source to the dominance of coal. Some scholars in environmental history and sociology refer to this as the 'metabolic rift' (Foster 2000; Clark and York 2005). This refers to a process of transition from circular movements of energy (where sources of energy renew themselves via biological processes), to linear movements, as the energy contained in first coal and then later oil and natural gas is released in a very short period of time, thus enabling apparently endless accumulation.

This transformation thus enables an extraordinary transformation of the modes of mobility that human societies can engage in. We shift from simple boats and ships, powered by wind or humans themselves, as well as carts drawn by horses or oxen, to a massive acceleration of ships (both in their construction and their own speed), the development of steam engines which eliminates the reliance on wind and that enables railways, the improvements in overland surfaces (road and rail) that eclipse water as the main medium of movement, and then in the twentieth century with the deployment of oil and electricity, the emergence of automobility, aviation, and so on.

So human mobility per se can be written as a material process of deploying energy derived from carbon molecules.

Mobilities of carbon I

As it enables mobilities of all sorts, carbon is simultaneously mobilized itself in this large-scale historical process. As the process unfolds, the sources of energy that are mobilized become progressively less globally ubiquitous. Wood is more or less universally available across the planet, coal is available in most places, but oil and gas only exist in a relatively small number of places. The mobilities of each source vary similarly. Wood travels locally, coal is moved around within what were at the same time becoming 'nations' – and the transport systems that emerge in the eighteenth century (canals, specifically) have the movement of coal as one of their principal aims. But coal, oil, and gas entail increasingly global flows of the embodied energy they contain. Oil in particular is one of the most mobile commodities globally, as well as being central to the global flows of most other commodities.

Geopolitics has simultaneously been dramatically affected by this shift in sources of carbon and energy, in at least two senses. On the one hand, in the twentieth century the US's pre-eminence as a global power was underpinned by its early and aggressive automobilization (Rupert 1995; Paterson 2007); the manner with which it deployed oil via automobiles was central to both its productivity advantages over other states and to its pattern of growth around high degrees of physical mobility for its citizens, with both economic and cultural consequences.

On the other hand geopolitics was transformed by the search for the sources of this new energy source. The sites where it was most concentrated, notably the Middle East, became sites of intense conflict and competition for control over the resources, either to secure access, or more commonly to secure profits, from them. The decision by the British navy to shift from coal to oil in 1912 is often taken as a key moment in this transformation (Klare 2001: 30). Engendered here therefore are other sets of mobilities – of armies, finance, cultural symbols (imperialism, freedom, etc.) – set in train by the search for the source of the economy's primary means of physical mobility.

Contradictory mobilities

Focusing on the carbonified character of our mobilities also enables us to illustrate their problematic socio-ecological character. As the mobility of people, food, and other commodities has increased exponentially, dependent on and generating similarly explosive expansion in carbon consumption, it has engendered a whole series of recurrent crises, on a progressively expanding scale. Injunctions against coal burning in urban areas go back to the European Middle Ages. But from the 1940s onwards, a series of crises produced by such carbonified mobilities have erupted. These have ranged from the smog in American and European cities from the 1940s onwards that has since globalized, through to climate change since the late 1980s, with concerns about land and water degradation, health, toxic chemicals, acid rain, and many others in-between.

Many of these have generated social mobilizations to mitigate their effects. They have most frequently operated however in a way that attempts to do so without challenging the underlying normativity of (auto)mobility itself (Rajan 1996). They do so by framing the problems as questions of technology rather than a broad system organized around carbonified mobility. We remove lead from petrol, we introduce catalytic converters to eliminate nitrogen oxides (that cause acid rain) and various gases that generate smog, and so on. At the most ambitious, we imagine decarbonizing our mobility systems, powering them instead with biofuels (where the carbon emitted is equivalent to the carbon absorbed by the plants growing), electricity (generated from renewable sources), or hydrogen (from water split by electrolysis). But none to date has eliminated these crisis tendencies of carbonified mobility.

The difficulty in challenging mobility arises out of two political characteristics of such mobility (see Paterson 2007 for a fuller elaboration of the argument that follows). On the one hand carbonified mobility has been central to capital accumulation since the Industrial Revolution. From railways and the steamship in the nineteenth century, to automobility and aviation in the twentieth century, the deployment of coal and oil to generate movement of people and goods has been central to increasing productivity and production, consumption, trade, and imperial military control, and thus the expansion of the global economy as a whole. Automobility in particular is often regarded to have dramatically re-shaped the economy, involving highly extensive backward and forward linkages from raw materials through to insurance, as well as being the site of highly innovative developments in production regimes, consumption patterns, and economic management, known collectively under the rubric of 'Fordism.'

On the other hand, mobility has been routinely invested with enormous symbolic power, notably through its ideological connection to freedom. Freedom of movement was an important rallying cry in the French Revolution, and has remained a standard element in the liberal ideological set of fundamental freedoms. But freedom always has this ambivalent character – while it can express freedom, overcoming feudal or other barriers, it can at the same time become a 'dictatorship' (Virilio 1986). Much effort has thus been expended to organize mobility such that it might have a chance of being experienced as freedom. Hence the symbolic significance of the word automobile: a machine that moves itself autonomously but simultaneously enables the driver to move autonomously. The fundamental contradiction here (Böhm *et al.* 2006) is obvious, but fails to undermine the ideological success of this articulation. Much effort has however also been spent on developing this phenomenology of driving as freedom – in advertising, clearly, but also in film, popular music, government propaganda, and so on (Paterson 2007: ch. 5). The effect has been the enormous cultural-political inertia of automobile-dominated mobility systems, which acts as a block to the challenges made by carbonified mobilities' various contradictions. In other words, while automobility entails and enables many forms of mobility, it is itself highly immobile as a system, reproducing itself stably over time and resisting shifts to alternative regimes (see also Dennis and Urry 2009).

Climate change is the most large-scale and systemic of these crises. Its global character arises out of the more or less absolute mobility of GHG molecules in the atmosphere: the CO_2 emitted from a power plant in the US or China rapidly mixes across the globe so that the concentrations of GHGs are roughly uniform globally. And its dynamics have been at the heart of what might be the biggest challenge to carbonified mobility itself – to decarbonize it while maintaining the heart of its political economic and cultural-political dynamism.

Mobilities of carbon II

It is in the conceptualization – or perhaps reification, or fetishization is even better – of carbon that a whole set of novel mobilities have been enabled. Climate change has been the principal impetus for this reframing. In other words, the new mobilities of carbon entailed in carbon trading arise precisely out of socio-ecological contradictions generated by older forms of carbonified mobilities – automobility, aviation, and the like.

But while the socio-political dynamics of climate change display extraordinary complexity, in many contexts they have been reduced to the single signifier of carbon. The logic of this process is worth tracing out.

First, climate change has been reduced to a question of reducing the emissions that generate it. This has two sorts of framing effects. On the one hand, adapting to climate change is neglected (although this has been partially redressed since around 2005 with renewed attention to such adaptation, and through the *force majeure* of climate impacts). On the other hand, and perhaps more importantly for the present argument, the anthropogenic causes of climate change are framed as simple chemical outputs (CO_2, CH_4, N_2O, CFCs, etc.) rather than complex social processes from which such outputs are merely the end result. Power plants, airplanes, cars, air conditioners, forests, and the varied social practices that they enable and sustain, are ignored – a classic case of commodity fetishism (Lohmann 2010).

Second, these multiple gases, each with their own characteristics, are reduced to a single measure. In the late 1980s and early 1990s, when large-scale scientific and political discussions of climate change started in earnest, a move was made (the normal narrative is that such a thing was 'necessary') to combine all the greenhouse gases into a single measure, which became known as the Global Warming Potential (GWP – for histories of this, see MacKenzie 2009 or Paterson and Stripple 2012). This itself was an adaptation – a generic concept made mobile if you like – of the Ozone Depletion Potential developed in the mid-1980s to compare the impacts of various gases on ozone depletion. With the GWP, all of the gases were to be reduced to a single metric so that, for example, the relative contribution of each to climate change could be indicated, as they were in the first IPCC report in 1990 (Houghton *et al.* 1990). As carbon dioxide was the numerically dominant gas (in the 1990 IPCC report it was judged to account for around 60 percent of climate change – that proportion has since gone up), the GWP became measured in relation to CO_2. CO_2 has a GWP of 1; everything else is a ratio to that number. Very quickly, overall greenhouse gases were being measured either in terms of millions of tonnes of CO_2-equivalent, or in terms of millions of tonnes of carbon.[2] Carbon had been mobilized effectively as an empty signifier, standing in for a whole range of specific greenhouse gases (carbon on its own has no greenhouse gas characteristics, indeed it is not even a gas at normal earth temperatures) and the social practices that generated them.

Carbon, thus framed, has then been reinscribed and reified in all sorts of contexts. Carbon counters, carbon offsets, carbon markets, low-carbon diets, carbon detox, carbon footprint, carbon disclosure – all sorts of 'lexical compounds' (Nerlich *et al.* 2011) have flowed from this framing. In some contexts it generates novel mobilities for carbon itself, notably in carbon capture and storage, where the GHG emissions from projects (normally CO_2 from large, single-point sources like power plants or oil sands operations) are pumped underground to where the coal or oil came from in the first place. But more important, so far at least, has been the mobilization of carbon emissions rights embodied in carbon trading.

Perhaps the most important moment was the shift from the aggregate measures of overall emissions towards the individual tonne as the primary measure. The aggregate measures mattered to IPCC scientists because they were interested in modelling various scenarios of climate change to determine the impacts of reductions in emissions of specific greenhouse gases over various timescales. Aggregate measures were also important to states that wanted to measure their own overall 'national' share in global emissions. But the shift to the individual tonne enabled the emergence of markets in carbon emissions, as it provided the basis for the single unit that could then be traded.

This was a framing effect of the Kyoto Protocol. A prominent dynamic of the Kyoto negotiations was to promote a series of institutional innovations that enabled countries, in various ways, to meet their obligations to reduce their emissions via investments abroad. Known as the 'flexibility mechanisms,' these are essentially the mechanisms that led to what we know now as carbon markets. The important framing effect however is in the transformation of aggregate state emissions into a series of individual tonnes that can be unbundled and traded. So, for example, a target to reduce overall emissions by, say, six percent (Canada's obligation) becomes an allocation of 94 percent of Canada's 1990 levels. These emissions are then unbundled into a number of tonnes (433 mt CO_2e, in Canada's case), which became referred to as 'assigned amount units' (AAUs) that could either be traded directly, through the emissions trading system (UNFCCC 1997: Article 17) or via one of the two carbon offset systems, Joint Implementation (Article 6) or the Clean Development Mechanism (Article 12). In the negotiations for the detailed rules guiding the implementation of Kyoto, agreed in Marrakesh in 2001, the credits from these mechanisms, as well as the AAU, all became measured under the single measure of the tCO_2e – carbon's ultimate fetish object.

Once inscribed, the tCO_2e became a highly mobile signifier. In other sites where emissions trading or carbon-offset systems were becoming entrenched as the principal policy tool to address climate change, this measure became rapidly reinscribed through a logic of mimesis and systemic adaptation.[3] In the financial markets that have emerged around emissions trading, it has become the short-hand through which all the various specific allowances, credits, and the acronyms by which they are known (AAUs, ERUs, CERs, EUAs, and so on[4]) are unified, thus enabling their mobility across the different 'asset classes' they represent. One carbon trading firm was even called for a while simply CO2e.com, reflecting the symbolic power the term had attained, and its capacity to signify a whole set of other equivalences, from the narrowly financial through to the ethical connections to action on climate change.

The rapid spread of these symbols, and the regulatory practices that they fed off, helped to sediment a space within financial markets whereby the rights to carbon emissions (or the promises not to emit carbon, in the case of offset projects) became themselves highly mobile. The main aim itself of emissions trading is to create some sort of mobility as to the location of emissions reductions themselves. A biomass, energy efficiency, or wind energy project in, say, India would become equivalent to a certain amount of emissions from a coal-fired power plant in, for example, Sweden. More rapid emissions reductions by a power company in the UK, triggered by a switch from coal to natural gas, would enable the purchase of allowances by a cement company in Spain to continue emitting at its existing level.

This level of mobility in carbon emission rights is itself designed into the system. But financial actors have taken this initial logic and expanded it enormously, with the development of a range of (relatively simple) derivative instruments (futures, options, swaps), as well as simple arbitrage and speculative practices trading between the different sorts of carbon instruments (AAUs, ERUs, etc.). These carbon markets have been in crisis since 2009, due largely to the economic crisis's direct impacts on greenhouse gas emissions and thus on carbon prices, but also a broader legitimacy crisis due to this financialized mode of governance of climate change (Paterson 2013; Helleiner and Thistlethwaite 2012). But prior to that they were the fastest growing financial markets in the world, more or less doubling in size every year, and still seem set to expand further, with expansions in the European system but also new systems starting in Australia, South Korea, and probably China. Nevertheless, carbon markets returned to growth in 2011, reaching $176bn in trading volumes (World Bank 2012). Such expansions raise the possibility of ever-more elaborate (and problematic) mobilizations of carbon by financial traders.

Mobile and immobile carbon

The story of carbon's novel mobilities can be read in a number of ways. As in many aspects of the 'new mobilities' literature, there is a distinct relationship between mobility and immobility (e.g. Hannam *et al.* 2006). The rapid growth of carbon markets depends first on reducing the various practices involved in producing greenhouse gas emissions (driving, flying, heating, etc.) to a simple question of which greenhouse gas they produce. It then depends on fixing a ratio of equivalency between these gases, culminating in a single, highly abstracted figure, the tCO_2e, that then enables a proliferation of specific commodities that represent it in particular institutional and market contexts.

This can be understood perhaps as similar to other generic processes in the mobilization of commodities. Most capitalist markets entail a relationship between a fixing – notably the establishing of private property rights – and the mobilization of the commodity in the market exchange. To sell my pig, it is presumed that I own the pig, and I am legally required to keep records that demonstrate my ownership of the pig. Similarly, to sell a carbon credit you have to go through a (much more elaborate) process that establishes your right to sell that credit. While the concept of the carbon credit has been fixed at an abstract level through the invention of the tCO_2e, for any specific credit, the project developer that seeks to sell credits from a project needs to develop an elaborate report that shows the likely emissions without the project, measure the emissions with the project, claim a certain amount of emissions forgone as a consequence, and then persuade the bureaucratic process involved in the governance of the offset project (the CDM, or one of the certifying systems involved in the voluntary carbon market).[5] At the same time, the emissions themselves have, in the project, a particular, local quality, fixed to the site itself, while the process of abstraction that turns them into carbon credits simultaneously renders them highly mobile via investment and then financial markets. Making this mobility possible requires a large range of infrastructural services to make it possible (consultancy firms, financial services, legal services, often environment or development NGOs, government agencies), and considerable organizational work (project developing, certifying and verifying, contract making, and so on) to assemble it in a way that enables the fixing of carbon to make it mobile (cf. Adey and Bissell 2010: 1–2).

The relationship between 'spatial fixes' and accumulation has a similar dynamic (e.g. Harvey 1989, 2003). In this narrative, in order to generate cycles of accumulation, capital must seek to create relatively closed spatial contexts of production, exchange, and consumption, within which money can then become highly mobile to generate accumulation. Carbon markets can themselves be understood as certain sorts of spatial fixes, linking together disparate parts of the globe in particular ways to create particular forms of accumulation (Bumpus and Liverman 2011).

But while this relationship between mobility and immobility of carbon does operate in a way that promotes the circulation of novel carbonified financial instruments, it should not be read as a simple linear, functional story. It is not possible to write, for example, a history of the tCO_2e that shows that it was invented *in order to* enable these commodification processes. It rather has a complex, messy history of scientists developing a way of analyzing GHGs to be able to compare their role in climate change, national governments needing aggregate measures of their GHG emissions, negotiators and administrators trying to create short-hand ways of simplifying the rapidly complexifying character of the Kyoto Protocol negotiations, and investors seeking to imagine how to generate business strategies around what would result (Paterson and Stripple 2012). Each element here entails not only instrumental calculations by actors, but inherent ambiguities: for example, how to decide on the equivalence between different GHGs when they stay in the atmosphere for different periods of time, or whether and how to include sinks (activities that fix carbon from the atmosphere into soils, plants, or seas) in national accounts of GHGs. In all of this, the qualities of 'carbon' molecules themselves intrude – such as the different atmospheric lifetimes of different GHGs. Carbon is at times, as Adam Bumpus puts it, 'uncooperative' (2011).

Conclusion

Mobile carbon has emerged as a purported 'solution' to the problems of carbonified mobilities. Whether it can in fact address its intended target adequately is of course hotly contested. It may of course be simply a means of moving carbon around rather than reducing its production. Those opposing carbon markets, such as Carbon Trade Watch or Durban Climate Justice, often explicitly invoke the alternative as 'keeping the oil in the soil and the coal in the hole' (e.g. Bond 2009), a framing where it is precisely the mobilization of fossil carbon that needs to be stopped. Discursive shifts within carbon market politics also give hints as to this contested mobility of carbon; witness a general shift from 'emissions trading' as the main metaphor (which could be read as simply moving carbon around) to 'cap and trade' (implying the limit to movement, the intention to keep some oil in the ground).

Whether it can do its purported job or not, carbon's novel mobilities attest to the organization of contemporary societies around mobility itself. Indeed it could be argued to help illustrate not only this but that mobility remains a generalized social imperative; the broadly political-economic analysis underpinning this chapter helps illuminate that when problems are identified, pressure is generated to create new forms of mobility, as such forms generate novel sites of accumulation which can simultaneously be invested with affective desire (Descheneau and Paterson 2011). This is fundamentally a continuity in social organization, as mobilities of all sorts have been similarly invested as a general social imperative since at least the late eighteenth century in Europe. And via carbon, the new mobilities of carbon share with other mobilities their particular sorts of materiality. While older mobilities depend on and are enabled by the chemical transformation of carbon molecules to release energy, the new mobilities depend on the abstraction of rights to carbon emissions from their socio-ecological consequences via their financialization. These nevertheless entail the mobilization of 'real' carbon, as they shape the development of projects in energy, forestry, agriculture, and beyond, and in many cases enable the affluent to continue their high-carbon lives via practices like carbon offsetting.

Notes

1 Of course other processes are entailed here, specifically the release of specific elements or molecules that bodies require for specific functions (iron for the blood, etc.). But it is the transformation of energy that is nevertheless the central function of digestion.
2 These numbers are not the same. For a tonne of carbon emissions, you get around 4 tonnes of CO_2, given the atomic mass of each element.
3 Systemic adaptation, in that many wanted to organize their systems so that the specific sorts of credits or allowances they were creating could themselves be mobile – trading allowances between the EU and the Kyoto system, between Australia and the EU, and so on. The significant limit to this mobility has been in the US, whose hegemonic presumptions, relative isolationism, and continued use of Imperial measures have combined to mean that both proposed federal cap and trade systems and those existing at the subfederal level (the Regional Greenhouse Gas Initiative in the North-East US) operate on the short tonne.
4 AAUs are Assigned Amount Units, the basic unit in the Kyoto Protocol. ERUs are Emissions Reduction Units, the credits created in the Joint Implementation mechanism in Kyoto. CERs are Certified Emissions Reductions, created by the Clean Development Mechanism. EUAs are European Union Allowances, created by the EU Emissions Trading System. There are also others in existence, for example in the Regional Greenhouse Gas Initiative, in New Zealand, in New South Wales, and others are in development in Australia, the Western Climate Initiative, South Korea, and perhaps China. The 'acronymization' is important to the performativity of the specific commodities, rendering them immediately recognizable and rapidly processable by traders, thus enabling their further proliferation into derivatives.
5 On the voluntary carbon market and its certification systems, see Bumpus and Liverman (2008) Newell and Paterson (2010).

References

Adey, P. and Bissell, D. (2010) 'Mobilities, Meetings, and Futures: An Interview with John Urry,' *Environment and Planning D: Society and Space*, 28(1): 1–16.
Böhm, S., Jones, C., Land, C. and Paterson, M. (eds) (2006) *Against Automobility*, Oxford: Blackwell.
Bond, P. (2009) 'The State of the Global Carbon Trade Debate,' *The Commoner*, Winter. Available online at www.durbanclimatejustice.org/articles/the-state-of-the-global-carbon-trade-debate.html (accessed 8 May 2012).
Bumpus, A. (2011) 'The Matter of Carbon: Understanding the Materiality of tCO_2e in Carbon Offsets,' *Antipode*, 43(3): 612–638.
Bumpus, A. and Liverman, D. (2008) 'Accumulation by Decarbonization and the Governance of Carbon Offsets,' *Economic Geography*, 84(2): 127–155.
Bumpus, A. and Liverman, D. (2011) 'Carbon Colonialism? Offsets, Greenhouse Gas Reductions and Sustainable Development,' in R. Peet, M. Watts and P. Evans (eds) *Global Political Ecology*, London: Routledge, 203–224.

Clark, B. and York, R. (2005) 'Carbon Metabolism: Global Capitalism, Climate Change, and the Biospheric Rift,' *Theory and Society*, 34(4): 391–428.

Dennis, K. and Urry, J. (2009) *After the Car*, Cambridge: Polity.

Descheneau, D. and Paterson, M. (2011) 'Between Desire and Routine: Assembling Environment and Finance in Carbon Markets,' *Antipode*, 43(4): 662–681.

Foster, J. B. (2000) *Marx's Ecology: Materialism and Nature*, New York: Monthly Review Press.

Hannam, K., Sheller, M. and Urry, J. (2006) 'Mobilities, Immobilities and Moorings,' *Mobilities* 1(1): 1–22.

Harvey, D. (1989) *The Condition of Postmodernity*, Oxford: Blackwell.

Harvey, D. (2003) *The New Imperialism*, Oxford: Oxford University Press.

Helleiner, E. and Thistlethwaite, J. (2012) 'Subprime Catalyst: Financial Regulatory Reform and the Strengthening of US Carbon Market Governance,' *Regulation and Governance*, early version available online: doi:10.1111/j.1748-5991.2012.01136.x.

Houghton, J. T., Jenkins, G. J. and Ephraums, J. J. (1990) *Climate Change: The IPCC Scientific Assessment*, Cambridge: Cambridge University Press.

Klare, M. T. (2001) *Resource Wars*, London: Palgrave Macmillan.

Lohmann, L. (2010) 'Commodity Fetishism in Climate Science and Policy: In Which Various Men with Beards are Enlisted to Help Explain Why Official Efforts to Address Climate Change Have Reached an Impasse.' Available online at www.thecornerhouse.org.uk/resource/commodity-fetishism-climate-science-and-policy (accessed 6 June 2012).

MacKenzie, D. (2009) 'Making Things the Same: Gases, Emission Rights and the Politics of Carbon Markets,' *Accounting, Organizations and Society*, 34(3–4): 440–455.

Nerlich, B., Evans, V. and Koteyko, N. (2011) 'Low Carbon Diet: Reducing the Complexities of Climate Change to Human Scale,' *Language and Cognition*, 3(1): 45–82.

Newell, P. and Paterson, M. (2010) *Climate Capitalism: Global Warming and the Transformation of the Global Economy*, Cambridge: Cambridge University Press.

Paterson, M. (2007) *Automobile Politics: Ecology and Cultural Political Economy*, Cambridge: Cambridge University Press.

Paterson, M. (2013) 'A Climate of Crisis: The Impacts of the Economic Crisis on EU Climate Change Policy', in J. DeBardeleben and C. Viju (eds) *The Economic Crisis in Europe: What it Means for the EU and Russia*, Houndmills: Palgrave Macmillan, 133–153.

Paterson, M. and Stripple, J. (2012) 'Virtuous Carbon,' *Environmental Politics*, 21(4): 563–582.

Rajan, S. C. (1996) *The Enigma of Automobility: Democratic Politics and Pollution Control*, Pittsburgh: University of Pittsburgh Press.

Rupert, M. (1995) *Producing Hegemony: The Politics of Mass Production and American Global Power*, Cambridge: Cambridge University Press.

Sheller, M. and Urry, J. (2006) 'The New Mobilities Paradigm,' *Environment and Planning A*, 38(2): 207–226.

Stephan, B. (2012) 'Bringing Discourse to the Market: The Commodification of Avoided Deforestation,' *Environmental Politics*, 21(4): 621–639.

UNFCCC (1997) *Kyoto Protocol on Climate Change*, New York: United Nations.

Urry, J. (2011) *Climate Change and Society*, Cambridge: Polity Press.

Virilio, P. (1986) *Speed and Politics*, New York: Semiotext(e).

World Bank (2012) 'New Initiatives Give Hope to a Carbon Market Facing Challenges,' Press Release, World Bank. Available online at http://web.worldbank.org/WBSITE/EXTERNAL/NEWS/0,,contentMDK:23206021~menuPK:34463~pagePK:34370~piPK:34424~theSitePK:4607,00.html (accessed 6 June 2012).

32

Passports

Lily Cho

In 2007, the Canadian Federal Court of Appeal rejected Eliyahu Veffer's claim to list 'Jerusalem, Israel' as the place of birth on his Canadian passport. Veffer was born in the western part of Jerusalem and then later became a Canadian citizen. When Passport Canada, the office responsible for issuing Canadian passports, refused to designate both the city and the country of his birth under the place of birth line on his passport, Veffer claimed that his rights to freedom of religion and equality as protected by the Canadian *Charter of Rights and Freedoms* had been violated.[1] While the court decided against Veffer, his case points to one way in which the place of birth designation on the contemporary passport is not merely an issue of identity and identification, but also one that is freighted with political issues. What is the importance and relevance of place of birth information on the contemporary passport? What does its purpose and place on the passport reveal about the relationship between culture and citizenship? In considering these questions, this chapter argues that the use of the place of birth reveals a problematic relationship between culture and citizenship, and a privileging of *jus soli* citizenship.

Citizenship appears, in many ways, to be culturally neutral. Holding a passport for a particular country should, regardless of the bearer's race, religion, or gender, signal that person as a citizen of that country. However, the designation of place of birth on the passport differentiates naturalized citizens from birthright citizens. One acquires citizenship through birthplace (*jus soli*), the nationality of one's parents (*jus sanguinis*), or naturalization, which, as Ayelet Shachar notes, also 'reflects the iconography of lineage,' and derives etymologically from the *nasci*, Latin for 'to be born' (2009: 128–9). Between *jus soli* and *jus sanguinis*, and the iconography of birth underpinning naturalization, citizenship acquisition is over-written by the genealogical. Further, most states limit the reach of *jus sanguinis* such that parents cannot pass citizenship to children born abroad without demonstrating residency in the country.[2] Thus, even *jus sanguinis* has embedded within it the conditions of connection to the soil and the primacy of place of birth. This privileging of birthplace signals an unevenness between foreign- and native-born citizens that is made explicit in the place of birth designation on contemporary passports.

Every passport issued includes place of birth information and yet this information seems to have very little function in terms of identification. My Canadian passport will tell you that

I was born in Edmonton, Alberta. This information should not distinguish me from Canadians born in, for example, Moose Jaw, Saskatchewan, any more than it should those who are born, as my father's passport states, in China. As Renato Rosaldo notes, 'Citizenship is often understood as a universal concept. In this view, all citizens of a particular nation state are equal before the law' (1999: 253). Or, as the US Customs Service puts it more ruefully in terms of potential terrorist threats in relation to US citizens born outside of the US, 'the fact that the passport states United States of America on the front poses the principal danger. Deleting the place of birth on the inside of the passport would have little effect on terrorists once "United States" is seen on the cover' (GAO 1987: 11). The cover of the passport, regardless of the information inside the document, renders its bearer equally potentially benign, and equally potentially dangerous. And yet, if citizenship is truly equal, if the nationality on the cover of the passport obviates any foreignness that might be indicated inside its pages, why does the place of birth designation continue to be used on contemporary passports? It does not seem crucial for ascertaining individual identity. As I will discuss in detail later in this chapter, it is clearly marked as an optional category of information in the international guidelines for passports. Its status as a discretionary item on the contemporary passports suggests that it is not considered to be vital information for assessing the identities of those wishing to cross national borders. And yet, the continued use of the place of birth designation raises the question of its purpose.

One might argue that place of birth, as biographical information, might help border agents and immigration officials to establish the identity of the bearer of the passport. And yet, not only is it considered optional information by international passport authorities, its usefulness as a tool for distinguishing one citizen from another is arguably limited. How does knowing that I was born in Edmonton, Alberta help to identify me as a citizen of Canada in a way that would be different if I had been born in another city, or another country? Surely, the identification photograph, as well as other biometric information such as fingerprint and iris images that may come into use in future passports,[3] distinguishes me much more definitively than data regarding my place of birth? This contradiction between the limited utility of birthplace information, and its widespread use, suggests something more than the persistence of mere convention. Passports did not always include birthplace information. However, passports did emerge out of a profound suspicion leveled at those who do not want to remain in their places of birth.

As the history of the passport reveals, it is a document of suspicion rather than recognition. Identification documents must be produced where there is cause, imagined or otherwise, for suspicion. They are in demand when there is some doubt regarding the person and the identity they claim. What is more, there is a long history of suspicion leveled at those who leave their place of birth. Beginning with the early modern period in Europe, John Torpey shows that the state attempted to regulate the movement of peoples with regards to the economic advantages of a particular area and military service (2000: 18). He points to a law passed by the English monarch Charles II that 'empowered the local authorities to remove to their place of legal settlement anyone "likely to be chargeable to the parish" – or, to put it in terms that would become familiar in American immigration legislation, anyone "likely to become a public charge"' (ibid.). The 'Act for the better Reliefe of the Poore of this Kingdom' of 1662 responded to 'the desire of the destitute to turn up more generous rates of poor relief than were available in their native villages' (ibid.). For Torpey,

> These laws governing movement helped to codify in law – and to implement in practice –
> a distinction between 'local' and 'foreign' poor, and notably referred to the place to

which illegal settlers should be removed as their 'native' residence. The act of removing oneself from one's place of birth thus appears to have been regarded as an anomaly, and may indeed have constituted a violation of the law without proper papers.

(ibid.)

Over time, it was not just being poor that would lead to possible charges of criminality, but also that of being found somewhere other than one's birthplace.

With the French Revolution, passport controls became more entrenched and defined even though the early period of the revolution attempted to do away with passports. Torpey observes that in 1791, with the victories of the revolution still fresh, the French National Assembly voted to abolish passport controls in favor of cosmopolitanism and freedom of movement (2000: 27). Only a year later, passport controls were reinstated and increasingly refined, thus laying the foundation for the contemporary passport. Torpey argues that the invention of the passport emerged as a response by an increasingly suspicious state in order to control and identify the enemies that it saw everywhere but could not easily mark.

Well into the twentieth century, the passport was understood to be a punitive document. 'The 1921 conference of the International Parliamentary Union in Stockholm expressed its condemnation of the passport system and called for greater freedom of movement' (Torpey 2000: 27). While the passport may seem relatively benign, indeed desirable, in the contemporary period the consolidation of its usage attests to a substantial history of state suspicion leveled with particular acuity upon anyone who does not want to stay put.

This bias against the mobile body, especially one that is devoid of an accompanying passport, has become particularly acute in the contemporary period. As Liisa Malkki observes, with regard to what she identifies as a sedentarist metaphysics that privileges staying in place, 'The pathologization of uprootedness in the national order of things can take several different (but often conflated) forms, among them political, medical, and moral' (1992: 32). In terms of morality, she observes that World War Two 'refugees' loss of bodily connection to their national homelands came to be treated as *a loss of moral bearings.* Rootless, they were no longer trustworthy as "honest citizens"' (1992: 32). Malkki connects morality and mobility (or lack thereof) with citizenship. The moral body, and the body that deserves the rights and privileges of citizenship, is an immobile one. Relatedly, writing of the 'widely diverse contexts' of Libyan Sanussi rebels under Italian rule, migrant camps established by the US Farm Security Administration during the Roosevelt era, and the treatment of Gypsies in Britain, Tim Cresswell notes that 'we see strikingly similar reactions to mobile people. Their mobility is seen as a threat, and the thinking that goes into planning for them emphasizes legibility and order' (2006: 42). As a document that turns precisely upon making the mobile body legible and orderly, the passport reinforces the metaphysics of sedentarism and punishes those whose bodies are perceived to be inconsonant with the nation.

In the United States, one of the clearest indications of reliance upon the passport as a punitive document emerges in the differential treatment of white and non-white travelers. Racial difference remains one of indication of a discrepancy between place of birth and nationality and this difference was cause enough for a demand for documentation. Craig Robertson observes in his history of the passport in the US that restrictions on immigration in the nineteenth and early twentieth centuries made the passport an increasingly important document for delineating those who belonged to the nation and those who did not. Noting 'the racialized othering that concerned much of the emergence of the modern documentation of individual identity,' Robertson points to ways in which documentation such as passports was not even necessary for those whose bodies read as white:

> In the early 1920s the equation of citizenship with a particular definition of whiteness (and its association with respectability) meant that in certain circumstances personal appearance was still accepted as evidence of US citizenship in lieu of paper documents.
>
> *(2010: 102)*

In contrast, for those who did not read as 'respectable' – that is, those whose bodies did not appear consonant with the nation's view of itself – identification documents were not optional. The foreignness of the racial other's presumed place of birth was immediate cause for suspicion and intense scrutiny.

Even though every passport issued by any of the United Nations member states includes it, place of birth is marked as an optional category by the International Civil Aviation Organization (ICAO). Established by the United Nations in 1944, ICAO sets the standards for civil aviation throughout the world. One of its responsibilities is to produce the standards that govern international passports. These standards are outlined in Document 9303, *Machine Readable Travel Documents*, approved and published under the authority of the Secretary General of the United Nations. Document 9303 is a manual for member states and outlines all of the specifications and requirements for passports used in international travel.

In addition to outlining such items as the type of paper, ink, and font to be used on a passport, Document 9303 lists several mandatory data elements that must be found on each passport: the name of the issuing state or organization; the type of document ('passport' in the language of the issuing state, as well as 'passport' in either English, French, or Spanish); the document code (a capital 'P' to designate a passport and, at the discretion of the issuing state, an additional letter to designate special passports such as diplomatic passports); the name of the issuing state or organization; the passport number; the name of the bearer; a primary identifier (predominant components of the bearer's name); a secondary identifier (secondary components of the bearer's name); nationality; sex; date of issue; authority or issuing office; date of expiry; and the holder's signature or usual mark. Document 9303 is explicit about optional data elements: profession, personal number issued by the state, and place of birth (ICAO 2006a: iv–11). Despite being clearly designated as an optional category, and unlike profession or personal number, place of birth remains in use in passports the world over.

It was not always the case that place of birth was universally used on the passport. In response to a rising number of terrorist attacks in the 1980s where passports were used to single out victims for hijackings and hostage-takings, a number of nation-states considered removing the place of birth designation from their passports. Ultimately, Austria was the only one to do so, taking action in 1986. However, upon joining the European Union, Austria reverted to listing place of birth in order to follow the same standards as other EU member states. In Canada the option to remove the place of birth designation was made available, also in 1986, and it continues to be an option today. As the Federal Court of Appeal justices noted in *Veffer v. Canada*:

> The Passport Canada policy explains that the place of birth is 'a feature to assist in identifying the bearer of the passport and, for the majority of travelers, may prevent further questioning at entry or exit points.' An applicant who omits his or her place of birth is required to sign a statement titled 'Request for a Canadian Passport without Place of Birth' and is advised to contact the representatives of the countries to be visited in order

to determine if difficulties will be encountered in entering those countries without having that information disclosed in the passport.

(2007: [10])

Even though this policy remains in place, as the justices note of the process involved in obtaining a passport without place of birth, the Canadian Passport Office makes clear that anyone who desires such a passport risks becoming a subject of suspicion. Traveling without such information on a passport is not the norm and abnormalities lead to additional paper-work at best (the need to contact countries to be visited prior to arrival at the border) and outright difficulties at worse.

The United States seriously considered removing place of birth from its passports and its deliberations on this issue offer some particularly revealing insights regarding the perception of the utility of place of birth information. In 1987, the United States General Accounting Office (GAO) submitted a report to Congress, *Passports: Implications of Deleting Place of Birth on US Passports*. This report continues to be the authoritative reference for current US policy and is cited in the most recent (November 2010) edition of the US Foreign Affairs Manual, *7 FAM 1300 Appendix D: Place of Birth Names on Passports*, as the authority for cur-rent US policy on this issue. The report notes that the US passport began to include place of birth in 1921 (GAO 1987: 6). However, this information did not become mandatory until 1928 (ibid.). In 1979, the US permitted foreign-born citizens to list their town or city of birth instead of their country of birth (ibid.). In considering deleting place of birth information from US passports, the GAO report surveyed every US agency that might be affected by the removal of place of birth on US passports: the Federal Bureau of Investigation (FBI), the Central Intelligence Agency (CIA), Immigration and Naturalization Services (INS), the Drug Enforcement Administration (DEA), and US Customs Service.

Of these agencies, three vociferously objected to removing birthplace information on US passports. Neither the FBI nor the CIA objected and both agencies were happy to follow the directions of the others being consulted. The INS argued against deleting birthplace from passports, noting in their formal submission to the GAO that "'a thorough and readily avail-able pool of biographic information is an essential tool . . . Without question, the place of birth is one of the most vital of the biographical data'" (GAO 1987: 9). The INS also worried about the effect of such a policy on other countries and observed that "'the elimination of the place of birth data from its passports, and perhaps encouraging other countries to follow suit would seriously undermine law enforcement efforts to detect abuse of US passports'" (ibid.: 10). Similarly, the DEA noted that place of birth is "'essential to any investigation is [sic] any and all information concerning any individual trafficker or group of traffickers. Therefore, all identifying data, including the place of birth information, is useful'" (ibid.: 10). While the GAO noted that the DEA had conducted no studies and had no statistics verifying its claims, it also pointed out that this information was used in assessing foreign passports in order to aid 'in investigating potential violators of drug laws and foreign drug couriers' (ibid.: 10). Like the DEA and the INS, in their submission the US Customs Services were "'strongly against'" removing birthplace from US passports. It noted that "'the knowledge that a person was born in a foreign country where he may have extensive family or business contacts could be a critical factor in determining the degree of inspection or investigation'" (ibid.: 11).

For all of the agencies that objected to the removal of birthplace information on passports, this information was declared to be essential for determining the potential criminality of those attempting to enter the country. These agencies use information regarding par-ticular birthplaces as flags for further scrutiny. Their submissions make clear the way in which foreign-born citizens – those whose places of birth do not correspond directly with their nationalities – are particularly subject to suspicion. Even though place of birth is not considered a vital category of identification according to ICAO, the persistence of this category on the contemporary passport signals its punitive function for citizens born abroad.

Where you are born matters. Citizenship is different for those who are born outside of the country of their nationality. As Audrey Macklin suggests, 'One cannot but speculate that a Canadian passport listing "place of birth" as Winnipeg (or even Vienna) routinely attracts less attention than one indicating a Karachi birthplace' (2007: 365–6).

'Indeed,' she goes on to argue, 'the fact that Canadian passports still identify the place of birth reveals something about lingering differences in the heft of citizenship for the birthright versus naturalized citizen' (2007: 366). In her argument, Macklin draws a connection between naturalization and racial difference by pointing to a pilot study conducted by the British Home Office on the decision-making processes of British Immigration Officers at UK ports. The 2007 study examined the rate at which Immigration Officers issued an IS81 (a form indicating that a passenger will be held for further questioning) to white and non-white passengers from an ethnically diverse country such as Canada. In the case of Canadian travelers at UK ports, only four white passengers were stopped for every 10,000 passengers. In contrast, 35 non-white passengers were given IS81s. The authors of the study further adjusted their numbers for socioeconomic status in case non-white travelers were being discriminated against on the basis of presumed low socioeconomic status rather than race. Surprisingly, the number of non-white Canadian passengers stopped actually increased to 54 out of every 10,000 passengers once the socioeconomic factors were evened out (Woodfield et al. 2007: 43).[4] As Macklin argues with reference to the experience of non-white Canadian passport holders in this study, 'Race and class (and race as a proxy for class) apparently diminish the heft of what is otherwise one of the most substantial citizenships in the world' (2007: 34). While there is not necessarily a positive correlation between place of birth and racial difference, they are also often connected. The differential treatment of non-white Canadians in this study suggests that a lack of correlation between place of birth and nationality can play a significant role in treatment at the border.

The passport as a document verifying identity has a history that mattered more to racial others than to those whose bodies appeared to be more consonant with the nation. The reliance upon the passport itself suggests a certain faith in the notion that people are who their documents declare them to be. 'With the widespread use of a similar passport,' Mark Salter notes, 'the examination at the border came to be centered on whether *documents* – rather than the traveler herself – were in order' (2003: 28). However, that notion of documentary orderliness only came to matter after the state began to favor the reliability of reading documents over that of reading bodies. As Robertson notes of the United States, prior to World War I the state found documents particularly unreliable for ascertaining the identities of racial others. Indeed, as with the case of Chinese immigrants, 'immigration officials found the problem posed . . . to be the identification of some*body*, not some*one* – the articulation of an individual to a racial group or set of behavioral traits via their body or personal appearance' (Robertson 2010: 171). As Robertson observes, for those who appeared 'respectable,' there was no need for documents at all (2010: 102). That respectability was shorthand for whiteness.

In predominantly white countries where immigration often meant the arrival of non-white communities, the correlation of whiteness with citizenship emerges with particular clarity around the standardization of the passport as a document of identity. In the early part of the twentieth century, William Williams, then the commissioner of immigration at Ellis

Island in the US 'assumed that the status of native-born citizens could be easily and effectively verified through appearance' (Robertson 2010: 180). Of course, a major part of his assumption rested upon the presumed whiteness of native-born US citizens. However, changes to immigration laws in the late nineteenth century complicated his presumptions. For example, in 1898 the US Supreme Court recognized the birthright citizenship of children born to Chinese immigrants in the US (even though Chinese people could not be naturalized at the time). The presumptive correlation between citizenship and whiteness became destabilized. 'With the increasingly problematic association of citizenship and whiteness, the beginnings of a practical need for documents appeared' (Robertson 2010: 180). The passport, along with birth certificates, naturalization certificates, and so on, came to matter at precisely the point when racial difference complicated the presumed whiteness of the nation.

Despite the seemingly racially and culturally neutral claims of citizenship, further examination reveals that it is very much a reflection of dominant culture. At the conclusion of his study of the genealogies of citizenship, Engin Isin argues 'citizenship is that particular point of view of the dominant which constitutes itself as a universal point of view' (2002: 275). That universal point of view has racial inflections. As Leti Volpp argues in *The Culture of Citizenship*, citizenship and racial otherness are simply not necessarily confluent. Indeed, they are more likely to exist in opposition to each other. Volpp suggests that 'citizenship is both a cultural and an anti-cultural institution, by which [she] mean[s] that citizenship positions itself as oppositional to specific cultures, even as it is constituted by quite specific cultural values' (2007: 574). As Volpp recognizes, even those specific cultural values that seem universal are actually racialized. For example, freedom in relationship to citizenship, as Volpp notes, is most often related to the French and US Revolutions of the eighteenth century and not connected with the black emancipation of the Haitian Revolution (2007: 584). For Volpp, 'the citizen emerges through distinction from the cultural other, who is repudiated from citizenship through total identification with an unassimilable cultural difference, and through simultaneous denial that the citizen might share similar cultural values' (2007: 585). Volpp discusses a range of examples of this perception of unassimilable difference: nineteenth-century US perceptions of Chinese Americans and the more recent debates about the headscarf in France. These examples circle back to what Rosaldo calls 'cultural citizenship,' a concept that 'operates in an uneven field of structural inequalities where the dominant claims of universal citizenship assume a propertied white male subject' (1999: 260). Citizenship is neither culturally nor racially neutral. Instead, its insistence upon universality obscures it as an expression of dominant culture.

The continuing use of place of birth designations on the contemporary passport reveals citizenship as deeply culturally invested. The cover of the passport offers the possibility of equality for all its bearers, but the information within the passport suggests that there are inequalities at play for those whose country of birth differs from their declared nationalities. The function of birthplace information inside the passport is not primarily that of identification. As the 1987 US GAO report highlights, the place of birth designation allows government agencies and border agents to target individuals with foreign birthplaces for potential criminality. They do not claim to use this information to ascertain whether or not that bearer of the passport is, to borrow Robertson's phrasing, some*one*, but rather to focus on the potential threats of some*body*. That is, birthplace information may have little use in differentiating one specific citizen from another, but it can be used to distinguish one group of citizens – for example, those who are born in foreign countries that raise the suspicions of border agents and immigration officials – from another.

This focus upon bodies as opposed to individual identities runs counter to the current trend in passport technologies where the body has been broken down precisely so that it can be correlated with the specificities of individual identity. As Peter Adey observes with regard to the biopolitics of airport security,

> The unity of the body is undone by focusing in on pieces of it. These pieces stand for the whole, for the whole of an identity. For instance, pattern recognition filters use finger prints. Palm recognition and now iris recognition technologies are deployed in many instances of facilitating airport priority passengers and frequent flyers who are pre-enrolled.
>
> *(2009: 277)*

Even without turning to fingerprint and iris scans, the photographic images currently used on all passports have themselves become standardized so that the facial recognition technologies can be used to translate the image into an algorithm (ICAO 2006a: ii–8). Given the increasing emphasis upon transforming the body into discrete units of information, the continuing use of information that relies not only on the body as a whole (one person born in a particular place), but also that body as it connects to other bodies (other people born in that particular place) seems almost anachronistic. 'To plot only "places of birth" and degrees of nativeness is to blind oneself to the multiplicity of attachments that people form to places through living in, remembering, and imagining them' (Malkki 1992: 38). Place of birth reveals little about individual identity and arguably obscures individuality by binding one person to a group of others.

The place of birth designation on the contemporary passport is neither the product of convention, nor a practical means of discerning individual identity. It is the residue of the inequalities and alterities that are foundational to citizenship. As Isin argues,

> citizenship and its alterity always emerged simultaneously in a dialogical manner and constituted each other. Women were not simply excluded from ancient Greek citizenship, but were constituted as its other as an immanent group by citizens. Similarly, slaves were not simply excluded from citizenship, but made citizenship possible by their very formation.
>
> *(2002: 4)*

The foreign-born citizen is not simply one kind of citizen. She safeguards the primacy of the birthright citizen. One need look no further than inside her passport to see that her difference matters.

Notes

1 A very similar case will be going before the US Supreme Court in November 2011. In Menachem B. Zivotofsky vs Clinton, US Supreme Court, No. 10–699, the parents of Zivotofsky, who was born in Jerusalem in 2002, want Secretary of State Clinton to list 'Jerusalem, Israel' on their son's passport. The case differs from Veffer vs Canada in that Veffer made a rights claim, whereas Zivotofsky relates to the authority of the judiciary to dictate US foreign policy.

2 For example, Canadian citizens born abroad cannot pass on citizenship to their children if they are also born abroad; the US requires that citizens demonstrate residency in the US for a specific period of time before they are able to pass on citizenship to children born abroad; German citizens born after 1999 cannot pass on citizenship to children born abroad if their permanent residence is not in Germany; Chinese citizens may not pass on their citizenship to foreign-born children unless they

permanently reside in China. There are exceptions in all of these cases for children of diplomats, government workers, and military personnel. Most countries also have exception for cases where the child would be rendered stateless.

3 The current guidelines for international passports as set out by the International Civil Aviation Organization allow for 'optional data elements' such as fingerprints and iris scans in future iterations of the passport. The specific guidelines for these elements are outlined in Document 9303, vol. 1, part 2.

4 The pattern was similar for South African passengers: 14 out of every 10,000 white South Africans were stopped as opposed to 148 non-white South Africans; adjusted for socioeconomic status, the number of non-white South Africans stopped increased to 254 (Woodfield *et al.* 2007: 43). Despite the striking differences in treatment for Canadian and South African non-white passengers, the authors of the study found only negligible differences in the treatment of white and non-white US passengers (two white US passengers were given IS81s, as opposed to five non-white ones for every 10,000 passengers (Woodfield *et al.* 2007: 43)). While this finding may seem anomalous given the Canadian and South African numbers, the authors of the study also noted that the study is limited given the relatively small data sets that they were working with.

Bibliography

Adey, Peter (2009) 'Facing Airport Security: Affect, Politics and the Preemptive Securitisation of the Mobile Body,' *Environment and Planning D: Society and Space* 27: 274–95.

Cresswell, Tim (2006) *On the Move: Mobility in the Modern Western World*. New York: Routledge.

General Accounting Office (GAO) (United States) Comptroller General (1987) *Passports: Implications of Deleting Place of Birth on US Passports*. Washington, DC: US General Accounting Office.

International Civil Aviation Organization (ICAO) (2006a) *Machine Readable Travel Documents*, Document 9303, Part 1, Vol. 1. United Nations: Secretary General.

International Civil Aviation Organization (ICAO) (2006b) *Machine Readable Travel Documents*, Document 9303, Part 1, Vol. 2. United Nations: Secretary General.

Isin, Engin (2002) *Being Political: Genealogies of Citizenship*. Minneapolis: University of Minnesota Press.

Macklin, Audrey (2007) 'Who is the Citizen's Other? Considering the Heft of Citizenship,' *Theoretical Inquiries in Law* 8: 333–36.

Malkki, Liisa (1992) 'National Geographic: The Rooting of Peoples and the Territorialization of National Identity among Scholars and Refugees,' *Cultural Anthropology* 7.1: 24–44.

Robertson, Craig (2010) *The Passport in America: The History of a Document*. Oxford: Oxford University Press.

Rosaldo, Renato (1999) 'Cultural Citizenship, Inequality and Multiculturalism' in Rodolfo T. Torres, Luis F. Mirón and Jonathan Xavier Inda (eds) *Race, Identity and Citizenship: A Reader*. London: Blackwell, pp. 253–61.

Salter, Mark (2003) *Rights of Passage: the Passport in International Relations*. Boulder, CO: Lynne Reiner.

Shachar, Ayelet (2009) *The Birthright Lottery: Citizenship and Global Inequality*. Cambridge, MA: Harvard University Press.

Torpey, John (2000) *The Invention of the Passport: Surveillance, Citizenship and the State*. Cambridge: Cambridge University Press.

United States, Department of Foreign Affairs (2010) 'Place of Birth Names in Passports,' Appendix D in *Foreign Affairs Manual*, 7 FAM 1300. Washington, DC: US Dept. of Foreign Affairs.

Veffer v. Canada (Minister of Foreign Affairs) (FCA) (2007 [2008]) FCA 247, 1 FCR 641.

Volpp, Leti (2007) 'The Culture of Citizenship,' *Theoretical Inquiries in Law* 8: 571–602.

Woodfield, Kandy *et al.* (2007) *Exploring the Decision-Making of Immigration Officers: A Research Study Examining Non-EEA Passenger Stops and Refusals at UK Ports*. London: Home Office Online Report.

Section Five
Introduction: Subjects

One of the critical tasks of mobilities research is to differentiate life on the move. Many have pointed out that in earlier work on spaces of flow, the implicit mobile subject that inhabits these mobile milieus is often a white, male, able bodied, western ego (see Crang, 2002). The experience of this caricatured illusory composite clearly does real violence by occluding the diverse plurality of subjects through which mobilities become enacted. Much mobilities research has since been concerned precisely with this multiplicity of experience, and is powerfully illustrated through volumes on gendered mobilities (Uteng and Cresswell, 2008) and mobilities and inequality (Ohnmacht *et al.*, 2009) for example, which seek to attend to this plurality. This work also reminds us that the task is not just one of differentiating mobilities, but also of tracing something of their relational constitution. Through the idea of a power-geometry, Doreen Massey (1993) famously reminds us that the mobility of some people is contingent on the relative immobility of others. Pivoting around this crucial observation, the chapters in this section work hard to foreground the relational constitution of a variety of specific mobile figures. But each of these chapters also reveals the challenges involved in developing typologies that might be suggestive of 'generic' figures. In contrast, the chapters in this section demonstrate research that helps to articulate singular, thoroughly socially and geopolitically contextual lifeworlds. In doing so, they draw into view particular configurations of temporalities, capacities, proximities, knowledges and distributions, each of which provides the structure of this introduction.

Spotlighting the importance of temporalities, much work in mobilities research underscores the importance of duration by historicizing mobilities. This is refracted in multiple ways in this section not just in terms of the personal, biographical histories that constitute individuals and collectives on the move, but also the more extensive histories of the practices and spaces that mobile subjects are bound up with. The temporalities that this section spotlights are multiple and diverse. As Scott McCabe's chapter shows, some of the temporal arcs implicated in being a tourist might be short but repetitive, as in an annual family holiday, whereas Rachel Woodward and K. Neil Jenkings's chapter shows that being a soldier involves much more drawn-out durations of movement and stasis. Pointing to rather different temporal logics, Kim Sawchuk spotlights some of the more sudden cuts and thresholds that might immobilize people in the context of impairment through accident or illness. Alternatively,

Juliana Mansvelt examines some of the more incremental mobility transformations that are particularly characteristic of older age. The cross-cutting relations between these different temporal logics are also illustrated by the pedagogical processes of learning to be mobile in particular ways. In the context of the soldier, Woodward and Jenkings underscore the gradual development of corporeal capacities through specific training exercises. Alternatively, Mansvelt demonstrates how attenuated corporeal mobilities in later life require experimenting with new ways of getting the daily chores done. Many of the chapters in this section express some of the different extents to which subjects are constituted in part by the temporalities of particular mobility systems. Tim Dant's chapter gestures to the coercive flexibility that the car affords, whereas Woodward and Jenkings's pinpoints the more rigid, timetabled character of military tours.

The differential capacities of mobile subjects is a key thread that weaves through each of the chapters in this section. This might be about the knotty relationship between mobility and social inclusion. For example, echoing some of the qualities of Elliott and Urry's (2010) 'globals', James Faulconbridge's chapter on executive mobility points to how aeromobility providers in particular have come to facilitate easy and streamlined passage that helps these subjects sustain powerful networks, whereas Roger Keil's chapter on infrastructure provision in relation to urban homelessness and TB illustrates how different access to material and economic resources and services can serve to radically immobilize underprivileged urban inhabitants. Alternatively, resonating with debates on 'network capital', it might be about the capacity to mobilize others, as demonstrated by Mansvelt in terms of homemaking practices of elders. The chapters together work hard to spotlight some of the broader political transformations that generate some hugely powerful capacities, such as the powers of the executive that Faulconbridge describes, which have developed in relation to new economic discourses and practices. Other chapters, such as Mansvelt's on elder mobility, point to the more 'micropolitical' powers that mobile bodies enact where the differential capacities of bodies on the move are much more fleeting and contextual, borne of situated encounters with other people and things. Indeed, J.-D. Dewsbury's chapter gives us one of the primary exemplars of subversion – a line of flight – through the 'inoperative mobility' of loitering that disrupts or withdraws from societal, cultural, economic and contextual rules, norms or expectations.

While many of the chapters here emphasize the hugely significant topologies of race, class and gender at play in mobile lives – splinterings that are particularly evident in Roger Keil's chapter on disease – at the same time, Sawchuk's chapter on the relationship of impairment to the urban form reminds us that mobile subjects cannot be reduced to aggregate markers of identity. Sometimes mobility relates to the maintenance of particular capacities, as illustrated in Woodward and Jenkings's chapter on the soldier. On the other hand, McCabe's chapter hints at how tourism might involve a series of much more fragile – even suspended – capacities. Discussion of new technologies, such as that in Tim Dant's chapter on the driver and passenger, demonstrates how new automobile technologies can simultaneously augment some capacities whilst depleting others.

Many of the chapters in this section describe some of the changing landscapes of proximity that systems of mobility generate. Faulconbridge's chapter, for example, describes how the corporate mobility of executives takes place in order to sustain particular business relationships which require face to face meetings. In a rather less productivist milieu, Mansvelt's chapter describes how the significance of face to face encounters is one of the imperatives that threads the lives of elders, providing vital connections to the world beyond the home. Furthermore, for Clare Holdsworth, the proximities engendered by family car travel can become important sites of negotiation. Faulconbridge also points to the parallel rise of virtual mobilities, in particular the mobile phone and internet, which have reshaped how proximity is enacted and experienced: something that Mansvelt reminds us is as important for elders as it is for businesspeople. Yet proximity is an ambivalent quality. Keil's chapter on homelessness and TB, for example, reminds us that a powerful politics of risk plays out through the fear of particular forms of contact. Here proximity is all about exposure to the more fickle mobilities of disease that intensify the threat of infection and contagion. In a very different context, McCabe's chapter alerts us to how certain forms of tourism might be contingent on removal from the proximity of others. Indeed Faulconbridge reminds us of the variegated nature of proximity through the figure of the executive, for whom 'entubulated' (Bissell and Fuller, 2011) passage is an infrastructural effect that permits proximity to other business types but is contingent on insulation from other people on the move. Such variegated proximity clearly invites us to examine the various visibilities and invisibilities that these mobile subjects enact. Whilst the mobility of the executive and soldier might be rather stealthy and fly under the radar for many, in contrast, it is the hyper visibility of the tourist that often becomes the cause of socio-cultural antagonism, leading many to self-consciously dis-identify with such a subjectivity, as McCabe suggests.

The mobile subjects that are the focus of this section are all in part constituted by the knowledges that they develop and enact. Knowledges might be generated through particularly scripted regimes of training and exercise, as Woodward and Jenkings show in their discussion on the soldier. Or they might be much more improvisatory and experimental, as Holdsworth discusses in relation to the child. Some of the chapters are particularly attuned to the embodied, sensate knowledges relating to physically moving about – for example, for a mobility-impaired person, as Sawchuk alludes to. Similarly, Mansvelt's chapter works hard to draw attention to the sometimes painful but often intense sensate landscapes that are threaded through everyday practices such as shopping for elders, where pains and anxieties are ways of knowing the world, sculpting perception and moulding attention. The desirability of some pleasurable sensations might be what sustains certain mobilities, as Faulconbridge describes in relation to the executive, and McCabe in relation to the tourist. Some chapters draw attention to the more self-consciously reflexive knowledges that are tethered to the development of specific mobile identities. Faulconbridge's executive is suggestive not just of a mode of being mobile, but more broadly an entire lifestyle. McCabe, on the other hand, describes how certain forms of tourism involve individuals engaging in a kind of reflexive self-styling to distance themselves from other forms of (mass) tourism, itself based on specific ways of knowing and performing. This is where attitudes and dispositions developed through practices become significant. Knowledges of mobile subjects are also significant for many of these chapters. The data doubles that permit easy passage for Faulconbridge's executive figure contrast with the techniques of surveillance that help to constrain Keil's diseased figures. Furthermore, Woodward and Jenkings's patrolling solider enacts a very different mode of searching and finding to that implicated in McCabe's tourist.

Finally, each of these chapters invites us to ask some crucial political questions concerning distributions of agency for mobile subjects. Overturning assumptions that agency resides only with human subjects, many of the chapters in this section carve out a much more distributed understanding of agency, which involves examining the human–non-human assemblages that compose mobility systems, or the volatile emergence of will and action as seen in Dewsbury's writing on the loiterer. All this is particularly striking in Dant's chapter on the driver and passenger, which sidesteps easy assertions of the driver being the figure in control and the passenger being relatively powerless. Dant demonstrates how mobile subjects are not bound by fleshy bodies but are much more distributed through knowledges, automations and prostheses that devolve agency to other parts of the car system. Furthermore, Sawchuk's chapter on impairment emphasizes the importance of thinking about bodies and spaces as being brought into being simultaneously. But it is in Dewsbury's chapter where we see one of the most ardent critiques of agency and subjectivity in current mobilities research. Dewsbury aims to subvert the assumption of a singular, purposeful mobile subject whose will, he argues, is not so simply their own but an expression of the drives and forces that are both interior and exterior to the mobile body.

Dant's development of a more nuanced conceptualization of intentionality is also discernible in Mansvelt's chapter on the elder and Holdsworth's chapter on the child, where each of these mobile subjects is often meshed into complex webs of allegiance, obligation and duty that sidestep any easy distinctions between voluntarism and coercion. Whilst distributive agencies can pinpoint modes of governance and control, they also permit certain freedoms – something that Dant develops through the notion of 'mobility capital'. Yet, at the same time, Holdsworth's chapter on the child and Mansvelt's chapter on the elder both spotlight how independent mobility has come to be an imperative of much planning and policy work in these areas. Other chapters emphasize how distributions need to be understood in terms of mobility collectives. Woodward and Jenkings's chapter clearly spotlights how moving together is not just about moving together with other troops, but with families too. As McCabe reminds us, the attractions and repulsions of moving together are also, of course, a key trope of writing on the tourist.

References

Bissell, D. and Fuller, G. (eds) (2011) 'Stillness unbound', in D. Bissell and G. Fuller (eds) *Stillness in a Mobile World*, London: Routledge.

Crang, M. (2002) 'Between places: producing hubs, flows, and networks', *Environment and Planning A*, 34: 569–574.

Elliott, A. and Urry, J. (2010) *Mobile Lives*, London: Routledge.

Massey, D. (1993) 'Power-geometry and a progressive sense of place', in J. Bird, B. Curtis, T. Putnam, G. Robertson and L. Tickner (eds) *Mapping the Futures: Local Cultures, Global Change*, London: Routledge.

Ohnmacht, T., Maksim, H. and Bergman, M. (eds) (2009) *Mobilities and Inequality*, Aldershot: Ashgate.

Uteng, T. P. and Cresswell, T. (eds) (2008) *Gendered Mobilities*, Aldershot: Ashgate.

33

Tourist

Scott McCabe

Over the last thirty-five years, the tourist has become the focus of intense scrutiny, initially amongst sociologists and social-anthropologists, and subsequently amongst a burgeoning field of scholars within tourism (or tourist) studies, giving rise to an eponymous journal along the way. The reason for this interest is partly at least that the tourist has become a perfect symbol of postmodernity. The opportunity for participation in tourism, as witnessed through tourism's continued global expansion in emerging regions, marks a transition into economic modernity, but also highlights the role and significance of tourism within the mobilities paradigm (Urry and Sheller 2004). The tourist epitomizes all that it means to be mobile and all that it means to be modern. In *Liquid Modernity*, Baumann (2000) described how technologies have compressed space and time to enable distant friends and relatives to feel 'closer' to each other, and to transform how we understand other places and cultures, de-exoticizing and demythologizing them. The improvements in technological capabilities underpinning mobilities outlined in other chapters of this volume have intensified the flow and speed of such changes almost into the realms of science fiction.

Therefore the fundamental geo-political, financial, technological and infrastructural conditions that led to the emergence of the mobilities paradigm both facilitated and were facilitated by incremental, inexorable increases in the numbers of people actually traveling for all sorts of reasons, with tourism being a principal component, evidenced by the latest figures showing that numbers of international tourists surpassed the one billion mark in 2012 (UNWTO 2012). The movement of people for non-leisure reasons is dealt with in other chapters of this handbook, so the focus here is on the phenomenon of leisure travel – the tourist. The tourist voluntarily displaces him or herself from the relative safety of the home environment at some significant expense, and often no small measure of discomfort, to experience an unfamiliar area, and possibly to meet people from other cultures. This voluntary character provides the potential for great insights into the social mores and concerns of the tourist's home culture and society. This was the overarching aim of early social theorists of the tourist. As MacCannell in his introduction to the 1999 version of *The Tourist* states, "a study of tourists . . . as a method of gaining access to the process by which modernity, modernisation, modern culture was establishing its empire on a global basis" (1999: xv). And Urry in the third version of *The Tourist Gaze* states that the study of the tourist "presupposes a system of social activities and signs which locate the particular tourist practices, not in terms of some intrinsic characteristics, but through the contrasts implied with non-tourist social practices, particularly those based within home and paid work" (Urry and Larsen 2012: 3). And yet, tourism and the tourist in particular has often been cast as symbolizing the more negative aspects of modernity, whilst at the same time the nature of tourist experience has been transformed by the very same global processes of mobility and modernity.

However, early social theorists have been criticized for constructing the tourist as a one-dimensional figure, and it is clear that there is a need to think reflexively about how the concept of 'tourist' is constructed and deployed to make claims about people and social activities (Uriely *et al.* 2002; McCabe 2005). At a basic level of description, a tourist is some-one who undertakes a journey to a place outside his or her usual environment for leisure purposes. Recent changes in global mobilities highlight a pressing need to develop new theorizations of tourists. For example, formerly it was relatively easy to differentiate tourist spaces from non-tourist spaces, and therefore relatively easy to determine who was a tourist amongst a range of other categories of persons (such as migrant, laborer, and so on). Now, everywhere is a tourist destination, at least potentially, as tourism has become hardwired into the planning and development of localities, regions and nations. Similarly, tourists tended to be more visible because their apparel, accoutrements and activities marked them out as distinct from locals and other inhabitants of tourist spaces. Yet now we all carry cameras on our mobile phones, engage in leisure practices in workaday spaces, and so on. Tourist-ness used to be characterized in binary, oppositional dualisms: host–guest; tourist–traveler; familiar–strange; home–away. However, the effect of postmodernism has led to the concept of the post-tourist (Feifer 2005), who playfully and knowingly subverts the norms and expectations of the tourist experience, engendering a multiplicity of forms and norms, types and stereotypes, conforming and resisting behaviors, which make any essentializing characterizations difficult to sustain and legitimate.

The tourist has become a multiplicity of tourists. The tourist industry has salami-sliced the tourist into ever more fragmented segmentations, resulting in more complex niche forms of tourism with increasingly varied combinations of experiences (e.g. business travelers bolting a short holiday onto a business trip, or the rise of the 'staycation'). Thus, it has become increasingly difficult to identify who is a tourist in the post-industrial landscapes of the developed world (Bianchi 2000). At any time and in any given place, tourists might be expected to be doing similar things in similar places to a whole range of other categories of persons, from bankers to prostitutes. How do we make sense of this complexity of people and activities?

The aim of this chapter is to reflect on the concept of the tourist, revealing how changes brought about through the processes of mobility provide an opportunity to reassess how the tourist is constituted. Through a review of recent research on the tourist, the discussion aims to address the implications that global mobility processes hold for developing new understandings of tourists and of how tourism connects to technological, social and spatial mobilities.

Situating the tourist

Early theories of the tourist developed classifications based on observed similarities in attributes or behaviors, producing typologies of tourist. Cohen developed a fourfold typology of tourist experiences – the organized mass tourist, the individual mass tourist, the explorer and the drifter (Cohen 1972) – based on behaviors as well as interactions with the organizing practices of the tourist industry and the degree of familiarity/strangeness sought. He went on to link together types of experiences to a range of tourist roles, proposing a range of tourist roles with common characteristics such as: permanency, voluntary-ness, direction, distance, recurrence and purpose of trip (Cohen 1974). Cohen's (1979) later analysis concerned tourists' orientation to Turner's (1973) notion of the 'center' in pilgrimage, which determined the types of experiences sought along a spectrum, where attachment to the home society influenced the type of experience. Tourists could then be classified along a spectrum of modes of experience from recreational to existential types.

Forms and types of experience have provided the framework for subsequent analyses whereby differences in qualities and attributes have provided the basis for knowledge production (e.g. Pearce 2005 in relation to the differences in behaviors between tourists and backpackers, Uriely *et al.* (2002) in relation to different forms of the 'backpacker' tourist experience). The main focal point of analysis remains the backpacker. Primarily constructed in direct contrast with more institutionalized forms of tourist experience – i.e. the packaged tour – theorizing about backpackers has developed to account for heterogeneity of forms of experience. Recent research has noted new forms of backpacker, the 'flashpacker' for example, which Hannam and Diekmann note "has greater disposable income, visits more 'off the beaten track' locations, carries a laptop, or at least a 'flash drive' and a mobile phone, but who engages with the mainstream backpacker culture" (2010: 2). Cohen (2011) also differentiates between backpackers and 'lifestyle travelers' who spend many years traveling, but who often spend periods of time working to sustain travel opportunities. Thus tourist research has aligned with a more general shift towards postmodernist thinking, which emphasizes the subjective, multiple and negotiated characteristics of individuals' experiences over more reductionist approaches in the social sciences (Uriely 2005).

However, there is growing criticism of this narrow focus on particular types of tourist experiences, which often overlooks the main styles and motivations underpinning activities, and thus tourists' own perspectives. Small (2008), for example, bemoans the almost total invisibility of the 'child' in tourist studies. Obrador argues that tourism research overlooks the 'thick sociality' of familial relations that typify tourist experiences: "Although tourism is intensively group based, figurations of the tourist emphasize a solitary, disembodied subject without family, children or friends" (Obrador 2012: 402). In another example, Andrews (2006) has interrogated how space is produced and consumed to meet particular, working-class representations of British identities in mass, packaged holiday resorts. Researchers in tourist studies are gradually moving away from the white, middle-class, educated view of the tourist as the subject for theorizing.

Alternative approaches are based on tourists' own perspectives on their practices. Jacobsen (2000) draws on Goffman's role theory in his study of Mediterranean charter vacationers, asking them how they see themselves in relation to their stated attitudes towards other vacationers. This study first identified that tourists' descriptions of their own experiences contrasted with how other people might characterize and describe them. Jacobsen called this an 'anti-tourist' attitude, described as an expected or perceived shallowness of experience of place within traditional tourism, and a tendency to condemn the superficiality of tourist experience (or 'role'), typified by brief stops in each place. The concept of role distance was deployed to define how tourists display both attachment and commitment to tourist activities and behaviors, whilst simultaneously distancing themselves from the identity that accompanies it (following Goffman 1959). Role distance therefore 'constitutes a wedge between the individual and the role, between doing and being' (Jacobsen 2000: 286).

This tendency for research participants to classify their own touristic activities as *anything but* touristic is evident in many studies. Tourists' use of the term 'tourist' is frequently pejorative, full of incumbent moral associations and emotive attributes (McCabe 2005). McCabe and Stokoe (2004) found that tourists were constructed negatively as people who *swarm* about, consuming places inappropriately, and who *collect* experiences of places and sites speciously. Uriely *et al.* (2002) found that backpackers, in contrast, described the activities and experiences of other backpackers in a largely positive light, which they contrasted with mass tourists. However, backpacking was only deemed to be positive when the experience conformed to certain characteristics, which signify their identity, whereas those who deviate from these norms are considered "fake" or "not serious" (Uriely *et al.* 2002: 534).

Therefore people using the same tourist infrastructure, inhabiting the same tourist spaces, may exhibit a range of different motivations, desires, and individualized meanings attached to their activities. And yet tourism is also tribal. Tourists do identify and affiliate themselves through their travel choices and experiences. This is particularly so in backpacking communities, but also in mass tourism in family resorts, singles holidays, senior citizens, and so on. The experiential dimensions of tourists' activities continue to unfold in ever more nuanced analyses, but remain inconclusive in their ability to articulate a unified theory of what it means to be a tourist. The concept 'tourist' is a contested representational device, a member's category full of incumbent meanings and associations, thus making the tourist a fascinating and ephemeral focus for social theorists. The tourist is inextricably linked to identity, and thus becomes an interesting lens through which to understand the contemporary social world.

The metonymic tourist

In this section, I want to return to the previous discussion of the way the tourist has been constructed by social theorists as being the perfect representation of modernity, becoming a metonym for contemporary social mores. I argue that this has contributed greatly to our understanding of tourists' activities and behaviors, but also at the same time, this work has selectively focused on certain types of tourist activities or phenomena, which whilst useful at the time, now needs to be broadened to reflect the changes in global mobilities and to reinvigorate theorizing on the tourist.

Enzensberger (1958) first theorized tourism as he sensed it was emerging as an important aspect of modern culture. Mass tourism was driven for many people by a romantic interest in the far away, the exotic, the pristine environment and a desire to escape a suffocating and confining social reality. Yet there is a paradox in that in trying to escape we become harnessed by processes and structures of society, and furthermore, in reaching the authentic and untouched we transform it, which ultimately leads to its destruction. Gemünden sums up this dialectic at the heart of Enzensberger's theory: "Thus the revolutionary notion of tourism remains paralyzed between the implicit critique that motivates its escapism and a nostalgia that mourns the loss of an untouched nature and longs for pre-industrial conditions. Unable to see through these dialectics, tourists are condemned to ever more subtle forms of confinement and exploitation" (1996: 113).

This dialectic provided the basis for subsequent theorizing on the tourist as a metaphor for modernity focused on the search for authenticity. Initially, MacCannell (1999) framed his analysis of the tourist in a critique of Boorstin's (1964) observation that tourism is a pseudo-event in which tourists seek inauthenticity in reaction to the meaninglessness of modern life. MacCannell argued alternatively that alienation brought about by modernity drove a search for meaning in tourist experiences. Wang subsequently developed a range of perspectives on authenticity (1999), differentiating between objective, subjective and existential forms of authenticity to allow for a range of meanings attached to tourist motivation. Rickly-Boyd (2012) applies the Benjaminian concept of 'aura' to extend the relationality of authenticity as a concept, which is established through ritual and tradition. Cohen and Cohen (2012) return the debate into a matter of processes of authentication recognizing that consensus has not been reached about the role and relationship between authenticity and tourist experience. Thus the concept of authenticity has been used to frame relations between tourists and modernity.

The second concept is that of the gaze (Urry and Larsen 2012). As mentioned previously, Urry's original purpose was to try to understand contemporary society through an analysis of what people engage in, and how, in tourist practices. He argues that tourist experiences are fundamentally visual in nature. Applying Foucault's analysis of the organizing processes and systems in the clinic, which he terms 'the medical gaze', Urry and Larsen argue that the tourism industry similarly constructs and directs mass tourists in particular ways: "It is the gaze that orders and regulates the relationships between the various sensuous experiences while away, identifying what is visually out-of-the-ordinary, what are relevant differences and what is 'other'" (2012: 14). It is not just that tourist practices generally involve taking photographs that makes tourism so fundamentally visual and ocular-centric. Rather it is the whole organizational process of mass tourism – including the numbers and scales of people involved in relation to the space, the object and character of the gaze, and the relational gazes between hosts and guests and their differences – that makes tourist practices such an inviting lens through which to explore contemporary social relations. Urry's thesis has spawned a long and detailed debate concerning the ways in which the concept of the gaze can be applied to analyze relations, and this has been particularly fruitful in the context of power imbalances between hosts and guests, and how tourism can be a site of resistance (Cheong and Miller 2000; Hollinshead 1999).

The third perspective is on the tourist as a performance practice. The key reference work here is that of Edensor (2000), who argues that in addition to tourism being a series of staged events and spaces, it is also an array of performative techniques and dispositions. In critiquing earlier work on typologies of tourists, Edensor argues that tourist practices are processes, and are therefore dynamic, contextual and constantly being refigured in praxis; here Edensor draws on Goffman's (1959) ideas of social life as a set of dramaturgical performances, whereby social actors orient their identities relationally in time and space, and contingently depending on the social context. Edensor argues that the features of tourist performances can be summarized as including ritualized times and spaces, stages – which he describes as 'enclavic' (prescribed and regulated) or 'heterogenous' (more varied and less clear-cut, where a diverse range of activities can occur) – and modes of performance, which are defined as being either disciplined and ritualized, improvised, or totally unbounded. The concept of the tourist as a performer sits well within postmodern theorizing since it focuses on praxis, ordinary people's actions, and specifically because it recognizes that tourism is just one of a number of social practices of play and ritual. This has also inspired a range of richly detailed and insightful analyses of performances (e.g. Haldrup and Larsen 2010).

This necessarily brief overview of three dominant discourses of tourist theory identifies some common elements. First, that tourist practices are diverse, which makes generalization difficult. Second, that tourism is meaningful to tourists, and relates to how people define themselves – their self-identity. And third, that theorizations of the tourist have attempted to explore how tourism reflects changes in broader society. I now want to go on to briefly outline some new issues that show how changes in society brought about by the frame conditions of mobilities affect what it means to be a tourist.

New perspectives on the tourist

On becoming a tourist

Like all social activities, tourism is learned. Following Berger and Luckmann (1966), we can see ourselves as socialized into tourism often through our experiences in childhood, and through the auspices of the tourism industry. Tourism is an important way in which we can learn about the world and other cultures (Mitchell 1998). Tourist experiences often are integrated into long-term memory and help to define our sense of who we are, contributing to identity (Cohen and Cohen 2012). However, as noted in other chapters in this book, mobility is not universal and the processes of mobilities can work to deepen inequalities in opportunities for travel. Tourist studies have often overlooked those who cannot participate in travel for tourism (Haukeland 1990). However, recent research has sought to understand exclusionary practices within tourism (Sedgley *et al.* 2012), highlighting that even in advanced economies growth in tourism statistics are powered by increasing participation amongst middle-class citizens. The changing demographic structure of society (in the west), with an increasing proportion of older people, changing family structures, and increased numbers of people living in cities, has led to a growing realization that tourism can bring important benefits to people who were previously unable to participate through 'social tourism' (McCabe 2009).

The current global financial crisis has resulted in general cuts in social welfare budgets, increased unemployment, rising transport costs and pressure on retirement incomes (in Europe), which will have long-term effects on tourism participation. The increasing use of self-service and Internet-based technologies to provide access to tourism products and services may provide further constraints to certain groups. There is an increasing potential that in developed economies whole sections of society will become disenfranchised from tourism opportunities. If this is prolonged, then generations of people in disadvantaged communities or social groups may 'forget' how to be a tourist. In work with social tourism practitioners in the UK, we found that some clients need a great deal of support to develop the skills and competencies to be tourists. These skills include time management (getting to the bus stop or train station), packing for a holiday and planning for leisure activities at the destination. This, of course, is counterbalanced by an increasing democratization of tourism opportunities in the emerging economies of the world, but here we also see deep, structural and relational inequalities to tourism opportunities being thrown into the spotlight. Across the world, there is a danger that tourism will become the preserve of the moneyed classes. Therefore, in order to become a tourist, we need to learn what is appropriate and how to perform tourism.

Being a tourist

As mentioned earlier, a tourist is often defined as someone who leaves the home environment for a period of time, generally overnight, for a leisure purpose. Harrison (2003) provides a detailed account of the reasons for tourism: a search for connection with others and intimacy; to explore what 'home' means to us; and to explore our sense of self. These are in many ways similar ideas to those discussed in the previous section, which explored the meaning of travel. However, these categories of tourist are rapidly changing. The 'staycation' is an example of how conceptions of a holiday are becoming less about physical movement and more about a psychological state of being. Although we might characterize the staycation as something of a tourism industry construction, introduced with the aim of encouraging more people to holiday nearer to home rather than going abroad, the concept highlights that tourist practices are greater than the sum of performances. Hom Cary captures this idea in her analysis of the 'tourist moment', "which conditions a spontaneous instance of self-discovery and communal belonging. It is a moment that simultaneously produces and erases the tourist-as-subject, for at the very instant one is aware of and represents oneself as 'tourist', one goes beyond 'being a tourist'" (2004: 63).

Being a tourist can also be interpreted as adopting a touristic attitude. The tourist attitude can remove the need to be in a designated tourist space, such as a hotel or tourist resort, for example. In this way, being a tourist can be achieved through doing typically tourist-like activities, such as sightseeing, or other pleasurable activities which might be associated with a tourist mood. In this sense, the duration of tourist time also becomes more flexible. It may be possible to be a tourist during a couple of hours in between other activities within a place. People are traveling more for non-tourism purposes – commuting, making business trips and going to meetings, for example – but if there is available time within such journeys or places to engage in leisure, then the adoption of a tourist frame of mind can allow us to envisage touristness as being more episodic, and much less structured.

Integrating tourism

Perhaps one of the most powerful arguments that explain the rise of tourism as a social phenomenon is that which links tourism to a quest for discovery and exploration. Dann (1996) links these aspects of tourism discourse to debates on Orientalism and on strangerhood. However, one of the effects of the World Wide Web has been to render the entire world as knowable from the confines and comforts of our homes and offices. What is left to explore? Is there any purpose now for travel? Yet there are ever-increasing numbers of tourists. Tourism has become integrated into the cultural psyche of many nations, so much so that it has become aligned into everyday life activities. Flexible working practices enable some people to live the majority of their lives in holiday destinations, returning to the homeland to attend work meetings when necessary. The increasing numbers of people searching online at home for new romantic liaisons in foreign countries must travel to meet corporeally.

Another example is provided by the phenomenon of couchsurfing (Germann-Molz 2011). Couchsurfing provides new forms of reciprocal hospitality exchanges and a site of resistance to the organizing power of the tourism industry by offering, through the medium of social networking technologies, to coordinate new social relations in new places, opening up new avenues for tourist experiences in non-traditional as well as conventional tourist places. However, as Germann Molz argues, couchsurfing offers researchers a new lens through which to understand how strangers negotiate relations of difference and intimacy, power and control, when they meet online and face-to-face. Ordinary people become informal tourism workers (sometimes willing to act as tour guides as well as accommodation service providers).

In terms of exploration, we also see new forms of activity, which shows the integration of tourism within everyday life. One such example is this of 'urban exploration', defined as the discovery and exploration of unseen parts of the built environment, with a focus on derelict places (Garrett 2011). Returning to the idea of trespassing, urban explorers aim to gain access to and explore areas and aspects of the city that are not generally available to the public. Recent examples included the London Consolidation Crew's scaling the Shard, London's newest highest building, as well as disused areas of the London underground network. More than simply acts of touristic resistance, Garrett argues that urban exploration offers opportunities to experience the past in a radically powerful, unique sense, to gain an understanding of an industrial past through its post-industrial present. These ways of seeing places are deeply emotional and make us confront debates of authenticity and the representation of heritage and material culture. Exploration is possible in the home environment and there are many ways in which under-used places can become the focus for tourist activities. Touristness can become integrated into home spaces, and disrupt their conventional uses. Also tourist behavior becomes integrated into everyday life and social activities.

Conclusion

This chapter sought to elaborate the idea of the tourist, and to outline how contemporary mobilities have reconfigured what it means to be a tourist, as well as tourist practices. Whilst the tourist is just one form of person on the move, tourism is one of the most significant and pervasive forms of mobility. The voluntary character of tourist practices and their importance as leisure practices marks them out as an exemplar of modern social life, and people use tourism to integrate their identities. This chapter outlined the main debates in tourist studies concerning the tourist experience and meanings attached to tourism, as a basis to discuss how mobilities are shaping and re-defining tourist practices of the future. The processes of global mobilities continue to influence relational inequalities in access to opportunities to tourism. At the heart of these processes is network technology, which presents sites of resistance to the organizing structures of the tourism industry, but also offers new forms of social relationships through tourism, and new modalities of being a tourist. Figurations of the tourist need to be re-examined to incorporate tourists' own perspectives and identities, to take into account that the touristic attitude is somewhat independent of conventional notions of activities within prescribed time and spaces, and to recognize that technologies now mediate personal and social relations within tourism experiences.

Bibliography

Andrews, H. (2006) 'Consuming pleasure: Package tourists in Mallorca', in Meethan, K., Anderson, A. and Miles, S. (eds) *Tourism, Consumption and Representation: Narratives of Place and Self*, Wallingford: CAB International, pp. 217–235.

Baumann, Z. (2000) *Liquid Modernity*, Cambridge: Polity Press.

Berger, P. L. and Luckmann, T. (1966) *The Social Construction of Reality*, New York: Doubleday.

Bianchi, R. V. (2000) 'Migrant tourist-workers: Exploring the "contact zones" of post-industrial tourism', *Current Issues in Tourism*, 3(2): 107–137.

Boorstin, D. (1964) *The Image: A Guide to Pseudo Events in American Society*, New York: Harper.

Cheong, M. S. and Miller, L. M. (2000) 'Power and tourism: A Foucauldian observation', *Annals of Tourism Research*, 27: 371–390.

Cohen, E. (1972) 'Toward a sociology of international tourism', *Social Research*, 39: 164–189.

Cohen, E. (1974) 'Who is a tourist? A conceptual review', *Sociological Review*, 22: 27–53.

Cohen, E. (1979) 'A phenomenology of tourist experiences', *Sociology*, 13: 179–201.

Cohen, E. and Cohen, S. (2012) 'Authentication: Hot and cool', *Annals of Tourism Research*, 39(3): 1295–1314.

Cohen, S. (2011) 'Lifestyle travellers: Backpacking as a way of life', *Annals of Tourism Research*, 38(4): 1535–1555.

Dann, G. (1996) *The Language of Tourism – A Sociolinguistic Perspective*, Oxon: CAB International.

Desforges, L. (2000) 'Travelling the world: Identity and travel biography', *Annals of Tourism Research*, 27(4): 929–945.

Diekmann, A. and McCabe, S. (2011) 'Systems of social tourism in the European Union: A comparative study', *Current Issues in Tourism*, 14(5): 417–430.

Edensor, T. (2000) 'Staging tourism: Tourists as performers', *Annals of Tourism Research*, 27(2): 322–344.

Enzensberger, H. M. (1958) 'A theory of tourism', *New German Critique*, 68: 117–135.

Feifer, M. (2005) *Going Places: The Ways of the Tourist from Imperial Rome to the Present Day*, London: Macmillan.

Garrett, B. L. (2011) 'Assaying history: Creating temporal junctions through urban exploration', *Environment and Planning D: Society and Space*, 29: 1048–1067.

Gemünden, G. (1996) 'Introduction to Enzensberger's "A Theory of Tourism"', *New German Critique*, 68(Special Issue on Literature, Spring–Summer): 113–115.

Germann Molz, J. (2011) 'Couchsurfing and network hospitality: "It's not just about the furniture"', *Hospitality and Society*, 1(3): 215–225.

Goffman, E. (1959) *The Presentation of Self in Everyday Life*, London: Penguin.

Haldrup, M. and Larsen, J. (2010) *Tourism, Performance and the Everyday: Consuming the Orient*, London: Routledge.

Hannam, K. and Diekmann, A. (2010) 'From backpacking to flashpacking: Developments in backpacker tourism research', in Hannam, K. and Diekmann, A. (eds) *Beyond Backpacker Tourism: Mobilities and Experiences*, Bristol: Channel View Publications, pp. 1–7.

Harrison, J. (2003) *Being a Tourist: Finding Meaning in Leisure Travel*, Toronto: University of British Columbia Press.

Haukeland, J. (1990) 'Non-travellers: The flip-side of motivation', *Annals of Tourism Research*, 17(2): 172–184.

Hollinshead, K. (1999) 'Surveillance of the worlds of tourism: Foucault and the eye-of-power', *Tourism Management*, 20: 7–23.

Hom Cary, S. (2004) 'The tourist moment', *Annals of Tourism Research*, 31(1): 61–77.

Jacobsen, J. K. S. (2000) 'Anti-tourist attitudes: Mediterranean charter tourism', *Annals of Tourism Research*, 27(2): 284–300.

MacCannell, D. (1999) *The Tourist: A New Theory of the Leisure Class*, Berkeley and Los Angeles: University of California Press.

McCabe, S. (2005) 'Who is a tourist? A critical review', *Tourism Studies*, 5(1): 85–106.

McCabe, S. (2009) 'Who needs a holiday? Evaluating social tourism', *Annals of Tourism Research*, 36(4): 667–688.

McCabe, S. and Stokoe, E. H. (2004) 'Place and identity in tourist accounts', *Annals of Tourism Research*, 31(3): 601–622.

Mitchell, R. D. (1998) 'Learning through play and pleasure travel: Using play literature to enhance research into touristic learning', *Current Issues in Tourism*, 1(2): 176–188.

Obrador, P. (2012) 'The place of the family in tourism research: Domesticity and thick sociality by the pool', *Annals of Tourism Research*, 39(1): 401–420.

Pearce, P. L. (2005) *Tourist Behaviour: Themes and Conceptual Schemes*, Clevedon: Channel View Publications.

Rickly-Boyd, J. M. (2012) 'Authenticity & aura: A Benjaminian approach to tourism', *Annals of Tourism Research*, 39(1): 269–289.

Sedgley, D., Pritchard, A. and Morgan, N. (2012) '"Tourism poverty" in affluent societies: Voices from inner-city London', *Tourism Management*, 33: 951–960.

Small, J. (2008) 'The absence of childhood in tourism studies', *Annals of Tourism Research*, 35(3): 772–789.

Turner, V. (1973) 'The center out there: Pilgrim's goal', *History of Religion*, 12: 191–230.

UNWTO (2012) *World Tourism Barometer*, volume 10, January 2012. Available online at http://dtx-tq4w60xqpw.cloudfront.net/sites/all/files/pdf/unwto_barom12_01_january_en_excerpt.pdf (accessed 11 September 2012).

Uriely, N. (2005) 'The tourist experience: Conceptual developments', *Annals of Tourism Research*, 32(1): 199–216.

Uriely, N., Yonay, Y. and Simchai, D. (2002) 'Backpacking experiences: A type and form analysis', *Annals of Tourism Research*, 29(2): 520–538.

Urry, J. and Larsen, J. (2012) *The Tourist Gaze*, 3rd edn, London: Sage.

Urry, J. and Sheller, M. (eds) (2004) *Tourism Mobilities: Places to Stay, Places in Play*, London: Routledge.

Wang, N. (1999) 'Rethinking authenticity in tourism experience', *Annals of Tourism Research*, 26(2): 349–370.

34

Soldier

Rachel Woodward and K. Neil Jenkings

The soldier is always mobile. From *Gilgamesh* onwards, the warrior lifestyle has been associated with the vagaries of a mobile occupation and the self-discovery this offers. *The Odyssey* is synonymous with the travails of the travelling soldier, and the traveller in general. Our university is sited on the course of the Roman Wall in England, which acted not only as a barrier to the northern tribes of Britain, but also as a defendable route along which Rome's soldiers could travel with speed between Britain's east and west coasts. The accounts of soldiers from Julius Caesar's *The Conquest of Gaul* (1963) to T. E. Lawrence's *The Seven Pillars of Wisdom* (2004) to Ed Macy's *Apache* (2008) testify to the centrality of mobilities in the execution of soldiers' military duties and their experiences of war.

In this chapter we use the term 'soldier' as shorthand for a range of military personnel and occupations including land, naval, marine and air forces personnel, who use and embody a wide range of mobilities. Caesar's invasion of Britain was by sea, Lawrence travelled by sea, air and camel during the Arab Revolt and Macy flew with the Army Air Corps in Afghanistan. But significantly our designation 'soldier' is not just about the warrior but is inclusive of all military personnel. It includes people working in occupations ranging from infantry to intelligence to explosive ordnance disposal, from medical care to communications to navigation to engineering. The point is that whilst popular imaginations of soldiers as mobile will focus on those whose personal mobilities are obvious – the patrolling soldier, the flying fighter-jet pilot, the sailor aboard a ship at sea – the very structure and organisation of armed forces is necessarily predicated on a much wider configuration of tasks and responsibilities, the ultimate aim of which is the maintenance of a mobile capability and a capacity for the deployment of lethal force over space, through time and to specified locations. Consequently, military mobilities are not uniformly acquired, deployed and experienced; they are diverse and unique to individual personnel and to their specific military roles. Furthermore, soldier mobility is composed of multiple, intersecting mobilities which operate at different scales – from mass movements in formation across space to subtle modes of bodily comportment.

Also worth noting at the outset is that much of the existing social science literature about military personnel focuses on a limited range of specific issues. If we consider the armed forces of advanced capitalist economies, we can identify a body of knowledge about ethnicities, gender relations, identities, citizenship issues, embodied practices, military occupations, force composition changes, and force management and organisation (see, for example, Segal, 2007 and Jenkings *et al.*, 2010). With key exceptions, the dominant analytic approaches to the soldier have been structuralist and quantitative, and result in us knowing far less about the day-to-day and often prosaic professional practices through which military action is conducted. Yet found in these quotidian actions and their underpinning logic is much of the informative detail about soldier mobilities. However, the mobilities turn in the social sciences has yet to catch up with the soldier despite recognition of the mobilities of war and securitisation, and so our intention here is to write expansively and speculatively with a view to establishing an agenda for mobilities-informed research on military personnel.

This chapter suggests a range of possible ways in which military activities, occupations and practices are mobile. Soldiers' mobilities, within both academic and lay civilian discourse on military personnel, are often assumed but rarely examined for what they might mean. Here, drawing on sources such as our own research on military identities and military memoirs, published accounts by others using ethnographic and auto-ethnographic data, and our own observations and experiences of military life, we trace some of the ways in which the mobilities of military life and experience define the category of the soldier. Our exploration is structured around the career course of the soldier, from the start of initial or basic training, through specialist skill-at-arms training and exercises, and on to deployment on active operations. We conclude with some observations about legacy and future mobilities, and consider what an exploration of the figure of the soldier through the mobilities paradigm might bring to wider sociological and geographical understandings of military personnel, military activities and military priorities.

Enlistment and initial training

Soldiers join armed forces at a young age. Leaving aside the deployment of paramilitary child soldiers, which we do not cover here but are a case in point, if we consider regular, all-volunteer and conscript armed forces, we see that personnel enlist in their late teens or early adulthood. The transition from a civilian to military environment involves physical movement from the family home, often for the first time unaccompanied over large distances, to the training camp and barrack block. This all-encompassing institutional transformation builds on the act of dislocation, involving formalisation in dress, hairstyle, living practices, routines, and styles of deportment and regimented movement in which belonging and collective group identity are developed through corporeality and mobility. During basic training, the recruit is mobile and immobile according to the dictates of training regimes and military regulations; he or she learns to move, or not, when ordered. The new military body learns, formally and informally, how to be moved by military transport. It learns to move in new ways through marching, through the techniques of the Tactical Advance to Battle ('tabbing'), through to running and swimming with kit and weapons. It learns the finely tuned collective movements of drill, of movement in accordance with symbolically laden choreographies scripting length of step, shifts of weight and balance required for starting, stopping, turning, standing and poise (see McNeill, 1995). It learns and adapts even to new ways of walking down the spaces of a barracks corridor or entering a commanding officer's office. The enlistment and basic training that all soldiers go through are times of transition, and these transitions are effected through mobility, through the adoption of new meaningful ways of being mobile, which militarise the once-civilian body.

When not in constant motion (many personnel recall or write about their first military experiences as a flurry of physical activity), recruits are immobilised, confined to barracks and military bases for an initial, designated period of time. This mooring (Adey, 2010) is intentional and meaningful in institutionally marking out the separation of the recruit from his or her former civilian life. Although a 'total institutional' separation is not permanent, changes occur in the individuals' mobilities and capabilities, which mark them out as soldiers. Informal practices are also at work:

> recruits emerging from total confinement now come into contact with other recruits in more advanced stages of the . . . training process who pass on knowledge which both adds to and reinforces the unofficial potency and legitimacy of unofficial 'ways' in common usage.
>
> *(Hockey, 1986: 49)*

'Freedom of movement', then, has military utility even when presented as an earned privilege, as it exposes the recruit to unofficial practices and modes of being. This is useful for inculcating social norms and behaviours in the recruit. Eddy Nugent's 'anti-memoir' of the enlistment, training and first posting of an infantry soldier in the British Army of the 1980s is a story of learning to cope with and transcend (often through subversion) the routine of movements forced upon an often-unwilling body. His transgressions are physical, spatial and mobile – for example, sneaking in and out of military spaces in contravention of orders, formative acts of movement for the young squaddie (Nugent, 2006). Although both Hockey and Nugent deal specifically with the British Army, the wider applicability of the practices they describe can be found in accounts from the USA (Fussell, 1996; Key and Hill, 2007).

In training camps and army bases the recruit is also inducted into new ways of moving through the civilian world. In the UK, new forms of access to the civilian public transport system are provided through travel warrants and military railcards, which prescribe routes and modes and specify (and limit) times of movement and behaviour. Civilian modes of travel using personal vehicles are tempered to the demands of the training regime; personnel invest time in directionless travel purely to keep car batteries charged during periods when wider personal mobility is limited. Military mobilities are extensive but restricted, facilitated but subject to military order.

Exercises

The trained, enlisted soldier continues to hone his or her skills in accordance with the requirements of their chosen military occupation. This is undertaken through exercises – the repetition of individual and collective tasks which, as many military memoirists attest, fine-tune military capabilities so that in combat operations 'the training just kicks in'. This is the case whether they are front-line or rear-echelon soldiers. Anna Simons, in her ethnography of a platoon of US elite forces, reveals something of the significance of the endless patrolling undertaken by the group under her observation. This is not only a rehearsal of the mobilities required to exercise lethal force, but also a mechanism for alerting patrol commanders to the (in)efficiencies of the individuals and their cohesion as a group. Forcing mobility onto the group avoids both stasis and the complaints and grumbles of the group that always seem to arise out of stasis (Simons, 1997: 17). The act of patrolling is a distinctive and specific form of military mobility. It requires the ability to assert dominance over space, and to transcend the obstacles of those spaces. Ballinger's account of marches over the training areas of the Brecon

Beacons describes the avoidance of roads, tracks and footpaths, the infrastructure of enabled movement, and the inculcation of the soldier's ability to cross rough ground, overcome natural obstacles (streams, hedges, ditches, rock), and to do so unseen and undetected (Ballinger, 1994). Patrolling and exercise activities are practised to a degree whereby the physical performance of such tasks becomes automated: 'head down, bergen on, mind in neutral', as Hockey (2002) puts it. Patrolling differs in mobilities terms with the type of terrain to be covered (whether woodland, desert, jungle or built environment), with formation and mode (foot patrol, vehicle convoy, small boat or ski patrol), and size and objective. Soldier mobilities are distinctive and specific, and developed still further in specialist roles such as reconnaissance and sniper work, which involves a tactical approach, stasis and invisibility (Swofford, 2004) to the extent that micro-movement such as the act of breathing must be controlled, as movement influences the accuracy of the shot (Lande, 2007). Stasis is part of the soldier's mobility; mooring (Adey, 2006) and stillness (Bissell and Fuller, 2010) are necessary components of the task and action.

Military roles across land, sea and air are not only about the facilitation of the movement of one's own force but also about the denial of movement to the enemy. In our own research with soldiers involving discussions of their military identities and experiences, a common theme amongst those who had served in commando, tank, artillery and infantry roles was that of the adrenalised motion of practising these techniques combined with the experience of tedious stasis (Woodward *et al.*, 2010). Respondents' personal photographs drawn on to make this point included the interior of an observation sangar, a collection of tanks painted in distinctive colours on a training area, and groups of military personnel sitting around with cups of tea, waiting for the next set of orders. But even a static guard is rotated.

Military roles also involve considerable logistical challenges in the transportation of personnel and matériel as a precondition for the exercise of lethal force. Whilst increasingly the resupply activities required by modern armed forces are out-sourced to private civilian companies, it is a truism that many of the principles and practices of logistics planning, management and execution in the civilian world are military in origin. Systems for the mobilities of people and objects may overlap with civilian practices, but remain distinctively military in that they are about fighting forces and the means by which force can be asserted. This overlap with the civilian is illustrated in Robin Watt's diary of the 1991 Persian Gulf War when part of the 1st British Division was forced to move using civilian Saudi buses and drivers to a concentration area to form up for attack (Watt, 1994).

We could also consider here how military roles in which the mobility of the operative is foregrounded in their job title, e.g. Swimmer Canoeist (Special Boat Service) or Paratrooper Fast Jet Pilot, shape status hierarchies within armed forces. Higate, reflecting on his role as an administrator within the British Royal Air Force points to ways in which certain RAF occupations, specifically those involving flight, become hegemonic. His analysis is focused on the hierarchy and hegemony of different military masculinities, and he considers postings where he was the only administrator working with jet pilots and RAF fire-fighters. 'In these contexts, clerking was belittled as worthless and unmasculine . . . "real men" perceived me as a worthless secretary' (Higate, 2003: 33–34). Our point here is that those occupations which accord with hegemonic ideals of military masculinity are also those where the mobility of the operative is foregrounded too. For example, the Special Boat Service (SBS), the special forces branch of the Royal Marines, are badged as swimmer-canoeists.

Finally, we should consider the mobilities of those whose lives are bound up with the soldier. Spouses (most commonly wives) and children of military personnel are, famously, highly mobile. Again, there is a wider issue for consideration here beyond the question of familial movement in response to a husband or father's change of posting. As the limited existing research on military families suggests, the consequences of frequent family moves for spousal employment and sociality, and for the education and socialisation of children, can be profound. They are also cross-cut by factors such as the management and administration of families' housing and welfare services, which recognise the fact of frequent movement, and which may – or may not – provide mechanisms for support for those living what are, for some, highly nomadic lives (Ender, 2002).

Combat operations

Armed conflict is a complex of mobilities, and beyond the soldier there are mobilities, shaped by war and its technologies and practices, which constitute an additional set of mobilities beyond the subject (see for example Kaplan, 2006; Virilio and Lotringer, 1997). Our focus here, however, is on the person, the soldier. The conduct of active operations involves, for the soldier, not only the mobilities so far described, translated to the theatre of war, but additional imperatives around movement and its meanings. The waging of war is a dangerous occupation, and this is of course recognised by soldiers themselves. Many memoir accounts of military participation evidence reflections of the time of initial deployment, when antici-pation and fear are remembered as being tempered by intense activities as the military body and its equipment are made ready for the move to the theatre of operations. The soldier's intense longing for deployment to the theatre of war, to put training into practice and to go on active operations, is especially often recounted at the initiation of a new war – although the reality of war rarely maintains such enthusiasm (Fussell, 1996). The practice of covering ground, of moving tactically up to and over a start line is now undertaken for real. In soldiers' accounts of their Falklands War experiences, the narrative arcs of different accounts tell the familiar story of the trained soldier transported thousands of miles by sea, landed on a beachhead and required to march across rough peaty ground and into battle. What is strik-ing, if we see these stories as accounts of mobilities, is the physical cost of these actions, the levels of exhaustion experienced, compounded by foul weather. What is also striking is the ways in which transcendence of pain and discomfort is invoked as lying with the collective identity, camaraderie or *esprit de corps* of the combined mobile unit. The mobility of the infantry, paratroop or marine body in these accounts is movement given meaning not just because of the tasks those bodies are called upon to perform but also because of the collective, shared understanding of that endeavour (see, for example, Lukowiak, 1993; Bramley, 1992; Ely, 2003; and also Woodward, 2008).

As in training and on exercises, military action on the ground is about the control – and lack of control – of movement across physical space. Following deployment of NATO troops to Afghanistan from 2002, and in significant numbers from 2006, we see this as the funda-mental basis for all military activities in both observation-based journalist accounts and in the published and online accounts from serving personnel. In *Restrepo*, a documentary film released in 2010 by Sebastian Junger and Tim Hetherington about a US army platoon, or in Janus Metz Petersen's 2011 documentary *Armadillo*, about a Danish unit, mobility is central. Mobilities, in these films, are deadly; to patrol is to risk and experience death, and to be static, manning an observation post, is to be, by virtue of the restricted mobility, a static target for Taliban mortar fire and equally dangerous. In his accounts of his tours of duty with British forces in Afghanistan, Doug Beattie raises repeatedly his desire, as a unit commander charged with mentoring Afghan personnel, to assert the idea of military presence through being kinetic, through moving through space and being seen to be moving through space,

however deadly the consequences (Beattie, 2008, 2009). Whilst many of the tactics and practices deployed are familiar and well-rehearsed, the challenges of military operations in the
context and terrain of Afghanistan and the mobilities they require prompt modifications to
existing ways of soldiering. Pilots charged with close air support learn to read the arid and
irrigated areas over which they fly at speed, in ways that make sense of an unfamiliar landscape. Mark Hammond's account of an operational tour as a Chinook helicopter pilot in an
Immediate Response Team details not the skills required for flying the aircraft per se, but
rather the demands of doing so on evacuation missions always with the threat of immediate
immobilisation because of Taliban fire or (equally deadly) the dust storms blown up by each
take-off and landing of the aircraft (Hammond, 2009). In his account of working as a Parachute regiment patrols platoon corporal tasked with mapping the territory of Helmand and
scouting out locations, Jake Scott explains the efforts he makes, as a navigator, to box around
settlements, cover ground which the enemy would not anticipate as crossable, and to take
complex detours as a deliberate feint to conceal a real destination (Scott, 2008). There are
echoes for the reader, in Scott's descriptions of his mobile observations across space,
of the insights for the researcher using a go-along methodology (Kusenbach, 2003; Jones
et al., 2008).

The memoirs of British forces in Afghanistan highlight the deadly meanings that mobility
entails in this theatre of war. The exponential increase from 2006 onwards in the use of
improvised explosive devices (IEDs) by Taliban fighters as a deliberate tactic to limit NATO
force movements is the clearest example of this. Doug Beattie describes one of many patrols
slowed to a crawl by the necessity for checking and neutralising IEDs:

> There was no quick way of doing it. Slowly, ever so slowly, men walked forward sweep-
> ing the area ahead of them with metal detectors. At the merest hint of anything suspi-
> cious it was then down on to their belt buckles, first gently dusting away loose sand and
> dirt with bare hands, then prodding the ground with bayonets, feeling for enemy devices.
> Every so often the WMIKs [vehicles mounted with machine guns] would push forward
> along the latest section of the road to have been made safe, before stopping again to cover
> the ground ever further south.
>
> *(Beattie, 2009: 52–53)*

The prices paid in the lives and limbs of NATO troops are high. Indeed, that is the point of
such devices – to limit an enemy's movement not just by blocking routes but also by creating
for them the distraction of having to care for and extract casualties, which requires the ceasing of mobility, compromising the achievement of objectives. Mobilities are about the limitations and constraints enacted by groups on others (Cresswell, 2006), and here we see this in
deadly, tactical form.

Mobile legacies and mobile futures

Military personnel inhabit mobile bodies. They operate according to strategies and tactics
which are explicitly and implicitly about the assertion of the mobility of the self and allied
forces (and friendly civilians) at the expense of the mobilities of the enemy. They are also the
inheritors of legacies of past mobilities and mobility traditions, through regimental memories
of 'glorious' cavalry charges, for instance. Similarly, whilst the likelihood of airborne infantry deployments by mass parachute drop is minimal, the British Army's Parachute Regiment
maintains a distinctive identity based on this increasingly obsolete mode of deployment, their

air-mobility increasingly helicopter based. Mobile legacies shape the wider organisational distribution of bases, barracks, airfields, communications stations and naval ports and impact on current mobility activities. In the UK, the concentration of RAF bases in East Anglia and Lincolnshire reflects both Second World War and Cold War strategies for aerial warfare against continental European neighbours. Now fading from sight, the remnants of anti-invasion fortifications on the British coastline and the internal Stop Lines and GHQ lines in southern England show past mechanisms for at least giving an appearance of taking an invading enemy's mobilities seriously, even if only for the sake of civilian morale during the Second World War. For US forces, the ring of US military bases around the Pacific Rim reflects both past attempts for a pan-Pacific presence and contemporary desires for global military dominance.

Naturally, mobilities of military forces will be a focal point for the evolution of military technologies (see Kaplan, 2006). The Unmanned Aerial Vehicle (UAV) is a case in point, with commentators on the development and consequence of this new technology pointing to the distanciation between machine and operator. UAVs are designed as an ultra-mobile mechanism for the conduct of military operations, primarily through surveillance and the delivery of aerial firepower (see Williams, 2011). They also render the military operative utterly sedentary as well as distanciated, sitting in an office environment far from the theatre of operations, immobilised in front of a screen, echoing the stance and stasis of the player of computer games. The immobility of the operator, though, is not without its problems; anecdotal evidence from the deployment of UAVs in Afghanistan and on the Pakistan border area suggest symptoms akin to PTSD amongst UAV operators, precisely because of their immobility in front of the scenes of carnage which they are responsible for unleashing. Other more basic technologies emerge in response to different demands, such as the developments in vehicle protection prompted by the vulnerability of soft-skinned, all-terrain vehicles to IED attack; the British Army's adoption of the Jackal, a light-weight armoured patrol vehicle, is a case in point, developed specifically because of the immobilities imposed on armed forces by Taliban fighting strategies in Afghanistan. Technology also plays a major part in the recuperation of the soldier whose mobility has been compromised by injury; increasingly, high-specification limb replacements have been used to allow soldiers back to military duty, and the success of such technologies also placates those voices whose concerns could prevent, delay or shorten military deployments.

The mobilities turn and the study of the soldier

Soldiers have always been mobile, in that the practices of armed personnel charged with the execution of lethal violence across space requires not just acts of movement, but the understanding of that movement as purposeful, contingent ultimately on state territorial ambitions and the control of people, goods and services. The question that follows, then, concerns how the arguments of the mobilities turn might shape how we study the soldier.

Certain facets of military experience and practice are either revealed anew or come to greater prominence as a consequence of viewing them through a mobilities lens – an example would be the conceptualisation of military force as a group effort. Military personnel operate in groups; the pursuit of armed activities is never a solo effort. Many military tasks are undertaken by small groups spread through space in hostile terrain and rely on group mobility skills. One of the truisms which conversations with soldiers reveal is the idea of the individual team on a mission, the success of which ensures a larger operation and the missions of other groups. To paraphrase one of our research interviewees, the soldier is just a small cog driving a small part in a much bigger military machine, but it is essential to understand that small cog's mobility as part of the professional expertise which contributes to the whole, and the identity of the soldier is bound up with this (see Woodward and Jenkings, 2011). Identities are indeed produced through networks of people on the move (Cresswell, 2010; Urry, 2007). The mobilities lens prioritises this notion, and emphatically spatialises the practices, often very prosaic, both front-line and rear-echelon, which contribute to wider mission success (or failure) and to the soldier's sense of self as a professional operative.

An example here would be Jake Scott's account of his path-finding with Patrols Platoon with 3 PARA in Helmand, undertaking reconnaissance work to facilitate the much bigger task of moving a new turbine to the Kajaki dam site on the Helmand River in Afghanistan (Scott, 2008). The mobilities lens draws our attention to the array of spatial observation, monitoring, data collection and ground-clearing strategies undertaken by this small platoon as part of the wider action. Without the space through which the turbine had to be moved being constituted as 'safe', the task would not have been achieved. Because it was achieved, coalition forces were able, for a short time at least, to claim a small measure of success in their stated objective of securing and stabilising the province to enable economic development to take place. In focusing on the mobile practices around operations such as this (although ultimately it failed to bring significant reconstruction in its wake) our attention turns from the wider objectives of the NATO presence in Afghanistan and judgements of success and failure, towards the specificities of actions on the ground and their meanings for the soldier concerned. The mobilities turn, in a way, humanises the soldier because it draws focus on the practical experiential aspect of soldiering.

Bibliography

Adey, P. (2006) 'If mobility is everything then it is nothing: towards a relational politics of (im)mobilities', *Mobilities*, 1: 75–94.
Adey, P. (2010) *Mobility*, London: Routledge.
Ballinger, A. (1994) *The Quiet Soldier: On Selection with 21 SAS*, London: Orion.
Beattie, D. (2008) *An Ordinary Soldier*, London: Simon and Schuster.
Beattie, D. (2009) *Task Force Helmand: A Soldier's Story of Life, Death and Combat on the Afghan Front Line*, London: Simon and Schuster.
Bissell, D. and Fuller, G. (eds) (2010) *Stillness in a Mobile World*, London: Routledge.
Bramley, V. (1992) *Excursion to Hell*, London: Pan.
Caesar, J. (1963) *The Conquest of Gaul*, Harmondsworth: Penguin.
Cresswell, T. (2006) *On the Move: Mobility in the Modern Western World*, London: Routledge.
Cresswell, T. (2010) 'Mobilities I: catching up', *Progress in Human Geography*, 35: 550–558.
Ely, N. (2003) *For Queen and Country*, London: Blake Publishing.
Ender, M. (2002) *Military Brats and Other Global Nomads: Growing up in Organization Families*, Westport, CT: Praeger.
Fussell, P. (1996) *Doing Battle: The Making of a Sceptic*, New York: Little Brown.
Hammond, M. and MacNaughton, C. (2009) *Immediate Response*, London: Michael Joseph.
Higate, P. (2003) '"Soft clerks" and "hard civvies": pluralizing military masculinities', in P. Higate (ed.) *Military Masculinities: Identity and the State*, Westport, CT: Praeger.
Hockey, J. (1986) *Squaddies: Portrait of a Subculture*, Exeter: University of Exeter Press.
Hockey, J. (2002) '"Head down, bergen on, mind in neutral": the infantry body', *Journal of Political and Military Sociology*, 30: 148–71.
Jenkings, K. N., Woodward, R., Williams, A., Rech, M., Murphy, A. and Bos, D. (2010) 'Military occupations: methodological approaches and the military-academy research nexus', *Sociology Compass*, 5: 37–51.
Jones, P., Bunce, G., Evans, J., Gibbs, H. and Ricketts Hein, J. (2008) 'Exploring space and place with walking interviews', *Journal of Research Practice* 4: D4.

Kaplan, C. (2006) 'Mobility and war: the cosmic view of US "air power"', *Environment and Planning A*, 38: 395–407.

Key, J. and Hill, L. (2007) *The Deserter's Tale*, New York: Atlantic Monthly Press.

Kusenbach, M. (2003) 'Street phenomenology: the go-along as ethnographic research tool', *Ethnography*, 4: 455–485.

Lande, B. (2007) 'Breathing like a soldier: culture incarnate', *The Sociological Review*, 55: 95–108.

Lawrence, T. E. (2004) *The Seven Pillars of Wisdom: The Complete 1922 Oxford Text*, Fordingbridge, Hants: J. and N. Wilson.

Lukowiak, K. (1993) *A Soldier's Song: True Stories from the Falklands*, London: Secker and Warburg.

Macy, E. (2008) *Apache*, London: Harper Press.

McNeill, W. (1995) *Keeping Together in Time: Dance and Drill in Human History*, Cambridge, MA: Harvard University Press.

Nugent, E. (2006) *Picking Up the Brass*, Enstone, Oxon: Writersworld.

Scott, J. (2008) *Blood Clot: In Combat with the Patrols Platoon, 3 PARA, Afghanistan, 2006*, Solihull: Helion and Co.

Segal, D. (2007) 'Current developments and trends in social research on the military', in G. Caforio (ed.) *Social Sciences and the Military: An Interdisciplinary Overview*, London: Routledge.

Simons, A. (1997) *The Company They Keep: Life Inside the U.S. Army Special Forces*, New York: The Free Press.

Swofford, A. (2004) *Jarhead: A Soldier's Story of Modern War*, New York: Scribner.

Urry, J. (2007) *Mobilities*, Cambridge: Polity.

Virilio, P. and Lotringer, S. (1997) *Pure War*, New York: Semiotext(e).

Watt, R. (1994) *A Soldier's Sketch-Book*, London: National Army Museum.

Williams, A. (2011) 'Enabling persistent presence? Performing the embodied geopolitics of the Unmanned Aerial Vehicle assemblage', *Political Geography*, 30: 381–390.

Woodward, R. (2008) '"Not for Queen and Country or any of that shit . . .": reflections on citizenship and military participation in contemporary British soldier narratives', in E. Gilbert and D. Cowan (eds) *War, Citizenship, Territory*, London: Routledge.

Woodward, R., Winter, T. and Jenkings, N. (2010) '"I used to keep a camera in my top left-hand pocket": British soldiers, their photographs and the performance of geopolitical power', in F. MacDonald, K. Dodds and R. Hughes (eds) *Observant States: Geopolitics and Visuality*, London: Routledge.

Woodward, R. and Jenkings, K. N. (2011) 'Military identities in the situated accounts of British military personnel', *Sociology* 45: 252–268.

35

Drivers and Passengers

Tim Dant

Who is a driver? The question brings to mind the car driver, the person who will get behind the wheel, start the car and 'drive off'. The term also fits easily with those who do something similar with trucks, trains, buses and other vehicles, usually with wheels. Who is a passenger? In our contemporary culture we think of the passenger as a person who gets into the vehicle and is driven away by someone else (the car driver, bus driver or train driver). The driver is an active subject and the passenger a passive one; the driver initiates and steers mobility, the passenger gives themselves up to mobility steered by someone else. These are two contrasting subject positions associated within mobility in the twenty-first century, but their social and material relations are undergoing changes and are even converging. Because embodied mobility (as opposed to virtual mobility) is so often tied up with wheeled vehicles, I will take the driver and passenger in the car as the paradigm case. Most passengers in trains or aeroplanes could not become the driver, but the passenger in a car is also often a driver and the driver sometimes a passenger. In this paper I want to explore the connections between these two positions, and in particular what happens when technology turns the driver into a passenger. No doubt there are other modes of mobility in which there is similar potential for the exchange of role between passenger and driver because both share similar skills and competence (the horse-drawn carriage and the bicycle rickshaw perhaps), but the ubiquity and familiarity of the car makes it the ideal example.

The motoring industry is beginning to adjust to what appears to be a downturn in the popularity of the motorcar as a means of transport.[1] Since 2007 there is some evidence of a decline in the number of cars being registered and the number of people who are passing the driving test.[2] It may be that the status and convenience of the car is in decline, it may be that the appeal of being in control of a car is fading as roads become more congested, or it may be that the cost of insuring a car is becoming prohibitive, especially for young people. It would be particularly interesting if this decline in enthusiasm for the car and the changing status of becoming a car driver were linked to the academic criticism of this means of transport for modern societies (Whitelegg 1977; Dant and Martin 2001; Sloman 2006; Böhm *et al.* 2006; Conley and Tigar McLaren 2009). It is more likely however that declining car consumption is linked to the economic downturn, which may be in itself a good reason for increasing the critique of the car in modern lives to push car culture beyond its 'tipping point' (Lutz and

Lutz Fernandez 2010).[3] Just what a 'car' is is in flux, as the technology and practices around the car, its control and the road are changing (Dennis and Urry 2009). The technology of cars and roads has developed, with mechanical, electrical and now digital innovations making the task of driving an 'easier' as well as a more efficient means of mobility, which is much less likely to kill people. Most recently, the responsibilities of the driver have begun to be transferred to digital control systems in the car and the 'intelligent' road – developments which have the potential to turn all drivers into passengers.

Traditional roles

The traditional meaning of the word 'driver' is as much about impulsion as steering; the driver of a horse, mule or elephant impels the beast with whip, spurs or stick to go faster or to keep going when it is tired. In a sailing yacht it is the force of the wind captured through the sails that drives the boat, and a 'driver' is a fore-and-aft sail over the rudder on a square-rigger that provides extra impulsion when turning. In a modern ship, drive comes from behind, through propellers, and the origins of the word 'drive' from German are to do with 'pushing from behind'; this makes sense of the mule driver, the driver sail, as well as the slave driver and the golfer's 'driver', a heavy club that 'pushes' the ball a long way. For psychologists, drives are internal forces pushing in the direction of a person's needs and instincts, and in a computer a 'driver' is a programme that pushes instructions from the central processor to a peripheral device such as a printer or screen. But the human subject of the car driver does anything but push from behind! Ironically the cyclist, who does provide the driving force as well as control the vehicle, is simply a rider and not a driver.

The passenger is altogether less confusing; anyone being conveyed by a means of transport, whether it is a rickshaw or an aeroplane, a car or a ship, is a passenger . . . as long as they are not the driver (or pilot, or captain). The passenger is someone whose mobility is powered from outside themselves and, most importantly, the control and direction of travel is independent of them. The pedestrian and the cyclist cannot be passengers, but the person in an air balloon's gondola or the howdah on an elephant can be. The English word passenger derives from the French 'passager' (Old French passageor), with meanings of 'passing by' as well as 'traveller'. This suggests a more autonomous mobility than the passive role in modern usage, and indeed the root 'pass', also from the Old French, refers to 'step', or 'pace'. Passengers do have a strong interest in where they are going and usually like to face the front, seated and relaxed, much like a driver. An emerging topic of interest for researchers in the transport geography and mobilities fields is the idea of the passenger not simply as a subject 'contained' or 'cocooned' in material ways, but also subject to bureaucracy and government (Bissell et al. 2011). This new thinking about the passenger is exploring the changing sociality as well as the emotional and material experience of passengering (see the papers on airline, coach, ferry and illegal passengers in the Special Issue of the Journal of Transport Geography (Bissell et al. 2011 and Adey et al. forthcoming).

In all the mobility possibilities I've mentioned (cars, trains, animals, ships, aeroplanes, bicycles) there is a necessary material interaction, a direct engagement of a human body with another material entity in a series of actions and reactions. These are often routine, habitual practices (getting on the bus and finding a seat, sitting behind the wheel and starting the engine) that are unremarkable until something goes wrong, but they are changing in ways that are altering the roles of the passenger and the driver. These material interactions involve different types of agency, which is what is sociologically interesting about the changing roles. When I get up from my chair, leave the house and walk to the shop to buy a loaf of bread,

I am clearly the agent of my actions. I have formed the wish to buy the bread, chosen the moment to act, and I control my body's movement in space as well as exert the muscular force necessary to get out of the chair and do the walking. I can choose the route (I might go the scenic way), go quickly or slowly, invite a companion, and I can manage the interaction with the shop and sales assistant at the other end of the walk. No other agency need be involved until I get to the shop; I can provide the motivational, intellectual and bodily power that is needed. These are precisely the embodied capacities of agency that are restricted in those suffering from a mobility or mental impairment. When other things – equipment of various sorts – become involved in a trip to get bread (horse and trap, bicycle, motorcar, bus, electric scooter), then the various aspects of agency are distributed throughout an assemblage of mobility components that is put together from what has been accumulated. I want to argue here that there are three dimensions of mobility – assemblage, agency and mobility capital – that are necessary to distinguish between the roles of passenger and driver and to understand how these roles are changing.

Assemblage

Even before the human child can walk it is often equipped with shoes and for most human beings some form of footwear – from flip-flops to waterproof hiking boots – is added to the body to enhance its native capacity as it becomes mobile. The conjunction of different types of components to form an entity that operates as a whole but which can at some point be disassembled, is best thought of as an 'assemblage'.[4] The human with shoes, then, is a simple 'mobility assemblage' with different capacities; running spikes with flat heels will increase traction for acceleration and turning, whereas spike heels will make running very difficult but will increase height and exaggerate the shape of the torso. The mobile human is almost always part of an assemblage that includes material objects that are gathered together for particular types of mobility. A cyclist is a human being in material interaction with the equipment of a bicycle and the specific capacities that it enables; it may be a folding bike, a mountain bike or a touring bike. The driver–car forms an assemblage that includes at least a driver and a car that can be started and controlled by the driver; it may also include passengers or bags, or other types of equipment included for the journey (Dant 2004).

The connection between the various components of mobility assemblages could be thought of as a 'hybrid' or an 'actor-network', but the drawback of these concepts is the downplaying of the particular capacities that the human component brings to the mobile assemblage. This has two key dimensions: the intentionality that motivates the mobility and the intentionality that directs it. I am using intentionality here in the phenomenological sense of consciousness that is directed towards something (Husserl 1999: 33). It is a human property that points to the range of possibilities that are open and on which consciousness works to direct the human being into the future. Various forms of motor technology have supplemented or replaced the motor capacity of the human body, but digital technology intrudes into human capacity for consciousness and alters, even relocates, the intentionality for mobility elsewhere in the assemblage.

Agency

The possibility of mobility is a mode of intentionality that the driver shares with the passenger but never completely with the equipment of the car or the bicycle. If instead of walking I use my car to get to the bakers, I lose none of the agency of choice or intention but I give

369

up some of the agency of embodied motility as the car does most of the work. If instead of walking I call a taxi or get a bus, then even more of my agency is given up – not just that of embodied motility but also the fine tuning of timing, route and pace. These different practices of mobility – walking, driving and being a passenger – involve different degrees of agency or control over intentions and movement. I shall call the directing of consciousness to where the mobile subject is to go *intentionality of purpose*, while the directing of consciousness to how mobility will be realised I will call *intentionality of progress*. The driver always has intentionality of progress and the willing passenger always has intentionality of purpose, but both modes of intentionality are present in the person who is their own agent, such as the driver using their car to get bread. But if the driver is the agent of someone else (the taxi-driver, chauffeur, or bus-driver, for example) then they only have intentionality of progress.[5] Intentionality of purpose fits with the common-sense notion of having an intention in that it is formed in consciousness by some sort of thought process such as making a decision or making a choice after deliberating on consequences or expectations. Intentionality of progress may be a more background process of consciousness involving a habitual exercise of skill such as driving a car. Fully attentive conscious intention is needed to acquire the skill, but once it is embodied it requires varying levels of conscious attention according to the unfolding situation.

Put simply, the intentional agency in the motorcar is within the human driver and together the driver–car forms the assemblage that brings together the various capacities needed to enact that agency through the material interaction that we call 'driving' (Dant 2004). The driver's consciousness is directed towards mobility, to the process of progressing towards the chosen end. Even when intentionality of purpose is formed in the mind of the driver ('I must get to Preston') there remain a series of possibilities that conscious intentionality must work on progressively. At an early stage some decisions about route are important – whether to go by the A6 or the M6 – and these may be dealt with through conscious deliberation about traffic, travelling times or short cuts, but may be dealt with by habitual patterns. But then there are possibilities that must be continuously negotiated: the management of speed and braking, choosing the lane on a motorway or at a junction, keeping a safe distance from other vehicles, and looking out for obstructions, especially those that are moving. These are the aspects of consciousness that the passenger is relieved of; their intentional consciousness can be directed to talking on the telephone, reading, daydreaming or looking out of the window at the scenery. Passengers can even doze or sleep. And these are the sorts of things that the driver cannot do since their intentional consciousness is preoccupied with progressing mobility. Some drivers do become skilled at 'multi-tasking' and can have complex conversations with passengers or on mobile phones, and even looking at maps or documents while they are driving (Laurier 2004). The driver may co-opt the passenger into the agency of driving as conversation is interspersed with pauses for driverly attention, at a junction for example, or for commentary on other road users (Laurier *et al.* 2008; Laurier and Dant 2012).

The history of automobile technology has evolved towards the driverless car (Dant 2012) in a series of stages through which intentionality of progress is given up to the car itself. The traditional motorcar is a tool of the driver who controls the engine, the steering, the gears and the brakes through his or her motor capacities. These four systems are designed to realise the driver's intentionality of progress and are 'equipment', in the Heideggerian sense, within the assemblage. Equipment is not a 'mere thing' like a stone that is found, and neither is it an artwork created by a human; it is in-between because it has the thingness of a mere thing but it has usefulness, that is to say, it is produced by human intentionality, directed towards something. For Heidegger an artwork has the properties of a thing but it has no purpose or use – it is sufficient in itself – whereas: 'A being that falls under usefulness is always the product of a process of making. It is made as a piece of equipment for something' (Heidegger 2001: 28; see also Verbeek 2005: 83–5). The motorcar is a thing but it is made up of things, each of which is 'equipment' with usefulness as well as aesthetic qualities (the bodywork, for example, is intended to protect the occupants as well as look good). It is intentionality in the design and making of these things that makes them 'equipment' directed towards the use or purpose of enhancing the mobility of the whole assemblage.

The many subsystems within the thing of the car developed initially through redesigned mechanical systems (such as rack and pinion steering, which improved the precision and sense of feedback over the recirculating ball system), and later through servo systems that redirect power from the engine to add force to that applied by the driver (as with power steering). Some equipment, such as an automatic gearbox, removes a whole subsystem from the driver's material interaction. The agency for deciding on the route may, for example, be handed over to a passenger, to the driver of a taxi or to a 'satnav' system. Intentionality of purpose is in the mobile person but they may hand over responsibility for achieving it – the intentionality of progress – to other people or systems. Cruise control, introduced in the 1950s as a mechanical system that maintains a steady speed without the need for constant pressure on the accelerator, began the move towards the car controlling itself. Since becoming an electronic system in the 1970s, cruise control can be linked to sensor-based warning systems and digital management systems. These can be set to take over control when warnings to the driver about being too close to the car in front fail to prompt a response. Sensor-based digital control systems can be very precise – quicker and more accurate than a human driver's response to the situation – allowing intentionality of progress to be transferred from the driver to the car. Once the satnav guidance system capturing the intentionality of purpose is linked to the control systems responding to the traffic situation, the driver's agency gives way to a passenger mode of agency in the 'driverless car' (Dant 2012).[6] But the agency of mobility in a digital environment may not be exclusively in the on-board systems in the car. The 'convoy system' turns the driver into a passenger at the moment they join the convoy and give up their intentionality of progress to the lead driver controlling the convoy. The 'intelligent road', however, offers the possibility of a continuous stream of information both from other nearby vehicles and a road management system that is monitoring the state of the traffic on relevant routes. Even the agency of the passenger to select their route may be restricted once intentionality of progress is managed on a collective rather than an individual basis.

Mobility capital

Mobility capital lies with whoever has the ultimate power to realise intentionality of purpose through the agency of the assemblage (Dant 2004: 76). It is the accumulation of the wherewithal to move people and things and may be in the possession of individuals, households or organisations including companies, local authorities and governments.[7] It is useful to think of the means of mobility as capitalised since money has to be accumulated and invested to access almost all forms of mobility. Mobility capital is a sub-form of cultural capital, as described by Pierre Bourdieu (1986), that has an embodied state in the driver and passenger, an objectified state as mobility equipment, and an institutionalised state in the legal, bureaucratic and organisational context of mobility. As Bourdieu made clear, the various forms of capital are no more than accumulated labour appropriated by agents or groups of agents, and their control is an expression of power (see Jensen 2011 for an analysis of mobility as power). As Bourdieu puts it: 'To possess the machines, he only needs economic capital; to appropriate them and use them in accordance with their specific purpose (defined by the cultural capital, of scientific or technical type, incorporated in them), he must have access to embodied cultural capital, either in person or by proxy' (1986: 50). The businessman who owns a car and employs a chauffeur may be a passenger, but he deploys his mobility capital to bring together an assemblage that gets him where he wishes to go. Bus companies and taxi firms gather equipment and people into sub-assemblages of vehicles and drivers who deploy intentionality of progress on behalf of passengers whose intentionality of purpose is realised in exchange for the fare. Car clubs, on the other hand, accumulate mobility capital in an intermediary corporation that is then deployed by 'drivers' who add their intentionality of progress as well as intentionality of purpose. The complex institutional systems that manage and control mobility – tax, insurance, policing, fuelling and repairing systems, for example – are themselves accumulations of capital in the form of people, buildings, equipment and files.

Mobility capital has three aspects: material equipment, energy and intelligence. Firstly, the material aspect lies in the ownership or control of equipment of all sorts: shoes, wheelchairs, bicycles, prams, as well as cars, helicopters and ships. The mobility capital in material equipment includes its various capacities for speed, comfort, range and volume, but it also includes its readiness and state of repair as well as any subsidiary equipment such as trailers, caravans and racks. The capacity to store mobility equipment when it is not in use (garage, parking space, bicycle shed) is an extension of the capital that also needs to be accumulated. Mobility equipment can be shared (e.g. the school minibus) or owned by a corporation whose employees use it for the corporation's purposes. Collectively accumulated mobility capital such as railtracks, airports and roads, with all their complex equipment (signage, surfaces, controls, buildings), are assemblages without which most vehicles are useless. Secondly, the energy for propulsion must also be acquired and accumulated. Walking and cycling requires the investment and accumulation of food energy and the preparation of motor capacity in key muscles in the human body. The energy for motor vehicles is accumulated in a limited way in the petrol or diesel in the on-board tank, or the electricity in a battery, but is accumulated in a more substantial way by corporations that store fuel in tanks of various sorts. Wind and solar energy can be converted into electricity for storage, and used for driving equipment which moves through water, on land or through the air. But both wind and solar energy can also be used as a directly propulsive force on boats, land vehicles and even aeroplanes without any prior accumulation. Finally, the 'intelligence' necessary for mobility is the capacity to realise intentionality of purpose through controlling and directing progress. Most human beings learn to walk and many human beings develop the capacity to control and direct motor forces beyond their body in riding a bicycle, steering a pram and driving a car. Intelligence and memory are also involved in learning how to find and follow paths and routes, though this capacity may be in a passenger who can be co-opted into the mobility assemblage as a navigator. Mobility intelligence can also be enhanced or even replaced by material capital: maps and satnavs, speedometers and digital control systems. These systems still require programming and interpretation – a residual human contribution that requires little mobility capital.

There are overlaps between the way I have discussed 'mobility capital' and the concepts of 'motility' (Kaufmann 2003; Kaufmann et al. 2004), 'network capital' (Urry 2002; Larsen et al. 2006) and 'mobility potential' (Kesselring 2006). All three concepts lay much more emphasis on social capital and the decisions of the individual and less on the formation of assemblages than I have. Although social capital is a third form of capital described by Bourdieu, after economic and cultural capitals, the largely descriptive ways in which it is discussed mean that it loses the dimension of class power that is implicit in Bourdieu's theory of the forms of capital. Kaufmann's concept is explicitly intended to link social and spatial mobility and identifies access, competence and appropriation as elements of individual motility. He and his colleagues claim motility as a form of capital that can 'be mobilized and transformed into other types of capital (i.e. economic, human and social capital)' (Kaufmann *et al.* 2004: 754). Their claim for motility as a concept that works at the micro- (household, individual), meso- (groups, networks) and macro- (business corporations, nations) levels ambitiously seems to encompass all aspects of mobility as a social and geographic topic. Kesselring's concept of 'mobility potential' is more focussed on the individual's access to the resources to cope with the 'mobility imperative' (2006: 271) and is derived from Kaufmann's initial formulation of motility as: '. . . the system of mobility potential. At the individual level, it can be defined as the way in which an actor appropriates the field of possible action in the area of mobility and uses it to develop individual projects' (Kaufmann 2002: 1, quoted in Kesselring 2006: 272). In their concept of 'network capital' Urry (2002) and his colleagues (Larsen *et al.* 2006) more specifically link mobility to the social capital that comes from the networking enabled by being mobile. The business and social contacts made through real or virtual travel contribute to the wealth and power of those involved. Urry (2002) emphasises the social value of 'meetingness' and the importance of social networking for social and economic life, but not the inequality of access to mobility that amplifies power differentials. Social networks, Larsen *et al.* argue, are becoming 'more distant' and the investment in social relations through a blend of travel and communication extends sociality to produce a new form of capital: 'network capital' (Larsen *et al.* 2006: 168). This is a form of social capital linked to a 'sociality with objects' that includes not only means of transport but also those of communication. In these various conceptualisations of mobility as a social resource that is realised in a variety of ways by different actors, there is much common ground. However, the term 'mobility capital' that I have chosen to use is intended to emphasise spatial mobility and to connect specifically with Bourdieu's forms of capital in emphasising their role in the class formation of contemporary societies. Mobility capital is a privilege that is not available to everyone equally and is linked to wealth and power and the ways that these are passed on in class-structured societies.

Conclusions

Is it better to be a driver or to be a passenger? I have argued that how mobility assemblages distribute agency distinguishes the driver from the passenger. The driver must have a mode of agency that I've called *intentionality of progress* and the passenger must have a mode of agency that I've called *intentionality of purpose*. For any person to realise mobility in the late modern world, they have to either accumulate or gain access to mobility capital that can form an assemblage that can realise both modes of agency. A collective organisation such as a transport authority can make mobility capital available that matches the intentionality of purpose of those who wish to be mobile and have sufficient money to buy a seat. But the lack of capacity for controlling and directing the mobility capital means that the bus passenger has a very different mobility status than the chauffeured business executive. To maximise the capacity to realise intentionality of purpose the individual may prefer to accumulate personal mobility capital. At best this will involve handing over responsibility for progress to other agents (car and chauffeur, driverless car, taxi, bus), retaining as much control over the deployment of capital as can be afforded. Taking on responsibility for progress in an assemblage may increase control over mobility, provided the individual has accumulated sufficient mobility capital (car owner, cyclist, shoe wearer).

In this brief account of the difference between drivers and passengers I have not been able to address the pleasures and possibilities associated with driving a car (Hagman 2010) or those associated with being a passenger (Bissell 2010; Watts 2008). The driver has an emotional orientation to interaction within the car, with other road users and to the road itself, that is an aspect of the skill needed for intentionality of progress (Katz 1999). These skills confer social status on the driver (Best 2006), who is then drawn into the complex social organisation of driving (Redshaw 2008); so it is not surprising that in Saudi Arabia women feel that it is worth risking imprisonment to claim the independent status of being a driver. But as the socio-technical culture changes in western societies with less 'freedom' to drive due to road congestion, speed restrictions, and the increasing capacity of the car to drive itself, we will have to look to other social and material arrangements to acquire status and pleasure. It is not so surprising that the numbers of new drivers and new cars are falling.

Notes

1 'Number of cars declines for the first time since the Second World War', David Millward, *Daily Telegraph*, 7th April 2010, www.telegraph.co.uk/motoring/news/7563297/Number-of-cars-declines-for-the-first-time-since-Second-World-War.html (accessed 5th October 2011); 'The end of motoring' Alex Rayner, 25th September 2011, www.guardian.co.uk/politics/2011/sep/25/end-of-motoring (accessed 5th October 2011).
2 After rising from the 1950s to a peak of over 3.2 million new registrations in the mid-2000s, the number dipped to 2.4 million in 2009, the lowest figure since 1995. After rising to a peak in 2005–6 of 1.8 million practical driving tests taken, the number fell to about 1.5 million in 2009–10. The average annual mileage of four-wheeled cars has decreased from 9,700 miles in 1995/97 to 8,420 in 2009. Transport Statistics Great Britain Vehicles: 2010 DOT, www2.dft.gov.uk/pgr/statistics/datatablespublications/tsgb/latest/tsgb2010vehicles.pdf (accessed 5th October 2011).
3 An economic downturn with global effects began in a number of industrialised countries in 2008, and by 2013 recovery from recession has not been sustained, leaving many western economies in an austerity mode as state sectors shrink, real wages and pensions fall and private investment is very cautious.
4 Deleuze and Guattari's (1988) notion of the 'machinic assemblage' points to the ways in which human beings are combined with material components to form entities with different properties, both material and social, that are greater than the sum of the component parts. Their concept is more extensive and fluid than the way that I am using the term here; theirs builds from the multiplicity of entities, social and material that together have desire and direction, speed and agency and act as an interface between strata.
5 The person in the police van who has been arrested or the air passenger who is the subject of 'special rendition' has no intentionality of purpose or of progress; they are simply prisoners of someone else.
6 'Google tests cars that drive themselves' BBC News, www.bbc.co.uk/news/technology-11508351 (accessed 19th October 2011).
7 The term has also been used in a rather different way in migration studies, apparently coined by Gesser and Olofsson (1997): 'cosmopolitans possess "mobility capital" – resources, knowledge and abilities that facilitate social as well as geographical mobility (formal education seems of particular importance in this regard)' (Gustafson 2006: 245).

References

Adey, P., Bissell, D., McCormack, D. and Merriman, P. (forthcoming) 'Profiling the passenger', *Cultural Geographies*.
Best, Amy L. (2006) *Fast Cars, Cool Rides: The Accelerating World of Youth and Their Cars*, New York: New York University Press.
Bissell, D. (2010) 'Passenger mobilities: affective atmospheres and the sociality of public transport', *Environment and Planning D: Society and Space*, 28: 270–289.
Bissell, D., Adey, P. and Laurier, E. (2011) 'Introduction to the special issue on geographies of the passenger', *Journal of Transport Geography*, 19: 1007–1009.

Böhm, S., Jones, C., Land, C. and Paterson, M. (eds) (2006) *Against Automobility*, Oxford: Blackwell.

Bourdieu, P. (1986) 'The forms of capital' in J. Richardson (ed.) *Handbook of Theory and Research for the Sociology of Education*, New York: Greenwood.

Conley, J. and Tigar McLaren, A. (eds) (2009) *Car Troubles: Critical Studies of Automobility and Auto-Mobility*, Farnham, Surrey: Ashgate.

Dant, T. (2004) 'The driver–car', *Theory, Culture & Society*, 21(4): 61–79.

Dant, T. (2012) 'True automobility' in E. Casella, G. Evans, P. Harvey, H. Knox, C. Mclean, E. Silva, N. Thoburn and K. Woodward (eds) *Objects what Matters?*

Dant, T. and Martin, P. (2001) 'By car: carrying modern society' in A. Warde and J. Grunow (eds) *Ordinary Consumption*, London: Routledge.

Deleuze, G. and Guattari, F. (1988) *A Thousand Plateaus: Capitalism and Schizophrenia*, London: Athlone Press.

Dennis, K. and Urry, J. (2009) *After the Car*, Cambridge: Polity Press.

Gesser, B. and Olofsson, P.-O. (1997) *Samhällsmoral och Politik: Exemplet Helsingborg*, Gothenburg, Sweden: Daidalos.

Gustafson, P. (2006) 'Place attachment and mobility' in N. McIntyre, D. Williams and K. McHugh (eds) *Multiple Dwelling and Tourism: Negotiating Place, Home and Identity*, Wallingford, Oxfordshire: CAB International.

Hagman, O. (2010) 'Driving pleasure: a key concept in Swedish car culture', *Mobilities*, 5(1): 25–39.

Hammond, M. (2009) *Immediate Response*, London: Michael Joseph.

Heidegger, Martin (2001) 'The origin of the work of art' in *Poetry, Language, Thought*, New York: HarperCollins Perennial Classics.

Husserl, E. (1999 [1950]) *Cartesian Meditations*, Dordrecht: Kluwer Academic Publications.

Jensen, A. (2011) 'Mobility, space and power: On the multiplicities of seeing mobility', *Mobilities*, 6(2): 255–71.

Katz, J. (1999) *How emotions Work*, Chicago: University of Chicago Press.

Kaufmann, V. (2002) *Re-thinking Mobility: Contemporary Sociology*, Burlington: Ashgate.

Kaufmann, V., Bergman, M. M. and Joye, D. (2004) 'Motility: Mobility as Capital', *International Journal of Urban and Regional Research*, 28(4): 745–56.

Kesselring, Sven (2006) 'Pioneering mobilities: new patterns of movement and motility in a mobile world', *Environment and Planning A*, 38(2): 269–279.

Larsen, J. Axhausen, K. W. and Urry, J. (2006) 'Geographies of social networks: meetings, travel and communications', *Mobilities*, 1(2): 261–283.

Laurier, E. (2004) 'Doing Office Work on the Motorway', *Theory, Culture & Society*, 21(4): 261–278.

Laurier, E. and Dant, T. (2012) 'What else we do while driving: towards the "driverless car"' in M. Grieco and J. Urry (eds) *Mobilities: New Perspectives on Transport and Society*, Farnham, Surrey: Ashgate.

Laurier, E., Brown, B. A. T., Lorimer, H., Jones, O., Juhlin, O., Noble, A., *et al.* (2008) 'Driving and passengering: notes on the natural organization of ordinary car travel and talk', *Mobilities*, 3(1): 1–23.

Lutz, C. and Lutz Fernandez, A. (2010) *Carjacked: The Culture of the Automobile and its Effect on our Lives*, Houndmills, Basingstoke: Palgrave Macmillan.

Redshaw, S. (2008) *In the Company of Cars: Driving as a Social and Cultural Practice*, Aldershot, Hampshire: Ashgate.

Sloman, L. (2006) *Car Sick: Solutions for our Car-addicted Culture*, Dartington, Devon: Green Books.

Urry, J. (2002) 'Social networks, travel and talk', *British Journal of Sociology*, 54(2): 155–175.

Verbeek, Peter-Paul (2005) *What Things Do*, Pennsylvania: University of Pennsylvania Press.

Watts, L. (2008) 'The art and craft of train travel', *Journal of Social and Cultural Geography*, 9: 711–726.

Whitelegg, J. (1997) *Critical Mass: Transport, Environment and Society in the Twenty-first Century*, London: Pluto Press in association with WWF.

36

The Executive

James Faulconbridge

Introduction

The remit of this chapter is to develop a theoretical framework for analysing how, for the executive, mobility has become a normalized way of doing business. Specifically, the chapter explains the normalization of executive aeromobility by drawing on work on social theories of practice (Reckwitz, 2002; Schatzki, 1996; Shove, 2003; Shove and Pantzar, 2005). The aim is to reveal the complex interdependencies that both explain the year-on-year growth in executive aeromobility and the difficulties executives face when trying to limit their mobility in the context of financial (recession, spiralling travel costs), social (stress, work–life balance) and environmental (global warming, peak oil) pressures.

The rise and explanation of executive mobility

Despite speculation that the information communications technology revolution might reduce the need for executive mobility, there is widespread evidence that mobility is now more firmly institutionalized as a business practice than before the arrival of email and videoconferencing. For example, The Barclaycard Business Travel Survey, which has been running since the mid-1990s, has charted an almost continuous year-on-year increase in the average number of miles travelled by the executives surveyed. By 2006 a 32-percent increase had occurred compared with 1996, where the executives surveyed were each travelling on average over 600 miles per month (Barclaycard, 2006). Indeed, over 50 percent of those surveyed in 2008 said that despite the effects of the global recession, and growing concerns about the environmental impact of business travel, they expected to travel more in 2009 than in previous years. Other surveys, such as the American Express Survey of Business Travel Management Practices and the PrivateFly Travel Survey confirm such trends and corroborate the findings of academic research which suggest that the 'mobile lives' (Elliott and Urry, 2010) of executives are increasingly taken for granted.

Studies contributing to the 'mobilities turn' in the social sciences explain the continued growth of executive mobility through reference to the now well-documented interdependence between corporeal and virtual forms of mobility (Urry, 2007) – i.e. the simultaneous reliance on travel, email, telephone and videoconference to conduct business (Faulconbridge *et al.*, 2009; Haynes, 2010). The role of corporeal hyper-mobility has predominantly been explained through reference to various 'compulsions of proximity' associated with the doing of business (Boden and Molotch, 1994; Millar and Salt, 2008; Urry, 2003). Building on the typology of Davidson and Cope (2003), three interrelated compulsions of proximity can be identified. First, mobility is associated with what might be described as '*transactional*' obligations. Such obligations involve an individual fulfilling a functional need, such as attendance at a particular place to repair a piece of machinery or install computer software. Second, mobility in particular to attend meetings is associated with fulfilling '*socio-economic*' obligations to other human beings, whether they are colleagues, clients or suppliers. Socio-economic obligations relate to sociologies of trust and intimacy, with compulsions stemming from the association between embodied encounters, seeing the whites of one-another's eyes, and the development of strong ties through which effective economic relationships can be built and profits generated. The third category in Davidson and Cope's (2003) typology – mobility to attend exhibitions, trade fairs and conferences – draws attention to the fact that the division sketched above between transactional and socio-economic obligations is not rigid. For example, participating in a trade show can both allow a transactional need to be fulfilled – a display can be interacted with, learned from and the insights gained used to inform future work (see Faulconbridge, 2010) – whilst socio-economic compulsions might also be fulfilled – a new client is met and a relationship developed that leads to future contracts (see Power and Jansson, 2008).

It would be tempting to read-off from analyses of compulsions an explanation of executive hyper-mobility that solely emphasizes the functionality of mobility. After all, both transactional and socio-economic compulsions are ultimately tied to profit generation and the facilitation of business exchanges. However, taking such an approach has its limitations. It ignores the complex array of cultures, logics and technological systems of provision that have come together to make mobility a taken-for-granted way of doing business. Without these coming togethers the kinds of productive activities associated with compulsions would not be possible and mobility would not have become an ingrained business practice. With this assertion in mind, the rest of the chapter considers the implications for understandings of contemporary executive mobility of beginning not only with questions about what mobility allows, but also with more fundamental questions about how mobility has emerged as a normalized socio-technical business system. The theoretical framing provided by work on social theories of practice is used to develop this argument.

A social practice interpretation of executive mobility

Social theories of practice have become an increasingly popular way of examining taken-for-granted forms of consumption and everyday activity. Practices are defined as a 'temporally unfolding and spatially dispersed nexus of doings and sayings. Examples are cooking practices, voting practices, industrial practices, recreational practices, and correctional practices' (Schatzki, 1996: 89). Three core elements make up any practice:

Meaning: practices are associated with and driven by particular mental maps, emotions and understandings of legitimate ways of being (Reckwitz, 2002).
Competency: practices become widespread when, first, knowledge of how to complete the required actions associated with a task (Reckwitz, 2002) and, second, knowledge of how to engage in the practice in a way that others consider legitimate (Shove and Pantzar, 2007) is shared by many individuals.

Materials: the availability of particular objects, knowledge about how to use them (Shove and Pantzar, 2005), and the intimate tying of objects to meanings (e.g. the car to convenience and comfort – see Warde, 2005) is central to the institutionalization of a practice as a way of being/doing.

Here I want to suggest that by the early 2000s, because of the 'hanging together' of a range of meanings, competencies and materials, and not just because of what it functionally enables, executive mobility had become a taken-for-granted practice – i.e. a routinized way of doing business. To develop such a line of analysis, I begin by sketching out the trajectory of change in one practice of executive mobility – aeromobility – and then consider what a practice-informed interpretation of this trajectory reveals about the causes of contemporary normalized executive aeromobility. I choose aeromobility for two main reasons. First, aeromobility is perhaps the most studied form of executive mobility (see Adey *et al.*, 2007; Bowen, 2010; Cwerner, 2009; Derruder *et al.*, 2011) and the existing literature provides a useful starting point for developing an interpretation of its normalization as a way of doing business. Second, aeromobility is a practice that has received most attention both in terms of its detrimental social impacts on executives (Espino *et al.*, 2002; Gustafson, 2006) and its related environmental impacts in terms of greenhouse gas emissions (Cohen, 2010). Any new insights that a practice perspective can provide into the normalization of aeromobility will, thus, be potentially useful as part of attempts to reconfigure mobility systems so as to minimize their harmful effects.

International aeromobility: the birth and growth of a normalized practice

As has been previously documented (see Beaverstock and Faulconbridge, 2010), there is a surprisingly limited supply of data about business travel. The UK International Passenger Survey (IPS) is thus used here to chart the growth in executive aeromobility to/from the UK between 1977 and 2010 because it is one of the few sources of data allowing comparisons of volumes of travel over time. The limitation of using this dataset is, however, that it does not provide any basis for comparing the UK with other countries. Nonetheless, the trends revealed by the data do appear to correspond with others' analyses of different national contexts (see for example the similar trends reported by, amongst others, Bowen, 2010; Lassen, 2006), giving some indication that the data is representative of broader trajectories of growth in executive aeromobility.

Figure 36.1 reveals that that there has been significant absolute growth in aeromobility since 1977, but that this growth has been uneven over time, being most dramatic between 1990 and 2007. Post-2007 the global recession led to a marked decline in mobility, confirming at the most fundamental level the now intimate relationship between travel and revenue generating business activities. In what follows I sketch out the developments leading up to 1977, the earliest year for which IPS data was available at the time of writing, and since 1977, which explain the growth detailed in Figure 36.1 and the associated gradual normalization of aeromobility as a way of doing business.

Foundations: circa 1960–1980

To understand contemporary executive aeromobility, it is necessary to begin any story at the point of the birth of the commercial aviation industry itself. Bowen (2010) offers a rich analysis which reveals a number of important points in this regard. The late 1950s heralded a

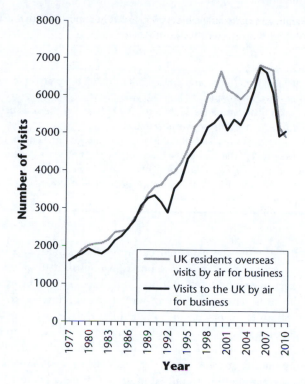

Figure 36.1   Volumes of executive aeromobility in the UK, 1977–2010 (Source: International Passenger Survey, various years)

major shift in aeromobilities, primarily because of the invention of the jet engine, the impact of which was twofold. First, the jet engine accelerated air travel, allowing speeds of around 500 miles per hour, compared with 300 miles per hour in propeller aircraft. Second, it made long-haul travel more feasible and less unpleasant because of the range and enhanced acoustics of the jet. Consequently, the 1960s and early 1970s saw the emergence of many of the components of the technical systems that now permit executive aeromobility. Table 36.1 summarizes a number of the other key developments in this period.

The work of the airlines in making executive aeromobility a way of doing business was not, however, simply to provide the required technological capabilities. The airlines also set about actively constructing cultures of executive aeromobility. Two discrete approaches to creating such cultures can be noted – both of which are documented by Bowen (2010: 178–179) through reference to the work of Hudson (1972). First, airlines attempted to shift executives from car, rail and other modes of travel to air. This involved using publicity materials to make an economic case for aeromobility as opposed to other forms of mobility, with the time-savings offered by air travel being focused on intensely. Second, airlines attempted to distinguish business travel from leisure travel. Exemplifying such attempts, Hudson (1972: 126) documents how a British Overseas Airways Corporation advert sought to generate such distinctiveness by arguing that 'If you want a man to do a first-class job, give him a first-class ticket'. This logic was supported in the advert by a description of the physical, psychological and ultimately economic benefits accrued from not travelling in economy class, thus generating an image of the successful executive being the aeromobile executive who is productive because of what the luxury and experience of travelling (in first or business class)

Table 36.1 Key developments in the airline industry in the 1960s and 1970s that provided the technological advances needed for executive aeromobility

Year	Development
1965	Jumbo Jet commissioned (first commercial flight in 1970): the piece of technology that made long-haul air travel affordable.
1968	Boeing 737 makes first commercial flight – the 'work horse' of the skies because of how it makes short/medium-haul air travel affordable.
1976	Concorde makes first commercial flight. Business travellers leaving London in the morning and arriving in New York at the start of the business day exemplify the benefit of this innovation.
1978	First business-class service offered by Pan AM – with all other major airlines introducing such services soon after. The start of the provision of services that enhance and enable executive mobility.

Source: Bowen, 2010

allows them to achieve. Note the gendered nature of the executive in this establishment phase – something that has begun to change but arguably still inflects many of the images and logics tied to executive mobility (Gustafson, 2006; Presser and Hermsen, 1996).

In many ways, the initial strategies of the airlines to lure executives into the skies could be said to be successful. Between 1960 and 1970 the airlines saw the largest growth in passenger miles travelled ever witnessed, with executives playing a significant role in this growth (Bowen, 2010: 43). Yet, the executive market would be inherently limited by the relatively small number of corporations that operated in spatially distributed markets in the 1960s and early 1970s. Put simply, aeromobility is only important if companies are operating in multiple places separated by significant metric distance. In the UK context and many parts of Europe this meant, in particular, that the number of transnational corporations (TNCs) was a key determinant of executive mobility volumes, whilst in the US the larger size of the union meant the number of corporations with operations stretched across the entire country mattered. In the rest of this chapter, in line with the use so far of UK data on changes in volumes of executive aeromobility, it is the relationship between the activities of TNCs and UK executive aeromobility that is focused upon.

The making of a market: circa 1980–2000

Figure 36.2 confirms that the surge in the number of and in the intensity of the activities of TNCs – measured using the proxy of foreign direct investment into/from the UK – correlates with growth in executive mobility in the UK. At one level, this relationship might be explained by the airlines' strategies outlined above and the capabilities that aeromobility provided corporations seeking to operate across space. However, when the wider economic context of the late 1970s and the 1980s in particular is examined, developments outside of the airline industry also become obviously important in explaining the establishment of aeromobility as a way of doing business. These developments act as elements in the co-evolution of various cultural, economic and technical systems that together generated both growth in the number of TNCs and the normalization of executive mobility.

Element 1: new economic discourses and practices

The ideological discourse of neoliberalism that has pervaded political-economic circles since the late 1970s especially has been particularly influential in the production of executive

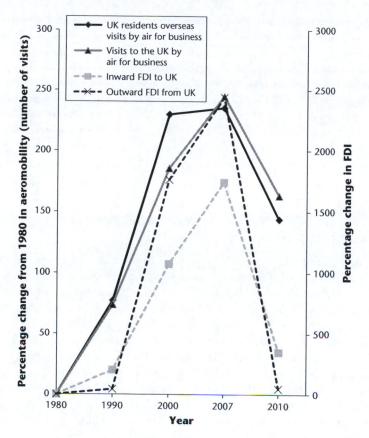

Figure 36.2 The relationship between the globalization of economic activity, measured as levels of FDI, and executive aeromobility in the UK (Source: International Passenger Survey, various years and UNCTAD, various years)

mobility systems. Of most relevance here are liberalization initiatives such as the General Agreement on Tariffs and Trade (GATT). For instance, the Tokyo Round of negotiations, concluding in November 1979, negotiated the biggest single set of trade barrier reductions ever achieved by the GATT – worth US$300 billion in 1980. This opened the way for significant rises in the number of TNCs in the 1980s with subsequent rounds of negotiations, and the expansion in the 1990s to include services through the General Agreement on Trade in Services (GATS), underpinning the continual growth in foreign direct investment through the period between 1980 and 2007.

But it was not just the functional effect of roll-back neoliberalism and initiatives such as the GATT and GATS that was important for normalizing executive aeromobility. It was also the discourses that accompanied such initiatives. Larner (2000) outlines how neoliberal projects are as much concerned with gaining ideological hegemony as they are with changing particular policies. This hegemony leads to the logics of neoliberalism pervading the consciousness of business leaders and ultimately shaping economic logics and decision making. For Larner (2000), this is a form of Foucauldian governmentality which encourages executives to conform to the norms of neoliberal markets. One particularly significant governmental effect has been to instill into the consciousness of executives the need to continually seek-out opportunities to cut costs (for example by relocating low-skilled activities to developing countries) and grow revenues (for example by entering new markets). Such financialized logics encourage globalization and executive hyper-mobility as individual workers are charged with managing more and more spatially dispersed operations, requiring their constant mobility between subsidiaries – what Wickham and Vecchi (2009) call 'nomadism'.

The emergence of particular socio-economic logics relating to business practice as a result of neoliberal reforms and their effects on the spatiality of the operations of firms is, therefore, I claim an important component in explanations of the growth in aeromobility in the UK in the 1980s and 1990s and its ultimate normalization as a business practice. However, this is not the only element in the story. The development of additional systems of provision is also important.

Element 2: new systems of provision facilitating and responding to new economic practices

As Dicken (2011) notes, the 1990s and 2000s were characterized by one of the most significant technological advances of the twentieth century: the emergence and boom of the internet. And as already noted, the explosion of corporeal mobility can only be explained if its relationship to virtual – principally internet-enabled – mobility is considered. Specifically, rather than being a way of reducing mobility, virtual communications (email, video conference, document sharing, etc.) should be seen, to use the words of Haynes (2010), as 'mobility allies' with corporeal business travel. The most notable effect of this allegiance is that the internet revolution has actually generated new needs for executive mobility. The internet allows firms to market their goods and services internationally, and to more closely control and coordinate the activities of spatially dispersed subsidiaries. Both of these developments enabled and encouraged more firms to engage in international business, something which in turn ultimately led to growth in demand for aeromobility, in the first instance so as to fulfill the kinds of compulsions of proximity outlined earlier in the chapter.

Moreover, other technological developments in the 1990s also helped institutionalize business travel because of the new affordances they offered to the mobile executive. For example, the laptop and batteries that provide several hours of work time helped ensure that mobility meant working on the move and not losing productive time in transit (Holley et al., 2008). In addition, the mainstreaming of mobile telephone communications in the 1990s, progressing into the 2000s with the development of the smartphone, is a further example of how communication technologies that might reduce the need for face-to-face interaction have actually driven the growth in business travel. Not only do such devices offer the ability to coordinate meetings whilst on the move (cf. Licoppe, 2004), they also allow executives to stay in touch with the office via voice calls and email, thus minimizing the chance that travelling results in missed business opportunities or the slowing down of 'fast' capitalist activities (Middleton, 2008).

In addition to communications technologies revolutions, changes within the airline industry systems of provision in the 1980s and 1990s were also part of the co-evolutionary process that led to executive aeromobility becoming a normalized practice. Increased capacity on existing routes and expansion in the number of city pairs served from hub airports made aeromobility more convenient. Moreover, reflecting the growing need of executives to travel to ever more dispersed subsidiaries, the formation of a series of airline alliances made inter-continental multi-leg travel smoother (Fan et al., 2001). There are now well over 500 formal alliances between airlines. The most significant are those that now claim to offer

Table 36.2 The development of key allied executive aeromobility industries and their role in the normalization of aeromobility

Industry	Role
International airport and business hotel chains	Provision of meeting and work spaces for mobile executives.
Corporate travel management companies and in-house travel management departments	Translating an executive's list of destinations into a series of flight codes and hotel bookings that minimize travel time and maximize work time.
Executive intelligence services	Magazines/websites (e.g. *Business Traveller*) and guides (e.g. *The survivor's guide to business travel*) (Collis, 2000). Providing executives with the competency to effectively manage their mobility and minimize personal (stress, work–life balance) and corporate costs (expense, travel time).

globally integrated coverage and access to virtually any airport worldwide through a partner carrier. For example, Star Alliance, major members including Air Canada, United Lufthansa, and Thai International, formed in 1997 and serves 900 destinations. At the same time, a new breed of low–cost carrier transformed short–haul aeromobility in the late 1990s, leading to falling prices and the development of ever greater numbers of routes to key business destinations (Mason, 2000).

A third element in the system of provision that has been vital in the co-evolution of the executive aeromobility system is the emergence in the 1980s and 1990s of an array of industries dedicated to making executive mobility as hassle-free as possible (see Table 36.2). The birth of each industry further ensured executive aeromobility was feasible and economically productive, thus helping expedite its normalization.

Aeromobility as a way of being and doing business: a practice perspective

The main contention here is that the institutionalization of executive aeromobility as a way of business life is a result of the co-evolutions outlined above in aeromobility technologies, neoliberal logics, the internet and mobile communication technologies, as well as in the allied services outlined in Table 36.2. To interpret the implications of such developments, Table 36.3 deploys the practice theory terminology outlined earlier in the chapter to explain how, between 1960 and 2000, the core elements of meaning, competency and materials associated with executive aeromobility came to hang together to generate a normalized practice. Each of the core elements of the practice, which result from one of the developments charted above, on their own are not capable of generating the normalized state of executive aeromobility that exists in the early twenty-first century. But together the various elements have combined to enable mobility performances that generate an institutionalized, robust and apparently indispensable way of doing business.

One of the most important contentions of work on social practice is that once normalized, any practice such as executive aeromobility becomes so taken for granted that decisions are not rationally made about whether to and how to engage in the practice. Rather, the practice becomes part of what Bourdieu describes as the *doxic* realm – an unconscious way of being and doing. Hence the implication of conceptualizing executive aeromobility, or any other executive mobility associated with the doing of business (e.g. travelling sales people, train

Table 36.3 The core components that 'hang together' to render executive aeromobility a normalized practice of doing business

Element of practice	Factors generating executive aeromobility as practice	Contribution to the compulsion of aeromobility
Meaning	*Airlines*: defining the economic rationality and the status of aeromobility.	Air is the right way for executives to travel.
	Neoliberalism: the need to seek-out new markets.	Aeromobility becomes essential to fulfill new cultures of corporate internationalization.
	Mobility markers: corporate discourses about the aeromobile executive as successful, ripe for promotion and a profit generator.	Demonstrating aeromobility (e.g. days on the road; elite status on frequent flyer programmes) is essential for career success; clients expect executives providing goods and services to be mobile and visit them in-situ.
Competency	Knowledge about how to become and minimize the costs of aeromobility gained from:	Acceptable ways of being mobile develop, with common ways of acting and using systems of provision being associated with legitimate (cost effective, culturally normalized) aeromobility practice.
	Colleagues in the workplace *Publications* that provide intelligence *Employers* – training schemes and in-house travel support departments.	
Materials	*Airlines*: providing executive aeromobility infrastructures (from the business-class cabin to the executive lounge; geographically expansive network coverage).	Aeromobility made possible and economically viable with materials designed to produce/meet particular logics of executive travel.
	Communication technologies: allies allowing the coordination of mobility and spatially dispersed business.	Executives made efficient and negative economic impacts (e.g. lack of coordination of subsidiaries; working-time lost on the move) overcome.

travel), as a routinized and taken-for-granted practice is to challenge the idea that 'compulsions of proximity' (Boden and Molotch, 1994) or the pleasure, experiences and perks of travel (Lassen, 2006) can alone explain hyper-mobility. Also important are particular meanings and logics that render mobility the 'right' way of doing business, in line with popular expectations and thus a tacitly routinized and embedded way of doing business. Hence there are compulsions of *mobility* as much as there are compulsions of proximity. It is not enough to think about what mobility allows when explaining its normalization. It is also necessary to think about what mobility means, the technologies that make mobility possible, and how together such influences lead to the construction and sustaining of a taken-for-granted business practice. This does not mean that executives and their employers do not reap economic rewards from the work achieved thanks to mobility. But it does means that the economic value added is only one of the meanings of mobility, and not necessarily more significant in generating compulsions of mobility than the other meanings and logics. For instance, the logic that the mobile executive is the successful executive results in embodied mobility, rather than virtual interaction or immobility, being viewed as the legitimate and expected way of doing business. The practice perspective also does not deny that the executive might experience forms of pleasure, benefit from perks such as visiting friends, or enjoy memorable experiences during travel. But, again, it does suggest that such factors need to be viewed as one constituent of a wider assemblage that includes competencies (the ability to do mobility with minimal economic cost) and associated materials (airline networks and mobile work/communication tools), without which the performance of the normalized social practice that is executive (aero)mobility would not occur.

Conclusions

This chapter has sought to explore what a practice perspective can do to develop understanding of the normalization of executive mobility. Using the case of aeromobility, an analysis has been developed that reveals the complex 'hanging togethers' that result in executive aeromobility being normal and a central part of the doing of business in the twenty-first century. In particular, the discussion reveals that normalized aeromobility results not simply from functional need, but also particular meanings and systems of provision that help to render aeromobility practice as taken for granted. This suggests that the future of aeromobility and executive mobility practices more generally is likely to be determined by a number of interrelated variables associated with the elements that make up mobility practices. For instance, in the context of climate change and peak oil, and associated attempts to reduce absolute volumes of mobility, it is likely to be not strategies that simply overcome the functional need for mobility that have most impact on mobility practices, but strategies that also change one or more of the elements of executive mobility practice, for instance the meanings attached to mobility. For example, and most radically, future crises such as oil shortages that lead to many of the material elements (and aeroplanes especially) central to executive mobility practices becoming unavailable could lead to transitions away from current hyper-mobility. Or, alternatively and less radically, the practice of executive mobility could be rendered extinct by the creation of meanings, competencies and systems of provision that lead to mobility substitutes such as videoconferencing becoming the 'new' normalized way of doing business. Or put another way, a practice perspective suggests that virtual mobility via videoconference has yet to become a taken-for-granted practice because shared meanings, competencies and materials are absent and prevent its normalization as a way of doing business.

The approach developed here is valuable, then, because it takes the first steps towards a new way of thinking about the causes and management of executive mobility. But, a practice-informed analysis does also generate many new questions. For example, all practices are spatially and temporally situated. Consequently, the relevance of the UK-biased analysis developed here in different national contexts is unclear. Meanings, competencies or materials may be replicated or may be different between situated communities of executives. Further analysis is thus needed to understand how widely the practice of executive mobility described here has diffused and how the practice may vary between situated contexts. There are also important questions about ways of changing practices that have only been touched upon here. For example, how work on transitions management in socio-technical systems (e.g. Geels, 2010) can be used to further understand the rise and potential future decline (naturally or as a result of disruptive interventions) of executive mobility is an obvious line of analysis that could complement the discussion here. As such, this chapter is only a starting point for the development of a practice perspective on executive mobility.

Acknowledgements

The ideas developed in this chapter emerged as part of research funded by the EPSRC under the auspices of a Research Councils UK Energy Programme project, grant EP/J00460X/1.

References

Adey, P., Budd, L. and Hubbard, P. (2007) 'Flying lessons: exploring the social and cultural geographies of global air travel'. *Progress in Human Geography*, 31, 773–791.

Barclaycard (2006) 'Business Travel Survey 2006'. Available online at www.barclaycardbusiness.co.uk/information_zone/travel/index.html (accessed 07/06/07).

Beaverstock, J. and Faulconbridge, J. R. (2010) '"Official" and "unofficial" measurements of international business travel to and from the United Kingdom: trends, patterns and limitations'. In Beaverstock, J., Derruder, B., Faulconbridge, J. R. and Witlox, F. (eds) *International business travel in the global economy*. Farnham: Ashgate, 57–84.

Boden, D. and Molotch, H. (1994) 'The compulsion of proximity'. In Friedland, R. and Boden, D. (eds) *NowHere. Space, time and modernity*. Berkeley: University of California Press, 257–286.

Bowen, J. (2010) *The economic geography of air transportation: space, time, and the freedom of the sky*. London and New York: Routledge.

Cohen, M. J. (2010) 'Destination unknown: Pursuing sustainable mobility in the face of rival societal aspirations'. *Research Policy*, 39, 459–470.

Collis, R. (2000) *The survivor's guide to business travel*. London: Kogan Page.

Cwerner, S. (2009) *Aeromobilities*. London and New York: Routledge.

Davidson, R. and Cope, B. (2003) *Business travel*. Harlow: Pearson.

Derudder, B., Beaverstock, J. V., Faulconbridge, J. R., Storme, T. and Witlox, F. (2011) 'You are the way you fly: on the association between business travel and business class travel'. *Journal of Transport Geography*, 19, 997–1000.

Dicken, P. (2011) *Global shift* (6th edition). London: Sage.

Elliott, A. and Urry, J. (2010) *Mobile lives*. London: Routledge.

Espino, C. M., Sundstrom, S. M., Frick, H. L., Jacobs, M. and Peters, M. (2002) 'International business travel: impact on families and travellers'. *Occupational & Environmental Medicine*, 59, 309.

Fan, T., Vigeant-Langlois, L., Geissler, C., Bosler, B. and Wilmking, J. (2001) 'Evolution of global airline strategic alliance and consolidation in the twenty-first century'. *Journal of Air Transport Management*, 7, 349–360.

Faulconbridge, J. R. (2010) 'Global architects: learning and innovation through communities and constellations of practice'. *Environment and Planning A*, 42, 2842–2858.

Faulconbridge, J. R., Beaverstock, J. V., Derudder, B. and Witlox, F. (2009) 'Corporate ecologies of business travel in professional service firms: working towards a research agenda'. *European Urban and Regional Studies*, 16, 295–308.

Geels, F. W. (2010) 'Ontologies, socio-technical transitions (to sustainability), and the multi-level perspective'. *Research Policy*, 39, 495–510.

Gustafson, P. (2006) 'Work-related travel, gender and family obligations'. *Work, Employment and Society*, 20, 513–530.

Haynes, P. (2010) 'Information and communication technology and international business travel: mobility allies?' *Mobilities*, 5, 547–564.

Holley, D., Jain, J. and Lyons, G. (2008) 'Understanding business travel time and its place in the working day'. *Time & Society*, 17, 27–46.

Hudson, K. (1972) *Air travel: a social history*. New Jersey: Rowman and Littlefield.

International Passenger Survey (various years) 'Visits to/from the UK by air'. Available online at www.statistics.gov.uk/statbase/tsdataset.asp?vlnk=683 (accessed 15/12/2011).

Larner, W. (2000) 'Neo-liberalism: policy, ideology, governmentality'. *Studies in Political Economy*, 63, 5–25.

Lassen, C. (2006) 'Aeromobility and work'. *Environment and Planning A*, 38, 301–312.

Licoppe, C. (2004) '"Connected" presence: the emergence of a new repertoire for managing social relationships in a changing communication technoscape'. *Environment and Planning D: Society and Space*, 22, 135–156.

Mason, K. J. (2000) 'The propensity of business travellers to use low cost airlines'. *Journal of Transport Geography*, 8, 107–119.

Middleton, C. A. (2008) 'Do mobile technologies enable work–life balance? dual perspectives on BlackBerry usage for supplemental work'. In Hislop, D. (ed.) *Mobility and Technology in the Workplace*. London and New York: Routledge, 209–224.

Millar, J. and Salt, J. (2008) 'Portfolios of mobility: the movement of expertise in transnational corporations in two sectors – aerospace and extractive industries'. *Global Networks*, 8, 25–50.

Power, D. and Jansson, J. (2008) 'Cyclical clusters in global circuits: overlapping spaces in furniture trade fairs'. *Economic Geography*, 84, 423–448.

Presser, H. B. and Hermsen, J. M. (1996) 'Gender differences in the determinants of work-related overnight travel among employed Americans'. *Work and Occupations*, 23, 87.

Reckwitz, A. (2002) 'Toward a theory of social practices: a development in culturalist theorizing'. *European Journal of Social Theory*, 5, 243–263.

Schatzki, T. R. (1996) *Social practices: A Wittgensteinian approach to human activity and the social.* Cambridge: Cambridge University Press.

Shove, E. (2003) *Comfort, cleanliness and convenience: the social organization of normality.* Oxford and New York: Berg Publishers.

Shove, E. and Pantzar, M. (2005) 'Consumers, producers and practices: understanding the invention and reinvention of Nordic walking'. *Journal of Consumer Culture*, 5, 43.

Shove, E. and Pantzar, M. (2007) 'Recruitment and reproduction: the careers and carriers of digital photography and floorball'. *Human Affairs*, 17, 154–167.

UNCTAD (various years) 'Foreign Direct Investment'. Available online at http://unctadstat.unctad.org/ (accessed 15/12/2011).

Urry, J. (2003) 'Social networks, travel and talk'. *British Journal of Sociology*, 54, 155–175.

Urry, J. (2007) *Mobilities.* Cambridge: Polity.

Warde, A. (2005) 'Consumption and theories of practice'. *Journal of Consumer Culture*, 5, 131–153.

Wickham, J. and Vecchi, A. (2009) 'The importance of business travel for industrial clusters – making sense of nomadic workers'. *Geografiska Annaler: Series B, Human Geography*, 91, 245–255.

37

Diseased

Roger Keil

There are many transient pains in Derek's life. He is weak and withdrawn and passive, most of the time, and he has been beaten on the streets for saying strange things, he has been robbed of his disability cheques on several occasions, his nose has been broken. He does not expect much better from the world, and he doesn't think much, or for long, about all the small terrors and abuses.

(Helwig 2008: 232)

★   ★   ★

Do you experience any sort of pain on a regular basis?

No. Just sadness in my heart. That's about it.
(Homeless respondent (2007 interview series))[1]

Introduction

Disease has often been associated with immobility and the inability to distance oneself from what was or was believed to be the origin and cause of infection, chronic disease or the conditions that contribute to these origins. We can assume that this is generally the case for poor and exploited people. The idea of social determinants of health is expressive of how the relationships of wealth and poverty in a given society influence the well-being of individuals and communities. For Canada, Juha Mikkonen and Dennis Raphael have found:

> The primary factors that shape the health of Canadians are not medical treatments or lifestyle choices but rather the living conditions they experience . . . Furthermore, our wellbeing is also determined by the health and social services we receive, and our ability to obtain quality education, food and housing, among other factors. And contrary to the assumption that Canadians have personal control over these factors, in most cases these

living conditions are – for better or worse – imposed upon us by the quality of the communities, housing situations, our work settings, health and social service agencies, and educational institutions with which we interact.

(Mikkonen and Raphael 2010: 7–8)

Poor health and disease is often associated with the living conditions in certain locations and places, as for example in the assumption that people in rural poverty and cities of the Global South are trapped in conditions that don't allow them to avoid the consequences of ill physical health. This includes both the vulnerability to chronic illness and the exposure to infectious disease. It is also presumed here that in those places unhygienic conditions prevail or that they are induced or exacerbated by processes such as rapid industrialization or urbanization (or their opposite: deindustrialization and urban decline). In the wealthier cities of the Global North, in recent debates on the future of urban form and the continuing or re-emerging socio-spatial inequalities in cities, concerns have been raised about an "obesity pandemic" among immobile children and teens; and "walkability" indices have been used to help describe the link between socio-economic status and health in urban and suburban neighbourhoods (Toronto Public Health 2012). Health linked to urban form and structure is now an accepted part of the overall debate on "social exclusion, mobility and access" in urban communities, rich and poor (Cass *et al.* 2005; Young and Keil 2010). The literature on the subject has spoken of "rural" or "urban" health penalties depending on the respective environments in which diseased or vulnerable populations reside (Van de Poel *et al.* 2009; Vlahov *et al.* 2005; Vlahov *et al.* 2004).

In this chapter, I take these complex relationships between health and mobility as a starting point. Concerning myself with the threat of new or re-emerging diseases to urban life, specifically tuberculosis among the homeless, I push beyond the inherent determinism in the relationships between space, place and bodies as they are related to (im)mobilities. I acknowledge instead that (im)mobilities are facilitated and conditioned by intricate socioecological relationships and metabolisms. In sum, one can speak of the political pathology of disease. The "diseased", therefore, may be subject to compromised health for reasons of immobility or reasons of mobility, both physical and social. Being a perceived danger to society as a whole has historically put the diseased body into a precarious position vis-à-vis the community from where disease often springs. Causality is often easily ascribed to the social environment of individuals. It is now common sense that certain social and environmental conditions cause or exacerbate ill health. But saving the diseased from the consequences of those conditions – a life of compromised health, social exclusion, or even death – is not as easily done. This is partly true due to the fact, as Philipp Sarasin (2008: 268) reminds us, that "[s]trategies to ward off the threat of infection have, since antiquity, been integral to the technologies of power. These strategies were almost always spatial strategies, and they are intimately linked to the construction of states, territories and cities."

Health, (in)security, (im)mobility

Health has been a prime area in which to study the changes that western societies have undergone since the end of the Fordist–Keynesian period. While national health systems were considered bulwarks against the age-old curses that have plagued humankind and infectious disease was considered 'conquered', newly emerging diseases (such as HIV/AIDS, SARS and Ebola) and old infections (such as TB) have threatened communities, cities and states to a degree unimaginable just a generation ago. Health has become an area in which we have had to learn to live with insecurity in an increasingly mobile world.

Enhanced global mobility is the most immediately plausible cause of heightened inse-curities around health, as boundaries are increasingly being punctured by the accelerated air travel of our times. But while perforated borders expose localities to potentially devas-tating disease outbreaks, local public health systems have been decimated by neoliber-alizing reforms and a more market-oriented delivery of health services. In addition, the highly differentiated populations of this era's global cities with their diaspora communities are both agents and victims of globalized flows of pathogens as well as targets of newly emerging racializations that are attached to the re-emergence of disease (Ali and Keil 2008; Ali 2012).

Whereas the 2003 global SARS outbreak like no other infection brought these new 'truths' about the dialectic of mobility and insecurity home to the booming metropolises of East Asia and North America, it is really HIV/AIDS and tuberculosis that symbolize the tremendous insecurities we have experienced now for a generation. HIV/AIDS has expanded its destructive path from its initial recognition among the (mostly) gay male community in the 1980s to a much broader spectrum of populations (with its most devastating impact in southern Africa). TB – once considered eradicated – has been a failsafe mirror of the deteri-oration of social conditions for large parts of the urban inhabitants of the West. The disease is now endemic in poor neighbourhoods and somewhat of an epidemic among cities' growing homeless populations.

Part of this paradigmatic shift is in the recognition of a rescaled, reterritorialized reality in a globalizing world which makes other-than-national levels of governance central to ques-tions of regulation of work, health and citizenship (McCann and Ward 2011). Some have also noted the increasing "unboundedness" of such relationships (Ali 2010). The urbanization of most of the world's population in particular opens up new questions of the place and desti-nation of mobility and (in)security. Post-Westphalian forms of governance, both below and above the nation state, have pushed to the fore of territorial and topological forms of human organization. These shifts are both material (in terms of changing built environments, metabolisms, etc.) and institutional (in terms of the changing forms of governance and dis-course that guide those material processes).

Here lies the truth of the 2011 Hollywood blockbuster *Contagion*, a film that draws a por-trait of a globally linked world in which capital, information and bodies move freely until it all comes to a grinding halt in a SARS-like pandemic outbreak. Consequently the diseased and the healthy are caught in a web of interdependencies that change the ways in which they can (re-)establish modalities of interrelating that destroy and make human, community and spatial realities. Diseased bodies step out of the realm of the 'normal' into a 'new normal' of uncertainty where the world they know is turned upside down. Here also lies the historical reality of the continued treatment of the diseased as "foreign bodies", through an often racialized, phantasmagoric representation that treats the sick body of an individual as an intruding threat to the supposedly healthy national body (Sarasin 2006). Of course, in most cases, the alleged intruder is already there, and is little else than the hidden victim of social inequalities of any given society. What is unusual for the subjects in *Contagion* and what is now considered the new normal for the world's mobile and uprooted populations, is com-mon for those that have already been immobilized socially and spatially through the revan-chist realities in the neoliberalized city. For the remainder of this chapter, I will discuss a particular diseased population in light of the dialectic of mobility and immobility that they experience as their urban everyday.

The enduring articulation: homelessness and tuberculosis

One of the perplexing and disheartening facts about the geography and political economy of homelessness in Western cities is its stubborn persistence as a social phenomenon, regardless of, or even because of, continuing waves of urban regeneration and social welfare and medical reform. Being homeless always entails a level of sequestration and segregation that is beyond the imagination and experience of housed populations. The forms of exclusion vary over time and so do the relationships with housed communities as well as with the state apparatuses in welfare, health and police. The state has historically and geographically structured urban space and society in ways that make the conduct of conduct possible in disease governance, particularly in situations of re-emerging disease epidemics.

Yet, some principles remain in place. While the "service dependent ghetto" (SDG) (Dear and Wolch 1987) had a specific origin in the deinstitutionalization of mental health patients in the 1980s in the United States, the principle of bundling service agencies in a particular part of the city in order to serve a street-dependent population holds for many places that were not immediately affected by deinstitutionalization as a specific practice. Not all homeless are mentally ill or in need of services related to mental illness. Nor has the SDG had an enduring presence everywhere. In fact, one can speak of a tendency for the SDG to be dismantled "in the wake of urban renewal, redevelopment and gentrification" (Yanos 2007: 672). In addition to threats to the institutional "landscape of despair" there has been a distinct tendency towards the peripheralization and suburbanization of "housing of people with mental illness" (Yanos 2007: 673).

More differentiated concepts have since been put forth to describe the urban sociospatiality of homelessness. Among them is the recent notion of the "homeless city", as advanced by Cloke *et al.* (2010). This notion adds the dimension of "performativity" to the institutional geography implied in the SDG. In sum, "for homeless people the city becomes reconstituted as a 'homeless city', the contours of which are shaped by a variety of institutional (and some noninstitutional) spaces … homeless people negotiate these regulatory processes in often creative ways, developing a range of tactics that rework the spaces of the homeless city in new ways" (Cloke *et al.* 2010: 242). In this shifting geography of the homeless city, we find spaces of performativity, rationality and affect that characterize the world of homeless urbanites more completely than concepts put forward previously. This makes room for "other aspects of homeless people's lives – such as care, generosity, charity, and anger. These emotions are not necessarily governed by such rationalities but nevertheless help to shape both the lives of homeless people and, as a consequence, the contours of the homeless city" (Ibid.). Cloke *et al.* (2010: 245) note that the lives the homeless lead in the "homeless city" are more complex than conventionally ascribed to them. They propose to add "the affective worlds of homelessness" to the maps of the homeless spaces. The more material places that dot the homeless landscapes – for provisioning, personal care, rest – express as much the mobility patterns of the homeless as the "regulatory strategies" of the state and the shadow state. They are supplemented with the "embodied and emotional interactions" of the homeless that define certain "geographies of performativity and affect" and give a more complete picture of the "homeless city".

Before we get too deeply into the strategies and tactics of the homeless city itself, let's consider another rather constant presence in the changing city: *tuberculosis*. Once thought of as a consequence of poverty and lack of hygiene in particular marginalized populations of the industrial city (Gandy and Zumla 2003; Roberts 2009), TB is now conceptualized more in the context of security and is understood as an external threat implicating "immigrant populations and border security in an age of globalization" (Craddock 2008: 187). Global cities with their "allure" of opportunity are focal points for the new TB (Craddock 2008: 193). But not all global cities are alike. Local difference matters. The argument has been made, for example, that high TB infection rates have more to do with a lack of efficacy of urban public health policy than with poverty or deprivation itself. This explains, for example, why New York, with its extreme social polarization has lower TB rates than more socioeconomically even Tokyo. The exemplary effort by New York public health to contain the disease over the past two decades makes the difference here, rather than the more obvious social determinants of health (Rodwin 2008: 38–9). Yet, there are some groups in the cities in the Global North that continue to experience heightened levels of TB infection regardless. Among them are the homeless in large cities.

Homelessness and TB are not naturally linked. They are socially and spatially articulated in the most enduring way. While for the housed population in northern cities TB is not usually a threat, it remains so for the homeless. Much of it has to do with the special vulnerabilities stemming from the homeless's tactical mobilities in a space that is strategically structured against them. While the homeless city is like a foraging terrain for survival in the city, the housed city does not share its privileges easily and voluntarily. Tireless work is involved on the side of the homeless. Clearly, as Harris Ali has demonstrated, social space is linked with mobility and access: "Literal social exclusion confounds tuberculosis control strategies because medical treatments can only be effective if cases and contacts can be found: and this is of course simply not possible if cases and contacts are well-hidden." This leads to the question: "How does the politics of mobility create specific situations of risk to tuberculosis infection?" (Ali 2010: 20).

Infectious fear

Later, as he walked through Davisville Station on his way home, he saw a woman in a tailored coat wearing a surgical mask over her mouth, and on the train, which was not as full as usual, another mask on the face of a man holding a newspaper. But otherwise the journey was normal, someone eating french fries from a cardboard container, someone reading *Shopaholic Takes Manhattan*, everyone pretending not to notice the man in the mask.

(Helwig 2008: 75)

In his book *Infectious Fear* (2009), Samuel Kelton Roberts Jr. presents a historiography of TB in Baltimore, Maryland, in the latter part of the nineteenth and early part of the twentieth century. The narrative is intertwined with the formation – and ultimately unmaking – of the African-American ghetto in that city. The book's subtitle *Politics, Disease, and the Health Effects of Segregation* suggests an intricate relationship between the career of disease as a social phenomenon with the construction of urban built and social environments. There are similar relationships between racialization, racism and segregation as social processes and the formation of particular actor constellations that drive and challenge these processes. The occurrence, spread, persistence and ultimately defeat of tuberculosis have been imbricated consistently with the racialization of the diseased, the segregation of housing, and the building of municipal institutions. The making of urban segregation – while emerging on a plane of the production of space in a capitalist city through markets and politics – has immediate roots in the biopolitical effects of spatialized public health strategies. Systematic forces of meaning-making collude to produce the relationships of (healthy or sick) bodies and space in which the perception of the North American city is still built today. While ostensibly about the "politics of race, reform and public health" in Baltimore (Roberts 2009: 6), the book can teach us something about the continuing neglect that homeless people experience in the context of disease containment, especially when it comes to TB, which is found more frequently among them than among the general population.

Roberts engages with the microgeographies of TB: we are led into the houses of the ailing, into the laboratories of public health, into the lives of the suffering, which reveals a repulsive process of racialized, gendered and classed campaign against 'consumption'. Throughout the tale of "politics, disease, and the health effects of segregation" we can see the basic 'modernity' of the thrust of establishing institutions to rule people, neighbourhoods and ultimately cities and societies through scientifically informed 'enlightened' discourses and practices. Those are often tainted by the most stunning fundamentalist beliefs in the essential differences among humans, which are deliberately translated into policies with the unsurprising effect of confirming those stereotypes. While we may think that we have overcome the crudest forms of such racializing practice, Roberts's book sounds a warning: "Contagion is a social relation to be measured not solely by its medicalization. The metaphorical language of blight containment employed after 1940 by white property owners and makers of housing policy – describing the movement of crime, vice and social pathology – was not far removed from the uses of house infection that also had little basis in science" (Roberts 2009: 219). The gentrification of inner-city "creative" districts today often coincides with a particular colonizing gesture through which the displacement of poorer (often racialized) residents (housed and homeless) is enacted. And infectious disease, once thought to be a problem of the past, has made a re-appearance in urban life, whether it is through the "white plague" of TB itself or through newer plagues such as SARS and HIV/AIDS. The imbrication of urban change, planning and health policy engineering opens some neighbourhoods for certain select people, and displaces others, immobilizing them in a web of physical exclusion and biopolitical (often racialized) segregation. This throws a spotlight back on the diseased bodies that populate those contested spaces.

Spatial justice

If the politics of race, health and segregation conspired in Roberts's tale about TB in Baltimore to produce a register of injustice and spatial inequity, of restriction of mobility and lack of control over space, we can take some advice from another perspective on how to mobilize space to reverse these trends through a politics of spatial justice. In its most recent incarnation, the idea of spatial justice derives from Edward Soja's book *Seeking Spatial Justice* (2010). While neither Roberts nor Sofa focused on homelessness nor on disease, Soja's perspective can be brought into application fruitfully here.

Soja foregrounds space, spatial consciousness and a spatial perspective in how he views the world in general and the city in particular. In that, he includes various registers of territorial, topological, scalar and other relationships which have a spatial dimension and create inequalities and injustices of all sorts. Viewing justice not just as an institutional or interpersonal outcome, but as a process engrained in the spatialization of urban life itself, opens our view towards the possibility of recognizing the tremendous spatial inequities that exist and need to be remedied. Importantly, urban space is inhabited and used by people with very different access to resources. The spatial justice perspective allows us to see the complex intermeshing of processes that play out in various spatial relationships. The microgeographies (Ali 2010) and micro-architectures (Cloke *et al.* 2010) of homelessness are suspended in two webs of spatialities that are constituted largely but not entirely behind the actors' backs: rescaling and reterritorialization in networks of topological relations that reach beyond the everyday experience of the individual homeless person. Not only do the micro-worlds in which our everyday takes place relate to realities beyond those worlds. They also have both a material and a discursive existence. If we consider networks, for instance, we can see them as objective realities of interconnected and even causal relations (e.g. disease transmission along certain lines of contact); but they also work, as King has pointed out, as *"powerful metaphors for interpreting the causes and significance of those problems"* (King 2008: 210; emphasis in the original). Realizing that the networks of opportunity and dependency through which the homeless navigate the homeless city are potentially contributing to the spread of disease in their midst is one thing; addressing these networked interdependencies through state or institutional action is another thing. It bears in it the danger of colonization and risks losing the capacity to act (King 2008: 210).

★   ★   ★

Space is never to be localized. It is always constituted through multiple scales and networks (Craddock 2008: 195). To find spatial justice in this context certainly needs a careful evaluation of which spatial boundaries should be maintained between what is considered healthy and what is considered infectious, and between the housed and the homeless, for example (Craddock 2008: 195). This involves, as Craddock notes, perceptively citing Deleuze and Guattari (1987), that "the administration of a great molar security has as its correlate a whole micromanagement of petty fears, a permanent molecular insecurity" (cited in Craddock 2008: 199). The microgeographies and micro-architectures of the homeless city have no autonomy from the geographies and architectures of the housed city, yet the reverse also applies. They are intertwined in myriad ways through all manner of spatial strategies that are more or less open or impervious to including notions of justice. This is the discursive terrain, the policy battleground, the site of negotiation for spatial justice. Who holds the power? How can one intervene? Who will intervene?

Socioeconomic inequalities and institutional reactions to them have to be seen in spatialized context in order to be fully understood. It is clear that "targeting of vulnerable populations makes epidemiological and economic sense, as it enables cash-strapped municipalities to focus resources on a limited set of subpopulations . . . It can also be beneficial when communities themselves are engaged in planning and implementing appropriate interventions" (Craddock 2008: 191). The problem ensues when such spatialized interventions occur under guidance of – in the larger sense – "tropical thinking". Denoting both "locale" and "designation", *tropical* can be used here in the sense that one part of society, in our case the housed population (with its social and state institutions) treats the "homeless city" as the "location of disease" (Craddock 2008: 192).

TB infection is often "the result of the complex interplay of individual agency and . . . 'structural violence' – that is, how the social structure of society, informed largely by economic criteria related to the unequal distribution of resources and power, results in the constraining of individual agency of subaltern people, thereby placing them in harm's way" (Ali 2010: 6). The discussed work on justice adds a distinct spatial dimension to this institutional and structural view. (Im)mobility and disease are mutually reinforcing aspects of that dimension.

The homeless city/The sick city

Rather than treating the diseased and the homeless as purely "acted upon", we need to begin seeing them as possessive of agency. This will cast light on what the experiences are of the homeless with the institutions of the state in general and health care institutions in particular. We ask: What does service density mean for the homeless? How do they use services offered in fixed locations for their health needs in general and their TB-related needs in particular? What other spatial strategies do homeless people pursue (go 'back home' to spaces including aboriginal reserves; use ambulant services, etc.)?

The homeless city is, in the first instance, recognizable from the outside as an institutional-built environment of service delivery. Its emergence is not a linear process but it is itself subject to changing relationships of the homeless to their city. One homeless person observed in an interview:

> What came first? People congregate around this area because there's all these shelters or are the shelters here because there's so many homeless? What causes what? I mean there's probably . . . like I used to live in Vancouver . . . and people go there a lot of times. And then all [there is the] Sally Ann, they're all there now. And now people are going there in the summer so it's like what came first? The shelters or the homeless?

The homeless co-construct the "homeless city" as a constantly shifting set of hubs and spokes through which they stay alive. The hubs are defined geographically and temporally as needed. They offer themselves as a tightly regulated and policed landscape but they also are somewhat open to tactical negotiation, purposeful or not.

In terms of how TB fits into this landscape of performativity, one can see a somewhat resigned realization that it is one disease that is present here and not beyond the homeless city's borders. The institutions of the homeless city itself, such as the shelters, enable the disease to do its work and allow the homeless little room to move into a space of relative protection.

Conclusion

Both the homeless city and its tubercular reality are usually portrayed as spaces of "helpless-ness and chaos", very much like the Global South, which is always under some design for development (Craddock 2008: 194). This portrait is ultimately debilitating and disempower-ing as the homeless and the patients are acted upon rather than collaborated with. Yet, on closer inspection, the "homeless city" is less chaotic and the homeless less "helpless" than what the common image suggests. In fact, there is perhaps both more structure and more agency in the homeless city than we might expect. The conditions under which injustices are being produced, and under which homelessness and disease are articulated into a difficult set of issues in the everyday of many people in the city, are as ambiguous as the networks we discussed above (King 2008). They are fluid and constantly renegotiated. As Soja says with reference to Edward Said: "[U]njust geographies of political power can also be enabling, creating the foundations for resistance and potential emancipation. It is important to remem-ber this double-sidedness, how the spatiality of (in)justice can be both intensely oppressive and potentially liberating" (Soja 2010: 37).

The intersection of urban space, homelessness and disease explored in this short essay has proven to be a fertile ground for the understanding of the dialectics of mobility and immo-bilization that is at the root of the current shift in the liquidity regime cities are undergoing. The traditional, sectoralized, segregated and sequestered nature of both the political ecology and political pathology of urban lives has given way to new mobility regimes into which the diseased are reinscribed in novel ways. The homeless who have been the subject of this essay are a prime group of urbanites whose topologies have been upended by urban regeneration, gentrification and a more interventionist punitive state. The homeless city has been shown to be resilient as the homeless have reoriented their urban everyday to deal with these new demands. Nonetheless, spatial justice has been elusive as the persistent chronic and infectious disease continues to be a sharp marker of difference between the housed and the homeless. The dialectic of *mobility* (the unbounded innovative pathways beaten by the homeless in criss-crossing the homeless city) and *immobility* (the continued framework of restraint that characterizes both the state's policing and the health care system's institutional landscape) persists as the central contradiction of the homeless diseased. The (diseased) homeless and the homeless city afford a glimpse into a mobility regime that is generalized in a moment of *contagion*.

Note

1 Interviews referenced in this chapter were conducted as part of the SSHRC Research Development Initiatives program-funded research "Attending to Social Vulnerabilities in Tuberculosis Transmission Dynamics: Toward a Synergistic Model of Qualitative and Quantitative Methods" under the leadership of Stephen Gaetz at York University (2006–2008).

Bibliography

Ali, S. H. (2012) 'Infectious Diseases as New Risks for Human Health'. In S. Kabisch, A. Kunath, P. Schweizer-Ries and A. Steinführer (eds) *Vulnerability, Risks and Complexity: Impacts of Global Change on Human Habitats*. Göttingen: Hogrefe, 13–25.

Ali, S. H. (2010) 'Tuberculosis, Homelessness and the Politics of Mobility'. *Canadian Journal of Urban Research* 19(2), 80–107.

Ali, S. H. and Keil, R. (eds) (2008) *Networked Disease: Emerging Infections in the Global City*. Oxford: Wiley-Blackwell.

Cass, N., Shove, E. and Urry, J. (2005) 'Social Exclusion, Mobility and Access'. *The Sociological Review* 53(3), 539–555.

Cloke, P., May, J. and Johnsen, S. (2010) *Swept up Lives? Re-envisioning the Homeless City*. Oxford: Wiley-Blackwell.

Craddock, S. (2008) 'Tuberculosis and the Anxieties of Containment'. In: S. H. Ali and R. Keil (eds) *Networked Disease: Emerging Infections in the Global City*. Oxford: Wiley-Blackwell, 186–200.

Dear, M. and Wolch, J. (1987) *Landscapes of Despair: From Deinstitutionalisation to Homelessness*. Oxford: Polity Press.

Deleuze, G. and Guattari, F. (1987) *A Thousand Plateaus: Capitalism and Schizophrenia*. Minneapolis: Minnesota Press.

Gandy, M. and Zumla, A. (eds) (2003) *The Return of the White Plague: Global Poverty and the 'New' Tuberculosis*. London: Verso.

Helwig, M. (2008) *Girls Fall Down*. Toronto: Coach House Books.

King, N. B. (2008) 'Networks, Disease, and the Utopian Impulse'. In: S. H. Ali and R. Keil (eds) *Networked Disease: Emerging Infections in the Global City*. Oxford: Wiley-Blackwell, 201–213.

McCann, E. and Ward, K. (2011) *Mobile Urbanism: Cities and Policymaking in the Global Age*. Minneapolis: University of Minnesota Press.

Mikkonen, J. and Raphael, D. (2010) *Social Determinants of Health: The Canadian Facts*. Toronto: York University School of Health Policy and Management.

Roberts, S. K. Jr. (2009) *Infectious Fear: Politics, Disease, and the Health Effects of Segregation*. Chapel Hill: University of North Carolina Press.

Rodwin, V. G. (2008) 'Health and Disease in Global Cities: A Neglected Dimension of National Health Policy'. In: S. H. Ali and R. Keil (eds) *Networked Disease: Emerging Infections in the Global City*. Oxford: Wiley-Blackwell, 27–48.

Sarasin, P. (2008) 'Vapors, Viruses, Resistance(s): The Trace of Infection in the Work of Michel Foucault'. In S. H. Ali and R. Keil (eds) *Networked Disease: Emerging Infections in the Global City*. Oxford: Wiley-Blackwell, 267–280.

Sarasin, P. (2006) *Anthrax: Bioterror as Fact and Fantasy*. Cambridge, MA and London, UK: Harvard University Press.

Soja, E. W. (2010) *Seeking Spatial Justice*. Minneapolis: University of Minnesota Press.

Toronto Public Health (2012) 'The Walkable City: Neighbourhood Design and Preferences, Travel Choices and Health'. April.

Van de Poel, E., O'Donnell, O. and Van Doorslaer, E. (2009) 'The Health Penalty of China's Rapid Urbanization'. Tinbergen Institute Discussion Paper, Tinbergen Institute Rotterdam, 1–41.

Vlahov, D., Galea, S. and Freudenberg, N. (2005) 'The Urban Health "Advantage"'. *Journal of Urban Health: Bulletin of the New York Academy of Medicine* 82(1), 1–4.

Vlahov, D., Gibble, E., Freudenberg, N. and Galea, S. (2004) 'Cities and Health: History, Approaches, and Key Questions'. *Academic Medicine* 7(9), 12 (December), 1133–1138.

Yanos, P. T. (2007) 'Beyond "Landscapes of Despair": The Need for New Research on the Urban Environment, Sprawl, and the Community Integration of Persons with Severe Mental Illness'. *Health Place* 13(3), 672–676.

Young, D. and Keil, R. (2010) 'Reconnecting the Disconnected: The Politics of Infrastructure in the In-between City'. *Cities* 27, 87–95.

38

Elders

Juliana Mansvelt

For elders, a term often used to refer to people over the age of 65, mobility is often framed in terms of physical movement. The acknowledgement that personal mobility may decline in later life has meant mobility for older people tends to be seen in terms of a bodily 'deficit', particularly within bio-medical discourses. However, recent work in the social sciences has challenged such views through highlighting the ways in which elders may engage in varying and productive forms of mobile practices as part of their engagement in familial, leisure, friendship, organizational and work networks (Cass *et al.* 2005).

This chapter examines older people's personal mobility and advocates a 'more-than-physical' and 'more-than-human' (Whatmore 2006: 600) conception derived from the interdependence of, and connections between, people, knowledges and things. Such a perspective can assist in illuminating the hegemonic power inherent in sociocultural values, institutions, networks and spaces that is associated with being physically mobile (Imrie 2000). In shifting the emphasis of mobility from elders themselves to the ways in which socio-technical assemblages enable and disable capacities for movement and stillness, I reflect not only on the different ways in which elders' mobilities are produced, but also the ways in which doing mobilities differently might be productive of new and empowering geographies of everyday life.

Elders' mobility as more than physical: moving from bodies to networks

The bulk of the literature on elders' mobility tends to focus on the physical and functional aspects of older people's bodies and their capacity to displace space, whether this is the ability of limbs, heads, hands and feet to function through a normal range of movements, or the ability of older people to move across a variety of scales. Gerontological research, for example, supports a view of mobility as 'the ability to move oneself (e.g. by walking, using assistive devices or by using transportation) within community environments that expand from one's home, to the neighbourhood, and regions beyond' (Webber *et al.* 2010: 443).

The power inherent in conceptions of human mobility in contemporary societies often becomes more visible in later years through the discursive framing of 'elder mobility' as an area of both medical and social-scientific concern. Studies of in-home mobility, for example, have shown how people's ability to undertake basic activities of daily living may be negatively affected with advancing age (Katz 1983). An emphasis on the challenges faced by older people in transgressing the boundaries of home-space, and in physically accessing community spaces has also characterized literature on elder mobility (Ayis *et al.* 2007; Banister and Bowling 2004; Metz 2000; Rowles 1983; Stalvey *et al.* 1999). This research has identified that elder mobility is influenced by a wide range of intersectional characteristics (including health conditions and individuals' social, physical and emotional needs, family circumstances and social networks, and material standards of living) and environmental factors (Metz 2000), and that social and spatial exclusion may result from a person's relative immobility (Kenyon *et al.* 2002). Such approaches have provided the basis for political, policy and practical interventions which promote the independence, health, wellbeing and social integration of older people, facilitating their mobility through such things as appropriate service provision and transportation, and engineering more inclusive built environments (Carder 2002; Davey 2007; Laws 1993; May *et al.* 2010).

However, the notion of elder mobility conceived of in terms of individual physical mobility and deficit can be problematic. In focusing on the maximization of physical movement much gerontological research has privileged travel and more formal and public types of transport (Cass *et al.* 2005), with elders' potential to move (motility) and ability to do so bound in notions of activity, independence and the displacement of space. This may have the effect of disempowering the 'stillness which punctuates the flow of all things' (Bissell and Fuller 2011: 3) and othering less-mobile elders.

Work emerging from the new mobilities paradigm (Sheller and Urry 2006; Urry 2007) has encouraged scholars to reflect on the ways in which things, ideas and information move across space and time. With a conceptualization of mobility as 'the fragile entanglement of physical movement, representation and practices' (Cresswell 2010: 18), scholars have been encouraged to think not only about the ways in which human movement is experienced, conceived and practised, but how this is entangled in shifting relationships between people, things and places. Ziegler and Schwanen (2011), for example, advocate a conceptualization of elder mobility which attends to the ways people travel and connect with new spaces through the transference of aspects of the material and imagined self through electronic, social and psychological spaces.

Moving beyond individuals' communicative, cognitive and corporeal ability to displace space, actor network approaches (Latour 2007; Murdoch 1997) enable an understanding of mobility as the outcome of shifting relations between human and non-human entities (which may exist in physical or dematerialized forms, e.g. digital data). Here mobile practices become the premise and products of a more-than-human world comprised of heterogeneous socio-technical assemblages through which people, things and imaginaries flow, stop and are rendered still.

The remainder of this chapter endeavours to recognize the complex cognitive, social, representational and material attributes of elder mobility, raising questions about the ways in which relationships between ageing bodies and mobility might be conceptualized. In drawing on research conducted with home-based elders I argue for a relational view of mobility which decentres the corporeality of human movement by placing it within its wider social and material relations.

Researching the mobilities of 'home-based' elders: a contradiction in terms?

The research upon which this chapter draws forms part of a multi-disciplinary research project[1] aimed at exploring older New Zealanders' experiences of engaging with and interacting with a range of public, private and voluntary sector organizations. The initial phase of the research involved the recruitment of 53 'active elders' aged over 65. A second group of 19 'home-based elders' were recruited. These home-based elders (15 female, 4 male) were aged 70–96 years and were primarily urban dwellers who 'found it difficult to leave home, except with the assistance of others' (participant recruitment advertisement). In one-off interviews ranging from 1–1.5 hours these participants were asked to reflect on their experiences of managing and interacting with a range of service providers and organizations.

Many of these participants had medical conditions and significant bodily, eyesight and hearing disabilities which made leaving home difficult. However, during the process of interviewing I began to feel increasingly uncomfortable at the positioning of these older people in relation to the 'active' elders. While the 'home-based' elders did find it challenging to leave their dwellings, they were keen to shape a sense of themselves as differently-mobile, active and engaged outside the home. In addition, the analysis of data from the 'active' elder group demonstrated that forms and moments of corporeal immobility also punctuated the narratives of these participants. Nevertheless, while the categorization of elders as 'home-based' can be problematized for its emphasis on the deficit of corporeal mobility and parallel assumptions of inactivity and sedentarism, understanding the mobile practices of these home-based elders provided compelling and novel understandings of what happens when taken-for-granted modes of being mobile in the world fail; when the capacities of actor networks do not easily allow for the operation of differently-mobile practices; and when the topology of movement and its representational framing alters. The remainder of the chapter explores these ideas through four themes.

The revelation of relative (im)mobility to elders through the disruption of habits

The taken-for-granted ways in which socio-technical networks function through their often-hidden power geometries may be revealed by both the failure and shifts in the operation of actor networks. Analysis of participant talk revealed that when previously habitual mobile practices are disrupted (for example when reaching, walking or brushing one's teeth becomes difficult), these practices and the material things which enable them become registered as the subject of narratives which are storied. Alice's medical condition had worsened gradually over the years and she now no longer could use her hands and used a wheelchair to move around the house. Here, and unprompted, Alice (aged 79) begins a story about the enabling power of a bidet during a conversation about the challenges of phone banking, a story I overlooked at the time:

Alice: Yeah. But with the phone banking see, I've got to touch.
Juliana: Oh I see. Gotcha.
And I've got the most wonderful toilet. Want to have a look at it?
Oh I might later.
She is fabulous.
Oh that's great.
Oh if you know of anyone who has got problems, it is, well they didn't want me to come out [of hospital], I was in rehab and they didn't want me to come home and not be able to look after myself personally wise like that. So my son, you know, got this bidet, what do you call them?
Bidets, yeah, yeah.

Type of thing. Well I've got a concrete floor and we couldn't think how we'd get that in. But he found a firm in Auckland and they send this one down that attach you on the toilet. Fabulous! Absolutely fabulous!

On reflection, I realized that my 'ablest' preconceptions about what constituted legitimate forms of informational and material networks that would enable Alice's body and mind to travel and connect with other organizations and flows (such as phone banking) prevented me from engaging with her story. Alice's conversation revealed that her bidet mattered, enabling her to move out of rehab, continuing to extend her distance from its discursive and material power as a place of relative dependence. Her son's purchase of the bidet allowed her to retain mobility within her own home and to reclaim a sense of agency and control over who and what services came in, and assisted toileting to continue as a personal and private habit (albeit one that was altered from its previous form).

Analysis of transcripts also showed, as Ziegler and Schwanen (2011: 768) found in their study of mobility and wellbeing in later life, that practices such as 'going to town' or 'using the phone' were formed of a collection of multiple acts, moments and relations involving different mobile practices (using steps, opening letter boxes, reaching, dialling numbers). For some, the failure of their everyday habits, repetitive practices which require little cognitive thought (including thinking itself, see Bissell 2011) had been gradual, thereby making the adaption easier. But for others the more sudden onset of 'disability' had meant they were abruptly confronted by their relative immobilities. Nevertheless, Faith (96 years), despite many years of 'disablement', still talked with some frustration about how she felt her body denied her previously held mobile possibilities. For Faith, movements of bending, sitting and seeing were no longer habitual, revealing the thought and bodily effort now applied to simple movements and a corporeality which she believed limited her capacity for social inclusion:

> And I'm so slow in getting round now so, I used to belong to the Herb Society. I enjoyed that. I was on the steering committee that started the one in Upper Hutt before we came here. I really enjoyed that but, gardening I enjoyed, but that, and I can only deadhead roses now. I can't do anything else. I can't bend. I mean I daren't sit on the low chair. I can't get up. These muscles have gone apparently. Well I've had a heart attack and a stroke and I've had a bad back for 70 years. So I mean I know what it is to be impeded by my body.

Participants' experiences revealed how mobility is not simply about movement through physical space but also through cognitive and social space. Participants' narratives powerfully demonstrated the fragility of previously habitual modes of living (Bissell 2010). When asked about her mobility, Olwyn (aged 70–74) highlighted the ways in which she felt her relative lack of mobility was altering her worldly relations:

> I just feel that with my health problems causing me to be dependent on this and not driving, my life has become very much constricted if you like. No not constricted. There's no sense of, of rebelling against it. How do you?
> *Juliana: But you do notice the difference? Is that what you are . . .?*
> . . . Well I do sometimes and you, you feel oh, I don't want to ask (my daughters) to take me such and such a place. The feeling of being dependent is hard to come to terms with. But you just have to.

As Bissell (2013) argues, the skilful proficiencies which emerge through habit are not so much the product of individual bodies but are contextual and relational, located in time and place contexts in which bodies and environments are entangled. For participants with limited sight, for example, habits taken for granted at home (like finding one's way around) become subject to disruption in less familiar environments (streets, shops and buildings), which in turn become known, felt and imagined with much more apprehension. As Bissell (2013) suggests with regard to the phenomenon of 'the yips' in sport, proficiency and the conservation of action engendered by the habitual always exists in relation to the threat of its annihilation. For some elders, imminent threats to their mobility and body-mind vulnerabilities were made real not only through their awareness of their declining physical capacities with age but also through the potential failure implicit in interactional engagements in virtual and real spaces – environments such as malls, streets, shops and buildings. These were spaces where bodily habits could no longer be taken for granted, and where the consequences of their failure (bladder or bowel accidents, getting lost, falling, holding up queues of people using an ATM) might be more visible.

The necessity of moorings for elders

Olwyn's earlier quote about the increased constriction of her social world also alludes to the ways in which moving imaginatively, virtually and physically was premised on what Hannam *et al.* (2006) describe as 'moorings' – with fixity in time and place necessary in order to make corporeal bodies, information and material things flow. Despite her sense of disempowerment, which arose from her dependence on her daughters and their vehicles for outings, Olwyn recognized that she had greater independence and mobility because of their intervention and the assistive technologies she relied on. She later went on to state:

> I don't like them, having to use them [raised toilet seats and shower stools] but . . . But the other thing, the other way of looking at it is that because of those things, you are able to be independent.

For a number of participants, seating, bench tops, door frames and rails allowed for moments of stillness as part of the co-constitution of their mobile practices. Here, moments of stopping were productive, allowing body-mind to rest, recuperate and prepare for movement. This was a stillness (and therefore a mobility) which could often only be achieved through the enrolment of other people and/or things in particular spaces. Ella (aged 86), for example, noted how resting on trolleys enabled her to steady herself and move around the supermarket without difficulty:

> *Juliana: So how do you find pushing the trolleys around?*
> Oh that's no problem. It's a help to me, having something steady, what I think that's steady to hold on to. That's no problem.

Similarly, Nina (aged 72) relied on the moments of rest and stability provided by chairs that were placed strategically around her home:

> And I have chair in the hall and I have a chair in the kitchen so I can get from Point A to Point B and if I need to sit it's there, so that's why there's odd chairs in places round the place.

Nina's need to explain to me the spatial arrangement of chairs within her house also brought to light the relative invisibility of moments of rest and stillness in normative conventions of walking. Volunteering such information, Nina suggests a felt recognition of her corporeal vulnerability with the explanation becoming a means of framing her experience of being a differently-mobile but coping person. Despite her narration of her mobile practice and her home environment as abnormal, she recognized the mobile opportunities afforded by the material arrangements of her home and the sense of autonomy and control that this spatial arrangement provided.

The capacities of virtual and imaginative mobilities for elders

While 'home-based' elders recognized that they faced challenges in moving within and outside the borders of their homes, they sought to establish, maintain and capitalize on actor networks (both within and beyond the home) which allowed them to engage in a range of differently-mobile practices. Research suggests it is not simply one's actual ability to be physically mobile, but also one's expressed desire to be mobile and the potential ability to be so which are important for elders (Mollenkopf *et al.* 2011; Banister and Bowling 2004). So strong are the imperatives to be active and mobile as part of ageing 'successfully' that participants would often resist constructions of themselves as sedentary. Isobel (aged 80), whose bodily movement was severely limited, suggests that she is always active in response to a question on voluntary work:

> Juliana: *And would you like to be doing any work on a voluntary . . .*
> No. I'm too busy with my reading and . . . keeping my brain going.

For many of these home-based elders the enabling capacity of imaginative, communicative and virtual mobilities was significant. This mobility of the self or the 'will or psychological disposition to connect with the world and others, with people and places beyond oneself, one's household or one's residence' (Ziegler and Schwanen 2011: 763) was also evident in participant talk, expressed through such things as participating in an online community, talking to others on the telephone, an awareness of people and place issues through listening to radio, and travelling imaginatively to other places through watching film or television. While talk was often around connection to people and environments outside the home, a mobility of the self was also to be found in what came into their homes (library books, DVDs, emails, letters, friends, carers, and representatives from organizations).

For three participants, 'networked sociality' (Urry 2007) was achieved through the mobilities enabled by information technologies. Facebook, email and university study enabled these participants to travel imaginatively and to interact across distanced spaces with more friends and relatives than corporeal travel would permit (Burnett and Lucas 2010). Such practices also produced a subjective sense of self that was less defined by physical immobilities or the home space. Nina (aged 72), who was studying for a university degree, talked about the ways in which her computer life empowered her to move money, ideas, information and consumer goods across home boundaries. Here she described the pleasure to be had from spending time on the computer and the way it had enabled her to interact with a whole range of organizations:

> Juliana: *What's your preferred way of dealing with these organizations?*
> For me (for) everything – the computer is fantastic. I mean I'm computer literate. I've been on computers for 20 years . . . [and later]

I'm happier at home than out really, I've got my computer, I spend a lot of time on the computer and I'm perfectly happy doing that or reading.

However for some, their inability to use a computer was a further reminder of their 'home-based' status, a lack of a connectivity and relative immobility. Pam (aged 81) told me how she was terrified of computers:

And everyone can use a computer in the world. Little children and old, old people but I can't. And I feel . . . so I blank out on that.

Thus the imaginative, social and virtual capacities which constituted a mobility of self were experienced differently for this participant. Participants' capacity to be mobile and the possibilities and products that such mobile practices permit, together with the extent to which they were able to control movements of self and other people, things and information varied greatly, potentially giving rise to both social inclusion *and* exclusion (Kenyon *et al.* 2002). Regardless of whether participants travelled much outside their home, their motility, or potential to travel, was impacted by a whole range of factors related to access to resources, personal aptitudes and their cognitive appropriation (Kaufmann 2010). For example, the ability to travel virtually was influenced by access to computers, broadband, finances, skills and personal competency using digital technologies, together with their cognitive understanding of the real and representational possibilities and problems of doing so.

The significance of network capital for elders

Network capital is the power to command and manage the mobility of self and others, and is a major axis of social inequality in contemporary society (Urry, interviewed by Adey and Bissell 2010: 7–8). While it might be easy to assume that the home-based elders would possess relatively little network capital (having more limited possibilities for face-to-face communication and less freedom to determine the modes, timing and spatial extent of one's travel) the importance of the network capital they possessed was striking in their narratives. For many participants the importance of policing, enabling and managing the mobility of other people, information and entities to their home was critically important in giving rise to a sense of autonomy and social inclusion. Mary (67) notes the personal contact she has with others, proudly telling me that her home is sometimes more akin to a train station:

Juliana: I've learnt you know, that it's the person coming in, it's not just the service . . .
Oh it makes a huge difference, it's the human contact.
Yes, so that's been good to learn about.
Yeah well sometimes here it's like Paddington Station!

Controlling who and what passed through home territory thus gave participants a sense of autonomy and empowerment, but also provided a connection to those outside one's household and to the wider community. Pam's interaction with her home help, gardener, home librarian and the meter reader provide companionship, connection and pleasure, helping her to feel 'at home' in part because of the people she has around her.

You know you mentioned the meter readers coming in and I . . .

Yes. So nice. Well you see I, I feel I'm so spoilt in many ways. These lovely people all around who, I haven't struck any duds really.

And later, in talking about her relationship with the home-based librarian, Pam states:

But, so that service of the public library, the housebound service has been a joy to me. It really has.

The significance of 'intercorporeality', or how the 'body is lived out and spoken about with other bodies (human and nonhuman) and our own embodied past' (Macpherson 2009: 1052) was evident in the experiences of elders particularly in relation to care. A number of participants talked about the enabling and/or disabling relations that they had with caregivers. Where a caregiver sensed and understood the older person's body, the mobile practices they engaged in together (such as shifting from bed to wheelchair) were experienced as relatively seamless movements. But the experience with caregivers who were inexperienced or lacked the ability to feel and know the series and synergy of movements necessary to achieve tasks or use equipment was seen as frustrating and served to magnify the relative disablement of the older person.

The role of non-humans in actor networks as part of the experience of intercorporeality was significant. Ella (aged 86) had lost her sight through macular degeneration, leaving her with only a small amount of peripheral vision, which also affected her ability to walk and balance. Ella's tale of this sudden and traumatic event was a reminder of the ways in which motion and emotion, felt and sensed body are co-constituted (Sheller 2004). Ella strongly believed that continuing to live in her own dwelling was dependent on her mobility and her capacity to wield network capital in order to manage flows of goods, money and information in and out of her house. Below are a series of excerpts from her conversation with me about the challenges of shopping – challenges which visibly and publicly shaped her as 'impaired' and less mobile:

Juliana: So how often would you need to get taxis anywhere?

Oh, well just if I wanted to go, well I can't really go shopping now by myself. I've got, that's my problem, I've got nobody, I'll have to tell the Blind Foundation, they may be able to help me there but I, I don't want to buy any clothes now but when I do, I can't, you know I can't go fossicking on the racks. And neither can I, because I, my balance is not good, and so I need, and of course I can't cross the road unless it's at a pedestrian crossing.

As for shopping, it was terrible. Because you see I didn't want to ask anybody. I can't read the labels.

And how do you manage now with your grocery shopping?

Well I can manage fruit and vegetables no problem, but of course I've no idea what they cost, which is a . . .

You can't read it?

No.

So, but now I sort of know which, pretty well, which aisle it is, and then I hope to find an assistant and they, they are marvellous there. If you ask them they'll help you. If not I grab the nearest person.

And I keep my white stick in the trolley and if anybody says anything, I say well I'm sorry but I've got very poor eyesight.

But . . . Another thing I can't see to use the EFTPOS thing.

Ella's narrative reveals the complex conjunctions of some of the human and non-human entities that are necessary for successful shopping: money as cash, pedestrian crossings, taxis, drivers, devices to access money, price labels, trolleys, her white sticks, passers-by, shop assistants, EFTPOS (point of sale card transaction) machines and supermarket layouts. While Ella sees her relative slowness, difficulty in reading labels, poor navigation and inability to use the EFTPOS machine as a product of her own embodiment (hence why she displays her white cane prominently, as if to justify any obvious inabilities as arising from her difference), the excerpts reveal the disabling effects of normative social-technical networks (Schillmeier 2007). The built environment of the supermarket, pricing systems and point of sale card machines are part of efficient and predictable networks for some, but may be inflexible and not easily adapted to the varying corporeal competencies of other individuals. Through such networks Ella's bodily impairments are rendered visible and known, and she is dis-abled from making information, money and commodities flow. However, also evident in Ella's account is her fortitude and her resourcefulness in the ways in which she is able to employ network capital. Despite her reluctance to ask others to help, Ella does enrol others (passers-by and shop assistants) to enable her to select and purchase her groceries. Ella's experiences, in common with all of the other participants, demonstrate the enabling power of network capital.

Though the accounts of elders revealed the frustration of being differently-mobile, they were simultaneously narratives of resilience: of success in spite of difficulty; of mobility in spite of friction; and of the pleasures to be found in overcoming mobility challenges.

Conclusion

The stories of these home-based elders reveal that being a body that is mostly confined to domestic space does not necessarily involve living in a way removed from other social life (Williams 1983). Despite their relative physical immobility, these home-based dwellers resist the notion that they are immobile, inactive or unproductive. The taken-for-granted assumption in much elder research that mobility for elders is constituted by physically 'getting out' did have some resonance with participants. But this assumption was also heavily contested through a multiplicity of spatial, temporal and social practices which involved a mobility of self beyond the body and the 'letting in' of flows of people, knowledge and things. The analysis of interviews indicates the significance of socio-technical networks in shaping mobile practices. It demonstrates the necessity of understanding elder mobilities as more than physical and more than human through the recognition that motility and mobility of the self arises from relations between people and technologies which may be both proximate and distant.

Understanding mobilities through moments, spaces and practices of connection between people, things and spaces provides new possibilities for developing practices that accommodate the ways in which elders desire and practise mobility of the self. In revealing that differently-mobile people may mobilize things differently, this study of the experiences of home-based elders highlights the need for organizational practices to provide flexibility in the ways they accommodate and enable corporeal difference. Beyond that, it is my hope that researchers might continue to critique neo-liberal visions of ageing citizenship which connect successful and responsible ageing with individual competence, physical activity, independence and self-reliance (Ziegler and Schwanen 2011; Peace *et al.* 2011). Instead, an openness to different and interdependent ways of being and becoming mobile in one's later years could, as Hansen and Philo (2007: 49) argue with regard to disability, shift the emphasis for home-based elders from doing things 'normally' to enabling 'the normality of doing things differently'.

Note

1 The research on 'Engaging Senior Stakeholders: Positive Ageing at the Organisation–Elder Interface' was funded by the New Zealand Foundation for Research Science and Technology (2009–2012). The research team, led by Professor Ted Zorn (Massey University), comprises a multi-disciplinary team of scholars: Dr Mary Simpson, Dr Margaret Richardson, Professor Peggy Koopman-Boyden, Dr Michael Cameron (Waikato University) and Juliana Mansvelt (Massey University).

Bibliography

Adey, P. and Bissell, D. (2010) 'Mobilities, meetings, and futures: an interview with John Urry', *Environment and Planning D: Society and Space*, 28(1): 1–16.

Ayis, S. A., Bowling, A., Gooberman-Hill, R. and Ebrahim, S. (2007) 'The effect of definitions of activities of daily living on estimates of changing ability among older people', *International Journal of Rehabilitation Research*, 30(1): 39–46.

Banister, D. and Bowling, A. (2004) 'Quality of life for the elderly: the transport dimension', *Transport Policy*, 11: 105–15.

Bissell, D. (2010) 'Vibrating materialities: mobility–body–technology relations', *Area*, 42(4): 479–86.

Bissell, D. (2011) 'Thinking habits for uncertain subjects: movement, stillness, susceptibility', *Environment and Planning A*, 43(11): 2649–65.

Bissell, D. (2013) 'Habit displaced: the disruption of skilful performance', *Geographical Research*, 51(2): 120–29.

Bissell, D. and Fuller, G. (2011) 'Stillness unbound', in D. Bissell and G. Fuller (eds) *Stillness in a Mobile World*, London: Routledge, 1–18.

Burnett, P. and Lucas, S. (2010) 'Talking, walking, riding and driving: the mobilities of older adults', *Journal of Transport Geography*, 18(5): 596–602.

Carder, P. C. (2002) 'The social world of assisted living', *Journal of Aging Studies*, 16: 1–18.

Cass, N., Shove, E. and Urry, J. (2005) 'Social exclusion, mobility and access', *The Sociological Review*, 53(3): 539–55.

Cresswell, T. (2010) 'Towards a politics of mobility', *Environment and Planning D: Society and Space*, 28(1): 17–31.

Davey, J. A. (2007) 'Older people and transport: coping without a car', *Ageing & Society*, 27(1): 49–65.

Hannam, K., Sheller, M. and Urry, J. (2006) 'Editorial: mobilities, immobilities and moorings', *Mobilities*, 1(1): 1–22.

Hansen, N. and Philo, C. (2007) 'The normality of doing things differently: bodies, spaces and disability geography', *Tijdschrift voor Economische en Sociale Geografie*, 98(4): 493–506.

Imrie, R. (2000) 'Disability and discourses of mobility and movement', *Environment and Planning A*, 32(9): 1641–56.

Katz, S. (1983) 'Assessing self-maintenance: activities of daily living, mobility and instrumental activities of daily living', *Journal of the American Geriatrics Society*, 31(12): 721–27.

Kaufmann, V. (2010) 'Mobile social science: creating a dialogue among the sociologies', *The British Journal of Sociology*, 61, 367–72.

Kenyon, S., G. Lyons and Rafferty, J. (2002) 'Transport and social exclusion: investigating the possibility of promoting inclusion through virtual mobility', *Journal of Transport Geography*, 10(3): 207–19.

Latour, B. (2007) *Reassembling the Social: An Introduction to Actor-Network-Theory*, Oxford: Oxford University Press.

Laws, G. (1993) '"The land of old age": society's changing attitudes toward urban built environments for elderly people', *Annals of the Association of American Geographers*, 83(4): 672–93.

Juliana Mansvelt

Macpherson, H. (2009) 'The intercorporeal emergence of landscape: negotiating sight, blindness, and ideas of landscape in the British countryside', *Environment and Planning A*, 41(5): 1042–54.

May, E., Garrett, R. and Ballantyne, A. (2010) 'Being mobile: electric mobility-scooters and their use by older people', *Ageing & Society*, 30(7): 1219–37.

Metz, D. H. (2000) 'Mobility of older people and their quality of life', *Transport Policy*, 7(2): 149–52.

Mollenkopf, H., Hieber, A. and Wahl, H. W. (2011) 'Continuity and change in older adults' perceptions of out-of-home mobility over ten years: a qualitative-quantitative approach', *Ageing & Society*, 31: 782–802.

Murdoch, J. (1997) 'Inhuman/nonhuman/human: actor-network theory and the prospects for a non-dualistic and symmetrical perspective on nature and society', *Environment and Planning D: Society and Space*, 15(6): 731–56.

Peace, S., Holland, C. and Kellaher, L. (2011) '"Option recognition" in later life: variations in ageing in place', *Ageing & Society*, 31(5): 734–57.

Rowles, G. D. (1983) 'Geographical dimensions of social support in rural Appalachia', in G. D. Rowles and R. J. Ohta (eds) *Aging and Milieu: Environmental Perspectives on Growing Old*, New York: Academic Press, 111–30.

Schillmeier, M. (2007) 'Dis/abling spaces of calculation: blindness and money in everyday life', *Environment and Planning D: Society and Space*, 25: 594–609.

Sheller, M. (2004) 'Automotive emotions: feeling the car', *Theory, Culture & Society*, 21(4/5), 221–42.

Sheller, M. and Urry, J. (2006) 'The new mobilities paradigm', *Environment and Planning A*, 38(2): 207–27.

Stalvey, B. T., Owsley, C., Sloanne, M. E. and Ball, K. (1999) 'The life space questionnaire: a measure of the extent of mobility in older adults', *Journal of Applied Gerontology*, 18: 460–78.

Urry, J. (2007) *Mobilities*, Cambridge: Polity Press.

Webber, S. C., Porter, M. M. and Menec, V. H. (2010) 'Mobility in older adults: a comprehensive framework', *The Gerontologist*, 50(4): 443–50.

Whatmore, S. (2006) 'Materialist returns: practising cultural geography in and for a more-than-human world', *Cultural Geographies*, 13(4): 600–9.

Williams, R. (1983) *Towards 2000*, London: Chatto and Windus.

Ziegler, F. and Schwanen, T. (2011) '"I like to go out to be energised by different people": an exploratory analysis of mobility and wellbeing in later life', *Ageing & Society*, 31(5): 758–81.

39

Impaired

Kim Sawchuk

We all move. How we move is a distinct aspect of our personal and social identity. We may recognize each other because of the color of our hair and eyes or by the sound of our voices. But we are also identifiable through our comportment, the ways that we physically navigate through space, and the technologies we use to assist our movements. A pair of running shoes, high heels; a walker, a walking stick; a hearing aid, a pair of crutches, a cane; a bike, a car, a scooter; a mechanical wheelchair, a motorized wheelchair. These devices for movement-assistance, what David Bissell terms "mobile prosthetics" (Bissell 2009), actively mediate our relationship to our environment.

Philosophers and psychologists underscore the centrality of our capacity for physical, bodily movement to the processes of learning and thought. Dance theorist Maxine Sheets-Johnstone, for one, emphasizes that cognitive processes are founded upon a "kinetic bodily logos" and asserts that, quite simply, we learn by moving and by listening to our own movement (1999: 198). From this purview our sense of self in the world around us is constituted in and through tactility and our embodied *relation* to our environment that utilizes all of the senses: sight, smell, taste, touch, hearing and that very strange sense known as proprioception, or our intuitive sense of the body's relation to its space.

This intertwining of movement, body, and thought in our communication with others is a captivating idea. Yet there are many possible ways to get from A to B. People are never simply abstract entities-in-movement. We learn and cultivate unique movement–repertoires comprised of distinct gestures and practices that change through any number of processes: age, exercise, illness, accident or injury. We execute these movement-gestures utilizing our corporeal capacities in our cities, towns or villages. We look, we listen, we wend our way through landscapes that continually shape and re-shape our movement-abilities. These environments favor some bodies over others. We are differentially mobile.

If indeed we experience the world as we move through it, then how we move through it – by foot, bike, car, wheelchair – and at what speed, in what form, and using what practices in those environments, matters. Movement is relational. Movement is differential. These relational and differential aspects are one of the reasons that contemporary mobility studies make a distinction between movement and mobility.

In this brief contribution I bring the idea of "differential mobility" into conversation with the terms "impairment and disability." The first part of the paper engages in a theoretical discussion and overview of these terms; the second section reflects on differential and relational impairment through a series of "movement-scenarios," my analytic interpretation of what Doreen Massey calls "stories-so-far" (2005: 130). Organized around different encounters with steps and stairs, these reflections are drawn from field-notes, observations, participatory action research on accessibility, formal and informal conversations and examples from the critical disability studies literature.

These observations on differential impairment assert, following Peter Freund (2001) and Irving Zola (1989: 401), that we are inter-subjectively related and that our bodies are simultaneously unique and in constant transition. As such, impairment is physical and experiential, but it is not an unchanging ontological condition, but rather an "ontogenetic" process. As Freund argues of social models of disability, "the social model needs to acknowledge the 'near' universality of the possibility of having a temporary or permanent impairment," a proposition intended to end the perpetuation of "segregated and unequal spaces" (Freund 2001: 704). At some point in our existence, our bodies age, get sick, suffer. We will become impaired.

This perspective on impairment as an ontogenetic process is intended to dismantle the binary system of normal/abnormal, impaired/healthy, abled/disabled. Not all impairments are equally severe. Some are long lasting. Some are painful. Others are life threatening. This demands an acknowledgement of difference and, as Freund and others suggest, an understanding of our potential impairment, as well as differential mobilities as concepts to put to work collectively towards greater accessibility for all.

Differential mobilities

Within mobility studies Tim Cresswell argues that the term *movement* – like the categories of 'space' and 'time' in philosophy – is an abstraction sundered from a living context. In contrast, mobility is understood to be socially produced, rife with relations of power, and located in a specific and unique set of spatial and temporal conditions. Mobility, states Cresswell, "is a fact of life" and "a capacity of all bodies," but it "does not exist in an abstract world of absolute time and space, but in a meaningful world of social space and social time" (Cresswell 2006: 4). He adds that "to be human, indeed to be animal, is to have some kind of capacity for mobility. We experience the world as we move through it. Mobility is a capacity of all but the most severely disabled bodies" (Cresswell 2006: 22). Mobility is about meaning and the production of an array of mobile practices (Cresswell 2006: 5). A sudden lurching motion or a body running haphazardly in our direction carries a different signification and invokes a different response than a hand reaching slowly towards us. While one may agree with Cresswell's discussion of mobility and power, what is less convincing is the division that he makes between movement and mobility.

Peter Adey, for one, proposes that the 'politics of mobility' revolves around two main ideas: "first, that movement is differentiated – that there is a politics to these differentials. In other words, that power is enacted in very different ways. And second, that it is related in different ways in differing social circumstances" (Adey 2006: 84). Adey is not alone in asserting that a politics of mobility must take into account differential relations of power. In his examination of networking and communicational aspects of differential mobility, Jordan Frith argues, "One of the most valuable aspects of this focus on mobility has been to show that mobility is a resource distributed unequally among social groups" (2012: 134). What is common amongst the work of these theorists is an attention to what the study of movement through space, and of blockages and obstacles to access, may tell us about the instantiation of relations of power that are social, material and systemic, and oft-times contingent upon specific contexts. Arguably, what is vitally important is to understand that movement and mobility are embodied and intertwined in a systemic and structural manner in existing societies to create, as Doreen Massey has written, "uneven geographies of oppression" (Massey 2008: 260).

As Massey proposed in "A Global Sense of Place," paying attention to differential mobility demands that researchers unearth the "uneven geographies of oppression" which are "evident in people's differential abilities to move" (2008: 165). For Massey, the turn in social theory to more 'nomadic' or processual forms of thought asks that we differentiate between capacities for movement and mobility, as "some are more in charge of it than others; some initiate flows and movement; some are more on the receiving end of it than others, some are effectively imprisoned by it" (2008: 161). What is critical, from Massey's point of view, is the idea that differential mobility points to the distribution of resources and capacities as a "zero-sum" game, where choices will be made and politics will be involved. For example, in the case of Montreal, building codes are often interpreted with the preservation of "architectural heritage" as a primordial value over the transformations of the exterior of buildings to make them accessible, particularly in the "heritage locations" such as Old Montreal. In other words, if space is considered as a "resource," then its organization into a set of codes that enhance or diminish access for those in motorized wheelchairs creates an *uneven distribution of resources* that weakens one person's movements and their mobility while it enhances access for others, a point also underscored by Adey (2006: 240). Through geographies of disability, and the construction of disabling environments, we exacerbate exclusion based on both impairment and disability.

If we have relatively easy access to public space we rarely pause or reflect on the taken-for-granted experience of everyday mobility, but this changes when our own bodies become impaired. Even such temporary experiences of impairment may remind us that those who have a form of disability are not alone or separate. They are systematically separated, distanced and alienated by architectures of inaccessibility. For this reason philosopher Celeste Langan calls for a linguistic change to abandon the problematic category of the "physically disabled" in favor of an alliance among the "mobility-impaired" (Langan 2001: 16). Yet, how do we understand "impairment"?

Impairment, disability and disablement

In common parlance, impairment is considered to be a bio-mechanical, physiological or cognitive condition, while disability is the experience of impairment as it is structured into a society. Britain's Union of the Physically Impaired Against Segregation (UPIAS), for example, defines impairment thus: "lacking part of a limb, or having a defective limb, organism or mechanism of the body" (UPIAS 1976). Lists of sanctioned impairments include a wide range of conditions such as AIDS, alcohol dependency, Alzheimer's, blindness, cerebral palsy, diabetes, Down's syndrome, drug dependence, epilepsy, paraplegia and schizophrenia (Deal 2003: 901; see also Butler and Parr 1999: 4). Impairments can include amputations, cerebral palsy, dwarfism, limb deficiencies, muscular dystrophy, osteogenetic imperfections, multiple sclerosis, polio, paraplegia, multiple sclerosis, quadriplegia and visual impairments (Butler and Parr 1999: 4).

If impairment is described as a biomechanical 'condition,' then disability is often understood as socially produced. As the UPIAS document says, disability is distinct from impairment: it is "the disadvantage or restriction of activity caused by a contemporary social organization which takes no account of people who have physical impairments and thus excludes them from mainstream social activities" (quoted in Butler and Parr 1999: 4). In these official institutional definitions impairment is to disability as sex is to gender.

Just as feminist scholars have questioned the distinction between sex and gender, critical disability scholars have questioned the hard and fast line between impairment and disability (Butler and Parr 1999). Debates rage on the relationship and meaning of these two terms; however, as critical disability scholars have so cogently put it, while people may have different impairments, we live in social contexts that produce or reproduce conditions that marginalize those with a disability or disabilities. In her extraordinary overview of impairment and disability, Vera Chouinard examines how "disability" and "impairment" emerged as *foci* within feminist geography and critical geography and inquiries in the 1990s (Chouinard 1997, 1999, 2001). This literature on "the geographies of disability" (Gleeson 1996, 1999) is part of a general turn to a social model of disability (Oliver 1990; Imrie 1996, 2001; Kitchin 2000) that is likewise critical of the dominance of biomedical definitions of disability. Rob Imrie, for one, suggests that the problem with the term *impairment* is that it tends to focus on *individuals* and that it *medicalizes* all conditions of corporeal difference as in need of treatment, like a 'disease.' As such, people with impairments or disabilities become "patients" and are pathologized; at the same time, such a perspective absolves us, socially, of our collective responsibility to create inclusive public spaces and to confront our complicity with disability discrimination. As Imrie puts it:

> The dominant strands of theory individualize the nature and experiences of disability, suggesting that it is akin to a medical condition that requires treatment and/or a cure. In this way, any negative experiences, which disabled people encounter in, for instance, moving around their environments or failing to obtain employment, is conceptualized as linked to individual impairment rather than resulting from forms of social and political discrimination.
>
> *(Imrie 1996: 397)*

Others such as Ruth Pinder (1997) question too extreme a view of disability as a social construct. Such a position, for Pinder, does not take into account that a disability is both physiological, embodied impairment and sociological. The study of disability and impairment must acknowledge "complexity of individual experience" (1997: 275). While Vera Chouinard questions the individualization and medicalization of illness (2000), she too suggests that impairment and disability may be a site of identity construction for subjects with corporeal differences (Crooks and Chouinard 2006: 347; Chouinard 2010). Echoes of this position can be found in the reclamation, by some critical disability activists, of the term "crippled" (Ervin 2013). But, as well, more recent disability scholarship questions the anthropomorphic, limited "species–centered" assumptions that may guide the discourse of critical disability studies from a radically transhumanist perspective (Wolbring 2008a) or from a position that acknowledges the liminality of the disabled subject (Campbell 2008). As Ferrier and Muller write in their introduction to a special issue "able,"

> The able–ist perspective produces disability in terms of lack and deviance from the human norm (which Wolbring calls 'species typical'). This able–ist production of disability – with its sense of lack and revulsion for the aberrant body/mind – is a powerful undercurrent informing our understanding of human agency. It underpins legitimizing

discourses which define humanity, particularly modernist discourses of medicine and technology which address the 'improvement' of human lives and promise to eradicate disability.

(2008: 2)

While within critical disability studies there are a range of positions on the relationship between disability and impairment, what is undeniable is this: as societies we need to under-stand how impairment can lead to *disablement* in specific social contexts, and find ways to dis–able able-ist cities through an identification of "the socio–spatial forces" at work that produce "material lived and imagined differences" between the abled and the disabled (Crooks and Chouinard 2006: 346). As Chouinard contends, disablement is "an embodied process of becoming and being ill in places(s) and over time in ways that have disabling outcomes for individuals" (Crooks and Chouinard 2006: 346). There are "relational processes of *differencing*," as Crooks and Chouinard (346), citing the work of Audrey Kobayashi (1997), so cogently state.

It is in this sense that the term "differential mobility" is germane for the thinking of how some movement-repertoires that give preference to bodily norms that create hierarchies of corporeal differences are structured into the built environment, so that those with disabilities are understood as *ipso facto* existing in a "diminished state of being" (Campbell 2001: 44). Fiona Kumori Campbell defines able–ism as "a network of beliefs, processes and practices that produces a particular kind of self and body (the corporeal standard) that is projected as the perfect, species-typical and therefore essential and fully human" (Campbell 2008: 153). From this point of view, people who have disabilities must either strive to become that bodily norm or find themselves distanced from the 'able-bodied' and excluded from the world that does not allow them to move through it with any ease.

What able-ism thus presumes is that *disability* is inherently an undesirable condition that must be overcome, most often through corrective medical treatment. While one would not deny the need for someone with a particular condition to receive medical attention, there is an "authority" and system of "legitimacy" at work that implies that, for example, if assistance is required for travel then one's disability must be medically sanctioned each and every time. Able-ism, as Campbell suggests, propounds that having a disability is a failing rather than a consequence of human diversity such as race, ethnicity, gender or sexual orientation. From an able-ist perspective, those with a "disability" can never quite "measure up" to the norma-tive yet power fiction of the fully abled body. As Crooks and Chouinard (2006) argue, if able-bodiness is presumed as the norm, then those with disabilities are marginalized and marked as inevitably other (see also Wolbring 2008a).

When one considers the question of differential mobilities from the perspective of able–ist systems of values, it becomes evident that hierarchies of power that are structured into our built environments influence our everyday lives and create differential access to spaces and places for some. While over 200,000 people are estimated to be living with a physical disa-bility in the city of Montreal, for instance, the relative inaccessibility of cultural centers, movie theatres, galleries, libraries, bars, cafes, terraces and restaurants renders those with mobility impairments absent and invisible (Gouvernement de Québec 2010). Just as city streets in North America have been built to favor the smooth circulation of automobile traf-fic, our streets and buildings are also structured to favor those on foot rather than those in wheelchairs. These points have been documented in projects such as "megaphone.net," in which participants in wheelchairs use cell phones to photograph the myriad of ways the built environment, most notably steps and stairs, sustains marginalization and exclusion from

413

public space (Sawchuk 2008). Differential mobility addresses the relations of power that hinder or enable movement, a system of preferential access to space that discriminates against those who have an "impairment."

Thinking of impairment in relational terms acknowledges that any impairment is not a fixed or static entity. Impairment is experienced within a "textured weave of connections," connections that constitute the morphological features that become the built environment, differentially experienced by some (Bissell 2009). From this point of view, understanding disability with respect to disablement, as a social and material process, can be brought into conversation with the term "differential mobilities," a perspective informed by Campbell's call for the cultivation of "disability imaginaries" that "think/speak/gesture and feel different landscapes not just for being-in-the-world, but on the conduction of perception, mobilities and temporalities" (2008: 9).

Temporality and impairment: movement-scenarios

The study of disability and impairment from the perspective of differential mobilities asks researchers to be attentive to able-ist presumptions of systems of design and architecture that assume a singular bodily norm and the "movement-flows" that reveal disabling environments. Conceptualizing impairment and disability as relational and in terms of difference situates individual subjects in 'inter-subjective' terms: as members of society where all are accountable to each other (Levinas 1985a). This constitutes an important challenge to the dominance of a biomedical model of impairment, which treats the impairment of functional abilities – a person's ambulatory, cognitive capacities – as individual problems that can be rectified through treatment. It also challenges the idea of a normal human body – or subject – that is then seen as lacking.

While differential mobility and the analysis of environments as "disabling" are vitally important, one alternative way to grasp the implications and dynamics of impairment and disability is to reflect on their temporal aspects. To return to Freund and Zola's point, we are ontogenetic subjects and are always potentially impaired. If this is so, then how might we describe impairment in temporal terms, rather than strictly biomedical categories? What does it mean not only to move through the city as an elderly person walking, driving, or taking the train or the bus? What does it mean to live in a city plagued by winter with a putatively public transportation system that does not allow you, in your wheelchair, easy access or entry into the subway system? If impairment is not a static biomedical condition, but situational, differential, experiential and relational, then what might we learn from thinking of impairment as permanent, sudden, temporary, gradual or occasional? Consider the lessons to be learned through different composite "fictive" encounters of steps and stairs, fictive encounters based on actual observations, discussions, experiences and field notes.

Consider the following typical scenario that describes a situation of occasional impairment: a woman enters a Montreal metro station with a stroller. If she is lucky, she may find herself in a station where one of the escalators might be working. If they are not, then she will be forced to pick up her stroller and carry it up these flights of stairs. If she is luckier, someone will help her with the task at hand and assist her in carrying the stroller. If she is young, strong and fit, then the stairs are an obstacle that merely impedes her ability to use the stroller. Despite this obstacle, there is a way, albeit a cumbersome way, to move on. Movement and navigation of the multiple flights of steps is hazardous, but it is not insurmountable.

In this "occasional impairment," impairment is contingent upon the completion of a routine daily task, through what Ingold calls a "taskspace" (2000). The twenty flights of stairs and lack of access to the subway do not pose a complete inhibition of movement, but a condition that one encounters 'from time to time' within a day, or within a week. While it is chronic (that is, related to chronos, or time), its severity is also distinct. Those who are occasionally impaired suffer a temporary inconvenience to their movements, however it is not of long duration. While there are elements of functional impairment, this is not a permanent condition of disablement. Occasional impairment occurs in the accomplishment of tasks on a daily or weekly basis. It's chronic, but not persistent.

Peter Freund suggests that "an able-bodied mother pushing a pram or a delivery person a hand cart, can both benefit from the same ramp that makes the built environment user-friendly for a wheelchair user. Transport accessibility, thus, is also a concern for people other than those with a disability (2001: 693). Spatial–temporal arrangements impact on virtually every 'body.' While this is no doubt the case, the same set of stairs do not pose the same set of challenges for those who are in a motorized wheelchair, for example, and experience an impairment that is not occasional, but an integral part of existence. In this case, the stairs represent only one instance of a larger set of systemic problems of movement. Transportation accessibility may be of concern for us all, however the creation of spaces for wheelchairs and prams does not necessarily lead to alliances between different constituencies of users. In London, for example, the Channel 4 special on transportation and accessibility, "No Go Britain," reported conflicts between wheelchair users and parents with prams for the limited space available on buses (Razzal 2012).[1]

In the case of a permanent impairment, particularly for those who live in and with a mobility aid, such as a wheelchair, every step and sill is literally shouting: "stay out stay away, do not enter." Every move must be calculated when planning any journey and options for entry and exit are extremely limited, but can also be obfuscating and not take an entire system into account: a major metro station in Montreal, Lionel Groulx, is marked as "wheel chair accessible," yet an elevator connects different platforms. Such scenarios are not only indications of who is barred from public space, in ways that are often extremely contradictory or ironic, but they also indicate *whose* time is valued, and how. As Brendan Gleeson writes:

> Often journeys have to be planned several days in advance, to allow time to book provision. For example, it is not possible for wheelchair users to travel on the London underground without pre-booking 24 hours in advance, and then travel is restricted to stations with a lift. Disabled people often have to travel circuitous routes and are denied the same spatial choices as 'able-bodied' people. Consequently, access to employment and social events can be denied.
>
> *(1996: 393)*

For Rob Imrie, the dominant underlying ethos is one that follows the State's line of integration or assimilation "to bring people back to 'normality'" (1996: 398). As such, policy is aimed at trying to make disabled people more 'normal,' rather than changing the system to accommodate disabled people for who they are. And while Gleeson and Imrie underscore the spatial aspects of discrimination, Gleeson's powerful analysis points to the issue of time and the temporal aspects that undergird not only the experience of impairment, but what it means to have an impairment in the current context.

This example of occasional impairment and permanent impairment differs from the experience of temporary impairment. Take, once again, the example of the stairs and lack of elevator, this time from the London Underground. A young man on the opposite platform hobbles towards the steps. He has a single crutch to brace himself. His foot is in a cast. In his other hand is a cell phone, which he glances at, awkwardly, to make a call. He is accustomed to walking and talking at the same time. However, his broken foot impedes his ability to communicate seamlessly while on the move. The phone is put into a pocket. He makes his way towards the steps. Steps are difficult, so he must grab the railing, dodging the stream of passengers who move against the flow. Taking care not to drop his crutch he hops up the stairs, eventually abandoning it. He literally pulls himself up the steps until the top is reached. He is temporarily impaired by an injury. As soon as the cast is off, his movements will not be impeded.

In this instance, temporary impairment is not a permanent condition of his body: it is a momentary crisis where movement is impeded for a fixed duration: until the cast comes off. It may leave behind traces depending on the damage. A temporary impairment may involve the experience of an injury or illness that will eventually heal. In this case the stairs are not viewed as a chronic problem that must be dealt with on a daily basis. There is an expectation that the bone will heal and one's identity isn't necessarily transformed, unless, of course, the injury never heals.

In other instances, impairments may be gradual, leading to a transformation of subjectivity and identity over a long temporal duration. And here we can think of the process of ageing with respect to a set of subway stairs. We feel and experience change with age; we may move from glasses to bifocals. We may notice that it is harder to keep lean muscle mass. None of these are impossible to manage or inevitable, or so we are told. For example, an elderly woman, in her early 90s, has until recently been a healthy, active senior, yet she has noted her recent limitations in mobility, and the difficulties she has in going up and down the stairs to her apartment. She must rely on the assistance of others to take longer treks, although she continues to descend a treacherous flight of stairs every day to fetch her paper. She no longer takes part in local fitness classes, is unable to volunteer for her local women's group. Every ten years she explains, "you must reconcile yourself to the idea that you are a new self." She adds, pausing, "I am not liking this decade, so much." A lack of energy and difficulties in moving impedes her desire to continue to partake in the world. The stairs become more and more of a struggle. She is becoming "gradually impaired," gradually altering the movement sphere of her interactions. In this case, the stairs represent a gage of changes in her mobility.

Such gradual changes are distinct from the impairments that may result in a moment's notice: a car accident may lead to a permanent condition of physical impairment; a disease may strike, leading to sudden and incurable damage that may lead to a loss of the ability to hear, to see or to move. In both of these instances, an identity suddenly shifts, categorically. You may find yourself, newly labeled within bio-medicine, as a "person with a disability," whose status and future life plans have changed irrevocably. Subjected to regimes of health management, the incurably impaired person suddenly faces a new direction of life, their expectations and future movements transformed. Crooks and Chouinard write: "women's experiences of chronic illness and impairment are outcomes not only of physically and mentally impaired bodies, but also of socially and spatially constituted barriers to inclusion and well-being" (Crooks and Chouinard 2006: 345). There is no turning back when one is suddenly, incurably impaired. Suddenly those parts of the built environment that were never a problem, barely considered, become an obstacle and reminder of an ability that once was. But unlike the gradual impairments that may come with age, and ageing, that may be an accumulation and relatively minor for a long duration, what is significant about a sudden experience of impairment is that the transition is sudden, shocking and world-changing in an instant. And as disability scholars such as Deal (2003) have examined through interviews with differently impaired subjects, there are hierarchies and differences within the disability community.

These everyday examples speak to the idea of impairment as a means to question our assumptions about the normal, or, to follow from Foucault, the "normativities" that structure our everyday lives. It introduces temporality into the issue of impairment within a specific social context and range of possible movements. Whether one is permanently impaired or suddenly impaired, what becomes clear is this: cities and towns in many parts of the world, including North America, are badly adapted to accommodate those who are impaired. These relational conditions of impairment are temporal in another sense. They create a form of differential impairment and access to the city which is augmented by the harsh winters, and the increasing reluctance of the city to properly clear sidewalks, making it not only treacherous for those in wheelchairs, but also for the elderly, for whom every slip on the sidewalk implies a possible broken bone and months in hospital. While these factors bring these subjects into "alliance," this is not to say that their bodies or challenges are the same (Parent 2013: 581; Veilleux 2013).

One must be very careful, when speaking of impairment, not to quickly categorize subjects into an identity that is totalizing. The person in a wheelchair may have trouble negotiating the streets of his city in winter, but at the same time have 'perfect' vision and excellent hearing. What creates his impairment is not a body condition but rather a body in relationship to the environment in which one moves. Impairments also highlight the complexity of our existence as embodied beings in the world.

In response to a biomedical model of impairment, critical disability studies propose a distinction between an individual's impairments (the bodily dimension) and the disability which is socially produced (exemplified in the barriers society unfairly creates for the person with impairments) (Goggin and Newell 2003). Critical disability studies demands that we pay attention to the ways that impairments are structured into the built environment. Yet this model of impairment, as Goggin and Newell write, has its own limitations that must be addressed. From their purview, other contingencies are equally relevant and require an understanding of the range of impairments and disabilities that are experienced by subjects. Goggin and Newell call for what, following a feminist framework, could be understood as an "intersectional" approach to the study of disability. As they suggest, it is equally important to acknowledge the interaction of gender, sex, race, class and age in the social relations and cultural dimension of disability. Their perspective proposes the key role of technology in transforming bodily capacity, or diminishing it, in the analysis of contemporary social relations of disability (Goggin and Newell 2003: 99).

Conclusion

Impairment is neither simply subjective, nor medical, nor a part of the built environment. It is a state of perpetual being that is relational, contingent, material and temporal. It reminds us, all of us, of how our existence as bodily subjects is never fixed, but in constant transition. Not all conditions of impairment or disability are the same. They may be distinguishable on the basis of "type," as identified by formal agencies for medical or insurance purposes, but also to provide needed assistance. However, they may also be understood in temporal terms. If we are impaired, or become impaired occasionally, temporarily, suddenly, gradually or permanently, it is not in the same context or with the same consequences. There are degrees of impairment – or disability – that intersect with our capacities to harness the resources we need to continue to move, engage, and be with and in different environmental contexts.

There are also ways that sensory impairments are "corrected" through technologies such as glasses, hearing aids, computers (for memory), or crutches and wheelchairs (Wolbring 2008b).

To quote Cresswell, "when devices are taken into account, citizens are no longer just bodies separated from the world but thoroughly social bodies" (2006: 167). We become, as he suggests, "prosthetic citizens," who are not abstract universals or mobile subjects, but subjects whose capacities "for mobility depend on the constraints" and, we might add, affordances "of the public sphere" (2006: 167). This is why I speak of differential mobility and relational impairment. "Difference as not absolute but relational" (Cresswell 2006: 179). This attention to how mobility is both relational and differential may facilitate a nuanced sense of how to describe the many ways that we move within spaces and locations: the variations in speed, the movement-gestures and repertoires, the temporal changes in an environment, as well as those that are a part of our bodies.

One term, "the relational," points to our imbrication in complex networks of shifting relations to others and to our contexts. The other term, "the differential," points to questions of power and privilege that hinder or hamper access. Differential impairment questions the binary system that divides the world into that of those who are impaired and those who are unimpaired. It adds a temporal aspect to the issue of impairment, pulling us away from impairment as a state or condition that is only considered in relationship to a geographic space, to one that takes time into account.

Note

1 The research on 'Engaging Senior Stakeholders: Positive Ageing at the Organisation–Elder Interface' was funded by the New Zealand Foundation for Research Science and Technology (2009–2012). The research team, led by Professor Ted Zorn (Massey University), comprises a multi-disciplinary team of scholars: Dr Mary Simpson, Dr Margaret Richardson, Professor Peggy Koopman-Boyden, Dr Michael Cameron (Waikato University) and Juliana Mansvelt (Massey University).

Bibliography

Adey, P. (2006) 'If mobility is everything then it is nothing: towards a relational politics of (im)mobilities,' *Mobilities*, 1: 75–94.

Bissell, D. (2009) 'Conceptualising differently-mobile passengers: geographies of everyday encumbrance in the railway station,' *Social & Cultural Geography*, 10: 173–195.

Butler, R. and Parr, H. (1999) 'New geographies of illness, impairment and disability,' in R. Butler and H. Parr (eds) *Mind and Body Space: geographies of illness, impairment and disability*, Abingdon: Routledge, 1–24.

Campbell, F. A. K. (2001) 'Inciting legal fictions: disability date with ontology and the ableist body of the law,' *Griffith Law Review*, 10: 42–62.

Campbell, F. A. K. (2008) 'Refusing able(ness): a preliminary conversation about ableness,' *M/C Journal*, 11. Available online at http://journal.media-culture.org.au/index.php/mcjournal/article/viewArticle/46/0 (accessed 22 August 2013).

Chouinard, V. (1997) 'Making space for disabling difference: challenges to geographies,' *Environment and Planning D: Society and Space*, 15: 379–387.

Chouinard, V. (1999) 'Body politics: disabled women's activism in Canada and beyond,' in R. Butler and H. Parr (eds) *Mind and Body Space: geographies of illness, impairment and disability*, Abingdon: Routledge, 269–294.

Chouinard, V. (2000) 'Getting ethical: for inclusive and engaged geographies of disability,' *Ethics, Place and Environment*, (March) 70–80.

Chouinard, V. (2001) 'Legal peripheries: struggles over disabled Canadians' places in law, society and space,' *Canadian Geographer*, 45: 187–192.

Chouinard, V. (2010) 'Impairment and disability,' in T. Brown, S. McLafferty and G. Moon (eds) *A Companion to Health and Medical Geography*, Oxford: Wiley-Blackwell, 242–257.

Clear, M. (1999) 'The "normal" and the monstrous in disability research,' *Disability and Society*, 14: 435–448.

Cresswell, T. (2006) *On the Move: mobility in the modern western world*, London: Routledge.

Crooks V. A. and Chouinard, V. (2006) 'An embodied geography of disablement: chronically ill women's struggles for enabling spaces of health care and daily life,' *Health and Place*, 12: 345–352.

Deal, M. (2003) 'Disabled people's attitudes toward other impairment groups: a hierarchy of impairments,' *Disability and Society*, 18: 897–910.

Deal, M. (2007) 'Aversion disablism: subtle prejudice towards disabled people,' *Disability and Society*, 22: 93–107.

Ervin, M. (n.d.) 'Smart Ass Cripple: Expressing pain through sarcasm since 2010.' Available online at http://smartasscripple.blogspot.ca (accessed 12 February 2013).

Ferrier, L. and Muller, V. (2008) 'Disabling able,' *M/C Journal*, 11. Available online at http://journal.media-culture.org.au/index.php/mcjournal/article/viewArticle/58 (accessed 22 August 2013).

Freund, P. (2001) 'Bodies, disability and spaces: the social model and disabling spatial organizations,' *Disability & Society*, 16: 689–706.

Frith, J. (2012) 'Splintered space: hybrid spaces and differential mobility,' *Mobilities*, 7: 131–149.

Gleeson, B. (1996) 'A geography for disabled people?' *Transactions of the Institute of British Geographers*, 21(2): 387–396.

Gleeson, B. (1999) 'Can technology overcome the disabling city?' in R. Butler and H. Parr (eds) *Mind and Body Space: geographies of illness, impairment and disability*, Abingdon: Routledge, 98–118.

Goggin, G. (2006) *Cell Phone Culture: mobile technology in everyday life*, London: Routledge.

Goggin, G. and Newell, C. (2003) *Digital Disability: the social construction of disability in new media*, Lanham, MD: Rowman and Littlefield.

Gouvernement de Québec (1975; 1982) *Charter of Human Rights and Freedoms*, updated January 2013. Available online at www2.publicationsduquebec.gouv.qc.ca/dynamicSearch/telecharge.php?-type=2&file=/C_12/C12_A.html (accessed 12 February 2013).

Gouvernement de Québec (2010) *Vivre avec une incapacité au Québec: unportrait statistique à partir de l'Enquête sur la participation et les limitations d'activités de 2001 et 2006*, Québec: Institut de la Statistique du Québec. Available online at www.stat.gouv.qc.ca/publications/sante/pdf2010/rapport_EPLA.pdf (accessed 12 February 2013).

Imrie, R. (1996) 'Ableist geographies, disabilist spaces: towards a reconstruction of Golledge's "Geography and the Disabled,"' *Transactions of the Institute of British Geographers*, 21: 397–403.

Imrie, R. (2001) 'Barriered and bounded places and the spatialities of disability,' *Urban Studies*, 38: 231–237.

Ingold, T. (2000) *The Perception of the Environment: essays in livelihood, dwelling and skill*, London: Routledge.

Kitchin, R. (2000) 'The researched opinions on research: disabled people and disability research,' *Disability and Society*, 15: 25–47.

Kobayashi, A. (1997) 'Paradox of difference and diversity (or, why the thresholds keep moving),' in J. P. Jones III, H. J. Nast and S. M. Roberts (eds) *Thresholds in Feminist Geography*, London: Routledge, 3–9.

Langan, C. (2001) 'Mobility disability,' *Public Culture*, 13: 459–484.

Levinas, E. (1985a) *Totality and Infinity: an essay on exteriority*, trans. Alphonso Lingis, Pittsburgh, PA: Duquesne University Press.

Levinas, E. (1985b) *Ethics and Infinity: conversations with Philippe Nemo*, trans. Richard A. Cohen, Pittsburgh, PA: Duquesne University Press.

Massey, D. (2005) *For Space*, London: Sage.

Massey, D. (2008) 'A global sense of place,' in T. Oakes and L. Price (eds) *The Cultural Geography Reader*, London: Routledge, 257–263.

Milner, P. and Kelly, B. (2009) 'Community participation and inclusion: people with disabilities defining their place,' *Disability and Society*, 24: 47–62.

Oliver, M. (1990) *The Politics of Disablement*, London: Macmillan.

Oliver, M. (1996) *Understanding Disability*, London: Macmillan.

Parent, L. (2013) 'The Politics of Snow,' paper presented at *Differential Mobilities: movement and mediation in networked societies*, Montreal, May 13, 2013. Available online at www.mobilities.ca (accessed 22 August 2013).

Parviainen, J. (2002) 'Bodily knowledge: epistemological reflections on dance,' *Dance Research Journal*, 34: 11–26.

Pinder, R. (1997) 'A reply to Tom Shakespeare and Nicholas Watson,' *Disability & Society*, 12: 301–305.

Razzal, K. (June 12, 2012) 'Paralympic transport will make London look stupid', Britain: Channel 4 News. Available online at www.channel4.com/news/paralympics-transport-will-make-london-look-stupid (accessed 22 August 2013).

Sawchuk, K. (2008) 'The paradox of mobility,' *Zexe.net: une cartographie numérique du monde*, Genève: Centre d'Art Contemporain Genève, 76–78.

Shakespeare, T. and Watson, N. (1997) 'Defending the social model,' *Disability & Society*, 12: 293–300.

Sheets-Johnstone, M. (1999) *The Primacy of Movement*, Philadelphia: John Benjamins Publishing Company.

UPIAS (1976) *Fundamental Principles of Disability*, London: Union of Physically Impaired Against Segregation.

Veilleux, M. (4 March 2013) 'Un service handicapé,' La Presse. Available online at www.lapresse.ca/debats/a-votre-tour/201303/01/01-4626861-un-service-handicape.php (accessed 22 August 2013).

Wolbring, G. (2008a) 'Is there an end to out-able? Is there an end to the rat race for abilities?' *M/C Journal*, 11. Available online at http://journal.media-culture.org.au/index.php/mcjournal/article/viewArticle/57 (accessed 22 August 2013).

Wolbring, G. (2008b) 'Oscar Pistorius and the future nature of Olympic, Paralympic and other sports,' *Scripted: Journal of Law, Technology and Society*, 5: 139–160.

Zola, I. K. (1982) *Missing Pieces: a chronicle of living with a disability*, Philadelphia, PA: Temple University Press.

Zola, I. K. (1989) 'Toward the necessary universalizing of a disability policy,' *The Milbank Quarterly*, 67: 401–428.

40
Child

Clare Holdsworth

In June 2011 the Australian government announced a softening of its much-criticised attempts to send un-accompanied child asylum seekers to Malaysia, as part of its programme to deter migrants from travelling to Australia. The government had been criticised by both the UN and Human Rights agencies for its attempts to send children to Malaysia. As the Chief Executive of UNESCO in Australia commented, it made the administration look 'callous and lacking in all forms of compassion' (The Guardian, 2011). Earlier in the same year the UK coalition government was accused of failing to deliver on its promise to end the detention of child asylum seekers when it announced plans for new centres to detain families refusing to leave the UK (Brown, 2011). These two policy announcements, and the criticisms levelled at governments in how they treat child asylum seekers, reveal underlying tensions about children's mobility. On the one hand a child embarking on a dangerous and risk-taking journey across international borders unaccompanied is at odds with an ideal of childhood as a time of stability and rootedness. Thus from this perspective children's mobility would appear to concur with Cresswell's (2006) notion of a 'sedentary metaphysics' of mobility, in which movement is opposed to the need for stability and belonging. The Australian government's attempt to deport children to Malaysia is deemed callous as children are assumed to be too vulnerable to embark on this kind of journey and it is appropriate to show more compassion towards child asylum seekers. Yet, locking up children is equally abhorrent. Childhood might conjure up ideals of stability, but it is also associated with freedom – that is, freedom to move around and play away from the surveillance of adults and freedom to develop one's own sense of self-hood in preparation for adulthood.

Yet these images of children either forced into taking perilous journeys or having their freedom restricted also reveal another quintessential character of children's mobility, that is that these practices are framed in relation to adult conceptions and behaviour. The very reference to *children's* mobility suggests a particular form of movement that is distinctive from adult practices, yet is still constrained by and performed within adultist spaces. In recent years academic interest in children's mobilities has sought to challenge how this mobility has been both conceptualised and empirically understood as part of a wider academic engagement with children sometimes referred to as the 'New Sociology of Childhood' (Holloway and Valentine, 2000; James and James, 2004; Matthews and Limb, 1999; Skelton, 2009). The fundamental premise of this re-engagement is that children should not be objectified by academic discourse, but that children's agency needs to be at the centre of academic theorisation and practice. This has initiated the development of participatory methodologies that seek to engage with children in diverse ways and situate children at the centre of data collection and analysis where appropriate. Geographers have responded to this re-conceptualisation and re-engagement, and there is now a substantial literature on children's mobilities, with recent special editions in *Population, Space and Place* (Holt and Costello, 2011), *Journal of Ethnic and Migration Studies* (White *et al.*, 2011), *Childhood* (Ní Laoire *et al.*, 2010) and *Mobilities* (Barker *et al.*, 2009), while the journal *Children's Geographies* has also promoted scholarship on children's migration and mobilities.

Existing scholarship on children's mobilities considers forms of migration, mobility and movement at different temporal and geographical scales. Research considers children's experiences in developed and less developed countries, as well as transnational events, and incorporates the significance of both everyday micro-mobilities as well as long-distance migration. Yet it would be inaccurate to present this as a niche of mobilities research. Rather, drawing on theoretical debates around inter-sectionality and inter-generationality, the child as a subject of mobility is integral to many varied forms of movement. As Barker *et al.* state, 'social studies of mobilities must – always, already – attend to the importance of age, ageing, and lines of aged difference which are part-and-parcel of so many mobilities' (2009: 7). This requirement applies to both mobility researchers, who must engage with age and generation, and researchers working with children, who must not situate their experiences in isolation from other mobilities as children's movement is experienced in relation to and constructed by diverse mobilities. Yet this is a very real challenge in children's mobilities literature. A common criticism of research on children's mobilities is that this scholarship has become ghettoised and has failed to engage with more mainstream accounts of mobilities (Holt and Costello, 2011). Moreover, children are assumed to be outside of mainstream empirical experiences and theorisations; the mobile actor is taken to be an adult unless otherwise stated.

The aim of this chapter is not to provide a detailed review of children's mobilities literature, not least because this narrative is developed in other reviews, particularly the special editions referenced above. Rather, this chapter considers three spheres of mobilities: children's mobility with families, mobility within families, and independent mobility. However this is not to suggest that children's mobility can be neatly compartmentalised within these types, as they imply each other. Rather this division is used to reveal the underlying tensions within children's mobility outlined in the beginning of this chapter: those between rootedness and dependence on the one hand, versus freedom and autonomy on the other.

Children's mobility with families

To start with an account of children's mobilities as part of family practices might at first seem out of line with a conceptualisation of children's mobilities that emphasises children's agency. In accounts of family mobility the subject of interest is often not the child but adults who arrange and engage in mobilities on behalf of children. For example, empirical analysis of residential moves demonstrates that couples move in anticipation of fertility (Kulu, 2008; Michielin and Mulder, 2008). Couples are motivated by the ideal that children need a stable family home with room to grow and play, hence couples' residential mobility anticipates children's future needs and assumes their future immobility. As Rossi (1956) described over 50 years ago, there is a logic to this process of mobility associated with family formation followed by stasis. Families with children are expected to move for strategic reasons; this could be for a larger house, to move closer to schools, or to follow parents' (usually the father's) career, thus augmenting family income. Yet this neat conceptualisation of family mobility not only objectifies children, but also reifies forms of mobility that are exclusionary. A common assertion is that parents want to maximise the opportunities for their children and will engage in forms of mobilities to achieve this. Relocating to access better schools, or bussing children long distances for education or extra-curricular activities creates not only complex mobilities for those involved, but also entrenches social cleavages; it is only families with access to appropriate resources that can engage in these kinds of strategic mobilities. These mobilities not only distort housing markets but can also bring about transformations within cities. The linkages between the process of gentrification and provision of schooling in urban areas are dynamic and have significant impacts on the fabric of city life, as well as entrenching differential access to high-achieving schools (Butler, 2003). Thus mobility that is practised *for* children may have much wider impacts than those for children themselves.

Yet there are other ways in which children's mobility with families are more celebrated. Take for example the 'family' holiday and the recognition in modern industrialised societies that families need to spend time together away from home, 'reconnecting' with each other (Obrador, 2012). Not being able to afford a holiday is increasingly recognised as a meaningful deficit, and in recent years the concept of welfare tourism has developed to promote the ideal that all families (and for this we should read families with children) deserve a holiday. The advantages of family holidays are uncontroversial, promoting well-being, improving family communication and consolidating family ties *through* mobility away from home.

This objectification of children through family mobility misses the reality of how this mobility is experienced. In particular, notwithstanding the significance of holiday mobility, the ideal of immobility for children is often reproduced in family life, and this has implications for other family members. An unspoken assumption of research on family mobility is that the aim of mobility is to achieve stability. Yet this focus on stasis is often misplaced. Rather as Green observed in the 1990s, household immobility is maintained by hyper-mobility (Green, 1997). Green's research focussed on the practices of dual-career couples, and children were absent from her analysis. Yet she demonstrates how the solution of reconciling the competing demands of family life, that is to establish a stable and fixed family home, was supported by hyper-mobility practices of family members, including mobility of parents to work, of children to school and of all family members to leisure activities (see also Dowling, 2000). Rootedness within childhood and children's restricted mobility are, therefore, often experienced through the mobility of others.

Children's mobility within families

If children are not to be treated as immobile bodies within families this suggests a re-conceptualisation of mobility relations within families. In recent years children's mobility within families has received more scrutiny. In particular, studies of 'the school run' seek to place this form of mobility on a par with commuting and other forms of adult mobility. Thus transport studies have now embraced children's mobilities and especially children's need to access transport in order to move between home and school. Yet the school run remains a compartmentalised form of mobility that is subject to very different scrutiny in comparison to other forms (Barker, 2003). For example the school run is often blamed for causing congestion and interfering with the movement of adults commuting to work or the delivery of goods and services. The vulnerability of children is also highlighted, and the regulation of traffic around schools imposes more stringent speed limits and parking restrictions, while at the same time children's mobility is intensively surveyed and regulated (Kearns and Collins, 2003). The ideal that children and automobility are counterpoised is reinforced by the practices and regulations of school-run mobility.

Yet while a focus on children's family mobility can reinforce distinctions between adults and children it can also challenge how mobility is experienced. The school run is more than just getting from A to B; the very act of movement and experience of transport is part of family life – and one in which children can resist being objectified (Kullman and Palludan, 2011). Clearly children have limited capacity for independent mobility; if they travel by car they are dependent on being driven, but this does not necessarily mean that they are objectified by mobility. Journeys can be important times of family interactions; as Laurier *et al.* (2008) demonstrate, time spent in the car is not wasted time but provides opportunities for sociability and more mundane practices of 'doing' family. These are not always positive; part of the holiday ritual is often the boredom and arguments of the journey to holiday destinations, but to treat all actors within family mobility as passive is too limited. Children in cars in particular are not just objects to be carried around; for example, children are involved in car purchase, sometimes explicitly, but very often implicitly. The popularity of MPV vehicles is driven by the assumption of the need for space in family cars, and the marketing of the 'family' car promotes both adults' and children's needs. Children need to be carried, as does the increasing baggage that children's mobilities necessitate – from baby carriers to booster seats, children appropriate space within the car, even when they are not present. Children can also influence the kinds of in-car entertainment, and the competing needs of drivers and child passengers have resulted in more emphasis on personalised space within the car. Thus, as Barker (2009) argues, the car has become a site for play, relaxation, homework, companionship, technology and the consumption of commodities.

Cars are also sites for family negotiations; arguments about space and privacy are part of children's experience of automobilities – not only concerning where they sit but their opportunity to control their own space. Technological development of in-car spaces means that there is more to control in terms of heating and lighting, as well as entertainment. The drawback of visioning the car as a site of negotiation is that it ignores the limitations of children's car travel experiences. Though children are certainly not silent and compliant passengers, they have to experience car travel as a form of dependency. Relations between parents and children configure children's experiences as passengers; moreover the design of in-car space incorporates corporate ideals of family space and interactions.

Returning to one of the main themes of this chapter – that children's mobility is not a niche form of mobility distinctive from that of other subjects – it is important to recognise that children are subject to similar processes, opportunities and constraints to those of adults through their family mobilities. Yet often this is ignored in family migration studies. We can consider this observation with reference to research on transnational migrants. As White *et al.* (2011) discuss, while trafficked children or child asylum seekers have come under the spotlight of migration research, children who move as part of a family group are often absent from the literature. Yet children are confronted with the same kinds of issues that are documented for adults. Moreover, when their experiences are considered it is often in relationship to their 'neediness' and vulnerability. Transnational migrant children's lives are associated with the disruption of mobility, thus emphasising the ideal linking childhood with rootedness. Other accounts accentuate the importance of children's integration, for example how children adapt to new educational systems and their ability to learn new languages – as such, their experience as *transnational* migrants can be overlooked. Yet children are not invisible actors in transnational research. Not only can children be active in family migration decision-making processes (Ackers, 2000; Bushin, 2009) but they can also be 'cultural mediators' moving between their host community and other family members (de Block and Buckingham, 2007). Yet their absence in academic studies also reflects their status in public policy – as White *et al.* (2011) remark, transnational children can be disadvantaged because of their invisibility. Policies that conceptualise the migrant as an adult worker ignore the realities of children's experiences; only when called to public attention do they redirect their attention, but then usually this is only towards the most needy and vulnerable groups such as unaccompanied children (Akers and Stalford, 2004).

A further limitation of this focus on children's mobility with families is that it takes a somewhat limited perspective on both family structure and form. The nuclear family, headed by a couple, or maybe a lone parent, tends to dominate how the family is operationalised in these accounts, but also relies on a rather inert interpretation of children's role within families. While we have discussed how children can shape mobility practices in the planning stage and through their experience of mobility, children remain very much located within family groups. One way of developing this is to consider how family life, and the complexity of both family structures and practices, is sustained by children's mobility. Children's mobilities are not just framed within families, but through engaging in mobility children can make an active contribution to family practices. This dimension can be revealed in a number of specific examples; I will outline two. The first is children's mobility in the global South. As writers such as Punch (2002) argue, the westernised ideal of childhood as a time of innocence, education and leisure cannot be sustained in most contexts in less-developed economies. In the global South, children are expected to contribute to household economies. They are engaged in daily practices, for example fetching water and looking after livestock, and the mobilities that these practices entail are essential to family life. Yet these mobilities also afford children time away from adult supervision – the task of collecting water can also provide opportunities to play, for example – and thus the boundaries between work and play are often blurred. In other contexts children's mobility makes a more direct contribution to household economies. This dimension of children's mobility is illustrated in van Blerk and Ansell's (2006) account of children's mobility as a strategy that households can adopt in response to adult household members' HIV/AIDS morbidity and mortality. Mobility can be used as a way of making sure that both children's needs and those of other household members are met. In this context children are often involved in complex mobility practices oscillating between exile and return to the family household, and these practices will vary according to the child's age and gender.

A second observation of children's mobility within and between families is that of the experience of children moving between different parental homes after parental separation. Again, children engaged in this form of mobility are often conceptualised as needy and vulnerable, and may be referred to as coming from a 'broken home'. Normative expectations that children need stability and permanency are often called upon in explaining how this form of mobility is both resisted and experienced. For example, parents might deny another parent access or overnight residency on the grounds that children need a unique home. Yet more recent interpretations have challenged the assumption that children miss out through their mobility between different homes. Writing from a Norwegian perspective, Jensen (2009) argues that children who move between different homes may acquire important skills through their mobility that they will take with them into adulthood. These children, in contrast to their more settled peers, will be normalised to mobility practices but will also acquire skills of negotiation in the movement between different households. It is also worth pointing out that it is not just children who experience parental separation who move

425

between different households. Many children spend time at other family members' houses, especially grandparents. As Jarvis (1999) argues, families are reliant on complex webs of mutuality and support, and at times these will be sustained by children's, as well as adults', mobilities. Children do not necessarily travel from school to home, but may go to friends' or other family members' homes along the way. In many cases family networks are materialised through the movement of children between different households.

Independent mobility

A central motif in both academic literature and popular discourses about children's mobility is that their opportunities for independent mobility have diminished in recent years. This decline in independent mobility has been concomitant with greater mobility but also increasing reliance on car travel as well as other institutionalised mechanisms for child-specific mobilities, such as school buses or walking buses (Barker *et al.*, 2009; Hillman *et al.*, 1990). Thus while children might be more mobile, the ways in which this mobility is realised are becoming more dependent on both adults and mechanised forms of mobility.

The observation that children are denied freedom in late modernity, that childhood necessitates innocence and dependency and thus children need to be protected and therefore denied expressive mobility, has been made by both academics and writers appealing to more popular audiences. Sibley (1995) argues that parents' fear for children's safety is misguided and warped, and has resulted in children leading sedentary lives, cocooned in home environments, rather than allowed to play outside and roam without adult supervision (see also Valentine and McKendrick, 1997).

Writers such as Louv (2005) and Palmer (2006) have contributed to popularly voiced concerns about the cosseted child. Palmer writes about toxic childhood – a condition that she equates with 'unhealthy' development – and top of her six areas for concern is the decline of outdoor play. Louv campaigns against denatured childhood in which children are denied direct experience of wilderness and nature, which he directly associated with rises in obesity, attention disorders and depression. His campaign for a re-engagement with nature emphasises the learning potential in children's freedom to move and escape from both adult control and the confinements and risks of urban life.

The association of childhood with escape and adventure is an essential theme of children's imaginary geographies, and is central to some of the most celebrated works of children's fiction. For example from Alice's imagined journey through Wonderland to the children in many of Enid Blyton's books, or in Arthur Ransome's *Swallows and Amazons* series, children in literature not only had fun and adventure but inhabited a space where adults were shadowy figures, or those that were present needed to be regulated and chastised by the children themselves. Moreover, these freedoms are sanctioned by parents, even if there is initial scepticism about children's desire for adventure. In *Swallows and Amazons* the children have to request permission from their absent father (he is away in the navy) to take the boat out on the lake. The father replies famously in a telegram that 'better drowned than duffers if not duffers wont drown' (Ransome, 1930: 12). Independent mobility therefore reveals the character of the children, as they find and prove themselves through their mobility and adventure.

Other literature uses mobility, and particularly mobility imposed on children by adults, as a motif for exploring the tensions, disappointments and hopes of childhood. Many of Jacqueline Wilson's very popular books deal with children coming to terms with parental neglect, domestic violence and parental separation. The eponymous heroine of *Lola Rose* (Wilson, 2003) for example, runs away from her abusive father with her mother and brother and has to learn to come to terms with her mother's chaotic lifestyle. The family escape not only feeds Lola Rosa's imagination and desire for family stability, but enables her to develop new friendships and build a new relationship with her mother and brother. Her mobility engenders both freedom as well as new responsibilities.

Conclusion

The story of *Lola Rose* takes us full circle back to children's mobility within families and their objectification within these processes and practices. The difficulty of taking the child as a subject of mobility is that children's mobility is governed by expectations of what is best for children, and that children themselves are not capable of bringing this about by themselves. Thus governments are faced with the dilemma of child asylum seekers constrained by their status as dependents and excluded from normative mobility practices, yet state agencies have to deal in a compassionate way with children who do make these challenging and dangerous journeys. Children's mobility is conditioned by their status as dependents within families, but also as learners. A child's body is in development, thus mobility is not just about getting from A to B, but is fundamental for children's learning and development about both their own corporeal ability and their relationships with others. Many of the first development milestones for children are defined by their capacity for mobility and separation from adults. Thus it is difficult to conceptualise the child as a moving subject without reference to how this movement is distinctive from that of adults as well as fashioned by adult mobility.

Thus the child as a mobile subject reveals how mobilities are shaped through relationships and dependencies with others. Yet this is not a characteristic that is particular to children. In recognising the child as a mobile subject the aim should not be to isolate this movement and to treat the child in her own terms, but rather to develop an intergenerational approach that considers how adult mobility is shaped by relationships with children and *vice-versa*. For example 'adult' journeys to work also involve returning home, yet are rarely conceptualised in this way. The overarching interpretation of adult commuting emphasises the need to maximise efficiency in getting to work rather than sustaining family life. Yet in the same way that children's mobilities are now treated as an area of importance for both mobilities research and transport policy, it is too limiting to ignore how adult mobility entails similar relationalities to that of children's mobility. An intergenerational approach would foster a reading of mobility in which age produces relational mobility rather than demarcating distinctive forms.

Bibliography

Ackers, L. (2000) 'From "Best Interests" to Participatory Rights: Children's Involvement in Family Migration Decisions', *Child and Family Law Quarterly*, 12(2): 167–184.

Ackers, L. and Stalford, H. (2004) *A Community for Children?: Children, Citizenship and Internal Migration in the European Union*. Aldershot: Ashgate.

Barker, J. (2009) '"Driven to Distraction?": Children's Experiences of Car Travel', *Mobilities*, 4(1): 59–76.

Barker, J. (2003) 'Passengers or Political Actors? Children's Participation in Transport Policy and the Micro Political Geographies of the Family', *Space and Polity*, 7(2): 135–151.

Barker, J., Kraftl, P., Horton, J. and Tucker, F. (2009) 'The Road Less Travelled – New Directions in Children's and Young People's Mobility', *Mobilities*, 4(1): 1–10.

Brown, J. (2011) 'New Centres "To Detain Child Asylum Seekers"', *The Independent* 3rd February 2011.

Bushin, N. (2009) 'Researching Family Migration Decision-Making: A Children-in-Families Approach', *Population, Space and Place*, 15(5): 429–443.

Butler, T. (2003) 'Plotting the Middle Classes: Gentrification and Circuits of Education in London', *Housing Studies*, 18(1): 5–28.

Cresswell, T. (2006) *On the Move: The Politics of Mobility in the Modern West*. London: Routledge.

de Block, L. and Buckingham, D. (2007) *Global Children, Global Media: Migration, Media and Childhood*. Basingstoke: Palgrave Macmillan.

Dowling, R. (2000) 'Cultures of Mothering and Car Use in Suburban Sydney: A Preliminary Investigation', *Geoforum*, 31(3): 345–353.

Green, A. E. (1997) 'A Question of Compromise? Case Study Evidence on the Location and Mobility Strategies of Dual Career Households', *Regional Studies*, 31(7): 641–657.

Hillman, M., Adams, J. and Whitelegg, J. (1990) *One False Move: A Study of Children's Independent Mobility*. London: Policy Studies Institute.

Holloway, S. and Valentine, G. (2000) 'Children's Geographies and the New Social Studies of Childhood', in S. Holloway and G. Valentine (eds) *Children's Geographies: Playing, Living, Learning*. London: Routledge, pp. 1–28.

Holt, L. and Costello, L. (2011) 'Beyond Otherness: Exploring Diverse Spatialities and Mobilities of Childhood and Youth Populations', *Population, Space and Place*, 17(4): 299–303.

James, A. and James, A. (2004) *Constructing Childhood*. London: Palgrave.

Jarvis, H. (1999) 'The Tangled Webs We Weave: Household Strategies to Coordinate Home and Work', *Work Employment and Society*, 13(2): 249–273.

Jensen, A.-M. (2009) 'Mobile Children: Small Captives of Large Structures?', *Children & Society*, 23(2): 123–135.

Kearns, R. and Collins, D. (2003) 'Crossing Roads, Crossing Boundaries: Autonomy, Authority and Risk in a Child Pedestrian Safety Initiative', *Space and Polity*, 7(2): 193–212.

Kullman, K. and Palludan, C. (2011) 'Rhythmanalytical Sketches: Agencies, School Journeys, Temporalities', *Children's Geographies*, 9(3–4): 347–359.

Kulu, H. (2008) 'Fertility and Spatial Mobility in the Life Course: Evidence from Austria', *Environment and Planning A*, 40(3): 632–652.

Laurier, E., Lorimer, H., Brown, B., Jones, O., Juhlin, O., Noble, A., Perry, M., Pica, D., Sormani, P., Strebel, I., Swan, L., Taylor, A. S., Watts. L. and Weilenmann, A. (2008) 'Driving and "Passengering": Notes on the Ordinary Organization of Car Travel', *Mobilities*, 3(1): 1–23.

Louv, R. (2005) *Last Child in the Woods*. New York: Algonquin Books of Chapel Hill.

Matthews, H. and Limb, M. (1999) 'Defining an Agenda for the Geography of Children: Review and Prospect', *Progress in Human Geography*, 23(1): 61–90.

Michielin, K. and Mulder, C. (2008) 'Family Events and the Residential Mobility of Couples', *Environment and Planning A*, 40(11): 2770–2790.

Ní Laoire, C., Carpena-Méndez, F., Tyrrell, N. and White, A. (2010) 'Introduction: Childhood and Migration – Mobilities, Homes and Belongings', *Childhood*, 17(2): 155–162.

Obrador, P. (2012) 'The Place of the Family in Tourism Research: Domesticity and Thick Sociality by the Pool', *Annals of Tourism Research*, 39(1): 401–420.

Palmer, S. (2006) *Toxic Childhood: How the Modern World is Damaging our Children and what We Can Do about It*. London: Orion.

Punch, S. (2002) 'Youth Transitions and Interdependent Adult–Child Relationships in Rural Bolivia', *Journal of Rural Studies*, 18(2): 123–33.

Ransome, A. (1930) *Swallows and Amazons*. London: Jonathan Cape.

Rossi, P. H. (1956) *Why Families Move*. Glencoe, IL: Free Press.

Sibley, D. (1995) *Geographies of Exclusion: Society and Difference in the West*. London: Routledge.

Skelton, T. (2009) 'Children's Geographies/Geographies of Children: Play, Work, Mobilities and Migration', *Geography Compass*, 3(4): 1430–1448.

The Guardian (2011) 'Australia to Send Child Asylum Seekers to Malaysia', *The Guardian*, 3rd June 2011.

Valentine, G. and McKendrick, J. (1997) 'Children's Outdoor Play: Exploring Parental Concerns about Children's Safety and the Changing Nature of Childhood', *Geoforum*, 28(2): 219–235.

van Blerk, L. and Ansell, N. (2006) 'Children's Experiences of Migration: Moving in the Wake of AIDS in Southern Africa', *Environment and Planning D: Society and Space*, 24(3): 449–471.

White, A., Ní Laoire, C., Tyrrell, N. and Carpena-Méndez, F. (2011) 'Children's Roles in Transnational Migration', *Journal of Ethnic and Migration Studies*, 37(8): 1159–1170.

Wilson, J. (2003) *Lola Rose*. Reading: Random House.

41

Loiterer

J.-D. Dewsbury

I too would be where I am not.
I too survey that endless line
Of men whose thoughts are not as mine.
(A Shropshire Lad –
by A. E. Housman, 2010)

To be where you are not: it would seem to indicate a state where you are in place somewhere, but your mind is elsewhere; it seems to suggest an uneasy agitation in situ, somewhere where you don't quite belong; it could mean, too, that you are neither here nor there both in terms of your physical presence, restlessly on the move, and in terms of your presence of mind, aimlessly directed this way and that, getting nowhere fast. Are these not the characteristics that encapsulate the loiterer? But to suggest then that loitering seems to be a form of distraction and disorientation is perhaps to miss the central tenet of the act of loitering, namely that it is a mode of being that is quite content with its own terms of reference. It is not then a state of being that is unintentionally distracted or disorientated from some other imposed structure. It is a paradoxical mobility, at once deliberate in its act of seemingly non-instrumental movement whilst equally being in a state of some uncertainty.

To loiter is to suggest a movement in being that is unintentionally intent, a sentiment captured in that notion of surveying that endless line, an action which is categorically an impossible task if it is to be judged by its completion, its purpose and its perspicacity. As a potentially important figure in the mobilities paradigm, the loiterer is perhaps too readily dismissed by being defined in reference to "a logic of practical action," where its quintessential qualities are conceived dismissively to be "without investment, without allegiance, without trajectory" (Bissell and Fuller, 2011: 7). Crucially then the loiter is deemed illegible on everything but its own terms. If such an activity is less acutely and keenly attuned to such means–ends calculation, then the mere act of surveying, of wandering in thought, of simply being there, has its own rights and validation. Loitering is then not an arbitrary act; it has its own logics and exists as a specific determination of time and space inhabitation. Like many mobilities that seemingly carry their passenger (Adey *et al.*, 2012), loitering is no different: the act of loitering propagates intensities that take over the cognizant aim of the body creating different oscillations of more or less self-aware moments of being in the act of doing something, even if that doing is a mere flicker of activity, that unconcerned shuffle-like resonance of the loiter itself.

In one sense, this flickery activity of the loiter moves us to exist alongside thoughts not as one's own in its very contradictions around the question of its agency. If, as Foucault instructs us, we see ourselves as constituted subjects in ways whose very subjectivity is framed by the terms of reference we falsely deem to be our own, then the loiter disposes us to stand aside from such self-constituting protocols. In loitering, we stand aside from the impatient certitudes of society's mainstream; we critique, however wanly, the specialized criteria set down before us in ways which delimit the topographical freedoms available; we reject the abstractions that matter socially, namely those Capitalist evaluations that value more productionist occupations over other ways of occupying time like just hanging around. The loiterer can thus be defined quite reasonably as an exemplification of Gilles Deleuze and Félix Guattari's line of flight, a movement (deterritorialization) that acts as a withdrawal from the mainstream ideology determining the kind of world we live in; thus, more precisely, and to concentrate upon one's own subject position or constitution of a subjectivity, to loiter acts as a withdrawal "from the subjective situation of being determined as a subject for others" (Lambert, 2012: 105). The figure of the loiterer is thus disquieting, deviant, vagabond (Cresswell, 2010). If as the prevailing Western subject we are all too predictable in adhering to the Capitalist values that constitute the subjectivities that we become, then exposing ourselves to the thoughts that are not as one's own, precisely in their disquietude, is a vital political gesture. The loiterer functions then as a heterodox figure for our times, a schizoanalytical soft subverter (after Guattari, 2009).

Such concerns have been at play in the social sciences for some time. For instance, Karl Marx disparaged a heroic indolence whilst Charles Baudelaire presented the vita contemptiva over that of the vita contemplativa, both sentiments considered in tandem within Walter Benjamin's argument that "experience is the outcome of work; immediate experience is the phantasmagoria of the idler" (1999: 801; see also Buck-Morss, 1986). Perhaps we can say then that one of the key characteristics of the loiterer is that it operates solely within the realm of immediate experience? I certainly think that its place as a figure within mobilities studies is important for the way in which it centralizes the perspective of immediate experience: the loiterer worries less about the conditions of the past that determine the social protocols expected to be adhered to in the present, and equally concerns itself less with any sense of miserly calculation of what they are currently engaging in as some metered anxiety about what they are achieving for some perceived future they are aspiring towards. The aspirations of the loiterer are different – like Herman Melville's Bartleby, they are an inoperative mobility (2009).

The figure of the loiterer seems then to challenge the mobilities paradigm by arguing that mobilities research is being too social-scientific. In "Becoming Undone," Elizabeth Grosz argues that the social sciences are unable to compass the qualitative nuances that only the humanities address, namely "the human as a literary, artistic, philosophical, historical, and culturally variable being" (2011: 15). Isn't the loiterer such a variable being, not as an empirical instance well attended to but as a figure that cuts into any easy subscription of the mobile subject? In this chapter, then, in drawing upon the trajectories underlying the three lines of Housman's 'A Shropshire Lad' quoted above, I want to use the act of loitering and the figure of the loiterer to problematize the way in which mobility as a conceptual trope for framing research tends to determine the role of spatial context, underdetermine the expansive nature of temporality, and overdetermine the centrality of the subject.

Stuttering space

Do we even know if we are loitering? Do we have a perception of it as an activity, even if it is understood as an unproductive one? In his presidential address before the American Psychological Association in December 1904, William James proposed a radical empiricism to the question of our experience of activity. His oration still challenges us today:

> Have we perceptions of activity, and if so, what are they like, and when and where do we have them? . . . Is there a fact of activity? And if so, what idea must we frame of it? What is it like, and what does it do, if it does anything? . . . Whence do we know activity? By our own feelings of it solely? or by some other source of information?
>
> *(James, 2003: 83)*

These questions do go straight to the heart of the mobilities paradigm where mobility in part gets referred to as "the brute fact of movement taken together with the social narratives that attach meaning to it and insert it into frameworks of power" (Cresswell, 2006: 735). Here we have an emphasis on how those 'other sources of information' frame seemingly brute activity with social meaning in ways which performatively reenact those frames of reference, and the codifications that they perform, in ways which are clearly laden with expressions of power. The act of loitering in this performative regard has meaning attached to it by the spatial relations that both constitute it and which it challenges. A performative is a citational iteration of the status quo which at the same time demonstrates the fragility of that status quo given the ongoing need for it to be performatively reenacted to exist. The loiter is such a performative, and it is performative in a very geographical way in that it pivots off a key tension at the heart of geography, namely that of the polarization of place and space (Doel, 1999: 9). The loiter is a movement that is in space but which gets its definition by being seemingly out of place. Thus it is that the most prevalent idea of loitering is often defined by questions of our access to public spaces, particularly in our cities, where dependent upon your gender, race, age, ability, sexuality, and class you are differentiated with limited and conditional access. Framed then through the idiom of safety the very act of loitering is strategized against in the infrastructure of many urban spaces. In this way it is perhaps the most performatively sustained and noticed mode that precisely reveals "how particular modes of mobility are enabled, given license, encouraged and facilitated while others are, conversely, forbidden, regulated, policed and prevented" (Cresswell, 2006: 735).

The potential in Doel's neologism of 'splacing' works against the loiter being an action that is out of place as unsettling and displacing because for Doel we are always already "disjoined, disadjusted, and unhinged" (1999: 9), such that an act of spatial movement is less a challenge to the sense of place, with its rules and protocols of historicized context and belonging, than an argument about our ongoing constitution of being human. In proposing a Derridean counterargument to Doel, Wainwright and Barnes argue that in recognizing that "we are bound by space and place and their opposition" the loiter explores the very difference between space and place (2009: 971); in a sense then it is not just a condition of being but a particular act that flags up precisely the way in which social narratives give a positive inflection of meaning to some forms of movement and not to others (Pinder, 2011). Arguing more with Doel, productionist, male, safe, straight, legal and assumed normal movements through the urban environs, whilst defining the conditions for the loiterer to emerge, define the loiter is itself as an agrammatical formula which is neither of movement nor stillness, as someone who spaces but never settles into place (nor then conforms to any sense of a place's protocol). To loiter with intent is then a somewhat threadbare phrase, there are no necessarily internal intentions but more likely external codifications that generate and ascribe any sense of intent upon the loiterer.

★ ★ ★

Thus in commonsense understandings of loitering we come to know if we are loitering in a negative way given that it seemingly needs the act of being policed by external codifications to become manifest in particular places where such policing is explicitly spatial and quite inventive. Take the case of the restaurant Stables in Towneley Park, Burnley: according to a BBC report on Radio 1 on 12th February 2008, "two weeks ago, it wasn't unusual to find 80 or 90 teenagers hanging outside . . . But with the help of Lancashire police, the manager installed a Mosquito[1] and he's had no trouble since" (must get one installed outside my office door in time for dissertation season).

Equally, however, the movements of the loiterer do not designate a discernible territory like the walker on the pavement, the footballer on the pitch, the shopper in the mall (Smith, 2010); rather they evoke an atmosphere of uncertainty, nuisance, threat, and idleness, their presence highlighting within the ordinary a heightened sensation of immediate experience. As an atmosphere of presence as opposed to a territory of location, it seems that whilst you can repeat the practice of loitering you cannot repeat a loiter. That is to say that loitering doesn't attune itself to cues from previous experiences so that the past can be traced into the immediate experience of the present to guide towards the next action, much like the runner who paces the race course better or the hunter who learns how to pay attention to the traces of the animal she is following. The loiter emerges in situ within the atmosphere it creates. Benjamin has already cautioned us to be attentive to such classifications of activity and the inherent worthiness that such classifications ascribe: "in place of the force field that is lost to humanity with the devaluation of experience, a new field of force opens up in the form of planning. The mass of unknown uniformities is mobilized against the confirmed multiplicity of the traditional" (1999: 801).

Thus, like Deleuze and Guattari's concept of nomadicism, loitering pertains to "groups whose organization is immanent to the relations composing them" (Holland, 1999: 183). Loitering is a stuttering in space that acts as a becoming-minor of any spatial identification. The loiterer does not then just challenge the architectural choreography of the movement patterns and the indication of social type they imply; becoming-minor is far more significant. In becoming-minor the loiterer introduces into mobilities a stuttering, not just a stuttering in movement, but a refashioning of movement itself and how we understand it. Movement as an emergent operation of individuation of speed and rest is not to be understood as in conflict but as in mutual co-production of a state of being. The idea of the loiter is then a minor-movement, a spacing as well as an action defined by spatial protocols and boundaries, a deterritorialization of movement, a connection of the individual to a political immediacy, and a collective assemblage of enunciation (Deleuze and Guattari, 1986: 16–18).

Confounding time

Like surveying an endless line, loitering suggests a limitless task and in so doing raises the question of temporality and duration in the experience of loitering. I am less interested here in any sense of repeated behavior of loitering, which studies do relate to activities such as stalking as these are as much an architecture of spatial presence as they are repetition. Instead

I want to ask how any paradigmatic instance of mobility gains definition by means of the temporality it exhibits. Take commuting: at once a drag (temporal sludge) which one would want to cut down but also a practice that affords a meantime (temporal oasis) between home and work for uninterrupted reading and thinking (Bissell, 2010a; Edensor, 2011). Extrapolating to journey times more broadly, Urry intimates that there is a subconscious sense that you don't have enough time to be just on the move, enough time "to unwind and switch codes – from work to home; home to leisure" (Adey and Bissell, 2010: 6). This raises the question then as to how we get inculcated to feel the passing of time. In this regard, the loiterer tasks mobility studies to be more expansive in its sense and sensibility of time. How might we grasp this expansiveness? In *The Body Artist* Don DeLillo contrasts the protagonist going out of the house to sit in her car (no explanation is given for this move, it is as if she had just loitered into it) with the scene at her bird feeder sometime later:

> She didn't know how long she was there. Maybe a long time. The rain beat hard on the roof and hood. How much time is a long time? Could be this, could be that . . . There were five birds on the feeder and they all faced outward, away from the food and identically still. They weren't looking or listening so much as feeling something, intent and sensing.

> *(2002: 53–55)*

Both human and bird echo this seemingly unproductive, out of place, occupation of space with their displacing preoccupation that takes them away from the expected use of the familiar milieu of car and feeder; it is not the space of the action that is confounded as much as it is the time taken that is confounding.

Bernard Stiegler isolates three domains of temporality that I want to take forward as important ways for expanding new perspectives of time within mobility (2003: 155). The first he defines as physical temporality – the time of entropy and the time of the expanding universe that is the time of becoming: the loiter perplexes our ease of living with time because we worry about wasting time given we only have a finite amount of it, that some experiences of life only have their window of time and are intensified and qualified to be precisely what they are by the borders of entropy that encroach upon them, and that in a becoming world opportunities can be missed. The second Stiegler sees as a temporality of living, a temporality that fights against the entropic, that denial of change and those practices that seek to extend the status quo of the present, be that unwrinkled skin, nostalgias for the past, or unattributed fears for the future – I wouldn't read this temporality as negative but it is where culture intervenes in codifying ourselves away from living in the present with its entropic heartbeat, and that is not always helpful in the long run. Finally, and the temporality which is most particular to his philosophy, Stiegler proposes the temporality that he calls technics, where living beings including the human are constituted by technical developments within a technical system. Crucially this means that the human agent of any mobility is prosthetic, reliant upon artifacts (from infrastructural assemblages to symbolic codifications[2]) that constitute the experience of mobility and thereby the human, but these are artifacts which at the same time the human is itself capable of altering. He writes that we are less predestined then and more destined to decision, "a capacity to make a difference, a capacity imposed by a lack of origin, by our original default" (ibid.: 156). The loiter confounds those technics of already-constituted action that architectures such as walkways, highways, and piazzas contain as solicitations within them, solicitations that choreograph movement from us which we enact without thinking as if such movement was our own.

Exemplary of the temporalities in a loiter is Bartleby's "I would prefer not to" event:[3] an event situated as "a stereotypic utterance and highly poetic expression, and (which) at the same time, would be neither one nor the other" (Lambert, 2012: 129). In other words, in translating this scene into an act of loitering, we have to be careful not to turn the act of loitering into a cliché. Bartleby's utterance seems mechanically commonplace but it is equally its singularity that makes it so well known; so too then I would be wary about seeing the loiterer and evaluating its impact as a generic act rather than as a specific presence. First, Bartleby's formula of neither affirming nor denying anything determinate doesn't say precisely what it is that he would prefer not to do, and thus he "inserts a space or interval between the requested action that is expected of his position (a scrivener, a legal writer, a copyist) and his response, even his 'respons-ibility'" (ibid.). So too the loiterer, who, as a particular writer of space, suspends the expectation of a body's movement through public space. Like a halo that grows ever more visible, the more one witnesses a body loitering, the question 'what is it not doing?' calls more urgently for an answer. This act then mitigates against the loiterer gaining identification as a subject that another body moving through the space might relate to. It is as if the loiterer is saying 'I would prefer not to' to any suggestion of identification that could be made of their act and which would put them in place and indeed make the space hold a less uneasy atmosphere. Time is crucial to the power of this act and indeed to the Bartleby formula. Not only does there need to be a sense of time, a duration to the movement of the loitering body for there to be any sense of that body taking time to be discernibly loitering and not just waiting or pausing; but equally there is the sense that this act might end. 'I would prefer not to' means more 'I would prefer not to now' rather than 'I would prefer not to ever.' The tension here is precisely because of this potential to act (and not just to unpause or have what was being waited for turn up), and because this current failure to do so leaves open the concern as to what kind of action might follow. In this sense loitering seems to renege on public responsibility simply because it creates a failure to identify, and to identify even what that failure is. Even if it just blurs societal identification creating a sense of unease, should we seek to hold the loiterer to account? Does the loiterer have a legitimate claim to the city? To exist? Cyclists do even if they mount pavements. Car drivers do even if they jump red lights. Rail drivers do even if their assemblage demands steel to be laid down through 'our' green and pleasant land. Pilots do even if their assemblage creates localized air-quakes that rip apart the peaceful quiet of a morning. The loiterer just somehow bugs us. It could be said then that it raises far more pertinent and awkward questions about the kind of basic human animal we want to be.

Asignifying desire

In *Anti-Oedipus* Deleuze and Guattari argued for a theory of society based on a theory of flows (1984: 262) such that it seems "that it is the business of every society to code these flows, and the 'terrifying nightmare' of any society would be a flow that eludes its codes, that is a decoded or uncoded flow" (Smith, 2012: 160). As we have seen, loitering is such a decoding flow, terrifying in its promise of uncoding our spatial and temporal order. Central to Deleuze and Guattari's argument is their posit that political economy and libidinal economy are one and the same thing,[4] the goal of the 'schizoanalysis' proposed thus being to "analyze the specific nature of the libidinal investments in the economic and political spheres, and thereby show how, in the subject that desires, desire can be made to desire its own repression" (1984: 105). Loitering here performs a minor disruption to the repression of desire in confounding the general flow of society. In this it contributes to the critique of the idea of mobility being a flow without restriction, to articulate instead mobility as something that contains both moments of stillness and experiences of less than ecstatic on-flow (Bissell, 2008). This disruptive capacity, as a singular moment, also points towards the asignifying capture of the evental performance of mobility, and as such opens up this ontology of mobility as flow with a sense of politics that goes beyond those questions of policy and the legal governance of the material production of mobilities and the (un)equal access to all forms of mobile freedom. It does this because the discrete individual subject is now less the centre of attention.

Daniel Smith points out that Deleuzian subjects are the interceptors of flows: "I am the point of destination for numerous flows, which I intercept; and I am also the point of departure for the production of new flows, and it is precisely the synthesis and production of flows that Deleuze terms desire" (2012: 169).

> Desire does not take as its object persons or things, but the entire surroundings that it traverses, the vibrations and flows of every sort to which it is joined, introducing therein breaks and captures . . . [to] intervene only as points of connection, of disjunction, of conjunction of flows whose libidinal tenor of a properly unconscious investment they translate.
>
> *(Deleuze and Guattari, 1984: 292–293)*

Crucially, desire exists within and outside the moving body, as well as the flow of the moving body itself. In other words, once we move away from understanding the drives and meanings of a moving body as something singularly determined by the representational codes that enframe it, we see in addition a way of understanding mobile bodies in more pluralist and multiplicitous ways. So, in loitering, what are we conscious of as we decide to go this way rather than that? Instead of thinking about loitering as a precise sense of conscious thought where we weigh up, even with a hint of hesitation, abstract possibilities reduced and focused to representational and historically authenticated moves, think towards an occasionalist world, one within which there are distributed agencies where even the most tenuous and fugitive differentiating energy deflects life's course (see Stengers, 2011: 208). This spotlights less the relationalities at play in Urry's call for the more methodological capture of the differential capacities of an individual's ability to move and more the capacities themselves: capacities that are not then forged out of relationships between discrete individuals with their differential position within mobility infrastructures but that rather emerge through the different molecular resonances within and beyond individual bodies (Adey and Bissell, 2010: 7). It is less then a question of "Who is moving? Who is moving who? Who has to move? Who can stay put?" (ibid.). In French, 'qui' (who) has a dual use, meaning both 'who' but also 'the one which' – a distinction that is precisely at the heart of Deleuze's Nietzschean inspired dissolution of the subject (Hardt, 1993: 30). The loiter then does not speak to a determination of movement in terms of answering a question as to what movement is as something possessed by a singular subject. Rather, like Nietzsche's alternative to the categorical question of truth – 'what does the one who seeks the truth want' (Deleuze, 1983: 94) – the loiter asks 'what really is it in us that wants to move'? Moving is a mixture of thinking, willing, and feeling, understood as forces or drives that move us and dispose us this way and not that, less then as emanations from an intentional knowing core and more as "only the relationship of these drives one to another" (Nietzsche, 1990, \$36: 66). Desire as the flow of internal and external forces presents a different cartography for understanding loitering as a distinct drive and not one synthesized from an understanding of movement already framed dialectically to a representational framing. This understands movement under the auspices of passivity and doesn't then judge the loitering activity in terms of some willfully central individual consciousness (Bissell, 2010b), which would overemphasize the level of intentionality in an act of movement. Such intentional emphasis silences, with a violence and purifying logic, the confused actuality of what Leibniz has called those 'little perceptions' (1991: 71). To loiter is to dwell in those thoughts that are not 'as mine,' those lures that act latently as "the minuscule folds" of perception "that no one of our thresholds of consciousness could sustain in a normal state" (Deleuze, 2006: 106).

Codas towards an ethics of loitering

The loiter lacks an anthem to its movement that would be at once confident and encompassing, and which would immediately invite others to join in. It does though still hold passerby witnesses to its beat in effecting an affective atmosphere that is more uncertain. Where Deleuze writes of stuttering in language, a stuttering that I have argued befits the leitmotif of the loiter, Derrida writes of the tremble, "a meditation on the fault, the fault-line" (Peeters, 2013: 533) which solicits thought as "a singular experience of non-knowing," an experience of passivity "in the face of an irreversible past as well as in the face of an unpredictable future" (Derrida, 2006: 97; quoted in Peeters, 2013: 533). The loiter poses this first ethical question to the mobilities paradigm: *some of the most important aspects of life take place in the loiter, on the fault-line between past codifications and new habits, in the moment of seemingly undirected non-knowing that nonetheless gets us to where we need to go.*

Derrida also aligns the tremble with the shudder, a convulsion that confounds any quick pursuit of movement's flow. This is not burdensome but acts as something that can be "light," as on the surface of things. Derrida pursues a poetic evocation of this shudder in space-time as something physical, material and desiring: "Water, they tell us, shudders before it boils, which is what we called seduction" (Derrida, 2006: 98; quoted in Peeters, 2013: 533). As I have suggested in relation to Deleuzian flows as desire, the loiter in thought, as in space, presents an important pause, a second moment of ethics: *an ethics of (di)stilling the more instrumental idea of movement as achievement, that of reaching a destination, with one of not quite achieving something; and in the spacing of this 'not quite' a blissful experience on its own terms exists, the tipping point towards the next moment when something does actually happen with a sense of something having happened.*

Finally, from the social sciences to the humanities of poetry, philosophy, and prose and back again, how does loitering refit the social science agenda of the mobilities turn? Alfred North Whitehead alerts us to a false economy of judgement in our thinking with his argument that "the methodology of rational interpretation is the product of the fitful vagueness of consciousness" (1985: 15). It is not so much that the figure of the loiterer subjects us in uncomfortable ways – the waste in its unproductivity, the threat in its apparent intent, the deviance in confounding the norm – but rather we subject it lazily in our codifications of its meaning to make it fit. A final ethical thought then is to be wary of overlooking the loiterer, overlooking it by depending on one point of view, by overemphasizing your excess of subjectivity:

> *Elements which shine with immediate distinctness, in some circumstances, retire into penumbral shadow in other circumstances, and into black darkness on other occasions. And yet all occasions proclaim themselves as actualities within the flow of a solid world, demanding a unity of interpretation.* Philosophy is the self-correction by consciousness of its own initial excess of subjectivity.
>
> *(Whitehead, 1985: 15; my italicization)*

Notes

1 The Mosquito is a small speaker that produces a high frequency sound much like the buzzing of the insect it's named after. This high frequency can be heard by young people aged roughly between 13 and 25 years old.
2 An example of this kind of technics, Stiegler argues that the 'copy and paste' technology of our times alters negatively the constitution of the human in its thinking capacities to synthesize ideas and become capable of critical reflection and judgement (see Beardsworth, 2010).
3 Bartleby is the scrivener in Herman Melville's short story "Bartleby the Scrivener," who when asked to carry out one of his daily tasks at work replies, "I would prefer not to" (Melville, 2009; see Agamben, 1999: 243–271).
4 "The truth of sexuality is everywhere: the way a bureaucrat fondles his records, a judge administers justice, a businessman causes money to circulate; the way the bourgeoisie fucks the proletariat; and so on" (Deleuze and Guattari 1984: 293).

References

Adey, P. and Bissell, D. (2010) 'Mobilities, meetings, and futures: an interview with John Urry,' *Environment and Planning D: Society and Space*, 28, 1–16.
Adey, P., Bissell, D., McCormack, D. and Merriman, P. (2012) 'Profiling the passenger: mobilities, identities, embodiments,' *Cultural Geographies*, 19, 169–193.
Agamben, G. (1999) *Potentialities*, Stanford, CA: Stanford University Press.
Beardsworth, R. (2010) 'Technology and politics: a response to Bernard Stiegler,' *Cultural Politics*, 6(2), 191–199.
Benjamin, W. (1999) *The Arcades Project*, Cambridge, MA: Harvard University Press.
Bissell, D. (2008) 'Comfortable Bodies', *Environment and Planning A*, 40(7), 1697–1712.
Bissell, D. (2010a) 'Passenger mobilities: affective atmospheres and the sociality of public transport,' *Environment and Planning D: Society and Space*, 28, 270–289.
Bissell, D. (2010b) 'Thinking habits for uncertain subjects: movement, stillness, susceptibility,' *Environment and Planning A*, 43(11), 2649–2665.
Bissell, D. and Fuller, G. (2011) 'Stillness unbound', in David Bissell and Gillian Fuller (eds) *Stillness in a Mobile World*, London, UK: Routledge, pp.1–17.
Buck-Morss, S. (1986) 'The flaneur, the sandwichman and the whore: the politics of loitering,' *New German Critique*, 39(Autumn), 99–140.
Cresswell, T. (2006) 'The right to mobility: the production of mobility in the courtroom,' *Antipode*, 38, 735–754.
Cresswell, T. (2010) 'Towards a politics of mobility,' *Environment and Planning D: Society and Space*, 28, 17–31.
Deleuze, G. (1983) *Nietzsche & Philosophy*, London, UK: The Athlone Press.
Deleuze, G. (2006) *The Fold*, London, UK: Continuum.
Deleuze, G. and Guattari, F. (1984) *Anti-Oedipus: Capitalism and Schizophrenia*, London, UK: The Athlone Press.
Deleuze, G. and Guattari, F. (1986) *Kafka: Toward a Minor Literature*, Minneapolis, MN: University of Minnesota Press.
DeLillo, D. (2002) *The Body Artist*, London, UK: Picador.
Derrida, J. (2006) 'Comment ne pas trembler,' *Annali*, 97–8.
Doel, M. (1999) *Postructural Geographies: The Diabolical Art of Spatial Science*, Edinburgh, UK: Edinburgh University Press.
Edensor, T. (2011) 'Commuter: mobility, rhythm and commuting,' in T. Cresswell and P. Merriman (eds) *Geographies of Mobilities: Practices, Spaces, Subjects*, Farnham, UK: Ashgate, pp.189–203.
Grosz, E. (2011) *Becoming Undone: Darwinian Reflections on Life, Politics, and Art*, Durham, NC: Duke University Press.
Guattari, F. (2009) *Soft Subversions: Texts and Interviews 1977–1985*, Los Angeles, CA: Semiotext (c).
Hardt, M. (1993) *Gilles Deleuze: An Apprenticeship in Philosophy*, London, UK: UCL Press.
Holland, E. (1999) *Deleuze and Guattari's Anti-Oedipus: Introduction to Schizoanalysis*, London, UK: Routledge.
Housman, A. E. (2010) *A Shropshire Lad and Other Poems: The Collected Poems of A. E. Housman*, London, UK: Penguin.

James, W. (2003) *Essays in Radical Empiricism*, New York: Dover Publications, Inc.

Lambert, G. (2012) *In Search of a New Image of Thought: Gilles Deleuze and Philosophical Expressionism*, Minneapolis, MN: University of Minnesota Press.

Leibniz, G. W. (1991) *Discourse on Metaphysics and Other Essays*, Indianapolis, IN: Hackett Publishing Company.

Melville, H. (2009) *Billy Budd, Sailor and Selected Tales*, Oxford, UK: Oxford Paperbacks.

Nietzsche, F. (1990) *Beyond Good and Evil*, London, UK: Penguin.

Peeters, B. (2013) *Derrida: A Biography*, Cambridge, UK: Polity Press.

Pinder, D. (2011) 'Errant path: the poetics and politics of walking,' *Environment and Planning D: Society and Space*, 29, 672–692.

Smith, D. W. (2012) *Essays on Deleuze*, Edinburgh, UK: Edinburgh University Press.

Smith, P. (2010) 'The contemporary derive: a partial review of issues concerning the contemporary practice of psychogeography,' *Cultural Geographies*, 17(1), 103–122.

Stengers, I. (2011) *Thinking with Whitehead: A Free and Wild Creation of Concepts*, Cambridge, MA: Harvard University Press.

Stiegler, B. (2003) 'Technics of decision: an interview,' *Angelaki*, 8(2), 151–168.

Wainwright, J. and Barnes, T. (2009) 'Nature, economy, and the space-place distinction,' *Environment and Planning D: Society and Space*, 27, 966–986.

Whitehead, A. N. (1985) *Process and Reality*, New York, NY: Free Press.

Section Six
Introduction: Events

Moving is by definition an event: it begins and ends, it has a measure and a tempo, it is infused with rhythms and breaks. If mobility is often described as a kind of network of linkages across space, it is also a "network in time," with turning points, hinges, and eventful punctuation points (Abbott 2001). Mobility depends on speed, velocity, aerodynamic flows, miles per gallon, bits per second; it also necessarily revolves around stop-and-go blockages, congestion, turbulence, friction, and disruptions. Movement intertwines diverse temporalities through the choreography of events, passages, and exchanges, yet there is so much more about the event of mobility that remains to be investigated. What are its affective qualities as an embodied experience, as a habit, or as a staging of encounters? How do different events of moving, slowing, staying, passing, pausing, or rushing inform the meaning and experience of mobility?

Perhaps the most familiar juxtaposition of different temporalities of mobility is the quest for the "holiday," a time set apart from everyday routine. Löfgren reminds us that the vacation is also a kind of "*rite de passage*," structured around leaving, journeying, arriving, and returning. It is not just about modes of travel, but also moods of travel, which are informed by all of the traveling objects and patterns of moving that inform travel: travel fever, anxiety, fidgeting, juggling things, but also comfort, convenience, and ease. Löfgren's history of the holiday suggests how the rituals and aesthetics of the journey had to be learned in different periods and contexts. Here the packing of luggage emerges as an interesting technology for managing temporal events, while producing the nervous worries of loss. Lightness and the use of specially designed travel gear mark the holiday as a special event, one requiring special tourist "skills, routines and reflexes." Thus we can think of "holiday moves" as the mastery of a special configuration of timing mobility.

The timing of mobility events is equally informed by more routine moves. Modern mobility systems are historically grounded in changes in capitalist systems of production that separated home from work, and gave rise to the phenomenon of "the commute." Aldred traces the shifting configurations of walking and cycling commutes, the rise of railways in the nineteenth century and eventually car cultures and "mass motorisation" in the twentieth century, alongside public transport systems. Both of these chapters therefore speak to the importance of historical approaches to mobility studies, another aspect of its temporality.

While commute times in the UK have remained relatively stable over more than a century, the distance of the daily commute increased steadily over the twentieth century. Even though commuting does not constitute the majority of trips, it nevertheless has often disproportionately influenced transport planning. Building on the work of Lyons on travel time-use (see also Chapter 14 in this volume), Aldred explores how the event of the commute can be valued in different ways, leading to different kinds of cost–benefit analyses. Thus rethinking the event of the commute has important implications for planning.

How people go to work, whether they work from home, and how they use their time while commuting are all important aspects of understanding transitions to sustainable mobility, which in itself is a kind of event-in-progress that often puzzles transport planners. How do patterns, infrastructures, and cultures of mobility change over time? Have transport planners focused too much on the problem of congestion, rather than considering the broader timing of moving, slowing, pausing, and staying still as potentially productive moments of social encounter?

Congestion is often imagined as the key challenge faced by the commuter, trying to navigate as smoothly and quickly as possible through crowded sidewalks, streets or stations. But Butcher reminds us that congestion can also be imagined as a question of diversity and proximity, an embodied experience of being "too close" to others. Rapid urbanisation presents problems of maladjustment, such as traffic jams, smells, noise, and crowds. Thus the physicality of the city is a kind of event, full of affective responses, and rules for navigating congested streets. And congestion is also managed by withdrawal into protected spaces, ranging from withdrawal into the home, into the segregated neighborhood, or into the gated community. In moving within and through different kinds of crowds, Butcher argues, there emerges a "micro-politics" of mobility and immobility. Being in the midst of congestion, paused amongst mobility, is not necessarily a bad thing.

The Occupy movement, like other social movements before it, has leveraged this micro-politics of blockage to create a politics of occupation, or presence in public space. Beyond the disruptions caused by congestion or traffic jams, the disruption of "normal" mobility has long been a repertoire of social protest. Graham also brings out the significance of disruption as a kind of flip side of the infrastructures of mobility that manage our flows of water, waste, people, information, etc. If these systems work seamlessly and become the invisible background, as noted in the Spaces, Systems, Infrastructures section of this Handbook, it takes disruption for them suddenly to leap to the foreground: "infrastructure disruptions render the arcane worlds of technically facilitated mobility as both momentarily visible and highly political." Yet in the Global South, Graham notes, the challenges of precarious access to mobility systems and fragmented services already bring infrastructures to the social and political foreground. Disruption is both an event in the contestation of urbanism, and an "opportunity for learning" that the city is a process, disruption being an everyday experience for those who live on the precarious margin.

Blomley gets down to the level of the sidewalk to really unpack the contestation of urban space. He reviews different ways of understanding the sidewalk. In the civic humanist tradition it is a public space of encounters, a city made on foot, an agora in motion where meeting strangers creates "vital frictions," complex patterns of interaction, reciprocity, and potential association. In contrast to this "traffic code" of self-organised civic encounter, there is also a politics of obstruction played out on the sidewalk. Notions of "obstruction and encroachment" frame the event of the sidewalk encounter in a different way, as a more legalistic prevention of possible harms. Blomley considers this protection of unencumbered passage as a valuing of "pedestrianism," a rationality at odds with civic humanist visions. Thus in the event of the encounter we might see a juxtaposition of different rationalities that conceptualise the space of the sidewalk, and the event of the encounters or obstructions that happen there, in very different ways. Does freedom lie in unencumbered mobility, or the right to assemble?

If Blomley encourages us to interrogate assumptions that equate smooth mobility of the pedestrian with freedom (when freedom might in fact hinge on the vital frictions of the crowded sidewalk), Bissell pushes us to rethink assumptions about habit. Habit is often presumed to be a brake on transformation, a kind of locked-in stasis built up into conservative *habitus*. Instead, he argues, we might draw on process theories that envision habit more as a productive relation, based on the shaping of action via repetition: "What were initially movements that were clumsy, difficult and required effort, through habit become increasingly precise, graceful and effortless. It is through habit that mobility competencies take shape through the efficiencies that habit affords where only those movements useful for the action are retained." Habit, then, is not simply about the routines of everyday mobility, or locked-in cultural patterns such as thoughtless car-driving, but involves an ontological investigation of transformative dynamics. Ultimately, for Bissell, habit "becomes a way of refiguring the mobilities–moorings relation in a more temporal, processual manner which invites us to consider what changes and what is retained, rather than what moves and what stays still."

As events that go, that begin and end, that rush and slow, mobility seems to evade easy capture and diagnosis; mobilities are not so easily stopped. And yet, Eric Laurier shows us that mobilities (see also Cresswell 2006) have so often been drawn into the realm of representation and signification by efforts to slow them down and hold them immobile, held still within the frame of a photo, video camera, and as we will see in the later section, a range of representational methods of expression. As events are so easily missed, or forgotten, or too quickly apprehended, Laurier shows how video techniques – which allow us to anticipate the following section on mobile methodologies – mean that mobility events can be restored or recovered, even if they only provide a very partial record.

Together these chapters offer many new ways to approach mobilities research, moving it beyond some common tropes of "living in a mobile world." Mobilities offer a rich field for philosophical investigation, and for thinking through the relations between being and becoming, agency and structure, individual and social field, temporality and stasis, historicity and futurity.

References

Abbott, A. (2001) *Time Matters: On Theory and Method*, Chicago: University of Chicago Press.
Cresswell, T. (2006) *On the Move: Mobility in the Modern West*, New York: Routledge.

42

Holidays

Orvar Löfgren

Modes and moods

Towards the end of the twentieth century there was a discussion about how new media and virtual realities would change tourism, creating a generation of couch surfers, who with the help of cutting edge technologies could travel around the world in their living rooms. Would there be any need to leave domestic comfort for expensive and cumbersome actual travel? In 2011 there were over 15 million Google hits for couch surfers, but they were about something entirely different. By then couch surfing had become the term for a rapidly growing form of non-profit tourism where one, with the help of the new social media, could find private lodgings at a tourist destination, make friends with the locals and take up their offer of a living room couch or a spare guest room, be it in Istanbul or Barcelona (see, for example, Germann Molz and Gibson 2007: 65 ff.).

If there's a general theme in the history of vacationing it is about *going elsewhere*. In the search for elsewhereness the role of physical – not only mental – mobility is central. It doesn't have to be a long journey, but the *rites de passage* of leaving, journeying and arriving are crucial in ways that virtual travel cannot offer.

I remember interviewing a fisherwoman in a village on the Swedish West Coast in the 1970s, where the coastal tradition of renting out the house to summer visitors had been well established since the early twentieth century. It fitted in with an older rural tradition of living in summer quarters, a more primitive or simpler living in the backyard houses. She told me that the day the family moved across the yard – a journey of 30 feet – felt like an adventure. They became a different family, a holiday family.

There are all kinds of long or short journeys that organize this transition into the holiday mood, from early globetrotting or later generations of backpacking in exotic destinations, to moves to summerhouses, camping sites or package tour hotels. In the following I will explore some aspects of the social and cultural organization of such movements.

My argument is that we need to take a closer look at the microphysics of different kinds of mobilities in order to understand the European tourist experience of the last two centuries. It is the intense materiality of holiday movements that interests me – uses and experiences of travel technologies, from choices of transportation to the battle with luggage. Looking back on a decade of research, Rebecca Solnit has reflected on the ways in which the body in motion has remained, on the whole, a highly theoretical entity rather than provoking an actual discussion of bodily sensations and practices:

> we seem to be reading about the postmodern body shuttled around by airplanes and hurtling cars, or even moving around by no apparent means, muscular, mechanical, economic or ecological. The body is nothing more than a parcel in transit, a chess piece dropped on another square, it does not move but is moved.
>
> *(Solnit 2001: 28)*

Mobility in such studies is often seen as frictionless, more of a mental than a physical process. This also used to be the case for tourism research, which calls for closer attention to be paid to the necessary and often irritating material conditions of tourist travel: the missing boarding pass, the ill-fitting walking shoes, the overloaded travel bag, the dead camera battery or the sun's reflection through the bus window. How do seemingly banal and insignificant objects like suitcases, train seats, earphones, waiting rooms and tickets shape travel experiences and what kinds of skills are needed to handle this material world?

I will use a historical perspective to capture tourist moves as a process of cultural learning. Each generation develops new patterns of mobility: learning the tourist gait, sightseeing from the car, handling fellow passengers in the train or on the coach trip, lining up for a charter flight. What interests me is the ways in which modes and moods of travel are interwoven. I am thinking of the ways in which certain daydreaming moods can be shaped by gliding through a landscape in a train, the sensualities produced by the combination of sand, sun and sea on the beach or how different a cityscape is experienced by walking as opposed to driving in a car.

Travel fever

"I'm travelling in some vehicle, I'm sitting in some café . . . I am porous with travel fever", sings Joni Mitchell in *Hejira*, but what kind of fever is that? The equivalent Swedish concept *resfeber* is a label for the specific 'structure of feeling', to borrow a term from Raymond Williams (1980), that many tourists experience when travelling. It is a nervous mix of anxiety and anticipation, that combines longing with fear and fascination of the unknown, the exhilaration and dread of letting go, moving out. Travel fever is epidemic and contagious – you can observe it in trains stations, airports and traffic jams, in people walking, waiting, driving. It is a state that combines motion, emotion and materiality. Travellers try to control their anxiety by pacing the floor, shifting their balance or seeking temporary security on a bench in a corner. There is a constant fidgeting with luggage, passports or exact change. Small objects become magically important and reassuring, because of their stubborn materiality in this world of flux and flow. In their footloose state people hold on to comforting objects like a handbag or a cell phone, or feel every second minute for the ticket in the breast pocket. There is a constant sensual interaction with the surrounding world, as the eye scans flashing notice boards and the ear tries to de-mystify loudspeaker messages. Furthermore, there are all kinds of bodily sensations shaping the situation: muscles aching from dragging too much luggage, nervous limbs and too much diffuse energy. There is also a split between body and mind, because in their thoughts tourists may already be at their destination, daydreaming about everything (pleasant or unpleasant) that lies ahead or nervously thinking about if they locked the door back home. There are a lot of multitasking skills needed here to juggle stuff, emotions, thoughts and bodies and such skills change with travel technologies (see Löfgren 2008).

Early locomotions

This interaction between modes and moods of travel surfaces when you look at the tourist interaction with travel infrastructures in different eras. In the nineteenth century the railways provided the first transport system for tourist travel on a larger scale. The train quite quickly became the tourist transportation alternative for the urban working class, with cheap excursion fares out to the coast or into the countryside. Train travel brought tourists of different classes into contact, on platforms and in trains, although the elaborated system of railway classes was developed to keep them separated. One had to learn where one belonged – first, second or third.

Middle-class observers often resented the collectivity of working-class excursions and the ways in which not only stations but the tourist landscape was appropriated by "the lower classes". The following British observation from the early twentieth century is not untypical:

> The excursion train used to vomit forth, at Easter and in Whitsun week, throngs of millhands of the period, cads and their flames, tawdry, blowsy, noisy, drunken; the women with dress that aped "the fashion," and pyramids of artificial flowers on their heads; the men as grotesque and hideous in their own way; tearing through woods and fields like swarms of devastating locusts, and dragging the fern and hawthorn boughs they had torn down in the dust, ending the lovely spring day in pot-houses, drinking gin and bitters; or heavy ales by the quart, and tumbling pellmell into the night train, roaring music-hall choruses; sodden, tipsy, yelling, loathsome creatures, such as make a monkey look a king, and the newt seem an angel beside humanity.
>
> *(Bailey 1978: 104)*

In the 1930s, when legislations about statutory paid holidays were underway in many European settings, new forms of mass tourism evolved. In the media there were worried debates: could ordinary people really handle the new freedom of holiday life? In the summer of 1936 the new left government of the *Front Populaire* in France passed a legislation for two weeks paid holiday, and in August 600,000 French workers travelled on their first vacation by train thanks to a 40 per cent price reduction on the National railways (Furlough 1998).

If the train became one form for mass travel during this early period, the bike was another. In Sweden workers got their first two-week vacation in 1938. The car was still a very exclusive mode of transport in Europe. In 1930 only one Swede in sixty owned a car, but one in six had a bicycle. The 1930s and 1940s were the great periods of biking holidays. A shipyard worker from southern Sweden remembers his first holiday back in 1938. He describes the fantastic feeling of freedom, with two empty weeks ahead, just packing his stuff, getting the bike out and hitting the road. Biking was combined with the newfangled technology of camping, offering an affordable holiday.

Families on the road

In the USA holidays by car were much more common than in Europe during the years between the two world wars.

> Some sunny Sunday very soon, just drive an Overland up to your door – tell the family to hurry the packing and get aboard – and be off with smiles down the nearest road – free, loose, and happy – bound for green wonderlands.
>
> *(Lynd and Lynd 1929: 261)*

This 1929 advertisement from *Saturday Evening Post* is quoted in the classical sociological study of Middletown, a study which captures the excitement the car brought to urban life and leisure. "Vacations in 1890?" said one Middletowner in 1929, "Why, the word wasn't even in the dictionary!" In pre-automobile Middletown, vacations for most people would be the rare Sunday outing with horse and carriage or a train excursion to Chicago (Lynd and Lynd 1929: 257). With the car, even working-class families could start to arrange short vacation trips, sleeping in the car or in tents. Vacations were not something you had to save up for or plan long in advance, and in your private car you didn't have to put up any appearances.

In Europe motor tourism didn't really expand until the 1950s and 1960s. The car fostered new modes of perception and sensuality in travel, but also remodelled family life. The family could be squeezed into its own, private moving space, filled with all the props offered by the new leisure industry – everything from portable radios and camping equipment to leisure-wear and leisure food. Campsites emerged everywhere in new, and what were often seen as far too uncontrolled, forms. The reaction of the traditional tourist industry to the post-war expansion and increasingly mobile tourism was mixed. Some felt that it threatened the traditional, established tourist pattern, with fixed weeks in boarding houses, rituals of shared meals, and well-worn paths for daily walks.

Now, more and more adventurous tourists ventured across borders, Germans driving into Italy, Brits into France, Scandinavians into Germany. The institution of the summer motor holiday was documented in photo albums and collections of souvenirs, with memories of the exciting ritual start of leaving home with a loaded car, break-downs in the middle of nowhere, and interesting contact with fellow campers. An infrastructure of gas stations, roadside cafeterias, motorist handbooks, road maps and camping grounds emerged. In the USA and later in Europe the idea of the family car became important, or as a middle-class Middletown woman put it: "I never feel as close to my family as when we are all together in the car" (Lynd and Lynd 1929: 257).

Learning to be a tourist, experiencing exotic places and strange food customs was now often taught within the framework of "the family vacation" and the family car. This mode of travelling also became an instruction in "how to be a family". The close living, the common project of holiday-making, developed new forms of togetherness but also of conflicts, and made the family stand out much more clearly in the social landscape (see Löfgren 2000: 60 ff.).

Catching a flight

The aeroplane remained a dream vehicle well into the advent of mass flight travel in the 1960s and 1970s. During the early twentieth century tourists from all over the Western world flocked to airports and air shows to watch flying machines and dream of becoming a pilot, hovering in the air, free as a bird, but with full control and detached from the mundane worries down below.

When cheap flights and package tours became a new tourist alternative the romance of air travel was transformed into a more mundane activity. People learned to handle the very special settings that airports were turning into. Anthony Vidler (2001) has compared the airport with two other spaces for waiting: the hotel lobby and the unemployment office. He focuses on the combination of 'demoralized waiting' and 'anonymous passage'. At the airport the travellers may experience the same powerlessness as at the unemployment office, he argues, thinking of the many micro-technologies for producing feelings of uncertainty and lack of control. You are not in control of your destiny, but feel herded like cattle.

This was not always the case. When flying was something for the wealthy few, airports had a much more informal and pampering atmosphere. The new travel form did not imitate the railways, but what during the 1920s were seen as the icons of modernity and luxury: the ocean liners. In the 'clippers of the sky' the flight crew took their titles and uniforms from the shipping world. The rituals and aesthetics of the journey were a scaled-down emulation of the ocean crossing, with champagne served by stewards (and later stewardesses) in navy blue.

This changed with mass travel. During the latter part of the twentieth century airports became large-scale machines for handling great numbers of bodies. "The passenger, a mobile unit, must be controlled and guided for safety and operating efficiency, in his own interest", as the official language put it (Zukowsky 1996: 51). The airport experience started to become very different from experiences in other transit spaces. In the 1970s the new fears of hijacking and international terrorism led to an even more radical restructuring of the airport into a defence system. Airports became "the perfect field for intense control and high surveillance experimentation" (Virilio 1986: 16), and this tendency was even more marked with the new threats of terrorism during the 1990s and early 2000s. Tourists had to learn that mundane objects from nail clippers to soda bottles would be confiscated by the security personnel.

At the same time airports became part of the new experience economies, with great energy put into designing them into 'event-spaces' of shopping, indulgence and entertainment (see Löfgren 1999). This tension makes the airport a scene of mixed emotions and moods. What kind of place is this, a paradise of hedonist shopping, reeking of perfume, malt whiskies, rich chocolate and pure silk? A stress laboratory, a no man's land between the nation state and the world, a surveillance machine for automated bodies, shepherded from control station to control station?

The package tour system reintroduced a collectivity in tourist travel, creating a temporary community of fellow travellers, sharing the flight, but also hotels and excursions. In many ways the package tour Gemeinschaft was modelled on the earlier tradition of coach trips by road, Scandinavians visiting the sins of Paris or the tulip fields of Holland, Germans invading the Italian beaches. The organized tour created a safety net of tour guides and pre-arranged activities. This made it possible for new kinds of tourists to venture abroad and this also made them learn what to bring along.

Luggage

"When George is hanged, Harris will be the worst packer in this world", Jerome K. Jerome ([1889] 1957: 34) writes in his classic description of how "Three men in a boat" prepare for their holiday on the river. Their endeavours to decide what to bring and how to squeeze it into the suitcases turn more and more chaotic.

The question of luggage – what to bring along and how – is an important part of holiday preparations and an intensely material one. During the history of modern tourism there has been an endless flow of advice and debate on what should go into the suitcases. In a sense, packing is a micro-journey in itself. As things pile up, the whole journey is anticipated – there is a lot of mental travel going on. Do I really need this? What have I forgotten? The needs and potentials of the upcoming vacation are materialized in the sorting and handling of all sorts of stuff. "Three men in a boat" belongs to a period of rapidly expanding tourism, in which the question of packing was ardently discussed.

In the introduction to Jules Verne's novel *Around the World in Eighty Days* from 1873, the master returns home to tell his surprised valet that they are about to embark on a world tour.

"'But what about trunks?' gasped Passepartout, unconsciously swaying his head from right to left. 'We will have no trunks. Just a carpet bag. Inside two woollen shirts, two pair of stockings. The same for you. We'll buy along the way.'" (Verne 1873: 10).

This was a radical solution for a globetrotting gentleman. Travel was still a question of dragging along all sorts of luggage. The infrastructure of servants, porters and luggage services meant that early upper-class travellers could bring along mountains of luggage as they arrived by train to the hotels of Nice for a long vacation in the mild winter sun, or by steamer to coastal resorts all over Europe.

But the battle with luggage could still be stressful, as in this description of a railway station scene from the 1870s: Porters are shouting, 'Claim your luggage, claim your luggage!' A harried pater familias on route for the seaside with many children, a dog and a number of pieces of luggage, is trying to claim all his stuff. Are they correctly labelled? This stressful scene is found in *Our Railways* from 1878, a book that discusses all the problems of the vast amounts of luggage carried by train and the problems of keeping track of it, as well as the newfangled institution of the lost property office, with its wealth of umbrellas, hats, small parcels and many more and stranger items (Parsloe 1878: 103 ff.). Travel nerves made passengers lose all kinds of belongings.

A whole industry of trunk makers developed, producing all kinds of containers for travel. The greatest innovator of them all was Louis Vuitton, who started his firm in Paris in 1854. His early experience of packing for upper-class households gave him insights that were useful when he turned to develop new kinds of luggage pieces for affluent travellers (see Pasols 2005).

As Giuliana Bruno (2002: 373 ff.) has pointed out, Vuitton's focus on fashion and women also put a focus on travel as a female possibility. His advertisements show women posing with new kinds of luggage, from shoe boxes to collapsible travel beds, or a voyageuse at her travelling desk, with a portable writing table and library.

Women pioneers demonstrated that women now could travel on their own, with the help of the new infrastructure of local guides and Thomas Cook representatives. One of those pioneers was the journalist Nellie Bly, who embarked on a trip around the world to beat the 80 days of Phileas Fogg in 1889. Like the hero, she decided to travel light, with one bag. "Packing that bag was the most difficult undertaking of my life; there was so much to go into such little space", she wrote,

> One never knows the capacity of an ordinary hand-satchel until dire necessity compels the exercise of all one's ingenuity to reduce every thing to the smallest possible compass. In mine I was able to pack two travelling caps, three veils, a pair of slippers, a complete outfit of toilet articles, ink-stand, pens, pencils, and copy-paper, pins, needles and thread, a dressing gown, a tennis blazer, a small flask and a drinking cup, several complete changes of underwear, a liberal supply of handkerchiefs and fresh ruchings and most bulky and uncompromising of all, a jar of cold cream to keep my face from chapping in the varied climates I should encounter.
>
> *(Bly 1889: 1)*

Bly's account is an early example of a now firmly established tradition repeated again and again in travel advice. "Travel light and pack smarter – it gives a wonderful feeling of freedom", writes a travel journalist in a Swedish newspaper in 2010. "Shrink your world, khaki-green for clothes are perfect, stains will not show. Combine day and night face cream, don't forget a roll of duct tape for repairs" (*Dagens Nyheter*, December 14, 2010, p. 45).

"Travelling light" became a motto already in the early twentieth century, even for the wealthy. The market started to produce miniature and lightweight travel items. The 'overnight bag' gained ground.

★ ★ ★

As the social base of international tourism slowly was broadened after the Second World War, the advice industry was intensified. A Swedish guide, *How to Travel in Europe* (Strömberg 1951: 49 ff.), was aimed at new middle-class groups ready to take the brave step of going abroad. At last the continent was open for leisure travel again. The backside blurb promises that the book will give the reader "a powerful travel fever!" Reading the long introduction of travel preparation is a bit nerve-racking, so much to think about.

Suitcases shouldn't be more than you can carry yourself and not look too fancy, because this will make hotel porters 'more hungry for tips', the author states. He preaches the need for travelling light, but goes on to suggest lists of necessary items that cover several pages, from a miniature iron and a silk robe for walking to the bathroom in the hotel corridor to an extensive medicine chest. Reading the long list of medicines and remedies (always bring extra toilet paper, it is a scarce commodity abroad), the reader might have second thoughts about daring to leave home. This anxiety is not lessened by the detailed chapter on customs problems and border passages, where the author starts by stating "thoughts about the customs make travellers terrified" and then produces impressive lists of customs duties and currency regulations in Europe. "How many gramophone records or how much coffee is one allowed to bring across the border? Don't forget that art works are taxed according to the weight of the frame" (Strömberg 1951). To be a tourist abroad is to be exposed to complicated regulations, a lot of paperwork and the whims of local officials. Here we are light-years away from the informal world of Lonely Planet travel guides.

Moving bodies, roving minds

The history of luggage gives insights into the changing ideas of what's needed for a perfect holiday, the musts and necessities of travel, but also the ways in which there has been a constant development of travel paraphernalia. The portable, the collapsible, the scaled-down and lightweight have been in focus for innovation and design, producing the watercolour box, the folding map, the handy guide book, the transistor radio, the pocket camera, the picnic set, the practical leisure wear.

In understanding the making of holiday experiences we need to explore how modes of transport and travel props, but also holiday media interact. Holiday moves are strongly mediated, images and texts go back and forth between home and abroad, now and then, adding new dimensions to tourist movements. What does it mean to see the world from a train window or through a camcorder, choosing a picture postcard to send home in 1910 or posting holiday snapshots on Facebook a century later? Performing in front of cameras or other tourists, clowning in a holiday video or posing as a family on the hotel balcony became a part of holiday moves.

Moving limbs and roving minds interact, as for example in the highly developed tourist skill of daydreaming, an activity where again we can see how the mental and material come together (see the discussion in Ehn and Löfgren 2010: 123 ff.).

In the history of tourist locomotion it is possible to see how new technologies of transportation reorganize earlier ones. The railway created a longing for walking, and the collectivity of the train journey made the automobile a symbol of the return of individual adventure and exploration, a much more sensual travel mode in which the speed was felt as the wind against the face and the vibrations of the surface. Some forms of transport are then trivialized into transit experiences: you can't wait to get out of the plane or the car to start travelling. Old transport technologies are rejuvenated as the new ones turn into routine or monotony. Increased travel comfort can also be experienced as pampering or sheltering. The wanderer descends from the train with boots and backpack ready to start the real holiday journey; the car driver unhinges the mountain bike out in the country to begin the adventure.

Technologies and trends come and go but it is the different ways in which they are put to work that are important here. Holiday-making means acquiring special tourist skills, routines and reflexes. Some of these skills have a very long history and a marked conservatism, like sightseeing, while others may be here today and forgotten tomorrow. To catch these processes of learning and unlearning holiday movements, a historical perspective and a generational comparison is helpful. Today many tourist skills have been naturalized into invisibility; once, they were challenging novelties one had to learn to master.

Bibliography

Bailey, P. (1978) *Leisure and Class in Victorian England: Rational Recreation and the Contest for Control.* London: Routledge and Kegan Paul.

Bly, N. (1889) *Around the World in Seventy-Two Days.* New York: The Pictorial Weeklies Company.

Bruno, G. (2002) *Atlas of Emotion. Journeys in Art, Architecture, and Film.* London: Verso.

Ehn, B. and Löfgren, O. (2010) *The Secret World of Doing Nothing.* Berkeley: University of California Press.

Furlough, E. (1998) 'Making Mass Vacations: Tourism and Consumer Culture in France, 1930–1970s'. *Comparative Studies in Society and History*, 40(2): 247–286.

Germann Molz, J. and Gibson, S. (eds) (2007) *Mobilizing Hospitality: The Ethics of Social Relations in a Mobile World.* Aldershot: Ashgate.

Jerome, J. K. ([1889] 1957) *Three Men in a Boat.* London: Everyman's Library.

Löfgren, O. (1999) 'Crossing Borders: The Nationalization of Anxiety'. *Ethnologia Scandinavica*, 29: 127.

Löfgren, O. (2000) *On Holiday: A History of Vacationing.* Berkeley: University of California Press.

Löfgren, O. (2008) 'Motion and Emotion. Learning to be a Railway Traveller'. *Mobilities*, 3(3): 389–409.

Lynd, R. S. and Lynd, H. M. (1929) *Middletown: A Study in American Culture.* New York: Harcourt, Brace.

Parsloe, J. (1878) *Our Railways.* London: Kegan Paul.

Pasols, P.-G. (2005) *Louis Vuitton: The Birth of Modern Luxury.* New York: HNA Books.

Solnit, R. (2001) *Wanderlust: A History of Walking.* London: Verso.

Strömberg, C. A. (1951) *Hur man reser i Europa.* Stockholm: Strömbergs förlag.

Verne, J. (1873) *Around the World in Eighty Days.* Available online at *www.online-literature.com/verne/aroundtheworld* (accessed 2 October 2002).

Vidler, A. (2001) *Warped Space: Art, Architecture, and Anxiety in Modern Culture.* Cambridge, MA: MIT Press.

Virilio, P. (1986) 'The Overexposed City'. In Michel F., Naddoff, R. and Tazi, R. (eds) *Zone: Fragments of a History of the Human Body*, pp.15–31.

Williams, R. (1980) *Marxism and Literature.* Oxford: Oxford University Press.

Zukowsky, J. (ed.) (1996) *Building for Air Travel: Architecture and Design for Commercial Aviation.* Chicago: The Art Institute of Chicago.

43

The Commute

Rachel Aldred

All change: birth of the commute

The word 'commute' is said to come from the 'commuting' of fares paid by nineteenth-century Americans regularly travelling to work by train (OED 2012). The commute to work as a mass phenomenon is tied to the separation of home and work, characteristic of the shift from feudalism to capitalism, and specifically to the later rise of mass transit enabling the large-scale greater separation of the two. Hence the commute should be seen in the context of structural changes in the organisation of production, as well as structural changes in gendered relations to spaces of paid and unpaid work inside and outside the home. This relates not just to the movement of people but of things, the railways initially being developed for freight purposes (Wolmar 2007). Rail freight enabled factories to be located further away from raw materials (such as coal and limestone, often found inconveniently far from existing population centres). Being able to move raw materials (and finished goods) longer distances gave employers more flexibility in locating factories and reduced the need to provide new housing for workers.

As rail became more widely used for passenger transport, employers' locational flexibility increased: people could travel further to work, and workplaces became less closely tied to the location of labour as well as materials. The development of transport technologies and systems in the context of capitalist expansion and competition forms the basis for the 'time-space compression' (Harvey 1990) which transformed existing spatial and social orders. There have been various waves of this compression, with impacts varying by region, nation, and social group. The first, in the nineteenth century, generated patterns of development that were then built on in subsequent waves. The railways inaugurated a new age that set transport costs on a long-term downwards course, generating centralised 'economies of production' at greater and greater spatial scales (Faith 1990).

As production became dependent on mass transit, there was debate then, as now, about the cost of the commute. Much of the British public transport industry was in the hands of private companies, whose guiding aim was profit, rather than supporting the development of other sectors by providing affordable travel. Following Parliamentary debate the Cheap Trains Act, 1883, required railway companies serving cities 'to provide proper and sufficient workmen's trains at such fares and at such times between six p.m. and eight a.m. as may appear to the Board of Trade to be reasonable' (Roberts undated: 9; UK Parliament 1883). As the nineteenth century drew to a close, public transport came under renewed state scrutiny, again focusing on the commute and the need to provide for the rising numbers of middle- and working-class commuters. Increasing regulation resulted in the creation by the twentieth century of private transport oligopolies, overseen by the British state (Wolmar 2007).

Around the turn of the century, in addition to the omnibus and the bicycle, discussed further below, overground rail networks were transforming travel to work in many cities. But in the UK capital major rail stations were located at the edge of the city (for reasons related to class, competition and property ownership), leaving gaps between entry to the capital and workplace locations. London's tram network remained under-developed and from 1863 it was instead the Tube (underground) that, alongside buses, tended to fill this gap. The Tube commute became a symbol of London, immortalised in Anthony Asquith's 1928 film *Underground*. At first, the new underground lines were greeted with mixtures of horror, fear and excitement. Cartoons portrayed the 'hellish' nature of the new system, with steam power, crowded trains and platforms, and (later in the nineteenth century) passenger smoking combining to give a sense of an underworld. When the Circle line opened in 1884, *The Times* commented: 'A journey from King's Cross to Baker Street is a form of mild torture which no person would undergo if he could conveniently help it' (quoted in LT Museum undated). Another journalist compared his Circle line trip to the inhalation of gas before having a tooth drawn.

While the underground nature of the system was particularly disconcerting, overground railways had earlier in the nineteenth century generated similar unease. While the workings of horse and foot power were transparent, the 'iron horse' was different. For its movement, it relied upon a power source stored in fossil fuel form, rather than upon direct and visible physical activity. The railway seemed to deny previously existing and apparently 'natural' limits to land movement, and so to challenge the received social order of things. In this it represented the irresistible force of the industrial world (Hobsbawm 1975). Across the globe, the railways were recognised as generating social and spatial transformation, challenging old divisions and producing new ones, with particular national and regional characteristics. Part of this challenge was the restructuring of relationships between home and work, a restructuring that has continued since.

The second wave: changes in twentieth-century commuting

In the UK, the spatial relationship between home and work was transformed again over the twentieth century, albeit unevenly. In the first half of the century, many people outside large cities continued to walk to work. A large study using oral history found that '[f]rom 1890s to the 1930s walking to work was the most common experience' (Pooley and Turnbull 2000: 14). Pooley and Turnbull's evidence suggests that in the early twentieth century distances to work remained relatively short in towns with less than 100,000 people. There, in the twenty-year period before World War Two around two-thirds of people walked or, increasingly, cycled to work. This contrasts with London, where (currently low) cycling rates are as high as they ever were. In 1900, most Londoners already used public transport (power sources were various, including electricity, horse, and diesel/petrol), indicating substantial separation between homes and workplaces. But outside London many people were still walking, and to a lesser extent cycling to work (in 1900 bicycles were relatively expensive).

Between 1930 and 1939 the number of licensed cars and other light goods vehicles in the UK doubled from one to two million, representing the spread of car ownership into the middle classes – although car ownership then declined slightly during the war years. Pooley and Turnbull (2000) report that in the 1930s and 40s car owners were often still willing to travel to work by public transport. Cars were still a luxury item owned by a small minority, rather than necessarily being seen as an everyday mode of transport, particularly as public transport was then both widespread and widely used. However, by the 1960s and 70s things had changed and male car owners, at least, had become much more attached to using their cars to commute. This represents a dramatic attitudinal shift away from the car as one means of transport (for the privileged, in some contexts) among many, to the car perceived as *the* solution for everyday travel.

In the US this shift happened early, with mass motorisation taking place before World War Two, with the result that by 1960 70 per cent of commuters were driving to work (Department of Transportation, United States 2011). In other countries this happened later and less decisively. In the UK it was only after World War Two that the proportion of journeys to work by private car topped 10 per cent; and even by 1960 most British people were still travelling to work by public transport or non-motorised modes. Yet like other European countries Britain followed the US in terms of commuting trends while not (as yet) catching it. Similarly, men led the trend towards car-based commuting, with women following, although differences remain. Pooley and Turnbull (2000: 22) comment that in Britain women were twenty years behind men 'in adopting motor vehicles as their principal means of commuting'. This is, they argue, partly due to cost and access issues, but also 'deeper attitudinal differences between men and women with respect to driving'. However, they found that in the 1980s women's attitudes to driving had become closer to men's.

Transport Statistics Great Britain (DfT 2011) confirms a substantial shift in women's access to cars over this period. In 1975/76 51 per cent of all men classified themselves as a 'main driver', but only 13 per cent of women did. By 2010, the figure for men had risen slightly to 62 per cent, but had dramatically increased to 50 per cent of women. As Pooley and Turnbull (2000) point out, the transformation of women's employment over the twentieth century has helped to drive this shift. Women's employment rates have converged with men's, and women have increasingly aspired to independent use of a car, especially as women's trips are often more complex than men's due to domestic and family responsibilities. Clearly, the availability of other alternatives (primarily public transport) plays a role: across Britain in 2009/10, 32 per cent of households had two or more cars or vans, but this falls to 16 per cent in London, where the public transport system is comprehensive and relatively reliable (and where commuting is dominated by public transport – see below). In rural areas, many of which have now become commuter villages with little public transport, more than half of all households own two or more cars or vans (DfT 2011).

Commuting today: regularity and variation

Viewed in terms of number of trips, commutes to work only account for a small minority of total journeys undertaken in the UK, and this figure has steadily decreased. In 2009, commuting accounted for 15 per cent of all trips, and business trips accounted for 3 per cent of trips. These trips account for 19 per cent and 8 per cent of total distance travelled (DfT 2011a) as they tend to be longer than other regularly undertaken trips (e.g. shopping, escort trips). The commute does possess a relative stability that supports its cultural importance. Around half of all people (more men than women) say that the commute also represents their most regular trip (Lyons and Chatterjee 2008), whereas (for example) trips for leisure and sociali-sation purposes may be more varied in terms of destination.

The UK Department for Transport (DfT 2011a) reports that since 1995/97, the number of commuting trips has fallen by 16 per cent to 147 (one-way) trips per person per year and the number of business trips by 22 per cent to 30. However, these figures are for all persons, not all employees – so include people not in employment. DfT (2005) reports the number of commuting trips per employee in 2002/03 as being 329 (i.e. 165 round trips), while the 'all persons' figure was 150. It is becoming increasingly common for employees to work flexibly to some extent, such as working one day a week from home. Lyons and Chatterjee (2008) cite a survey of 1014 full-time workers in Britain showing that only 62 per cent travelled to work on all weekdays in the survey reference week.

While commute distances have steadily increased over the twentieth century, commute time has remained more stable. The average commute time in the UK (as in the US) is under half an hour, as are the majority of commutes: analysing *Social Trends* data, ONS (2011) found that 75 per cent of workers in October to December 2009 took half an hour or less to travel from home to work. (However, these figures may disproportionately exclude some groups, such as undocumented immigrants, who are likely to have longer commutes.) The official statistics contain a small minority for whom time spent is much longer: 5 per cent of workers spend over an hour travelling from home to work. Given the importance of London as an employment centre within the UK economy, alongside its high house prices, many of those people will live in the London commuter belt and travel in by rail and Underground, or by a mixture of car and public transport. While the one-hour-plus commuters may be extreme outliers, even for those with an average commute time spent travelling to and from work adds up to nearly 200 hours a year (TUC 2011), equivalent to approximately five weeks' work if taken in a block.

There is a clear divide in the UK between London and non-London commutes; outside London, under 10 per cent of workers use any form of public transport to get to work, while inside London public transport is dominant. However, all regions are dominated by public or private motorised transport. Before mass transit (and before the bicycle became popular and affordable), the limits imposed by walking had helped to limit the spatial separation of home and work. Walking substantial distances for utility purposes then was more socially accept-able than it is now, but even so, most workers could not have been expected to travel the current average trip length of 8.6 miles to and from work by foot (a round trip if walking of over five hours). However, once longer distances became possible, and especially with more automobile commuting, workers could be expected to get to work whatever the distance.

Table 43.1 Trips and distance travelled by journey purpose, Britain

Trip purpose	% of trips	% of distance
Other escort/personal business	20%	14%
Shopping	20%	12%
Visiting friends	16%	20%
Other leisure	15%	22%
Commuting	15%	19%
Education (inc. escort)	11%	4%
Business	3%	8%

Source: DfT 2011 Personal Travel Factsheet.

In other words, worker mobility has become not just enabled but expected (expressed in contractual terms such as 'you may be expected to work at other sites' and through job advertisements stating 'essential driver' or 'essential car owner'). Getting employees to work has become a problem for the worker rather than the employer, with a concomitant cost burden. In the US, households spend 16 per cent of their annual expenditure on transport – that's approximately $148 per household per week (Bureau of Labor Statistics 2011). In Europe, the percentage is slightly lower: in 2008 the EU-27 average was 13.4 per cent and the EU-15 average was 13.5 per cent (European Commission 2010). The UK DfT reported that in 2010 households spent 13.7 per cent of their income on transport – £77.10 per week (DfT 2011).

The political importance of the commute is bolstered by its visibility in statistical releases. Commuting is relatively easy to measure, while mode split (proportion of overall journeys by mode) is less well recorded. For example, the UK Census of population records 'main mode of travel to work' but does not seek information about other journeys. The 'main mode' (by distance) under-records cycling and walking components of commutes, and in terms of transport statistics more generally, cycling and walking remain particularly badly measured. Comparable national European statistics for all journeys exist for motorised modes only: with respect to distance travelled by passenger land transport in 2008, the EU-27 average showed cars with an 83.3 per cent share, buses with 9.4 per cent, and railways, trams and metros with 7.3 per cent (Eurostat 2011). Only in Slovakia, Hungary and Turkey was the share held by the private car under 75 per cent.

As a regular activity, with often relatively fixed origin and destination (although often attached to other trips and not undertaken every single work day) the commute does however offer substantial scope for diversity of mode within a broadly motor-dominated system. Within Europe, cities have very different commuting patterns, despite often similar levels of car ownership and use for journeys considered more broadly. A survey in 75 European cities (Eurobarometer 2009) found vastly different levels of car commuting: from 13 per cent (Paris, France) to 91 per cent (Lefkosia, Cyprus). Cycling levels among the surveyed citizens varied from 60 per cent in Copenhagen (Denmark) and Groningen (The Netherlands) to zero in Lefkosia, Sofia and Burgas (Bulgaria), Valletta (Malta), Barcelona and Oviedo (Spain), Irakleio (Greece), Istanbul, Ankara and Diyarbakir (Turkey), and Braga (Portugal), with much variety in between.

What the commuting figures demonstrate is the extent to which the journey from home to work can be decoupled from an overall reliance on the private car. Substantial differences also exist within countries. England has a high level of car dependence, but London is very different both for commuting and transport more generally, having seen both an overall dominance of public transport and, within private modes, a gradual fifteen-year shift away from the private car towards the bicycle (Transport for London 2011). Also striking in London is the importance of the bicycle within the city's inner boroughs: while the bicycle mode share is stuck at around 2 per cent for all trips in Greater London, 8.3 per cent of Inner London residents cycle to work. This has increased the political visibility of cycling, which draws strength from understandings of the commute as an important journey as well as the take-up of cycling by professional employees and City workers.

Rationalising the commute: from time wasted to productive time?

The broader definition of the commute as a political issue continues to be shaped by class and income. Higher-income employees have longer commutes, an ONS analysis of the 2001 Census finding that '[m]anagers have much longer average commuting distances than elementary workers' (Office for National Statistics 2008: 1). In 2005, people living in households in the highest income quintile in Britain travelled more than twice as far to work as people in households in the lowest income quintile (ONS 2008: 2). With the rise of sophisticated statistics on commuting, concern has grown among policy-makers that expensive people are wasting large amounts of their valuable time commuting. The imputed cost of congestion (calculated from time spent stuck in traffic multiplied by the 'value' of the travellers' time) assumes time spent travelling is 'lost' to the economy and that time is converted into money by individuals making decisions over how and where to travel.

In accordance with this, traffic models used by policy-makers seek to minimise the amount of time that commuters spend travelling (at least those travelling by motor vehicle – bicycle travellers are poorly included in many such models, particularly in low-er-cycling countries where cycling has historically been associated with poverty and hence had low political importance). The UK Department for Transport's Transport Analysis Guidance (WebTAG) gives details as to how to calculate the value of time for different transport users. For working time, the figures are derived from average wages paid to users of different modes of transport. (Cycling advocates have complained that the figures are based on out-of-date statistics that do not reflect the uptake of cycling by middle-class commuters.)

For commuting and other 'non-work' time, the 'market prices' of £6.46 per hour for commuting (2010 prices and values) and £5.71 per hour for other time are derived from calculations of people's willingness to pay to avoid travel time. In other words, because 'productive time' is rewarded by wages it is prioritised over 'free' time spent by employees, commuting or not. These figures are used within transport modelling to calculate 'costs' and 'benefits' of transport schemes. Transport campaigners have criticised how these models deliver high 'benefits' by summing very small travel time reductions for a very large number of travellers (Monbiot 2011). Moreover, in WebTAG reduced fuel consumption is still included in modelling as a negative feature because of the reduced tax take, although it is now described as a 'benefit reduction' rather than a cost increase. The inclusion of reliability remains at an early stage, although 'the majority of studies find that travel time variability is valued more highly than travel time itself' (Batley et al. 2008: 84). When modelling commute decisions, people are assumed to make 'rational' choices, minimising 'generalised' costs of travel, principally with reference to costed time savings and to monetary cost. They are

Table 43.2 Values of working time per person, 2010 prices and values

Vehicle occupant	Market price (£)
Taxi/Minicab passenger	57.06
Rail passenger	47.18
Underground passenger	45.90
Walker	37.83
Car driver	33.74
Bus passenger	25.81
Cyclist	21.70

Source: DfT 2012.

not assumed to take time benefits as distance – for example, moving further away from work because the commute is quicker – although the history of 'the commute' tells us this is what has happened on a societal scale.

In the UK, assumptions about the value of travel time have contributed to the approval of HS2, the multi-billion-pound project to speed up rail travel between Birmingham and London. Long-distance rail travellers tend to be relatively affluent, therefore the time they could save travelling on work business is prioritised, the assumption being that time they spend in the office is highly valuable but the time they spend on a train is value-less. Yet this is undermined by a shift towards conceptualising the commuter (and the business traveller) as productive, supported by recent research (Lyons and Chatterjee 2008). Business travellers often occupy peak-time First Class compartments, but rather than 'doing nothing' they are frequently making business calls, using laptops and reviewing documents. Their time on trains may well be spent 'creating value' for their employers, and this is one reason why they might choose the train over car travel. However, Laurier's (2004) research found car travellers also spending time working, for example making business calls while stuck in traffic jams.

Other research has uncovered the wide array of non-work activities that people participate in while travelling: such as watching a film, socialising with friends, reading a book, or listening to music. Increasingly networked public transport users may now not socially interact with those in their immediate vicinity, but rather with friends, family and followers via Twitter, Facebook and other applications. Even rail travellers gazing out of the window or snoozing may feel that their time is well spent (Lyons and Chatterjee 2008). This is because travel can provide emotional (as well as mental and physical) benefits. My research has found multiple emotional benefits to cycling, including the creation of personal space apart from often busy and stressful work and home lives. While the assumption embedded in traditional transport modelling is that the ideal commute would be zero, commutes may be perceived to be too short as well as too long.

These new approaches have led to calls to value time spent travelling. Valuing travel time could provide additional reasons for relieving public transport overcrowding (and might mitigate the pressure to reduce congestion). However, Lyons and Chatterjee (2008) point out that valuing travel time positively might lead to encouraging longer commutes, which might not be beneficial for environmental reasons. More fundamentally, the assumptions that would remain embodied in transport modelling and calculations can be critiqued, as the extent to which people appreciate (or not) different types of commuting journeys will be shaped by cultural, political and infrastructural factors that may be subject to dramatic change on a societal level. The calculation of individual preferences can also be seen as a strategy of governance; (imputed and/or predicted) individual choices apparently guide decisions, rather than political priorities.

Unsustainable and future commutes

I want to end by reflecting on the commute in the context of unsustainable transportation (Banister 2008). A growing focus on the commute as environmentally damaging has been given impetus by climate change, yet 'local' issues of air pollution and traffic danger often seem more immediately relevant to people living in the vicinity of heavy motor traffic. Taking sustainability seriously requires being critical of technical fixes, recognising the importance of related and deeply embedded social practices, and paying attention to how change might impact on inequalities. In societies where most workers commute, the commute helps to structure everyday lives, with other decisions made in tandem with commuting choices. Commutes are often predominantly individualised, in terms of people travelling alone by car. However, the commute remains communal in that this 'personal timetable' (Urry 2008) is still to a large extent publicly shared – hence 'rush hours' based around work and school commutes when traffic comes to a standstill.

Often, organisational or technological trends are seen as heralding an answer to the 'unsustainable commute'. However, such trends may be incorporated into problematic systems of practice and/or aggravate them. One example might be the increase in occasional teleworking, which might actually support the continued lengthening of commute journeys, through making such journeys more bearable if they are only undertaken three or four days per week. Shorter and more diverse working weeks may be an attractive solution to a range of policy problems (NEF 2011), yet if commutes become less regularised this may make it harder to create the varied and less car-based solutions seen currently, which depend on a certain regularity. And while public transport can be seen as a 'green' alternative to the car, this depends on the type of public transport and the role it plays within systems of production and consumption. Long-distance high-speed rail commutes are not necessarily sustainable even though they are more energy-efficient per passenger kilometre than those by car.

Full-time home working – another mooted solution to the commute problem – has disadvantages including the lack of contact with others, the loss of demarcation between home and work, health and safety issues, and potentially increased physical inactivity. One possible alternative might be the use of remote office centres to allow desk-based employees to work relatively locally in office environments. Such arrangements are diverse and currently poorly monitored: some call centres might be an example of this, but are not necessarily counted as remote offices, while on the more 'informal' end people may use café wi-fi as an alternative to working from home, yet be recorded as 'home' workers.

As work patterns continue to change, so will relationships between 'work' and 'home' – already complicated by school, educational, and shopping trips. The potentially greater use of home- and remote-working could transform and/or deepen divides between different groups of employees. For those whose presence is necessary at the workplace (e.g. for cleaning, catering, caring and manufacturing jobs), the commute will remain compulsory. Potentially there could be a turnaround where more elite groups increasingly E-work and so do less commuting, but where commuting becomes a burden placed on working-class employees whose physical presence is required. This could be further complicated by disparities in house prices preventing lower-income workers from moving nearer employment centres in some locations.

Because commutes are complex and also involve travelling to non-work locations, changes in shopping and educational provision will shape the future journey to work. If distance learning becomes more popular, this will shape educational and related commutes; online shopping may change people's travel needs on journeys to work (through reducing the need to carry goods). Policy related to school provision and 'school choice' will affect how parents are able to plan their work journeys. The resultant changes in commuting patterns will then themselves shape the way that people view their home and work lives. In a world where oil dependency is still increasing, yet is ever more unsustainable, will the ability to commute, or the ability not to commute, become seen as a luxury? If systems of production are forced into greater localisation, will this be accompanied by increased or decreased inequality (Dennis and Urry 2009)? The 'commute problem' will not be solved by a technical fix to the existing system, if at all.

Bibliography

Banister, D. (2008) 'The Sustainable Mobility Paradigm'. *Transport Policy*, 15: 73–80

Batley, R., Grant-Muller, S., Nellthorp, J., de Jong, G. and Watling, D. (2008) *Multimodal Travel Time Variability: Final Report to the Department for Transport*. Leeds: Institute for Transport Studies.

Bureau of Labor Statistics, US (2011) 'Focus on Prices and Spending: Consumer Expenditure Survey 2010'. Available online at www.bls.gov/opub/focus/volume2_number12/cex_2_12.htm, accessed 9/2/2012.

Dennis, K. and Urry, J. (2009) *After the Car*. Cambridge: Polity Press.

Department for Tourism (2012) 'TAG UNIT 3.5.6 Values of Time and Vehicle Operating Costs'. Pdf file. Available online at www.dft.gov.uk/webtag/documents/expert/pdf/u3_5_6-vot-op-cost-120723.pdf, accessed 28/5/13.

Department for Transport, UK (2005) *Focus on Personal Travel*. London: DfT.

Department for Transport, UK (2011) 'Transport Statistics Great Britain 2011'. Web document. Available online at www.dft.gov.uk/statistics/series/transport-statistics-great-britain/, accessed 9/2/2012.

Department for Transport, UK (2011a) 'Personal Travel Factsheet: Commuting and Business Travel'. Pdf file. Available online at http://assets.dft.gov.uk/statistics/series/national-travel-survey/commuting.pdf, accessed 9/2/2012.

Department of Transportation, United States (2011) 'Journey to Work: National Summary'. Available online at www.fhwa.dot.gov/planning/census_issues/ctpp/data_products/journey_to_work/jtw1.cfm, accessed 9/2/2012.

Eurobarometer (2009) 'Perception survey on quality of life in European cities'. Pdf file. Available online at http://ec.europa.eu/public_opinion/flash/fl_277_en.pdf, accessed 9/2/2012.

European Commission (2010) 'Energy and Transport in Figures Part 3: Transport'. Pdf file. Available online at http://ec.europa.eu/transport/publications/statistics/doc/pb2010_3_transport.pdf, accessed 9/2/2012.

Eurostat (2011) 'Passenger Transport Statistics'. Available online at http://epp.eurostat.ec.europa.eu/statistics_explained/index.php/Passenger_transport_statistics#Source_data_for_tables_and_figures_.28MS_Excel.29, accessed 9/2/2012.

Faith, N. (1990) *The World the Railways Made*. London: Pimlico Press.

Harvey, D. (1990) *The Condition of Postmodernity*. Oxford: Blackwell.

Hobsbawm, E. (1975) *The Age of Capital*. London: Abacus.

Laurier, E. (2004) 'Doing Office Work on the Motorway'. *Theory, Culture & Society*, 21: 261–277.

London Transport Museum (undated) 'Object: Metropolitan Railway A class 4-4-0T steam locomotive No. 23, 1866'. Available online at www.ltmcollection.org/museum/object/link.html?_IXMAXHITS_=1&IXinv=1981/535&IXexpand=journeys, accessed 9/2/2012.

Lyons, G. and Chatterjee, K. (2008) 'A Human Perspective on the Daily Commute: Costs, Benefits and Trade-offs'. *Transport Reviews*, 28(2): 181–198.

Monbiot, G. (2011) 'An Answer to the Meaning of Life'. Available online at www.monbiot.com/2011/06/06/an-answer-to-the-meaning-of-life/, accessed 9/2/2012.

New Economics Foundation (2011) *21 Hours: Why a Shorter Working Week Can Help us All to Flourish in the 21st Century*. London: NEF.

Office for National Statistics, UK (2008) 'Commuting Patterns as at the 2001 Census, and their Relationship with Modes of Transport and Types of Occupation'. Pdf file. Available online at www.neighbourhood.statistics.gov.uk/HTMLDocs/images/Commuting%20by%20Occupation%20and%20Transport%20-%20Final%20for%20pdf_tcm97-70153.pdf, accessed 9/2/2012.

Office for National Statistics, UK (2011) 'Three Out of Four People Work within 30 Minutes of Home'. Pdf document. Available online at www.ons.gov.uk/ons/rel/social-trends-rd/social-trends/social-trends-41/index.html?format=print, accessed 9/2/2012.

Oxford English Dictionary (2012) 'Definition for Commute'. Available online at http://oxforddictionaries.com/definition/commute, accessed 9/2/2012.

Pooley, C. and Turnbull, J. (2000) 'Modal Choice and Modal Change: The Journey to Work in Britain since 1890'. *Journal of Transport Geography*, 8: 11–24.

Roberts, M. (undated) 'Congestion and Spatially Connective Infrastructure: The Case of London in the 19th and Early 20th Century. Pdf file. Available online at www.landecon.cam.ac.uk/staff/publications/mroberts/Spatial_Connectivity-Historical_London.pdf, accessed 9/2/2012.

Trades Union Congress, UK (2011) 'Commute Times Add up to Five Extra Weeks Work a Year'. Available online at www.tuc.org.uk/workplace/tuc-20275-f0.cfm, accessed 9/2/2012.

Transport for London (2011) 'Travel in London Report 4'. Available online at www.tfl.gov.uk/assets/downloads/corporate/travel-in-london-report-4.pdf, accessed 9/2/2012.

UK Parliament (1883) 'The Cheap Trains Act 1883'. Pdf file. Available online at www.railwaysarchive.co.uk/documents/HMG_ActCheap1883.pdf, accessed 9/2/2012.

Urry, J. (2008) *Mobilities*. Cambridge: Polity Press.

Wolmar, C. (2007) *Fire and Steam: A New History of the Railways*. London: Atlantic.

44

Congestion

Melissa Butcher

The city has become a productive space to explore the impact of human mobility, and its juxtaposition, congestion. It is a site where interaction is unavoidable, generating both conflict and conviviality, as transnational and local flows of people, technology, capital and media become imbricated, adding to the city's complexity and physical and affective sense of congestion. On a daily basis infrastructure and forms of transport must be negotiated, along with crowds that roil through streets and transit stations, dispersing into suburbia, estates, slums, terraces and the condominiums of gentrifying neighbourhoods. Residents, deploying competencies acquired over time, go with the flow, step to the side to avoid collision, or watch for breaks in the traffic and interstitial breathing spaces. These negotiations are inflected by personal dispositions of, as Bauman (2007) puts it, mixophilia and mixophobia: the love of the city and all its crowds, and its inverse proposition, the fear of the city with all its strangers.

The experience of the congested city is then above all else, as this essay will argue, an affective process, expressing embodied experience, for example, excitement and/or discomfort, of things too close and too unpredictable, as we slide between the human and non-human. To alleviate these sensations, governments target infrastructural transformation, such as traffic plans and housing redevelopments. But local authorities also deploy diversity programmes and social cohesion narratives centred on multi-culturalism to manage, to 'decongest', our entangled lives.

It will be argued here that managing diversity is the key thrust of policies that ostensibly target congestion, as the result of affective responses to the close proximity of difference and what it represents, namely, unpredictability. These infrastructural and intercultural capacities can enable the navigation of diverse, crowded urban space, but are developed and deployed within extant frameworks of pre-existing power relationships that can also shift the burden of congestion onto others. These responses to congestion, both material and cultural, will be the focus of this essay, which begins with an overview of the relationship between congestion and mobility in urbanisation, then highlights the affective dimension of this process and how cities have responded.

It has become axiomatic to refer to the increasing urbanisation of social life, with much of the population shift occurring in the global South. As countries such as India and China deregulate, their cities become the drivers of economic growth, pulling internal and transnational immigrants towards them in their wake. By the middle of this century, it is estimated that 5.3 billion people in the developing world will reside in urban centres; over 60 per cent will be in Asia and nearly a quarter of the world's urban population will be in Africa (UN Habitat 2008). This movement is a response not only related to the opportunities provided by new economic activities, but also to the impossibility of continuing to survive in old ones.

The North has shared similar dynamics in its own path to urbanisation, but a new hierarchy of 'world cities' marks out centres such as London and New York as the archetypal global hubs. These cities attract mobile transnational capital, human resources and technology, as well as directing these flows, with a concomitant concentration of political and economic power (see for example Knox 2002). Behind this evolution is the reality that urban centres have a capacity to lower transaction costs, acting as critical engines of economic development, industrialisation, and the dynamic concentration of people. Almost one-third of urban growth in the global North is accounted for by immigration (UN Habitat 2008).

However, cities can strain and buckle under a haphazard pattern of expansion and the need to modernise. This pressure is driven not only by the demand for infrastructure to manage congestion but also by the demand to be incorporated into the contemporary discourse of 'world city', with its associated gains in terms of economic investment and global flows. For example, housing provision has lagged behind demand in many urban centres, leading to a lack of affordable homes, squatter settlements, and homelessness even in global cities of the North. Security of tenure is an issue for the urban poor – for example, in Delhi's redevelopment in the 2000s, some 150,000 were evicted as 'illegal' settlements were demolished (Dupont 2008). In Beijing, an estimated 300,000 lost their homes in preparation for the 2008 Olympic Games (Broudehoux 2009). These are deliberate measures taken by local authorities to decongest urban space, which, as a consequence of the importance placed on mobility and room to move, increases in value.

One of the most visible signs of urban maladjustment is the traffic congestion that chokes city roads, from Bangkok to London. To this end, a key concern of city authorities is decongesting streets and public transport. Mass, rapid transport systems are appearing in the growing cities of the South, such as Bangkok's Skytrain (Richardson and Jensen 2008) and Delhi's Metro (Butcher 2011b). Cities such as London and New York are increasingly integrating 'alternative' means of mobility, such as cycling, as part of their mainstream traffic plans (Spinney 2009). But the outcomes of human–non-human interactions within these infrastructures indicate that it is not only faster or more spacious transport simply for the sake of instrumental mobility – for commuting, for example – that urban residents require. The 'good' city is one in which mobility is easy and comfortable, that is, in which movement takes into account interpersonal and psycho-social responses to the built environment and to diverse others who use these public forms of transport.

It is in this sense that congestion is above all else an affective experience within city spaces, which also contain a geography of emotions (see Kothari 2008; Wise 2005). Affective, embodied responses to smells, noises, crowds and the behaviour of others are implicated in how urban space is used and developed. The centrality of the corporeal experience in the formation and understanding of urban space is highlighted by Rose et al. (2010) and Latham and McCormack (2004), who suggest that the city assembles both buildings and bodies as much as it is built by the latter (see also Pile 2010; Anderson 2009; Amin 2008; Jiron 2008; Montserrat Degen 2008).

Take, for example, descriptions of mobility through Delhi, a city formed in movement, association, planning and belief of the local authorities in its potential for 'world class' status

(Brosius 2008). Mobility is marked by unpredictability, delays and blockages created by increasing congestion on the roads (Butcher 2011b). Bus routes suddenly change, diversions appear overnight as a result of construction, and delays are caused by VIPs crossing the city. Commuters at times travel backwards to go forwards (to avoid crowded Metro stations, for example). Mobility, or the lack of it, across Delhi engenders affective responses to the travails of congestion, including frustration and pleasure, nostalgia and fear.

The physicality of the city is documented in the 'pushing' and 'shoving' of encounters in its crowded space. Narrative descriptions of riding on buses include disgust as sweat and smell permeate the commute, and as passengers fall first one direction then another as corners are turned or brakes hit too hard. The overcrowded Metro at times leads to a sense of suffocation, but also pleasure in the potential for encounters with the new (foreign tourists, for example), or for the resurgence of good memories (travelling with a former boyfriend, for example). Frustration, on the other hand, is generated in interactions with other passengers and road users who do not behave 'properly', that is, do not follow communally defined and subjectively interpreted codes of civility (see for example Fyfe *et al.* 2006; Phillips and Smith 2006).

These affective responses to congestion in the city are rooted in cultural frames of reference, that is, an accumulation of knowledge that delineates who, what and how many is permissible in which space and when, and that engenders what is civil and uncivil behaviour. This knowledge is in turn bound to subjectivity, that is, to a sense of self and place in the order of urban life. This can be seen in the circumscribing of boundaries in the city based on a sense of place within an existing order, and the sense of discomfort generated when those boundaries are challenged. Subjective identity referents, aligned to ethnicity, class, gender, age, etc., supply the template from which affective reflexes are generated, and are the mechanisms by which judgements are made and boundaries are set. This 'template for civic and political behaviour', as Amin (2008: 5) describes it, is transposed onto the relationship between the human and non-human, such as the built environment and transport infrastructure, and is part of a cultural framework that forms the rules for navigating crowded, contested streets.

The very perception of congestion, of how many makes a crowd to begin with, and its management is based on this cultural knowledge of places and accessibility, permissibility and acceptability. Processes of management of congestion can, therefore, range from the instrumental (e.g. 'no cycling in the park') to affective responses that engender geographies of avoidance of those spaces that are marked out as uncomfortable or even dangerous. However, the two forms of boundary construction are entangled. Physical zones of exclusion such as gated communities and gentrification projects are designed to remove uncivil spaces of congestion that cause discomfort (see Anjaria 2009; Lees 2008). In these spaces, as Herbert (2008: 661) argues, 'freedom from fear rests, rather paradoxically, upon self-confinement'.

In this sense, the affective discomfort generated in the perception of congestion creates urban planning that enforces the contestation of space use. High-rise, low-income estates are pitted against terraces and manor homes. Local markets, in streets of left-over vegetable waste and cardboard boxes, are gentrified or out-manoeuvred by clean shopping malls that enable the easy flow of traffic within and without. Space becomes privatised, regulated and surveilled to contain or exclude congestion, 'while spaces for spontaneous play and interaction, for rubbing along with unknown others' diminish (Watson 2006: 156). Those that are perhaps excluded from such spaces generate their own affective boundaries. In a lower-income neighbourhood in London, the private space of home has become a place of 'negotiated exclusion' (Massey 2005), as long as an 'ethos of mixing' is adhered to in public space

(Wessendorf 2009). For young men in Clayton's (2011) Leicester study, there is a sense of 'nationalism of the neighbourhood', a demarcation of place to manage feelings of exclusion from other parts of the city.

Therefore, the transforming shape of the urban impacts on the trajectories of residents, their ability to be mobile, to interact or to avoid not only association, but also forms of conflict. If, as Watson (2006: 161) argues, streets are 'essential for the enactment of rituals which provide an opportunity for a society to narrate a story about itself', then the form of those streets, access to them, and just how crowded they are, impacts on that story as well (see Clayton 2011; Noussia and Lyons 2009; Pinder 2008; Valentine 2008 for their discussion on the intersection between the built environment and social interaction). Writers have suggested that conflict in congested cities that enforce intimacy is unavoidable, and indeed sometimes it is a necessity to transform social relations (see for example Harris 2010; Landau and Freemantle 2010). Increasing mobility within parts of a city adds to the instability of normative notions of community and to the sense of crowding and congestion. Boroughs in London, for example, are marked by the ebb and flow of transitory populations (Wills 2010) driven by social mobility, economic downturn, urban renewal and the search for a sense of home. Notions of belonging as familiarity and 'community', which underpin much of government and local authority programmes to manage diversity and the sense of congestion that comes with it, have been destabilised by the volatility of movement into and out of these spaces.

One school of thought argues that this perception of community breakdown, physically embedded in residential segregation, equals a decline in trust, exacerbating conflict (e.g. Uslaner 2010). Yet the city is also demarcated as a space of conviviality and cosmopolitanism (e.g. Glick–Schiller et al. 2011; Watson 2006). This complexity is demonstrated in research that highlights the potential for both resentment and co-operation in the same place (Karner and Parker 2011; Bloch and Dreher 2009). Congestion, it seems, in the sense of the close physical proximity of different ideas of space use inflected by accumulated cultural knowledge, has the potential to produce both openness and withdrawal from diversity (Datta 2009).

However, others have indicated that it is not difference per se that generates conflict but affective responses to the nature of crowds, of congestion itself, as humanity is squeezed together. Describing the experience of the city, Raban (1974: 117) argued that the source of the city's basic dynamic is not speed or consumption but that 'we live in constant and close proximity to strangers', which generates intimate, ambiguous, contradictory, often unavoidable contact. Anxieties are magnified by the perception of the other as a crowd, especially when judged an uncivil crowd because of its breaching of cultural frames of reference that establish boundaries of comfort. While the fear of the stranger stems from his/her ambiguity, fear of the crowd stems from its size and unpredictability. For London, Wessendorf (2009) gives the example of conflict over the use of the local park in a gentrifying part of the city, as young 'hipsters', predominantly white and middle-class, take over the space in the summer. Their numbers, and the perception of an unwillingness to engage beyond their own circle of familiarity, generated discomfort for others.

There is an undefined critical mass, a tipping point past which this affective discomfort is generated. The talk turns to 'invasion' and feeling 'crowded out' (Bloch and Dreher 2009). These anxieties linked to migration and subsequent change are repeated across countries and throughout history, as indicated by McKeown's (2008: 168) research into the establishment of migration control from the sixteenth century, in the face of assumed 'vast hordes of . . . people crowding in upon us' (see Crozier and Davies 2008, for a contemporary example in Britain). Affective anxiety, however, appears to be most correlated with crowds associated with dirt and noise, equated with disorder and class distinction that embodies the ambiguity and unpredictability of difference. Encounters are, therefore, inflected with unequal economic, material and social conditions, framed within an 'interaction order' (Noble 2011) that ensures congestion occurs in some areas and not others.

A third approach to the examination of the outcomes of engagement with congested spaces can stem from Canetti's (1960) view that there is nothing we fear more 'than the touch of the unknown', but that 'it is only in a crowd that man (sic) can become free of this fear of being touched'. Not just any crowd though, I would suggest. A crowd in which we lose our fear of being touched by the unknown is a crowd that is already dense with familiarity. This is a closed crowd – a crowd that sets its boundaries, and desires permanence at the expense of disorderly change. Familiarity repels the other no matter how densely packed. Perhaps then the tensions that infiltrate congestion are found in the dynamics of closed and open crowds, order and spontaneity, where congestion can lead to creative impulse and dissent. Their meeting can be fraught, as incursion into each other's territory is unwittingly made in congested space. The closed crowd may not even appear on the streets. Its adherents appear silent, invisible in cultural frameworks dominated by established social hierarchies (for example, men, capitalism, Englishness). Its boundaries are of course always contested (for example, by women, youth or other cultural frames of reference) and sometimes breached by the open crowd. But the open crowd's impermanent nature may not provide any lasting infrastructure on which to build equality and can also block a thoroughfare as easily as any gated community.

The essay finishes, therefore, by focusing on the means to navigate through this complex assemblage of human and non-human interactions in order to establish and maintain a sense of well-being in the midst of urban congestion. As noted above in the example of gated communities, material infrastructure is not always the best means to manage the paradox of simultaneous congestion and estrangement, and indeed, may exacerbate the anxieties generated in affective responses to congestion. New research on complexity is focusing on interior infrastructures – notions of personal resilience that comprise the capacity and competencies to manage the 'mental costs' of negotiating complex urban spaces (Valentine 2008; Yeoh and Willis 2005). Arguments have been made that urban populations develop a complex repertoire of skills, including an ability to negotiate complexity that renders 'the strange familiar . . . and the familiar strange' (Amin 2008: 9; see also Robins 2008; Massey 2005). These mechanisms for managing well-being in a crowded city can be referred to as competencies developed and deployed in order to manage diverse spaces, to negotiate the use of space and to establish place sharing protocols. They can be used to differing degrees, in different places and to manage affective responses to the unfamiliar and unexpected (see for example Butcher 2011a; Collins and Friesen 2011; Glick-Schiller *et al.* 2011; Noble 2011; Bloch and Dreher 2009; UNESCO 2009).

Outside the realm of the social sciences, international human resources management studies and cross-cultural psychology literature has detailed arguments for a set of specific competencies to manage mobility and interactions with difference (see for example van Woerkom and de Reuver 2009; Peltokorpi 2008; Chang and Tharenou 2004; Graf 2004). These include cognitive, behavioural and affective abilities such as flexibility, tolerance for ambiguity, patience, a willingness to engage with difference, problem-solving capacities and reflexiveness, managing emotions and stress, and the imaginative ability to empathise. These capacities are developed in interactions with others and are essential for discovering ways to flow through urban space that can have implications for conflict management and urban planning.

To co-exist in the congested city requires the capacity to make ourselves, and our responses to others, legible. However, these skills are not necessarily about forging links across difference. As noted above, at times negotiating encounters do not occur under equal or apparently very tolerant or cosmopolitan conditions. But using these 'practical logics', complex and changing spaces are negotiated every day by 'finding points of connection through the accumulation of knowledge across forms of order' (Noble 2011: 837). For example, *ad hoc* alliances can resolve local, specific conflicts (e.g. Karner and Parker 2011; Gow 2005); and social practices are adapted and recreated to maintain attachments to the past, to ensure continuity, as well as create meaningful patterns of relationships in the present with individual differences according to context and personal disposition.

Developing a sense of a shared life can also occur in banal, everyday interactions, in which skills for sharing space become unremarkable for local residents. Wessendorf (2009), for example, points to in-between, interstitial spaces where belonging is constructed, such as civility in public interactions. This implies a sense of mixing not necessarily resulting in lasting networks, but meaningful nevertheless to manage the anxieties that can come with a congestion that contains both crowds and diversity. However, the fleeting nature of these interactions can also generate and deepen prejudice and conflict, or require particular spaces (such as shops or workplaces) that not all members of a locality can access (e.g. the unemployed; see Matejskova and Leitner 2011). Affective responses to congestion are neither static nor linear processes, but impacted by time, trust, disposition and the history of relationships in a neighbourhood constructed in response to hierarchies.

Therefore, while social and economic segmentation remains – exemplified by urban centres that concentrate global capital, poverty, boundaries of inclusion and exclusion, and crowds of difference – the spaces within which inhabitants operate overlap and are not mutually exclusive or immutable. Herbert (2011) argues for the fluid nature of boundaries, and a rethinking of their capacity for positive affect – enabling security for those within them, for example. Decades earlier, Canetti (1960) wrote of the individual's sense of transcendence when subsumed into a crowd, now free of the burden of distance from others. So while power is inscribed into the movement of people into and through cities, into the technologies of mobility and social organisation framed by cultural norms that can direct and influence the experience of congestion, as Barker *et al.* (2009: 7) note, it is possible to negotiate constraints and opportunities. There is a 'micro-politics' of mobility and immobility. Such thinking about congestion and urban space is supported by the use of congestion as protest, as the Occupy movement (2011) has attempted to do, shifting the micro-politics of mobility from fringes and interstitial spaces to the centres of cities. This understanding of the malleability of congestion incorporates experiences of belonging, space-use and power in the realities of feeling comfortable in a place defined as home, in which we have a stake. Adding to our repertoire of skills, then, that as individuals we deploy to navigate the city, we find a means to move, like water, sliding between the cracks of space that mysteriously open up once some unseen pressure of presence is applied to the crowd.

References

Amin, A. (2008) 'Collective culture and urban public space', *City*, 12(1): 5–24.

Anderson, B. (2009) 'Affective atmospheres', *Emotion, Space and Society*, 2(2): 77–81.

Anjaria, J. (2009) 'Guardians of the bourgeois city: citizenship, public space and middle class activism in Mumbai', *City and Community*, 8(4): 391–406.

Barker, J., Kraftl, P., Horton, J. and Tucker, F. (2009) 'The road less travelled – new directions in children's and young people's mobility', *Mobilities*, 4(1): 1–10.

Bauman, Z. (2007) Keynote Address, *BodyTalkCity, conference* organised by Dublin Docklands Development Authority, 17 November 2007, Dublin, Ireland.

Bloch, B. and Dreher, T. (2009) 'Resentment and reluctance: working with everyday diversity and everyday racism in southern Sydney', *Journal of Intercultural Studies*, 30(2): 193–209.

Brosius, C. (2008) 'The Enclaved Gaze: Exploring the Visual Culture of "World Class-Living" in Urban India', in J. Jain (ed.) *India's Popular Culture: Iconic Spaces and Fluid Images*, Mumbai: MARG.

Broudehoux, A.-M. (2009) 'Seeds of Dissent: The Politics of Resistance to Beijing's Olympic Redevelopment', in M. Butcher and S. Velayutham (eds) *Dissent and Cultural Resistance in Asia's Cities*, Abingdon: Routledge.

Butcher, M. (2011a) *Managing Cultural Change: Reclaiming Synchronicity in a Mobile World*, Farnham: Ashgate Publishing.

— (2011b) 'Cultures of commuting: the mobile negotiation of space and subjectivity on Delhi's Metro', *Mobilities*, 6(2): 237–254.

Canetti, E. (1960 [1973]) *Crowds and Power*, trans. Carol Stewart, New York: Farrar, Straus & Giroux.

Chang, S. and Tharenou, P. (2004) 'Competencies needed for managing a multicultural workgroup', *Asia Pacific Journal of Human Resources*, 42(1): 57–74.

Clayton, J. (2011) 'Living the multicultural city: acceptance, belonging and young identities in the city of Leicester', *England, Ethnic and Racial Studies*, Online, DOI:10.1080/ 01419870.2011.605457.

Collins, F. and Friesen, W. (2011) 'Making the most of diversity? The intercultural city project and a rescaled version of diversity in Auckland, New Zealand', *Urban Studies*, 48(14): 3067–3085

Crozier, G. and Davies, J. (2008) '"The trouble is they don't mix": self-segregation or enforced exclusion', *Race, Ethnicity and Education*, 11(3): 285–301.

Datta, A. (2009) 'Places of everyday cosmopolitanisms: East-European construction workers in London', *Environment and Planning A*, 41(2): 353–370.

Dupont, V. (2008) 'Slum demolitions in Delhi since the 1990s: an appraisal', *Economic and Political Weekly*, 43(28): 79–87.

Fyfe, N., Bannister, J. and Kearns, A. (2006) '(In)civility and the city', *Urban Studies*, 43(5): 853–861.

Glick-Schiller, N., Darieva, T. and Gruner-Domic, S. (2011) 'Defining cosmopolitan sociability in a transnational age. An introduction', *Ethnic and Racial Studies*, 34(3): 399–418.

Gow, G. (2005) 'Rubbing shoulders in the global city: refugees, citizenship and multicultural alliances in Fairfield, Sydney', *Ethnicities*, 5(3): 386–405.

Graf, A. (2004) 'Screening and training intercultural competencies: evaluating the impact of national culture on intercultural competencies', *International Journal of Human Resource Management*, 15(6): 1124–1148.

Harris, A. (2010) 'Young people, everyday civic life and the limits of social cohesion', *Journal of Intercultural Studies*, 31(5): 573–589.

Herbert, S. (2011) 'Contemporary geographies of exclusion III: to assist or punish?', *Progress in Human Geography*, 35(2): 256–263.

— (2008) 'Contemporary geographies of exclusion I: traversing skid road', *Progress in Human Geography*, 32(5): 659–666.

Jiron, P. (2008) 'Mobile Borders in Urban Daily Mobility Practices in Santiago de Chile', paper presented at the 38th World Congress of the International Institute of Sociology, Central European University, Budapest, Hungary, 26–30 June, 2008.

Karner, C. and Parker, D. (2011) 'Conviviality and conflict: pluralism, resilience and hope in inner-city Birmingham', *Journal of Ethnic and Migration Studies*, 37(3): 355–372.

Knox, P. (2002) 'World Cities and the Organisation of Global Space', in R. J. Johnston, P. J. Taylor and M. J. Watts (eds) *Geographies of Global Change: Remapping the World*, 2nd ed., Oxford: Blackwell Publishing.

Kothari, U. (2008) 'Global peddlers and local networks: migrant cosmopolitanisms', *Environment and Planning D: Society and Space*, 26(3): 500–516.

Landau, L. and Freemantle, I. (2010) 'Tactical cosmopolitanism and idioms of belonging: insertion and self-exclusion in Johannesburg', *Journal of Ethnic and Migration Studies*, 36(3): 375–390.

Latham, A. and McCormack, D. (2004) 'Moving cities: rethinking the materialities of urban geographies', *Progress in Human Geography*, 28(6): 701–724.

Lees, L. (2008) 'Gentrification and social mixing: towards an inclusive urban renaissance', *Urban Studies*, 45(12): 2449–2470.

Massey, D. (2005) *For Space*, London: Sage.

Matejskova, T. and Leitner, H. (2011) 'Urban encounters with difference: the contact hypothesis and immigrant integration projects in eastern Berlin', *Social & Cultural Geography*, 12(7): 717–741.

McKeown, A. (2008) *Melancholy Order: Asian Migration and the Globalisation of Borders*, New York: University of Columbia Press.

Montserrat Degen, M. (2008) *Sensing Cities: Regenerating Public Life in Barcelona and Manchester*, London: Routledge.

Noble, G. (2011) 'Bumping into alterity: transacting cultural complexities', *Continuum: Journal of Media and Cultural Studies*, 25(6): 827–840.

Noussia, A. and Lyons, M. (2009) 'Inhabiting spaces of liminality: migrants in Omonia, Athens', *Journal of Ethnic and Migration Studies*, 35(4): 601–624.

Peltokorpi, V. (2008) 'Cross-cultural adjustment of expatriates in Japan', *International Journal of Human Resources Management*, 19(9): 1588–1606.

Phillips, T. and Smith, P. (2006) 'Rethinking urban incivility research: strangers, bodies and circulations', *Urban Studies*, 43(5–6): 879–901.

Pile, S. (2010) 'Emotions and affect in recent human geography', *Transactions of the Institute of British Geographers*, 35(1): 5–20.

Pinder, D. (2008) 'Urban Interventions: Art, Politics and Pedagogy', *International Journal of Urban and Regional Research*, 32(3): 730–736.

Raban, J. (1974) *Soft City*, London: Hamish Hamilton.

Richardson, T. and Jensen, O. (2008) 'How mobility systems produce inequality: making mobile subject types on the Bangkok Sky Train', *Built Environment*, 34(2): 218–231.

Robins, K. (2008) 'The challenge of transcultural diversities', *Transversal Study on the Theme of Cultural Policy and Cultural Diversity*, Strasbourg: Culture and Cultural Heritage Department, Council of Europe.

Rose, G., Degen, M. and Basdas, B. (2010) 'More on "big things": building events and feelings', *Transactions*, 35(3): 334–349.

Spinney, J. (2009) 'Cycling the city: movement, meaning and method', *Geography Compass*, 3: 817–835.

UNESCO (2009) *Investing in Cultural Diversity and Intercultural Dialogue*, Paris: UNESCO Publishing.

UN Habitat (2008) *State of the World's Cities 2008/2009*, London, Sterling, VA: Earthscan.

Uslaner, E. (2010) 'Segregation, mistrust and minorities', *Ethnicities*, 10(4): 415–434.

— (2008) 'Living with difference: reflection on geographies of encounter', *Progress in Human Geography*, 32(3): 323–337.

Valentine, G. (2008) 'Living with difference: reflection on geographies of encounter', *Progress in Human Geography*, 32(3): 323–337.

Van Woerkom, M. and de Reuver, R. S. M. (2009) 'Predicting excellent management performance in an intercultural context: a study of the influence of multicultural personality on transformational leadership and performance', *International Journal of Human Resources Management*, 20(10): 2013–2029.

Watson, S. (2006) *City Publics: The (Dis)enchantments of Urban Encounters*, London: Routledge.

Wessendorf, S. (2009) 'Commonplace diversity and the "ethos of mixing": perceptions of difference in a London neighbourhood', MMG Working Paper 11–09, Gottingen: Max Planck Institute for the Study of Religious and Ethnic Diversity. Available online at www.mmg.mpg.de/workingpapers (accessed 1 November 2011).

Wills, J. (2010) Keynote Address, *Alternative Urbanisms*, Urban Geography Research Group conference, University College London, 11–12 November 2010.

Wise, A. (2005) 'Hope and belonging in a multicultural suburb', *Journal of Intercultural Studies*, 26(1/2): 171–186.

Yeoh, B. and Willis, K. (2005) 'Singapore and British transmigrants in China and the cultural politics of "contact zones"', *Journal of Ethnic and Migration Studies*, 31: 269–285.

45

Disruptions

Stephen Graham

The secret ambition of design is to become invisible, to be taken up into a culture, absorbed into the background. . . . The highest order of success in design is to achieve ubiquity, to become banal.

(Mau 2003: 3–4)

"Cities are the summation and densest expressions of infrastructure, write urban historians Robert Herman and Jesse Ausubel (1988). Or, more accurately, a set of infrastructures, working sometimes in harmony, sometimes with frustrating discord, to provide us with shelter, contact, energy, water and means to meet other human needs."

(Herman and Ausubel 1998: 4)

By sustaining flows of water, waste, energy, information, people, commodities and signs, massive complexes of contemporary urban infrastructure are the embodiment of western, Enlightenment dreams of the social control of nature through advances in technology and science. They are a prerequisite to any notion of modern 'civilization'. They are at the heart of the ways in which cities act as the main centres of wealth creation and capital accumulation through extending their control and appropriation of labour power and of resources over distant territories, people and ecosystems. They have tended to become inexorably woven into notions of the modern state and modern identities associated with nationhood. And infrastructure networks are always at the centre of discussions about urban futurity and the 'impacts' that new waves of technological innovation will have on our rapidly urbanizing planet.

On our rapidly urbanizing planet, the everyday life of the world's swelling population of urbanites is increasingly sustained by vast and unknowably complex systems of infrastructure and technology stretched across geographic space. Immobilized in space, they continually bring into being the mobilities and circulations of the city and the world. Energy networks connect the heating, cooling and energising of urban life through infrastructure to both far-off energy reserves and global circuits of pollution and global warming. Huge water systems sate the city's insatiable thirst whilst waste water and sewerage remove human and organic wastes from the urban scene (at least partially).

Within cities, dense water, sewerage, food and waste distribution systems continually link human bodies and their metabolisms to the broader metabolic processes through which attempts are made to maintain public health. Global agricultural, shipping and trade complexes furnish the city's millions with food. Highway, airline, train and road complexes support the complex and multi-scaled flows of commuters, migrants, tourists and refugees, as well as materials and commodities, within and through the global urban system and its links with hinterlands and peripheries. And electronic communications systems provide a universe of digitally mediated information, transaction, interaction and entertainment which is the very lifeblood of digital capitalism and which is increasingly assembled based on assumptions of always being 'on'. The vital material bases for 'cyberspace' are largely invisible and subterranean. They also link intimately both to the electrical infrastructures which allow the digital to function, and to the other infrastructural circuits of the city as they themselves become organized through digital media.

Whilst sometimes taken for granted – at least when they work amongst wealthier or more privileged users – energy, water, sewerage, transport, trade, finance and communication infrastructures allow modern urban life to exist. Their pipes, ducts, servers, wires, conduits, electronic transmissions and tunnels sustain the flows, connections and metabolisms that are intrinsic to contemporary cities. Through their endless technological agency, these systems help transform the natural into the cultural, the social and the urban.

As the great demographic and geographic shift of global urbanization intensifies, humankind will become ever more reliant on functioning systems of urban infrastructure. Indeed, the very nature of urbanization means that every aspect of people's lives tends to become more dependent on the infrastructural circuits of the city to sustain individual and collective health, security, economic opportunity, social well-being and biological life. Moreover, because they rely on the continuous agency of infrastructure to eat, wash, heat, cook, light, work, travel, communicate, and remove dangerous or poisonous wastes from their living places, urbanites often have few or no real alternatives when the complex infrastructures that sometimes manage to achieve this are removed or disrupted.

Infrastructural edifices thus provide the fundamental background to modern, urban everyday life. This background is often hidden, assumed, even naturalized. This is most common in wealthier, western cities where basic access to a suite of communication, energy, water and transport systems has been to some extent universalized as the basis for modern, urban citizenship. Once initially completed and universalized, the water, sewerage and electricity systems of the city tended to become "buried underground, invisible, banalised, and relegated to an apparently marginal, subterranean urban world" (Kaika and Swyngedouw 2000: 122).

In conditions where continuous access to key infrastructure circuits has been broadly universalized, anthroplogists Geoffrey Bowker and Susan Leigh Star stress that "good, usable [infrastructure] systems, disappear almost by definition. The easier they are to use the harder they are to see. As well, most of the time, the bigger they are, the harder they are to see". Within social scientific writing about cities especially, the vast infrastructural circuits of the city have often emerged as little more than "the forgotten, the background, the frozen in place" – a merely technical backdrop that is the preserve of engineers only. Bowker and Leigh Star (2000: 33) offer the banal and often universal experience of uninterrupted electricity services to power a simple reading light as an example of how infrastructures have a tendency to become taken for granted. "Unless we are electricians or building inspectors", they write, "we rarely think about the myriad of databases, standards, and inspection manuals subtending our reading lamps, much less about the politics of the electric grid that they tap into".

When infrastructure achieves such a status as a 'black box', few modern urbanites venture to understand the inner workings of the technology or the giant lattices of connection and flow that link these network access points seamlessly to distant elsewheres. How many of the world's burgeoning billions of urbanites, after all, routinely consider the extraordinary assemblages of fuel sources, generating stations, transmission wires and transformers that push electrons through the myriad electrical artefacts of contemporary urban life? Or the mass of servers, satellites, glass fibres, routers – and, indeed, electrical systems – that bring our 'virtual' worlds of play, socialising, e-commerce or communication into being? Or the globe-straddling systems of communication, data processing, financial transaction, or risk profiling that bring airliners into the sky? Or the vast subterranean worlds that bring the fresh water to the tap or faucet, or remove the human waste from the toilet once flushed? Or the global supply chains that populate supermarket shelves with produce, or fill the gas or petrol station with the hydrocarbon products of the decayed forms of billions of ancient life forms?

In many cities of the global south, by contrast, access to energy, water, waste, communications and transport services is anything but assumed – enormous efforts to continuously innovate mean that basic infrastructural politics infuse urban life in such contexts. It is crucial to stress that, beyond the discourses of the powerful, infrastructure services have "always been foregrounded in the lives of more precarious social groups – i.e. those with reduced access or without access or who have been disconnected, as a result either of socio-spatial differentiation strategies or infrastructure crises or collapse" (McFarlane and Rutherford, 2008: 63).

It is equally important that western histories whereby relatively standardized and ubiquitous infrastructure grids have been more or less constructed are not generalized as representing an inevitable trajectory or history for all cities everywhere. In many global south cities, for example, access to networked infrastructures has always been highly fragmented, highly unreliable and problematic, even for relatively wealthy or powerful groups and neighbourhoods.

In contemporary Mumbai, for example, many upper-middle-class residents have to deal with water or power supplies which operate for only a few hours per day. Their efforts to move into gated communities are often motivated as much by their desires for continuous power and water supplies as by hopes for better security. The pervasiveness of such infrastructure disruptions in Mumbai is in turn used by the City's boosters to invoke major infrastructural edifices and massive demolitions of informal settlements as they strive to overcome continuous infrastructural disruptions and so become 'more global' or 'the next Shanghai'.

This means that, in many cities, infrastructural circulations are *not* rendered as mere 'technical' issues which merge into the urban background. Far from it: their politics dominate urban life and urban political discourses to a powerful extent. Colin McFarlane and Jonathan Rutherford write that "it is clear that from the viewpoint of Bombay or Ulan-Ude [in Russia] infrastructures have rarely, if ever, been concealed or technical issues" (2008: 363).

The startling point about the rendering of taken-for-granted energy, communication, transport and water grids as 'normal', culturally banal, invisible, even boring is that it takes the sudden interruption or disruption to such systems to make them visible on the urban scene. Such events render the huge material systems of infrastructure as instant, albeit often temporary, ruins of modernity. When the website is not available; the volcanic ash prevents the airline from flying; electricity is blacked out; the fuel is unavailable for the food supply, water pumps or school run; the subways fail to move; or the tap fails to deliver clean water – the infrastructural backstage of urban life becomes startlingly visible. Whether through technical malfunctions, interruptions in resource supplies, wars, terrorist attacks, public health crises, labour strikes, sabotage, network theft, extreme weather or other events usually considered to be 'natural' (floods, earthquakes, tsunami, etc.), disruptions to the flows of energy, water, transportation, communication and waste that are the very lifeblood of the contemporary city quickly breed a sense of emergency. The 'black box' of the infrastructure system is thus momentarily opened; the politics of infrastructural assemblages become a sudden preoccupation within media and public debate.

It is worth considering a few examples to help illustrate this point. In Spring 2010, the interruption of global airline systems by the Icelandic volcanic eruption filled the world's newspapers with detailed technical analyses of how jet engines deal with ingested dust. The cascading disruptions and devastations of urban Japan through the earthquake–tsunami–nuclear catastrophe a year later filled the same newspapers with detailed cross-sections of different styles of nuclear reactor, highlighting their various levels of resilience to power outages. And the unintentional severing of a transoceanic fibre optic line off the coast of Egypt by an Egyptian fishing trawler in February 2008 – which instantly brought to a halt much of the digitally mediated economy of Dubai, Mumbai and beyond – fleetingly revealed the global strands of interurban glass which bring the supposedly 'virtual' world of the Internet into being.

As well as being experiences which tend to destroy any prevailing myths about the 'technical' nature of infrastructure, infrastructure disruptions render the arcane worlds of technically facilitated mobility as both momentarily visible and highly political. But infrastructure disruptions also present a major opportunity to understand cities better. For, by removing the complex, stretched-out flows that continually sustain modern urbanism, such events, paradoxically, work to make such flows more visible – before they are rendered into the urban background once 'normal' service is resumed. Critical analysis of city life needs, therefore, to exploit infrastructure disruptions as what sociologists call 'heuristic devices' – opportunities for learning in ways that render the banal and ordinary as contested worlds of dynamism and action that are absolutely crucial in constituting the contemporary city as process.[1]

Note

1 An earlier version of this essay appeared in M. Gandy (ed.) (2011) *Urban Constellations*, Berlin: JOVIS Verlag.

Bibliography

Bowker, G. and Leigh Star, S. (2000) *Sorting Things Out: Classification and its Consequences*, Cambridge, MA: MIT Press.

Graham, S. (ed.) (2010) *Disrupted Cities: When Infrastructure Fails*, New York: Routledge.

Herman, R., and Ausubel, J. (1988) *Cities and Their Vital Systems – Infrastructure Past, Present and Future*, Washington, DC: National Academy Press.

Kaika, M. and Swyngedouw, E. (2000) 'Fetishising the modern city: The phantasmagoria of urban technological networks', *International Journal of Urban and Regional Research*, 24(1), 122–148.

Leigh Star, S. (1999) 'The ethnography of infrastructure', *American Behavioral Scientist*, 43(3), 377–391.

Mau, B. (2003) *Massive Change*, London: Phaidon.

McFarlane, C. and Rutherford, J. (2008) 'Political infrastructures: Governing and experiencing the fabric of the city', *International Journal of Urban and Regional Research*, 32(2), 363–374.

46

Sidewalks[1]

Nicholas Blomley

The police say that there is nothing to see on a road, that there is nothing to do but move along. It asserts that the space of circulating is nothing other than the space of circulation. Politics, in contrast, consists in transforming this space of 'moving-along' into a space for the appearance of a subject: i.e. the people, the workers, the citizens. It consists in refiguring the space, of what there is to do there, what is to be seen or named therein.

(Rancière 2001: 22)

Introduction

'The first step to wisdom is calling a thing by its right name,' noted the judge, upholding a Seattle sidewalk use ordinance that prohibited a person from sitting or lying on a sidewalk in commercial areas during business hours. Side*walks*, it seems, are just that: 'Whoever named "parkways" and "driveways" never got to step two; whoever named "sidewalks" did.'[2] Sidewalks, he concludes, are obviously for walking. Given that the state has a legitimate interest in 'protecting public safety by keeping the sidewalk clear of pedestrian interests,'[3] the ordinance must be upheld.

For the critics, this is yet another example of mobility being put to work in a punitive and exclusionary fashion. The Seattle ordinance seeks to install a 'consumptive public sphere,' for one, which ascribes to spaces such as the sidewalk 'a single, natural, pre-given purpose: the circulation and movement of goods and persons' (Feldman 2006: 40). The bodies of homeless people, recumbent on the sidewalk, are clearly an affront to such a logic, which seeks to 'exclude abject poverty from "prime" consumption spaces' (43).

Mobility scholarship is also alert to the ways in which mobility is framed and regulated by the state (Richardson and Jensen 2008; Hannam *et al.* 2006). Urban spaces, like Seattle's sidewalks, are said to be framed according to 'governing logics' (Jensen 2011) or 'mobility regimes' (Sheller 2008), that are sometimes expressed as forms of governmentality (or 'governmobility,' Bærenholdt 2008). As with mobility more generally, such logics are deemed indelibly social and political, to the extent that they represent and seek to produce desired forms of movement. All too often, it is feared, the motion of certain bodies – such as the purposeful consumer – is advanced over those of others, such as members of the public poor, who are compelled to 'move on.'

For far from a space of freedom and political possibility, the sidewalk is intensely regulated, often in pursuit of unfettered pedestrian mobility. Blumenberg and Ehrenfeucht (2008), for example, document the highly detailed 'sidewalk-control strategies' at work in Las Vegas, ranging from 'no-obstruction zones,' sweeping prohibitions on particular uses (begging, sitting/sleeping, prostitution, the placement of 'structures') and more specific time/place/manner restrictions on certain uses, such as news racks and parades. Others note the use not only of 'hard' regulatory restrictions on the sidewalk and its uses, but also 'soft' control practices, such as landscaping and beautification (Loukaitou-Sideris *et al.* 2004). Historical accounts of sidewalk regulation also note the manner in which certain uses (such as union activity, hucksters, the poor) have been targeted in sidewalk pogroms, often justified according to the need to promote circulation and flow (Ehrenfeucht and Loukaitou-Sideris 2007). Such interventions are frequently seen as illiberal in effect or in intent, threatening individual liberties and curtailing 'sidewalk democracy' (Loukaitou-Sideris *et al.* 2004).

The value of such accounts rests on the recognition of sidewalks as far from inert slices of urban infrastructure, but as political sites, shot through with power relations. However, my aim here is to try and complicate such treatments. I do not doubt that sidewalk regulation can have illiberal effects, or that it is sometimes motivated by objectionable beliefs. However, I want to take seriously the particular work of urban law in framing mobility and sidewalk space on its own terms. Legal logics of sidewalk mobility, I wish to suggest, do quite particular work. As Valverde notes, '[t]he legal bits are as much part of the fabric of street life as the cultural, the economic, and the architectural bits' (2009: 180).

But while the legal must be thought of with reference to the other 'bits,' they are not necessarily commensurable. My contention here is that urban law, while clearly 'social' and 'political,' should not be too quickly subsumed within generalized accounts of 'power' or 'the state,' or with reference to big abstractions such as 'neoliberalism.' Similarly, I wish to suggest that legal strategies to regulate the sidewalk need to be understood on their own terms (Valverde 2003). To do so requires that we suspend (temporarily, at least) any agenda-seeking impulse, for it may cause us to miss such specificities. At work here, I contend, is a particular logic of mobility, which I term 'pedestrianism.' This has its own institutional and historical specificity, and is powerfully sustained through deeply engrained networks of jurisprudence, bureaucratic practice, municipal law, 'level of service' indices, and administrative codes (Ben-Joseph 2005), and materialized in a built landscape of kerb cuts, street furniture and buffer lanes (Blomley 2011). Pedestrianism, of course, is not entirely autonomous. However, it constitutes mobility in distinctive and significant ways, and thus requires treatment on its own terms.

Most immediately, it departs from an alternative framing, present in Feldman's critique and much recent mobilities scholarship. Elsewhere, I have termed the principles underlying this account as a form of 'civic humanism' (Blomley 2011). By this, I mean first a view of mobility on the sidewalk as serving valued collective ends, promoting human flourishing and the production of a public; second, an emphasis on the person in motion, and the productive encounters that occur between people and their environment as we move on the sidewalk; and, third, a view of the sidewalk as 'public space' – that is, as given meaning and having value to the extent that the sidewalk is used, occupied and possessed by the people, necessarily set apart from institutions such as the state or the private market.

While fixated on sidewalk mobility, pedestrianism is markedly different. Rather than an emphasis on the public ends of mobility, the focus is more functional, such that mobility is valued as an end in itself. This view, second, is non-humanist in that it does not take the person as its primary focus. Rather, it is interested in the arrangement of things in space, whether these are people or objects. Finally, it views the sidewalk not so much as 'public space' than as 'municipal space,' over which the state acts as trustee, acting so as to advance generalized 'police' goals such as 'safety' and 'public welfare.'

I hope to flesh out the distinctions between these two perspectives in relation to sidewalk mobility through the example of a legal dispute in Vancouver. I do so as I fear that mobility scholars are in danger of overlooking both the specificity, and the pervasiveness and reach of pedestrianism. In the purview of lowly and rarely studied urban actors, such as engineers, it appears mundane and rather uninteresting. Its primary domain, the sidewalk, appears as an obvious, inert piece of urban infrastructure. But pedestrianism has real effects, constituting mobility and the sidewalk in particular ways. To understand the complicated work that it does requires us to treat it on its own terms (Riles 2005).

The humanist sidewalk

Pedestrianism is easily overlooked by scholars, perhaps due to the prevalence of civic humanist accounts of urban walking and the sidewalk. There is a longstanding celebration of walking – including that which happens on the sidewalk – in terms of its productive value. It is said to build freedom, democracy, community, human enjoyment and a public: '[s]ocial relations . . . are not enacted *in situ* but are paced out along the ground' (Ingold and Vergunst 2008: 1). Walking is thus seen as inherently sociable. It is not simply an end in itself, or a mode of transportation, but charged with social and communicative values (Knox 2005). Walking is an 'enlightened everyday practice' that offers the potential for enchantment and empowerment (Lavadinho and Winkin 2008: 155). Histories of walking reveal its density and complexity, as illustrated by a comparison between the religious pilgrim, the Romantic wanderer, the urban flaneur and the rebellious mob (Amato 2004).

Walking is valuable for civic humanists as it creates opportunities for encounters with others. Such mobile encounters work upon our interior lives in collectively productive ways. This can include the production of political practice, to the extent that the agora can be constituted while in motion (Jensen 2009). For Solnit (2000: 176) it is through walking 'that the citizen knows his or her city and fellow citizens and truly inhabits the city rather than a small privatized part of it.' The mass march is a means by which we carve out a public sphere: 'a lot of history has been written with the feet of citizens walking through their cities . . . [Walking signifies] the possibility of common ground between people who have not ceased to be different from each other, people who have at last become the public' (Solnit 2000: 217).

Walking is also said to be constituted by, and productive of, the spaces within which it occurs. We do not simply walk through space; by our walking, we make space. Walking in the city is given a particular emphasis, whether through explorations of the 'urban explorations' of the Situationists (Pinder 2005) or the pedestrian practices of the 'ordinary practitioners of the city,' noted by de Certeau (1984), for whom walking constitutes a spatial order, but also challenges it: 'Walking affirms, suspects, tries out, transgresses, respects, etc. the trajectories it "speaks"' (99). The city itself, in this sense, is made on foot: 'People not only observe the city whilst moving through it, rather they constitute the city by practicing mobility. The meaning of places in the city is constituted by the movement as much as by their morphological properties' (Jensen 2009: 140).

For civic humanists, the spaces in which urban mobility occurs need to be carefully considered if they are to meet these valued collective ends. Such sites 'are more than functional, they are emotional: they provide us with places to grow and to remember, places to sit back and relax and enjoy life, places to meet people that we care about, places to fall in love with' (Lavadinho and Winkin 2008: 166). As such, sidewalks are given particular significance by some scholars. They are, for Jacobs (1961: 29), 'the main public places of a city . . . its most vital organs.' Sidewalks and that which happens upon them, it seems, are thus freighted with considerable social weight. They are 'not merely footpaths,' but are a space 'that manufactures and maintains civilized social discourse.. . . On the sidewalk, we become who we are as a function of the city, just as the city becomes the mirror of our humanity' (Nelligan and Mauro 2008: 11).

As such, they should not be designed simply to facilitate flow. Indeed, some urban designers point to the importance of creating stickiness and complexity in order to facilitate mobile encounters. William Whyte (2000) celebrates the 'vital frictions' and 'amiable disorder' of the street based on encounters with other people and objects. People actively seek out disorder and congestion, he argued. For Jan Gehl, public life is to be valued to the extent that it 'offers an opportunity to be with others' (2001: 19). Encounters between such persons are seen as rich with inter-subjective possibility. While such encounters with strangers can be unsettling, many would also argue that such 'vital frictions' are ultimately productive of urban public life. Thus, for Sennett (1994: 310), '[t]he body comes to life when coping with difficulty.'

The micro-geographies of such 'frictions' and 'difficulties' are deemed highly significant. As we move through these spaces, we engage in a form of 'sidewalk ballet,' to borrow from Jacobs (1961), based on highly patterned, yet un-programmed, complex forms of interaction and convergence. The others that we encounter are not to be understood as impediments to be avoided, or obstacles to be navigated, but as socially productive urban moments. For Jacobs, such mobile encounters constitute networks of reciprocity and association. As such, sidewalks and their users 'are active participants in the drama of civilization versus barbarism in cities' (Jacobs 1961: 30). For Goffman, the everyday encounters that occur between strangers as they navigate the sidewalk are not collisions with 'obstructions,' but the means by which relations of trust and reciprocity are learned and reproduced. Goffman refers to the intricate, tacit and informal rules of mutual comportment and movement as a 'traffic code,' reliant upon an implicit contract: 'City streets provide a setting where mutual trust is routinely displayed between strangers' (1971: 17; cf. Ross 1901/1969). This need not simply entail polite encounters between social equals. Indeed, for some, encounters with those who break the 'traffic code,' like the importuning panhandler, are the basis for a valuable inter-subjective moment. Such an appeal 'breaks down the wall between speaker and listener and engages [the panhandler's] interlocutor in a social interaction' (Hershkoff and Cohen 1991: 913).

The obstruction

Yet, while, as Solnit (2000) notes, protest is often produced through acts of collective urban walking, politics is also made through forms of organized stillness. One striking case concerns a long-standing vigil outside the Chinese consulate on Vancouver's Granville Street, a major thoroughfare, conducted by Falun Gong adherents to protest the Chinese state's crackdown against their organization. Because of the advanced age of many of the protestors, and Vancouver's inclement environment, a 'meditation hut,' approximately one meter by two meters in size, was erected on the sidewalk. Surrounding the hut were a series of large bill-boards, eight feet high and a hundred feet long, emblazoned with protest messages designed to be read by speeding commuters.

The billboards and the hut were located on a small grassy strip of the City street that abutted the private property of the Chinese Consulate on one side, and the City sidewalk on the other.

How are we to understand the effect of these structures in relation to the mobile sidewalk? For the civic humanist, presumably, this is a site of encounter, rich with inter-subjective possibility. Rather than a transient moment, the longevity of the site was particularly significant. The Falun Gong was there for the long haul: initiated in 2001, the hut was in place until 2009. For the Falun Gong, this was a vigil, a physical witnessing of dissent and moral disapproval predicated on permanence. Marching on the streets, holding placards or chanting, the Falun Gong pointed out, sends a 'distinctly different message.'[4] A vigil, it was noted, implies an extended period of waiting.

> An integral part of the vigil by the Falun Gong is that the message it is expressing be continued until the Falun Gong is satisfied that the human rights issues it raises are heard by the public and the Chinese government, and the alleged human rights issues addressed. Without the consistency of a vigil that has been underway now for seven years, 24 hours a day, seven days a week, in rain, sun, snow and hail, the expressive content of the Falun Gong's message will be diminished.[5]

As such, this was a meditation designed to speak outwards, rather than inwards. Charged with political and ethical meaning, it was intended to engage with others. Commuters traversing Granville Street[6] became used to the sight of a solitary meditator inside the shelter, legs crossed in a lotus position, maintaining a permanent presence. While the words and

Figure 46.1 Falun Gong Protest, Granville Street, November 2006 (photo by author)

images on the posters were loud with passionate appeals to justice, it was our encounters with the silent, meditating protestor – permanently present – that were characterized as meaningful. For one observer, the meditator's 'complete silence is discomfiting. It speaks louder than any bullhorn' (McMartin 2009: A1). For the Falun Gong, the hut itself also served as a form of speech, its physical form evoking the information kiosk and the religious shrine simultaneously.

But despite such grandiose claims, in itself the shelter was a modest thing. For its defenders, this was 'a peaceful vigil by one person on a patch of dirt that no one uses.' Of the hut they said 'it is unlikely a less intrusive shelter could be conceived of.'[7] The City of Vancouver, however, felt otherwise. The City authorities had nothing against the protest *qua* protest, they insisted, despite extensive lobbying by the Chinese Consulate. They did object, however, to the structures involved, and their location. In particular, they were deemed a violation of section 71(1) of the City's Streets and Traffic By-law,[8] which forbids any person from placing any 'structure, object, substance or thing which is an obstruction to the free use' of the street or sidewalk or 'which may encroach thereon' without official authority, and sought to enforce an injunction against the Falun Gong to that end. In their supporting argument to the BC Supreme Court, the City characterized the boards and hut as just that – 'encroachments' and 'obstructions':

> Section 71 of the By-law prohibits construction of structures on City streets that obstruct the free use of the street or encroach on the street. The Respondents have conceded that the structures that are the subject of this petition are on a street and that they encroach on the street. . . . However, the City submits that, in addition, the structures constitute an obstruction to the free use of the street . . . Streets constitute a finite public resource that is shared by a number of competing interests. In addition to being used for the movement of vehicles and pedestrians, City streets have many other uses. These uses include both static and moving elements. Respondents' structures occupy part of the street. That part of the street is no longer free for another use while these structures are there. Thus, the structures obstruct a free use of the street.[9]

This administrative framing of the sidewalk deserves more careful attention – in particular, the notions of obstruction and encroachment (and related conceptions of use, moving and static elements, and the public) that the City invokes (Blomley 2011), for these have distinctive meanings. While this is also a mobile sidewalk, it is a quite particular one, informed by a pedestrianist logic.

Obstruction and encroachment rely upon a particular sensibility, which views the sidewalk as a surface upon which are arranged a set of objects in order to achieve what the City termed 'orderly and well managed streets.'[10] At work here, I think, is a rationality of 'police,' an ancient and deeply engrained logic, concerned with the maintenance of 'the good order and constitution of a state's persons and things' (quoted in Dubber 2004: 140; cf. Iveson forthcoming). The commissioned police officer is only one manifestation of a pervasive concern with the distribution of objects in order to achieve salubrity, order and general welfare. While generally manifest, the quintessential police site is the city. The indictment of blockage and the facilitation of flow, moreover, are one of their primary concerns (Levi 2008; Blomley 2012). Police charge the state with the protection of the community from often open-ended 'threats.' Similarly, we cannot rely, it seems, upon the 'traffic code' – the Goffmanesque abilities of street users to self organize. The sidewalk is to be governed by law, through a logic of legal permissions, whereby any 'structure, object, substance or thing' upon the sidewalk is *prima facie* illegal. Further, unlike the humanist, the primary object of police law is not the person, but urban objects more generally, whether persons or things. While in this case the City detaches things from people (distinguishing between the rights of the protestors to peacefully assemble and the obstruction occasioned by the meditation hut), in other cases it is the human body that is deemed an obstruction (Blomley 2007). Obstruction, moreover, does not require actual obstruction, just the possibility of obstruction.[11] At work here, it seems, is a form of prudentialism, dedicated to the prevention of possible harms, rather than a criminological logic that seeks to punish harms after they have occurred.

It is in this context that the idea of the 'obstruction' begins to become intelligible. Rather than a site of productive encounter – such that the meeting between the Falun Gong protestor ensconced in her shrine and the passing citizen becomes a moment charged with communicative possibility – the shelter is deemed an 'obstruction.' What does an obstruction do that renders it objectionable? Put another way, what is the function of a sidewalk that is compromised by the obstruction? As we have noted, for a civic humanist an 'obstruction' is potentially a moment of encounter, laden with value and social meaning. As the Falun Gong's lawyers pointed out, '[t]here are many circumstances where an encroachment or obstacle is not only tolerated, but welcomed and valued as part of our civic culture and society.'[12] Conversely, for the City the sidewalk is not a productive space, but one of zero-sum competition between multiple, opposed 'uses': 'City streets constitute a finite public resource that has to be shared by many competing interests.'[13] The by-law, the City argued, does not 'pitch the state against the individual. Rather, it concerns the orderly administration of public space for the benefit of the public at large. To that extent, it is concerned with the balancing of competing *individual* interests existing on that space.'[14] The City's self-identified job is to arbitrate between these interests. In so doing, it draws a striking distinction between what it terms 'static and moving elements.' The principal function of the sidewalk, it turns out, is to facilitate 'moving elements.' 'Static elements,' consequently, are viewed as potential obstructions that impede movement. Objects on the sidewalk (whether people or things) must be so arranged so as not to impede circulation. The primary function of the sidewalk, therefore, is to facilitate a smooth and unencumbered passage.

So, echoing some contemporary scholarship, mobility is good, it seems. Why is mobility good? Well, not because it is 'good,' ethically speaking, but because it is functional. Flow is valuable simply as an end in itself. There is no attention to the interior life of the person in circulation, including that which happens when she encounters an 'obstruction.' Obstructions are bad simply because they impede flow (on occasion, an appeal is made to 'safety,' but this seems frequently reducible to the prevention of impedance). It would seem that the 'space of circulating is nothing other than the space of circulation,' to borrow from Rancière (2001: 22). This is evidenced by pedestrianism's frequent characterization of the pedestrian as moving 'from point A to point B.' *Why* she is moving is not an object of concern, or what it is about point B, as opposed to C, that makes it a worthier, more valuable location. Nor does pedestrianism worry about *who* is moving. It could be the protestor, on his way to a rally, or the executive, on her way to her limo. This desubjectification becomes even more evident in the urban engineering shorthand for the mobile person: the 'ped.' A ped is essentially an administrative unit, an object-in-motion. What is significant about the ped is not its soul, but its proportions, motion and lack of impedance.

For the civic humanist, as noted, a sidewalk has a significance that private spaces, like my hallway, do not. These are 'public spaces,' sites in which we encounter and help form a public sphere that is, of necessity, set apart from market or state imperatives. The Falun Gong protest not only occupies a sidewalk, where as we circulate we are likely to encounter it, but a *public* sidewalk, a site of speech, difference, and democratic dialogue. The City's view, however, differs. The sidewalk is part of a unitary property holding, held by a public corporation. The sidewalk is municipal property, held in trust by the City, to serve 'public ends,' of which, as noted, the most significant is circulation. But there's another interesting dimension to this. The reported 95 cm of public sidewalk taken up by the Falun Gong's hut is objectionable not only because it (potentially) 'obstructs,' but also because it 'encroaches.' It works a sort of expropriation of property by sectional interests. Without regulation, it is said, the sidewalk will 'degenerate into chaos,'[15] as multiple 'private' interests battle for it. The protest structures – whose purpose, we assume, was to engage with the public, in public – amounted to 'expropriation of public space for private use. Such permanent occupation by an individual or a group is incompatible with the very nature of public space which, although vested in the City, belongs to the public as a whole.'[16] Far from an attempt to open the sidewalk to the needs of private capital, in pursuit of a consumptive public sphere, the City claims to be acting in defense of the 'very nature of public space.'

The subsequent judicial evaluations of sidewalk mobility proved interesting, revealing the presence of both civic humanist and pedestrianist logics. Initially, the courts sided with the City (as is their wont), closely echoing their submission. While the Falun Gong's structures were expressive, 'the erection of permanent structures on a street . . . is incompatible with the principal function of the street,' understood as the facilitation of movement.[17] On appeal, however, the court characterized the structures as supportive of 'the values of democratic discourse and self-fulfillment.'[18] Departing from the City's view that 'democratic discourse must occur in a manner consistent with the proper functioning of a municipality,' the court characterized sidewalks as 'spaces in which political expression takes place.'[19] Given that the by-law amounts to a blanket ban on political protest structures, it is unconstitutional. But lest we imagine that the court had embraced a fully humanist view of the sidewalk, it should be noted that the court, echoing police, concluded that what is needed is not more fully 'public' space, but a more carefully organized 'municipal space.' What is required, the court notes, is an appropriate regulatory framework for 'political structures.'

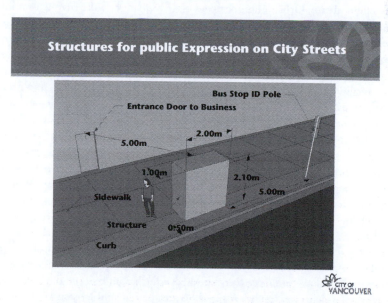

Figure 46.2   Falun Gong Protest, Granville Street, November 2006 (photo by author)

The City, accordingly, responded with a revised policy that, not surprisingly, remained firmly wedded to a pedestrianist logic of permissions, and predicated on a suspicion to the 'obstruction' and the 'encroachment.' What is significant about the structure is not its political value, it seems, but its dimensions, location and permanence.

It is still not a site of 'encounter,' but an object that must be carefully positioned so as not to unduly 'obstruct.' Sidewalks are still essentially for circulation, egress and unencumbered flow. At time of writing, the Falun Gong, predictably, has objected to the revised by-law, and petititioned the BC Supreme Court to strike it down as unconstitutional.

Conclusions

What, then, are we to make of this, in terms of an understanding of mobility and the sidewalk?

★   ★   ★

The first point is to underscore that mobility relies upon diverse rationalities or logics. This is not the same as saying that mobility serves different ends (organized commuter or consumer circulation versus oppositional forms of walking), but rather that it is differently conceived. I've tried here to trace some of the significant, perhaps ontological, differences between a civic humanist and pedestrianist rationality. For the latter, walking is an end in itself that requires no particular justification. What must be guarded against, however, is the obstruction that impedes, particularly when it constitutes a form of 'encroachment.'

Both, however, are pro-mobile, but for very different reasons. As such, one should be cautious of the view that 'to be free is to be mobile' (Pritchard 2000: 50; cf. Sager 2006; Sheller 2008). While, following de Certeau, we are not necessarily confined by the circulatory logics of the state, and, whether moving or static, we can rework the space of the sidewalk to other ends, mobility scholars should be cautious of the uncritical embrace of sidewalk mobility as a desired end. Urban engineers and civic humanists alike invoke mobility, but in quite distinctive and potentially opposing ways.

For these two sidewalk rationalities do not necessarily coexist. As this dispute demonstrates, they can collide. For the City, the protest hut was a 'structure' that obstructed and encroached. The Falun Gong sought to frame their buildings and hoardings as valuable sites of encounter, echoing Rancière's observation, quoted in the epigraph, that '[p]olitics . . . consists in transforming this space of 'moving-along' into a space for the appearance of a subject.' The Falun Gong case is a relatively minor one. However, the pedestrianism that is at work here is reflected in an extensive corpus of similar sidewalk case law, in which municipal authorities invoke pedestrianist logics in conflicts with encroaching merchants and homeowners, pickets and protestors, sleeping homeless people, and newspaper proprietors. Strikingly, however, such disputes usually are resolved in favor of 'moving-along' (Blomley 2011).

The protestor or beggar, one may complain, may not particularly care why he or she is moved on. Put another way, what difference does it make that the Falun Gong's hut was torn down in the name of pedestrianism? I suspect, however, that it does make a difference. Deeply lodged in legal practice and discourse, pedestrianism has considerable institutional purchase. A lexicon of obstruction, encroachment and circulation appears to be remarkably powerful and 'common-sensical,' and is successfully invoked in such contexts and deployed in resultant decisions. It becomes hard to argue against – how can one defend 'obstruction,' for example?

It thus becomes tempting to ascribe some sinister hidden agenda to pedestrianism. The

Falun Gong insisted (unsuccessfully) that the City was in cahoots with the Chinese Consulate. As noted, in other cases when, for example, homeless sidewalk encampments have been broken up, or regulations preventing people from sitting or lying on the sidewalk have been introduced, progressives similarly point to commercial or neoliberal agendas. Yet while mobility may be invoked to serve such ends, pedestrianism cannot be simply reduced to such imperatives. For while the 'static elements' targeted by law may, indeed, be protestors or the public poor, they may equally be sidewalk cafes, newspaper boxes, merchants' produce displays, or sandwich boards. While this does not, of course, preclude an examination of mobility law's relationship to other logics or social projects, it must first be treated carefully on its own terms, with a close examination of how it constitutes the sidewalk.

Notes

1 Thanks to Clive Ansley and Mathew Van Den Hooven of Ansley & Co.
2 Roulette vs City of Seattle [1994] 850 F. Supp. 1442.
3 Ibid., 1448, quoting Seeley vs State [1994] 850 F. Supp. 1442.
4 Appellants factum, 2009, paragraph 43, copy with author.
5 Written argument of the petitioners [Response to petition], p. 35, copy with author.
6 It should be pointed out that this stretch of Granville Street sees very few pedestrians (an interesting irony given what is to come) but many car and transit users.
7 Appellants factum, 2009, paragraphs 15, 19, copy with author.
8 A by-law is a municipal law within Canada.
9 Reply submissions of the City of Vancouver, 2011 paragraphs 5, 6, 7, copy with author.
10 Reply submissions of the City of Vancouver, 2011, paragraph 81, copy with author.
11 Both the Falun Gong and other observers noted the fact that the shelter was hardly a factual obstruction. One editorialist ridiculed the mayor for making 'Granville Street safe for pedestrians again, despite the fact there was room to drive a Buick down it' (McMartin 2009 A1).
12 Appellants factum, Court of Appeal, paragraph 34, 2009, my copy.
13 Appellants factum, Court of Appeal, paragraph 39, 2009, my copy.
14 Reply submissions of the City of Vancouver, 2011, paragraph 55 (original emphasis), copy with author.
15 Reply submissions of the City of Vancouver, 2011, paragraph 41 (original emphasis), copy with author.
16 Reply submissions of the City of Vancouver, 2011, paragraph 43, copy with author.
17 Vancouver v Zhang 2009 BCSC 84 paragraph 51.
18 Vancouver v Zhang 2009 BCSC 84 paragraph 40.
19 Vancouver v Zhang 2009 BCSC 84 paragraph 39, 41.

References

Amato, J. (2004) *On foot: a history of walking*, New York: New York University Press.
Bærenholdt, J. Ø. (2008) 'Mobility and territoriality in making societies: approaching "governmobility".' Paper presented at the European Urban and Regional Studies Conference, Istanbul, 18–21 September 2008.
Ben-Joseph, Eran (2005) *The code of the city: standards and the hidden language of place-making*, Cambridge, MA: MIT Press.
Blomley, N. (2007) 'How to turn a beggar into a bus stop: law, traffic and the "function of the place"' *Urban Studies*, 44: 9, 1697–1712.
Blomley, N. (2011) *Rights of passage: sidewalks and the regulation of public flow*, New York: Routledge.
Blomley, N. (2012) 'Coloured rabbits, dangerous trees, and public sitting: sidewalks, police and the city' *Urban Geography*, 33:7, 917–935.
Blumenberg, E. and Ehrenfeucht, R. (2008) 'Civil liberties and the regulation of public space: the case of sidewalks in Las Vegas' *Environment and Planning, A*, 40: 303–322.
City of Vancouver (2011) 'From humanism to pedestrianism – how to turn politics into police. Structures for expression on city streets' from Staff presentation to Standing Committee on Planning and Environment, City of Vancouver, 7 April 2011. Copy with author.

De Certeau, M. (1984) *The practice of everyday life*, Berkeley: University of California Press.

Dubber, M. (2004) '"The power to govern men and things": patriarchal origins of the police power in American law' *Buffalo Law Review*, 52: 4, 101–66.

Ehrenfeucht, R. and Loukaitou-Sideris, A. (2007) 'Constructing the sidewalks: municipal government and the production of public space in Los Angeles, California, 1880–1920' *Journal of Historical Geography*, 33: 104–124.

Feldman, Leonard C. (2006) *Citizens without shelter: homelessness, democracy and political exclusion*, Ithaca: Cornell University Press.

Gehl, J. (2001) *Life between buildings: using public space*, Copenhagen: Arkitektens Forlag.

Goffman, I. (1971) *Relations in public: microstudies of the public order*, New York: Basic Books.

Hannam, K., Sheller, M. and Urry, J. (2006) 'Editorial: mobilities, immobilities and moorings' *Mobilities*, 1: 1, 1–22.

Hershkoff, H. and Cohen, A. S. (1991) 'Begging to differ: The First Amendment and the right to beg' *Harvard Law Review*, 104: 4, 896–916.

Ingold, T. and Vergunst, J. L. (2008) 'Introduction,' in Ingold, T. and Vergunst, J. L. (eds) *Ways of walking: ethnography and practice on foot*, Abingdon: Ashgate, 1–19.

Iveson, K. (forthcoming) 'Policing in the city,' in Davidson, M. and Martin, D. (eds) *Urban politics: critical approaches*, London: Sage.

Jacobs, J. (1961) *The death and life of great American cities*. New York: Vintage.

Jensen, A. (2011) 'Mobility, space and power: On the multiplicities of seeing mobility' *Mobilities*, 6: 5, 255–271.

Jensen, O. B. (2009) 'Flows of meaning, cultures of movement – urban mobility as meaningful everyday life practice' *Mobilities*, 4: 1, 139–158.

Knox, P. (2005) 'Creating ordinary places: slow cities in a fast world' *Journal of Urban Design*, 10: 1, 1–11.

Lavadinho, S. and Winkin, Y. (2008) 'Enchantment engineering and pedestrian empowerment: the Geneva case,' in Ingold, T. and Vergunst, J. L (eds) *Ways of walking: ethnography and practice on foot*, Abingdon: Ashgate, 155–167.

Levi, R. (2008) 'Loitering in the city that works: on circulation, activity and police in governing urban space,' in Dubber, M. and Valverde, M. (eds) *The new police science: the police power in domestic and international governance*, New Haven: Stanford University Press, 178–99.

Loukaitou-Sideris, A., Blumenberg, E. and Ehrenfeucht, R. (2004) 'Sidewalk democracy: municipalities and the regulation of public space,' in Ben-Joseph, E. and Szold, T. S. (eds) *Regulating place: standards and the shaping of urban America*, New York: Routledge, 141–161.

McMartin, P. (2009) 'Dissent loses ground on the boulevard' *Vancouver Sun*, Feb 3 A1.

Nelligan, M. and Mauro, N. (2008) 'Introduction,' in Nelligan, M. and Mauro, N. (eds) *Intersection: sidewalks and public space*, Oakland: Chainlinks.

Pinder, D. (2005) 'Arts of urban exploration' *Cultural Geographies*, 12: 383–411.

Pritchard, E. A. (2000) 'The way out west: development and the rhetoric of mobility on postmodern feminist theory' *Hyapatia*, 15: 3, 45–72.

Rancière, J. (2001) 'Ten theses on politics' *Theory and Event*, 5: 3.

Richardson, T. and Jensen, O. B. (2008) 'How mobility systems produce inequality: making mobile subject types on the Bangkok sky train' *Built Environment*, 34: 2, 218–231.

Riles, A. (2005) 'A new agenda for the cultural study of law: taking on the technicalities' *Buffalo Law Review* 53, 973–1025.

Ross, E. A. (1901/1969) *Social control: a survey of the foundations of order*, Cleveland: The Press of Case Western Reserve University.

Sager, T. (2006) 'Freedom as mobility: implications of the distinction between actual and potential traveling' *Mobilities*, 1: 3, 465–488.

Sennett, R. (1994) *Flesh and stone: the body and the city in western civilization*, New York: W. W. Norton and Company.

Sheller, M. (2008) 'Mobility, freedom and public space,' in Bergmann, S. and Sager, T. (eds) *Ethics of mobilities: rethinking place, exclusion, freedom and environment*, Abingdon: Ashgate, 25–38.

Solnit, R. (2000) *Wanderlust: a history of walking*, New York: Penguin.

Valverde, M. (2003) *Law's dream of a common knowledge*, Princeton: Princeton University Press.

Valverde, M. (2009) 'Laws of the street,' *City & Society*, 21: 2, 163–183.

Whyte, W. (2000) *The essential William Whyte*, New York: Fordham University Press.

47

Habits

David Bissell

The paradoxical status of habit is what characterises so many mobile lives. Habit haunts the temporalities of the endemic, eases our everyday routines, and sculpts our tastes, aptitudes and desires. But habit also dulls excitement and sense, saps our creative impulses and attenuates our horizons. Habit at once provides the material grips on the world that we require to form attachments and allegiances; whilst at the same time provides the bedrock against which we can fashion new stimulations.

Within mobilities research the trope of habit has been articulated in relation to quotidian events such as the daily commute (Edensor, 2011). It is often tethered to specific modes of 'everyday' mobility such as walking (Middleton, 2011), driving (Thrift, 2004) and railway travel (Binnie *et al.*, 2007). But habit is pivotal to understanding how all kinds of mobile life unfold: from the experiences of transnational migrants (Frändberg, 2008), to the business practices of global elites (Elliott and Urry, 2010). Habit provides us with the comfort of familiarity. But it is the same force that often drives us to be mobile in other ways where we might travel to escape the confines of our routines. Yet whilst the realm of the exceptional would seem to be furthest from habit's orbit, these are very often the shapes of life that we fall back to when we are on holiday (Edensor, 2007).

Drawing out these tensions, in this chapter habit is not a supplementary 'dimension' of mobile life that can be splintered off from other domains of experience, but rather a force that orients all mobile life. It builds on process philosophies to describe how habit is a way of apprehending the torsion of change and stability that underpins the new mobilities paradigm. It invites us to be vigilant for new sites where habit is available to be worked on in subtle and powerful ways to generate new attunements to mobile life.

Habit and inertia

Transport research has often invoked habit to understand why people continue to rely on particular modes of travel, particularly in the face of multiple environmental crises that demand that we change the ways that we move about (Fujii and Kitamura, 2003). Habit is often deemed to be a powerful barrier that impedes the mobility transitions that are required to generate lower-carbon ways of moving, such as cycling, walking and public transport. It is also invoked as an explanatory variable to account for why people might travel in ways that are not economically optimal (Lyons, 2004).

This largely negative evaluation of habit is situated within a heritage of thought that has been suspicious of its insidious powers to stagnate life and disable more 'desirable' forms of action. Influential enlightenment thinkers apprehended habit as the unhelpful shackles on our existence that attenuate our freedoms. Within the mind–body dualism of Cartesian thought, habit firmly inhabits the bodily realm of necessity in contrast to the freedom afforded by the mind. For Kant, habits of the body represent unthinking, automatic repetition of the same, which jeopardise more moral, and therefore 'desirable', forms of action that can only emerge through deliberative thought. Thus, for enlightenment thought, habit presents an epistemological predicament in the way that it veils us from the world, obscuring our capacity to know it properly. Habit's automatisms thus form a barrier to self-knowledge and moral understanding, and result only in inauthentic modes of existence.

Remaining shackled to this logic, many contemporary mobility transition debates rooted in models of behavioural psychology have appealed to the liberatory capacities of deliberative thought through strategies of awareness-raising which aim to 'defrost' (Middleton, 2011) sedimented habits. Here again, habit is an intransigence that is rooted firmly within the individual as a force that stabilises rather than transforms. Contrary to assertions that our present is a liquid modernity characterised by overwhelming flux that necessitates increased reflexivity and flexibility, here it is the relentless seriality of habit that is figured as the obstacle to our thriving, locking us into patterns of life that are difficult to escape from.

Habit transformations

To understand habit as a resistance to change, however, is to overlook how it participates in processes of transformation. Bourdieu's writings on habitus have been particularly influential in underscoring the significance of changeability. Rather than focusing on the individual, as much behavioural psychology does, Bourdieu's unit of analysis is society at large, and 'habitus' describes the unconscious norms that underpin thought and action which are inscribed through different sites of learning. For Bourdieu habitus can change over time, either suddenly or more gradually, through its formative relation with the field. However, habitus is generally concerned with the reproduction of the social order and the preservation of conformity over deviation to achieve congruence between habitus and field. Whilst Bourdieu's is a body that '*enacts* the past, bringing it to life' (1990, 73), its tendency to appropriate the rule-like character of the habitus underplays its transformative potentials. Beasley-Murray goes further: 'habitus is conservative: it is history, literally, incarnate; it ensures the tired repetitions of social reproduction; it encourages us to wait for the familiar rituals of everyday life' (2011, 216).

For other thinkers, particularly those influenced by philosophies where processes are not subordinated to substances, habit is not mere repetition or continuity of the same but is instead implicated in processes of intensive transformation. For Erin Manning (2009), inertia, far from being a condition induced by a surfeit of habit, is a situation where there is *not enough* habitual action. Manning's is a much more dynamic understanding where habit is a force of transformation itself, where past actions feed movement into the next actions. Inertia is an *absence* of this forward movement from incipiency to displacement which results in continuity of the same. Manning is one of a number of thinkers who have sought to carve out an understanding of habit that fully implicates it within processes of transformation rather than a resistance that tempers change. One of those thinkers is Félix Ravaisson, whose writings on habit are highly germane for mobilities research given his substantive focus on what repetition does to movement. For Ravaisson, habit constitutes a *permanent change in disposition* that repetition or continuity of movement brings about. Thus Ravaisson places much more emphasis than Bourdieu on the question of futurity, where it is habit that *ensures* that change takes place continually.

At the heart of Ravaisson's theorisation of habit is a dual logic where the repetition or continuity of a movement, an active affection at first willed by the body, strengthens that movement. In contrast, the repetition or continuity of sensation, a passive affection at first felt as an impression on the body, weakens that sensation. Through this inverse law, active movements become increasingly automatic, removed from the sphere of conscious will, thereby becoming more passive. On the other hand, passive impressions are incorporated into the body and become desires, thereby becoming more active. Through this torsion of activity and passivity emerges a spontaneity that 'is at once active and passive, equally opposed to mechanical fatality and to reflective freedom' (2008, 55). Ravaisson calls this the 'obscure activity' of habit that 'increasingly anticipates both the impression of external objects in sensibility, and the will in activity' (2008, 51).

Habit understood as the development of these creative tendencies accounts for how movements over time and through repetition become transformed. What were initially movements that were clumsy, difficult and required effort, through habit become increasingly precise, graceful and effortless. It is through habit that mobility competencies take shape through the efficiencies that habit affords where only those movements useful for the action are retained. Here we might think of how the bodily movements required for sports or videogames become increasingly removed from the realm of cognitive effort (Ash, 2012); or how the daily commute progressively takes place on 'autopilot' (Middleton, 2011). At the same time, those sensations that were initially painful become attenuated and woven into the task to-hand. We might think of how, for some, the strains of the daily commute become easier to bear, where agitations that once impacted with force lose their capacity to affect. Furthermore, in the absence of certain stimuli that we have become habituated to, we might miss their presence such that those sensations become a desire in and of themselves. It is this aspect of habit that furnishes it with the 'infrastructural' properties that cocoon the mobile body as much as the more obdurate materialities that are traditionally understood as infrastructure, such as buildings or technologies of transit. The virtual infrastructures of habit are thus transitional and developmental and lend the body a 'container agency' (Bissell and Fuller, 2011). It is habit that generates the affects of comfort which provide a 'guarantee' for the body (Merleau-Ponty, 2002) whilst at the same time changing the phenomenal experience of proximity whilst on the move (Bissell, 2013a): something that Jirón's (2010) 'tunnel effect' of routine movement through the urban landscape describes well.

Creative syntheses of habit

Ravaisson bequeaths an understanding of habit that apprehends it as a process of transformation rather than something that keeps change in check. Habit enables an idea to be translated into matter, where an idea that begins in consciousness can become manifested through action which, increasingly removed from the will, becomes sustained by the 'obscure activity' of habit to form a *passive intentionality*. For Ravaisson, the strengthening of activity and weakening of passivity that habit gives rise to are not just 'prosthesis' and 'armour' that extend and guard an underlying, essential body, but permanent transformations of the relations that constitute body and world (Dewsbury, 2011). Unlike Bourdieu's more ideological understanding of habit, which, although very much corporeal, is more like the learned inhabitation of a set of codes and norms that regulate how we live with others, Ravaisson's work signals more a radical transformation in the affective, molecular constitution of life and its future orientation.

Although lacking the insights afforded by more recent developments in neuroscience and biology, Ravaisson speculates how this transformation could be accounted for 'by some change . . . in the physical constitution of the organs' (2008, 53). As Lalande remarks, 'one must not confuse the manifestation of habit, which renders it sensible to us, with the biological modification that constitutes it' (Lalande, 1956 cited in Toscano, 2006, 113). This is not a 'ductile' body that returns to an original form, but a 'plastic' body whose permanent disposition is changed. Whilst many of the empirical examples that Ravaisson gives hint at the phenomenal aspects of habit for lived bodily experience, what is radical about Ravaisson's understanding of habit, and the way that his ideas become extended and reworked by Bergson and later Deleuze, is the *impersonality* of habit. Habit is not coincident with 'individual' bodies but is part of the movement of life itself that brings bodies into being. Indeed the problem with many accounts of habit is that they tend to imagine bodies that are already-individuated prior to habit's work, rather than seeking to understand how habit is itself a force of individuation.

These individuations are often underplayed in practical accounts of mobile lives. Where 'practice' is of course central to both the constitution of subjects and a way of drawing out the significance of the wider assemblages within which practices take place, there is often a tendency to understand practice as only the *extensive movements in space that take place in time*. This overlooks the *intensive movements that time gives rise to*, which spotlights the ontogenetic folding of body with world that is habit. For some, practice is a helpful way of thinking about the collectives that are absent from more humanist renderings of habit. For example, Turner asserts that 'practices without sharing . . . are habits – individual rather than shared' (2001, 120). Yet this understanding appeals to a 'cult of interiority' that tethers habits to individual (human) subjects, rather than seeing habit as an impersonal, creative force that at the same time individuates and connects.

Whilst practices are a manifestation of the 'obscure activity' of habit, they are a specific manifestation amongst countless others that habit gives rise to. What this means is that to talk of a discrete habit belies how a movement practice such as 'the journey to work' is actually composed of thousands of interlocking habits across different forms of matter. One of Deleuze and Guattari's (1994) important contributions to our understanding of habit is how it is not something individual, or restricted to human or even organic life. To spotlight the transformative potentials inherent to all matter, they describe how all forms of organic and inorganic matter contract the forces that produce their particular form, taking from environments what they require to create new characteristics. Habit can thus be understood as a 'plastic' synthesis which involves both 'a form of contemplation – absorbing the environment, passively lending itself to what is given – and a kind of exercise, informing and transforming the surroundings, appropriating the given conditions for its organic functions' (Malabou, 2005, 60). This gives us a powerful way of understanding how events become enrolled into our constitution through habit, helping to sculpt who we are at the molecular level. José Gil describes this synthetic process wonderfully when he says that 'the singularity of the "individual" is not that of an "I" or a distinct body – with its organs, skin, affect, and thought separate from the rest of the community – but that of a body in communication with the whole of nature and culture, and all the more singular to the extent that it allows itself to be traversed by the greatest number of natural and social forces' (1998, 159).

Importantly, then, it is matter's inherent tendencies for elaboration which make the synthesis of habit creative. It is what makes events linger and sustain, where matter contracts the past, stores it up, and deploys it when needed. But it is not mere deployment of what went before. As Erin Manning describes, 'events do not perish into nothingness. Like memories, they can be reactivated. To reactivate an event is not to recreate the same movement again but to invent a new movement that calls forth a certain array of recognizable elastic points. This new movement will be virtually populated with the pastness that constitutes the experience of moving in that way. In relational movement, once I know that it is possible for my body to move in a certain way, it is much more likely I will experiment with that way of moving' (2009, 39).

So whilst phenomenologists have enhanced our understanding of the embodied experience of habit from the perspective of the lived body, Ravaisson's understanding of habit, which is developed by Bergson and Deleuze and Guattari, is much more post-phenomenological in the way that he is interested in the impersonal, ontogenetic forces that cross-cut bodies and their milieu, reforming both in the process. Indeed Ravaisson's signal achievement is the way he underscores the importance of an ontological investigation into habit, rather than just a phenomenological account of it, which reveals how bodies, organic and inorganic life are all involved in processes of contemplation and contraction, extending and elaborating their form – thus pointing towards an understanding of subjectivity as being constantly 'reactualized through events of the present passing' (Manning, 2009, 22). But where does this leave us as mobilities researchers? Rather than understanding habit as a discrete 'factor' which impacts on our mobility decisions, or a resistance to change that inheres within individual bodies, or an ephemeral mediator of style, habit becomes a much more expansive transformative dynamic that helps us to understand the torsion of obduracy and change that characterises all forms of mobile life. Habit thus becomes a way of refiguring the mobilities–moorings relation in a more temporal, processual manner which invites us to consider what changes and what is retained, rather than what moves and what stays still (see Hannam *et al.*, 2006).

The mobility politics of habit

One of the most significant implications of this ontological investigation of habit is that it problematises the question of agency that has been at the heart of thinking about the politics of mobility. One of the key axioms for thinking through the politics of mobility is whether movement is voluntary or coerced (Cresswell, 2010), and thus indicative of a surfeit or deficit of individual freedom. The issue of whether someone freely chooses to be mobile or not is an important one. But very often this issue is evaluated according to an understanding of a body that privileges an autonomous sovereign wilfulness heavily invested in the liberatory capacities of individual, deliberative thought (Bissell, 2011). Accordingly, this positions habit negatively as either a potential source of false consciousness, an obstacle to our thriving, or an ally for the sustenance of pervasive inequalities – and something that deliberative thought must somehow overcome. In contrast, what Ravaisson's account of habit demonstrates so well is that habit is not *opposed* to conscious, deliberative thought but instead participates fully in how thinking and moving become manifest. Habit is the productive relation through which desires become realised: where an activity that once required conscious effort, over time, becomes increasingly removed from the sphere of conscious willing, animated instead by habit's 'obscure activity'. At the same time, the affective, molecular changes that this transition initiates transform the nature of desire itself, thereby stimulating new activities and new futures. As such, *habit is the way that all movements stretch beyond themselves to condition future movements*. Thus rather than understanding the sovereign will as the point of origin, habit is primary – and willing is just a sub-component of habit's work. Ravaisson's understanding of habit as the creative engagement of living beings with worldly forces thereby demands that we entertain not only a more distributed notion of wilfulness, but also a more fluid and impersonal notion of desire – both of which complicate and expand our thinking for a politics of mobility.

More specifically, habit invites us to think about the relation between mobility and freedom in a rather different but no less politicised way. If we take it that habit is at the very core of our constitution, as Deleuze reminds us when he says 'we are habits, nothing but habits' (1991, x), it makes little sense to suggest that our freedom is conditional on the overthrowing of habit. Certainly the biopolitical potentials of habit have been instrumentalised into all kinds of practices of discipline and control that we might apprehend in negative ways and that we might want to be rid of. But such conceptualisations take us perilously close to the tradition that is built on a negative conceptualisation of liberty 'from' something where good habits are parsed from bad habits according to a moral schematisation: where freedom becomes merely a 'chosen' state that is attained once the shackles of bad habits have been severed. A less ideological and more ontological understanding of freedom acknowledges that 'it is not that subjects are or are not free; rather actions, those undertaken by living beings, may sometimes express such freedom' (Grosz, 2010, 147). Freedom is therefore something that is enacted: quite simply it is a capacity for *action*, where life transforms itself. *Freedom is the capacity to develop habits*. Acknowledging this fact is not the same as helplessly surrendering to the forces of life, but rather it opens up questions that are sensitive to the new ontological material politics that Ravaisson's understanding of habit sets into motion.

How might we evaluate habits differently?

Rather than regarding certain habits of moving and thinking as innately good or bad, we must instead consider how habit tempers our capacity to move forward in the world. This takes us away from a prescriptive, moral evaluation and closer to the immanent method of evaluation that Deleuze draws from Spinoza, where we evaluate our habits according to the ways that they extend or attenuate our capacities for action. Whilst this alerts us to the difficulties entailed in identifying and naming discrete habits or bundles of habits, carving out a mobility politics of habit requires attending to how 'habit ecologies' unfold, where different habits live together constituting the transitional relations that compose organic and non-organic life. Developing Massey's (1993) notion of a 'power geometry' in this context where different habits rub up against each other, whilst some habits might permit comfort, ease and efficiency for ourselves and others, these same habits might inflict hurt and debilitation on other forms of life. Complicating matters further, as Berlant (2011) persuasively reminds us, those habits that are life-enhancing and those which are life-denying often turn out to be one and the same thing.

How might we attend to habits?

This task of evaluation might be even more difficult given the tendency for habit to be concealed from both sensation and consciousness. Indeed if habit is involved in the attenuation of sensation, we need new ways of becoming receptive to habit's power. Whilst specific affects such as pain, discomfort and sorrow might be indicative of situations where certain habits demand our attention, the way that we work on these habits that we identify as being debilitating and thus want to change also requires a sensitivity to habit's slow-creep synthesis of matter. Exemplary here might be therapeutic spaces which involve movement practices that respect the speed of habit's transitions. Think here of how prayer, yoga and cognitive-behavioural therapy each involve fine-grained repeated bodily movements designed to foster, gradually and over time, new perceptual capacities. We might expand this question to ask: what forms of attention and new perceptual capacities are opened up by other forms of repeated movement such as those involved in the daily commute or in other forms of ritualised movement? An ontological understanding of habit thus exposes us to alternative sites for a mobility politics which might implicate art, aesthetics and spirituality.

How do different configurations of matter reveal different configurations of habit?

Whilst Ravaisson is keen to impress that habit is nothing less than the general movement of life, a metaphysics that comes freighted with transcendental overtones, we are charged with unpicking the intricate and subtle topologies of habit, exploring the sites where its power is differently manifested. Different habits demonstrate different strengths of engagement and we might be more susceptible to their duress under different conditions. This might be about identifying how different forms of habitual action are particularly susceptible to unfolding at different times of day. Are there times when the force of habit does not play out so strongly, where our material grips on the world subside? It might also involve identifying the sites where habit forms stronger attachments. Unpicking the concurrent obduracy and fragility of habit, we might draw inspiration from Nietzsche, who admits that 'I love my brief habits and consider them invaluable means for getting to know many things and states down to the bottom of their sweetness and bitterness' (1974, 236). As examples he cites cities, poems and music, amongst others. These he contrasts with his dislike of 'enduring habits' such as those 'owing to an official position' and 'constant association with the same people' (1974, 237). How might this distinction between transience and obduracy map onto unfolding relations of mobile life such as the oscillation between the transience associated with 'global roaming' and the 'banality of fixed relations' that Elliott and Urry (2010, 74) identify with new transnational working practices?

What shapes of life open up when habits are disrupted?

From this, we might want to ask: how are different forms of mobility implicated in disruptions to the force of habit? Such a question immediately brings to mind a rich history of mobility practices that owe their inspiration to the Situationist International, whose aim was to cultivate new modes of awareness through tactics that set out to defamiliarise the familiar (Wark, 2011). Whilst the imperatives of these practices vary, some subscribing to a more explicitly ideological politics of transgression, these experiments intentionally set out to disrupt habits of perception and sensing. Less-intentional disruption to mobility infrastructure is another privileged site in which habits might be revealed (Graham, 2009). Some habits might persist and endure through such events whilst others might not live on. That the attenuation of habit is not always comfortable is revealed in the clumsiness and fatigue that jet lag brings about (Bissell, 2014). Furthermore, we might consider how events of disruption become synthesised into habit's refrains, perhaps revealing themselves as either useful allies to cope with similar future disruptions, or in other possibly unwanted ways when we are least expecting it. An extreme example of this might be the unwilled flashbacks associated with post-traumatic stress disorder. How new mobile technologies serve to accommodate our existing habits, making them immediately intuitive and comfortable, whilst also modulating them in novel and often subtle ways (Sheller, 2007) is a key challenge for designers and architects of mobile spaces that points to questions regarding the transposability of habit.

How might habits generate their own disruptions?

However, to imagine habit as the gluey plateau of coherence, where transformation is of the order of slow-creep when compared with the more immediate event-like character of disruption that habit absorbs, is to neglect the more explosive disruptions that the force of habit generates itself. Habit participates in the development of bodily proficiencies through its capacity to refine and streamline movement. But we might consider how particular forms of obsession and addiction illustrate a more volatile habit-body (Bissell, 2012). In these instances, one particular habit might intensify and overwhelm others, gripping the world too tightly, such that it becomes increasingly unreceptive to and insulated from the lure of other ideas. Similarly, whilst habits might be tamed for the services of skill, they are not always so obedient to what we might desire. Here we might imagine how particular willed movements might generate their own convulsive habits that intrude on and endanger skilful performance as in the golf 'yips' or 'dartitis' (Bissell, 2013b). Indeed such incipiencies remind us how the skilfulness of the proficient performer emerges in part through a relation to its immanent disruption. As such, habit forces us to rethink the relation between mobility and resilience, not as the preservation of the same, but a transition that is characterised by slow-creep folding and sudden explosion (Malabou, 2005).

How might we cultivate receptivity for occasions where we need to change our habits?

Ultimately, one of the most significant politico-ethical challenges that we face is how we might cultivate a heightened receptivity to occasions where we need to change our habits of moving and thinking. Such a challenge recognises that our ideas and goals change, but rather than helping us realise them, it might be our current suite of habits that holds us back. William Connolly is instructive here when he says that 'a primary principle of ethics for us is the prescription to cultivate sensitivity to new circumstances and social movements that suggest the possible need to change entrenched habits. To accept that principle is to acknowledge the need to work periodically on your preliminary habits of thought and action by tactical means' (Connolly, 2011, 80). Under new circumstances, previously useful habits might become redundant. However, recognising the difficulties that come with working on our habits is not a diagnosis of our 'individual' failure or moral weakness, but rather of the nature of attachment that habit gives the world. As such, we must 'act forward in a world replete with uncertainty, sensitive to possible ways in which old habits may be out of touch with new developments' (Connolly, 2011, 157).

References

Ash, J. (2012) 'Technology, technicity, and emerging practices of temporal sensitivity in videogames', *Environment and Planning A*, 44: 187–203.

Beasley-Murray, J. (2011) *Posthegemony: Political Theory and Latin America*, Minneapolis: University of Minnesota Press.

Berlant, L. (2011) *Cruel Optimism*, Durham: Duke University Press.

Binnie, J., Edensor, T., Holloway, J., Millington, S. and Young, C. (2007) 'Mundane mobilities, banal travels', *Social and Cultural Geography*, 8: 165–174.

Bissell, D. (2011) 'Thinking habits for uncertain subjects: movement, stillness, susceptibility', *Environment and Planning A*, 43: 2649–2665.

Bissell, D. (2012) 'Agitating the powers of habit: towards a volatile politics of thought', *Theory and Event* 15(1). Available online at http://muse.jhu.edu/journals/theory_and_event/v015/15.1.bissell.html.

Bissell, D. (2013a) 'Pointless mobilities: rethinking proximity through the loops of neighbourhood', *Mobilities*, 8: 349–367.

Bissell, D. (2013b) 'Habit displaced: the disruption of skilful performance', *Geographical Research*, 51: 120–129.

Bissell, D. (2014) 'Virtual infrastructures of habit: the changing intensities of habit through gracefulness, restlessness and clumsiness', *Cultural Geographies*, forthcoming.

Bissell, D. and Fuller, G. (2011) 'Stillness unbound', in D. Bissell and G. Fuller (eds) *Stillness in a Mobile World*, London: Routledge.

Bourdieu, P. (1990) *The Logic of Practice*, Palo Alto: Stanford University Press.

Connolly, W. (2011) *A World of Becoming*, Durham: Duke University Press.

Cresswell, T. (2010) 'Towards a politics of mobility', *Environment and Planning D: Society and Space*, 28: 17–31.

Deleuze, G. (1991) *Empiricism and Subjectivity: An Essay on Hume's Theory of Human Nature*, New York: Columbia University Press.

Deleuze, G. and Guattari, F. (1994) *What is Philosophy?* Trans. H. Tomlinson and G. Burchell, New York: Columbia University Press.

Dewsbury, J.-D. (2011) 'The Deleuze-Guattarian assemblage: plastic habits', *Area* 43: 148–153.

Edensor, T. (2007) 'Mundane mobilities, performances and spaces of tourism', *Social and Cultural Geographies*, 8: 199–215.

Edensor, T. (2011) 'Commuter: mobility, rhythm, commuting', in T. Cresswell and P. Merriman (eds) *Mobilities: Practices, Spaces, Subjects*, Aldershot: Ashgate.

Elliott, A. and Urry, J. (2010) *Mobile Lives*, London: Routledge.

Frändberg, L. (2008) 'Paths in transnational time-space: representing mobility biographies of young Swedes', *Geografiska Annaler B: Human Geography*, 90: 17–28.

Fujii, S. and Kitamura, R. (2003) 'What does a one-month free bus ticket do to habitual drivers? An experimental analysis of habit and attitude change', *Transportation*, 30: 81–95.

Gil, J. (1998) *Metamorphoses of the Body*, Minneapolis: Minnesota University Press.

Graham, S. (ed.) (2009) *Disrupted Cities*, London: Routledge.

Grosz, E. (2010) 'Feminism, materialism, and freedom', in D. Coole and S. Frost (eds) *New Materialisms: Ontology, Agency and Politics*, Durham: Duke University Press.

Hannam, K., Sheller, M. and Urry, J. (2006) 'Mobilities and moorings', *Mobilities*, 1: 1–22.

Jirón, P. (2010) 'Mobile borders in urban daily mobility practices in Santiago de Chile', *International Political Sociology*, 4: 66–79.

Lalande, A. (1956) 'Habitude', *Vocabulaire Critique et Technique de la philosophie*, Paris: PUF, 392–398.

Lyons, G. (2004) 'Transport and society', *Transport Reviews*, 24: 485–509.

Malabou, C. (2005) *The Future of Hegel: Plasticity, Temporality and the Dialectic*, London: Routledge.

Manning, E. (2009) *Relationscapes: Movement, Art, Philosophy*, Cambridge: The MIT Press.

Massey, D. (1993) 'Power-geometry and a progressive sense of place', in J. Bird, B. Curtis, T. Putnam, G. Robertson and L. Tickner (eds) *Mapping the Futures: Local Cultures, Global Change*, London: Routledge.

Merleau-Ponty, M. (2002) *Phenomenology of Perception*, London: Routledge.

Middleton, J. (2011) '"I'm on autopilot, I just follow the route": exploring the habits, routines, and decision-making practices of everyday urban mobilities', *Environment and Planning A*, 43: 2857–2877.

Nietzsche, F. (1974) *The Gay Science: With a Prelude in German Rhymes and an Appendix of Songs*, trans. W. Kaufmann, New York: Vintage.

Ravaisson, F. (2008) *Of Habit*, trans. C. Carlisle and M. Sinclair, London: Continuum.

Sheller, M. (2007) 'Bodies, cybercars and the mundane incorporation of automated mobilities', *Social and Cultural Geography*, 8: 175–197.

Thrift, N. (2004) 'Driving in the City', *Theory, Culture & Society*, 21: 41–59.

David Bissell

Toscano, A. (2006) *The Theatre of Production: Philosophy and Individuation between Kant and Deleuze*, Basingstoke: Palgrave Macmillan.

Turner, S. (2001) 'Throwing out the tacit rule book: learning and practices', in T. R. Schatzki, K. Knorr-Cetina and E. von Savigny (eds) *The Practice Turn in Contemporary Theory*, London: Routledge.

Wark, M. (2011) *The Beach beneath the Street: The Everyday Life and Glorious Times of the Situationist International*, London: Verso.

48

Capturing Motion

Video set-ups for driving, cycling and walking

Eric Laurier

The sluggish imagination

Humans, animals and machines in motion can be hard to follow. As part of their quite ordinary practices their actions are done together and apart, in and out of synch. Borne ceaselessly forward their actions project, interrupt and align with one another. As we study them we find ourselves getting lost in amongst questions: What happened after that? Who did that? Did they do it at all? Methodologies for securing quite what did happen derived their impetus from a wager. Leland Stanford bets a considerable sum of money against John Isaac that while galloping, at certain points, a horse is no longer touching the ground. The photographer and camera-experimenter Edweard Muybridge is asked to provide evidence that will settle this wager one way or the other. One fast photograph of the ungrounded feet manages to settle the bet. The vestiges of that first inquiry remain with us in the photo-finish. That uncertain moment over, Stanford releases the resources to build the devices that allow Stanford and Muybridge to study galloping. The photographic mechanism for the proto-film recording is constructed from lines of still cameras along a track that are triggered by wires. The playback mechanism – called the zoopraxiscope – is another machine that then runs the images for the viewer. Muybridge tours the world with the zoopraxiscope, introducing the concept of the sequential film recording as a technology for an ambitious set of inquiries into the motion of humans and animals.

Ninety years later, the newly emergent group of ethnomethodologists adopted light-weight but time-limited film cameras and the longer-running, but barely portable, early video cameras (Hill and Crittenden, 1968). Why they did so is usually encapsulated in a brief quote from Harold Garfinkel (1967) which, in turn paraphrasing Herbert Spiegelberg (Maynard, 2012), describes video as an aid to the sluggish imagination: a remark that seems to push us in quite a different direction from the zoopraxiscope as a revelatory device, like the microscope or telescope, that allows us to see things in a detail unavailable to the naked human eye. What Garfinkel gestures toward is that when we have difficulty supplying the details of how mobile practices are organised and their organisation made visible, video will quicken our sociological imaginations. His early collaborator Harvey Sacks was also working with devices for recording, though in his case it was the tape recorder. Sacks also warns his students about the limits of their imagination (Sacks, 1992). His warning is not all that far from Garfinkel's remark, yet Sacks emphasises the surprises to be found in recordings. People accomplish astounding things, and do so in shared ways that our conventional accounts of what people do tell us they simply do not, or would not do, nor would they do it *that* way. Stanford wins: horses fly. In ethnomethodology and conversation analysis, the video recording and the action-replay are drawn into the dialectics of the imaginative structure of the world and matters of fact (Raffel, 1979).

Muybridge's first recording shows us that following things in flight, be they horses, dirty jokes (Sacks, 1978) or soil samples (Goodwin, 1999), can require quite a complex set-up of recording equipment. To settle the bet Muybridge had to make sure the hooves were not missed by the cameras; a primary concern of ethnomethodology and conversation analysis is not to lose the phenomenon in the recording (Garfinkel, 2002).[1] Muybridge stripped away the settings in which the motion, that he was interested in recording, was happening. His horses ran against a white wall for maximum visibility; his later studies of human motion were carried out against black walls with square grids marked out on them for easier measurement (Figure 48.1). His studies blocked out the social world to focus on physiology, to the point where his boxers, dancers and cleaners were stripped even of their clothes. By contrast ethnnomethodologists leave the clothes on, put back the furniture and find ways of filming in the organised mess of all manner of real-worldly places. Their desire is to follow human and animal motion in, and through, complex social settings, be they everyday (Ryave and Schenkein, 1974), workplace (Luff *et al.*, 2000) or scientific (Goodwin, 1997). In the fifty years since ethnomethodologists and conversation analysts first started using the recording devices to record, replay and re-witness all manner of practices, the audio-visual recorders have become themselves more suited to following things in motion.

What I aim to do in the rest of this chapter is to consider three common forms of mobility and the camera set-ups that have been assembled in order to try not to lose the thing, where losing it and finding it are ever-present issues. Driving, cycling and walking are practices that I have familiarity with through either having recorded them myself or being involved with discussions around what cameras to use, how to position them and the ensuing assessment of how those recordings turned out. As Luff and Heath note (2012: 256), "unlike methodological debates surrounding the accomplishment and use of interviews, fieldwork and even focus groups, the discussion concerning video is still constrained to a small number of issues." Their discussion of camera angles in video methodologies more generally parallels many of the concerns of this chapter on mobility in particular.

Figure 48.1   Selection from gymnastics studies (Muybridge, 1887)

Set-up 1: Handheld from the passenger seat – following the action

My first attempts to use video to record mobile practices arose out of a project with Chris Philo, studying how office work was being undertaken in cars (Laurier, 2004). At that time, mobile phones and portable computers were only just becoming commonplace for company employees, and were transforming the nature of what could be done during car journeys. Mobile ethnographies in, and of, multiple sites were coming to the fore and marking out a change from the tradition of the ethnographer settling for long periods into one fieldsite (Cook and Crang, 1995; Marcus, 1995). Geographers, anthropologists and others were becoming interested in doing ethnographies that followed people and/or things as they themselves moved from one place to another, sometimes inspired by actor-network theory (Latour, 1987) and sometimes not. For our project, the usual method of studying an organisation would be to spend time in its offices and so, to learn about the mobilising of the office that was part and parcel of regional service work, we located the ethnographer in the worker's car. The realities of an in-car ethnography are a little more peculiar, of course, because that places the ethnographer in close proximity in the passenger seat rather than at the safe distance of a spare desk.

Retracing the intellectual set-up of my video use, I was only just becoming interested in ethnomethodology via Lynch's (1993) work in science studies and conversation analysis for analyzing interview materials (Laurier, 1999). While they were not particularly video-friendly, I was still equally or more interested in the socio-material studies of Law (1991) and Latour (1987) and how they were being taken up by Thrift (1996), Hinchliffe (1996) and others in human geography. Alongside these intellectual concerns, cultural geography's engagement with experiments in representational forms through reflexive writing strategies (Ashmore, 1989), new media and visuality (Rose, 2001) was shaping both how I documented my fieldwork and how it was written up. The set-up of the theory did influence the plan for setting up the video recording workers in their cars from the passenger seat. Going beyond the audio would help make apprehensible the roles played by materials and new technologies. The camera itself should try and follow the things.

One thing we got right in that early project was that, while we had a brand new camcorder and were pretty keen to use it, we held back. Following the procedures established by Rod Watson (1999) studying truck drivers' work for the US Forest Service, I spent a week travelling with each mobile office worker and becoming familiarised with their routines before filming anything. The week was spent learning the basics of their work in the car and how it related to the other parts of the job, learning a little bit about their biographies and

Figure 48.2   Frame grab of Ally looking at an A to Z

letting them get used to my presence doing the kind of passenger-seat ethnography that Jack Katz was using to study road rage (Katz, 2001). I was becoming what Lave and Wenger (1991) called a 'legitimate peripheral participant' with a legitimate peripheral camera. What the first week also allowed me to do was prepare for the filming by planning and discussing with each participant what sorts of events in the cars I would like to video record over the next week.

During the week of filming I sat with the camcorder in my lap, ready to switch it on and begin recording the work activities as they happened. Another thing that we got reasonably right was trying to minimise the distraction and disruption created by filming (see also Esbjornsson et al., 2007). How I accomplished this in the car was by having the camera in such a position that it could always record, turning off the beep and the red light that signaled the beginning and ending of recording. Why do this? Because the starting and stopping of a recording raises questions for the person being recorded of 'why now?' Any ethnographer that has used a notebook will know that the very act of writing in the notebook distracts research subjects. They ask themselves, or you directly, 'why are you writing something down now? What did I do? What did I say?' These are all interesting questions to answer and could be answered at the time, but if they are, then whatever it was that you wanted to record has promptly evaporated.

However there were problems with the set-up that became apparent as the phenomenon we were following did not so much get lost as become abbreviated. By having the ethnographer start filming whenever an interesting event began happening, the event had already begun happening, and so how it first began would be missed (Heath et al., 2010). Following the thing with the camera systematically missed the beginnings of the movement and routinely provided an incomplete record (Luff and Heath, 2012).

Set-up 2: A pair of fixed cameras – the participants and what they see

When five years later I had the opportunity to record car-based practices for a second time as part of the Habitable Cars project (http://web2.ges.gla.ac.uk/~elaurier/habitablecars/) with Barry Brown and Hayden Lorimer, we rethought the earlier approach (Laurier et al., 2008). Breaking what had been continuous fieldwork into two stages, the passenger-seat ethnography now ran for a first week and, when it was complete, the cameras were given to the participants to film themselves. As with the previous single-camera set-up for mobile office workers, during the first week I had a chance to get to know the car's occupants, their relationships to one another, their accounts of why they drove the way they did, and so on.

A common solution in workplaces like offices for creating a more complete record is to use fixed cameras that provide a mid-shot (Luff and Heath, 2012), however the restricted space of the car removes that possibility. Our solution was to adopt and adapt a dual camera set-up for filming within cars, developed by Lorenza Mondada (2012) on the Espace, Mobilités, Interactions, Corps (EMIC) project. One camera was filming the road ahead while the other was pointed inwards toward the car travelers. In film terminology the former is called a "point of view" shot, and that nicely describes its utility for studying the viewpoint that this form of mobility relies upon. The latter, as we have already noted, is somewhere between a mid-shot and a medium close-up. With a short distance and a wide field to capture, Mondada's original set-up used fish-eye lenses and attached the cameras to the dashboard using sticky-backed velcro. The small adaptations used for Habitable Cars were to insert the cameras into foam cubes and attach semi-fish-eye lenses rather than full fish-eye lenses. The foam cubes made placing the cameras within the car quick and easy. The foam also reduced vibration from the road. The rearward-forward set-up provided a degree of access to the

Figure 48.3   Twin-camera set-up

perspective available from the front seats of the car, while also recording the front seats of the car and limited parts of the backseats (see Figure 48.3 above). Recently this set-up has been made more straightforward, not to mention smaller, through the manufacture of a series of cameras that are built with rearward and forward-facing lenses.

As you can see from Figure 48.3, the front-facing camera provided a limited access of the view of the road ahead. This view is frequently central to making sense of the talk and gestures of driver and passenger and, indeed, the larger course of action that the car is involved in (e.g. cornering, waiting at traffic lights, cruising on the motorway, etc.). Moreover, when combined with the shots of the driver and passenger, the front view then allowed us to analyze what they were looking at, and when and how visible features were brought to the attention of one another. It was not entirely irrelevant to everyday activities either, since the landscape, or events, ahead of the car were often a resource in establishing topics for discussion or, indeed, moving into the closings of various conversations as destinations were reached and so on (Laurier *et al.*, 2008). What was missing in leaving the camera with this fixed perspective on the road ahead was the view out of the side windows, which was often all the more likely to be topicalised by rear seat passengers (e.g. 'did you see that cute little dog mum? Mum, can we get a dog? Can we?'). While the rear-view camera set-up captured a great deal, it was by no means a panoptic device and the car is certainly not a panoptic architecture. Quite what children were up to, in left- and right-sided positions in the backseat, was hidden. These seats were blind spots that many of the children knew and utilised for naughtiness, or treated as inferior for the purposes of seeking parental attention.

The lenses themselves also had their own peculiarities. Full fish-eye lenses produce perspectival shifts that make it "difficult to recover the orientation of the participants, both where they were looking at any moment and what objects they might be looking at" (Luff and Heath, 2012: 260). Even a semi-fish-eye lens bent the visual field and usually made it appear that the driver and passenger were facing away from one another when actually they had been facing ahead. Given that the project was interested in the gestural and embodied aspects of their interactions, the stance produced by turning away from one another rather than being side-by-side is consequential.

Set-up 3: Multiple mini cameras – a shifting patchwork of perspectives

Over the last decade attaching cameras to helmets has become part of recording the excitement of mountain-biking and street-racing. The resulting recordings are then usually heavily edited and set to music to dramatise the accomplishments and hazards of these extreme sports. For ethnographers of mobility the existing video-velo-culture has made using head-cams to study extreme cycling minimally disruptive because it fits into an existing ecology of the leisure practice. Moreover the project of recording the cycling has established an immediate purpose and point of commonality in a shared desire to work out camera set-ups, thereby easing ethnographers into the study of these practices (Brown and Spinney, 2009). Katrina Brown *et al.* (2008) and Justin Spinney (2011) have led the field in collecting video recordings from, and of, extreme cycling.

The head-cam set-up seems to promise a perspective from the eyes of the cyclist, though Brown and Spinney (2009) are quick to alert us to the fact that the camcorder's field of view is not convergent with where the cyclist is looking. As with the fixed, front-facing cameras earlier, the head-cam has a narrower field of view and, for the cyclist, it is trained upon the direction of their helmet rather than their eyes. The cyclist's work of watching-where-they-are-going involves flicking their gaze up and down between the immediate terrain under the wheels and the more distant features of road or track that they are approaching. As Brown and Spinney (2009) also argue, it is not only that this set-up misses what the cyclist looks at, and how they go about monitoring the way ahead, it misses that they use their hearing, their balance, their kinaesthesia and more, together to make sense of their mobile environment (Ingold, 2011).

As much as it misses it also captures, recording otherwise missed details of what happens at high speed and without rest (Büscher, 2006). It is the familiar settling of the bet by Muy-bridge but this time against the ethnographer's pen and whether it might be able to stay on the page. What Brown and Spinney also used their video for was to review the recordings with cyclists in order to elicit more detailed descriptions of cycling practices from their participants. Their rather lovely twist is that when their cyclists talked about visual materials from the camcorder they played down the visual aspects of the recording in favor of the detailed description of embodied practices. Muybridge's apparatus of capture is finally returned to its subjects, allowing their "fleeting and ephemeral movements to be played back, what was previously deemed impossible to reflect upon or seemingly insignificant can be dissected in detail" (Spinney, 2011: 167).

Trials riding (a sort of parkour-on-bicycle) offers itself for recording from a third-party perspective to catch the spectacular skills of cyclists jumping, balancing and flipping their bicycles across all manner of urban features (Saville, 2010). In considering how to capture trials riding, Spinney shifted back to recordings of the bike riders from a distant shot rather than from a headcam worn by the researcher or participant. Once again his set-up neverthe-less copies the pre-existing recording practices of the cyclists and their moves. Spinney (2011) also used a third form of recording, a return to earlier set-ups that had not worked quite so well with extreme cycling but did work more effectively in this circumstance. The researcher followed the cyclist as they travelled along a familiar route, again the purpose being to use the recording as a way of reflecting upon the journey with the participant.

Recording the cyclist themselves has only really been accomplished as part of road-bike racing coverage, by filming from a vehicle ahead of the cyclist. The disruption and complex-ity of filming cyclists has set this approach aside as unusable outside of sports coverage and professional film-making. What Spinney's approach begins to outline is a set-up that might allow the capture of moments of cycling as they happen.

It is Paul McIlvenny (2013) who has recently established a camera set-up that captures how we cycle together. His set-up does not work for the lone cyclist but has provided the means to record a number of settings where groups cycle together. These are, anyway, settings of

Figure 48.4   Bike-to-bike camera set-up (McIlvenny, forthcoming)

great interest to scholars of mobility: cycling in traffic, cycling as a family, commuting on bicycle together, etc.

In initial studies of a child learning to ride in the city in 2010, McIlvenny utilised the unusual construction of Danish Christiana bikes to mount several cameras on one bicycle to provide perspectives of himself and his daughter and the road ahead and behind (Figure 48.4). Alongside recording father and daughter on the same bike, he also began experimenting with recording his daughter riding her bicycle beside him. In his second series of vélo studies he drew upon lessons from the first studies to then mount multiple small, wide-angle cameras, designed for recording extreme sports, on multiple bikes. The recording of cyclists is thus done from the frame of each bike, providing a large enough distance to bring other cyclists into shot. The shifting placement of the bikes in relation to each other did mean that they slipped out of shot fairly regularly, yet there was still a large enough collection of episodes collected for analysts of vélomobility to study later.

What I also want to cover briefly in this section is how McIlvenny's approach can be borrowed for recording walking practices. It is not incidental that the road movie is a conventional cinematic genre and the pavement movie is not. Filming and recording conversations inside vehicles is relatively easy because people stay roughly where they are, close enough to camera and microphone. Filming people on the pavement, walking across moorland or even just walking down an office corridor requires either cameras themselves on tracks and wheels following the walkers or multiple set-ups. None of those professional requirements bode well for social scientists interested in recording walking.

The classic early studies of pavement life in US cities by William H. Whyte (Whyte, 1985, 2009) were shot from parapets above the urban pedestrians. Whyte's camera set-up of the 'view from slightly above' was returned to by ethnomethodologists with a concern for the organisational practices used by walkers to make their walking intelligible and accountable (Lee and Watson, 1993; Ryave and Schenkein, 1974). More recent studies with a concern for the looks of the environment from the walker's perspective reproduced it by following their movements with a handheld camera (Weilenmann *et al.*, 2012). Like Spinney's following-on bike set-up, this is reliant on the researcher maintaining the perspective; it provides limited perspectives and is not really practical for extended recordings of walking practices.

Recording walking practices at ground level has become technically possible with the arrival of micro video cameras. These tiny cameras can use human clothing and luggage as the moving bipod equivalent of McIlvenny's bicycle-tripod. Groups of pedestrians are fitted with clip-on cameras, cameras on lanyards (Figure 48.5) and/or cameras in spectacles or hats that then provide multiple perspectives on their fellow walkers (Brown *et al.*, 2013). This particular set-up appears to provide relatively stable shots, ongoing audio, if a shifting patchwork of perspectives. As cameras grow yet smaller and their image stabilisation more effective we can look forward to being able to capture more of what happens while we walk and the related temporal features and spatial organisation of all manner of varied pedestrian practices.

What's still missing

Having begun with Muybridge's early recordings and continued from there I have attended to the visual and almost entirely ignored the capture of the auditory aspects of mobility. I am guilty, as many videographers are, of leaving the audio to take care of itself. Unlike the visual field, the audio field from most consumer camcorders seems wide enough to capture the background noise, the vocal utterances and more. There is, though, an equally fine art to capturing the details of audio that are perceptible to moving subjects. In the car the details of the backseat conversations go unheard, just as what else it is that goes on there goes unseen. Cyclists hear motor vehicles approaching them from behind and may adjust speed or location or simply glance over their shoulder. There is, simply, more to what we can hear, where we hear it and how it is heard, from one person to another in a group.

There are other things that will inevitably be missing. While smaller, lighter and higher-resolution recordings of mobile practices seem to offer the opportunity to capture ever more of the visual embodied organisation of mobile practices, we should not forget that recordings always and inescapably lose their phenomena. It is in the video recording's nature as a recording rather than the thing itself (Raffel, 1979). That recordings always leave something out does not obviate us from trying to record the world at all nor from our exercising our skill and thought in the selection and handling of our recording devices.

Finally, in studying mobile practices with video I would suggest we need to rephrase if not give up the slogan that video is an 'aid' to the sluggish imagination. Yes, it does help in confronting the student of mobility with a far more complex and finely organised set of human, animal and machine practices than they could have imagined. But, it is easy enough for the sluggish mind to fail to respond with imagination, to look past or away from what is before it, especially when it looks so like their everyday mobilities rendered onto a screen. What video also requires is for us to exercise our imagination in responding to the glimpses, breaths, over-steers, near-misses and family homework that it records in overwhelming detail. It is a motion recording of mobility that is far, far from the temporary fix of the tick-box summary of travel by car [ ], bicycle [ ], or on foot [ ]. Instead we could think of it as filling in the phenomenological bracket and providing the detailed descriptions of [driving], [cycling] and [walking].

Note

1 David Good provides a more detailed history of Muybridge and the rise of videography in his unpublished appendix to Goode 2007 (copies available from the author).

References

Ashmore, M. (1989) *The Reflexive Thesis.* London: University of Chicago Press.

Brown, B., Laurier, E., and McGregor, M. (2013) 'Mobility, Maps and Mobile Device Use.' *Proceedings of CHI 2013.* New York: ACM.

Brown, K. M., Dilley, R., and Marshall, K. (2008) 'Using a Head-Mounted Video Camera to Understand Social Worlds and Experiences.' *Sociological Research Online*, 13(6). doi:10.5153/sro.1818.

Brown, K. M., and Spinney, J. (2009) 'Catching a Glimpse: The Value of Video in Evoking, Understanding and Representing the Practice of Cycling.' In B. Fincham, M. Mcguiness, and L. Murray (eds) *Mobile Methodologies*. Hampshire: Palgrave MacMillan, pp. 130–151.

Büscher, M. (2006) 'Vision in Motion.' *Environment and Planning A*, 38(2), 281–299.

Cook, I., and Crang, M. (1995) *Doing Ethnographies*. London: RGS-IBG Catmog.

Esbjornsson, M., Juhlin, O., and Weilenmann, A. (2007) 'Drivers Using Mobile Phones in Traffic: An Ethnographic Study of Interactional Adaptation.' *International Journal of Human–Computer Interaction*, 22(1–2), 37–58.

Garfinkel, H. (1967) *Studies in Ethnomethodology*. New Jersey: Prentice Hall.

Garfinkel, H. (2002) *Ethnomethodology's Program*. London: Rowman & Littlefield Pub Incorporated.

Goode, D. A. (2007) *Playing with My Dog Katie. An Ethnomethodological Study of Canine–Human Interaction*. West Lafayette: Purdue University Press.

Goodwin, C. (1997) 'The Blackness of Black: Color Categories as Situated Practice.' In L. B. Resnick, R. Säljö, C. Pontecorvo, and B. Burge (eds) *Discourse, Tools and Reasoning: Essays on Situated Cognition*. New York: Springer, pp. 111–140.

Goodwin, C. (1999) 'Practices of Color Classification in Professional Discourse.' In A. Jaworski and N. Coupland (eds) *The Discourse Reader*. London: Routledge, pp. 474–491.

Heath, C., Hindmarsh, J., and Luff, P. (2010) *Video in Qualitative Research: Analysing Social Interaction in Everyday Life*. London: Sage.

Hill, R. J., and Crittenden, K. S. (eds) (1968) *Proceedings of the Purdue Symposium on Ethnomethodology*. Lafayette, IN: Prude Research Foundation.

Hinchliffe, S. (1996) 'Technology, Power, and Space – The Means and Ends of Geographies of Technology.' *Environment and Planning D: Society and Space*, 14, 659–682.

Ingold, T. (2011) *Being Alive: Essays on Movement, Knowledge and Description*. London: Routledge, pp. 1–289.

Katz, J. (2001) *How Emotions Work*. London: University of Chicago Press.

Latour, B. (1987) *Science in Action*. Milton Keynes: Open University Press.

Laurier, E. (1999) Geographies of Talk: "Max Left a Message for You". *Area*, 31(1), 36–46.

Laurier, E. (2004) 'Doing Office Work on the Motorway.' *Theory, Culture & Society*, 21(4–5), 261–277.

Laurier, E., Lorimer, H., Brown, B., Jones, O., Juhlin, O., Noble, A., Perry, M., Pica, D., Sormani, P., Strebel, I., Swan, L., Taylor, A., Watts, L., and Weilenmann, A. (2008) 'Driving and "Passengering": Notes on the Ordinary Organization of Car Travel.' *Mobilities*, 3(1), 1–24.

Lave, J., and Wenger, E. (1991) *Situated Learning*. Cambridge: Cambridge University Press.

Law, J. (1991) *A Sociology of Monsters: Essays on Power, Technology and Domination*. London: Routledge.

Lee, J. R. E., and Watson, R. (1993) 'Methodological Orientations in the Analysis of Public Space.' In *Interaction in Public Space: Final Report to the Plan Urbain*. Paris: Plan Urbain, pp. 17–31.

Luff, P., Hindmarsh, J., and Heath, C. (2000) *Workplace Studies*. Cambridge: Cambridge University Press.

Luff, P., and Heath, C. (2012) 'Some "Technical Challenges" of Video Analysis: Social Actions, Objects, Material Realities and the Problems of Perspective.' *Qualitative Research*, 12(3), 255–279. doi:10.1177/1468794112436655.

Lynch, M. (1993) *Scientific Practice and Ordinary Action*. Cambridge: Cambridge University Press.

Marcus, G. E. (1995) 'Ethnography in/of the World System: The Emergence of Multi-sited Ethnography.' *Annual Review of Anthropology (1995)*, 95–117.

Maynard, D. W. (2012) 'An Intellectual Remembrance of Harold Garfinkel: Imagining the Unimaginable, and the Concept of the "Surveyable Society".' *Human Studies*, 35(2), 209–221. doi:10.1007/s10746-012-9226-0.

McIlvenny, P. (forthcoming) 'Vélomobile Formations-in-Action: Biking and Talking Together.' *Space and Culture, forthcoming* .

Mondada, L. (2012) 'Talking and Driving: Multiactivity in the Car.' *Semiotica*, 191(1/4), 223–256. doi:10.1515/sem-2012-0062.

Muybridge (1887) Selection from Gymnastic Studies in Muybridge's Human Figure in Motion (2007). Dover Electronic Clip Art.

Raffel, S. (1979) *Matters of Fact*. London: Routledge.

Rose, G. (2001) *Visual Methodologies*. London: Sage.

Ryave, A. L., and Schenkein, J. N. (1974) 'Notes on the Art of Walking.' In R. Turner (ed.) *Ethnomethodology: Selected Readings*. Harmondsworth: Penguin, pp. 265–274.

Sacks, H. (1978) 'Some Technical Considerations of a Dirty Joke.' In J. N. Schenkein (ed.) *Studies in the Organization of Conversational Interaction*. New York: Academic Press, pp. 249–269.

Sacks, H. (1992) *Lectures on Conversation Vol 1*. Oxford: Blackwell.

Saville, S. J. (2008) 'Playing with Fear: Parkour and the Mobility of Emotion.' *Social and Cultural Geography*, 9(8), 891–914.

Saville, S. J. (2010) *Playing Towards Contact: Doing Parkour, Bike Trials and Capoeria*. Aberystwyth University.

Spinney, J. (2011) 'A Chance to Catch a Breath: Using Mobile Video Ethnography in Cycling Research.' *Mobilities*, 6(2), 161–182. doi:10.1080/17450101.2011.552771.

Thrift, N. J. (1996) *Spatial Formations*. London: Sage.

Watson, R. (1999) 'Driving in Forests and Mountain.' *Ethnographic Studies*, 4, 50–60.

Weilenmann, A., Normark, D., and Laurier, E. (2012) 'Managing Walking Together: The Challenge of Revolving Doors.' *Space and Culture*, 1–23.

Whyte, W. H. (1985) *The Social Life of Small Urban Spaces*. New York: Project for Public Spaces.

Whyte, W. H. (2009) *City*. Philadelphia: University of Pennsylvania Press. 2 http://web2.ges.gla.ac.uk/~elaurier/habitable_cars/.

Section Seven
Introduction: Methodologies

One of our students recently complained about the problem of doing research outside and of how her recordings with respondents had 'background noise' which made it difficult to transcribe interviews. While there are computer programmes which will seek to minimize such 'background noise', we contend that such 'noise' is very much part and parcel of doing mobilities research. It is this noise which makes the recordings more intelligible, not less, providing valuable insights into the frictions and turbulence created by mobile people and things. Rather than eliminating or complaining about the noise, we would encourage researchers to actually research the noise, as this is the very stuff of mobilities research. Doing mobilities research thus involves paying attention to how people, things and seemingly intangible entities such as ideas are on the move, as well as to how environments themselves make a difference. Law and Urry (2004, p.403) have argued that existing methodologies:

> deal, for instance, poorly with the fleeting – that which is here today and gone tomorrow, only to re-appear again the day after tomorrow. They deal poorly with the distributed – that is to be found here and there but not in between – or that which slips and slides between one place and another. They deal poorly with the multiple – that which takes different shapes in different places. They deal poorly with the non-causal, the chaotic, the complex.

It has been argued that if we are to adequately understand the ontology of contemporary mobilities then we also need to have mobile methodologies not necessarily to 'capture' but to keep pace with the fluid (dis)order and (dis)embeddedness of (de)territorialized social life (D'Andrea, 2006). First, "researchers will benefit if they track in various ways – including physically travelling with their research subjects – the many and interdependent forms of intermittent movement of people, images, information and objects" (Büscher and Urry, 2009, p.103). Second, "as a consequence of allowing themselves to be moved by, and to move with, their subjects, researchers are tuned into the social organization of 'moves'" (Büscher and Urry, 2009, p.103).

It has been argued that specific methods of data collection need to become much more "flexible, informal and context dependent, partly mimicking mobile subjects being studied in their own suppleness" (D'Andrea, 2006, p.113). By expanding his or her own viewpoint, the researcher "will then perceive and experience the trembling of slowly moving entities running at high-speed through blurred surroundings" (D'Andrea, 2006, p.114). Such research may provide a new critical window on the mobilities, immobilities and moorings of contemporary social life by utilizing innovative, experimental and increasingly sophisticated technologies (Hannam *et al.*, 2006; Fincham *et al.*, 2010; Büscher *et al.*, 2011). However, we also need to make sure that we do not over-animate social life and that we pay attention to both established and innovative methods beyond the social sciences which allow us to examine other histories and artistic and scientific practices (Merriman, 2013). It is equally important to recognize that "[s]tillness, waiting, slowness and boredom may be just as important to many situations, practices and movements as sensations and experiences of speed, movement, excitement and exhilaration" when doing research (Merriman, 2013, p.16). Mobile methodologies add to our repertoire of techniques for gathering data, rather than replacing those which already exist, and this is evident throughout the chapters in this section of the Handbook.

In his chapter on *Histories* George Revill reflects on historical methods for mobilities research and contends that it may be initially difficult for researchers using mobile methods to analyse some historical situations where all we may have are relatively silent infrastructures and their representations. He argues for the importance of considering the role of infrastructures in constituting and enabling mobile experiences, where the reverberations of infrastructural histories and memories are seen as an important starting, standing and continuation point for mobilities research.

In his chapter on *Mappings* Martin Dodge takes our methodological discussion in a more overtly spatial direction. Mapping is a major challenge of visualizing mobilities in a meaningful form, as certain characteristics of mobilities are seen to be unmappable. He goes on to discuss the novel solutions to this problem in terms of: innovative graphic designs, the use of animation and the use of digital technology. The use of digital technology is also considered by Debbie Lisle in her chapter on *Photography*. Photography has conventionally been seen as a technology which stills movement or captures stillness, however Lisle shows how stillness is complex, "polyvalent, pluralistic and heterogeneous", giving rise to and being associated with specific ontologies rather than simply being the undesirable or problematic 'other' to mobilities. Her research explores two aspects of mobility with respect to the photograph: the first in terms of the manner in which photographs physically move between different contexts, technologies and people, through activities such as posting, downloading and file sharing. Second, she discusses more epistemological questions surrounding the mobility of meaning and the pathways of interpretation between photographs and viewers.

In his chapter on *Video* Paul Simpson focuses on the use of mobile video methods as one possible solution to the challenge of gaining access to aspects of mobile practices. Importantly, he discusses the use of video in combination with other more established methods such as interviews. He thus concludes that video methodologies do not necessarily present 'the answer' in and of itself in the pursuit of a better understanding of the playing out of mobile practices 'as they happen', but can provide a 'helping hand' in gaining insights into the mundane happenings of movements that might not necessarily be accessed in the same way through talking-*only* methodologies.

Jennie Germann Molz's chapter discusses the use of online technologies in mobile methods. She notes that "information and communication technologies have become increasingly *networked* in the shift from Web 1.0 to Web 2.0". The first iteration of online communications composed primarily of relatively static web pages has been replaced by more complex hyperlinked and decentralized online communication networks of interactive virtual worlds, user-generated social media, and social networking platforms. More significantly, perhaps, information and communication technologies that were originally tied to land-line telephones and desks have become mobile and converged into the smartphone. Moreover, she notes how these technologies provide mobility researchers with new tools and capacities "for recording, collecting, storing, managing, analyzing, interpreting and disseminating data".

In terms of data analysis Ole Jensen discusses the relationship between semiotics and research on mobility studies. Using airports as an example, he focuses on "mobile geo-semiotics", examining how mobilities may be seen to be "staged" by both a range of experts and mobile subjects in everyday life. Finally, Cristina Temenos and Eugene McCann focus on "policy mobilities", which they discuss in terms of the actors, practices and infrastructures that affect the mobility of policies across space and time. In their chapter, they draw our attention to what happens to policies while they move and they suggest that mobile methods may provide a fruitful way forward to inform the impact of mobilities research on policy debates.

References

Büscher, M. and Urry, J. (2009) 'Mobile Methods and the Empirical', *European Journal of Social Theory*, 12(1), 99–116.

Büscher, M., Urry, J. and Witchger, K. (2011) 'Introduction: Mobile Methods', in M. Büscher, J. Urry and K. Witchger (eds) *Mobile Methods*. London: Routledge, pp.1–19.

D'Andrea, A. (2006) 'Neo-Nomadism: A Theory of Post-identitarian Mobility in the Global Age', *Mobilities* 1(1), 95–119.

Fincham, B., McGuinness, M. and Murray, L. (2010) 'Introduction', in B. Fincham, M. McGuinness and L. Murray (eds) *Mobile Methodologies*. Basingstoke: Palgrave Macmillan, pp.1–10.

Hannam, K., Sheller, M. and Urry, J. (2006) 'Editorial: Mobilities, Immobilities and Moorings', *Mobilities*, 1(1), 1–22.

Law, J. and Urry, J. (2004) 'Enacting the Social', *Economy and Society*, 33(3), 390–410.

Merriman, P. (2013) 'Rethinking Mobile Methods', *Mobilities*, forthcoming.

49

Histories

George Revill

Mobility studies are often defined in terms of their primary focus on the practices and experiences of being a mobile subject. In this sense John Urry (2000, 2007) has eloquently argued for mobilities as a paradigmatic way to address social relations and subjectivities within present day societies made in and through mechanised mobility and telecommunications systems. Yet, theorising the historical specificity of mobile experience remains problematic for a mobility studies shaped substantially by recent experiences of mechanised mobility, networked and broadcast telecommunications. Much innovative work in mobilities studies has, for example, been in the field of mobile methodologies which challenge conventional approaches to meaningful experience as consciously symbolically structured or open to textual forms of analysis. Drawing on qualitative, participatory and multi-media data collection, such techniques provide novel means of accessing the flux and flow of mobile experience (Spinney 2006; Hein *et al.* 2008; Fincham *et al.* 2010; Revill 2010). Yet such methods cannot simply be adapted to historical situations where we do not have direct access to the immediate responses of past actors; very frequently all that remains available to mobility historians are the apparently mute buildings, structures and machines of transport archaeology and second-hand accounts in print and visual media. Neither do such methods enable us to readily locate specific mobilities historically and geographically within broader systems of socially situated meaningful experience. However, since the criticisms of travelling theory by Cresswell and others in the late 1990s many have recognised the importance of locating the experience of mobility geographically and historically if mobilities are to be recognised as producers of difference, differential experiences and uneven socio-material relationalities (Wolf 1992; Cresswell 2001a, 2001b, 2006, 2010, 2011; Cresswell and Verstrate 2002; also Adey 2006). Such processes of location necessarily implicate infrastructures, equipment and technologies equally along with practices, knowledges and social relations in the shaping of mobile experience.

   This chapter argues that a prerequisite for recognising the historical specificity of mobile experiences has to begin with a theorisation of the role of infrastructure as an integral part of that experience. It argues that in this regard it may be useful for mobilities studies to embrace current re-workings of communications theory within the philosophy of technology figured as post-, critical or cultural phenomenologies. Thought of in terms of communication theory, the experience of mobility is simultaneously one which is to a degree given shape by the infrastructures, technologies and equipment which provide media by which we come to know parts of the world in particular ways. At the same time the embodied actions and activities of movement are themselves active practices which draw on such media in the processes of sensing and making sense of self and world. The chapter concludes by discussing some of the implications of this for studying the experience of mobility as historically situated.

Mobility infrastructure, situating the experience of mobility

Infrastructures sometimes seem to form an apparently passive background to human practices lived in the moment – whilst at other times they form the focus of attention and attachment located in reflexive historical senses of meaning, culture, belonging and identity. Infrastructures are often obdurate and deeply embedded in social and material life, but at the same time our encounters with them are frequently experienced as either transitory, just in passing as we move through the ticket barrier or take the phone call – or, superficial to the extent that our attention lies beyond the technology itself and on the task or action it enables or facilitates. Infrastructures often appear almost transparent; they run unnoticed in the background until system failure brings us up sharp with their existence and our dependence on them (Law 2003). In a present-day context, for example, Bissell (2009a, 2009b, 2009c) adopts the infrastructures of rail travel as a container or context in which to explore aspects of embodied experience such as boredom and temporality, whilst Adey (2004, 2008) shows how passenger experience is actively shaped and indeed manipulated by airport designers and operators. However, the technologies and infrastructures of mobility also have a distinctive and sometimes high profile and iconic presence in popular imaginations and public histories. From this position for instance the authors in Miller (2001) examine the highly racialised, gendered and status-bound experiences of owning and driving automobiles as these have developed through the twentieth century. Transport infrastructures and related iconic machinery continue to play highly charged and richly layered symbolic roles in histories of modernity, imaginings of nation building, social, economic and cultural progress, and narratives of individual self fulfilment (for example, Bishop 2002, 2008; Divall and Scott 2001; Divall and Revill 2005; Merriman 2004, 2005a, 2005b, 2008; Revill 2012).

Histories of specific technologies can certainly help begin to unpack such complex ramifications, associations and implications, but it is only too easy to overdraw the impact of any particular technology or piece of equipment. The theoretical resources available to mobility studies do not necessarily provide readymade frameworks which address infrastructure and equipment as active participants in the making of historically situated mobile experience. Notions of anchoring and mooring developed by Urry and others are helpful to the extent that they suggest both contingency and exchange (Hannam *et al.* 2006). Yet the clear separation between that which is mobile and that which is static, and the dependency of that which is mobile and moored to an anchoring fixity suggested by these terms may be less rather than more helpful if infrastructures are to be understood as co-constructive of the experience of mobilities. This may be particularly problematic if accounts of mobility are to address the ways in which the experience of mobility is shaped by engagement with specific systems, practices and technologies of mobility located within particular histories and geographies. The idea of mobility regimes is derived partly from the Foucauldian conception of 'regimes of practice'. It provides a useful way of conceptualising the subjective experience of mobility given form within broader systems and practices which include infrastructures broadly defined as equipment, technologies, physical structures, legal systems, techniques of monitoring and surveillance. The concept of regime seems most useful as a means of engaging mobilities infrastructures in the context of mobility systems which are significantly defined by processes and practices of regulation (Shamir 2005; Verstraete 2010). A focus on historical mobility regimes may be useful for understanding the disciplining of mobile bodies as drivers, passengers and pedestrians (Merriman 2005b, 2008), or indeed rivers, sailors and cargoes (Revill 2007), yet it does not necessarily provide sufficient scope to address the creative and expressive dimensions of mobile experience. In this context Cresswell (2010: 18) has characterised mobility as 'a fragile entanglement of physical movement, representations, and practices'. For Cresswell such 'constellations of mobility' are formed from three elements. In turn these are: particular patterns of movement, representations of movement, and ways of practising movement. In concert they constitute entities or systems which 'make sense together'. In this way Cresswell seeks to bring together the apparently disparate components of mobility as meaningful experience, drawing together sensitivity to the affective experience of movement with a critical politics of cultural representations.

Cresswell's formulation has proved effective and appropriate in a variety of historical contexts (see 2001a, 2006). However, because his formulation is centred on the mobile subject and deals with infrastructures, technologies and equipment only to the extent that mobile subjects pass through and engage with them, there remains work to do in order to more fully theorise relationships between the shaping of experience and embodied sense-making. Some authors look to the work of Henri Lefebvre (1991), an important influence on Cresswell's tripartite formulation, for a fully articulated understanding of the relationships between bodies, infrastructures, technologies and equipment. In particular, Lefebvre's (2004) rhythmanalysis informs both historical and contemporary studies of walking, cycling, and public transport. Many of these studies focus on the ways in which the polyrhythms of motion, stasis, engagement and detachment forge specific embodied experiences of movement (Hein *et al.* 2008; Bissell 2009a, 2009b; Edensor and Holloway 2008; Edensor 2009; Fincham *et al.* 2010). Yet as Burgin shows, Lefebvrian-derived rhythmanalysis is not as comfortable with the meaningfulness of reflexive cultural experience as it is with regulatory structurings and embodied affectivities. In this context, Burgin (1996: 30) has forcefully argued that a major stumbling block is Lefebvre's essentially passive understanding of perception. In this context rhythm is something which is done to people and rhythmanalysis remains firmly grounded in the search for a geology of underlying truth lying beyond historical specificity (Revill 2013).

So an important issue here is to find a theoretical perspective able to manage the relationship between routine and purposive action, and habitual and reflexive conscious action through which embodied mobile subjects experience mobility systems as historically situated beings. More fully historicised accounts of the experience of mobility require approaches which are better able to engage and negotiate infrastructures and materialities in relation to practices and experiences. This is of practical as well as theoretical importance for historical accounts of mobile experience. In the absence of recorded oral testimony researchers have to work with what materials remain: the built forms, material artefacts, documentary evidence, and literary, visual and sonic representations of past mobile practices. To engage with this material requires the mobility historian to move beyond a sense that the term *infrastructure* suggests passive sedentary and externalised structures or contexts, which seems to be the antithesis of the experiential richness and fluid, contingent, creative socialities and material engagements which characterise mobility studies' engagement with embodied movement.

Communications, post-phenomenology and the specificity of mobile experience

In contrast to Lefebvre's search for underlying truths in rhythm, more recent theorists have figured rhythm in relation to an active sense of reception suggested by the term *listening* rather than a passive model of perception suggested by the term *hearing*. This begins to figure infrastructure and mobile experience as a much more active, engaged and co-constructed set of practices. For Nancy, the sense of reverberation, the interference patterns created by the interaction between mobile bodies and their material context, actively produce rather than simply reflect. Thus, Nancy (2007: 5) argues in favour of a conception of sensing which has important implications for the study of mobile experience. In this case *to sense* is *to make sense*, it is an active conscious process of sensible being in the world which operates across a range of registers, from the habitual and affective to the reflexively conscious and conventionally representational. The intimately interconnected conceptions of sense-making and shaping suggested by Nancy is itself echoed in Ihde's (2003, 2009) self-styled 'post-phenomenology' of technology. By styling this as a 'post' phenomenology Ihde seeks to distance himself from the search for universal qualities in human experience, which he argues characterise the phenomenologies of Merleau Ponty and others. Key to this perspective, according to Verbeek (2005: 112), is the fusion of an existential phenomenology concerned with the ways in which human beings locate themselves and find and make meaning in the world, and a hermeneutical phenomenology concerned with the ways in which systems, structures and equipment enable, constrain and shape experience. In this context Michel Foucault's musings on the 'extraordinary' nature of the railway as a cultural product and producer of modern mobile life as at once environment, practice and experience, are surprisingly pertinent. The train, he said:

> is something through which one goes, it is also something by means of which one can go from one point to another, and then it is also something that goes by.
>
> *(1986: 23–24)*

To a certain extent Foucault is merely reflecting ideas developed by media and communications theorists during the 1960s and encapsulated in McLuhan's slogan 'the medium is the message' (1964). Yet there is more to his comment than this apparent simplicity might suggest. As simultaneously subject, object, representation and practice, the cultural experience of mechanised travel challenges the model of passive consumption, developed by early theorists concerned with radio, TV and film, from one of submissive hearing to active listening and fuses its metaphor of mediation with one of envelopment and immersion. Foucault's sense of the technological shaping of experience as alternately engendering subjects as traveller then bystander, participant then spectator, is echoed by others concerned with phenomenologies of technology. Miller (1987, 2005; see also Michael 2000), for example, adds a sense of active materiality derived from Hegel's *Phenomenology of Spirit*, to the social shaping of meaningful encounter taken from Goffman's symbolic interactionism and the technical framing of experience attributed to the art historian Ernst Gombrich. For Miller (2005: 8), Hegel justifies an approach which denies any a priori separation between humanity and materiality. Peters (1999: 118) casts this formulation in the context of communication conceived as both a form of material/social exchange and a medium of sense-making:

> Hegel invites us to see subjects as intertwined with objects, selves as intertwined with others, and meaning as public rather than psychological . . . The problem of

communication for Hegel is not so much to make contact between individuals as it is to establish a vibrant set of social relations in which common worlds can be made.

The sense of communication as an immersive socio-technical medium shaping and giving meaning simultaneously to experience and material form, suggested by Foucault's musing on the train, is echoed by Ihde's call for a reworking of the post-phenomenology of technology as a theory of 'communicative interaction' (Langsdorf 2006). Perhaps it is not surprising that Ihde's approach is also informed by his earlier work on listening (Ihde 1976). Echoing interpretations of Hegel by Peters and Miller, Ihde's notion of communicative interaction is placed in direct contrast with the idealised rule-governed terrain that Habermas (1984) figures as the ground for meaningful dialogue in his theory of communicative action. Rather, a version derived from Ihde suggests communication as a 'discursive materiality' (Barad 2003, 2007), something messy, contingent, mutable and engaged across a wide range of affective and reflexive practices and through a heterogeneous assembly of materialities. In many respects thinking of mobilities through the notion of communication has a long and relatively conventional history. Histories of transport have long been situated within a wider history of communications, which includes postal and newspaper services, and subsequently telegraph and telephony (Mattelart 2000). To this extent Urry's characterisation of a contemporary world built jointly on globalising patterns of movement and media, individual mobility and networked communications technologies builds on these older historiographies (Kern 1983; Urry and Elliott 2010). However, the broader sense of communication as both medium by which we experience the world and tools by which we come to understand it gives this reworked conception of communication new vitality. Such a notion is implied by Urry's formulation, if only to the extent that individuals in contemporary society come to understand themselves and their relations to others as variously immediate and distanciated, whether privileged, fluid and connected, or disempowering, fixed and isolated. In this respect mobility studies' relationship to communications theory might have more in common with historical studies of situated subjectivity such as Connor's (1997) characterisation of the 'modern auditory "I"'. Thus for Connor, the making of identity within the modern world is a product of modernity's communications networks. For him this is characterised by an auditory dynamic that locates us within 'the switch-board experience' of modern life, found initially in early telephone systems, radiophonic broadcasting, and cinematic matter, which necessitate a new shuffling between 'rapture and capture', sight and sound.

The active, spatio-temporally specific and socially situated conception of sensing and sense-making suggested by the idea of listening implies both an openness to the heterogeneity of sensory experience and a sensitivity to the ways in which particular events, actions, activities, artefacts and materials become meaningful within the spatio-temporal specificity of individual events (or utterances). This approach is characteristic of what has been variously termed as a cultural, post-, or critical phenomenology in which active, mediated conceptions of sensing and reception replace substantially universalised physiological models of perception (Connor 1999; Clucas 2000; Ihde 2003, 2009; Sterne 2003; Born 2013). From this position Ihde suggests a fourfold register for the spectrum and varieties of the human experience of technologies (Ihde 2009: 42). There are clear resonances here with Miller's formulation derived from Goffman, Gombrich and Hegel to the extent that Ihde embraces both performative social relations, and relations of technological framing within the context of fluid interactive and co-constructed conceptions of the social and the material. For Ihde, *embodiment relations* concern the ways in which material technologies or artefacts are incorporated into taken-for-granted bodily experience as prosthetic extensions of the senses, or as tools which are ready to hand. In contrast, *hermeneutic relations* engage one's more linguistic, meaning-orientated capacities. In this case, though engagement remains *active*, the process is more analogous to our *reading or interpreting* than to bodily action. *Alterity relations* suggest the ways in which humans engage with technologies as quasi-objects or quasi-others, perhaps admitting room for issues of alienation, estrangement and objectification, and fetishisation of particular technologies and technological systems. And finally, *background relations*, which later bring into prominence the infrastructural qualities of technologies – that which is hidden or taken for granted (Ihde 2009: 43–4). In these ways Ihde constructs his own way of conceptualising the fragile entanglements identified by Cresswell, which are characteristic of our engagement with communications technology. Thus his formulation recognises some of the specificities of human engagement with technology, the possibility of alienation, its unacknowledged routine presence, and the practicality of tools, whilst at the same time alluding to some of the concern with spaces of embodied experience, reflexive consciousness and symbolic representation evident in Cresswell or indeed Lefebvre. Most importantly Idhe champions what he calls a relational, or in his terms 'inter-relational', ontology which is tuned to historical specificity.

> Technologies transform our experience of the world and our perceptions and interpretations of our world, and we in turn become transformed in this process. Transformations are non-neutral. And it is here that histories and any empirical turn may become *ontologically* important, which will lead us to the pragmatist insight that histories are also important in any philosophical analysis as such.
>
> *(Ihde 2009: 44)*

Thus Ihde's fusion of precepts and concepts from phenomenology and pragmatism reject the transcendental and the universal as a starting point for a theoretical space that both starts from and takes seriously the lived qualities of experience. His approach to technologically mediated experience is open to the ways in which this experience is shaped by a wide range of material, embodied, symbolic and historical processes, affordances, traits, traces and inscriptions.

Mobile experience and spatio-temporal specificity

The implications of taking the historically situated experience of mobility as an ontological starting point, in the context of an approach to infrastructures, equipment and technologies informed by ideas of communicative interaction, might usefully be reviewed with regard to Schivelbusch's (1986) well-known discussion of 'panoramic perception'. Schivelbusch shows how early rail travellers reported that they found looking out from a train disturbing and even nauseating. In his account, the new habit of reading whilst travelling helped transform perceptual experience. Now, travellers read a little and occasionally gazed passively over their reading matter out of the window and into the middle distance. By this means the reading matter rather than the landscape formed the focus of attention. Consequently, the disorientating blur of the passing scene beyond the train was reduced from a main focus of attention to merely an occasional distraction. According to Schivelbusch, railway travel was thus transformed into a substantially routine event that reorganised the perceptual space of the journey as one of detachment, objectification, alienation and theatricality. Thought of in terms of communicative practice, the framed window of the coach running along level track is both what the traveller knows and is the way in which the traveller comes to understand their experience. The act of reading and gazing into the middle distance both shapes what is known about the social environment of the carriage and provides a set of resources and practices which enable the traveller to understand and give meaning to the experience within the carriage and world beyond the railway. Thus, using Idhe's terminology, the story of panoramic perception can be understood through the *embodied relations* bound into the routine boredom of the journey and the ensuing sense of nausea in terms of *hermeneutic relations* including the cultural specificity of landscape perspective and the coping behaviour associated with social mixing in railway carriages. Subsequently the account connects *background relations*, which include both the straight, level track running on bridges and embankments and the window framing the view, to a set of *alterity* relations, which include the objectifying contents of the book and the subsequent sense of distance from and spectacularisation of landscape created by the assemblage of book, soft sprung upholstery and framed, glazed window.

Though Schivelbusch, like Ihde and others concerned with the relationships between infrastructures, technologies and experiences, takes historically situated mobile experience as an ontological starting point, his phenomenology ultimately produces a univocal assertion of the experience of rail travel (Revill 2011). Though the idea of panoramic perception has become a dominant way for academics to think about the phenomenology of the railway journey, this is only one of a number of possible ways of thinking about or experiencing the railway journey, either historically or geographically. For those not necessarily familiar with the dominant western aesthetic of landscape perspective, or those experiencing the conviviality, crowding and sometimes rowdiness of third-class travel in nineteenth-century Europe, contemporary Asia and Africa, or for urban commuter trains, panoramic perspective does not necessarily define the experience of the train journey as an experience of detachment, isolation and ultimately alienation (Revill 2012). Each of Ihde's registers call for a more clearly articulated and situated understanding of the shaping of experience within a historical context informed by pre-existing conventions concerning, for example, landscape observation and the cultural and social expectations of travel. Such historically and culturally specific conventions both initiate and give meaning to this changing mode of experience. The notion of communicative 'interaction' is important here not because it reduces experience to text but because it highlights the multi-dimensional qualities of sense-making as they work through a variety of practice and media, and an active conception of the way experience is shaped by the multiple specificities of media and practice. Most importantly, the notion of communication also highlights the sequential and enfolded qualities of experience. It recognises experience made through a temporally complex multiplicity of situating practices which, like acts of talking and reading, are informed simultaneously and chronologically by memories of the past and anticipations of the future, as well as senses of being in the moment.

If thinking about mobility systems as communicative assemblages enhances sensitivity to the historical specificity of mobile experience, then this also suggests both the need to work with ways of experiencing the world which are current for specific peoples at specific times and to build theoretical understanding from concepts, ideas and understandings which are current in the historical moment of their experiencing. Though substantially focusing on the present within mobility studies perhaps one of the most useful examples of how this might be achieved is presented by the extensively researched topic of 'automobility'. Work on 'automobility' illustrates the ways in which studies of mobility and travel can forge a constructive engagement between the embodied and affective experience of mobility, its cultural representation, and the structuring and organisation of transport technologies. As Sheller and

Urry put it (2000: 739), automobility is 'a complex amalgam of interlocking machines, social practices and ways of dwelling' (see also Urry 2007; Featherstone *et al.* 2004). Automobilisation 'creates independence and liberates its subject from spatiotemporal constraints, it also formulates new dependencies re-embedding its users (and nonusers) into another, highly mobile, yet equally structured way of life' (Beckmann 2001: 600–601). Thus Beckmann (2001: 602) claims:

> As a result, the subject of automobilisation becomes its object. Rather than a self-determined subject, the car-driver is subjected to the expert systems framing this hybrid, which gradually turn him or her into the object of this very mobility paradigm.

Beckmann's formulation clearly resonates with Foucault's characterisation of the experience of rail travel to the extent that it suggests characteristics shared with other communicative systems. These include twin senses of shaping and sense-making, the complex enfolding and mutual dependence of both subject and object, and immersive and reflexive experience. Thus the complex entanglements suggested by automobility engage with a mode of inhabitation that structures experience and shapes expectations to the extent that, for many, it has become impossible to think of life without and beyond the automobile. For 'automobility' the intersection of medium and message, shaping and sense-making, are fundamental to the well-known set of social and environmental problems which constitute automobility as a set of issues which define substantial areas of debate around current and future mobility. Yet, focus on the current and future impacts of automobility has diverted attention away from the importance of automobility as a historically specific formulation. Following the example of 'automobility', an important first move for researchers concerned with historically situated studies of mobile experience is to find an appropriate 'vehicle', medium or hermeneutical device which resonates with and connects specific mobility technologies with broader cultural formations and modes of habitation as simultaneous media for the shaping and sense-making of experience. The mobilities literature suggests that many other forms of mobility can be productively thought of in this way. To cite only a few examples with more or less historical currency for specific mobile subjects, one might think of 'Aeriality' (Adey 2010), 'Velomobility' (Pesses 2010), or perhaps early nineteenth-century romantic ideas of walking encapsulated in the 'Peripatetic' (Jarvis 1997; Solnit 2001), Ingold's (2007: 76–85) contrast between wayfaring and navigation in early modern Europe, or indeed Cosgrove's (2003) work on the transformative qualities of images of the earth from space. Recasting these and other such mobility regimes as communicative assemblages might begin to facilitate a constructive engagement between theories of embodied mobility and material histories of infrastructures, technologies and equipment in ways which historically situate experiences of mobility.

Conclusion

This chapter began by considering the relationship between the apparently solid material histories of infrastructures, technologies and equipment, and the fleeting ephemeral histories of mobile experience. It then examined the complex ramifications of these for the construction of mobile experience and looked at the ways in which mobilities studies engages with notions of infrastructure and equipment in this context. Drawing on Don Ihde's self-styled 'post' phenomenology of technology, the chapter then examined the ways in which thinking about mobility systems in terms of communicative assemblages might help provide a more active and co-constructed sense of mobile experience. It is argued that refiguring mobility regimes in this way provides a way of theorising the experience of mobility which is sensitive to and congruent with the lived experience of historical actors. Mobilities studies consciously or otherwise sets itself against the undue focus on the infrastructures, equipment and material technologies of historical transport systems which for so long fascinated transport historians (Mom 2003; Mom *et al.* 2009). This chapter argues that it might be time for mobility historians to engage with and reclaim important dimensions of those often discarded histories if we are to more fully situate the historical experiences of mobility.

References

Adey, P. (2004) 'Surveillance at the airport: surveilling mobility/mobilizing surveillance', *Environment and Planning A* 36 1365–1380.

Adey, P. (2006) 'If mobility is everything then it is nothing: towards a relational politics of (im)mobilities', *Mobilities* 1 75–95.

Adey, P. (2008) 'Airports, mobility and the calculative architecture of affective control', *Geoforum* 39 439–351.

Adey, P. (2010) *Aerial Life: spaces, mobilities, affects* (Wiley-Blackwell: Oxford).

Barad, K. (2003) 'Posthumanist performativity: how matter comes to matter', *Signs: Journal of Women in Culture* 28(3) 801–31.

Barad, K. (2007) *Meeting the Universe Halfway: quantum physics and the entanglement of matter and meaning* (Duke University Press: Durham and London).

Beckmann, J. (2001) 'Automobility – a social problem and theoretical concept', *Environment and Planning D: Society and Space* 19 593–607.

Bishop, J. P. (2002) 'Gathering the land: the Alice Springs to Darwin rail corridor', *Environment and Planning D: Society and Space* 20 295–317.

Bishop, P. (2008) *Bridge* (Reaktion Books: London).

Bissell, D. (2009a) 'Travelling vulnerabilities: mobile timespaces of quiescence', *Cultural Geographies* 427–445.

Bissell, D. (2009b) 'Visualising everyday geographies: practices of vision through travel-time', *Transactions of the Institute of British Geographers* 34 42–60.

Bissell, D. (2009c) 'Conceptualising differently-mobile passengers: geographies of everyday encumbrance in the railway station', *Social and Cultural Geography* 10 173–195.

Born, G. (2013) 'Introduction' in G. Born and T. Rice *Music, Sound and the Reconfiguration of Public and Private Space* (Cambridge University Press: Cambridge).

Burgin, V. (1996) *In/different Spaces: place and memory in visual culture* (University of California Press: Berkeley and London).

Clucas, S. (2000) 'Cultural phenomenology and the everyday', *Critical Quarterly* 42(1) 7–34.

Connor, S. (1997) 'The modern auditory I' in R. Porter (ed.) *Rewriting the Self: histories from the Renaissance to the present* (Routledge: London) pp 203–223.

Connor, S. (1999) 'CP: or, a few don'ts by a cultural phenomenologist', *Parallax* 5 (2) 17–31.

Connor, S. (2000) 'Making an issue of cultural phenomenology', *Critical Quarterly* 42(1) 2–6.

Cosgrove, D. (2003) *Apollo's Eye: a cartographic genealogy of the earth in the western imagination* (Johns Hopkins University Press: Baltimore).

Cresswell, T. (2001a) *The Tramp in America* (Reaktion: London).

Cresswell, T. (2001b) 'The production of mobilities', *New Formations* 43 11–25, 13.

Cresswell, T. (2006) *On the Move: mobility in the modern western world* (Routledge: New York).

Cresswell, T. (2010) 'Towards a politics of mobility', *Environment and Planning D: Society and Space* 28(1) 17–31.

Cresswell, T. (2011) 'Mobilities 1: catching up', *Progress in Human Geography* 35(4) 550–558.

Cresswell, T. and Verstraete, G. (eds) (2002) *Mobilizing Place, Placing Mobility: the politics of representation in a globalized world* (Rodopi: Amsterdam).

Divall, C. and Revill, G. (2005) 'Cultures of transport: representation, practice and technology', *Transport History* 26 1.

Divall, C. and Scott, A. (2001) *Making History in Transport Museums* (Leicester University Press: London and New York).

Edensor, T. (ed.) (2009) *Geographies of Thythm: nature, place, mobilities and bodies* (Ashgate: Farnham, Surrey).

Edensor, T. and Holloway, J. (2008) 'Rhythmanalysing the coach tour: the Ring of Kerry, Ireland', *Transactions of the Institute of British Geographers* 33(4) 483–501.

Featherstone, M., Thrift, N. and Urry, J. (2004) *Automobilities*, Sage: Theory, Culture & Society series (Sage: London).

Fincham, B., McGuiness, M. and Murray, L. (2010) *Mobile Methodologies* (Palgrave Macmillan: Basingstoke, Hants).

Foucault, M. (1986) 'Of other spaces', *Diacritics* 1 22–7.

Habermas, J. (1984) *The Theory of Communicative Action: Vol 1 Reason and the rationalization for society* (trans. T. McCarthy) (Polity Press: Cambridge).

Hannam, K., Sheller, M. and Urry, J. (2006) 'Editorial: mobilities, immobilities and moorings', *Mobilities* 1(1) 1–12.

Hein, J. R., Evans, J. and Jones, P. (2008) 'Mobile methodologies: theory, technology and practice', *Geography Compass* 2(5) 1266–1285.

Ihde, D. (1976) *Listening and Voice: a phenomenology of sound* (Ohio University Press: Athens Ohio).

Ihde, D. (2003) 'If phenomenology is an albatross is postphenomenology possible?' in D. Ihde and E. Selinger (eds) *Chasing Technoscience: Matrix of Materiality* (Indiana University Press: Bloomington) pp 117–130.

Ihde, D. (2009) *Postphenomenology and Technoscience: the Peking lectures* (SUNY Press: Albany, NY).

Ingold, T. (2007) *Lines: a brief history* (London: Routledge).

Jarvis, R. (1997) *Romantic Writing and Pedestrian Travel* (Macmillan: Basingstoke, Hants).

Kern, S. (1983) *The Culture of Time and Space* (Weidenfeld and Nicolson: London).

Langsdorf, L. (2006) 'The primacy of listening: towards a metaphysics of communicative interaction' in E. Selinger (ed.) *Postphenomenology: a critical companion to Ihde* (SUNY Press: Albany, NY) pp 37–47.

Law, J. (2003) 'Ladbroke Grove, Or How to Think about Failing Systems', published by the Centre for Science Studies, Lancaster University, Lancaster LA1 4YN, UK. Available online at www.comp.lancs.ac.uk/sociology/papers/Law-Ladbroke-Grove-Failing-Systems.pdf.

Lefebvre, H. (1991) *The Production of Space* (Blackwell: Oxford).

Lefebvre, H. (2004) *Rhythmanalysis: space, time and everyday life* (trans. S. Eldon and G. Moore) (Continuum: London).

Mattelart, A. (2000) *Networking the World: 1794–2000* (University of Minnesota Press: Minneapolis).

McLuhan, M. (1964) *Understanding Media* (Routledge: London).

Merriman, P. (2004) 'Driving places: Marc Augé, non-places and the geographies of England's M1 motorway', *Theory, Culture & Society* 21(4–5) 145–167.

Merriman, P. (2005a) '"Operation motorway": landscapes of construction on England's M1 motorway', *Journal of Historical Geography* 31 113–133.

Merriman, P. (2005b) 'Materiality, subjectification and government: the geographies of Britain's Motorway Code', *Environment and Planning D: Society and Space* 23 235–250.

Merriman, P. (2008) *Driving Spaces* (Blackwell: Oxford).

Michael, M. (2000) *Reconnecting Culture, Technology and Nature: from society to heterogeneity* (Routledge: London).

Miller, D. (1987) *Material Culture and Mass Consumption* (Blackwell: Oxford).

Miller, D. (ed.) (2001) *Car Cultures* (Berg: Oxford).

Miller, D. (ed.) (2005) *Materiality* (Duke University Press: Durham, NC).

Mom, G. (2003) 'What kind of transport history did we get? Half a century of *JTH* and the future of the field', *Journal of Transport History* 3rd ser. 24 121–138.

Mom, G., Divall, C. and Lyth, P. (2009) 'Towards a paradigm shift? A decade of transport and mobility history' in Mom, G., Piries, G. and Tissot, L. (eds) *Mobility in History: The state of the art in the history of transport, traffic and mobility* (Éditions Alphil-Presses universitaires suisses: Neuchâtel).

Nancy, J.-L. (2007) *Listening* (Fordham University Press: New York).

Pesses, M. W. (2010) 'Automobilty, velomobility, American mobility: an exploration of the bicycle tour', *Mobilities* 5(1) 1–24.

Peters, J. D. (1999) *Speaking into the Air: a history of the idea of communication* (University of Chicago Press: London, Chicago).

Revill, G. (2007) 'William Jessop and the River Trent: mobility, engineering and the landscape of eighteenth century "improvement"', *Transactions of the Institute of British Geographers* 32 201–216.

Revill, G. (2010) 'Mobilities' in J. Agnew and J. Duncan *Companion to Human Geography* (Wiley-Blackwell: Oxford).

Revill, G. (2011) 'Perception, reception and representation: Wolfgang Schivelbusch and the cultural history of travel and transport in mobility' in P. Norton, G. Mom, L. Milward and M. Flonneau (eds) *History: Reviews and Reflections T2M Yearbook* (Éditions Alphil-Presses universitaires suisses: Neuchâtel) pp 31–48.

Revill, G. (2012) *Railway* (Reaktion: London).

Revill, G. (2013) 'Points of departure: listening to rhythm in the sonoric spaces of the railway station', *Sociological Review Monographs* (in press).

Schivelbusch, W. (1986) *The Railway Journey: the industrialization of time and space in the 19th century* (Berg: Leamington Spa).

Shamir, R. (2005) 'Without borders? Notes on globalization as a mobility regime', *Sociological Theory* 23(2) 197–217.

Sheller, M. and Urry, J. (2000) 'The city and the car', *International Journal of Urban and Regional Research* 24(4) 737–57.

Solnit, R. (2001) *Wanderlust: a history of walking* (Verso: London).

Spinney, J. (2006) 'A place of sense: a kinaesthetic ethnography of cyclists on Mont Ventoux', *Environment and Planning D: Society and Space* 24 709–732.

Sterne, J. (2003) *The Audible Past: cultural origins of sound reproduction* (Duke University Press: Durham, NC).

Urry, J. (2000) *Sociology Beyond Societies: mobilities for the twenty-first century* (Routledge: London).

Urry, J. (2007) *Mobilities* (Polity: Cambridge).

Urry, J. and Elliott, A. (2010) *Mobile Lives* (Routledge: London).

Verbeek, P.-P. (2005) *What Things Do: philosophical reflections on technology, agency and design* (University of Pennsylvania Press: Pennsylvania).

Verstraete, G. (2010) *Tracking Europe: mobility, diaspora, and the politics of location* (Duke University Press: Durham, NC and London).

Wolf, J. (1992) 'On the Road Again: metaphors of travel in cultural criticism', *Cultural Studies* 7 224–239.

50

Mappings

Martin Dodge

Introduction

Mapping how things move through space is a significant challenge. Creating workable cartographic representations that can meaningfully display particularities of movement and also aid the investigation of the patterns and different processes of mobilities has stretched mapping practice and is, in many respects, still an unresolved challenge for cartographers, information designers and visualisation programmers. Producing aesthetically pleasing and analytically useful maps of spaces of mobility has become one of the key research frontiers in cartography and geovisualisation (Andrienko *et al.* 2008; Dodge *et al.* 2009; Dykes and Mountain 2003).

Mapping as a process of knowledge creation is more than just drawing lines on the page or displaying dots on screens and, as such, a major aspect of the challenge of visualising mobilities in a meaningful form comes before epistemological actions (data symbolisation and graphic inscription), and instead lies in ontological decision-making around what is deemed mappable in a given domain, and then which data is actively selected for mapmaking. As has been well documented, mapping as a process of abstracting reality, operating with both technological constraints and socially determined values, works by selection and classification to construct a partial but believable representation that provides a convincing solution to a particular problem. What is chosen to be mapped is as important as the cartographic design or the utility of the finished representation. This ontological basis of mapping is easily overlooked but is very much evident in the cartographies of movement. Only certain aspects of mobility are deemed mappable and fewer still are selected for survey, classification and inscription.

Mapping the structures of what outwardly appear to be material objects to human eyes and hands at microscopic, atomic or now subatomic scales, reveal that physical things are not solid but composed of the incessant motion of waves/particles of energy. At another scale, the ground under our feet appears fixed, but we know from geological evidence that the earth's surface is made up of moving tectonic plates (continental drift of the Eurasian plate is about 20 mm per year, imperceptibly slow in human terms but sufficient to completely reshape the Earth over a few million years). What's more, the periodicities of the day, months and the

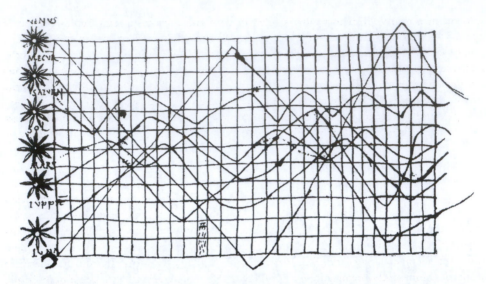

Figure 50.1 An early spatial graphing of moving object. Dating from the tenth century it was designed to plot the cyclical motion of seven planetary bodies across a grid of time intervals. Graph found in the appendix to commentaries by Macrobius on In Somnium Scripionus (Funkhouser 1936)

seasons of the year, demonstrate that we are all riding on a planet in very rapid rotation and orbital motion.[1] And if we accept conventional astronomic theory, premised upon Edwin Hubble's (1929) ground-breaking observations, all matter in the visible universe is moving outwards at the speed of 77 kilometres per second per 3.26 million light-years from the time-space 'big bang' origin. Indeed, some of the first mapping representations produced in recorded history were quasi-religious diagrams plotting observed celestial motion and granting power to priests to predict future occurrences in the sky (Figure 50.1).

Closely coupled to spatial movement at multiple scales in terms of the ontological challenges in mapping is that everything is in process in terms of temporal change. As with space, much of the passage through time occurs at scales too short or too long for unaided human perception. The apparent fixity of terrestrial geomorphology is an artefact because the processes of change work beyond human lifespans, but when mapping at longer timescales the surface of the planet is ceaselessly changing, driven by the inexorable, transforming forces of volcanism and weathering. So much of movement in space, change through time, and the general dynamism of objects in time-space are never deemed mappable, captured or inscribed in cartographic products.

Static cartography – fixing space, freezing time, stopping motion

The ontological difficulties in mapping mobility are multiplied because of the common media of representations for topographic cartography, and scientific diagramming more generally, have been static inscriptions fixed on paper. Conventional mapping practice has typically dealt with the fact that everything moves and everything is changing by actively denying this reality in the process of abstraction. The working solution of most mapmakers down through history has often been to represent phenomena and process by artificially freezing time at some arbitrary point and halting movement or simply ignoring things that were mobile. As a consequence, nearly all cartography is fixed in time and provides a static representation of space. This is so obvious that it is easy to overlook when using conventional map products.

The lack of temporal sensitivity in most cartographic design means that so much of the spontaneity and serendipity of everyday events that make places feel alive is not conventionally deemed representable in topographic maps. Maps are a lifeless media. Beyond narrow technical concerns for legible inscriptions, this freezing has important ideological implications because the resulting maps inherently privilege the status quo and entrench power-relations that are most easily 'frozen'.[2] Such fixity of things and the locking-down of events into regular time slots is really a cartographic fiction, and it gives an artificial sense of permanence to the world that is really working as a series of dynamic, overlapping and often contested processes.

Static maps are inherently and particularly selective in what they can show and crucially in what is not chosen to be shown. The surveyor's gaze has always favoured things that appear fixed in the landscape (or those with relatively long durations to human sensibilities). According to Bunge (1971: iv) the result is that "[m]aps attempt to integrate over time, that is, maps assume an average span of time. This means that nothing that moves is mapped, and therefore property is inherently preferred over humans". As things that move or change quickly and unpredictably tend not to get mapped,[3] this is clearly problematic for constructing worth-while and workable representations of many aspects of human culture – like the daily flux of cities – as the actual work and social activities are never mapped. Look at the largest-scale urban mapping available and there is evidently a high level of detail of physical structures but nothing on the changing social and economic relations transacted every day or the myriad of mobile bodies, objects and flows that inhabit the spaces and beckon places into being.

How things can move is neither simple nor singular in nature. There are many kinds of movements and an unknown number of patterns. In developing suitable mapping approaches and cartographic design metaphors, it can help to start to make sense of the plethora of kinds of movement by imposing taxonomic categories. This is beginning to happen with useful work in cognitive cartography, transport studies and GIScience (e.g. Hirtle *et al.* 2010; Schwanen and Kwan 2012), but as yet there appears to be no widely agreed taxonomy for mobility that can be readily exploited by mapmakers. Figure 50.2 presents one of the more useful efforts: a summation which displays a quite detailed (but probably not exhaustive) hierarchical classification of patterns of movement in terms of differing underlying motives for the activities. While the GIScience researchers acknowledge it is incomplete, they claim "classification and formalization of patterns is necessary to give guidelines for the development of visual and interactive methods that are expected to enable users to detect and explore patterns" (Dodge *et al.* 2008: 2). These different patterns, resulting from distinct drivers, may well require different kinds of visual representations to communicate meaning, especially to a non-expert audience. Effective visual mapping of distinct kinds of mobility could also help to better determine the causation and perhaps even the real meanings that people attach to their journeys. What is causing an observed convergence motion of a group of people, for example, or is the rapidity of divergence of a set of objects due to something significant (a flight from a new risk?). It seems likely that growing taxonomic sophistication will be useful to inform more appropriate mapping and will be important to meeting the challenges of understanding mobilities.

In real-world applications such mapping can swiftly become a technical challenge in terms of the sheer data volumes involved in tracking potentially millions of individual objects or aggregated points of movement at fine granularity in space and through time. Dealing with realistic scales of data has indeed been one pragmatic reason why much mobile and temporally

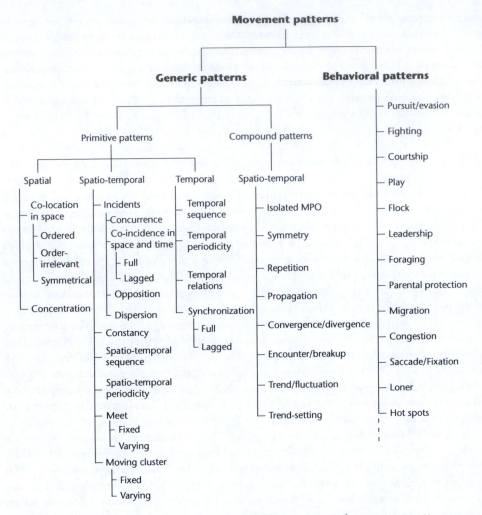

Figure 50.2 A useful attempt to taxonomise the different types of movement patterns as a preliminary to more effective visualisation of mobility (Dodge *et al.* 2008)

dynamic phenomena have never been mapped.[4] In addition to the 'big data' challenge, there have also been serious aesthetic concerns, as designers and mapmakers have struggled to develop a meaningful and effective visual language to display motion on static media of distribution. In many respects existing representational solutions for envisioning space, such as the conventions within topographic cartography (e.g. familiar graphic palettes of points, line and area styles on 'default' British maps produced by the Ordnance Survey), and thematic mapping (with its shaded polygons and proportionally sized symbols), have lacked the semiotic capability to really convey the dynamic nature of physical mobility or temporal change.

Solutions to mapping mobilities

The ontological and technical challenges of representing physical movements and temporally dynamic processes have spurred cartographers, and latterly researchers in geovisualisation and information visualisation, to develop novel solutions. These solutions can be broadly grouped into three kinds of mapping: first, extending static, single, cartographic images through clever graphic designs; second, making maps that change through the medium of animation; and third, using digital technology to deliver ego-centred maps that are interactive and dynamically updated in harness with the person's movement. We will review each of these approaches in turn, considering a range of exemplars.

Developing clever graphical designs

Whilst acknowledging the general weaknesses of much conventional cartographic design in adequately capturing a world of moving objects and representing dynamic change, there have been some notable attempts to develop creative solutions to display mobility through static spatial imagery. Here we will consider, in particular, flow maps and 'fish-tank' time geography diagrams as some of the more sophisticated design innovations, and while these are not widely deployed in real-world contexts, they do nonetheless show what can be done with ingenuity and skill. As such they may seem unusual and unconventional ways of representing geography and spatial patterns, and are typically not well covered, if at all, in mainstream cartography textbooks. What's more, they don't form part of the default palette of semi-automated designs afforded in mapping software and GIS suites.

Flow mapping can be defined as the production of a graphic "on which the amount of movement along a linear path is stressed, usually by lines of varying thickness" (Dent 1995: 234). As a mapping technique it emerged in the nineteenth-century creative 'explosion' of thematic cartography developed purposefully for the needs of state to understand the increasingly complex economic and social make-up of industrialising nations, with their rapidly growing populations and expanding cities (cf. Robinson 1982). Conventionally the first flow map is credited to Henry Drury Harness, who had the task of representing the pattern of passengers travelling on Ireland's new railway network for a report to Parliament (Robinson 1955). Although he is now acknowledged as an innovative designer, it is unclear how widely seen or influential Harness's railway flow maps of 1837 were. Another more widely known mapping of the spatiality of flows also arises from the 'golden age' of inventive thematic cartography in the nineteenth century. It was created by a retired civil engineer, Charles Joseph Minard, in 1869. It seems simple at first glance, but it provides a surprisingly sophisticated mapping of the movement of the French army in the Russian campaign of 1812/13, in which over 400,000 soldiers under Napoleon's command either deserted or died. His *Carte Figurative* provides a distinctly diagrammatic form of mapping, and a highly effective and efficient representation of a complex, multi-dimensional set of data, recording the movements of a massive army over many months and several thousand miles from the River Niemer in present-day Poland to occupy Moscow, before being forced to retreat again (cf. Friendly 2006; Robinson 1967).

Flow maps as a cartographic design solution that can tie together the scale of movement with spatial location and direction remain a distinctive and somewhat specialised approach, although they have been developed since the work of nineteenth-century pioneers such as Drury and Minard. A contemporary deployment of flow mapping has been conducted by quantitative human geographer Danny Dorling as part of his extensive and ongoing analysis of inequalities in British society. Dorling has a deep interest in developing creative and clever maps and diagrams to visualise the latent socio-spatial pattern locked in large demographic datasets such as the UK national censuses. In particular, Dorling has exploited cartograms to radically distort spaces of representation to show more clearly social reality (see some of his recent books for copious examples, such as Dorling 2012; Dorling and Thomas 2011). As the pre-eminent data source for the state, documenting the social makeup of the nation, censuses tend to privilege fixed populations in space and time (people are tied to a single 'night-time' residential address as recorded on midnight on one designated census day). More recent decennial censuses in the UK have, however, asked employed people about their daily 'journey to work' and also recorded previous addresses one year before the census date to try to capture some measure of residential migration. These questions have provided the raw variables to create unique population-level movement datasets that can be analysed as flow matrices between zones and mapped as flow maps.

Dorling has experimented with how such large and complex patterns of aggregate movement might be visualised, and two exemplars of his work in this direction, exploiting data from the 1981 census for England and Wales, are displayed in Figure 50.3. In trying to synthesise and visualise such a large volume of data on a single flow map there are clearly challenges of legibility of detail for individual zones, in spite of the exaggeration of geographic scale by the use of the cartogram projection. However, such mapping does capture some of the essence of mobility at a societal level by detailing the sheer complexity of daily commuting and the significant number of multi-scalar annual residential moves. Mapping the dynamic nature of social space through movement at the national scale is often never seen and can therefore be perceived as somewhat unconventional. Instead the vast majority of official reports and academic analyses of the structure of society rely on a small trope of descriptive statistics, a narrow range of charts and the tyranny of the choropleth as default thematic cartography.[5]

The amount of information encoded in the flow map with variable sized bands and movement arrows can be increased by exploiting other graphic variables for these symbols, most obviously shading styles and colour hue. A colour ramp may be used to indicate varying speed along the line of movement or intensity of traffic. The effective nature of this approach can be seen in real-world applications to visualise shipping traffic movements in the busy sea lanes of the North Sea (Figure 50.4). The visualisation used a historic database of tracking data generated by the Automatic Identification System (AIS) – a GPS-based status radio beacon fitted to all commercial vessels and routinely collated by Coast Guards for both real-time safety monitoring, and analysis and forward-looking planning. The researchers developed existing density measures showing the volume of traffic to incorporate indication of velocity of movement.

Flow line maps are not the only way to visualise movement through space. Another quite different means to represent movement is equally distinctive because it is little seen in comparison to the default designs of thematic cartography. This method of mapping exploits perspective drawing to create a sense of a third dimension on a flat image that can be used to represent time, and thus movement. These pseudo-3D maps are termed space-time cubes (STC) – or what could be thought of as 'fish-tank' diagrams – and the design metaphor arose principally out of Torsten Hägerstrand's influential work in the 1970s developing the approach to human activity known as 'time geography'.

Mapping time-space by 'fish-tank' diagrams focuses attention on the paths that individuals or groups take as they go about their daily activities, as well as highlighting the places they dwell in-between periods of movement. The projection of movement up into the z-dimension above the x, y ground plane is a quite simple concept in visual design terms but can prove effective in revealing personal mobility (cf. Lenntorp 1978; Kwan 1999). People's accessibility is mappable via this method in relation to the social structures of modern living and physical constraints of moving the corporeal body which shape everyday spatiality, in often

Daily Commuting Flows Between English and Welsh Wards in 1981.

The line width of flows involving more than 1000 people is drawn in proportion to the magnitude with direction indicated.

Flows of more than 1 in 30 of the two area's participating populations drawn as thin lines.

43.6 % of all movements shown on a population cartogram.

(b)

Yearly Migration Flows Between English and Welsh Wards 1980/1981.

1,352,520 migration flows shown

The width of line is in proportion to the number of people moving, direction is indicated by arrows.

Population cartogram

Colours show the distribution of occupation by place of origin.

Quartile levels by ward of:

Professional

Supervised

Intermediate

Figure 50.3 Innovative mapping of movement at the societal scale produced by geographer Danny Dorling to visually demonstrate the complicity of flows between thousands of places in England and Wales (Source: Dorling 2012)

VESSEL TRAFFIC ON THE NORTH SEA

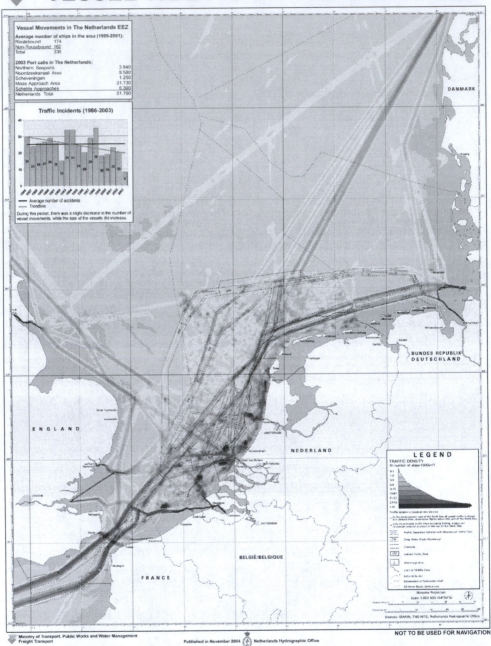

Figure 50.4   An example of a sophisticatedly designed static flow map able to convey the aggregation of vessel movement and varying intensity across space denoted via thickness, opacity and colour of the route lines (Source: Netherlands Hydrographic Office)

subtle ways (e.g. the provision of free workplace car parking or stopping points along public transport routes and the frequencies of service, the timings of the school day and the shift patterns set forth by employers).

Space-time cubes can become surprisingly complex to draw in practice, as questions of geographical scale present a representational challenge when trying to map out real lives, as well as a result of the legibility required of the base map to facilitate interpretation. Also, thought needs to be given to how best to scale the time axis and the granularity of units to appropriately capture the changes, but also to cope with long periods of little or no mobility. Yet effectively designed STCs can show the ratio of being motionless to mobile in daily life, along with the innate creativity in the sequencing and chaining-together of activities in time and space to facilitate solutions to daily tasks. Most people's daily mobility is habitual, citational and strictly local in scale; and much is about going to specific places for face-to-face interaction. STCs are particularly useful for showing so-called 'coupling constraints' which tie people together at agreed points in space and time. Such practical constraints limit others' scope of potential travel.

The significance of different transport infrastructures and communication technologies to everyday mobilities – and people's differential access to them – can be effectively displayed using STCs. For example, in his doctoral research David Mountain (2005) visualised his movement paths, recorded via GPS tracklogs, and used colour coding in his 'fish-tank' diagrams to delineate different modes of travel (walking, cycling, public transport) (cf. Dykes and Mountain 2003). Equally, the more expansive spatial flexibility (seen by some as 'freedom') of the private car can radically extend personal mobility in comparison to someone tied to public transport timetables. In the 'fish-tank' diagrams, the vectors of travel are intuitively mapped by the length of the path in the horizontal plane equating to geographical distance and the slope of the line indicating the speed of movement. Steeply sloping paths provide records of slow physical movement, while a shallow gradient represents rapid travel. What is harder to visually encode is the cost of movement, the degree of sustainability or otherwise of travel patterns dependent on fossil fuels. There is also scope to visualise the distance-traversing nature of telecommunication, although how to fit more complex online activity, which is potentially multi-scalar in nature, is more difficult because the 'wormhole' effects created by virtual interaction cannot be represented within the coordinate space of the single 'fish-tank' (see, however, efforts by Kwan (2000)).

Analysis conducted within time geography has often been based on small samples of individuals, using primary data gathered by intensive qualitative methods, and the results presented by hand-drawn diagramming practice. This approach has been quantitatively extended in the last decade or so by exploiting the automatic capture of time-stamped movement data (via GPS and the tracking of mobile devices), making it possible to efficiently map out many people's activity space. Displaying the time-space paths of hundreds or thousands of people at a city-wide scale required a shift from hand-crafted cartography to computerised mapping. The work of Mei-Po Kwan (cf. 1999, 2000; Kwan and Lee 2003) is especially noteworthy in this regard where she has exploited geovisualisation concepts to chart masses of individual space-time paths in a three-dimensional GIS. An example is shown in Figure 50.5, in which the local 'fish-tank' metaphor is remade into a city-wide 'aquarium', with potential to show something of the mobile throng of daily activity that brings urban space alive. As Kwan and Lee (2003: 51) note, "unlike quantitative methods that tend to reduce the dimensionality of data in the process of analysis, 3D geovisualization may retain the complexity of the original data to the extent that human visual processing is still capable of handling". There is additional flexibility of visualising the STC within 3D GIS because it enables the user to

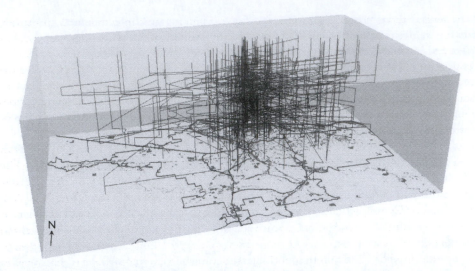

Figure 50.5 An example of Mei-Po Kwan's work exploiting the power of 3D GIS to extend the single STC to visualise many people. In this case the time-space 'aquarium' is showing paths of a sample of African and Asian-American people in the city of Portland, USA (Source: Kwan and Lee 2003, courtesy of Mei-Po Kwan)

interactively select and classify what is shown, along with the ability to query individual paths (and stations along paths) and crucially to control the viewing perspective by panning and zooming. The potentialities of geovisualisation provide a much greater scope for the display of large data volumes, but this cannot necessarily overcome the fundamental limits of this metaphor for mapping individual movement (cf. Kraak 2003), most particularly regarding legibility issues within congested urban centres at peak times, with over-plotting of multiple paths into a bewildering mess. This mode of mapping also struggles when the temporal dimension expands beyond the daily or weekly, and with the difficulty of showing the wide spatial scale of occasional long–distance trips, overseas holidays or events like a spell of hospitalisation.

Developments in map animation to show movement

Beyond the clever graphic symbology of flow mapping and the technical sophistication involved in plotting 3D pathways in time-space 'fish-tanks', perhaps the most obvious way to show the physical movement of objects and material change in the landscape is to make an animated map. The development of animation in film is testament to the potential for showing life-like change by displaying a sequence of still images in rapid progression. There are many different components to an animation that can be modified (and manipulated) to produce very different visual effects. While map animation would appear to be ideally suited to showing mobile phenomena, and has obvious advantages over a conventional static cartographic image – fundamentally because the mapmaker is able to display *additional* spatial data over and above one single map – research has questioned whether people can read map animations as easily as they can a single map solution, and how far they can reliably cognise spatial information when images are only visible to them for a fraction of a second (Harrower 2004).

In general terms there are three major kinds of map animation: temporal animation, showing change (such as 'canned' 24-hour weather forecast animations widely seen on television and the web); motion-focused animation, showing moving objects (such as tracking websites for buses and train and planes); and the dynamic viewpoint animation, where the camera (the viewer's perspective) seems to move (the virtual flight over a map landscape or zoom from space to ground-level satellite imagery beloved by news media). The basic types can be combined to create more complex movies, and, when used with interactive display controls, then cartography crosses over into the realm of geovisualisation.

As noted above, the tracking of people's movement has become much more feasible with digital devices, GPS and cellular communication networks. The movement databases can be usefully represented via map animations and the possibilities were well-explored in an innovative experimental art project conducted by Esther Polak and the Waag Society in 2002. Called *Amsterdam RealTime*, the initial project was to track a small sample of volunteers as they moved about the city, with an updating map displayed in the Waag Society gallery as part of a larger public exhibition. The project developed its own tracking hardware system to do this by adapting a PDA to link to a GPS and share the location coordinates continuously by mobile phone protocols. Tracking the volunteers throughout Amsterdam showed how surprisingly detailed spatial patterns of urban circulation could be built over several weeks, which were shown in short map animations.

The act of animating multiple map frames can be a powerful visualisation technique for mobile objects and dynamic phenomena. It can reveal things that would be unseen in single, static cartographic displays, but one needs to be careful that what is revealed is actually 'real' and not merely an artefact emerging from the map animation process itself. A particular challenge in this regard is how cartographers handle scaling of the time dimension when making map animations. Most often real-time needs to re-scaled by either speeding up movement or slowing down change to make a feasible display for viewers.

Animating maps to show mobile spatial phenomena has potential but may raise as many challenges as it solves for the cartographer, including issues in the practicality of design. For example, how do you convey details of the passage of time on the map key that informs but does not distract the viewer? Can map animations show multiple parameters for rapidly moving objects, given that viewers cannot dwell on details or easily make comparisons with a complex legend? In this regard map animations are often grossly simplified in comparison to the amount of data that can be effectively conveyed on well-designed single thematic maps which can be considered at length. Therefore they might not be an efficient way to map spatial phenomena. In the future the development of more effective map animations could perhaps learn much from cinematography. As map animations become more sophisticated in terms of their visual design and modes of user interaction, then perhaps their intrinsic cartographic basis is morphing into something distinct from 'a map'. Here one might argue that cartographic approaches remain valuable even as more interactive visualisation becomes possible, in much the same way that photography – based on single, static images – remains a powerful visual media in spite of the availability and sophistication of cinematography and interactive video.

Emergence of ego-centred, dynamic mapping

The availability of and easy access to very detailed urban mapping, largely for free,[6] has become taken-for-granted in many countries over the past few years, reflecting a radical shake-up of the political economy of cartographic production, and efficiency gains from online delivery. Many people today are carrying around mobile devices with sophisticated mapping capabilities that were the preserve of the best-equipped elite military forces only a decade or so ago.[7] This is remarkable because most people regard it as unremarkable! The availability of such detailed cartography on–demand and taken everywhere with the user is quite clearly contributing to new mappings of mobility, and is perhaps itself even changing how and why we move.

Mobile maps are challenging mapmakers and interaction designers to develop effective cartographic design solutions that can convey meaning on small screens and often in adverse viewing conditions. Beyond issues of design, there are also deeper conceptual changes to the fundamental nature of the map in this age of wireless access, as the map becomes ego-centred and generated from dynamic 'real-time' data. The result is that mapping seems to be much more personal and much more present – this makes it potentially much more useful for mapping mobile societies. There is a perceptible and significant shift with people no longer being consumers of a fixed range of cartographic products; instead they are becoming mapmakers able to enrol increasingly sophisticated spatial data (like satellite imagery and panoramic photography) to envision their own geographical context in a relevant way.

As noted in the introduction to this chapter, conventional maps were static and tended not to show things that moved or changed, but now they are becoming dynamic, carried on mobile devices and using cartographic data that updates in time according to the person's spatial context. Map use is no longer fixed to particular places (e.g. sitting at a library desk or in front of an expensive graphics workstation). Cartography appears to be more flexible and mutable when rendered on-demand from a GIS database, with the addition of feature query and spatial searching, quite unlike carrying a trusty, printed A–Z street atlas with its fixed geographical extents tied to one preset scale and the size of the printed page, along with its alphabetical index of road names at the back in a tiny hard-to-read font. The satnav capability of mobile mapping, with its keyed destination, calculated route and especially the reassurance of turn-by-turn directions, is potent and potentially changing how people engage with urban space (cf. Axon *et al.* 2012).

These different informational arrangements have been characterised in terms of the emergence of 'ubiquitous cartography' (Gartner *et al.* 2007), being premised upon new, quicker and cheaper modes for capturing geospatial data, including the rise of volunteered and crowdsourced mapping (Dodge and Kitchin 2013). As important is the increased coverage, reliability and transmission bandwidth of wireless networks that are now easily taken-for-granted, but have to be engineered and maintained.[8] Equally significant for mobile mapping are the transparent mechanisms for continuously generating spatial positioning, which are good enough to put the user's dot at about the right spot on their map. The capability of handheld devices is growing and evolving novel interface controls, coupled with continuous access to software services that seem to exist magically 'in the cloud'. The result is that smartphones, combining communication and computation, are highly functional and peculiarly compelling, acting as personal 'helpers' that many people now find indispensable – they are carried lovingly everywhere, positioned in prime spots on tabletops and are the first thing many people look at when waking in the morning. They are arguably the most significant technology of the age, able to extend bodies and augment cognitive abilities. This techno-human hybrid is most evident in the ways that mobile devices help in navigating space more efficiently, find the right places and locate the people they want to meet. These abilities, labelled as 'location-based services' (LBS), constitute one of the 'killer apps' that have made smartphones so seductive to their owners and promise many commercial opportunities for those able to monetise mapping and spatial search services.

These mobile devices and LBS are forming a new kind of map, what one might call the 'me-map', which always positions the viewer at the centre of the mapped world and crucially can update the orientation and location in relation to their movement through space (Dodge *et al.* 2009). "Unlike the geocentric maps that serve many purposes and many users in a balanced manner", according to Meng (2005: 12), "an egocentric map is intended for an individual person for his task at hand". Importantly, the attribute data displayed on the base map can be context-relevant, showing only selected aspects that are important to a person at that time and at that particular location. In this sense the ego-centred nature of the map is more than just getting the x, y location; it is about delivering mapping that fits the moment. The touch-screen interaction of the latest smartphones is also significant because it shifts the role of map from 'surface' representation to a tactile interface to spatial information, with people caressing the screen, almost massaging the map. This ability to control the me-map in such an intimate way hints at its perceptual power and deepens the connection between screen display and embodied activity.

The rise of 'me-maps' as one of the most deeply mobile forms of media currently seen is significant for how people interact with the world and as such should also be subject to critical scrutiny for the risks and threats that might result from the undoubted opportunities and benefits in LBS. First, as such mobile mapping is so intuitive and becomes in many respects ubiquitous, then people become over-dependent on it. And with such dependence comes the risk that a few dominant LBS providers, as key 'ring-holders' for ego-centric cartography, will hold undue power to determine what people see on their maps (and crucially what they don't see). This monopolistic control of the map databases is compounded especially when the few alternative cartographic products cease to be available, as is apparent in the rapid decline in the quality of printed maps. As we come to rely on the smartphone screen as our sole source of information, do we and should we trust the mapping presented to us – remembering the suppliers are unaccountable and profit-motivated companies like Google, Apple and Microsoft? They are often more secretive about their practices than state agencies, claiming the right of commercial confidence. It could be argued that on-demand egocentric mapping has greater scope for deceptive manipulation because it is more matched to the individual user than are mass-printed map products. The spatial search at the heart of LBS can also be easily and covertly distorted to highlight features like favoured businesses and to deny the existence of others (see analysis by Zook and Graham 2007). While there is no tangible evidence of such overly discriminatory practices, one can imagine mobile mapping algorithms that work to deny access to the 'wrong' kind of people but deliberately direct the 'right' people to more expensive, profitable places. This is plausible because the intrinsic, personalised, locative nature of 'me-maps' is such that they can completely invade an individual's spatial privacy. Many people do not consider their smartphone screen to be a two-way medium, so that while it maps for you it is also mapping you for those who control the service. Mobile mapping arguably breaches people's commonsense notions of freedom of movement and anonymity of activity.

The depth of this intensive and intimate surveillance within dynamic me-mapping, and the risks to personal identity and the autonomy of self, is clearly indicated by the number of powerful interests seeking to exploit mobile phone tracking data. Mobile network operators have also proved reluctant to reveal what data they store, what they can do with it and with whom they share it or sell it onto. This was illustrated by German politician Malte Spitz, who challenged the regulation around the retention of personal transactional data by large companies by suing his mobile phone provider Deutsche Telekom to release some 35,000 data records on his activity from August 2009–February 2010. To highlight this issue he presented his own data online: "Seen individually, the pieces of data are mostly inconsequential and harmless. But taken together, they provide . . . a profile – a clear picture of a person's habits and preferences, and indeed, of his or her life" (Biermann 2011).

Major demographic and marketing corporations are keenly interested in such continuous profiles created by mobile devices. So too are a number of academics working together with network operators and LBS companies (e.g. Ratti *et al.* 2006). The micro-geography of movement and its relatively easy availability from mobile devices has also been a boon to law enforcement agencies. The suspect's mobile phone is now seen by police as one of the most vital pieces of evidence to be seized during an arrest, and a whole new branch of digital forensics is developing to strip the data and analyse it (see, for example, Nutter 2008).

The voluntary carrying of smartphones everywhere and their seductive, egocentric mapping services takes individual surveillance to a new level of granularity by observing people continuously through space-time, along with the capacity to link movement patterns and positions of dwelling to information searches, pictures taken, payments made and social communications sent and received. This kind of matrix of data on material activity and daily behaviours has the potential, when analysed appropriately, to reveal some parts of people's identity and the meanings they attach to places and events. Such intensification of spatial surveillance, often seen as an essential and unavoidable part of participation in the mobile society, is creating a digital shadow of people's lives, of unparalleled detail, in the databases of massive corporations that run the networks, control the handset software, and offer alluring free mobile services.

In many respects the continuous tracking of people's movements and physical activities through their mobile devices is just the tip of the iceberg for automated real-time tracking of moving objects. It is widely predicted that in the near future everything that moves and has significant value will be uniquely tagged with RFIDs and tracked by a dense mesh of sensors (Kitchin and Dodge 2011). Tracking all shipping containers around the world is routine today, but soon there will be complete tracking of everything manufactured within these millions of shipments, of how the goods move through the distribution channels, retail sites and places of consumption, and then of where they are disposed.

Conclusions

In conventional form, the map is a poor means to represent the world in motion; it has been a static medium unsuited to showing change and movement. Maps typically seek to present a timeless view of space, arguably as part of their denial of their subjective and partial nature, and to project an aura of objectivity, suggesting that they represent reality in an accurate and trustworthy fashion. There has been considerably creative design work by cartographers and others to overcome these limitations, with some of the most promising developments being in terms of flow mapping and the more experimental work with animation techniques to make short map movies. In appearance, the most novel design solutions are the so-called 'fish-tank' diagrams that can provide a revealing mapping of time geography and, when carefully drawn using real data, they have potential to display the daily choreography that is hard to represent on conventional 'flat' maps.

Despite significant developments in the past decade or so, with greater volumes of detailed tracking data and the rapid development of ego-centred 'me-maps', there are many challenges in mapping movement. It is an exciting area of research in academia and an active frontier for applied science by industry. Finding the right way to map mobility that can expose something of the underlying causes and the real social meaning or economic value attached to it will be very useful in understanding and coping with a changing world. It raises profound ethical issues regarding privacy of movement and autonomy of activity, with the 'spy' behind the smartphone screen potentially watching – and recording – everywhere that people go. Yet one must acknowledge a duality here, because such intensive and intimate mappings of the movements of people can undoubtedly have positive applications; in applied research, for example, to better guide transport planners, property developers and architects to effect structural change in cities that is in harmony with major social drivers of mobility and can also shape future travel pattern in ways needed to meet other beneficial goals (like sustainability, safety or social inclusion). As such, being better able to map mobility could contribute to meeting significant environmental, social and economic challenges facing contemporary societies.

Notes

1 The rotational spin of the Earth is around 1,000 miles an hour at the equator, and the annual procession around the Sun is at the velocity of 107,300 km/h.

2 Of course, the elements of the landscape that are deemed permanent and mappable are themselves culturally contingent and vary over time. Topographic maps in the nineteenth century often indicated watering places for horses, for example, reflecting the dominant mode of transport of the time. Many 'general' purpose maps today would highlight petrol stations above bus stops, reflecting the dominant interests of car drivers above other forms of travel.

3 Governmental concern over the last couple of centuries with evermore detailed mapping of the weather is an interesting exception to the rule. Efforts to map (and in some senses, thereby, control) future weather patterns is clearly useful to many hegemonic interests, not least the military (cf. Monmonier 1999).

4 This is changing due to the well-documented improvements in computation, the automation of data capture and the declining costs of storage (cf. Kitchin and Dodge 2011). Following on the coat tails of natural sciences and biomedical science, there is much interest in the humanities and social sciences in tackling analysis with 'big data' that was previously considered impractical or completely unfeasible.

5 This is comparable to the dominance of Excel, with its design defaults and helpful wizards which tend to diminish the diversity of ways in which data is charted. Similar arguments are made about the pernicious influence of PowerPoint on how presentations are made (cf. Tufte 2003).

6 It is far from free, of course. The huge capital costs of granting no-cost public access to high-resolution satellite imagery are being met, in part, by revenues from geographically targeted advertising, but it is also being heavily subsidised at the moment by large corporations like Google and Microsoft as they seek to entice users to their sites and to dominate the marketplace for online mapping. There is no guarantee that no-cost user access will continue to be provided by such corporations in the future.

7 At least for the affluent minority in industrial economies, with the right devices and technical savvy to work them. The long-standing issues of 'digital divides' remain unresolved.

8 It is somewhat ironic that flexible, mobile mapping is also dependent on a fixed and immobile infrastructure. The network hardware needed to support mobile services is substantial but hidden, with wireless telecommunications dependent on a dense forest of antennas connected to broadband and fibre-optic cables.

References

Andrienko, G., Andrienko, N., Dykes, J., Fabrikant, S. I., Wachowicz, M., 2008, 'Geovisualization of dynamics, movement and change: key issues and developing approaches in visualization research', *Information Visualization*, 7: 173–180.

Axon, S., Speake, J., Crawford, K., 2012, '"At the next junction, turn left": Attitudes towards sat nav use', *Area*, 44(2): 170–177.

Biermann, K., 2011, 'Data protection: Betrayed by our own data', *Zeit Online*, 26 March. Available online at www.zeit.de/digital/datenschutz/2011-03/data-protection-malte-spitz.

Bunge, W., 1971, *Fitzgerald: Geography of a Revolution* (Schenkman Publishing Company, Cambridge, MA).

Dent, B., 1995, *Cartography: Thematic Map Design, Fifth Edition* (McGraw-Hill, New York).

Dodge, S., Weibel, R., Lautenschutz, A-K., 2008, 'Towards a taxonomy of movement patterns', *Information Visualization*, 7: 1–13.

Dodge, M., Perkins, C., Kitchin, R., 2009, 'Mapping modes, methods and moments: A manifesto for map studies', in Dodge, M., Kitchin, R., Perkins, C. (eds), *Rethinking Maps: New Frontiers in Cartographic Theory* (Routledge, London), pp. 311–341.

Dodge, M., Kitchin, R., 2013, 'Crowdsourced cartography: mapping experience and knowledge', *Environment and Planning A*, 45(1): 19–36.

Dorling, D., 2012, *The Visualization of Spatial Social Structure* (Wiley, Chichester, England).

Dorling, D., Thomas, B., 2011, *Bankrupt Britain: An Atlas of Social Change* (Policy Press, Bristol).

Dykes, J. A., Mountain, D. M., 2003, 'Seeking structure in records of spatio-temporal behaviour: Visualization issues, efforts and applications', *Computational Statistics & Data Analysis*, 43(4): 581–603.

Friendly, M., 2006, 'Visions and re-visions of Charles Joseph Minard', *Journal of Educational Behavioral Statistics*, 27: 31–61.

Funkhouser, H. G., 1936, 'A note on a tenth century graph', *Osiris*, 1: 260–262.

Gartner, G., Bennett, D. A., Morita, T., 2007, 'Towards ubiquitous cartography', *Cartography and Geographic Information Science*, 34(4): 247–257.

Hägerstrand, T., 1970, 'What about people in regional science?', *Papers of the Regional Science Association*, 24: 7–21.

Harrower, M., 2004, 'A look at the history and future of animated maps', *Cartographica*, 39(3): 33–42.

Hirtle, S., Richter, K. F., Srinivas, S., Firth, R., 2010, 'This is the tricky part: When directions become difficult', *Journal of Spatial Information*, 1. Available online at http://josis.org/index.php/josis/article/viewArticle/17.

Hubble, E., 1929, 'A relation between distance and radial velocity among extra-galactic nebulae', *Proceedings of the National Academy of Sciences of the United States of America*, 15(3): 168–173.

Kitchin, R., Dodge, M., 2011, *Code/Space: Software and Everyday Life* (MIT Press, Cambridge, MA).

Kraak, M. J., 2003, 'The space-time cube revisited from a geovisualization perspective', *Proceedings of the 21st International Cartographic Conference*. Available online at www.itc.eu/library/Papers_2003/art_proc/kraak.pdf.

Kwan, M-P., 1999, 'Gender, the home-work link, and space-time patterns of non employment activities', *Economic Geography*, 75(4): 370–394.

Kwan, M-P., 2000, 'Human extensibility and individual hybrid-accessibility in space-time: A multiscale representation using GIS', in Janelle, D. and Hodge, D. C. (eds), *Information, Place and Cyberspace: Issues in Accessibility* (Springer, New York), pp. 241–256.

Kwan, M-P., Lee, J., 2003, 'Geovisualization of human activity patterns using 3D GIS: A time-geographic approach', in Goodchild, M. F., Janelle, D. G. (eds), *Spatially Integrated Social Science* (Oxford University Press, Oxford), pp. 48–66.

Lenntorp, B., 1978, 'A time-geographic simulation model of individual activity programmes', in Carlstein, T., Parkes, D., Thrift, N. (eds), *Human Activity and Time Geography* (Edward Arnold, London), pp. 162–180.

Meng, L., 2005, 'Egocentric design of map-based mobile services', *The Cartographic Journal*, 42(1): 5–13.

Monmonier, M., 1999, *Air Apparent: How Meteorologists Learned to Map, Predict, and Dramatize Weather* (University of Chicago Press, Chicago).

Mountain, D. M., 2005, 'Exploring Mobile Trajectories: An Investigation of Individual Spatial Behaviour and Geographic Filters for Information Retrieval' (Unpublished PhD Thesis, City University, London). Available online at www.soi.city.ac.uk/~dmm/phd/.

Nutter, B., 2008, 'Pinpointing TomTom location records: A forensic analysis', *Digital Investigation*, 5: 10–18.

Polak, E. and Waag Society, 2002, *Amsterdam RealTime*. Available online at http://realtime.waag.org/.

Ratti, C., Frenchman, D., Pulselli, R. M., Williams, S., 2006, 'Mobile landscapes: Using location data from cell phones for urban analysis', *Environment and Planning B: Planning and Design*, 33: 727–748.

Robinson, A. H., 1955, 'The 1837 maps of Henry Drury Harness', *The Geographical Journal*, 121(4): 440–450.

Robinson, A. H., 1967, 'The thematic maps of Charles Joseph Minard', *Imago Mundi*, 21: 95–108.

Robinson, A. H., 1982, *Early Thematic Mapping in the History of Cartography* (University of Chicago Press, London).

Schwanen, T., Kwan M-P., 2012, 'Critical space-time geographies', *Environment and Planning A*, 44(9): 2043–2048.

Tufte, E. R., 2003, *The Cognitive Style of PowerPoint* (Graphics Press, Cheshire, CT).

Zook, M. A., Graham, M., 2007, 'Mapping digiplace: Geocoded internet data and the representation of place', *Environment and Planning B: Planning and Design*, 34: 466–482.

51

Photography

Debbie Lisle

In analysing the characteristics, contours and limits of contemporary mobility, scholars have been careful to pose the increasingly frenetic movement of modern life against a number of immobilities, 'moorings' and forces of rootedness (Adey, 2006, 2010; Cresswell, 2010; Hannam, Sheller and Urry, 2006; Urry, 2007). They remind us that the ability, freedom and capacity to move are not universally available or applicable, and that the condition of possibility for some people's movement is the immobility of others. As Adey explains, 'Mobility, like power, is a relational thing' (2006: 83). From the start, then, the 'mobility turn' has been constituted by a structuring tension between movement and stasis, and while the politics of mobility – its capacity to entrench, rearrange and disperse power – has always been at the forefront of this research agenda, it is only recently that scholars have asked about the political possibilities of stillness (Bissell and Fuller, 2011). Usually framed as some form of stubborn resistance to the rapid changes, speeds and circulations of modern life, stillness is now being understood as something more polyvalent, pluralistic and heterogeneous – a disposition with its own ontology and not the silenced and difficult Other of mobility (Bissell and Fuller, 2011: 3) Building on research that questions the constitutive antagonism between mobility and immobility, and taking seriously the political possibilities embedded in stillness, this chapter uses the photograph – the most still of visual objects – to expand and develop the remit of mobilities research. It explores two registers of mobility with respect to the photograph: the first (and most obvious) is the manner in which photographs physically move between different contexts, technologies and people, especially within digital cultures via activities such as posting, downloading and file sharing. The second register involves more epistemological questions about the mobility of meaning and the prevailing pathways of interpretation created between photographs and viewers. Certainly it is important to analyse how the digital revolution has dramatically expanded the capacity for photographs to be developed, posted, sent, copied, circulated, downloaded and re-circulated. But that only accounts for one aspect of a photograph's mobility. What needs further examination is whether and how the capacity to circulate photographs so quickly, widely and constantly changes the way viewers interpret and make meaning out of these images. In our increasingly mobile and networked world, how does meaning *move* between photographs and viewers? How is it generated, circulated, re-circulated and fixed? Which established interpretive pathways does it travel along, and which does it refuse? And what happens to issues of meaning when the bounded nature of both material photographs and embodied viewers is challenged?

This paper tracks the evolution of thinking about mobility and photography in order to show how successive understandings have increasingly shed the prevailing idea that photographs are still, inert and immutable objects, and embraced the possibility that these objects *move* in a variety of ways. Traditional understandings of photographs as truthful forms of evidence or symbolic repositories for our emotions and memories do not offer much scope for thinking about mobility. However, a more relational approach that positions photographs within existing networks and digital cultures opens up the possibility of tracking the physical circulation of photographs and the new pathways of interpretation that arise as a result. This paper builds on those insights to suggest a further area to explore: the breaking down of the powerful anthropocentrism which underscores our claims about both photography and mobility. It is only once the boundaries between the human, viewing subject and the material, immutable object are problematised, critiqued and re-imagined that we can begin to understand mobility as a properly heterogeneous, permeable and networked practice. As insights from Actor-Network Theory, Non-Representational Theory, New Materialism and Posthumanism suggest, our interactions with photographs are best understood as temporary subject–object assemblages through which various networks intersect and flow. For me, assemblages are not simply constellations of already formed subjects and objects; that is, they do not accumulate and glue discrete bodies together in a larger collective. Rather, assemblages create the conditions under which the most foundational boundaries we take for granted – the corporeal and the material – are valued for their porosity, vulnerability and openness, rather than their resilience. Subjects and objects do not simply move within networks: the conditions of mobility itself render corporeal and material boundaries permeable, thereby threatening the notion that some bounded subjects and objects remain still while others move.

This future area of research poses challenging questions for the way we study mobility more generally. If subjects and objects are bounded entities, it is possible to track and even measure their movement, speed, force and accumulation. In short, we can apply all kinds of traditional and innovative research methods to entities that have clear boundaries, limits and edges, be they subjects (e.g. migrants, border guards, business travellers, locals, refugees, city dwellers, children) or objects (e.g. aeroplanes, viruses, data, cars, genomes, guns, passports). But once the corporeal and material boundaries of these entities are deconstructed – once subjects and objects are understood as porous, mobile assemblages – we need to ask different questions. What happens to political, democratic and public life when non-human objects are afforded agency, vibrancy and potential? Some very interesting research is currently being undertaken here on non-human objects that have a direct impact on political life – for example, viruses that continually mutate as they spread across the world, biological agents used for terrorist purposes, sub-atomic particles manipulated by nanotechnology, and the intertwining human and natural forces contributing to climate change (Bennett, 2010; Braun and Whatmore, 2010; Bingham *et al.*, 2008; Kirksey and Helmreich, 2010). Photographs, of course, do not express such direct political impact, but taking them seriously as 'vibrant matter' (Bennett, 2010) contributes to a wider project of dethroning the corporeal and material boundaries that continue to underscore so much mobilities research.

The singular truth

Since its inception, photography has always carried what John Tagg (1988) has helpfully described as the 'burden of representation'; that is, photographs are understood as truthful evidence and documentary 'proof'. Although this evidentiary understanding of photography has been soundly critiqued by Tagg and others (Barthes, 1982; Benjamin, 1972; Sontag, 1979; Tagg, 1988, 2009) who demonstrate the histories, social relations, institutions, cultural forces and power relations that construct notions like 'photographic truth', it remains a predominant and seductive trope. We still want to believe that the camera never lies and that photographs give us direct access to the truth by capturing a fixed reality and delivering it to us in an unchanged form. This assumes not only that there is a more 'real' world existing prior to acts of representation, but also that photographs themselves are static and inert objects faithfully representing that fixed reality to viewers. Within this approach, a photograph's physical mobility – defined by how widely and systematically it is disseminated, and through which technologies, media platforms and outlets – is of secondary importance to the manner in which the photograph is able to deliver an unambiguous, truthful and objective message to the viewer. Because this mobility of meaning is both singular (i.e. wider notions of accuracy produce a correspondence between reality and photographic representation) and unidirectional (i.e. that singular meaning travels from the photograph to the viewer), the potentially infinite significations and interpretive journeys of a photograph are arrested and channelled through the narrow causal chains of truth-telling and objectivity. The result, of course, is that the viewer either gets the message right (i.e. accurately) or misinterprets its singular, unambiguous 'truth'. With such a truncated account of the way meaning is generated and disseminated, the evidentiary approach positions photographs as inert and immutable products of a purely technical procedure. The camera – a scientific instrument – allows the photographer to record truth and reality accurately, and the photograph – an objective document – delivers that truth unhindered to the viewer. This characterisation of the photograph as a mute and passive vehicle for singular meaning is further reinforced when compared with cinema; indeed, photography is often understood as cinema's constitutive form, but it is also understood as lacking the key ingredients of movement, time and narrative (Beckman, 2008; Campany, 2008; Lisle, 2011: 145; Green and Lowry, 2006). This stillness is not a hindrance to the truth-value approach because the photograph's immutability is precisely what secures the singular and unidirectional construction of meaning. Within such a controlled conceptual landscape, there is no need to ask whether the breadth of a photograph's global dissemination increases or decreases the likelihood of counter-meanings and misreading. Rather, it is assumed that the photograph's singular meaning retains its integrity throughout its journey to different viewers in diverse contexts.

Emotions and memories

The opposite of the evidentiary approach is the claim that photographs always exceed their truth-value, and are therefore more important as symbolic containers of our emotions and memories. Here, both the technical aspects of photography as well as its artistic and compositional elements are less important than its affective power: its capacity to invoke physical, emotional and visceral responses in the viewer. A highly treasured photograph could be blurry, indistinct and off-centre, but its value is primarily in the subject matter of the image and how that affects the viewer. Like the truth-value approach, there is a similar lack of concern with the physical mobility of the image itself – the technical aspects of its production, dissemination and reproduction. Unlike the truth-value approach, however, understanding photographs as containers of our emotions and memories offers a much broader account of how meaning is generated between photographs and viewers. Barthes's *Camera Lucida* (1982) provides one of the most nuanced accounts of this position. Ruminating on questions of love, death, time and memory, Barthes explains how photographs – especially those of people who are no longer living – often overwhelm and astonish him (1982: 76, 82). This he famously attributes to the photograph's *punctum* – the element of the image which shoots out and pierces, or wounds, the viewer (Barthes, 1982: 26). Here, the photograph's mobility travels in the same direction as it did in the truth-value account of photography – from the picture to the viewer. But Barthes's account of the *punctum* explains that this movement is neither singular nor contained. Rather than the truth being captured and delivered unchanged to the viewer, the 'shooting out' and 'piercing' capacity of a photograph is a much more unruly affair. Indeed, we may declare that we are 'moved' by a photograph, but that moving occurs in a variety of ways. While many overarching social discourses such as pity, empathy and anger seek to access the power of our emotional responses and harness them to ideological goals, these responses do not necessarily follow any instrumental logic. For example, stereo-typical images of famine often used to increase charitable donations may cause some viewers to feel sadness, pity and guilt and be moved to give money, but they may cause others to feel boredom, irritation and disgust.

Understanding photographs as containers of our emotions and memories requires an additional mobility that travels in the opposite direction to Barthes's *punctum*: this time from the viewer to the image. Rather than the mute and passive subject simply being injected with (and uncritically accepting) the truth-value of a photograph, or even its powerful *punctum*, viewers in this approach are given more agency. Emotional responses to photographs are not just reactive because viewers are not always fixed in 'responsive' mode; rather, viewers are pro-active in their interpretations because they project their own histories, experiences and desires onto photographs. In this sense, photographic interpretation requires a two-way mobility: meaning is produced by the *punctum* shooting out of the image, but also by the viewer projecting his/her desires onto the image. While this doubled-mobility expands both the remit of what a photograph could possibly mean and the number of interpretive pathways along which photographic meaning could travel, the photograph itself – its materiality – remains a bounded object. It is either the generator of meaning (through the *punctum*), or the receptacle of it (absorbing the viewer's projections). Similarly, the corporeal limits of the viewer also remain intact, as their activities are restricted to either receiving meaning from, or projecting meaning onto, the photograph. While some critical work pushes these boundaries through notions of haunting, spectres, fantasies and imaginings (Liss, 1998; Lury, 1997; Sutton, 2009), most conventional accounts of emotions, memory and photography only offer a fixed and bilateral route through which meaning moves (i.e. back and forth between the photograph and the viewer).

Circulations

Partly because the 'truth-value' and 'emotional impact' theorisations of photography were developed in a pre-digital age, neither approach properly acknowledges that the physical dissemination and circulation of photographs has an impact on the way meaning is generated and secured. As a consequence, the understanding of mobility in these two approaches focuses primarily on how meaning emerges, circulates and vacillates back and forth between the viewer and the picture, rather than how these two entities *themselves* circulate. This is where the 'new mobilities paradigm' offers productive new avenues of research that help us track how digital photographs are taken, stored, sent, posted, circulated, disseminated, downloaded and re-circulated around the world. It has prompted an engagement with technological developments such as the ubiquity, size, portability and affordability of digital camera technology; the presence of digital cameras within mobile phones; the breadth and ease of digital storage capacity; the immediacy of the digital screen which allows instant viewing and deleting; and most importantly, the widespread access to the internet which allows people to post, share and disseminate digital images (Larsen, 2008: 146–152; Haldrup and Larsen, 2006; Rubenstein and Sluis, 2008; Sutton, 2010). This suggests that traditional questions about photographic meaning must be analysed alongside newer questions about the digital construction of photographs, their virtual presence, and most importantly, their mobility and circulation within global networks and screen-based digital cultures. For Larsen, this means bridging the chasm between the social and the technical that has marked conventional understandings of photography, and re-ordering the hierarchy that has tradi-tionally privileged social, historical and ideological analyses of photography at the expense of concerns about technology, materiality and mobility (2008: 144).

By foregrounding the technological aspects of photography, non-human objects in the network (e.g. photographs) are valued just as much as human agents (e.g. viewers). Conse-quently, agency is no longer the sole domain of the subject because it is transferred, dispersed and shared out to objects who can, in Thrift's words, answer back (2008: 9). This conceptual shift acknowledges the powerful connection between human viewers and material photo-graphs, but affords the photograph itself – as an object – much more capacity for action, and therefore a much fuller role in the generation of meaning. As Edwards and Hart (2004: 4) argue: 'objects themselves can be seen as social actors, in that it is not the meanings of things *per se* that are important but their social effects as they construct and influence the field of social action'. Because this dispersal of agency to non-human objects is a shift away from hierarchical relations which privilege the human subject and into networked relations of mobility (what some might call a rhizomatic shift), it requires us to re-think our understand-ing of encounters between viewers, cameras, photographs and digital technology. Sometimes temporary and fleeting, sometimes drawn out and repeated, these encounters are moments of pause in a networked flow when humans and non-humans construct hybrid formations such as 'photographer-camera-iconic landscape', or 'viewer-screen-photograph'. As Larsen's work on tourist photography suggests, these hybrid constellations emerge for the entire dura-tion of photographic practice, from framing an image in a viewfinder, clicking the shutter, viewing the image on the camera's back screen, uploading it, sending and posting the image, printing the image and finally to viewing it (2005, 2008: 146–52).

The elevation of the photograph's materiality, its enhanced agency, and the positioning of both subjects and objects within mobile networks poses challenging questions to the traditional way we understand the production and circulation of photographic meaning. Analysing how photographs and viewers *themselves* move within networks automatically widens the possibilities of what can happen during their encounters (e.g. brief glimpses, long moments of contemplation, bored dismissal), reveals the infinite pathways of interpre-tation along which photographs can potentially signify, and opens up a wider horizon for the mobility of meaning (i.e. its multiple sites of generation, where and how quickly or slowly it circulates, and how it changes as a result of its travels). Studying photography within the 'new mobilities paradigm' offers a productive way out of the subject/object logic by releasing viewers and photographs from their fixed, bilateral positioning. It helps us understand photography as a mobile visual practice rather than an immutable vehicle for truth or a static mirror of our emotions. More importantly, by putting photographs and viewers into circulation, this approach turns its critical lens on the unexamined everyday practices of taking, disseminating and accessing photographs rather than on a general dis-embodied theory of photography.

Porous assemblages

The 'new mobilities paradigm' makes two persuasive and necessary claims: first, that photographs and viewers are now understood to be constantly moving and encountering one another within networks; and second, that during these encounters subject–object hybrids are formed in which a dispersed and co-dependent agency is formed. Larsen's work is the most productive here (2005, 2008), and his invocation of Actor-Network and Non-Representational Theories rightly suggests that we need to understand the relationship between viewers and photographs within mobile digital networks as co-constitutive and co-dependent. The problem remains, however, that this is a largely accretive account of photography and mobility; that is, photographs and viewers are simply *added together* to form subject–object hybrids, then disaggregated and dispersed throughout the network before coalescing once again into a different hybrid formation. This process of coalescing, disaggregating and dispersing does provide a relational account of mobile subjects and objects, but it does not fully question the corporeal boundaries of the viewing subject or the material boundaries of the photograph itself. My concern is that Actor-Network and Non-Representational Theories are not taken far enough in terms of understanding what is at stake when viewer agency is radically dispersed onto photographs, or even when agency itself is understood as 'a relational achievement between humans and non-humans' (Larsen, 2008: 145). Part of the problem is that the outdated term 'hybrid' still allows an accretive framework to operate. If we accept Latour's claim that we should not start with the essences of either subjects or objects (Larsen, 2008: 145), then we must equally accept that we should not start with the corporeal limits of subjects or the material limits of objects.

Larsen makes a revealing claim in his discussion of digital photography and mobility: that 'While digital camera screens have a material tactility, the photographs they display are images, not physical objects' (2008: 149). But this claim only holds if we discount both the minute objects that constitute the digital camera screen itself (e.g. pixels, triads, phosphor dots, light particles, currents, voltages, glass, plastic, conductors, electrodes) and the way our other senses enhance the act of looking. When we *do* take these into account, two shifts immediately occur. First, by focusing on different scales of materiality from the very small (e.g. nanoparticles) to the very large (e.g. global systems) it becomes quite difficult to claim with any certainty what is, and what is not, an object. Thus, Larsen's claim that the digital storage of photographs actually *de*-materialises them (2008: 149) is hard to sustain. Surely a more significant question here is about scale: about what counts as 'material' and what doesn't (i.e. how large and how small), and how that material/non-material boundary is produced, secured and policed. Second, by bringing our other senses fully into the act of looking, we begin to understand that seeing is also a process of touching – an optic/haptic practice that fuses bodies to photographs in ways that go much further than the concept of the hybrid allows (Edwards and Hart, 2004: 9; Hansen, 2001). My point is that while Larsen and others are right to draw on Actor-Network and Non-Representational Theory to re-imagine the relationship between photography and mobility, these efforts are often hampered by a lingering reliance on fixed notions of corporeality and materiality. In this sense, recent work on New Materialism, Posthumanism and affect offers a productive way forward because it does not assume that things or people are bounded entities with unbreacheable limits (Bennett, 2010; Coole and Frost, 2010; Hayles, 1999; Massumi, 2002; Wolfe, 2009). Here, human/non-human assemblages are not understood as accretive collections, but rather as entities that are always already amalgamated, entangled and interlaced, as well as porous, open and vulnerable.

Forward motion

Once the sanctity of corporeal and material boundaries is challenged, the foundational tension between mobility and immobility must be questioned. As I have argued elsewhere, 'Once this terrain is opened, the photograph no longer remains still: it is now unavoidably part of the haphazard, multilevel and instantaneous production of meaning that continually loops and circulates through affective, emotional and ideological registers' (Lisle, 2011: 151). In short, when the material boundaries of the photograph and the corporeal boundaries of the viewer are shown to be permeable (and here I mean more permeable than notions like hybrid allow), it makes no sense to talk of the photograph as a still, inert or immutable object, or the viewer as a bounded subject with a monopoly on agency. Likewise, calling corporeal and material boundaries into question also challenges the tendency within the 'new mobilities paradigm' to privilege the physical mobility of objects over questions of meaning (Larsen, 2008: 146). Understanding that photographs physically move through virtual and digital cultures is not enough: we need a critical account of photography that foregrounds more dispersed, contingent and unbounded encounters between viewers, images and their networked environment that *doesn't* reproduce the foundational binary between stillness and mobility. If photographs *themselves* have agency, capacity and potential, the privileged and anthropocentric account of the viewer is unseated and the relationship between human subjects and non-human objects is re-imagined in a more horizontal and democratic formation. As Bennett argues, taking 'thing power' seriously and puncturing the anthropocentric hegemony of the subject has significant implications for the way we understand self-interest, collective political action and the public sphere (2010). Photographs have long been important components of public culture; the challenge now is to work out how that significance changes in a condition of mobility. As this chapter has argued, photographs can no longer be understood as static, inactive objects brought to life by privileged viewers. Rather, what needs to be explored is the way these images move through actual, digital and virtual worlds and suture themselves – no matter how temporarily – to equally mobile and porous viewing subjects. Only then can we start to delineate and resist the new constellations of power and hegemony that are taking hold in contemporary visual culture.

References

Adey, P. (2010). *Mobility*. London: Routledge.

Adey, P. (2006). 'If Mobility is Everything Then it is Nothing: Towards a Relational Politics of (Im)mobilities'. *Mobilities*, 1(1): 75–94.

Barthes, R. (1982). *Camera Lucida: Reflections on Photography*. Trans. Richard Howard. London: Jonathan Cape (re-printed 2000).

Beckman, K. (2008). *Still Moving: Between Cinema and Photography*. Durham: Duke University Press.

Benjamin, W. (1972). 'A Short History of Photography'. *Screen*, 13(1): 5–26.

Bennett, J. (2010). *Vibrant Matter: A Political Ecology of Things*. Durham: Duke University Press.

Bingham, N., Enticott, G., and Hinchliffe, S. (2008). 'Biosecurities: Spaces, Practices and Boundaries'. *Environment and Planning A*, 40(7): 1528–33.

Bissell, D., and Fuller, G. (eds) (2011). *Stillness in a Mobile World*. London: Routledge.

Braun, B. and Whatmore, S. (2010). *Political Matter: Technoscience, Democracy and Public Life*. Minneapolis: University of Minnesota Press.

Campany, D. (2008). *Photography and Cinema*. London: Reaktion Books.

Coole, D. and Frost, S. (eds) (2010). *New Materialisms: Ontology, Agency & Politics*. Durham: Duke University Press.

Cresswell, T. (2010). 'Towards a Politics of Mobility'. *Environment and Planning D: Society and Space*, 28(1): 17–31.

Edwards, E. and Hart, J. (eds) (2004). *Photographs Objects Histories: On the Materiality of Images*. London: Routledge.

Green, D. and Lowry, J. (eds) (2006). *Stillness and Time: Photography and the Moving Image*. Brighton: Photoforum/Photoworks.

Haldrup, M. and Larsen, J. (2006). 'Material Cultures of Tourism'. *Leisure Studies*, 25(3): 275–89.

Hannam, K., Sheller, M. and Urry, J. (2006). 'Editorial: Mobilities, Immobilities and Moorings'. *Mobilities*, 1(1): 1–22.

Hansen, M. B. N. (2001). 'Seeing with the Body: The Digital Image in Postphotography'. *Diacritics*, 31(4): 54–82.

Hayles, K. (1999). *How We Became Posthuman: Virtual Bodies in Cybernetics, Literature & Informatics*. Chicago: University of Chicago Press.

Kirksey, S. E. and Helmreich, S. (2010). 'The Emergence of Multispecies Ethnography'. *Cultural Anthropology*, 25(4): 545–76.

Larsen, J. (2008). 'Practices and Flows of Digital Photography: An Ethnographic Framework'. *Mobilities*, 3(1): 141–60.

Larsen, J. (2005). 'Families Seen Photographing: Performativity of Tourist Photography'. *Space and Culture*, 8(4): 416–34.

Lisle, D. (2011). 'Moving Encounters: The Affective Mobilities of Photography'. In D. Bissell and G. Fuller (eds) *Stillness in a Mobile World*. London: Routledge (pp. 139–54).

Liss, A. (1998). *Trespassing Through Shadows: Memory, Photography & the Holocaust*. Minneapolis: University of Minnesota Press.

Lury, C. (1997). *Prosthetic Culture: Photography, Memory and Identity*. London: Routledge.

Massumi, B. (2002). *Parables for the Virtual: Movement, Affect, Sensation*. Durham: Duke University Press.

Rubenstein, D. and Sluis, K. (2008). 'A Life More Photographic: Mapping the Networked Image'. *Photographies*, 1(1): 9–28.

Sontag, S. (1979). *On Photography*. London: Penguin.

Sutton, D. (2010). 'Immanent Images: Photography after Mobility'. In D. N. Rodowick (ed.) *Afterimages of Gilles Deleuze's Film Philosophy*. Minneapolis: University of Minnesota Press (pp. 307–325).

Sutton, D. (2009). *Photography, Cinema, Memory: The Crystal Image of Time*. Minneapolis: University of Minnesota.

Tagg, J. (2009). *The Disciplinary Frame: Photographic Truths and the Capture of Meaning*. Minneapolis: University of Minnesota Press.

Tagg, J. (1988). *The Burden of Representation: Essays on Photographies and Histories*. London: Macmillan.

Thrift, N. (2008). *Non-Representational Theory: Space, Politics, Affect*. London: Routledge.

Urry, J. (2007). *Mobilities*. Cambridge: Polity.

Wolfe, C. (2009). *What is Posthumanism?* Minneapolis: University of Minnesota Press.

52

Video

Paul Simpson

Recently, I have been researching the experience of cycling in Plymouth, UK. In particular, I have been interested in how the things cyclists encounter on a day-to-day basis in undertaking their commutes and other routine journeys have implications for their experience of cycling through Plymouth's various urban environments. I've been interested in how mundane things like road surfaces, hills, helmets, traffic lights, cycle lanes (or a lack thereof), buses, cars, other cyclists, and pedestrians; ephemeral happenings like gestures, glances, shouted words and passing comments, rain, and wind; and sensations of speed, slowness, proximity, and space, are all enrolled in the production of the experience of cycling.

One comment that has been made again and again by the cyclists involved in this research is that much of their time spent cycling is: 'not very interesting, is it?'. While nothing could be farther from the truth for many researchers of mobile practices like cycling (Fincham *et al.* 2010a), getting cyclists to see this and discuss such routine experiences is not easy. When I first met with the various cyclists involved in the project, many were quick to mention the relatively rare, and at times spectacular, events from their recent experiences of cycling. Many excitedly recounted near misses with traffic, being knocked off their bikes by white vans, or being 'cut-up' on the way to work that morning. Many also were quick to mention particularly bad roads, difficult junctions, or problematic cycle-infrastructure. And these are obviously important aspects of their experiences. However, the rest of the routine and uneventful travel that constitutes the majority of their past, present, and likely future commuting experiences was not so readily offered up for discussion.

Based on these experiences of researching cycling, this chapter is going to focus on the use of mobile video methods as one possible solution to the challenge of gaining access to those aspects of mobile practices which either may at first seem to many of lesser importance as compared with the more spectacular aspects of being 'on the move', or equally may be less easily talked about (the felt, embodied aspects of travel experiences). As such, the chapter will unfold over four main parts. First, I will provide some context to the use of video in mobilities research and discuss some recent debates related to the development of methods that can attend to various aspects of the experience of being mobile. From there, I will provide further background to the research project this discussion emerges from and the specific methodological approach employed in trying to gain an understanding of cycling experiences. Third,

I will draw out some specific aspects of cyclists' experience uncovered in this research and, in doing so, illustrate the usefulness of a mobile video-elicitation approach. This will be followed by a brief conclusion, where I will make some suggestions as to how the methodological approach taken here might be taken forward in future work on the experience of undertaking various forms of mobile practices.

Mobile video methods and the study of mobile practices

The mobilities turn in the social sciences has posed significant questions about the study of everyday mobile practices (see Buscher *et al.* 2011; Fincham *et al.* 2010b). How can researchers engage mobile individuals and groups when they are actually on the move, and when such movements might often appear insignificant to them given their mundane regularity? It may not always be practical to make observations at the point of mobility itself or, likewise, to engage with those being studied while they are undertaking these movements (Brown and Spinney 2010; Urry 2007). Equally, participants often think researchers are after something 'interesting', and so that the humdrum aspects of their daily movements can't (or shouldn't) be of interest given their apparent insignificance and banality. This all becomes even more pressing when we factor in the related focus within mobilities research on the "actuation of mobility itself" (Adey 2010: 133). This is the case as such a focus directs us towards the extra-discursive, felt, and embodied aspects of how mobility which "exceed our capacities to . . . think about and represent them" happens (Adey 2010: 142). How then can we research the actual experience of mobility when: i) we are rarely aware of the movements we routinely make; ii) we do not necessarily reflect on them as they actually happen; and iii) our descriptions of such movements generally fall short of fully accounting for the movement itself (Adey 2010; also see Thrift 2000)?

This has all led to a frustration amongst some mobilities researchers "regarding the ability of a narrow range of methods to explain particular aspects of . . . [various] forms of movement" (Spinney 2011: 163). As Hitchings (2012: 61) notes, some have argued that "everyday practices are . . . so habitually done that potential respondents are probably unable to comment" on their involvement in them and so, the argument goes, traditional social science methods like interviews, for example, "can only ever provide an unsatisfactorily washed out account of what previously took place".

Responses to these frustrations and perceived methodological limitations have often been focused around the interrelated issues of how to 'be there' when 'there' is not a static location (Brown and Spinney 2010; Laurier 2010; Murray 2010), and how we can attend to the singular and ephemeral, yet equally routine, nature of mobile experiences in doing so (D'Andrea *et al.* 2011: 155). In approaching this, such work has argued that there is a need to get beyond (solely) "verbalised accounts of practice divorced from the context of doing that is so fundamental to the creation of meaning in mobile practices" (Spinney 2011: 163), and so to "develop and hone techniques and strategies for eliciting embodiments, affects, practices, meanings, institutions and structures of mobility" (D'Andrea *et al.* 2011: 155).

One technology that has been increasingly presented as providing opportunities to develop such strategies and techniques is digital video. While there is a significant tradition of using video to study aspects of social and communal life in disciplines like anthropology (for a review see Garrett 2011), the use of video in many social sciences is less prominent (see, however, Ash 2009, 2010; Kindon 2003).[1] That said, the work of scholars like Eric Laurier and Justin Spinney has raised the profile of the use of video in the study of everyday and mobile practices, having illustrated in various ways how "ordinary and fleeting aspects of everyday life can be apprehended where they were previously missed or glossed over in the production of more static texts" (Spinney 2011: 166; see also Brown and Spinney 2010; Laurier and Philo 2006b, 2006a, 2006c; Spinney 2009).

One critical point that has been raised here, though, relates to the situation of more traditional social sciences methods (such as interviews) in relation to these developments. It has been asked whether we really need 'new' methods to engage these mobile practices, or whether it is in fact possible to 'tweak' existing methods to attend to the experience of mobility (Shaw and Hesse 2010; also see Latham 2003). For example, while Lorimer (2010: 242) argues that the generation and analysis of video allows researchers to witness various knowledges, skills, and embodied practices that "escape text- and talk-based approaches" and Rosenstein (2002: 6) claims that video can "capture the 'sparkle' and 'character' of an event", Hitchings (2012: 65 [emphasis added]) contends that the routines that form a key part of everyday practices, while by no means easily accessible, "*are* feasibly dragged into discursive consciousness", and so that talk-based methods such as interviews should not be dismissed so easily. Taking this further, Dewsbury (2010: 325) suggests that "[a] well conceived set of interview questions might well be far more effective [than video] at capturing the tension of the . . . body" and so we need to remember that video "records only a partial print of the innumerable and complex dimensions of the performance [of mobility] itself" (Adey 2010: 143).

In light of these debates, in this chapter I do not want to suggest that traditional methods like interviews are redundant when it comes to attending to mobile practices. Nor do I want to suggest that video provides 'the answer' to studying them. Rather, and more simply, I want to suggest that video opens up certain opportunities in attending to and foregrounding the fleeting, ephemeral, and mundane aspects of mobile practices. This is particularly in terms of the ways that it might prompt participants to discuss their experiences of being mobile by making their movements more expressly present as part of the research process. It is not necessarily the case that video 'captures' affects or felt relations (Brown *et al.* 2008), but rather that, in the least, it *provides useful resources in facilitating the reflection upon aspects of the experience of undertaking mobile practices which might be passed by if it were not for the detailed record of events video generates* (see Simpson 2011).

More specifically, the approach taken here seeks to draw on this potential of video *in combination* with more established talk-based methods like interviews. As such, this forms part of a broad call for moves towards innovative elicitation-based methods which, in their combination of various texts and media with in-depth interview discussion, have potential to get at the routine and felt aspects of mobile experiences, and so behind the overtly 'eventful' aspects of everyday life (see Brown and Spinney 2010; Duffy and Waitt 2011; Latham 2003).[2] For the researcher, the footage produced "can capture aspects of social situations that are difficult for the researcher to notice" through more traditional forms of observation and note taking (Brown *et al.* 2008: section 5.3), and so allow them to include these into discussions with the participants. Equally, this then allows for "a step by step re-making of . . . mobile experiences" by the participant and so allows them to "reflect on their representations of their journeys by watching the video recording" (Murray 2010: 16). As such, this provides a means "to capture the taken-for-granted, mundane elements of everyday life" (Murray 2010: 24) which might, though not necessarily, be lost in taking a more straightforward talk-based approach. Therefore, in this chapter I will illustrate how this sort of video-elicitation approach "expands the possibilities for describing, dissecting and interpreting the various mobile techniques, experiences and settings enacted" in the undertaking of mobile practices (D'Andrea *et al.* 2011: 152), and in the study of the practice of cycling in particular.

Video elicitation and cyclist experiences

As mentioned above, this chapter emerges from a research project undertaken in Plymouth, UK, in 2011 that examined the embodied experience of cyclists as they move through the city and their sensory perception of the urban environment as they do so.[3] In particular, a key objective of the research was to develop understandings of the relation between the planning of the built environment for cycling and its actual embodied experience by cyclists by examining how cyclists experience, perceive, and attend to the environments as they cycle. As such, the study focused on uncovering the ways in which the experience of cycling, and commuter cycling in particular, was produced through the interrelation of cyclists, other road users, pedestrians, infrastructure, legislation, and both the literal and metaphorical/ affective atmospheres encountered through this.

In approaching these themes, the study drew on the experiences of 24 cyclists of varying age and ability; a variety of routes through the city were analysed using a combination of head cam video recording and interview methods. Cyclists were recruited through various cycling groups (primarily Plymouth University and Plymouth City Council's respective Bike User Groups, and the Plymouth Cycling Campaign) and were provided with a head cam and asked to cycle their usual commuting route to and/or from their place of work. The head cam was fitted to their helmet (where worn) or worn on a 'head-strap'. Each cyclist produced between 40 and 60 minutes of video, depending on the length of their journey and the number of times it was undertaken with the head cam (individual journey times varied from 10–15 minutes to one hour). Cyclists were not asked to provide a running commentary on their journey, though some did occasionally make comments to the camera. From there, the recorded footage was watched and a specific interview schedule developed for each participant based on the events recorded on their journey(s).

The interviews with these cyclists lasted on average one hour and consisted of watching a selection from the participant's head cam video (a mix of complete journeys and specific clips) and both asking the participant to volunteer anything they thought was significant to their experiences of cycling in Plymouth as they watched, and asking the questions identified as outlined above. It was a case therefore of "employing video as a way of retaining and evoking some of the context and detail of the practices under scrutiny whilst allowing the researcher to talk through [such] practices 'as they happen' during playback with participants" (Spinney 2011: 166). Once completed, all interviews were fully transcribed. These transcripts were then emailed to participants, who were given the opportunity to amend or add details to them. In many places participants provided additional reflections, having thought further about the topics discussed and things which they previously had not necessarily considered.

Given the scope of material covered in these interviews, I am going to focus here on one aspect of these journeys relevant to two particular cyclists involved in the study that specifically highlights the utility of video in engaging the mundane and felt aspects of their journeys that might have been passed over were it not for the reflection facilitated by the video: the implications of passengering on approaching the journey and the experiences brought about through this more overtly sociable form of cycling.

Sociable cycling and cyclist (dis)position

As part of this research, two cyclists (Brian and Sophie[4]) each cycled from different residential areas of Plymouth to work in the centre of the city – both via childcare, and both with their child on their bike. Brian cycled with a child seat attached behind his saddle, and Sophie cycled on a tandem bicycle. One notable aspect of the experience of undertaking these journeys that the use of video methods allowed a particularly clear insight into was the mundane social interactions that took place between Brian and Sophie and their respective passengers (their pre-school-aged sons), and particularly how there were significant emotive and felt interactions taking place between parent and child (see Barker 2009; Barker *et al*. 2009). It is evident that this forms a key aspect of 'how mobility really happens' here, and so is felt, by those moving.

Mechanical diggers and pirate stories

Throughout Brian and Sophie's journeys with the camera, a range of conversations with their passengers took place (see Barker 2009). Many of these were relatively mundane. Conversations involved discussions of day-to-day activities, checking the child was OK on the back of the bike, and so on. However, some of these conversations gave a particularly clear insight into how these banal interactions are in fact a key aspect of the experiences of both riders moving through the city and have a significant impact on how this is approached.

> Son: "Can I have a story now mum? Please??"
> Sophie: "Right ok, so you want a story do you, which one do you want?"
> Son: "em . . . THE PIRATE ONE!"

[Pause for a few seconds as crosses a junction (see image), looking side to side for traffic as does so]

> Sophie: "The pirate one, yeah? OK. Sorry, microphone, but I'm going to tell my son a story . . ."

(Transcript from video of Sophie's commute)

Figure 52.1 Story telling

The exchange in Figure 52.1 took place after Sophie and her son had left the busy roads that they start their journey on and were cycling through a network of back lanes that they use to cycle on to avoid further busier roads. As Sophie noted while watching the video of this, her son commonly liked to be told a story on their way to his childcare:

> I sometimes tell him a story, but if there's anything complicated I won't, I'll just stop and he'll nag me for a minute and I'll just say 'No in a minute, in a minute, in a minute'. So yeah, it does affect your concentration, but as long as you're just cruising along you don't really . . . there's nothing else to think about really . . . I do it a lot and I don't have to think too hard. It's when you're fiddling around in traffic I don't like talking too much – I don't talk to him very much when we're in traffic. But on quiet roads it's quite sociable, quite nice to chat.
>
> *(Interview)*

While Sophie was initially a little reticent, and even potentially a little embarrassed, to be talking about this relatively intimate aspect of her interaction with her son while undertaking this journey (and so joked about it on the video), it became evident that it was an integral part of her commuting practices. We can also see how, while having to manage them within the context of navigating through her route (not engaging in this when she is on busy roads and, equally, pausing the story at various points when she has to shift her attention towards potential hazards, and so on), she enjoys these conversations and that they add something to her experience. While it might be the more problematic aspects of navigating this route – so as to avoid busy roads, steep hills, and awkward junctions – that constitute the more forthcoming aspects of discussions about her experience of her route and key features of that, through the video footage it became possible to gain more of an insight into how this journey is actually experienced by Sophie and her son.

Further, turning to Brian's experience, a number of conversations also took place between Brian and his son, again on the quieter sections of their route. For example, as they cycled alongside a disused railway line brief conversations took place about never seeing trains there, and how, when passing a building site, "the big digger's not working!" (Son, transcript from video) because "they're all having their bacon sandwiches and cups of tea, aren't they?" (Brian, transcript from video). As Brian noted when watching this back, "This is more like more of my sort of weekend cycle if you like, with children. Yeah, it is a completely different experience than if I was commuting on my own. More pleasurable" (Interview). While not something that would necessarily come up in a general conversation about their experiences of cycling in Plymouth, given its everyday nature – Brian, like many others, had been quicker to mention the dramatic problematic events when I first met with him than these more micro-scale interactions – this proved to actually be of great significance to Brian. Again, as he went on:

> it's about the social thing, I want my boy to be . . . I'm looking forward to going out cycling with him. And then it's not about getting from A to B as quick as possible, it's about the experience and enjoying it. Yeah hopefully this will give him an appreciation of it, and it's something that we will continue to do for a long long time.
>
> *(Interview)*

This gives a particularly clear example about the importance of the mundane occurrences in the playing out of the mobility itself to the broader experience of cycling, particularly given the proud and emotive way it was articulated in relation to the bonding practices of a father and son. While the video doesn't *show* these affects or feelings, it does help to raise their presence and significance through discussion of the footage.

Speed, route, and purpose

From discussions with Brian and Sophie, it was also evident that the presence of a passenger on these journeys had significant implications for the approach taken to the journey and to some extent the disposition of the rider. This was both in terms of what might be described as the 'purposefulness' of approach adopted and in terms of the connected subtle and not so subtle variations in the specific route chosen.

The filming undertaken by Brian included both that of his journey with his son discussed above, but also the equivalent journey without the passenger. Notable in the first instance is that, even taking into account a slightly more direct route (based on cycling more in traffic), the 18-minute journey time with his son was slashed to 12 minutes without him. However, more subtle differences and justifications for this came up when watching both of these journeys together in the interview.

One of the key points at which this comes up is when Brian joins the first busy road-based section of the journey, where he joins up with the A397 (the main route into Plymouth city centre from Plymstock) (see Figure 52.2). When riding with his son, Brian stayed off the road, avoided going on the roundabout (instead crossing via the pedestrian/cyclist islands), and used a shared cyclist and pedestrian path (the images down the left of Figure 52.2). However, when it came to riding alone, Brian stuck to the road route across the roundabout and used a shared bus and cycle lane, before joining the same shared cycle and pedestrian path alongside the dual carriage way (shown in the images to the right of Figure 52.2). As Brian noted while watching the latter clip:

> I try and keep away from the road as much as I possibly can [when his child is on the bike]. And if I do go on the roads they're usually quiet back roads that I know, and I know well . . . Cos I just don't want to take that risk . . . I'm aware of how vulnerable you are on a bike and how vulnerable he is on the back, cos he's completely strapped in. So if I drop the bike he's attached to that bike. Whatever happens to that bike, he's attached to it. So um . . . yeah my cycle is much slower with him on the back.
>
> *(Interview)*

As such, connecting back to the sociable aspect of his journeys with his son discussed above, it's a case for Brian of "cycling and talking with him, and yeah finding quieter and slower routes. Whereas [his] normal commute is just as fast as [he] can" (Interview). When cycling with his son, a key feature of this experience is enjoying the time with his son, and so avoiding unnecessary risk and finding ways of undertaking the journey that facilitate a sociable journey. Without him, it became a case of speed, potentially more risk, and making the journey interesting through challenging his own fitness.

Further, though in a slightly different sense, this was also the case with Sophie's cycling. While the heaviness of the tandem bike, and in turn there only being one person to power it, meant her approach to cycling having dropped her son off at childcare did not change quite so much as in Brian's case, some impact did come out following the interview. As Sophie noted in email correspondence (in response to the transcript being sent to her for approval):

> in the interview you asked if I cycle differently with . . . (my son). I didn't really think that I did, but actually, now that he has started school and I cycle in on my own on my

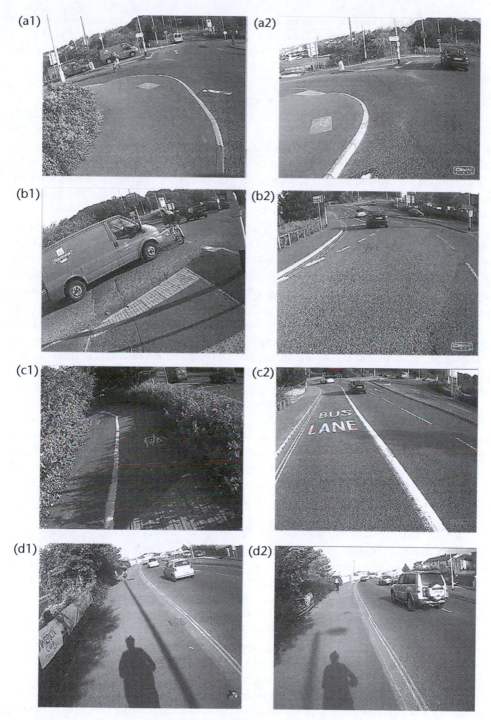

Figure 52.2 Route variation by Brian. (*a1, a2*) Approaching the roundabout; (*b1, b2*) Navigating the roundabout; (*c1, c2*) Taking a different path; (*d1, d2*) Emerging in the same spot

Note The images on the left show Brian's route while carrying his son and the images on the right show the route taken when not carrying the passenger.

mountain bike, I cycle a) much faster and b) am more likely to take the shorter, hillier routes than I ever was when I was carrying him. I occasionally also cycle on Mutley Plain [a busy street many cyclists said they deliberately avoided] – though I still cycle on the pavement when going up Mannamead road. So yes, having a lighter and more manoeuvrable bike does change the way I cycle sometimes. If I have time I will still go the longer way around, but this feels like more of a choice than a necessity now.

(Email correspondence)

As such, while it had not necessarily occurred to her at the time, following the interview and having watched her journey on the tandem, this (in addition to further evolutions in her cycling practices) had encouraged Sophie to reflect further on her approach both with and without her son and the implications this has for cycling experiences.

Conclusion

To conclude, I want to turn to a pertinent question posed by Fincham *et al.* (2010a) in a recent collection on mobile methods. They ask: "Can existing social science research methods that slow down and freeze experiences (the interview, the focus group, the survey) adequately capture mobile experiences, practices where the context of movement itself may be crucial to understanding the significance of the event to the participant, rather than simply being 'read off' from destination points and origins?" (Fincham *et al.* 2010a: 2). In response to this question, based on the preceding discussion, I would suggest the answer is both yes and no.

No, in that 'traditional' interviews do risk losing the context of the practices taking place and so potentially risk missing something important to the experience of the playing out of the mobile practices they seek to understand. As Brown and Spinney (2010: 132 [emphasis added]) suggest, "many of the experiences that make cycling [and other such mobile practice] meaningful are fleeting, ephemeral and corporeal in nature and do not lend themselves to apprehension by language *alone*". It is the 'alone' here though that I want to emphasize. As such, the 'yes' comes in that such methods can be invigorated in various ways to make it possible to re-present something of the context of mobility through the use of technologies like video when employed in an elicitation-based mode.

While not necessarily actually presenting the experience in its totality, or necessarily 'capturing' the affective relations that take place in their playing out (see Simpson 2011) – feelings of care, concern, and enjoyment amongst riders – this kind of footage can provide a detailed record of the events that took place, such as the subtle variations in route choice, differences in the speed of the ride, mundane everyday conversations between participants, and so on. In this way, it can be used to encourage participants to discuss those aspects of their mobility that they might not normally be quite so forthcoming about or able to talk about. "The benefit of video in this sense" then "is that it is capable of conveying a greater depth and richness of content . . . which in turn can enable participants to talk about sensory experiences in ways and in detail previously prohibited" (Spinney 2011: 176).

As such, I would suggest that video does not present 'the answer' in and of itself in the pursuit of a better understanding of the playing out of mobile practices as they happen. Rather, and more modestly, I would argue that when used in certain ways mobile video methods can provide something of a helping hand in gaining insight into the mundane happening of movement and its experience that might not necessarily be accessed in the same way through talk-*only* methodologies.

Notes

1 There is not space here to review work in the arts that has engaged mobility through video. However, see Merriman and Webster (2009) for a discussion of a range of key points here.
2 That is, of course, not to ignore the potential such video methods also present in being used to examine such eventful occurrences, particularly in terms of their ability to present a different perspective on the unfolding of such an event and so encourage participants and researchers to reflect on them in different ways.
3 This project was generously funded by an RGS–IBG Small Grant.
4 These names have been changed to preserve anonymity.

References

Adey, P. (2010) *Mobility*. Routledge, London.

Ash, J. (2009) 'Emerging spatialities of the screen: Video games and the reconfiguration of spatial awareness'. *Environment and Planning A*, 41, 2105–2124.

Ash, J. (2010) 'Teleplastic Technologies: Charting practices of orientation and navigation in videogaming'. *Transactions of the Institute of British Geographers*, 35, 414–430.

Barker, J. (2009) '"Driven to distraction?": Children's experiences of car travel'. *Mobilities*, 4, 59–76.

Barker, J., Kraftl, P., Horton, J. and Tucker, F. (2009) 'The road less travelled – New directions in children's and young people's mobility'. *Mobilities*, 4, 1–10.

Brown, K., Dilley, R. and Marshall, K. (2008) 'Using a head-mounted video camera to understand social worlds and experiences'. *Sociological Research Online*, 13. Available online at www.socresonline.or.uk/13/6/1.html.

Brown, K. and Spinney, J. (2010) 'Catching a glimpse: The value of video in evoking, understanding and representing the practice of cycling'. In Fincham, B., McGuinness, M. and Murray, L. (eds) *Mobile Methodologies*. Palgrave Macmillan, Basingstoke.

Buscher, M., Urry, J. and Witchger, K. (eds) (2011) *Mobile Methods*. London, Routledge.

D'Andrea, A., Ciolfi, L. and Gray, B. (2011) 'Methodological challenges and innovations in mobilities research'. *Mobilities*, 6, 149–160.

Dewsbury, J.-D. (2010) 'Performative, non-representational, and affect-based research: seven injunctions'. In DeLyser, D., Aitken, S., Craig, M., Herbert, S. and McDowell, L. (eds) *The SAGE Handbook of Qualitative Research in Human Geography*. Sage, London.

Duffy, M. and Waitt, G. (2011) 'Sound diaries: A method for listening to place'. *Aether: The Journal of Media Geography*, 7, 119–136.

Fincham, B., McGuinness, M. and Murray, L. (2010a) 'Introduction'. In Fincham, B., McGuinness, M. and Murray, L. (eds) *Mobile Methodologies*. Palgrave Macmillan, Basingstoke.

Fincham, B., McGuinness, M. and Murray, L. (eds) (2010b) *Mobile Methodologies*. Palgrave Macmillan, Basingstoke.

Garrett, B. L. (2011) 'Videographic geographies: Using digital video for geographic research'. *Progress in Human Geography*, 35, 521–541.

Hitchings, R. (2012) 'People can talk about their practices'. *Area*, 44, 61–67.

Kindon, S. (2003) 'Participatory video in geographic research: A feminist practice of looking?' *Area*, 35, 142–153.

Latham, A. (2003) 'Research, performance, and doing human geography: Some reflections on the diary-interview method'. *Environment and Planning A*, 35, 1993–2017.

Laurier, E. (2010) 'Being there/seeing there: Recording and analysing life in the car'. In Fincham, B., McGuinness, M. and Murray, L. (eds) *Mobile Methodologies*. Palgrave Macmillan, Basingstoke.

Laurier, E. and Philo, C. (2006a) 'Cold shoulders and napkins handed: Gestures of responsibility'. *Transactions of the Institute of British Geographers*, 31, 193–208.

Laurier, E. and Philo, C. (2006b) 'Natural problems of naturalistic video data'. In Knoblauch, H., Raab, J., Soeffner, H.-G. and Schnettler, B. (eds) *Video-Analysis: Methodology and Methods*. Peter Lang, Oxford.

Laurier, E. and Philo, C. (2006c) 'Possible geographies: A passing encounter in a café'. *Area*, 38, 353–364.

Lorimer, J. (2010) 'Moving image methodologies for more-than-human geographies'. *Cultural Geographies*, 17, 237–258.

Merriman, P. and Webster, C. (2009) 'Travel projects: Landscape, art, movement'. *Cultural Geographies*, 16, 525–535.

Murray, L. (2010) 'Contextualising and mobilising research'. In Fincham, B., McGuinness, M. and Murray, L. (eds) *Mobile Methodologies*. Palgrave Macmillan, Basingstoke.

Rosenstein, B. (2002) 'Video use in social science research and program evaluation'. *International Journal of Qualitative Methods*, 1. Available online at www.ualberta.ca/~ijqm. Accessed 20/11/09.

Shaw, J. and Hesse, M. (2010) 'Transport, geography and the "new" mobilities'. *Transactions of the Institute of British Geographers*, 35, 305–312.

Simpson, P. (2011) '"So, as you can see. . .": Some reflections on the utility video methodologies in the study of embodied practices'. *Area*, 43, 343–352.

Spinney, J. (2009) 'Cycling the city: Movement, meaning and method'. *Geography Compass*, 3, 817–835.

Spinney, J. (2011) 'A chance to catch a breath: Using mobile video ethnography in cycling research'. *Mobilities*, 6, 161–182.

Thrift, N. (2000) 'Afterwords'. *Environment and Planning D: Society and Space*, 18, 213–255.

Urry, J. (2007) *Mobilities*. Polity Press, Cambridge.

53

New Technologies

Jennie Germann Molz

The 'new' in 'new technologies' has a surprisingly long shelf life. After all, most of the technologies encompassed in the term 'new technologies' – phones, cameras, wireless communications, computers, global positioning systems and the Internet – can hardly be considered new anymore. When we talk about new technologies, then, we are in many cases referring not to the technology itself, but rather to the disruptive effects of technological innovation on the social landscape. As Hesse-Biber (2011: 4) explains, new or emergent technologies are those technologies that 'introduce a significant break in the way individuals, groups and society as a whole conduct their everyday activities, as well as add new dimensions to our understanding of the social world.' Telephony, photography and computing may not be new, strictly speaking, but three related and relatively recent technological innovations have renewed these old technologies in ways that have significant practical and epistemological implications for mobile methods.

To begin with, information and communication technologies have become increasingly *networked* in the shift from Web 1.0 to Web 2.0. The first iteration of online communication, which was composed primarily of static web pages and marked by a one-way flow of information, has been replaced by a complex, hyperlinked and decentralized online communication network made up of interactive virtual worlds, user-generated social media and online social networking platforms.

Second, communication and information technologies that were originally tied to landlines and desktops have become *mobile*. The un-tethering of telephony and computing from fixed locations has enabled users to take their networked lives on the road and facilitated the nearly ubiquitous connectivity that characterizes contemporary social life. The mobility of these networked devices is aided by a range of other developments, including advances in battery performance, the regularization of international roaming plans, the proliferation of wireless access points, digitization of information and images, and the miniaturization of personal technologies (Elliott and Urry 2010). An additional effect is that these technologies have become more affordable and accessible for the mobile public (including researchers).

Third, in recent years we have seen a *convergence* of technological functions into a single device: the mobile smartphone. Today's programmable smartphones combine the functionality of a telephone, digital camera, video and audio recorder, Internet-enabled computer and

GPS in one handheld device. Convergence constitutes another major shift, this time to Web 3.0. As Hein *et al.* (2008: 15) explain:

> If Web 2.0 was built on social networks and sharing content across platforms, Web 3.0 seems to be concerned with spatialising those data – not just sharing a photograph on Flickr, but also allowing viewers to see precisely where it was taken. There is a change in public consciousness about location and mobility that is being driven by these technologies.

Smartphones are thus more than the sum of their parts. By facilitating location-aware mobile communication among dispersed groups, the convergence of location-based software, like Google Earth, with photography, telephony or online networking affords new spatializations of sociality, new mobile configurations of togetherness and new qualities of interaction.

As information and communication technologies become increasingly networked, mobile and converged, their methodological implications across and beyond the social sciences become ever more complex. A complete account of these implications is beyond the scope of this chapter (for a fuller treatment of the intersection between new technologies and mobile research methods, see Büscher *et al.* 2010a; D'Andrea *et al.* 2011; Hesse-Biber 2011). Here, I provide a general overview of the frameworks and debates that have engaged mobilities researchers' imaginations as they experiment with new possibilities and cope with new problems posed by these technologies. I begin with the fact that new technologies constitute both an object of research *and* a means of social inquiry. Embodying a dual role as both 'technology' and 'technique,' mobile technologies engender new empirical realities as well as new methods of observing, generating, ordering and interpreting social data. Next, I describe the way new technologies have been deployed in a broader project of 'mobilizing' ethnography. Finally, I outline a few of the practical challenges and ethical dilemmas that scholars have identified as pressing issues for mobilities research in the twenty-first century.

Mobile technologies/mobile techniques

Mobile methods stem from the premise that social life is produced through various intersecting mobility systems and experiences: corporeal travel, the physical movement of objects, imaginative travel, virtual travel and communicative travel (Urry 2007). In this formulation, new technologies are both conduits of mobility and hinges that link these interdependent mobilities together. Mobility thus 'engenders new kinds of researchable entities, a new or rediscovered realm of the empirical' (Büscher *et al.* 2010a: 2) even as it also produces new sorts of questions, new ways of knowing and new kinds of knowledge about the world. Emerging technologies are central to the way moving and knowing intersect as a new empirical realm. A whole range of technologies now combine with various embodied and mediated mobilities to shape the contours of social life and to open up 'new avenues for critique' (ibid.: 2). In this sense, new technologies are complicit with mobility more generally in producing both the empirical objects of mobilities research and, in a very practical sense, providing new tools for conducting that research.

New technologies produce new empirical realities by calling into question existing sociological categories – such as intimacy, togetherness or personhood – as well as by generating altogether new kinds of social phenomena. With built-in location-aware, networked and communicative features, smartphones and mobile computing devices afford new articulations of togetherness and remoteness and new combinations of proximity and distance on the move. SMS and GPS enable new intimacies between distant friends and loved ones (Raiti 2007; Morel and Licoppe 2010). The tiny screens in the palms of our hands allow us to toggle back and forth between friends' updates on Facebook and face-to-face interactions with physically co-present friends. Texting, blogging, tweeting, updating, friending and following have become synonyms for relating. Even familiar mobility practices, like backpacking or tourist photography, take on new social possibilities. Backpackers carrying digital devices become 'flashpackers,' perpetually plugged in to their social networks even while far from home (Germann Molz 2012). And instead of snapping photos to share with friends and family upon her return home, the tourist equipped with a networked digital camera in her mobile phone can share photos in real-time, producing instant, image-based interactions at a distance and on the move (Larsen 2008). Meanwhile, 'cyborg' technologies that meld onto the body extend the sensory capacities of the mobile body and enable new expressions of identity, shifting our understanding of what it is to be a self or to be human (Büscher *et al.* 2010a; Hesse–Biber 2011).

Emerging technologies also complicate social space in various ways, altering our definitions of place, presence and absence. Online, we find ourselves in the virtual spaces of 'second' worlds and the connected spaces of social networking sites. Offline, we find our physical spaces shot through with hotspots and augmented at various scales by information and communication technologies (de Souza e Silva 2006; de Souza e Silva and Sutko 2009; Aurigi and De Cindio 2008). With a smartphone in hand, the material environment of the city becomes a hybrid landscape of physical spaces overlain with digitized links, stories, images and information. These hybrid places are made by – and make possible – altogether new social practices such as location-based social networking and spatial annotation activities like placelogging (Kottamasu 2007) and mobile geotagging (Humphreys and Liao 2011), and technical platforms like MoSoSo's (mobile social software). Novel forms of co-presence – such as 'comobility,' the sense of being mobile with others at a distance – become possible thanks to the latest generation of locative media applications that allow users to share their geographical location data in real time with distant friends (Southern 2011). These new patterns and spatializations of mobile sociality call for innovative methods that allow researchers to 'capture, track, simulate, mimic, parallel and "go along with" . . . and shadow the many interdependent forms of intermittent movement of people, images, information and objects' (Büscher *et al.* 2010a: 7)

In many cases, the very same technologies under investigation in these emerging social worlds also serve as useful tools of inquiry. These devices offer mobilities researchers enhanced technical capabilities for observing and participating in social practices, for monitoring and interviewing respondents, and for recording, collecting, storing, managing, analyzing, interpreting and disseminating data about mobilities while on the move. Mobile phones with built-in digital cameras, video and voice recording and embedded GPS and location-aware capabilities become powerful instruments for mobile research, simplifying the technical practicalities of recording, storing, managing and transporting data even as they engender ever more complex mobile realities.

The use of mobile phones as sensors is an example of how new technologies can be used to capture and track respondents' movements. Researchers underscore the dramatic potential posed by the nearly ubiquitous uptake of mobile telephony worldwide. Eagle (2011: 492) observes that 'the possibilities are staggering now that billions of people are essentially carrying pocket-sized networked computers throughout their daily lives.' Here, the emphasis is not solely on what people *do* with those mobile phones but rather how researchers can capitalize on this distributed computing power. Eagle outlines a series of techniques for using mobile phones as sensors, pointing out how triangulating mobile service provider data with location-based handset data provides an enormous amount of real-time information that can be used to track, chart and monitor individuals and groups. Mobile phones have been used as sensors to map everything from the daily movements of urban commuters (Licoppe *et al.* 2008; Ahas 2010) to the spread of cholera in post-earthquake Haiti (Bengtsson *et al.* 2011). Along with mobile positioning methods, researchers are also developing methods of conducting phone-based surveys, questionnaires and interviews with large samples (Vicente *et al.* 2009).

In these cases, GPS-enabled mobile phones are used to produce massive amounts of quantitative data, but they are also being used in qualitative research as well. Thanks to the convergence of digital audio, video and photographic recording features, smartphones serve as affordable and handy recording devices to capture daily interactions, conversations, and moving and still images in the ethnographic field. For example, in their study of mobile video telephony, Morel and Licoppe (2010) use an innovative combination of 'video glasses' (worn by users) and video capture of mobile screens to study the way individuals orient themselves to the device and to one another during video calls. In a project titled 'Rescue Geography,' a study of people's perceptions of places facing radical urban regeneration, Hein *et al.* (2008) use GPS to add a layer of geographical location data to their qualitative walking interviews with local residents. In both cases, the device both generates and records social data.

In these contexts, the nature of the relationship between methods of recording and the data recorded takes on renewed significance, even though this is by no means a new theme in research. From pen and pad to typewriters to computer keyboards and now mobile phones, 'what we record is indeed surely influenced by the technology we use to record it' (Vergunst 2011: 207). However, emerging methods produce particular kinds of 'mobile' data. For example, using mobile phones as sensors translates embodied mobilities into coordinates and maps of 'moving dots' (Ahas 2010: 197). Meanwhile, a project like Hein *et al.*'s (2008) 'Rescue Geography' produces 'micro-geographies of interview locations' as well as personalized 'story maps' linking people's narratives and memories with specific locations. These kinds of techniques frame nodes, connections, spatialities, proximities, choreographies and itineraries as units of knowledge. New technologies do not just produce new kinds of data, but new amounts of it as well. The ubiquity of mobile phones and the exponential increase in portable computing power produces unfathomably large volumes of data, now measured in petabytes, which in turn require new analytical tools for sorting, mining and searching data. It is in the context of such sheer masses of data that new logics like algorithms and 'qualculation' take on methodological resonance as forms of building and ordering knowledge (Büscher *et al.* 2009; Germann Molz 2010).

In order to address the links between new technologies, mobility and methodology, some scholars have found it useful to think about the relationship between technology and technique. Put simply, technologies are *objects* of inquiry. We might think of technologies as the 'things' mobilities researchers study: objects such as digital devices, software platforms or mobile applications and the various social practices that surround these technologies. Technique, on the other hand, refers to *ways* of investigating these objects. As Vergunst (2011) notes, 'the question here is not so much about the content of ethnography as the way it is done, or in other words, the techniques of ethnographers' (205).

With mobility and technology, however, the very things that constitute the empirical realm serve also as ways of knowing. In research on walking, for example, it is difficult to draw a line between technology and technique. Walking is both the social practice under investigation and the mode of inquiry. It is perhaps no surprise that a range of methods such as walking interviews (Jones *et al.* 2008), 'walking whilst talking' (Anderson 2004; Moles 2008) and auto-ethnographic walking (Lee and Ingold 2006) have entered the repertoire of mobile methodologies. In these studies, walking is a technique both for the researcher and the researched – it is a way for researchers to 'move with' respondents as these individuals encounter landscapes and know the world. Many of these studies also involve a range of technological devices that are employed by both researchers and respondents to navigate, map, track and record the walks. The correlation between technology and technique is apparent as researchers use mobile positioning techniques to study how people use mobile positioning technologies to coordinate their movements and their day-to-day social lives. In these cases, the knowledge-producing techniques of researchers overlap with those of their respondents, each informing the other in a complex assemblage of movement, technology and knowledge. This complexity might be summed up by Mauss's (2006 [1948]) distinction between technique, as embodied skill or knowledge which is learned and collective, and technology, which for Mauss is not solely a reference to human–made objects, but a science which deals with the study of technique (cited in Vergunst 2011: 206). Technology and technique thus constitute a self-referential system of objects, methods, embodied practices and knowledge.

Vergunst offers his study of recreational hill walkers in north–east Scotland as an example of the complex relationship between movement, technology and knowledge. He notes that even 'low-tech' walkers will occasionally 'stop and take photos, or, on a hill walk, take a GPS reading' (Vergunst 2011: 210). These practices are contained, however, by walkers' comments that mark some GPS uses as good (such as confirming that the group is where it should be or marking the achievement of a particular elevation) and others as not so good (such as coming to depend on the device rather than one's own navigational skills). For Vergunst, what is interesting in these moments of technological engagement is 'not the result (the photo, or the GPS reading ... in an objective sense), but the *technique*, or in other words, the way the person interacts with their surrounding objects and landscapes according to their shared and learned habits and gestures' (ibid.: 210). What Vergunst participates in and observes on these walks involves the embodied use of mobile technologies, the technologically augmented mobility of bodies and the social analysis of both. For Vergunst, however, it is embodied movement – not the portable recording and locative technologies he carries with him – that remains the most significant methodological technique in his fieldwork. He argues that the researcher's body is the primary 'instrument' and because ethnography involves multisensuous and learned bodily skills that cannot be replaced by technologies of representation, it must be practised *in situ* by the ethnographer. Like Vergunst, many researchers have found ethnography to be quite suited to the study of mobilities, due not least of all to its emphasis on sustained immersion in respondents' lived experiences, on-going participation, and detailed observations of social and material practices (Haldrup and Larsen 2010). However, his emphasis on the ethnographer's embodied engagement – on being there and moving with respondents – raises more questions than it answers. As we will see in the next section, new technologies fundamentally problematize what 'being there' and 'moving with' mean in ethnographic research settings.

Mobilizing ethnography

Many of the methodological metaphors now appearing in mobilities research are adaptations of ethnographic techniques. Efforts to repurpose ethnography to the study of mobile phenomena can be traced back to two key scholarly developments in the 1990s, both of which arose, at least in part, in response to emerging media, and information and communication technologies. The first was anthropologist James Clifford's (1997) assertion that ethnographers should pay attention to the way places and communities are produced through 'routes' as well as 'roots.' Arguing against sedentary ethnographic techniques that privileged place-based dwelling and face-to-face interaction over mediated communication, Clifford sought to reconceptualize the ethnographic field in terms of 'travel encounters,' sets of connections, relations and embodied practices through which communities were both grounded *and* linked to the world beyond. Along similar lines, George Marcus (1995, 1998) called for a shift from conventional 'single-site' ethnographies to 'multi-sited' ethnographies designed not around place-based locales, but around 'chains, paths, threads, conjunctions, or juxtapositions of locations' (1998: 90). These approaches involved tracking ethnographic subjects – including people, objects, stories and metaphors – beyond the confines of geographically bounded communities, through intersecting networks, and across spatial and temporal boundaries.

This understanding of the ethnographic field as fluid and reticular rather than static and bounded aligned well with a second key development in the late 1990s: the application of ethnographic techniques to new Internet-based social phenomena. In fact, Marcus (1998: 88) noted that multi-sited ethnography was especially evident in media studies, including research on what were, at the time, new modes of electronic communication via the Internet. With the Internet transforming the social landscape, Internet researchers adopted and adapted ethnographic techniques to study newly emerging forms of online social life such as virtual communities, multi-user domains, and interactive discussion forums. Eventually, researchers proposed new methodological models – cyberethnography (Correll 1995; Ward 1999; Gajjala 2002); virtual ethnography (Hine 2000); and, more recently, digital ethnography (see Murthy 2008) – to work through the practical and theoretical implications of doing ethnography with social groups that coalesce, at least to some degree, around digital and computer-mediated interactions. These models involved ethnographic practices like sustained immersion online and ongoing interaction with social groups, but further challenged the notion of the field as a culturally and spatially bounded entity. In this literature, 'connectivity' rather than place became the central metaphor for describing online and hybrid online–offline research fields (Hine 2000) and researchers spoke of an 'ethnography of networks' that focused not just on 'nodes' but on the flows and connections between these nodes (Wittel 2000). The ethnographer's participation also shifted from one of embodied immersion in a distant field site to a kind of mediated or 'experiential rather than physical displacement' (Hine 2000: 45). Internet-based ethnographies were not originally intended as mobile methodologies per se, but in reimagining the field and the researcher's immersion in it, they pried open the fundamental concepts behind ethnography in ways that would prove extremely useful to mobilities research.

In his description of an 'ethnography of networks,' Wittel (2000) acknowledges that thinking of the research field in terms of networks and connections meant that other core presumptions of ethnography – an emphasis on the researcher's embodied co-presence, for example, or what constitutes sustained immersion in the field – would also have to be revised to attend to new possibilities posed by online interactions. As he puts it, whether 'co-presence requires one single shared space is a problem worth discussing, particularly in the context of online-ethnographies' (2000: para. 8). This is a problem that researchers have been discussing ever since. The networks Wittel refers to have now gone mobile and converged with other technological features like digital photography and location-aware software, developments that further trouble our sense of place and presence in ways that animate these methodological debates once again. Mobilities research adheres to the ethnographic ethos of 'being there' and 'moving with' research subjects as a way of generating thick descriptions of embodied, material and social mobilities, however what terms like 'there' and 'with' signify cannot be taken for granted. What or where is the research field in a mobile, mediated and networked social world? How do researchers engage with the field? What does it mean to be co-present with one's research subjects or to be immersed in the field? And what does participant observation consist of in these contexts?

To begin with, the research field is, as Clifford (1997) and Marcus (1998) note, mobile and multiple. New technologies are, by design, portable objects on the move with mobile people. The fields of social interaction they produce are similarly mobilized, but not just across multiple physical locations. Multi-sited ethnographies involving new technologies may well take place among various geographical locations, but they also take place in virtual domains, in-between online and offline spaces, and in hybrid environments. For example, in their ethnography of tourism mobilities, Haldrup and Larsen (2010) studied Danish tourists in their homes before departure and upon their return and travelled with them to observe them on holiday at the beach or beside the hotel pool. But as Haldrup and Larsen note, these embodied practices cannot be cordoned off from the mediated and online interactions that are so thoroughly woven into everyday practices of moving, communicating and connecting. It is on these interdependent mobilities and connected communications that they focus their multi-sited ethnography:

> Unlike traditional ethnography, which defines sites as *material* dwelling places, multisited ethnography also deals with *virtual* sites such as databases and blogs, not in an isolated cyberspace, but in relation to physical everyday places such as internet cafés, work places and private living spaces, as virtual worlds and material worlds are not separate entities (Wittel 2000). Multisited ethnography privileges routes rather than roots; connections and networks.
>
> *(Haldrup and Larsen 2010: 46)*

In addition to physically moving with tourists, Haldrup and Larsen interacted with their respondents in several virtual and communicative field sites as well, including the digitized photo albums tourists produced, personal homepages and blogs online, and flows of online and on-the-phone communication. In many cases, the field is a hybrid assemblage of physical mobilities, online portals and communication flows, evidenced by spatially annotated urban landscapes or location-based social networking where geographical spaces are augmented by digitized stories or electronic connections (see de Souza e Silva and Sutko 2009).

The connectivity that constitutes the research field also involves intersecting immobilities, moorings and disconnections. Haldrup and Larsen (2010: 50) argue that mobile ethnography must pay special attention to the way tourism performances are 'constructed through routes *and* moorings, connecting home and away as well as physical, object, imaginative, virtual and communicative mobilities.' Physical and virtual mobilities alike rely on a vast material infrastructure that provides the relatively fixed platform on which bodies and data move – from airports and railways to coaxial cable systems and cellular towers (Hannam *et al.* 2006). In practice, mediated connections can moor travelers as well as mobilize them, as demonstrated in Paris's (2010) account of the way online networking sites and personal websites serve as 'virtual moorings' for backpackers. Likewise, doing ethnography on and through new technologies involves intermittent moments of movement and stillness, of connecting and disconnecting.

Thinking of the research field in terms of connectivity has significant implications for how researchers move 'with' people or become immersed in their lived experiences of mobility. For one thing, new technologies subject research relationships to the same crisis of co-presence as other social relationships. Terms like 'absent presence' (Gergen 2002), 'virtual proximity' (Bauman 2003), 'connected presence' (Licoppe 2004) and 'ambient virtual co-presence' (Ito and Okabe 2005) refer to the new forms of sociality under investigation, but they also signal new ways for researchers to be co-present in a field of connectivity. These forms of presence may include embodied immersion, but the tropes of 'being there' and 'immersion' are themselves too sedentary to account for the complex mobilities of bodies, objects, information, images and communications that characterize these new empirical realities. In place of immersion, then, mobilities researchers draw on more fluid metaphors of engagement like tracking, simulating and mimicking (Sheller and Urry 2006), shadowing (Jirón 2010), following (Haldrup and Larsen 2010; Germann Molz 2012) and experimenting (Büscher *et al.* 2010b).

According to Haldrup and Larsen (2010), foregrounding routes and connections in the ethnographic field requires the researcher to 'follow flows.' Following flows involves a variety of techniques, including analyzing the circulation of place myths, following the objects tourists carry with them abroad or bring home, traveling with tourists and following the 'communication flows' of digital and virtual travel in order to examine 'what communication technologies travel with tourists and how they are used in practice [to produce] tourists' "connected presence" with people and places at home or elsewhere' (ibid.: 52). Following the flows of people, objects, stories, images and communication entails a similar level of sustained engagement as immersion, but attends to the fluid, mobile and intersecting qualities of the social phenomena under investigation. Indeed, following – as a new form of mobile sociality – may *be* the very thing mobilities researchers are studying. 'Following' as a method thus simulates a broader shift in which interactions within new social media platforms are increasingly patterned around status updating and interpersonal monitoring. The steady stream of status updates posted on blogs and networking sites like Facebook and Twitter reproduce sociality in terms of 'following.' On Twitter, subscribers are literally referred to as 'followers' and this terminology now pervades the social media space as a way of describing how people interact with each other online and on the move. The matter-of-fact tone with which the term 'follow' is invoked in popular discourse surrounding social media like blogs, Facebook and Twitter belies the nuances of social connection and power that following suggests. At stake here are not only new patterns of intimacy and togetherness, but also new articulations of control and surveillance that mobilities researchers must also address, as we will see in the concluding section.

In addition to 'following,' 'experimenting' has become a significant methodological metaphor for sustained engagement with mobile, mediated and networked research fields. According to Hein *et al.* (2008: 15): 'One of the more exciting things about using mobile methods is the potential to experiment with new technologies . . . Mobile methods represent an almost unique opportunity to explore cutting edge theory and technology simultaneously.' Mobilities research makes room for experimental art and design interventions, interdisciplinary collaboration among scholars, engineers, computer scientists and software designers, and public participation. In many cases, experimenting involves playful interaction with prototypes of mobile technologies and new mobile software applications. Southern's (2011) work on 'comobility' is an example of this experimental approach. As both an artist and a scholar, Southern became interested in using locative media and GPS to produce shared walks between distant people in motion. Working with a fellow artist, she designed an iPhone app called 'Comob' that mapped social and spatial relationships together. She describes her approach as a hybrid practice of locative arts, mobilities research, speculative design and analysis combined with the development, production and use of locative media (Southern 2011: 3). In this case, experimenting extends as well to the dissemination of the research. Southern shares her project with audiences in various ways, in some instances presenting the Comob app at workshops, arts festivals and conferences and in others making walks herself using the Comob application to 'experiment with sharing [her] location with a distant and distributed audience' (ibid.: 4). Participants in the workshops and performances are then engaged in the coproduction and refinement of the application. This experimental and participatory approach to mobilities research gestures toward another implication for ethnographic research: the presentation and dissemination of research.

Even as ethnography goes digital, its epistemological remit remains much the same: 'Ethnography is about telling social stories' (Murthy 2008: 838). Indeed, storytelling is the ethnographer's stock-in-trade. It is through stories that knowledge is produced and shared, and it is precisely because ethnographic techniques generate such rich, vivid and complex accounts of lived experience that mobilities researchers have turned to these methods. However, new technologies afford new ways of sharing these stories, in the process extending the reach of social research to different, and perhaps unlikely, audiences (Hein *et al.* 2008; Murthy 2008). Interactive networking and multimedia websites like blogs, Twitter, Facebook, Academia.edu, YouTube and Flickr provide free, user-friendly platforms for researchers to share their findings as well as their work-in-progress with an interactive audience. For example, some scholars have used blogs to collaboratively produce scholarly knowledge. An example is the multi-authored review piece 'Geographies of food' based on an online blog conversation among various scholars (Cook *et al.* 2011a, 2011b). Research practice and dissemination can also become intertwined in new ways, as in Southern's (2011) presentation on and experiments with co-mobility. Sharing research generated by or about mobile technologies thus becomes wrapped up in the same self-referential system that binds technology to technique.

Ethnographic techniques have been adapted to the study of new mobile technologies, and in the process, new technologies have transformed the foundational metaphors around which ethnographic research is imagined. Our conceptions of what constitutes the field, the nature of the research relationship, how researchers engage in a deep and sustained way with the mobile social worlds they study and how they share that knowledge have all been revised against a backdrop of new mobile technologies. While there is undoubtedly a special affinity between mobilities research and ethnography, new technologies are by no means limited to ethnography, or even to qualitative research. Indeed registering the implications of mobile technologies across qualitative and quantitative as well as micro- and macro-level research is one of the challenges facing mobilities research more generally (D'Andrea *et al.* 2011). In the concluding section, I summarize three specific methodological dilemmas that emerge around new technologies.

Conclusion: dilemmas and challenges

As new technologies augment mobile methodologies in a variety of ways, they also draw attention to ongoing methodological concerns that continue to provoke debate. First is the issue of representation. Mobile methodologies emerged out of a key problematic: how do we study mobile phenomena without freezing them in place, thereby destroying the very thing that fascinates us? It was initially out of dissatisfaction with the immobilizing effects of conventional social research methods like interviews, surveys or place-based ethnographies that the current conversations around mobile methodologies emerged. As the methodological innovations described throughout this chapter suggest, researchers have come a long way in developing a set of practical techniques that mobilize research. However, the struggle over how to represent this research continues. Despite the innovative dissemination channels discussed previously, much research inadvertently fixes the very mobilities it aims to analyze, often producing static accounts of mobile phenomena. For example, representations produced using mobile positioning technologies tend to parcel human movements into coordinates or dots and lines. As Vergunst (2011: 211) notes, the issue at stake 'is whether points on a map marking progression can ever actually encapsulate a trajectory or route.' Even as new technologies enable researchers to generate new kinds of data, there are technical limitations to the form this data can take. Here, technology may also be the solution. For example, Hein et al.'s (2008) 'Rescue Geography' used GPS technology to produce meaning-laden 'story maps' with participants. And participatory experiments like Southern's (2011) performative co-mobility walks represent the research as it is made. New technologies also offer other interactive, participatory and multimedia outlets for the presentation of mobilities research that may be able to more accurately capture and represent the rhythms and movements of daily life.

The second concern involves the ethics of privacy and surveillance. This concern is certainly not new in social science research, but it is amplified by mobile observation methods like following, tracking, 'sociological stalking' (Büscher et al. 2010a: 8) or using mobile phones as sensors. For researchers and participants alike, these techniques tap into anxieties over a hyper-monitored Orwellian future. Tracking respondents using locative software or following their blogs and Twitter feeds mimics precisely the sociable practices researchers aim to study, but this means that the same connotations of power and control related to such interpersonal surveillance cannot be escaped in the research relationship. If anything, research-based surveillance is all the more problematic in contexts where surveillance has become such a normalized aspect of everyday social interactions. Furthermore, as Southern (2011: 3) points out, the fact that 'GPS is often relatively hidden or in the background within mobile devices makes it particularly difficult for individual users to monitor where data is sent.' Participants may not realize they are being tracked, or in their apparent lack of concern with the spatial data their mobile practices produce, may implicitly agree without fully recognizing the research implications. Büscher et al. (2010b: 130) argue that 'citizens and designers need more methodological innovation to ... enable people to question the invisibility [of tracking technologies] and to grasp the complexity of the technologies involved.'

Addressing these concerns may not be as simple as devising new standards for protecting respondents' privacy or gaining their informed consent. Some scholars argue that the very meaning of privacy has been fundamentally reconfigured in a surveillance-saturated society, to the extent that we can no longer think of privacy as an individual right to be protected. As Burbules (2009) suggests, what is at stake in this context is not just the application of existing ethical guidelines to new social phenomena, but an altogether new ethical sphere that is unprecedented in its complexity, uncertainty, ubiquity and interdependence. What is required, according to Burbules, is not an ethics applied to new technological practices, but rather a new form of 'networked ethics' designed to cope with the complexity and uncertainty of a networked environment in which distinctions between 'good' and 'bad' are not clear-cut. He observes that 'in the same way that the networked environment is a collaborative knowledge space, it is also a collaborative moral space' (Burbules 2009: 545).

A third concern has to do with the distancing and dividing effects of new technologies. Even as new technologies enable novel forms of togetherness, community and inclusion, mobilities researchers worry about the ways in which these technologies distance researchers from respondents, reproduce existing social divisions or create new ones. New technologies may afford new ways for researchers to be co-present with respondents, but they do not guarantee that this togetherness will be productive. Vergunst worries that new technologies may actually get in the way of building relationships in a research community, arguing that 'technologies that isolate the researcher from the rhythms and intersecting sensory and material perceptions of movement are likely to result in a loss of sensitivity in fieldwork situations' (Vergunst 2011: 214). In negotiating these new combinations of proximity and distance, however, researchers often find themselves simulating precisely the emerging patterns of sociality they aim to explore. The connecting effects of new technologies are often accompanied by new forms of disconnection and distancing that must be negotiated in the research setting just as in social life more generally. Researchers must also negotiate a 'digital divide' that persists between those who have access to new technologies and those who do not (Murthy 2008). According to statistical data compiled by the International Telecommunications Union (ITU), a United Nations agency, Internet access remains stratified, and although mobile phone usage is quite nearly universal, there remains a stark divide between those who have access to the 3G networks and those who do not (ITU 2010). In some countries, access to mobile phones and the Internet may be relatively widespread, and yet tightly constrained by political controls over network infrastructures and content. The digital divide is not just about who has access to these technologies and who doesn't; the metrics of inequality also include issues of speed and lags, of technical savvy and economic opportunity, and of social inclusion and political participation (Mossberger *et al.* 2003; Warschauer 2004). Researchers have also highlighted the existence of what we might call a 'mobilities divide' between those in the 'fast lane' who have access to and control over their own mobility, and those in the 'slow lane' who do not (Bauman 1998; Cresswell 2006). Much of the research that focuses on the mobile social landscapes emerging around new technologies is skewed toward groups doubly advantaged by their access to mobility *and* the latest technologies, an issue that must be taken into account as researchers design and implement innovative mobile methodologies.

Mobile information and communication technologies have created unparalleled research opportunities by engendering new empirical realms, new possibilities for researchers to connect with respondents, and new instruments of inquiry. At the same time, they have generated new ethical dilemmas that are endemic to the very social worlds under investigation. These dilemmas, much like the technologies and techniques around which they revolve, must be seen not merely as research concerns but as social concerns. As researchers journey with respondents, participate in hybrid social worlds, and intervene in these new dilemmas, they bring our awareness to the intimate ways in which mobile methods shape the very worlds they explore.

References

Ahas, R. (2010) 'Mobile Positioning,' in *Mobile Methods*, ed. by M. Büscher, J. Urry and K. Witchger. London: Routledge, pp. 183–199.

Anderson, J. (2004) 'Talking whilst Walking: A Geographical Archaeology of Knowledge,' *Area*, 36(3): 254–261.

Aurigi and De Cindio (eds) (2008) *Augmented Urban Spaces*. Aldershot: Ashgate.

Bauman, Z. (1998) *Globalization: The Human Consequences*. New York: Columbia University Press.

— (2003) *Liquid Love: On the Frailty of Human Bonds*. Cambridge: Polity Press.

Bengtsson, L., Lu, X., Thorson, A., Garfield, R. and von Schreeb, J. (2011) 'Improved Response to Disasters and Outbreaks by Tracking Population Movements with Mobile Phone Network Data: A Post-Earthquake Geospatial Study in Haiti,' *PLoS Med*. 8(8): e1001083. doi:10.1371/journal. pmed.1001083.

Burbules, N. C. (2009) 'Privacy and New Technologies: The Limits of Traditional Research Ethics,' in *The Handbook of Social Research Ethics*, ed. by D. M. Mertens and P. E. Ginsberg. Thousand Oaks, CA: Sage, pp. 537–549.

Büscher, M., Coulton, P., Efstratiou, C., Gellersen, H., Hemment, D., Mehmood, R. and Sangiorgi, D. (2009) 'Intelligent Mobility Systems: Some Socio-technical Challenges and Opportunities,' in *Proceedings of EuropeComm 2009*, pp. 140–152.

Büscher, M., Urry, J. and Witchger, K. (2010a) 'Introduction: Mobile Methods,' in *Mobile Methods*, ed. by M. Büscher , J. Urry and K. Witchger. London: Routledge, pp. 1–19.

Büscher, M., Coulton, P., Hemment, D. and Mogensen, P. H. (2010b) 'Mobile, Experimental, Public,' in *Mobile Methods*, ed. by M. Büscher , J. Urry and K. Witchger. London: Routledge, pp. 119–137.

Clifford, J. (1997) *Routes: Travel and Translation in the Late Twentieth Century*. Cambridge: Harvard University Press.

Cook, I. *et al.* (2011a) 'Geographies of Food: "Afters",' *Progress in Human Geography*, 35(1): 104–120.

— (2011b) *Geographies of Food: 'Afters'* blog. Available online at http://food-afters.blogspot.com/.

Correll, S. (1995) 'The Ethnography of an Electronic Bar: The Lesbian Cafe,' *Journal of Contemporary Ethnography*, 24(3): 270–298.

Cresswell, T. (2006) *On the Move: Mobility in the Modern Western World*. New York: Routledge.

D'Andrea, A., Ciolfi, L. and Gray, B. (2011) 'Methodological Challenges and Innovations in Mobilities Research,' *Mobilities*, 6(2): 149–160.

de Souza e Silva, A. (2006) 'From Cyber to Hybrid: Mobile Technologies as Interfaces of Hybrid Spaces,' *Space and Culture*, 9(3): 261–278.

de Souza e Silva, A. and Sutko, D. M. (2009) *Digital Cityscapes: Merging Digital and Urban Playspaces*. New York: Peter Lang.

Eagle, N. (2011) 'Mobile Phones as Sensors for Social Research,' in *The Handbook of Emergent Technologies in Social Research*, ed. by S. N. Hess-Biber. Oxford: Oxford University Press, pp. 492–521.

Elliott, A. and Urry, J. (2010) *Mobile Lives*. London: Routledge.

Gajjala, R. (2002) 'An Interrupted Postcolonial/Feminist Cyberethnography: Complicity and Resistance in the "Cyberfield",' *Feminist Media Studies*, 2(2): 177–193.

Gergen, K. (2002) 'The Challenge of Absent Presence,' in *Perpetual Contact*, ed. by J. Katz and M. Aakhus. Cambridge: Cambridge University Press, pp. 227–241.

Germann Molz, J. (2010) 'Connectivity, Collaboration, Search,' in *Mobile Methods*, ed. by M. Büscher, J. Urry and K. Witchger. London: Routledge, pp. 88–103.

Germann Molz, J. (2012) *Travel Connections: Tourism, Technology and Togetherness in a Mobile World*. New York: Routledge.

Haldrup, M. and Larsen, J. (2010) *Tourism, Performance and the Everyday: Consuming the Orient*. London: Routledge.

Hannam, K., Sheller, M. and Urry, J. (2006) 'Mobilities, Immobilities and Moorings,' *Mobilities*, 1(1): 1–22.

Hein, J. R., Evans, J. and Jones, P. (2008) 'Mobile Methodologies: Theory, Technology and Practice,' *Geography Compass*, 2: 1–20.

Hesse-Biber, S. N. (2011) 'Emergent Technologies in Social Research: Pushing Against the Boundaries of Research Praxis,' in *The Handbook of Emergent Technologies in Social Research*, ed. by S. N. Hess-Biber. Oxford: Oxford University Press, pp. 3–22.

Hine, C. (2000) *Virtual Ethnography*. London: Sage.

Humphreys, L. and Liao, T. (2011) 'Mobile Geotagging: Reexamining Our Interactions with Urban Space,' *Journal of Computer-Mediated Communication*, 16(3): 407–423.

Ito, M. and Okabe, D. (2005) 'Technosocial Situations: Emergent Structuring of Mobile Email Use,' in *Personal, Portable, Pedestrian: Mobile Phones in Japanese Life*, ed. by M. Ito, D. Okabe and M. Matsuda. Cambridge, MA: MIT Press, pp. 257–273.

ITU (International Telecommunications Union) (2010) 'Mobile Telephony' and 'Internet Users.' Available online at www.itu.int/ict/statistics.

Jirón, P. (2010) 'On Becoming "La Sombra/The Shadow",' in *Mobile Methods*, ed. by M. Büscher, J. Urry and K. Witchger. London: Routledge, pp. 36–53.

Jones, P., Bunce, G., Evans, J., Gibbs, H. and Hein, J. R. (2008) 'Exploring Space and Place with Walking Interviews,' *Journal of Research Practice*, 4(2) Article D2. Available online at http://jrp.icaap.org/index.php/jrp/article/view/150/161 (accessed 2 December 2009).

Kottamasu, R. (2007) 'Placelogging: Mobile Spatial Annotation and its Potential Use to Urban Planners and Designers,' Masters Thesis, Department of Urban Studies and Planning, Massachusetts Institute of Technology.

Larsen, J. (2008) 'Practices and Flows of Digital Photography: An Ethnographic Framework,' *Mobilities*, 3(1): 141–160.

Lee, J. and Ingold, T. (2006) 'Fieldwork on Foot: Perceiving, Routing, Socializing,' in *Locating the Field: Space, Place and Context in Anthropology*, ed. by S. Coleman and P. Collins. Oxford: Berg, pp. 67–86.

Licoppe, C. (2004) '"Connected" Presence: The Emergence of a New Repertoire for Managing Social Relationships in a Changing Communication Technoscape,' *Environment and Planning D: Society and Space*, 22: 135–156.

Licoppe, C., Diminescu, D., Smoreda, Z. and Ziemlicki, C. (2008) 'Using Mobile Phone Geolocalisation for "Socio-Geographical" Analysis of Co-ordination, Urban Mobilities, and Social Integration Patterns,' *Tijdschrift voor economische en sociale geografie*, 9(5): 584–601.

Marcus, G. E. (1995) 'Ethnography in/of the World System: The Emergence of Multi-sited Ethnography,' *Annual Review of Anthropology*, 24: 95–117.

Marcus, G. E. (1998) *Ethnography through Thick and Thin*. Princeton: Princeton University Press.

Mauss, M. (2006 [1948]) *Techniques, Technology and Civilization*. Ed. by Nathan Schlanger. New York: Berghahn.

Moles, K. (2008) 'A Walk in Thirdspace: Place, Methods and Walking,' *Sociological Research Online*, 13(4): 2. Available online at www.socresonline.org.uk/13/4/2.html (accessed 14 May 2011).

Morel, J. and Licoppe, C. (2010) 'Studying Mobile Video Telephony,' in *Mobile Methods*, ed. by M. Büscher , J. Urry and K. Witchger. London: Routledge, pp. 164–182.

Mossberger, K., Tolbert, C. J. and Stansbury, M. (2003) *Virtual Inequality: Beyond the Digital Divide*. Washington, DC: Georgetown University Press.

Murthy, D. (2008) 'Digital Ethnography: An Examination of the Use of New Technologies for Social Research,' *Sociology*, 42(5): 837–855.

Paris, Cody M. (2010) 'The Virtualization of Backpacker Culture: Virtual Mooring, Sustained Interaction and Enhanced Mobilities,' in *Beyond Backpacker Tourism: Mobilities and Experiences*, ed. by K. Hannam and A. Diekmann. Clevedon: Channel View, pp. 40–63.

Raiti, Gerard C. (2007) 'Mobile Intimacy: Theories on the Economics of Emotion with Examples from Asia.' *M/C Journal* 10.1 (2007). Available online at http://journal.media-culture.org.au/0703/02-raiti.php (accessed 25 September 2011).

Sheller, M. and Urry, J. (2006) 'The New Mobilities Paradigm,' *Environment and Planning A*, 38(2): 207–226.

Southern, J. (2011) 'Co-mobility: An Experiment in Mobilities Research and Locative Art Practice,' paper presented at the Mobilities in Motion: New Approaches to Emergent and Future Mobilities conference, Philadelphia, PA, 21 March 2011.

Urry, J. (2007) *Mobilities*. Cambridge: Polity Press.

Vergunst, J. (2011) 'Technology and Technique in a Useful Ethnography of Movement,' *Mobilities* 6(2): 203–219.

Vicente, P., Reis, E. and Santos, M. (2009) 'Using Mobile Phones for Survey Research: A Comparative Analysis Between Data Collected Via Mobile Phones and Fixed Phones,' *International Journal of Market Research*, 51(5): 613–633.

Ward, K. J. (1999) 'Cyber-ethnography and the Emergence of the Virtually New Community,' *Journal of Information Technology*, 14(1): 95–105.

Warschauer, M. (2004) *Technology and Social Inclusion: Rethinking the Digital Divide*. Cambridge, MA: MIT Press.

Wittel, A. (2000) 'Ethnography on the Move: From Field to Net to Internet,' *FQS: Forum: Qualitative Social Research/Sozialforschung*, 1(1): Art. 21. Available online at http://qualitative-research.net/fqs.

54

Mobile Semiotics

Ole B. Jensen

This chapter is about how to understand the mobile condition of contemporary life with a particular view to the signifying dimension of the environment and its 'readability.' The chapter explores the potentials of semiotics and its relationship to the new mobilities literature as a way into the analysis of mobilities in motion. The theoretical scope is therefore an attempt to 'mobilize' semiotics by drawing on a central body of theory within and adjacent to the discipline. The chapter is arguing for the inclusion of semiotics into mobilities research, as well as that semiotic analysis of cities and material environments needs to be sensitive to movements and flows.

In architecture and urban design theory the study of cities and buildings 'as signs' has long been discussed and seen as an opportunity to explore the symbolic meanings of the material environment (Venturi and Scott Brown, 2004; Venturi *et al.*, 1972). Here we shall engage the more general assumption that 'humans read their environments.' This is by no means an attempt to reduce the material and physical world to signs or texts but rather to claim that all our environs need some kind of interpretation to answer the key question: 'what is going on here?' The theories of Goffman (1959, 1963, 1972) will prove to be unavoidable in this context, but the idea in this chapter is to connect Goffman's interaction perspective to notions of semiotics to see if this will add a new dimension to our theorizing and conceptualizing of mobilities (Jensen, 2010a). It is important to understand that 'mobile semiotics' is not only an analysis of sign systems and road signs. Much more is read as signs (everything, in fact). However, we need also to delimit ourselves in this exploration. This chapter will therefore deal only with the designed and staged systems of signs created to control, afford, facilitate, and coordinate mobilities. The chapter foregrounds semiotics as a precondition to mobilities and discusses the semiotic systems that afford circulation and friction within the city. The chapter thereby presents new ideas about a 'mobile geo-semiotics' and mobilities and is theoretically based on the works of Scollon and Scollon (2003), Lynch (1960), Gottdeiner (1995), and Peirce (1994), as well as theories within the 'mobilities turn' by Adey (2010), Cresswell (2006), Elliott and Urry (2010), Sheller and Urry (2006), and Urry (2000, 2007).

The chapter contains four sections. The first section introduces the theme. Section two proceeds to discuss theories of relevance to frame a 'mobile semiotics' under the heading of 'staging mobilities.' Hereafter, the frame is discussed with an eye to an empirical example in section three. The chapter ends with some concluding remarks in section four.

Staging mobilities

The notion of a 'mobile semiotics' concerns how signs (in their broadest possible sense) afford, process, and coordinate (or obstruct) the physical circulation and movement of people, vehicles, and goods in more or less codified systems of infrastructure. Furthermore we shall think of this as taking place in sites and spaces of mobility. Thus we argue that we are looking at the semiotic dimension of the more general process of 'staging mobilities' (Jensen, 2013). This is to be understood as an analytical perspective on mobilities that engages with how mobility is being 'staged' by planners and designers, as well as how humans 'stage themselves' in daily mobility practices. The term proposed is 'staging mobilities,' which makes an attempt to link mobilities research to the work of Erving Goffman in particular (Jensen, 2006, 2009, 2010a, 2010b, 2013).

The key idea is that mobilities are carefully and meticulously designed, planned, and 'staged' (from above we might say). However, they are equally importantly acted out, performed and lived, as people are 'staging themselves' (from below so to speak). 'Staging mobilities' is a dynamic process between 'being staged' (as, for example, when traffic lights command us to stop, or when timetables organize our routes and itineraries) and the 'mobile staging' of interacting individuals (as, for example, when we negotiate a passage on the sidewalk, or when we choose a particular mode of transport in accordance with our self-perception). The theoretical cornerstones of the 'staging mobilities' framework link material spaces and mobile practices with the staging of embodied social interactions. This we argue takes place in infrastructures and technologically mediated networks full of semiotic systems. 'Staging mobilities' is about how mobilities and places are coded and valorized due to their affordances for social interaction and cultural meaning. The notion of a 'mobile semiotics' presented in this chapter should therefore be understood as a part of this more general theoretical framing.

Semiotics

Semiotics is the study of signs and signification in general. Moreover, it is the study of the conditions of potential meaning production. So semiotics is concerned not so much with *what* a phenomenon means as *how* it may mean something (Jørgensen, 1993: 13). As such, semiotics is a part of understanding human communication, but also at a more profound level a part of understanding human knowledge, meaning and culture. Charles Sanders Peirce is seen as one of the founders of semiotics. To him semiotics was a 'form of logic' (1994: 93). The art of making sense of signs predates the thinkers involved in this chapter. Most often, classic Greek medicine is mentioned as the birthplace of semiotics. In particular, Hippocrates in the fifth century BC is cited as having founded medicine on a simple theory of signs connecting symptoms in the patient with an assumption of underlying causes for the illness (Jørgensen, 1993: 15). There are different trajectories and thinkers to follow within the broad discipline, but here we shall take the work of Peirce as a point of departure since the pragmatic philosophy of this perspective lends itself with particular relevance to the study of the material world (Gottdeiner, 1995: 9; Scollon and Scollon, 2003). To Peirce, a sign is something which stands to somebody for something in some respect or capacity (Peirce, 1994). The sign works, according to Peirce, as a triadic relation between a sign, an object, and an interpretant. Peirce argued that signs may either be icons (defined by their resemblance to an object), indexes (defined by some direct and existential connection with the object) or symbols (where the relation to the object is a matter of social convention) (Peirce, 1994: 100). The Italian semiotic theorist and cultural analyst Umberto Eco makes a distinction between 'intentio auctoris' (the intention of the 'author'), 'intentio operis' (deciphering the image) and 'intentio lectoris' (the interpretation by the user) in his discussion of visual semiotics (Wagner, 2006: 313). In this chapter we shall be interested in this nexus of the intentions derived from the 'sign maker' and the sense made of it from the 'sign reader,' with a particular emphasis on the fact that all signs and meanings are materially situated in the world and that the moving human body creates particular challenges and complexities to this 'mobile sense making.' In particular the understanding of how signs and semiotics systems 'create mobile subjectivities' (Richardson and Jensen, 2008) is interesting, as 'signs turn individuals into crowds' (Fuller, 2002: 235). We shall explore sites of particular importance to strict control and exercise of power in the way that semiotics systems orchestrate and order mobile bodies in space (Fuller and Harley, 2004: 126). The 'performative capacity' of signs can be understood as the way semiotic systems may 'create mobilities' through their ability to direct, organize and steer the flow of people, goods and vehicles.

'Geosemiotics'

Since the aim of this chapter is to understand the material and physical movements in space, we are interested in semiotic conceptualizations that orient more towards the material and physical world than linguistic systems as such. For the purpose of understanding mobilities as well as in order to connect to the level of social interaction, the 'geosemiotic' perspective is rather ideal. According to Scollon and Scollon, geosemiotics is: 'the study of the social meaning of the material placement of signs and discourses and of our actions in the material world' (2003: 211). Put very simply, there is a difference between the 'road work ahead' sign on the back of a municipal van being moved to the site of its placement and its final destination on a street corner. We all know not to pay attention to it if we are driving behind the van, but also to do so if we meet it on the street corner. The same sign may even be placed in a local art gallery and then the relevant semantic frame for making sense of the sign shifts again. Geosemiotics is thereby granting primacy to the 'index dimension' of the sign as we saw it in Peirce's semiotic theory. The physical and material location of the sign becomes the pivotal point of departure for the analysis since *all signs must be located in the material world to exist* (Scollon and Scollon, 2003: vii). In this respect the perspective also lends itself to mobilities studies as we are interested in how flows of goods and people are orchestrated and coordinated by using signs. The signs and sign systems are however not only affording and creating circulation; they are also distributed across the urban landscape themselves. Thus the approach defines two different dimensions of semiotics – a centrifugal distribution of signs and discourses, and a centripetal concentration of signs and semiotic systems (Scollon and Scollon, 2003: 168). Geosemiotics connect the visual signs to their physical placement in order to comprehend which actions and interactions are afforded and encouraged, as well as which are dismissed or refused. More importantly, these bundles of infrastructure, sign systems, building complexes, and commercial and leisure activities are understood from the vantage point of the interacting, situated and moving human body (Scollon and Scollon, 2003: 15). Beyond this level the perception and the ability to 'make sense' of the world (and its signs) meet challenges as we increase the speed of our bodily movement. In his seminal study 'The Image of the City,' Lynch coins the notion of 'legibility' and ideas about how humans 'map' their environs mentally or cognitively. This concerns how the cityscape is seen, understood and made sense of on the basis of its visual properties (Lynch, 1960: 2–3). Moreover, Lynch also coined the term 'wayfinding' (1960: 4) to capture how city dwellers orient themselves and find their way through the city. Needless to say, the complexity of 'data' and information that the brain has to process in order to orient let alone make sense of the situation is rising with the increasing speed of the body (Appleyard *et al.*, 1964; Cullen, 1996; Gibson, 1986).

Semiotics and mobile assemblages

The semiotic systems modify and interact with the human body and sensations as the person moves, and thus affords particular motions, directions, speeds, modes and routes. This perspective relates to ideas about 'assemblages,' large technical systems and actor–network theories in urban studies and mobilities research (e.g. DeLanda, 2006; Deleuze and Guattari, 2003; Farias and Bender, 2010; Graham and Marvin, 2001; Latour, 2005; Thrift, 2008). Here we do not have the space for unfolding this theoretical perspective, but the key issue is how such 'systems and networks' assemble human and non-human agents in an attempt to create and 'stage' mobilities. For the purpose of this chapter's theme we are especially interested in the semiotic properties of such systems and how signs and the semiotic dimension play an active part in producing and re-producing mobilities. Coming from a theoretical perspective of a 'relational and mobility oriented' understanding of places (Jensen, 2009) we argue that the signage and semiotics of network systems are important features of the contemporary mobility landscape. Put differently, 'an arrow is a sign that has no referent; it assembles movement, it doesn't identify things' (Fuller, 2002: 233). In a description of the semiotic systems Fuller furthermore speaks of 'decision points' as the sites where sign systems mediate physical routes demanding crucial decisions to be made (e.g. 'something to declare?' at the customs, or the off-ramp on the freeway). In such points, finding one's way requires plotting predictable paths and 'decision' points within the signage systems (Fuller, 2002: 235). Airports are 'critical points of contact' (Jensen and Morelli, 2011) where global transit flows of people, goods and aircrafts meet and merge with leisure activities, lifestyle consumption chains, shopping goods, jet fuel, etc and are all mediated and coordinated by means of semiotics systems and networks. Thus the semiotic system may be understood as a vital part of the urban assemblage facilitating and filtering mobilities (Fuller, 2002: 238). Or in the words of Deleuze and Guattari:

> Semiotic systems depend on assemblages, and it is the assemblages that determine that a given people, period, or language, and even a given style, fashion, pathology, or minuscule event in a limited situation, can assure the predominance of one semiotic or another.
>
> *(Deleuze and Guattari, 1987: 119)*

The sign system as interface between the orchestration of mobilities 'from above' and lived mobile experiences seen 'from below' is the pivotal point of contact in the 'staging mobilities' frame that we argue will be useful as an overarching umbrella for the analysis.

The airport and its mobile semiotics – a short empirical illustration

There are a very large number of potential cases one could explore if the issue is the study of signs and sign systems facilitating mobilities. I am using the airport as illustrative example.

This is deliberate, since much research has been done on airports and readers therefore will be able to relate the mobilities semiotics to a well-known example.

Airports

Airports have their own particular logic to them, as they are mobility-circulating machines par excellence. Their size and complexity illustrate a new scale of mobility and network city. They are huge socio-technical systems embedding cosmopolitan lifestyles as well as transnational migration patterns and global cargo flows. Some even argue that the airport is the city of the future (Gordon, 2004; Güller and Güller, 2002; Koolhaas, 1995). One of the things that make airports particularly interesting is that they are completely and strictly designed, planned and staged mobility sites. So studying the relationship between mobility and semiotic systems becomes very clear in the contemporary airport (Figure 54.1). Apart from being the 'critical point of contact' between national territories and international airspaces the airport also contains a number of semiotic systems similar to the 'real city' (e.g. directional, informational and commercial signs, etc.). However, being a 100-percent surveilled landscape, the airport is (mostly) without, for example, transgressive signs such as graffiti and other subversive semiotic utterances.

Airports therefore lend themselves to an understanding of an almost fully controlled example of 'staging mobilities' from above. Speaking about the Dutch Schiphol airport, Cresswell notices that the signage designer Paul Mijksenaar has become a 'global transport

Figure 54.1 Airport semiotics

sign design guru,' working through the simplistic and legible airport signage system that has become an international reference work (Cresswell, 2006: 241). In the airport there are of course directional signs guiding passengers through the system towards their gates and flights. But no small dimension of the contemporary airport is now dedicated to commercial usage and shopping. According to airport designers the general rule of thumb concerning commercial signs versus directional signs is to put the former parallel to the flows and the latter at a right angle to the flow (Cresswell, 2006: 242). In this way there is installed a hierarchy of facilitating flow before shopping, reflecting that the key rationale of airports still is mobility. The semiotic dimension of airports may best be described as a 'spectacle':

> Airport signage is a spectacle, an interface for social exchanges between humans and technology. Signage virtualizes the social relations of individuals onto the anonymity of crowd control, reconfiguring territories of geophysical/architectural/cultural space into territories of recognition and action that speak to a productive power of language that exceeds representation.
>
> *(Fuller, 2002: 233)*

Airport signage is regulated at national and international levels just like the road signs regulations. The US Federal Aviation Administration's 'Guidelines for Airport Signing and Graphics' of 1994 is one such influential example, as is the 'British Airport Authority (BAA) Signs Manual,' both setting international standards for airport semiotics (Fuller, 2002: 234). Interestingly Fuller argues that the colors, fonts, lighting, placement and sizing of airport signs are moving towards an internationally homogeneous semiotic language – what she terms a 'mono–language' (ibid.). The 'mono–language' of international airport semiotics is however not unbiased (Fuller, 2002: 235). The 'language' of airport semiotics might at first glance seem transnational and universal, as an 'Esperanto of airspace.' However, if one looks closer at the actual pictograms, we see that, for example, restaurants are depicted by knives and forks not bowls and chopsticks, a female wearing a knee-long skirt is the sign for the women's restroom, and the arrival/departure arrows follow the logic of left–to–right literacy systems (Fuller, 2002: 235). All in all, small and often unnoticed indications of the fact that the 'international' dimension of airport semiotics is predominantly dominated by Western perspectives can be seen (however, there are examples of Asian variations on these models):

> Like all interface systems, alphanumeric and pictographic signage stabilizes both system and user. You may not need to speak the language of the country to get around; but you do need to know the techno–cultural dialect of English – the international language of the airport.
>
> *(Fuller and Harley, 2004: 31)*

The experience of 'being processed' by the semiotic system may be present in a number of settings, but the airport still remains a special place in the sense that the strict security and surveillance systems are making the mobile subject vividly aware of the mobile processing to a much higher degree than, say, a walk on a municipally signed sidewalk:

> Nowadays we are increasingly all travelers, suburban shoppers, global citizens or refugees, following arrows and signs, trying to efficiently navigate the procedures that synchronize daily activity and collective behavior. We move through and by these

semioticised acts: the forms, the arrows, the prohibitions, the diagrams and the maps . . . we obey the signs . . .

(Fuller, 2002: 237)

This points towards an 'airport syntax' and seems to suggest an underlying 'mobile semiotics grammar' as a set of rules regulating and specifying how best to orchestrate and facilitate the flows of passengers. Much more could be said about the airport, which truly is an interesting site for studying mobile semiotics, but here it was meant only as a short empirical illustration of the applicability of mobile semiotics.

Conclusion

This chapter started out by inquiring how to comprehend the mobile condition of contemporary life with a particular view to the signifying dimension of the environment and its 'readability.' In the chapter the potentials of semiotics and its relationship to the new mobilities literature has been explored. We argue that it makes sense to incorporate the semiotic dimension of mobilities into the analysis, and that we therefore need to incorporate theoretical inputs from the theories of semiotics into the mobilities theory. In particular we have found that the perspective of 'geosemiotics' lends itself well to the mobilities analysis. In relation to this we may speak of a 'mobile semiotics.' By this is meant how signs (in their broadest possible sense) afford, process and coordinate (or obstruct) the physical circulation and movement of people, vehicles and goods in more or less codified systems of infrastructure. Thus the semiotic layer must be added to the understanding of mobilities.

As a prolongation of the theoretical fusion of mobilities and semiotics in general, we find that the approach from 'geosemiotics' is even more appropriate in terms of analyzing mobilities. By 'mobilizing' geosemiotics we shall talk about the meaning of material locations as signs, as well as the fact that signs are interpreted in motion and that moving makes different interpretations possible. The different mobile interpretations point towards the inclusion of signs into the analysis of mobilities in order to capture the very way mobile subjects understand the built environment. What takes place is a 'mobile sense-making' where signs and materially situated meanings connect to the moving human body and thus create particular challenges and complexities of making sense of the world. In a more specific way we shall argue that the systems and socio-technical networks that 'host' contemporary mobilities are complex and large material environments where technologies, humans, software, codes, semiotic and communicative systems, objects and artifacts are assembled in a specific combination, facilitating and affording certain practices and restricting or preventing others.

'Mobile assemblages' specific to particular modes of transport mix and relate to the material design and manifestation of contemporary mobilities in ways that must be understood relationally and in semiotic terms. The key issue is how 'systems and networks' assemble human and non-human agents in an attempt to 'stage' mobilities. The semiotic system understood as a vital dimension of the 'mobile assemblages' modifies and interacts with the human body and sensations as the subject moves and thus affords particular motions, directions, speeds, modes and routes.

Here we have made a first attempt to raise the issue of including the semiotic dimension into the mobilities research in general, as well as tried to offer a few beginning concepts from what may become an emerging vocabulary of a mobile semiotics within the mobilities-turn literature of the future. As already mentioned, the key idea is that mobilities are carefully and meticulously designed, planned and 'staged' (from above). However, they are equally importantly acted out, performed and lived as mobile subjects are 'staging themselves' (from below). 'Staging mobilities' is a dynamic process between mobile subjects 'being staged' and the 'staging' of mobile subjects. The theoretical cornerstones of the framework link material spaces and mobile practices with the staging of social interactions. This we argue takes place in technologically mediated networks and infrastructure spaces full of semiotic systems. 'Staging mobilities' is about how mobilities and places are coded and valorized due to their affordances for social interaction and cultural meaning.

Acknowledgement

This chapter is written in great respect and admiration for the late Ron Scollon, who taught me about 'geosemiotics' as well as inspiring true cross-disciplinary curiosity. I am thankful for the many debates and exchanges we had over issues of how to understand the relationship between material spaces and cultural meaning. This chapter is dedicated to his memory.

References

Adey, P. (2010) *Mobility*, London: Routledge.
Appleyard, D., K. Lynch and J. R. Myer (1964) *The View from the Road*, Cambridge MA: MIT Press.
Cresswell, T. (2006) *On The Move: Mobility in the Modern Western World*, London: Routledge.
Cullen, G. (1996) *The Concise Townscape*, Oxford: Architectural Press.
DeLanda, M. (2006) *A New Philosophy of Society: Assemblage Theory and Social Complexity*, New York: Continuum.
Deleuze, G. and F. Guattari (1987) *A Thousand Plateaus: Capitalism and Schizophrenia*, London: Continuum.
Deleuze, G. and F. Guattari, (2003) *A Thousand Plateaus*, Minneapolis: University of Minneapolis Press.
Elliott, A. and J. Urry (2010) *Mobile Lives*, London: Routledge.
Farias, I. and T. Bender (eds) (2010) *Urban Assemblages. How Actor-Network Theory Changes Urban Studies*, London: Routledge.
Fuller, G. (2002) 'The Arrow – Directional Semiotics: Wayfinding in Transit,' *Social Semiotics*, vol. 12, no. 3, pp. 231–244.
Fuller, G. and R. Harley (2004) *Aviopolis: A Book about Airports*, London: Black Dog Publishing.
Gibson, J. J. (1986) *The Ecological Approach to Visual Perception*, New York: Psychology Press.
Goffman, E. (1959) *The Presentation of Self in Everyday Life*, New York: Doubleday.
Goffman, E. (1963) *Behaviour in Public Places: Notes on the Social Organisation of Gatherings*, New York: The Free Press.
Goffman, E. (1972) *Relations in Public: Micro Studies of the Public Order*, New York: Harper & Row.
Gordon, A. (2004) *Naked Airport. A Cultural History of the World's Most Revolutionary Structure*, Chicago: University of Chicago Press.
Gottdeiner, M. (1995) *Postmodern Semiotics: Material Culture and the Form of Postmodern life*, Oxford: Blackwell.
Graham, S. and S. Marvin (2001) *Splintering Urbanism: Networked Infrastructures, Technological Mobilities and the Urban Condition*, London: Routledge.
Güllerm, M. and M. Güller (2002) *From Airport to Airport City*, Barcelona: Editorial Gustavo Gill.
Jensen, O. B. (2006) 'Facework, Flow and the City – Simmel, Goffman and Mobility in the Contemporary City,' *Mobilities*, vol. 2. no. 2, pp. 143–165.
Jensen, O. B. (2009) 'Flows of Meaning, Cultures of Movement – Urban Mobility as Meaningful Everyday Life Practice,' *Mobilities*, vol. 4, no. 1, pp. 139–158.
Jensen, O. B. (2010a) 'Goffman and Everyday Life Mobility,' in M. H. Jacobsen (ed.) *The Contemporary Goffman*, London: Routledge, pp. 333–351.
Jensen, O. B. (2010b) 'Negotiation in Motion: Unpacking a Geography of Mobility,' *Space and Culture*, vol. 13, no. 1, pp. 389–402.

Jensen, O. B. (2013) *Staging Mobilities*, London: Routledge.

Jensen, O. B. and N. Morelli (2011) 'Critical Points of Contact – Exploring Networked Relations In Urban Mobility and Service Design,' *Danish Journal of Geoinformatics and Land Management*, vol. 46, no. 1, pp. 36–49.

Jørgensen, K. G. (1993) *Semiotik: En Introduktion*, København: Samlerens Bogklub.

Koolhaas, R. (1995) 'The Generic City,' in R. Koolhaas and B. Mau (1996) *S, M, L, XL*, New York: Monacelli Press, pp. 1239–1264.

Latour, B. (2005) *Reassembling the Social*, Oxford: Oxford University Press.

Lynch, K. (1960) *The Image of the City*, Cambridge MA: MIT Press.

Peirce, C. S. (1994) *Semiotik og Pragmatisme*, København: Gyldendal.

Richardson, T. and O. B. Jensen (2008) 'How Mobility Systems Produce Inequality: Making Mobile Subject Types on the Bangkok Sky Train,' *Built Environment*, vol. 34, no. 2, pp. 218–231.

Scollon, R. and S. Scollon (2003) *Discourses in Place: Language in the Material World*, London: Routledge.

Sheller, M. and J. Urry (eds) (2006) *Mobile Technologies of the City*, London: Routledge, pp. 137–151.

Thrift, N. (2008) *Non-Representational Theory: Space, Politics, Affect*, London: Routledge.

Urry, J. (2000) *Sociology beyond Societies: Mobilities for the Twenty-First Century*, London: Routledge.

Urry, J. (2007) *Mobilities*, Cambridge: Polity.

Venturi, R., D. Scott Brown and S. Izenour (1972) *Learning from Las Vegas: The Forgotten Symbolism of Architectural Form*, Cambridge MA: MIT Press.

Venturi, R. and D. Scott Brown (2004) *Architecture as Signs and Systems: For a Mannerist Time*, Cambridge MA: The Belknap Press.

Wagner, A. (2006) 'The Rules of the Road, A Universal Visual Semiotics,' *International Journal for the Semiotics of Law*, vol. 19, pp. 311–324.

55
Policies

Cristina Temenos and Eugene McCann

Certain policy models that are anointed as 'best practices' seem to quickly gain political currency across the globe. In parallel, cities that are defined as successful places for policy invention, implementation, and emulation become part of a global discussion. These inter-referential and comparative impulses are evident in municipal decision-makers' attempts to attract the 'creative class,' enhance downtown business areas, become the 'greenest' city, or implement new forms of transit. Indeed, references to models from elsewhere empower particular interests, regimes, and constituencies as they engage in local politics and governance. Yet, we should not assume that the policies themselves, or their proliferation, are somehow naturally or unproblematically good or 'best.' What is important is not so much that they move around in some abstract sense, but that *people move them around* for particular purposes. New planning and design strategies, economic development models, etc. are social products, built up from the ground over time and bearing the imprint of the interests involved in producing them (McCann, 2008, 2011a, 2011b; McCann and Ward, 2011a; Peck and Theodore, 2010a; Ward, 2006).

The global proliferation of particular policy models reflects and constitutes not only the local contexts in which they are operationalized and experienced but also important yet understudied global geographies of knowledge circulation and territorialization. How, then, might we characterize, conceptualize, and research these policy movements and mutations? How are these circulations activated, sustained, and directed? Through which spaces do they move and what sorts of infrastructures facilitate and channel their movement?

Contemporary thought in geography has employed the notion of 'policy mobilities' as a frame through which to analyze the practices and power relations inherent in the way that a particular policy intervention, defined as a best-practice model with wider applicability, is then mobilized through global circuits of policy knowledge, and appears in mutated forms elsewhere (McCann and Ward, 2011a). This approach is characterized by a concern for the actors, practices, spaces, and infrastructures that affect the (re)production, adoption, and travel of policies and best practice models across space and time. Attention to what happens to policies while they are 'in motion' is another important focus, since the paths traveled and the things that happen to policies along the way are just as important as the policies themselves and the places they affect (McCann, 2011a).

A research agenda has begun to emerge that offers a rich conceptualization of ongoing practices, institutions, and ideas that link global circuits of policy knowledge and local policy practice, politics, and actors (McCann, 2011a; McCann and Ward, 2011a; Peck and Theodore, 2010c). This conceptual work informs, but also benefits from, detailed empirical research into how the local and sometimes immobile or fixed aspects of place interact with policies mobilized from elsewhere. Indeed, it can be argued, building upon Harvey (1982) and Massey (1991), that the tension between policy as fixed, territorial, or place-specific, on the one hand, and dynamic, global, and relational on the other is not a problem for conceptualizing policy mobilities. Rather, it is precisely this tension and its productive effects on policies and places that should be our research focus (Massey, 2011).

Circulating policies: spaces, mobilities, infrastructures

The policy mobilities approach develops detailed empirical analyses of the contexts and practices of policy mobilization, critical analyses of inter-local policy mobilizations that seek to maintain a focus on wider contexts, an attention to policy mutation, hybridity and emergence, and rich accounts of the politics of policy mobilities. Space does not allow a full discussion of these aspects (but see Peck and Theodore, 2010c; McCann and Ward, 2011a, in press). Here we focus on how the policy mobilities approach draws upon the wider mobilities discussion and on how geographers conceptualize the actors, places, and infrastructures that facilitate the circulation of policies.

Mobilities and policy mobilities

Attention to notions of mobilization, as well as assemblage and mutation, in critical policy studies stems from a dissatisfaction with a longstanding literature in political science which focuses on policy *transfer*. Geographers have critiqued that literature for its narrow focus on only some policy actors and institutions and its tendency toward a literal and somewhat flat notion of transfer, in which policies are assumed to move fully formed from point a to b (see McCann and Ward (in press) for a summary of the critique, and Marsh and Evans (2012) for a response).

Reference to the mobilities approach has allowed a shift in the terms of debate from policy transfer to 'policy mobilities.' Conceptually, mobilities scholars reject both understandings of places as natural steady-state containers of socio-spatial processes and also as the glamorization of free-flowing movement as the new 'unsteady-state' of globalization. Thus, they question received spatial binaries like global/local or near/far and emphasize the importance of connections. Furthermore, they take issue with the 'black-boxing' of the powerful socio-spatial relations that constitute the connection between the beginning and end-points in any displacement process. While these end-points are important, powerful, and meaningful, so is what happens *in transit* among them (Cresswell, 2010; Sheller and Urry, 2006). Mobilities are, nonetheless, tied to and facilitated by various 'moorings,' organizing nodes, or fixed infrastructures. They "entail distinct social spaces that orchestrate new forms of social life around such nodes, for example, stations, hotels, motorways, resorts, airports, leisure complexes, cosmopolitan cities, beaches, galleries and roadside parks" (Sheller and Urry, 2006: 213).

The study of policy through a mobilities frame adds spaces of knowledge production and circulation, including the Internet, social media, the 'geoweb,' conferences, mega-events, and sites of protest to the spaces that most mobilities scholarship has addressed (but see Larsen *et al.*, 2006). These are sites of encounter, persuasion, and motivation. They are places where mobilized policy knowledge must touch down in one sense or another to gain fuel and traction, as in the case of conferences where encounters around ideas direct and invigorate policy circulation (Adey, 2006; England and Ward, 2007; Cook and Ward, 2012; McCann, 2011c). Furthermore, a focus on policy emphasizes and elaborates the role that states at various scales play in shaping geographies of knowledge circulation. Tracing the travels of policies allows us to disrupt common conceptualizations of states as territorially, politically, and socially bounded entities. Instead, we can conceptualize interconnections among 'unbounded' states and state actors as crucial circulatory infrastructures, while simultaneously emphasizing the continued importance of territorial fixity and embeddedness – of both state actors and other policy actors – in powerful geographies of knowledge production.

Informational and institutional infrastructures

'Informational infrastructures' (McCann, 2004, 2008, 2011a; Cook and Ward, 2011) are institutions, organizations, and technologies that frame and package knowledge about best policy practices, successful cities, and cutting-edge ideas for specific audiences. There are at least four sub-sets of these infrastructures:

1   States, from the local to the national, and related international organizations play crucial roles in defining and directing flows of knowledge about policy. State actors, from politicians to bureaucrats, engage with global circuits of policy knowledge, learning new models or promoting their own innovations to others. They have the power to implement the new ideas in their jurisdictions, thus lending them legitimacy (when they can be defined as successful).
2   Educators and trainers formally educate new generations of policy actors, usually in institutions of higher education and subsequent professional development training. They frame knowledge by turning their students' attention to particular 'hot' policy models, gurus, and exemplary cities. This knowledge frame is legitimized through networks of credentialization.
3   Professional and activist organizations also frame, codify, and facilitate the circulation of policy knowledge through their professional publications, information clearinghouse websites, email lists, awards, conferences, workshops, and field trips (e.g. see McCann's (2011a) discussions of UN Habitat and Ward's (2006, 2007, 2010b) analysis of institutions spreading the model of Business Improvement Districts). Through their activities, these organizations anoint certain policies and cities as worthy of notice and emulation.
4   The popular media also frame and channel knowledge about urban policy. Their dissemination and repetition of narratives about what constitutes good or bad policies, policy gurus, and exemplary cities shape the mental maps of policy actors, thus partly defining and directing popular and political policy discussions and agendas (McCann, 2004).

In combination, these actors and institutions compose the "fragile relays, contested locales, and fissiparous affiliations" – the socio-spatial infrastructures of policy mobilization (Rose, 1999: 51).

Placing policy mobilities

How, then, have geographers and others working on policy mobilities understood these spatialities and infrastructures? Following Massey (1991), they understand urban places as unbounded, as nodes within networks of relations, or as "the coming together of the previously unrelated, a constellation of processes rather than a thing . . . open and . . . internally multiple" (Massey, 2005: 141, 2011). They are assemblages of policy models and expertise drawn out of circulation and gathered in local contexts. Yet, these policy assemblages (Prince, 2010) tend to be constrained and conditioned by various forces, legacies, and pre-existing conditions, including infrastructures. The range of opportunities for a city with a particular heavy industrial heritage and a declining population and tax base, for example, are likely to be quite different from those for a city with a booming economy and a growing population.

Critical research on policy-making seeks to grapple with the tension-filled relationships between territorial fixity and place specificity and global flows, relations, and interconnections. Similarly, researchers balance studies of the wider conditioning contexts and ideologies that delimit and define 'best' practice models with serious consideration of the role of individuals and small groups of policy actors in mobilizing and operationalizing policies.

Conditioning contexts and 'middling' technocrats

Policy mobilities researchers reject the notion of policies as unitary objects, found in particular places and then moved in complete form across space. Rather, geographers consider "power relations . . . [conditioning] what is seen, and what counts, in terms of policy innovations, preferred models, and best practices" Peck (2011a: 791).

Peck and Theodore's (2010b) analysis of the travels of 'conditional cash transfer' (CCT) anti-poverty programs pays attention to "institutional and ideological conditions that variously enable, envelope, and energize [the] purposeful mobilization" of policies (Peck, 2011a: 793). CCT policies have been in place across the Global South for over a decade, are promoted by the World Bank, and were adopted by New York City after local policy actors studied Mexico's federal *Oportunidades* program. It was distilled, translated, and mobilized by Mexican technocrats, then adopted in localities elsewhere. Peck notes that CCTs "have been actively co-produced with the new [global institutional] 'consensus' on poverty alleviation and as such can be seen as mobile and somewhat self-fulfilling affirmations of that evolving consensus" (Peck, 2011b: 176). CCTs then, become 'best' practice models not so much as a result of their inherent qualities, but because they are produced by and reflect the ideological/institutional context, or infrastructure, in which they have emerged.

Larner and Laurie (2010) go further in their study of individual policy actors. "Travelling technocrats," they argue, are not only high-level agents of elite institutions like the World Bank. "'[M]iddling' technocrats" play a crucial role in the spread and, crucially, the implementation of new policy ideas, since "[t]hey are . . . on the ground as employees, contractors or consultants, rather than occupying high status roles in international think tanks, government offices or executive boards of transnational corporations" (Larner and Laurie, 2010: 219). Similarly Kuus (2011: 1144) argues that the study of bureaucratic actors allows "a closer examination of the interconnections between geopolitical practices and the agents of these practices." From both perspectives, the 'policy actors' who both utilize and constitute the institutional spaces and informational infrastructures of policy mobilities are not only those elites who write the policies; nor are they only "the hegemonic institutions and actors, and NGOs and transnational social movements, who feature in most existing accounts" (Larner and Laurie, 2010: 224–225). Rather, they are also those 'middling' actors who engage in the seemingly banal technocratic (infrastructural) work of teaching and spreading new models.

Inter-urban policy mobilities and policy tourism

Many policy models that gain popularity are associated, to varying degrees of accuracy, with particular cities (e.g. Bogotá for transportation, Porto Alegre for participatory budgeting, Copenhagen for bicycle lanes) and, certainly, most traveling policy models journey through cities in one way or another. It is perhaps not surprising then that most of the work on policy mobilities has an urban orientation. Ward's (2006) study of Business Improvement Districts is a clear example (see also: Ward, 2007, 2010b, 2011, and Cook 2008, 2009). BIDs are areas of cities where businesses have agreed to be taxed at a higher rate and to use the revenue to fund place-specific governance strategies like private security, extra street-cleaning, or advertising. They are a particular mobile policy model that is representative of both the activities and priorities of contemporary urban business leaders and politicians, and also of the wider institutional and ideological context of global neoliberalism. Ward traces the BID model's development in one city, its circulation through particular infrastructures – government institutions, professional bodies, specific places – and its adoption in modified form elsewhere.

Ward highlights the role New York has played as a destination and learning site for those interested in seeing how BIDs are operationalized. These trips are important elements of policy mobilization and, in them, we can see the intersection of the policy mobilities notion of informational infrastructures with the more traditional idea of physical infrastructures underpinning movement, as discussed by mobilities scholars. Institutional and informational infrastructures of knowledge mobilization create road maps for policy entrepreneurs as they look to study policy models in the field while their physical travels are facilitated and mediated by infrastructures like airports, conference facilities, etc.

These trips are a form of 'policy tourism,' in which the tours on which visiting delegations are taken and the places they visit are carefully regulated by their organizers; thus, the knowledge generated through this practice is relationally produced and packaged. Yet, contemporary policy tourists regard seeing a policy operating in its 'natural environment' as an effective learning experience (González, 2010) as have generations of policy actors before them (Clarke, 2011a, 2011b). In this sense, the 'touristic' aspect of policy mobilization – fact-finding trips, site visits, and conferences attendance – resonates with Hannam *et al.*'s (2006: 12–13) assertion that "the time spent traveling is not dead time," but involves inspiring activities. Such policy travel ideally provides a focused retreat-like context to share ideas with peers and study on-the-ground manifestations of policy models. On the 'supply side,' cities that are popular destinations for delegations of policy actors often develop protocols and narratives that make dealing with policy tourists efficient and edifying, and also convey a consistent message.

These combinations of routeways, encounters, and stories are forms of infrastructure since one of the purposes of infrastructures is to facilitate and direct repeated actions, processes, or movements in a way that is predictable and largely invisible. Again, these informational infrastructures are interconnected with the material infrastructures of physical travel and it is worth emphasizing that these infrastructures are themselves conditioned by wider ideological fields that define which policies, which cities, and which policy gurus are appropriate objects of tourism and learning.

Local politics and global infrastructures

Identifying these nested hierarchies of ideological, institutional, informational, and physical infrastructures does not mean that the definition of a policy as a 'best' practice or the definition of a city as a worthy 'model' for others is a straightforward matter, however. The critical question is, best for whom? Every policy and every policy infrastructure serves particular interests more so than others. For some, a policy encouraging dense condo living around a downtown core is a beneficial form of 'revitalization.' Yet, for others, the same model of new urbanism threatens to gentrify existing neighborhoods and displace vulnerable populations. The question of whether such a model is good for a city then becomes not a technical question of zoning bylaws, green building technologies, and rapid transit, but a political one of social justice, equity, and community resilience.

The study of policy mobilities, like the study of all mobilities, must then be the study of politics and power. In general terms, when a locally developed policy becomes a global 'model' by receiving accolades and being copied by others, we might ask whether this positive attention is likely to confer weight and legitimacy on its advocates and thus increase their influence in the local politics of policy-making. When a 'best practice' policy model is brought into a city from elsewhere, is it somewhat armored against local criticism and questioning by its global renown, even though it has to be modified to the local context? Furthermore, when local policy-making is 'globalized' in these ways, does local politics also take on a partially global character as those involved in debating the pros and cons of a new policy direction in a specific city seek to characterize and evaluate how, in whose interests, and with what outcomes it operated in cities elsewhere?

In this regard, policy experts and consultants whose travels spread 'best practice' models are not only members of a growing 'consultocracy' (Saint-Martin, 2000) who help to constitute infrastructures of policy knowledge, but they are also political actors. Temenos and McCann (2012), for example, chart how a sustainability framework originally associated closely with a particular consultant and originally developed for the corporate sector was introduced into a municipal planning process because its precepts dovetailed with local political elites' desire to both educate the local population in growth management planning and recycling practices and also develop and market a brand for their municipality as a model of sustainable development.

An analysis of the local politics of policy-making also highlights how activists hoping to radically change cities can also be transfer agents, using similar infrastructures and strategies as business and political elites to spread their own particular 'best practices' – a process Purcell (2008) dubs 'fast resistance transfer.' For example, the development in Vancouver, Canada, of a drug policy at the turn of the current century involved significant changes in local discourses around injection drug use, public health, and the (de)merits of criminalizing users of illicit drugs. In a few years, a standard criminalization approach was replaced by a strategy in which drug use was defined as primarily a public health issue, and a new facility was established to allow users to inject under supervision and in relative safety. This new 'harm reduction' strategy was modeled on several European cities via Internet and document searches, fact-finding trips, conferences, guest experts, lectures, workshops, etc. (McCann, 2008). During this time, local politics became framed by points of reference elsewhere. Critics of the harm reduction approach opposed its implementation in Vancouver by articulating different stories of its impacts in European cities, while also offering up other places as alternative models (McCann, 2011b). The local politics of policy-making is, then, also a global(ized) politics. It is one that tends to be driven by hegemonic elites, but, like any hegemony, it can be challenged and restructured.

Conclusion

The purpose of this chapter has been both to outline the notion of policy mobilities and also to discuss the actors, institutions, spaces, and infrastructures that activate and direct policy mobilities. We have shown how geographers with an interest in the critical study of policy utilize the notions of mobilities and infrastructures as part of an analysis of the spatialities of knowledge. We suggest that the informational infrastructures that underpin the global circulation of policy models work at different levels of abstraction to condition the possibilities of policy change; we point out that these infrastructures are social and can best be understood through a lens that focuses closely on micro-practices and micro-sites of policy-making, as well as on larger ideological and institutional contexts; and, finally, we argue that, as a social process, policy mobilization is fundamentally about power and politics.

The policy mobilities approach is recent and, therefore, will continue to be fleshed-out conceptually and empirically through debate, critique, and empirical application. Certainly, questions of how policies move or don't, what happens in the process, and what are their socio-spatial implications remain to be fully answered. More specifically, three issues are likely to shape much future discussion in the literature. First, there is a question of methodology. Researchers have largely employed a number of 'standard,' qualitative case study methods – interviews, discourse and document analysis, participant or direct observation – but with an attention to literally and figuratively following policies and policy actors through particular spaces and infrastructures of knowledge production and political struggle/legitimation (Cochrane and Ward, 2012; McCann and Ward, 2012). More might be done to elaborate on these 'mobile methods' (Büscher *et al.*, 2011). Second, Robinson (2011a) and Massey (2011) rightly argue for a more serious consideration of the policy innovations and productive connections developed in Global South cities in order to "draw us towards alternative maps of causality [and] differently constituted cases for comparison" (Robinson, 2011a: 13; see also Clarke, 2011a, 2011b; Peck and Theodore, 2010b; Roy and Ong, 2011). Third, there is the question of immobility, failure, and disconnection. Not all policies are mobilized and not all mobilized policies find receptive audiences elsewhere. Furthermore, geographies of policy mobility are as uneven as any other geographies and this reflects power differentials in access to policy networks and communities. Like physical infrastructures, informational infrastructures channel, delimit, and prohibit flows in ways that reflect long-standing legacies of power relations. Thus, attention must be paid to immobilities so we do not normalize or glamorize movement (Adey, 2006; Sheller and Urry, 2006). As Jacobs (2011: 8) notes, "Sites of failure, absence and mutation are significant empirical instances of differentiation."

Commonalities, we suggest, among policies are not the result of happenstance. They are, in part, the product of purposeful mobilizations and their social and physical infrastructures. Mobilities and infrastructures of all types facilitate and channel interconnections, but they also delimit and contain flows and access to flows. Thus the policy mobilities approach seeks to analyze the inherent fixities and mobilities of policy-making as powerful socio-spatial formations that deeply impact everyday life.

Acknowledgements

This chapter is a substantially modified version of a paper for *Geography Compass*. We would like to thank that journal's editor, Andy Wood, and also Valorie Crooks, Byron Miller, and Janet Sturgeon for comments on an earlier version. The chapter is influenced by discussions with colleagues working on policy mobilities, including Tom Baker, Nick Clarke, Allan Cochrane, Ian Cook, Sara González, Jamie Peck, Russell Prince, Jennifer Robinson, Ananya Roy, Nik Theodore, and Kevin Ward.

Bibliography

Adey, P. (2006). 'If mobility is everything then it is nothing: towards a relational politics of (Im)mobilities,' *Mobilities* 1(1), 75.

Allen, J. and Cochrane, A. (2007). 'Beyond the territorial fix: regional assemblages, politics and power,' *Regional Studies* 41(9), 1161–1175.

Anderson, B., McFarlane, C. (2011). 'Assemblage and geography,' *Area* 43(2) 124–127.

Benson, D., Jordan, A. (2011). 'What have we learned from policy transfer research? Dolowitz and Marsh Revisited,' *Political Studies Review* 9(3), 366–378.

Brenner, N. and Theodore, N. (2002). 'Cities and the geographies of "actually existing neoliberalism",' *Antipode* 34(3), 349–79.

Brenner, N., Peck, J., and Theodore, N. (2010). 'Variegated neoliberalization: geographies, modalities, pathways,' *Global Networks* 10(2), 182–222.

Buroway, M., Blum, J., George, S., Gille, Z., and Thayer, M. (2000). *Global Ethnography: Forces, Connections, and Imaginations in a Postmodern World.* Oakland: University of California Press.

Büscher, M., Urry, J., and Witchger (eds) (2011). *Mobile Methods.* London: Routledge.

Clarke, Nick (2011a). 'Urban policy mobility, anti-politics, and histories of the transnational municipal movement,' *Progress in Human Geography* 35(4), 1–19.

Clarke, Nick (2011b). 'Globalising care? Town twinning in Britain since 1945,' *Geoforum* 42(1), 115–125.

Cochrane, A. and K. Ward (eds) (2012). 'Theme issue: Researching policy mobilities: reflections on method,' *Environment and Planning A* 44(1), 5–51.

Cook, I. R. (2008). 'Mobilising urban policies: The policy transfer of US Business Improvement Districts to England and Wales,' *Urban Studies* 45(4), 773–795.

Cook, I. R. (2009). 'Private sector involvement in urban governance: the case of Business Improvement Districts and Town Centre Management partnerships in England,' *Geoforum* 40(5), 930–940.

Cook, I. R. and Ward, K. (2011). 'Trans-national networks of learning, mega-events and policy tourism: the case of Manchester's Commonwealth and Olympic Games projects,' *Urban Studies* 48(12), 2519–2535.

Cook, I. R. and Ward, K. (2012). 'Conferences, informational infrastructures and mobile policies: the process of getting Sweden "BID ready",' *European Urban and Regional Studies* 19(2), 137–152.

Cresswell, T. (2010). 'Towards a politics of mobility,' *Environment and Planning D: Society and Space* 28(1), 17–31.

Cresswell, T. (2011). 'Mobilities II: still,' *Progress in Human Geography* 35(4), 550–558.

England K. and Ward, K. (eds) (2007). *Neoliberalization: States, Networks, Peoples.* Oxford: Blackwell.

Evans, M. (2004). 'Understanding policy transfer,' in *Policy Transfer in Global Perspective.* Aldershot: Ashgate, 10–42.

González, S. (2010). 'Bilbao and Barcelona in motion. How urban regeneration "models" travel and mutate in the global flows of policy tourism,' *Urban Studies* 1–22.

Hannam, K., M. Sheller, and J. Urry (2006). 'Editorial: Mobilities, immobilities and moorings,' *Mobilities* 1, 1–22.

Hart, G. (2002). *Disabling Globalization: Places of Power in Post-Apartheid South Africa.* Berkeley, CA: University of California Press.

Harvey, D. (1982). *The Limits to Capital.* Chicago: University of Chicago Press.

Jacobs, J. M. (2011). 'Urban geographies I: still thinking cities relationally,' *Progress in Human Geography* 36.3(2012), 412–422.

Jessop, B., Brenner, N., and Jones, M. (2008). 'Theorizing sociospatial relations,' *Environment and Planning D: Society and Space* 26(3), 389–401.

Kuus, M. (2011). 'Policy and geopolitics: bounding Europe in Europe,' *Annals of the Association of American Geographers* 101(5), 1140–1155.

Larner, W. (2002). 'Globalization, governmentality and expertise: creating a call centre labour force,' *Review of International Political Economy* 9(4), 650.

Larner, W. and Le Heron, R. (2002a). 'From economic globalization to globalizing economic processes: towards post-structural political economies,' *Geoforum* 33, 415–419.

Larner, W. and Le Heron, R. (2002b). 'The spaces and subjects of a globalizing economy: a situated exploration of method,' *Environment and Planning D: Society and Space* 20, 753–774.

Larner, W. and Laurie, N. (2010). 'Travelling technocrats, embodied knowledges: globalising privatisation in telecoms and water,' *Geoforum* 41(2), 218–226.

Larsen, J., Urry, J., and Axhausen, K. W. (2006). *Mobilities, Networks, Geographies.* Aldershot: Ashgate.

Marsh, D. and M. Evans (2012). 'Policy transfer: coming of age and learning from the experience,' *Policy Studies* 33(6), 477–481.

Marston, S. (2000). 'The social construction of scale,' *Progress in Human Geography* 24(2).

Massey, D. (1991). 'A global sense of place,' *Marxism Today* (38) 24–29.

Massey, D. (2005). *For Space.* London: Sage.

Massey, D. (2011). 'A counterhegemonic relationality of place,' in McCann, E. and Ward, K. (eds) *Mobile Urbanism: Cities and Policymaking in the Global Age,* 1–14.

McCann, E. (2004). '"Best places": inter-urban competition, quality of life, and popular media discourse,' *Urban Studies*, 41(10), 1909–1929.

McCann, E. (2008). 'Expertise, truth, and urban policy mobilities: global circuits of knowledge in the development of Vancouver, Canada's "four pillar" drug strategy,' *Environment and Planning A* 40(4), 885–904.

McCann, E. (2011a). 'Urban policy mobilities and global circuits of knowledge: toward a research agenda,' *Annals of the Association of American Geographers* 101(1), 107–130.

McCann, E. (2011b). 'Points of reference: knowledge of elsewhere in the politics of urban drug policy,' in McCann, E. and Ward, K. (eds) *Assembling Urbanism: Mobilizing Knowledge & Shaping Cities in a Global Context.* Minneapolis: University of Minnesota Press, 97–122.

McCann, E. (2011c). 'Situated knowledge on the move? Reflections on urban policy mobilities/immobilities.' Paper given at IAG Conference Wollongong, July 3–6.

McCann, E. and Ward, K. (2010). 'Relationality/territoriality: toward a conceptualization of cities in the world,' *Geoforum* 41(2), 175–184.

McCann, E. and Ward, K. (eds) (2011a). *Mobile Urbanism: Cities & Policy-Making in the Global Age.* Minneapolis: University of Minnesota Press.

McCann, E. and Ward, K. (2011b). 'Introduction,' in *Mobile Urbanism: Cities & Policy-Making in the Global Age.* Minneapolis: University of Minnesota Press.

McCann, E. and Ward, K. (2012a). 'Assembling urbanism: following policies and "studying through" the sites and situations of policy making,' *Environment and Planning A* 44(1), 42–51.

McCann, E. and Ward, K. (2012b). 'Policy assemblages, mobilities and mutations: toward a multidisciplinary conversation,' *Political Studies Review* 10(3), 325–332.

McCann, E. and Ward, K. (In press). 'A multi-disciplinary approach to policy transfer research: geographies, assemblages, mobilities and mutations,' *Policy Studies.*

McFarlane, C. (2011). 'The city as a machine for learning,' *Transactions of the Institute of British Geographers*, 1–37.

Mountz, A. and Curran, W. (2009). 'Policing in drag: Giuliani goes global with the illusion of control,' *Geoforum* 40(6), 1033–1040.

Nicholls, Walter (2009). 'Place, networks, space: theorizing the geographies of social movements,' *Transactions of the Institute of British Geographers*, 78–93.

Peck, Jamie (2011a). 'Geographies of policy: from transfer-diffusion to mobility-mutation,' *Progress in Human Geography* 35(6), 773–797.

Peck, Jamie (2011b). 'Global policy models, globalizing poverty management: international convergence or fast-policy integration?' *Geography Compass* 5(4), 165–181.

Peck, Jamie (2011c). 'Creative moments: working culture, through municipal socialism and neoliberal urbanism,' in McCann, E. and Ward, K. *Mobile Urbanism: Cities & Policy-Making in the Global Age.* Minneapolis: University of Minnesota Press.

Peck, J. and Tickell, A. (2002). 'Neoliberalizing space,' *Antipode* 34(3), 380–404.

Peck, J. and Theodore, N. (2010a). 'Mobilizing policy: models, methods, and mutations,' *Geoforum* 41(2), 169–174.

Peck, J. and Theodore, N. (2010b). 'Recombinant workfare, across the Americas: transnationalizing "fast" social policy,' *Geoforum* 41(2), 195–208.

Peck, J. and N. Theodore (eds) (2010c). 'Mobilizing Policy, special theme issue of *Geoforum*,' 41(2), 169–226.

Peck, J. and Theodore, N. (2012). 'Follow the policy: a distended case approach,' *Environment and Planning A* 44(1), 21–30.

Prince, R. (2010). 'Policy transfer as policy assemblage: making policy for the creative industries in New Zealand,' *Environment and Planning A* 42(1), 169–86.

Purcell, M. (2008). *Recapturing Democracy: Neoliberalization and the Struggle for Alternative Urban Futures.* New York: Routledge.

Robinson, J. (2005). *Ordinary Cities: Between Modernity and Development*. New York: Routledge.

Robinson, J. (2011a). 'The spaces of circulating knowledge: city strategies and global urban governmentality,' in McCann, E. and Ward, K. (eds) *Mobile Urbanism: Cities & Policy-Making in the Global Age*. Minneapolis: University of Minnesota Press.

Robinson, J. (2011b). 'Cities in a world of cities: the comparative gesture,' *International Journal of Urban and Regional Research* 35(1), 1–23.

Rose, N. (1999). *Powers of Freedom: Reframing Political Thought*. Cambridge: Cambridge University Press.

Roy, A. and Ong, A. (eds) (2011). *Worlding Cities: Asian Experiments in the Art of Being Global*. Malden, MA: Wiley-Blackwell.

Saint-Martin, D. (2000). *Building the New Managerialist State: Consultants and the Politics of Public Sector Reform in Comparative Perspective*. Oxford: Oxford University Press.

Sheller, M. and Urry, J. (2006). 'The new mobilities paradigm,' *Environment and Planning A* 38, 207–226.

Stone, D. (2004). 'Transfer agents and global networks in the "transnationalisation" of policy,' *Journal of European Public Policy* 11, 545–566.

Temenos, C. (2012). 'Geographies of harm reduction: urban health policy as post-political negotiation or social justice movement?' Presentation given at Royal Geographical Society–Institute of British Geographers Annual Conference, Edinburgh, UK.

Temenos, C. and McCann, E. (2012). 'The local politics of policy mobility: the education of attention in developing a municipal sustainability fix,' *Environment and Planning A* 44, 1389–1406.

Urry, J. (2000). 'Mobile sociology,' *The British Journal of Sociology* 51(1), 185–203.

Urry, J. (2007). *Mobilities*. Cambridge: Polity.

Ward, K. (2006). '"Policies in motion," urban management and state restructuring: the trans-local expansion of business improvement districts,' *International Journal of Urban and Regional Research* 30, 54–75.

Ward, K. (2007). 'Business improvement districts: policy origins, mobile policies and urban liveability,' *Geography Compass* 1(3), 657–672.

Ward, K. (2008). 'Towards a comparative (re)turn in urban studies? Some reflections,' *Urban Geography* 29, 405–410.

Ward, K. (2010a). 'Towards a relational comparative approach to the study of cities,' *Progress in Human Geography* 34, 471–487.

Ward, K. (2010b). 'Entrepreneurial urbanism and Business Improvement Districts in the State of Wisconsin: a cosmopolitan critique,' *Annals of the Association of American Geographers* 100(5), 1177–1196.

Ward, K. (2011). 'Policies in motion and in place: the case of the Business Improvement Districts,' in McCann, E. and Ward, K. (eds) *Mobile Urbanism: Cities and Policy-Making in a Global Age*. Minneapolis: Minnesota University Press, 71–96.

Epilogue

Oil, the American Suburbs and the Future of Mobility[1]

John Urry

Oil and money

It is often said that money makes the world go round, as trillions of dollars, euros, yen, yuan and other major currencies circulate around the world at dizzying speed. The scale of this predominantly digital movement dwarfs the income and resources available to individuals, most companies and many countries.

But there is another powerful mobile force in the world and that is oil. Žižek writes about its origins: 'Nature is one big catastrophe. Oil, our main source of energy – can you even imagine what kind of ultra–unthinkable ecological catastrophe must have happened on earth in order that we have these reserves of oil?' (Žižek 2008). Ancient fossilized organic materials settled on the bottom of seas and lakes and were buried. As further layers were laid on top, intense heat and pressure built up and this caused the organic matter ultimately to change into liquid and gaseous hydrocarbons. The long hydrocarbon chains of oil are in effect 'preserved sun', and only the sun exceeds oil in its energy. This was a unique gift, but like most gifts it is finite and irreplaceable.

This oil is central to 'western civilisation'. Oil as much as money makes the world go round. It is remarkably versatile, convenient, mobile and for most of the twentieth century exceptionally cheap since it first gushed out of the ground at Spindletop in Texas in 1901. At $100 a barrel, the world's known oil reserves are currently worth $104 trillion, or forty times the value of the UK economy (Singh 2011)!

Oil makes fast movement possible. It provides almost all transportation energy in the modern world (at least 95 per cent) powering cars, trucks, planes, ships and some trains. It thus makes possible the mobile lives of friendship, business life, professions and families. Oil also moves components, commodities and food around the world in trucks, planes and vast container ships, as well as oil itself in large tankers (WWF 2008). Oil is also an element of most manufactured goods and much packaging and bottling worldwide (95 per cent). It is crucial to at least 95 per cent of food production and distribution for a rising world population through providing power for irrigation, moving food and providing pesticides and fertilizers (Harvey and Pilgrim 2011). Oil is also used for much domestic and office heating, especially within oil-rich societies, and is crucial in providing back-up power and lighting.

Overall, oil generates around a third of all greenhouse gas emissions and is a major category currently increasing across the world. Besides being itself mobile, oil is energy-dense, storage-able, and non-renewable. The geologist M. King Hubbert, who discovered the problem of 'American peak oil' in the 1950s, noted its problem: 'you can only use oil once . . . Soon all the oil is going to be burned' (Heinberg 2005: 100).

Many suggestions and prototypes are being developed to produce alternative energy, especially nuclear, solar and wind. But these do not replace oil and what has been called 'oil civilization' (Owen 2011). Economies and societies worldwide became utterly dependent upon this source of mobile power. Moreover, all alternative fuels have a much poorer ratio of energy returned on energy invested, or EROEI. Furthermore, as oil's price rises there is not necessarily more produced and delivered to the market place. Currently its supply seems relatively fixed and intermittent rapid increases in price are certain. Moreover, most energy innovations take a very long time to develop, often decades. An energy transition from one type of energy to another only happens once a century or so (Smil 2010).

It was thus contingent carbon resources and especially 'oil' that enabled the 'west' to dominate the long, highly mobile twentieth century. It was less the Enlightenment or western science or liberalism that secured western civilization. It was its carbon resources and especially the mobile energy resource of oil that generated an exceptional 'modern, mobile' civilization based on fast movement. Owen writes how: 'Oil is liquid civilization' (Owen 2011: 77). Beginning in the US, the west consolidated its power and influence in the world.

Cheap, plentiful oil was central to American economic, cultural and military power. The US accounts for one-third of global wealth, 22 per cent of world energy consumption and one-quarter of total carbon emissions (the population is only five per cent) (Burman 2007; Heinberg 2005). If the American Dream was to be experienced by the world's population, it would take five planets to support it (Hulme 2009). American production and consumption got there first, especially because it initiated and monopolized the manufacture of 'Large Independent Mobile Machines', or LIMMs. LIMMs carry their own energy source and given the denseness and historic cheapness of oil this was highly efficient in generating the US's 'addiction to oil' (Rutledge 2005). Globally there are nearly one billion cars and trucks and almost one billion international air journeys a year.

But it is a huge problem for one resource to be the basis of these modern systems and societies. The future of oil is the future of modern societies set upon their pathway during the momentous twentieth century. This had a dramatic effect in exploiting the earth's resources. 'We have deployed more energy since 1900 than all of human history before 1900' (McNeill 2012). The twentieth century used as much energy as the previous hundred or so centuries of recorded human history. And in using those resources to engender fast movement, that century generated carbon dioxide emissions that will remain in the atmosphere for hundreds of years.

The oil exploring, producing and using industries are a huge economic enterprise containing many of the world's largest and richest companies. This 'carbon capital' consists of western-based oil 'super majors' (ExxonMobil), state oil companies mainly found in producing countries (Saudi Aramco, the world's most valuable company), car and truck producing corporations (Toyota was the world's largest until 2011), huge engineering and road construction companies (Bechtel), and many corporations providing services to car-drivers and passengers (Holiday Inn, McDonalds). This capital made the mobile twentieth century.

Further, finance and oil are intertwined. Oil is speculated upon in financial markets. Its price movements now stem from this speculation, as from changes in the supply of and demand for oil for transportation and manufacturing. A major Report for Lloyds of London shows how speculation de-stabilizes supply and price and further reduces energy security (Froggatt and Lahn 2010). There are now over seventy-five crude oil financial derivatives. while fifteen years ago there was just one. This Lloyds Report maintains that extensive growth in financial trading in oil makes oil prices higher and more unstable (Dicker 2011). Oil prices are exceptionally sensitive to even small changes in demand.

And according to the Chief Economist of the International Energy Authority, the peaking of global oil supplies is not for the future but already occurred in 2006.[2] This chapter shows how that peaking has had major economic and social consequences. The world economic crash of 2007–8 onwards was partly brought about by oil shortages and price increases as mobilities were especially slowed down in distant American suburbs.

Neo-liberalism

Crucial here is neo-liberalism, which became the dominant global orthodoxy of economic and social policy from around 1980. It moved from its birthplace within the Economics Department at the University of Chicago (Harvey 2005). Even by 1999 Chicago School alumni included 25 Government Ministers and over a dozen central bank presidents through-out the world (Klein 2007).

Neo-liberalism is a doctrine and set of practices that asserts the power and importance of private entrepreneurship, private property rights, the freeing of markets and the freeing of trade. These objectives are brought about by deregulating private activities and companies, privatizing previously 'state' or 'collective' services especially through low taxes, undermin-ing collective powers of workers and professionals, and providing conditions for the private sector to find ever-new sources of profitable activity. Neo-liberalism especially minimizes the role of the state in order to readdress the balance it observes between the 'bad' state and 'good' markets. Neo-liberals hold that states are always inferior to markets in 'guessing' what should be done. States are thought of as inherently inefficient and easily corrupted by private interest groups. Markets are presumed 'natural' and will move to equilibrium, if unnatural forces or elements do not get in the way.

However, states are often important in eliminating 'unnatural' forces, destroying sets of rules, regulations and forms of life that slow down economic growth and constrain the private sector. Sometimes that destruction is exercised through violence and attacks upon democratic procedures. The 'freedom of the market' is brought about through 'shock treatment', the cre-ation of an 'emergency' which enables the state to wipe the slate clean and impose free-market solutions (Friedman 2002). Klein describes how the disaster of Hurricane Katrina in New Orleans in 2005 provided conditions for the large-scale privatization of the New Orleans school system (Klein 2007). Never let a good crisis go to waste is a neo-liberal mantra.

Harvey summarizes neo-liberalism as involving 'accumulation by dispossession' (Harvey 2005). Peasants are thrown off their land, collective property rights are made private, indigenous rights are stolen and turned into private opportunities, rents are extracted from patents, general knowledge is turned into intellectual 'property', the state forces itself to sell off or outsource its collective activities, trade unions are undermined, and financial instruments and flows redistribute income and rights towards finance and away from productive activities.

Since 1980 neo-liberalism became the dominant global discourse. It especially involves the light regulation of banks and financial institutions and the resulting trillion-dollar growth in financial securitization. The distinction between commercial and investment banking has been undermined with the lowering of lending standards and the proliferation of innovative business models. There was the 'macho' domination of financial services and a privileging of competitive individualism implemented through a bonus culture rewarding indebtedness and dangerous risk taking.

There has also been the extensive movement offshore of revenues that ought to be taxed and used for providing collective services and benefits onshore. Shaxson describes tax havens or 'treasure islands' involving jurisdictions facilitating tax avoidance (legal) and tax evasion (illegal). There are around seventy or so secrecy jurisdictions. 'Offshore is how the world of power now works' says Shaxson (2011). This offshore world reduces the capacity of states to tax revenues in locations where companies and individuals generate their income and wealth. More than half of world trade now passes through tax havens, including much oil revenue. Eighty-three out of the US's top hundred companies have subsidiaries located in one or more tax havens. A quarter of all global wealth is held 'offshore' (Kochan 2006). Such movement of monies offshore is central to the enormous shadow banking system and the overwhelming imbalance between 'financialization' and the 'real economy', so much so that there is little of the world economy that is not now 'financialized' (Stiglitz 2007; Krugman 2008; Radice 2011). By September 2008 the global value of financial assets was $160 trillion, more than three-times world GDP (Sassen 2009). What, though, has this movement of money offshore got to do with oil and transport?

Sprawltown

Finance in the US, in the 1990s and early 2000s especially, flowed not into manufacturing industry but into many kinds of property development. In order for property to get built the private sector often cajoles national or regional states to create and pay for, often through borrowing, related mobility infrastructures such as motorways, high-speed rail links and airports. Property development is then undertaken by firms who borrow finance. The properties built are then purchased by buyers who also borrow to make the purchase. Loans are made to property purchasers who would not otherwise be able to buy. Thus there is a speculative funding of highly leveraged new developments that are leased or sold with indebtedness on all sides. Property developments here include suburbs, apartments, second homes, hotels, leisure complexes, gated communities, sports stadia, office blocks, universities, shopping centres and casinos, all built on the indebtedness of developers and purchasers, as well as states.

Central here is the speculative intertwining of property and finance involving new forms of 'finance'. The debts incurred are turned into commodities or 'securitized'. They are parcelled up, sliced and diced into financial packages which are sold on, with huge markets developing throughout the world for many of these 'products' which presuppose that property can only be worth more. This creates a financially complex 'house of cards' resting upon the 'bet' that property rises in value. During the 2000s an unsustainable 'bubble' of private, corporate and national indebtedness developed especially within the US.

Moreover, many new suburbs in the US from the 1980s onwards were built distant from city centres. They were not connected to city centres by mass or public transit. Such *Sprawltowns* depended upon car travel and hence plentiful cheap oil, so newly arriving residents could commute to work and drive about for leisure and social life (Ingersoll 2006). Only one-half of US suburbs have any access to public transport and residents are wholly dependent upon car travel and thus upon the price of oil.

Much of this suburban housing was 'sold' to people with 'sub-prime' employment, credit and housing histories, involving new financial 'innovations'. Although sub-prime housing is known to have been 'central' in the events that 'triggered' the crash of 2007/8, it has not been recognized how sub-prime suburbs were driven to the brink by a problem of mobility, by oil dependence *and* oil price spikes in the few years beforehand. Even Stiglitz's (2010) dissection of the American 'mortgage scam' does not grasp how energy resources can bite back and reverse what seemed at the time irreversible. How did oil reverse what appeared inevitable – that property could only keep going upwards in value?

There was cheap oil for much of the period since the early 1980s. The US index of petrol prices was in money terms 134 in 1990 and more or less the same in 2000 (138) (Cortright 2008).[3] The roaring 1990s, especially house price inflation, which ran two-and-a half-times the increase in per-capita income for Americans, was based upon the falling real price of petrol. Such petrol prices remained more or less constant in money terms until 2003 (145).

Indebtedness in the US in turn fuelled the huge growth in consumption as house prices rose. It became possible to cash in the 'rising values' of property, especially in 2002–4. That money was used to fund further consumer purchases, especially of goods manufactured in China and transported to the US in vast container ships. This generated a huge US current account deficit (Brenner 2006). Many Americans believed that they really were richer as house prices continued to rise and private debt skyrocketed. Also, many people were drawn into purchasing housing through mortgages that offered very low rates in the first few years, but much higher rates after that ('variable rate mortgages').

Writing during 2006, Brenner describes how financial speculation was producing a real estate mania. The total value of residential property in developed economies rose by more than thirty trillion US dollars between 2000 and 2005. This staggering increase was equivalent to 100 per cent of those countries' combined GDPs at the time (Brenner 2006). Indebtedness was thus built upon indebtedness. Such intersecting bubbles of asset prices seemed not to be understood by anyone, nor could they be 'governed'. George Soros, one of the financial 'masters of this universe', reports that no one understood the global system that they themselves were creating (Soros 2008; Tett 2009)!

Bubbles burst

Bubbles, however, burst and they burst most dramatically and painfully as they fill with more and more hot air. The bursting of this bubble, first in the US from 2005 onwards and then worldwide, had dramatic consequences for the real economy. This is where oil is central. Throughout the twentieth century soaring oil prices always generated economic crises. All recent major economic crises bar one have rising oil prices at their core. Murray and former UK Government Chief Scientist David King maintain that the events of 2007–8 were not just a credit crunch but an 'oil-price crunch' (Murray and King 2012).

In the middle years of the 2000s global shortages of oil led to a rapid rise in petrol prices worldwide, including in the US. The US imports two-thirds of its oil and now possesses only a tiny three per cent of global oil reserves (Hofmeister 2010). The US is twice as dependent upon imported oil as it was in the early 1970s. There was a five-fold increase in 'real' oil prices between 2002 and 2008. Over a longer period – between 1990 and 2007 – the price per barrel of oil increased over fourteen times, partly because the world output of oil and related products could not be raised beyond around 84 million barrels a day. Labban maintains that this 'oil crisis arrives as a financial crisis' (Labban 2010: 551).

Moreover, hurricanes Katrina and Rita hit the Louisiana coastline during 2005. These extreme weather events destroyed billions of dollars of gas and oil infrastructures through flooding the Mississippi delta. Other refineries around the world were working to full capacity and could not increase production when these Mississippi refineries were shut down. Rita led to the capsizing of a production platform. Such extreme weather events intersected with the crisis of oil supply. This illustrates Homer-Dixon's argument that: 'societies face crisis when they're hit by multiple shocks simultaneously or they're affected by multiple stresses simultaneously' (Homer-Dixon 2006: 1).

These hurricanes were the extreme events that showed the vulnerability of the world's 'oil civilization'. Without the capacity to replace Gulf of Mexico supplies, the price of oil skyrocketed. There will be many other occasions when floods or hurricanes or blowouts or revolutions will reduce supply, dramatically increase prices and devastate patterns of life including for those living in suburbs built upon 'easy oil', easy movement and the presumed rising price of property (Strahan 2007). These oil shortages were reflected in the US petrol price spiking in the 2000s. It reached 302 in 2007 and a peak of 405 in July 2008. The petrol price peaked 2007–8. By February 2009 the petrol index was still higher, at 186, than it had been in 2000.

But many living in these new American suburbs completely depended upon cheap petrol and cheap movement. Without it they could have no life. As petrol prices increased, so property owners were forced to reduce their expenditure on housing and other goods and services, including that on cars. Hamilton argues that: 'the oil price increase was one factor pushing home sales and house prices down' very rapidly (Hamilton 2009). In the heated atmosphere of the bubble, 'gas [i.e. petrol] price increases may have been the trigger that broke the expectations of continued growth' (Cortright 2008: 5). Suddenly it cost more to fill up an SUV's petrol tank than it cost to buy a week's groceries.

The American housing boom was thus brought to a shuddering halt through the escalating price of petrol in the middle years of the last decade. This increase tipped financially weak households over the financial brink. They could no longer afford the mortgage payments, which they anyway could only just manage to pay given their sub-prime standing. Ten thousand homeowners lost their homes to foreclosures every day. Millions of Americans received foreclosure notices and tens of billions in real-estate assets were written-off as losses by banks. This was a vicious circle. Foreclosures helped accelerate the fall of property values, helping to spur more foreclosures. The losses they created brought the financial system to the brink of collapse in the fall of 2008. The steep recession that followed led to greater homeowner foreclosures, as homeowners who lost their jobs often also lost their homes.

Many households thus defaulted on their mortgages, suburbs collapsed with much property for sale, financial institutions around the world were left holding huge amounts of bad debt (albeit rated AAA by the major ratings agencies), some banks went to the wall or were 'nationalized', and there was a global recession on an unprecedented scale, continuing into 2012.

There was a geographical distribution to these patterns. House price falls were the most marked in suburbs rather than in metropolitan cores, and they were especially steep in those distant 'oil-dependent' suburbs. House price reductions were greatest where there were no alternatives to the car and where the dependence upon the price *and* availability of petrol for almost all aspects of life was highest. Households were spending up to 30 per cent of their income on travel. Cheap oil was a necessity.

Because of increases in the cost of petrol the value of housing in commuter belts dropped very steeply. Many such suburbs turned into 'ghostburbs', full of foreclosures, for sale signs and empty housing. This meant that 'households [were] being made to rethink another cherished American institution – the white picket-fenced suburban dream home' (Ghazi 2008; Dodson and Sipe 2008; Rubin 2009: 291).

This all reduced US consumer spending, which is similar to what happened in 1990–1 during the first Gulf War. This reduction led to multiple defaults as banks realized that they held huge amounts of bad or toxic debt. This produced the escalating collapse of especially investment banks, first in the US, and then the rest of the world, which had also invested in many American mortgages. This house of financial cards came tumbling down – beginning, according to Stiglitz (2010), in these oil-dependent suburbs full of American households who had been sold 'sub-prime' mortgages through a vast 'scam'.

There were many consequences of this collapse, including a reduction in the distances that Americans now travel. This was the first downward shift of US mileage for thirty years or so (Cortright 2008: 17). Such reductions produced a marked decline in car sales, with at least 150,000 fewer people being employed in the US motor industry. Global oil production fell by two million barrels per day in 2009, or 2.6 per cent, the largest decline since 1982. Some speculate that this slowdown marks the beginning of the end for 'oil addiction', as it was in these American 'sub-prime', oil-dependent suburbs based upon cheap car-based movement where the collapse first occured.

Conclusion

In the last years of the last century, neo-liberalism ratcheted up the global scale of movement within the global North. Oil enabled this. This travel of people and goods is essential to most social practices that depend upon and reinforce a high-carbon society. Much of this high carbon production and consumption was based on indebtedness and on a greatly increasing significance of 'finance' within modern economies. Indeed money was increasingly borrowed from the rest of the world, especially China, so as to fuel this carbon extravaganza for the global rich.

But this extravaganza came to a shuddering halt when oil prices increased in the early years of this century. Suburban houses could not be sold, especially those in far-flung oil-dependent locations. Financial products and institutions were found to be worthless. Easy money, easy credit and easy oil had all gone together. And when oil prices hit the roof in these US suburbs, easy money and credit also came to a shuddering halt and the presumed upward shift in property prices was shown to be a false dream.

The financial house of cards had been built upon cheap oil and cheap mobility; but when the oil got prohibitively expensive the house of cards collapsed. This story of oil in the US provides a bleak vision of the future as 'easy oil' more generally will have run out by the middle of this century. The Chief Economist at HSBC Bank maintains that: 'Even if demand doesn't increase, there could be as little as 49 years of oil left' (Ward 2011). And of course demand is increasing very rapidly especially outside the 'west'. Elsewhere I show how we have not seen anything yet – that collapsing supplies and dramatically rising prices will wreak future devastation around the world in the decades to come. The twentieth century has left us with an utterly unsustainable civilization based on the mobilities of people and goods requiring this one resource of cheap, plentiful, easy oil.[4] Cannot live with oil, cannot live without it, we might conclude.

Notes

1 This chapter is drawn from John Urry, *Societies beyond Oil* (London: Zed, 2012).
2 www.good.is/post/international-energy-agency-s-top-economist-says-oil-peaked-in-2006/ (accessed 27.12.11).
3 These are end-of-year figures.
4 Much more detail is provided of multiple futures in John Urry, *Societies beyond Oil* (London: Zed, 2012).

References

Brenner, R. (2006) *The Economics of Global Turbulence*, London: Verso.

Burman, S. (2007) *The State of the American Empire*, London: Earthscan.

Cortright, J. (2008) *Driven to the Brink*, Chicago: CEOs for Cities.

Dicker, D. (2011) *Oil's Endless Bid*, New York: Wiley.

Dodson, J. and Sipe, N. (2008) *Shocking the Suburbs*, Sydney: UNSW Press.

Friedman, M. (2002) *Capitalism and Freedom*, Chicago: University of Chicago Press.

Froggatt, A. and Lahn, G. (2010) *Sustainable Energy Security*, London: Lloyd's and Chatham House.

Ghazi, P. (2008) 'Gas guzzlers and "ghostburbs"', *The Guardian*, 2008, July 2nd.

Hamilton, J. (2009) 'The oil shock and recession of 2008: Part 2', Econbrowser. Available online at www.econbrowser.com/archives/2009/01/the_oil_shock_a_1.html (accessed 10.03.09).

Harvey, D. (2005) *A Brief History of Neo-Liberalism*, Oxford: Oxford University Press.

Harvey, M. and Pilgrim, S. (2011) 'The new competition for land: food, energy and climate change', *Food Policy*, 36: S40–S51.

Heinberg, R. (2005) *The Party's Over*, New York: Clearview Books.

Hofmeister, J. (2010) *Why We Hate the Oil Companies*, New York: Palgrave Macmillan.

Homer-Dixon, T. (2006) *The Upside of Down*, New York: Island Press.

Hulme, M. (2009) *Why We Disagree about Climate Change*, Cambridge: Cambridge University Press.

Ingersoll, R. (2006) *Sprawltown*, New York: Princeton University Press.

Klein, N. (2007) *The Shock Doctrine*, London: Penguin Allen Lane.

Kochan, N. (2006) *The Washing Machine*, London: Duckworth.

Krugman, P. (2008) *The Return of Depression Economics*, Harmondsworth: Penguin.

Labban, M. (2010) 'Oil in parallax: scarcity, markets, and the financialization of accumulation', *Geoforum*, 41: 541–552.

McNeill, J. (2012) 'The history of energy since 10,000 B.C.' *The Globalist*. Available online at www.theglobalist.com/StoryId.aspx?StoryId=2018 (accessed 19.01.12).

Murray, J. and King, D. (2012) 'Climate policy: oil's tipping point has passed', *Nature*, 481: 433–435.

Owen, D. (2011) *Green Metropolis*, London: Penguin.

Radice, H. (2011) 'Confronting the crisis: a class analysis', *Socialist Register*, 47: 21–43.

Rubin, J. (2009) *Why Your World is About to Get a Whole Lot Smaller*, London: Virgin.

Rutledge, I. (2005) *Addicted to Oil*, London: I. B. Tauris.

Sassen, S. (2009) 'Too big to save: the end of financial capitalism', *Open Democracy News Analysis*. Available online at www.opendemocracy.net/article/too-big-to-save-the-end-of-financial-capitalism-0 (accessed 01.01.2009).

Shaxson, N. (2011) *Treasure Islands*, London: Bodley.

Singh, M. (2011) 'What's all the oil in the world worth?' Available online at www.fleetstreetinvest.co.uk/oil/oil-outlook/oil-world-worth-00027.html (accessed 23.06.11).

Smil, V. (2010) *Energy Transitions*, Santa Barbara, CA: Praeger.

Soros, G. (2008) *The New Paradigm for Financial Markets*, London: Public Affairs.

Stiglitz, J. E. (2007) *Making Globalization Work*, London: W. W. Norton & Company.

Stiglitz, J. (2010) *Freefall*, London: Penguin.

Strahan, D. (2007) *The Last Oil Shock*, London: John Murray.

Tett, G. (2009) *Fool's Gold*, London: Little, Brown.

Ward, K. (2011) 'Global Economics and Climate Change: Energy in 2050', *HSBC global research report*, London: HSBC.

Worldwide Fund for Nature (WWF) (2008) 'Plugged In. The End of the Oil Age, Summary Report', Brussels: WWF, March.

Žižek, S. (2008) 'World renowned philosopher Slavoj Zizek on the Iraq War, the Bush Presidency, the War on Terror & more', *Democracy Now*. Available online at www.democracynow.org/2008/5/12/world_renowned_philosopher_slavoj_zizek_on (accessed 20.05.10).

Index